More praise for

"The most comprehensive, up-to-date and cogently argued comparison yet published."   —Steven Merritt Minor, *New York Times Book Review*

"Impressive."   —William Grimes, *New York Times*

"This dense, comprehensive, scholarly investigation is more nuanced than most. . . . Overy's analytical strength and depth of knowledge emerge."
                                                              —*Publishers Weekly*

"This fine book is proof of years of contemplation of an important subject that has been excavated many times but which still rewards those who are eager enough to dig in overlooked parts of the terrain."
                                            —Robert Service, *The Guardian*

"A formidable addition to the literature of this period. . . . Indispensable."
                                                              —*The Telegraph*

"Overy's monumental comparative history is invaluable."
                                  —Michael Burleigh, *Sunday Times* (London)

"Engrossing, well written and wise."   —Sam Leith, *The Spectator*

"Original and thought-provoking."   —Peter Lewis, *Daily Mail*

"A superb work, comprehensive and written with rare fire and intelligence."
                                            —Neal Ascherson, *The Observer*

"Powerful and important. . . . [Overy] provides a detailed and nuanced comparative history of the structures and regimes these two notorious dictators created. . . . [The book] includes the most extensive comparative discussion of the treatment of Jews in Nazi Germany and Stalinist Russia I have ever read."   —*Jewish Book World*

"A very important comparative history of Nazi Germany and Soviet Russia."
                                                              —*Choice*

RICHARD OVERY

The Dictators

Hitler's Germany and Stalin's Russia

W. W. Norton & Company
New York London

For information about permission to reproduce selections from this book,
write to Permissions, W. W. Norton & Company, Inc., 500 Fifth Avenue,
New York, NY 10110

Manufacturing by RR Donnelley, Harrisonburg, VA
Production manager: Anna Oler

Library of Congress Cataloging-in-Publication Data

Overy, R. J.
The dictators : Hitler's Germany and Stalin's Russia / Richard Overy.
p. cm.
Includes bibliographical references (p.) and index.
ISBN 0-393-02030-4
1. Hitler, Adolf, 1889–1945. 2. Stalin, Josef, 1879–1953. 3. Dictators—Germany.
4. Germany—Politics and government—1933–1945. 5. Dictators—Soviet Union.
6. Soviet Union—Politics and government—1936–1953. 7. National socialism.
8. Communism. 9. Totalitarianism. I. Title.
DD247.H5O94 2004
943.086'092—dc22   2004056087

ISBN 0-393-32797-3 pbk.

W. W. Norton & Company, Inc.
500 Fifth Avenue, New York, N.Y. 10110
www.wwnorton.com

W. W. Norton & Company Ltd.
Castle House, 75/76 Wells Street, London W1T 3QT

4 5 6 7 8 9 0

'Human groupings have one main purpose: to assert everyone's right to be different, to be special, to think, feel and live in his or her own way. People join together in order to win or defend this right. But this is where a terrible, fateful error is born: the belief that these groupings in the name of a race, a God, a party or a State are the very purpose of life and not simply a means to an end. No! The only true and lasting meaning of the struggle for life lies in the individual, in his modest peculiarities and in his right to those peculiarities.'

Vasily Grossman, Life and Fate, p. 230

Contents

CONTENTS

List of Illustrations

SECOND SECTION

ILLUSTRATION ACKNOWLEDGEMENTS

The author would like to thank John Cunningham at the Society for
Co-Operation in Russian and Soviet Studies (SCRSS) and Marek Jaros
at the Wiener Library (WL), the Institute of Contemporary History,
for their help with the pictures in this book.

Copyright for the following pictures is held by the SCRSS: first section,
pictures 1–12, 14, 16–21, 23–36; second section, pictures 23–26, 31.

Copyright for the following pictures is held by the WL: second section,
pictures 12, 13, 20, 27. The following images were supplied by the WL,
copyright unknown: second section, pictures 1–10, 15–22, 28–30, 32.

Every effort has been made to trace copyright holders but this has not
been possible in all cases. If notified, the publishers will be pleased to
rectify any omissions at the earliest opportunity.

List of Tables and Maps

TABLES

MAPS

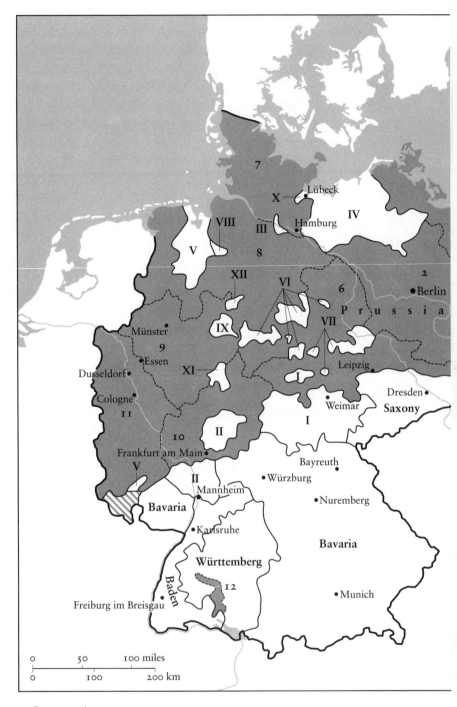

1 Germany in 1933

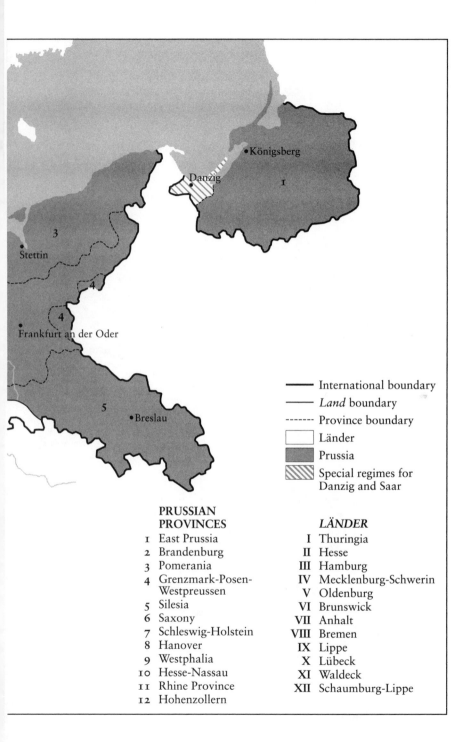

●Königsberg

Danzig●

I

3

●Stettin

4

4

●Frankfurt an der Oder

5

●Breslau

—— International boundary
—— *Land* boundary
------ Province boundary
☐ Länder
▨ Prussia
▨ Special regimes for
Danzig and Saar

PRUSSIAN
PROVINCES
1 East Prussia
2 Brandenburg
3 Pomerania
4 Grenzmark-Posen-
  Westpreussen
5 Silesia
6 Saxony
7 Schleswig-Holstein
8 Hanover
9 Westphalia
10 Hesse-Nassau
11 Rhine Province
12 Hohenzollern

LÄNDER
I Thuringia
II Hesse
III Hamburg
IV Mecklenburg-Schwerin
V Oldenburg
VI Brunswick
VII Anhalt
VIII Bremen
IX Lippe
X Lübeck
XI Waldeck
XII Schaumburg-Lippe

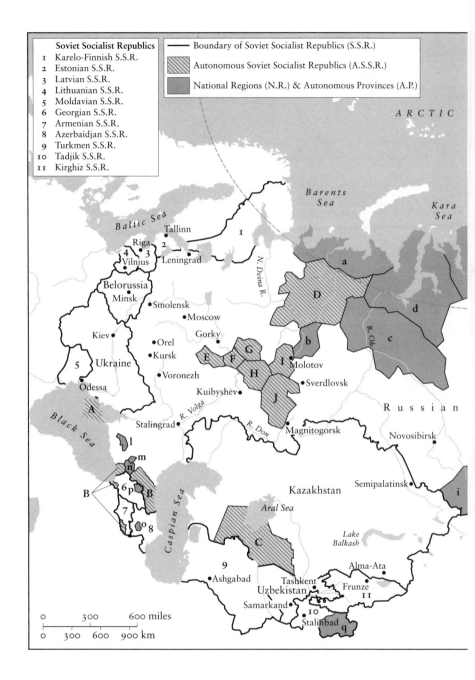

Soviet Socialist Republics
1 Karelo-Finnish S.S.R.
2 Estonian S.S.R.
3 Latvian S.S.R.
4 Lithuanian S.S.R.
5 Moldavian S.S.R.
6 Georgian S.S.R.
7 Armenian S.S.R.
8 Azerbaidjan S.S.R.
9 Turkmen S.S.R.
10 Tadjik S.S.R.
11 Kirghiz S.S.R.

—— Boundary of Soviet Socialist Republics (S.S.R.)

Autonomous Soviet Socialist Republics (A.S.S.R.)

National Regions (N.R.) & Autonomous Provinces (A.P.)

ARCTIC

Barents Sea

Kara Sea

Baltic Sea

Tallinn
Riga
Leningrad
Vilnius

N. Dvina R.

Belorussia
Minsk
Smolensk
Moscow

Kiev
Orel
Gorky
Kursk
Ukraine
Voronezh

Odessa
Kuibyshev
Molotov
Sverdlovsk

Black Sea

Stalingrad
R. Volga
R. Don
Magnitogorsk

Novosibirsk

RUSSIAN

Caspian Sea

Kazakhstan
Semipalatinsk

Aral Sea

Lake Balkash

Ashgabad
Tashkent
Uzbekistan
Samarkand
Stalinbad

Alma-Ata
Frunze

R. Ob

0   300   600 miles
0 300 600 900 km

2 The Soviet Union in the 1930s

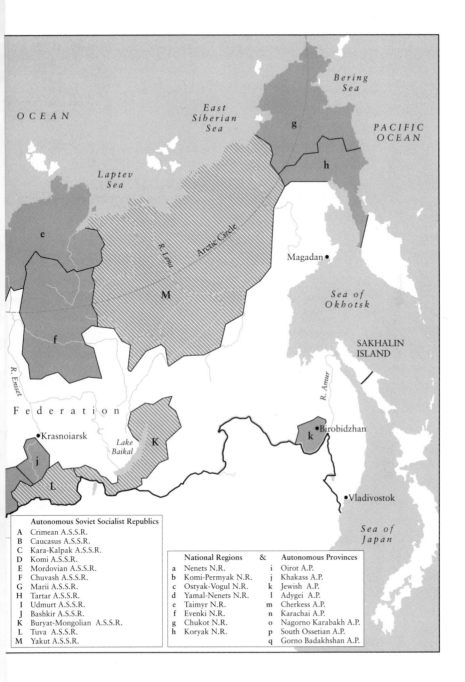

OCEAN

Bering
Sea

East
Siberian
Sea

g

PACIFIC
OCEAN

Laptev
Sea

h

e

R. Lena

Arctic Circle

Magadan •

M

Sea of
Okhotsk

f

SAKHALIN
ISLAND

R. Enisei

Federation

R. Amur

• Krasnoiarsk

Lake
Baikal

K

k

•Birobidzhan

j

L

•Vladivostok

Sea of
Japan

Autonomous Soviet Socialist Republics
A   Crimean A.S.S.R.
B   Caucasus A.S.S.R.
C   Kara-Kalpak A.S.S.R.
D   Komi A.S.S.R.
E   Mordovian A.S.S.R.
F   Chuvash A.S.S.R.
G   Marii A.S.S.R.
H   Tartar A.S.S.R.
I   Udmurt A.S.S.R.
J   Bashkir A.S.S.R.
K   Buryat-Mongolian A.S.S.R.
L   Tuva A.S.S.R.
M Yakut A.S.S.R.

National Regions   &   Autonomous Provinces
a   Nenets N.R.   i   Oirot A.P.
b   Komi-Permyak N.R.   j   Khakass A.P.
c   Ostyak-Vogul N.R.   k   Jewish A.P.
d   Yamal-Nenets N.R.   l   Adygei A.P.
e   Taimyr N.R.   m Cherkess A.P.
f   Evenki N.R.   n   Karachai A.P.
g   Chukot N.R.   o   Nagorno Karabakh A.P.
h   Koryak N.R.   p   South Ossetian A.P.
                            q   Gorno Badakhshan A.P.

DENMARK

• Kiel

Schleswig-
Holstein

Mecklenburg
Schwerin

Hamburg
Hamburg

Luneburg •
East Hanover

Oldenburg•

Wester-Ems

NETHERLANDS

Hanover• Wolfsburg

Magdeburg-
Anhalt

Münster
•
North Westphalia

South Hanover-
Brunswick

Dessau

Essen

Essen•
Düsseldorf•
Düsseldorf

Dortmund
South
Westphalia

Halle-

Halle •

BELGIUM

Cologne•
Cologne-Aachen

Kassel •
Kurhessen

Weimar •
Thuringia

Koblenz

Hesse-
Nassau
Frankfurt

Main-
Franconia
Würzburg

Bayreuth
•

Moselland

Mannheim •
Westmark

Nuremberg
•
Franconia

Bayerisch
Ostmark

Karlsruhe •

• Stuttgart
Württemberg-
Hohenzollern

Augsburg •
✠•
Munich

FRANCE

Baden

Swabia

Munich-
Upper Bavaria

SWITZERLAND

Innsbruck
•
Tirol-Vorarlberg

ITALY

0	50	100 miles
0	50	100 km

3 The Party organization in Germany

Königsberg

Danzig

East Prussia

Danzig-
West Prussia

Stettin

Pomerania

Mark
Brandenburg

Berlin Berlin

Posen

Frankfurt

Wartheland

Warsaw

Merseburg

Lower Silesia

Dresden

Breslau

POLAND

Saxony

Upper Silesia

Protectorate of
Bohemia and
Moravia

Linz

Lower Danube

SLOVAKIA

Vienna

Upper
Danube

Vienna

Salzburg

Salzburg

Styria

Graz

HUNGARY

Carinthia

Villach

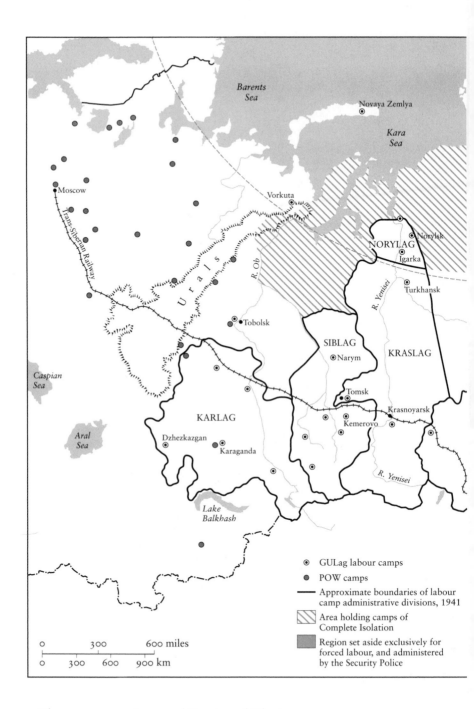

4 The camp system in central Russia and Siberia

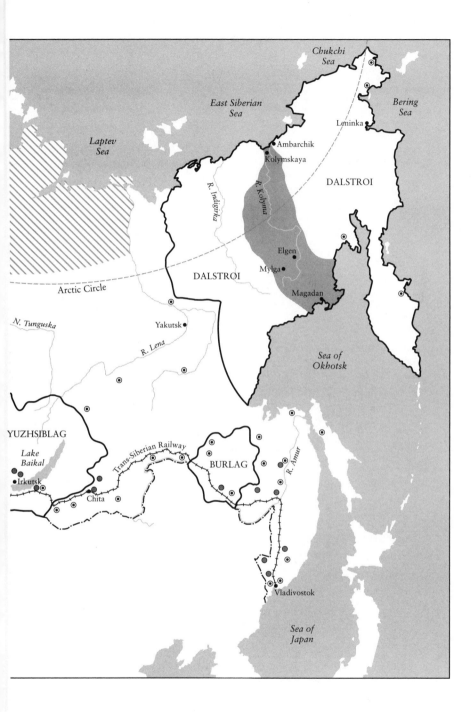

North Sea

DENMARK

Kiel-Nordmark

NETHERLANDS

BELGIUM

LUX.

FRANCE

SWITZERLAND

ITALY

Hamburg-Wilhelmsburg I ★
Bremen-Farge
Bremen-Sebaldsbrück
★ II
Oldenburg
Unterlüss

Wuhlheide
IX ★
Frohnau
Fehrbellin
Dreetz
Henningsdorf X ★
Falkensee-Finkenkreg Berlin
Genthin Groß-
beeren Gosen

Bentheim
Gronau
Ahaus
Dorsten
Gladbeck-Zweckel
Oberhausen-Holten
Duisburg
Krefeld
Düsseldorf
Leverkusen
Alsdorf
Aachen
Bonn
Ohrbeck
Gütersloh
Hamm
Dortmund
Unna
Essen Wetter
Solingen-Ohlings
Hunswinkel
Köln
Bad Godesberg
Liebenau
Lahde Langenhagen
Bad Hannover
Eilsen Ahlem
Beelen Hildesheim
Hönnetal
Meschede
Siegen
Kasse
Breitenau
Affoldern
Watenstedt- Magdeburg
Hallendorf
Hessen
Blankenburg Halberstadt
Eichenberg
Osendorf
Schkopau
Spergau
Kulkwitz
Lippendorf
Leitzkau
Piesteritz
★ VIII
Ragunn
Böhlitz-
Ehrenberg
Leipzig Dresden
Peres-Böhlen
Cossebaude
Weissig
Oederan
Freiberg
Chemnitz
Ober
Leutensdorf-
Maltheuern

★ III

★ IV
Kranichfield
Bibra
Zwickau
Plauen
Falkenstein
Johanngeorgenstadt

Neuwied
Hundstadt
Ettingshausen
Freiesneen
Römhild
Rieneck

Bacharach
Frankfurt-
Heddernheim
Mainz

VII ★ Pilsen-Karlow

Miroschau

St. Wendel
Etzenhofen
Neue Bremm
Ödheim
Karlsruhe Heilbronn
Rudersberg
Niederbühl Leonberg
Kniebis- Neckerhausen
Ruhestein
Neckartenzlingen
Oberndorf-Aistaig
Rotenbach (Schrezheim)
Fellbach Wasseralfingen
Heidenheim-Mergelstetten
Offingen
Ehingen
Augsburg
München-Berg am Laim ★ VI
München-Moosach

★ V

Innsbruck-Reichenau

Kraut

0 50 100 miles	
0 50 100 km	

5 The camp system in Greater Germany

Baltic Sea

Honebruch

Hägerwelle

Brückendorf ● Ortelburg
Schiemanen ● Snopki
Soldau ● Praschnitz
Mielau ● Scharfenwiese
Lauffen Nosarzewo
Sichelberg ● Zichenhau ● Macheim
Hohensalza ● Reichenfeld ● Ostenburg
Ostrowo ● Steinhausen Serock
Treblinka

Alt-Buchorst
Fürstenwalde
Schwetig ● Bretz ● Posen-Lenzingen
Chelmno ■
XIV ★
Grodziec
Christiastadt
Litzmannstadt-Sikawa ●
Sobibor ■
Wildfelde
Rothenburg
Rattwitz
Maidanek ★ ■
Radeberg ● Löbau
Bodenbach
Zittau ● Kleinschona ★ XIII
Reigersfeld
Blachstädt ●
Generalgouvernement
Belzec ■
Tetschen ● Morchentiern
Czalositz
★ XI
Nifke
Heyderbreck ●
Myslowitz ● ● Laband
Hradischko
Breschen ● ● Mlatkau
Auschwitz ★ ■ Birkenau
★ XV
Krehanitz
Jirowitz
Parduitz
Groß-Kunzendorf ● ● Mährisch-Ostnau
Tworschowitz
Janowitz Markt
Plan a.d. Lainsit

SLOVAKIA

Siebenharten
Oberlanzendorf ●
★ XII
Schörgenhub Moosnierbaum ●
St. Valentin

Frauenberg St. Dionysch
Niklasdorf
HUNGARY

★ Concentration camps
I Neuengamme
II Bergen Belsen
III Mittelbau-Dora
IV Buchenwald
V Natzweiler
VI Dachau
VII Flossenburg
● Work Education Camps (Gestapo)
VIII Sachsenburg
IX Ravensbrück
● Work Education Camps of firms and communes
X Sachsenhausen
XI Theresienstadt
◇ Several camps at same place/same city
XII Mauthausen
XIII Groß Rosen
XIV Warsaw
■ Extermination Camps
XV Plaszow

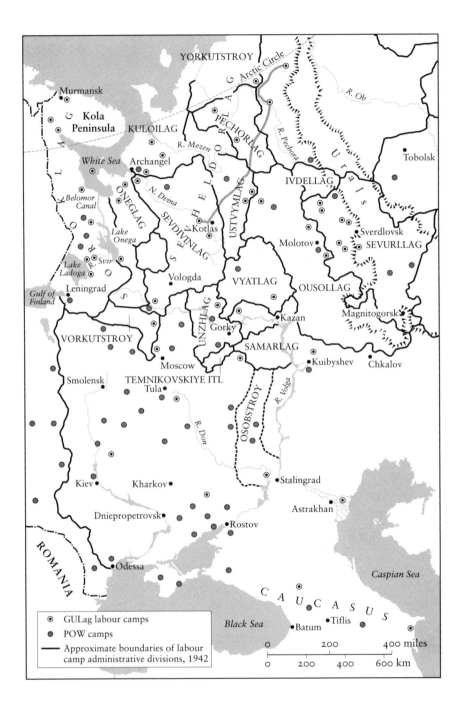

6 The camp system in the Western Soviet Union

Abbreviations

BA-B	Bundesarchiv-Berlin (Lichterfelde)
BA-MA	Bundesarchiv-Militärarchiv (Freiburg)
Cheka	Extraordinary Commission for Combating Counter-revolution and Sabotage
CPSU	Communist Party of the Soviet Union
DAP	Deutsche Arbeiter Partei (German Workers' Party)
DNVP	Deutschnationale Volkspartei (German National People's Party)
Freikorps	Free Corps (volunteer militia)
Gestapa	Geheime Staatspolizeiamt (Secret State Police Office)
Gestapo	Geheime Staatspolizei (Secret State Police)
GNP	Gross National Product
Gosplan	State Planning Commission
GPU	State Political Directorate
GUlag	Main Administration of Corrective Labour Camps
GUPR	Main Administration of Forced Labour
IG Farben	Interessengemeinschaft Farben AG (Interest Group Dyes)
ITK	Corrective Labour Colony
ITL	Corrective Labour Camp
IWM	Imperial War Museum (London)
KGB	Committee of State Security
Komsomol	All-Union Leninist Communist Youth League
NA II	National Archives II, College Park, Maryland
NI	National Income
NKGB	People's Commissariat of State Security
NKVD	People's Commissariat for Internal Affairs

NSDAP	Nationalsozialistische Deutsche Arbeiterpartei (National Socialist German Worker's Party)
OGPU	All-Union State Political Directorate
OKW	Oberkommando der Wehrmacht (Supreme Command of the Armed Forces)
PFI	Proof and Filtration Camp
POW	prisoner of war
PRO	Public Record Office, Kew, London
Rabkrin	Workers' and Peasants' Inspectorate
RSHA	Reich Sicherheitshauptamt (Reich Main Office of Security)
SA	Sturmabteilungen (Storm detachments)
SD	Sicherheitsdienst (Security Service)
SLON	Northern Special Purpose Camps
SS	Schutzstaffel (Protection Squad)
USSR	Union of Soviet Socialist Republics

NOTE ON TERMINOLOGY

Throughout the text the word ton refers to metric tonnes. Other weights and distances have been rendered in metric measurements where possible. The word billion is used to denote one thousand million (or milliard). I have chosen to use the term Soviet Union in preference to the acronym USSR throughout the text, chiefly on aesthetic grounds. I have also chosen in most cases to spell National Socialist in full rather than use the common term Nazi, which began life as a piece of political shorthand and was never used by the regime to describe itself. The term communist is used lower case where it describes the movement or ideology in general, but in upper case where it refers specifically to the Soviet Communist Party. There were many varieties of 'communist', even in the Soviet Union, and its use should not be taken to imply only the Soviet form.

Preface

Hitler and Stalin have been part of my life for far too long. I was interested in them as a precocious schoolboy and have worked on or around the two dictatorships for much of the last thirty years. As a student I was brought up under the old totalitarian school, which explained dictatorial rule as domination through fear by psychopathic tyrants. The two dictators were still treated differently – Hitler as an unmediated monster, Stalin as a man forced by necessity to preserve the 1917 revolution by savage means that were justified by the noble ends that Soviet communism claimed to represent. 'Did Stalin betray the Revolution?' was the essay title I was given, a question that suggested this was open to interpretation. No one would have set the question, 'Did Hitler betray the German people?' Hitler was a man apart, beyond discussion.

Thirty years on the two men are set in a very different context. This is not because they have been forgiven the terrible things that their systems did to their own and to other peoples, but because the systems were not simply a one-man show. For a long time now it has been possible, and very necessary, to write the history of these two dictatorships from perspectives in which the two dictators at the core play only a small and often distant part. These were large and complex societies whose values, behaviour, aspirations and development owed something to the overblown personality at the centre, but they were obviously constructed of many elements with their own trajectories, their own detailed social and political history, their own perpetrators, onlookers and victims. The more we know about the periphery, the clearer it is that the centre succeeded only to the extent that much of the population accepted and worked with the two systems, or constructed their lives in ways that avoided as far as possible direct contact with the dangerous powers of the state, or approved the moral purposes of the dictatorships and applauded their achievements. A life of Hitler and Stalin today has to be a history of life and times, or better still, a history that sets them in the societies that gave rise to them and explores the dynamics that held dictatorship together beyond the simplistic image of omnipotent despot.

The scholarship of the past twenty years has transformed our understanding of both Hitler's Germany and Stalin's Soviet Union because it has in large part focused on the many areas of state, society, culture, science and ideas which make up the history of this as of any other age. This has been a recent process, for several reasons. The opening up of former Soviet archives has provided a stream of Russian and western scholarship that has been challenging, original and informed in ways that were impossible with the rationed sources of the Soviet period. German archives from the Third Reich were, in general, open, but there was a reluctance to engage with much of the material in the long aftermath during which Germans came to terms with Hitler. Much of the best early history was written by non-German historians, but in the last decade or so there has been a veritable explosion of outstanding new research on every aspect of German society – from pre-Hitler to post-Hitler – by German scholars who no longer have any diffidence in confronting the historical truths. This analysis of the two systems would not have been possible without such an outpouring. Even an area so central to the history of the two systems as the story of the concentration camp has only been filled in properly in the last few years, with often surprising results. I would like to record the very great debt that I owe to all the authors whose work I have relied on here in order to supply the many missing parts of the jigsaw around the figures of the two dictators. Reading the many thought-provoking and innovative approaches to dictatorship has been one of the pleasures of writing this book.

I have many other scholarly debts to record. A great many people have listened to me think through the arguments presented here, not least the many students who have taken my Comparing Dictatorships course at King's College, London, with such interest and enthusiasm. Teaching them has been a stimulating experience, and I have modified my views in many places as a direct result of what they have written or said in class. I have many colleagues who have shared their own perspectives with me, sometimes agreeing with what I say but often, and thankfully, disagreeing as well. I would like to thank in particular Albert Axell, Claudia Baldoli, David Cesarani, Patricia Clavin, Gill Coleridge, Ulrike Ehret, Richard Evans, Isabel Heinemann, Geoffrey Hosking, Sergei Kudryashov, Stephen Lovell, Lucy Luck, Jeremy Noakes, Ingrid Rock, Robert Service, Lennart Samuelson, Jill Stephenson, Chris Szejnmann, Mikulas Teich, Alice Teichova, Nicholas Terry, Adam Tooze and Richard Vinen. I would like to give special mention to Olga Kucherenko and Aglaya Snetkov, who have both worked on Russian-language material for me. Finally, the team at Penguin, Simon Winder, Chloe Campbell, Charlotte Ridings and Richard Duguid, all deserve my grateful thanks.

Richard Overy
February 2004

Introduction
Comparing Dictatorships

'In Russia and in Germany – and wherever totalitarianism penetrated – men were fired by a fanatical faith, by an absolute unquestioning certainty which rejected the critical attitude of modern man. Totalitarianism in Russia and Germany broke the dikes of civilization which the nineteenth century had believed lasting.'   Hans Kohn, 1949[1]

The temptation to compare Hitler and Stalin is a compelling one. They are popularly regarded as the twin demons of the twentieth century, responsible for different reasons and in different ways for more violent deaths than any other men in history. They sit uneasily in comparison with other contemporary dictators or with those in earlier times. To set Stalin and Hitler side by side is to join company with two of the historical giants of the modern age, whose dictatorships met head-to-head in the greatest and costliest of all armed conflicts.

Two questions immediately arise: can the Stalin and Hitler dictatorships be compared? Should they be compared? Tzvetan Todorov, in a recent book on the crisis of the twentieth century, has answered yes to both questions, on the ground that they shared the common characteristics of a single political genus: totalitarianism.[2] This is an answer with a long pedigree. In the 1950s, when the West confronted Soviet communism so shortly after fighting Hitler, it was easy to see both men as 'totalitarian' leaders, dominating systems that tried to impose an absolute and ruthless authority over the populations under their central control. Western political scientists tried to fathom out how they had defeated one monstrous dictatorship, only to be faced with a second, apparently even more sinister and unyielding than the first. However, the development of a model for the ideal or typical totalitarian regime glossed over very real differences between systems classified as 'totalitarian'. The term itself came to be regarded as a description of the apparatus of power and repression, ignoring the regime's wider social, cultural and moral ambitions, which is what the term had originally encompassed when it was first coined in the 1920s in Mussolini's Italy. Historians by the 1960s generally turned their back on the idea of a generic 'totalitarian' system, preferring to focus on a narrative that emphasized the peculiar character of each national dictatorship, and played down the resemblances.

Since the collapse of European communism in 1989–91, discussion of the two dictatorships has been refocused. A more historically sophisticated definition of totalitarianism has been developed, one that highlights the extent to which the systems were driven by a positive vision of an exclusive social and cultural utopia (often described with the term 'political religion'), while recognizing that the political and social practices of the regime were often very different from the utopian aspirations. It is no longer necessary to rely on a crude political-science model of 'totalitarianism' to define the two dictatorships; over the past dozen years the detailed historical knowledge of both the German and the Soviet regimes has been transformed, thanks on the one hand to the *glasnost* revelations in the Soviet Union and the successor states, and on the other to a wave of critical scholarship in Germany that has opened up many aspects of the Hitler regime hitherto cloaked in silence. This research allows us to say with confidence, as Todorov does, that the two systems were also 'significantly different from each other', while sharing a common totalitarian complexion.[3]

The revelation of the scale and premeditated nature of Stalinist mass murder has contributed to the view that Stalin was no better than Hitler. 'Nazism and Communism, equally criminal' ran the title of an article published in France in 1997 by Alain Besançon. It has even been suggested that a calculus of evil might exist which could make it possible to determine with more scientific precision which of the two men was most wicked, though this was not Besançon's intention.[4] The shock to former Marxists and fellow-travellers of Soviet communism to discover that the Stalin regime really was built on blood unscrupulously spilled, and ideals distorted beyond recognition, produced a powerful backlash. The publication in France in 1997 of *The Black Book of Communism*, by former French Marxists, showed how far the left had moved in recognizing that Stalin's dictatorship was based on a savage criminality.[5] A recent study has no doubt that Stalin was a psychopath; studies of Hitler's 'mind' focus on the pathology of evil.[6] The implicit assumption – that both Stalin and Hitler were cut from the same bloodstained cloth – has blurred any real distinction between them. Yet such a comparison is just as intellectually barren as the earlier attempt to tar all dictatorships with the same brush of undifferentiated totalitarianism. No one doubts the horrors at the heart of the two dictatorships, but it is a futile exercise to compare the violence and criminality of the two regimes simply in order to make them appear more like each other, or to try to discover by statistical reconstruction which was the more murderous. The historian's responsibility is not to prove which of the two men was the more evil or deranged, but to try to understand the differing historical processes and states of mind that led both these dictatorships to murder on such a colossal scale.

This book is a contribution to that understanding. For all the efforts to define the Hitler and Stalin dictatorships as models of a shared totalitarian impulse, or a common moral depravity, equally guilty of unspeakable crimes, there has been remarkably little literature that offers a direct historical, rather than polemical comparison. Here it is necessary to explain what *The Dictators* is *not* about. The book is not a twin biography, though Hitler and Stalin feature throughout the narrative. Alan Bullock, in his monumental dual biography *Parallel Lives*, published in 1991, interwove the personal history of the two dictators, and this approach does not need to be repeated.[7] There are now excellent individual lives of both men, which have reconstructed every aspect of their biographies in careful detail.[8] Their life histories are among the most closely examined of any historical actors. Nor is *The Dictators* a straightforward narrative history of the two systems. There are many excellent accounts of both, which again require no reiteration.[9] *The Dictators* has been written with two purposes in mind: first, to supply an empirical foundation on which to construct any discussion of what made the two systems either similar or different; second, to write a comparative 'operational' history of the two systems in order to answer the large historical question about how personal dictatorship actually worked. The answer to this question is central to understanding how the two dictatorships emerged and what kept them both in being until the dictators' deaths.

Some areas of convergence are clearly visible, though the differences are no less striking. Both dictatorships emerged at a particular historical moment and owed something to historical forces which can usefully be compared. Both were representative in an extreme form of the idea of the 'super-personality', whose roots are said to lie in the work of the German philosopher-poet Friedrich Nietzsche. Both displayed obvious operational similarities, in the nature of the state security apparatus, the exploitation of the camp on a wide scale, the complete control of cultural production, or the construction of a social utopia on a mountain of corpses. These are not accidental comparisons. Both systems were aware of the other, and reacted to that knowledge. Hitler's dictatorship eventually launched a war of annihilation in order to eradicate Stalin's dictatorship. Both dictators also briefly reflected on what might have been if they had co-operated rather than fought each other. 'Together with the Germans,' Stalin is said to have remarked, 'we would have been invincible.'[10] Hitler, in February 1945, assessing the options he might have taken in the past, assumed that 'in a spirit of implacable realism on both sides' he and Stalin 'could have created a situation in which a durable entente would have been possible'.[11] Humanity was mercifully saved from this grim partnership because more divided than united the ambitions of the two men.

The dictatorships were not constructed and run by one man alone, however unrestricted the theoretical basis of his power. The recognition that dictatorship flourished on wide complicity, fuelled by a variety of motives from idealism to fear, makes greater sense of their durability and of the horrors both perpetrated. Both were regimes with wide popular backing as well as deliberate victimization. They were systems that in an extraordinarily short period of time transformed the values and social aspirations of their populations. They were both revolutionary systems which released enormous social energies and a terrible violence. The relationship between ruler and ruled was complex and multi-dimensional, not simply based on submission or terror. There is now no doubt that each dictatorship depended on winning the endorsement or co-operation of the majority of the people they ruled, and that they did not survive only from the fear that they inspired. They each developed a powerful sense of their own legitimacy, which was shared by much of the population; this sense of moral certainty can only be comprehended by unravelling the threads of the moral garb in which the two systems were dressed.

During the course of writing *The Dictators* it became clear how important it was to reconstruct as faithfully as possible the world in which they operated, however alien or fantastical much of it now appears sixty years later. To do this, it has been impossible to overlook the dictators' own words, either written or spoken. For most historical characters this might seem to be stating the obvious, but in these two cases there has been a reluctance to engage with the views of men whose actions appear to speak louder than their words. Hitler's writing is usually dismissed as irrational, muddled or unreadable. Stalin has always been regarded as an intellectual pigmy, with little or nothing to contribute to mainstream Marxism. Yet in each case the dictator said or wrote a great deal, and on an exceptionally wide range of subjects. They both saw themselves as figures on a very large historical canvas. They had views on politics, leadership, law, nature, culture, science, social structures, military strategy, technology, philosophy and history. These ideas have to be understood on their own terms, because they influenced the decisions both men took and shaped their political preferences, and, because of the nature of their authority, influenced in turn the wide circle of politicians and officials around them. They were not intellectuals (for whom neither man had much respect – 'They are totally useless and detrimental', Hitler once asserted[12]), but they did in each case define the parameters of public political discourse and exclude the ideas and attitudes of which they disapproved. Their role in shaping ideology was central, not marginal; so, too, was the role ideology played in shaping the dictatorships.[13]

These ideas did not develop in a vacuum. Neither dictatorship was imposed from outside like some alien visitation. Neither was a historical aberration, incapable of rational explanation, though they are often treated as if they were special, discrete histories, separated off from what went before and what came afterwards. The dictatorships have to be placed in context to understand the ideas, political behaviour and social ambitions that defined each. That context is both European and, more narrowly, Russian and German. They were the product of political, cultural and intellectual forces that were the common stock of early twentieth-century Europe. They were also, and more directly, the product of particular societies whose earlier histories profoundly shaped the character and direction of the two systems.

The common denominator was the impact of the First World War. Neither dictator would ever have achieved supreme power in two of the largest and most powerful world states without that upheaval. The war was massively traumatic for European society, but a more profound upheaval for German and Russian society than it was for the prosperous and politically stable states of western Europe and North America. Stalin was a creature of the Bolshevik revolution of October 1917, which transformed monarchist Russia in a matter of years; Hitler's radical nationalism was forged from the moral and physical disorder of defeated Germany as the old imperial order fell apart. Both states had much in common. They had both been defeated in the more limited sense that they had sued for an armistice because they could not continue the war effort. Failure in war opened the way in each state to a transformation of the political landscape. Russia went from Tsarist empire to communist republic in nine months; Germany went from authoritarian empire to parliamentary republic in less than a week. These changes provoked widespread political violence and economic crisis. The Bolsheviks only succeeded in consolidating control of the former empire in 1921, after four years of civil war and the establishment of an authoritarian one-party state. Germany experienced two different revolutionary movements, one communist, one nationalist; the second was used to defeat the first in the early years of the German republic, but was then stifled as the victorious Allies helped the republican government briefly to stabilize the new system. Both states experienced a hyper-inflation that destroyed the currency entirely and dispossessed anyone with monetary wealth. In the Soviet Union this served revolutionary purposes by ruining the bourgeoisie; in Germany it ruined a whole generation of German savers whose resentments helped to fuel the later rise of Hitler's brand of nationalism.[14] Both states were regarded as pariah states by the rest of the international community, the Soviet Union because it was communist,

Germany because it was held responsible for the outbreak of war in 1914. This sense of isolation pushed both states towards a more extreme form of revolutionary politics and the eventual emergence of dictatorship.

Germany and the Soviet Union reacted to the seismic shifts in politics and society ushered in by the Great War in ways that were determined by their different complexion. Germany was a more developed state, with two-thirds of its population working in industry and services, an established bureaucracy, an effective national system of schooling, and a world-class scientific reputation. Russia was predominantly rural, with some four-fifths of its people working in the countryside, though not all as farmers; welfare and education were both under-developed by the standards of the rest of Europe, and regional differences were more marked as a result of great variations in climate and the imperial character of Russian expansion across Asia in the nineteenth century. Yet in some important respects the division between Germany as a 'modern' state and Russia as a 'backward' state can be exaggerated. Russia had an extensive modern bureaucracy, a highly developed culture (Dostoevsky was particularly popular in Germany before 1914), a rapidly growing industrial and trading economy (which made her the fifth largest by 1914) and a small but high-quality scientific and engineering sector, among whose achievements was the first multi-engined heavy bomber, built in 1914.

In terms of political culture the gap was also less wide than might at first appear. Both were federal systems with a good deal of decentral-ized administration; neither was a full parliamentary state, though the Tsar enjoyed wider powers than the Kaiser; more important, in neither system did modern political parties enjoy the kind of political responsibility in government that prepared them adequately for what happened after the war. In each state there also existed a sharp polariz-ation in politics, and a language of political exclusion against the radical enemies of the empire; each state, dominated by conservative elites, had political police forces, and each regarded radical nationalism and Marxism as forces to be contained and combated. Though political liberalism of a more western kind existed in Russia and Germany before 1914, it was a powerful force in neither, and was soon swept aside in the 1920s. If the two states that gave rise to dictatorship had anything in common it was an ambivalent attitude to the western model of development. Under the unfavourable conditions of the 1920s important political forces in the Soviet Union and Germany turned their back on the victorious West and pursued a more revolutionary course. Dictatorship was not in either case an inevitable or necessary outcome of that history, but one that is comprehensible in terms of the political culture and moral outlook that preceded them, and of the failure of alternative models of historical development. Circumstances shaped the eventual emergence of dictatorship as much as the ambitions of their central actors. To recognize that the two dictatorships were products of a particular set of historical conditions reduces the temptation to see them only as a monstrous historical caesura, for which historians are obliged to use a special set of surgical instruments when they dissect them.

The structure of *The Dictators* is narrative in only a loose sense. It begins with the rise to power and ends with war and racism, but the matter in between is explored through a number of central themes essential to understanding how and why dictatorship functioned the way it did. Not everything is given equal weight. There is little here on foreign policy or on the actual course of the military conflict except where this is obviously relevant. Some familiar, and dramatic, episodes are not covered in detail where they do not contribute directly to the explanation. The thematic approach has one particular advantage. It has proved possible to disaggregate some important issues that are usually treated as a unity. For example, the 'Great Terror' of 1937–8 in the Soviet Union has many distinct components which have their own origins and trajectories. A coherent 'Great Terror' is a historical construct rather than a reality. The terror appears in most of the chapters that follow, a product of a number of distinct pressures and ambitions which combined to produce a deadly conjuncture in the mid-1930s. The same can be said of the Holocaust. German anti-Semitism also appears in every chapter, but the strands that contributed to genocide – biological politics, the world 'Jewish conspiracy', the war with 'Jewish-Bolshevism', issues of national definition and identity – become coherent only at the point in late 1941 and early 1942 when the key decisions were finally made to resolve these many different issues through systematic mass murder. Reality is more fractured and less historically clear-cut than much of the conventional narrative of the two dictatorships suggests.

Comparison is not the same as equivalence. Each of the thematic chapters has been structured in ways to make clear the contrasts between the two systems, not only the glaring differences of geographical and social circumstances, but less obtrusive differences in ideas, political practice and institutional development. There are clear differences between the two men: Stalin, obsessed with details of policy and the daily control of those around him; Hitler, a man of grand visions and sporadic, if decisive, interventions. No attempt has been made here to suggest that they were the same kind of personality (which they clearly were not), or that a generic 'dictator' or a generic 'dictatorship' can be deduced from just these two examples. There are, nonetheless, striking similarities in the ways the dictatorships operated, the way in which popular support was courted and sustained, the way in which state repression was set up and the legal system subverted, in the appropriation and exploitation of culture, in the expression of popular militarism and the waging of total war. For all the differences in historical circumstance, structure and political outlook, the patterns of complicity and resistance, terror and consensus, social organization and social ambition bear clear resemblances and, in some cases, a common European root. They were each the fruit of distinct violent, utopian revolutionary movements which defy neat political categorization.

There remains an essential difference between the two systems that no comparison should overlook. The Stalinist regime, and the Soviet system that produced it, was formally committed to building a communist utopia, and found thousands of communists outside the Soviet Union (whose varieties of Marxism often had little in common with the Soviet version or with Soviet reality) who were willing to endorse it because of their hostility to contemporary capitalism. Hitler and National Socialism hated Marxism, as did a great many Europeans outside Germany. Hitler was unswervingly committed to constructing a new European order based on racial hierarchy and the cultural superiority of Germanic Europe. Despite their common rejection of European liberalism and humanism, their revolutionary social ambitions, their collectivism – both exclusive and discriminatory – and the important role played by science in shaping their social ambitions, the ideologies were distinctively different, which explains the eventual hegemonic war between them. Soviet communism was intended to be an instrument for human progress, however imperfectly crafted it now appears, whereas National Socialism was from its very nature an instrument for the progress of a particular people.

This claim for the social ambitions of the Soviet Union may ring very hollow knowing what has now been revealed about the murderous character of Stalin's rule. Social development under Soviet dictatorship was, as the exiled Soviet writer Viktor Serge observed in his satirical novel of the Stalin years, completely ambiguous: 'There is sure progress under this barbarism,' reflects one of Serge's doomed communist characters, 'progress under this retrogression. We are all dead men under a reprieve, but the face of the earth has been changed.'[15] People in both dictatorships had to come to terms with the cost in political freedom or human dignity or truth that had to be paid so they could be included in the new society. Though the ideological destinations were distinctively different, each dictatorship exposed a wide gulf between the stated goal and the social reality. Bridging the gulf was a process that lay at the heart of dictatorship as it distorted reality and terribly abused those who objected. These processes were closely related in the two regimes, Soviet and German; they form the core of the analysis of dictatorship with which this book is chiefly concerned.

I

Stalin and Hitler:
Paths to Dictatorship

'. . . for a people's liberation from a great oppression, or for
the elimination of a bitter distress, or for the satisfaction of its
soul, restless because it has grown insecure – Fate some day
bestows upon it the man endowed for this purpose, who finally
brings the long yearned-for fulfilment.'

Adolf Hitler, *Mein Kampf*, 1925[1]

It is spring 1924. The plenum of the Central Committee of the All-
Union Communist Party (Bolsheviks) convened on 18 May a few days
before the Thirteenth Congress of the Party. That same day, Lenin's
widow handed over to the committee a sealed letter painfully dictated
by her invalid husband in December 1922. Five copies were made,
each closed with sealing wax. Lenin's instructions to his wife were to
hand the letter over to the next congress of the party in 1923, for he
was too ill to address the delegates himself, but she waited until after
his death a year later on 21 January 1924. The letter contained his
political testament. It was opened and read out to select members of
the congress delegations, and discussed by the Central Committee.
The testament is best remembered for Lenin's condemnation of Stalin:
'Comrade Stalin, having become General Secretary [in April 1922],
has concentrated unlimited power in his hands, and I am not convinced
that he will always manage to use that power with sufficient care.'[2]
Stalin knew the content even before it was opened; one of Lenin's
secretaries, worried by the potential impact of the testament, had
shown it to Stalin just after Lenin had finished dictating it. After
circulating it to a handful of party leaders, Stalin had issued a curt

instruction to Lenin's assistant to burn it, not realizing that four more copies had already been locked away.[3] What Stalin also did not know was that Lenin dictated an addendum a few days later, which might have ruined his political career. Angered by Stalin's coarseness and arrogance he advised the party 'to devise a means of removing him' and to appoint a replacement 'more tolerant' and 'less capricious'.[4]

Lenin's proposal, which might, so soon after his death, have carried some weight with the party faithful, was not put to congress. It was discussed at a closed meeting of the Central Committee. One eye-witness remembered Stalin sitting on the steps of the committee's rostrum while the testament was read out, looking 'small and pitiable'; though his expression was outwardly calm 'it was clearly discernible from his face that his fate was at stake'.[5] Grigory Zinoviev, backed up by the committee chairman, Lev Kamenev, who now sat at the table in Lenin's armchair, proposed that the testament be disregarded on the grounds that Lenin was not himself when he wrote it. Stalin, it is alleged, offered to resign, but was overruled by his allies in the party leadership. Some pretence was made at the Congress to encourage Stalin to take Lenin's censure seriously and to behave with greater decorum. Stalin was rescued not only by his own show of false modesty, but also by the realities of the leadership struggle after Lenin's death. Among the obvious successors little love was lost. Zinoviev and Kamenev did not want the flamboyant and gifted commissar for defence, Leon Trotsky, to inherit Lenin's mantle. By supporting Stalin, they thought they had an ally in the contest with their rival. It remains an open question whether a hostile reaction from the Central Committee and the Congress after reading Lenin's letter might have unseated Stalin, but there is no doubt that the decision to ignore Lenin's last request gave Stalin a fortunate political reprieve which he grasped with both hands. Twelve years later Zinoviev and Kamenev were executed after the first of the major Stalinist show trials.[6]

That same spring in Germany, at a court hearing held in the dilapidated classroom of a former infantry training school in a Munich suburb, Adolf Hitler waited to learn his fate for leading a coup the previous November against the Bavarian government. The *Putsch* of 9 November was intended as the prelude to an ambitious 'March on Berlin' to topple the republic and seize national power. The attempt was quashed in a hail of police bullets. Hitler threatened to shoot himself the following day in the house where he was hiding out, but was alertly disarmed by the mistress of the household, who had recently learned ju-jitsu.[7] He was caught that same day, and a few weeks later was sent for trial on a charge of high treason, alongside other leaders of his small National Socialist party and the veteran world war army commander Erich Ludendorff. The former Quartermaster-General of the German army had marched with Hitler towards the lines of policemen and soldiers blocking the path of the procession on 9 November and had not flinched even after the police opened fire and his companion had fled. High treason was a serious offence, which carried a possible prison sentence of twenty years' hard labour. After threatening a hunger strike, Hitler decided to exploit the trial as a way to publicize his brand of revolutionary nationalism. He was fortunate to be tried before the Munich People's Court (*Volksgericht*), which was scheduled for closure at the end of March 1924 alongside other emergency courts set up in the immediate post-war era. An extension of a month and a half was granted to allow what became popularly known as the 'Hitler-Trial' to take place in Bavaria rather than Berlin.[8] The trial lasted twenty-five days, from 26 February to the final judgment on 1 April. Outside the temporary courthouse armed troops stood guard behind rough barbed-wire barricades. Most of the space in court was taken up by three blocks of seats allocated to the press, who came to report the extraordinary political theatre that unfolded within.[9]

Hitler was allowed to talk at inordinate length in his own defence. He presented himself and his co-defendants as honest German patriots bent on saving Germany from the condition of 'permanent slavery' to which she had been betrayed at the end of the war in 1919 by those who had accepted the Versailles settlement. The presiding judge, Georg Neidhardt, was openly sympathetic with the nationalist right in Bavaria, and gave Hitler the oratorical space he needed. On the last morning of the proceedings Hitler dominated the court. The session opened just after nine o'clock and closed at 11.17. Although there were five other defendants, Hitler's final statement took up almost two-thirds of the morning. He ended with a rhetorical flourish on the theme of historical redemption: 'Might you pronounce your "guilty" a thousand times, this eternal goddess [History] of the eternal court

3

will laughingly tear up the petition of the state prosecutor and laughingly tear up the judgment of the court, for she pronounces us free!'[10] Even the prosecutor was seduced into describing Hitler as a man with a 'calling to be the saviour of Germany'. Neidhardt imposed a prison sentence of five years (three less than the state attorney had demanded) and a fine of 200 gold marks. He ought to have ordered Hitler's deportation since he was not yet a German citizen, but Austrian. Even a five-year sentence might have ended Hitler's political career, but, following a favourable report on Hitler's exemplary behaviour in Landsberg prison (where he was showered with food, drink and flowers from well-wishers, refused to take part in prison sports – 'A leader cannot afford to be beaten at games' – and dictated *Mein Kampf*), he was released on 20 December 1924.[11] Neidhardt was rewarded more generously than Zinoviev and Kamenev; following Hitler's appointment as Chancellor in January 1933 he was made president of the Bavarian high court, and at the celebration of his retirement in 1937 a letter from Hitler was read out praising the unstinting patriotism the judge had displayed throughout his career.[12]

Both Stalin and Hitler owed a good deal to luck in surviving the crises of 1924. Had the party leadership decided to honour Lenin's last wishes, Stalin's survival at the very heart of the party apparatus might have become more problematic; had Neidhardt been a less sympathetic jurist, Hitler might have ended up struggling to become Austria's *Führer*, not Germany's. Nevertheless neither man accepted that good fortune had any part to play in their political survival. In an interview with the American journalist Walter Duranty, Stalin reacted sharply to a question about how much his career owed to good luck. Uncharacteristically irritable, he banged his fist on the table: 'What do you think I am, an old Georgian granny to believe in gods and devils? I'm a Bolshevik and believe in none of that nonsense.' After a pause, he added: 'I believe in one thing only, the power of the human will.' Hitler habitually attributed the course of his career to the unseen hand of Fate. Writing just after the war, Albert Speer observed that Hitler 'had pieced together a firm conviction that his whole career, with its many unfavourable events and setbacks, was predestined by Providence to take him to the goal which it had set him'. This 'unshakeable faith', Speer continued, was Hitler's central, 'pathological' characteristic.[13] Yet the crises of 1924 are a reminder that the rise of neither man to dictatorship was in any sense preordained or irresistible. Hitler was no more the necessary outcome of German history than Stalin was the inevitable child of Lenin's revolution in 1917. Chance, as well as ambition and opportunity, governed their rise to supreme power.

There can be no doubt that Hitler and Stalin were very different personalities. There are superficial similarities, but any inferences drawn from the coincidence of certain factors in their biography have to be made with great care. Both, it is said, were beaten unmercifully by a tyrannical father: Stalin's a drunken cobbler, Hitler's a petit bourgeois martinet. Each formed a close attachment to their mothers. Both rebelled against an early religious education. Both were outsiders, socially and nationally, from mainstream Russian or German society, Stalin a Georgian, Hitler an Austrian. Each kept a strong accent that helped to identify them as distant from the mainstream. Both embarked on careers in the political underworld as terrorists, Stalin in the Russian Social Democratic Party before 1914, Hitler in the shady world of radical nationalism in Germany after 1918. Each served time in prison for their political beliefs. None of these comparisons was remarkable or unique. Hundreds of Europeans in the early part of the century were imprisoned for their beliefs; many were 'outsiders', whether on the left or the right of politics. Most Europeans had some kind of a religious education; few boys in the late nineteenth century avoided a beating, but regular and brutal abuse, which both Stalin and Hitler suffered, was also widespread. On most other comparisons of personality traits, daily habits or routines the two men were unalike.

Stalin's biographer has to overcome two hurdles: on the one hand there exists a wide chasm between the real history of Stalin's revolutionary career and the mendacious life that was constructed in the hagiographies of the 1930s; on the other, the surviving accounts of Stalin's personality gravitate wildly between the image of an implacably cruel despot, devoid of human qualities, and the portrait of a quiet, unassuming, warm human being, the kind of man whose knee, as the American envoy Joseph Davies put it, 'a child would like to sit on'.[14] Stalin was a man with different faces, and those faces changed through time. Capturing the 'real' Stalin is to recognize that the fixed points in any description are, in reality, determined by the time and circumstances when the account was made. The quiet, churlish, watchful Stalin that features in many accounts by contemporaries of his political adolescence grew into the avuncular, reserved and capricious statesman of the 1940s. The details of his early life are well known. Born on 6 December 1878 in the small Georgian town of Gori, in the distant Caucasian borderlands of the Russian Empire, the son of a shoemaker and a washerwoman, Stalin's was a remarkably unprepossessing origin for a man who climbed to the pinnacle of power fifty years later. He began life as a proletarian revolutionary should, disadvantaged and unprivileged. He attended a local school, where his remarkable memory struck his teacher as significant enough to get him a place at a seminary school in Georgia's capital, Tiflis. Here the thin-faced young boy, pock-marked from an early bout of smallpox, slightly bandy-legged, with a left arm four centimetres shorter than it should have been thanks to a debilitating ulcer, made his first contact with the Russian social democratic movement.[15]

He joined the movement aged eighteen and was expelled from the seminary. He was attracted to the uncompromising revolutionary outlook of Russian Marxism and the simple lessons of class warfare. He joined the underground movement and lived in its dimly lit and dangerous catacombs for the next seventeen years of his life. Here he learned to survive by erasing his own person; Josef Dzhugashvili, the name he was given at birth, became first 'Koba', then at times 'David', 'Nizhevadze', 'Chizhikov', 'Ivanovich', until finally, at some point shortly before the outbreak of war in 1914, he took the Russian word for steel, 'Stalin'. He was absorbed entirely in the struggle, read widely, wrote more than his later detractors were prepared to admit, and robbed banks to fund the cause. He was arrested at least four times and exiled to Siberia. He escaped, which from Tsarist exile meant little more than boarding a train and heading west. He was a delegate to party conferences abroad, including the Fourth Congress in Stockholm and the Fifth in London, but crucial for his later elevation was his decision to side with the Bolshevik or 'majority' faction when the Social Democratic Party split in 1903 over revolutionary tactics. Stalin remained in the branch led by the young lawyer Vladimir Ulyanov, whose *nom de révolution* was Lenin. In 1912, though in prison, he was appointed to the Bolshevik Central Committee, the governing body of the party, and remained a member, save for a brief sabbatical during the Great War, for the next forty years. In 1913 he began a four-year exile in Turukhansk on a government stipend of 15 roubles a month; here he passed much of his time hunting and fishing. A fellow exile in 1916 recalled the 36-year-old, by now an ageing veteran of the youthful revolutionary struggle: 'Thick-set, of medium height, a drooping moustache, thick hair, narrow forehead and rather short legs . . . his speech was dull and dry . . . a narrow-minded, fanatical man.' Stalin was disdainful and taciturn, his attitude towards the people around him 'rude, provocative and cynical'.[16] Stalin's personality was now set in terms still recognizable in the later dictator.

The revolution of February 1917 made Stalin. He returned from Siberia to Petrograd and became one of a cohort of experienced activists hoping to use the collapse of the Russian monarchy as a stepping stone to social revolution. The heroic version of Stalin's revolutionary contribution written in the 1930s has Stalin everywhere, in the thick of crisis. He became Lenin's closest collaborator and worked unstintingly to prepare the way for the Bolshevik seizure of power in October.[17] The reality was different, though Stalin was not as unobtrusive in the revolutionary year as later revisions of his role suggest. He placed himself behind Lenin's policy, announced in April 1917, of no compromise with the Provisional Government. His articles and speeches show a restless, uncompromising revolutionary, exposing the dangers of counter-revolution by less single-minded or opportunist socialists, and urging the party and the population to seize the initiative by transferring power to the toilers of Russian society. His narrow views on party unity and a single party line, characteristic of the 1930s, were fully developed in the ideological and organizational turmoil between the two revolutions. In the soldiers' *Pravda* in May he called for 'one common opinion', 'one common goal', 'one common road'.[18] It was Stalin who delivered the report of the Central Committee in July 1917 that called for a break with the other socialist parties, the Mensheviks and Socialist-Revolutionaries, for supporting the 'bourgeois' government. His speeches demonstrate a clear grasp of political realities and a consistently revolutionary course. When the final crisis of the Provisional Government arrived in October 1917

Stalin voted with the majority in the Central Committee in favour of a coup. His speech, recorded in a brief minute, ended with the following prescription: 'we must firmly and resolutely take the path of insurrection'.[19]

Some of this revolutionary enthusiasm may have been injected later when Stalin's collective works were published in the 1940s. The coup in October 1917 did not need Stalin for it to be successful, but there can be no doubt that in the bright air of politics above ground, Stalin flourished. No one has ever doubted that he was a committed revolutionary who, throughout 1917, saw revolution in terms of transferring power to ordinary men and women and destroying utterly the society of privilege that exploited them. This was his *métier*, his reason for living. When the first Bolshevik government was formed on 26 October 1917, Stalin was rewarded with the Commissariat of Nationality Affairs. This was, in the context of a disintegrating multi-ethnic state, an important post, which Stalin exploited to prevent the non-Russian borderlands, including his native Georgia, from seceding from the new revolutionary community. His firm policy brought him into major conflict with Lenin in 1921, who preferred a looser federation, and contributed to the unflattering references in the testament. Stalin was one of a dozen or so who formed the Bolshevik leadership corps. In October 1917 he was chosen as a member of a seven-man 'Political Bureau' of the Central Committee, forerunner of the formal Politburo set up in 1919, which Stalin also joined. In November he was named as one of four party leaders, together with Lenin, Trotsky and Yakov Sverdlov, who could decide on emergency issues without wider reference.[20] His office was close to Lenin's, and he worked for him as a political chief-of-staff in the critical early years of a regime confronting civil war and economic collapse. In 1919 he was given the additional post of Commissar for the Workers' and Peasants' Inspectorate (*Rabkrin*) to try to ensure that the state apparatus functioned effectively and to field the complaints of ordinary people. These many responsibilities made him an unsurprising choice as General Secretary of the party in April 1922, when it was decided that the apparatus that serviced and supported the Central Committee should be strengthened.

There are many conflicting accounts of Stalin during the early period of his public career, but most of them focus on Stalin as a political nonentity or lightweight. The origin of this damning judgement lies in the memoirs of a non-Bolshevik, Nikolai Sukhanov, published in 1922, who famously defined Stalin as a 'grey blur'; it was sealed by Trotsky's later waspish description of Stalin as the party's 'outstanding mediocrity'.[21] The view that Stalin's personality was flat and colourless and his mental powers limited was widespread. In exile together in Siberia during the war, Kamenev dismissed what Stalin had to say with 'brief, almost contemptuous remarks'.[22] Lenin, it was said, justified appointing Stalin to a government post in October 1917 because 'no intelligence is needed'; Stalin's name came last on the list of twelve recommended commissars drafted by Lenin.[23] The image of the dull bureaucratic time-server was captured in an early nickname, 'Comrade filing cabinet', 'tovarishch kartotekov'.[24] Stalin's own behaviour and personality lent weight to this image. He was outwardly modest and unassuming, lacking the flamboyance and intellectual confidence of many of his colleagues. His voice was remembered as 'toneless'; his oratorical skills were feeble, reading slowly from prepared scripts, with occasional pauses and stutters and just sufficient inflection to add emphasis where needed to texts that were methodical or formulaic. Later critics found that he talked like yesterday's *Pravda* editorial, which he had probably written.[25] At meetings he was often observed sitting to one side, saying little or nothing, smoking cigarettes or a pipe filled with foul-smelling tobacco, but watchful and attentive.

It is easy to see why so many of his peers underestimated the man sheltering behind the mask of awkward modesty and intellectual diffidence. Stalin was a master at dissimulation. Where some saw only a blank mind, there existed a shrewd, informed, cautious and organized intelligence. Stalin was not stupid. He read voraciously and critically, marking his books with queries, comments and underlining. In the 1930s his library counted 40,000 volumes.[26] He wrote extensively both before 1917 and in the 1920s, works and speeches that ran to thirteen volumes when they were published. His Marxism was thought out carefully and presented in apparently clear, logical, consistent and measured arguments. His prose, though later held up as a model of socialist clarity, was pedestrian and unimaginative, though just occasionally spiced with an arresting metaphor, made more so by the turgid passages that surround it. He favoured what he called in 1917

9

a 'creative Marxism', and the body of his own political thought shows a mind willing to adapt Marx to existing realities as readily as Lenin had done.[27] From the central issue of creating a communist society he never wavered. His view of communism was single-minded rather than narrow-minded. Early on in his public career he saw communism as a historical necessity, even though the real history confronted by the Bolsheviks in the 1920s made communism look simply utopian.

If Stalin was not stupid, neither was he an 'intellectual', a term that he turned into one of abuse. His personality in the 1920s was, by the standards of a Lenin or a Trotsky, more obviously plebeian. He was coarse and direct; he swore often, even at Lenin's wife, which occasioned the damaging addendum to the testament. Swearing separated off the real underclass in the movement from the educated and genteel Bolshevik intelligentsia, and became endemic to the new ruling group that Stalin surrounded himself with in the 1930s. Unable to suffer politeness, quite ungroomed socially (at an inter-Allied dinner in 1943 he had to ask in embarrassment how to use the array of cutlery besieging his plate), with little physical presence, Stalin resorted instead to a brusque, even autocratic manner.[28] Unassuming to those he wished to beguile, he could be irascible, vulgar, aloof or overbearing to subordinates, and implacably cruel to those he regarded for his own reasons as enemies. Stalin may have been by nature vengeful and insecure; he may have borrowed the culture of vendetta from his native Georgia; he was said by Kamenev to have read and re-read Machiavelli during his Siberian exile – nothing is quite certain about the origin of his view of political relationships.[29] But as a politician he brought to a high art the use and misuse of men.

There is a telling anecdote, which may have been embellished (since its source was Trotsky), that after a dinner in 1924 Stalin, Kamenev and the head of the security service, Felix Dzerzhinsky, challenged each other to say what they most liked. Stalin chose the following: 'The sweetest thing in life is to mark a victim, prepare the blow carefully, strike hard, and then go to bed and sleep peacefully.'[30] True or not, the story reveals a central element in Stalin's political make-up. His view of other people was cynical and opportunistic: those who were useful to him he indulged as long as he needed them, those in his way he did not confront but outmanoeuvred. His habit of watching was the habit of a predator understanding its prey. Stalin was secretive and disloyal, though quite capable of winning trust from the same individual he was in the process of bringing down. 'Watch Stalin carefully,' Lenin was said to have repeated. 'He is always ready to betray you.'[31] Stalin made few close friends, though he could be jovial and comradely when he chose to be so. Throughout his career he carried a profound distrust of other people that bordered later in life on the pathological. His instincts were, as a consequence, vengeful and capricious, even if his public persona in the 1930s radiated the image, according to one of many foreign visitors charmed by Stalin, of 'a pleasant, earnest ageing man'.[32]

Stalin was an evident product of the long years of underground politics, where trust was hard to establish, police spies and provocateurs everywhere, secrecy and self-reliance a second nature, and betrayal a daily fact of life. He absorbed the values of the underworld and brought them, honed by the harsh experiences of the civil war, to the practice of high politics. In the 1930s and 1940s, as the Soviet Union's dictator, he behaved as if infiltration, concealment, betrayal and bitter, party-splitting arguments over ideology and tactics – the material world of underground politics – somehow functioned still in the mature environment of a one-party state. Nonetheless the older Stalin became a more effective and settled personality than the angry young man of the underground. He exploited the limitation of his personality. His glumness became imperturbability; his awkward diffidence was transformed into unaffected modesty; his stilted speech-making evolved into a slow, deliberate, wry presentation, which could last for three or four hours. His facial expressions gave few clues to the state of mind beneath. Only his yellowish-brown eyes, which never lost the habit of darting to and fro, as though searching for the vulnerabilities of those he met, revealed to guests the alertness of the mind behind the outward calm.[33]

His working methods evolved with his personality. He was never the mild party clerk of popular myth, the bureaucrat-turned-dictator. Nikolai Bukharin, the editor of *Pravda* in the 1920s and a principal victim of Stalin's later purges, picked out 'laziness' as Stalin's chief trait, a view that fits ill with the image of a tireless official outdistancing his rivals by dint of administrative stamina.[34] Stalin worked tirelessly, but politics was his work. He neglected his commissarial duties to such an extent that he was publicly censured by Lenin. He disliked bureaucracy and in 1924 withdrew from both his commissariats. The routine work of the party secretariat was carried out by a large team of officials and assistants assembled by Stalin after 1922. Stalin was an activist and a revolutionary, and remained so as long as he was able. His personal routine in the 1930s has often been contrasted with that of Hitler, but there were resemblances. He rose late and retired late; meetings and correspondence punctuated most days, but he could also be absent at his dachas and in the 1930s took long vacations. The evenings might involve a dinner, perhaps a film in the Kremlin cinema, and late-night discussions. He drank little, usually a light Georgian wine, but enjoyed watching the inebriation of his guests. He welcomed the company of women, to whom he could be charming to the point of gallantry. Otherwise he would eat simply in the modestly furnished three-room apartment set up for him in the Kremlin. He married twice, but the suicide of his second wife in 1931, which deeply affected him, left him alone for the period of his dictatorship, though seldom celibate.[35] He never used his power for ostentation, which he disliked and ridiculed in others. His hatred of privilege remained with him, though the elder statesman and world politician of the years after 1945 dressed more formally and displayed a greater dignity than the party politician of the 1930s.

Any account of Stalin's life raises the question of what it was that impelled him forward. His first post-*glasnost* Russian biographer, Dmitri Volkogonov, assumed, as common sense might dictate, that it was power: 'the more power he accumulated and kept in his hands, the more power he wanted'.[36] Robert Tucker, in his classic biography, assumed that what Stalin wanted was not only power, but fame: 'Glory . . . remained his aim.'[37] Bukharin and Trotsky saw Stalin driven by profound defects of personality: envy, jealousy, petty ambitions.[38] Stalin left almost no account of his own motives. He once remarked during the civil war, at the successful defence of the Volga city of Tsaritsyn, that he would willingly sacrifice 49 per cent if he could 'save the 51 per cent, that is, save the revolution'.[39] He may have been driven by envy to ruin more successful or ambitious men around him, he may have liked the plaudits of dictatorship (though there is much evidence that he deprecated his extravagant glorification), but the one consistent strand in all his activity was the survival of the revolution and the defence of the first socialist state. Power with Stalin seems to have been power to preserve and enlarge the revolution and the state that represented it, not power simply for its own sake. The ambition to save the revolution became for Stalin a personal ambition, for at some point in the 1920s, perhaps after Lenin's death, Stalin came to see himself as the one Bolshevik leader who could steer the way with sufficient ruthlessness and singleness of purpose. His instinct for survival, his unfeeling destruction of thousands of his party comrades, his Machiavellian politics, point not to a personality warped by self-centred sadism, but to a man who used the weapons he understood to achieve the central purpose to which his life had been devoted since he was a teenager. The consequences of that singleness of purpose for Soviet society were profound and harrowing, but for Stalin they must have seemed justified by the one overriding historical imperative to construct communism.

Hitler's biography is a more open one. The details of his life are better known and his views on a great many issues have survived in his writing and recorded conversations. The Hitler legend elaborated in the 1930s was closer to the truth than the official version of Stalin's past. Yet the innermost thoughts, which might have been poured out in a diary or a regular private correspondence, remain as sealed with Hitler as they do with Stalin. Understanding Hitler's personality is an extraordinary challenge. The gulf between the awkward, undistinguished, very private individual and the public political Hitler, demagogue and prophet, seems all but unbridgeable, whereas in Stalin private character was reflected in public persona. So remarkable is the contrast in Hitler's case that there has always been speculation that he possessed some rare, scarcely understood psychological or physical element that fascinated and entranced both those in his direct physical orbit and the crowds he began to harangue from the early 1920s. Not even the supernatural was ruled out. Two British guests at a Hitler rally in Berlin in 1934, seated in the stadium just feet behind him, watched him captivate his listeners with the familiar rising passion and jarring voice. 'Then an amazing thing happened,' continued the account: '[we] both saw a blue flash of lightning come out of Hitler's back ... We were surprised that those of us close behind Hitler had not all been struck dead.' The two men afterwards discussed whether Hitler was actually possessed at certain moments by the Devil: 'We came to the conclusion that he was.'[40]

Adolf Hitler was born on 20 April 1889 in the small Austrian town of Braunau am Inn, the fourth child of his father's third marriage, though his three older siblings all died in infancy. His father was a customs official, and the family solidly lower middle class. He died in 1900, and Hitler's mother, Klara, in 1907. He attended local schools, where he showed some aptitude, but at his senior school in Linz he lost interest in learning. Like Stalin, Hitler was blessed with an exceptional memory. He left school at sixteen and moved from Linz to Vienna, where he hoped to become an artist or an architect. He was not, as he later claimed, in poverty, but lived from a sizeable legacy, and from the sale of his pictures, mostly townscapes, which were displayed in local galleries. In 1907 he was rejected by the Vienna Academy of Arts. His days were spent with an assortment of Viennese drifters, and his evenings at concerts, where he heard Wagner operas interpreted by the composer Gustav Mahler.[41] There are few clues to the later politician in the five years he spent as an adolescent in Vienna; he was interested in popular politics and attracted to Pan-German nationalism, but it is not clear at this early stage that his nationalism was also explicitly anti-Semitic. Yet the shy, polite, socially gauche young man, who could at other times be rudely opinionated, devious, self-centred and insensitive towards his friends, was recognizably the divided self of the 1930s.

In May 1913 Hitler fled from Vienna to Munich to avoid Austrian military service. The authorities caught up with him, but for almost a year he managed to avoid deportation until, in February 1914, the 24-year-old artist was forced to return to Salzburg, where the medical inspectors pronounced him 'unfit for military or auxiliary service' and free to return to Germany.[42] In August that year Hitler heard the announcement of the outbreak of the First World War standing in the Odeonplatz in Munich. Two days later he volunteered to fight with the German army, which found him fully fit. After a brief two months of training Hitler was sent to the campaign in Belgium and northern France. Like thousands of other young Europeans who flocked to fight,

Hitler confessed to being 'tremendously excited'.[43] The war made Hitler, as revolution made Stalin. Hitler was promoted to corporal after a month, and won the Iron Cross, Second Class after two ('The happiest day of my life,' wrote Hitler to his Munich landlord). The Iron Cross, First Class, was finally awarded in August 1918. He was personally courageous and exhilarated by the extreme nature of the demands conflict made of every soldier: 'risking my life every day, looking Death straight in the eye'.[44] That he survived for four years, while he watched thousands of his colleagues killed, was mere chance. The war was a far more formative influence than the years in Vienna. In *Mein Kampf* Hitler called it 'the greatest and most unforgettable time of my earthly existence'.[45] He merged himself psychologically with the struggle; he inured himself, on his own confession, to the demobilizing fear of death. There is no reason to doubt that as a young soldier who had experienced relentless years under the abnormal and brutalizing conditions of the front, the fact of defeat was unendurable. Hitler may have embroidered his description when he recalled the armistice night in which was born a fiery hatred for those who had surrendered Germany to the Allies, but throughout his subsequent career his political behaviour suggests a complete inability to separate his own psychological state from the historical reality he was trying to confront. He understood national defeat as if it were a direct personal humiliation. He bore within him an uncontrollable lust for vengeance that bordered at times on the deranged.[46]

Hitler began post-war life as an army agitator in Munich, employed to inform on radical politics and give the occasional talk about the dangers of Marxism and the Jews. In September 1919 he joined a small Munich political party founded on 9 January that year by a watchmaker, Anton Drexler, who had previously been a member of the Fatherland Party set up in 1917 by a cross-section of radical nationalist and Pan-German politicians to rally support for war. Hitler was member number 555 of the German Workers' Party (enrolment began with number 501); in November 1919 he was appointed its propaganda leader. In February 1920 the party changed its name to the National Socialist German Workers' Party, and the twenty-five-point party programme was published. The following year, on 29 July 1921, he was elected chairman of the party and in this capacity launched the

Putsch that landed him in 1924 in Landsberg fortress, turning him overnight into a national political figure. Impressions of the young politician vary widely. Those who heard him speak, or were drawn to his circle, described him in terms that might have been applied to a popular preacher with the power of revelation. 'There was an unknown fire that burned inside him,' recalled his close friend Max Amann.[47] But much of the testimony suggests that Hitler was regarded as a misfit; his appearance and behaviour when he was not in performance were dull and unremarkable, and his attempts to pose as the tribune of a betrayed people often ludicrous. The hallmark scruffy raincoat, the narrow dark moustache, the floppy fringe of hair, the pale and slightly puffy face, even the grey-blue eyes that could look vacant and expressionless, all made Hitler easily recognizable, but no less unprepossessing.

There is a revealing recollection of a meeting with Hitler in 1920 at the Munich villa of the composer Clemens von Franckenstein which captures the mixture of social insecurity and strident demagogue exactly. Hitler came with other theatrical and artistic guests. He wore gaiters and a floppy hat, carried a riding whip, though he could not ride, which he used as a prop by intermittently cracking it against his boots. He also brought his dog. He looked 'the stereotype of a headwaiter'; he sat with awkward reserve in the presence of his aristocratic host. In the end he snatched at a cue and began a political monologue in a style that stayed with him all his political life. 'He went on at us like a division chaplain in the army,' recalled another guest. 'I got the impression of basic *stupidity*.' Uninterrupted, Hitler began to shout instead of preach. Servants rushed in to protect their master. When he had left, the guests sat, so it was recorded, like a group of railway passengers who had suddenly realized they were 'sharing a compartment with a psychotic'.[48] The sense of profound awkwardness or embarrassment that Hitler could produce in anyone not captivated by the display made it difficult to silence him once a discourse was under way. Hitler learned to use this as a form of defence against contradiction or objection, battering his interlocutor into submission. Hermann Rauschning, a party leader in Danzig, observed later, in 1933, that Hitler's tirades represented 'a conquest of inhibitions', which explained 'how necessary to his eloquence were shouting and a feverish tempo'.[49]

Somehow, in the 1920s, Hitler succeeded in turning the unattractive private rant into the triumphant public oratory that became his most striking attribute as leader of the party and, later, as dictator. He was conscious of the impression he left, and had too little humour to brook criticism, inattention or laughter. According to Heinrich Hoffmann, his photographer, who was never allowed to picture Hitler wearing glasses, or in swimwear, Hitler 'had a horror of appearing ridiculous'.[50] The speeches were carefully rehearsed and choreographed. At first he wrote them himself, as Stalin did, but later dictated them. He would perform the speech as he intended his audience to hear it and expected his secretaries to reproduce it as he spoke, without notes. His speech for the tenth anniversary of the dictatorship was written this way. His secretary strained to hear the first minutes as Hitler began to talk slowly and quietly, pacing up and down. By the end he was shouting at the wall, his back turned, but completely audible.[51] He went over his speeches until he was satisfied that the total performance worked. From very early in his career he recognized the power of his thick, rasping voice with its strong Austrian accent, one moment deliberate and even-paced, next moment strident, noisy and indignant, occasionally, but just briefly, hysterical. He thought that speaking always outdid writing in politics: 'the power which has always started rolling the greatest religious and political avalanches in history,' he wrote in *Mein Kampf*, 'has from time immemorial been the magic power of the spoken word.' Political passions could be aroused only 'by the firebrand of the word hurled among the masses'.[52]

Among the many historical perspectives on Hitler, there is a widespread assumption that the content of his speeches mattered less than the form in which they were delivered. Hitler's ideas are conventionally treated as derivative and ill-thought out, the product of a lazy intelligence and dilettante tastes. *Mein Kampf* is widely regarded as a mixture of self-serving and mendacious biography and the turgid plagiarism of ideas other than his own. 'Hitler was the type of the half-educated,' wrote his former Economics Minister in 1945. 'He had read a tremendous lot but had interpreted all that he had read according to his own lights . . . without improving his knowledge.'[53] This is only a half-truth. Hitler did read to support his own ideas; his surviving library shows that he read widely in modern popular philosophy, political science and economics and carefully underlined or indicated in the margin passages that he liked or disliked. He read Schopenhauer; he read Lenin; he read Paul de Lagarde, the nineteenth-century apostle of the 'leader principle'; he read Houston Stewart Chamberlain, perhaps the most widely known of the generation of late nineteenth-century race theorists.[54] But it is evidently the case that Hitler thought out from these many sources his own world view, and his own ideas about political practice and behaviour. These became in most cases *ideés fixes*, and they coloured his later political career as much as Stalin's creative Marxism governed his. That Hitler was narrow-minded and selective, blind to rational or critical objections, intellectually naïve or banal does not reduce the value of his ideas as a historical source in understanding his rise to power and the dictatorship that followed. *Mein Kampf* remains an invaluable source for understanding Hitler's window on the world.

The world view is quickly sketched. He clung to its major contours all his life, though the details changed through time. Hitler believed that he was witnessing one of the periodic upheavals of world history, prompted by the French Revolution and the age of unbridled individualism and economic egoism which followed it. The division of European society into classes, which suited the interests of the bourgeoisie, created class envy and the worship of money, alienated the working classes from the nation and encouraged a revolutionary internationalism that threatened to undermine European civilization. The key to survival was to recognize that history progressed through racial rather than class struggle, and that a proper understanding of the importance of race (or nation) was the key to transcending the age of class and ushering in the national revolution.[55] The race, and the culture and social institutions that the racial community generated, had to be preserved above all. This was, in Hitler's view, the central task of politics. His radical nationalism went beyond simply reasserting the national interest, which was common to nationalists of all descriptions. Hitler wanted the nation to represent a particular kind of community, with 'race comrades' instead of classes, an economy controlled in the name of the people, and common blood as the defining form of allegiance, a combination deliberately captured in the term 'national socialist', which owed as much to Hitler's Austrian heritage as it did to the German milieu of radical nationalism.[56] The enemy of these ambitions was, principally, the Jew. At some point at the end of the war Hitler absorbed the popular anti-Semitic argument that the Jews were to blame for German defeat: either as Marxists preaching an ideology of festering social decomposition, or as capitalists pulling the strings of the world market, or as a biological challenge to the purity of blood, Jews and Jewishness became for Hitler a historical metaphor explaining Germany's crisis.[57]

His view of political practice was cynical and manipulative. The crowds moved by his rhetoric mattered only to the extent that they would give a revolutionary momentum to the political movement. Hermann Rauschning remembered a conversation with Hitler on the secret of his success with the crowd: 'The masses are like an animal that obeys its instincts. They do not reach conclusions by reasoning ... At a mass meeting, thought is eliminated.'[58] Hitler saw human relationships in terms of a struggle of personality: 'Mastery always means the transmission of a stronger will to a weaker one,' which followed, he believed, 'something in the nature of a physical or biological process'.[59] His view of race was narrowly exclusive, rejecting any human material that did not qualify. 'All who are not of good race in this world,' he wrote in *Mein Kampf*, 'are chaff.'[60] The contempt for much of humankind mingled with a deep hatred for anyone defined as the enemy. Hitler's language was always peppered with expressions that reflected the absolute quality of these obsessive animosities: 'eradicate', 'annihilate', 'destroy'. Anyone who crossed him became an outcast; like Stalin he had a long and vengeful memory. In Hitler's politics other people were either to be seduced and mastered, or excluded and eliminated.

These were the views and attitudes that Hitler carried with him as he was transformed from radical nationalist agitator into head of state and dictator. The mature politician displayed greater decorum and a self-conscious gravitas, though his outbursts of fierce temper persisted. The rages came to be used as a political instrument, turned on and off deliberately for the effect they had in negotiations, though Hitler continued to be capable of a complete loss of self-control that was quite unfeigned. He exhibited a profound nervous tension, which manifested itself in numerous medical conditions, both real and imagined.[61] Though he applauded decisiveness as a political virtue, he was observed often to be in a state of indecision and nervous uncertainty. He was equally capable of sudden moments of certainty and 'iron resolution' arrived at abruptly after days of hesitation or summoned up with an impulsive energy, but in either case rendered incontrovertible once they were pronounced. The appearance of a profound capacity for intuitive judgement was one of the techniques Hitler developed to reinforce popular perceptions of him as Germany's messiah. In his daily intercourse Hitler played on the distinction between his outward ordinariness and the exceptional nature claimed for his personality. Modestly but smartly dressed, Hitler would disarm guests and visitors with an apparently placid normality. His smiled greeting, followed by a handshake, 'the arm held straight and low', would then be followed by a silence both disconcerting and unexpected. This was the moment when Hitler would gaze fixedly into the eyes in front of him with a searching intensity. The effect could be hypnotic, as though a rabbit had been transfixed by the stare of a snake. The eyes remained, observed one of Hitler's interpreters, 'fixed steadfastly' on the victim; 'those who could withstand this gaze were accepted', those who wilted or were indifferent dismissed.[62]

The gap between the messianic pretensions of the dictator and the humdrum nature of the personality grew wider with time. The Hitler who could overturn the Versailles settlement, revive German military power, declare war on half the world and annihilate millions was incomprehensibly different from the small-minded, moralistic, petit bourgeois Hitler, whose favourite meal of the day was afternoon tea. The ordinary Hitler was fussy and fastidious, his cultural tastes limited and safe, his personal regime prim and ascetic, and became more so during the war. After 1933 Hitler led a life that was bound by banal routine. He became more isolated and his lifestyle habitual and carefully, even obsessively, controlled. After the suicide of his niece, Geli Raubal, in 1931, to whom he had a deep attachment, he kept women at a distance. The contrast with Stalin, earthy, coarse and gregarious, is striking. Hitler loathed smoking; Stalin smoked all his life. At Hitler's residences – the chancellery in Berlin and the alpine retreat in the Bavarian township of Berchtesgaden – there were separate rooms for smokers and non-smokers to retire to after meals. No one dared smoke comfortably in his presence. Hitler was almost a teetotaller (he allowed himself a little brandy in milk to help him sleep, and was observed with a glass of champagne the morning Japan attacked the United States at Pearl Harbor); he preferred mineral water at meals, infusions of camomile or lime flowers at other times.[63] Hitler was a vegetarian who hated hunting; Stalin ate generous quantities of meat, drank wine or vodka, and was said to be at his most relaxed with a shotgun or a fishing rod.[64] Hitler could be obsequiously polite, a gentleman with the opposite sex, and swore so seldom that when he cursed the Italians for surrendering to the Allies in September 1943 a secretary could still recall it in her post-war memoirs.[65] Though Hitler saw himself as an artist turned politician, his tastes were anything but bohemian. His favourite opera, despite Wagner, was Franz Lehár's *The Merry Widow*; he enjoyed the Wild West stories of the German author Karl May; among Hitler's cultural possessions discovered hidden in a salt mine in 1945 was a copy of the song 'I'm the Captain in my Bathtub'.[66]

Some explanation for the wide gulf between the dull private self and lowbrow tastes and the strenuous public life lived self-consciously in the midst of world history can be found by interpreting the motives for power. Hitler, like Stalin, did not pursue power simply for its own sake. The trappings of power seem to have meant very little; Hitler's brittle personality may have been psychologically buttressed by power after years of resentful failure, but it was power for a particular purpose. Hitler regarded the power he enjoyed as a gift of Providence for the German people, to be exploited only to rescue Germany from her state of debilitation and shame. 'This is the miracle of our times,' he told a party rally in November 1937, 'that you have found me, that you have found me among so many millions. And I have found you. That is Germany's fortune.'[67] Hitler saw himself as Germany's saviour; his personal power was a power assigned by world history, his humble beginnings and simple life merely a reflection of the fact that Hitler was chosen for his mission by a discriminating Providence from among the masses themselves. Shortly after the crisis that led to the purge of Ernst Röhm in June 1934, he made a grave claim in the Reichstag: 'in this hour I was responsible for the fate of the German people . . .'[68] Hitler was as single-minded about the salvation of the German nation as Stalin was about the survival of the revolution. He came to the

conviction that he was the instrument of history to secure that salvation, as Stalin was convinced that he was indispensable for building
communism. This profound sense of a destiny fulfilled is consistent
with Hitler's whole political career, from the early post-war years
when his speeches and writing betray an unsophisticated but uncon-
ventional mind wrestling with the lessons of world history, to the final
testament dictated in 1945 in which Hitler claimed his place in that
history: 'I have sown the good seed. I have made the German people
realize the significance of the struggle they are waging for their very
existence . . .'[69]

Hitler and Stalin were neither of them normal. They were not, as far
as can be judged, mentally unbalanced in any clinical sense, however
tempting it has been to assume that monstrous acts and madness
should go hand-in-hand. They were men with exceptional personalities
and an extraordinary political energy. They were driven in each case
by a profound commitment to a single cause, for which, and for
differing reasons, they saw themselves as the historical executor. In the
face of such a destiny, both men developed an exaggerated morbidity.
Stalin had a profound fear of death, and as he got older feared what
his loss might mean for the revolution he thought to protect. Hitler,
too, became consumed by a fear that he would not live long enough.
'Oppressed by a terror of time,' observed the Hamburg party leader
Albert Krebs, 'he wanted to compress a century's development into
two decades.'[70] Each was ruthless, opportunistic and tactically flexible,
their political practice focused uncompromisingly on their personal
survival. Both were underestimated by colleagues and rivals, who
failed to see that personalities so unobtrusive and modest when at rest
disguised a hard core of ambition, political ruthlessness and amoral
disregard for others when engaged in the work of politics. They were
both absorbed by the daily challenges of political life; both had to
construct their road to dictatorship through their own efforts, and in
the face of resistance. The singleness of purpose and powerful will
displayed by both men in the 1920s did not automatically bring them
to the position of unrestricted authority each enjoyed by the 1930s.
Dictatorship was not preordained. It is unclear exactly when Stalin
realized that his personal power might be a more certain route to
secure the revolution than collective leadership – perhaps in the final

months of Lenin's life. Only during the sojourn in prison in 1924 did Hitler come to identify himself, tentatively at first, as the figure sent to save Germany. Such self-images took time to evolve, and even longer to communicate convincingly to wider circles of party or public. The starting point for both Stalin and Hitler was to master their own parties before they could make any wider claim to power.

'We are against questions of Party leadership being decided by one person,' wrote Nikolai Bukharin in 1929. 'We are against the replacement of control by a collective with control by a person . . .'[71] The Bolshevik Party in the 1920s after Lenin's death was intended to be a party run by its central caucus. In the first few years after 1924 no one figure dominated in the Central Committee or the Politburo. Decisions on policy were taken after discussion in the central institutions of the party. Stalin's voice was one among many. The core of the central leadership consisted of Zinoviev, Kamenev, Bukharin, Trotsky and the premier appointed to succeed Lenin after his death in 1924, Alexei Rykov. Yet by 1930 all of them had been driven out of the party's top rank and Stalin was widely regarded as the 'boss', the single most important figure in the leadership. 'When he makes his entry,' claimed an early biography, published in 1931, 'backs straighten, attentiveness concentrates: the audience is in the presence of the great leader . . .'[72]

The five years between 1924 and 1929 were decisive in Stalin's career. During this period he exploited his position as General Secretary to outmanoeuvre and outdistance his colleagues. His first weapon was to appropriate the legacy of the dead Lenin. In October 1923, as Lenin's health slowly declined, Stalin suggested to other party leaders that Lenin's body should be embalmed after his death, but was ridiculed by Trotsky and patronized by Bukharin, who rejected the idea as 'an insult to his memory'.[73] However, by the time of Lenin's death four months later Stalin had succeeded in winning over a majority in the Politburo for the idea. Lenin's preservation was supervised by a Stalin ally, Felix Dzerzhinsky. Stalin was one of the two principal pall-bearers at Lenin's funeral. Three months later, at the Sverdlov party university in Moscow, he gave a series of lectures on Lenin's contribution to Marxist theory. Published as *Foundations of Leninism*, the work gave coherent shape to Lenin's thought and displayed Stalin as the one party leader who claimed to understand it fully. The book was dedicated to the generation of new young communists who were entering the party since the revolution, for whom a single, clear guide to the Leninist foundations of the revolutionary state was essential. Stalin succeeded in identifying himself in the popular mind as the single authentic executor of revolutionary theory.[74]

Stalin needed Lenin's legacy to underscore the importance of party unity and of party leadership. Stalin made the attack on factions and splitters a central plank in securing his primacy in the party. In his address to the Congress of Soviets, which met just two days after Lenin's death, Stalin gave pride of place to uncompromising solidarity: 'Departing from us, Comrade Lenin enjoined us to guard the unity of our party as the apple of our eye.'[75] In *Foundations of Leninism* Stalin powerfully reiterated Lenin's resolution passed at the Tenth Congress of the party in 1921 'On Party Unity', though his own writings from the revolutionary period were also full of exhortations for a single party line. The party required 'unity of will' and 'absolute unity of action'; this united will, wrote Stalin, 'precludes all factionalism and division of authority in the Party'.[76] Stalin almost certainly believed that this was the cornerstone of political strategy, but it also suited his own political interests to present himself as the apostle of unity. All those whose authority in the party he undermined in the 1920s were charged with factionalism, an accusation that Stalin introduced insidiously into his speeches and articles to isolate his rivals and to undermine the ground of their resistance.

Above all, Stalin identified himself with the wider interests of the party rank-and-file. Stalin had the advantage of his genuinely plebeian past. He always defined the party as an organization of workers and poor peasants, though much of its leadership was drawn from the more advantaged intelligentsia. His speech on Lenin's death began with the statement 'We communists are people of a special mould', but went on to define the ideal party members as 'the sons of the working class, the sons of want and struggle, the sons of incredible privation'.[77] In the Sverdlov lectures he gave notice that intellectuals and other petit bourgeois elements who entered the party as opportunists bent on ideological fragmentation should be expelled by true proletarians through 'ruthless struggle', a strategy that he pursued relentlessly against the party's intellectual elite in the years that followed.[78] Stalin was able to promote the proletarianization of the party partly through his growing control of personnel appointments in the party apparatus. Stalin's supporters were placed in the offices of the Central Committee and the secretariat responsible for organization and the allocation of appointments. Stalin was always alive to the details of the balance of power in committees and assemblies, although the extent to which this produced a tame Stalin party machine can be exaggerated. Most office-holders were formally appointed by the Central Committee, not by Stalin. A surer explanation for his success with the new party faithful lay in his ability to appear to be the one leader who consistently put the party first before political self-interest or ambition. In committee he developed a tactic that allowed him to have the final say, but to appear to be the spokesman of the party line. 'At meetings Stalin never took part in a discussion until it was ended,' reported Boris Bazhanov, who worked with Stalin in the Kremlin. 'Then when all had spoken, he would get up and say in a few words what was in effect the opinion of the majority.'[79] In larger congresses he posed as the voice of party common sense, and parodied, ridiculed and insulted any hint of deviation from a party line that was, in reality, capable of creative distortion when it suited him. Stalin came to be regarded by much of the rest of the party as the loyal representative of the party line and the most reliable champion of party unity.

There were, nonetheless, real issues of revolutionary strategy that divided the party leadership. Well before Lenin's death Trotsky, who had led Soviet forces during the civil war as Commissar for the Workers' and Peasants' Army, became identified with political positions that put him outside the Leninist mainstream. He remained wedded to a greater degree of party democracy and genuine debate over the party line; he was hostile to the New Economic Policy introduced in 1921 as a means to restore a functioning market economy in agriculture and small-scale trade, and instead favoured socialized food production and rapid, large-scale industrialization; finally Trotsky believed that the international work of the revolutionary movement ('waiting for the world revolution, by giving it a push') was essential to the task of building socialism in the Soviet Union, whose system would otherwise be merely 'temporary'.[80] Trotsky was an ambitious protagonist who, during 1924, began to distance himself from Leninism and reduce the legend of Lenin's role in 1917, at just the time that Stalin was cementing his own claim as Lenin's successor. Zinoviev and Kamenev, who had supported Stalin over Lenin's testament, also began to turn against him as they came to realize he might undermine their own prospect of leadership. However, by late 1924 Stalin felt strong enough to launch a savage public attack. In a lecture on 'Trotskyism or Leninism?' he accused Trotsky of founding a centre for the 'non-proletarian elements' in the party committed to destroying the proletarian revolution.[81] A month later Stalin published in *Pravda* a letter written by Trotsky in 1913, which had been discovered in old police files. The letter, to a Georgian Menshevik, was dismissive of Lenin: 'the whole edifice of Leninism at the present time is built on lying and falsification.'[82] The letter severely damaged Trotsky's moral authority in the party, and in January Trotsky asked to be relieved from his post as defence commissar.

For the following two years Stalin relentlessly pursued both Trotsky and his erstwhile allies Zinoviev and Kamenev. They came to be identified by Stalin and his supporters in the party as a 'United Opposition', bent on splitting the party by trying to push the pace of economic change and denying the ability of the Soviet Union to build an independent socialist system. Stalin's tactical skill lay in his close attention to details and the slow and deliberate way in which he allowed those details to gnaw away the reputation of his victims. In 1924, for example, he arranged that no further towns, farms or factories should be named after Trotsky. He ordered Trotsky's name to be removed from army political education pamphlets that described him as the leader of the Red Army.[83] Anonymous rumours and street libels were spread about Trotsky that played on the fact that he had been a Menshevik for most of his career, joining the party only in 1917. The same tactics were employed with Zinoviev and Kamenev, whose failure to endorse the party's call for an insurrection in October 1917 was turned by Stalin into an example of revolutionary sabotage. By the time of the Fourteenth Party Congress in December 1925 Stalin's rivals had been forced into a position of self-defence, which was weakened by the tendency of all three men to attack Stalin personally, where Stalin always appeared to attack them in the more abstract terms of their threat to the revolution. When Kamenev began a speech condemning Stalin as a party leader, he was shouted down by the congress delegates chanting 'Stalin! Stalin!'.[84] In a speech a year later Stalin opened with the disarming comment that he would try as far as he could 'to avoid the personal element in my polemic', and then launched into a savage personal attack on his target.[85] Stalin employed crude but effective rhetorical devices to avoid the appearance that this was simply a squabble amongst unruly aspirants for Lenin's throne. During speeches he often spoke of himself in the third person, as if he represented the party even against his own interests.

The opposition grasped one more desperate opportunity to try to outflank Stalin, though it was scarcely the 'cross-roads in history' later described by Trotsky in his autobiography.[86] In October 1927, already expelled from the Politburo and denied any state office, a Central Committee plenum convened to expel Trotsky and Zinoviev from among their number. Trotsky used the occasion to circulate a long letter on party history, in which he exposed those parts of Lenin's testament that damned Stalin and called for his removal. Copies were reprinted and distributed secretly. On 23 October 1927 there occurred a last dramatic confrontation on the floor of the plenum. Trotsky rose to denounce Stalin in passionate terms as the real danger to the party, a centralizing, bureaucratic ogre who should have been shed by the movement when Lenin had invited it to do so. He was interrupted by regular shouts of 'slander!', 'factionalist!'; others listened with little attention. Stalin, angry and defensive, aware that there had already been awkward questions about why Lenin's testament had been suppressed from wider circulation, gave a reply which, for all Trotsky's accusations that he could not articulate his thoughts or sustain an argument, displayed a controlled resentment of such power that he entirely outbid Trotsky's final plea. He welcomed the attacks on his person: 'I think it would be strange and offensive,' he told delegates, 'if the opposition, which is trying to wreck the Party, were to praise Stalin, who is defending the fundamentals of the Leninist party principle.'[87] He accepted unequivocally that he fitted the description from Lenin that he was 'too rude', but turned the argument on its head: 'Yes, comrades, I am rude to those who grossly and perfidiously wreck and split the party.' Stalin urged the plenum to accept that 'rudeness' was a necessary attribute, not a vice. He called for the expulsion of those who had denounced him, and asked the plenum to rebuke him for his earlier mildness towards them. To amused shouts of 'That's right, we rebuke you!' and stormy applause, Stalin carried the day.[88] The opposition was expelled from the Central Committee, and the following month from the party. In January 1928 Trotsky was exiled to central Asia and, a year later, to Turkey.

For much of the period of struggle against the so-called 'left opposition' Stalin had relied for support in the Politburo and Central Committee from a cohort of leaders around the party economist and editor of *Pravda*, Nikolai Bukharin. He was a popular figure in the party and the very opposite of Stalin. Unaffected, sociable, open-minded, polite, distinguished by his red hair, trim moustache and goatee beard, Bukharin had a remarkable intelligence and encyclopaedic knowledge. A teacher's son who studied economics at Moscow University, he joined the party in 1906, fled abroad in 1910 and returned to Russia after the revolution. A party radical in 1917 and during the civil war, in favour of revolutionary war to spread communism in Europe and a rigid and coercive economic mobilization, he changed in the years 1922–3 into a party moderate, in favour of the New Economic Policy and modest industrial development at a pace that the petit bourgeois tradesmen and peasant farmers could accept, a balance captured by his insistence that 'the city should not rob the village'.[89] He was politically inept and guileless, but during the mid-1920s Bukharin was widely regarded as the foremost thinker in the new Soviet system and a likely successor to Lenin. He was on friendly terms with Stalin, but had also been a close intellectual companion of Trotsky. His circle included the Moscow city party leader Nikolai Uglanov, the trade union chairman Mikhail Tomsky and the premier, Alexei Rykov. They did not constitute a clear faction or platform, but they shared a commitment to balanced economic growth and a stable post-revolutionary society, which has come to be seen as the acceptable face of Russian communism and a desirable alternative to Stalinist dictatorship.[90]

It may be that Stalin had always intended to bring down Bukharin because he saw him as a threat with his reputation as a popular and likeable figurehead, but the issue that divided them was doctrinal as much as personal. Stalin had never been happy with the implications of the change in economic direction made necessary in 1921. In a long conversation with Bukharin in 1925 on economic prospects, Stalin had stressed that the New Economic Policy would 'stifle the socialist elements and resurrect capitalism'.[91] Stalin favoured faster growth of industry to build a proper proletarian state, but in the contest with Trotsky's ideas on 'super-industrialization' he had to play a cautious middle position. In the winter of 1927/8, with the United Opposition defeated, Stalin was able to move towards the position of rapid industrial development for which he had always harboured a strong preference. This meant exacting a greater surplus from the peasantry; in the spring of 1928 Stalin finally pushed through emergency measures of grain collection that formed the first stage of the revolution in the countryside with which Stalin has always been associated. This was the point at issue with Bukharin, and it led to his elimination and the destruction of the remaining group of national leaders around him.

Stalin played a game of political chess with his new victim. Gradually Stalin dropped hints into his speeches to indicate that a new opposition faction was forming, opposed to the economic revolution. Lacking any broad power base or appeal to the more proletarian elements of the movement, Bukharin and his allies found themselves isolated. In Moscow, where Bukharin did have support, Stalin manipulated the city committee elections to gain a majority, and the city's leader, Uglanov, was sacked in November. In January 1929 Stalin finally defined Bukharin as the representative of a platform 'in opposition to party policy'.[92] That same month Bukharin made the mistake of reminding Stalin once again of Lenin's unflattering judgement. In a *Pravda* article titled 'Lenin's Political Testament', Bukharin outlined what he saw as true Leninism, and he accused Stalin of undermining Lenin's commitment to party democracy. In a statement issued on 30 January Bukharin boldly stated that the 'Stalinist regime is no longer tolerable in our party'.[93] Stalin worked to achieve a majority in the Central Committee and then demolished remaining resistance. At a Central Committee plenum in April Bukharin's supporters attacked Stalin and his record in the party. To each personal slight Stalin remarked 'this is trivial', but then concluded in his own defence by citing Lenin's damning indictment of Bukharin in the testament, that his Marxism was scholastic and unorthodox. The committee voted to remove the 'right opposition' from their posts. Bukharin lost his Politburo seat in November 1929 and the editorship of *Pravda*. He, Rykov and Tomsky were forced to write an obsequious letter confessing their errors. Tomsky was removed from the chairmanship of the trade unions, and Rykov's place as premier was taken by Stalin's close ally Vyacheslav Molotov, in December 1930. The 'right opposition' as an organized platform was largely a fiction, but there did exist real differences of opinion over political strategy. Stalin did not believe that Bukharin really understood the revolutionary drive at the core of Leninism. In an angry exchange on the eve of Bukharin's expulsion Stalin snarled at him: 'Your lot are not Marxists, you're witch-doctors. Not one of you understood Lenin!'[94]

In December 1929 Stalin's fiftieth birthday was celebrated country-wide; the list of Politburo members, which had always been given in *Pravda* in alphabetical order as an indication of the collective leadership of the party, was changed to distinguish Stalin as 'Lenin's first pupil' and the party's guide. This was a first and necessary step to establishing the personal rule of the 1930s.[95]

Hitler's mastery of his party took place in a very different context. There was no question that he was prepared to tolerate 'collective leadership' in any formal sense. When he emerged from Landsberg jail in December 1924 his object was to restore his position as undisputed party leader forfeited during his incarceration. Hitler, unlike Stalin, had to master a restless party far from any prospect of power, while Stalin was a senior member of a governing party. The period in prison left Hitler in a difficult position. His party was banned in all German provinces except Thuringia.[96] In July 1924 he gave up political activity altogether until his release at the end of the year. Outside, the small groups of National Socialists split into different factions, some joining a radical nationalist umbrella organization in northern Germany, others a small pan-German association in Bavaria. The first group, the National Socialist Freedom Party, chose the elderly General Ludendorff as a substitute leader in Hitler's absence, but the Bavarian wing would not accept him. The movement that greeted Hitler when he returned to politics in 1925 was tiny and divided; the party publishing house in Munich, the Eher-Verlag, employed only three people.[97] Hitler reorganized the party largely around allegiance to his own person. His first public address on 27 February 1925 was in the same beer cellar in Munich where the *Putsch* had been launched. Thousands surrounded the hall, unable to get seats. Inside he called for loyalty to his personal authority. Local nationalist leaders, who clustered around Hitler when he had finished, 'reached out the hand of reconciliation', one witness observed, by placing themselves under him 'unconditionally'.[98]

The following two years were a watershed in Hitler's career. He began his renewed ascent to party domination from unpromising foothills. The radical nationalist wing of German politics was small and fractured. Hitler enjoyed the unqualified support of a few thousand Bavarian nationalists; the northern German organization was dominated by revolutionary nationalists who were less enthusiastic about Hitler's authoritarianism; Ludendorff was still a large personality on the fringes of the movement; and there existed the looming figure of an ambitious young pharmacist, Gregor Strasser, who, during Hitler's absence, had began to act as the 'trustee' for the imprisoned *Führer*. Strasser was Bukharin to Hitler's Stalin. Though he is often portrayed as representing a 'northern' wing of the party, Strasser was a Bavarian, born in 1892 into a devoutly Catholic family. His father was a minor civil servant. Strasser, like Hitler, fought throughout the war, also winning the Iron Cross First and Second Class; like Hitler he regarded the war as the central experience of his life. His personality was, in many ways, the antithesis of Hitler's. Strasser was naturally gregarious, cheerful, open and humorous; his large frame and strong voice, his ready smile and air of unforced authority made him a born leader and a popular figure both inside and outside the party. His view of politics was shaped by the trench experience: a powerful revolutionary nationalism that rejected the old imperial order entirely in favour of an organic national community, based not on class divisions and privileges but on common labour for the nation. 'Because we had become nationalists in the trenches,' he told an audience in 1924, 'we could not help becoming socialists in the trenches.'[99] Hitler's movement was a natural home for Strasser. He joined the party in 1922, and in March 1923 took over a Bavarian regiment of the party's paramilitary organization, the *Sturm-Abteilung* (SA). When Hitler was in prison Strasser emerged as one of the leading members of the radical nationalist bloc set up to contest elections in the absence of the banned National Socialist party, and was elected to the Reichstag in December 1924. Unlike a number of prominent right-wing radicals, Strasser decided to rejoin Hitler in February 1925, but to do so as 'a colleague' not a 'follower'.[100]

Hitler accepted Strasser's collaboration in rebuilding the emaciated party, but he remained unambiguously committed to the idea that he alone could lead it to future triumphs. This conviction had hardened in the months in prison, fed by the sycophantic attentions of his secretary and amanuensis Rudolf Hess, who shared prison with a leader whom he dubbed 'the Tribune'. After the re-founding meeting, Hess noted his master's 'unshakeable belief in his own destiny'.[101] Hitler's view of party organization rejected ideas of party democracy favoured by some party officials; his conception of the movement was based entirely on the idea that he was the potential saviour of Germany whose ideas and political behaviour should not be subject to the will or advice of others. On 14 February 1926 Hitler summoned the senior party leadership to a conference in the northern Bavarian city of Bamberg. Among the leaders sat party radicals who preferred a revolutionary path to power. These were loosely organized in a work group set up the previous July by Strasser to co-ordinate the strategy of the party outside Bavaria; Strasser had also drawn up a modified version of the party programme of 1920, which he hoped the party might adopt. Hitler spoke relentlessly for five hours. He insisted that the party programme was unalterable ('the foundation of our religion, our ideology'); he rejected a path of revolutionary struggle in favour of a parliamentary path to power; above all, he made it clear that he was indispensable to the success of the movement.[102] Five months later, at the first congress since the party was re-founded, held on 4 July in the city of Weimar, Hitler's personal authority in the party was accepted by the majority and his position as party *Führer*, a title formally approved at Weimar, rendered for the moment unassailable.

There is no doubt that Hitler exploited his personal appeal and charismatic image ruthlessly in order to clear away any possible challenges to his leadership and to simplify the process of working out party strategy. Nonetheless there existed real differences in the party over major issues of doctrine and tactics. Strasser represented the party circles who favoured an assertive 'Germanic' form of socialism: 'We are socialists,' he wrote in 1926 in a pamphlet setting out the future tasks of the movement, '[and] are enemies, deadly enemies of the present capitalist economic system.'[103] There were circles equally hostile to the idea that the party should focus all its efforts on becoming the nationalist representative of the urban working classes. This difference was reflected in a disagreement over tactics: the 'socialist' wing favoured more uncompromising hostility to parliament, the moderates argued for the legal path to power. It is tempting to compare Hitler's approach to the argument with Stalin's tactics in the debate on Soviet industrialization. Both men opposed the radical option because it was associated with party circles that represented a possible threat to their own political position. Hitler largely shared, and continued to promote in the 1930s, the Strasserite view that the old economic order was bankrupt and unjust, and should be replaced by an economic system based on 'achievement' for the nation.[104] But he recognized that uncompromising revolutionism would alienate electors and might, in the end, sweep him away as well.

The strength or coherence of the opposition Hitler faced can be overstated. There was no equivalent of the 'United Opposition', since most party leaders came to accept that without Hitler the party would look indistinguishable from the other radical nationalist splinter groups jostling for survival. The evident differences in political outlook and ideology reflected the heterogeneous origin of the many nationalist groups and associations that were absorbed into the party. Such differences could be overcome only through uncritical allegiance to Hitler, just as the no-less-diverse ideological positions in the Soviet communist party of the 1920s were eventually united by reliance on Stalin's party line. Both parties were broad ideological, political and social coalitions, not monolithic movements. Hitler devoted a large part of his political energy before 1933 to the task of managing the party, smoothing over differences, expelling dissidents, binding local party leaders with a constant round of conciliatory visits, face-to-face encounters and uplifting talks. There were, nevertheless, objections to the idea that a party could rely chiefly on the manufactured myth of a German messiah. Artur Dinter, a consistent opponent of a Hitler-centred movement, and former party leader in Thuringia, introduced a resolution at a major party conference on organizational reform in August 1928 intended to limit Hitler's authority with the appointment of a party senate. In the subsequent vote Dinter was the only one to register approval. In October he was expelled from the party, and Hitler sent a circular letter to all party leaders to sign, confirming their rejection of any limitations on his authority. All returned their signatures.[105]

Other serious challenges were provoked by the revolutionary wing of the movement, whose views were reinforced when the 1928 Reichstag elections showed that the legal path to power had achieved strikingly little. The National Socialists won only twelve seats, and polled fewer votes than the nationalist bloc had done in 1924. Party policy shifted from the struggle to win the workers away from Marxism to a search for votes among farmers and small-town middle classes. The urban strategy was not abandoned, but the socialism became less obtrusive. This raised particular problems with the paramilitary wing of the movement, since the SA was predominantly urban and had a large proportion of manual workers in its ranks. It was re-founded later than the party, in autumn 1926, and led by a former Freikorps leader, Franz Pfeffer von Salomon. He became a champion of an SA organization independent of the central party apparatus, and he shared the uneasiness of many SA leaders about the overblown personal leadership imposed on the movement by Hitler.[106] In 1930 that resentment boiled over into an open rupture. In July 1930 Gregor Strasser's brother Otto, who represented a small group of uncompromising anti-capitalist revolutionaries, seceded from the party with a formal announcement that 'the socialists leave the NSDAP'.[107] In August von Salomon resigned in protest at the failure of the party to support the aspirations of the SA to become a proto-army to rival the established armed forces. Hitler calmed the subsequent crisis by declaring that he would take over the SA himself, and offering some small concessions. However, the following spring a full-blown rebellion broke out among the SA in eastern Germany, led by Walther Stennes, who briefly overturned the party leadership in Berlin on 1 April and declared the SA in control, only to be swept aside after an emotional appeal by Hitler on the absolute necessity for loyalty. A subsequent purge suspended all SA members, subject to political vetting. Hitler centralized control over SA appointments in the party headquarters, and forced all SA leaders to swear a personal oath of obedience to him. The SA was finally taken under the control of another former Freikorps leader, Ernst Röhm, who had been Hitler's superior officer in 1919, and a fellow defendant in 1924.[108]

Hitler faced one remaining obstacle before he was offered the chancellorship in January 1933. Though Gregor Strasser never denied his personal loyalty to Hitler, he remained a colleague rather than an assistant. In 1928 he was made Organization Leader of the party, and rationalized and streamlined its structure and procedures to cope with the large increase in party members provoked by the economic crisis after 1929. He was a popular and widely respected politician and the party's most effective and notorious parliamentary figure. From 1930 onwards he began to shift away from the more socialist elements in his thinking to focus on the need for real political power. He explored contacts with other political parties and their spokesmen; unlike Hitler, who would brook no compromise coalitions that failed to deliver him the chancellorship, Strasser feared that Hitler's stubbornness would lose the party any opportunity of power, shared or otherwise. In the summer of 1932 failure loomed as large as success and Strasser became impatient. In October he advocated a bloc with the trade unions and other nationalist parties: 'whoever wants to go along with us is welcome'.[109] He negotiated with the Catholic Centre Party; he negotiated with army leaders, and became an ally of Kurt von Schleicher, the defence minister and an advocate of a broad national-social alliance to which leaders other than Strasser were also attracted. When the election of November 1932 showed a sharp slump in the National Socialist vote, Strasser moved towards an open rupture, hopeful that he could bring important elements of the party with him, or persuade Hitler to accept a coalition and collective leadership. On 3 December Schleicher offered Strasser the vice-chancellorship in a coalition government; after ten years in opposition there was evident temptation. In a tense face-to-face confrontation in the Kaiserhof Hotel in Berlin, Hitler ordered Strasser to stop any further negotiations. Instead of splitting the party and joining the government, on 8 December Strasser abruptly resigned and withdrew almost entirely from politics, unable himself, at the last moment, to deny the importance of Hitler to the national revolution he wanted to see fulfilled in Germany.[110]

Strasser and Bukharin have both come to be regarded as genuine historical alternatives to the dictatorships that swept them both aside. Had Strasser succeeded in reducing Hitler's authority, or replacing him altogether in a nationalist coalition early in 1933, the personal dictatorship might perhaps have been averted. Had Bukharin exploited the position described in Lenin's testament as 'the favourite of the entire party' to promote his own version of the revolution successfully, then Stalin might have been unseated or forced to accept a partnership.[111] There can be no doubt in either case that the history of Germany and the Soviet Union would have been different if they had won their parties' confidence. But it is important not to see either alternative as the acceptable face of communism or National Socialism, moderate shadows of the fanatical reality. Strasser was an extreme anti-Semite, a bitter opponent of Marxism, a revisionist in foreign policy and an anti-parliamentarian in his politics. Bukharin began his Soviet career on the extreme revolutionary wing, and his commitment to economic caution did not make him any more of a democrat; as a senior member of the Politburo he gave his support to the full range of authoritarian provisions introduced in the 1920s. They were not so much alternatives to Hitler or Stalin as varieties.

In the event neither Bukharin nor Strasser was a strong enough personality to overcome the grave weaknesses confronting all opposition to the future dictators. Both men were direct and uncomplicated personalities, whose straightforwardness was a handicap in dealing with the covert or devious political manoeuvrings they confronted in Stalin and Hitler, both of whom relished the art of politics and were ruthless in its practice. Neither had the ambition or singleness of purpose or willpower to seize the leadership, as they demonstrated through their limp reaction to the confrontation when it eventually came. Their doctrinal differences with their dominant rivals have been exaggerated by historians keen to highlight other possible outcomes to the crises of the 1920s.[112] Above all, neither man succeeded in convincing either the party mass or the wider population that they could deliver key political pledges more effectively. Hitler and Stalin both appealed over the heads of the cohort of party leaders to the mass of ordinary members who came to identify them as indispensable to the party's future. Strasser and Bukharin were condemned to a grisly fate, nonetheless, for representing a genuine sentiment in both parties critical of the style of leadership adopted by Hitler and Stalin. Strasser was arrested at his home on 30 June 1934 on the pretext that he was conspiring to overturn the state, and was shot by an SS captain a few hours later in a cell in the secret police headquarters in Berlin. Bukharin clung on to a limited career in the party, humiliated by Stalin for eight years until he was finally made to stand trial in March 1938 as a counter-revolutionary terrorist. Condemned to death, he wrote a brief note to Stalin on the night he was shot, 15 March 1938: 'Koba, why do you need me to die?'[113]

Mastery of the party was not enough to explain the coming of dictatorship, though it was an essential precondition. The transition to personal dictatorship can best be explained as a product of two periods of intense crisis, one in the Soviet Union, one in Germany. The crises were historically distinct but both were revolutionary in character. In the Soviet Union the years from 1928 witnessed an exceptional social upheaval with the onset of collectivization, the Five-Year Plans and a prolonged assault on the culture, ideas and expertise defined as 'bourgeois' which the regime had tolerated or exploited in the 1920s. The so-called 'second revolution' returned to the radical trajectory and social conflicts of the early post-revolutionary years of civil war so as to speed up the creation of socialism. In Germany the exceptional social and political crisis ushered in by the slump in 1929 spawned a nationalist revolution which rejected entirely the political system, culture and social values of the republic and sought an authentic 'German' national community. This revolution was also hostile to 'bourgeois' values, which were regarded as western, cosmopolitan and divisive. National regeneration was regarded as a return to the trajectory of national self-assertion interrupted by war and defeat.

Hitler and Stalin emerged from the political in-fighting of the 1920s as the supreme representatives of the two revolutions and of the circles in both populations that endorsed and participated in them. Neither upheaval was simply orchestrated by Stalin or Hitler, though both played important roles in promoting crisis and exploiting the political opportunities that it offered. The revolutions were the result of social forces and historical circumstances that were difficult to predict or to control; they generated violence and political conflict on a wide scale. The instability of both societies, deep in the throes of crisis, encouraged the search for figures of political stature who could be trusted to end the disorder, while, at the same time, securing the revolutionary outcome. Stalin and Hitler relied in the passage to full dictatorship on popular support and a widespread perception, even among those who were not eager converts, that they might be a source of political stability, a representation of revolutionary order. Neither man could usurp power in any crude or direct way. The dictatorships were the fruit of a unique historical conjuncture in which the pretensions of the two leaders matched, if imperfectly, the aspirations of those they sought to represent.

The 'second revolution' in the Soviet Union was the product of the evident paradox at the heart of the post-revolutionary settlement in 1921, when Lenin pushed through the New Economic Policy. The decision to permit private agriculture and private trade had obvious repercussions in a society where four-fifths still worked the land and many 'workers' were still craftsmen and small shopkeepers. The decision in the same year to end factionalism and stamp out any alternative political forces left a predominantly urban revolutionary party, formally committed to building a modern workers' state and large-scale industry, in charge of a community where modernizing socialism was difficult to impose. This contradiction was unavoidable once it was recognized by much of the party that revolutions were not going to occur elsewhere in Europe in the 1920s. The battles between Trotsky and Stalin were about the implications to be drawn from this reality. Trotsky represented a narrow constituency that saw the revolution ultimately doomed if it could not spread; Stalin was the leading spokesman of the rest of the party, which came to accept that the exemplary construction of socialism in the Soviet Union was the prelude to encouraging revolution elsewhere. Trotsky's defeat left the party to face the logic of its own position. Social and economic conditions had to be radically and swiftly transformed if the Soviet Union alone were to demonstrate what a socialist society looked like. In a speech to industrial managers in February 1931, echoing comments he had already made at the Central Committee in November 1929, Stalin presented economic transformation as a fundamental question of revolutionary survival: 'We are fifty or a hundred years behind the advanced countries. We must make good this distance in ten years. Either we do it, or we shall go under.'[114] Stalin reminded his listeners that the transformation of the Soviet Union was the model for the world proletariat, who would look at the modernized state and declare, 'There you have my advanced detachment, my shock brigade, my working-class state power, my fatherland!'[115]

The process of constructing the model socialist state was in reality violent, socially destructive and often chaotically supervised. The turning point came in the years 1927 and 1928. During the winter of 1927 grain supplies to the cities fell sharply. In November and December they were half the levels of 1926.[116] The grain crisis was caused partly by the failure of industry to supply enough consumer goods; peasants held on to their grain to increase their bargaining power with the state. Yet at the same time the state economic planners had produced the outlines of what became the First Five-Year Plan to try to raise overall levels of industrial production, particularly heavy industry, more rapidly. The grain crisis compromised the industrial plan; it also demonstrated that the market forces at the heart of the New Economic Policy threatened to shift the balance in Soviet society to the large segments engaged in private trade and production. By the spring of 1928 there was a rising tide of party opinion against peasant speculators, or kulaks, and in favour of more rapid industrial growth. In January extraordinary measures had been introduced under Article 107 of the Criminal Code on speculation, in order to extort more grain from the peasantry and punish those who held on to it. During 1928 the Five-Year Plan was begun with an emphasis on heavy industry rather than consumer goods; party agents were sent out to the villages to reduce the threat of hoarding from farmers resentful at the lack of things to buy. 'We cannot allow our industry,' Stalin announced early in 1928, 'to be dependent on the caprice of the kulaks.'[117]

The result was an end to the social collaboration and moderate economics of the 1920s. In the countryside party activists, resentful of a peasantry that might hold the revolution to ransom, launched a new class war against any peasant who was defined as a capitalist, often on the most slender evidence. The poorer peasantry and rural workers were mobilized to push through a social revolution in the countryside. The traditional village assembly, or *skhod*, was exploited as an instrument to isolate the 'rich' peasants and opponents of state policy, and increase their quota of state supplies to levels that would eliminate their market power. Traditional carnival and rituals of humiliation were encouraged against kulaks, who were paraded through the village streets, made to wear tar collars, or publicly beaten.[118] The strategy to use the peasantry itself to push through what the party wanted – called by Stalin the 'Urals-Siberian method', where it was first successfully practised – produced a revolutionary momentum that opened out in 1929 into open and violent class warfare and, by the end of the year, a formal policy of 'dekulakization'. During the year the party moved in favour of collectivized agriculture – large state-organized farms in place of small private peasant plots, and the destruction of the independent market in agricultural products. Mass collectivization began in October; a month later Stalin announced what he called 'the Great Turn' in the process of building a modern, socialized agriculture. He saw the crisis as central to revolutionary survival: 'Either we succeed,' he told the Central Committee plenum, 'or we go under.'[119] On 27 December 1929 Stalin finally called for an uncompromising policy of 'liquidating the kulaks as a class'. The language of violent class warfare permeated all rural policy.

The renewal of revolutionary class war moved forward on other fronts, encouraged by those party leaders who, like Stalin, feared that the era of the New Economic Policy would lead to a slow revival of capitalist society. In March 1929 the maximum industrial plan was confirmed by the Supreme Soviet, marking the onset of a programme that physically transformed the Soviet Union and led to a mass exodus from the countryside into the new industrial centres. The party used the social upheaval to launch an aggressive proletarianization of Soviet society. Hundreds of thousands of new party members were drafted in from the factories, swamping the older generation of pre-revolutionary Bolsheviks. Cultural production was controlled to exclude more experimental forms of expression, which were defined as formalist or bourgeois, and authentic proletarian art patronized. The cultural revolution was one facet of a sustained war against the remnants of the bourgeois class and bourgeois values, which was signalled in March 1928 with a show trial of engineers from the Shakhty coal mines in the southern Ukraine. The fifty-three engineers were accused of deliberate sabotage and counter-revolutionary 'wrecking' activities. Most were found guilty and five were executed. The trial marked an end to the period in which so-called bourgeois experts were regarded as welcome collaborators. In April 1928 Stalin argued that the trial exposed a new form of bourgeois counter-revolution 'against pro-letarian dictatorship'. The fear of renewed 'offensives against Soviet power' from domestic capitalist forces was used as the excuse to harass, arrest, imprison or execute thousands of the old intelligentsia at work in industry and bureaucracy, including a number of the country's top economists and statisticians who had made possible the industrial planning of the late 1920s.[120]

The effects of the renewed revolutionary class war were, in the short term, disastrous. The old generation of experts was replaced by hastily trained cadres of proletarian substitutes. Industry expanded, but in a frenzy of half-finished projects, unfulfilled quotas and poor-quality output, which encouraged successive waves of persecutions for wrecking. The most damaging consequences were felt in the countryside, where millions of peasants resisted the sudden transformation of their existence violently, turning parts of the rural Soviet Union into a state of undeclared civil war. Equipment and buildings were destroyed or burned down. Farmers destroyed their livestock rather than let them fall into the hands of the state: between 1928 and 1933 the stock of cattle fell 44 per cent, the number of sheep by 65 per cent, the number of horses, vital for ploughing in a pre-tractor age, by more than half. Grain output fell, but central procurement rose, leaving much of the countryside desperately short of food.[121] Peasant resistance provoked a spiralling violence as communist party members, officials and police-men fanned out into the provinces from the cities to combat peasant sabotage. Violent clashes and acts of terrorism rose from a little over 1,000 incidents in 1928 to reach 13,794 by 1930. That year there were 1,198 murders and 5,720 attempted murders and serious assaults, most directed at party activists and peasants who voluntarily joined the collectives. Riots and demonstrations multiplied as well, reaching more than 13,000 in 1930, involving, according to official estimates, an aggregate of more than 2.4 million peasants.[122] The authorities wilted under the assault and in March 1930 Stalin announced a temporary pause, blaming communist activists for being 'dizzy with success' in the countryside. By October the proportion of collectivized farms in Russia dropped from 59 per cent to 22 per cent.[123] The regime regrouped, and the following year collectivization was pushed through by force: more than 2 million farmers were deported to the labour camps of the north and east, and 2 million more deported within their own region.[124]

In 1932 the crisis finally produced massive famine. In a vast swathe of population from Kazakhstan through the northern Caucasus to the Ukraine, as a consequence of excessive procurement levels, loss of manpower and horses, peasant demoralization and resistance, an estimated 4–5 million died of malnutrition and hunger-induced disease in the winter of 1932/3. That year the crisis ushered in by the second revolution reached its peak. Industrial output slowed and inflation rose. A strike movement broke out among the Moscow industrial workforce in April in reaction to food shortages. The situation in the Ukraine, where the party insisted on extracting the maximum quotas as a punishment for peasant resistance, was so desperate that it prompted Stalin to remark, in an urgent letter written in August 1932, 'we may lose the Ukraine', though his reaction was, characteristically, to insist on tougher measures against saboteurs and criminals.[125] In March 1932 a group of communists grouped around Martem'ian Ryutin, a Central Committee candidate, produced a 200-page document titled 'Stalin and the Crisis of the Proletarian Dictatorship', which analysed in detail the failures of the second revolution. In September the so-called Ryutin platform circulated to the Central Committee a 'Letter of the Eighteen Bolsheviks', which called on all party members to get the country 'out of the crisis and dead end' through 'the liquidation of the dictatorship of Stalin and his clique'.[126] They were all expelled from the party in October 1932, though their views reflected a broader anxiety in the party about the rural crisis. Though Stalin called for Ryutin's execution, the Politburo demurred. Stalin had to accept a prison sentence for him instead.

The regime kept control during the crisis of the second revolution partly because of the popular support given to what was widely regarded as a real effort at last to bring the revolution back to its essential socialist principles. Mass resistance in the countryside was also accompanied by greater enthusiasm from poorer or landless rural workers, who co-operated in denouncing those alleged to be kulaks. The new cadres of more proletarian party members, who formed brigades of revolutionary 'shock workers' in the factories, or toured the villages bearing revolutionary good tidings, welcomed the new direction because of the advantages it promised to a working class that had seen little benefit from the New Economic Policy. Molotov, who became premier in 1930, encouraged the *'unleashing of the revolutionary forces* of the working class and poor and middle peasants'.[127] The chief beneficiary of this movement was Stalin himself, who deliberately threw his weight behind the new wave of class war. He came to be seen as a figure indispensable to the party and the country during the critical years of revolutionary reconstruction. 'It happened,' complained Bukharin in 1936, 'that he became a kind of symbol of the party, and the lower ranks, the workers, the people believe in him.'[128] Even those who disliked what Stalin represented were drawn to support his revolutionary activism. 'I cannot bear inaction,' wrote Ivan Smirnov, a former Trotsky supporter. 'I must build!'[129] Stalin succeeded in establishing his authority as a symbol of solidity in a changing world. Even in 1932, at the height of the crisis, this sense that he was necessary outbid Ryutin's belief that he was not. 'Loyalty to Stalin,' wrote Alexander Barmin later, 'was based principally on the conviction that there was no one to take his place . . . to stop now or attempt a retreat would mean the loss of everything.'[130] The first revolution was identified with Lenin; the second revolution was a broad movement forward to complete the processes unleashed by the first. It came to be identified as Stalin's revolution, and his claim to supreme authority grew with the crisis itself.

The 'national revolution' in Germany has always been identified with Hitler and National Socialism, since the end product was a Hitler dictatorship; hence the efforts made by historians to identify the reasons for the party's electoral success and the precise nature of its social constituency as explanations for its rise to power. Yet in reality Hitler became the representative of a much broader movement of political nationalism, which emerged well before the National Socialist

43

party became electorally significant, and which collaborated with National Socialism after it became a mass movement. Significant numbers of Germans who were not convinced party members or voters welcomed the end of the Weimar Republic and the rebirth of Germany; the early years of Hitler's government were years of nationalist coalition. Hitler came to power only because a group of conservative nationalists around the ageing president, Field Marshal Paul von Hindenburg, elected as a symbol of the nation in 1925, judged, reluctantly, that Hitler was essential to carry the broader national revolution through to its conclusion. The years of crisis after 1929 were exploited by National Socialism more successfully than any other nationalist movement, but in the main that success rested on the ability of the party to speak a language of social revival and national assertion that enjoyed a wide popular resonance. Hitler depended for his ultimate political authority on the representativeness of his appeal.

The economic crisis can only ineffectively be conveyed as a series of sharply falling graphs. In the course of four years the world's second industrial power saw trade fall by more than half, two-fifths of the workforce jobless, the rest on short time or falling wages, shopkeepers and small businesses impoverished, the state near the point of declaring its bankruptcy.[131] Most Germans had experienced only two or three years since 1919 in which economic growth reached pre-war levels, and the sudden economic collapse that followed produced profound shock waves of social hardship and political crisis. The Reichstag coalition, made up of liberals and social-democrats, fell apart in 1930 in arguments about social security payments, and from then until 1933 government was based on emergency presidential decree and administrative action by the Chancellor. Reichstag elections in 1930 and in the summer of 1932 only illustrated the decline in the electoral fortunes of moderate opinion and the rise of parties committed to anti-parliamentary and extra-parliamentary activity: the combined share of the vote taken by National Socialism and the German Communist Party rose from 31 to 52 per cent between the two elections. The revival of communism played an important part in rekindling popular memories of the post-war German revolution; the economic collapse inspired wide fears that the end of capitalism might mean social disintegration and civil war. 'It was depressingly familiar,' wrote one witness, '[it] had the smell of 1919 or 1920.'[132] Politics was perceived to be about fundamental issues concerning the future of Germany. The political violence and rising crime that marked the years after 1929 were viewed as symptoms of a profound moral crisis. In 1932 alone 155 people were killed in political clashes, including 55 National Socialists and 54 communists.[133] Thousands more were wounded or threatened. Gregor Strasser was suspended from parliament for assaulting a fellow deputy. The police system struggled to contain the violence. Guns were regularly used to settle disputes. At times Hitler himself carried a loaded pistol. Political sentiment degenerated into expressions of deep resentment and violent hatreds.

Nationalist forces in Germany often spoke about the need for 'revolution'. It was a word frequently used by Hitler to describe the destruction of the existing order and the party's plans to build a new Germany.[134] However, nationalism was divided in the 1920s, not only by personality, but by differing versions of the nation. Until 1929 National Socialism was a small part of the nationalist political establishment, distrusted by other nationalists. 'Most people looked upon us as immature hotheads,' explained an SA man in an essay for the social researcher Theodore Abel written in 1934, 'sacrificing their time and money for a chimerical cause.'[135] Hitler, recalled another witness, 'was still widely regarded as a somewhat embarrassing figure with a dismal past'.[136] The nationalist constituency included the German National People's Party, led from 1928 by the press baron Alfred Hugenberg, the German People's Party and a fringe of smaller parties and lobby-groups that shared much of the outlook of German nationalists. There were paramilitary and veterans' organizations numbered in millions, the largest of which was the Stahlhelm, or Steel Helmet, led by Franz Seldte. There were trade associations and unions, like the large German-national Commercial Employees Association, whose views were broadly nationalist. There was an influential radical nationalist intelligentsia whose spokesmen shaped the expectations for national regeneration and social reform, very few of whom were National Socialists. These many groups were united by hostility to republican politics, an enthusiasm for authoritarianism, militarism and treaty revision and, in some, though by no means all cases, the desire to construct a new social order.

This was the diverse nationalist constituency that struggled to find a political solution after 1929 that would avoid a return to parliamentary rule, and could protect the nation from communism, while reviving Germany's economy and power. In the summer of 1929 a national 'Reich Committee' was established, combining Hugenberg's nationalists, Seldte's veterans and the conservative nationalist Pan-German League under Heinrich Class. Hitler's movement was also linked to it, but during the course of 1930 and 1931 National Socialism sought to outbid its allies by promoting a more strident and radical nationalist message. Many of the smaller movements merged with Hitler's party, or instructed their members to vote for National Socialist candidates. By 1932 National Socialism, by dint of its effective propaganda and organization, had become the largest element of the nationalist movement. The central appeal rested on the projection of Hitler as the man Germany had been looking for. In November 1932 the election posters declared: 'Hitler, Our Last Hope'. The drop in the National Socialist vote in those elections did not necessarily reflect the ebbing of enthusiasm for a national rebirth, only in the ability of Hitler to deliver it.

Hitler was rescued by the growing fear among conservative nationalists, many of whom were repelled by the street violence and populism of the movement, that the unresolved political crisis of 1932 would open the way further to communism and civil war. He was invited to form a 'Cabinet of National Unity' on 30 January 1933, in which National Socialists would have only three seats. Hitler's appointment did not usher in dictatorship, but it did signal the point at which a national revolution moved from aspiration to reality. During the following year and a half a process that was described as 'co-ordination' (*Gleichschaltung*) took place across Germany; thousands were removed from their posts because they had not been part of the national revolutionary struggle, and thousands more ended up in prisons and camps, victims of a wave of unrestricted brutality and intimidation. The civil war mentality distinguished not between National Socialists and others, but between nationalists and others, and the violence that scarred the first months of the regime was directed at the alleged enemies of the nation, principally socialists, Jews and Christians who actively opposed the movement. The national revolution was driven forward by a broad coalition of nationalist forces that began to crystallize into a more specifically National Socialist version of the revolution only with the abolition of all other political parties in the summer of 1933. Even after this, the coalition with conservative nationalists persisted. The nationalist banker Hjalmar Schacht held the important economics ministry, Seldte became Minister of Labour, and the finance minister was a career bureaucrat. None was a member of the party.

Hitler was evidently the chief beneficiary of the nationalist revolution. The development of a mass following for the party legitimized his claim to represent that revolution. Hitler's popularity with around one-third of the electorate in 1932 gave him a stronger claim to political leadership than any other figure in the nationalist movements. Strasser's hesitancy in challenging Hitler in 1932 stemmed from his private belief that he would damage the prospects for Germany's future if he split the party. Like Stalin, Hitler played on fears of class war to enhance his claim. The more he preached the threat from communism, a tactic that peaked in the spring of 1933 when he won the legal means to destroy the communist movement, the more Hitler emerged in the popular mind as the man who would save Germany. Crisis was essential to that purpose. In 1929 Strasser had recognized this reality when he said 'we want catastrophe ... because only catastrophe ... will clear the way for those new tasks which we National Socialists name'.[137] Even those who distrusted Hitler, like the Catholic politician Franz von Papen, who was instrumental in persuading the President to appoint Hitler to the chancellorship, thought that only Hitler held the key to the rallying of the fractured nationalist forces in 1933. In the March 1933 election the National Socialists won 44 per cent of the vote, but the nationalist parties together won a majority – 52 per cent. Many nationalists retained their distaste for the social radicalism and racial violence of Hitler's followers, but very few wanted Germany to return to the economic chaos and political civil wars of the early 1930s.[138] In this sense Hitler's widening authority, like Stalin's, rested on evaluations that were both positive and negative. For those who endorsed dictatorship, some did so with enthusiasm, some with reluctant and calculated complicity, from fear that the alternative might plunge the system backwards, losing the gains of the second revolution or undermining the salvation of the nation. Prolonged crisis was inseparable from this process; in each case the ambitions or the sense of destiny that drove Hitler and Stalin forward allowed them at the critical juncture to pose as the representative of all those who hankered for change with stability. Without crisis it is more difficult to believe that either politician could have been transformed into the larger person of dictator.

When did they become dictators? This is a question that has no clear historical answer. Stalin's dictatorship is conventionally dated from the point in December 1929 when his birthday was extravagantly celebrated in the pages of *Pravda*. This point certainly marked his mastery of the party machine, but he was still regarded among the public as one among a number of party figures, perhaps *primus inter pares* but not yet the unrestricted authority of the later 1930s. When one of the porters at a Moscow university was asked in 1929 whom he meant when he talked about the 'new Tsar', he named the Soviet president, Mikhail Kalinin.[139] The projection of Stalin as the figure who would build the new socialist community evolved during the second revolution, but he was never called 'dictator' except by his detractors. Hitler's dictatorship, by contrast, appears to rest on more solid ground. His appointment as Chancellor on 30 January 1933 is often taken as the starting date of a 'Hitler dictatorship', even though he was chancellor in a cabinet composed largely of non-National Socialist nationalists, under a President who retained emergency powers to overrule his chancellor, or to prorogue parliament if he had good cause to do so. Hitler's government was granted emergency powers to make laws under an enabling act passed in March 1933, but it was unclear whether this was a right to be exercised by Hitler alone or by the government as a collective body.[140] Hitler's unrestricted personal authority, which he had long exercised in his party, also evolved in the course of the national revolution. Historians have plucked at different dates to define the moment of dictatorial power for both men, but the choice clearly rests on the definition of personal dictatorship.

A good case can be made for the year 1934 as the turning point. Ten years after the crises which might have spelt the end of their political careers, Stalin and Hitler dominated the congresses of their

48

respective parties. Both occasions were used as opportunities to sum up the recent revolutionary past. The communist party's Seventeenth Congress, the 'Congress of Victors', which assembled in January 1934 in Moscow, heard Stalin announce that anti-Leninism was over: 'there is nothing left to prove and, it seems, no one to fight. Everyone can see that the line of the party has triumphed.'[141] In a bizarre charade Stalin permitted all his former enemies, including Zinoviev and Bukharin, to make speeches filled with fawning praise for Stalin ('*our* leader and commander', insisted Kamenev).[142] In September 1934 the National Socialists celebrated the 'Congress of Unity, Congress of Power'. Hitler's triumphant address was read out by the party leader of Bavaria, Adolf Wagner, to an ecstatic crowd in the Zeppelin Field in Nuremberg. 'The German form of life,' intoned Wagner, 'is definitely determined for the next thousand years. For us, the unsettled nineteenth century has finally ended.'[143]

Yet it was not the two congresses in 1934 that signalled the coming of personal dictatorship, but two murders. The first was the murder of Ernst Röhm, the head of the SA, who, on Hitler's orders, was shot in a cell in Stadelheim prison in Munich on the afternoon of 1 July 1934. The second was the assassination of the popular secretary of the Leningrad communist party, Sergei Kirov, on 1 December 1934, as he walked to his office in the Smolny Institute. In each case, Hitler and Stalin used the deaths as an opportunity to demonstrate that they were now above the law; this expression of unrestricted personal power was the essential element that defined the authority of the two men as dictatorial.

The appointment of Röhm to head the SA in 1930 had been made to reward an old party fighter and to end the mutinous grumbling of the revolutionary elements in SA ranks. The result was quite the reverse. Röhm built up a much larger and more militarized organization, and saw himself, like Strasser, as a colleague rather than a mere lieutenant. In 1933 the SA was unleashed in a wave of official and unofficial violence against the enemies of the movement. SA men expected the national revolution to reward them with office or employment, but many remained unemployed; there was talk of the SA taking over police functions, even the role of the German army, which, with only the 100,000 men permitted under the Versailles settlement, was now only one-twentieth the size of the party militia. Hitler hesitated to alienate his conservative allies in the national coalition and reined back the SA in the summer of 1933. But over the following year, Röhm's ambitions for a greater national revolution expanded. He openly courted the idea of an SA army and SA air force to take over the Reich's defence; SA men began to applaud the cult of their own leader rather than Hitler. By the summer of 1934 the mood of much of the SA was one of resentful radicalism.[144]

Hitler faced a difficult choice, since the SA had grown up with the movement and symbolized its long and bloody struggle for power. Threats from the army leadership in June 1934 that they would act if he did not, pushed him reluctantly to accept that he should eliminate Röhm. The secret police had a thick dossier on the flamboyant homo-sexuality of the SA leadership, and of Röhm's contacts with von Schleicher, the conspirator who had tried to lure Strasser into govern-ment in December 1932. Hitler, supported by the rest of the inner leadership, planned a coup for a day late in June 1934 on the pre-text that Röhm was about to overthrow the government and deliver Germany into the hands of foreign powers (an accusation worthy of the Stalin purge trials). On 30 June, amidst scenes of extraordinary drama, SA leaders were dragged to prisons in Berlin, Munich and other cities and there shot by men of the *Schutzstaffel* (SS), Hitler's bodyguard. Schleicher, Strasser and a host of other prominent critics and opponents were murdered on the same day on the pretext that they too were part of the plot. A total of eighty-five murders have been identified, but the number was almost certainly greater as party leaders settled old scores.[145]

Hitler himself arrested Röhm. He dashed by plane to Munich and by car to Bad Wiessee, to the hotel where Röhm and Edmund Heines, SA leader from Breslau, were staying. Hitler burst into the SA chief's bedroom brandishing a revolver and screamed at him, 'You are under arrest, you pig.' The startled Röhm was handed to two SS men, who thrust clothes at him and bundled him into a waiting coach for a journey to Munich's Stadelheim prison. He was among the last to die. Hitler found it difficult, now in colder blood, to order the death of a very old comrade. He remembered the time ten years before when he and Röhm were on trial together in Munich for high treason: 'He once stood next to me in the People's Court,' he complained to Hess.[146] The following day he decided to allow Röhm to shoot himself. A gun was left in his cell and he was given ten minutes to decide. Hearing no shot, the SS commandant of the local Dachau concentration camp, Theodor Eicke, entered the cell and shot the bare-chested Röhm at point-blank range. That day the army leader, Colonel Werner von Blomberg, announced to the army that Hitler had saved the nation from treachery 'with soldierly decisiveness'.[147] At a cabinet sitting on 3 July a law was agreed that the murders without trial were 'lawful for the necessary defence of the state'. The Justice Minister, Franz Gürtner, an elderly lawyer and a non-National Socialist, confirmed that what Hitler had done was unquestionably legitimate.[148] In the Reichstag on 13 July Hitler explained the fantastic dimensions of what was, in reality, a non-existent plot. He announced that everyone should know 'for all time', that whoever raises a hand against the state 'his fate is a certain death'. The Reichstag president, Hermann Göring, who had organized the purge of the SA in Berlin, told the assembled delegates that 'We all approve, always, whatever our *Führer* does.'[149] Hitler was publicly and explicitly above the law, able, without restriction, to order life or death.

Kirov may have been murdered on Stalin's orders, but the weight of evidence so far assembled suggests that he was the victim of a lone assassin. The significance of Kirov's death, like that of Röhm, is that he represented the last possible barrier to Stalin's unrestricted exercise of authority. Sergei Kostrikov, a clerk's son, who chose the name Kirov as his Bolshevik pseudonym, was a little younger than Stalin, with a long and respectable revolutionary career that brought him to head the Leningrad party in February 1926 as Stalin's emissary to root out the left opposition. He was an inspiring leader, hard-living (and drinking), energetic, good-looking with a wide, boyish face, and a speaker who was, according to one who heard him in his early days in Leningrad, 'passionate, convincing, inspiring'.[150] During the 1930s he was regarded as a loyal Stalin supporter, and, like Röhm, made extravagant displays of that loyalty in public. His private view was more critical. Before the Congress of Victors, it is claimed that a group of senior Bolsheviks tried to encourage him to compete for Stalin's post, but he refused. At the Congress, however, he sat not on the stage, which his office allowed, but with the Leningrad delegation. When he gave his speech, laced with the usual hyperbole about Stalin, it was without notes, fiery and exciting, whereas Stalin's was solid and unglamorous. Kirov received a tumultuous standing ovation. After the votes for the Central Committee elections had been cast, it was announced that Stalin had received 1,056 out of 1,059 votes, and Kirov 1,055. But later testimony revealed that perhaps as many as 289 ballots with Stalin's name erased and Kirov's approved were destroyed, which would have left Kirov as a clear winner, and Stalin's authority challenged, though not overturned. Stalin never put himself up for election again as General Secretary, and from then on neither party nor state documents referred to him by this title.[151]

During 1934 Stalin became more wary of Kirov. The ovation he had received at the congress was normally reserved only for Stalin. A few weeks later Stalin invited Kirov to come to Moscow to join the Central Committee secretariat there, under closer scrutiny. Kirov bravely refused, and his decision was supported by others in the Politburo. Kirov seems to have had little fear of Stalin. In 1932 he had argued in defence of Ryutin, when Stalin had wanted him executed. He disagreed at times with Politburo decisions. He was incautious in his private remarks about Stalin.[152] During the year Kirov was overburdened with assignments from Moscow. Stalin insisted on seeing him regularly, and in August, against Kirov's inclinations, he had to accompany Stalin for a long holiday at Stalin's dacha at Sochi. Kirov's health declined. When he returned from supervising the harvest in Kazakhstan in October 1934, he found that his office on the third floor in the party headquarters in the Smolny Institute had suddenly been moved, without his knowledge, from the main corridor to a room around the corner at the far end of a long passageway, next to a small side-staircase.[153] It was here, just after 4.30 in the afternoon, that Kirov was shot in the neck at close range by Leonid Nikolaev, an unemployed party member with a poor record of discipline and a starving family, who had tried to get Kirov to re-employ him without success. He was a shabby and desperate assassin, whose diary entries showed him wrestling for weeks with the idea of assassination in terms reminiscent of Dostoevsky. The truth may never be known, but no evidence has emerged that links Stalin directly with Kirov's death. That same evening Stalin rushed by train to Leningrad, and the following day took the unusual step of interviewing Nikolaev on his own, ostensibly to get him to confess the names of his accomplices. Three weeks later Nikolaev was executed.[154]

Stalin used the Kirov murder to force through an extraordinary decree. That same day, without the usual discussion in the Politburo, or the ratification by the Supreme Soviet, as the constitution required, Stalin hastily drafted and signed a law that allowed the secret police to arrest terrorist suspects, try them in secret and *in absentia*, without defence or right of appeal, and to execute them at once.[155] The so-called 'Kirov Law', like the law pushed through by Hitler two days after the murder of Röhm, was used by Stalin to put himself effectively above the law. It became the instrument for destroying thousands of party members unmasked as enemies of the people over the following three years. More than 1,100 of the delegates who had applauded Kirov with such unguarded enthusiasm at the Congress of Victors were dead or imprisoned four years later. Ryutin, languishing in prison already, was executed in 1938. A close colleague of Stalin later recalled his leader's reaction at a Politburo meeting when news of the Röhm purge arrived in Moscow: 'Hitler, what a great man! This is the way to deal with your political opponents.'[156]

The path to dictatorship travelled by both men was unpredictable and unplanned. Both were driven by a remarkable determination to fulfil what they saw as a necessary place in history, but that remorseless will was married to an obsession with the tactical details of political struggle, an unnatural resentment towards anyone who compromised or obstructed their political ambitions, and an unprincipled pursuit of public esteem. This was a merciless combination. It is easy to deplore the weakness of the opposition that they confronted, but it is impossible not to recognize how difficult it was to find ways to obstruct or outmanoeuvre men who felt they carried the weight of history on their backs and were willing to use it, if they could, to crush the men or circumstances in their path. Though unforeseen opportunities and straightforward chance played a part in explaining their personal histories, Stalin and Hitler were not accidental dictators.

2

The Art of Ruling

'True democracy means, not a helpless surrender to cliques, but submission to a leader whom the people have elected themselves.'   Max Weber, 1922[1]

'There is definitely no contradiction in principle between the Soviet democracy and the application of dictatorial power by individual persons.'   Lenin, 1918[2]

At 6.30 in the morning of 12 December 1937 the wife of a Soviet professor of railway engineering wrote down in her diary an account of how she had voted just half-an-hour before in the national elections for the first Supreme Soviet under the recently ratified Stalin Constitution. Her diary entry shows her in a state of evident elation. The evening before, she and her husband had agreed that they would try to be first in line at the polling station on their precinct, but when they left home, a little before six o'clock, there were already figures hurrying along the street to vote. The polling station was filled with 'slogans and flowers', and helpful electoral literature. The two managed to get to the front of a queue of twenty-five people, and the doors opened promptly at 6.00. Inside helpers hustled about, organizing the voters. In a second room officials handed out ballot slips. There were two envelopes, to ensure the secrecy of the vote, and two papers, one for local and one for national elections, each printed with the name of one candidate from the only permitted political party. The pair entered the booths, each covered by a red calico curtain, ticked the papers, sealed them in envelopes and tucked them into two ballot boxes. Nearby a crèche had been set up so that mothers could leave their offspring while they engaged in the serious task of voting. The professor's wife felt a 'kind of excitement in my soul'. She had slept only two hours that night in anticipation that she and her husband would be 'the very first of the first voters at the first such election in the world'.[3] The two sat for some time comparing their experience. Her sister wrote later that she, too, had managed to vote after scrambling to register in time, having just got a residence permit three days before the election. As she pushed her envelope into the ballot box she was overcome by sentiment in recollecting an ancient saying, which seemed to sum up her belief that the most modest of citizens now had a great democratic power: 'The tiniest little fish can stir the depths of the ocean.'[4]

It is easy to scoff at the simple-mindedness of Soviet voters, faced with a single party and one or a number of approved candidates elected unopposed, though not completely unanimously, by a submissive electorate. These educated Russians thought they were taking part in a real democratic experiment. At one pre-election discussion group in Leningrad a listener asked if they could take their ballot paper away with them on the day and think about the choice. Mischievous though the question may have been, the answer was serious enough: 'Of course you have the right to go home, sit down and spend a few hours discussing all the ramifications.'[5] The Soviet Union under the new constitution – 'the most democratic constitution in the world' – claimed to be a democracy, and persuaded millions inside and outside its borders that this was indeed the case. The electoral process dominated much of the life of the party, and was repeated at every level of state and party organization. Even Stalin himself went electioneering in the days before each general election in the Moscow *raiony* he represented, too grand for the hustings, but not too grand for a walkabout and handshakes. His election in December 1947 was won with 131 per cent of the popular vote, as electors from neighbouring districts added their unauthorized support.[6] The elections were the occasion for widespread celebration – fireworks, flypasts and festivals.

Preparations for the new constitution began in February 1935 with the appointment of a Constitutional Commission of thirty-one members, chaired by Stalin himself. After a year of drafting, five months were set aside for the public discussion of the constitution.

According to official figures, an extraordinary 623,334 meetings were held nationwide, covering around four-fifths of the electorate. A grand total of almost 170,000 alterations and suggestions were received from cities and villages across the Union, though only 48 found their way into the constitution.[7] There was wide interest in the issues raised by a document that promised full civil rights, including freedom of speech, assembly and conscience; many ordinary people saw the popular discussion as a genuine attempt to involve the people democratically in the construction of their future, and took the opportunity to raise awkward issues about the apparatus of repression under which they actually lived.[8] Despite its evidently restricted character, the elections in 1937 were perceived by many ordinary people as an opportunity to participate in framing a new constitutional order. The turnout reached 96.8 per cent of the electorate. Some ballots were spoilt. In one district 97 per cent of votes cast were valid, the remainder defaced in some way, or the candidate's name erased. In Novosibirsk region the name 'Trotsky' was written in on one ballot, 'I am voting for the heavenly Tsar' on another, and 'We are not voting' on a third.[9] But the great majority of votes were cast according to procedure, and the democratically elected Supreme Soviet assembled a few days later.

The German dictatorship made less public show of democracy, but popular mandates continued to be sought after the last multi-party Reichstag elections in March 1933, in which the National Socialists won 44 per cent of the popular vote, a larger share than any party since Germany was founded in 1871. Between 1933 and 1938 Germans went to the polls a further four times, three times for Reichstag elections held on the same day as a national plebiscite, once for a plebiscite alone, in August 1934. Neither the Weimar republican constitution nor the national parliamentary system was abolished or replaced after 1933. National votes were presented as an opportunity for the German people to express their commitment to the new national cause in a direct way, and in all but one case well over 90 per cent of the population turned out to vote. During 1933 and 1934 this included a fraction still prepared to express their opposition. The Reichstag election of 12 November 1933 returned the first completely one-party parliament; the same day the German people were asked to approve Germany's withdrawal from the League of Nations. All but 5 per cent of the electorate voted, and of those 89.9 per cent said 'yes' to the plebiscite. A smaller proportion, 87.7 per cent, voted for the National Socialist parliament, with over 3 million ballots counted as spoilt because they did not bear the simple cross required against the candidate's name.[10] For the plebiscite a year later, approving Hitler's decision to fuse together the office of Chancellor and President into the single and unique office of *Führer*, the rules were relaxed to allow voting slips which had either a cross or written words to indicate assent. This time only 84 per cent of the electorate turned out to vote, nine-tenths in favour of the proposition, but the sum of spoilt ballots and non-voters reached 7.2 million, the last time any significant body of voters registered their apathy or disapproval.[11]

For the two subsequent elections, called on 29 March 1936 and 10 April 1938, the rules were changed on spoilt ballots. All ballot papers left blank were to be counted as votes for National Socialism, in the absence of any other party. Only those voters who bothered to write in 'no', or crossed out the candidate's name, would count as votes against. The 1936 election was the first to record an almost unanimous vote, 98.8 per cent; in some districts 100 per cent was recorded, though local officials almost certainly discounted spoilt ballots altogether. For the 1938 election the rules were changed again. A single voting paper was produced to cover the Reichstag election and a plebiscite asking for approval of the union with Austria, completed by force on 12 March 1938. The election was a simple acclamation, 'yes' or 'no' for the '*Führer*'s list', to avoid the danger that support for the National Socialist party might be less than for the person of Hitler. The paper had 'yes' in a large circle, 'no' in a small circle. In one polling station voters were told to go into the polling booth only if they intended to register a negative vote. Local party officials tried to isolate potential 'no' voters even before they reached the polling stations to exclude them from voting. Even then the announcement of a 99 per cent 'yes' vote did not tally with the (unpublished) results as they came in from the constituencies. The poorest result came from the commune of Visbek, where only 68 per cent of the electorate said 'yes'; one recorded 75 per cent, and eight others under 87 per cent.[12] However, for the party faithful, the act of participation and affirmation was enough: 'Our way to the ballot box,' observed the novelist Werner Beumelburg of the election in March 1936, 'is thus no election or plebiscite, but on the contrary a serious, celebratory, ineffable declaration to the fate which we serve and of the man to whom this fate is entrusted.'[13] This was a description of what was commonly called 'German democracy' by the jurists and political scientists who defined the nature of the new political order after 1933.

Neither Hitler's Germany nor the Stalinist Soviet Union was recognizable as a democracy in the conventional liberal sense. Yet both assumed that they had a democratic complexion, indeed that their form of democracy was identifiably superior to the western model, which was regarded not only as the source of inherently inefficient governance, but as the product of self-interested class forces that failed to represent the interests of the whole society. 'But what is democracy?' asked Stalin when he announced the new Soviet Constitution in November 1936. 'Democracy in capitalist countries . . . is, in the last analysis, democracy for the strong, democracy for the propertied minority.'[14] The problem with conventional parliamentary democracy was the existence of parties or factions, whose purpose in Soviet eyes could only be to undermine the revolutionary state and divide popular opinion, or, in the German case, to splinter and weaken the nation in the throes of its rebirth. The Soviet people, Stalin continued, only needed one party because there was no longer division between 'capitalists and workers, landlords and peasants'.[15] A few months later, in April 1937, Hitler gave a long speech on the nature of democracy to local party leaders in which he, too, explained that only one party was needed in a society united with one will: 'But we cannot tolerate an opposition above all, for it would certainly always result again in decomposition.'[16] Multi-party systems were seen as expressions of social turmoil and divided loyalties, rather than free political choice.

In each case democracy was defined as the absence of political division and the true representation of popular interests. The Bolshevik Party inherited from Lenin the idea of democratic centralism. This apparent oxymoron reflected Lenin's argument that the party would have to be the directing force of the revolution, while at the same time acknowledging the participation of the broad masses of party and non-party members whose views the party should consider before arriving at a firm conclusion. The mixture of participation and representation was exemplified, at least in theory, in the discussions surrounding the framing of the constitution in 1936. Stalin praised the 'thoroughgoing democratism' of the new constitution, because it gave the vote to all without discrimination, creating the powerful illusion that the state genuinely represented the interests of the entire working people of the Soviet Union.[17] The illusion was sustained by the assertion that the party represented the people as a whole, and not merely an interest-group or social elite as happened elsewhere.

The idea of representation was central to the concept of 'German democracy': National Socialism represented nothing more than the united people or *Volk*; Hitler its ideal personification. The idea of regular plebiscites was introduced into law on 14 July 1933. Their purpose, Hitler explained in a speech in March 1933, was to ensure that the acts of the new government ultimately received their 'lawful legalization' (*sic*) from the *Volk* itself in a more direct form than the medium of parliamentary elections usually permitted. Under National Socialism the people had to see itself as the real 'lawmaker', and Hitler as the man trusted to safeguard the 'historic task of the *Volk*'.[18] In his 1937 speech, Hitler contrasted parliamentary democracy, in which everyone has a voice and nothing can be decided, with his conception of Germanic democracy, in which a single figure emerges to supply firm, uncompromising national leadership for the entire German people. 'In my eyes,' continued Hitler, 'that is the most beautiful and most Germanic democracy. What can there be more beautiful for a people than the realization: out of our ranks can the very best, without regard to origin or birth or anything else, reach the very highest office.'[19] The ideal of the leader chosen from the people to personify their united will existed in the work of Max Weber and numerous other German intellectuals before 1933. Hitler claimed to supply that ideal. 'Democracy basically means,' wrote a young National Socialist jurist in 1935, 'nothing other than the self-rule of the *Volk* . . . The authorization to lead comes from the *Volk* itself.'[20]

The attempt to present systems dominated by the will of a single individual as in some sense a democracy had evident political purposes. Each regime was presented as if it were the people's choice, representing and mediating on their behalf. 'We go far beyond any parliament on earth,' Hitler was reported to claim, 'in our constant reference to the will of the people.'[21] This was an act of intellectual subterfuge, but it created a popular public belief that the dictatorships represented the people collectively in ways that liberal parliamentary systems either had not in the past or could not now. The bond between population and leader was a complicit one; neither Hitler nor Stalin simply exercised naked power in defiance of any popular interests. 'Socialist democratism' (as Stalin named it) and 'Germanic democracy' were intended to describe forms of rule whose stated purpose was to defend the interests of the whole community, or at least of those not otherwise outlawed on grounds of race or class enmity. Specious though the reality might now appear, the populist foundations of dictatorship were powerful instruments of legitimization.

The concern with democratic credentials highlights the fact all too often overlooked in descriptions of the two systems that both the Soviet Union and Germany had a formal constitutional structure throughout the life of the dictatorships. The existence of a constitution did not effectively limit either dictator, but personal rule was never a case of straightforward despotism, regardless of established procedures or constitutional norms. Hitler and Stalin were forced by the existence of a constitutional apparatus to develop forms of authority that were, in effect, extra-constitutional, or which distorted out of recognition existing constitutional provisions. It is here that the heart of dictatorial authority is to be found.

The first Soviet state constitution was published in December 1922, but it gave a poor guide to the actual processes of government because the communist party played the leading role in formulating and dictating policy. The party Central Committee was the chief source of authority, but in practice, since the committee met irregularly, its political sub-committee, or Politburo, was the most important element in the system. Established in 1919 with five members, the Politburo quickly became the arena where all major issues of policy were argued out and decided. By 1930 the membership of this inner cabinet had risen to ten. In 1919 a second sub-committee was added for party organization and personnel matters, the Orgburo. A party secretariat was established at the same time with one party secretary; in 1922 the number was expanded to three and Stalin made the senior member as

General Secretary. This structure remained in being until 1952, when Stalin abolished the separate Politburo and Orgburo and replaced them by a single party Praesidium. Throughout the existence of the Soviet state, the party Central Committee and its subordinate organs assumed responsibility for initiating or for approving policy, though the balance of power between state and party altered over time in the state's favour.

The formal constitutional structure in 1924 was a parliamentary state based on a mixture of direct and indirect election. The people voted directly for the Congress of Soviets of the Union; the Congress then selected a Central Executive Committee made up of 500 to 600 delegates divided into two chambers, a Council of the Union and a Council of Nationalities. The first represented the whole state, the second was made up of delegates from each of the major national components of the Soviet Union, selected on a proportional basis. The Congress also elected a Praesidium, whose president was automatically the Soviet head of state, and a Council of People's Commissars (the equivalent of a ministry), whose chairman became the country's premier. The Council had five members only in the 1920s, eight in 1936.[22] This structure was rationalized in the 1936 Stalin Constitution, which was, at least on paper, a model of representative government. The Congress was replaced by a directly elected Supreme Soviet composed of two legislative houses, one with deputies from the whole union, one with deputies representing the nationalities. Either house could initiate legislation, which became law on the basis of a simple majority in both parliamentary houses. The Supreme Soviet elected the Praesidium as before, but appointed, or 'formed' (in the language of the constitution), the Council of People's Commissars, which was the highest executive and administrative agency of the state. The Praesidium could dismiss commissars, but only on the recommendation of the premier, for whose dismissal no provision was made in the constitution.[23] In March 1946 the commissariats were renamed ministries, and the chairman became President of the Council of Ministers, assisted by six vice-presidents and a larger cabinet of ministerial specialists.

Hitler's Reich failed to generate a constitution of its own; throughout its twelve-year life the constitution of the republic, ratified at Weimar in 1919, remained the German constitution. The former structure of Reich institutions remained, on paper, largely unchanged, though the processes of law-making were altered radically and the distribution of authority changed so fundamentally as to nullify the provisions of the constitution entirely. The result was the emergence of a 'dual state', a concept first elaborated by the German lawyer Ernst Fraenkel in 1940, two years after he fled from Germany to the United States. This was very different from the dualism of the Soviet system, between party and government; the National Socialist Party never produced a central committee, or a political bureau, though it did come to play an increasingly important part in generating policy and subverting state authority as the dictatorship wore on. The 'dual state' represented a division between the existing constitutional structure and a system of extraordinary administrative and executive powers that operated outside or in contradiction to the established norms.

The Third Reich inherited a formal parliamentary system based on two directly elected legislative houses: the Reichstag, composed of deputies representing the whole country, and a Reichsrat or national council, representing the separate provinces (*Länder*) that composed the larger German state. The President was directly elected, but his executive authority was limited. The key political figure was the Chancellor, appointed by the President but responsible directly to the Reichstag. The Chancellor was premier and chairman of a cabinet of ministers, also responsible to parliament. This ministerial apparatus, with its long-established bureaucratic tentacles, remained in being throughout the dictatorship, though the context in which it functioned altered substantially.

The constitutional arrangement was already collapsing well before Hitler came to power. From 1930 no parliamentary majority could be found to support the government, which came to rely not on the Reichstag, which met seldom, but on emergency decrees published by the President under Article 48 (II) of the constitution. Parliament could still bring a government down, but the appointment of Hitler in January 1933 with no parliamentary majority was evidence that the existing parliamentary system no longer functioned as the designers of the constitution had intended. After 1933 only the constitutional shell remained. National Socialist plans to transform the Reichstag into an advisory senate, which Hitler had openly discussed well before coming to power, were abandoned in 1934 and parliament remained technically responsible for passing laws, though it lost the right to initiate legislation, and gave up the practice of criticizing it.[24] However, on 30 January 1934 an act was passed permitting the government to 'make new constitutional law', and as a result the second chamber, the Reichsrat, was abolished by the Law for the Reconstruction of the Reich; at the same time all provincial parliaments lost their right to draft local legislation. Law-making powers had already been transferred to the government under the passing of an Enabling Act (Ermächtigungsgesetz) on 24 March 1933. This oddly titled Law for Remedying the Need of People and State allowed the government to make laws on its own behalf in defiance of the constitution. The law was to remain in force for four years. It occasioned a great deal of debate among constitutional lawyers, some of whom argued that the precise wording did not change the constitution, but merely suspended it. The right to make law was nonetheless the central issue, for unlike the Soviet system, where the separation of powers remained a formal reality, the German government united, in effect, legislative and executive powers together. The act was hailed as the 'Basic Law' (Grundgesetz) of the new regime, or, in the words of the academic jurist Carl Schmitt, 'a provisional constitution'.

The direct fusion of executive and legislative functions was made explicit on 2 August 1934 when, following the death of President von Hindenburg that very morning, a Law concerning the Highest State Office of the German Reich was promulgated, allowing Hitler to take over the role of President without a direct election. The law had been agreed by the cabinet the day before, and was intended to come into force 'from the moment of the Reich President's demise'. The joint responsibilities of President and Chancellor were amalgamated into the single office of 'The Leader', Der Führer. This simple title was adopted as the letterhead for Hitler's official correspondence as head of state (though until 1942 chancellery officials stubbornly persisted in adding '. . . and Chancellor' to the documents they drew up for his signature).[25]

There are obvious differences in the way Stalin and Hitler subverted the existing constitutional structures to achieve personal dictatorship.

The source of Stalin's power in the 1930s was informal and extra-constitutional; he did not hold supreme state office or enjoy the official sanction of special law-making powers. Hitler's authority, on the other hand, derived explicitly from high public office and the terms of the 'provisional constitution' defined by the enabling legislation. The precise nature of Stalin's power as General Secretary of the party defies clear definition, yet from the late 1920s until he assumed high state office for the first time as Chairman of the Council of Commissars in 1941, Stalin came to be regarded as the principal source of authority. Writing in *Pravda* in January 1938, Vyacheslav Molotov, Stalin's predecessor as Soviet premier, described a unique relationship between government and dictator: 'In all important questions, we, the Council of People's Commissars, seek counsel and instruction from the Central Committee of the Bolshevik Party and, in particular, from comrade Stalin.'[26] Stalin himself never accepted that he was a dictator. When the American reporter Eugene Lyons asked him to his face in 1931, 'Are you a dictator?' he received the following disingenuous reply: 'No, I am not a dictator . . . No one man or group of men can dictate. Decisions are made by the party and acted upon by its chosen organs, the Central Committee and the Politburo.'[27] The word 'dictatorship' seems to have been especially troubling for Stalin. Marginal notes from his personal copies of Lenin's works have revealed his private distaste for Lenin's regular and sometimes casual use of the terms 'dictatorship of the party' or 'dictatorship of the proletariat'.[28] In the 1930s Stalin's name appeared below Molotov's on formal decrees; he seldom signed a document without co-signatories in order to retain the fiction that governing was still a collective activity.

It was precisely here, in the work of the Central Committee and the Politburo, that Stalin was able to develop the principle of customary authority on which his power ultimately rested. He was not a dictator in the conventional sense, flaunting as Hitler did the public spectacle of supreme power; his was an ascribed power, derived from habitual deference to his views rather than the necessity of formal obedience. The roots of this power lie in the political manoeuvring of the 1920s already described, and on Stalin's ability to make himself the indispensable defender of Lenin's revolution even in the process of transforming it. But this was a slow and unpredictable process; in the 1930s Stalin consolidated an authority that ultimately rested on the intangible respect or fear that he aroused in the circles around him who had survived the political conflicts of the 1920s. During the 1930s the main institutions of the party went into steady decline. The Central Committee plenum was called less and less regularly, and was often little more than a stage for a piece of Stalinist theatre. During the 1940s it met only a dozen times, and on only one occasion, in 1947, did it engage in serious political discussion. In seven of the years between 1941 and 1951 it did not meet at all.[29]

More significant was the decline in the role of the Politburo. The committee put together in 1930 was staffed largely with Stalin's loyal supporters and the Politburo remained a Stalin fief until his death. Stalin had long before developed the means to circumvent discussion by controlling the agenda and applying administrative action to any items for which too little time was allowed for debate. In 1932 an important change in procedure took place, when the normal forty or fifty issues for each meeting were reduced down to fifteen. Of necessity, many items had to be agreed outside the forum of the committee and, in effect, by Stalin's secretariat. Additional closed or extraordinary meetings took place, where business was conducted without minutes and secretly among a small group. The regular Politburo meetings declined in number, and the volume of protocols based on decisions taken outside the committee or between meetings grew larger and their circulation more restricted.[30] There were 153 meetings between 1930 and 1934, 69 between 1934 and 1939, and 34 in the next three years. In the post-war period the Politburo as the central cabinet of the system fell rapidly into desuetude, meeting on average only eight times a year.[31] Stalin preferred to organize small sub-committees or special commissions, whose members he could appoint and whose deliberations he could monitor. The ability of Politburo members to know everything that was under consideration declined for every member save Stalin, who dominated it for thirty-four years from its inception in 1919 until his death in 1953.[32]

The wealth of continuous administrative experience that Stalin carried with him cannot be discounted as a formidable factor in his domination of the political process in the 1930s. The recently published correspondence between Stalin and the Soviet premier Molotov, and between Stalin and one of his closest colleagues, Lazar Kaganovich, reveal the extensive grasp that Stalin had of even the most trivial affairs of party and state. They also illustrate the extent to which the Soviet leadership by the early 1930s habitually came to look to Stalin for directives on almost every aspect of policy. When Stalin was absent for a brief holiday or at one of his dachas, the letters reveal the suppressed anxiety of men, used to obtaining immediate and direct sanction from the General Secretary, forced to wait for the pace of the mail.[33] The letters also reveal the extent to which key recommendations or decisions on personnel and policy were conducted independent of the formal structures of party or state committees. Stalin's suggestions did not have the force of law, but by the 1930s they were instructions ignored at peril. When Stalin complained about grass growing on Moscow's pavements, workers were said to have been sent scurrying about the city to remove every plant in view.[34] The development of informal avenues for decision-making and discussion was by no means a uniquely Soviet phenomenon, but Stalin exploited them to subvert the formal arenas of policy-making where some level of general discussion or criticism would have been unavoidable. He disliked what he called 'bureaucratism', which was in his view sterile and slow-moving. Stalin came to prefer discussions among a few trusted colleagues, even face-to-face conversations in the quiet of his study, rather than endure hours spent in committee. His appointment diary in the 1930s has revealed a long list of private meetings where much of the business of state was undoubtedly conducted. His personal attendance at meetings declined from the 1930s, leaving those present the unenviable task of second-guessing Stalin's own view. Politics continued at his dacha or his Kremlin apartment, over lunch or dinner, hidden from colleagues and, regrettably, permanently lost to historians.[35]

This opaque form of authority, separate from the regular procedures of both party and state, was reliant upon Stalin's unique control of the networks of secret communication and secret intelligence whose subterranean arteries were tunnelled out beneath the foundations of every institution of the state and party apparatus. The covert structure of the Soviet system was a political instrument of the greatest importance, and one that Stalin's secretariat had enjoyed close control over since the early 1920s. The hub of the system was the communist party headquarters at number 4, Old Square in Moscow. On the fifth floor was the inner sanctum of Stalin's party secretariat, where all save Politburo meetings were held. It was here that Stalin built up a secret chancellery under his direct personal control. The Secret Department (*sekretayi otdel*) was first established in 1921. It had offices for the Politburo and Orgburo secretaries, held the archive of all top-secret documents, the internal codebooks for secure communication and Stalin's personal secretarial assistants, most of whom ended up as senior politicians in the 1930s.[36] The documents were kept in fireproof steel safes, and the whole office shielded by a heavy steel door and armed guards. Only a favoured few, thoroughly checked for loyalty, were allowed access to the files. The Secret Department prepared the Politburo agenda and checked that its decisions were implemented; it was responsible for sending out central party instructions in carefully sealed top-secret packets using heavily armed couriers from the state security service, which by the 1930s had 1,325 communication centres countrywide. The thousands of dossiers on party leaders, full of past indiscretions and current foibles, were housed in its rooms and could be accessed by Stalin whenever he needed.[37]

In 1934 the system was overhauled to make secrecy as absolute as possible, and to centralize the gathering of all classified information. The office was renamed the Special Sector and placed under a faithful gatekeeper, Alexander Poskrebyshev. A short, unprepossessing, balding bureaucrat, who had risen from male nurse to Central Committee assistant by 1924, allegedly chosen by Stalin because of his terrifying looks, he became head of the secret chancellery for almost twenty years.[38] His job was to prepare agenda, arrange documents for Stalin to sign and to control the flow of secret information around the system. He was unpopular with the rest of the party leadership, since he barred the way to Stalin; he was teased and abused by Stalin, and ended as a victim of the dictator's caprice in 1952 when he was sacked for failing to detect a (non-existent) plot to poison the state's leaders.[39] The Special Sector had smaller offices all over the Soviet Union that supplied secret information to Moscow and received secret information from the centre. Every Soviet and state office had a Special Department with the same responsibility. All the secure lines of communication and intelligence ended in Stalin's own chancellery. The principle was observed that no one, save Stalin, should know any more than they needed to know at any moment, a situation replicated in the administrative practice of Hitler's Reich.[40] A most secret index was kept in which all lapses of party discipline or manifestations of opposition were recorded. Stalin, it must be presumed, was privy to it all, armed against any eventuality well in advance.

The secret structure brought Stalin into close contact with the security system, though the exact nature of this relationship still remains hidden from view in the archives. Knowledge that Stalin had unrestricted access to the system's entire stock of secrets must have been alarming enough to anyone in the political establishment who feared for their future. In Viktor Serge's novel of the Stalinist 1930s, a doomed character reflects on the power of the secret file: 'He knew . . . that a dossier, KONDRATIEV, I. N., was making its way from office to office, in the illimitable domain of the most secret secrecy . . . Confidential messengers laid the sealed envelope on the desk of the General Secretariat's secret service . . .' Eventually, speculated Serge, who was imprisoned for three years in the 1930s, 'The Chief looked over the sheets for a moment.'[41] The extent to which Stalin's authority in the 1930s and 1940s ultimately rested on the threat of arrest, imprisonment or death has never been seriously doubted. Among the body of new evidence on the persecutions of the 1930s, which reached their peak with the execution of almost 700,000 in 1937 and 1938, there is ample archival testimony to Stalin's responsibility, together with Molotov and others, for signing the death warrants of thousands of victims, though this followed their arrest, interrogation and trial, and was not the result of secret state murder. The threat of demotion or arrest hung over every head among the party and state elite, a threat that came not only from Stalin, though his approval was probably required for the removal of anyone senior. State security worked closely with the covert apparatus centred on Stalin's chancellery and its many subordinate outposts in the provinces; security men guarded the offices, delivered secret correspondence and shared the intelligence gathered countrywide. Collusion was routine. Stalin's capacity to issue instructions to the security police placed him outside rather than above the law, just as his habitual endorsement of policy lay outside rather than above the formal constitution of the state. Yet customary authority, for all its secretiveness and arbitrariness, required the compliance of the many who acknowledged it. This was a position Stalin enjoyed long before the onset of the violence of the mid-1930s, which suggests that fear was only one of the factors that underlay Stalin's exceptional powers.

Hitler's power may have existed on a more formal foundation of authority but, like Stalin, he exercised it in ways that defied political convention. An element of customary authority characterized Hitler's dictatorship; so, too, the development of a secluded sphere of politics where ideas were tested and decisions made, shielded from all public scrutiny, and, all too often, devoid of any surviving historical record. With Hitler there was none of Stalin's diffidence, though Hitler too did not willingly call himself a dictator, a term he stopped using early in the 1920s. The unique office of *Führer* was nonetheless unashamedly described in terms of supreme, untrammelled power. The term was chosen not only because it distanced the new political order from the established political vocabulary of presidents and premiers, but because the term, meaning not only 'leader' but 'guide' or even 'chief', suggested the idea of a lawgiver or prophet granted by history herself, whose destiny was to lead his people unswervingly towards the future. Ernst Huber, describing the National Socialist constitution in 1939, explained that the office of *Führer* was not a 'state office' but an 'all-embracing and total' authority, incorporating the will of the entire people.[42] Hitler's conception of political leadership had always been rigidly authoritarian. He was fond of banal analogies – the commander of a regiment, the captain of a boat, the architect of a building – to demonstrate that only absolute power was rational. The slogan 'Authority of the leader downwards, responsibility of the followers upwards' became a defining element of the National Socialist revolution.[43] This relationship was not, it was claimed, a description of despotism or tyranny. There was supposed to exist an 'unconditional affinity' between leader and followers (*Gefolgschaft*); trust in the leader was expressed in irrational terms of absolute, unmediated, mystical obedience to a genius risen from among their own ranks. The personal bond between leader and led was captured linguistically by adding the word 'my' to 'leader': *mein Führer*.[44]

These abstractions were commonplace assumptions in Hitler's

Germany. But they did not define with any clarity or legal preciseness the practical extent of Hitler's authority. The arguments surrounding the introduction of the Enabling Act in March 1933 hinged on how to define the ascription of law-making authority to the new government. The final draft gave 'the Reich government' the right to 'decide' on laws on its own behalf, but the original draft, prepared by the new Interior Minister, Wilhelm Frick, had spoken of 'measures' rather than laws, which would have given the government still wider powers of initiative. In either case, 'government' was also an ambiguous term. The government was a coalition of party and non-party ministers, with Hitler as Chancellor, forced initially to play the part of a chairman of cabinet. The act of March 1933 did not give Hitler alone the authority to pass laws. Four years later, when the act was up for renewal by the Reichstag, Hitler sought to redraft the wording so that only he could make the law: 'Reich laws are enacted by the *Führer* and Reich chancellor.' There followed a flurried argument with officials from Frick's Interior Ministry, who wanted the government as a whole to retain a larger say, and the Reichstag to continue to give formal assent to laws. Hitler abandoned the change after he was persuaded to wait until a complete National Socialist constitution could be drafted, and on 30 January 1937 the existing version of the Enabling Act was passed by the Reichstag, and renewed again for the last time two years later. The formal legal principle was retained that laws were approved by 'the Reich government as a collegium', not by Hitler alone.[45]

In reality Hitler had long before abandoned the pretence that the state was governed by a collective leadership. Instead, he issued decrees and directives on his own behalf, which were given the force of law because the rest of the system came to accept them as such. 'In the formulation of the law,' wrote Hans Frank in 1938, 'the historical will of the *Führer* is implemented.' A *Führererlass*, or decree, could legally be published as an emergency measure, 'not contingent,' Frank continued, 'on any prerequisites of the laws of the state'. Increasingly the publication of administrative directives came to assume a permanency in the system that permitted Hitler to act as if he were the sole lawgiver, without the legal obligation to consult ministers or seek the (uncontested) approval of the Reichstag. A Hitler decree was treated by the rest of the system as a special category of law, in a real sense more imperative than any formal act of parliament. During the war years, out of 650 major legislative orders, only 72 were formal laws; 241 were *Führer* decrees, 173 *Führer* orders. Of this number almost two-thirds were secret. The same force of law could extend even to unwritten orders. Objections expressed by officials to the genocide of the Jews in 1941 and 1942 could be silenced by the reply 'It is a *Führer* order', though it is unlikely that any single document signed by Hitler expressed it.[46] Obedience to Hitler moved from the realm of constitutional normality to forms of habitual deference to the leader's will in whatever form it was expressed.

The abandonment of 'collective' decision-making was made explicit by the decline in the role of the cabinet. Hitler attended less and less regularly after 1934, and the number of meetings fell away to just six in 1937 and one, final, meeting on 20 February 1938. Smaller groups of ministers met together, but not routinely or often. Hitler was uncomfortable with committee meetings and, like Stalin, preferred affairs to be discussed with one or two people at a time, sometimes face-to-face in his official study, sometimes at his Bavarian mountain retreat at Berchtesgaden, or over lunch or dinner. From 1936 onwards most of Hitler's discussions of political affairs took place in informal sessions, without minutes or protocols. In late August 1936, for example, Göring was summoned south to Bavaria, where his appointment as head of a powerful new economic planning agency was discussed and agreed on a long walk through the alpine countryside. In 1941 the newly appointed party leader in Vienna, the former Hitler Youth leader Baldur von Schirach, was invited to lunch with Hitler. Before the meal, Hitler took him to one side in the open air, out of earshot of anyone else, to instruct him on the expulsion of Vienna's Jewish population.[47] The diaries and appointment calendars of senior ministers – Himmler, Goebbels, Speer, Göring – reveal regular meetings behind closed doors, the content of which survives, if at all, only in remembered snatches of conversation. Like Stalin, much of the business of governing surrounded the figure of the dictator himself; the entourage became accustomed to an irregular, secretive and fragmentary political process that shielded their leader from any sense that he was the head of a committee. 'I am certainly no chairman of a board of directors,' Hitler told the audience of party leaders, assembled in 1937 to hear his views about leadership.[48]

Hitler's authority relied less than Stalin's on the manipulation of the secret state. He had access to regular intelligence reports, and the party's headquarters in Berlin and Munich kept routine dossiers on all party members, but his public image as the people's leader and his formal and informal law-making powers gave him a more secure grasp of power than Stalin enjoyed in the 1930s. His personal chancelleries, one for his state responsibilities, one for the party, were used as filters to keep his workload and the volume of visitors under control, but not to construct a separate, secret state. As the dictatorship was consolidated, the party chancellery came to play a more important part in helping to initiate or organize those few aspects of policy, particularly race policy, that were to be kept secret from the rest of the apparatus.[49] In 1934 the Chancellery was run by Philipp Bouhler in collaboration with Hitler's deputy, Rudolf Hess. Following Hess's flight to Scotland in May 1941 it was placed under Martin Bormann. Bormann was Hitler's Poskrebyshev, chosen for his bureaucratic qualities and grim personality, disliked by most of the cohort of ministers who had to worm their way past him to Hitler. Under Bormann's guidance the party chancellery encroached more and more on the conduct of the government, until by 1944 all state legislation had to be presented to and approved by the chancellery before publication.[50] Bormann's secretariat became an important adjunct to the exercise of Hitler's power, just as the secret chancellery in the Kremlin became an indispensable tool for Stalin's more oblique domination of the Soviet state.

Different though their approach to dictatorial power was, there were common features in the way Hitler and Stalin exercised that authority. Both developed a pattern of governance that relied on their direct physical presence in defined locations, in much the same way that royal authority in the age of absolutism was exercised. Their authority travelled with them. In September 1935 the body of Reichstag deputies was physically transported to Nuremberg so that they could ratify laws which Hitler wanted to announce to the party congress.[51] When Stalin retired briefly to his dacha at Kuntsevo late in June 1941, following the German invasion, the governmental system was thrown briefly into confusion until his colleagues persuaded him to return to the Kremlin.[52] A verbal instruction from either came to be sufficient to secure action. Closed meetings, unrecorded telephone calls, casual and informal conversations may have left only the lightest fossil traces, but almost certainly came to play a significantly larger part in the art of ruling than the formal committees and correspondence which lie embedded in the archive record. This was not a 'hidden' authority, since it was real enough to those who learned to work in the shadow of dictatorship, but it was largely ascriptive, since it depended on the psychological readiness of the rest of the formal apparatus of government or party to accept the expression of dictatorial will as a substitute for the normative processes of government and law-making. The very use of familiar and popular titles, *Führer* or *khozian* ('boss'), underscored how distinct was this relationship from the world of conventional politics.

Ascribed power was not something that happened automatically. The development of customary authority was, above all, a process, as its name implies. Both Hitler and Stalin were more unrestricted in their power by the late 1930s than they were in 1934; Stalin's authority was greater after victory in 1945 than in 1941. The process was a complex one, in which the two dictators played a central part in identifying the achievements of the regime with their own person to legitimize their unique claims to power. The extent to which that power relied on the manipulation of public opinion and dictatorial image, or on the fiction of popular 'representation', or the political activism of the party, or the threat of state persecution forms the subject-matter of much of the rest of the book.

How absolute was the power that Hitler and Stalin wielded? This is a question that early accounts of either dictatorship took for granted. Both men were described as wielding unlimited, total power. However, the paradigm of completely unrestricted power, exercised in a coherent, centralized polity by men of exceptional ruthlessness who brooked no limitations or dissent was, and remains, a political-science fantasy.

As historical research has abandoned the image of total, centralized power, both Stalin and Hitler have come to be regarded as in some sense 'weak' dictators. The process began first with Hitler. The evidence that other power centres existed in the Third Reich, competing for access to Hitler, engaged in endless bureaucratic squabbles to defend their fiefdoms, developing policy initiatives that promoted more radical solutions than Hitler might have wanted (a process described by the German historian Hans Mommsen with the term 'cumulative radicalization'), intent on subverting the regular routines of government in their own interest, all suggested that Hitler was never a complete master in his own house.[53] The evident absence of anything like a regular pattern of ruling – no central cabinet or executive committee, a supreme authority often absent from Berlin, accumulating paperwork that remained unread or unsigned, unpredictable and irregular schedules – paints an image of a disorderly, even chaotic dictatorship, demonstrably distant from the ideal of total power on which Hitler's political image once rested.[54] The portrait of the artist-ruler, more interested in architecture than administration, rising late in the morning, watching films until late at night, though in reality a caricature of Hitler's working habits, has promoted the view that Hitler was a dilettante dictator, whose art of ruling was self-destructive and whose state was confusion rather than order.[55] Since the fall of communism in Eastern Europe, Stalin's rule has been subjected to the same critical review. The evident chaos and incompetence integral to the modernization drive of the 1930s, and the confused and discordant voices emerging from the central political apparatus as it wrestled to master that chaos, have opened a new window on to a system which once boasted of unity and clear lines of command. Stalin has emerged as a more fearful, reactive and uncertain political magnate than the conventional image of ruthless centralizer and unrestricted despot once suggested.[56]

Some of this new historical image is incontestable, but the idea of 'weak dictatorship' succeeds only to the extent that this history is set alongside a putative ideal of absolute, total authority exercised with supreme coherence by men with planned ambitions. Measured against the exaggerated expectations of generic 'totalitarianism', dictatorship must always be something less: the more these abstract notions of absolute, unrestricted and premeditated power are regarded as a manifestation of 'strength', the weaker the historical reality will seem. This dichotomy is logically absurd. Dictatorial power is not incompatible with systems of rule which are decentralized, or depend upon extensive delegation, or whose patterns of decision-making are ill-defined or discordant, or whose social reality fails to synchronize with the political ambitions of the regime. The dictatorships might achieve their ends in ways less contradictory or socially inefficient, but the power relationship between the dictators and the people they lead or represent lasts as long as they continue to claim it, and the people continue to ascribe it. This power may not be unrestricted, not least to the extent that popular dictatorship seeks its legitimization in the acclamation of the people, but it remains above or outside the law, like Thomas Hobbes' all-mighty Leviathan. Neither Stalin nor Hitler was an ideal absolutist, but the perfect dictator is an invention beyond history.

The character of both dictatorships was shaped, above all, by historical realities that determined the restless, dynamic, often un-coordinated or contradictory features of each system. Both dictator-ships were developed and sustained for the most part against a background of exceptional crisis. Stalin's dictatorship was born in the so-called 'second revolution' after 1928, was consolidated during the period of collectivization and political terror, then plunged into the war with Germany, and ended with the reconstruction of a country ravaged by one conflict and confronted with the onset of a Cold War against a hostile West. Hitler was the offspring of the German slump and political civil war; the regime consolidated the national revolution slowly, before embarking on massive rearmament and military expansion, a war of extraordinary proportions and ambitious plans to remodel Europe around a German 'New Order' after 1939. Some of these circumstances were generated by the dictators' own extravagant long-term ambitions, some not; much of the time the dictators had to react to the unexpected, rather than plan and execute any dictatorial blueprint. The dictatorships were impelled forward by crisis, and the dictators' personal power enlarged by it. Strategies of what is now called 'crisis management' were built into the two regimes, but the consequence was the development of emergency political and adminis-trative systems forced to chase problems and find solutions that were innovative, improvisatory and, at times, contradictory. In the Soviet Union in the 1930s the exceptional measures adopted to cope with the economic and social upheaval after 1928 became institutionalized.[57] In the Third Reich established institutions and administrative procedures jostled with new offices and party appointees to deliver what Hitler wanted, or to resolve temporary setbacks. The result was all too often a disorganized scramble for priority status and a search for methods that circumvented red tape or avoided the widespread phenomenon of *Doppelarbeit*, of two offices overlapping the same work.[58] In neither system was there ever a period of equilibrium. A sense of crisis, of obstacles to overcome, of social wars and military wars, was used to keep both societies in a state of almost permanent mobilization.

The second reality ought to be self-evident. Both states possessed large, complex and multi-layered structures of law, security, administration and economic management, where officials laboured in their own way to turn policy into reality. Though much of what they did ultimately rested on policy decisions, or ideological prescriptions generated from the centre, the intermediate and peripheral rings of administration had to interpret these instructions and translate them into legal or social or economic reality. There existed throughout the system ample opportunity for subjective interpretation, limited local improvisation, jurisdictional wrangling, even conscious disloyalty. The detailed evidence from the execution of the Five-Year Plans in the 1930s shows that in many cases managers would have failed to meet central targets if they had not illegally bribed workers, procured unofficial supplies or falsified their statistical returns.[59] There was no expectation that either dictator could directly supervise the formation of all policy and oversee its implementation. These routine limitations on implementing policy were almost impossible to avoid, even in the Soviet Union, where control commissions proliferated precisely to try to verify degrees of fulfilment.[60] In this respect the two dictatorships were little different from any other complex modern state. Competition between offices, arguments over policy, the gap between central plan and local practicalities, or independent initiatives by office-holders remote from the heart of the system is little more than a description of the regular discordances of the modern state, as evident in Roosevelt's America as in Hitler's Germany. The operational details of the regime are of little help in assessing the degree of authority enjoyed by the principal holders of power, though they will explain why the fulfilment of some policies proved to be so much more difficult than others.

One circumstance more than any other responsible for the idea of 'weak dictatorship' is the contradiction between the centralizing tendencies of dictatorial power and the reality of widespread delegation. This conclusion must also be treated with caution. Delegation was self-evidently unavoidable, but it did not necessarily reduce the degree of personal power enjoyed by either Hitler or Stalin, even if it necessarily compromised the degree of direct responsibility they enjoyed for executing policy. 'Stalin did not work alone,' Molotov reminded an interviewer years later. 'Around him he gathered rather a strong group.'[61] A feature of each system was the necessity for the two dictators to create a close circle of loyal colleagues and subordinates who formed a leadership corps in which the dictator remained unquestionably the master. 'Many of them were very able people,' Molotov continued, 'but at the pinnacle Stalin alone stood out.'[62] The inner circles remained remarkably constant over the life of both dictatorships, though the balance of power among the entourage and their degree of access to the dictator remained less stable. In the two courts of dictatorship the ruling clique jostled for preferment as eagerly as any of the courtiers of Louis XIV.

The ruling groups were composed entirely of men; they were drawn almost exclusively from the party leadership, though most held an official ministerial or commissarial portfolio as well. Their party provenance was the primary link with the dictator, usually pre-dating their acquisition of state office, and it defined them as an elite distinct from the formal structures of government and state, while simultaneously illustrating how important a role the parties played directly and indirectly in running the two regimes. In most, though not all cases, the inner group were also intimate as friends. The habit among Stalin's circle was to use the epithet 'friend' between themselves, but to describe Stalin as 'our great friend'.[63] The Politburo members all lived close together in the Kremlin compound, or near to it. Hitler's circle was less privileged, and their lives led more separately. In some cases he did not use the familiar German 'Du' even with intimate colleagues. His style of leadership was more distant and formal than Stalin's; he was 'my *Führer*', not a friend. Where Stalin saw his close circle almost every day, when he could, there were often long intervals in the time spent between Hitler and his colleagues. They, in turn, treated an interview or meal with Hitler as a special therapeutic event, which would inspire or invigorate, or sometimes overawe them.[64] From both groups Hitler and Stalin expected unconditional loyalty, which they received in return. Even after their deaths and the exposure of the murderous regimes they ran, the inner circle generally remained loyal. In the interrogations before the Nuremberg Tribunal only one of the defendants, Albert Speer, a latecomer to Hitler's inner circle, condemned that loyalty, while acknowledging its overpowering character.[65] In the 1970s, the ageing Molotov, whose Jewish wife had been a victim of Stalinist repression, remained loyal regardless: 'Despite Stalin's mistakes, I see in him a great, an indispensable man! In his time there was no equal!'[66]

Vyacheslav Molotov, the son of an accounting clerk, was the most senior of the men that surrounded Stalin. He had briefly served as 'responsible secretary' of the party (forerunner of the post of General Secretary) for the twelve months before Stalin took over. A pre-war Bolshevik, who adopted the Russian word for 'Hammer' as his revolutionary pseudonym, he was a stolid, widely read, rather puritanical man who dressed more conventionally than the rest of the Bolshevik leadership in suit and tie, with little sense of humour and a habit of speaking remorselessly and at length in order to secure his point of view, for which he was rewarded with the less flattering epithet 'stone-arse'.[67] He remained a member of the party secretariat under Stalin in the 1920s, and was appointed premier at Stalin's instigation in 1930. In 1939 he also became Commissar for Foreign Affairs, a post that he held until 1949, when Stalin, increasingly forgetful, capricious and paranoid, began to ease Molotov out of the inner circle after more than twenty years. The only other person to have served Stalin longer was Kliment Voroshilov. A former metalworker, who joined the party in 1903, he was one of the few genuine proletarians in the party leadership in the 1920s. He became part of Stalin's circle after fighting in the civil war to save the city of Tsaritsyn (later Stalingrad) under Stalin's political direction. In 1925 he was appointed Commissar for Defence, a post he held until his evident lack of military or administrative competence brought his demise in 1940. He was universally regarded as irredeemably stupid. His eager, smiling face, much like a small rodent, grins out of innumerable photographs behind Stalin's shoulder. Stalin ridiculed him without mercy, exploiting him as a court jester. Voroshilov drank heavily. His weak personality and unsophisticated intellect did not prevent him becoming a heroic military figure in the public eye. He was too little a threat for Stalin ever to get rid of him, and after Stalin's death he became President of the Soviet Union, a story of rags to riches achieved solely on mediocrity.[68]

The third figure from the 1920s, who also began his career in Stalin's secretariat, was Lazar Kaganovich. A bootmaker from central Asia, who entered the party in 1908, he was a tall, coarse, hard-working and tough administrator, with a reputation for exceptional harshness that earned him the nickname 'Iron Lazar'. He met Stalin in 1918, and joined him in Moscow in 1922 as head of party education; he joined the Politburo in 1925, where he remained a member throughout the dictatorship. Though poorly schooled and politically unoriginal, he rose rapidly and in the 1930s was one of a small handful of leaders who met with Stalin almost every day. He had to bear the suicide of his older brother, whom Stalin had marked down at the height of the terror in the 1930s as a political deviationist. He was used by Stalin as a troubleshooter, coping with problems and crises as Stalin's special emissary, but with wide latitude to act as he saw fit.[69]

Kaganovich, Voroshilov and Molotov were the longest survivors, working with Stalin from the early 1920s, and living on until well after his death. In the 1930s a second cohort of close collaborators emerged, all but one of whom also survived the dictatorship: Andrei Zhdanov, Georgi Malenkov, Lavrenti Beria and Nikita Khrushchev. Zhdanov was, according to Molotov, held 'in exceptionally high esteem' by Stalin.[70] A plump, pretentious personality, 'with expressionless eyes' and dandruff, who drank inordinately, Zhdanov was one of the few Soviet leaders who pretended some education and familiarity with culture. Stalin used him as his cultural overseer in the 1930s and 1940s until, tense, overweight, and suffering from chronic high blood pressure, he died of a heart complaint in 1948, just at the point when Stalin had begun to withdraw his patronage.[71] Malenkov was even less prepossessing than Zhdanov; pudgy-faced, pear-shaped, relentlessly obedient to Stalin, he was constantly jealous of others in Stalin's entourage. He began work in Stalin's secretariat in the late 1920s, and remained close to him throughout the dictatorship, favoured for his blind loyalty and brutality and his organizational skills. Beria and Khrushchev were relative newcomers who were chosen by Stalin in the late 1930s from their reputations as tough scourges of local party branches. They both survived to fight out the succession following Stalin's death.

The inner circle lived in close proximity within the Kremlin walls. Stalin insisted on knowing where they all were each day; he watched their conversations and distrusted any independent social life they enjoyed. The atmosphere of the Kremlin was stifling and menacing, broken by regular practical jokes of stunning childishness. Pepper was liberally sprinkled on dinnertime dishes; tomatoes were put on chairs; vodka substituted for drinking water.[72] Stalin observed his circle closely, and played one off against another when it suited him to do so, shifting responsibilities and extending or withdrawing patronage to avoid any one figure from dominating, or posing a threat to his own ascendancy. He remained as loyal as he was able to the central group around him, which was reduced only by death, suicide or assassination – Kirov in 1934, Grigorii 'Sergo' Ordzhonikidze (Commissar for Heavy Industry) in 1937, the ageing president Mikhail Kalinin in 1946, Zhdanov in 1948. This image belies Stalin's reputation as a man so paranoid that no other communist leader could survive for long. Research on the survival rate of the party leadership has shown that the inner circle had a much higher chance than the outer ring of younger, more educated communists throughout the dictatorship, very few of whom entered the inner sanctum, and those who did, like the outstanding young economist Nikolai Voznesensky (killed in 1950 on Stalin's orders), were distrusted as potential usurpers.[73]

Hitler, like Stalin, was surrounded in the 1930s by a group of party leaders who had worked with him from the 1920s, and who constituted a relatively stable establishment throughout the life of the dictatorship. The most important politically was Hermann Göring, the son of a diplomat who had joined an elite Prussian regiment before the First World War, fought with distinction as a highly decorated pilot during the war, joined the party in 1922 after listening to Hitler speak and was severely wounded in the groin during the November *Putsch* in 1923. He fled abroad, but returned under amnesty in 1928 in time to become one of the twelve party deputies elected that year. He was

President of the Reichstag by 1932, and one of the few National Socialists to join Hitler in government in January 1933, first as Minister without Portfolio, then as Aviation Minister and, in 1935, commander-in-chief of the newly founded German Air Force. An ebullient, loud, unscrupulous but unreservedly loyal lieutenant, Göring was a large political personality; he was ambitious and vain, but shrewd enough to slake his thirst for advancement in the dictator's shadow. In December 1934 he was officially declared to be Hitler's successor, and by the late 1930s his role in German domestic affairs and foreign policy was conducted with a good deal of independence, though not insubordination. During the war his role was superseded increasingly by Hitler himself, and in the last days of the conflict he was condemned to death by Hitler for daring to suggest that he should take over a government that Hitler could no longer control from his embattled bunker in Berlin.[74]

Another survivor from the early days of the movement, Joseph Goebbels, stayed with Hitler to the end, when he and his whole family killed themselves. The son of a Düsseldorf worker who rose briefly to be a plant manager, Goebbels was a short, slightly built figure with finely defined features and a sharp wit, handicapped by a club foot, and viscerally hostile to the established elite of pre-war Germany. He was one of a number of party leaders who could boast a university doctorate. He joined the party in 1925 and made his reputation in the Berlin of the late 1920s as a propagandist and political terrorist, and a man with the power to move an audience almost as remarkable as Hitler's. In 1933 he was rewarded with the portfolio of Propaganda and Popular Enlightenment. He probably met with Hitler more regularly than any of the others of the inner circle, though his influence as one of the more radical party leaders is hard to gauge. In 1944 he was chosen by Hitler as Special Commissioner for Total War for his loyalty, ruthlessness and optimism. His emotional dependence on Hitler, whom he regarded uncritically as the German messiah, was profound – a bond powerful enough to provoke suicide.[75] The third of the close inner circle was Heinrich Himmler, who rose to head the entire Reich security system and the SS, the black-uniformed elite of the movement, which in the late 1920s had supplied Hitler's personal bodyguard. Himmler came from a respectable Catholic Bavarian family, but in the aftermath of German defeat in a war he missed serving in by only a few weeks, he threw himself into radical nationalist politics, joining the party in 1923, where he developed a reputation for efficient, over-orderly organization and an obsession with the biological survival of the Nordic peoples. He was a thin, pale-faced, unobtrusive individual with a quiet voice, a limp chin, and lips whose regular, almost reflex smile seemed to observers both cordial and menacingly insincere. He suffered a private complex about his own physical credentials and masculinity, which he shielded with a veneer of exaggerated hardness in front of his men. In 1936 he became commander of all German police and security forces and in 1939 a special commissioner for the protection of the German race, two tasks that he combined in his role as the the organizer of mass deportations and genocide during the war. In the war years Himmler drew closer to Hitler as Göring's star waned, but like Göring he tried to supplant Hitler in the final days of the Reich.[76] Both men committed suicide: Himmler when he was caught by the British on 21 May 1945, Göring to avoid execution on 15 October 1946 after he had been condemned to death by the International Military Tribunal at Nuremberg.

The ring of other leaders round Hitler lacked the political stature, skills and ruthlessness of the inner core. Rudolf Hess was out of his depth in the competition for influence. Robert Ley, who headed the German Labour Front, set up in 1933 to replace the trade unions, ran the party's national organization and was another party 'old fighter' who remained in office throughout the dictatorship, arguing relentlessly with his colleagues over issues of political responsibility. The Baltic German Alfred Rosenberg, one of the first party members, was the party's self-styled philosopher. His face with its staring, dark-rimmed eyes gave an impression of permanent and uneasy resentment; he hovered on the edge of the circle, sometimes favoured by Hitler, but often the butt of his colleagues' intrigues. Newcomers to the party, whose membership dated only from the early 1930s, were rarer in the inner group. Joachim von Ribbentrop, foppish, humourless, relentlessly self-important, became the party's foreign affairs spokesman, and, in 1938, Foreign Minister, dominated entirely by Hitler, but arrogant and conceited towards everyone else. Albert Speer, who joined the party in 1931, had a special place in Hitler's affections as the man responsible for realizing many of Hitler's architectural dreams. In 1942 he was made armaments minister, a post that brought him into regular contact with Hitler. He was drawn into the private inner circle of the adjutants, servants and secretaries favoured with long evenings of dinner, films and monologues, though he was not close to others in the leadership corps, who successfully schemed in 1944 to reduce his influence. In the final months of war it was the 'old fighters' in the entourage, who had worked for the movement for twenty years or more, who still dominated the system.

Hitler retained to the end a myopic faith in the quality and loyalty of the party establishment around him. 'My imagination boggles,' he is reported to have said in April 1945, just weeks from his suicide, 'at the idea of a Germany henceforth deprived of her elite which led her to the very pinnacles of heroism . . .'[77] But in reality Hitler's personality dominated his entourage, which became every bit as acquiescent as the prudent or fearful men around Stalin. 'One thing is certain,' wrote Albert Speer shortly after the end of the war, 'all his associates who had worked closely with him for a long time were entirely dependent and obedient to him.' In Hitler's presence they became 'insignificant and timid' and had 'no will of their own'. But once removed from the source of their own psychological emasculation, 'the more brutal and egocentric they were . . . towards their subordinates'.[78] Hitler was no doubt aware of the competition between the members of his entourage and, like Stalin, may have played a game of divide and rule with them, but there is slender evidence that he deliberately orchestrated the tensions among them (or that they needed his prompting). Speer observed during the years he spent in Hitler's immediate shadow that he gave or withdrew his favour intuitively or impulsively, freezing out those who showed any open manifestation of contradiction and arbitrarily rewarding those who won his trust. Hitler was capable of recognizing threats to his own position, as he did with Röhm, and was later to do when he refused to enlarge Göring's already substantial responsibilities when the War Ministry fell vacant in 1938, but in general he tolerated the inner core of the party leadership however unqualified, dissolute, incompetent or delusional some of their number may at times have been.

*

It has been widely accepted that the existence of the competitive, power-seeking elites around Hitler placed inherent limitations on his exercise of dictatorship. The term used to describe the system of authority that resulted is 'polycratic rule', a political state of multiple power centres, and the antonym of 'autocracy'. Such a structure, so it is argued, reduces the independence or freedom of manoeuvre of the dictator, while simultaneously challenging the coherence of the system and inhibiting its capacity to fulfil policy.[79] On this account delegation, though unavoidable, was also self-defeating because it encouraged separate power blocs to build up around members of the inner elite, whose unrelenting political egotism, jealous guardianship of responsibility and institutional insecurity undermined the ground for the delegation of tasks in the first place. This interpretation raises fundamental issues about the exercise of dictatorship that could as well be applied to the Soviet Union. Yet in neither case can 'polycracy' easily be demonstrated. Power should not be confused with responsibility. There were no other power centres in either dictatorship separate from the will of the central figure, whose authority, customary or otherwise, was capable of overruling any decision taken elsewhere in the system. That this was never done routinely resulted from the complexity of each governmental system, but the absence of permanent central review did not affect the principle which allowed Hitler or Stalin to insist on a matter if they felt it merited their intervention. The immediate entourage in both dictatorships was subject to close political control. Beria's son watched Stalin's court in operation for more than a decade: 'Stalin succeeded in subduing all the men around him . . . everyone was ruled by a rod of iron.' In his recollections, Molotov, though proud of the 'strong group' assembled around Stalin, admitted 'we were like teenagers' in his presence: 'He guided, he was *the* leader.'[80] The effect of Hitler on men who were otherwise, as Speer put it, capable of 'forceful behaviour in their own sphere of influence', was numbing. On a number of occasions Göring, who was widely regarded as the Reich's largest political personality after Hitler, was observed leaving a private and disagreeable interview with him in tears or pale and incoherent.[81] Neither dictator brooked serious or sustained contradiction; it is implausible that either would have tolerated a system of rule based on the explicit exercise of independent power in multiple centres.

It is worth examining more closely what Hitler and Stalin *did* expect from the rest of the leadership. First, they supplied a sounding board and a stimulus for the dictator's ideas. The close circle was necessary for both men, for neither dictatorship was exercised in isolation. In the Kremlin there was discussion on a great many issues; Stalin encouraged his colleagues to express their views, argued with them and sought their explanations and justifications. He liked to sum up a discussion at the end, making it clear what his own view was and excluding others. Hitler had almost no capacity for listening to others for any length of time, but he needed other people to listen to him. One of his interpreters, Eugen Dollmann, who observed him over a number of years, described a man who was 'quite without any gift for conversation at any time'. He would stand awkwardly with guests, or sit saying little at table 'until suddenly a topic would be touched upon in which he was interested, whereupon he would launch into a discourse sometimes lasting several hours'.[82] Speer recalled the sight of Hitler pacing up and down, bombarding his adjutants with 'endless and repetitive discussions' in order that he might be clear in his own mind about an issue in 'all the details from every angle'.[83] Speer was one of the very few who could contradict Hitler and explain his own view without prompting a tirade in return, but this was largely explained by the narrowly technical nature of the issues on war production or building design that the two men discussed.[84]

In the second place, the inner circle was used as a political task force to deliver solutions to problems of particular urgency or significance. The granting of special commissions was not an admission of weakness but the consequence of a form of personal rule in which the failure, inadequacy or resistance of normal state channels for enforcing policy were transcended by the appointment on exceptional terms of trusted members of the inner circle. The priority for each dictator was not the survival of sound or rational procedures resting on respect for bureaucratic practice or traditions of demarcation: their priority was action appropriate to achieve particular results. The inner circles contained men with their own strong views and political ambitions, and they were left room for personal initiative. If allocation of fresh responsibilities brought conflict with established institutional interests, this mattered little as long as the new organization and its organizer could deliver what was promised. It is this system of agency that gave to each dictatorship the appearance of chaotic misallocation of administrative effort and permanent tension between centre and periphery.

There are numerous examples of appointments that were defined by particular targets and exceptional powers. In the Soviet Union Stalin made Zhdanov responsible for the introduction of a narrow cultural conformity in the 1930s; Khrushchev was dispatched to the Ukraine in 1938 to destroy the remnants of the Ukrainian communist party and bring the region under closer control from Moscow; Kaganovich was sent to Kazakhstan to do the same; in 1945 Beria was given the most secret assignment: to produce a Soviet atomic bomb in three years, and to spare no expense. The Soviet system inherited from the years of civil war the habit of irregular, coercive intervention by representatives of the central authority armed with special powers, but it did not make these delegates a source of power in their own right. Their power was on loan from the central authority, and was strengthened precisely because of that umbilical connection.

In the Third Reich the establishment of special commissarial powers became commonplace only from the mid-1930s. The model was the establishment of the Second Four-Year Plan, passed into law on 18 October 1936, which gave Göring, who was to be its plenipotentiary, a unique form of authority, defined in the decree as 'full power' (*Vollmacht*) to remove any political or institutional obstacle in the path of achieving the plan.[85] This power was real enough, and its recipient used it to ride roughshod over the objections of the ministerial, military and business leadership to accelerated rearmament and economic reconstruction, but it was power, as the decree made clear, derived from Hitler himself. Other irregular appointments followed on key issues: Himmler for questions of race and resettlement, Ley for the social and welfare policies of the German New Order, Fritz Sauckel, *Gauleiter* of Thuringia, to expropriate the labour resources of Europe for the German economy, Goebbels as Plenipotentiary for Total War. For all these appointments – sometimes as plenipotentiary, sometimes as commissar (a title not entirely tarnished by its Soviet connotations), sometimes as commissioner – the power to enforce the government's will was derived from the central authority but was not independent of it. It was the improvisatory and untested nature of this kind of delegated authority that produced so much political tension; although backed directly with Hitler's power, the new officeholders still had to battle across hostile bureaucratic terrain already inhabited by established interests in order to deliver what the centre wanted.

There was no question that both dictators could do all this for themselves from the apparatus under their direct daily supervision. Hitler signed a great many of the papers placed on his desk without paying them close attention. Some areas of state policy were of less direct interest to him, though it would be a mistake to suggest that Hitler was ignorant of or uninterested in them when it came to issues of real significance. His wartime decrees, laws and orders show that he also approved and endorsed domestic policy issues despite the pressures of supervising the military effort. During the war Hitler worked with a fanatical determination until Speer judged that he had become 'work's slave'.[86] Stalin also worked long hours but could only deal directly with a portion of the business presented to him each day, estimated by one biographer to be between 100 and 200 documents. Many decisions were made without anything formal written down. Stalin would add a tick or initials in thick blue pencil if he approved, or wrote 'agreed'.[87] Molotov remembered seeing large string-bound bundles of unsigned documents lying unopened at Stalin's dacha 'for months'. Decrees were published over his printed signature. Otherwise, continued Molotov, 'he simply would have become a bureaucrat', a fate Stalin had never wanted.[88] Hitler feared the same. 'I cannot imagine anything more horrible,' his valet overheard him saying, 'as sitting in an office day in, day out and there to squat over documents and eke out my life this way.'[89] Both men concentrated their efforts on those issues of high policy that were of particular significance in their own or other people's judgement. When documents were presented to him Stalin asked 'Is it an important question?' and if he received the answer yes, 'he would pore over it to the last comma'.[90] Hitler focused his attention on those areas of policy that he considered the proper preserve of a leader and guide: military preparation and military conflict, foreign policy, an enduring architectural legacy, and racial survival.

Here, in the priority areas of state activity, both Stalin and Hitler were faced with a wide range of problems to be solved and impediments to be removed. Their preferences were not capable of easy solutions. The efforts to construct a new economic order, to remodel society, to combat religion, to arm for war, and to win it when it came, are all explored in detail in what follows. The outcome was always something less than the optimum, but was nonetheless significant. Without visible achievements neither dictator would have been able to make the same claim to supreme authority. 'But he did a great deal,' remarked Molotov, in justifying Stalin, 'and that's the main thing.'[91] The path to achievement meant resolving similar issues in both systems. For example, tensions between centre and periphery produced a persistent centralizing urge to prevent either centrifugal pressures or sheer inertia from obstructing the fulfilment of policy. Much of the political conflict in the Soviet Union in the 1930s and the savage terror that it provoked derived from the efforts of Stalin's government to break the independent influence of local party leaders, and to establish instruments of central communication and supervision that would produce a better match between the stated aims of policy and the eventual outcome.

In Hitler's Germany the issue was complicated by the inherited social power or political influence of institutions that stood in the way of his priorities. The political conflicts of the 1930s were a product not of a deliberate or involuntary institutional Darwinism imposed on the party leadership, but of a conflict between the party leadership and the forces of conservative nationalism and conservative social power, concentrated in the traditional army leadership, the section of the business community representing the old heavy industrial sectors, the diplomatic corps and the surviving non-National Socialist remnants of the nationalist coalition forged in 1933. The tension between these established institutions and the aspirations of the National Socialist movement represented the main barrier to the realization of a more radical racial and national policy.

The crisis was resolved in a prolonged political contest in the years between 1936 and 1938. The beginning was signalled by the creation of the Four-Year Plan in October 1936, and the end came with the creation of the Supreme Command of the Armed Forces in February 1938, under Hitler's direct jurisdiction. In both cases what Hitler aimed to do was not to multiply, deliberately or otherwise, the number of institutions responsible for the same task, but the opposite: to centralize decision-making and to simplify the execution of policy in place of a fragmentary and competitive process of policy fulfilment. The appointment of Göring personified the transition from an economic and military policy dictated by the army leadership and the economics ministry, under the conservative banker Hjalmar Schacht, and opened the way to large-scale rearmament and a military command economy.[92] The decision to make himself supreme commander of the armed forces in 1938 was prompted by Hitler's frustration at the lukewarm attitude of the military leadership to a more active and violent foreign policy. The new office gave him central control, in practice, of most issues of military and foreign policy and broke any possibility that conservative circles could any longer obstruct the drive to war.[93] During the eighteen-month period Schacht was compelled to resign in November 1937, the army leadership was forced out of office in January and February 1938, and the non-National Socialist foreign minister Constantin von Neurath was sacked the same month. The crisis was not planned in advance but proceeded step-by-step by means of a subterranean power struggle, the net result of which was to end the formal coalition with conservative opinion and to produce a political establishment filled with leading party figures.

This example demonstrates how important it is to see the dictatorships not as fixed, ideal systems of centralized authority, that were then undermined by extensive 'limitations' imposed by the social and institutional reality they each embraced, but to turn this approach on its head. The role of the dictators was to try to remove restrictions on the exercise of power and the formation of policy from an initial position where their power was still far from absolute. Hitler's power did not become weaker as the dictatorship developed, but stronger; Stalin was a more absolute figure in the aftermath of the crisis of economic modernization than he was in its midst. The process of centralization involved identifying, compromising with or removing the limits to policy formation. The consequence was a process in which the dictator continuously appropriated more unrestricted authority, not a system in which a theoretically unlimited dictatorship was continuously compromised by restriction.

*

Two examples will serve to illustrate the extent to which both dictators succeeded in overcoming these limitations and reducing constraints on their decision-making. Both were made in a context where important figures from the political and military establishment disagreed with the dictator's viewpoint, and both decisions led to an outcome that proved the rest of the establishment right and the dictator wrong. The first is Hitler's decision to make war on Poland in September 1939, convinced that the conflict would be localized. The second is Stalin's decision to take no serious action to anticipate a German attack in the summer of 1941 in the conviction that Hitler was neither in a military position to take action against the Soviet Union, nor willing to forgo the political agreement made between them in August 1939, a week before Hitler's attack on Poland.

The decision to prepare for war against Poland and the eventual order for German troops to cross the frontier were made by Hitler alone. They were not taken in isolation from the international order, which fuelled Hitler's perception of the opportunities presented by apparent western feebleness in the face of dictatorial willpower. Some case might be made for the argument that German irredentism in the Polish borderlands pushed Hitler to take a strong stand against Poland, but this, too, would miss the point that Hitler was determined to have a small war in 1939, if he could, and kept up pressure on the Poles to make it impossible for them to accept a settlement short of conflict; the preparatory details of the campaign were worked out by the armed forces, who at this stage could still get their way on matters of merely technical significance. The decision to go to war was nonetheless taken by Hitler on his own behalf when on 3 April, following the failure to get the Polish government to accept voluntarily territorial transfers to Germany in March 1939, he ordered the armed forces to prepare 'Case White' for the invasion and occupation of the whole of Poland later that summer. The war, he argued in his directive, would 'root out the threat' from Poland 'for all time', but the precondition for war was Polish diplomatic isolation. Hitler's own perception of the war was a local German–Polish conflict, with, at most, protests and threats from the West.[94]

The conviction that the West would not intervene to save Poland remained central to Hitler's view of the war throughout the summer of 1939. Troops were ordered into position on 12 August 1939 and X-Day for the invasion set for 26 August. The issue was not the war with Poland, for which there was some popular support, but the problem of keeping it localized. Over the summer months the French and British governments made it clear that if Poland were invaded, they would declare war. A general war was not welcome either to the German public, or to the military and party leadership. Hitler stuck rigidly to the judgement that the West was too militarily weak, politically divided and spineless to oppose real demonstrations of political will – 'Our enemies are little worms; I saw them at Munich' – and the intelligence community supplied him with material from which he took the evidence he wanted to see to support these suppositions.[95] As the crisis came to a head, the uncertainty about western reactions affected even Hitler. A pact was hurriedly signed with the Soviet Union on 23 August to guarantee her neutrality. Hitler used this to demonstrate triumphantly to his entourage that the West now had no hope of preventing his conquest of Poland. He hesitated again on 25 August when the order should have gone out to invade; X-Day was postponed until 1 September. In the last days the members of the inner circle expressed their doubts. Göring complained to Goebbels that they had not worked successfully for six long years 'in order to risk it all in a war'. Goebbels' diary records his own fears that Hitler had misjudged the mood, but also Hitler's assurance, expressed the day before war: '*Führer* does not believe England will intervene.'[96] On 31 August the order for invasion was given and not withdrawn; three days later Britain and France declared war on Germany.

The decision to attack Poland in defiance of all the evidence that invasion would provoke a general war, which Hitler did not want (war with France, his army adjutant heard him say in late August, 'was a problem for later'; Poland 'will remain isolated'), must be understood as an expression of Hitler's own perception of his authority. A year previously, he had planned another small war, against Czechoslovakia, but had been compelled by fear of western intervention, unenthusiastic public opinion and the direct intervention of Göring, in a dramatic meeting at the chancellery on the morning of 28 September, to accept what became the Munich Conference and a settlement by agreement. He regarded this not as a victory for diplomatic bullying, but as a defeat for his plans for war. '*Führer* has finally given in, and thoroughly', observed one witness in his diary. In 1939 Hitler was determined not to repeat this public climbdown and abandon war a second time as Germany's Supreme Commander, whatever the dangers. 'I have always accepted a great risk in the conviction that it may succeed,' he told his commanders. 'Now it is also a great risk. Iron nerves. Iron resolution.' He was observed to be 'exceptionally irritable, bitter and sharp' with anyone around him advising caution in August 1939.[97] When on the day of the German invasion of Poland Ribbentrop told him about warnings from Paris that France would fight, Hitler replied: 'I have at last decided to do without the opinions of people who have misinformed me on a dozen occasions . . . I shall rely on my own judgement.'[98] In September 1939 he defied the evidence that a general war was unavoidable, and ignored any restraints on his authority from party, armed forces, public opinion or foreign statesmen. The war against Poland was a classic expression of wilful dictatorship.

So too was Stalin's insistence in the spring and summer of 1941 that there was no fear of a German attack. Here, too, there was some rationality in the judgement. Hitler was at war with the British Empire and had been drawn into a conflict in the Balkans by his Italian ally. Stalin, according to the Soviet ambassador in Washington, Maxim Litvinov, thought it 'madness' for Hitler to attack 'such a powerful land as ours' before finishing the war in the West.[99] In April 1941 the Soviet Union concluded an agreement with Japan to guarantee her neutrality, freeing the Soviet Union to concentrate more forces in its western areas. Stalin ordered the punctual and full delivery of supplies to Germany under the terms of trade agreements concluded between 1939 and 1941, and the Soviet Union gave limited assistance to German forces attacking Britain from the air and at sea. In the spring of 1941 he wrote a personal letter to Hitler, which remains unpublished, asking for reassurance that German troop build-up in the East had no hostile intent; Hitler replied that they were resting in readiness for an invasion of Britain. But alongside this plausible interpretation of German intentions was an overwhelming quantity of evidence of all kinds that Germany was preparing a massive assault. German plans were covered by an elaborate deception, but the gradual movement of 3 million men and their equipment towards their eventual battle stations could not be permanently concealed. There was ample intelligence, some of it from communist sympathizers on the German side of the line who crossed on to Soviet territory with their news, to indicate German intentions. At least eighty-four warnings arrived in Moscow, but they were regarded at Stalin's prompting as deliberate provocation or misinformation, spread by the British to try to get the Soviet Union involved in war. At a meeting of the Central Committee war section on 21 May the intelligence was greeted so nervously that members forgot the customary applause when Stalin's name was mentioned. But all efforts by those around Stalin to get him to take the intelligence seriously were ruthlessly rejected. When General Proskurov, head of Soviet intelligence, argued personally with Stalin he was arrested and shot.[100]

Stalin's conviction hardened into an obsession. According to some accounts Stalin had a profound fear of mobilizing to meet the German threat because the Tsarist mobilization in July 1914 provoked the crisis that led to the First World War. He rejected the suggestion of the army chief-of-staff, General Georgi Zhukov, to place Soviet forces on alert on 14 June with the words: 'That's war!'[101] By this stage Soviet spies and sympathizers abroad had supplied details of the precise date for the German attack, the size and scale of the assault. Even Stalin had doubts, as Hitler had done in August 1939. But the more those doubts assailed him, the more determined he was to assert his authority. Though Red Army soldiers on the frontier could, by the middle of June, see glimpses of the forces assembling opposite them, and Soviet observers catalogued 180 reconnaissance flights by German aircraft deep into Soviet territory, Stalin remained blind to it, and was supported by those in his entourage who sought his approval. Years later Molotov still defended Stalin: 'Provocateurs everywhere are innumerable. That's why you can't trust intelligence.' The nature of Stalin's domination provoked self-inflicted damage. Beria, whose task it was as head of state security to root out the provocateurs and defeatists spreading false rumours of German bellicosity, wrote to Stalin on 21 June, hours before the largest invasion in history: 'My people and I, Josef Vissarionovich Stalin, firmly remember your wise prediction: Hitler will not attack in 1941!'[102]

Stalin's decision was as public an assertion of his dictatorship as

Hitler's had been two years before. Both decisions were on issues of the highest importance; both were taken in defiance of the facts; both were taken against doubts expressed by leading military and civilian figures; both were taken despite, or perhaps because of nagging self-doubt. The consequences were grave, but in neither case was the dictatorship weakened by the public evidence of wilful miscalculation. 'Stalin,' remarked Molotov later, 'was still irreplaceable.' Hitler was privately shaken. 'It was plain to see how shocked he was,' wrote one witness.[103] He raged at what he saw as western stupidity and arrogance. His entourage displayed 'a perplexed dismay'.[104] Stalin's reaction was fury, with Hitler's duplicity, but also with himself. 'Lenin founded our state,' he muttered, after leaving a briefing on disastrous Soviet defeats a week after the invasion, 'and we've fucked it up.'[105] The public and the armed forces were rallied in both states. War was presented as something for which others were to blame: Britain and France for encircling Germany again and launching an unjustified war, Germany for an act of unprovoked fascist aggression. In Germany a number of senior officers had toyed with the idea of overthrowing Hitler in a coup, but withdrew from the attempt because of his evident and widespread popularity. Stalin's broadcast to the Soviet people on 3 July 1941, his first public speech since the invasion, which called on his 'brothers and sisters' to resist aggression with everything in their power, was widely greeted with relief by the population. Hitler dictated an address at once, on 3 September 1939. He began, perhaps inadvertently, with the words 'dear party comrades', but then substituted 'To the German people', an appeal to wage war to the death.[106] Neither dictator was diminished in the public eye by failure, an outcome that illustrates how unrestrained was their power even in the most adverse of circumstances.

Not every decision taken by the two dictators was so unambiguously their own. The important point about the two described here is that they were in a real sense a test of the limits of dictatorial power. Neither Hitler nor Stalin could afford to back down from the stance they had taken without damaging the image of their authority, but nor were there individuals or institutions with the means to restrain them had they been more amenable to reason. The two crises revealed the inhibiting effects not of too little power, but of too much. If there existed weaknesses in the two dictatorships, they stemmed not from the failure of the centre to exert a 'total' control over the societies they ruled, which was self-evidently not possible, but from the extraordinary authority the dictators actually did have to influence policy and events when they chose to do so. They were exceptional rulers, exerting a form of direct, customary authority based on widespread popular acclamation that was unique in the history of both countries, before or since; and the two dictators saw themselves as exceptional, called to perform a historic task in times of crisis.

Such forms of authority have to be described with a political vocabulary distinct from the language of conventional politics. This mode of ruling dispensed with open and systematic forms of decision-making and policy formation; much of the process was secretive, deliberately concealed or compartmentalized. The imposition of policy rested not on clearly established lines of authority and responsibility, but on the extent to which the dictators' agents could use states of emergency or exceptional, and usually coercive, powers to translate the will of the dictator into literal policy where the official apparatus of state was either incompetent or resistant. This subversion of a regular system of government was simplified through the absence of any clear consensus on the nature of political authority in the period that immediately preceded the two dictatorships. The fundamental weakness at the heart of Marxist politics was the failure to describe the source of authority with any clarity. Even Lenin's insistence on the 'dictatorship of the proletariat' under the 'directing force' of the party left open the issue of how that authority was to be established and exercised. Stalin's dictatorship was the first example of many subsequent communist states where a system of authority had to be artificially constructed on the foundation of a doctrine that specifically avoided issues of power. In Germany the concept of political authority was in crisis in the 1920s as millions rejected the republican system because they saw party politics as something inherently incapable of exercising decisive power. Both men exploited the vacuum that opened up in the 1920s by developing unique and exceptional forms of popularly endorsed but absolute authority, with which much of the population could identify.

Neither leader was seriously constrained in the exercise of that power. They did not interfere everywhere, they could take advice, they sometimes listened to objections and they closely followed public opinion. Yet none of this detracted from the power they were able to exert on issues that mattered to them. Although the traditional image of the all-powerful, all-seeing despot at the hub of a well-oiled political machine has been sensibly discredited, both men nonetheless held potentially unlimited power (and the means to secure it through popular approval and the delegation of responsibility). Without that power the grim achievements of either system cannot be understood. The unique nature of this form of authority was clear from the problems of its reproduction. Hitler gave much thought to the succession in the 1930s, as well he might in a system described by one National Socialist political philosopher as one in which 'not the "office" but the "personality"' was decisive. He issued instructions in 1934 that Göring should succeed him if he died or was killed; in 1939 he added the unlikely figure of Hess ('one of the great cranks of the Third Reich', as Speer put it), who was to succeed if anything happened to Göring.[107] But succession was in no sense hereditary: Hitler insisted that the next *Führer* would have to seek the popular approval of the people and the party through a plebiscite and a special party electoral college. Future leaders, Hitler believed, would have to emerge from the people, as he had done, in ways that defied any written constitutional rules.[108]

The Soviet situation is usually assumed to be different, since a party-dominated authoritarian state both preceded Stalin and followed after his death. But here, too, the special authority enjoyed by Stalin was never reproduced. Even before his death his potential successors began to dismantle the instruments essential to personal dictatorship. The secret chancellery was made into a formal department that served the whole system and not just the First Secretary of the party. Stalin was pressured into calling a party congress in 1952, the first since 1939, and the Central Committee began to meet more regularly. After Stalin's death collective leadership was agreed. When Khrushchev, made First Secretary in 1953, emerged clearly as Stalin's successor in 1956, his powers, though very large, were not unlimited. Eight years later the Central Committee unseated him.[109] In neither Germany nor the Soviet Union was the customary authority enjoyed by Hitler and Stalin, and the personal and arbitrary governance that went with it, capable of reproduction. Both were the product of a particular moment in history that permitted the development of a unique bond between population and leader which survived as long as they remained alive.

3

Cults of Personality

'There is no similar name on the planet like the name of Stalin. It shines like a bright torch of freedom, it flies like a battle standard for millions of labourers around the world; it roars like thunder, warning the doomed classes of slave owners and exploiters . . . Stalin is today's Lenin! Stalin is the brain and heart of the party! Stalin is a banner of millions of people in their fight for a better life.'

Pravda, 19 December 1939, for Stalin's 60th birthday[1]

'My Führer! Thus I stand this day before your portrait. How powerful, strong, beautiful and exalted it seems! So simple, kindly, warm and unpretentious! Father, mother, brother, all in one and even more . . . You are the Führer, though you utter no commands. You live and are the Law. You are Love, you are Power.'

Das Schwarze Korps, April 1939, for Hitler's 50th birthday[2]

When Josef Stalin died on 5 March 1953 the whole nation mourned. Only a few hours after his death he was taken to the laboratory attached to Lenin's mausoleum to be prepared for the lying-in-state. He was to be embalmed, like Lenin, and laid in a catafalque by the side of the father of the revolution. Vast crowds, with ashen, tear-stained faces, gathered around the House of Trade Unions to glimpse the corpse. So many, it turned out, that hundreds were asphyxiated in the crush and a number of policemen's horses were trampled to death. Even those who hated Stalin were aware of the power of the cult that sustained him. 'Somehow,' wrote Andrei Sinyavsky, 'I was mentally able to resist that incredibly powerful magnet whose epicentre radiated lethally throughout the city . . . that night his presence was more palpable in the streets than in there with the wreaths and the honour guard.'[3] For true believers, like the soldier Peter Grigorenko, Stalin's death was 'a great tragedy'. Stalin remained 'faultless' amidst a bevy of corrupt or vicious advisers. The young Peter Deriabin later recalled his mother-in-law's anguished question when news of Stalin's death arrived: 'What shall we do now that Comrade Stalin is dead? What shall we do?'[4]

Hitler committed suicide on 30 April 1945, by shooting himself through the mouth. His body was dumped unceremoniously in the back garden of his chancellery, doused with petrol and burned beyond recognition. The SS men who guarded his bunker in Berlin got drunk on the remaining supplies of alcohol. Albert Speer, Hitler's armaments overlord, who had contemplated assassinating Hitler a few weeks before to prevent the utter destruction of Germany, but could not bring himself to do it, took out the signed photograph Hitler had once given to him and openly wept at the news of his leader's death: 'Only now was the spell broken, the magic extinguished,' he later wrote.[5] There was no funeral, no memorial. Within weeks all of Germany knew of the horrors perpetrated by the regime. The Allied fear that a Hitler cult would survive on after defeat was found to be misplaced, but British censors intercepted letters written between Germans at the end of the war that displayed desperate desires that he might still be alive, and in one case the fervent hope that somewhere in Germany at that moment a baby was being born, who would arise to avenge Germany.[6] A survey of young Germans carried out in October 1945 found 48 per cent who believed a new *Führer* was the answer to German revival; as late as 1967 one-third of a poll of West Germans thought Hitler would have been among the greatest of German statesmen had it not been for the war.[7] During the war, millions of Germans died for *Führer* and Fatherland, millions more died for Stalin and the Motherland. Though different in death, Hitler and Stalin each enjoyed a popular loyalty of exceptional power and intensity during their lives.

The source of that popularity lies to a considerable extent in what has come to be called the 'cult of personality'. The systematic adulation of the two leaders was a defining feature of both dictatorships, and was understood to be so at the time. The artist and novelist Wyndham Lewis wrote about *The Hitler Cult* in 1939; in 1937 there appeared in Zurich a book under the title *Der Mythos Hitler* (The Hitler Myth), which compared Hitler to Mohammed and his followers to Muslim fanatics.[8] Contemporary critics of Stalin's regime focused on the bizarre exaggerations of Stalin's person, 'the legendary leader'.[9] These extravagant forms of political worship, evident too in the case of Mussolini, made the dictatorships distinct from other forms of authoritarianism, for example military dictatorship or unconstitutional monarchy, because they flourished only by virtue of political artifice, through the construction and communication of the cult, and not by virtue of force or habitual deference. The projection of the 'super-personality' was both the cause and effect of their power.

The two dictators approached the cult of personality from opposite directions. For Hitler, personality was the defining criterion of leadership; it was central to his entire political outlook. In *Mein Kampf* he devoted a whole chapter to the subject. Hitler argued that the chief purpose of the state was to promote the higher personalities to positions of authority: 'it builds not upon the idea of majority, but upon the idea of personality'. An effective modern state 'must have the personality principle anchored in its organization'. Hitler assumed that the 'superior minds' were not chosen, but that they somehow emerged in the course of the struggle for existence within a given people, 'life alone giving the examinations'. These higher beings were by their very nature set apart from the masses: 'Extraordinary geniuses permit of no consideration for normal humankind.' In the early days of the movement Hitler was too diffident to see himself as this exceptional figure. 'We need a dictator who is a genius,' he announced in 1920.[10] Only after the failure of the 1923 *Putsch* did he come to believe that he was, indeed, the personification of his argument that great men emerge from societies in crisis. *Mein Kampf* was an expression of the idea of struggle as the school of genius. In 1926, when he was confirmed by the party as *Führer*, he presented himself as living proof that personality, not aptitude, wealth or title, was the key to supreme political leadership. During the Third Reich the cult of personality was for Hitler a natural outcome, not a historical aberration.

Hitler saw the idea of *Führer* as a unique form of leadership appropriate to a modern age in which the people as a whole should have a say in choosing who led them. In his recorded conversations during the war, Hitler returned a number of times to the question of the best way to describe the leading personality. He dismissed the term 'chancellor' because it implied that there was some 'supreme chief' above him. The term 'president' he also dismissed: 'You can imagine it! President Hitler!' He was deeply hostile to the idea of royal authority, and welcomed the fact that with the popular term '*Führer*' he had put an end to the 'last vestiges of servility, those survivals of the feudal age'. He thought the example of the last Kaiser, Wilhelm II, showed 'how one bad monarch can destroy a dynasty', and he refused any idea after 1933 that the Kaiser should be allowed back to Germany from his exile in the Netherlands. He considered hereditary monarchy to be 'a biological blunder'; weaker links in the line led inevitably to the 'weakening and decay' of the state. 'In the hereditary monarchies,' continued Hitler, at a dinner in March 1942, 'there were at least eight kings out of ten who would not have been capable of successfully running a grocery.'[11] The hostility was reciprocated. When Wilhelm II published a book on eastern symbolism in 1934, he pointed out that a swastika with its arms turned to the left (as it was in Hitler's Germany) symbolized night, misfortune and death.[12]

Stalin emerged from a revolutionary movement committed to eradicating the personal rule of the Tsar and creating the dictatorship of a mass party that was at least formally representative of the ordinary people. 'Soviet power,' wrote Stalin in 1924, while Hitler was busy dictating *Mein Kampf* in Landsberg jail, 'has a most pronounced mass character and is the most democratic state organization of all possible.'[13] The few passages on leadership in his writing are the very antithesis of Hitler's. They focus on the role of the party in leading and preparing the mass of toiling workers and peasants for the transition to a collectivist and democratic future, and on the collegial character of decision-making. This was conventional Leninism. The only clue to Stalin's later status as the object of extravagant adoration can perhaps be found in a rhetorical question that he posed in the same remarks on Soviet power: 'who can give correct guidance to the proletarian millions?' Stalin's answer was based on Lenin's view of the Bolshevik party as the vanguard or directing force, but he went further to suggest that the party should also develop its own inner core, dictating to the rest of the party. It may be possible to detect here the seeds of his later uncompromising personal domination even of these upper party cadres. In periods of crisis, he wrote, history demands 'the concentration of all the forces of the proletariat at one point, the gathering of all the threads of the revolutionary movement into one spot'.[14]

The emphasis in all Stalin's theoretical writings on the necessity of a single party line, of iron discipline, of complete centralization, are certainly all compatible with the idea that at some stage a single leader might create these conditions, but there is little evidence that Stalin actually thought that way in the 1920s. By 1931, when the German biographer Emil Ludwig asked him in an interview how he justified his elevated position in the communist hierarchy, Stalin told him that Marxism 'has never denied the role of heroes'. Although he added, more modestly, that 'Somebody else could have been in my place,' he did not deny that a heroic figure was necessary; quite the contrary, 'for somebody had to occupy it'.[15] Stalin made no attempt, however, to provide any theoretical grounding for a cult of heroic personality. He read widely on the history of Russia's great rulers, particularly Ivan IV (the Terrible) and Peter the Great, both of whom were rehabilitated in the 1930s as Russian heroes from history at Stalin's encouragement. He admired Dostoevsky, whose *Crime and Punishment* explored the idea that world historical figures could act as they pleased, regardless of the prevailing moral or ideological restraints. Stalin is remembered for the very un-theoretical remark, 'the people need a tsar', which is often taken as an explanation for the shift away from collective to single-man leadership.[16]

Yet there are many witnesses from the years of personal dictatorship who recall Stalin's apparent unease at the cult status popularly ascribed to him. 'At first,' Molotov later recalled, 'he resisted the cult of personality', he 'did not entirely like this adulation'. Only later, after the war, did he come 'to enjoy it a bit'. Molotov considered the later Stalin to have become rather 'conceited'.[17] In a speech given in November 1937 Stalin insisted that 'personality is not the crux' and that he was not an 'outstanding man', but a hard-working and conscientious servant of the people.[18] In a letter Stalin wrote in February 1938 to a children's publishing house, he complained that a proposed book of 'Stories about Stalin's Childhood' was 'full of factual errors, distortions, exaggerations, undeserved praise'. This was not, in his view, the worst of it: 'the book has a tendency to engrave in the minds of children (and people in general) the cult of personalities, leaders, sinless heroes'. His instruction was to burn the book.[19] In the end, Stalin may have exploited the cult not because it could be ideologically justified, but because it secured his role as the chief legatee of Lenin's revolution, and satisfied popular yearning for a strong central figure. There are no grounds for thinking that he did not understand and enjoy the evident political benefits to be derived from the development of the cult, but his view of it was opportunistic and cynical, whereas Hitler's was deadly earnest.

To explain either cult historically it must be placed in the wider cultural and political context of the age, for the idea of 'personality' was one of the critical discoveries of *fin de siècle* Europe. The German philosopher-poet Friedrich Nietzsche, writing in the 1870s and 1880s, rejected what he described as the prevailing 'herd mentality' of modern, industrialized mass society. He valued individuals who could transcend the prevailing ethos of a dull social order and stifling convention and express their moral autonomy and psychological independence from the values and institutions of the modern world. He called these unique personalities '*Übermenschen*', or 'Overmen'. The term became one of the key words of the early twentieth century. The vulgar reception of Nietzsche soon translated the concept into the realm of social theory and politics, which is not what he had intended. Many European intellectuals believed that modern societies should reject the crude egalitarianism of the left and liberalism and try to create social incubators for the outstanding 'personality'. Ernst Bertram's book *Nietzsche, Attempt at a Mythology*, first published in 1918 and reprinted seven times in the 1920s, highlighted the idea of a prophet sent to save the nation from itself.[20] Another German, the social theorist Max Weber, one of the most influential thinkers of his generation, originated the idea that the most desirably authentic form of political authority in the modern age derived from promoting what he called the 'charismatic personality', instead of relying on inherited deference or simple merit.[21]

Weber defined what he saw as the essential characteristics of this form of leadership. He believed that the successful leader had to be independent of the limitations of circumstances and to rely on his own psychological strength and willpower. 'He knows,' Weber wrote, 'only inner determination and inner constraint.'[22] He had to transcend the selfish interests of class or corporation and be trusted to act on the basis of his own will, with 'decisiveness'. Weber thought that the British nineteenth-century prime minister, William Gladstone, was a clear example. In 'The Nature of Charismatic Domination', published in 1922, Weber argued that a strong, popular leader, drawn from the people but not submerged by it, was the product of periods of crisis: 'the "natural" leaders in times of spiritual, physical, economic, ethical, religious or political emergency were . . . those who possessed specific physical and spiritual gifts which were regarded as supernatural'.[23] These powers had to be acknowledged by the mass of the population because they were the only source of legitimacy. Weber recognized that in the modern age the powerful will of the exceptional individual could be expressed as political power only as long as he 'is certified as charismatically gifted by the belief of his followers', in some plebiscitary way. If those he seeks to rescue 'do not recognize his mission', then he remains an outsider. If they do accept him, 'he remains their master' as long as proof of his singular powers can be sustained. This form of leadership was, Weber concluded, 'characteristically *unstable*'.[24]

The idea of the exceptional, wilful personality became central to many disciplines besides political science. Eugenicists applied it to ideas of race-breeding; social theorists – Vilfredo Pareto in Italy, Joseph Schumpeter in Austria – used it to explain the way modern political and industrial elites emerged; psychologists extrapolated from Nietzsche the idea that the truly great personality could only be nurtured among a few exceptional individuals. In 1934, the year both Hitler and Stalin consolidated their personal dictatorships, the Swiss psychologist Carl Jung published an essay on 'The Development of Personality', in which he argued that the prevailing popular interest in personality derived from the historical fact that the great deeds of world history came from 'leading personalities' and never from 'the inert mass'. Jung endorsed the belief that authentic personalities were few and far between, driven by 'brute necessity' to become a law unto themselves, and, eventually, 'a *leader*'.[25]

The popular reception of the idea of personality in Germany fitted with a profound rejection of western ideas of individualism, which were regarded as shallow and materialist. The First World War encouraged the fragmentation of the liberal bourgeois world view, with its emphasis on civic equality and the solid, actively responsible citizen. Out of the experience of war and defeat came the longing for national redemption around a heroic personality, 'the Man to Come', as Franz Haiser described him.[26] There was no popular demand for the restoration of the discredited emperor. Those who expressed a longing for a German messiah in the 1920s focused on the idea of a man drawn from the common people. The desire developed quite independent of Hitler, who was, however, able to exploit it for his own purposes. When the economic slump came after 1929 it was widely regarded not simply as the bankruptcy of unfettered economic individualism, another plank of the liberal age, but of conventional parliamentary politics and the prevailing bourgeois elites. In 1932 the economist Werner Sombart, one of the founders of the German Democratic Party in 1919, told an audience of businessmen that Germany should now search for a single strong-willed leader: 'without him we will sink into chaos'.[27] Hitler's cult of personality was not something grafted on to German political culture, but derived its appeal from a wide, though by no means universal, expectation of a German redeemer.

The impact of Nietzsche in Russia was equally profound. His idea of the heroic rejection of the present found an enthusiastic audience among a section of the Russian Marxist movement. The novelist Maxim Gorky expressed the longing for a Russian 'superman' who would sweep away the old order for good. The idea of the heroic individual pitting himself against the corruption of the Tsarist system and the passivity of the mass appealed to a revolutionary movement committed to ideals of party activism.[28] The literature of pre-revolutionary Russia had a strongly apocalyptic tone; expectations of revolution mingled with romantic ideas of redemption and the idealized personality. The idea of a redeemer, rescuing Russia from the clutches of debauched Tsarism, had other roots in popular mythology: peasants expected the 'White Tsar' to rescue them from poverty and to redistribute the land; sectarian Christians expected the Second Coming; radical intellectuals, repelled by scientific socialism, married their revolutionary aspirations to older traditions of messianic belief. The expressionist poet Alexander Blok echoed the Biblical disciples in his poem about a group of revolutionaries, 'The Twelve', written in 1918: 'And wrapped in wild snow at their head/Carrying the flag blood-red . . . Ahead of them Christ Jesus goes.'[29] Not even the Bolshevik party remained immune to the appeal of symbolism, myth and the cult of the exceptional being. Anatoly Lunacharsky, who became the first Commissar for Enlightenment in 1918, was the most prominent representative of the so-called 'god-building' movement in the party, who sought to link Russian religion and Russian socialism by postulating the creation of the 'perfected organism' or 'superman', the god-like hero of a revolutionary movement that Lunacharsky described as 'the most religious of all religions'.[30] Though Nietzsche's books were banned from Soviet libraries in 1922 on grounds that they were an expression of bourgeois mysticism, the idealized view of personality survived among the 'god-builders'.

Russia also had the Tsar. A tradition of systematic adulation existed long before 1917. Popular monarchism in Russia, particularly that of the peasant majority, perceived the Tsar as essentially good and just, vengeful against the enemies of the people, a protective 'little father' who would save his children from corrupt officials and greedy landlords.[31] This perception wore thin in the years before 1914, and was eroded rapidly during the First World War, but the culture of popular adulation survived the revolution, transferred to the new leaders. The idea of 'Tsar' became a revolutionary metaphor; in place of the monarch there were revolutionary leaders sitting far away in Moscow, caring day and night for their people, meting out tough justice to class enemies, little fathers solicitous for the children of the new Russia. 'Moscow is asleep,' ran a poem published for Stalin's birthday in 1939, 'Stalin is the only one awake/At this late hour –/ He thinks of us . . . He can even hear the song/Which a shepherd sings in the steppe/The little boy will write a letter to Stalin/And will always receive a reply from the Kremlin.'[32] Lenin deplored the survival of these pre-revolutionary habits of mind, but not even his colleagues were immune. 'Leader by the grace of God', wrote Zinoviev of Lenin in 1918.[33]

Lenin provoked the first cult of personality in post-revolutionary Russia. This was not a surprising outcome. His personality – ascetic, hard-working, orderly – set him apart from the many free (and freer) spirits in the socialist movement. His overpowering conviction that he understood the course of revolutionary struggle better than anyone else manifested itself in a remarkable struggle for self-assertion within the movement, and an intolerant rejection of anything he regarded as schismatic or intellectually shallow. After the October revolution, Lenin was the driving force of the new system. He set up his office in the Kremlin palace in Moscow, where peasants and workers who came to see him had to go through a disinfectant room before being ushered into his presence.[34] Despite himself, Lenin appeared to be the image of the good tsar – simple, modest, willing to mix with ordinary people and share their problems, but at the same time the god-like creator of the new order. He was first described by the term *vohzd*, or 'leader' (traditionally applied to military commanders), in 1918, and the term came into popular usage in the 1920s when it was applied to all the senior party figures as collective *vozhdi*.[35] A popular reverence for Lenin proved impossible to suppress, and in the crisis of the civil war the party itself exploited the growing cult for its own political survival.

The symbolic world created in the first years of revolutionary Russia was strongly influenced by Russia's religious past. The civil war became a Manichean contest between the forces of good and evil, revolutionary saints and counter-revolutionary demons. Lenin only gradually came to be seen as the senior saint, author, as one poet put it on May Day 1918, of 'The Holy Bible of Labour'.[36] After an attempt on his life in August 1918 the cult began to take firmer shape. Zinoviev spoke in Petrograd a week later about Lenin the apostle and evangelist of Russian socialism: 'He is really the chosen one of millions . . . He is the authentic figure of a leader such as is born once in five hundred years in the life of mankind.'[37] Until his death in 1924 Lenin was able to prevent official propaganda from adopting the exaggerated religiosity that was increasingly evident in popular attitudes to Lenin as Christ-like redeemer, but with his death the popular cult was joined by an official 'Lenin cult', which persisted throughout the subsequent history of the Soviet Union.

At the core of the official cult was the decision to embalm Lenin's body and to display it in a grand communist mausoleum in Red Square. Stalin was said to have been the source of the idea, in October 1923, months before Lenin's death, though there is no direct record of the meeting. By the time a special 'Funeral Commission' was set up by the Central Committee on the day of Lenin's death, the ambition to preserve the dead leader was already embedded in the discussions about the body's future. The Commission was headed by Felix Dzerzhinsky, chief of the security police, and made up of senior party members (though not Stalin). There were bitter arguments about what to do with Lenin's remains, which, following an autopsy, had been temporarily preserved for the lying-in-state. The Commission had already sent out official 'mourning statements' throughout the Soviet Union, which presented a less-than-truthful rendering of the life of Lenin for public consumption. There was no dispute about using the leader's death to reaffirm the revolutionary achievement among the population at large, or about presenting Lenin in terms likely to encourage a popular cult.[38] The dividing line came over the issue of embalming.

Those who favoured embalming argued on grounds of political expediency. Dzerzhinsky recommended displaying Lenin to the Soviet masses as the symbolic incarnation of the revolution. Others objected to the strongly religious symbolism of sanctification and reliquary typical of the Russia Lenin had fought to overturn. While the bickering went on, workers blasted out with dynamite the foundations of a temporary, wooden mausoleum in Red Square in ground as hard as stone. Soon the body began visibly to deteriorate; the skin darkened and wrinkled, the lips began to shrink. In a panic, the Commission, now renamed 'for the Immortalization of the Memory of Lenin', hunted for scientists who knew enough biology to save him. In March two were found, and the decision was finally taken that Lenin would be displayed in perpetuity in a new and grander mausoleum. The wooden structure, completed in 1924, was finally replaced by a magnificent granite building in 1930.[39] Lenin was reborn in almost Christlike terms; martyrdom, resurrection and immortality were the themes of the Lenin cult, 'Lenin lives!' its watchword. The first giant statues of Lenin appeared in Stalingrad in 1925 and at Leningrad's Finland Station in 1926. All over the Soviet Union in the years immediately following his death, small shrines – so-called 'Lenin Corners' – were set up in offices, factories and villages, designed according to guidelines issued by the party in February 1924. Lenin Evenings were organized to celebrate his birthday. Lenin kitsch appeared in the shops, souvenirs for the thousands of communist pilgrims who shuffled past the wax-like body of the great leader, year in, year out.[40] The party encouraged a ritual veneration that would become, a decade on, the hallmark of the new cult of Stalin.

It is evident that Hitler and Stalin were the political beneficiaries of two separate strands of political messianism whose roots lay in the nineteenth century. The contemporary discourse on the unique, power-seeking personality was transformed in post-revolutionary Russia and post-war Germany into metaphors of the redeeming saviour, but one drawn from the people, understanding and mediating their suffering, struggling against inert and malign historical forces. 'The hero, the leader, the saviour,' wrote Jung in his 1934 essay, 'is one who discovers a new way to a greater certainty.'[41] Without such fertile cultural soil, the cults surrounding Hitler and Stalin would never have grown so tall.

All cults of personality are more or less fictions. The exaggerated image of both dictators had to be created. This is not to imply that without the image Hitler and Stalin were nonentities, since the history of their rise to power already described, when the cults were in their infancy, shows that they possessed many other political and personal skills, quite independent of the cult, which they exploited. The problem both men faced was that this was all they had. They were not monarchs, or successful military commanders, or men of high national achievement, whose claims to leadership were self-evident. Whatever the strengths of personality and will they displayed, both men understood that their claim to supreme, customary authority had to be artificially stimulated and sustained and in some sense made 'larger than life'.

The self-conscious construction of political images is a common-place in an age of spin-doctors and television; in the 1930s it was a novelty. Yet image was all-important for two leaders whose claim to authority derived from public acclamation. They were never simply themselves in the public sphere. 'This little brown-coated man, Herr

Adolf Hitler,' wrote Martha Dodd, daughter of the American ambassador, 'is a fairy-tale.'[42] The fiction was constructed in a host of trivial ways. Hitler, it is well known, spent hours rehearsing his speeches on great public occasions. His exaggerated theatricality was never as spontaneous as it appeared. One of his secretaries, Christa Schroeder, interrogated after the war, recalled how Hitler rehearsed his speeches endlessly, going over the language time and again, pausing to rehearse 'with the same kind of voice, and acting' that he would use when the time for the speech finally came.[43] Much of his public behaviour was calculated. He refused to be seen or photographed wearing glasses (only one such picture has survived; Hitler was so long-sighted that, to avoid wearing glasses, papers had to be typed in large print on the so-called '*Führer*-typewriter'). His personal behaviour in public, though it lacked the boldness of the strutting, gesturing image projected by Mussolini, was self-consciously that of the Chosen One.[44] Martha Dodd observed how the 'slender body, pale, soft, neurotic face, modest bearing' of the pre-1933 days gave way by stages to a figure 'insolent and arrogant, with shoulders flung back pompously, who walks and marches as though he had made the earth under his feet'.[45]

Hitler's overblown, sometimes almost hysterical behaviour on a rostrum in front of thousands of onlookers was the apotheosis of the image. These events were stage-managed in every detail and displayed to as wide an audience as possible. The 1933 party rally was made into a film under the title *The Victory of Faith*, and watched by 20 million in German cinemas. It was not an entirely successful vehicle for the cult, for not only was Hitler regularly to be seen side-by-side with Ernst Röhm, but the finale featuring his closing address could not be filmed for technical reasons.[46] The following year the young actress and film director Leni Riefenstahl was invited to make a cinematic record of the 1934 rally. In the subsequent film, *Triumph of the Will*, Hitler was no longer ordinary. His closing speech crowned the film with scenes of remarkable dramatic power and emotional intensity. The second film displayed more adequately than the first the ritualized image of an adoring, expectant public and their sole heroic redeemer. This juxtaposition supplied the core representation of the cult throughout the 1930s. The American journalist Virginia Cowles left a vivid eyewitness account of one of these rallies, in a vast stadium of 200,000 people:

As the time for the Führer's arrival drew near, the crowd grew restless. The minutes passed and the wait seemed interminable. Suddenly the beat of the drums increased and three motor-cycles with yellow standards fluttering from their windshields raced through the gates. A few minutes later a fleet of black cars rolled swiftly into the arena: in one of them, standing in the front seat, his hand outstretched in the Nazi salute, was Hitler.

Then Hitler began to speak. The crowd hushed into silence, but the drums continued their steady beat. Hitler's voice rasped into the night and every now and then the multitude broke into a roar of cheers. Some of the audience began swaying back and forth, chanting 'Sieg Heil' over and over again in a frenzy of delirium. I looked at the faces around me and saw tears streaming down people's cheeks.

The success in making Hitler seem so much larger than life was magnified by the disconcerting image of the man who then left the rostrum. Cowles saw the public star suddenly become 'drab and unimpressive'.[47] Though he found Hitler capable of displaying moods of 'savage admonition', Wyndham Lewis also concluded that away from the stage and the microphone 'a more prosaic person it would be difficult to find'.[48]

Stalin's public image was far removed from the dramatic and emotionally charged confrontations staged in Germany between leader and led. He appeared seldom in public, and when he did so the atmosphere was less sensational. He preferred to sit at the edge of the room at meetings, a quiet observer rather than the prima donna. He often chose to speak last, not as triumphant finale, but as modest coda. He perfected an avuncular style (though only Americans called him 'Uncle Joe'), underlined by the thick moustaches and the pipe, and the slow and deliberate way of speaking. It is alleged that during the 1930s he consulted members of the Moscow State Theatre for lessons on his style of dictatorial image. He was advised to be a larger version of himself, using his pipe as a prop, talking slowly, with long pauses pregnant with suspense, and the occasional sardonic smile.[49] When he did speak in public, he was unhurried, sometimes hesitant. The stenographic reports indicate no swaying, tearful crowds but 'laughter' or 'loud laughter', and occasionally 'loud and prolonged applause'. People were allowed to interrupt when Stalin spoke, though often only to underline the leader's sentiments ('The swine', called out a sympathetic listener, on hearing of kulak resistance). At the end of speeches Stalin can be seen on newsreels applauding his audience as they stand and applaud him.[50]

Yet in some important respects the two dictators approached the construction of their images in very similar ways. Both presented themselves as modest, simple men, carved from the common people. They dressed unostentatiously, in simple tunics and jackets. Hitler wore only his Iron Cross, first class; Stalin his badge as Hero of Soviet Labour. Only supreme command in the war altered this preference, when both men wore full military dress on formal occasions. But Stalin was never happy with his title of Marshal of the Soviet Union awarded in 1943, nor with the resplendent white uniform that went with it: 'What do I need all this for?' he asked Molotov. He refused the award of Hero of the Soviet Union offered to him in 1939.[51] Stalin disliked outward show and distinction, and made his unpretentiousness a virtue. Hitler liked to pretend that he had shared the life of the common labourer when he talked to crowds of German workers. He eschewed anything that made him appear flamboyant or privileged or indulgent.

The image of unsophisticated men-of-the-people was deliberate, almost certainly sincere, and entirely different from the pomp and ceremony of the pre-war emperors. This pose allowed both men to appear to be simultaneously accessible and distant to their public. On the one hand, people could identify with the leader-figure as someone who shared and understood their problems; on the other, both dictators cultivated the idea that they were, despite their political humility, forced to separate themselves from everyday life while they ran the nation's affairs. Hitler saw more of his people in the 1930s than Stalin did, but during the war both men progressively cut themselves off from contact with the wider population. Their private lives were shielded from the public gaze. Hitler deliberately chose to remain single, in part because he wanted to show that he was wedded to the historic task of rebuilding Germany, in part perhaps because he wanted to encourage German women to harbour some faint, lingering hope that he would choose one of them.[52] His mistress, Eva Braun, was forced to live a shadowy existence. Stalin did have a family, but he made a clear distinction between his private affairs and his role as dictator, even to the point of sacrificing one of his sons who fell into German captivity during the war.

This mix of approachability and detachment was illustrated by the development of Hitler's new Reich Chancellery building, constructed in the mid-1930s and completed in January 1939. The monumental building had at its core a vast study with an enormous, uncluttered desk. Its purpose was scarcely a workroom. It was the place where Hitler received individual guests. When they arrived, after parading along the high-ceilinged corridor to the study door, they would see the lonely figure of the *Führer*, almost lost in the vast room where he was said to work tirelessly for Germany's future. Hitler would then rise and come forward to greet the new arrival, to put him at his ease. The theatrical effect was acute – intimate and intimidating at one and the same time. The link between the two sensations was the idea of the representative individual. Hitler was one of the people, but at the same time he was more than one of the people. He told the workers who had built the new residence, 'Whenever I receive anyone in the Chancellery, it is not the private individual Adolf Hitler who receives him, but the Leader of the German nation – and therefore it is not I who receive him, but Germany through me.'[53]

This complex idea was central to the fictions at the heart of the cult of personality. Both Stalin and Hitler presented themselves as somehow distinct from the everyday world of politics (in which they actually took a lively and regular part) by virtue of their historic roles as leaders. Instead they promoted the idea that they were guiding the states they ruled on behalf of the people, above politics yet capable of interpreting and mediating the people's will. Both leaders were habitually referred to by the term 'guide' as well as leader. The central myth of Hitler's dictatorship was the claim that he possessed a unique affinity with the German people, an intimate relationship that made the leader, in the words of Carl Schmitt, Germany's leading constitutional lawyer, an 'immediate or real presence' for the millions of Germans who followed him.[54] At the party rally at Nuremberg in 1934 Hitler himself explained the nature of his bond with the people: 'Our leadership does not consider the people as a mere object of its activity; it lives in the people, feels with the people, and fights for the sake of the people.'[55] This 'continuous and infallible contract' allowed the will of each to be subsumed by the leader's will. The people were 'personified in the *Führer*', who would guide them to a historic destiny.[56]

Stalin's claim to be guiding the people's destiny derived from political circumstances peculiar to the Soviet Union. Where Hitler deliberately presented his leadership as something rooted in sensations of affinity and psychic unity with the German people, Stalin's cult was rooted in the very practical issue of preserving Lenin's revolution. Stalin identified himself with the legacy of the dead leader immediately after Lenin's death in January 1924. In the series of lectures delivered at Sverdlov university in April 1924, later published as *Foundations of Leninism*, Stalin set down his view that the party and its leadership had a historic obligation to preserve the 'party of Leninism' at all costs, and outlined and defended every aspect of Lenin's contribution to revolutionary thought.[57] It is difficult to date the precise point at which Stalin began to present himself as Lenin's heir, leading and guiding the party, seeing further than the working class, yet sustaining the myth that he was the true representative of the people, the personification of revolutionary endeavour, but it was an attitude well entrenched by the end of the 1920s when the term *vozhd* began to be used to denote Stalin alone, 'leader and teacher' like Lenin.

From this time on Stalin was regularly referred to as Lenin's devoted pupil and constant companion. The anniversary of Lenin's death in 1930 was merged with celebrations for Stalin's fiftieth birthday. During the early 1930s Stalin succeeded in presenting himself as the primary interpreter of Leninist doctrine. Images of Lenin were set side-by-side with portraits of Stalin in posters and newspapers, but slowly the artistic representation of the two men began to alter. In the 1920s, posters with both men had Lenin prominently illustrated, with a smaller Stalin behind him, in some cases partially obscured. The posters of the 1930s first depicted the two men as visually equal, but these gave way, by the middle of the decade, to posters in which Lenin was a face on a banner, or a ghostly presence in the corner or the background, smiling on his successor, whose stolid form now dominated the picture. Posters of Stalin were regularly issued in runs of 150,000 or 200,000, while Lenin seldom merited more than 30,000. In one of the most famous poster images of the dictatorship, produced by Viktor Govorkov in 1940, 'Stalin in the Kremlin Cares about Each

One of Us', Stalin is seated at his desk busy writing under the light of a lamp, late into the night, but there is no image of Lenin in sight. In one of the last posters of the dictatorship, Viktor Ivanov's 'Great Stalin – Beacon of Communism', Lenin has been reduced to just his name, conspicuously written on the front of the book Stalin is holding. In the large bookcase, directly behind Stalin, the only name clearly visible on the spines of the books is 'J. Stalin'.[58]

By the mid-1930s the Lenin cult was in decline, sucked dry by the new cult of Stalin. 'Stalin is the Lenin of today', ran the party slogan. On New Year's Day 1934, *Pravda* carried an article by Karl Radek, a former party leader demoted during the power struggles of the 1920s, under the title 'Stalin, Architect of Soviet Society'. Radek, a close friend of the 'god-builder' Lunacharsky, presented Stalin as Lenin's true successor as the party's supreme being. The article was published in pamphlet form in a print-run of 225,000 copies, giving wide publicity to the formal construction of the new cult of Stalin.[59] During the 1930s Stalin was referred to more often than Lenin as the people's revolutionary mentor. In 1934 schools were all issued copies of Stalin's address to the Seventeenth Party Congress, with instructions to explain the enthusiasm of the party as a whole 'in proclaiming their attachment to their guide, Comrade Stalin'.[60] 'Inspired guide of all the proletariat, Stalin the Great', ran a *Pravda* headline in 1935; 'Master of Wisdom', 'Wisest man of our times' appeared in 1936. In the 1937 film *Lenin in October*, Stalin is the senior partner, advising Lenin's every move.[61] Stalin never abandoned entirely the connection he had constructed between himself and the legacy of the dead Lenin, which he used to protect himself from criticism. He refused to allow the use of the term 'Stalinism' to describe his contributions to theory.[62] However, he did appropriate the popular veneration that had sustained the Lenin cult in the 1920s.

The idea that Stalin was now the principal guide of the revolution in succession to Lenin implied a myth of omniscience and infallibility, claims that were also present in the constructed myth of the *Führer*. The leader as guide, remote and all-seeing, yet somehow ever-present, was an image underlined by the iconographic status of the two dictators. The visual image was essential to the communication of the cult. Portraits of Hitler were supposed to be hung in every public building, and in 1934 the Interior Minister, Wilhelm Frick, announced that funds from the state would bear the cost of installing approved photographic images of the *Führer* in every office.[63] Busts, picture postcards, cheap posters, all made Hitler exceptionally visible to his public, but in ways that were carefully selected. From early on in his career Hitler was aware of the importance of portraiture. The first official portrait appeared in three formats in September 1923. This photograph, and most subsequent pictures, was taken by the photographer Heinrich Hoffmann, one of Hitler's closest companions. Great care was taken with the expression and the pose in all Hitler's public images. In the 1920s in Germany there was a lively interest in the culture of facial representation, partly a result of growing interest in racial biology, partly aesthetic. A popular volume published in Germany in 1927 by Ernst Benkard under the title *The Eternal Countenance* contained images of the death masks of the famous displayed on a plain black background, including the composer Richard Wagner. Hitler borrowed the idea for one of the most striking posters of the 1932 election campaigns – a photograph just of Hitler's face set on a plain black background with the single word 'Hitler' in large letters at the foot.[64]

The presentation of Hitler as the personification of the German race faced the self-evident problem that Hitler lacked the firm profile, tall stature and blond hair of the racial stereotype he sought to preserve. Max von Gruber, president of the Bavarian Academy of Sciences, and a eugenicist, wrote after seeing Hitler for the first time: 'Appearance and head of bad race, half-breed. Low sloping forehead, unattractive nose, broad cheekbones, small eyes, dark hair.'[65] Hoffmann tried to present Hitler in the best light by concentrating on his eyes, which had a dreamy, visionary appearance in many images. After 1933 the official portraits focused on a more withdrawn, austere, unsmiling image of the seer-statesman in smart uniform or suit. Paintings of Hitler abandoned all pretence of presenting the real man in favour of idealized images of a taller, more robust and distinguished Hitler in the pose of soldier, prophet or statesman. In 1936 Hoffmann published a set of photographs in book form. *Pictures from the Life of the Führer* sold two million copies. In 1939 Hoffmann published 200,000 copies of a second, smaller book, simply titled *The Countenance of the Führer*, which contained sixteen portraits covering Hitler's political life from 1919. The images had first been shown together in the party paper *Illustrierte Beobachter* in 1936 under the title 'a face forged by struggle' to counter unflattering comments about Hitler's physiognomy in the exiled satirical magazine *Simplicissimus*, but they could have done little to stifle the view that Hitler's was not the ideal face for the New Order.[66]

Stalin's face was also used exhaustively to promote the cult of his personality. The propaganda apparatus from the mid-1930s poured out an endless stream of images of Stalin in paternal poses with children or workers, or Stalin as party philosopher, book in hand, gazing into the socialist future. The leader's visibility was a perpetual, omnipresent reminder of the cult, but the images were also carefully constructed to maximize their impact. As early as 1918 Lenin originated the idea of public representation of socialist heroes in the forms of statues, busts or bas-reliefs, though he had in mind chiefly dead heroes.[67] From 1924 poster art, public portraits and statuary began to incorporate living Bolsheviks. The turning point for Stalin may have been the May Day Parade of 1932, when in Moscow's Pushkin Square colossal but equal-sized portraits of Lenin and Stalin were hung side-by-side. From then on portraits of Stalin appeared everywhere in public spaces, and in a great many homes (though anyone foolish enough to hang one in the lavatory risked prosecution). Unlike the images of Hitler, early Stalin portraits could show him smiling or at ease, though with no hint of the pock-marked skin or swarthy complexion. Only later in the dictatorship did the stiff, statesmanlike images predominate; Stalin can be seen in numerous portraits staring steadfastly into the distance, unmoving, rock-like.[68] In 1935 the official journal *Art* published guidelines 'On Portraits of Leaders', which carefully described what was and was not permissible in representing Stalin. The same effort went into the publication of popular histories or picture-books. In 1939 further instructions were issued for Stalin's sixtieth birthday celebrations on 'What to Write about the Life and Activities of Comrade Stalin'.[69] In 1929 *Pravda* had announced that a simple popular biography of Stalin would soon be available 'for every worker and peasant who can read',[70] but it was not produced for another ten years. For Stalin's birthday in 1939 there finally appeared an authorized *Short*

Biography, followed by a second edition eight years later which, like books on Hitler, had portraits from youth to mature statesman, starting with an earnest image of the young seminarian and ending with a greying, plumper Stalin in the uniform of wartime generalissimo. The last seven pages of a book bought by millions of Soviet citizens describe all the ingredients of the cult of personality – the link with Lenin, the heroic guide and father to his people, the scourge of enemies, the single-handed builder of Soviet communism, the sober philosopher-leader.[71]

Alongside the pictures and statues, there were the leaders' own words. Hitler's *Mein Kampf* became a bestseller, and the party bible. First published in two volumes in 1926 and 1927 at the then substantial cost of twenty-four marks, the book sold modestly. In 1930 a single-volume version was published at eight marks and sales began to rise, reaching more than a million by the end of 1933. In April 1936 registrars were instructed to issue copies to all newly-weds. By the end of the Third Reich an estimated 8 to 9 million had been sold.[72] Stalin wrote much more than Hitler. His books were sold in cheap party editions in numbers that dwarfed even Marx and Lenin. In 1932–3 the public bought 16.5 million books and pamphlets by Stalin, 14 million by Lenin. In the 1940s an official edition of Stalin's collected works was published in thirteen volumes, an honour enjoyed until then only by Lenin. By the time of his death Stalin had sold 706 million copies, Lenin 279 million, and Marx and Engels a mere 65 million.[73] Among these works was the *History of the Communist Party of the Soviet Union: Short Course*, which was written under Stalin's direction in 1937 and published in 1938. Although Stalin's name does not appear in the long table of contents, the book was filled with lengthy quotations from Stalin's works (twenty-six in the last hundred pages), and an entirely mendacious reworking of revolutionary history, in which Stalin is given responsibility 'to direct the uprising' of October 1917.[74]

The writing of the *Short Course* demonstrated the extent to which the legends and myths that surrounded the dictators could be deliberately created by rewriting history. The cults of personality ensured that the new history would bear little relation to reality, nor was it intended that it should do so. The object was to demonstrate that two ordinary men had assumed extraordinary historical roles. Still joined to the people, Hitler and Stalin were nonetheless presented as men burdened by high office, working ceaselessly for the nation or the revolution, all-seeing, all-knowing, above all good shepherds, tenderly caring for their flocks, vigilant in their defence against the wolves who might otherwise devour them. The dictators became allegorical representations of the systems they dominated, but the power of the cults rested on the willingness of the German and Soviet populations to recognize and accept the fictionalized version of personality on which the allegory was founded.

It has often been suggested that the German and Soviet populations were victims of some form of mass hypnosis, in which they mutely followed whither their unscrupulous leaders took them. This has never been a convincing argument. The success of the two cults of personality relied on the active and willing participation of millions, who suspended their disbelief and endorsed and magnified the overblown personalities constructed by the authorities. Cults flourish in two directions, from above and from below, as Weber had recognized. The evidently voluntary character of adulation in these, as in other modern dictatorships, is a significant indicator of how popular dictatorship works. There is an act of complicity between the ruler who projects the image of mythic hero and the followers who sanctify and substantiate it. The emotional bond created by the act binds both parties. Dictators cannot freely step outside the performance they have helped to produce. 'Stalin too had no right to divest himself of either his pensive pipe or his candy moustache,' wrote Andrei Sinyavsky later in the Soviet period. Doomed to do everything 'worshippers demand of their god', Stalin was no longer a person, 'he had become a portrait'.[75]

Sinyavsky's point is critical if sense is to be made of the cult of personality. The dictators created necessary metaphors of themselves, but they swiftly became the property of the whole people, to be accepted or rejected, as Sinyavsky well understood: 'Who's pulling the strings? Maybe we do it ourselves, without noticing.'[76] It was popular, enthusiastic endorsement that moulded the cults into the grotesque forms they assumed at their apogees. Some of the momentum for this transformation was doubtless generated by the propaganda and party apparatus, which saw it as part of their function to ensure that Hitler and Stalin were worshipped the right way. Stalin closely monitored what was printed in *Pravda* and *Izvestiia*, day by day. When a young author, Alexander Avdeenko, was rebuked for ending a speech 'thank you, Soviet power', he was told that Soviet power 'was above all, Stalin'.[77] A few weeks later, in February 1935, *Pravda* reprinted a second speech by Avdeenko whose absurdly fulsome phrasing would have been recognized in a less earnest political culture as satire:

The men of all generations will call on Thy name, which is strong, beautiful, wise and marvellous. Thy name is engraven on every factory, every machine, every place on the earth, and in the hearts of all men . . .[78]

This is an extreme example. Yet it demonstrates the extent to which the cult was appropriated and reflected back by an audience that understood its own part in the construction of myth.

Cults are conventionally religious rather than political phenomena. In both Germany and the Soviet Union the distinction between the two became blurred in the public mind. The Hitler cult was the more self-consciously religious of the two. Hitler was described either as god himself, or a gift from god. Alois Spaniel, a party leader from the Saar, described Hitler as 'a new, a greater and a more powerful Jesus Christ'. The Church minister Hans Kerrl described Hitler as 'the real Holy Ghost'. Among the thirty-point programme of the pro-National Socialist German Christian movement, set up in 1933, could be found the following:

the greatest written document of our people is the book of our Führer, *Mein Kampf*. [The movement] is completely aware that this book incorporates not only the greatest, but also the purest and truest ethics for the present life of our people.[79]

The National Socialist movement developed its own liturgy, complete with creed, baptism and marriage service. Small 'Hitler altars' were set up in public places and private homes, like the Lenin Corners of the Soviet cult.[80] Funerals of public party figures were opportunities for exaggerated displays of religiosity. The martyrs to the cause, who were remembered every year on the anniversary of the November *Putsch* of 1923, were honoured as saints.

In the Soviet Union direct reference to Christian imagery was more difficult in a state that was at least officially atheist. Nevertheless the development of the popular cult was permeated, as in Germany, with metaphors that were unashamedly sacred. The ideas of Stalin as saviour, as the source of a supernatural power, as prophet or redeemer, were borrowed from traditions in Russian popular religion with which most ordinary Russians were still familiar, even if they were hostile to them. Some of the early images of Lenin had strong iconographic echoes, and Lenin Corners unabashedly copied the tradition of sacred corners in the households of the Orthodox faithful. In the 1930s Stalin was sometimes presented with his arm raised on a red background, like iconographic images of Christ. Images of Stalin staring directly out of a photograph, rather than obliquely as had been conventional in the 1920s, may also have echoed religious imagery.[81] Eulogies to Stalin reflected the new religiosity. 'Thy incomparable genius mounts to the heavens', wrote one poet in 1936; 'But Thou, O Stalin, are more high/ Than the highest places of the heavens', wrote another. 'O Great Stalin, O Leader of the Peoples/ Thou who didst give birth to man/ Thou who didst make fertile the earth' appeared in *Pravda* in August of the same year.[82] A letter written to President Kalinin simply stated, 'You are for me like a man-god, and I. V. Stalin is god.'[83]

Religious imagery also flourished in another area of traditional Russian culture, the folktale. During the 1920s the Soviet authorities frowned on the Russian oral tradition of fables and fairy stories as a manifestation of cultural backwardness. But in the early 1930s the folklorist Yuri Sokolov suggested that folktales could be made to serve as a bridge between traditional society and the modernizing party. In 1932 he was appointed to head the folklore section of the Union of Soviet Writers. Under his guidance folklore was mobilized for the party. The traditional epic poem (*bylina*) was revived, alongside traditional folksongs in a modern Soviet form (*noviny*), and their authors were encouraged to think in terms of a new generation of popular revolutionary heroes. The celebrated folksinger Marfa Kryukova was sent on countrywide tours to find inspiration for new songs about Stalin, and in 1937 a national anthology of folk writing, poems and songs was published.[84]

Not all of the new folktales and folksongs were about Stalin, but those that were underlined the cult. 'Glory to Stalin will be eternal' was the theme of one *novina* in 1937, in which Stalin meets Lenin and decides to found the Bolshevik Party. The song encapsulates the idea of Stalin as far away in Moscow, yet ever present among his people: 'And from that [Kremlin] tower day and night/ In his military dress/ With a telescope in his hand/ With a gay smile/ He looks and rules his country with care.' In a traditional lament, a widow is advised, 'Go to Stalin's city:/ Il'ich [Lenin] gave to Joseph,/ All his knowledge to Joseph.'[85] The most famous of the Soviet generation of fable writers, I. F. Kovalev, invoked the world of sorcery, wizards and demons to political ends. Lenin and Stalin fight with a magic sword and a destroyer-ball weighing 1,000 poods. In the tale of 'The Hero with Black Curls', Stalin drives a magic post into the ground in order to make the earth move in the opposite direction, and rids Russia of the Tsar, priests and soldiers.[86]

The popular development of the cults took many other forms, but all of them shared a common culture of political hyperbole that came to assume an existence of its own, independent of the real object of adulation, as writers, artists and officials vied with each other in giving expression to the metaphorical superman. Hero-worship infected all areas of public life. In Germany new days of celebration were created: the Hitler-Day to mark his birthday on 20 April; a Day for the German Mother on the birthday of Hitler's mother; the day of remembrance on 9 November for those who died fighting for the cause of National Socialism; extravagant celebrations every 30 January to mark the day that Hitler became Chancellor. All over Germany streets and squares were renamed after the *Führer*; Hitler-Oaks were planted; thousands of unfortunate young German boys were christened Adolf, a name, according to one enthusiastic philologist, 'composed of "*ath*" (divine or spiritual act) and "*uolfa*" (creator)'.[87]

In general the cult of Hitler was neither as remorseless nor as unsophisticated as the Stalin cult appeared in the Soviet Union. Once public adulation for Stalin was officially permitted, the USSR witnessed extravagant bouts of unrestrained, though not always unorchestrated, sycophancy. Soviet literature in the 1920s still incorporated critical portraits of Stalin, but from the early 1930s all literary forms adapted themselves to the cult of personality. Few were more ironic than a folk tale from the Nenets region in Siberia, *Stalin and Truth*, published in 1936, in which a young Stalin is exiled to the tundra by the Tsar because of his friendship with Truth. In his icy exile he shows himself to be a true hero, leading the common people to a happier, tsar-less future.[88] Another novel published that same year, *In the East*, recalls a more mature leader, as the heroine listens to 'the voice of our motherland, the simple, clear, infinitely honest, boundlessly kind, un-hurried and fatherly voice of Stalin'.[89] At least some of this adulation had traditional roots in Asian societies, where the unbridled flattery of rulers had a recognizably symbolic significance. One of the first unashamedly cultic poems was by the Iranian poet A. A. Lakhuti: 'Wise Master, Marxist gardener/Thou art tending the vine of communism'.[90] Even flattery had its limits. In August 1936, at the height of the first wave of the cult, an editorial in *Izvestiia* candidly confessed that when it came to Stalin 'writers no longer know with what to compare you, and our poets have no longer sufficient pearls of language to describe you'.[91]

Local officials competed with each other in ascribing Stalin's name to villages, towns, theatres and collective farms. By the 1940s the map of the USSR showed, besides Stalingrad, the cities of Stalinsk, Stalinogorsk, Stalinbad, Stalinski, Stalinograd, Stalinisi and Stalinaoul. In 1937 several letters to the party suggested renaming Moscow 'Stalin-odar' or 'Stalindar' (gift of Stalin). Another enthusiast suggested chang-ing the calendar so that it would be dated from Stalin's birth, not that of Christ. This proved too much for Stalin, who refused both proposals.[92] In the years immediately before the outbreak of war, the cult was deliberately played down. An anonymous letter from a sympathetic communist, sent in July 1938 to Andrei Zhdanov, over-lord of the arts in the Soviet Union, complained that 'Everything is Stalin, Stalin, Stalin . . . In the end this sacred and beloved name – Stalin – may make so much noise in people's heads that . . . it will have the opposite effect.'[93] The reduced intensity of the cult was, however, only relative. When Stalin's name was mentioned at Central Committee meetings before the war, all those present were said to have clapped. The war and victory brought a renewed wave of unrestricted idolatry. Between 1945 and 1953 the cult became institutionalized, and no one challenged the image of Stalin as the father of his people and architect of victory, even when the producers of the film *The Fall of Berlin* showed Stalin alone poring over staff maps, planning Hitler's defeat.

Under high Stalinism it was possible to believe that the Stalin of pre-war myth had become the reality of post-war hero-statesman.

The sheer irrationalism of both cults in the 1930s begs the question of belief. Even for those who accepted the leadership cults as an act of faith, the exaggerated enthusiasm of the faithful and the fabulous qualities ascribed to both leaders possessed an evident metaphorical character. It is plausible to argue that both dictators could have retained their power with a considerably lower level of idolatry. Why, then, did both actors and audience indulge in these extravagant forms of political theatre? What purposes were served by the cult of personality?

Most attempts to answer these questions begin with the dictators themselves. Their motives are not entirely explicit. Stalin's efforts to play down the cult are seldom taken seriously, since there are numerous examples of Stalin's direct intervention in encouraging or sustaining it. For Hitler the cult was entirely consistent with the idea that the new 'Leader-State' was based upon the principle of personality. The cult in Germany was understood to be a necessary corollary of the idea of leadership (*Führung*) and following (*Gefolgschaft*); absolute authority from above, absolute obedience from below.[94] It is Stalin who is the anomaly.

The temptation is to explain Stalin's cult in terms of his own weaknesses of personality. Stalin has been variously described as insecure, greedily ambitious and vain. In this account, the cult of personality was not an extension of the political system, but a psychological prop. Stalin needed his fragile self-esteem to be puffed up by crude expressions of glorification. There may be some truth in this characterization, though it is impossible to substantiate. Stalin, like Hitler, rose from an unprepossessing background to exercise supreme power over one of the great states of Europe, a success story that might have needed constant reiteration in the dictator's mind. However, there is too little historical evidence to support the idea that the cult was a reflection of a fragile psychology. Stalin's reluctant acceptance of the cult rested on a political calculation of its advantages. A more convincing explanation for the cult's development can be found in the way the political system was constructed in the 1930s, and the growing importance of personal rule within it.

Here, once again, there is common ground between Stalin and Hitler. The contexts in which personal rule arose were different; so too was the substance of that dictatorship – Hitler as redeemer of the German nation, Stalin as guardian of Lenin's revolutionary legacy – but the purpose of the cult in both cases was to underpin and secure the dominant political position of the two dictators. The devices used to achieve this were broadly similar: ritual adulation, perpetual visibility or 'presence', the construction of heroic myths, the deflection of criticism, a deliberate juxtaposition of immanence and distance. The cults were carefully constructed works of political artistry, which played on the prevailing political longing for the strong leader (Carl Jung once more: 'our age calls for the redeemer personality, for the one who can emancipate himself from the inescapable grip of the collective'[95]), and legitimized their calling.

The mobilization of cults to endorse personal rule brought other political dividends. Both Stalin and Hitler were freed from moral restraint. The idea that politics could be reduced to expressions of the leader's will allowed the construction of a distinctive moral universe. The rightness of both dictators was assumed from the myths of infallibility and omniscience generated by the cults of personality. The remark 'It is an order from the *Führer*' eliminated all discussion in the Third Reich (though it did not necessarily stifle opinion). Although Stalin continued to work formally through the Central Committee of the party and the Council of People's Commissars, no major decisions could be taken without his approval. The idea of moral certainty extended to justifying ostensibly immoral acts. When Stalin interfered with the making of Sergei Eisenstein's film about Tsar Ivan IV ('the Terrible'), he told the producer: 'you must show that it was necessary to be ruthless'.[96] The *Short Biography* celebrated Stalin's 'merciless severity', and 'extraordinary firmness' towards those who challenged the moral and political unity of the party.[97] When Gottfried Feder, who drafted the National Socialist party programme, described the nature of the *Führer* he did so in the following terms: 'an inward drive; moral earnestness; passionate will ... The dictator must be entirely free from all unnecessary restraints and scruples ... In the pursuit of his aim he must not refrain even from bloodshed and war.'[98] The cult of personality both magnified the exercise of personal will and justified the dictators when what they willed was vicious and repressive.

The myths of infallibility could also be exploited as instruments of political management and social control. The period of personal rule brought to an end the existence of fundamental divisions within both parties on ideology and tactics, and reinforced the idea of social and political integration. Though the party line was never set in concrete, it was understood that Hitler and Stalin were the final arbiters on issues of ideology. The 'Great Debate' over revolutionary strategy in the Soviet Communist Party in the 1920s was never repeated under Stalin. The defeat of the National Socialist revolutionaries in 1934, with the murder of Ernst Röhm, left Hitler free to dominate the ideas of the party. Indeed, the cults of personality bestowed on both men an almost oracular power. Those around them listened to what they said rather than waiting for written instructions or orders. This simplified the task of managing both political parties. Party officials and members, whatever individual misgivings they might have had, played an important part in constructing and communicating the cults of personality to the wider public. The more elevated the status of each dictator, the more dependent the respective parties became on sustaining and reinforcing the cults to secure their own acceptance; the more successful the cult, the less room for manoeuvre for other political actors. 'It is clear that in communist circles there is now a struggle going on for the president's seat,' claimed a Soviet academic (wrongly) at the height of the Stalin cult in 1936. 'I am almost sure that the president will be Stalin, who will that way be transformed into Joseph the First, the new all-Russian emperor.'[99]

The relationship between leader and led was also greatly simplified by the projection of an exaggerated leadership image. The role of guide or redeemer ascribed to the two dictators reduced the need for more conventional forms of political loyalty, and helped to overcome the paradox between the flesh-and-blood ordinariness of the two men and the fantastic historical role ascribed to them. More credulous or enthusiastic supporters accepted the central myth that Hitler and Stalin could be trusted to protect the nation and preserve its people. The result was a widespread and willing political abdication, evident even among social or political groups previously hostile to the new regimes. In Hitler's Germany that abdication was ritualized in the introduction of the party 'Heil Hitler' salute. On 13 July 1933 the greeting became compulsory for all public employees; it was also compulsory during the singing of the national anthem and the party hymn, the 'Horst Wessel' song. Germans unfortunate enough to be unable to raise their right arms through disability were allowed to raise the left.[100] All public correspondence was supposed to carry the words 'Heil Hitler!' instead of 'sincerely' or 'best wishes', and the archive shows that officials began to do so almost immediately after Hitler assumed the chancellorship.

The Stalin cult could scarcely go so far, but ritual affirmation of the great leader was evident at party meetings and public events, and the absence of such references, deliberate or accidental, invited rebuke. So, too, did any criticism publicly expressed, or humour. Jokes certainly circulated about both Hitler and Stalin, but they generally remained behind closed doors. The two leaders had to be treated with an evident reverence; failure to take them seriously could be regarded not simply as foolish or rash, but as political blasphemy. Those who broke the magic spell and voiced aloud their misgivings or hostility ran the very real risk of arrest and conviction for treasonable defamation. The link between the cults and the systems of terror showed what little space existed in either society for those who refused to be seduced by the pervasive atmosphere of adulation.

The public reaction to the cult was, nonetheless, far from monolithic. Public complicity with the cults masked a wide variety of motives. Cynical opportunists and true believers may outwardly behave in the same way. No special intuition was needed for the party official or member to grasp that the cult could be exploited in their interest too. It might be mobilized to secure compliance in the local party branch or social unit; properly used it could mean promotion; at the least, enthusiastic endorsement could be expected to show positive results (though in the Soviet Union the regular purging of the party showed that even Stalin-worship was no protection). All this could be done by individuals whose private opinion of the object of adulation was less flattering.

Popular attitudes to the cults also changed with changing circumstances. Stalin's cult developed very slowly in the early 1930s, emerged more powerfully in 1933–4 at the point where the personal dictatorship was being secured, reached a peak in 1936–7 during the Great Terror, and re-emerged in strengthened form as the defeat of Germany became clear by 1943. Then for ten years, until Stalin's death, the cult remained a central feature of the system. The peaks and troughs were partly explained by deliberate efforts from the centre to deflect popular hostility away from Stalin – for example over collectivization, or the German–Soviet Pact of 1939. The strength of the Hitler cult also reflected the ups and downs of the regime. It peaked in 1933–4, declined during the years of consolidation, and then rose steadily during the period of foreign policy and military successes, reaching a second peak in the summer of 1940 when millions of Germans rejoiced at Hitler's historic victory over the French. Thereafter Hitler still commanded a fanatical loyalty and belief, but bombing and the imminence of defeat reduced the appeal and exposed his fallibility in the last year of war.[101]

There were also many Germans and Soviet citizens who refused to accept or endorse hero-worship. This was more evident in the Soviet Union, where the cult fitted less well with the evolution of party politics in the 1920s. Despite the traditions of royal adulation and religious mysticism, which were deliberately invoked in communist garb to support first the cult of Lenin, then that of his successor, the fact remained that the whole Soviet experiment had been predicated on destroying a monarchical system based on the Tsar-cult. In the 1930s grass-root criticism of the cult certainly existed. One worker complained: 'everyone is praising Stalin, they consider him a god, and no one makes any criticism'.[102] Other grumbles focused on the comparison with Hitler, or the link with the age of the tsars. 'Now the time has come when the leaders have become gods and are carried like icons,' observed another worker after the 1937 Soviet elections.[103] Some of those who opposed Stalin, like the poet Osip Mandelstam, felt compelled for their own safety to play the part of worshippers, despite all their better instincts. In the winter of 1936/7 Mandelstam composed an *Ode to Stalin*. His wife later recalled that to write the ode, the poet had to 'get in tune, like a musical instrument, by deliberately giving way to the general hypnosis' and 'putting oneself under the spell of the liturgy'.[104] Other writers disguised their views as irony or fable, though the censors proved remarkably alert to the slightest hint of irreverence. The only Soviet writer to publish open criticism of Stalin before the leader's death, the poet Naum Mandel, escaped execution because the authorities assumed he was mad.[105]

With the passage of time it is the true believers who appear more psychologically complex. Their devotion to the cause is sometimes compared with the bond between rock star and fans of a later age, but this is a trivial and historically inept comparison. The true believers are more commonly regarded as a secular congregation, experiencing the same enthusiasm and denial of self associated with ecstatic states of religious belief. Neither cult disguised the exploitation of religious imagery; at least some of the states of belief in both dictatorships had strong religious overtones. However, neither cult was metaphysical. They relied on a bond, real or imagined, that was essentially political, an expression of a relationship of power between leader and follower. It was a relationship that was in a real sense immediate and physical, not other-worldly. Consider this diary entry written by a witness of Stalin's visit to a young communist congress in April 1936:

And HE stood, a little weary, pensive and stately. One could feel the tremendous habit of power, the force of it, and at the same time something feminine and soft. I looked about: Everyone had fallen in love with this gentle, inspired, laughing face. To see him, simply to see him, was happiness for all of us.[106]

A post-war painting by Robert Sturua of a peasant girl, surrounded by an awe-struck circle of her family, was simply titled *She Saw Stalin*.[107]

The bond with Hitler was also a relationship of political power. Albert Speer observed, in one of his post-war interrogations on the subject of Hitler's personality, that his immediate circle of loyal supporters became in his presence 'insignificant and timid . . . They were under his spell, blindly obedient to him and with no will of their own.' The physical presence of the leader exerted, Speer observed, a remarkable effect on those more distant from the inner circle: 'there existed in the minds of the people a very powerful general conviction of Hitler's greatness and mission'; people approached him with 'feelings of reverence for his historical magnitude'.[108] There was in the Hitler cult also an element of sexual power, almost entirely lacking in Stalin's case. Women wrote to Hitler asking him to father their children. One woman wrote that her marriage had broken down because of her commitment to the leader: 'From the first moment when I heard of Adolf Hitler, he gave me a new faith, he brought me strength and power and love. He is my idol, and I will devote my life to him.'[109] Women, so it was claimed, were to be seen at Hitler's Bavarian retreat at Berchtesgaden eating handfuls of the gravel that the *Führer* had just walked across.[110]

The exaggerated enthusiasm for both men owed much to the image they projected and the power that this implied. But it can also be explained in terms of the historical context in which the two dictatorships arose. Both populations had been exposed to prolonged periods of political uncertainty, civil war, violence and economic deprivation. The degree of crisis was acute and prolonged and disorientating. The longing for salvation was one of its consequences. Both leaders exploited and were sustained by the psychological insecurity of their populations and the sense of certainty that the leader-image bestowed. The cults of personality were in some sense necessary fictions, in worlds where 'normal' politicians had been exposed as incompetent, traitorous, or simply overwhelmed.

Near death both men betrayed a revealing anxiety about the future. Each claimed at one point in their careers to have contemplated retirement, Hitler to a quiet life in Linz, Stalin as a simple pensioner, but they remained wedded to their mission. Hitler, in his final recorded monologues in the spring of 1945, asked himself how Germany would cope without their fallen leader. After the war Stalin despaired for his Central Committee colleagues when he would no longer be there to guide them: 'What will become of you? The imperialists will strangle you.'[111] In neither state did the overblown cult of personality survive their deaths. In February 1956 Khrushchev announced to a stunned party leadership that Stalin had abused his power and needlessly oppressed the Soviet people. The Central Committee published a resolution 'Concerning the Setting Aside of the Personality Cult and its Consequences' to ensure that nothing like the idolatry granted to the person of Stalin would be repeated.[112] His body was removed from the

Lenin mausoleum in Red Square in 1961 and reburied unostentatiously in the Kremlin wall. The Soviet national anthem, introduced in 1943, after Stalin had corrected and approved the lyrics, contained the phrase 'Stalin raised us – faithfulness to the people/Work and heroic deeds he inspired in us'. After 1956 the anthem was played but no longer sung until, in 1977, Lenin's name was substituted for the disgraced Stalin's.[113] In rural Russia, which had been the butt of Stalinist oppression, myths developed in the 1960s that Stalin's ghost was the source of malign hexes.[114] In Germany the denigration of Hitler's reputation was completed in the war crimes trials held at Nuremberg from November 1945. No attempt was made subsequently to revive the ideal of the charismatic hero, though pale versions of the Stalin cult could be observed in the communist German Democratic Republic. Uninhibited worship of personality was confined to a brief dozen years of German history.

4

The Party State

'Party and state are not one and the same thing, for their tasks are different. The party commands the state but it is not the state! The party is the political leadership, the state the function of administration.'   Otto Dietrich, September 1936[1]

'The Party exercises the dictatorship of the proletariat . . . In this sense the Party *takes* power, the Party *governs the country* . . . This does not mean that the Party can be identified with the Soviets, with the state power. The Party is the core of this power, but it cannot be identified with the state power.'

Josef Stalin, January 1926[2]

Nothing taxed the semantic and conceptual ingenuity of the two dictatorships quite as much as the problem of defining the party and its precise relationship to state and society. The party was nonetheless the central institution of both systems. Hitler was the party's *Führer* far longer than he was Germany's, twenty-four years in all, if the year in prison is included; Stalin's personal authority derived not from high state office, but from his position as General Secretary of the party, which he held for thirty-one years, most of them as the party's unofficial 'boss' (*khoziain*). Neither dictatorship is conceivable without the activity and complicity of the mass party, yet the role of the parties in explaining the operation and survival of the dictatorships has generally been neglected in favour of the dominant personality at their core.

The term 'party' is itself misleading. Though both began life as one party among many competing for members and votes and parliamentary seats, Hitler and Stalin did not see either National Socialism or Soviet communism as a party in the conventional European sense. In 1934, at the annual party congress, Hitler gave a long closing speech on the nature of political parties in Germany. The old parliamentary parties, supplanted in 1933, he viewed as electoral machines representing only the narrow confessional or economic interests of a fraction of the population, but never the whole people. They were none of them inspired by a 'true world view' because they were prepared to make ideological compromises with other parties to share power, or chose simply to remain in opposition, a prey to factionalism and class conflict.[3] Stalin dismissed the parties of pre-revolutionary Russia, too, as nothing more than 'election machines adapted for parliamentary elections and parliamentary struggle', which put self-interest and power-seeking before political resistance, and would have led Russia's masses to 'hopeless despair and inevitable defeat'.[4] What had been necessary, he wrote in 1924 in *Foundations of Leninism*, was a new kind of party, uncompromising, united, revolutionary and exclusive, a party to transcend party. Hitler described the infant National Socialist movement – he preferred the term 'movement' (*Bewegung*) to the pejorative 'party' (*Partei*) – in almost identical terms. It was set up, he told his congress audience, to accept no compromise, to represent a unitary and revolutionary will, and to hold 'power on its own'.[5]

Both dictators looked back from the secure vantage point of established single-party rule, but their analysis of what they believed to be the distinctive character of the two parties says much about the position each enjoyed under dictatorship. Rather than representing an economic interest or a class faction, National Socialism and Soviet communism claimed to stand for the whole community, imbued with a sense of the people's deeper historic interests. Communism was the 'directing force' or 'vanguard' of all the forces of social revolution in Russia; National Socialism was, in Hitler's term, the 'racial core' (*Rassenkern*) of the entire German people, responsible for safeguarding the racial future.[6] Each party was supposed to attract into its ranks the finest elements of the population, whose social commitment and intelligent activism set them apart from the mass. The party, continued Hitler, was composed of the minority of 'worthwhile elements' committed to fighting and sacrificing on behalf of the entire *Volk*. Communists represented, in Stalin's view, 'the finest elements of the working class' destined to play the part of leaders to the rest of their class.[7] The party faithful were not, on either account, to be separated from the rest of the population, but were a form of 'transmission belt' (Lenin's term) or 'connecting link' (Hitler's) between the dedicated core and the distant edges of the non-party population. Through the party, according to Hitler, 'the whole people become National Socialist', while the party 'incorporates the will of the German people'; for Stalin the party imbued the entire population with a revolutionary 'spirit of discipline and endurance'.[8] The ideal of a populist movement of selfless and self-conscious political activists, drawn from the people and representing their most profound and general interests, was the founding myth of both parties.

The exact relationship between party and state was more difficult to define. In both cases there was no sense that the party could become the state, substituting its own bureaucracy, procedures and personnel for the inherited structures of administration and policing, even where these were, as in Russia after 1917, weak or non-existent. Yet neither was a conventional parliamentary party, willing to sit back while the task of governing was delegated to a small ministerial circle and an independent bureaucracy. The dilemma was resolved by regarding the party as the source of political leadership and inspiration and seeing the state as its executive arm. 'The party *governs* the country,' Stalin wrote, but the institutions of state 'are organizations that rally the labouring masses' under party leadership and guidance, compelling obedience when necessary.[9] The need to coerce, to exercise what Lenin described as 'power based directly on the use of force', was the separate function of the state; it would be absurd, Stalin argued, for a workers' party to be seen to use force against the working class.[10] The same distinction was made in Germany. In Hitler's Reich the party was presented as the source of political leadership, and of political leaders, but the administration of policy was the responsibility of the state, whose officials became, in Hitler's words, 'the obedient and honourable officers of the movement'. The two, party and state, had identifiably separate functions, but the party was, at least in theory, the senior partner: 'As long as the National Socialist party is there, there can exist nothing other than a National Socialist state.'[11]

These ideals were not without substance. No other party was permitted in either system, and factionalism within the party was fought against resolutely and violently. Political leadership was exercised by the top ranks of the party, joined in many cases to high state office. Both parties saw themselves as a representative elite. However, the relationship to the state and to the wider society from which the party rank-and-file was recruited was both more complex and more ill-defined than the neat division of responsibility outlined by the party leaders. The parties themselves were not passive actors, manipulated exclusively from above. The role, structure and significance of the parties changed over time as the nature of the dictatorships changed. The functional disparity between state and party was a process of adjustment and compromise rather than agreed demarcation. The social bond between party and people was not a frictionless unity, but the product of political agitation, constant supervision and, when required, open coercion.

Both parties grew from modest roots into gigantic organizations embracing large segments of each population. The Bolshevik fraction of the Russian Social Democratic Labour Party had 8,000 members in 1905, shortly after its foundation, and 26,000 members when the Tsar was overthrown in February 1917; at Stalin's death in 1953 the Communist Party of the Soviet Union, a title it was given only a year before, superseding the less elegant 'All Union Communist Party (Bolsheviks)' by which it had been known since 1924, boasted a membership of almost 7 million. The National Socialist German Workers' Party, successor in 1920 to the tiny German Workers' Party, had around 3,000 members in 1921, but in 1945 an estimated 8 million.[12]

The pattern of growth in the two parties was irregular – long periods of consolidation or slow expansion punctuated by periods of rapid inflation or deflation. The two parties closely controlled the number and quality of those who applied for entry, for membership was regarded as a privilege, not an automatic entitlement. Applicants were frequently rejected. In the Soviet Union a compulsory period of probation as a 'candidate member' was formally introduced in 1922, though a brief period of apprenticeship had first appeared in 1919. Each prospective member had to be introduced by at least three party referees, each with a certain number of years of party service behind them. Until 1939 workers and peasants were at an advantage, with short probation periods of six months or a year, while non-workers had to wait two years and find five members willing to vouch for them. In 1939 a standard candidacy system was introduced, with one year's probation for all.[13] The National Socialist party initiated a two-year probationary period in 1933, after which members received, in addition to the party card, the coveted party record book; each candidate was assessed for their political reliability, and files were kept on every successful applicant. The party card was presented at official ceremonies in each dictatorship, to indicate its solemn significance. In the Soviet Union party members could sometimes be distinguished by the small canvas purse hanging from a chain round their necks, containing the precious document. Loss of the party card had serious repercussions, and might even lead to exclusion or a period again as a candidate.[14]

One of the first and most important duties was to pay monthly contributions to the party, without which neither organization could properly function. Communists paid 2 per cent of their earnings when they were admitted to the party, and then a regular contribution based on monthly income. In 1934 the poorest members paid 20 kopeks a month, the better-off 3 per cent of their earnings; in 1952 a sliding-scale was introduced from 0.5 per cent to 3 per cent of income.[15] The National Socialist party introduced a sliding scale of 2 to 5 marks a month according to income in 1934, but for those members who joined before May 1933 the pre-1933 rate of 1.50 marks was kept. Failure to pay these modest sums punctually was one of the most frequent justifications for expulsion from the party.[16]

The growth of communist party membership in the 1920s was governed mainly by the urgent necessity of getting as many workers and poorer peasants as possible into the party to create a more genuinely proletarian character. Recruitment campaigns in 1924 and 1925, the so-called 'Lenin Enrolment', brought in 200,000 new members, and a third 'October Call' in 1927 added a smaller number. However, the most rapid expansion of the party with younger workers and peasants coincided with the First Five-Year Plan, when over a four-year period some 1.8 million new members were hastily recruited, doubling the size of the party. From 1933, conscious that the scramble to engross new members during the period of the plan had been almost undiscriminating, the party suspended further recruitment and initiated a series of purges, which reduced the party by 1.6 million. From November 1936 a new membership drive was permitted, but against a background of continuous and vicious purging its effects were slight. Only from the summer of 1938 did the party begin to grow again rapidly (see Table 4.1), and although the war brought the expansion briefly to a halt, millions of soldiers who distinguished themselves in battle were given a short-cut to party membership as a reward. Even in the battle zone, the routines of admission and verification continued. In Sevastopol, besieged by German forces in the spring of 1942, subjected to regular bombardment and shelling, fifty-seven new civilian members were welcomed to the party in the first three months of the year.[17] In January 1946 1.8 million members were transferred from the armed forces into the civilian party, but because many had been battlefront admissions the authorities in July 1946 began a renewed drive to vet members for reliability. Admissions ran only a little ahead of expulsions, and for the last six years of Stalin's dictatorship the party grew at a modest average of 1.8 per cent a year.[18]

The development of National Socialist membership was less of a roller coaster, but it was still subject to deliberate periods of restriction. When the party achieved power in 1933 recruitment expanded rapidly, and in the wake of the March 1933 election victory the so-called *Märzgefallene* ('March windfalls') flooded the party, bringing it to a total of almost 850,000 and forcing the party to declare a moratorium from 1 May. The party offices could not cope with the additional processing work; recruitment, except for members of affiliated organizations (SA, SS, Hitler Youth, etc.), was suspended until May 1937, when the organization was better prepared to absorb additional numbers, and the party was in need of more funds.[19] The new wave was confined to those Germans who had already demonstrated their affinity with the movement by membership of one of its many affiliated and associated branches, or who had rendered some 'special service'

Table 4.1 Membership of the Communist Party of the Soviet Union 1917–1953

Year*	Full Members	Candidates	Total
1917	24,000	—	24,000
1919	350,000	—	350,000
1920	611,978	—	611,978
1921	732,521	—	732,521
1922	410,430	117,924	528,354
1923	381,400	117,700	499,100
1924	350,000	122,000	472,000
1925	440,365	361,439	801,804
1926	639,652	440,162	1,079,814
1927	786,288	426,162	1,212,450
1928	914,307	391,547	1,305,854
1929	1,090,508	444,854	1,535,362
1930	1,184,651	493,259	1,677,910
1931	1,369,406	842,819	2,212,225
1932	1,769,773	1,347,477	3,117,250
1933	2,203,951	1,351,387	3,555,338
1934	1,826,756	874,252	2,701,008
1935	1,659,104	699,610	2,358,714
1936	1,489,907	586,935	2,076,842
1937	1,453,828	527,869	1,981,697
1938	1,405,879	514,123	1,920,002
1939	1,514,181	792,792	2,306,973
1940	1,982,743	1,417,232	3,399,975
1941	2,490,479	1,381,986	3,872,465
1942	2,155,336	908,540	3,063,876
1943	2,451,511	1,403,190	3,854,701
1944	3,126,627	1,791,934	4,918,561
1945	3,965,530	1,794,839	5,760,369
1946	4,127,689	1,383,173	5,510,862
1947	4,774,886	1,277,015	6,051,901
1948	5,181,199	1,209,082	6,390,281
1949	5,334,811	1,017,761	6,352,572

Table 4.1 *Continued*

Year*	Full Members	Candidates	Total
1950	5,510,787	829,396	6,340,183
1951	5,658,577	804,398	6,462,975
1952	5,853,200	854,339	6,707,539
1953	6,067,027	830,197	6,897,224

* Figure for 1 January except for 1919–21 when the date is March.
Source: T. H. Rigby *Communist Party Membership in the USSR 1917–1967* (Princeton, 1968) pp. 52–3; M. Fainsod *How Russia is Ruled* (Cambridge, Mass., 1967) p. 249, who has lower figures for 1917–21 as follows: 23,600, 251,000, 431,400, 576,000.

to the Reich. From a figure of 2.7 million in 1937, membership reached 3.9 million by the end of 1938. Applications were briefly suspended again, but in 1939 it was decided to open the doors to all-comers to try to recruit at least one-tenth of the population into the party's ranks. The party swelled to 5.4 million in two years, until, once again, the doors were barred. In 1942 new members were to be recruited only from the Hitler Youth to try to change the age profile of the movement, and young Germans supplied a steady flow of new blood until Germany's collapse in 1945, when almost 10 per cent of the population were party members (see Table 4.2).[20]

The number who undertook party work of some kind was greater in both cases than the aggregate figures suggest. In the Soviet Union a network of 'sympathizers' was set up in the early 1920s, then suspended, and finally reintroduced in the 1930s to back up party officials in areas where party recruitment was scarce. In Germany too, the shortage of high-quality organizers forced the party to employ non-members in party posts.[21] Members could also resign, die, face expulsion or be killed. The pressures on party members were considerable and failure to meet the high standards expected carried with it the penalty of demotion, or worse. The Soviet communist party was always in the process of renewing itself. The rapid turnover of membership meant that many Soviet citizens were communists for only a short time before the privilege was withdrawn. The purge of 1933 removed

Table 4.2 Membership of the National Socialist Party 1919–1945

Year	Members	Year	Members
1919	55	1937	2,793,890
1921	3,000	1938	3,900,000
1923	55,287	1939	4,985,400
1928	96,918	1940	5,339,567
1930	129,563	1942	7,100,000
1933	849,009	1944	7,600,000
1935	2,493,890	1945	8,000,000

Source: M. Kater, *The Nazi Party: a Social Profile of Members and Leaders, 1919–1945* (Oxford, 1983), p. 263; D. Orlow, *The History of the Nazi Party: Vol 2, 1933–1945* (Newton Abbott, 1973), p. 206 for figure for end of 1938.

800,000 members; the purges in 1934 removed a further 340,000. In 1935 a two-year campaign of verification of party documents removed a further 350,000. By the end of the 1930s the party was considerably smaller than in 1933, but much of the membership was now new. An estimated 40 per cent of all members had joined since 1937, 1.1 million in 1939 alone.[22] The result of the purge policy was to remove large numbers of 'old Bolsheviks' who had joined the party before 1917. In 1930 69 per cent of party secretaries were from the pre-1917 generation; in 1939 over 90 per cent had joined the party after 1924.[23] The war then produced a second massive transfusion of new members. An estimated 3.5 million communists were killed during the conflict, and over 5 million new candidates admitted. On 1 January 1946 only one-third of the party's survivors had been members before June 1941, and of this fraction at least half had been in the party for less than three years before the war. The situation in the Ukraine, occupied by Axis forces, was extreme. There had been 521,000 members in 1940, but when the area was recaptured only 16,816 were left, and the party cadres had to be rebuilt from scratch.[24]

The war also affected National Socialism, with hundreds of thousands of party members transferred into the armed forces. Some 40 per cent of party 'block' or cell leaders had been drafted by 1943.[25]

During the war membership rose by approximately 3 million, but with losses in combat or through bombing the number of new joiners was certainly greater. By 1945 at least 65 per cent of party members had entered the party since 1938.[26] Party members were also expelled for infractions of party rules or misconduct: in 1934–5 there was a wide purge of party members who had supported, or were suspected of supporting, the revolutionary ambitions of Röhm's SA in 1934. One-fifth of the party's 203,000 political officers in office in 1933 had left or were purged by 1935, and in areas where SA sympathies had been strongest the purge accounted for almost one-third.[27] The balance between the German equivalent of the Old Bolsheviks, the party's *alte Kämpfer*, and the newcomers to the party also strongly favoured the post-1933 generation of members. By 1935 71 per cent of all block leaders and 60 per cent of all political officers had joined since Hitler came to power.[28] In both parties the hard core that fought the political battles of the 1920s were swamped by new waves of recruits who entered the party under the dictatorships.

The parties underwent fundamental changes as they grew into mass movements. Both started life as small protest groups, strongly anti-state and inveterately hostile to the competing parties around them. As they metamorphosed into larger organizations they attracted, alongside the committed core, many members who had once belonged to rival movements. The parties were forced to become coalitions, absorbing weaker political groupings and turning their supporters into authentic communists or National Socialists. The Soviet party in the 1920s was a mixture of former Socialist-Revolutionaries, Mensheviks, anarchists and nationalists, blended together by a new commitment to communism. The strenuous efforts to impose party unity and to outlaw factions in the early 1920s reflected the movement's mongrel origins. Only by the 1930s were new recruits the product of an undeniably communist upbringing. The National Socialist party was a cocktail of former nationalist fringe movements, peasant parties and associations of radical anti-republican protest. In 1933 it absorbed members from the defunct right-wing parties, the German Nationalist People's Party and the Bavarian People's Party. Even former communists and social-democrats could be found among the wave of new recruits in 1933.[29] Only by the late 1930s could new members, drawn predominantly and deliberately from young age-groups, be regarded as political virgins, unsullied by past politics.

Both parties were also social and geographical coalitions, drawing support promiscuously from across the social spectrum and from every region. The composition of each party had evident traits: the Soviet communist party was weaker in the countryside than in the cities, National Socialism the reverse; neither party recruited extensively among women, though communism more so of the two; both parties had around the same proportion of manual working-class members by the 1940s; both parties had a preponderance of members under thirty-five years of age. The early members joined from many motives, attracted to the ideas or the social promises or the violent activism of the movement, or seduced by the personality cult. The millions of newcomers in some cases shared that enthusiasm, but the social and geographical spread of the parties drew into their ranks those with more practical or prudent ambitions, who could see the social and political advantages of joining. Still others joined involuntarily, because they were asked to do so because of their job or position. At the height of the First Five-Year Plan whole factory workshops were asked to sign a multiple application form and then inducted by the cell meeting the following day, without any investigation into their political past or degree of commitment.[30] Schoolteachers in Germany were under persistent pressure to take up membership; so too were German bureaucrats. The swollen volume of membership by the 1940s was no clear indication that millions who had not previously been communists or National Socialists had become so as enthusiastic volunteers.

The surviving statistics on the social structure of each party are incomplete and the social categories employed generally too blunt, but they do permit a number of conclusions. The prejudice in the Soviet Union against candidates who were not drawn from the toiling masses produced by the early 1930s a party apparently composed overwhelmingly of workers and peasants, who made up all but 8 per cent of membership in 1932. But party statistics were based on social origin rather than current occupation; in 1932 38 per cent of the party were non-manual workers, and only 43 per cent were actually engaged in industry. Stalin initiated the movement in the mid-1930s to involve more technical intelligentsia in the party under the slogan 'cadres decide everything', and to purge many of the workers and peasants sucked in by the priorities of the First Five-Year Plan. These changes slowly turned the party into a predominantly white-collar movement, based on a cohort of educated technicians and intellectuals. In 1947 they comprised half the membership, while only 32 per cent of the post-war party were workers, a proportion that continued to fall.[31] By Stalin's death in 1953 more than half the party were white-collar workers. The party remained very under-represented in the Soviet countryside. The purges of the 1930s bit deep into peasant recruitment, and by 1939 the 243,000 collective farms mustered only 12,000 party cells and 153,000 members. After the war, in Kalinin province north of Moscow, there survived only 167 party cells on the region's 6,940 farms, a rate of 2.4 per cent.[32] A sustained drive to bring the party into the countryside increased the rural membership to a little over one-quarter of the whole, but many of the new rural members were local officials or technicians sent out from the cities, who ought more properly to be counted among the party's white-collar constituency.

As the communist party became less proletarian, National Socialism became more so. Hitler's movement drew support before 1933 from all areas of German society, but its manual working-class element expanded rapidly during the economic slump after 1929, reflecting the movement's populist character. Many of the workers attracted to National Socialism were drawn from rural areas or small craft shops or from less organized sections of the factory proletariat, but the rising support among workers was unmistakable. Saxony, the most densely industrialized province in Germany, also had the densest support for the party.[33] Between 1930 and 1932 the proportion of manual working-class recruits was 36 per cent of the total. This proportion rose steadily over the course of the Third Reich to more than 40 per cent by 1944, constituting the largest social element in the movement. Around one-fifth of members were white-collar workers, 10 per cent peasants, and the rest drawn from the professional intelligentsia and the business community.[34] The party was less well represented in towns than in the countryside, where in 1933 some 43 per cent of new members were recruited – some farmers, some workers, some commuters to city jobs.[35] Despite the increasingly plebeian composition of the party, there existed a large gap between the occupational status of the rank-and-file and the party officials. Among senior posts only one-tenth were held by workers in 1935. A similar gap opened up in the Soviet Union. Delegates to the party congress in 1930 were largely manual workers; the congress in 1939 had over half its audience made up of the intelligentsia, and in 1952, at the Nineteenth Congress, the figure was 85 per cent.[36] Both parties were led by an apparatus drawn largely from a class of officials, teachers, managers and technical-intelligentsia, who reproduced in their political careers inherited patterns of social demarcation.

The age and gender profile of the parties says much about the social reality of both dictatorships. The two parties were largely male and mainly young. Women were able to join the National Socialist party if they played some role in the movement's ancillary organizations, but by 1935 there was still only one woman in every twenty party members. This ratio increased from 1938 as more young women came through the youth movement, and during the war the loss of men to the front gave more opportunities for women and raised their statistical proportion in the party, but the leadership posts were dominated by men. The number of women is known more precisely in the Soviet case: 15.9 per cent of the party in 1932, 17 per cent in January 1945, and 21 per cent in 1950.[37] In the Soviet Union leadership posts were almost exclusively male. The rapid turnover of communist party members also ensured that the party never grew old under Stalin. In 1927 just over half the members were under thirty years of age; in 1946 two-thirds were under thirty-five.[38] In Germany the party started young, but a slower turnover meant that it aged as the dictatorship aged. In December 1934 some 37 per cent were under thirty, two-thirds under forty. By the war many members had reached their forties, and the increasingly middle-aged complexion of the party explains the enthusiasm for introducing more Hitler Youth graduates into the movement after 1942. Nonetheless, office-holders were still relatively young. The average age of party district leaders in 1943 was only forty-five.[39]

The organizational structure of the parties was little different from the conventional mass parties elsewhere in Europe: it mimicked the administrative divisions of each state, and was organized in a clear hierarchy. The National Socialist party was founded on the principle of 'leadership' and 'following'; orders from higher officers had to be obeyed unconditionally by those below. But the communist party was no less authoritarian in principle. Its statutes made clear that obedience to instructions from above was to be unequivocal.[40] The building block of both parties was the cell, thousands of which made up the larger party organism. Though it stood at the foot of the party structure, the cell was of central importance, reflecting perhaps the parties' own origins in networks of tiny, often isolated groups. In the communist party a cell could be as small as three members, but they were usually much larger. Each cell elected a committee and a secretary (though by Stalin's time the candidates were usually selected beforehand, and were subject to the approval of the party hierarchy). As the party membership increased, the cells were split into three categories and re-named 'primary party organizations': cells with fewer than 15 people did not qualify for a committee, cells of 15 to 500 members elected a bureau and secretary, while only cells of more than 500 members enjoyed the structure of a full party committee and a full-time, paid official as secretary. Each cell committee had four departments to deal with its separate functions – one for organization, one for party recruitment, one for culture and propaganda, and one for mass agitation. In 1931 there were 51,185 cells established in factories, farms, soviets, universities and transport industries; by the 1950s there were over 200,000.[41]

Directly above the party cell were the district or town organizations, each with their own committees, *raikomy* or *gorkomy*, 10,900 in total in 1939. They registered all cell members, controlled recruitment and communicated central directives out to the fringes of the movement. Above these were the 137 regional, or *oblast* committees, which were the principal territorial organizations, responsible in most cases directly to the Central Committee of the party in Moscow. Six autonomous provinces, or *krai*, had their own provincial committees, to which the *oblasty* on their territories were subordinate. The higher committees were in turn subdivided into numerous departments and sub-committees dealing with party finances, the local economy, education, propaganda and culture. In 1935 full-time paid officials were introduced into a party of volunteers to cope with the workload and professionalize practices, but their exact number is not known.[42] At the apex of the vast party pyramid stood the Central Committee, with its all-powerful secretariat and lines of command running down to the thousands of party cells.

The primary organization in National Socialism before 1933 was the *Ortsgruppe*, or 'local group', which could be any size and was run by a local group leader. In July 1932, to cope with the growth of the party into a genuinely national movement, the primary group was redefined. Members in every street or apartment house would constitute a party 'block', and a group of blocks would be a 'cell' of between 11 and 50 members. In rural areas, where the party was more thinly spread, the blocks were to form a base (*Stützpunkt*) with the same number of members as a cell. The *Ortsgruppe* was made up of a number of cells or bases, and could hold between 51 and 500 members.[43] By 1935 there were 21,283 of them, sustaining a network of 269,501 cells, bases and blocks. At regional level the local groups were responsible to 855 *Kreis* organizations, equivalent to the *raion*, or district, in the Soviet system, and 30 party *Gaue*, the leading organizational units of the party. Each *Kreis* and *Gau* supported a large permanent staff and numerous departments responsible, like the *oblasty*, for education, propaganda, the local economy, culture and party organization.[44] At the party apex was the office of the party chancellery and a small group of twenty-one national party leaders (*Reichsleiter*), each responsible for a division of party affairs – propaganda, organization, publications, ideology, agriculture and so on.[45]

On May Day 1936 the party introduced a radical reform of its organization and function. Until that point the structure embraced all party members and managed the party's affairs. From 1936 the party assumed ambitious responsibility for the entire German population. Each local group, cell and block was assigned a fraction of urban or rural territory where it was responsible for the political outlook, education and morale of every inhabitant, members or not. Each block looked after 40 to 60 households; each cell had from 4 to 8 blocks. To cope with the anticipated extra workload each block was further subdivided into units of 8 to 15 houses, under the eye of a 'block helper' or 'house guardian', who was not necessarily a member of the party. Under new regulations drawn up in May 1938, the *Ortsgruppe* was assigned between 1,500 and 3,000 households; many of the groups had to be reduced in size, expanding their aggregate number to 30,601 by 1941, and the total of cells and blocks to a remarkable 657,411, smothering the country with party units far more thoroughly than in the Soviet Union.[46] Each primary organization had to ensure that there were enough party members in each area to carry out the necessary functions, but for all intents and purposes the German people were involuntarily co-opted into a vast, all-inclusive national movement.

The work of supervising an entire population was eased by the development of numerous mass organizations, linked closely to the National Socialist party but composed in the main of non-members. Each party promoted a rich associational life designed to win allegiance to the party among broader circles of German and Soviet society. By far the most important was the recruitment of young people. In 1918 a communist youth organization was formed in Russia, radical in temper and largely independent of the party. The radicalism was stamped out by 1926, when it became the All-Union Leninist Young Communist League, usually known as *Komsomol.* In 1939 it was directly affiliated with the party, on whose organization it was closely modelled. Entry to the youth league was controlled like that to the party. Members needed a communist sponsor, and served a period as a candidate. Only in 1936 were entry rules that favoured the children of workers and poor peasants relaxed, and from then on the movement grew rapidly from 4 million members to more than 9 million in 1939, and 16 million by the time of Stalin's death.[47] Membership started at the age of fifteen (changed to fourteen in 1949) and went up until twenty-one. In the 1920s a junior association of Pioneers, from the ages of ten to fifteen, was introduced, which by the 1940s absorbed most school-age children.

The network of affiliated associations in Germany was much larger, more varied and less exclusive than the Soviet model. The paramilitary SA and SS involved more than 4 million men. The Hitler Youth (*Hitler-Jugend*) was formally established in 1926 and integrated into the party structure. In 1928 the youth sections were divided into two age groups, the Hitler Youth for 15–18-year-olds and junior units for those aged 10–14, which in 1931 became the *Deutsche Jungvolk.* A few girls belonged to associated 'sister groups' in the 1920s, but in June 1930 an official organization, the League of German Girls (*Bund deutscher Mädel*), was set up, with a junior section for 10–14-year-old girls. At the start of the dictatorship the youth groups mustered little more than 100,000 members, but as other youth associations were closed down or absorbed by the party, the numbers grew rapidly. In 1936 there were 5.4 million members, 46 per cent of them girls, by 1939 7.7 million.[48] They were organized territorially like the party, but their internal organization had more in common with the army. Entry was controlled to ensure that the healthiest or most racially aware got priority, but by the late 1930s the net was spread very widely. The party also established a separate organization for women in October 1931, the *Nationalsozialistische-Frauenschaft*, and in 1936 an umbrella association for all German women's groups, the *Deutsche Frauenwerk*, which numbered about 4 million in 1938. There was a National Socialist Car Corps for party enthusiasts on wheels, and separate professional organizations for academics, students, lawyers, doctors and dentists. The second-largest organization behind the youth movement was the movement for National Socialist Welfare (*National- sozialistische Volkspflege*). Founded unofficially in Berlin in 1932, the charity was absorbed into the party as an affiliate in May 1933 and turned into an army of volunteer collectors, distributors and supporters numbering, by 1943, more than 7 million.[49] It was here, in the diverse and widespread associational life of the movement, that much of the population was monitored, organized and recruited for active service in the cause of the party.

The parties had many purposes, but their first responsibility was to organize, discipline and educate their own members so that those purposes could be properly realized. Since each party was a coalition, embracing a variety of outlooks, social origins and personalities among the many millions of their members, the establishment of a workable consensus and clear rules of conduct was the precondition for the wider effort to integrate and dominate the non-party masses. Each party developed an apparatus to impose internal party justice and to ensure that individual party members displayed the ideal character- istics befitting the 'best elements'. Lenin originated the idea that the party should be ceaselessly vigilant against any slackers or traitors who might worm their way into the movement: 'Our statutes,' wrote

Lenin in 1904, 'represent organizational mistrust on the part of the party towards all its parts.'[50] The party was scarred permanently by a culture of institutional suspicion that produced a perennial condition of investigation and self-criticism, and resulted in the routine purging of those who were judged unworthy any longer of membership.

Communist party purges have often been misinterpreted as a short period of deliberate bloodletting in the mid-1930s, to strengthen Stalin's position in the hierarchy and to secure a party that was consistent with his description of 'a monolithic organization, carved from one piece'.[51] In fact the formal process of purging long pre-dated Stalin's dictatorship; the purge was a generic term that covered a number of distinct forms of party self-discipline. Every member was under permanent surveillance, and at regular intervals had to present to a review board evidence of their continued commitment and activity, and display a certain level of political literacy. Members knew that this was a requirement, and prepared in advance for the ordeal. An American visitor to the household of a skilled worker in Moscow in 1932 watched him laboriously reading the works of Marx and Lenin every night in preparation for the purge board. Just days before the review, his wife tested him on his version of his curriculum vitae and helped him cram for the political theory test. The co-tenant of their small worker's apartment had been demoted from member to 'sympathizer' for ignorance of theory, but in this case all went well on the day. The vindicated communist, dismissed with 'a congratulatory nod' by the party tribunal, returned home 'looking ten years younger', with bottles of wine and vodka under each arm. The entire family and their friends consumed as lavish a feast as they could muster, with endless toasts to the party and the Five-Year Plan, and bouts of wild dancing.[52]

In October 1924 the party laid down a number of what were called party 'illnesses', for which the remedy of purging may seem a peculiarly apt metaphor. There were seven in all: careerism; 'marrying or close contact with petty-bourgeoisie'; expanding economic assets; excessive personal habits; alcoholism; sexual licence; and religious attendance. Any one of these charges could bring dismissal. The first major purge of party cells in city soviets came in 1925; there were two more major purges in 1926 and again in 1929–30. Following the party's rapid growth from the late 1920s, the Central Committee ordered a major review of party membership in 1933, beginning that year with ten major *krai* or *oblast* areas, and then in 1934 extending the review to the whole party. The decree of 28 April 1933 pointed out that too many careerists, 'double-dealing elements' and political illiterates had been allowed into party ranks during the collectivization and industrialization drive, which was certainly true.[53] The party *chistka*, as it was called, was a formal affair, held in local public buildings in front of a three-member purge board. Local communists were called forward in turn to stand and declare their social origins, their activity for the party and to confess any dereliction of duty in a spirit of 'self-criticism'. Then witnesses would be called to offer corroborating statements, or to expose failures. The commission took written statements and cross-examined those who complained about each party member, before deciding on one of a range of recommendations, from confirmation of status to expulsion.[54]

The following year a purge of a different kind was undertaken. On 13 May 1935 the Central Committee issued a second order 'on Disorders in the Registration, Issuance and Custody of Party Cards'. The campaign for the verification of documents, to make sure that party cards were not being used illicitly and had been correctly issued, was to culminate in a third purge wave, in December 1935, when the party leadership ordered an exchange of existing party cards for a new card between 1 February and 1 May 1936. The withdrawal of the party card could be justified on many grounds. In the city of Smolensk 455 were taken away in 1935, some under very unspecific charges ('people who do not inspire political trust' – 28 per cent; 'those from a class-alien milieu who concealed their past' – 22 per cent), some under particular misdemeanours ('agents of the enemy' – 1.5 per cent; 'deserters from the Red Army' – 2.6 per cent), some on grounds of moral turpitude, embezzlement, swindling or a hidden criminal past.[55] The purge then continued through 1937 and 1938 on instructions from the centre, issued on 29 July 1936, to unmask political enemies sympathetic to Trotsky and the disgraced party opposition. It was this purge that finally unleashed the mass killings familiar as the Great Terror, which is dealt with in a later chapter, but it is important to be clear that the act of purging was not necessarily a cue for arrest and execution. The purge was a distinct element of party self-discipline, not a judicial process. Its object was to tighten central control over local party cadres, and to root out incompetent or corrupt officials. Expulsion from the party was exercised in the 1930s as it had been since the 1920s, and was to continue for the rest of the Stalinist period and beyond. The subsequent victimization of former party members was carried out by agents of state security and by state interrogators and state courts, who investigated what they viewed as actual crimes rather than poor party performance. Plenty of the victims of the state terror were arrested while they were still party members, and were never formally purged. On the other hand, it was possible to be purged and later reinstated, or purged for behaviour that violated party rules, such as drunkenness (which seems, from contemporary accounts, a far from uncommon failing), but was not a state crime. The party purge was a formal procedure designed to ensure that high standards of committed political activism should be maintained by the survivors of a remorseless process of internal party inspection. In practice, it was often used to ensure that party officials remote from Moscow did not challenge the political monopoly of the centre.

Strict party discipline against corruption, laziness or insubordination was not confined to communism. Hitler introduced party courts into the movement as early as 1921, when it was still a tiny organization. They were responsible for verifying membership, expulsions and purges, but also acted as courts of honour where members accused by colleagues of malpractice could vindicate themselves. There were permanent courts at both *Gau* and *Kreis* level. Like Soviet purge commissions they consisted of a three-member board, summoned members to justify themselves, listened to witnesses and investigated alleged party crimes. They too had a range of judgments: innocent, guilty with a verbal reprimand, guilty with a written warning, guilty and expulsion (*Ausstossung*) from the party.[56] The party courts were headed from 1927 by a retired soldier, Major Walter Buch, a tall, ascetic Hitler fanatic, who shared the party's extreme anti-Semitism (but had the temerity to caution Hitler in 1928 that he possessed 'a contempt for humanity', which filled Buch 'with grave uneasiness').[57] He oversaw the development of a national system of party courts in the 1930s. A law of 17 February 1934 gave them judicial status and the right to investigate and punish party crimes, including the right to recommend confinement in extreme cases. Their work was monitored by a system of *Gau* Inspectors, who kept watch on party discipline for the national leadership. The courts dealt with hundreds of cases, most of them petty issues: failure to pay dues for three months, immoral behaviour, a criminal record, or simply 'loss of interest' in party affairs.[58]

The courts could also investigate more serious criminal offences. In 1939 party courts tried thirty party, SA and SS men for rape, theft and murder during the anti-Jewish pogrom of 9 November 1938; twenty-one murders were excused as the result of Jewish provocation, but three men who raped Jewish girls were imprisoned – not for their sexual violence, but for contaminating the race. The courts could even bring party leaders to book; in theory Hitler, as a party member, had to accept their jurisdiction and respect their judgments, though in practice he overruled them when it suited him. In 1938 the *Gauleiter* Wilhelm Kube was stripped of his office and sent to a camp for two years for falsely accusing Buch's wife of being Jewish. The notoriously anti-Semitic *Gauleiter* of Franconia, Julius Streicher, was brought before the court in 1940 accused of embezzlement, adultery and malicious gossip and was sacked from his post. Josef Wagner, *Gauleiter* of Westphalia-South, was accused in 1941 of pro-Catholic sentiment because he had sent his children to a Catholic school and his Catholic wife had objected to her daughter's marriage to an SS man. Although the High Party Court in Berlin found the case not proven, Hitler overturned the verdict and eventually insisted that Wagner be sent to a concentration camp.[59]

Discipline went hand-in-hand with political education. Party members in both systems were the object of continuous instruction on the party line and means to self-improvement as a party activist. Communists were expected to read and learn their political classics as a matter of course. The man who danced after passing the purge commission told his American guest: 'Without political theory, one cannot understand what goes on in this country. A Communist must set the pace in study . . .'[60] The education of party members was the responsibility of the Central Committee Department of Propaganda and Agitation. At the top of the system in the 1920s were party universities, the 'evening university' of Marxism-Leninism and the

Sverdlov Communist University, which was set up in 1921 to train around 1,000 future communist leaders a year, and the Marx-Engels Institute; in 1936 they were all grouped under the Communist Academy of Sciences, renamed the Academy of Social Sciences after a major reorganization of party education in 1946. There were Higher Party Schools set up in the 1930s in the capital and in the separate republics, which taught three-year courses in organization and propaganda to the prospective party elite, and below them thousands of smaller political schools (*politshkoly*) and study circles for political literacy. There were 52,000 of them in 1930, 210,000 by 1933, where 4.5 million students, including non-party sympathizers, were given brief seminar courses in the basics of historical materialism. When the *Short Course* on the history of Bolshevism was published in 1938, students of politics were expected to use it as the indispensable guide to understanding communism. Study circles met every two weeks over an academic year of eight months, with between ten and twenty-five political students in each class. After the war the party sought to raise levels of party education following the post-war rebuilding of party cadres. Following the Central Committee resolution in 1946 'On the Training and Retraining of Leading Party Workers', some 400,000 were pushed through the Higher Party Schools.[61]

National Socialism did not educate members so systematically or with such high intellectual ideals. The party schools involved a good deal of physical exercise, with the object of turning out a biological elite rather than one steeped in political economy. The training of party cadres in Germany was the responsibility of the Reich Organization Leader, the former chemist Robert Ley, a squat, loud-mouthed fanatic with a reputation for drink and women, and an obsession with creating physically ideal Germans. He set up training centres, grandly called *Ordensburgen* or 'order castles', where party officials were given brief training courses in German history and the party's world view, and made to do early-morning callisthenics, shooting and running. The castles were officially established on 24 April 1936, but training schools existed at *Gau* and *Kreis* level well before that, supervised by a party Main Office for Schooling. In 1937 three-year schools were based in the 'castle' system to educate the next generation of party officials.[62] They drew on the products of a number of special schools set up for boys chosen for their racial good looks and leadership potential. The first were the National Political Education Institutes (Napolas) set up in 1934, which took boys who were blond, clever and athletic from age ten to eighteen; the second, set up in April 1937, were the Adolf Hitler Schools for boys aged twelve to eighteen. Both emphasized the building of personality through paramilitary training and competitive sport; political instruction was, like the Soviet *Short Course*, based on a thorough familiarity with the party's history. Hitler Youth members had to master a number of set themes on which they would be tested by oral examination. These included 'The struggle for Germany', 'Causes of German Collapse in the First World War', 'The *Volk* and its Blood Source', 'Measures of the National Socialist State for Keeping German Blood Cleansed' and so on.[63]

The object of political education was to turn out better communists and National Socialists, able to grasp the party line and, in turn, to make it comprehensible to wider circles of the public. In reality an elite of dedicated and informed party members was difficult to build. Many communists were purged or reduced to candidate status because of their political illiteracy, some because they were completely illiterate. Though denunciations of party members were often malicious, local party officials could and did abuse their position. Criminality, drunkenness and careerism were present in both parties. So rapidly did the two parties expand and so volatile was their membership that there was always a shortage of competent officials. In both parties a gap opened up between the ordinary rank-and-file membership and a hard core of more dedicated activists. Around one-third of National Socialists by the late 1930s had party posts that compelled them to engage in party work almost every day. The communist party by the 1930s recognized that the so-called *aktiv*, the members who did something, represented an elite within an elite, holding party office and often meeting separately and more often than the regular membership.[64] They too made up an estimated one-third of the party. For the more dedicated activist work was never-ending. 'That's what it means to be a communist,' explained one woman member, whose married life in the 1930s consisted of being posted to parts of the country remote from her husband. 'Your life isn't your own.'[65]

Party members were expected to do a great deal more than become models, however inadequate, of a racial or revolutionary ideal. In 1935 Hitler announced at the party rally that the party's role as a body of 'activists and propagandists' was 'to educate and to supervise' the rest of the German population.[66] The party rules adopted at the Soviet Communist Party Congress in March 1939 laid down the responsibility of the party to lead the rest of the population in the task of constructing communism, to help push through party policy and to 'daily strengthen links with the masses' by explaining and communicating party decisions.[67] It was in the mundane daily routines of the party, rather than in the periodic set-piece festivals and rituals, that the real political significance of the party lay. The introduction of the cell and block into German society brought the party into every household. The local block leader, responsible for approximately forty to sixty households, was helped by a number of other local block officials or helpers, representing other party associations: the German Labour Front, the Women's Association (which supplied 280,000 block leaders and helpers in 1938) and National Socialist Welfare. The local Hitler Youth and *Bund deutscher Mädel* (BDM) groups were also recruited to help collect donations in money or scarce raw materials, or to distribute party literature.[68] The cell and block members were charged with a number of tasks: they had to monitor their households for evidence, in Ley's words, of 'the opponent or enemy of our idea'; they had to hand round propaganda and educational material, if possible through a personal visit to every household under their supervision once a month; they were supposed to compile a dossier of political reliability on each household, observing their behaviour, checking the degree of flag-waving; they listed all known Jews in their area, catalogued all Jewish property and noted down those non-Jews who continued to maintain contact with Jews in the neighbourhood; finally they were regarded as the frontline of the home front, preparing the people for war and mobilizing enthusiasm for the war effort once war had broken out.[69]

This formidable array of tasks was co-ordinated through a regular monthly meeting, 'a block evening' or a 'cell evening', where the work plan for the following month was worked out, party literature reviewed and occasional lectures presented.[70] The details of the household list or card index, made compulsory in the organizational reform of 1936, were also updated, and families whose morale or behaviour raised questions were scheduled for additional visits or received detailed questionnaires on their attitude to the new Germany. The system was difficult to operate, partly because party organizations loaded the cell and block leader with too much routine, non-political administration, partly because even the most enthusiastic local activist found the remorseless cycle of morale-boosting visits and form-filling a chore. Nevertheless, the household index was an invaluable tool for the exercise of party social control and the pursuit of the racial and security aims of the regime. It also supplied essential information for the system of 'political judgements' that the party employed ruthlessly to ensure that jobs in both the public and private sector were filled with candidates sympathetic to the regime, or welfare granted only to politically acceptable applicants, or licences approved only for those with an unblemished record. The judgement was based on a standard form held on file by the *Kreis* office, based on information supplied by the local party branches and, above all, by the cells and blocks.[71]

The political judgement was a general-purpose tool of the party apparatus. There was no appeal in cases where the party's verdict was disapproval. The judgements had to be applied for by any public agency where decisions might be affected by the political standing of an applicant. In April 1939 an agreement between the party and the Economics Ministry opened the way to supplying judgements in areas of private employment too, and in some localities these made up one-quarter of all requests.[72] Beside the personal details, each form contained information about past political allegiance, religious conviction, contributions to party charities, current political outlook and behaviour, and a final box for the party's recommendation. The judgements often used crude measurements. Failure to give the Hitler salute was taken as *prima facie* evidence of hostility to the regime; in one unfavourable judgement it was recorded that only half a salute was given on purpose, 'Heil' instead of 'Heil Hitler'. Regular religious attendance was suspect; so too was opportunistic conversion from social-democracy or communism.[73] The records of the Berchtesgaden *Kreis* show what impact a hostile judgement could have. Business licences were withdrawn from a man with a Jewish wife; another was denied on grounds of 'political unsuitability'; withdrawal of all subsidies was recommended for a farmer judged negatively; a teacher was refused promotion because he 'has not forsworn his religious affiliation'.[74] Some were approved, but warned that they must take up some active role in one of the many affiliated branches of the movement. The political judgement gave local party organizations exceptional and arbitrary power to include and exclude whom they chose, to monitor the local political mood and to isolate potential troublemakers.

The communist party was less thoroughly organized at local level because its personnel was spread too thinly over a vast territory and lacked the skills or equipment or time necessary to establish a household-by-household survey, or even to fulfil the tasks of agitation and surveillance expected by the party rules. Many communist party members held down government or industrial appointments, which made it difficult to leave time enough for monitoring the wider non-party population. Meetings of party cadres were generally closed meetings. In the rural areas party organization was particularly weak, and direct day-to-day party control harder to operate than in Germany. Much activity in the villages was delegated to cells of communist youth, who set up 'red corners', helped found village soviets and stocked village libraries. Nevertheless, educational and propaganda work were essential activities for the party faithful. Party instructors toured factories and villages discussing party initiatives, offering advice and monitoring compliance. The party also recruited non-party spokesmen who were educated in the party schools. There were 130,000 agitators in 1933; the party claimed 3 million by the war.[75] Their work was run by local branches of the national department of agitation and propaganda, which issued regular memoranda for speakers. In the Moscow district after the war these were distributed two to three times a month in batches of 135,000; each one gave details of three or four main topics, with instructions on how they were to be presented to the public. The Soviet population was confronted with these subjects in meetings organized simultaneously across the country in halls and workshops festooned with banners, slogans and red flags. Attendance was compulsory and persistent absenteeism was interpreted as a political protest. The meetings were rudimentary and the propaganda primitive. *Pravda* reported a meeting called to discuss the Stalin Constitution in November 1936 at which the only question from a somnolent audience was from a woman: 'Why aren't there any galoshes in the shops?'[76] Even the smaller discussion circles organized after the war sometimes lacked rigour. At a circle in the city of Torzhok the teacher trained the students to respond to simple questions based on the *Short Course*: 'Could the tsarist government satisfy the workers and peasants?' to which the class responded in unison, 'No.'[77]

The party rank-and-file played a more important role in the institutions in which they worked rather than the households in their neighbourhoods. Party cells were based on individual factories, farms, offices or colleges and it was here that the non-party masses were monitored for their commitment to communism and social behaviour. The factory meeting was the means not only to communicate new policy initiatives, but to seek the views of the workforce, to denounce shirkers or class enemies or to give help where possible to those who needed schooling or welfare. These meetings were, like the propaganda and agitation sessions, largely staged affairs. One overseas worker at the Elektrozavod plant in Moscow witnessed a mass meeting where a middle-aged technical inspector was tested on his knowledge of communism. He proved to be woefully ignorant. He thought Stalin was president of the Soviet Union; that Comintern (The Third International) was a radio station; that the communist international trade union organization was an opposition faction. But as a close friend of the party cadre, he avoided anything worse than the laughter of his peers.[78] The factory or farm meeting was also an opportunity for non-party workers to voice their complaints. Though the system could discipline as un-Soviet those who moaned, and mark them down for further surveillance, it was also possible for complaints to be forwarded, even to provoke action. The party cell acted as the chief agent between people and leaders, centre and periphery, mobilizing support, assessing local opinion and penalizing those identified as potential enemies or misfits in much the same way as the German party controlled their neighbourhoods.

The parties became an integral part of the societies they led because they were a product of those same societies. Many party members knew their localities and workplaces intimately, and that information was central to the efforts of the party apparatus to mobilize and to monitor the large majority who were outside the party. In both systems the party became very quickly a central element in daily life, impossible to avoid or ignore except in the more remote regions of the Soviet countryside. The effect was to produce a supervised integration of society, increasing the pressures to conform, isolating and identifying deliberate acts of dissent or political defiance, and penalizing those who refused to accept the new system. This form of popular, local supervision was more effective and more intrusive in Germany than in the Soviet Union, where cell and block leaders were encouraged to confront their supervisees 'across the kitchen table'.[79] In Germany the party introduced small but important ways of compelling public demonstrations of party loyalty, whatever the individual's private thoughts might have been. The party welfare collectors went from door to door, collecting donations or selling badges and trinkets, and recording those who refused; subscribers kept a record book of their contributions.[80] Young Germans were subjected to rigorous schedules to encourage party-mindedness. Each BDM member, for example, was given a printed 'General Service Plan' covering a four-month period, with instructions on a monthly party project, the monthly song, the monthly social evening on special themes ('The inner Reich', 'We carry and build the Reich', etc.), party work to be done at home, and a final column for special duties.[81] The communist party sold newspapers, distributed pamphlets, organized Soviet youth and moulded the public life of the community as far as it could, but it never succeeded in placing a party official in charge of every 150 Soviet inhabitants.

The effectiveness of the party presence was compromised in some measure by deficiencies in party education and the difficulty of finding enough competent organizers. The parties themselves were, despite the exaggerated public image of a united and wholesome servant of the people, constantly concerned to eradicate corruption and incompetence in their own ranks and to mask the routine disputes and personal rivalries that organizations of such size and heterogeneous character could scarcely avoid.[82] The dictatorships needed to centralize and discipline the party as part of the effort to unite the population with the regime. This was a separate process from the extensive and irreversible partification of the social and institutional life of the two states, which developed its own local dynamic and was not simply imposed from above. The evidence from both systems shows how seriously and enthusiastically many party members set about the task of mobilizing those for whom they were responsible. Being a member of the party also brought privileges, status and career opportunities, alongside the less glamorous routines of party labour, and these gave party branches additional incentives to sustain their smothering influence on local affairs. These social advantages were very real in both systems, sometimes complementing, sometimes substituting for the idealism that party members were supposed to display. The party became the means to create new structures of social power and local political influence, and the instrument to exclude or emasculate alternative forms of identity, social status or institutional autonomy.

The party was no less important in the sphere of the state. The relationship between the two – state and party – was moulded by historical circumstances. For Soviet communists the 'state' as a set of institutions, regulations and personnel defined by a body of constitutional law disappeared after the Bolshevik revolution. In practice the party ruled Russia while the task of constructing an alternative, communist state run by a national system of state soviets was slowly completed. The new state was defined in the 1924 constitution, which formally established the Soviet Union, and redefined in the 'Stalin Constitution' published in December 1936. Under Stalin the size of the state apparatus and the responsibilities of state institutions continuously expanded. The communist party played a key part in leading and operating the new state, but its position altered relatively as the state grew in importance, size and experience. The state to which the party gave birth became, by the 1940s, an independent-minded adolescent.

The state taken over by the National Socialist regime was, by contrast, a powerful set of administrative and judicial institutions, rooted in a body of established constitutional law, run by a large population of federal and provincial bureaucrats with a strong sense of collective identity and moral purpose, served by an elaborate, long-established body of procedural regulations.[83] National Socialists confronted the issue of how to control or limit a state apparatus for which they were not responsible and whose standards of impartiality, habits of routine and institutional inertia ill-fitted the more radical and utopian aspirations of the party. Over the course of the dictatorship the state was brought increasingly under party influence, its responsibilities subverted or circumvented, and its legal and procedural foundations modified. By 1945 the 'normative' state was a hollow relic of the state inherited in 1933.

In each system the relationship between party and state was dependent on patronage. The parties developed formal and informal ways of securing the appointment of state officials to ensure that party members, or known sympathizers, were preferred. In the Soviet Union the lists of those offices in the party gift was institutionalized in the *nomenklatura* system. Its origins lay in Lenin's insistence after 1917 that the party would only succeed in building socialism if its supporters were at the same time state office-holders. The heart of the system was a Central Committee card index of all party members based on the return of a standard questionnaire, which helped to decide where to allocate party workers. The Record and Assignment Department of the Central Committee (Uchraspred) catalogued all the established posts in the party organization, trade unions, Soviets and commissariats. In June 1923 formal lists were drawn up of posts that could only be appointed by the party's central offices; similar lists were compiled for lower-level appointments by provincial party authorities. Stalin wanted the party to control appointments in 'all branches of administration without exception'.[84] In 1926 the Central Committee was responsible for appointing a total of 5,100 senior posts. The system expanded in the 1930s and 1940s to embrace all areas of public life. In 1936 party members supplied 55 per cent of officials in local soviets and state enterprises, and 68 per cent of officials in the regions and republics of the Soviet Union. At the heart of the apparatus of state, the Central Executive Committee and the Congress of Soviets' Praesidium, the proportion was almost 100 per cent.[85] As the state sector expanded, it became impossible to fill every post with a communist; instead, appointees could apply for membership once in office. The total proportion of state office-holders who were party members is not known, but among academics in the 1940s the figure was approximately three-quarters, and among senior army officers the same.[86]

National Socialism did not develop a formal *nomenklatura* system, but state appointments at all levels came to be dominated by the party. The pre-1933 German state was decentralized, with ministries and officials appointed at provincial as well as national level, and it was at this lower level of the state that local party bosses launched a brief, and often violent, campaign in 1933 to oust state officials, ministers or mayors who were regarded as out of temper with the 'national revolution'. In Marburg, for example, the mayor (*Oberbürgermeister*) was sent on leave by the party in March 1933, and replaced in 1934; the job of senior administrator (*Landrat*) was taken over by the party *Kreis* leader; professors were suspended at Marburg university; municipal workers who had supported left-wing parties were sacked, and party supporters were nominated to lead the local swimming and gymnastics clubs.[87] In Baden the local administration was unsympathetic to the party. After the March 1933 election the *Gauleiter*, Robert Wagner, declared himself a local commissar, ousted the ministers and replaced them with party members, purged the police force and filled the freed positions with party supporters. The senior state administrators were forced to take on *Kreis* leaders as advisers, principally on matters of personnel appointment; fifteen out of the forty Baden administrators joined the party by 1935. By the same date almost 14 per cent of the Baden party comprised state appointees.[88] The party did not need here, as elsewhere in the Reich, to control all appointments; it was enough to place members in key positions, and to ensure that personnel policy could be reviewed by party offices.

At national level the party began early in 1933 to pursue a policy of purging and discrimination throughout the entire state apparatus. The central instrument was the Law for the Restoration of the Professional Civil Service announced on 7 April. Under the provisions of the law any professional state employee could be dismissed on the vague grounds that they had not worked unreservedly to help establish the new national state. Jewish employees could be sacked for being Jewish. Although only 2 per cent of all state employees were removed, among higher grade officials the proportion was higher. In Prussia 12 per cent of senior office-holders were retired.[89] The party concentrated its efforts on senior appointments because they could influence the structures subordinate to them without the wholesale and damaging removal of thousands of junior staff. In Prussia by 1937 all 12 of the *Oberpräsidenten* (the highest civil service post) had been appointed since 1933, together with 31 out of 34 of the next rank *Regierungspräsidenten*, all but one of the 46 vice-presidents and 97 *Landräte*. By 1941 nine-tenths of all senior appointments in Prussia were National Socialists. In the Reich as a whole 60 per cent of top bureaucratic jobs, and two-thirds of all state posts filled since 1933, went to party members.[90] On 26 January 1937 a second German Civil Service Law extended the influence of the central party over state appointments, though less extensively than many party officials would have liked. The new law allowed promotion only for those awarded a positive political judgement (which gave the party certificate the full force of law); it also allowed party members who were state officials to communicate problems in their work directly to their party superiors rather than their employers; finally paragraph 71 allowed the removal of any official who could no longer guarantee to 'stand up at any time for the national socialist state', though by this stage most officials who did not comply with the new regime had already been replaced.[91]

The ability to influence state appointments in the smaller municipalities and districts was also extensive. At first there was little regulation from above, and a tough or ambitious *Kreis* or *Ortsgruppe* leader could impose a miniature seizure of power without much reference to his superiors. By 1935 in Bavaria almost half (44.6 per cent) of all mayoral posts had been taken over by the district party leader, who fused the two jobs together.[92] Non-party mayors were expected to support the new regime. 'It is useless,' wrote one Bavarian *Kreis* leader in 1933, 'if here and there a district . . . believes it is in a position to get a mayor who is not liked by the NSDAP.'[93] Most mayors were party members – 69 per cent in Bavaria, 61 per cent throughout the Reich. On 30 January 1935 a Decree for the Structure of the German Commune was published, which gave the force of law to party interference in the primary unit of urban and rural administration. Each commune was to have a 'party plenipotentiary' appointed by the Party Chancellery, whose responsibility was to approve all office-holders at communal level. Like the Soviet system, party leaders were no longer expected to act in an executive role, but to rely on the plenipotentiary to recommend men and women committed to the national cause. The plenipotentiary was usually the *Kreis* leader, who now enjoyed the legal right to interfere in each and every public appointment, and to choose the members of each commune advisory board, which were soon filled by party workers and their friends.[94] Although, in February 1937, the Party Chancellery removed the right of local party leaders to hold the post of mayor or *Landrat* simultaneously with an official party appointment, in order to permit local party leaders to focus more on party work and political leadership, the influence of the local party bosses on all the affairs of the local community was in most cases a fact of life. A legal instrument to secure the direct responsibility of the *Kreis* leader to make all appointments and to control the local budget was prepared by the Party Chancellery, but never put into force.[95]

Alongside the official and unofficial pressure to appoint party members and fellow-travellers to public office, each party produced a 'shadow state' within their own organizations. The number of full-time officials working for each party represented in itself a countervailing bureaucratic structure to the normative state. The National Socialist party had 1,017,000 officials by 1935 in all its many branches; by the war there were an estimated 2 million.[96] The number of permanent officials in the communist party and its affiliates is not known with any precision during the Stalin period, but it was more than 500,000 by the 1960s. Some sense of the perpetual inflation of the party bureaucracy can be gleaned from the numbers of permanent officials attached to the Central Committee: 30 in 1919; 534 by 1929; around 1,500 by Stalin's death.[97] Many of these officials worked on matters internal to each party, but the organizational structure of the parties included departments that shadowed state offices and responsibilities, where the role of the party can have been nothing other than prescriptive.

The shadow state began at the very summit of the two parties. The Party Chancellery in Berlin was physically situated in the heart of the government district, on Friedrich-Wilhelm Strasse. Directly subordinate were the offices of the *Reichsleiter*, many of which dealt with state issues – propaganda, law, colonial policy, agriculture, local communes, security. A few streets away, near the Foreign Office, was the department of Hitler's deputy, where more office heads sat dealing with major political issues: finance, taxation, constitutional law, foreign policy (run until 1938 by the party's opinionated and effete foreign affairs expert, Joachim von Ribbentrop), education, construction (a post held by the party's chief architect, Albert Speer), technology, health policy, race issues, and culture. Only one of the twenty specialized departments was devoted specifically to 'internal party affairs'.[98] The role of these party offices was not an executive one, but nor were they entirely decorative. Department heads and *Reichsleiter* were regularly invited to discussions on policy issues with ministerial colleagues; party views on policy were channelled through the party chancellery, whose energetic and ruthless organizer, Martin Bormann, rose to be one of the most powerful political players in the last years of the Reich.

Below the chancellery, the separate levels of party organization each had departments responsible for major areas of public life as well as party business. By the mid-1930s the *Kreis* organization had no fewer than thirty separate departments; those for race policy, health, bureaucracy, education, law, agriculture, handicrafts, economics, technology and communal affairs all dealt with areas of activity external to the party.[99] In 1936 regular district party conferences and events were introduced, where local party functionaries met with the local leaders of affiliated groups – Hitler Youth, German Women's Association, SA, etc. – and representatives from the local institutions of state, economy and culture. They served as propaganda tools, but also as a means to link local communities and the party more closely together. In the party districts of upper Bavaria, over 1.3 million people attended one form or other of local party function during the course of 1938. These included nine district party conferences, capped by an eleven-day conference in Munich. Though the meetings involved a good deal of party jamboree, they had a distinct political purpose in making evident to local officials and community elite, through lectures, exhibitions and the many opportunities to discuss issues of policy in a convivial atmosphere, the reality of party political leadership.[100]

The cornerstone of the shadow state was the *Gau* organization. The party regions had large permanent offices most of which dealt with major areas of policy, which made unavoidable regular contact between the party's regional elite and the local state organization. The *Gauleiter* held, in many cases, the office of Reich Representative

(*Reichsstatthalter*), which was established by law on 7 April 1933 as an instrument to centralize the political structure of the Reich. Hitler appointed himself Reich Representative for Prussia, but by a law of 27 November 1934 the Prussian *Oberpräsidenten*, the senior regional officials, were given the same responsibilities as the other Reich Representatives. These, too, were mainly *Gau* leaders. Their duties were poorly defined, and their executive responsibility unclear, but the object was to ensure the political co-ordination of the Reich using the most senior party leaders to oversee not only party organization and personnel policy, but the territorial organs of state under their control.[101] In 1939 the *Gauleiter* were appointed Reich Defence Commissars, responsible for co-ordinating labour and economic mobilization, civil defence and welfare in their regions, at the expense of military authorities who had assumed blanket responsibility for the local war effort during the First World War, but who now found themselves forced to work side-by-side with party leaders. The *Gauleiter* were regarded, and regarded themselves, as the aristocracy of the party's political leadership. Their power at local level derived principally from their party position; the local *Gau* offices, like the numerous communist party headquarters all over the Soviet Union, became more significant power centres than the emasculated provincial state authorities, not through the exercise of local administrative and executive authority, but because no political initiatives inconsistent with party policy or disapproved of by the *Gauleiter* were allowed to materialize within the boundaries of their fief.

At national level, party leaders held regular assemblies at which major issues of policy were discussed. These conferences involved both *Gauleiter* and *Reichsleiter*. They were organized by the Party Chancellery; Hess, Hitler's deputy, was always present until his flight to Scotland in May 1941, when he was replaced by Bormann. Hitler attended many of them, even if he did no more than give a concluding speech. Participants were sworn to secrecy, and no written records have survived of their proceedings. There were twenty-seven meetings between 1933 and 1939, lasting anything from one to three days, and a further nineteen during the war. They coincided in many cases with key points in the dictatorship – the 1934 party crisis, the re-occupation of the Rhineland, the Austrian takeover in 1938, and so on. Some fragments of evidence indicate the subject-matter: Himmler lectured on the homosexual threat in 1937 and on the party's role in the East in 1939, Hitler on the Jewish question in 1941. The conferences were no doubt opportunities for sociability and expressions of party solidarity, for resolving conflicts and mollifying inflated egos, but their very secrecy suggests that these were also occasions where the political leadership revealed their private political agenda, or communicated more sensitive issues of policy and future strategy to the party's most important corps of leaders.[102] The *Gauleiter* were the only group among the party and ministerial elite vouchsafed regular assemblies throughout the whole life of the dictatorship. It is inconceivable that the conferees did not discuss policy, appointments or state affairs while they had the chance to do so, absent briefly from the daily pressures of their other responsibilities.

The Soviet Communist Party was less clearly organized to match the activities of the state established in the 1920s. The Central Committee secretariat was the central party agency. Its organizational structure was modified regularly in the 1930s and 1940s as party leaders searched for the most functionally effective form of central control. Only the form introduced in 1948 was designed deliberately to shadow the structure of the Soviet state, with departments for trade unions, heavy industry, agriculture, trade, finance, foreign affairs, military, transport, light industry and propaganda.[103] But throughout the Stalin dictatorship the Central Committee secretariat monitored state performance, communicated party policy to local soviets, and placed communists in key positions in the state sectors. These responsibilities were reproduced organizationally at each level of the party apparatus. The *oblast* organization, like that of the German *Gau*, had departments responsible for all major spheres of state and economy: finance, agriculture, education, light industry, trade, communal economy, roads and pavements, health, social services and communications.[104] But unlike the German party, the senior communist regions also had responsibility for local economic planning and for the distribution of the budget; these functions gave the *oblast* secretary and committee wide powers to regulate and verify what the state agencies were doing. At every level of the Soviet state, Control Commissions watched the performance indicators of policy and monitored fulfilment. Local censorship boards supervised all regional cultural production. Few public activities did not prompt investigation by party officials. The relationship between party and state was, at this level, as intimate and ubiquitous as it was in Germany.

In both systems the party acted as a political doorman, enabling or empowering state officials, checking their credentials, monitoring their behaviour and outlook, and imposing penalties on failure or dissent. This was a messy, unplanned process. The neat organizational charts masked endless institutional bickering, arguments over jurisdiction and protocol, confused responsibilities and uncertain duties. The tendency of party workers, constrained by their advisory or poorly defined leadership role, to seek real executive responsibility led to regular disputes and persistent tension. The parties generally wanted their members to lead rather than administer; state officials wanted to be able to act without the party always peering over their shoulder, but even the party faithful placed in state posts had to be monitored. The 1937 Civil Service Law in Germany established the right of the party courts to investigate and punish any lapse on the part of party members in state office.[105] Communists appointed to state posts were in the political frontline, constantly watched by their colleagues at work, appraised almost daily by their party sections. The extent of party influence over the state depended not so much on neat expressions of constitutional demarcation, but on the struggle at the grassroots to push through party policy. In every town, commune and village, the terms of party power and the limits of party influence differed one from another, the product of a complex web of personal relations, political ambitions and social tensions.

If the relationship between state and party was messily defined at ground level, this was because the two dictatorships were uncertain about the practical terms of the relationship themselves. These were hybrid systems in which party and state both had a role to play, but where the party was supposed to be the senior partner. Most accounts of the Soviet system regard it as a 'party-state', where the state was entirely hostage to a dominant 'totalitarian' party. The institutionalization of the *nomenklatura* system and the shadowing of all state activity by the party certainly produced a system of party primacy while the state was in the process of construction in the 1920s and

1930s. Major policy was decided by an inner party clique. Yet under Stalin the party began a slow process of relative decline as the state structure matured, a shift in the balance of power that Stalin did nothing to reverse – rather the opposite. In the 1920s the Party Congress and the Central Committee met regularly; they were the senior decision-making bodies of the party according to the party statutes.[106] During the Stalin dictatorship the Congress was assembled only three times, in 1934, 1939 and 1952, and in only the first was there any serious discussion of policy issues. The Central Committee plenum, which was supposed to meet, according to the 1939 statutes, three times a year, met only three times altogether between 1941 and Stalin's death in 1953: in January 1944, February 1947 and August 1952.[107] The influence of the party was also profoundly affected by the purges of the 1930s, which removed, along with poorly educated or careerist communists, thousands of the political vanguard that had run the Soviet Union since the revolution. New cadres emerged, but they fitted obediently into an existing economic and administrative system, rather than becoming the architects of a new one.

The role of the party at local level was subject to a great many practical constraints, as well as the constant rounds of political and military bloodletting. The party structure was thinly spread geographically. Even in the 1940s the typical mode of transport for the party secretaries outside the cities was a bicycle or a horse; telephones and typewriters were in short supply. Party officials were overloaded with work, first for the party, which was a priority, then the many responsibilities for local economic, cultural and social life, the collection of accurate statistics and the compilation of local political intelligence. These tasks would have taxed an organization heavy with office equipment and secretaries. So anxious did party officials become about fulfilling the economic plan or matching the objectives of the party centre that they also became embroiled in running the day-to-day affairs of local factories or farms to keep them up to plan. In 1948 Khrushchev launched an attack on district party officials for their failure to stick to the task of leadership, and their readiness to manage affairs best left to state officials.[108]

The root of this problem was the inflated size of the state sector. White-collar employment expanded rapidly in line with the strategy of economic modernization: 3.9 million in 1928, 8.6 million by 1940, 15.5 m by 1960.[109] The party was faced in the 1930s with large state organizations with their own vested interests to defend, including the soviets, the trade union structure, the commissariats, the military and the security system. These had been organizationally primitive in the 1920s, dependent on the input from educated party members for real guidance in policy, kicked along by party inspectors to work more effectively. By the 1930s they had become much larger, with a body of procedural rules worked out (regulations governing the rights and obligations of bureaucrats were first laid down in December 1922) and offices properly organized. In 1931 Stalin warned party cadres to stick to 'concrete and operational leadership' and to leave the fulfilment of policy to the state apparatus.[110] Significantly, it was the state security division of the interior commissariat that undertook the arrest and execution of party members between 1936 and 1938. The process of consolidating state institutions continued during the war. The armed forces succeeded in downgrading the role of the party military commissar from the autumn of 1942. The national commissariats were divided up into ever-more specialized sectors so that the technical expertise of the permanent officials gave them the capacity to mould or even initiate policy. As if to confirm the changing nature of the Soviet state, the commissariats were renamed ministries in 1946. Above all, Stalin himself decided in 1941 to accept high state office for the first time. He spent the last twelve years of his dictatorship as Premier as well as General Secretary, a change in status that reflected the more profound change in the nature of the Soviet state apparatus that the communist party had built up: a 'normative state' different from the 'emergency state' of the early revolutionary years. Though the party organization continued to play an important agitational and monitory role in every sector, it was one among a number of institutional heavyweights – the armed forces, the security apparatus, the ministerial structure – all state organs in which technical competence came to count as much as, if not more than, party loyalty.

Accounts of the German dictatorship have usually presented the opposite image: the party after 1933 was pushed into the background, and its radical political claims frustrated, Hitler refused to sanction a widespread reform of the state, and the old ministerial and institutional structures remained in place. There is a limited truth here. The party did not provide a clear forum for party leaders to decide policy; nor did Hitler agree to a radical reform of the Reich structure which might have strengthened the party's executive role.[111] The decline of the normative state was, nonetheless, a reality after 1933, and the beneficiary was the party. This was not a planned process but a piecemeal erosion of state functions, public morality and legal norms. The bureaucracy was forced to forswear impartiality in 1933 when the League of German Bureaucrats was transformed into a new Reich League, which was to abandon its distinct corporate identity and educate its members in obedience to National Socialist values.[112] Judges, lawyers and soldiers were made to swear oaths of loyalty to the *Führer*. The security apparatus, dominated by party leaders and the SS, subverted the rule of law from 1933 onwards. Local party officials, though short of money and personnel like their Soviet counterparts, were not so overburdened with party work, nor constantly engaged in formal procedures of verification and assessment, nor under constant threat of exclusion or demotion if they could not remember *Mein Kampf* quite clearly enough. Many of them saw it as their responsibility as National Socialists to harass and challenge any institution or individual not acceptable to the party; they were aided in this by a large army of affiliated organizations, particularly the Hitler Youth and the SA, which could bring direct, coercive pressure to bear if necessary.

The confrontation between state and party, where it occurred, was the consequence of the existence of a large state apparatus before 1933 that had been entirely independent of National Socialism. The party did not have to build up a state, but to break one down. The Soviet project was constructive, the German one transformative. Important areas of public activity were independent of the traditional state: the Labour Front, the SA, the SS, the Hitler Youth, from 1936 the Four-Year Plan for German war preparation, the National Socialist women's movement. Key areas of state activity were subverted by the party. The judicial, security and police system was defended for some time against party encroachment by the National Socialist Minister of the Interior, Wilhelm Frick, a former bureaucrat himself, but in June 1936 Heinrich Himmler won the right to operate the system on

National Socialist terms. The SS was the most predatory and ambitious of the party institutions. During the war the SS consolidated its position as a law unto itself, and began to spread its influence into other areas of state. The security apparatus was a central element in challenging the traditions of the normative state and transforming the surviving ministerial apparatus into a more pliable tool of the movement. By 1944 Himmler was Minister of the Interior, the SS judge Otto Thierack was Minister of Justice, and high-ranking SS officials were operating important parts of the war economy. The gigantic task of planning the post-war German order devolved on to SS and party leaders.[113]

Hitler had misgivings about creating an over-bureaucratic party structure, but just as Stalin did nothing to reverse the growth of a consolidated state in the Soviet Union, so Hitler did not reverse the transformation or dismantling of the old state. Stalin needed the state in order to control the party; Hitler needed the party in order to control the state. These differing political priorities were expressed in the way the dictators approached the issue of a constitution. The Stalin Constitution of 1936 was a description of state institutions and state power, in which the directing role of the party was mentioned only twice, and then obliquely.[114] The efforts to construct a formal reform of the state in Germany foundered on the hostility of a leader who, unlike Stalin, feared that fixed written rules would circumscribe the exercise of dictatorship.[115] The Soviet project was realized in a rigidly bureaucratic, administratively top-heavy Soviet state that survived for a further forty years; the new German state disappeared in 1945, still in the process of definition, but enough was achieved by that date to show that the structure at every level in Germany was closer to the idea of a 'party-state' than it was in the Soviet Union.[116]

The 'one-party' system was a novelty in inter-war Europe. No European state before 1914 had been dominated and led by a single political party. Despite the confident pronouncements about the role of the party, both Bolshevism and National Socialism were experimental movements, not pre-packaged systems. They were run in the main by ordinary Germans and Russians who had in many, perhaps most cases no previous experience of political organization and limited or non-existent administrative expertise. This explains the strenuous efforts made at the self-discipline and education of the two parties to turn them into more effective and unitary movements. It also explains why party officials were sometimes rightly perceived by their populations to be corrupt, venal and incompetent; party members were to be found in the concentration camps of both systems. Both parties were self-taught; they survived the learning process because any alternative had been forcibly removed, but also because much of the wider population shared the party's ambitious idealism to construct a new society.

These caveats might make it seem unlikely that either party could be regarded, as they so often are, as 'totalitarian' parties.[117] This is a term much misused. 'Totalitarian' does not mean that they were 'total' parties, either all-inclusive or wielding complete power; it means that they were parties concerned with the 'totality' of the societies in which they worked. In this narrower sense both movements did have totalitarian aspirations, and never were simple parliamentary parties. There were few areas of public life that did not come under party review, or had to be co-ordinated with the party, or eliminated. The public was subjected, willingly and unwillingly, to permanent party surveillance. The party events, for example, organized in Upper Bavaria in 1939 covered, so it was estimated, some 70 per cent of the regional population.[118] Party officials were supposed to visit party cells and households on a regular basis. In the Soviet Union, district instructors were ordered if they could to visit their local party cells every single day to keep themselves abreast of every development. One instructor in a rural district worked out a ten-day cycle of visits, which would take him to two or three different localities on three- or five-day shifts in order to get to every cell.[119] These were demanding schedules, requiring exceptional individual commitment. They were the result of party instructions that saw the party perpetually enrolled in mobilizing and engaging the population, and, above all, in providing ligaments to join the peripheral population to the central political apparatus.

No statistics can indicate how successful or otherwise that process of mobilization was, but there is no reason to doubt that the party did invite widespread voluntary participation, nor to doubt that there were grumblers and dissenters, who participated, if they had to, with reluctance. The role of the party should not be underestimated in either case. It is significant that the parties were able to dominate the local and national skylines regardless of popular criticism or periods of unpopularity. There was no alternative to the immanence of party life in either system. Both parties were open to public rebuke where party members violated their own standards or abused their position, though public redress was seldom automatic. When a young NKVD (security force), lieutenant on leave in a village in Kalinin province, found that the local collective farm was run by a cabal of permanently drunk communists, who gave jobs to their relatives, he immediately complained to the district party, who refused to discuss the case. He took it up to *oblast* level, where he was finally told that drunkenness and nepotism would have to be tolerated since the farm had more than fulfilled its quota.[120] The sense of 'them' and 'us' generated by the development of an often unmerited elite mentality among party members certainly existed in elements of the non-party majority, but there were no outlets for a broader rejection of party power, and dangerous consequences for those who persisted.[121]

The totality of the German system was certainly the greater of the two. The party had a larger and more stable body of activists, with higher levels of education; German society was more geographically compact; there was a rich and widespread associational life linked with the party machine. For an average German family regular contact with the party youth groups, the local SA, the party welfare collections, or the women's associations was unavoidable. Party symbols and language were pervasive. Encouraging party slogans and banners hung from factory and office walls or decorated party buildings. The party's presence was visible and demanding. The Soviet party had many of these characteristics, but lacked the personnel to cover the wide territories of the Union. Millions of the population in the countryside saw the party irregularly at best. In the cities the party offered a diet of political culture and education, youth work and civil defence volunteers, interspersed with festivals and party visits. It was visible enough, but not until the 1950s and 1960s did the expansive, all-embracing culture of party life become a state-wide reality. The communist party was the beneficiary of the absence of any alternative cultural or institutional life in much of the new Russia; the German claims to totality were made in the context of a society with many alternative outlets before 1933, which explains why National Socialism was so much more intrusive and exacting. The communist German Democratic Republic, set up in 1949, owed much more of its organization and values to the National Socialist system it replaced than to the Soviet one it emulated. In all three systems the parties – integrative, supervisory, persuasive and coercive – supplied the practical means to bind the population to the dictatorship.

5

States of Terror

'It should be remembered and never forgotten that as long as capitalist encirclement exists there will be wreckers, diversionists, spies, terrorists, sent behind the frontiers of the Soviet Union ... not the old methods, the methods of discussion must be used, but new methods, methods for smashing and uprooting it.'   Josef Stalin, 1927[1]

'It will be one of the most important tasks of the Movement to declare a relentless battle against the destroyers of the people's power of resistance and to wage this battle until they are utterly annihilated or subdued.'   Adolf Hitler, 1933[2]

Terror has always been regarded as a defining characteristic of modern dictatorship; fear, it is supposed, held in its chill grip the millions not seduced by propaganda. State terror, so the argument goes, was indiscriminate and ubiquitous. The German and Soviet people were imprisoned by the apparatus of terror. The temptation is to see the two systems divided between an army of secret policemen on one side and a mass of victims on the other.

Violent repression on a wide scale certainly existed but it was never called 'terror' in either system. The words 'terror' and 'terrorist' were applied not to the policemen and security agents who enforced state repression, but to those who opposed the dictatorships. Both systems saw themselves at the forefront of a war against international terrorism. What is now defined as ruthless state terror was viewed by Hitler and Stalin as state protection against the enemies of the people. This very different perception of 'terror' is central to an understanding of the relationship between the security forces and society. For much of the life of both dictatorships the public war against terror won widespread approval and even co-operation from the two populations. Though fear might now seem the most rational of responses to what were, by any standards, fearful regimes, that fear was projected onto the victims of discrimination and state repression. 'Terrorists' were excluded and persecuted not only by the organs of state security, but by a population made anxious through orchestrated programmes of public vilification.

Repression under Hitler and Stalin was never pursued simply for its own sake, to induce a general obedience from fear. Repression was targeted at groups or individuals who were isolated as a threat to the predominant political priorities of the two systems. In the Soviet case this meant protecting the proletarian revolution from its alleged bourgeois, counter-revolutionary enemies at home and abroad; in the German case it meant protecting the German nation or race from apparent threats of biological defilement and spiritual decay. Enemies in both cases were defined as particularly intransigent, cunning and vicious in order to lend weight to the anti-terrorist struggle and to justify the most ruthless methods of suppression. In each case the prevailing mentality was more akin to that of civil war.

Hitler and Stalin, who were themselves both former political terrorists, played a key part in creating the idea of the perpetual enemy. Stalin's whole political outlook was shaped by a central dualism between virtuous Bolshevik revolutionary and counter-revolutionary opponent. 'We have internal enemies. We have external enemies,' announced Stalin in 1928 during the Shakhty show trial: 'This, comrades, must not be forgotten for a single moment.'[3] State security was necessary, Stalin argued in a speech in 1927, 'for the purpose of protecting the interests of the revolution from attacks on the part of the counter-revolutionary bourgeoisie and their agents'. Enemies were always defined as part of a network of terror: 'plotters, terrorists, incendiaries and bomb-throwers'.[4] The accused in the first of the major show trials of the 1930s, the Zinoviev-Kamenev trial of August 1936, were supposed to have operated a 'Terrorist Centre'. Bukharin, at his show trial in March 1938, asked whether he was in favour of terrorist acts, was forced to confess 'I was'.[5] Stalin saw the terrorist as a particularly dangerous opponent. He told the German biographer Emil Ludwig, in an interview in 1931, that the regime had at first betrayed the interests of the working class by excessive mildness: 'We learnt from experience that the only way to deal with such enemies is to apply the most ruthless policy of suppression.'[6] Stalin reserved his most intemperate public vocabulary for the enemy terrorist: 'shoot them, destroy them,' he urged in November 1937. 'They are worldwide provocateurs, the most vile agents of fascism.'[7]

The watchword of Stalinist repression was vigilance. After years of activity in socialist politics, Stalin seems to have habitually assumed that party divisions, ideological divergence and tactical squabbles were the result of infiltration by alien political forces. The terrorist network operated from within the party, as well as outside. His call in 1937 to turn the party into 'an impregnable fortress' was directed at the army of agents, 'wreckers' and traitors within its own walls; 'double-dealers' (*dvuruzhniki*) were to be unmasked and exterminated.[8] The enemy was always in the pay of a malign foreign power. In the 1920s the enemy was some representative of the worldwide anti-communist bourgeoisie; in the 1930s enemies were defined as agents of fascism (until the German–Soviet pact of August 1939 forced prosecutors to shift the blame for terrorism back to imperial Britain and France); after 1945 the enemy became an agent of American imperialism, or international Zionism, or merely 'cosmopolitan'. The alien image of the enemy simplified the act of isolation and exclusion, and lent repression enhanced plausibility in the public mind, despite the often ludicrous character of the accusations. In the final major show trial in March 1938, the defendants (all committed communists) were accused of organizing a conspiracy with foreign states (in this case Germany and Japan) with the object of 'provoking a military attack . . . dismembering the USSR' and 'restoring capitalism'.[9]

Hitler's attitude to the enemy shared the inflammatory language and alien characterization of the Soviet model. In a speech in 1934 he told the audience that his movement had saved the German people 'from Red terror'. After the Röhm purge he gave vent to the following bloodthirsty outburst: 'Beasts, criminals, conspirators, traitors, well-poisoners – bloodily, swiftly destroy and shoot them, burn out these ulcers to the raw flesh, grasp them ruthlessly and bloodily.'[10] The enemy was sustained, in Hitler's view, by alien forces, predominantly by Jews and Bolsheviks, who worked to undermine the National Socialist state at the behest of foreign interests. These were the same enemies who, in November 1918, through 'their mad or criminal action' had brought Germany its misfortunes.[11] Hitler told the Reichstag in 1934: 'The National Socialist state in its domestic life will exterminate and annihilate even these last remnants of this poisoning and stultification of the people.'[12]

The watchword of Hitler's repression was vengeance; revenge not only against the betrayal of Germany by Jews and socialists in 1918 – the notorious idea of 'the stab-in-the-back' – but revenge against all the enemies of the movement and traitors against the new Germany. Political repression was not intended to be indiscriminate; the enemy was defined and excluded, just like the class enemy in the Soviet Union. In the first years of the regime that enemy was overtly political: the remnants of German communism and social-democracy, opponents in the German churches. By the mid-1930s the principal menace to national survival was defined in terms of a political biology. The alien enemy was concealed, like the masked anti-Bolshevik, though in the body of the nation, not the party. Non-German (particularly Jewish) blood, hereditary genetic defects of mind and body, sexual perversion and deviation, or socio-pathological behaviour were used to define the many categories of racial threat. Political and biological victimization sometimes overlapped. Popular psychological theory postulated the argument that there was a direct connection between psychiatric disorder, racial inadequacy and communist sympathies.[13] Repression of race-enemies became the central objective of the German security services, a priority that ended in the 1940s with genocide.

State discrimination and violence in both dictatorships derived from a specific, if broad-ranging sense of who the enemy was. The identification of enemies owed much of its inspiration to the political convictions of the two dictators. Both regimes presented the apparatus of state security as an instrument to protect the great majority of both populations who did not engage in subversive activity. By deliberately exaggerating the nature of the counter-revolutionary threat in the one case or the Jewish-Bolshevik menace in the other, both systems succeeded in presenting state repression as a form of popular political justice with which ordinary people could identify. The use of a violent, exterminatory rhetoric accustomed the public to accept ruthlessness on the part of the regime in waging the relentless war against subversion or national decay. This unrestrained and deadly war was waged in the name of the people. Terror became representative.

State repression was the responsibility of police forces and security agencies, working closely with the judiciary. However lawless or random repression now seems, both dictatorships provided a legal basis and developed a formal institutional framework through which they could isolate and persecute all those defined as enemies of the people. This was by no means a new process in either state. Political police forces existed throughout Europe during the late nineteenth century. In Tsarist Russia the state political police, supervised by a Special Section (*osobyi otdel*) set up in 1898, fought an underground war against political opposition to the monarchy.[14] In Germany every provincial police authority had a political section that monitored local politics and investigated cases of treason, political defamation or terrorism. In the 1920s political crime in Germany escalated sharply with the rise of radical parties with paramilitary wings. In 1932 alone 250 people were sentenced for high treason; there were hundreds of political prisoners in German jails on the eve of the Hitler regime, many of them National Socialists convicted of murdering and maiming their opponents.[15] Political police forces found themselves compiling card indexes on political radicals and supplying forensic evidence of politically inspired crime.

The direct forerunner of the Stalinist security apparatus was set up on 20 December 1917 under the clumsy title of the All-Russian Extraordinary Commission for Combating Counter-Revolution, Speculation, Sabotage, and Misconduct in Office. Better known as the Cheka, the new security force became a virtual law unto itself during the civil war, when an estimated 250,000 were executed at its hands.[16] In 1922, anxious to restore some sense of revolutionary legality after the violence of the civil war, the Soviet government replaced the Cheka with the State Political Administration (GPU), directly responsible to the Commissar for the Interior, but the name 'chekist' remained in common use. With the formal creation of the Soviet Union the GPU became the All-Union GPU, or OGPU. Its activities were supervised by the Commissar of Justice, and political crimes had to be heard before Soviet courts in all but the most exceptional cases. The most serious cases of treason were heard before the senior army court, the Military Collegium. Throughout the 1920s the OGPU pursued as enemies social remnants from the old order, socialist renegades and foreign spies. When the collectivization drive began in 1929, the OGPU undertook to round up recalcitrant 'rich peasants' and to deport them to camps and labour colonies. The notorious three-man courts or *troiki* were set up to cope with the vast workload in the countryside. The activity of the security service closely matched the political priorities of the party; Stalin's secretariat established and nourished close links with the OGPU, though it was by no means simply Stalin's creature.[17]

In the summer of 1934 the whole security apparatus underwent a major transformation in order to bring the political police under the closer scrutiny of the state authorities following regular complaints about the abuse of justice. In reality the system that was constructed provided a more effective and centralized instrument for the intensification of repression, and it lasted for the remainder of Stalin's dictatorship. The OGPU was taken over directly by the Commissariat for Internal Affairs (NKVD) under Genrikh Yagoda; with the title of State Security (*Gosbezopasnost*) it became one of the commissariat's major divisions. The ordinary police, or militia, were unified under the NKVD at the same time. In November of the same year a national network of labour camps, usually known by the acronym GUlag, was set up under the NKVD, bringing every arm of state repression and policing under one roof. The *troiki* were suspended with the reform, but the NKVD retained its so-called Special Sessions – tribunals that sat in judgement on counter-revolutionary and terrorist crimes, without calling witnesses, or even the accused.[18]

The chief legal instrument for dealing with anti-state terrorism was Article 58 of the Russian criminal code of 1926. The article defined, though never very precisely, an extensive range of counter-revolutionary and terrorist crimes, which carried sentences ranging from three months in prison to execution. The definitions were vague, catch-all provisions, whose flexibility was ruthlessly exploited by the officials of state security. In 1934 the opportunity came to make state security a virtual law unto itself. In the hours following the murder of Sergei Kirov on 1 December, Stalin dictated a new law on 'terrorist organizations and terrorist acts'. The law was approved two days later by the Politburo. Its provisions were a recipe for state lawlessness. Terrorist acts were to be investigated for no more than ten days; there would be no prosecution or defence attorneys; no appeals; all those guilty (there was in reality no presumption of innocence) were to be executed 'quickly'.[19]

The heart of the security apparatus was the notorious building on Lubyanka Square, which housed the bureaucrats, detectives and guards of the State Security division. It was here that political suspects were brought in large black police vans. Sometimes the vehicles were decked out in an innocent livery of bright colours; sometimes they masqueraded as tradesmen's or bakers' vans so as not to alert the victims beforehand or alarm the neighbourhood. The arrestees were placed in overcrowded cells, unbearably stuffy in summer, freezing in winter. They were stripped, searched, finger-printed and photographed on arrival. Terrorist suspects were kept apart from other more innocuous counter-revolutionaries. Once in the cells prisoners were either interrogated so that they could compromise others, or judged *in absentia* by the NKVD Special Session and removed to prison or execution, or taken to a military *troika* where the case would be heard and sentencing carried out within twenty-four hours, under the terms of the law of 1 December 1934. Torture was not officially sanctioned except at the height of the repression in 1937–8, when detectives wanted quick answers, but interrogators were generally free to make their victims stand for hours (Bela Kun, who had led the unsuccessful communist revolution in 1919 in Hungary, was forced to stand on one leg for days until he confessed to being a fascist agent), and to deprive them of sleep, and to subject them to a torrent of slander and abuse.[20] Supervision of lower rank guards and interrogators was scanty, and the margin for abuse a wide one. Few prisoners could withstand mistreatment for more than a few days. Most 'confessions' were fabricated and altered by the interrogating officer using the bulging file of evidence and extorted confessions supplied by other prisoners. I. A.

Pyatnitsky, secretary of the executive committee of the Comintern until his arrest in July 1937, finally confessed for no more than fifteen minutes after months of torture, but was then presented with a twenty-nine-page transcript of his confession to sign.[21] Accounts of interrogation suggest that the police officers believed what they were told about their prisoners, since many had no grounds to disbelieve it.

The trial that followed was a cursory investigation at most, based on evidence that was generally not made available or known to the prisoner. Prisoners were given copies of an indictment, which was the basis on which they were to confess their guilt. The trials were a mockery of justice. Evgenia Ginzburg, who survived to write an account of her own seven-minute hearing, was brought in by two guards, who sat either side of her as she faced three judges and a court secretary. She was charged under Article 58 and the Kirov law. Her accusers revealed bored, expressionless faces. 'You plead guilty?' asked the presiding judge. When she said no, the judges refused to discuss the case. After listening to her protestations of innocence, they withdrew to consider the verdict and sentence; two minutes later they were back, to impose ten years in a labour camp.[22]

The overcrowded cells and conveyor-belt justice were the consequence of a very great increase in cases of political repression, which peaked in 1937–8. During the period known generally in the West as 'the Great Terror', and in the Soviet Union as the *Ezhovshchina*, named after the Commissar for Internal Affairs, Nikolai Ezhov, a member of Stalin's secretariat appointed at his insistence in September 1936, State Security were given additional powers to combat a nationwide 'terrorist organization' operating in the party itself. The nature and consequences of the frenzied repression under Ezhov are examined below. The inspiration for the sudden escalation of terror against enemies was, without question, Stalin. From the autumn of 1936 to the Central Committee plenum held in June 1937, Stalin pushed his entourage into a final battle with masked 'class enemies'. He personally instructed courts to shoot those they convicted. At the end of a lengthy Central Committee plenum in February and March 1937, where party vigilance against wreckers and terrorists was the main item for discussion, Stalin published his own plenum speeches under the title 'Measures to Liquidate the Trotskyists and other Double-Dealers'.

The word 'liquidate' was added to the title of the speech for publication deliberately; its meaning was for once unmistakable in a country used to having to read the codes in everything their leader wrote or said. Stalin warned that the final battle – 'the sharpest form of struggle' – had arrived against all those subversive forces that had threatened the revolutionary state since the 1920s.[23] This apocalyptic vision became hideously magnified by the state security forces and party secretaries, always over-eager to demonstrate that they, at least, were virtuous revolutionaries.

The additional powers granted to State Security officers reveal much. At some point in 1937 (the document has never been found) interrogators were instructed by the Central Committee to use physical torture to extract confessions. According to Kaganovich, when asked to recall it in the 1950s, Stalin himself drafted the handwritten order and got other members of the Politburo to sign it. A special group of 'breaker-investigators' (*kolol'shchiki*) was recruited, whose title speaks for itself. The number of detectives quadrupled under Ezhov; so short-staffed did the system become that interrogators lacking even the usual slender qualifications – including police drivers and boilermen – were recruited to beat out confessions.[24] The *troiki* were revived in November 1936, and their use expanded again in the summer of 1937. It was these small kangaroo courts, dispensing what was taken to be revolutionary justice, that worked overtime to fulfil NKVD orders 00446 and 00447 of July 1937, to 'put an end once and for all to the foul subversive work against the foundations of the Soviet state'.[25] The orders were handed down from the Politburo with instructions that the guilty were to be shot, not imprisoned. For the year that followed, State Security had virtually unrestricted power to kill anyone who came into their hands.

During the second half of 1938 the wave of state executions began to subside as Stalin sent out signals to show that the emergency was past; he sided with those who now argued that the terror had run its course to excess. In November Ezhov was sacked and succeeded by Lavrenti Beria, a Georgian like Stalin, who cut his teeth on savagely purging the party organization in the Caucasus, before being moved to Moscow as Ezhov's deputy and Stalin's stalking-horse in the NKVD. He was very different from the slightly-built, wan-faced

Ezhov, perpetually drunk and habitually tense by 1938; Beria was a solid policeman, whose calm, expressionless eyes gleamed out behind pince-nez glasses (Stalin made him add a chain to them, to appear less bourgeois). He had a ferocious temper and a foul mouth, combined with remarkable political cunning. He survived as head of the NKVD for six years, and avoided the fate of his predecessors, Yagoda and Ezhov, both of whom were shot on characteristically implausible charges.

Although Beria has been remembered by history as a corrupt and cynical ogre, a reputation it would be hard to fault, he brought the NKVD back to the more modest levels of repression before the *Ezhovshchina* and introduced reforms in police practice. Torture was reduced and proper investigative procedures introduced. On 31 December 1938 the Supreme Court of the USSR ruled that cases could only be brought under Article 58 where intent to commit counter-revolutionary or terrorist crimes could be demonstrated. The *troiki* were suspended once again, and so too the Special Sessions, where many State Security prisoners had been condemned to death in indecent haste.[26] Beria wanted to transfer responsibility for investigation to the Commissariat of Justice, but the Central Committee vetoed it, and the NKVD continued to apprehend political suspects and investigate their cases.[27] He established a Department for the Investigation of Specially Important Crimes, and this took over the major political cases down to the end of the dictatorship, including that of his predecessor. During the course of 1939 a number of public trials were held of State Security men accused of fabricating evidence and perverting the course of justice, almost certainly the only show trials where the evidence and accusations were substantially true.

The security services maintained a state of revolutionary vigilance nonetheless. Beria did little to overturn the traditions of trumped-up charges, forced confessions and summary justice; torture was never eradicated; Article 58 and the Kirov law remained on the statute-book until after Stalin's death in 1953. Alleged counter-revolutionary crimes continued to bring hundreds of thousands of Soviet citizens into the security net. Under Beria the organization became larger, more efficient and more bureaucratic. The impromptu police violence of the 1930s was replaced by a more methodical and systematic programme of surveillance. In April 1943 the enormous NKVD empire was split again; the State Security division, responsible for political police work and the camps, was upgraded to a full commissariat of state security, the NKGB, and placed under Beria's former deputy in the Caucasus, Nikolai Merkulov. Beria survived as Internal Affairs Minister until 1946. That year the commissariats were transformed into ministries. The new MVD was taken over by Sergei Kruglov; the MGB by a career policeman, Viktor Abakumov. Beria survived to take over a reunified MVD/MGB organization briefly following Stalin's death in 1953, but was removed within weeks by his former colleagues, and shot in circumstances that still remain uncertain.[28]

In Germany the establishment of a police and judicial apparatus of repression had to be undertaken in quite different circumstances. When Hitler assumed power in 1933, the judiciary was independent, the rule of law still effective and the political police departments obliged to operate along constitutional lines. The first wave of political violence unleashed in January 1933, as the party and the SA took swift and bloody revenge against their opponents, was outside the law. The wave of beatings and murders were beyond police control and flimsy efforts to contain it broke down. The SA set up small internment camps for their victims, and interrogation centres where prisoners were savagely tortured. Hermann Göring, who was appointed Minister of the Interior in Prussia in February 1933, instructed an assembly of police officials that same month to ignore the evidence that the terrorism, directed predominantly at the left-wing parties, 'conflicted with the present rights and laws of the Reich'.[29]

The wild and public violence of the Nazi movement was slowly converted into a violence officially sanctioned by the state, and eventually into institutionalized state repression. On 11 February 1933 the SA in the Rhineland were sworn in as police auxiliaries, and eleven days later they were given police authority throughout the whole of Prussia.[30] The opportunity to legalize repression was provided a week later when, late at night on 27 February, fire could be seen enveloping the German parliament building. The following day Hitler asked President Hindenburg for emergency powers to contain the threat of communist revolution, for which the burning of the Reichstag was supposed to be the signal. So fortuitous was the moment that it has always been tempting to assume that the arsonists were National Socialists, and not the simple-minded Dutch communist, Marinus van der Lubbe, who was caught at the scene. But like the Kirov murder, which triggered the savage emergency powers of the Stalinist dictatorship, the Reichstag fire was almost certainly the work of a lone terrorist.

The Reichstag fire decree 'for the protection of people and state' was published on 28 February 1933 under Article 48 (2.2) of the German constitution granting the President emergency powers. The decree supplied the major legal instrument for state repression until the end of the dictatorship, though at first parliament went through the constitutional charade of renewing it each year. Its provisions were nothing if not candid. Major articles of the constitution guaranteeing civil rights (114, 115, 117, 118, 123, 124 and 153) were suspended. This permitted 'limitations of personal freedom' and restrictions on 'the right of free speech', as well as curbs on press freedom, the violation of the privacy of telephone and postal communication, house searches and property seizures. The decree introduced the death penalty for those guilty of a range of crimes from acts of treason to the sabotaging of railway lines, all of which had previously been punishable by hard labour. Death also awaited those who carried out terrorist murders of state officials or government figures, or who incited murder, or 'discussed it with another person'; crimes against public order involving a weapon; and kidnapping of hostages for political purposes (all crimes routinely perpetrated without punishment by the SA).[31] At the end of March a law on the death penalty was published, which allowed it to be imposed retrospectively on crimes committed before 28 February, and on the unfortunate van der Lubbe, who was hanged a few days later.[32]

The legal instruments necessary to impose political repression were completed with two further emergency decrees on 21 March. The first concerned what was defined as 'malicious gossip' (*Heimtücke*) – the spread of defeatism or demoralization, defamation of political figures or the party, or remarks likely to cause 'foreign policy difficulties'. It was replaced with a new 'Law against malicious slander of state and party and to protect party uniforms' on 20 December 1934, which additionally allowed the arrest of anyone wearing uniforms without permission or making fun of them. These offences, designed to muzzle all public political criticism by the vagueness of their formulation, carried long jail sentences, or, in extreme cases, the death penalty. Also on 21 March the regime introduced 'special courts' (*Sondergerichte*), in which cases of political crime, defined under the emergency laws, could be heard without the usual safeguards in legal procedure. These were not a complete novelty: special courts had been used to deal with political unrest in the years between 1919 and 1923. A *Sondergericht* was set up on 6 October 1931 to deal with the many cases of political violence. Yet taken together with the emergency decrees, they consti-tuted one of the most important steps in permitting the regime to circumvent the traditional judicial system and impose its own form of people's justice. The special courts could work faster, dispense with the usual procedures for the defence, and restrict appeals. By 1935 there were twenty-five of them, spread across the Reich.[33] On 24 April 1934 a supreme special court was created, with its seat in Berlin, to take on the most serious cases of treason. In 1936 the People's Court (*Volksgerichtshof*) was placed under Otto Thierack, one of the many German judges to join the party before 1933. Ruthless and intem-perate, he had little respect for the traditional legal system. In his hands the People's Court became an instrument of narrow political justice.[34]

The dictatorship still lacked its secret policemen. In the early months of the regime the existing political police departments were purged of known political opponents; many had been willingly pursuing the radical left long before Hitler came to power and needed little encour-agement to exploit the wider powers supplied by the emergency decrees. One of them, a young Prussian detective called Rudolf Diels, suggested to Göring that he convert the Prussian office into a new secret police force. On 26 April 1933 the Secret State Police Office (*Geheime Staatspolizeiamt*) was formally established, with Diels as its first director. The acronym GPA was thought to be too close to the Soviet GPU. A postal official suggested the abbreviation 'Gestapa' and the police force became known as the 'Gestapo', the Secret State Police. On 20 April 1934 the organization was transferred to the jurisdiction of Heinrich Himmler, who in a year had risen from the office of political police chief in Bavaria to become responsible for political police forces throughout most of Germany. The Gestapo headquarters were established in Berlin at 8, Prinz Albrechtstrasse, and the organization placed under the direction of a brutal and ambitious Bavarian policeman, Heinrich Müller. This building, which closely resembled the Lubyanka in Moscow, with its flat, grey unremarkable façade concealing the sound-proofed cells in the basement, became the hub of the system of political repression.

In the first years of the regime the ordinary police and courts continued to play an important role in political repression, using instruments already available in the penal code to safeguard the state against public order offences and treasonable actions. By 1935 there were 22,000 more political prisoners in the regular prison system than in the camps, most of them communists or social-democrats. In the regular prison in Chemnitz, in Saxony, three-quarters of all prisoners in 1934 were political prisoners; in Dortmund, in the Ruhr, prisoners in the hard-labour penitentiary were at one point exclusively political.[35] The factor that distinguished the political police force from the rest of the police apparatus was the right to take suspects into protective custody (*Schutzhaft*). This right was first granted under the emergency powers following the Reichstag fire, and it was central to the work of repression, but it was a right that had to be renewed and carefully defined. By July 1933, there were, according to the Interior Ministry, 26,789 in protective custody; in effect this meant confinement in a concentration camp or prison without the right to a court hearing. There were regular complaints from officials and from the public about the evident abuses such a system entailed. Most of the irregular camps, set up by the SA in 1933, were closed down. On 12 April 1934 the Interior Minister Wilhelm Frick, a National Socialist lawyer to whom the police were still, in theory, subordinate, published secret guidelines on 'protective custody' to ensure that unitary regulation operated throughout the Reich. Though the unfortunate prisoners now enjoyed the right to be informed in writing within twenty-four hours of the reasons for their confinement, no limit was placed on their imprisonment as long as they continued to constitute 'a threat to public security and order'. Despite Frick's own reservations, this was a definition left largely to the discretion of the secret police authorities, who continued to insist that they should have the right to hold prisoners without trial. On 25 January 1938 a second protective custody decree was drawn up, which lasted down to the end of the war. Responsibility for operating the system was given over completely to the Gestapo.[36]

The Gestapo retained the primary right of arrest throughout the dictatorship. The popular image of the black-uniformed SS man as the symbol of state terror has obscured the reality that arrest, investigation and deportation were the responsibilities of the political police force, not of the SS. The popular image of the Gestapo is, on the other hand, broadly true. Detectives did arrive early in the morning (usually in pairs), knock on the door and politely invite suspects to accompany them to police headquarters. When the Munich editor, and later founder of *Picture Post*, Stefan Lorant was arrested in March 1933, he was taken to his newspaper office where the two policemen searched for evidence. When Lorant asked them what they were looking for they realized that they had no idea, and telephoned their inspector, who told them to hunt for 'caricatures likely to bring the government into contempt'. He was next taken to prison, searched, fingerprinted, photographed from the front, side and with his hat on, and thrown into a small communal cell. The search of his office had revealed a picture postcard sent by a friend on a visit to the Soviet Union, who had innocently written on the front 'I am reading Marx and Engels'. Lorant was charged with 'Bolshevist intrigue' and kept in jail; a few weeks later his wife was arrested and placed in the women's wing. After seven months, without a court hearing, and together with his wife, he was deported to Hungary, where he had been born.[37]

The political police had few restraints on their activities, even in cases as incompetently handled as Lorant's. Party agencies came to play an increasingly important part in the security apparatus, at the expense of the formal police and judicial system. Lorant witnessed SA bullies allowed into the political prison to club and kick prisoners senseless. Unlike the Soviet system, where the NKVD enjoyed control over the State Security division during the high period of state repression, the German Interior Ministry found itself excluded, step-by-step, from any effective supervision of the security apparatus. In February 1936 a new law was agreed on the Gestapo that freed the secret police entirely from administrative judicial review, and allowed them legally to decide who was a political criminal, and what constituted political crime.[38] Four months later Hitler agreed to a comprehensive reorganization of the security services under Himmler. On 17 June 1936 he was officially appointed Reich Leader of the SS and Chief of the German Police. His new title made explicit the fusion of party and security interests. Himmler was now able to construct a highly centralized, national system of police power. Under his control came the ordinary police, led by Kurt Daluege, a senior SS officer; the criminal police and secret state police (which were amalgamated on 26 June into a new force of 'security police', *Sicherheitspolizei*) under Himmler's SS deputy, Reinhard Heydrich; and the concentration camps, which had been handed over to SS control in March of that year. Heydrich also remained director of the party's own security service (*Sicherheitsdienst*), whose primary task was to monitor public opinion and identify potential resistance both inside and outside the party.

The new organization, though nominally under the umbrella of Frick's Interior Ministry, became its own master. As party sympathizers and SS men were appointed to key police functions, and to posts in the Interior and Justice ministries, the entire judicial and police system came to reflect more and more closely the political will of the party leadership. Shortly after the outbreak of war the entire apparatus was raised to the level of a ministry under the title of Reich Security Main Office (*Reichssicherheitshauptamt*), and Himmler and Heydrich given ministerial status. One of the RSHA's first acts was to issue guidelines to allow the Gestapo to take anyone guilty of weakening the war effort into custody and to execute them, or send them to a camp, without reference to the courts. This status was given the euphemistic title 'special handling' (*Sonderbehandlung*); this was the point at which the security police won an unlimited and formal right to kill their victims if they chose to. Early in 1943 Himmler recommended that in place of a trial a quaintly worded formula be recited to camp prisoners immediately before their judicial murder: 'The delinquent has done such-and-such and has therefore on account of the crime forfeited his life. To protect people and Reich he is to be conveyed from life to death. Judgement will be imposed.'[39] On 30 June 1943 the Gestapo won the additional right to decide whether *any* criminal or political case should proceed to trial or straight to confinement, but by that stage such legal niceties were irrelevant in the face of the unlimited power enjoyed by the security forces in the fight against what Himmler called 'the natural enemy, international Bolshevism, led by Jews and Freemasons'.[40]

There are some evident similarities between the apparatus of state security in both dictatorships. Both evolved over time into heavily centralized, bureaucratic police systems, culminating in separate state security ministries – the MGB in the Soviet Union and the RSHA in Germany. Both closely reflected the political priorities of the two regimes; 'It is the function of the police only to deal with what the Government wishes to have dealt with,' wrote the security police official, Werner Best, in 1937.[41] State Security in the Soviet Union remained slavishly sensitive to signals from the central party and state apparatus. In both regimes the security apparatus slowly accumulated legal instruments that allowed it to bypass the existing justice system. In the Soviet Union, however, those instruments were regularly reviewed, and from the late 1930s (with the exception of arbitrary military justice during the war years), State Security was supposed to operate within its own legal limits, even if this made slight difference to those ensnared in its tentacles.

It is the utterly lawless character of state repression in Germany by the end of the dictatorship that marks the chief difference between the Soviet and German security systems. For all its evident injustices and incompetence, its arbitrariness and legal sophistry, the Soviet system operated on an agreed legal foundation. Political prisoners were put on trial and their cases painstakingly, often viciously investigated, sometimes for years. This was a system open to massive and regular abuse. Political 'enemies' were secretly murdered, so that it has become impossible to establish with certainty whether the death of public figures from suicide, accident or natural causes was aggravated state repression or not. State Security was also able to operate its own courts, and to conduct its own investigations, so that the legal forms adopted were not part of the normative judicial system, much though the Commissariat of Justice would have liked to control them. Once in the system it was almost impossible to be released without conviction, though a higher authority could, and very occasionally did, overturn a few among the thousands of unsound judgments. Yet State Security, even at the height of the *Ezhovshchina*, never claimed the right simply to seize prisoners for internment or execution without a hearing or a charge.

The German system also produced a gradual bifurcation of state security and the normative judicial system. State security was endowed with special legal instruments, special courts, and the right to investigate cases on its own terms. Both systems routinely used torture to extract confessions or incriminating intelligence; both systems set up camps for political prisoners. The chief distinction was the Gestapo's right to take people into protective custody, and to recommend 'indefinite confinement', even for prisoners who had been granted a lesser sentence by a regular court, or had already served their sentence. (Paradoxically, administrative autonomy also gave the Gestapo the right to release people with nothing more severe than a warning and no threat of court action, which seldom happened in the Soviet system once proceedings had begun.) Protective custody, first granted at the outset of the dictatorship, was flagrantly and systematically abused, and it eventually gave the security police, ignoring even the special courts, the right to decide between life and death, not only for political prisoners, but for millions of innocent Germans and Europeans victimized and murdered not for any crime they had committed but because of their race.

One of the most difficult things for historians to establish is just how many victims of state repression there were. The Soviet security system generated a mass of secret statistics, most of which have become available since the fall of European communism. The Third Reich was less statistically fastidious, and more secretive. While record-keepers in the NKVD laboriously wrote down every conviction and sentence, German camp and prison records were not so scrupulously maintained, or were deliberately destroyed every few months. At the end of the war bonfires of security papers blazed all over the Reich. Even with the better Soviet records, it stretches belief to assume that every victim was recorded, or that some were not recorded twice by rival agencies keen to demonstrate that they were over-fulfilling their norms, particularly under the exceptional conditions during the *Ezhovshchina* and the war. The two dictatorships incarcerated and murdered prisoners in millions, not hundreds. A statistically precise figure of the victims of either dictatorship is beyond historical recovery, and it is in the nature of murderous repression that it should be so.

The existing figures do, nonetheless, give a clear indication of the scale and character of the repression. For years the figures circulating in the West for Soviet repression were greatly inflated. Anton Antonov-Ovseyenko, the son of a leading party victim of the 1930s, claimed in memoirs written in 1980 that Politburo sources indicated that 18.84 million people were sent to Soviet prisons between 1935 and 1940, and that 7 million of these were shot; some 16 million were said to be in camps; the number of dead in the 1930s from famine and repression he calculated to be 41 million.[42] Some of these figures were accepted and reproduced in the West, where estimates ranging from 8 to 20 million arrests and 9 to 40 million deaths have been widely circulated.[43]

The archive shows a very different picture. Aggregate statistics of arrests, convictions and executions were compiled in 1953 after Stalin's death. Those arrested, convicted and sentenced by the NKVD agencies between 1930 and 1953 total 3,851,450.[44] The total executed, according to these figures, was 776,074, which is very close to the figure of 786,098 for those sentenced for execution between 1930 and 1953 published under Gorbachev in 1990. The full record is set out in Table 5.1. These figures are substantially lower than the more speculative pre-*glasnost* estimates. The statistics for those sent to camps are consistent with what is now known from the archives of the GUlag, about the size and composition of the camp population. In 1940 there were 4 million in the various penal institutions: approximately 1.3 million in the GUlag camps, 300,000 in prison, 997,000 in special settlements and 1.5 million in deportee camps.[45]

The exceptional years are 1937 and 1938. In the two central years of the *Ezhovshchina* are to be found 35 per cent of all convictions between 1930 and 1953, and 88 per cent of all executions, a total in two years of 681,692 victims. The average for those executed in the 'normal' years 1932–6, 1939–40 and 1946–53 is 1,432. A sentence in camp or prison was the usual fate, and the camp populations rose steadily after the war as killing on a large scale declined. By 1950 there were 6.45 million in the various parts of the camp empire. Total deaths in the GUlag camps from 1934 (when accurate records start) to 1953 numbered 1,053,829, in the most part from disease, overwork, frost-

Table 5.1 Sentences of Cases brought to Trial by State Security 1930–1953

Year	Death	Camps	Exile	Other	Total
1930	20,201	114,443	58,816	14,609	208,069
1931	10,651	105,683	63,269	1,093	180,696
1932	2,728	73,946	36,017	29,228	141,919
1933	2,154	138,903	54,262	44,345	239,664
1934	2,056	59,451	5,994	11,498	78,999
1935	1,229	185,846	33,601	46,400	267,076
1936	1,118	219,418	23,719	30,415	274,670
1937	353,074	429,311	1,366	6,914	790,665
1938	328,618	205,509	16,842	3,289	554,258
1939	2,552	54,666	3,783	2,888	63,889
1940	1,649	65,727	2,142	2,228	71,746
1941	8,011	65,000	1,200	1,210	75,421
1942	23,278	88,809	7,070	5,249	124,406
1943	3,579	68,887	4,787	1,188	78,441
1944	3,029	73,610	649	821	78,109
1945	4,252	116,681	1,647	668	123,248
1946	2,896	117,943	1,498	957	123,294
1947	1,105	76,581	666	458	78,810
1948*	—	72,552	419	298	73,269
1949	—	64,409	10,316	300	75,025
1950	475	54,466	5,225	475	60,641
1951	1,609	49,142	3,452	599	54,802
1952	1,612	25,824	773	591	28,800
1953	198	7,894	38	273	8,403

* Capital punishment was abolished in 1947, but was reintroduced in 1950 for particularly severe cases.
Source: J. P. Pohl, *The Stalinist Penal System* (London, 1997), p. 8.

bite and malnutrition. Some of the NKVD executions were carried out in the camps, and may be double counted in the global total of NKVD killings. More difficult to assess is just how many of the cases tried under the security agencies were in fact criminal cases (like the case of two unfortunate peasant boys sent to mind the collective farm cows, who were caught eating three cucumbers and were each sentenced to eight years in a camp).[46] Nor is it possible to calculate how many cases in the ordinary justice system were in fact raised under Article 58 and punished by execution or imprisonment. The numbers who died in transit to camps, in overcrowded wagons, short of food and water, in sub-zero temperatures can only be hazarded. The full reckoning of the victims of Soviet repression is certainly larger than the figures show, though by hundreds of thousands rather than millions. Executions and camp deaths between them total 1,829,903; this figure should be treated as a minimum. It need hardly be said that aggregate figures mask millions of stories of human suffering beyond the immediate circle of victims: women and men left without a partner, children without parents, families uprooted and loyal friendships obliterated. For the traumas of repression, statistical exactitude is an irrelevance.

When it comes to the Third Reich the ground is less solid. The statistical material is fragmentary and incomplete, though it indicates very much lower figures than in the Soviet Union. Between 1933 and 1939 there is an estimate of 225,000 sentenced and imprisoned for crimes defined as political, with punishments ranging from short periods in prison or camp to indefinite confinement. However, the numbers in the camps at any one time before 1939 suggest lower figures: 25,000 at the peak in 1933, 10,000 by 1936, 25,000 again by the outbreak of war. Only in the last three years of the war, when the camps became swollen with prisoners-of-war, Jews and forced labourers, did the numbers reach the hundreds of thousands.[47] The camp figures for the 1930s are also difficult to reconcile with high estimates of the number held under 'protective custody', which in one case suggest a total 162,000 in 1939. The figures that are known from Interior Ministry estimates are much lower: 27,000 at the peak in summer 1933, 3,000 in 1934, 4,000 in June 1935. Since those arrested under protective custody would expect to end in a camp by 1939, the figure of 162,000 is clearly a distortion. Exact statistics on all those arrested and imprisoned by state security have been lost with the destruction of the records and are unlikely to be reconstructed, but they now appear to have been, like Soviet figures, more modest than was once believed.

The total number killed by the German security system has also never been satisfactorily computed. There are archive records of those convicted and executed by the People's Court for treasonable offences: up to the war the court condemned 108 to death, from 1940 to 1944 a total of 5,088.[48] This pattern is reflected in the number of death sentences handed down from the Düsseldorf Special Court: one case each year from 1937 to 1939, 5 in 1940 and 7 in 1941, but then followed by 74 cases with a death sentence in the last four years of war. There are additional statistics on the numbers executed for both political and criminal offences by the ordinary courts between 1938 and 1945 – a total of 16,080.[49] It is not known what proportion of these executions was for ordinary crimes, but since most of the victims were non-Germans it can be assumed that most were foreign workers or prisoners-of-war accused of sabotage, miscegenation or murder. Beyond these raw numbers were thousands of victims of random brutality, SS terrorism in the last months of the war, political murder by party thugs, and thousands of non-Germans who were killed for resistance and sabotage throughout occupied Europe, under the terms of the notorious *Nacht und Nebel* (Night and Fog) decree published by Hitler on 7 December 1941, which allowed the Gestapo to dispose of their prisoners without trace.[50]

The exceptional years for the German security system came between 1941 and 1944. During the years of conflict with the Soviet Union the RSHA masterminded the mass murder of millions of men, women and children. The great majority were Jews brought from all over Europe; an estimated 5.7 million. Around 3.6 million were exterminated in purpose-built camps, a further million and a half were murdered in the villages and cities of the western Soviet Union in the first year of the Soviet–German war.[51] The concentration and labour camps also became sites of mass murder, deliberate neglect and a regime of punitive, debilitating labour. The total number of deaths has been estimated at 1.1 million, including a high proportion of Jews who laboured until they died.[52] The terrible aggregate of all those who were killed, who died of disease and malnutrition, or who were worked to death by the German security system cannot be rendered precisely, but is unlikely to be much less than 7 million, most of them non-Germans.

The overwhelming majority of all the millions of victims of both dictatorships were innocent. Their 'crimes' were trivial, or, in most cases, not crimes at all. They were also, in the main, defenceless – ordinary men and women and children seized at home or at work, sometimes singly, sometimes in great security sweeps. In both systems the families of suspects were hauled into the net. When Stalin railed against the counter-revolution in November 1937, he promised to eradicate not just enemies of the people but their 'kith and kin' as well. This had to be done, Molotov explained to Russian journalist Feliks Chuev years later: 'Otherwise, they would have spread all kinds of complaints . . . and degeneration . . .'[53] The vendettas of the Soviet security system snared friends, mere acquaintances, room-mates and colleagues, as if 'counter-revolutionary' activity were some kind of contagious disease. Evgenia Ginzburg was condemned to the camps because she had once worked years before with a fellow academic who was now an unmasked Trotskyist. She was expelled from the party for lack of vigilance, but by the time she was arrested in February 1937, the system had turned her into an arch-criminal. 'Death would be too good for you,' shouted her arresting officer. 'You turncoat! You agent of international imperialism!'[54]

Thousands of victims in both systems were turned, like Ginzburg, from respectable, even loyal, citizens into criminals and outcasts. Stefan Lorant, whose only 'crime' was not to support National Socialism, underwent a slow metamorphosis in Gestapo prison from a successful, middle-class professional to an abject prisoner, in dirty unkempt clothes, desperate to avoid the punishment cell and the malevolence of the party guards, treated by the political police with contempt. Random though victimization often was, the system turned innocence into apparent guilt, citizens into prisoners. Some of those persecuted under both regimes were opponents or critics, though few were terrorists or political criminals. Most were stigmatized and punished to satisfy the powerful fantasies of conspiracy woven by the two dictatorships. The paradoxical, often absurd character of the victimhood that these fantasies provoked can be illustrated by the remarkable spectacle of *both* regimes repressing communists in the 1930s.

The pattern of victimization in the Soviet Union can be explained by a conspiracy theory central to the existence of the communist state. The theory was shaped, like so much in the infant Soviet system, by the experience of the civil war. There remained an ever-present fear that Soviet society would be the object of an international plot hatched between the forces of world bourgeoisie and their surviving allies inside the Soviet Union. This was not entirely irrational given the history of western intervention on the side of the counter-revolutionary armies in 1919 and 1920. The conspirators were always portrayed as a fifth column of foreign spies and provocateurs in league with the remnants of the old classes and oppositionists in the party. Their purpose, so it was claimed, was nothing less than the destruction of the revolutionary achievement and the restoration of capitalism. Their methods were always defined in the same rhetorical terms – sabotage, wrecking and terrorism. Their involuntary accomplices were the slack or opportunist officials and party members who failed to 'unmask' the subversives in their midst. With periodic shifts of emphasis, this remained the central political text of the Stalin years from the late 1920s to the dictator's death in 1953. Whether it was believed or not by the thousands of lesser police officials and party hacks who fought against conspiracy was immaterial. What mattered was the insistence of the party leadership that counter-revolutionary conspiracy was a public political reality.

Almost all the victims of the regime can be defined within these terms of reference. The party line on conspiracy was formulated at the centre, but it rippled out to the edges of the vast Soviet pool. Take, for example, the fate of the Red Army 57th Special Corps, sent to Mongolia in 1937 to prevent incursions by the Japanese from neighbouring Manchuria. The soldiers were billeted in squalid conditions on the bleak, remote Mongolian plain. Morale was poor, accidents were frequent and equipment regularly broke down. But in the summer of 1937, following the unmasking of a 'conspiracy' in the Red Army high command, the long arm of Soviet law reached across the Soviet Union to the distant 57th Corps. An NKVD Special Department arrived to 'expose and liquidate participants in the military conspiracy'. They unearthed a fabricated plot in every single unit of the army corps, one after another. Investigations continued for thirteen months, as each conspiracy unearthed a fresh conspiracy in other units. NKVD reports defined the unmasked enemy in a bewildering variety of ways, even when, as in the following case, they all came from the same unit: 'son of a kulak', 'served with Kolchak [commander of White armies in the civil war]'; 'is a sycophant'; 'participant in a counter-revolutionary Trotskyite organization'; 'military-fascist conspiracy'; 'conducting sabotage'; 'had ties with enemies of the people'; and so on.[55] The corps' commissar, A. P. Prokof'ev, was recalled all the way to Moscow and arrested as he sat for an appointment in the waiting room of the Defence Commissariat. His replacement was sent all the way to Mongolia, only to be exposed as a fascist conspirator a few months later, and sacked.[56]

The fate of the 57th Special Corps was repeated all over the Soviet Union during the 1930s. The witch-hunt was more frenzied during the two years of the *Ezhovshchina*, but the directives to unmask the fifth column pre-dated the height of the terror and persisted on into the 1950s. The OGPU had already constructed what it called 'The Case of the All-Union Trotskyist Centre' in 1934, and hundreds were arrested as alleged members of the centre during late 1934 and 1935 and afterwards shot.[57] In 1936 government commissars were asked to report to the Central Committee the number and category of employees unmasked in their own fiefdoms. Lazar Kaganovich, Commissar for Transport, reported the dismissal of 485 former tsarist policemen, 220 former Mensheviks and Socialist-Revolutionaries, 572 Trotskyists, 1,415 former White officers, 285 wreckers and 443 spies. All of them, reported Kaganovich, had ties to the 'Right-Trotskyist Bloc' of conspirators and wreckers.[58] Revelations of subversive activity then carried the strong risk of subsequent accusations of a lack of vigilance. Kaganovich survived, but thousands of other communist officials were imprisoned or executed for what they had failed to do rather than for what they had done.

Membership of the party was no protection. The most dangerous place to be was close to the centres of power. During the *Ezhovshchina* the upper levels of the party were decimated. Five of Stalin's Politburo colleagues were killed, and 98 out of 139 Central Committee members. Of the Central Committee of the Ukraine Republic only three out of 200 survived; 72 of the 93 members of the *Komsomol* organization Central Committee perished. Out of 1,996 party leaders at the Seventeenth Congress in 1934, 1,108 were imprisoned or murdered. In the provinces 319 out of 385 regional party secretaries and 2,210 out of

2,750 district secretaries died. The party rank-and-file in general fared better, though in Leningrad a zealous Zhdanov was said to have expelled nine-tenths of party members.[59] The pattern of repression in the city shows that senior officials, party or not, were most vulnerable. From a sample of those purged, 69 per cent were over 40 and only 6 per cent under 30; among the smaller number of women purged, 75 per cent were over 40 years old, almost half over 50.[60] This generational pattern suggests that the purges directly benefited the cohorts of younger communists and workers who had grown to adulthood since the revolution.

Distrust was strongly in evidence in the case of those party members who came into contact with foreigners, or were foreigners themselves. A xenophobic fear of foreign contamination and infiltration was characteristic of communist political culture from the late 1920s onwards. The Communist International worked from offices in the Hotel Lux in Moscow, but its network stretched worldwide. In the early 1930s it jealously maintained its immunity from contamination by other socialist or social-democratic movements abroad. But after Stalin, with considerable reservations, accepted the idea that foreign communists should co-operate with other socialists in a 'Popular Front' against fascism (a shift in revolutionary strategy formally announced at the Comintern international congress in Moscow in July 1935), he came to suspect that spies and fascist agents would use collaboration as an opportunity to infiltrate the Comintern apparatus. In February 1937 Stalin warned its general secretary, Georgii Dimitrov: 'all of you there . . . are working in the hands of the enemy'.[61] During 1937 and 1938 the communities of foreign communists in the Soviet Union, and the Comintern organization itself, were destroyed. The German Communist Party in exile lost 7 of its Politburo members (only 5 had been killed under Hitler) and 41 out of 68 party leaders. The Polish Communist Party in exile, whose members had been under State Security scrutiny since 1929, lost its entire Central Committee, and an estimated 5,000 members, all killed as agents of the 'Polish secret services'.[62] The party was formally wound up in August 1938 for lack of any members who were not compromised as crypto-fascists. Lack of vigilance in exposing the conspiracies led to the repression of 700 working in the Comintern headquarters. For the next fifteen years, until Stalin's death, links with the outside world, however tenuous or casual, could end in death or imprisonment.

The roll-call of victims beyond the party core reflected the many manifestations of the alleged conspiracy. Anyone unmasked as a former class enemy, whether a kulak, a 'White guard', or the child of a bourgeois or gentry, particularly if they had gone to the sensible lengths of concealing their identity, always ran the risk of repression, though only during the period 1937–8 did they risk almost certain death. The idea of counter-revolutionary sabotage was revived (an accusation that could be traced back to the very first show trial, of Countess Sofia Panina, accused in 1918 of revolutionary treason).[63] During the period of collectivization and industrial reconstruction after 1928, sabotage was regularly used to describe the most trivial dereliction of duty, accident or mechanical failure. Careful statistics of accidents were kept as political evidence. At moments of heightened party vigilance, accident rates could be used as evidence. In the 57th Special Corps the number of accidents multiplied during 1938 (2,728 in nine months) as unskilled or incompetent workers were brought in to replace the drivers and skilled mechanics who had been swept away in the first purge. These accidents became grounds for yet further accusations of sabotage.[64]

The victims were more likely to be the elite than the luckless worker. In the industrial economy it was the plant directors and the engineers who bore the brunt of the criticism for failures to meet the schedules of the Five-Year Plans. Accusations of economic failure, generally described as wrecking activity, also had a very long pedigree, back to the trials of experts in the late 1920s, but in this case failure was exploited as part of a heightened class war in the factories. Workers were encouraged to denounce managers and supervisors. In 1936 alone 14,000 industrial managers were arrested for wrecking and revolutionary sabotage. At the vast Kirov iron and steel plant in the Donbass industrial region the director, G. V. Gvakhariya, the model of a modern manager, efficient and innovative, was asked by his local party in March 1937 to account for a number of technical problems in the works that held up production. He was accused of wrecking and arrested. By April the press had labelled him a 'fascist agent' as well; he was tried and shot. A few months later it was announced that

Gvakhariya had sabotaged the plant to increase the possibility of German and Japanese victory in a future war. His colleagues soon followed him. By 1940 only two of the engineers and thirty-one of the technicians employed in the huge plant in 1937 were still working there.[65]

The purges hit all areas of institutional life, with the higher echelons suffering most. Thousands of diplomats, senior officials and army officers were killed. Out of approximately 24,000 priests and church leaders in 1936, only 5,665 were still alive five years later.[66] In the end the conspiracy devoured the conspirators. NKVD and State Security officials were purged in their turn in 1939 for wrecking in the party. Ezhov was first demoted late in 1938, then arrested in April 1939 and accused of being a British and Polish spy. After a spell drying-out in a clinic, he was subjected to the same barbarous routine he had imposed on his victims. Badly beaten and forced into a confession by interrogators who only months before had worked to his orders, he was taken before the Military Collegium in February 1940, where he withdrew his confession and announced in his own defence that during twenty-five years of party work he had 'fought honourably against enemies and exterminated them ... used everything at my disposal to expose conspiracies'.[67] He was shot the following day for espionage.

Conspiracy served the same function in Hitler's Reich in defining the enemy and justifying his exclusion or extermination as it did in the Soviet Union. There were two distinct, though related conspiracies, which derived from the experience of defeat in 1918. The first focused on the Marxist enemy, whose internationalism and pacifism had poisoned Germany during the First World War and sapped her national spirit and military vitality, and whose continued existence posed a perpetual threat of treason to national revival and redemption. The betrayal of the national ideal was the litmus test for exclusion and repression. 'We assuredly wish to annihilate anything,' announced Göring in March 1933, 'which opposes the people and the Nation.'[68] The second conspiracy concerned the Jews. They too, in National Socialist discourse, had conspired to wreck Germany's war effort, impose revolution in 1918 and encourage racial decomposition to open the way for the Bolshevization of Germany and the rest of Europe. These enemies, it was believed, continued to work away to keep

Germany disarmed and divided and would undermine the military and political revival of the new Reich. There was genuine fear that another 'stab-in-the-back' might be repeated in the next war. It is in this light that Hitler's comment in *Mein Kampf* about avoiding defeat in 1918 by gassing 10,000 Jews should be read.[69] Eliminating the enemy was about ensuring victory. In Himmler's address to senior officers in 1937 about the role of security in a future war, he argued that the home front was a theatre of war against the inner enemy, 'the ideological (*weltanschauliche*) opponent', who would conspire to rob Germany of victory once again. It was the job of state security, continued Himmler, 'to keep our blood and our people healthy' in order to secure military triumphs in the future.[70]

The majority of victims of state repression in the first years of the regime were communists, trade-union officials, social-democrats and intellectuals hostile to National Socialism. Unlike the unfortunate victims unmasked by the NKVD, these were real opponents. But the idea of a communist revolutionary conspiracy in 1933 was as fanciful as the 'Trotskyist-fascist centre' invented in Moscow. Communists were rounded up and tortured to reveal the networks of communist agents, the plans for revolution and the secret caches of weapons and explosives hoarded for the purpose. Violent clashes between communists, policemen and SA auxiliaries flared up as communist political activity was suppressed. On the day following the Reichstag fire an estimated 1,500 communists were rounded up in Berlin, 10,000 throughout Germany. The exiled communist party announced in 1935 that 393 party members had been murdered since January 1933.[71] Communists and social-democrats were the majority in the first camps set up in 1933 and 1934.

The other victims of political repression were drawn from a wide circle of critics and opponents whose anti-Nazism was now defined as treason. The political police were indifferent to class, rank or reputation. Known anti-Nazis among the clergy, the professions and the conservative political parties were given short doses of prison or camp. Many, like Stefan Lorant, were entirely guiltless. Others imprisoned with him were the victims of private grudges. Fritz Gerlich, the publisher of a Catholic paper in Munich, was kept in a darkened cell and beaten by SA men to make him reveal the source of his allegations about Ernst Röhm's homosexuality. An elderly Jewish doctor, who had once instructed a pension board to reduce a disability award for a war veteran and National Socialist, was beaten with rubber truncheons for one minute every hour until he collapsed. The driver of the car that took Hitler to serve his sentence in Landsberg prison in 1924 was interrogated about unflattering comments he had made at the time about the future *Führer*.[72] Most of those rounded up in the first weeks of the regime under protective custody were released by the summer of 1933. Some of the early victims were Jewish, but German Jews were not yet the systematic target of the state security apparatus. They were the victims of intimidation, occasional physical assault, wrongful arrest, theft and compulsory redundancy. Like communists, they were counted among those to be excluded from the new Germany as enemies of the German ideal.

By the mid-1930s the racial priorities of the regime came to define the nature of state repression in Germany. Political opposition had been so ferociously cauterized that it was now limited and easily curtailed. It was the second strand of conspiracy, the fear that German revival and triumph would be weakened by biological contamination and decomposition, which brought the state security system into the heart of the regime's policy on race. The great majority of German victims of state repression between 1936 and the end of the war were biological victims, imprisoned or murdered not for political crime, real or imagined, but to protect the race. Among the first to be caught in the security net were so-called 'asocials' (*Asoziale*). They included, according to a police circular from Heydrich in December 1937, 'beggars, tramps [gypsies], whores, alcoholics' and 'the work-shy'.[73] The first major sweep was made in March 1937. Some 2,000 were taken into protective custody and many transferred to concentration camps.[74] Some were compulsorily sterilized to prevent the transfer of the recessive genes alleged to cause the asocial personality. Recidivist criminals were treated in the same way. They were placed in secure (indefinite) confinement in the prison system, but during the war, at Hitler's insistence, asocials and habitual criminals in prisons were transferred to camps and 20,000 worked to death.[75]

Sexual offenders were also victimized. Homosexuals were particularly singled out. Himmler was fanatically homophobic ('pederasty is an aberration of degenerate individuality', he once confided to his student diary).[76] When the police system was reorganized in 1936, Himmler introduced a new department for the 'combating of homosexuality and abortion', both deemed to be positive threats to racial development, but even before that homosexuals had been subject to intimidation and arrest by the Gestapo rather than the regular police force.[77] From 1936 onwards homosexuals began to be transferred to camps, though victimization was arbitrary, often dependent on denunciation. In July 1940 Himmler issued a decree ordering all homosexual offenders with more than one partner to be transferred to camps indefinitely as degenerates of evident incorrigibility; in 1943 Kaltenbrunner, head of the RSHA, tried to introduce a law for the compulsory castration of all convicted homosexuals. An estimated 5,000 died in police custody and the camps.[78]

Other sexual offences became the preserve of the security system. Following the law on the protection of German blood in 1935, 1,680 German Jews were convicted of race defilement.[79] During the war the Gestapo extended its activities to monitoring sexual relations between Germans and foreign workers. Male Poles and Russians caught 'defiling' German women could expect to be executed or sent to a camp, but the woman also ran the risk of protective custody and a camp sentence. Paedophiles also gravitated towards the camp system. Some 2,079 sexual offenders were castrated between 1933 and 1939, most for child abuse.[80] For those that the regime regarded as a threat to racial health, compulsory sterilization was introduced in 1933, and was routinely imposed in prisons, secure hospitals and the camps. Between 1933 and 1945 an estimated 400,000 people were sterilized, both men and women.[81] At the same time abortionists, in a country where abortion rates ran at more than a million a year by 1932, were also victimized as enemies of the healthy regeneration of the race, and after 1936 became the subject of detailed Gestapo investigation.

During the war, state security became the principal agent of more radical race persecution. The chief victims were the Jewish populations of Germany, Austria and the occupied and satellite territories in Europe. The Gestapo was given responsibility for compiling all the information on the size and distribution of Jewish populations, as well as dossiers on prominent Jews. In September 1939 a young SS officer,

Adolf Eichmann, was brought to Berlin from his post organizing Jewish emigration in Vienna and Prague, to head a newly created office of Jewish affairs within the recently established RSHA. Office IV D4 (soon to be renamed IV B4) became the hub of the entire programme of Jewish persecution, from the registration and political monitoring of Jewish populations, to their eventual round-up and deportation to the ghettos and extermination camps in the East.[82]

A great deal of the effort of state security during the war years was devoted to organizing the Jewish genocide. Race policy defined Jews as enemies of the Reich, and the Gestapo treated Jews as if they were, in reality, political opponents. They applied to the task of identifying and deporting Jews the same methods of police detective work, political intelligence and heavy-handed violence that they had used on communists in the early 1930s. Occasionally a Jew who was also a communist fell into their hands. In March 1940 an émigré German Jew, Josef Mahler, together with his wife, was expelled from the Netherlands to Germany, where they were arrested under protective custody by the local Gestapo. He had been an active communist since 1932, and from 1937, when he left Germany, had passed on information about conditions in Germany to foreign communist contacts. Violently interrogated for a year, neither he nor his wife divulged anything. They were sent to the Westerbork concentration camp in April 1941, from where Mahler's wife was shipped to her death in the eastern camps. The police continued their remorseless investigation. They found the Mahlers' illegitimate daughter and extracted from her the testimony they wanted. Mahler was hauled back to the Gestapo cellars in Düsseldorf, but refused to confess after months of torture. On 2 September 1943, unable to unearth the conspiratorial net they were looking for, he was killed in the prison.[83]

Thousands of police hours were spent investigating alleged Jewish crimes, or simply hunting down Jews who were in hiding, or had tried to disguise their identity, like the former kulaks and bourgeoisie in the Soviet Union. Non-Jews could be victimized for sheltering Jewish neighbours or concealing Jewish children, though thousands bravely did so across occupied Europe. In 1941 it became a political crime in Germany to be seen talking to anyone Jewish, or engaging in trade or intercourse with Jews.[84] It was a crime for Jews not to wear the distinguishing yellow Star of David made compulsory in Germany on 15 August 1941. With dogged persistence, the Gestapo tracked down Jews all over Europe simply for being Jews, and treated anyone who obstructed them as criminal accomplices. The operation bore the mark of a terrible literalness. In a town in remote Belorussia one woman in a crowd of Soviet Jews standing by the pit they had just dug, waiting to be shot, was saved at the last moment by an officer who confirmed that she was an ethnic Russian. The German officials let her go, though it could have made no difference to them, in hostile territory hundreds of miles from the Reich, whether the woman was shot or not.[85]

The majority of victims of the German apparatus of terror during the war were murdered on grounds of race. Most were killed not by state security but by the SS, the armed forces, or local anti-Semitic militiamen. The RSHA acted as the impresario, organizing, classifying and supplying the millions of victims. The rest of the German population, though still obliged to observe the laws about defamation, defeatism or demoralization, was less scrupulously monitored by the security system. Only 13 per cent of those investigated for listening to foreign broadcasts were prosecuted.[86] Much of the casual grumbling overheard and reported to the police carried little more than a warning. Only for those defined as enemies and social outsiders, like the counter-revolutionary 'enemy' in the Soviet Union, did the apparatus of repression work remorselessly and tirelessly, to fulfil its mission. Some of those caught in the security net were genuine opponents (though others could survive undetected). Yet for the millions of guiltless individuals victimized by both regimes there remains a terrible historical irony. Most of the work of state security in bringing enemies to justice was entirely wasted labour. The conspiracies were phantoms.

The day in Stefan Lorant's prison when Dr Fritz Gerlich dragged himself back to his cell, almost senseless and covered in blood from the bludgeoning given him by the SA, he heard an SS officer shouting out: 'You richly deserved what you got.'[87] This episode captures an important reality about the relationship between the apparatus of repression and the society it seeks to repress. If repression is to work, a substantial section of society must identify with or even approve its activities. Stalin was not being altogether disingenuous when he rejected Emil Ludwig's observation during an interview in 1932 that the Soviet people were simply 'inspired by fear': 'Do you really believe that we could have retained power and have had the backing of the vast masses for fourteen years by methods of intimidation and terrorization?'[88]

In both dictatorships the apparatus of repression was part of society, not an abstraction. It was run by police officials and policemen who were recruited from the population, not external to it. In both dictatorships many of those who ruthlessly hunted down Trotskyites or Jews had long careers performing ordinary police work beforehand; many had police careers that successfully continued after the dictators were dead. In the Soviet Union to be a 'Chekist' carried with it a certain status. 'I felt satisfaction, I was even proud,' recalled one recruit to the NKVD in 1938. Most of his fellow policemen were 'simple boys, who have been told that "enemies of socialist society" try to wreck our Soviet system ... The fellows do what they are told and quietly accomplish their job.'[89] Some were party members, a higher proportion in Germany than in the Soviet Union, but even the chief of the Gestapo, Heinrich Müller, was not a party man, and joined only in 1938. Others found themselves in the security police by chance, drafted in from regular police work, or party organizations. Many of them were, in Christopher Browning's description, 'ordinary men', brutalized by the system they worked for. Few of them were sociopaths. They were callous rather than bestial. One of the psychiatrists who examined Adolf Eichmann after his capture by Israeli secret agents in 1960 pronounced him entirely normal: 'more normal, anyway, than I am after examining him'.[90]

For the vast majority who were not the direct victims of repression, daily life was also more normal than the popular image of either dictatorship suggests. It was possible to live in Germany throughout the whole period of the dictatorship and perhaps witness an incidence of state repression on no more than two or three occasions in twelve years – an SA bully beating a worker in March 1933, a garrulous anti-Nazi neighbour taken off for an afternoon to the police station to be told to hold his tongue in November 1938, the town's Jewish dentist sent off for 'resettlement' in September 1942. A Soviet worker could pass the twenty years of Stalin's dictatorship with only a few hours disrupted by State Security – the arrest of the technical director one day in March 1937, the disappearance of a fellow-worker with a German name in 1941, a gang of prisoners repairing the factory roads for a week in 1947. No one in either system could be unaware that State Security was out there, but for the ordinary citizen, uninterested in politics, lucky enough not to belong to one of the groups stigmatized as enemies, the attitude was as likely to be prudent respect, even approval, rather than a permanent state of fear.

The state security apparatus was never large enough in either system to maintain a permanent and ubiquitous review of the whole population. They focused their efforts on the fraction of the population defined in the regime's terms as 'enemies of the people' or, in the German case, 'alien to the people' (*Volksfremde*). The few examples of Gestapo records that have survived show that the number of secret policemen was tiny in relation to the size of the population they monitored. At its peak in the 1930s the whole Gestapo numbered only 20,000 in a population of 68 million, and this number included the clerks and typists, as well as the detectives. The city of Frankfurt-am-Main had just forty-one political policemen in 1934. In 1935 the Dortmund Gestapo, responsible for the eastern industrial area of the Ruhr valley, employed seventy-six, spread out between headquarters and small sub-stations. The Düsseldorf office, responsible for 4 million inhabitants of the western Ruhr valley, had 281 political police in 1937.[91] Many of the employees were desk-bound policemen. The Gestapo was hostage to the traditions of German bureaucratic practice, and precise record-keeping was mandatory.[92] The sheer volume of work with which the Gestapo was entrusted compelled many officers to chase paper trails rather than subversives. Only during the war, as senior officers were drafted away to work in occupied Europe and younger, more Nazified replacements brought in, does it appear that paperwork declined in favour of summary justice and extorted confessions.[93]

The NKVD faced many similar problems. Its employees in 1939 totalled 366,000, but the great majority were border guards, regular policemen and the internal security militia. The NKVD was responsible for maintaining the security of the transport system, and running the state fire service. The number of political policemen in the total was very small. One estimate suggests 20,000 for a population of approximately 170 million.[94] The evidence from local State Security offices indicates a sparse presence. The average number of employees for each district or *raion*, according to a former NKVD official, was between eight and fifteen. One district in the Smolensk regional administration had eight workers, including a secretary and a building inspector. Murmansk region fielded eight to ten officers. Leningrad, with almost 3 million people, was said to have no more than thirty.[95] Less populated districts had sub-stations with three to five operatives; some areas had no presence at all. Given the many subordinate tasks devolved to State Security – pursuing ordinary criminal cases, unmasking venality and corruption, even making sure that the harvest was gathered in according to the rules – detectives had the same pressures faced by Gestapo agents in balancing the demands of bureaucratic exactitude, operational efficiency and effective surveillance. Like the Gestapo, who under the pressure of a great increase in workload during the war years found ways of cutting red tape and processing victims rapidly and summarily, Soviet State Security at the height of the panic in 1937 and 1938 abandoned routine, wrote out confessions in advance or fabricated the flimsy evidence required for conviction.[96]

Both state security forces relied in their work on the active collaboration and collusion of the societies they were policing. The first link was the police informer. The Gestapo inherited the system from the pre-1933 political police, who had used police spies as a way to penetrate communist organizations. Informers, or *Vertrauensmänner*, were recruited by the Gestapo to monitor left-wing political resistance, but they could also be used to supply a variety of other forms of political intelligence. A small number of informers played a central role in breaking up the major communist networks that survived in Germany after the initial wave of repression in 1933.[97] No record exists of their number. Police informers, *sekretnye sotrudniki*, were also widely employed by Soviet security to gather intelligence or to act as agents provocateurs, much as Tsarist secret policemen had done with the illegal Bolshevik movement before 1917. The city of Khar'kov had, according to one estimate, around fifty informers working in 1940.[98] Most major factories or institutions had an informer who reported to the local Special Department. Party workers in both dictatorships played something of the same role, watching their local neighbour-hoods and passing information on to party offices and policemen.

The second source of information was voluntary denunciation. In both dictatorships state security was inundated with unprompted reports from the general public. In the Soviet Union denunciation was linked to the traditional practices in Russian society of petitioning higher authority for redress of local grievances against corrupt officials. But under the revolutionary regime, the exposure of corruption or abuse was just one source of complaint. Many of the letters were welcomed as 'signals from below' (*signaly s mest*) from a vigilant communist public, rather than as malicious denunciation (*donos*), a term which carried strong echoes of acts of betrayal from the Tsarist period.[99] The public was encouraged to expose examples of political crime through the regular party pronouncements on the vigilant unmasking of enemies. The Young Pioneer Pavlik Morozov, who was said to have denounced his own father only to be murdered by his grand-father in revenge, became a public martyr to the cause of telling tales. NKVD files have even revealed the case of a zealous camp prisoner who wrote more than 300 letters of denunciation from prison.[100]

In Germany the Gestapo relied overwhelmingly on denunciation. The thousands of letters focused predominantly on new categories of political crime – intercourse (both commercial and sexual) with Jews, malicious gossip, political defamation. Robert Gellately's pioneering analysis of the casework of the Würzburg Gestapo has shown just how extensive denunciation was. In cases to do with the isolation of Jews, 57 per cent were the result of communications from the public, and a further 17 per cent from information supplied by party organs and the regular police force. Only one case out of 175 was actually unearthed by the political police themselves.[101] In Saarbrücken 87.5 per cent of cases of malicious gossip came from public reports (though it is difficult to see how the Gestapo could have acquired this knowledge any other way); more menacingly, 69.5 per cent of all cases defined as treason or high treason, for which the death penalty was mandatory, began life as denunciations.[102] Almost all the case studies of Gestapo operational activity reveal proportions of between a half and two-thirds of all cases derived from public denunciation. The detectives themselves discovered in general fewer than 10 per cent of the cases on file.[103]

Public collusion has a number of possible explanations. Many of the denunciations were intentionally malicious, even fraudulent. The Gestapo kept a separate in-tray for denunciations where the motive was suspect. Occasionally the denouncers would themselves become the victim of police investigation. One NKVD case file revealed that a notorious denouncer was arrested 'for anti-soviet activities . . . drunkenness, hooliganism, slander of honest workers . . .'.[104] Many letters made little pretence of being anything other than self-motivated, like the following letter written in Eisenach to the local Nazi party office in January 1940: 'I would like to know why the Jew Fröhlich . . . is still able to share a six-to-seven room apartment . . . There must be some *Volksgenosse* worthier than a Jew who could live in his apartment.'[105] It is not always easy to disentangle the public informers with a grudge or vendetta from those genuinely concerned to uphold the goals of the regime. In some cases motives may have conveniently overlapped. Collective farmworkers, for example, used denunciation of 'class enemies' to get back at farm organizers and officials whom they resented. The pleas sent in by farmworkers – 'help us purge the *kolkhoz* of these rascals' or 'deliver us from these enemies of the people' are just two examples – can be read a number of ways.[106]

There were without question those who denounced political crimes because they did identify with the particular political or social goals of the regime, and saw it as a civic responsibility not to hold back. Indeed such actions may well have reinforced the sense of being a social insider in a world where the terrible costs of social exclusion were evident. For millions in both societies it was safer, more prudent, often more personally advantageous to belong. The result was the existence of what might be called a 'soft terror' alongside the hard reality of direct state repression. In both dictatorships the public collaborated in numerous acts of self-policing. This could take many forms, from an innocuous reminder to a work colleague to sign his letters 'Heil Hitler', to the betrayal of a neighbour sheltering a Jewish child. During the drive against sabotage at work in the Soviet Union in 1936, the workers took affairs into their own hands in threatening managers with exposure. Thousands of those victimized in the *Ezhovshchina* were isolated by their social group or their peers, not by the political police.[107]

The complex process of self-policing not only helps to explain how the repressive apparatus could operate with such limited resources, but it exposes the extent to which both societies perceived repression not as a smothering blanket of regime terror, but as something necessary or even desirable in itself. The pervasive idea of conspiracy, on which repression rested, had its roots in patterns of popular belief that existed before the dictatorships. In Germany fear of the extreme left as enemies of the state (*Reichsfeinde*) can be traced back to the 1870s, perhaps even earlier. Modern forms of anti-Semitism as world conspiracy were widespread throughout Europe from at least the 1890s, and were sharpened in the 1920s with the popular identification of the Jewish threat with the revolutionary menace of Soviet communism.[108] In Russia a popular political culture of suspicion and conspiracy, of unmasking 'the other' long pre-dated 1917, and was taken up and dressed in communist garments for the war against counter-revolution. Hitler and Stalin were thus representing political conflict in ways which had a clear social resonance. The conspiracy theories that underlay repression were distorted projections of pre-existing patterns of social and political prejudice.

Repression could thus be disguised as a form of popular political justice, generated as much by pressure from below as it was by policy from above. In both regimes repression was routinely presented as if it reflected the popular will to protect society from internal forces of decay. 'Leaders come and go,' Stalin told a group of workers at the height of the *Ezhovshchina* in October 1937, 'but the people remains. Only the people is eternal.'[109] In a speech celebrating the anniversary of the seizure of power in January 1936 Hitler reminded his audience that the opposition was not directed just against National Socialism but were 'enemies of our people in their own land'.[110] No effort was made to disguise the repression. The first official concentration camp at Dachau was reported widely in the press, complete with pictures of the first communists sent there. The alleged communist plots were used to increase levels of public alarm, and to stimulate the sense that repression was to protect the public from real crime.[111] The choice of the term 'People's Court', and the description of enemies as 'alien to the people', were designed to reinforce the idea that regime and population were in the struggle against terror and conspiracy together.

Popular justice in the Soviet Union was made visible through the many show trials that took place, not just during the Great Terror but throughout the life of the dictatorship. These could sometimes take the form of small, provincial affairs. In Western Siberia, for example, 108 show trials were conducted in 1934 alone. The difference in 1937 was the likelihood that trial would result in execution, not prison. On 3 August 1937 Stalin ordered local officials in the countryside to use the arrest of enemies as an opportunity for local show trials. Some thirty to forty trials were held in an atmosphere of rural carnival. Farmworkers were allowed a day off to go to the trials, which were lubricated with supplies of vodka. Many of those on trial were unpopular officials and experts rather than ordinary workers, which enhanced the sense of popular revenge against people who had actually aroused real social resentment. When the Smolensk *oblast* committee reported to Stalin a successful rural trial late in August, he replied: 'I advise you to sentence the wreckers in Andreev *raion* to shooting, and to publicize the shooting in the local press.'[112] By comparison, the major show trials of the Old Bolshevik leadership between August 1936 and March 1938 were examples of political theatre for the whole population, whose purpose was not only to expose the malign depths of the counter-revolutionary plot, but also to demonstrate publicly the shared interest of regime and people in protecting society from subversion. Ilya Zbarsky and his father, both scientists close to the centre of power in Moscow, were given passes to the Bukharin trial in March 1938. In a long dirty-white courtroom in the House of Trade Unions, once used by the Tsarist nobility as a ballroom, Ilya heard a two-hour indictment listing in detail the long record of conspiracy. 'These statements,' he wrote in his memoirs, 'made such an impression on me that I became convinced that the men were guilty.' As Bukharin spoke, people in the courtroom cried out 'Swine!' and 'Liar!' to lend weight to the idea that he was the object of popular vengeance, though they were in all probability agents of the NKVD.[113]

The idea of popular justice against real enemies seems to have been widely believed and endorsed. In both populations the information available was manipulated and restricted by the authorities, but in many cases the belief derived from a network of popular prejudices directed at the targets of discrimination. In Germany the castration of paedophiles and the imprisonment of homosexuals and asocials pandered to conventional moral revulsion. The victimization of communists was widely approved, and by circles well beyond the party. The persecution and isolation of the Jews played on explicit images of Jewish ambition, corruption and deviancy and provoked little open opposition, even when Jews began to be moved out of Germany to the East. In the town of Eisenach the local party leader who in 1940 had received the complaint about a Jewish tenant welcomed the decision in September 1942 to ship the community's Jewish population to the East: 'very shortly a great pile of Jews will be on their way from Eisenach. This will free up housing.'[114]

In the Soviet Union too, the idea that state repression was both necessary and justified was widely accepted, sometimes even by those who felt they or their family had been the victims of a particular miscarriage of justice. Those arrested and tried were regarded as criminals or traitors, whose activities were dangerous, even supernatural. The death of livestock was treated not as natural accident, but the result of a counter-revolutionary hex, for which a named individual must be responsible. Fear of spies and subversionists played not on conventional moral scruples but on traditional superstition; communists could be seen as inheritors of the power of white magic to battle against black magicians, who now flooded fields and set fire to buildings in the guise of the modern wrecker. The traditions of popular myth and fable, expressed in crude divisions between good and evil, were exploited by ordinary people to justify the more modern and sordid manifestations of repression that they confronted.[115] The stigmatization of enemies also fitted with a more recent language of class conflict generated by the revolution, which pitted poor peasant against kulak, honest worker against masked bourgeois, the regular army recruit against the hidden White guard. At the so-called Industrial Trial in 1930, half a million people marched past the courthouse bearing banners inscribed 'Kill the wreckers', 'No mercy to class enemies'; their rhythmic chant, 'Death! Death! Death!' could clearly be heard by everyone in the court.[116] These class prejudices were actively manipulated in defining the enemy at home and abroad. The mix of millenarian myth and class division provided the cultural framework that sustained the permanent state of anti-conspiracy vigilance throughout the Stalin dictatorship.

The complex relationship between state repression and society goes some way to explaining the hideous crescendos of violence that descended on both systems, first in the Soviet Union in 1937–8, then in Germany between 1941 and 1945. In both cases the regime's leaders responded to what they perceived as an intensification of the conspiratorial threat – in Stalin's case the final stage of the class struggle against domestic terrorists and foreign powers, in Hitler's case against the Jews as the cosmopolitan enemy who would stab Germany in the back at home and wage merciless war from abroad. In both cases the existence of a large self-interested security apparatus tied closely to the party and the dictator offered an instrument to defeat the conspiracy, a task on which they had already been working before the escalation was ordered. Both Himmler and Ezhov were key figures in driving on and organizing the accelerated programme of destruction.

Neither excess was pre-planned or systematically orchestrated; both owed a good deal to the circumstances of the mid-1930s or the war years to which Stalin and Hitler and the agencies of state security reacted. Yet neither was intelligible without the language, ideas and practices already developed in the state's war against the fantasies of terror and subversion. The escalation of violence against 'enemies' was the product of a profound and dangerous symbiosis between leaders, policemen and people; it appeared to those who imposed the violence both necessary and legitimate. 'The sight of the dead,' wrote the commander of an SS killing-unit in the Soviet Union to his wife in 1942, 'is not very cheering. But we are fighting this war for the survival or non-survival of our people . . . wherever the German soldier is, no Jew remains.'[117] In October 1943 Himmler addressed SS commanders on the destruction of the Jewish population during the war. The genocide was 'a proud page in our history'. The death of millions was 'to preserve our people and our blood . . . Everything else we can be indifferent to.'[118] When Molotov reflected late in his life on the terror of 1937–8 he still accepted that it was a necessary step to prevent internal crisis: 'of course there were excesses, but all that was permissible, to my mind, for the sake of the main objective – keeping state power! . . . Our mistakes, including the crude mistakes, were justified . . .'[119]

6

Constructing Utopia

'The geopolitical importance for a movement of a vital physical centre . . . cannot be overemphasized. The existence of such a place, imbued as it must be with the enchanted and magical atmosphere that surrounds a Mecca or Rome, can alone in the long run give a movement that strength which resides in its inner unity . . .'   Adolf Hitler, *Mein Kampf*, 1925[1]

'Stalin, the architect of the new world [inspired a plan] almost a fairy tale, almost magical [to make Moscow] a new Mecca to which fighters for the happiness of mankind will stream from all ends of the earth.'   Nikolai Bukharin, 1935[2]

In December 1922, at the Communist Party Congress, Sergei Kirov announced to delegates crammed into the House of the Trade Unions that the party would build a magnificent new palace to the revolution, 'an emblem of proletarian might'.[3] Planning began in 1924, after Lenin's death, but only in 1930 did the Central Committee formally announce a competition for the design of a 'Palace of Soviets'. There were 160 entrants, including the celebrated modernist, Le Corbusier. A commission of judges under Molotov decided three years later that no one had won outright, but the team led by the Soviet architect Boris Iofan was given the chance to rework their submission. Their design for a colossal wedding-cake of a building was accepted by Stalin, and two years later work began in earnest on excavating massive foundations on the site of the demolished Cathedral of the Redeemer, near the Kremlin, in the heart of Moscow.[4]

The Palace of Soviets was to be the largest building in the world. It had a floor area of 110,000 square metres; its height, at 420 metres, was greater than the recently completed Empire State Building in New York. On its vast base – so large that the concrete for the foundations consumed 16 per cent of the annual cement production of the USSR – stood six layered towers, one on top of the other. The whole was capped with a monumental statue of Lenin, three times the size of the Statue of Liberty, over 90 metres in height. The effigy, stretching heavenwards a grotesque 35-metre arm with 6-metre fingers, could have been seen over sixty kilometres away.[5] Leading up to the over-powering pseudo-classical entranceway to the palace was a new road, in places 250 metres in width, which would run straight through the centre of Moscow. Inside, under a 100-metre dome, was a congress hall for 21,000 delegates of world socialism. The whole effect was to conjure up images of the ideal city from a pre-modern age, a monument to a new utopian civilization that could stand comparison with the seven wonders of the ancient world. 'We shall build it,' wrote one eulogist, 'so that it stands without ageing, eternally.'[6]

Though Stalin could not have known it, Hitler too was dreaming of a record-breaking building. Housed from 1937 in sealed and guarded exhibition rooms in the Berlin Academy of Art stood a model 30 metres long of a huge axial road through the centre of Berlin. At its mid-point stood a mammoth congress centre, the People's Hall (*Volkshalle*). The design was based on a sketch Hitler himself had made in the mid-1920s. He caused a secure passage to be built from the Reich Chancellery to the model-room, and at night he would take guests by flashlight along the path in order to show them what the new Berlin would look like.[7] At one point on the 120-metre-wide roadway – deliberately designed to be wider than the Champs-Elysées by one-third – was to be the world's largest triumphal arch, a monument to the German dead of the First World War, whose 1.8 million names were to be carved in granite on its 117-metre-high walls. The People's Hall was the centrepiece of the display; its vast meeting room was intended to house 200,000, making it the largest indoor gathering-place in the world. The dome had a diameter of 250 metres and a height of 74 metres, making it seven times larger than St Peter's in Rome. The building was tall, 290 metres high, though dwarfed by the Palace of Soviets, to Hitler's irritation. Like Stalin's monument to the revolution, Hitler's buildings were designed for a utopian posterity. They were to be built, Hitler told the party congress in 1937, not for the year 1940, not even for the year 2000, 'but should go on like the cathedrals of our past, thousands of years into the future'.[8]

Neither of these monuments to dictatorship was ever completed. The People's Hall was postponed with the outbreak of war, to be built after victory by a planned army of 3 million foreign forced labourers. The model disappeared from Berlin in 1945, looted or burnt.[9] The Palace of Soviets was founded on waterlogged land, fed by no fewer than 117 springs. The seepage was covered first with a layer of bitumen; then thousands of local gravestones were used to try to stem the flow. During the war the reinforced steel skeleton was torn down to use for tank traps. After the war Stalin ordered building to restart, but the technical problems could not be overcome. Postponed, rather than cancelled, in his lifetime, it was abandoned in the 1950s and in 1960 converted into a giant heated swimming pool.[10]

The construction of the world's most spectacular edifices was only one part of an even more imaginative programme to turn Moscow and Berlin into capitals that would overtake cities both ancient and modern in their monumental scale and symbolic significance. Beyond the capital cities there existed ambitious plans to remodel the urban and rural landscape of both states as a self-conscious expression of a new age. At the heart of these plans lay a clear utopian purpose: the society of the future would be integrated, shaped and engineered by the built environment of dictatorship. Berlin and Moscow were singled out as the nub of a new global order. 'Berlin,' Hitler remarked in 1941, 'will one day be the capital of the world,' and it needed buildings grandiose enough to reflect the power and achievements of a new German empire.[11] Moscow was regarded as the centre of world socialism, a New Jerusalem, where the ideal society would inhabit the ideal city.[12]

Neither dictator liked the capital cities they inherited. Hitler regarded Berlin as a typical modern 'mass' city, chaotically built, teeming with incipient Bolshevism and ruined by its self-interested bourgeoisie. The old Reich Chancellery was, he thought, 'fit for a soap company'.[13] At one point he toyed seriously with the idea of building an entirely new 'Ideal City' outside Berlin in Mecklenburg, a German

Brasilia, but thought better of it.[14] The plan for Moscow approved by Stalin described the old city as the victim of 'barbarous Russian capitalism' at its worst. He worried fussily that so many streets and squares were unevenly shaped.[15] Neither dictator approved of the architectural efforts of the 1920s to improve the two cities. Stalin was a driving force behind the Central Committee resolutions in 1930 against experimental styles of life and, in 1931, against what was called architectural 'formalism' – buildings that reflected the modernist fascination with simple, functional construction in glass, steel and concrete, exemplified by the work of the German Bauhaus school at Dessau. Many of the modernist proposals reflected a more general wave of cultural experiment and artistic utopianism in post-revolutionary Russia. One architect proposed a large communal dormitory, 'a laboratory of sleep', where a socialist consciousness would be induced among the slumbering masses by carefully selected noises and scents redolent of collectivism.[16] Another suggested large communal apartment blocks in which the inhabitants would operate according to a 'Graph of Life', with every minute of the day accounted for, from reveille at 6.00 in the morning to 'prepare to retire (a shower may be taken) – 10 minutes' at 10.00 in the evening.[17] Stalin dismissed these fancies as 'petit bourgeois'.

Hitler rejected architectural modernism as well. The Bauhaus was closed down in April 1933, when its offices were sealed by the Gestapo. Hitler's regime disliked unadorned, functional, glass-and-concrete buildings because in this case they were regarded not as a manifestation of bourgeois formalism, but of so-called 'building-bolshevism'.[18] In its place Hitler preferred an architecture that modelled itself on the idea of the organic community, blending town with countryside, modern techniques with classical models, party and people with their leader. The theory was seldom clearly formulated, but it would be wrong to see in Hitler's preferred style a yearning for rural simplicity and garden suburbs. His chief interest was in monumental urban architecture, designed to reflect the imposing grandeur and historical permanence of the new German empire. His conception was intended to be timeless rather than reactionary. The huge buildings had evident echoes of the classical past, but were clearly modern in their extravagant expression of power. The gigantic airport designed by Ernst Sagebiel for the

Tempelhof airfield, but never completed, was far from the clean, light designs of Weimar modernism, but was classical to only a limited degree, while its function was unmistakably futuristic.[19]

Hitler made explicit his commitment to the large city as the centre-piece of the new order at the party congress in September 1936, when he publicly announced the rebuilding of Berlin. On 4 October 1937 he issued a comprehensive law for 'the reconstruction of German cities', which gave priority to the capital. At the beginning of 1937 he appointed the party's favourite young architect, Albert Speer, to the long-winded post of Inspector-General of Building for the Renovation of the Capital.[20] Speer was only thirty-two, but he had caught Hitler's eye working on party buildings earlier in the 1930s. Tall, good-looking, rather gauche, the ambitious young man was able to establish a rapport with Hitler envied by other party leaders. Hitler gave the rebuilding of Berlin his detailed attention. Right up to the end of the war, when the model of the People's Hall was taken down into the *Führerbunker*, he spent hours with the plans. He saw himself as the German people's 'master-builder', building the German 'New Order' in a very literal sense.[21]

Stalin also paid close attention to the rebuilding of Moscow, after first approving the demolition of some of its largest and finest churches. Late in 1930, the party's Central Committee set up a commission to investigate the improvement of Moscow city services. Stalin, unusually, attended all its meetings; he listened carefully to engineers discussing water-supply, street-building, bridge-repair and slum clearance. Finally the commission agreed on major projects: a canal to link Moscow with the Volga river, a Moscow metro, and a master-plan for remodelling central Moscow, prudently christened the 'Stalin plan'.[22] Town planners and architects were granted a year from October 1931 to prepare a complete model for the capital of world socialism, which reflected Stalin's wish to build organically, 'according to a set plan'. His personal obsession with urban tidiness was demonstrated by the instruction that the plan 'defining the line of street and square' had to be 'an inviolable law'.[23] Again, none of the 150 entries satisfied the Soviet leadership, and in 1932 the town planner Vladimir Semonov was instructed to design Moscow without the experimental modernism and urge to de-urbanize characteristic of most of the failed designs. A gypsum model was ready by 1933, and after months of discussion it won cautious approval at a staged meeting in the Kremlin, where Stalin, standing in front of a large map of the capital, lectured the experts on his vision of the city of the future.

On 10 July 1935 Stalin and Molotov signed the Central Committee resolution 'On the Master Plan for the Reconstruction of Moscow'. It was a ten-year programme, which would more than double the area of the capital. The central quarters were to be characterized, like the new Berlin, by huge axial roads and open squares for popular assemblies. Along the new roads there were to be built monumental office blocks, commissariats, apartments in a style much influenced by the contemporary neo-classical French architect Auguste Perrot, adorned rather than functional, derived from the old, but exploiting the techniques of the new.[24] A clutch of new buildings sprang up between 1935 and the coming of war. All of them had to be presented to Stalin by nervous designers. So anxious were they to match the leader's vision as closely as possible that the huge Moskva Hotel, built with the same over-high classical portico found on the designs for Berlin, was constructed with two wings of completely different styles because Stalin had mistakenly approved as a single design two separate submissions placed on a table in front of him.[25]

The plans for Moscow were realized more fully than in Berlin. The Moscow–Volga canal was begun in 1933 and completed four years later by an army of camp labourers, thousands of whom died to build it. The canal labourers were nicknamed *zeki*, a term derived from their official title as canal-builders, but soon applied to camp labourers in general.[26] Zeks were used to build the Moscow underground as well. The first tunnel was begun in 1932, and the initial twelve kilometres opened by Stalin in May 1935. It was designed as a monument to the new socialist age, with cavernous neo-classical stations, mosaics and extravagant trim. The object was to impress all those who passed through it with the might of the proletarian state: 'every screw,' Kaganovich boasted, 'is a screw of socialism'.[27] After the war Stalin continued to take a close interest in the shape of the new capital. The high point of Stalinist monumentalism was reached with the so-called 'tall buildings' erected in the late 1940s, loosely based on a sketch made by Stalin himself. The vast Moscow State University, begun in

1949 and completed in the year of Stalin's death, was the last of the utopian buildings. Extravagantly constructed by prisoner-of-war labour housed in three camps on the outskirts of the city, the design had echoes of the unbuilt Palace of Soviets.[28]

The capital cities were the centrepieces of a more comprehensive and ambitious programme of national construction. In Germany the party generated a number of different visions of an ideal environment, but those who favoured urban decentralization and a focus on rustic village life as the expression of an authentic Germanic culture were to be disappointed. Hitler was irredeemably in favour of cities as centres of party power and expressions of German identity. He linked the building programme with the wider project to construct what was called a *Volksgemeinschaft* (People's Community). Buildings, he told an audience in 1937, would give people a sense of unity, strength and togetherness: 'they will psychologically fill the citizens of our people [*sic*] with a permanent self-consciousness, namely: to be German!'[29] Hitler's own preference was for an organic mix of village and city, bound together by a new network of modern highways. This spatial unity was defined by the author of the party programme, Gottfried Feder, in his book *Die neue Stadt* (*The New City*), published in 1939. Feder favoured an ideal township of 20,000 inhabitants, mixing 'the great city and the village'.[30] Albert Speer designed an ideal city, 'Stadt-X', in which an integrated town network was prettily interspersed with areas of park and woodland.[31]

National Socialist architecture reflected the concept of an organic environment, linked to a particular set of social and political principles. Under the law of 1937, which launched the rebuilding of Berlin, Hitler decreed a further seventeen sites as model cities for the future. The principal metropolises, designated as '*Führer* Cities', were Munich (where Hermann Giesler designed a dome for the new railway station even wider than the projected People's Hall), Linz, Hamburg and Nuremberg, and a greenfield industrial city at Wolfsburg, where it was intended to build 1.5 million cars a year in a model workers' city. There were, in addition, twelve '*Gau* capitals': Augsburg, Bayreuth, Breslau, Dresden, Düsseldorf, Cologne, Münster, Stettin, Weimar and Würzburg in Germany; Graz and Salzburg were added after the incorporation of Austria in 1938.[32] Each of these cities was to have, like the cities of the Roman Empire, a standard central construction: a wide axial roadway for marching to a central forum, where there would be a large square for popular assemblies, and a congress hall. The size of the squares and halls was prescribed to match the significance of each centre. Weimar's square was to hold 60,000, Dresden's 300,000 and Berlin's half a million; Weimar's people's hall was allotted a capacity of 15,000, Dresden got 40,000 and Berlin 200,000.[33] The ideal cities were to be built regardless of cost and regardless of the existing townscape. Speer estimated the city-building alone would have cost 20 billion marks. At Hitler's insistence private property rights were suspended in the interests of the 'people's community' where they clashed with the new building plans. Speculative gains caused by increasing urban property values in the new party cities were to be taxed away.[34]

Side-by-side with the urban building programme went a policy of extensive resettlement aimed at breaking down the chaotic, socially dangerous areas of the large industrial cities, which menaced 'not only civilization, culture, health and social peace, but above all reproduction'.[35] This threat was to be solved by creating new low-rise housing in suburban settings. These small cottages and homesteads were built in a traditional German style. They were designed to give ordinary German workers a sense of 'relationship with the soil', and to develop a proper 'sense of community'.[36] The project for building around 6 million homesteads, at the rate of 300,000 a year, was given to Robert Ley's German Labour Front in a Hitler decree published on 25 November 1940, 'The Basic Law of Social House Construction'. Hitler kept personal responsibility for deciding each year how many houses should be built. Priority was for families with children, since they were the most socially valuable workers. Hitler also approved a standard design and proportions. Houses were to have a minimum floor area of 62 square metres, to include a kitchen, two bedrooms, bathroom, hallway and balcony. Each was to have its own integral air-raid shelter built to withstand a direct hit and large enough to house everyone in the family.[37]

This idealized geography of power centres, model industrial cities and communal townships was extended seamlessly to the areas of German conquest after 1939. The area of eastern *Lebensraum* was intended as the principal site of German resettlement, where German farmers would transform the landscape, while German skilled workers and engineers organized the area stretching from the Austrian and Czech iron and coalfields through to the iron ore, manganese, coal and oilfields of southern Russia and the Ukraine.[38] Serious thought was given to a ring of garrison cities around the perimeter of the new empire, where a permanent armed presence would protect the construction of the Germanic utopia. The conquered areas would then supply construction materials and labour for a building programme of breathtaking scale and extravagance.[39] One of the few projects to get beyond the drawing board was the new German city to be built round the Polish town of Oswiecim, better known by its German name of Auschwitz.

More than a year before the camp at Auschwitz-Birkenau became the site for the mass murder of German racial victims the region was selected by Himmler as the location for a *Musterstadt* or ideal city. Here he intended to establish the largest European centre for agricultural research into plant and animal breeding. The decision taken in 1941 to transfer the chemical production of synthetic rubber to the town gave the unexpected opportunity to create an 'organic' unit – part industrial city, part model agricultural settlement. The original plan to settle 3,000 ethnic Germans in neat workers' suburbs was expanded by 1943 into an intended settlement area of 70–80,000 people.[40] The homesteads for farmers were to combine, on Himmler's instructions, the traditions of German farm design with the most modern farming techniques and equipment.[41] The work of preparing the site was to be done by concentration-camp labour. Over the next two years the ideal city took shape as an army of abused and starving prisoners struggled to widen rivers, install drainage in a waterlogged topography, build homesteads, farm buildings and workers' suburbs, and create a huge integrated chemical plant. The designers were much influenced by Feder's book on the new National Socialist town, and by the proposals of the town planner Carl Culemann for organic cities that imitated the structure of the party itself: a core residential group of 10 houses, an urban cell of 100 houses rising to a district area of 10,000 houses.[42] A plan was ready by 1941 and approved a year later. The model city was complete with a stadium, parade grounds, party buildings (these were to be erected on the site of the old city's Jewish quarter), an SS suburb, schools and playgrounds. The whole German-ized area was to be served by a permanent camp, whose 100,000 wretched labourers would be a visible reminder that this was an imperial city. The non-German population could, Himmler argued, live as they liked in hovels and huts; they were destined to become an army of helots serving the population of German citizen-soldiers.[43]

The Soviet Union also produced a building programme that went far beyond the capital city. 'As Moscow is rebuilt, so shall all our Motherland's cities be rebuilt', ran a press report in 1935.[44] In 1929 a national construction programme was described as a 'General Plan for Building Socialism'; town-planning was seen as a principal factor for 'organizing the psyche of the masses'. The general plan suggested an urban area that was somewhere between a town and a village, not unlike Feder's proposals except for the size, for the Soviet mixed city was to provide homes for 60,000 inhabitants.[45] There was, as in Germany, a strong belief that the cities inherited from an earlier age were degenerate and atomistic. Utopian town-planning favoured the decentralized city, full of green spaces and parks of socialist relaxation; Stalingrad was the finest example, strung out for sixty-four kilometres along the Volga (and, fortuitously, more difficult for an army to capture outright). However, Stalin, like Hitler, was a convinced urbanist, who rejected the 'petit bourgeois village' in favour of 'the socialist city'.[46] The emphasis was on 'scientific construction', as befitted a materialist state committed to social progress.[47] The new socialist city was sup-posed to reflect the social goals of the regime. Priority was given to party buildings, palaces of labour, assembly halls and squares for popular declarations of communal solidarity. Leningrad did get its House of Soviets, a monumental construction designed by the architect Noi Trotsky in a pseudo-classical style, with twenty towering Attic columns along the front supporting a vast frieze with carvings of heroic socialist struggle.[48] Housing was also designed to reflect collectivist priorities, with shared facilities and child-raising. One apartment block, completed in 1930, required tenants to sign a pledge to 'struggle resolutely against alcoholism, unculturedness, and religion' as a condition of their occupation.[49]

Soviet model cities were industrial rather than imperial. The jewel in the architectural crown of the new communist order was intended to be the city of Magnitogorsk, a sprawling new region of heavy industry and workers' housing built on a rich iron-ore field near the southern tip of the Urals, on 'magnetic mountain'. It was here that in 1929 the regime decided to build a monument to the new revolutionary state, which ten years later housed 200,000 people and hosted the largest integrated industrial complex in the Soviet Union. The new city was more than a response to the demands for rapid industrial and urban development prompted by the Five-Year Plans. Its ultimate purpose, according to a 1930 bulletin for the construction agency building the city, was 'the deep inculcation of the new socialist way of life'.[50] Alongside the areas of industrial and extractive development it was planned to build a 'socialist city', with a grand park and an effective greenbelt to shield the population from the permanent clouds of smog and fumes which hung over the whole area. Instead of the neat village homesteads built at Wolfsburg to house skilled workers at the Volkswagen plant, the skilled workforce of Magnitogorsk were to live in large apartment 'superblocks', each of which could house more than 8,000 people. Residents would cook, eat and wash together to permit women to undertake productive labour in preference to household drudgery; their children would be cared for in block crèches, their leisure time filled with visits to the cinema and local sports.[51]

The first superblock was completed in 1933, loosely based on a design by the celebrated German architect Ernst May. A shortage of sanitary equipment was compounded by the failure to build a sewage system, and the first residents were forced to brave temperatures as low as −40 degrees to reach temporary wooden shacks outside on the street, which served as toilets for thousands of people.[52] A second block was completed in 1937, but was so badly built that it could not be occupied. Most of the 200,000 people crowded into the grimy, hazardous areas around the factories lived in single-storey wooden barracks, or in tents and mud huts. Little thought had gone in to planning an instant city, and the result was little different from the improvised industrial townships of the first wave of industrialization under the Tsars. The only area of decent housing was in a large birch wood, where detached bungalows and larger villas had been built to house American engineers brought in to help establish the ironworks.

When the Americans left in 1932, the township was given to the local elite of managers and party bosses, who enjoyed a lifestyle and material privileges denied to the proletarian mass. The 'socialist city' failed to materialize around them. Only 15 per cent of the population could be housed in buildings made of brick. Pictures of the living conditions of the workers show tightly packed wood-built dormitories and dinners at long wooden trestles, conditions almost indistinguishable from those of the penal labour colony set up by the NKVD outside the town in 1932.[53]

The Soviet Union did build a new urban society despite the failure of the model city. The utopian aspirations of the 1920s gave way to the harsh realities of industrial construction, but there remained a strongly utopian core even to the more realistic dictates of Stalinist planning. It was assumed that the new cities were centres of proletarian culture and party power; palaces of labour supplanted princely palaces; churches were demolished to make way for party buildings; hospitals and schools, often housed in primitive wooden sheds and makeshift halls, were opened throughout the urban Soviet Union. The National Socialist building programme was also intended to create a sense of community, but one conscious of its racial heritage and imperial future. National Socialist model cities were filled with martial buildings and political monuments, designed in turn to overpower the public buildings of an unheroic bourgeois age. In both dictatorships, cities became the principal physical expression of a new society.

The social vision at the heart of both dictatorships was utopian in a very literal sense. Like the construction of Thomas More's ideal city, both pursued the perfect society by compelling their subjects to struggle against the imperfect present. The old order was supposed to grow under the transforming zeal of the regime into a new order, in which a former egoism was abandoned in favour of the collective 'we'. Perfection was to be achieved at the price of abandoning the present and embracing the time to come with an apocalyptic enthusiasm. 'The state must act,' wrote Hitler, 'as the guardian of a millennial future in the face of which the wishes and selfishness of the individual must appear as nothing and submit.'[54] The socialist project under Stalin was built on the idea of struggle against the surviving elements of class selfishness and the eventual triumph of a golden age of communist collectivism. Marxism itself, for all Marx's rejection of utopian thinking, has as its central ambition the creation of an ideal society brought about by the transforming qualities of revolutionary struggle.

The two systems did not pursue the same ideal state, but they were united by one common aim: to create a classless society. This was not an accidental identity of purpose. Both Stalin and Hitler were products of a powerful wave of post-war anti-bourgeois sentiment, which blamed the pre-war 'bourgeois age' for creating a class-riven society in the first place. Stalin, as a good pupil of Marx, hated the bourgeoisie as the embodiment of the social forces of repression; he was also deeply and genuinely hostile to bourgeois values, which he regarded as pretentious and dishonourable. Hitler's anti-bourgeois fulminations in the 1920s have often been regarded as beer-hall talk, gradually abandoned as the party became more respectable and power a real possibility. This is to underestimate the extent to which Hitler and much of the National Socialist movement saw themselves as successors to the bourgeois stage of history. In *Mein Kampf* Hitler called on young Germans to 'be final witness to the total collapse of the bourgeois order'.[55] Throughout the 1920s and 1930s hostility to the bourgeoisie was a central thread running through Hitler's writing and speechmaking. In a remark made in 1932 to Otto Wagener, one of the party's economic experts, Hitler observed that the business bourgeoisie 'know nothing except their profit. "Fatherland" is only a word for them.' At the party congress in 1936 he told the party faithful that what Germany needed were 'men of hard determination, not weak petit bourgeois'.[56] He privately applauded Soviet communism for getting rid of the Russian bourgeoisie, who were 'worthless for mankind'. At the end of the Third Reich, in January 1945, he told an audience: 'the age of the bourgeoisie has come to an end, never to return.'[57]

Hitler and Stalin meant something very particular by the term 'bourgeois'. It was often applied indiscriminately to embrace the old elites in general, both those more evidently bourgeois as well as landowners and aristocracy. In the Soviet Union the term was used to define anyone not evidently drawn from the poor peasantry or the manual working class. Since class identity was never very clearly defined after 1917, the word 'bourgeois' was used in a pejorative sense against all kinds of so-called 'former people' – priests, Tsarist army officers, civil war counter-revolutionaries, even the new wave of tradesmen and peasant speculators made possible by the New Economic Policy in the 1920s.[58] To be bourgeois was to be by definition a person interested in the selfish undermining of the new revolutionary order and a potential outcast. Hitler also defined bourgeois with calculated imprecision. He talked sometimes of the top 'ten thousand' or even 'hundred thousand' in German society, including not only industrialists and bankers, but princes, generals and landowners. He blamed the old elites for creating class envy by making naked material interest their chief ambition, indifferent to the social impact on those they employed. He disliked their political timidity – 'a bunch of cowardly shits', he called them in 1922 – and cultural arrogance. He was determined, like Stalin, to ensure that the bourgeoisie as the engineers of social fragmentation should be excluded from building the new political order.[59]

In place of class society both dictators pursued the ideal of an organic community. The distinction between 'society' (*Gesellschaft*) and 'community' (*Gemeinschaft*) had been elaborated by the nineteenth-century German sociologist Ferdinand Tönnies. By the 1920s the distinction was widely understood and popularly discussed. 'Society' represented a rational association of individuals organized to pursue sectional or class interests; 'community' was, by contrast, a social organism held together by the unselfish commitment of its members to the whole. Communism easily fell into the second category because of its ideal of a post-class community based upon social sharing and social collaboration. National Socialism also defined itself as a movement pursuing the ideal of community, but one founded upon common service to the nation or *Volk* and a shared racial identity. Both represented what the German writer Bogislav von Selchow described as the 'age of the we' or *Wirzeit*, in place of the defunct bourgeois 'age of the ego', the *Ichzeit*.[60] The community character of the two systems was encapsulated in the Soviet term 'comrade' and the German word '*Volksgenosse*' (member of the *Volk*), which superseded the individualist epithet 'citizen'.

The concept of the *Volksgemeinschaft* was central to the idealism of the National Socialist movement. The idea of an exclusive community organized on the principle of 'identity of kind', in which class ascription was overturned in favour of common service to the whole, had its roots in the nineteenth century, and was in wide currency by the 1920s. Hitler shared this utopian longing entirely. The principle of the new National Socialist state, he told an audience in November 1937, was to be found 'not in Christianity, nor in state theory', but 'in the unified people's community'.[61] The cause of that unity was the possession of a common blood and a common racial consciousness. It was this unifying principle that required individuals to suppress their egoism in favour of the long-term preservation of the community. Hitler again, in 1933: 'The lone individual is past, the people remains ... It is necessary that the individual slowly gets used to the idea that his personal "I" is insignificant measured against the being of the entire people.'[62] The slogan, 'the needs of the people before the needs of self', was repeated like a mantra throughout the life of the dictatorship.

This form of community was presented by the movement as a 'socialism of the race', an idea directly derived from the so-called 'national bolshevist' outlook of many German radical writers of the 1920s. The ideal of national service abolished conventional class distinctions: 'I recognize neither bourgeois nor proletarians,' Hitler declared in 1927, 'I recognize only Germans.'[63] The theme of common labour for the *Volk* was used to transcend the reality of social distinction. In the National Socialist community the worth of racially acceptable individuals was measured by their willingness to contribute to the general good of the people, regardless, in Hitler's words again, 'of social origin, class, profession, fortune, education . . .'.[64] The principal target for integration into the people's community was Germany's manual working class, which had to be won back from the alienating experience of class society and the seductions of communism.

The prospect of winning the worker away from Marxism had sustained the party's activities during the early years of the movement. The creation of a nationally minded workforce – 'the comrade with the red cloth-cap must become a comrade in the national community' – was regarded as the critical test for the new ideal state.[65] The creation of the German Labour Front on 10 May 1933, a vast corporation representing the entire workforce from labourer and skilled operative to manager, was intended gradually to reconcile worker and nation in a classless future. On May Day 1933, Hitler spoke publicly about the importance of manual work once it was filled 'with loyal and honest meaning', and the idea of the 'honour of labour', expressed in numerous symbolic ways, was intended to heal the wounds inflicted on ordinary workers by an insensitive employer class.[66] Throughout the 1920s Hitler had consistently preached the necessity of integrating the worker as representative of some kind of elemental life-force, 'the bearer of the living energy' of the people. Here, too, Hitler was out of step with those elements in the party who lauded the peasant as the fundament of the racial community.[67] The movement was in general more committed to the idea of the 'national' worker. Hitler preferred workers because, he told a party audience in 1938, they were ruled by instinct rather than by reason, 'and out of instinct comes faith'. The success of the party in attracting worker support was confirmed in the party census of 1935, which found that almost one-third of party members were manual workers, and a further 20 per cent white-collar employees.[68]

The ambition to create a classless community in the Soviet Union had a quite different issue to confront. Here the worker was included as a matter of course; the problem was to find ways to transcend class by including non-workers in the new system. Communists had no illusions after 1917 that they had abolished class. The aim of the revolutionary state was, in the long run, to produce a communist society in which there were no classes in the Marxist sense, but a single community based on social ownership and collective endeavour. The nature of this community was seldom articulated very clearly, since the reality in the Soviet Union was so evidently distant from the imagined future. With the abolition of classes, communism would be self-defining: a form of 'people's community' that excluded in this case class enemies; a socialist commonwealth based upon scientific principles of organization and a collectivist mentality.

In the 1920s class was still a live issue. The coming of the New Economic Policy had turned millions of peasants into potential rural capitalists; a new class of petty traders emerged; bourgeois experts had to be recruited, at home and abroad, to help with economic reconstruction. The urban working class only returned to the size of the Tsarist workforce by 1926. Together, the urban workforce, poor peasants and rural workers, and the non-bourgeois intelligentsia ('proletarians by conviction'), formed the core of a future communist community.[69] Only these 'toilers' were granted the vote in 1918. Soviet society remained curiously fractured along traditional lines of class distinction. Although the Tsarist order of legal estates (*sosloviia*) had been abolished in November 1917, the class identity of non-toilers was still expressed in the same pre-revolutionary categories. Only party members were not required to reveal their own, or their parents' *soslovie* when challenged. Those descended from class enemies, the so-called *lishentsy*, could not join party associations or attend higher education. When the campaign against the kulaks and private traders or 'nepmen' began in 1928, they were added to the list of class enemies, and suffered the same deprivations.[70] Four years later the regime finally abolished the one remaining vestige of the old social order, the labour collective or *artel*. These small work communities, common in the construction and mining industries, were a throwback to an earlier age. They were run by elected 'elders'; the men slept and worked together as a work team, and were paid from a common pot. Stalin disliked their independence. Under pressure from him all forms of collective or communal labour were scrapped and their members turned into brigades of revolutionary shock workers.[71]

From the early 1930s Stalin and his political allies embarked on a great utopian experiment of their own. The collectivization and industrialization drives were instruments to create the conditions for a Soviet community in which class was finally destroyed as a social category, to be replaced by a community based on heroic socialist construction.[72] Stalin warned repeatedly that during this dangerous period class enemies would become more desperate and the class struggle sharper. The 'dying remnants', as he told the Central Committee plenum in January 1933, were 'stealthily sapping and undermining', wrecking farms, stealing public property, injecting 'plague and anthrax into cattle'. The 'classless society' would only be achieved after the state had crushed the 'remaining detachments of the bourgeoisie'.[73] At the Seventeenth Party Congress a year later, delegates called for the creation of a classless socialist society by eradicating the residues of capitalist consciousness during the life of the Second Five-Year Plan. Stalin, in his final address to the Congress, laid out a programme of organized class struggle for the final aim of abolishing classes.[74]

Abolition meant the imprisonment and exile of millions of peasants, and a growing concentration camp population of alleged class enemies. At the same time the regime applauded the ennobling character of manual work in constructing the new order. Workers, so it was claimed, 'have a more concrete form of thinking . . . than bourgeois intellectuals'.[75] The image of the heroic labourer as the centrepiece of the drive to build a socialist tomorrow has much in common with the idealized image of the National Socialist worker. Both were held up as models to emulate; manual work was regarded in both systems as intrinsically rewarding and morally validating. Stalin, in a rare exposition on the nature of communism, defined it as a system in which all had 'an equal duty to work'.[76] At the end of 1936 Stalin finally announced that the struggle to forge a classless society had been successful. With the elimination of all exploiting classes there remained only workers, peasants and an intelligentsia, most of whose members were drawn from one of the two other categories. These groups, Stalin claimed, were not classes in the old sense at all, but were the architects of a 'new, classless, socialist, society', characterized by 'collective property' and 'collective labour' and the elimination of social antagonism.[77]

The construction of new forms of community, distinct from the old world that gave rise to them, did not mean the end of social differences in either system. In the ideal state, class differences formerly based on the nature of capitalist society were turned into functional categories. Both systems expected everyone included in the community to make a positive contribution to the whole by performing to the best of their ability. Even those who were excluded, in camps and penal colonies, were expected to contribute their labour power to the community that had isolated and punished them. In the Soviet Union the result was a rejection of crude egalitarianism in favour of a distribution of social tasks according to aptitude and technical capability. Equality, Stalin pointed out in the same speech to the Seventeenth Party Congress, came from an equal obligation to work and to be rewarded for it, but it did not mean that everyone did the same work or got the same pay, or lived identical lives. This was 'to slander Marxism'.[78] Under Stalin's

dictatorship different tasks earned different rewards; exceptional commitment to building socialism brought privileges and bounties.

In Germany, too, equal membership of the people's community did
not mean a simple egalitarianism. 'The highest value,' Hitler argued,
'is to be placed in him who is prepared to put all his activity into the
service of the community.'[79] The efficiency of a state was, in his
view, expressed in the extent to which the finer racial minds could
be identified and promoted, whatever their social origin. This was
supposed to produce not class competition, but a rational allocation
of social tasks. Worker or engineer, porter or plant manager were all
to be united by their willingness to work selflessly for the promotion
of the community. Hitler himself hoped that at some point gross
inequalities of income would be ironed out by a system of 'graduated
compensation', which reflected the nature of the contribution each
racial comrade made to the race as a whole, including 'the one who
sweeps the streets'.[80] This idealized community was an expression
of a socially efficient demarcation of function, where competence
(*Leistung*) determined the contribution an individual could make to
the whole. The rationalization of economy and society through the
proper utilization of human resources in the service of the community
was characteristic of the social aspirations of both systems.

The key figure in promoting the construction of the new society was
the man with practical expertise. The new built environment was
possible only through the efforts of engineers, architects, technologists
and town planners. The erosion of class identities and conventional
class power was designed to produce a more technocratic society
run by experts, who were driven by their desire to master technical
problems for the community rather than by the imperatives of institutional self-interest or class greed. These ideas were not confined only
to the two dictatorships. The notion that modern societies should be
engineered by a selfless elite of planners and technologists had advocates throughout the developed world.[81] Both Germany and the Soviet
Union needed technical skills to promote industrial development,
urban renewal and military build-up regardless of the nature of the
social experiments both were simultaneously engaged in. The deliberate assault on class, however, gave practical functionaries a greater
social prominence in both regimes.

Both dictators shared the conviction that technology was an essential instrument of social construction. Hitler's fascination with technical modernity is well known. 'I am a fool for technology,' he told his circle in 1942.[82] His interest in mass motorization, for example, fused together his conception of the 'people's community' with the practical issues of road-building and car construction. Hitler, who read Henry Ford's autobiography while in prison in 1924, saw himself as the German Ford, supplying the ordinary worker and farmer with an affordable small car, to erode the gulf between the wealthy car-owning public and the rest of society. In September 1933 he summoned the Austrian car designer Ferdinand Porsche to Berlin; here Hitler asked him to produce 'a low-priced family car . . . a car for the people'.[83] The subsequent revolutionary design of a small, squat car with a rear air-cooled engine was soon described as the 'people's car' or *Volkswagen*. The rest of the German motor industry dragged its feet over production plans and Hitler transferred the entire project to the German Labour Front. Plans for the car were followed by plans for a 'people's tractor', to speed up the technical modernization of German agriculture. At the same time a network of 6,000 kilometres of fast multi-lane motorway was planned; half of it was built by 1939 under the direction of Fritz Todt, an engineer and enthusiastic National Socialist.

Todt was the model of the new technocratic elite of the 'people's community'. A party member since 1923, Todt was a Hitler favourite. In 1934 he was made responsible directly to Hitler for all questions of technology; his formal post as General-Plenipotentiary for Construction gave him a central role in the physical remodelling of the new order in all its many aspects. His organization built not only roads, but the new cities and the *Westwall* fortifications along Germany's frontier with France, which alone in the winter of 1938–9 employed half a million workers and consumed one-third of all German cement production.[84] He also headed a new corporate organization of engineers, the Main Office for Technology, which drew under its umbrella the country's 300,000 engineers. Todt's view of technology was entirely consistent with the new views of a society based on achievement for the community rather than class ascription, in which Germanic technology would become 'a pillar of the total state',

supplying the technical means to ensure national survival and development, while at the same time healing the modernist rift between technique and culture.[85] The idea that technology represented a flourishing
of what was called 'the German essence', quite distinct from soulless
'American-Jewish' technique, seems to have been widely shared among
Germany's engineering community. The desire to integrate technology
into an organic community as a main instrument for its transformation,
the 'primacy of technology' (*Primat der Technik*) as one philosophic-
ally minded engineer put it in 1934, represented an important strand
of the prevailing anti-bourgeois sentiment of the pre-Hitler years.[86]

Stalin also recognized the indispensability of technique. The master-
ing of practical challenges was central to the construction of a scientific
socialism; there was no need to infuse technology with fanciful notions
of racial essence or spiritual health, since its primacy was self-evident.
'Technology in the period of reconstruction decides everything,'
claimed Stalin.[87] His favourite film was said to be the 1938 production
Volga! Volga!, a musical comedy that ends with the triumphant
completion of the Moscow–Volga canal by regiments of prisoner-
labourers, 55,000 of whom were generously granted amnesty after it
was finished, but unknown thousands of whom died in its construction.[88] The problem confronting the Soviet Union was the absence of
a large community of experts untainted, in the eyes of the regime, with
the residue of bourgeois idealism or the stigma of counter-revolution.
The establishment of a new category of expert had both a political and
a practical purpose: the building of the socialist community could be
carried out in the end only by an intelligentsia whose interests were
identical with the social ambitions of the regime. In 1928, at the start
of the First Five-Year Plan, Stalin called for a rapid programme to
train a new layer of technical experts drawn from the politically reliable
fraction of the population: 'from the working class, Communists, and
members of the Young Communist League'.[89]

The rejection of the 'bourgeois' engineer as the agent of social
modernization was a central feature of the wider struggle to construct
a classless society. In the Soviet model, the engineering intelligentsia
could not take the lead roles while workers languished in the wings.
In the late 1920s and early 1930s many engineers were either recruited
abroad, and hence suspect as a matter of course, or came from more

privileged social or educational backgrounds. The prevailing cultural stereotype was the expert as wrecker or saboteur. The paradox was resolved by pushing thousands of young Soviet men and women through crash training courses to make them effective *praktiki*, people with experience but no diploma, but whose proletarian credentials were unblemished.[90] By 1931, 3 million were undergoing technical training; the priority was a narrow practical schooling, linked directly with issues of production and construction. As industrialization deepened, the number of *praktiki* declined in favour of larger numbers of worker graduates from technical colleges and universities, which could supply a higher quality of training, but throughout the 1930s the generation of a technical intelligentsia that was both more practical and more socially modest in its origins continued. Between 1933 and 1941 the proportion of the technical and managerial intelligentsia drawn from higher education dropped from 22 to 17 per cent, while the proportion supplied by the *praktiki* rose from 59 to 66 per cent.[91] The exemplar for the new classless state was the heroic engineer-worker, and thousands were promoted into positions of responsibility previously held by those whose social background or education disqualified them during the purges.

The new classless societies were intended to develop functional rather than social elites. This was simpler in the Soviet Union, where social categories were very fluid in the first twenty years after 1917. Social mobility was an inevitable consequence of the destruction of older elites and social classes and the development of forced industrialization. Peasants moved into the cities and became workers; millions of both became low-level supervisors, managers and technicians; thousands more became managers and engineers; Stalin's Politburo, unlike Lenin's, had only one member not drawn from a plebeian background. The formation of a distinctly modern social structure allowed the Soviet Union under Stalin to create the social conditions for the abolition of the classes inherited from the pre-revolutionary period, an outcome that also facilitated the Stalinist ideal of a predominantly proletarian commonwealth. It is more difficult to decide the social outcome in Hitler's Germany, for here the idealists had to cope with an established social structure and inherited elites. Social analysis of National Socialism demonstrates that the principal social classifications of peasant, worker, white-collar employee, independent businessman and professional class persisted. The conclusion that the dictatorship therefore made little difference to the long-term structural evolution of the German population, that the worker remained a worker, the engineer an engineer, nonetheless ignores a significant acceleration in social mobility and, above all, the consolidation of a distinctive National Socialist elite that matched the social utopianism of the regime, just as the rise of the *praktiki* satisfied the projected image of a communist future.

Any of a hundred photographs of Hitler surrounded by clusters of uniformed officials, some military, some party men, some drawn from the myriad associations and corporations which sprang up after 1933, reveals the extent to which the party produced an elite that was definably different from anything that preceded it. The decision that everyone should wear a uniform was a self-conscious one, designed, in Hitler's words, 'so that Germans can walk together arm in arm without regard to their station in life'.[92] In uniform the visible divide between what Hitler called 'the crease in the trousers' and the 'mechanic's overall' disappeared. Uniforms easily displayed, through the intricate system of tabs and badges that adorned them, the function each performed. They blurred or transcended conventional class distinctions. As in the Soviet Union, the new elite in Germany were distinguished both by their practical function and by their political loyalty. Fritz Todt was an evident example, but there were many others. By the late 1930s Hitler promoted practical men with a party record. It is significant that he chose first Todt, and then his architect Albert Speer, as successive ministers for armaments during the war, though neither had any experience in the military field, while senior military officials were gradually pushed out of technical and economic responsibilities in favour of a young generation of loyal technocrats. The running of the vast German empire was, from 1939, dominated by party appointees in alliance with a cohort of junior officials whose technical competence and party card pushed them rapidly up the career ladder. The young Adolf Eichmann was a salesman and drifter in the 1920s. Membership first of the party, then of the SS, brought him to senior rank in the main security office by 1939; his malign efficiency in Jewish affairs made him into a central player in the organization of genocide two years later.[93]

There were thousands of Eichmanns in the party machine. The changing social composition in Germany derived from membership of the party and its subordinate institutions. Most were workers and white-collar workers, not very different from the upwardly mobile new workforce in the Soviet Union. One-third of all those in the SS were manual workers by origin; between 1933 and 1942 the proportion of workers joining the party each year rose from 30 to 43 per cent, that of white-collar workers from 26 to 32 per cent. By 1939 two-thirds of those who joined the party were workers or white-collar employees.[94] The great bulk of those who joined the party and party institutions were young. Half of those admitted into the SS were under thirty, 85 per cent under forty.[95] The social support for the National Socialist experiment came from the post-war generation who hoped to exploit the new institutional apparatus to increase their social status and responsibilities, not by moving from one conventional class to another, but by transcending class altogether. Eichmann did not derive his social identity after 1933 by scrambling out of the petite bourgeoisie on to some higher social plane, but from his role as an SS officer and race-bureaucrat. The party's elite actively sought to create a distinct social establishment where the old rules of social distinction and class snobbery were overturned. This new generation became a self-styled political caste, whose social claims and identity were based on loyalty to Hitler and National Socialism, on racial criteria of selection, or on ill-defined qualities of 'leadership', not on conventional class ascription.

The social consequences of building organic communities, led by a mixed party-technocratic elite and dominated by party institutions, were not the same under the two systems. The Soviet object was to create a community with greater social opportunities for peasants and workers to display their native aptitude in constructing socialism and abolishing classes. Social value was attached to the practical, hard-working and politically acceptable proletarian. The German ideal was a community of blood, in which service to the race or nation was a common obligation for its long-term preservation, and in which 'race-value' rather than merit was a measure of true social worth. Though evidently similar in form, the social utopias were profoundly divergent in purpose.

Nowhere was the social idealism of the two dictatorships more distinct than with the idea of the 'New Man' who would build the new society and stride through its new cities. Each social vision, communist and National Socialist, presupposed that the citizens of utopia would be different from the people of the present. Writing in 1926, a Leningrad professor, Nikolai Gredeskul, speculated on a Soviet future populated by transformed individuals: 'they will think differently, feel differently, have different characters, and different relations among themselves'. They would be Lunacharsky's 'beautiful Man of the Future', part worker, part thinker.[96] The expectation that people would be changed in positive ways by social revolution was central to its purpose. The 'plasticity of the organism', as Bukharin put it, would enable the new society to remodel its inhabitants to become active, conscious and virtuous members of the socialist community.[97]

The National Socialist obsession with the New Man is well known. The idea derived not from the reforming possibilities of social revolution, but the possibility of physically generating a new human breed. 'Creation is not yet at an end,' Hitler is supposed to have told Hermann Rauschning. 'Biologically regarded, man has clearly arrived at a turning point. A new variety of man is beginning to separate out.' The new form Hitler called the 'god-man', to which he attached attributes thought to be desirable for the tough tribe of future Germans (though impossible to generate biologically): 'fearless', 'formidable', 'dominating', 'brutal', 'intrepid'.[98] National Socialism was popularly identified with the idea of biologically engineering men and women of supreme physical aspect – so-called 'Aryans', tall, blond, blue-eyed, sharp of profile, gracefully proportioned, ideal inhabitants of Utopia. These beautiful men of the future Hitler deemed 'the pure and noble material' with which he could construct the new order.[99]

The ideal man clearly had utopian roots. In the late nineteenth century scientists began to apply theoretical breakthroughs in biology to human populations. The key lay with developments in evolutionary biology following the pioneering work of the British social biologist

Francis Galton, who, in 1881, coined the term 'eugenics' to describe the idea that human populations could be engineered to create a healthy gene-pool and sound demographic development. Scientific interest in controlled evolution produced a plethora of fantastic proposals for better breeding, including an ideal all-female collective serviced by a small number of racially selected male 'guests' responsible for propagating the species, but for nothing else. The German biologist Alfred Ploetz, describing his own version of a eugenic utopia, coined the term 'racial hygiene' (*Rassenhygiene*) in 1895 to describe the application of eugenic principles, and this term dominated the German debate about racial decline and racial invigoration down to the 1930s.[100] Eugenic science was genuinely international; it was welcomed as a modern, scientific means to prevent social degeneration, persistent patterns of hereditary disablement and even criminality. In the Soviet Union eugenics was taken up as a key to more general strategies of post-revolutionary social improvement. In 1921 a Russian Eugenics Society was founded; one of its first steps was to set up a commission to study the Jewish race.[101]

A central issue in evolutionary biology remained unresolved. Darwinism held that characteristics were inherited; the work of the French biologist Jean Lamarck, who preceded Darwin by a generation, had argued the case for acquired characteristics, a consequence of adaptation to environmental changes rather than genetic patterning. Those who followed Darwin assumed that nature was paramount in determining human biological development; those who favoured Lamarck believed that nurture ameliorated the human condition. In the early twentieth century this scientific debate became a live political issue. Socialists inclined to Lamarckian science because social improvement was clearly linked to changes in the socio-economic environment. Stalin himself, in his 1906 pamphlet *Anarchism or Socialism*, came down strongly in favour of a crude neo-Lamarckian interpretation of Marxism: 'If the ape had not risen to its feet, its descendant, man, would have been obliged to walk on all fours forever . . . First the external conditions change . . .'[102] In the 1920s Darwinian biology had provoked growing interest in genetics in the Soviet Union, but the political drift was in favour of environmental evolution. A German scientist and socialist, Paul Kammerer, tried to demonstrate

Lamarckian principles through experiments conducted on the Midwife Toad. When his results were exposed as a fake he killed himself, but in the Soviet Union his story was made, improbably, into a film, and Kammerer himself into a hero of revolutionary science. Genetics and Darwinism were condemned as idealist bourgeois science, and in 1930 the Eugenics Society was dissolved. The universities began to close down departments of genetic biology. The connection between genetics and racism in National Socialist thinking completed the break; Soviet scientists rejected these views as 'zoological' nonsense.[103] In the 1930s Stalin revealed himself as a committed disciple of Lamarck; he threw his weight behind the rise of environmental science, represented most notoriously by the peasant-turned-agronomist Trofim Lysenko, whose experiments to produce sturdy winter wheat by first soaking seeds in water were hailed as a model example of the triumph of environment over genes. Although the conclusions that were drawn from Lysenko's primitive experiment proved to be scientifically insupportable, his work was hailed as a breakthrough for practical proletarian technique against speculative bourgeois science, and Mendelian genetics was outlawed for a generation. With Stalin's backing, Lysenko became the leading spokesman of Soviet science after 1945.[104] Environmental biology also had implications for human development: in the new Soviet society man was to be nurtured, not bred.

In Germany, Darwin triumphed. Here the debate favoured the argument that characteristics were inherited, and that a strong and vigorous race could only be produced by natural selection. 'All human traits,' wrote Eugen Fischer, director from 1926 of the newly founded German eugenics institute, 'normal and pathological, physical or mental – are shaped by hereditary factors.'[105] Many German scientists and welfare experts assumed that the long-term tendency was for racial stock to degenerate unless, as the pro-Hitler Fritz Lenz wrote, 'the strong and the fit are given advantages in propagation'.[106] It is significant that Hitler shared this scientific conception entirely. Darwinism fitted with his presumption that all life was struggle and that life favoured the fittest. *Mein Kampf* is peppered with references to heredity and inner nature as the principal determinants of human evolution. For Hitler the only legitimate state was one that promoted its best racial stock: 'Politics today is completely blind without a biological foundation and biological objectives.'[107] Even if Lamarckian science had not been discredited experimentally in inter-war Germany, Hitler would still have promoted Darwinism at its expense. National Socialist new man was born rather than made.

The creation of the biological 'new man' had profound implications for German social and welfare policy. The propagation of healthy racial stock was an ideal rather than a reality in Weimar Germany. After 1933 the scientists and doctors who had promoted race hygiene found a regime whose central social ambition was to create a healthy, expanding, racially exclusive population as the foundation stone of the 'people's community'. The party's Office of Race Policy and the SS Race and Settlement Office, set up under Walther Darré in 1933, recruited doctors and academics who shared the view that race could only be protected effectively by coercive and direct medical intervention. The first step was to identify and classify those physical and psychological conditions that subverted the hygiene of the race. This was done quickly. The protection of the genetic heritage (*Erbgut*) by excluding the possibility of reproduction among groups identified as genetically unworthy was enshrined in the Law for the Prevention of Offspring with Hereditary Diseases, which was published in July 1933 and came into force on 1 January 1934. The association of habitual crime with biological deficiency added a second law, published in November 1933, to combat 'compulsive criminality'.[108]

Prevention meant compulsory sterilization or castration at the behest of state medical, welfare and penal authorities. The law drawn up by Dr Arthur Gütt, an Interior Ministry official and party enthusiast for racial hygiene, listed nine conditions that threatened racial health: feeblemindedness; schizophrenia; manic depression; hereditary epilepsy, alcoholism, blindness and deafness; hereditary physical disfigurement; and Huntington's chorea.[109] Officials working in education, health care and welfare were empowered to send those under their charge to new Hereditary Health Courts, which would decide whether compulsory sterilization was required in the long-term interests of the race. In most cases the courts upheld the recommendation. The most contentious category, 'feeblemindedness', allowed the authorities to sterilize thousands on grounds regarded simply as inimical to the community rather than the race as such – vagrancy, petty crime, sex outside marriage, disruptive and delinquent behaviour. In the first three years of the law 90 per cent of cases resulted in sterilization orders, the majority for alleged feeblemindedness. By 1945 an estimated 360,000 had been sterilized (and more than 2,000 sexual criminals castrated). A profile of the German population drawn up by racial statisticians suggested that hereditary conditions affected around 1.6 million of the population, all of whom should be sterilized to cleanse the gene pool.[110]

The only way to track down and exclude the biological 'degenerate' was through official screening of the entire population. This fantastic proposition was set in motion in 1934. All of those who came under medical or welfare supervision were to supply details for a genealogical and health databank, which was eventually to be extended to the entire population. On 1 April 1935 a nationwide network of clinics for racial hygiene was opened, where the data was collected and processed. Coloured cards indicated the sex of the individual, ethnic origin, four-generation genealogy, hereditary medical and psychiatric condition, and any criminal record. The success of the programme varied from region to region: Hamburg produced more than a million profiles, Thuringia half a million. Patients in psychiatric hospitals and homes throughout Germany were surveyed. In 1939 Himmler ordered genetic profiling as a regular procedure in all criminal investigations, alongside the habitual photograph and finger-printing. Hundreds of thousands of Germans applied to a new Reich Office for Family Research, set up in 1935, in order to prove their racial and genetic purity.[111] Heredity became a measure of inclusion for those who fitted the official template of racial health and affinity; for those who did not, it became a perverse instrument for social discrimination and biological penalty.

The same principles of heredity and racial health were soon applied to marriage. The race of the future relied on the wise choice of a marriage partner; the state reserved the right to prevent unwanted unions. In 1935 two laws were passed to ensure that marriage conformed to the biological imperatives of the race. The Law for the Protection of German Blood and Honour, announced at the party rally in September 1935 at Nuremberg, prohibited marriage or sexual intercourse between Germans and Jews; the following month marriage between race members with a clean bill of health and those with hereditary illness or disability was outlawed. Health and genealogical certificates were not made compulsory but were strongly encouraged, and registrars could refer anyone asking to get married to a racial health clinic if there were any doubts about their racial suitability. Those compulsorily sterilized were permitted only to marry infertile partners, but disqualification also extended to habitual criminals, alcoholics, medically classified psychopaths, and any of the estimated 750,000 Germans suffering from venereal disease. Even after a former VD-sufferer had successfully gone through the humiliating process of urine-sampling and blood-testing, he or she might still be denied marriage where there were any remaining doubts about cure. Victims of tuberculosis, diabetes, leukaemia and asthma could be rejected on the grounds that these were all medical conditions that might mar a happy marriage or debilitate its offspring.[112]

For the rest of the population marriage was represented by the regime as a singular commitment to the future of the German people, one to be taken only after long deliberation and prudent medical checks. The party's Office of Race Policy published a set of ten guidelines for prospective newly-weds that stressed that marriage was founded not only on love but on criteria of race and health: 'When choosing a spouse, inquire into his or her forebears!'; 'If hereditarily fit, do not remain single!'; and so on.[113] These same criteria were applied to the system of marriage loans introduced in June 1933 to help combat unemployment by taking women who married out of the job market. Within eighteen months 365,000 loans were paid out to those couples where there were no biological or social grounds for objection. Half of the rejected applications failed on grounds of physical or mental subnormality.[114] The principal purpose of marriage was child-bearing ('Hope for as many children as possible!' was the final injunction on the party list). Married couples without children were officially designated as households rather than families, and were liable to direct pressure from medical and welfare officials (and higher taxes) for their lapse. Generous family allowances were introduced: a single fixed payment for large families, as well as graduated monthly contributions that by 1941 cost the state more than a billion marks annually.[115] These, too, could be forfeit in families where social deviancy or physical abnormality could be demonstrated. By deliberately penalizing the weakest households, natural selection was given an artificial boost.

'In my state,' Hitler declared, 'the mother is the most important citizen.' The new woman was idealized in a hundred propaganda posters, a contented and competent helpmeet for her man, but, above all, a model of heroic fecundity. On 12 August each year, the birthday of Hitler's mother, thousands of child-bearers were presented with medals, bronze for four or five children, silver for six or seven, gold for eight or more.[116] The woman as mother and helper, the man as fighter and thinker were stereotypes of National Socialist rhetoric. Yet gender roles were more complicated than this. The woman as mother was also once the girl who went on long hikes organized by the party, who undertook her 'year of duty' (Pflichtjahr) working the land aged eighteen, and who imbibed the keep-fit culture common across inter-war Europe. In 1939 over 14 million women were included in the labour statistics, 37.3 per cent of the workforce. A striking image from a party calendar in 1939 shows ten tall, pigtailed teenagers in shorts and singlets each holding a javelin; beneath runs the caption 'Future Mothers'. The ideal new woman could also be strong, independent, a model of vitality and courage; if she did her national service breeding children, it was still regarded as national service. During the war years the SS even promoted the idea that unmarried women might bear children for the Fatherland without social stigma. In the SS Lebensborn maternity homes around half of the 12,000 babies were born to unmarried mothers.[117] On the other hand marriage, even for the racially fit, was not sacrosanct. In 1938 the government drafted new divorce laws to make them compatible with the priorities of the racial community. The object was to make divorce simpler, in the hope that it might lead to quick re-marriage and more children. In cases where one or other partner was guilty of racially dishonourable conduct, or had become mentally disordered, or had deserted the battlefield of births through involuntary sterility or a refusal to reproduce, divorce could now be approved.[118]

The family was the core unit of the people's community. But it was not an independent unit. During the period of the Third Reich family life was formally subordinate to the imperatives of the racial community. The emergence of the new man could not be left entirely to

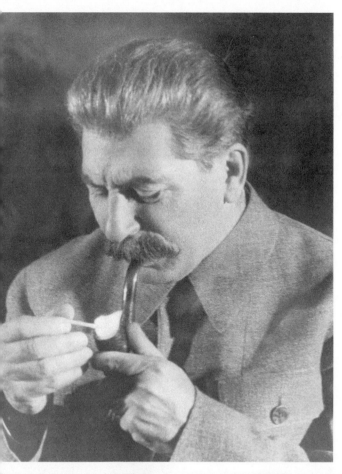

1 Josef Stalin at the height of his powers as dictator. He impressed the American envoy Joseph E. Davis as the kind of man whose knee 'a child would like to sit on'.

2 Stalin at a meeting of the Praesidium of the Supreme Soviet, with President Kalinin on his left. Stalin sat on all important committees so that he could monitor closely the work of party and state.

3 Stalin applauding his
audience after a speech on
the new constitution in
1936. A quiet, methodical
speaker, he developed an
oratorical style that
blended modesty and
authority together.

4 A poster of the two
leaders, c.1936. The cult of
Lenin was used to endorse
Stalin's own cult. Here
Lenin has already become a
pale shadow behind the real
Leader.

5 A propaganda session in the Soviet countryside, *c*.1930. Collective farmers listen to an agitator explaining state policy with the help of a booklet by Stalin. Over 2 million farmers were sent to labour camps between 1930 and 1932.

7 Andrei Vyshinsky in 1938 as Chief Procurator of the Soviet Union. As the most senior of Soviet lawyers Vyshinsky played a key part in the creation of the Stalinist judicial system and the development of Soviet legality.

He called for 'implacable hatred' against enemies of the revolution, though he himself had been a Menshevik in 1917.

A march past of athletes in Red Square in Moscow in 1937. The banner bears the portrait of Nikolai Ezhov, commissar of the interior and head of Soviet State Security. Under his authority almost 700,000 were executed as enemies of the people, a bloodbath that ended with his own execution early in 1940.

8 A diploma awarded in 1931 for denouncing rich peasants to the authorities. The recipient was rewarded with a silk dress.

9 The Praesidium building of the Supreme Soviet of the Ukraine in Kiev. The architect, V. I. Zabolotni, was awarded a Stalin Prize for the design, completed in 1939. In cities all over the Soviet Union the new built environment was intended as a monument to the Stalinist utopia.

Building the fourth section of the Moscow metro in the 1940s. The underground system in the capital was a prestige project. 'Every screw,' said Lazar Kaganovich, 'is a screw of socialism.'

11 *The Unforgettable Meeting* by V. Yefanov, painted in 1936 to celebrate an over-achieving woman worker. Social reality was presented as social fantasy, a parody of the harsh existence imposed on the Soviet workforce during the Five-Year Plans.

КОМСОМОЛ ЕСТЬ — ШКОЛА
ВСЕСТОРОННЕЙ
ГОСУДАРСТВЕННОЙ ДЕЯТЕЛЬНОСТ

12 A party member subjecting a group of Russian prostitutes to a course of political re-education. In the 1930s Stalinist morality frowned on sexual decadence and lauded the conventional, loving family unit.

13 Trofim Lysenko, the Soviet 'people's scientist', holding a vegetable aloft at a scientific conference. Lysenko rejected Mendelian genetics and argued instead for the primacy of environment over heredity, a view adopted by the whole Stalinist system.

14 The giant statue *Worker and Collective Farm Woman* by Vera Mukhina, on top of the Soviet pavilion in Paris in 1937. The German pavilion stood opposite with a giant statue of two naked Aryan men entitled *Comradeship*.

15 An anti-religious demonstration in Moscow in the 1920s. Workers carry a placard of an Orthodox clergyman with the slogan 'Down with the priests' imposture'. Thousands of churches were closed or destroyed and more than 35,000 priests either killed, imprisoned or forced into poverty.

16 A painting of the young Stalin talking to peasants in 1902 by A. Kutateladze. The picture uses unashamedly religious imagery despite the regime's violent anti-clericalism and atheism.

17 A group of Stakhanovite coal-miners pose after winning the national mineworkers competition. Millions of workers in the 1930s became 'over-achievers', entitled to extra pay and rations. Even in the labour camps high achievers were given more bread.

18 A couple playing draughts in the Gorky Park of Culture and Rest in 1937. Most ordinary people were untouched by the wave of terror in 1937–8 that swept away those in authority in party and state.

19 The writer Maxim Gorky after his return to the Soviet Union in 1932. In 1917 Gorky warned that Lenin's revolution would produce 'prolonged and bloody anarchy', but in the 1930s he became the mouthpiece for Stalin's 'socialist realist' art.

20 The writer Mikhail Bulgakov, whose work Stalin liked but would not allow to be staged or read. When Bulgakov's play about Stalin's early life was turned down in 1939, he became ill and depressed, and died less than a year later. His crowning achievement, the novel *The Master and Margarita*, was not published until 1968.

21 A Georgian woman learning to write using the new alphabet imposed in the late 1920s. By 1939 the regime claimed to have all but eliminated illiteracy. The printed word was the most important medium for political education.

22 The painting *At an Old Urals Works* by Johanson, which won first prize at the first all-Soviet art exhibition held in Moscow in 1939. Stalin liked the picture because of its clear class confrontation. The capitalist is painted in unmistakably anti-Semitic terms.

3 Tractors lined up at the Chelyabinsk Tractor Factory in 1935. Tractors symbolized the Soviet odernization drive of the 1930s. Motor Tractor Stations became the centres in the countryside for education, propaganda and party meetings.

24 Dividing up the landlords' land in the new Latvian socialist republic following the Soviet annexation of the Baltic States in 1940. In all the new areas the Stalinist model of economic development and social repression was imposed immediately.

25 The woman tractor driver Olga Marchevo, who became a Stakhanovite model for other women workers on collective farms. By 1945 four-fifths of the workers on the land were women, and one-third of all construction workers.

26 Architects and town-planners work on the reconstruction of Moscow in 1946. The war brought massive destruction to the western Soviet Union from bombing. More than 3 million captured Axis soldiers were used as forced labour to help with economic revival, some of them on the construction sites of the capital.

27 A 1936 poster on 'Fascism Means War'. In the 1930s Stalin encouraged the massive rearmament of the Soviet Union to counter the threat from Germany while trying to find ways to avoid a direct conflict.

28 An idealized image of mother and child confronting the threat of war: 'Accursed be the Warmongers! Mothers of the World Fight for Peace'. The emphasis on family values reflected a widespread rejection of the sexual liberation and social experiments of the 1920s.

29 During the war women made up more than half of the Soviet workforce. Here a former student checks shells in an arms factory. Supervisory jobs were still the preserve of men.

30 A group of women volunteers in 1941 fighting with partisans against the German invasion. Women flocked to join the militia when war broke out, but only four in every hundred survived the war.

31 In Leningrad thousands of women were compelled to build barricades and prepare the city's fences. After the city was surrounded in September 1941, it was subjected to regular bombing and elling. An estimated 1 million people perished in the city between 1941 and its liberation in 1944.

32 Soldiers of General Guryev's units kneel at the presentation of the Lenin Banner before departing for the Stalingrad front. Religious symbolism helped to rally the population in the middle years of the war when the Soviet Union faced defeat.

33 German soldiers pose with executed partisans. All over the occupied Soviet Union irregular forces were hunted down and killed. By 1943 an estimated 300,000 had joined the partisans to escape German brutalities or to avoid the fate of collaborators.

34 A train filled with Soviet Jews from Belorussia on their way 1932 to find industrial employment in the Kuznets region. The Soviet regime hoped to end a sense of separate Jewish identity by encouraging them to become workers and farmers.

35 After the war, the cult of personality reached its zenith. Here at Taganskaya station in Moscow a bas-relief shows an ageing Stalin surrounded by adoring citizens. By 1948 all but two of the entries for the Stalin Prize for art were pictures of the leader.

36 When Stalin died 1953 his body was embalmed and laid side-by-side with Len in the mausoleum. I 1956 Stalin was denounced by Khrushchev, and fiv years later his body was removed.

nature. The worthy family was supported by a network of welfare and health support to prevent further racial debilitation. Nationwide programmes to screen for tuberculosis, dental inspections for all children, regular checks on families with poor health records or low standards of hygiene were all designed to ensure that the biological end-product would more closely resemble the racial ideal. At schools the six-day teaching week was reduced to five to leave a day for organized sport.[119] The Hitler Youth was a school for the intrepid and instinctive, where strict discipline was combined with bouts of violent free play and paramilitary training. Special schools were set up where young boys who showed the qualities of outward form and inward drive defined in the many race manuals that appeared in the 1930s would be taken to be groomed for life as future leaders. Here, according to the education minister Bernhard Rust, they would learn 'to survive the contest of life'.[120]

The model new man was the party comrade and soldier-to-be whose virtues were martial and heroic, whose bearing was disciplined and tough, and whose instincts embraced self-sacrifice and racial ardour. Boys with glasses could not attend the special party schools. The SS was set up with these ideals in mind. Himmler, SS Reich Leader despite his spectacles, intended it to be the racial bearer of the nation, physically distinctive and utterly committed to the struggle for nation and blood.[121] Entry to the SS was restricted. A special race card was devised which was filled in for each applicant to assess his physical qualities, race and personality. There were nine physical categories listed, with bizarre bureaucratic thoroughness, from 'ideal' to 'deformed'. Unsurprisingly, only the first four guaranteed selection. Under each heading there were twenty-one physical characteristics used to define where on the physical spectrum the candidate was positioned – 'height', 'shape of head', 'colour of eyes' were listed alongside the more cryptic 'relative length of legs', 'eyelids', 'orbital creases'. A similar questionnaire was later used throughout occupied Europe in an SS-led screening of the population of the occupied territories to determine who might be recruited as honorary Aryans, and who should be exterminated.[122] For the SS, the screening was intended to produce men who were physically and mentally equipped to defend the racial utopia with a brutal indifference to the human cost and an utter disregard for any moral imperatives other than biological survival.

It was these 'new men' who helped to turn first Germany and then occupied Europe into a vast and lethal genetic laboratory. The unfortunate union of party racial politics and hereditarian science was cemented by the recruitment of doctors and scientists into the SS apparatus of racial cleansing and renewal. During the course of the 1930s the rhetoric of battle against the forces of racial contamination was ruthlessly applied to the people's community by a generation of scientific experts who enjoyed the political opportunity to turn scientific speculation into an iron reality. Some rejected the more radical versions of the racial utopia and were shunted aside. The cohort of experts that came to surround Hitler and Himmler were promoted because they shared the practical vision and moral certainties of the new racial community. This unholy alliance permitted not only compulsory sterilization and social exclusion, but eventually strategies of extermination.

The ideal of biological purity led logically to a policy of negative selection. The race professionals divided the population into those with race value and those deemed 'unworthy of life', who threatened to contaminate the whole. The metaphors adopted to describe the purification of the race were narrowly medical. The population became the 'body' (Volkskörper), which, like the human organism, was constantly menaced by diseases of every kind. This body required a cure, otherwise the result would be, as the Minister of the Interior put it in 1933 when he introduced the sterilization law, the death of the race (Volkstod).[123] The analogy with the human medical condition gave a spurious scientific legitimacy to the idea that all those deemed to be hostile to the body of the people (Volksfremde) had to be excised or purged in some way to secure the biological survival of the whole. Under these terms, which came to dominate the discussion of racial hygiene in the 1930s, the biological utopia became a community both exclusive and absolute, in which there was no room for those who constituted a demonstrable threat to the healthy organism.

Those perceived from their very physical presence to constitute a biological danger were not confined to victims whose hereditary condition qualified them for compulsory sterilization. Biological enemies came in many shapes, but they were all reduced in the perverted medical vocabulary of the day to 'bacilli' or 'cancerous growths' or bodily parasites. This imagery was applied with particular ferocity to the Jews. 'Our task here is surgical,' announced Joseph Goebbels, 'drastic incisions, or some day Europe will perish of the Jewish disease.'[124] Jews were regularly pilloried as the vehicles of bodily decomposition. Gerhard Wagner, head of the party's Race Office, told the party rally in 1935 that Judaism was 'disease incarnate'. Jews were blamed for other manifestations of degeneration – they were more criminal, more inclined to homosexuality, more pornographic, and more subject to hereditary feebleness of mind, myopia, diabetes and a host of other inherited conditions.[125] The idea of the Jew as disease-bearing parasite led to an ultimately fatal link between biological and chemical research in Germany. In 1935 the government ordered all chemical laboratories to report substances with high toxicity which would produce death when inhaled in small doses. At IG Farben's research centres experiments on highly toxic insecticides in the late 1930s produced not only the army's nerve gases 'tabun' and 'sarin', but a highly lethal exterminator made from hydrocyanic acid known as Zyklon B. Early forms of the product had been used during the First World War for delousing and for fumigating military installations and camps. Zyklon B was adopted to kill insect parasites at concentration and POW camps because of its exceptional toxicity. The gas was first used experimentally at Auschwitz in the autumn of 1941 on human victims, and from 1942 it was the chief agent for killing the Jews of Europe. 'Anti-Semitism,' Himmler is supposed to have said, 'is the same as delousing.'[126]

Jews were not the first victims of the idea that radical measures should be taken to cure the racial body, though they came to constitute by far the largest category of 'biological' victims. The threshold from sterilization to death was crossed in the course of 1939. In the spring Hitler authorized his personal physician, the SS doctor Karl Brandt, and the head of his personal chancellery, Philipp Bouhler, to organize the killing of handicapped children. This was a critical threshold; once crossed, it made possible the step-by-step extermination of all those deemed to be a biological menace – habitual criminals, sexual offenders, Jews, gypsy 'half-castes', the mentally ill. The decision for state murder derived from the logic of the biological politics of the regime and its hereditarian priorities. Following years of lobbying from the more extreme advocates of racial hygiene, who saw in the disabled a permanent biological blot, and from those who thought the welfare costs too high for those classified as having no race-value, Hitler finally approved the decision to allow what he and many others rationalized as a merciful release from suffering and a medical necessity for the 'racial body'.[127] The timing, however, owed much to the coming of war. Hitler had indicated years before that war would change the context of racial policy. Lives 'unworthy of life' diverted resources from the war effort and filled up hospital beds; above all, for Hitler war was a test of racial health and national virility, and thus a battle against internal degeneration as well as external enemies. Doctors and scientists became what Rudolf Ramm, a Berlin medical academic, described as 'biological soldiers'.[128]

This complex of professional pressure and dictatorial fantasy opened the floodgates of state-organized mass murder. Under the euphemistically titled Committee for the Scientific Registration of Severe Hereditary Ailments appointed on 18 August 1939, a programme to exterminate disabled children at twenty selected institutions was set in motion. In some cases they were given lethal injections or barbiturate overdoses; in others the children were denied medical aid and food until they perished. In the summer of 1939 Hitler extended the programme to include the adult disabled as well. Under a veil of complete secrecy, hand-picked officials and doctors set up offices in Berlin at 4 Tiergarten Strasse (the origin of the cover code T4 adopted by the project), where they ran what was called the Charitable Patient Transport Company. Its object was anything but charitable. In the winter of 1939 a room at Brandenburg prison was converted into a gasproof chamber with a small sealed window and a pipeway connected to a supply of carbon monoxide gas. Eight disabled men were led into the room and locked in. The gas was injected into the room and a crowd of medical experts and officials clustered round the small aperture to watch the death agonies of those inside.[129] The experiment was judged a complete success. Three more gas killing-centres were then established, at Grafenek, Hartheim and Sonnenstein, and late in 1940 two more at Bernburg and Hadamar. Around 80,000 physically and mentally handicapped Germans were murdered in these, the first of the gas chambers.

During the first years of the war the murder of biological victims expanded to include Jews, social deviants (known as 'asocials') and habitual criminals. In September 1940 the decision was taken to murder all Jewish mental patients. A group of 160 were first filmed as the subject of a propaganda film on race defilement, *The Scum of Humanity*, and then liquidated in the Brandenburg gas chamber. Early in 1941 all Jews, criminals and 'asocials' in hospitals were slated for extermination, and in April 1941 the concentration camps began to exterminate mentally-ill and criminal prisoners. This project, known as '14 f 13', was assisted by T4 officials at their gas-chamber sites. The procedures adopted mimicked medical practice. Victims were told that the chamber was for disinfection and cleansing; after they were ushered in, the process of gassing was supervised by medical personnel, one of whom administered the lethal dose of carbon monoxide. A doctor then officially pronounced the victims dead, and removed any organs needed for further medical research. Finally assistants, known quite literally as 'burners' (*Brenner*), took the bodies to a crematorium, after first removing any gold dental work, to be sent to Berlin by special courier and thence to the German Central Bank. This procedure was adopted in its entirety when T4 officials were invited to help set up extermination centres in the winter of 1941–2 at Chelmno, Sobibor, Maidanek, Treblinka and Belzec, where millions of victims – for the most part Jews and gypsies – were murdered to satisfy the imperatives of the regime's utopian biological vision. Genocide had other roots in political anti-Semitism and popular xenophobia, and in the circumstances of total war, but it also stemmed from the appropriation and perversion of hereditarian science in the name of a violent programme of racial cleansing. Genocide was consistent with the many other elements that made up the National Socialist biological utopia. The significance of scientific racism was reflected in the curiously expressive biological language (for example the use of the term 'physical extermination' instead of simply 'killing') which was used by race policy officials to describe the mass murder of the Jews.[130]

*

The Soviet Union generated a 'new man' of a quite different stamp. Rather than trying to draw out the innate, the primitive and the instinctive, Soviet society sought to restrain these impulses by constructing a social environment that would encourage a programme of personal development that was balanced, healthy and civilized. The ideological conviction that deviancy, sexual transgression, crime and poor health were socially induced meant that welfare and health policy should, in the words of a Soviet medical official, be primarily concerned with 'studying and constructing social life'.[131] There was a powerful imperative in Bolshevism to use science to mould the revolutionary future. The rhetoric of Soviet medical expertise echoed the German claim that the new community constituted a 'body' that was in need of therapy and healing, but the Soviet object was to identify and ameliorate the 'social illness' through the positive pursuit of prophylactic remedies, not to gouge out those elements through violent medical intervention.

The primacy of environment in explaining social development still left wide scope for discrimination. The Soviet community was also exclusive, but that exclusion was expressed in political rather than biological terms. The deliberate withholding of civil rights from all those whose previous social caste made it impossible for them to be classed as a 'toiler' defined the frontiers of the socialist utopia. Those who had been exploiters, or the children of former exploiters, were regarded as the victims of a social disease, which could not be allowed to contaminate the healthy new state. They were not allowed to hold official positions or attend higher education; children were forbidden from participation in communist youth groups. During the 1930s these rules were gradually relaxed, but all official forms required a statement of parents' occupation and status, and in practice the declaration of an unacceptable social heredity was penalized by prejudices deeply embedded in the system. During the 'Great Terror' of 1937–8 some 200,000 were imprisoned under the heading 'socially harmful'.[132] Thousands more were imprisoned as the spouse or relation of an enemy of the people, because it was expected that they too had been poisoned by the environment of deception and class enmity constructed by the primary victim. In 1947 all political prisoners were separated from the ordinary criminals in the camps and prisons because Stalin feared the effect that the climate of political resentment might have on criminals capable of recovering from their own 'social illness'. When political prisoners were released they were banned from most jobs and restricted geographically, away from the main centres of population. Only after Stalin's death were these restrictions eased, but by this time most of the victims of exclusion were old men and women.[133]

Social exclusion did not mean that there was no hope of redemption. In Germany Jews could not become 'Aryans', any more than a crippled child could learn to walk; their fate was sealed. But in the Soviet Union the whole object of social and welfare policy was to create the conditions that would eradicate crime and social deviancy and enhance health and social well-being. This commitment appeared in the 1920s to be as utopian as any of the biological paradises dreamt up in Germany. Under Stalin the widely publicized 'backwardness' of Soviet society was to be overcome by formal programmes of training, education and state-sponsored 'cultured behaviour'. The idea of influencing behaviour rather than breeding it was central to Soviet social policy. Peasants and workers were taught that their existences had been 'dark' before communism, and elaborate rituals of public shaming were introduced to teach new lessons. In one village in spring 1934 the arrival of a communist journalist with the 'cultural sled' had immediate results. He carried razors to shave off traditional peasant beards. He brought a magic lantern and blank glass plates; on these he drew cartoons of local villagers caught in the uncultured acts of drunkenness and wife-beating. At night in the village school he gave a show to bring home the message of 'culturedness', where the wife-beater was ridiculed and berated by his fellows.[134] Everywhere in the USSR in the 1930s officials and party members reminded people not to spit, not to remove their shoes and socks in public, not to lie across train seats, and not to urinate in the street. The emphasis on social hygiene was widely accepted as a central part of constructing the socialist utopia. 'Cleaning your teeth,' explained a *Komsomol* pamphlet, 'is a revolutionary act.'[135]

Changing attitudes to behaviour and social environment under Stalin went hand-in-hand with a changing attitude towards the family. Here the two dictatorships were at one. Unlike family policy in the 1920s, which assumed the gradual breakdown of the conventional family unit as the state supplied education and social support for the young, and men and women sought more collectivist modes of daily life, social policy under Stalin reinstated the family as the central social unit, and proper parental care as the model environment for the new Soviet generation. The rediscovery of the family as the instrument for 'moulding the children' was the inspiration of Anton Makarenko, who took over the camps and homes for orphans and street children in the 1920s. Strict military-style discipline, combined with a strongly co-operative ethic, transformed the children's lives, and Makarenko became a Stalin favourite. His posthumous *A Book for Parents*, published in 1940, instructed them to instil in their charges the values of heroic socialist labour, collectivism and faith in the party.[136]

Family policy was driven by two primary motives: to expand the birth rate and to provide a more stable social context in a period of rapid social change. Mothers were presented as heroic socialist models in their own right and motherhood was defined as a socialist duty. In 1944 medals were introduced for women who had answered the call: Motherhood medal, Second Class for five children, First Class for six; medals of Motherhood Glory in three classes for seven, eight or nine offspring; for ten or more, mothers were justly nominated Heroine Mother of the Soviet Union, and an average of more than 5,000 a year won this highest accolade, and a diploma from the Soviet President himself.[137] The ideal family was defined in socialist-realist terms as large, harmonious and hardworking. Husband and wife were supposed to give each other companionship and support. Socialist love was now contrasted with sexual licence: 'so called free love and loose sexual life,' preached *Pravda* in 1936, 'are altogether bourgeois'.[138] The greater sexual liberation evident in the 1920s was supposed to give way to conjugal responsibility and the sublimated urge to construct socialism. The party hero of Leonid Leonov's 1930 novel *Sot*, having given up cigarettes, alcohol and sex, sees his married life as 'merely a fuel to treble his strength' for the following day's political labours.[139]

In 1934 old-fashioned marriage was rehabilitated. Permission was granted to local authorities to recommence the production of wedding rings, banned since the 1920s. The ZAGS offices for registering marriages, births and deaths, set up in 1919, had replaced church ceremonies after the revolution. They were unappealing places, one bride recalled, the walls covered with lurid posters on alcoholism and venereal disease, offering the most peremptory of ceremonies for three roubles. These registries were brightened up and a longer and more solemn ceremony introduced.[140] At the same time the regime tightened up divorce. During the years after the revolution divorce was easy and thousands of men abandoned wives and family, leaving the state to support them. In 1936 a decree on divorce raised the cost to 50 roubles for the first, 150 for the second and 300 roubles after that, while absentee fathers were to be tracked down and forced to pay up to half their income to support children they had abandoned. Fathers who absconded without payment faced the risk that they would be caught by the police and fined or imprisoned.[141] For the many thousands of women coping with single parenthood and work, the state introduced extensive nursery provision. By 1940 there were places for 2 million infants from birth to age seven, and a further 4 million places for the children of seasonal workers.[142]

Tough measures were introduced for all those who failed to conform to the ideal of the happy, companionable, child-rich household. The Soviet authorities, like the German, regarded homosexuality as a challenge to their natalist priorities and criminalized it in 1934. Abortion, which had been legalized in November 1920, was outlawed in 1936. Though it was never made a capital offence, as it was in Germany in 1943, abortionists could expect between one and three years in prison, while the woman seeking termination was subject to a fine of up to 300 roubles. The change in policy on abortion was not as abrupt as it appeared. The decree legalizing it in 1920 described abortion as an evil made necessary by prevailing economic conditions. The Women's Division of the Party assumed in the 1920s that abortion would disappear as the economy prospered. It had little to do with emancipating Soviet women. The 1936 decision was justified by the regime on the grounds that abortion was both dangerous to female health and a deliberate act of selfishness in limiting the growth of the coming generation of Soviet 'new men'. Women, so it was argued, had no individual right to choose whether they would bear children for the Soviet Motherland or not; the 'right' they enjoyed was to expect society to provide a supportive environment for family life and motherhood.

257

One concession was made to genetic science: those with hereditary illnesses could apply for abortions.[143]

The model new Soviet man of the 1930s was a hero of socialist construction, animated not by the crude impulses of nature but by the rational desire to master and control those urges, to become 'a conscious lord over himself'.[144] This could be achieved by deliberate programmes of training and self-improvement to shape and develop a disciplined, cultured and technically proficient individual. Soviet psychologists rejected the idea that character was innate, for this could encourage the belief that there were naturally inferior classes or races; in 1934 they were forced by the regime to reject Freudian ideas of the unconscious as decadent bourgeois science, since it suggested that man was a mere plaything of his inner mind. Man, it was claimed, could shape his own personality through conscious self-discipline and proper schooling.[145] In May 1935 Stalin chose the occasion of a speech to graduates passing out from the army academies to signal that the nurture of properly trained individuals, dedicated to the communist cause, fearless in the face of any difficulty, was the 'main thing'. A few months later he called again for 'new people', masters of technique and heroes of labour, to sustain the communist utopia.[146]

On the night of 31 August 1935, at the Nikanor-East section of the Central Irmino coal mine in the Ukrainian Donbass coalfield, a young hewer named Aleksei Stakhanov was given the chance to show just what Soviet new man was capable of. His mine supervisor invited him to try a record-breaking shift. The norm was 6.5 tonnes per worker, per shift. In just five-and-three-quarter hours Stakhanov hewed 102 tonnes. He emerged in the early hours of the morning to be greeted by a hastily convened extraordinary party meeting, where his new world record was hailed as a political example to the world of Soviet new man in action.[147] Though he was helped by two labourers putting in the pit-props as he drilled coal, and by the generous assistance of his supervisor, it was Stakhanov who became within days a national hero. Other miners overtook his record within a week – 119 tonnes, then 125 tonnes – but Stakhanov was fortunate to have been first. The Commissar for Heavy Industry, Sergo Ordzhonikidze, read a report on his world record and told *Pravda* to use the miner as an example of one of the 'new people', and on 8 September the paper announced the birth of the 'Stakhanovite movement' for exceptional achievement at work.[148] Stakhanov was rewarded with a privileged apartment, a month's wages, and a pass for the local cinema.

Stakhanovites proliferated in weeks across the whole of Soviet industry and agriculture. There had been shock-worker brigades from the early days of the Five-Year Plans, whose task was to push industrialization forward by extravagant collective efforts, but the emphasis in the early 1930s was on the little man, on anonymous, ordinary workers pushing forward the frontier of Soviet modernization. From 1931–2, the last years of the First Plan, there was pressure from the authorities to change the emphasis from little man to 'hero of labour'. The use of the term hero became widespread, and was applied not only to workers but to successful athletes, aviators and explorers. In 1934 Soviet writers were told to develop the theme of 'heroization'.[149] Stakhanov possessed many of the attributes of the ideal 'hero', whose intense but joyful gaze stared out from posters and propaganda pamphlets in the mid-1930s. He was young, with a long, fine-featured face and a winning smile. He was a family man. Brought up in a village near Orel, he was typical of millions of young Russians who left for the industrial centres in the 1930s; typical, too, was the brief period of specialist training. Above all, Stakhanov had been a dauntless, resolute, uninhibited over-achiever. The Soviet obsession in the 1930s with greater scale – bigger buildings, giant factories, production records, stratospheric flight, journeys of remarkable length and endurance – was matched by a new generation of 'big' heroes, drawn from the ordinary people but rendered extraordinary by their deeds.[150]

The 'new man' could also be a 'new woman'. In 1928 there were 3 million women workers, in 1940 some 13 million. Though the regime came to emphasize family values and child-rearing in the 1930s, women of all ages worked, and more in the child-bearing age category of twenty to twenty-nine than in any other. The emancipation of women was itself part of the wider drive against the old class-based society, which Stalin considered over by 1936. In 1937 *Pravda* described Soviet woman as 'new woman' and quoted Stalin's remark that 'such women would never have existed and could not have existed before'.[151] There were women hero-workers in the Stakhanovite movement, including one Moscow farmworker who achieved an enviable world record for harvesting cabbages. In general there was a smaller proportion of female Stakhanovites, but in 1936 a quarter of all female trade unionists were classified as norm-breaking workers.[152] Most women workers worked in less-skilled sectors such as textiles or agriculture, where opportunities were fewer, but in 1939 one-third of all engineers were women, and a remarkable 79 per cent of doctors.[153] Though women were restricted in their access to the highest jobs and had to cope with the twin pressures of running a household and a job, they were regarded as an integral element in the construction of the new community. Stalin's rhetorical claim in 1938 that 'Woman in our country has become a great might', if it still disguised the social reality of discrimination, it nonetheless exposed a priority very different from that of the Third Reich.[154]

Nothing quite encapsulates the contrasting image of the new humanity in the two dictatorships more completely than two famous statues designed to adorn the German and Soviet pavilions at the Paris World Fair of 1937. In 1936 the expressionist Russian artist Vera Mukhina was invited to create a gigantic sculpture to stand atop the Soviet display. The result was *Rabochii i Kolkhoznitsa* (*Worker and Collective farm woman*). Cast in stainless steel, the statue was a representation of the new man and the new woman. Oversize, beautifully proportioned, youthful, the two figures press forward, arms aloft, clothed in workwear, the man with a hammer, the woman with a sickle. They gaze steadfastly in front of them, their faces both intense and ardent.[155] It is a statue of communist worker-heroes on the march. By contrast, the monumental statues in Hitler's Germany were male, soldierly and obtrusively physical. One of the best known was Joseph Thorak's *Kamaradschaft* (*Comradeship*), which was chosen to stand outside the German pavilion, directly opposite the Soviet one, and later adorned the new Munich Museum of German Art, opened in 1937. Two enormous naked male figures, models of so-called 'Aryan' man with bulging muscles and chiselled faces, stand defiantly side-by-side, one clasping the hand of the other in expression of a unique comradely bond between race brothers and soldier-companions. Their countenances are grim, unrelenting and proud; here is no forward movement, only implacable defence.[156] There is no female companionship, but instead a powerful homoeroticism. It is a statue of racial warriors.

Utopias do not and cannot exist. They are by their nature ideal but unattainable, just as Thomas More's *Utopia* was placed deliberately beyond the grasp of real men. Both the Soviet and German experiments in social reconstruction could as easily be defined as dystopias – producing not the ideal, frictionless, engineered community, but a nightmare of violence, discrimination, persecution and misrepresentation.

The gap between utopian fantasy and social reality was always self-evident. The Soviet city was a confusion of planning projects and improvised construction; during the 1930s and 1940s the new urban workforce was compelled to live in tiny, cramped apartments. Inhabitants in Moscow had an average four square metres each in 1940, a decline of almost 30 per cent since 1930.[157] Many lived in communal barracks in the new cities, or huts of mud and sticks. Living standards declined or stagnated. The Soviet 'new man' existed alongside growing violence and criminality – 'hooliganism' in Soviet language – and millions experienced spells in camps and labour colonies for the petty crimes that the socialist environment was supposed to eradicate. In Hitler's Germany the people's community defined 'the people' in narrowly prescriptive terms: it could not include those deemed to be biologically contaminated, criminal or socially deviant; Jews, gypsies, Slavs were later victimized and murdered in their millions in wartime. Women were breeders, not leaders. The party was stridently masculine and coercive, epitomized by the self-conscious brutality of the SS. The National Socialist 'new man' ended up during the war committing atrocious crimes across occupied Europe.

Under these circumstances the ideal community might be regarded as little more than a deliberate fiction constructed in order to clothe the naked reality of oppression and social dislocation. Yet this argument, for all its appeal, misses an important point: both dictators were committed to the idealized communities they hoped to build, and won widespread, even enthusiastic, support among their populations for constructing them. Both systems were predicated on the myth of perfectibility. They promised to eliminate the discordances of the past and to substitute a redemptive, utopian future. In the late 1930s in the Soviet Union the idea of 'no conflict at all' (*beskonfliktnost*) was added to the language of social construction.[158] Stalin famously defined the new age in November 1935, when he told an audience of worker-heroes: 'Life has improved, comrades. Life has become more joyous.'[159] Hitler, from at least 1935 onwards, talked as though the conflicts of the old class society had been replaced by a new social harmony in which present and future would merge into an ideal unity: 'Our revolution is a new stage . . . which will end by abolishing history.'[160]

In both systems the future ideal was never relegated to the status of mythology. Socialist construction meant remaking the social structure, eliminating the vestiges of the old order by deporting kulaks, blowing up churches, or imposing 'culturedness'. The German new order imprisoned, mutilated or murdered millions in the name of biological salvation, covered the German countryside with fast motorways, educated a young elite in party schools, and tried to replace the conventional structures of social identity with a party-led, racially determined technocracy. In both cases, there existed widespread popular enthusiasm for the new age that extended beyond the propaganda posters and docile newsreels. 'We were born to make fairy tales come true', ran the words of one popular Soviet song of the 1930s.[161] The young American socialist Seema Allan recorded dozens of encounters in the Soviet Union in the 1930s with people consumed with a simple idealism. One woman, struggling to bring up her children and manage the piggery on a collective farm, told her: 'I understand everything our country needs. I work with my whole soul!' She wanted Allan to tell the world outside that 'we are going from the dark into the light'.[162] No observer of German society after 1933 could fail to be struck by the widespread evidence of popular and enthusiastic longing for a new beginning and a new age.[163]

The pursuit of utopia can be explained in a number of ways. Both movements, Stalinist and National Socialist, were self-consciously revolutionary in nature. The juxtaposition of a golden future with a corrupt and decadent past was exploited to instil and sustain popular enthusiasm and identification with the regime. Stalin's object was not only to eradicate the bourgeois age but those vestiges of bourgeois or petit-bourgeois mentality that he detected in the culture, science and social policy of the previous decade. The communist vision of the 1930s was one of purification. This vision bore within it more menacing implications of social cleansing based on estimates of social or political worth; purging was justified by the regime in order to safeguard the revolutionary future. National Socialism also carried in its social idealism the notion of purification 'extended,' in Hitler's words, 'to nearly all fields'.[164] Revolutionary purity here also meant eradicating the decadence of the republican society of the 1920s; German culture, science and society were 'purged' in this case in the name of a racial idealism that justified the discrimination and violence that purification required. Both dictatorships sought their legitimacy in ends rather than means.

The two systems also shared a common commitment to the scientific reconstruction of society. In the Soviet Union the scientific character of the social experiment in the 1930s was its central intellectual foundation. Pure utopian social experiment was rejected in favour of a social ideal rooted in the scientific development of a socialist environment. The emphasis on Lamarck, the rejection of Freudian psychology in favour of the idea of the mutable personality, and the public support for Pavlov's experimental work on induced behaviour, all indicated the concern of the regime to root socialist construction in modern science. The obsession with planning derived from the same vision of rational social development.[165] The National Socialist experiment also had a modern, scientific underpinning, in the preoccupation of German sociologists, biologists and welfare experts with the pure social body, and the concern of psychologists with ideas of innate racial character. The creation of a pure race through eugenic policy and coercive welfare policies became a primary feature of the dictatorship; the concern with 'community' over society grew out of contemporary sociological idealism; the scientific preference for heredity over environment encouraged educational and welfare priorities to maximize the development of new elites with a racially defined personality.[166]

The exploitation of scientific discourse as a way of legitimizing the pursuit of the ideal future defines both dictatorships as 'modern'. The elements of social conservatism in both – the attitude to the family and motherhood, the persecution of homosexuality and abortion, the hostility to modernist architecture, the substitution of technocratic communities for class divisions – were justified not in terms of a return to the past, but in terms of the current demographic, sociological and geographical requirements of the new orders. There were, nonetheless, essential differences between the two systems. The Soviet utopia pursued under Stalin was a sociological utopia, whose object was to create a progressive society based around the satisfaction of human needs. The new buildings that sprang up in the bleak new industrial cities were palaces of labour, workers' clubs, state nurseries and technical colleges. The heroes of the new Soviet pantheon were modest workers and farmers; the villains were social reprobates subverting social progress.

The German utopia pursued under Hitler was a biological utopia, committed to the development of a pure racial body capable of reproduction on narrowly defined demographic lines. Individual worth and well-being were measured in terms of biological usefulness and race-value, above all the willingness to accept the sacrifice of the self for the survival of the species. The monuments of the German new order were war memorials, temples to party martyrs, 'Soldier-Houses', stadia for games and military tattoos. The heroes of the new Germany were political street-fighters and soldiers who had already died for the cause, or were willing to die in the future.[167] It is entirely fitting that the effort to construct such a utopia foundered on failure in war in 1945, for this was the logic of the vulgar Darwinism that underpinned the enterprise – victory or defeat in the struggle for existence. The Soviet experiment survived for longer and achieved more. By the time of Stalin's death the social structure and social provision had altered in substance from the 1920s, at vast social expense and with high levels of coercion and discrimination. After Stalin's death, the party reversed much. Abortion was legalized in 1955; modernist architecture replaced the revolutionary baroque; millions imprisoned as social or political deviants were released. But the ambition to create a communist community, exclusive and socially demanding, its members moulded by the 'concrete conditions' of the communist world, lived on until its final collapse in 1989.[168]

7

The Moral Universe of Dictatorship

'Our ethics are an instrument for destroying the old society of exploiters; a struggle for the consolidation and the realization of Communism is the basis of Communist ethics.'

V. Lenin, *Collected Works*, XXVI[1]

'The primary thing is not the formal law but the race; law and the life of the race are not to be separated from each other.'

Hermann Göring, August 1934[2]

There is one question that is seldom asked of the two dictatorships yet is fundamental to understanding how they could behave as they did towards the populations under their power: why did they think they were right? In neither case did those who ran the two regimes regard as criminal or immoral the vicious persecution unleashed against enemies, both real and imagined. It is unlikely that Stalin and Hitler spent sleepless nights tortured by the thought of the millions victimized at their behest. In neither case did the dictators display any outward doubts about the justice of their particular cause. The lack of conscience was not merely a consequence of exceptional power unscrupulously exercised, the expression of might as right. In each dictatorship a unique moral universe was constructed in order to justify and explain what appear otherwise to be the most sordid and arbitrary of acts.

Historians have been wary of trying to reconstruct the moral outlook of the dictatorships because their ethical claims are seldom taken to be more than rhetorical or demagogic devices to sweeten the sour taste of state repression. Yet the failure to take the ethical discourses of both dictatorships seriously distorts historical reality and undermines any attempt to understand the operation of the dictatorships on their own terms. Both regimes were driven by powerful moral imperatives that challenged and transcended the norms derived from the heritage of Roman antiquity and Christianity. They did not simply rely on the existence of a tough coercive power to enforce their values, but directly contested other moral claims that compromised their own claim to legitimacy and moral worth. The most evident examples of this moral contest can be found in their attitudes to organized religion and the law. Both institutions were rooted in moral traditions that long pre-dated dictatorship; both institutions offered a moral sphere, or a moral reference point, for those who wanted to stand outside the predatory ideology of the systems. The moral plane of dictatorship was not an irrelevance, but a battleground between differing interpretations of justice and moral certainty.

Both systems shared the conviction that moral norms are not universal or natural or the product of divine revelation. The moral universe of both dictatorships was founded not upon absolute moral values, but on relative values derived from particular historical circumstances. The only absolute reality the two systems acknowledged was nature herself. In the Soviet Union the whole system of Marxist-Leninist thought was predicated on the idea of 'dialectical materialism', a term that held an exceptional authority throughout the Stalin years. It was officially defined by Stalin himself in an essay on *Dialectical and Historical Materialism* that he published in 1938. Its philosophical essence was simple, even simplistic: everything in nature is part of an objective material world that is both completely integrated and constantly subject to change. The changes occur 'dialectically', a term first used in the modern age by the very un-Marxist nineteenth-century German philosopher Georg Hegel, to describe the dynamic contradictions that propel all phenomena from lower to higher forms of existence. Marxists asserted that dialectical materialism could be used to describe not only the development of the natural world but also the evolution of history as an unfolding succession of economic systems, each with its own social contradictions generated by class conflict. Stalin took from Marxism the idea that these changes could be defined in terms of observable, scientific laws of history, just as there were scientific laws governing the behaviour of the natural world. These laws, Stalin wrote in 1952, are 'the reflection of objective processes which take place independently of the will of man'.[3] The coupling of natural science and social history, first formulated by Lenin, made the emergence of communism not simply historical accident but historical destiny, a product of the essential nature of things.[4]

The laws of development gave the revolution an irresistible air of legitimacy. Communism was understood to be the most progressive and highly developed stage of history, and hence, by definition, ethically superior to all other forms of society. Soviet morality, according to Lenin, was determined by the historical struggle of the proletariat. What was moral was anything that served 'the interests of the class struggle'; what was immoral was anything that hindered the historic march to communism.[5] This formulation gave unlimited opportunity for the communist party, as the vanguard of the revolutionary struggle, to determine what forms of action and thought were most appropriate for the current stage of historical development. First Lenin, and then Stalin, subverted the central thesis in Marx that the superstructure of politics, culture, thought, etc. was determined entirely by the nature of the economic system. Stalin's most original contribution to Marxist philosophy was to insist that the construction of communism relied not only on concrete material conditions, but also on the subjective role of the party in 'organizing, mobilizing and transforming' society. These party functions involved acts of revolutionary will that were intended to reflect the underlying historical reality, and were therefore not merely capricious; but it was also possible on these terms to present any crime committed in the name of the state as no more than a timely initiative in the service of revolution.[6]

Hitler used nature and history differently. Where Marxists saw class struggle as the instrument of historical transformation, Hitler saw the conflict of races. He derived his historical vision from a crude Darwinism, almost certainly from the work of Ernst Haeckel, who interpreted Darwin for a German audience in the 1860s by stressing the importance of natural selection for human populations as for animal. The principal feature of nature for Hitler was not Stalin's interdependence of natural phenomena, but its exact opposite: 'the inner segregation of the species of all living creatures'. In nature species kept themselves biologically exclusive thanks, Hitler believed, to an overriding instinct for self-preservation. 'Racial purity the highest law', he wrote in his synopsis for an unwritten 'Monumental History of Mankind', drafted in the early 1920s.[7] The natural contest for food and territory described by biologists altered the balance of the species through time in favour of the more powerful. 'Nature is quite unbending,' Hitler continued, 'which means: Victory of the stronger.'[8]

Hitler applied the laws of nature indiscriminately to human history. Humanity was divided into races rather than species, but here, too, nature had forsworn 'the blending of a higher with a lower race'. When this happened the consequence was regressive breeding, a form of de-evolution. The predominant historical reality was always 'the nation's struggle for existence' against other races and the threat of biological contamination, a threat he associated in particular with the Jews.[9] History contained no eternal truths, but was conditioned by the perennial contest of higher peoples (what Hitler called 'culture-forming' or 'culture-bearing' races) against those weaker or more degenerate than themselves. The iron logic of history impelled those nations capable of achieving a healthy population and a superior culture to mimic the animal kingdom, by seizing territory and food. The nation or race was justified not by any external or absolute moral standards, which the philosophers of National Socialism unanimously rejected, but by the extent to which it could defend its own historical right to exist. Germany faced these historical imperatives like every other nation: 'self-preservation and continuance are the great urges underlying all action,' wrote Hitler in 1928.[10] But the difference was that the German, or 'Aryan' people, who had climbed the 'endless ladder of human progress', represented the pinnacle of historical achievement, just as communism for socialists represented the highest form of human evolution. Hitler's Germany faced an inescapable destiny, legitimized by the logic of nature and history. Hitler, too, believed that only by supreme acts of will would the Aryan people surmount the obstacles around them and complete their historic mission.[11]

In both cases dictatorship was justified not by subjective factors (the ambition of powerful men, for example) but by the objective laws of nature and history. The result was a moral displacement that relieved the regimes and their agents of direct responsibility for their actions:

it could be, and was, argued that biological or historical necessity, not human caprice, produced the new moral order and governed human behaviour. These historical forces were the source of what Stalin called 'authentic knowledge' and 'objective truth', or Hitler described as 'Nature's stern and rigid laws'.[12] Both men rejected the idea that their systems were historical accidents; they were 'right' for their time. Given the exceptional power exercised by both dictators, these personal world views came to supply much of the moral underpinning for both systems. Their overwhelming sense of historical certainty promoted the many abuses of dictatorship; but it also necessitated a contest for the moral field already occupied by the absolute ethics of organized religion and conventional jurisprudence.

Late in 1930, at a wayside shrine to the Virgin Mary in the western Ukraine, there occurred a miracle: the cast-iron statue was seen to be shedding tears of blood. Thousands of pilgrims streamed from the neighbouring villages in the autumn cold. Some died by the roadside. Eventually the local communist authorities put a fence round the shrine and posted guards, but the fence was pushed aside and the militiamen chased off. Next, a committee of scientists was sent to study the statue so that the miracle could be exposed as mere superstition and the multitude camped out in the surrounding fields might disperse. The experts discovered that the head was so corroded that rust-filled rain-water seeped through the face, creating the illusion of bloody tears. They arrived together at the site, armed with bottles of green, blue and yellow water. From the top of a ladder they poured the liquids into the head and the Madonna began to weep tears of many colours. The crowd was at first silent in the face of this new miracle, but when one of the scientists tried to explain that this was science not God, the peasant pilgrims assaulted them and beat two to death. A few days later troops arrived to protect a second scientific delegation. The crowd attacked at once and in the fight the statue was knocked over and shattered. A local simpleton was killed in the crush, and his funeral became the occasion for a vast procession headed by priests and monks carrying censers and sacred banners. This tested communist patience too much; the militia cleared the procession at bayonet point, so ran the reports, and hundreds were killed.[13]

The conflict between the two idea-systems was seldom as direct or bloody as this, but the arguments over miracles provided a very public airing of the contest between the scientific materialism of the new communist state and the enduring faith of much of the Soviet Union's population. Christianity was fundamentally incompatible with Communism. Nevertheless, the relationship between the revolutionary movement and religion was an ambiguous one. Before the First World War there were prominent socialists who argued that the original Christianity was socialist in nature, and that Jesus should properly be regarded as the first proletarian revolutionary.[14] Millennial movements proliferated in the last years of the monarchy, nourishing and nourished by the apocalyptic revolutionary struggle. Clergymen played a part in criticizing the social excesses of the old order and promising a redemptive political future.[15] Only the triumph of Bolshevism in November 1917 made it clear that the relationship would be confrontational. Lenin was implacably opposed to all religious sentiment, as was Marx. 'Any religious idea,' he wrote to Maxim Gorky in 1913, '. . . is the most dangerous foulness, the most shameful "infection".' Worship he dismissed as 'ideological necrophilia'. God was useful only as a means to *lull to sleep* the class struggle'.[16]

The new communist regime did not take the threat from Christianity very seriously. They interpreted religion in class terms; the churches were instruments of the old ruling order used to peddle illusions about the future. It was assumed that with the smashing of the old system religious belief would wither away. Churchmen were class enemies, but they were not regarded as rivals for the hearts and minds of the masses, which history would now make socialist. The terms of the battle were understood much more clearly by Russian Christians (and by the handful of messianic Bolsheviks led by Anatoly Lunacharsky and Nikolai Berdiaev). The *Sobor* (council) of the Russian Orthodox Church announced in November 1917 that Bolshevism was 'descended of the anti-Christ', and proceeded to anathematize the movement a few weeks later.[17] Clergy were reminded that Christianity was a 'singular truth' above the ebb and flow of politics. A letter published a few years later from a group of imprisoned bishops reiterated the Church's belief 'that the principles of Morality, of Justice and the Law are absolute and unchangeable', while those of communism were conditional and ephemeral.[18] The Church saw itself locked in a struggle long awaited between God and Satan for nothing less than the soul of Russia.[19]

The communist regime treated the Church as a political institution rather than as a set of beliefs. On 28 January 1918 the Russian Orthodox Church was formally separated from the state; religious belief was permitted as long as it did not threaten public order or trespass on political soil. Religious property was liquidated, and a twenty-year programme of church closures begun. Religion was banned from schools. The state and the party were officially atheist, though practising Christians could be found serving both. Religious faith, rather than the institutions of church life, was regarded as simple superstition destined to be swept quickly away by the revelations of modern science. Young revolutionaries revelled in a mischievous blasphemy. At Christmas *Komsomol* brigades toured the streets singing irreverent carols, and carrying red Christmas trees. In Baku a group of schoolchildren were encouraged to test the truth of the Bible when they were taken to a park and told to pray for their lunch. When nothing appeared they were told to call on Lenin, and within minutes trucks laden with bread, cheeses and fruit drove into the park: 'You see now,' they were told, 'it is not God who gives bread but Lenin.'[20]

The ridiculing of religion proved counter-productive. Gradually the regime came to realize that religious faith was a powerful moral reality that the years of revolution and civil war had done little to dispel. In 1921 the regime shifted from a policy of political repression to a battle of ideas. Lenin called for the party to adopt a programme of 'militant atheism' and 'militant materialism'.[21] Religion was to be defeated by the power of scientific explanation, which represented a 'single truth'. In June 1923 the party set up the League of the Godless led by Emilian Yaroslavsky, an Old Bolshevik who had briefly preceded Stalin as secretary to the Central Committee of the party and was the most openly atheist of the regime's new leaders. By 1929 the League had 9,000 cells of atheist agitators and 465,000 members.[22] A year later, in 1924, a Society of Militant Materialists was founded. The party launched a nationwide programme of atheist propaganda and scientific demonstrations. The tombs of fifty-eight saints were opened up to show local populations that they contained simply bones and dust (though St Sergius of Radonezh was said to have been found perfectly preserved, to the rapturous joy of the onlookers and the consternation of the monastery's communist custodian, who was subsequently beaten up by the crowd).[23] In 1922 the atheist weekly *Bezbozhnik* (*The Godless*) was first published, and soon had a circulation of hundreds of thousands; a monthly journal *Bezbozhnik ustanka* (*The Godless in the workplace*) was targeted at the proletariat; the magazine *Ateist*, launched in 1925, carried more sophisticated scientific articles to challenge the moral and metaphysical claims of the Church intelligentsia.

For most of the 1920s the two sides were locked in debate, often literally so. Face-to-face confrontations between atheists and churchmen were organized in Soviet universities and institutes, which gave religion a public platform it could scarcely have expected. The scriptures were subjected to a scurrilous deconstruction in the 1922 edition of a *Bible for Believers and Unbelievers*. Petr Pavelkine's pamphlet 'Is There a God?' contested the very foundations of belief. Anti-religious agitators were encouraged to raise awkward questions at meetings: 'is resurrection from the dead possible?'[24] The question of immortality was even subjected to scientific experiment. In the hope of demonstrating that science rather than religion could offer perpetual life, some Soviet biologists began to seek ways of halting the ageing process and 'revitalizing' human organs. Work at the Department of Living Matter in the Institute of Experimental Medicine focused on isolating the biochemical elements that would prevent decomposition. One of the prominent 'God-Builders', Alexander Bogdanov, died in 1928 during a blood transfusion undertaken to try to secure his physical immortality.[25]

At the same time the Soviet regime looked for ways to force the churches to accept the existence of the new order and to acknowledge their political subordination to it. In 1922 the government found an issue to test the balance of power between the two systems, which raised the stakes between the two sides dramatically and made a violent outcome almost unavoidable. The churches were ordered to hand over all their sacred treasures, including the chalices and vestments used for the holy sacrament. The ostensible purpose was to sell the goods to raise money for Soviet famine victims, but the issue was more evidently about the relationship between Church and state. Patriarch Tikhon reluctantly ordered compliance, save for the sacramental objects. The state then seized the objects by force. In the course of the expropriation over 8,000 clergy were killed and there were more than 1,400 violent clashes with angry parishioners. The regime staged fifty-five trials of recalcitrant clergy from all denominations, and executed a number of prominent churchmen, including Metropolitan Benjamin of Leningrad, a popular and modest churchman, noted for his loyalty to the poorest of his congregation.[26] The Patriarch himself was briefly imprisoned by the secret police for counter-revolutionary activity, but he emerged from prison after he agreed to sign a confession to be published in the government newspaper *Isvestiia*: 'I declare hereby to the Soviet authorities that henceforth I am no more an enemy to the Soviet government.'[27]

While Tikhon was in prison a group of radical clergy, who wanted a church more in step with the modern age, occupied the Patriarchal offices and declared a schism from Orthodoxy. They founded, with official government approval, the Renovationist or 'Living' Church, declared that Christianity was, after all, compatible with the moral aims of socialism ('every honourable Christian should . . . use all means to realize in life the grand principles of the October Revolution'), and introduced a modernized liturgy and democratic procedures.[28] Though by 1925 the Living Church had 12,593 parishes and 192 bishops, its born-again Christianity had little appeal to the faithful, and the government withdrew its support. Two years later, in 1927, Metropolitan Sergei Stragorodsky, who was the most senior prelate following Tikhon's death in 1925, was recognized as the acting head of the Russian Orthodox Church after he, too, had undergone the rigours of imprisonment and confession. On 29 July 1927 the Metropolitan issued a public declaration that the Church recognized the Soviet Union as its 'civil fatherland' whose 'joys and successes are our joys and successes'.[29] Hundreds of clergy refused to render unto Caesar that which was Caesar's; by 1930 an estimated one-fifth of all those imprisoned in the far-northern Solovki camp complex were clerical victims of religious persecution.

By the late 1920s religion had abdicated any political contest with communism, but the religiosity of much of the Soviet population was widely evident. It was said that Stalin was kept informed of the 'miracle' of the weeping Virgin and the outpouring of religious enthusiasm that it provoked. At the Sixteenth Party Congress in 1930 he announced ominously that religion was 'a brake on building socialism', but the Central Committee had already decided the previous year that the failure to eradicate religion by argument required a complete overhaul of the anti-religious campaign.[30] Under Stalin the cultural and institutional life of all the Soviet Union's religions was ruthlessly emasculated and thousands of clerics murdered or exiled. From 1929 onwards the ideological war against religion was intensified using crude inspirational slogans: 'beat religion on the head every day of your life'.[31] Religion was regarded as a principal obstacle to the modernization of Soviet society and the construction of a communist economy, and religious communities were treated as if they were political supporters of a vestigial capitalism.

The physical assault on religion meant the closure or confiscation of churches, chapels, mosques, synagogues and monasteries. Beginning in 1928 with the closure of a modest 532 religious houses, by 1940 the overwhelming majority had been dynamited, closed down or taken over by the civil authorities for a wide variety of other purposes. The famous Strastnoi monastery in the centre of Moscow was converted into the national anti-religious museum, where posters and artefacts drove home the message that all religion stemmed from an ancient fount of primitive superstition; smaller exhibitions of godlessness – Museums of Scientific Atheism – proliferated across the Soviet Union.[32] The closures hit every denomination. The Russian Orthodox Church had 46,457 churches and 1,028 monasteries at the time of the revolution; by 1939 estimates vary from 100 to fewer than 1,000 still operating.[33] In Moscow there were 600 religious communities of all kinds in 1917, but by 1939 only 20 survived. Not even the pro-communist 'Living Church' was spared. In Leningrad, where it had been most successful in winning adherents from traditional Orthodoxy, there was just one church still functioning in 1940. The number of officiating clergy also declined; from 290 Orthodox and 400 Renovationist bishops consecrated in the 1920s and 1930s, only 10 of each branch still held office in 1941. Some had died in prison camps, others had been executed for counter-revolution, unknown numbers were in hiding. The population of parish priests fell from an estimated 40,000 in the late 1920s to around 4,000 in 1940. Thousands of Catholic, Baptist, Jewish and Muslim clerics suffered the same fate.[34]

Stalin was also the driving force behind a magnified anti-religious campaign. The starting point was a new law on religious organizations that came into force on 8 April 1929. The legislation transformed the residual status allowed to religion in the constitutional arrangements of 1918. No religion was permitted any longer to engage in what was loosely called religious propaganda; all study groups and Bible circles, religious youth and women's movements, church reading rooms and libraries, all forms of religious education and formal proselytizing were banned. Clerics were only permitted to perform divine service and nothing more. Services had to be conducted in designated religious houses by priests who were resident in the immediate area, and no books other than the liturgy could be displayed or stored in the churches.[35] Tax levels were raised on all clergy to a point where they paid everything they earned to the state – 80 per cent income tax, and a further 20 per cent for failure to serve in the armed forces. Rules were altered on clerical residence rights, which left most clergymen forced to live off the generosity of those of their congregation who could offer a private room and a regular supply of food gifts. Priests who tried to buy food in state shops were forced to pay a special deposit before they could do so. A subsidiary law of 5 August 1929 ensured that indigent clerics should not become a financial burden on the state by removing all their rights to welfare, pensions or health insurance.[36]

The new law specifically endorsed the right of *anti*-religious propaganda, and during the 1930s the Soviet Union was flooded by a spring tide of atheist activity. The Central Committee set up what became known as the 'Cult Commission' on the same day as the new law on religious organization, whose task was to oversee the gradual liquidation of organized religion. Responsibility for the work of education was given to the League of the Godless, which in 1929 signalled its greater appetite for the ensuing struggle with religious faith by changing its name to the League of Militant Godless. The 465,000 members of 1929 were transformed by 1932 into a mass movement of 5.6 million. Anti-religious agitation – 'the agitators' companion' –

was handed down from the central propaganda apparatus of the state to be used in regular meetings staged by the League in every village, factory and office. 'Your task,' ran one ambitious party circular in 1937, 'is to explain to the wide masses the reactionary class character of Easter and religious feasts in general and of religion as a whole.'[37] In 1920 the party had organized only 230 anti-religious lectures; in 1940 there were 239,000 lectures delivered to an estimated audience of 11 million. Scientific materialism was promoted as the true path. Christmas Day was renamed a Day of Industrialization. Peasants were taught 'godless meteorology' and collective farms set up 'godless hectares' to demonstrate to sceptical or superstitious villagers that science could produce richer crops than prayer. In 1929 the 'continuous work week' was introduced to prevent church attendance; four days of work were followed by one day off and most Sundays became simply another workday.[38]

The new wave of atheist education and religious suppression had mixed effects. The churches survived by improvisation within the limited space allotted them. A visiting Dutch theologian in Moscow in 1930 found himself in a hotel opposite a small chapel. He observed how many passers-by made an unobtrusive bending of the head or their upper body as they drew level with the chapel. When he crossed the street to see for himself he found a large notice by the doorway bearing Marx's famous dictum 'Religion is the Opium of the People'. Inside, a priest in ragged vestments preached to a congregation in the face of constant braying and catcalls from a small group of young godless activists standing to one side. The priest told his visitor that the chapel was soon to be converted into a cultural centre; the neighbouring church of St Vladimir had been turned into a cinema, where filmgoers could still be seen crossing themselves in the foyer where there once hung an icon of the Madonna.[39]

Religious worship and religious belief persisted throughout the Stalin years. The 1937 census revealed that over half the population (57 per cent) still defined themselves as believers. The Soviet regime reacted uncertainly to this reality. Stalin called for a temporary relaxation of religious persecution in the early 1930s, yet in 1937 responded angrily to the failure of Yaroslavsky's League or the Cult Commission to erode religious belief more rapidly, and the League was savagely

purged alongside other party institutions. In 1936 the Stalin Constitution gave priests the right to vote, which they had lost in 1918, a
shift in policy that produced confusion among atheist communists.
It is sometimes argued that Stalin, a former seminary student, still
harboured residual religious sentiment which might explain the periodic lapses in an otherwise unremitting campaign against the religious
world view. There is no evidence to support such a conclusion. Stalin
remained a consistent advocate of the scientific and materialist base of
all knowledge. His concessions to religion were tactical and opportunistic, but they gave churchmen no immunity from the revolutionary
state. In January 1937 Metropolitan Sergei and fifty-one bishops were
officially recognized as the central authority of the Orthodox Church,
but during the course of the same year fifty bishops were arrested for
counter-revolution and spying and were shot or imprisoned.[40] The
'relaxation' of persecution detected in 1936 was followed by the most
intensive three years of church closures, clerical arrest and anti-
religious terror. For Stalin the Orthodox Church (though not the sects
or the schismatic church or Judaism) was useful as a tame instrument
of the regime. Any manifestation of a challenge to the world view of
Soviet communism was met throughout with a relentless hostility.

The opportunistic character of Stalinist religious policy was evident
in the revival of Orthodoxy in 1941 as a contribution to the patriotic
war effort and a means to seduce Soviet allies. Orthodox leaders
produced an English-language anthology titled *The Truth about
Religion in Russia*, where it was argued, under such lurid headings as
'Outrages against Sanctuaries and the Faithful' or 'The Fascists Took
a Blanket from a Child', that National Socialism was the true enemy
of religion. Under communism, wrote one obliging bishop, 'no one
prevents us from freely confessing our faith'.[41] Thousands were published, printed on the same presses used by the Godless League. It is
certainly the case that the authorities allowed the reopening of
churches; by 1947 there were an estimated 20,000, together with 67
monastic houses.[42] But the moral contest with religion scarcely relaxed.
In September 1944 the Central Committee called for a revival of
'scientific-educational' propaganda against religious belief, and in
1947 a Society for the Dissemination of Political and Scientific Knowledge was founded to carry on the work of the defunct League, which

had ceased operation in 1943. A group of students who met in 1948 to discuss the existence of God were arrested for submitting Marxism-Leninism to 'hostile criticism'.[43]

The contest with religion over fundamental questions about truth was never resolved under Stalin. Communists hoped that the physical eradication of religious institutions and the silencing of religious teaching would gradually erode the cultural backwardness of Soviet society and replace superstition with the certainties of natural and social science, and to a very considerable extent this was the case. The Soviet Union was not de-Christianized, but it was a thoroughly secular state in which all citizens were exposed to the dogmatic assertions of the communist world view; a survey of residents in Voronezh in 1964 found only 7.9 per cent willing to admit to being firm believers, and 59.4 per cent convinced atheists.[44] Those who professed religion did so on the defensive, always courting the risk of victimization. Metropolitan Sergei, in a private interview in 1936, admitted that he patiently awaited 'the day of Christ's triumph' in Russia, but in public the Orthodox Church hailed Stalin as 'God's chosen one'.[45]

The place of religion in the German dictatorship appeared to be very different. National Socialism was not formally an atheist movement, though many of its members were militantly anti-Christian. Article 24 of the party programme stated that National Socialism would be built 'on the base of a positive Christianity' and Hitler assured the churches in Germany shortly after he came to power, in March 1933, that religion was one of 'the most important factors in the preservation of the German people'.[46] The regime did not dynamite or confiscate German churches or impoverish the clergy. Religious observance was permitted throughout the dictatorship (except for German Jews and for Jehovah's Witnesses, who refused military service). Millions of party members were, and remained, Catholics or Evangelical Protestants. Many German Christians found little incompatible between their belief and their political affiliation and enthusiastically endorsed the national revolution. The enemy for many believing Germans before and after 1933 was godless Bolshevism. In 1939 the exiled wing of the Russian Orthodox Church, at its synod in Yugoslavia, published 'The

Address of Thanks to Adolf Hitler' for his fight against the Bolshevik Antichrist.[47]

The relationship between German religion and the dictatorship was, in reality, more complex and less compatible than the terms of its survival might suggest. The major denominations already faced serious problems long before 1933. From the late nineteenth century they faced the progressive decline of church loyalty and the reality of widespread secularization. Millions of Germans abandoned Christianity both formally and in practice. Under German law individuals could give notice of withdrawal from the confession with which they were registered. Between 1918 and 1931 2,420,000 withdrew from the Protestant Evangelical churches; 497,000 withdrew their Catholic allegiance. Figures for attendance at communion showed that millions more were at best passive Christians. In Prussia in 1933 only 21 per cent took regular communion, in Hamburg (the lowest figure) only 5 per cent.[48] In 1919 the Evangelical churches, the religion of two-thirds of Germans, were separated from the state and lost the support they had enjoyed since the Reformation. German Protestantism saw itself at a historic crossroads, reflected in the search for what the evangelical church leader Karl Barth called 'a theology of crisis' to cope with the moral relativism and lost values of the modern age.[49]

The troubled position of German Christianity provoked reactions not dissimilar from the Russian experience. Germany had its 'God-builders' who promoted the idea of a new man, whose heroic confrontation with life and profound spiritual strength would overcome the enfeebling longing for the afterlife and reveal how 'Man becomes God'.[50] Among younger theologians there was a strongly apocalyptic tone. 'In all the world we see no form of life that is not being dissolved,' wrote Friedrich Gogarten in an essay, 'Between the Times', written in 1920 in reaction to German defeat. 'This war is the dawn of the end of a period of history, indeed of an era of humanity.'[51] Some Protestant churchmen saw war and defeat as a judgement on Germany for failure to sustain belief in the God of the Germans. There was a long tradition in German Protestant piety of associating God and nation; service to the *Volk* was also service to a particular, historical God, not to the abstract, absolute values of a wider Christian commonwealth. After the war, nationalist piety revived. In 1925 a movement for a distinct German Christianity was founded. Calling itself the German Church (*Deutschkirche*), its principles included 'emphasis on thought of the German native land'.[52] They championed the idea of a Germanic saviour – 'Jesus the hero, the fighter for God' – in place of a cosmopolitan Jesus clothed in humility, pacifism and self-denial.[53] Nationalist theology saw God manifested in the soul and blood of the German people: 'the kingdom of heaven is within us,' wrote Ernst zu Reventlow, 'not outside us'.[54]

The radical nationalist wing of German Protestantism had much in common with National Socialist views on the primacy of the race and the unique mission of the German people. The German Faith Movement (*Deutsche Glaubensbewegung*), led by a Tübingen theology professor, Wilhelm Hauer, emerged in the late 1920s championing the idea that the German God was an expression of the particular spirituality of the German people, not 'the party God of the others'. Faith in a God revealed to the Germans replaced faith in an immanent, transcendent God. When Hitler came to power in 1933, the German Faith Movement had a following of half a million and petitioned, unsuccessfully, for full recognition as an official religion. Larger still was the movement of German Christians (*Deutsche Christen*), founded within the Evangelical Church in 1932 to represent the interests of National Socialism. The name was suggested by Hitler himself. Inspired by Pastor Friedrich Wieneke, one of the first National Socialist candidates to contest a municipal election, it was led from May 1932 by a young Protestant cleric and former Freikorps fighter, Joachim Hossenfelder. A party member since 1929, Hossenfelder became the party's national adviser on Church affairs. His view of theology was muscular and military: 'Christian faith is a manly, heroic affair'; God, he believed, spoke more powerfully through 'blood and race' than through 'the concept of *humanity*'.[55] A million Evangelical Protestants flocked into the movement by 1934 in the belief that a heroic national Christianity could march in step with National Socialism.

Hitler saw the relationship in political terms. He was not a practising Christian, but had somehow succeeded in masking his own religious scepticism from millions of German voters. Though Hitler has often been portrayed as a neo-pagan, or the centrepiece of a political religion in which he played the Godhead, his views had much more in common with the revolutionary iconoclasm of the Bolshevik enemy. His few private remarks on Christianity betray a profound contempt and indifference. Forty years afterwards he could still recall facing up to a clergyman-teacher at his school when told how unhappy he would be in the afterlife: 'I've heard of a scientist who doubts whether there is a next world.'[56] Hitler believed that all religions were 'now decadent'; in Europe it was the 'collapse of Christianity that we are now experiencing'. The reason for the crisis was science. Hitler, like Stalin, took a very modern view of the incompatibility of religious and scientific explanation. 'The dogma of Christianity,' he told Himmler in October 1941, 'gets worn away before the advances of science.'[57] There were no lies in science as there were in religious ideas of the afterlife; '[scientific] truth,' Hitler announced in an after-dinner conversation some months later, 'is the indispensable formulation.' There was nothing to offer anyone who looked for 'needs of a metaphysical nature' in the party. Truth lay in natural science, and for Hitler that meant the truths of racial biology – natural selection, racial struggle, 'identity of kind'.[58]

Hitler was politically prudent enough not to trumpet his scientific views publicly, not least because he had to maintain the distinction between his own movement and the godlessness of Soviet communism. Nor was he a thorough atheist. His public utterances are peppered with references to 'God' and 'spirit'. For Hitler the eschatological truths that he found in his perception of the race represented the real 'eternal will that rules the universe'; in the infinite value of the race and the struggle to sustain it men find what they might call God, an inner sense of the unity and purposiveness of nature and history.[59] Such views could be detected in the development of critical theology in Germany before the First World War, which suggested that God should be experienced as inner feeling rather than as external morality; they could also be found among the values of the German pre-war youth movement, where communion with nature, inward contemplation and group loyalties were designed to mould a secular spirituality. What Hitler could not accept was that Christianity could offer anything other than 'false ideas' to sustain its claim to moral certitude.[60]

The attitude of the rest of the party was far from uniform, but there existed in it a strong current of strident anti-clericalism. The anti-religious radicals around the party's self-styled philosopher, Alfred Rosenberg, disliked Christianity for its internationalism, pacifism and humanism, and for its 'oriental' roots in the work of the 'Jewish-Syrian' apostle Paul. Rosenberg, a Baltic German who fled west following the Russian revolution, and spent penniless months in 1919 in a Munich library reading everything he could about Jews, Freemasons and Bolsheviks as the 'enemies' of Germandom, was one of the few party leaders who defined National Socialism in terms of a historic clash between cultures and value-systems. In 1930 he finally published *The Myth of the Twentieth Century*, which became, alongside *Mein Kampf*, required reading for the party faithful. Rosenberg's identification of Christianity as *artfremd*, or alien, to German values encouraged party anti-clericalism, even paganism. The German Faith Movement rejected the 'Jewish' Old Testament and searched for traditional Germanic forms of religious expression, including Viking anthems and the symbolic sun-flag. 'The Cross must fall,' ran its propaganda, 'if Germany is to live.'[61] The attraction of heathenism and cultic rites, though restricted to an extreme wing of party religiosity, found echoes in the public ritual of the party and the outlook of many of its religious supporters, but not from Hitler, who had dismissed folk-cults as a lunatic fringe in *Mein Kampf* and publicly rejected any association with 'mystic cults' once in power.[62]

When Hitler became Chancellor in 1933 the relationship with religion required more urgent attention. Most German Christians, both Catholic and Protestant, did not support the more extreme religious nationalists, and many had not voted for Hitler. He wanted to neutralize any political threat from organized religion. The first step was to reach agreement with the German Catholic Church, whose theology was not susceptible to the new nationalist trends, and whose primary spiritual loyalty was to the Papacy. After three months of negotiations, a Concordat was signed in Rome on 20 July 1933; in return for an agreement not to interfere in German politics Hitler's government confirmed all the confessional rights of the church, and the right to Catholic education. Hitler's hope for German Protestantism was to mirror the agreement with Catholic Germany by creating a single Reich Church out of the twenty-eight provincial evangelical churches, which would be loyal to the new Reich and govern its own affairs.

The lead was taken by the German Christians who convened a council on 5 April 1933 in Berlin, where they issued a call for a unified Protestant Church faithful to the tenets of National Socialism, including the 'Aryan' cleansing of the Church. On 25 April Hitler appointed a prominent German Christian, a former army chaplain and enthusiastic National Socialist, Ludwig Müller, as his representative in the process of unification. Two months later Müller succeeded in drawing up a constitution for a new Reich Church which passed into law on 14 July. A National Synod met at Wittenberg on 27 September, where Müller was elected Reich Bishop of a united Evangelical Church. The former army chaplain, son of a railroad worker, and an enthusiast for no-nonsense military-style religion, arrived to confirm his election at the same *Schlosskirche* where Luther had nailed his Ninety-five Theses to the door four centuries before. He was preceded by Church banners and large swastika flags; behind him came religious leaders in brown SA uniforms, followed by a troop of soldiers in full marching dress bearing a green-bordered white badge emblazoned with a linked swastika and crucifix. A few weeks later, on the occasion of Martin Luther's 450th birthday, the new Reich Bishop told the congregation that the Protestant church looked on Hitler 'as a gift from the hand of God', behind whose government the church stands 'firmly and invincibly'.[63]

The reality was very different. The ambition to get the German churches to endorse the dictatorship unconditionally provoked almost immediate resistance. In May 1933 a group of evangelical churchmen established a working group – the Young Movement of the Reformation – which rejected state efforts to compel a unitary church and impose rules of ethnicity on church membership. In September 1933, in reaction to the election of the Reich Bishop, the former First World War submarine captain Pastor Martin Niemöller founded a Pastors' Emergency League, which had 7,000 members by early 1934, some 40 per cent of evangelical clergy.[64] Niemöller came from the same generation of front-line clerics as Müller; he had even joined the National Socialist party. He was a loyal patriot and was willing to respect a lawful state. What he and his fellow pastors could not accept was state insistence that the Church should conduct its affairs contrary to scripture and the Reformation confessions by, among other things, excluding Christianized Jews. The result was a Protestant schism. Rejecting the authority of the new Reich Bishop and the German Christians, representatives of almost half the evangelical churches met at Barmen in Westphalia on 30 May 1934, where they declared a breakaway 'Confessing Church' (*Bekenntniskirche*) founded upon a Theological Declaration drafted by Karl Barth and two young clergymen in a hotel room in Frankfurt-am-Main a few days before. The heart of the declaration was a reassertion of the moral power of scripture and a rejection of any other moral source. 'We repudiate the false teaching,' ran the first of six theses, 'that the church can and must recognize yet other happenings and powers, images and truths as divine revelation alongside this one word of God . . .'[65] During the course of the discussion Hans Asmussen, a pastor from Schleswig-Holstein, told delegates that 'the wisdom of the state in its present form is not God's wisdom'.[66]

The schism created a situation of complete confusion in church–state relations. The German Christians were a weakened force following an ill-judged speech by one of their number, Reinhold Krause, at the Berlin Sportpalast in November 1933. Krause expressed unconditional commitment to National Socialist laws and values, urged the rejection of the Bible as Jewish superstition ('stories of cattle-dealers and pimps') and rejected the injunction to 'love thy neighbour' in favour of a heroic, 'fighting Jesus'.[67] This proved too much for other nationalist Christians. Hossenfelder resigned a few weeks later. Bishop Müller could not be confirmed as head of the Reich Church despite the arrest and intimidation of hostile clerics, and in December 1934 he was finally replaced by a Minister for Church Affairs, Hans Kerrl. He appointed a Reich Church Committee on 24 September 1935 to supervise local committees set up for the separate evangelical churches, but all further attempts to create a unitary Protestant Church foundered on the profound theological and political differences provoked by reform. Hitler kept aloof from the internecine squabbles – 'Leave the religions to devour themselves,' he remarked during the war – but he could not remain indifferent to the moral challenge represented by Christian insistence that the only absolute values lay in Church teaching.[68]

Christianity was ultimately as incompatible with National Socialism as it was with Soviet communism. Article 24 of the party programme accepted 'positive Christianity', but also called on the churches to do nothing to offend 'the sense of morality of the German race'.[69] This injunction placed the moral outlook of the party above that of all religions. That moral outlook was rooted in 'the acknowledgement and ruthless exploitation of the iron laws of nature'.[70] The primary law, and the 'source of all genuineness and truth', was the unconditional defence of the race and its blood. Morality and truth were, in the words of an Italian Catholic critic, 'bound up with race and depend upon race'. For the 'Aryan', the moral certainty of his race 'holds good only for him'.[71] This was the world view contested by a great many German theologians. They followed Karl Barth's lead in asserting that neither nature nor science could provide an absolute morality: 'God alone is Lord.'[72] On 5 March 1936 the Confessing Church issued a declaration rejecting the National Socialist ambition to be 'the supreme and ultimate authority in all spheres of life' and invoking divine judgement on its pretensions. Though it was banned by the Gestapo, 700 pastors read out the declaration and were arrested.[73] The following spring the Papacy issued an encyclical 'with burning anxiety' (*Mit brennender Sorge*) that was read out in all Catholic churches on 21 March 1937. Much of it concerned breaches of the Concordat agreements on education and religious freedom provoked by party anti-clericals ('we expect a complete cessation to the anti-Christian propaganda'), but the encyclical also rejected the National Socialist moral position in favour of the absolutes of the natural law tradition, and called on Catholic communities to reassert 'truth' and a 'sense of justice'.[74]

The regime and party reacted to the moral contest much as the Soviet regime and the communist party reacted. On the one hand a policy of political repression and direct persecution, tempered by occasional political prudence in the face of widespread belief; on the other a direct contest in the field of education and propaganda. Political repression intensified as the regime consolidated its position, a shift exemplified by the fate of Martin Niemöller. When he was first arrested in January 1934 he was soon released in response to popular pressure. Following an outspoken sermon given in Berlin on 27 June 1937, in which Niemöller made clear a Christian's obligation to 'obey God rather than man', he was arrested for anti-state activity and sentenced to seven months in prison in March 1938; Hitler intervened to see to it that after serving his time in prison he should be sent to a concentration camp, from which he was fortunate to emerge alive in 1945. Over the course of the dictatorship more than 6,000 clergymen were imprisoned or executed on grounds of treasonable activity, some of them, like Niemöller, former party members.[75] The churches were subjected to regular Gestapo surveillance; in 1936 a separate branch for 'churches, sects and freemasons' was organized which mirrored the Soviet GPU 'division for religious affairs'. From 1938 Martin Bormann, head of the Party Chancellery and a prominent party atheist, took a leading role in trying to sever all state financial support for the churches, and to limit their legal status and activities, but the need to mobilize church support for the war effort from September 1939 led, as it did in the Soviet Union after 1941, to a limited political truce between Church and state.[76]

The churches abandoned the political contest as they did in the Soviet Union. Many Christians found themselves in a conscientious no-man's land between their hostility to party anti-clericalism and their sympathies with the movement's anti-communism and nationalism. When Stefanie von Mackensen, a party member but an activist in the Confessing Church, was called before a party disciplinary court for objecting when her local *Gauleiter* publicly described the churches as a 'big pigsty', she was asked directly whether in a conflict of conscience she would obey 'the Jew Christ or Adolf Hitler'. She replied 'Christ alone' and was asked to leave the party (though on appeal was allowed to keep her membership).[77] The church congregations, both Catholic and Protestant, party or non-party, responded defensively to political repression and anti-clericalism, unwilling to court further conflict, anxious about the survival of faith in a secular age and, in many cases, loyal to much of party policy. When a group of Catholic bishops tried in November 1941 to publish a Christian indictment of everything (except its anti-Semitism) that the regime stood for – 'what does conscience require? What does God . . . expect?' – publication was blocked by Cardinal Adolf Bertram, the senior Catholic prelate in Germany, on the grounds that it was politically inexpedient. Bertram remained blinded by Hitler's anti-Bolshevism; when in May 1945 he heard news of the *Führer*'s suicide, he drafted an order for his diocesan churches to hold 'a solemn requiem' for the fallen leader.[78]

From the mid-1930s the regime and party were dominated much more by the prominent anti-Christians in their ranks – Himmler, Goebbels, Bormann, Heydrich – but were restrained by Hitler, despite his anti-religious sentiments, from any radical programme of de-Christianization. Nonetheless the party began to limit religious teaching and promote its own idealism. Religious youth movements were closed down or merged with the Hitler Youth, from which all religious instruction was excluded. In August 1937 Himmler banned all Confessing Church seminaries and instruction. Dissident Protestants were barred from universities. State-sponsored denominational schools were closed by 1939, together with private ecclesiastical schools. Religious education by clergymen was eliminated. Religions were prevented from publicly collecting for charity.[79] The new generation of Germans was taught to despise the characteristics of Christian man as tainted with a degenerate, Jewish effeminacy and to seek within themselves the strength to assert and defend the race. The Prussian dissident Friedrich Reck observed the consequences of this clash of values during a stay in Munich in August 1936. He watched a Hitler Youth, who had been billeted in a school classroom during a party rally, glare at the crucifix on the wall and, with a 'young and still-soft face distorted in fury', tear it down and throw it from the window 'with the cry: "Lie there you dirty Jew"'. A few weeks later Reck ruefully reflected in his journal that 'God is asleep in Germany'.[80]

Germany was not de-Christianized under dictatorship any more than the Soviet Union. Religion was persecuted less systematically and violently in Germany because Hitler expected 'the end of the disease of Christianity' to come about by itself once its falsehoods were self-evident. During the war he reflected that in the long run 'National Socialism and religion will no longer be able to exist together'.[81] Both Stalin and Hitler wanted a neutered religion, subservient to the state, while the slow programme of scientific revelation destroyed the foundation of religious myth. In Germany this could be achieved more readily, since the process of secularization had gone further by the 1920s than it had in Russia; there also existed an evident overlap in the ideological outlook of many Christians in Germany with the ideology of the party, a convergence that was largely absent in the Soviet Union. Nonetheless in both cases the churches realized the historic character of the wider contest between Christian tradition and the moral claims of revolutionary or racial necessity, even if they were too politically cowed or fearful to contest it fully. In Germany and the Soviet Union, parties and leaders alike also recognized the deeper significance of the moral contest, but assumed that religious morality was the product of a fading stage of history destined to be overturned by scientific certainty and party enthusiasms.

The principal testing ground for the moral claims of both dictatorships was not the contest with religion, but the relationship between law and the state. It is here that the difference between modern dictatorship and modern liberal democracy is most clearly exposed. Under dictatorship the state was not subject to any form of judicial review. Those who made the law also enforced it. Law was unpredictable and unevenly applied. Judges were hostage to their political masters. Those unlucky enough to be ensnared in the Soviet or German judicial systems during the dictatorships found that court proceedings were weighted overwhelmingly in favour of the prosecution and that any punishment handed down could be altered at will by the political authorities. Western legal historians have no doubt that conventional western notions of justice enshrined in long-established traditions of natural law and civil rights were non-existent in both dictatorships. The moral argument seems in this case beyond question. The abuse of law has been the trademark of world tyranny.

This is not an opinion that many Soviet or German jurists would have accepted in the 1930s and 1940s. They perceived justice not in terms of abstract theories of right but as the product of a unique moment in history, which gave the law of dictatorship its own validation. There were judges, prosecutors and lawmakers (what proportion is uncertain) who shared the assumption that what they did was not only legal in formal terms but also fundamentally just. In their view the normative law of the liberal West had no greater claim to moral authority since it appeared to be based on western self-interest, and had nothing to offer to a revolutionary state. Soviet legal theorists defined all systems of law as an expression of a particular class society; they rejected the Russian legal heritage because Tsarist law, like Tsarist religion, was regarded as an institution designed to oppress the very classes that the revolution was supposed to liberate. The idea that there was any higher legal morality that transcended historical change and stood above the state was rejected as an idealist fantasy: states made and enforced the law on behalf of particular class interests, and had always done so.[82] 'Ideas about the moral and immoral, the just and the unjust, the good and the bad are not inborn,' wrote A. Denisovi in 1947, 'they cannot be deduced from so-called "eternal principles".'[83]

Long before 1933, legal theorists in Germany were turning away from the idea developed by nineteenth-century German liberals that states were bound by a set of external, abstract legal norms that guaranteed individual civil rights and an independent judicial system. This was partly a reaction to the willingness of the victorious Allies to impose in the name of international justice and a liberal diplomacy what many Germans regarded as the greatest injustice of all, the 'War Guilt' clause of the peace settlement of 1919. It also reflected the hostility of many legal theorists and judges to the way republican governments after 1919 had used the law to expand individual rights to welfare and protection at work. But the central issue was a growing division within legal theory, evident since at least the 1870s, which mirrored the arguments between internationalists and nationalists also being faced by German Christians. Much of the legal profession was nationalist and conservative in outlook. There were calls to return to a more authentically German form of law, in place of a legal tradition 'stamped', as one young jurist complained, 'with the spirit of the Enlightenment'.[84] Hans Gerber, an academic jurist, described the new spirit of German law after 1933: 'National Socialism insists that justice is not a system of abstract and autonomous values such as the various types of Natural Law systems.' Each state, Gerber continued, 'has its own concept of justice'.[85] National Socialists could refer to Article 19 of the party programme, drafted in 1921, which called for 'a common Germanic law' to replace the Roman law tradition 'dominated by a materialistic conception of the world'. The 1900 Civil Code, based on those traditions, was dismissed by party lawyers as 'oriental', even Jewish.[86]

The rejection of universal criteria of justice made law historically contingent, a product of its own time and place. In both dictatorships law was regarded not as something set in stone, but something that evolved and changed with altered historical circumstances. Historical reality, it was argued, dictated the nature of legal systems and governed their moral worth. States made the law they wanted in their own image. Such an argument still left unresolved the distinction between what was legal and what was legitimate, between law and justice. If states made laws of their own choosing, rather than laws derived from long-established legal traditions, they were not, by definition, just laws. The issue was resolved by elaborate tautologies. In the Soviet Union the revolution was just; law was promulgated by the revolutionary state; therefore law was also just. In the Third Reich the highest justice was the preservation of the life of the nation; the nation was the source of law; hence law was also just. These virtuous circles allowed both dictatorships to reject the moral absolutes of abstract right, while simultaneously asserting the moral absolute of their own law-making. It was on this foundation of casuistry that each system constructed the architecture of legitimacy.

Here the similarities end for the moment. The Soviet state had a legal *tabula rasa* in 1917. On 24 November Tsarist courts and legal codes were abolished. Soviet judges were told to make use of what they needed from old legislation, but to be guided by revolutionary consciousness when arriving at their judgments.[87] Law was seen as an extension of policy, which in a socialist state would soon take the form of mere technical rules, and eventually wither away as state power declined. 'Communism,' wrote Peter Stuchka, one of the most prominent legal theorists of the revolution, 'means not the victory of socialist laws but the victory of socialism over any law.' He assumed that once a classless society had been achieved 'law will disappear altogether'.[88] The central figure in Soviet legal theory in the 1920s, Evgeny Pashukanis, regarded the law of the transitional period from revolution to communism chiefly as a set of economic regulations that altered with economic priorities. Law was merely a problem that was '99 per cent political'; revolutionary legality possessed a flexibility and adaptability that reflected its temporary character.[89] With the coming of the First Five-Year Plan there were strong expectations that law would be transformed into a branch of economic planning, 'the administration of things', as Marx had described it.

This utopian conception of the law defied the reality that crimes continued to be committed, contracts had to be enforced and counter-revolutionary activity curtailed. The administration of justice, nominally operated by the Justice Commissar, Nikolai Krylenko, was rudimentary. Revolutionary tribunals were run by party appointees with little or no legal training; the courts depended on inconsistent and arbitrary interpretation of that 'revolutionary consciousness' on which Lenin had instructed them to rely in 1917.[90] It was soon found that legal codes were necessary again. A criminal code was introduced in the Russian republic in June 1922, a civil code four months later. Both had to be based to a considerable extent on pre-revolutionary models, and judges were instructed to use bourgeois rules in cases where they were sufficiently in keeping with the 'social aims' of the revolution.[91] By the late 1920s Soviet law pointed in two directions: Marxist legal theory confined formal systems of law to the dustbin of history; legal practice showed that law was more necessary than ever in regulating society and protecting it from crime.

The paradox was resolved by Stalin himself. He rejected the idea that either law or state would wither away while communism was still under construction; indeed at the Sixteenth Party Congress in 1930 he called for 'the highest development of state authority'. He freely admitted that this replaced one paradox with another ('Is this "contradictory"?' he asked rhetorically, 'Yes, it is "contradictory".'), but he argued that withering away could only occur in dialectical response to the 'maximum intensification' of state authority.[92] Stalin rejected the idea of law as a mere set of economic regulations; in the 1930s law was to become a set of norms determined by the party in the interests of the struggle to construct communism. Its legitimacy derived from this central revolutionary ambition: 'socialist law,' wrote Andrei Vyshinsky, the jurist who led the Stalinist transformation of law, 'does not know any other goals than to aid the destruction of the capitalist world and to build a new communist society.'[93] Under Stalin, history dictated that law was to be raised 'to the highest level of development' because it was the instrument of a 'higher law' of revolution whose virtue was unimpeachable. 'For the first time in history' – Vyshinsky again – 'legal provisions coincide with general moral principles, because Soviet law embodies the people's will.'[94] It was a will interpreted by the party, but in reality by Stalin himself.

Vyshinsky, more than any other jurist, shaped the legal theory of Stalin's dictatorship. He was fortunate to have survived so long, for everything about his background was wrong. He was of Polish extraction, the son of bourgeois parents, who qualified as a lawyer before the war; an active socialist, he joined the Mensheviks rather than the Bolsheviks, and served as a Menshevik deputy and militia leader under the Provisional Government, in which role he ordered the arrest of Moscow Bolsheviks after their failed coup in July 1917. In 1918 he was in turn arrested as a counter-revolutionary, escaped punishment, joined the communist party in 1920, but was then twice purged for unreliability before reinstatement.[95] He was something of a dandy; clean shaven, in his smart suits and shirts, Vyshinsky would not have been out of place in any western courtroom. He was the very model of the opportunist class enemy rooted out in their thousands during the purges of the 1930s. He survived because he was fortunate to read the signals from Stalin more clearly than his legal colleagues. In 1932 he wrote a book on *Revolutionary Legality in the Contemporary Period* in which he laid out the foundation of the legal theory that shaped the law of the Stalin era.

Vyshinsky began from the assumption that law was the direct product of the dictatorship of the proletariat: in essence, class law. As a consequence mere legal formalism was always subject to what he called 'party mindedness'. Legality was not of any value if it contradicted what the revolutionary moment required. In the early 1930s Soviet law needed to be strengthened not only in terms of the administration of justice and formal legal procedures, but as an active instrument for the construction of communist society. 'Law and state cannot be regarded apart from each other,' he wrote. 'The law obtains its power and content from the state.'[96] Law was not autonomous; its legitimacy derived from the fact that it was the revolutionary state that 'creates, guarantees, regulates and utilizes the law'.[97] It differed from bourgeois law precisely for this reason: in bourgeois systems law was a means to limit and regulate state power according to a higher concept of individual right; Soviet law was to ensure that the norms of the revolutionary state were ruthlessly enforced against the wilful behaviour of individual criminals and counter-revolutionaries. In 1934 Vyshinsky was rewarded with the post of deputy-Procurator and a year later became the Procurator-General of the Soviet Union, an office that allowed him to regulate, centralize and stabilize the judicial system and improve the technical capabilities of a profession in which only 1.8 per cent had attended advanced courses in legal education.[98] He also saw to it that the legal theorists of the 1920s, condemned during the purges as hopeless utopians or bourgeois legalists, or sometimes both, should be themselves the victims of his new brand of revolutionary legality. Pashukanis disappeared in January 1937; Krylenko was arrested and shot in 1938.

The Third Reich was quite a different case. In Germany there existed a settled body of law, codified in the 1871 Penal Code and the Civil Code of 1900. The judicial system was well-established and its personnel highly trained. Legal theory was argued over by a large corpus of academic lawyers, but few openly condemned the established virtues of the rule of law and judicial impartiality, even among the younger cohort of jurists who argued for a law based on national traditions. Germany was, above all, a *Rechtsstaat*, a state founded upon general principles of respect for the law and the legal protection of its citizens. During the republican 1920s legal reformers argued for a milder penal regime; civil and constitutional law bolstered the rights and opportunities of ordinary people. In 1922, the jurist Hans Kelsen published *The Theory of Pure Law*, arguing that law was based on a set of settled norms unaffected by the ebb and flow of politics or the moral enthusiasms of the moment.[99]

Almost all this rich heritage was overturned in the first years of the dictatorship, and the general principle of a state bound by law destroyed. Law was reduced to simplistic formulae derived from the world view of National Socialism: 'law is what is useful for the German people', or 'all law stems from the right to life of the people'.[100] The legal foundation of the state was reversed: law became in National Socialist jurisprudence an expression of the higher morality of the race – 'the absolute securing of the life of the nation' – and hence was subordinate to the will of the race and its political leadership.[101] 'Law,' remarked Franz Gürtner, Minister of Justice in Hitler's first cabinet, 'renounces its claim to be the sole source for deciding what is legal and illegal.'[102] The moral basis of law was instead to be the 'ethical order of the people' based upon their racial 'healthy common sense'. Morality and law, so it was argued, would only then coincide; National Socialist law represented 'the moral code of the nation'.[103] Race law played the role taken by class law in Soviet jurisprudence; both systems claimed that authentic justice could be derived only from the popular will interpreted and mediated by the state's supreme authority.

These ideas were not the offspring of party hacks trying to justify the rapid overturning of the rule of law made possible by the decrees granting the government emergency and enabling powers in February and March 1933. The intellectual foundation for the legal theory of Hitler's dictatorship was supplied by an important fraction of the community of academic lawyers who both shaped, and were shaped by, National Socialism. The most important of their number was Carl Schmitt, a 45-year-old professor of law at Berlin University, who had become an intellectual star of the radical right in the 1920s for his uncompromising hostility to parliamentary democracy and 'rootless' liberalism.[104] On 1 May 1933 he joined the party and by doing so publicly put his *imprimatur* on Hitler's legal and constitutional ambitions. Schmitt's idea of the state derived from the seventeenth-century English political philosopher Thomas Hobbes: sovereign power is indivisible and absolute, whoever makes the law, executes and judges it as well. 'The *Führer* is no organ of the state,' wrote Schmitt, 'but the highest judge of the nation and the highest lawgiver.'[105] Law was not some abstraction, he wrote in 1935, but should reflect 'the plan and aim of the lawgiver'. Above all, the law served to isolate and exclude the enemies of the state; the state defined who was 'friend' and who was 'foe' (*Freund oder Feind*), and the law imposed exclusion. Schmitt applauded the leader who could seize the moment at times of national crisis and act with iron decision to turn these aims into concrete legal provisions. Law reflected the primacy of political leadership, and thus supplied 'a more profound idea of legality'.[106]

There has been much debate about the extent to which Carl Schmitt was responsible for the destruction of the rule of law after 1933. He was certainly no Vyshinsky, exulting in the physical elimination of his former colleagues in the great purge trials. From 1936 he began to fall out of favour as more politically astute lawyers jostled for preferment. After 1945 Schmitt's indictment of liberal constitutionalism continued to be discussed and taught inside Germany, and his flirtation with Hitler came to be regarded as an aberration in a long and fruitful scholarly career.[107] There were other senior law academics who embraced the new regime with greater political enthusiasm and intellectual sophistry than Schmitt. He was, nonetheless, an academic leader and a distinguished public figure who willingly and unambiguously endorsed, with hundreds of his colleagues, the destruction of what he regarded as an outworn conception of legal right. In July 1934, a few days after Hitler announced to the Reichstag that he had from necessity acted beyond the law in ordering the murder of Ernst Röhm and a circle of alleged conspirators, Schmitt wrote an article in the journal of German jurists under the heading 'The *Führer* protects the Law'. He explained that Hitler combined in his person both supreme political and judicial power; the purge was thus not beyond the law but was an expression, in Schmitt's words, of 'the highest justice' dispensed by the nation's 'highest judge'.[108]

This topsy-turvy view of law was widely accepted. Ernst Forsthoff, a professor of law at Kiel with something of a liberal reputation, welcomed the new legal order as a first step to creating a real 'state based on law'.[109] The legal profession fell into line behind the new legality. In April 1933 120 out of 378 law academics were sacked on grounds of race or political outlook; they were replaced by much younger colleagues who willingly accepted the changed legal climate. By 1939 two-thirds of all law faculties had been appointed since 1933. In 1933 there were already 9,943 judges in the party; by 1942 there were 16,000.[110] Lawyers were required to join the League of National Socialist Jurists and those who remained aloof were starved of work and subject to constant political harassment. Around 1,500 were purged in 1933, mostly German Jewish lawyers in state employment; the remaining 1,753 German Jews still practising were barred from doing so in September 1938. All other lawyers were required to make an oath of direct fealty: 'I swear to remain loyal to Adolf Hitler, the leader of the German nation and people . . .'[111]

The new legality was to be codified. In 1935 a commission on the criminal law began its work, led by the ageing Minister of Justice, Franz

Gürtner, one of the few conservatives to survive in office into the late 1930s, thanks to his enthusiasm for the new state. His state secretary, Roland Freisler, came to play a central part in imposing National Socialist values while the commission completed its labours. In 1934 Freisler urged judges to abandon impartiality in favour of judgments made 'only in the spirit of National Socialism'.[112] A draft of the new People's Law (*Volksgesetzbuch*) was ready by 1942, but the final work of codification had to be suspended because of the war. Since much of the formal law was still based on the codes inherited from before 1933, Freisler reminded jurists that even without a new criminal code all legal concepts were to be handled in a way consistent with 'the highest possible life value for the Germanic community'.[113] In effect, the 'Germanic community' meant Hitler, as its representative figurehead. The law, wrote another jurist in 1939, is 'an order from the *Führer*'.[114] Hans Frank, the party head of the League of Jurists, asked lawyers to test every judgment as if they were Hitler himself: 'Formerly, we were in the habit of saying: this is right or wrong; today, we must put the question accordingly: What would the Führer say?'[115]

It is now possible to understand why legal theorists and jurists in both dictatorships thought that the system they operated was not only legal, but also legitimate. The consequences for the operation of the law were profound, and remarkably similar. Two general principles underlay the development of legal practice: the first was the unqualified assertion that the state was above the law. There was a distinction here between the communist state as the representative of the revolutionary masses, and the Third Reich as a state in which Hitler was 'the representative of the whole people'.[116] Though in reality Stalin played a dominant role in Soviet law-making, the fiction was maintained that 'state authority' or 'the dictatorship of the proletariat' was the source of law.[117] However, in neither case was the state subject to its own laws nor to judicial review, and in both cases state authorities could appeal to the demands of historic fictions – the 'law' of the revolution or the 'laws' of racial development – to explain their special status.

Under such a dispensation individual rights were always subordinate to the interests of the collectivity, whether that was the communist state or the racial community. 'You are nothing,' ran another Nazi slogan, 'the *Volk* is everything.'[118] The law was said to represent a fictive 'public will'; individual freedom derived not from rights which could be defended against the state but from the duties of compliance with this will and strict obedience to its rules. Judgments in individual cases depended on the political function of law: cases were heard not on their legal merit, but in terms of their consistency with what popular justice required. 'There might be collisions and discrepancies between the formal command of the laws and those of the proletarian revolution,' wrote Vyshinsky in 1935. 'This collision must be solved only by the subordination of the formal commands of law to those of party policy.'[119] Curt Rothenburger, court president in Hamburg, wrote approvingly of the demise of the 'neutral, non-political judge of the liberal epoch' and the birth of justices who were 'politically aware through and through, firmly bound to the world view of the lawgiver'. Judges were encouraged to pronounce judgment *contra legem* if their 'racial consciousness' dictated.[120]

The second principle was to view the law as an instrument in the war against the enemies of society. The law could define who deserved to be included in the class state or the racial community and who should be excluded. Carl Schmitt's concept of 'Friend or Foe' has had a universal validity for all modern dictatorships. Legal theory in the two systems was little interested in protecting the individual from the state, but it was centrally concerned with the protection of the community from individuals bent on crime or political deviancy. A traitor to the people was described in Germany as 'the most heinous of criminals'; the lawyer Georg Dahm even suggested that simple theft was disloyalty to the *Volk*. Criminal trials came to be seen as a litmus test for the defendant's prospects of remaining a member of the community at all.[121] In the Soviet Union theft *was* defined as a political act. The decree 'On Protecting and Strengthening Public (Socialist) Property' handed down on 7 August 1932 solemnly declared state property to be 'sacred and inviolable'; all thieves were by definition 'enemies of the people'. The maximum penalty was death by shooting, the minimum ten years in a camp.[122] Two years later, in June 1934, a comprehensive 'Treason Statute' was added to the 1926 Soviet Criminal Code, with a mandatory death sentence for the traitor and five years in Siberia for every member of a traitor's family.[123] Much of the law that was new in both dictatorships was concerned with finding and punishing enemies.

The 'enemy' was defined politically: counter-revolutionary in the Soviet Union, an enemy of the race and nation in Germany. To be certain that the law could deal with them even in cases where no criminal offence had actually been committed, both judicial systems introduced the legal principle of 'analogy'. The Tsarist courts had used the device to convict elements considered socially dangerous but who had not violated a specific article of the Criminal Code. Their behaviour was criminalized by 'analogy'. Abolished in 1917, the device was resuscitated in 1922 and used extensively to convict alleged political criminals during the 1930s. When Evgenia Ginzburg, a loyal party member, was arrested and charged with counter-revolution in 1937 she challenged her judges to tell her what actual crime she had committed. Nonplussed, they replied: 'Don't you know that comrade Kirov was killed in Leningrad?' Her protests that she had never been to the city, and that the murder had taken place three years before were impatiently brushed aside: 'But he was killed by people who shared your ideas, so you share the moral and political responsibility.'[124] The principle of 'analogy' gave the state almost unlimited opportunity to haul into the legal net anyone they judged to be a social menace. It was adopted into German law in June 1935. Until then 'analogy' had been specifically prohibited in the criminal code. A redrafted Paragraph 2 of the code now allowed prosecution in cases where 'popular opinion' deemed an act to be worthy of punishment even though it was not defined as illegal. 'If found that no particular criminal law is of use for the deed in question,' ran the amendment, 'then the deed is to be punished according to the law whose principles seem most relevant.' The traditional legal maxim that there could be 'no punishment without a law' was replaced, in Carl Schmitt's approving words, by the maxim 'no crime without punishment'.[125]

Both dictatorships practised what has been called 'a political jurisprudence'.[126] The law was made subject to the arbitrary will of the supreme state authorities, but its very arbitrariness was disguised by creating the illusion that Soviet or National Socialist law was the product of a higher justice that the state represented. Higher justice was said to derive ultimately from the popular will, or 'healthy public opinion'. This legally imprecise concept was used by jurists in both systems as a source of legitimation for legal practices that in reality emasculated individual rights and the public's prospect of legal redress. Neither system wanted simply to flout the law. Instead the moral foundations of the law were recast to make the public understand that judicial practice under dictatorship was just because it was rooted in 'people's justice'.

The dictatorships believed that they gave expression to a higher morality. The source of this moral presumption was the crisis of the First World War. The hostility displayed towards the liberal world view was a direct product of the conflict. At its end there was a profound sense that the moral certainties of the pre-war age had disappeared, to be replaced by competing moralities, of which western liberalism was one of many. The Soviet Union emerged from the war's messy aftermath in the belief that it was the most advanced state in the world. Communists understood that they represented the triumph of the last oppressed class; their new society was by definition the most progressive stage of history. It was capitalism, Marxists argued, that was responsible for the ills of the world, and it was capitalism that was therefore fundamentally immoral. Germany emerged from the war embittered by defeat and by what was almost universally regarded as an unjust peace. There was a strong sense that German values were under threat from western liberalism; the qualities that were thought to set German culture apart were regarded as morally superior to the values of the western states imposed through war. Beginning in 1918 with the publication of the first volume of Oswald Spengler's *The Decline of the West*, a cohort of German intellectuals called on German culture to redeem Europe by taking the lead in a moral revolution against communism and capitalism.

The rest of the world regarded the two countries not as moral beacons to the future, but as pariah states which would have to earn their moral passage back into the international community. This indictment was turned on its head in Germany and the Soviet Union: it was the liberal order that had demonstrated its moral bankruptcy in facing the challenges of the modern age. German nationalists and

Soviet revolutionaries were united by their conviction that they had nothing to learn from the West; both regarded 'bourgeois' values as corrupt and corrupting, promoting a socially destructive morality of unrestricted self-interest and hedonism, thinly veiled by a desiccated rationalism and universalism. 'The West has already said everything it had to say,' wrote the Russian novelist Mikhail Bulgakov in 1920. '*Ex oriente lux* [from the east, light].'[127] Neither regime saw any advantage in adopting an alien western morality for which there appeared to be little popular demand or social necessity. When, in 1947, the Soviet philosopher G. S. Alexandrov was rash enough to publish a history of western philosophy, Andrei Zhdanov called ninety academics together to discuss their colleague's failure to recognize that however progressive other systems of thought might look, Marxism was a philosophy 'differing qualitatively from all previous philosophical systems'.[128] 'Our morality,' wrote Zhdanov in an essay on Soviet ethics, 'censures . . . the bourgeois pursuit of pleasure and neglect of duty.'[129]

The distinctiveness and moral worth of German values was a commonplace assumption among Germany's educated elites. The philosopher Ernst Troeltsch contrasted the rational, mechanistic, humanitarian morality of the West with the unique vitality of the German 'historical and productive spirit'.[130] Wilhelm Stapel, a leading German Christian, argued that 'nations vary in character and therefore in ability and qualifications', from which he drew the conclusion: 'We Germans are not on a level with other nations; we have a right that cannot be compared with that of anybody else.'[131] Carl Schmitt contrasted the 'power of real life' expressed in the German response to the post-war crisis with the 'mechanism' of western universal values; another jurist, Wilhelm Siebert, described western approaches to moral issues as an 'expression of helplessness, rootlessness, and debility'; and so on.[132] The ethical claims of western liberalism were dismissed as self-serving and hypocritical: 'not till the Anglo-Saxons found it expedient was political moralism raised to "universal validity"', wrote one German critic, for whom western moral complacency was a mask for unscrupulous imperialism.[133]

The moral order was instead regarded as the product of specific historical circumstances unique to particular peoples and societies. The two dictatorships justified a moral outlook that rejected universal truths or values by asserting that the moral order was legitimized by the higher necessity of history. The result was a philosophical paradox: morality was determined by the course of history and was therefore relative, yet the value-systems produced by history possessed an absolute worth precisely because they were historical realities rather than abstract principles. This paradox was explained by a young National Socialist academic in 1935, when he argued that the only 'truth' was what profited the 'blood and life' of the race: 'without having to believe in absolute truths, one can acknowledge absolute values'.[134] The idea of absolute historical value is central to understanding how the moral universe of dictatorship could be applied with such fanatical rigour. When Roland Freisler urged his legal colleagues to accept National Socialist values into law, it was because historical necessity demanded it: 'history remains implacable and incorruptible – for it is the truth'.[135] Soviet ethics were based on a similar sense of historical certainty. The philosopher M. N. Rutkevich, writing in 1952, could comfortably reconcile the tensions between history and value: 'All the fundamental theses ... of Marxist-Leninist philosophy, economic science, and the theory of socialism and class struggle ... these are all *absolute* truths, so far confirmed by practice that nothing in the future can ever refute them.'[136]

The characteristics of the new morality in both systems represented a profound rejection of humanism. In defiance of an ethical outlook that promoted the intrinsic value of the individual and of personal rights, the two dictatorships constructed moral orders that preached the absolute value of the collective and the absolute obligation to abandon concern for self in the name of the whole. The German theologian Michael Müller welcomed the end of ethical relativism under Hitler because he had instilled in the German people the fundamental idea that 'the individual must serve the group' and the principle that 'life is not happiness but self-sacrifice'.[137] Disregard for the individual promoted a deliberate moral toughness. 'A Bolshevik must be hard, brave and unbending, ready to sacrifice himself for the party,' Kaganovich told a party comrade who complained of cases of injustice. 'Yes, ready to sacrifice not only his life but his self-respect and sensitivity.'[138] In 1961 the Soviet communist party formally published the twelve commandments of 'The Moral Code of the Builder of

Communism', which inscribed in stone some of the harsh principles of communist ethics inherited from the Stalin years: 'labour for the good of society – he who does not work, neither shall he eat'; 'an uncompromising attitude to the enemies of communism'.[139]

The assumed virtue of the collective gave moral force to the exclusive and brutal character of the two systems. Both dictatorships were marked by a profound historical resentment against those who thought differently, more marked and violent in the Soviet Union because it had to overturn organized religion and construct a judicial system almost from scratch. Retribution was clothed with righteousness. 'An irreconcilable hatred against enemies of the people,' wrote Vyshinsky in 1938, 'that is one of the most important principles of communist ethics.'[140] The hatreds of National Socialism were central to the regime's purpose, and the moral language of the dictatorship reflected it. The violence directed by both dictatorships against those whom they wished to exclude was deliberately presented as something that distinguished their moral values from the insipid humanism of the West. Victor Kravchenko, an industrial manager lucky to escape the purges himself, recalled being told at a party purge meeting that there was 'no room for "rotten liberalism" and "bourgeois sentimentality"' when unmasking 'enemies'. In the words of Himmler's protégé, the SS official Werner Best: 'in the epoch of the national state one law alone holds good: Be strong!' Rosenberg boasted that strong men were strong because they were '*absolutely* hard men'.[141] The imperative to victimization and exclusion was seen as one of the virtues of dictatorship, not one of its vices.

The moral certainties of dictatorship were not universally shared by their populations. It was possible to operate in both systems by paying lip-service to the official morality while keeping a private conscience; it was possible to regard some of what the regime did as an injustice, but to applaud the general world view; it was possible to fight against the prevailing moral climate, though the cost was inexorable punishment. For millions in both dictatorships the new moral order was accepted for what it was. Both systems displayed a fierce moral energy in constructing the new order and in destroying those who allegedly obstructed or subverted it. The warriors of the new morality were lionized as heroes by the regime. The young Nazis who died in political street brawls and bar fights before 1933 became the martyrs and saints of the movement. NKVD officials in the Soviet Union were awarded the coveted Hero of the Soviet Union medal for the endless misery they caused to their victims. The moral universe of dictatorship made the state's crimes explicable not as crimes but as necessary precautions to prevent a greater injustice. Indeed for Hitler and Stalin the greater sin would have been their failure to protect the race or the socialist state against the threat of destruction. This moral inversion made possible the most murderous regimes of the century.

Protected by this warped moral armour, the perpetrators of state crime carried out orders whose fulfilment is otherwise incomprehensible. During his interrogations at Nuremberg the commandant of Auschwitz, Rudolf Höss, was clear in his mind what was moral and what was not. When his interrogator accused him of pilfering Jewish possessions he reacted with real indignation: 'but it would have been against my principles . . . it would not have been honest'.[142] About the mass extermination of more than a million Jews, gypsies and Soviet prisoners at Auschwitz Höss displayed no remorse or sense of moral lapse. The higher morality dictated by the imperatives of history and nature was regarded as distinct from the treatment of conventional crime. Murderers and thieves were sent to prison in both systems, but those who murdered Jews in cold blood and looted their valuables for the state treasury, or those who confiscated church treasures and murdered the priests that resisted, were not. The dictatorships used this moral distinction to win popular approval, to legitimize the otherwise illegitimate exercise of state power, to applaud the brutality and lawlessness that state power unleashed, but, above all, because both assumed that the imperatives of history had made them right. 'Only necessity,' said Hitler in 1942, 'has legal force'; or Stalin in 1952: 'History above all does nothing essential unless there exists a particular necessity for it.'[143] Neither the dictatorships nor the behaviour of the dictators can be understood without recognizing that it was essential for them to be viewed as the moral instruments of an irrepressible and redemptive historical movement.

8

Friend and Foe: Popular Responses to Dictatorship

'Naturally, I myself am extremely cautious, since I am in a particularly dangerous position and have to think of my wife and children. When teaching my class I am not merely 100 per cent Nazi, I am 150 per cent. I lay it on so thick that even the dullest boys cannot help seeing how absurd it all is.'

German teacher, Bielefeld, August 1939[1]

In 1939 the German Freedom Party published in London a book of letters from Germans who were hostile to Hitler's Reich, under the title *Uncensored Germany*. One of the letters, from a schoolmaster, starts this chapter. Dated 14 August, just before the outbreak of war, it was a reply to a reproachful inquiry about why he, an opponent of the regime, should have joined the party. His response reveals much about popular attitudes to the dictatorship. His membership was not, he protested, sincere but was taken up from fear of the authorities. 'What would be the use,' he continued, 'of a false show of heroism, which would only be a form of suicide?' Everyone around him had adopted 'the habit of dissembling'. His pupils he divided into categories that could have been applied across the German population as a whole. Some were so enthusiastic for 'the heroic theories' of National Socialism that they dreamt of a second, even more radical wave of national revolution; the bulk of pupils he considered to be 'cynical opportunists', willing to work with National Socialism to improve their career prospects, sceptical and materialistic in outlook; finally came a small group of boys opposed to the regime, who, lacking any safe means of expressing their resistance, 'take refuge in the privacy of their personal lives' and read literature. Only one pupil, whose father shared the teacher's private sentiments, ran the risk of openly criticizing the regime.[2]

All the many problems of interpreting popular responses to dictatorship are present in this story. Under both Hitler and Stalin there existed those who became noisy sponsors of a system they did not necessarily believe in. Any analysis that takes evidence of explicit endorsement as its starting point has to expect an element of calculated dissimulation beneath the surface. In the Soviet Union such people were called 'radishes': red on the outside, white within. Alongside the enthusiasts for the movement, genuinely convinced of the rightness of their cause, these false friends are difficult to distinguish. To all appearances they belong at that point on the scale reserved for the convinced fanatic, even though their true feelings may have been of despairing but powerless hostility. The spectrum of attitudes in the school classroom, though not statistically verifiable either here or for the wider society under dictatorship, suggests a common-sense division in German society into four rough categories: those who believed; those who enjoyed or profited from or were happy to identify with the new order through opportunistic association; those who displayed an apathetic outward compliance, but inwardly sustained an unspoken conscientious objection; and finally those whose intolerance for the regime, from whatever cause, manifested itself in forms of dissent, opposition or resistance.

This summary fits much of the recent discussion of popular attitudes to the two dictatorships, which has compelled acceptance of the idea – so different from the traditional 'totalitarian' model of ruthless control over a captive populace – that broad sections of the German and Soviet public supported the dictatorships, often with enthusiasm and devotion, or at least with a general approval.[3] Neither system can be properly explained without accepting this conclusion, but the extent to which that enthusiasm was the product of genuine ideological identification or the product of political education and self-interest remains open to conjecture. The dictatorships depended on creating a strong sense of identity between the population and the aspirations of the regime by acting as though these ambitions represented popular interests and reflected popular prejudices, as, to a considerable extent, they did. Those who supported or went along with the systems acted out of complicity, not fear, and did so because they found their own expectations and beliefs reflected to some degree in the dictatorships.

This shifting perspective on dictatorship requires a different answer to the question which is so often asked of the two populations: 'Why was there so little opposition?' Where once the answer was simply to recite the openly terroristic nature of the two dictatorships, and the iron grip of the state, current interpretations rely much more on understanding the complex nature of the popular social response to dictatorship. There were many factors other than the state apparatus for repression that explain the reluctance to engage in direct confrontation, or more accurately, the widespread absence of any prolonged manifestation of popular hostility. Part of any explanation lies in the historical circumstances that shaped the dictatorships. In both states the 1920s were years of sharp social division and political argument, and the idea of 'dissent' or 'opposition' as the cause of economic crisis, or civil conflict or political instability – a view vigorously promoted by the dictatorships themselves – produced a wide popular consensus for a politics without conflict and a society without divisions. To be 'anti' rather than 'pro' came to be regarded popularly as an unacceptable challenge to the promise of social consent and political harmony. Both dictators placed the idea of unity at the centre of their view of politics: unity of the *Volk* and unity of the toiling Soviet masses. The expression of differentness was presented as if it were a betrayal of the rest of society, or of the nation; consent and compliance became social duties to prevent society from falling back into a state of damaging discord. This dichotomy was internalized by the two societies, placing those who genuinely opposed the regimes into a political no-man's-land.

Yet what did opposition amount to? It defies any simple definition. It was possible to resist the regime, even violently, as Soviet peasants did during collectivization, but not to be a political opponent of the regime itself. It was just as possible to be opposed to the dictatorships on political grounds but to avoid the risk of open resistance. There were relatively few examples in either dictatorship of political opponents who also actively resisted, and all were violently suppressed. None is well known from the Stalinist era. In Germany probably only the White Rose group of students, active briefly in Munich in 1942, is universally known. It was possible to resist or oppose a particular facet of the regime – German anti-Semitism or Soviet farm policy – but to be in general agreement with the other purposes of the dictatorship. This was the dilemma that faced the conservative opponents of the National Socialist regime who tried to assassinate Hitler in July 1944, who liked much of what the nationalist revolution had achieved. It was possible, and by far the most common, to engage in minor acts of non-compliance or insubordination or hostility, which are usually subsumed by the generic term 'dissent'.

Dissent is a problematic term. In the Soviet Union it has been used as a catch-all description for all forms of protest, non-conformity or intellectual independence, for those of a different mind from the rest of communist society. Soviet dissent might well have incorporated resistance and political opposition, but it is usually applied to those who rejected the regime on grounds of conscience or religion, but who did not engage in acts of political protest as such. Dissent in the history of the Third Reich has been defined more broadly as any manifestation of protest or dissociation short of acts of open political defiance or subversion. The width of this definition raises some awkward questions. Much of what might be taken for dissent was a product of complex layers of social, institutional and personal interaction, where some degree of friction or discordance was as unavoidable under dictatorship as under any other system. No social group, whether a neighbourhood or a factory or a classroom, can speak with a single voice, and in systems less obsessed with unity the grumbles and conflicts of everyday life can be regarded as nothing more than what they are, neither dangerous nor subversive. What turned these trivial manifestations of disapproval into dissent was the way they were treated by the regime, which defined those they detected as expressions of deliberate and challenging non-conformity. In most cases dissent, in this broad sense, went undetected or unpunished, but both populations got to know that there existed an element of risk every time a grumble was overheard or a rule ignored or the regime calumnied. Little of this, despite the sensitivity of the regimes, had any significant political content. Many acts of minor dissent were spontaneous, uncoordinated and unreflective.

The measurement of dissent is also fraught with problems; both regimes politicized actions and behaviour that in other situations would not be political crimes: listening to foreign radio broadcasts, playing American jazz, talking to Jews, pilfering from work, and so on. In such cases the regime's often fantastic definition of dissent bore little relation to the intention of those penalized by the system. The woman caught stealing ears of corn from the collective farm after harvesting was hungry, not a political saboteur. The bank director grumbling to a companion during a train journey across Germany about the course of the war was expressing a private, if imprudent, opinion, but was not a saboteur either. Yet both examples can be found in the record. The bank director was arrested and executed; the woman sent to the GUlag.[4] Even where dissent was genuinely expressed its impact was limited by numerous existential factors. Many acts of dissent were perpetrated by German or Soviet citizens who reacted against one aspect only of the regime, but who did not see their action as a rejection of the whole. This bifurcation was most obvious where an individual made a distinction between dictator and dictatorship: in favour of communism but hostile to Stalin, or enthusiastic about Hitler yet lukewarm about the party.[5] Acts of dissent were also a small part of any individual's relationship to the regime (which could change through time from enthusiasm to uncertainty and back again), but they were unlikely to be more than episodic, or trivial. Larger acts of non-conformity – religious refusal to acknowledge temporal power, for example – were treated as political resistance and heavily punished. But many dissenters slipped in and out of disillusionment, or found ways of making some kind of peace with the system. 'It is difficult to be brave every day,' wrote a German social-democrat about his brief flirtation with the opposition.[6] Ordinary citizens had to face a variety of pressures, of conscience, of fear for family, of shame, or the risk of public disapproval, which could inhibit dissent entirely long before thoughts of the concentration camp.

Dissent is an elastic and unquantifiable phenomenon. Though it evidently surfaced in a wide variety of contexts and degrees of intensity, the dimensions of dissent have been confused by state definitions of non-conformity and by the exaggerated expectations of historians. Popular attitudes to the two dictatorships were neither one-dimensional nor autonomous; dissent, enthusiasm and compliance rubbed shoulders in Soviet and German society. They could inhabit the same individual as he faced the differing things that society asked him to do, or as social and political obligations changed through time. When Alexander Solzhenitsyn was arrested for a chance remark in a letter intercepted by the military censor in 1945, he was an artillery officer with the Red Army, fighting to save the system he sneered at.[7] Dissent was often ambiguous, or camouflaged or hidden, and this, too, makes any estimation of its range and content difficult. The complicated mosaic of popular opinion in regimes where 'opinion' was officially orchestrated and controlled appears chiefly in police or party political intelligence reports, where the reporters were likely to distort the public mood by focusing principally on negative responses, or by using the regime's own fear of unrest or conspiratorial fantasies to frame their view of the population.[8]

Dissent, opposition and resistance nonetheless existed, not in watertight compartments but with permeable walls between them all. The weakness of any hostile political response to the two dictatorships and the evidence for widespread approval and compliance should not be taken to imply that the two dictatorships were entirely consensual. If they had been they would have spent far less time monitoring opinion and pursuing enemies. Nevertheless the frailty of the opposition in both dictatorships reflected not only the power of the state they faced, but the problem of working in societies that did broadly comply and resented social disruption. All of these issues of the scale, nature and effectiveness of popular responses to dictatorship surfaced in the relationship established between the regimes and the working classes.

A file on industrial sabotage among Soviet railway workers kept by the NKVD in 1933 reported the following overheard remarks: 'Everything that comes from the Kremlin strangles the working class'; 'There's a scandal – they don't treat us right. There must be another revolution . . .'[9] Soviet workers had a clear revolutionary tradition rooted both in the failed revolution of 1905 and the two successful revolutions in 1917; workers' opposition, hostile to the authoritarianism of the Leninist state, was ruthlessly crushed in 1921 at the end of the civil war. Stalin's security state kept close watch on workers to ensure that

that potential was never turned against their own 'workers' state'. The German dictatorship was also faced with a large factory working class, whose revolutionary potential was expressed briefly in the crisis after defeat in 1918 with the Spartacist uprising, and the short-lived Bavarian communist revolt in the spring of 1919. This insurrectionary potential haunted the nightmares of German nationalists down to the 1930s. The German industrial workforce was the largest and most organized in Europe; the German socialist parties between them polled more votes than National Socialism in 1932. When Hitler achieved power in 1933 he feared that a socialist-led general strike might paralyse the new regime. The savage persecution and outlawing of communists and social-democrats reflected that fear; throughout the 1930s the security and police apparatus reported weekly and monthly on the residual activity and situation of the Marxist parties, which were described routinely as *staatsfeindlich*, hostile to the state.[10]

Under both dictatorships the situation for workers changed greatly for the worse. The 1920s, by comparison, were a golden age. In Germany workers were closely involved, through trade unions and pay-bargaining agreements, in setting their own wage levels and conditions of work. Works councils set up during the First World War became institutionalized as a means of representing workers' views to management. The German republic was committed to a progressive welfare system and workers' popular culture was emancipated from the cultural ghetto to which it had been confined before 1914. The Social-Democratic Party was by far the largest political party in Germany before 1933, with more than 1.3 million members at its peak in 1923.[11] Soviet workers were a small but privileged social caste in the 1920s, regarded as the central engine of transformation for the proletarian state. Their material conditions slowly improved, generous welfare provisions and educational opportunities were extended, and workers were encouraged to join the communist party on easy terms of entry. They were protected by a new labour code and the eight-hour working day, and Soviet trade unions represented workers directly on the factory floor, arguing for improved conditions and defending worker interests against party and state.[12] By 1928 workers' living standards reached a level they were not to reach again until the very end of Stalin's dictatorship.

The changed circumstances for Soviet labour were signalled by the onset of the First Five-Year Plan in 1928. A public campaign was launched against workers as complacent slackers, persistently absent from work or drunk. To secure lower levels of absenteeism and to reduce high labour turnover, tough anti-labour legislation was introduced in the spring of 1929. That same year the trade union leadership, dominated by supporters of the Bukharinist wing of the party, was removed, together with two-thirds of the membership of factory union committees that supported an independent union movement. Trade unions were ordered to 'turn their face to production', disciplining and exhorting workers to work faster and more productively, but no longer to protect them, or to negotiate wage levels, which were set by the plant director in collaboration with rate-fixing commissions.[13] The Commissariat of Labour under another Bukharinist, V. Schmidt, was closed down. On 29 March 1929 a new law restored to factory managers complete authority (*edinonachalie*) to direct or punish the workforce without reference to the trade unions.[14]

There followed a torrent of labour legislation reversing many of the gains of the revolution: social security was reduced and entitlement made more conditional; a decree in October 1930 prohibited the free movement of labour, and a few months later labour exchanges were closed down; infringements of labour discipline or damage to tools were criminalized in 1931; in July 1932 Article 37 of the 1922 Labour Code was suspended, removing the right of workers to be transferred only with their consent; in November 1932 a single day's absence from work became punishable by instant dismissal; on 27 December 1932 the regime introduced internal passports for the urban population in order to be able, like the Tsarist state, to monitor the movement and whereabouts of its workforce.[15] On 15 January 1939 came a compulsory 'labour book' for all workers, in which were inscribed details of all the jobs they had held and any infractions of discipline, punishments and reprimands. No worker could change employment without written permission from his plant director in the labour book. A few months later a new discipline code required all plant directors to report anyone more than twenty minutes late for work to the local prosecutor's office. A list had to be compiled each morning, with the precise number of minutes late next to every name. The list was signed by the manager and dispatched to the prosecutor, and court hearings held almost immediately. Punishment was up to six months of correctional labour.[16]

The Hitler regime also set about dismantling the powers and rights enjoyed by the wage-labour force. The day after the May Day celebration of labour in 1933 the government dissolved the main trade union association, the German Free Trade Unions, occupied all its offices with the help of the SA and sequestrated its funds. (The Catholic Christian Trade Unions were liquidated later, on 24 June.) Many trade union leaders were arrested and taken to camps and prisons. On 10 May the organization and funds were taken over by the nationally organized German Labour Front, which neither represented labour interests directly nor helped to determine wage rates. Those functions were taken over by new state commissioners, Trustees of Labour, whose responsibility was to fix all wage agreements under the supervision of the Labour Ministry and without reference to the workforce. Also in May 1933, strikes were formally outlawed; the works' councils (*Betriebsräte*) were set aside in a law of 4 April. New labour relations were formally established in the 'Law for the Ordering of National Labour', published on 20 January 1934 from a draft by the mayor of Leipzig, and a future resistance leader, Carl Goerdeler. The law established for German managers the same absolute powers of leadership enjoyed by their Soviet counterparts. The plant *Führer* was able to fix work conditions and impose the wage levels agreed by the Trustee. Wage rates were fixed at the levels of the depression, and altered little during the course of the dictatorship. The works' councils were replaced in all firms employing more than twenty people by new 'trust councils' (*Vertrauensräte*), which were nominally elected after an agreed list of politically reliable candidates had been drawn up by the managers and the party cell in the plant.[17] Labour discipline was tightened up and in 1935 a labour book was introduced to help in monitoring the distribution of the workforce. Employers in iron and steel, engineering, construction and agriculture had the right to refuse to let a worker change employment under new legislation to restrict labour turnover, and in 1938 the state's right to conscript workers to tasks of national importance was introduced.[18]

The emasculation of rights, the increase in labour discipline, the strengthening of managerial authority and the loss of bargaining machinery were compounded with a wage policy and regular shortages of food and consumer goods that left most Soviet and German workers little better off than they had been before the First World War. Deprivation on such a scale did provoke unrest and opposition among both working populations, though its political effect proved to be modest and its capacity to defend labour interests negligible. In Germany the much-feared general strike did not materialize because in the early weeks of the dictatorship both the Social-Democratic Party and the trade union movement decided that discretion was the better part of valour. There was a widespread, and not altogether irrational, assumption that the Hitler government would in its turn be overthrown, and that nothing would be gained for an already weakened trade union movement by confronting a regime clearly bent on smashing any evidence of resistance. 'Organization, not demonstration, is the word for now,' announced Theodor Leipart, head of the trade union movement, on the day Hitler was elected.[19] In March the trade unions began negotiations with the National Socialist factory cell organization to see whether a single independent 'United Trade Union' could be constructed. When union leaders were arrested or sacked on 2 May, the organized labour movement had done little to preserve its substance.[20] After the liquidation of the unions, small cells of union activists remained in factories across Germany. In summer 1933 an attempt was made to set up an underground 'Reich Leadership for the Revival of Trade Unions', based on informal contacts between unionists, principally in the metalworking and railway sectors, and among port workers in Hamburg, but in the summer of 1935 the network was broken up by the Gestapo. Communist unionists tried to set up a rival Revolutionary Union Opposition in Berlin and Hamburg, publishing newspapers and recruiting members, but this, too, was penetrated by the Gestapo in 1934. In Hamburg 800 workers were imprisoned. The final wave of arrests came towards the end of 1937, when a network of around 1,500 railway trade unionists was broken up. In December all were given long prison sentences.[21]

The banned political parties also set up underground networks to maintain a skeleton organization for the moment when Hitler's government fell. Many social-democrats believed that they would be able to survive as their grandfathers had done under Bismarck's anti-socialist legislation in the 1880s, and they remained generally more passive than former communists. Active opposition was stifled by the effectiveness of police action. Of the 422 communist party leaders, 219 had been arrested and sentenced by the autumn of 1935, 125 had emigrated, 24 had been killed and 42 had left the party. Out of 60,000 remaining members, 18,243 were prosecuted between 1933 and 1935.[22] Communist networks were small, scattered and vulnerable. In Baden, for example, a communist cell organization survived in Mannheim, together with a local regional committee, until the police broke it up in 1935. The scope of their activity was presented in regular Gestapo bulletins, issued from the regional headquarters in Karlsruhe. The report for October 1934 shows limited propaganda activity, mainly 'from mouth to mouth', together with the distribution of a few flysheets. A communist paper – The Little Red Flag – appeared briefly in Oberhausen, but ended with the arrest of twelve former communist party members, who were given a short taste of special custody. A worker found with a copy of the parent Red Flag paper was arrested. But other activity was scarcely revolutionary: a peasant was arrested in Mannheim for saying that Hitler was 'a scoundrel'; a former Heidelberg communist was sent to a concentration camp for saying out loud, 'I am and remain communist, as long as I live'; in Konstanz a woman was arrested for smuggling in Swiss newspapers; and so on.[23] In the Ruhr a more developed communist network existed, which published two newspapers, Freedom and Revolutionary, in editions of 2,000 or more, but here too police activity, according to a Moscow-trained activist, left a residual organization in which 'independent activity is managed very little or not at all'. This network was also broken up in 1934.[24]

The workforce could also be prompted into spontaneous protests, though most were short-lived and the scale tiny. Gestapo records, though incomplete, show 25,000 strikers in 1935 in a workforce of 16 million, 4,000 of whom were given short spells in prison. In the month of September 1935 the police reported thirty-seven strikes in the Rhineland, Westphalia, Silesia and Württemberg. The last quarter of 1936 shows approximately 100 incidents nationwide. Throughout 1937 the Labour Front central office reported 250, but strike activity ebbed away thereafter. The strikes were always associated with just one plant, or part of a plant, and lasted only a few hours, sometimes a whole day. They were for the most part about wages, conditions of work or unfair dismissals. The Labour Front found political content in 40 out of the 250 strikes organized in 1937.[25] The Gestapo and the Labour Front together drafted a list of all 'unreliable members of the workforce' so that they could clamp down on known troublemakers and strike leaders, rather than resort to mass arrests. The Labour Front set up its own 'secret service', organized in two departments, one to investigate Marxism in the factories, one to prevent strike action. It co-operated closely with the SS security service in gathering political intelligence on the labour force. In 1939 the Gestapo set up Work Education Camps, where recalcitrant workers could be sent for a short, sharp re-education in how a worker should behave in the new Germany.[26] In each factory or mine of any size there was a Gestapo representative or a Labour Front overseer responsible for monitoring the behaviour of the employees. By 1935 surveillance had helped to overcome the first organized opposition. Political activity was reduced to maintaining small clandestine networks; incidents of sabotage or work stoppages amounted to a scattering of unco-ordinated and brief skirmishes.

The Soviet workforce was more difficult to discipline. During the First Five-Year Plan there were numerous small instances of dissent or protest, almost always a consequence of insupportable conditions or economic hardship, often very violent. The number of strikes nation-wide was not recorded, and in some cases managers were wary of reporting unrest from fear that they would bear the blame. There is evidence of local strike activity. In the Donbass city of Stalino twenty-five strikes were reported in 1928–9. They were small in scale and limited to very real economic grievances: shortages of bread, excessive deductions from wages for compulsory saving, or the high cost of union and co-operative dues. Strikes in 1932 were more common, in a reaction to the food shortages induced by the crisis of collectivization.[27] They were reported in Leningrad, Moscow, Gorky and the industrial regions of the southern Ukraine. Many were the so-called 'Italian strikes', *italianki*, where the pace of work was deliberately and collect-ively slowed down.[28] The link between the food crisis and industrial unrest was very direct, as it had been in 1917. In April 1932 the trade union general secretary, Nikolai Shvernik, warned Stalin that the workers were 'steeped in foul moods' from lack of bread.[29] But the limited effectiveness of industrial action was evident from the fate of one strike at the Teikovo calico works in the Ivanova Industrial Region outside Moscow.

Strike action began at the works on 8 April 1932 after workers heard that the already meagre food ration was to be cut again by a third or more. The director appeared in front of an angry crowd, announced 'It's a state decree, and there's nothing to explain to you' and refused to negotiate. The following day more workers downed tools. Those who tried to continue were bullied and jeered at; a group of women forced the few communist workers in their shed to stop work. On 11 April a march was organized to the local town to petition the party authorities for food. Outsiders joined the demonstration, but when one of them gave an impromptu speech calling on workers to 'overthrow the Soviet regime' he was shouted down by an angry crowd. The first few security troops sent to stop the march were swept aside, but on the way to Ivanova GPU agents picked out and arrested the strike leaders one by one. On 16 April the strike was called off without achieving anything. The report sent to Moscow talked of 'events' by class enemies, not a strike. In his diary one factory leader was dumbfounded by the stoppage: 'What a horror! The fifteenth year of the revolution, and suddenly . . . It simply can't be.'[30]

How widespread such incidents were can only be guessed at, but they were fuelled by real hunger, which ebbed after 1932. The GPU, like the Gestapo, kept files on known dissidents and activists so that they could act quickly in a crisis against the militant fraction. Each Soviet factory and mine had a 'special section' staffed by GPU agents who kept the workforce under surveillance. Soviet camps, like German, began to fill up with workers.

The subdued and fragmentary response of the two workforces to their conditions under dictatorship, involving a few thousand workers out of millions, could plausibly be attributed to the tough discipline and close policing imposed on them. Workers ran greater risks than other groups because they were watched so closely and their forms of protest were so conspicuous. There are, nonetheless, other explanations for the behaviour of the workforce which have little to do with state coercion. In neither society was 'labour' a collective social or political reality. It was socially heterogeneous, politically fragmented and regionally diverse. In Germany there existed a wide gulf between an impoverished craft worker in a small Bavarian workshop and a well-paid steelworker in the Ruhr valley. The German workforce was divided in its political allegiance: the left was split between social-democracy and communism, and social-democracy was itself split between a moderate and a radical wing; millions of Catholic German workers before 1933 supported the Centre Party; millions regularly voted in the 1920s for parties of the nationalist right, but then switched their support to Hitler after 1930.[31] The divisions within the workforce were evident in the last elections to the works' councils, held in April 1933, when National Socialist candidates took one-third of the vote of shop-floor workers and half the votes from industrial white-collar employees.[32] In the Soviet Union on the eve of the Stalin dictatorship could also be found very real differences between the old-established, skill-based industries, the numerous small-scale craft sectors, and daily hired labour, poorly trained and quite separate from the skilled workers. Worker identity was regional, even parochial. Political allegiance among older workers had also been divided, and a core of former Mensheviks and Socialist Revolutionaries existed in the industrial heartlands. Divisions in outlook and milieu were no less evident than in Germany, though the Soviet Union had no broad stratum of socially conservative or nationalist workers.[33]

The particular economic circumstances of the early 1930s also played an important part in shaping the popular response of labour to the dictatorship. The Soviet labour force underwent an exceptional transformation from the late 1920s onwards. The 3.1 million industrial workers of 1928 had become 8.3 million by 1940; the non-agricultural workforce as a whole grew over the same period from 6.8 million to 20 million. The old-established skilled workforce was diluted by a flood of largely unskilled or semi-skilled labour, much of it from the countryside, including a great many women and young workers uninitiated into labour politics. The new workforce predominated in the more modern industrial sectors. In the motor and aviation industries 57 per cent of the 1932 workforce had entered employment in the previous four years, in iron and steel 50 per cent, in the electro-technical industry 48 per cent. In these three sectors only around one-fifth of the workforce had been employed before 1917.[34] Around three-quarters of the newcomers had never had regular paid employment before, either coming straight from the farm, or from military service, or schooling. The number of women in the workforce increased from 2.4 million in 1928 to 7 million in 1933, when women made up exactly one-third of the industrial labour force; by 1937 they were 42 per cent of it. Much of the new workforce, both male and female, was very young: in 1930 a quarter of workers in heavy industry were under twenty-three, by 1935 over one-third. In the 1,500 factories built under the First Five-Year Plan the proportions were yet higher: 43 per cent at the ironworks in Magnitogorsk, 60 per cent in the giant 'Stalin' chemical works at Stalinogorsk.[35] Here in the teeming, chaotic industrial frontier cities the need for discipline was very real among workers who had had no experience of timekeeping, possessed limited skills and literacy and had none of the inherited solidarity of the old union-based industries. Disgruntled workers tended not to strike but simply to leave for another job. In the early 1930s, as the new working class gradually solidified, tensions persisted within the workforce between the older 'core workers' and the new recruits. A common identity could be found only in the context of the new industrial and social order, rather than in the persistence of habits of worker behaviour and worker expectations inherited from the pre-revolutionary age.[36]

Although Germany did not experience the same degree of dislocating social change, the outlook and structure of the workforce was also moulded by crisis. The factor that dominated worker expectations in the 1930s was the experience of long-term unemployment. At the height of the slump, the worst in Germany's history, more than a third of the workforce was without work, some for as long as three years, and millions more were on short time and sharply reduced earnings. The annual cohorts of young Germans coming onto the job market between 1929 and 1933 had no real experience of regular paid work. The impact of enforced idleness on this scale was immense. Trade union membership fell to its lowest level since the war – just 3.5 million in 1932 from a peak of 8.5 million a decade earlier.[37] After 1933 many of the workers who joined the labour force were young or had long severed close links with labour organizations. Older workers were passed over in the re-employment schemes; new categories of cheap labour service emerged to build roads and restore services that were subject to tough discipline and military-style conditions.[38] The country's extraordinary construction boom produced a large labour force of mobile young workers, and later of migrants from Italy and Poland, with few links to the organized labour traditions. Like the Soviet Union, Germany embarked on a large-scale programme of industrial restructuring and the new motor vehicle, aviation and chemical sectors attracted workers who broke away from traditional patterns of employment and labour practices. What united all workers in the first years of the regime was the prospect of a job. The re-employment policies produced full employment in four years; many workers identified with a regime that offered regular work and pay, and distanced themselves from the socialist trade unions and political parties that had signally failed to avert the disaster of the slump.[39]

The two regimes capitalized on these changing conditions to break down older forms of worker identity, and to reduce any residual sense of solidarity. This was achieved by promoting labour policies that fragmented the workforce and promoted a greater sense of individualism, while at the same time encouraging workers' integration into Soviet or German society. Both systems tried to project a positive image of the worker. After the 'anti-worker' rhetoric of the late 1920s, the Soviet regime again put workers at the centre of the campaign for socialist construction. From 1930 workers could earn extra money or bonuses as 'shock workers' organized in shock brigades, which competed with each other for special recognition and privileges. Shock brigades then became, in 1931, 'cost accounting brigades'; each of the 150,000 brigades was supposed to strive against the others to achieve more efficient production and cheaper output. In 1935 the brigades gave way to rewarding exceptional individual effort, pitting worker against worker. The Stakhanov movement separated off the more ambitious or skilled workers from the rest of the workforce; they sat in separate factory canteens, with better rations, and were granted the best of the generally poor housing available.[40] Training courses were widely offered to permit workers to educate themselves out of crude labouring jobs and into higher-paid, more skilled occupations. At one motor vehicle factory the number of unskilled workers fell from half the workforce in 1931 to just 18 per cent by 1938; skilled workers were 17 per cent of plant labour in 1931, 39 per cent seven years later.[41] The traditional skilled labour force supplied many of the expanding number of supervisors, plant administrators or party cell leaders; this differentiation allowed them to dominate the incoming mass of cheap unskilled labour more effectively.[42] The individual worker was presented with a web of incentives to identify with the regime and to measure his or her achievement at the expense of others.

The process of 'individualization' was paralleled by changes in the nature of production and the way in which work was rewarded. The modern factories of the Five-Year Plans broke production down into different stages and processes, each with its own specialized workforce, demarcated from the rest. Work was increasingly organized by time and motion experts, who set norms for production times for each separate group of workers. This, too, reduced a sense of solidarity in the plant workforce, a solidarity that had been previously linked to communal forms of worker organization, based on the tradition of the *artel* or labour collective. There were by 1930 232,000 separate norms set by Rates and Norms Bureaux, plant by plant. Workers were supposed to conform to standard methods tested under laboratory conditions on the basis of a new science of 'biomechanics'.[43] Norms were constantly raised, and workers challenged to meet defined levels of personal achievement. Pay was linked to norms. The majority of workers came to be paid on piece-rates – 70 per cent by 1935 – and these were regularly recalculated to speed up production. Piece-rates also encouraged a sense of competition between workers and made explicit the differences in aptitude and attitude. The payment of regular daily or weekly wages in the 1930s was also restructured to encourage the greater demarcation of the workforce. A wage-scale graded in seventeen major categories was introduced, and workers became ambitious to move up the wage ladder by overtaking their peers. The classification of skills produced an array of different measurements of status: the twelve separate categories of metalwork in 1930 became 176 by 1939; over the same period just three classes of electrical skill were transformed into 188.[44] All collective wage agreements were abandoned in 1935, and the calculation of rewards for every worker was decentralized to the individual factory or construction site. Class identity was replaced by identities derived from the particular workplace and the particular working group.

The German workforce experienced a similar process of individualization and decentralization. Cut off from union organization, and with wage rates determined by external adjudicators, workers were supposed to identify much more with the plant they worked in than with the rest of the workforce. The weekly *Betriebsappell* (factory assembly) brought the whole workforce together to listen to exhortations from management and to applaud the roll-call of factory high-achievers. The extensive use of piece-rates in German industry encouraged extra efforts for extra rewards, while the careful demarcation of skills produced the same pattern of fragmentation as in Soviet industry. The introduction of standardized work practices and production norms broke down the older classification of factory labour into unskilled, semi-skilled and skilled and replaced it with a system of differentiation based on the productive achievement and sex of the individual worker. Large-scale training programmes, organized under the Labour Front by the Office for Professional Education, provided opportunities for millions of workers – 2.5 million by 1936 – to move to more highly paid skilled jobs, or to move from low-wage consumer industries to the burgeoning armaments sector, where rewards were higher.[45] The Labour Front also organized a nationwide competition for skilled workers (*Reichsberufswettkampf*) that, by 1939, involved 3.5 million workers in local and national competitions. The finalists took part in a skill Olympics, where young workers vied with each other to build walls, turn pots and sew dresses better than the rest. The competition was widely popular, symbolizing the evident transformation of the outlook of younger workers from traditional collectivism to worker meritocracy.[46] The fragmentation of identity was accelerated by the same process evident in the Soviet Union, of recruitment of traditional core workers – the so-called *Stammarbeiter* – into supervisory or administrative roles that distanced them from the rest of the workforce. Older and more experienced workers were chosen to run training schemes or supervise the less-skilled, creating new structures of status and reward that split the natural leadership from the rank-and-file.[47] This process was accelerated during the war when millions of German male workers were replaced by redeployed female labour and foreign forced labour, which were dominated by male supervisors and foremen promoted from the established male work-force. By 1944 over one-third of the labour force in war industries was female and 37 per cent non-German.[48]

In both systems the individual plant became the source of additional rewards and opportunities. During the 1930s and 1940s the Soviet factory became, literally, the key to survival for millions of Soviet workers. Food was provided, often generously, in factory canteens and kitchens. A foreign worker in the Karbolit factory in Dubrovka in 1937 reported that the canteen offered a choice of three different soups, twelve or fifteen different meat dishes, with fruit, tea and black or brown bread all at a cost of two or three roubles a day from a monthly wage packet of 200 to 300 roubles. At the Hammer and Sickle Steel Plant in Moscow in the 1930s there was a closed shop for the workforce where they could buy fruit and other foodstuffs produced by the workers themselves on the factory farm twelve kilometres from Moscow. The same plant provided crèches, day-care centres and medical facilities. This was particularly important for the high number of female employees throughout Soviet industry, who were granted statutory leave not only for maternity but, on production of a medical certificate, severe menstrual cramps.[49] Factories all over the Soviet Union provided small allotments for their workers; many collective farms were allocated as suppliers to the local industries. The additional 'social wage' increased the longer a worker stayed loyal to his factory. In the 1930s it added an estimated one-quarter to the wages paid in cash. Social welfare depended on length of service, which for the new workers in the 1930s could mean very real differences in levels of amenity and assistance. Individual factory bosses could give discretion-ary loans to favoured or loyal workers from the plant's social fund, to finance holidays, medical expenses or a family crisis.[50]

In Germany workers could be given bonuses in kind, or supplemen-tary food supplies collected in company storehouses. The long tradition of business paternalism flourished in the 1930s as employers, particu-larly in the expanding armaments and heavy industrial sectors, explored ways of keeping the workforce loyal in a low-wage economy.

The social welfare payments made by large businesses to fund kindergarten, workers' housing or educational programmes increased steadily during the decade (they could also be set against corporation tax). The Labour Front itself offered workers regular and cheap holidays through the Strength through Joy organization. In 1933 only 18 per cent of German industrial workers took a holiday at all; in 1934 2.1 million took trips of a week or more to German destinations, in 1938 7 million.[51] The same organization offered medical facilities to try to cut back on the high levels of tiredness and absenteeism, particularly evident in the growing number of female workers who had to juggle the demands of home life, motherhood and work. Preventative medical care and improved standards of hygiene, promoted by the Beauty at Work programme, were linked to increased productivity levels; malingerers were regularly checked by medical staff to reduce above-average levels of absenteeism after 1933.[52]

The workforce in both systems adapted to the new conditions rather than confront them. This did not necessarily make them enthusiasts for either communism or National Socialism, though many were in each system. Workers were forced to search for strategies of survival of their own, sometimes through the complicity of a small group of co-workers, often as individuals. The atomization of the workforce, already evident in its heterogeneous character and changing structures, destroyed a collective public identity and encouraged workers to retreat to the private sphere of family or street. Neither regime wanted to promote the re-formation of an autonomous worker milieu which might deflect the new economic and political realities. In Germany a distinct worker identity survived in small urban pockets, where neighbourhood solidarity repelled the blandishments of the regime, but the associations that had helped to bind workers together inside and outside the factory gates – youth groups, co-operatives, drama clubs, the paramilitary brigades, etc. – were eliminated or closely monitored. From each of the many workers' choirs across Germany the SS security service recruited an informer to pass on details of anything suspicious overheard between the songs.[53] For the millions of workers who had not been active union or party members before 1933, National Socialism provided opportunities for social mobility and political responsibility or shaped new forms of status and identity.

In the Soviet Union integration with the prevailing system made obvious good sense, since it promised opportunities for social development and enjoyed a monopoly of institutional and cultural life.

Adaptation could also take more tangible forms. In both systems there existed some room for manoeuvre in setting wages and establishing new work practices. The decentralization of responsibility to the individual plant or factory put managers in the position where they relied on the workforce to fulfil plans and norms. In some cases this resulted in the factory authorities delegating the task of organizing work practices to the shopfloor workers and supervisors. In the Soviet Union norms were set at deliberately low levels to help the weaker workers and to encourage high bonuses for the workers who comfortably exceeded them. There were endless opportunities for malingering or returning false records of achievement; the poor system of distribution in industry often meant that workers were paid for doing nothing until their supplies turned up. At the Dinamo plant in Moscow the average working time each day in August 1933 was just four hours seventeen minutes; the rest of the time was spent waiting for parts or materials.[54] High labour turnover encouraged the factory authorities to turn a blind eye to many practices just to keep the workforce together and reasonably disciplined. Workers recognized their power to make life difficult for managers, who were under constant pressure to deliver on time. Stakhanovites were sometimes murdered, assaulted or boycotted because of the threat they posed to the less-motivated sections of the labour force. These complicit communities shielded workers from the full letter of the law and the remorseless demands for achievement.

Much the same happened in Germany. Workers found ways of resisting the setting of high norms for piecework by agreeing among themselves to work at a deliberately slow and thorough pace when the norm-setters were inspecting. Collective agreements to go slow in a workshop could pressure managers into conceding improvements or higher piece-rates. The wage-fixing authorities faced numerous problems in setting the pace of work factory by factory and preventing excessive pay increases. The Labour Trustee in Brandenburg, for example, was responsible in 1939 for no fewer than 330,000 firms; his office received 800 to 900 telephone calls a day and several hundred letters. Twenty officials worked until late in the evening and most Sundays to cope with the backlog of norm-fixing. Local factory owners did what they could to avoid controls and pay higher wages 'in order to hold onto their labour force'. One used special bonuses to get round official wage ceilings: 300,000 marks were paid out to workers on Hitler's birthday, 50,000 marks to celebrate the birth of a child, 150,000 marks at Christmas.[55] Although nominally the creatures of the factory authority and the Labour Trustees, the Trustee Councils could also become instruments to defend worker interests against management efforts to rationalize production; workers were appointed as Labour Front supervisors, and connived to improve conditions with the strength of the party behind them. Informal agreements and veiled threats, go-slows and bribes replaced the suspended machinery of wage-bargaining, strikes and lockouts.[56]

None of this amounted to a direct political challenge. Workers were concerned about issues of food, wages and the pace of work. The element of flexibility at the level of the individual plant provided the means to deflect militancy, and to encourage a greater sense of integration and adaptation. One of the regular 'Germany Reports' produced by the exiled social-democrats in Prague in 1936 observed that 'great parts of the labour force have come to believe through acceptance of the system that they can exchange freedom for security'.[57] The exiled socialists watched as German workers became rapidly depoliticized. 'The automatism with which the factory workers accept everything is frightening', ran another report from Saxony; 'political indifference has reached frightening proportions in the proletariat', ran another from 1936.[58] This conclusion fitted with the judgement made by the Gestapo a year before: 'the number [of workers] who stand for the *Führer* and his idea is steadily growing'.[59] Both sides had a tendency to exaggerate the pre-existing levels of political activism. Most German workers in 1932 did not belong to a trade union; millions of workers did not vote for and had never been active in the socialist movements. For them the transition to National Socialism left them enthusiastic, or cautiously sympathetic, or indifferent, but it did not make them any more politically engaged than they had been before. Former socialists and communists, who now lacked any secure means for protecting their interests, in the main abandoned politics and made some kind of compromise with the new order. Workers formed the fastest growing element among new party joiners throughout the late 1930s and the war.[60]

Soviet workers had even less experience of political activism than German ones. The overwhelming majority of the new young workers who entered the labour force after 1929 had known only the communist party. The small number of workers who flirted with Trotskyism or who retained loyalty to older ideas of Menshevik democracy was ruthlessly purged in the 1930s. The milieu of the Soviet labour force was shaped by the exigencies of the vast programme of industrial and urban construction. Many of the new towns were poorly resourced and barren; Soviet workers spent their private hours and energies trying to give greater shape and purpose to their local communities, and this could only be achieved through the agency of the party. The evidence of persistent dissent, expressed through indiscipline, grumbling and occasional violence, and sometimes through a real act of sabotage, was deflected by the regime into the search for political 'enemies', most of them imaginary, and countered by the endless promises of a utopian tomorrow. The gradual stabilization of the new urban and industrial communities created a sufficient sense of integration, as in Germany, to eliminate any widespread political threat from a wage-labour force whose means to define, co-ordinate or execute political opposition, rather than casual dissent, was effectively stifled.

The most direct and effective means of opposing dictatorship was to assassinate the dictator. Elements of the system would have survived the deaths of either man, but it seems unlikely that personal dictatorship of this type would have passed to a successor as absolute as the fallen leader. Assassination might have come from many directions: ambitious claimants to the dictators' thrones; disillusioned subordinates; opponents willing to carry out tyrannicide; a deranged protester. In Russia there was a long tradition of political murder as virtuous retribution.[61] Lenin was the victim of two attempts on his life. Many years later, a man was caught in the Lenin mausoleum trying to shoot the embalmed corpse.[62] It is all the more remarkable that no evidence has yet surfaced about a single assassination attempt against Stalin.

There were plenty of alleged plots confessed by prisoners beaten and tortured by the security police, but they were grotesque fantasies fuelled partly by Stalin's own paranoia about death. There were certainly unnumbered Russians who would have liked to see Stalin dead. A Soviet defector, Genrikh Lyushkov, who crossed into Japanese territory in June, 1938, was supposed to have been recruited by Japanese intelligence agencies to murder Stalin. A Paris-based group of émigrés discussed murdering Stalin in February 1937, according to the NKVD infiltrator in their midst. Another NKVD agent reported a remark made by Trotsky's son Lev Sedov, also in Paris: 'There is no point in hesitating any longer. Stalin has to be killed.'[63] Numerous jokes circulating in the Soviet Union had the death of Stalin at their core. The acronym USSR was said to stand for 'Stalin's Death will save Russia'.[64]

Stalin was well aware of the possibility of murder. His savage reaction after the assassination of Kirov in 1934 reflected that fear. The arrangements for his personal security became almost comically elaborate. Curtains had to be cropped to prevent anyone standing behind them unobserved. His official cars were heavily armoured and stripped of running boards to prevent assassins from jumping onto the side of the vehicle. It was said that Stalin never announced in advance in which bedroom he would sleep; rumours persisted that his food and drink was sampled before he touched it.[65] He was heavily guarded by militia and security men and exposed himself seldom to direct contact with the public. None of this should have deflected a determined assassin. Luck clearly played a part, but it was bolstered by the tactics of infiltration and surveillance practised by the security services. The remark by Lev Sedov was faithfully passed on to Moscow by a young Pole, Mark Zborowski, who became Lev's closest companion and confidant for six years, all the while working for the Soviet secret service. Stalin was informed at once. It was Stalin, not his protagonists, who ordered assassinations. Lev Sedov died in mysterious circumstances in a Russian hospital in Paris a year after his outburst. In 1937 Stalin personally ordered the murder of the elder Trotsky.[66]

Hitler was the target for assassination throughout his political career, from the two shots fired at him during a beerhall mêlée in Munich in 1921 to the plot hatched by his armaments minister Albert

Speer in 1945 to pour poison gas down the air vents of Hitler's Berlin bunker.[67] The number of attempts has been estimated at forty-two, though some were repeated by the same group, or sometimes the same person, some, like the Speer scheme, were never put into operation, and yet others may have escaped detection altogether. They were all united by failure. Hitler was grazed by a stone in an attack on his car in July 1932, and badly dazed, cut and bruised by the bomb that exploded in his headquarters on 20 July 1944, but otherwise remained unscathed. He interpreted his survival from shootings, at least eight bomb plots, one stoning and one mugging to the hidden hand of Providence 'directing me to complete my work'.[68] Good fortune certainly played its part – the bomb planted by a disgruntled SS man in 1929 could not be primed in time because he was stuck in a lavatory with a faulty lock; the bomb carefully concealed by Georg Elser, a Württemberg watchmaker, behind the wooden casing of a pillar in the Munich beer cellar where Hitler spoke to party 'old fighters' on the evening of 8 November 1939, exploded thirteen minutes after Hitler left, killing eight and wounding sixty-three.[69] Incompetence and hesitancy ruined other attempts. The young Swiss theology student Maurice Bavaud, sent from a seminary in Brittany to do God's work in killing Hitler for not being anti-communist enough, entered Germany with a gun in October 1938 obsessed with his mission. He followed Hitler to Berlin, back to Berchtesgaden and then to Nuremberg, where he succeeded in finding a front row place to watch Hitler march in the annual remembrance of party martyrs. He had practised firing the gun at trees in the local forests, but was accurate at only a few metres. Hitler walked by on the far side of the road from Bavaud, too distant for a shot. He was finally caught after he forged a letter of introduction from the French foreign minister and tried to use it to get a personal audience with the *Führer*.[70] Bavaud was executed, but Elser was sent to a camp and only killed towards the end of the war.

The closest anyone came to killing Hitler was in July 1944. The July Plot was distinguished by the fact that it was planned and carried out by insiders in the military establishment who had access to Hitler denied to almost all the other assassins. A circle of conservative army officers and officials, grouped around a former chief-of-staff of the army, Ludwig Beck, had conspired for several years to find a way of killing Hitler in order to save Germany from what they saw as certain disaster. In March 1943 two bottles of Cointreau primed with a British-made plastic explosive and British detonators, picked up from British parachute drops, were placed in Hitler's aircraft by General Henning von Treschkow, but failed to detonate. Plans to storm Hitler's headquarters, even to gun him down in cold blood, were discussed but never realized. Finally in 1944 a young staff officer, Count Claus Schenk von Stauffenberg, convinced that killing Hitler was a chivalric duty, volunteered to carry a bomb into Hitler's headquarters. He was handicapped by severe wounds received in the Tunisian campaign; with one eye, no right hand and two fingers blown off the left hand he somehow learned to prime the explosives. Twice before he carried his lethal briefcase into meetings with Hitler. On the first occasion Himmler, who was also a target, was absent; on the second Hitler left prematurely. However, on 20 July 1944, Stauffenberg succeeded in walking past three security posts on his way to a briefing meeting in Hitler's East Prussian headquarters. He set the timer, concealed the briefcase containing the bomb under a thick oak map table and made an excuse to leave. Outside he watched as the small cabin disintegrated in the explosion, throwing debris and bodies into the air. He bluffed his way out of the now buzzing compound, flew to Berlin and announced Hitler's death. Hitler survived only because another officer, irritated by the briefcase against his foot, pushed it further under the table, away from the dictator. Stauffenberg was arrested in Berlin that day and executed at once in the cobbled courtyard of the War Ministry.[71] Hundreds of his fellow conspirators were arrested, tortured, put on trial and either executed or sent to camps.

The July Plot was unique among the many assassination attempts because it was the outcome of a much broader plan to overturn the regime and establish a new form of government. There were almost no other examples under either dictator of a concerted and planned attempt to overthrow the dictatorship from within. Active political opposition in this sense remained extraordinarily confined. The German social-democrats finally called for revolutionary activity late in 1933 only after their organization had been destroyed. Newspapers were published, chief among them *Sozialistische Aktion*, which spelt out the break in social-democracy's long tradition of parliamentary legitimacy. 'Revolution Against Hitler' was one of their first illegal pamphlets.[72] But the efforts already described of the remnant of party activists remaining in Germany were focused on mere survival rather than on plotting the downfall of the regime. The party operated principally in exile. Its headquarters was set up first in Prague, later in Paris after the German occupation of Bohemia in March 1939, and finally in London. On Germany's borders the party set up a network of secretariats, six in Czechoslovakia, two each in Poland, Switzerland, France and Belgium, and one each in Luxembourg and Denmark. From here newspapers and pamphlets were smuggled into Germany, and regular radio broadcasts beamed across the frontier. There was no way to prevent the gradual disintegration of the residual party network within Germany. After the wave of arrests in 1934 and 1935 revolutionary activity generally ceased and members were forced into a policy of waiting for the dictatorship to collapse under its own weight. Two former social-democrat officials, Hermann Brill and Otto Brass, founded a separate 'German Popular Front' in 1936, with a ten-point programme for the re-establishment of democracy and a socialized economy, headed by point number one: 'Overthrow and destruction of the Hitler dictatorship.' They were caught two years later and each sentenced to twelve years in prison.[73]

The German communist party also kept up illegal revolutionary activity in the first few years, but, like social-democracy, had to concentrate its efforts on simply sustaining its etiolated apparatus, which was penetrated and destroyed by the Gestapo so often that some city cells were on to their sixth or seventh leadership by 1936. Most political activity was conducted outside Germany: the German politburo was set up in Paris under Wilhelm Pieck; Walter Ulbricht, the general secretary, and later leader of the communist German Democratic Republic, left Germany in September 1933 for Czechoslovakia, but spent long periods in Moscow. Away from the bitter reality of political life in Germany, they urged all German workers to refuse to pay taxes, rent, gas and electricity bills and to mount nationwide marches, strikes and demonstrations.[74] In 1935, consistent with the shift in the tactics of the Communist International to a policy of a 'popular front' against fascism, the exiled communists tried to establish links with social-democracy. A few 'United Front Committees' appeared here and there in Germany, but the old and bitter divisions between the two socialist movements were difficult to heal even in the face of a common enemy. The two sides met in Prague in November 1935, but the social-democrats refused collaboration on the ground that anti-communist workers would be driven into the arms of the dictatorship if they moved too far to the left. A second meeting in Paris in January 1939 exposed how far apart the two sides were. The good faith of German communists was not trusted by the rest of the German left; popular front rhetoric was regarded as a likely stepping stone to a rigid Stalinism.[75]

The weaknesses of political opposition from the left derived not only from police oppression but from deeply held inherited rivalries. Communists had the stronger revolutionary tradition, but their links with the Soviet system and espousal of direct, militant action had not appealed to most Germans before 1933, and did so even less in the dangerous political climate after 1933. Communism was turned into a marginal movement, isolated by the Hitler regime as the single greatest danger to the recovery of the German nation, and distrusted by social-democracy for its authoritarianism and violence. Both wings of German socialism suffered after 1933 from the necessity for organizations in exile. Relations between those who stayed and those who left were often strained: the exile movements were impatient for evidence of solidarity and resistance and were invariably disappointed; those activists left in Germany resented the exaggerated expectations of émigré authorities who seemed blind to the persistent danger to which domestic supporters were exposed. By 1939 left-wing activity in Germany had all but disappeared.

Conservative political opposition was very different. It was not based on any potential mass movement, or on the activity of former political parties. The numbers involved were very small and came, in the main, from those circles in German society where resistance was the most unexpected. Their activity was counter-revolutionary, not revolutionary. The handful of generals, landowners and senior bureaucrats, who came to decide in the late 1930s that Hitler represented a dangerous social experiment and a threat to the survival of 'old Germany', were drawn from those very conservative circles who had initially welcomed the new order in 1933 and were deeply hostile to the German left. The chief wartime conspirator, Ludwig Beck, described the dictatorship in 1933 as 'the first real ray of light since 1918'; Carl Goerdeler, the leading civilian among the conservative resistance, and regarded as Hitler's possible successor as Chancellor, had called in 1932 for an end to the party system and for 'a dictatorship lasting for years', and in 1934 wrote to Hitler endorsing the destruction of other political parties and the amalgamation of all authority 'in the hands of one person'.[76] The lawyer Fritz-Dietlof von der Schulenberg, one of those hanged in 1944, had joined the National Socialist party in 1932 and in 1933 applauded Hitler's triumph over 'the powers of Jewry, capital, and the Catholic Church'.[77] When the small circles of conservative opponents began to explore the possibility of a coup against Hitler in 1938, thoughts of a coalition with more 'moderate' National Socialists, including Hermann Göring, were seriously entertained. When the coup was launched on 20 July 1944, the putative new government included Albert Speer, a prominent National Socialist, and Hjalmar Schacht, a minister in Hitler's government.[78]

These authoritarian and nationalist sympathies handicapped the conservative opposition throughout its life. Before 1933 the German electorate had rejected the conservative vision of the nation in favour of Hitler's more radical promise of renewal. There was little popular desire to see the traditional conservative elite back in power, and conservative opponents, though, like Beck, they sometimes talked about the need to build a broad post-Hitler alliance, even with the German left, had almost no popular support among the wider German public. What drove many conservatives into opposition was not the necessity to restore democracy, but the danger posed to the future of the German nation by what they regarded as a dangerously wilful foreign policy and irresponsible warmongering. Conservative opponents were happy to accept the demolition of the Versailles settlement and the restoration of German armed power under Hitler; during the war they also regarded a strong and united Germany as an essential element in any post-war settlement and a bulwark against communism. Claus von Stauffenberg hoped that after he had slain Hitler, Germany would be allowed to play a full part as a Great Power, with its armed forces intact, with a political order that was 'soldierly' and 'totalitarian', run by true 'national socialists'.[79] Goerdeler, though sincerely repelled by the racism and oppression of the dictatorship, wanted Greater Germany, complete with Austria, the Sudetenland and the South Tyrol, guaranteed in any future peace settlement.[80] The opposition hoped that the western Allies would accept the necessity for a strong Germany with its face towards the Soviet menace. Adam von Trott zu Solz, generally regarded as a liberal among the opposition, and the chief emissary to the British during the war, still expected a free hand in the East and 'strong armour' against communism.[81] The result was a persistent rejection by the Allies of any of the advances from the conservatives, who were regarded as spokesmen for those same militaristic and nationalist circles that the West blamed for bringing Hitler to power in the first place.

The conservative opposition had also to come to terms with their new roles as conspirators and assassins. For many this meant breaking with ancient traditions of military loyalty and the defence of the state. Most senior officers and officials did not join the opposition; the oath of fealty sworn to Hitler placed powerful conscientious constraints upon them even in the face of the corruption and criminality of the regime. The July plotters wrestled with the inner voices telling them that the murder of their head-of-state and commander-in-chief was treason. They justified their actions in a variety of ways. For some it was enough to ensure that Germany and German values would survive the tyrannicide; others, including Claus von Stauffenberg, saw it as justifiable homicide vindicated by a higher, eternal law against injustice. Goerdeler, for all his patriotism and authoritarian leanings, was outraged, as were many of his co-conspirators, by the genocide of the Jews, which was, by 1943, common knowledge among them. The accusation of treason, at the height of a desperate war, was nonetheless an unappealing prospect. The conspirators' chance of creating a domestic consensus for a conservative-dominated government, created on the foundation of Hitler's murder, was slender. It was made more difficult by the establishment in the Soviet Union of two exile organizations, the communist-dominated 'Free Germany Committee', set up in July 1943, and, two months later, the League of German Officers, recruited from among German prisoners-of-war, both of which kept up an open propaganda war of leaflets and radio broadcasts in 1943 and 1944 to get the German army and the German people to overthrow Hitler. Their value to the Soviet war effort was transparently opportunistic, but the effect in Germany was to identify in the popular mind the military conservative opposition with the Soviet enemy and the 'traitors' they harboured. When Hitler announced on the day of the assassination attempt that the plotters had tried 'to stab Germany in the back', the wider population was inclined to agree, not necessarily from enthusiasm for Hitler, but from outrage at treason. A German communist broadcaster in the Soviet Union, Anton Ackermann, bemoaned the conspirators' failure to create 'a broad basis in the people'.[82]

Alongside overt political opposition there did exist throughout the life of the dictatorship regular acts of conscientious resistance. This form of protest was always treated by the regime as an act of political disobedience, but it seldom amounted to political opposition in any organized or coherent sense. Much of it was expressed in individual acts of defiance that ran counter to the formal attitude of the group or institution from which the protest emanated. Clergymen regularly denounced some aspect of party policy from the pulpit, even where the Church was not collectively opposed. Secret acts of defiance, the sheltering of German Jews from the authorities, for example, resulted from a basic humanity, not from any desire to fight for the overthrow of the system. There is no way of estimating how widespread such acts of conscientious protest were; some were discovered and penalized, but many were not. Some were sudden, impulsive acts, others more carefully thought through. Resistance was sometimes successful, in the sense that it went undetected, sometimes not, but it was a category of popular attitude distinct from opposition. The history of the White Rose movement is among the best known. The small group at Munich University took its name from a popular novel of the 1930s, set in Mexico. The key figures were Hans and Sophie Scholl, the children of a small-town mayor who lost his position in 1933. Hans was a member of the Hitler Youth, but left to become a member of a small youth protest group, an act for which he was briefly jailed. He did labour and military service in the Medical Corps, but in 1942 was in Munich, where, together with his sister and an academic expert in folk-music, Kurt Huber, he drafted six protest flysheets that were posted around the city denouncing the criminality of the regime and calling for non-compliance. Their position was philosophical as much as political. In one of the sheets they asked why their society had lost sight of its humanity: 'Why does the German people behave so apathetically in the face of the most dreadful and unworthy crimes?'[83] They were arrested on 18 February 1943 after a university porter saw one of the group scattering leaflets early one morning and telephoned the Gestapo; the Scholls were executed four days later, Huber in July. Hans was said to have died with the word 'freedom' on his lips.

Political opposition in the Soviet Union was inhibited by restrictions similar to those in Germany. Historians face evident problems in assessing not only the extent, but the very existence of active opponents to Stalin's dictatorship after the defeat of the Ryutin platform in 1932. The show trials suggested an extensive, co-ordinated opposition dedicated to overthrowing Stalin, introducing capitalism and shackling the Soviet Union once again to the imperial power system. These have always been regarded as the fantasies they were, dreamt up by State Security, beaten out of its prisoners or woven from a web of denunciation, innuendo and fabricated evidence. It is beyond question that there were communists in the Soviet Union under the Stalin dictatorship, as there were in the so-called opposition of the 1920s, who disagreed with Stalinist strategy, though most ended up in prison or were executed during the 1930s. But argument within the party did not disappear entirely. It can too easily be forgotten that it was possible to contradict Stalin in committee on issues of policy and to survive the experience. None of this amounted to concerted political opposition to rid the party of Stalin, or the Soviet Union of authoritarian communism. One oppositionist, the novelist Viktor Serge, described the impossibility of serious political activity: 'How could anyone conspire in these conditions – when it was scarcely possible to breathe, when we lived in a house of glass, our least gestures and remarks spied upon?' In the early 1930s Serge kept in touch with no more than twenty others, but they did nothing else than 'simply existing' and 'talking freely in each other's company'.[84] Occasionally leaflets or open letters were secretly printed calling for protest. One example from 1937 called on voters to use the elections to register their disapproval: 'Comrades! Protest against the unheard-of terror . . . At the elections put in clean bulletins, cross out all the names. Down with the bloody dictatorship!'[85] The impact of isolated acts of defiance appears to have been slight. On the present evidence, the conclusion must remain that under Stalin's dictatorship there was little active political opposition inside the Soviet Union committed to a change of leader or regime.

The political opposition, such as it was, worked outside the Soviet Union, which was the only possibility for conducting regular propaganda and an independent political life. Even then, independence was conditional, for Soviet assassins and agents provocateurs worked assiduously to betray or destroy any opposition outside Soviet frontiers as well as within. External activity was largely doomed to failure. It stretched from the extreme right to the communism of the exiled 'left' opposition around Trotsky. The exile communities were very large: in 1936 the League of Nations' refugee board counted 844,000 Russians abroad. Among them were former Kadets, Socialist Revolutionaries and Mensheviks, who reconstructed miniature versions of the banned parties in exile. The Mensheviks published a regular journal, *Socialist Courier*, in New York.[86] On the right, groups loyal to the Romanov dynasty, largely destroyed in the early 1920s by the Cheka, were replaced by nationalist and quasi-fascist organizations. In 1932 the National Alliance of Russian Solidarists was formed in Yugoslavia, sympathetic to Mussolini, and later to Hitler and Franco.[87] In Berlin in 1933 the Russian National Socialist Movement was set up by émigré White Russians; its members, each comically adorned with Hitler's familiar toothbrush moustache, and a uniform like that of a railway guard, were closely watched by the Gestapo, and the organization closed down in 1939.

Russian fascism's main home was outside Europe, in Manchuria. The Russian Fascist Party, modelled on Mussolini's movement, was founded in the city of Harbin in 1931. Here, on the remote reaches of the Sungari river, thousands of Russians who had fled from the revolution constructed a little Russia. In a city teeming with different nationalities, the Russians printed and read numerous papers in Russian, attended the Russian cathedral, sat in cafés along the smart Bolshoi Prospekt, and talked endlessly of the war of revenge against Bolshevism. The White community was fractious and diverse, and Soviet agents encouraged their squabbles. The Russian Fascists, under their own Mussolini, the young Siberian expatriate Konstantin Rod-zaevsky, were one among several nationalist groupings, numbering at most only a few thousand uniformed men. They were anti-Semitic, intensely nationalist ('Russia for the Russians'), Christian and corpora-tist.[88] In 1934 the party merged with another fascist group founded the year before in the town of Thompson, Connecticut, pretentiously titled the All-Russian Fascist Organization. It was commanded by Count Anastase Vonsiatsky, a Polish émigré who in the 1920s had flirted with the Paris-based Russian Armed Services Union (committed to terror attacks against the Soviet Union), married a wealthy American woman twenty years his senior, moved to New England and declared himself the Russian Hitler. His organization borrowed Mussolini's black shirt and Hitler's swastika. The party song was a Russian version of the National Socialist anthem, with jazz added. The flamboyant Vonsiatsky found it hard to share the role of *Führer* with Rodzaevsky, and in 1935 the two organizations parted company again. Vonsiatsky returned to the United States where he published forged copies of a journal *Fashist*, which, he claimed, was published in Moscow by fascist sympathizers; one of his Soviet fascist supporters was said to be responsible for the murder of Kirov.[89] Russian fascism was perman-ently at war with itself during its short life. Rodzaevsky, who at the end of the war converted from fascism to Stalinism ('Stalinism . . . is our Russian Fascism cleansed of extremes, illusions, and errors'), was caught and put on trial in Moscow, flanked by two rival fascist bosses and another sworn nationalist enemy. All were found guilty and executed. After serving a three-year prison sentence in America during the war on charges of spying for Germany, and later playing a great deal of golf, Vonsiatsky died in Florida in 1965.[90]

The principal political opponent of Stalin, until his murder in 1940, was Leon Trotsky. Throughout his period of foreign exile from 1929, he sought the active overthrow of his triumphant rival and the estab-lishment of a network of anti-Stalin communists committed to his vision of world revolution. He began his activity in the temporary room given to him in the Soviet consulate in Istanbul. Here he wrote the article that made him forever a marked man in Stalin's eyes: 'What is Stalin? This is the most outstanding mediocrity in our Party . . . His political horizon is extremely narrow . . . His theoretical level is primitive . . .'[91] He moved to the Turkish island of Prinkipo, where for four years he kept up a prolonged journalistic assault on his target. Trotsky founded the *Bulletin of the Opposition*, which for ten years was the main outlet for his vituperative and personal attacks on Stalin. It was edited by his son, Lev Sedov, but written largely by Trotsky himself. Copies were smuggled occasionally into the Soviet Union, but a copy of each edition was always supplied to Stalin by the Central Committee press office. Trotsky tried to keep up contact with sympathizers in the Soviet Union, but the risks they ran were great. One visitor to Prinkipo, Yakov Blyumkin, who was given two letters to hand on when he returned home, was arrested on his arrival in the Soviet Union and shot. In 1933 Trotsky announced his intention to establish a Fourth International to rival the Stalinist Comintern; it was launched eventually in Paris in June 1938 as the 'World Party of Social Revolution', but in December 1936 Trotsky had moved to Mexico and could influence events in Europe little. His family was decimated by Stalin. His mother, Alexandra, disappeared from Leningrad in 1936. His two sons were both murdered: Sergei Sedov, who stayed in the Soviet Union, was arrested in 1935 and executed in October 1937.[92]

Trotsky supporters were regular victims of assassination wherever they operated. Hundreds were murdered on the republican side in the Spanish Civil War by other communists and NKVD agents. The headless torso of one of Trotsky's former secretaries, Rudolf Klement, was found floating in the Seine in 1937; in September the same year Ignace Reiss, a Soviet diplomat in Paris and an acquaintance of Lev Sedov, was lured to a restaurant in Lausanne as he tried to defect, clubbed unconscious and his body riddled with bullets.[93] Trotsky's own life had long been forfeit. Elaborate plans were laid to assassinate him in his Mexican retreat. After a failed machine-gun attack, a lone assassin, Ramon Mercader, a fanatical Spanish Stalinist and a veteran of the internecine vendettas of the Civil War, disguised himself as a local Marxist journalist to gain regular access to the house. He arrived one hot sunny day in August 1940 in a hat and a thick raincoat; a suspicious Trotsky invited Mercader into his study, where he was clubbed to the floor with a small pick-axe concealed beneath the coat. He died of his wounds the following day, a victim of the terror tactics he had consistently advocated.[94] Opposition from abroad gave no sanctuary at any time for enemies of the Stalin dictatorship. Soviet security was more than a match for political activists, but the chief problem facing Trotsky and his allies, like the German exiles, was the absence of any secure public political space inside the Soviet Union. The vilification of Trotskyism by the regime in the 1930s made any public resonance for his assault on Stalin impossible.

The most direct threat presented to the Soviet system in the Stalin years came during the war from Soviet prisoners in German hands who, like the League of German Officers, were manipulated by their captors to try to undermine the political will of the enemy. At least three movements were sponsored, all nominally committed to the overthrow of Soviet communism. Two were founded in 1941 shortly after the German invasion. The Russian National Army of Liberation was led by a former Soviet engineer, Bronislav Kaminsky, whose 'army' became a byword for atrocity and crime as it fought a savage war against Red Army stragglers and Soviet partisans; the Russian National People's Army was formed near Smolensk by Russian émigrés patronized by the German occupiers, but was disbanded in 1943.[95] Kaminsky was used by the SS on assignments where the barbarity and rapacity of his followers was tolerated, but when his brigade was used to destroy the Warsaw uprising in August 1944 amidst scenes of indescribable carnage, Himmler ordered him shot and his followers were sent to join the Russian forces loosely organized as an unofficial Russian Liberation Army under the leadership of the former Soviet general Andrei Vlasov. The army never existed as an organization recognized by the Germans; the term was used to describe an assortment of anti-Bolsheviks, freebooters and proto-fascists used by the German army to supply liberation propaganda to weaken the resolve of the Red Army. Vlasov's first letter, dropped from the air over Soviet lines, called on soldiers to join the contest against 'the universally hated Stalinist system'; several thousand responded to the call.[96]

Like the German military conspirators, Vlasov started out as a staunch enthusiast for the system he served. He joined the Red Army in 1919, the party in 1930; he played an exemplary part in purging his own military unit during the *Ezhovshchina*; he was awarded the Order of Lenin and the Order of the Red Banner; he fought a distinguished war against the Germans in the retreat from Kiev in July 1941 and the counter-offensive around Moscow in January 1942. In June 1942 his 2nd Shock Army was annihilated trying to break the German ring around Leningrad and Vlasov was captured. Over the next six months he was transformed from loyal communist soldier to anti-communist crusader. In December 1942, as head of a putative liberation committee, he published the so-called 'Smolensk Declaration'. It bore the unmistakable stamp of the German army propaganda directors who worked closely with Vlasov, though his own conviction that communism was wrong for Russia seems to have been held with sincerity rather than opportunism. The Declaration called for political revolution: 'The overthrow of Stalin and his clique, the destruction of Bolshevism.' It also included thirteen generous pledges for a liberated Russia, among them the end of collectivization, intellectual and conscientious freedom, the abolition of the terror apparatus and social justice for all, but no commitment to political liberty.[97] Vlasov explained in an open letter published three months later that his ideological conversion came as he watched masses of ordinary Russians spilling their blood needlessly for a cause that ultimately served Anglo-American capitalism, whose stooge Stalin had become. This obscure reasoning led Vlasov to conclude that alliance with Hitler's Germany was the only way to secure the liberated Russian motherland.[98]

Hitler turned a blind eye to the activities of Vlasov's liberation movement, but only in September 1944 was it given formal German blessing when Himmler authorized the establishment of the Committee for the Liberation of the Peoples of Russia. In January 1945 two divisions of Russian volunteers were formed, but they saw action only briefly in Prague in April 1945, when Slav solidarity overcame their pro-German sentiments and they turned their guns on the SS to protect the Czech population from their final savage rampage.[99] Vlasov and his principal collaborators were caught at the end of the war and prosecuted a year later. Sentences of death by hanging were approved by the Politburo on 23 July, and the trial began a week later. It was said that Stalin ordered them hanged with piano wire like the executed victims of the failed July Plot, but the evidence indicates a simple rope.[100] Like the German military conspirators, Vlasov's liberation movement traded on fantasies about the extent of popular support for the overthrow of the regime, for which there was little evidence; the stench of treason could not be expunged as long as Vlasov publicly allied himself with the Germans. The movement was divided politically on a broad spectrum from anti-Semitic nationalists to reform communists, contradictions that could only be masked by focusing on the common ambition to remove Stalin and a shared loyalty to the motherland. A Vlasov government in Moscow would have faced the same problems in establishing its moral authority as a Goerdeler government in Berlin. Political opposition in both systems was hobbled by dependence on external support and the stigma of betrayal. The absence of any practical platform for public political debate through an independent press and a distinct party organization made opposition invisible to the overwhelming majority of the populations in each dictatorship, and forced opponents to rely on acts of terror that would distance them yet further from those they sought to emancipate.

The novelist Isaac Babel, arrested in 1939 and later shot, once remarked that the only privacy allowed in the Soviet Union was to be found at night, in bed, with the blankets pulled right over the head. Then, and only then, could a man and his wife enjoy a whispered conversation free from any fear of an eavesdropper.[101] Hans Frank, the National Socialist lawyer, boasted that the Third Reich only left its citizens alone when they were finally fast asleep. The exceptional restriction of free expression or free choice in societies where there was wide public approval of the regime did inhibit all forms of political opposition and severely circumscribed more modest expressions of non-conformity. Anyone in either dictatorship who chose overt or discreet expressions of difference operated, usually knowingly, on a scale of risk. Each occasion carried the same risk; one successful gesture of defiance did not reduce the odds that the second or third would go unpunished. The calculus of risk kept most German and Soviet citizens politically immobile.

This raises the question of what areas of personal autonomy remained under the dictatorships. If daily life had really been as restricted as Babel suggested, society could scarcely function. Areas of autonomy did exist; neither regime could pretend to control the daily lives of everyone they ruled, so they chose those key elements that, from ideological conviction or political prudence, they considered it necessary to control. This left most individuals, except those marked for distinct discrimination on grounds of race or social class, with the possibility of making choices about their personal lives, some large, some trivial, which remained relatively unencumbered by the state: when and whom to marry, family size, a job, where to live, when to go to the theatre or what to see at the cinema. Neighbourhood or milieu could still shelter small communities from the demands of public, political life. Choice was often closely circumscribed by the conditions of the job or housing market or by the family policy and cultural preferences of the regime, but within the permitted space it was still relatively free. A project undertaken at Harvard in the late 1940s to interview thousands of Soviet citizens who had stayed in the West after the defeat of Germany concluded that political acquiescence was the price Soviet citizens paid to be able to sustain other things that mattered to them: 'affection for their homeland, family, work, status, and the whole way of life to which they were accustomed'. Accommodation with the regime was accepted 'in order not to lose . . . that which they cherished'.[102] This was a natural choice for both the Soviet and the German populations, who learned to adapt to what the regime would or would not permit in order to inhabit a private sphere where they could construct a limited but independent existence. This act of complicity between regime and population allowed daily life to continue and cushioned daily experience against the abnormalities of political dictatorship.

Sometimes a lifestyle choice was a deliberate challenge to the regime as a substitute for a more direct political confrontation. This was particularly so with episodes of youth revolt in both regimes, which were explicit rejections of the conformist, smart and politically engaged image of young people projected by the Hitler Youth and the Soviet *Komsomol*, but were acts of political criticism rather than organized political revolt. This ambiguity made the state uncertain in its response, though ultimately repressive. There were many small, secret youth organizations in the Soviet Union before 1941 and again after the war. In Voronezh in 1948 an illegal youth organization was discovered led by the son of a local party official. The Communist Party of Youth (KPM) met and discussed political issues outside the permitted party parameters. They were betrayed and fifty-three teenagers ended up in the camps. Another group in Astrakhan between 1947 and 1949 met in a literary circle, where they discussed ways of making the system more collectivist rather than less; another group that flourished briefly in December 1945, who called themselves the Enlightened Communist Youth, argued that they represented a better kind of young communist, not a non-communist alternative. These small groups of idealists were also rounded up by State Security.[103] In other cases Soviet youth simply sought to opt out by listening to forbidden music (jazz in particular), or avoiding the remorselessly cheerful and laborious routines of *Komsomol* activity.

In Germany too, the institutionalization of the youth movement and the loss of radical momentum created disillusionment among young Germans, which emerged in the late 1930s and peaked during the war years. This could take the form of simple non-conformity – refusing to go on organized hikes, growing hair a little too long, listening to jazz, flaunting their sexuality – or the organization of gangs or 'cliques', as the regime called them, which were belligerently independent. Most of the alternative movements were composed of young, predominantly working-class teenagers from the industrial areas of the north-east, who described themselves by the general term 'Edelweiss Pirates'. The pirate groups each had their own name and their own rituals and songs. They met in their spare time, hunted out and beat up Hitler Youth patrols, and refused to do the many helpful things a proper German youth was supposed to do. Some of their songs show a close link between the gang violence and political rejection of the regime: 'Hitler's power may lay us low/And keep us locked in chains/But we will smash the chains one day/We'll be free again.'[104] In Düsseldorf in 1943 they scrawled 'Down with Hitler' or 'Down with Nazi Brutality' on city walls, but there was little evidence that they had a clear idea of a political alternative, except for the so-called *'Meuten'* gangs which flourished in the one-time communist strongholds in Leipzig in the late 1930s. The Gestapo tried a number of methods to combat youth rebellion. Some were given no more than a warning or brief weekend spells of 're-education'; others were sent to labour camps or young-offender concentration camps. In December 1942 a sweep was made of the Ruhr area which netted 739 boys and girls, but the authorities were never quite certain how to cope with a movement that was seldom overtly political beyond the desire to mock at or opt out of the lifestyle defined by the party.[105] Some of the protest was indistinguishable from later post-war manifestations of youth defiance and rock-music subcultures, but directed in this case at the exaggerated respectability and wholesomeness of official National Socialist images of childhood and family values. In both dictatorships such protest was treated as political, even though the few thousands who indulged in it were often driven less, or not at all, by ideas of political opposition, and more by a headstrong adolescent rejection of everyday life under dictatorship.

The public arena for protest or debate was closely restricted and monitored, though not inflexibly so. Popular opinion was not extinguished in either regime, but it was shaped by what was tolerated by the system and what was not, though this was never in itself entirely predictable. Opinion was neither uniform nor constant. Under dictatorship, public views ranged from enthusiastic approbation to conscientious outrage. Expressions of approval may have been self-interested or artificial, but could certainly be genuinely spontaneous as well. Thousands of letters were received from the public in both dictatorships, sent personally to Hitler or Stalin, or to newspapers or party offices, which gave advice, endorsed policies, lauded the leadership, expressed thanks, or offered congratulations. *Izvestiia*, the official Soviet government journal, received around 5,000 letters a day in the late 1930s.[106] *Pravda*'s letter pages were full of ritualized echoes of the party line. When news of the alleged conspiracy among the army leadership was released in June 1937, letters denouncing the traitors were dutifully published: 'execute the spies, despicable fascists and traitors!' ran one letter from a Moscow motor-vehicle plant; 'They ought to be shot like mad dogs! We all are to become the NKVD's volunteers', from a workers' meeting; and a poem written by Demyan Bednyi, 'Revolting is the hiss of spies!/Ugly is the enemy who walked among us!/We are ashamed for the mothers who gave birth/To such vile dogs!'[107] Such formal manifestations of solidarity should not be dismissed out of hand. There existed a layer of opinion that voluntarily identified with the system in the Soviet Union and in Germany, and letter-writing was a routine means of expressing it.

Letters, sometimes anonymous, also represented an important

medium for the expression of discontent. Written petitions and pleas from below dated back long before the revolution. The files of letters in Soviet offices were seldom about the government or the political system, but focused on personal hardships and injustices with a level of candour and indignation that is hard to match in the letters sent to German ministries or party offices. Many were from communists who wanted their regime to govern with greater justice. A letter over an illegible signature was sent to the government in 1938 to protest at mass arrests: 'Completely Soviet people, devoted people to the Soviet state, sense that something is wrong here . . . Comrades, none of this helps Soviet rule, but only alienates people.'[108] Letters, often poorly drafted autobiographies, highlighted the hardships of Soviet life. One worker in 1937: 'What is there to say about Soviet power? It's lies . . . I am a worker, wear torn clothes, my four children go to school half-starving, in rags'[109]; a widowed farmer in 1936: 'Lenin died too early. Now things are worse for us, poor widows, than they were before the Revolution . . . Why do the communists treat us so badly, in a way that the capitalists didn't?'[110] Letters could also endorse the regime's fantasies about the enemy within, while deploring the methods. A letter sent from Odessa in December 1938 complained that Ezhov had arrested the wrong people and 'overlooked real spies and saboteurs'.[111] The many letters that complained about NKVD excesses, or petitioned for clemency, were eventually used by Stalin as one spurious justification to remove Ezhov from office. To judge from contemporary accounts few letters were answered or achieved redress. They allowed individuals to let off steam in the privacy of correspondence, but they also reveal the depth of popular confusion and disgruntlement behind the public mask of unity.

Discontent and scepticism could be expressed out loud and in public through rumour, gossip and ridicule. Humour was used to ventilate opinions that were risky to express in more explicit ways; passed from mouth to mouth, jokes and doggerel formed a safety valve for individuals who had little intention of confronting the regime, but who wanted to collude with others in creating an independent discourse that the authorities could police only with great difficulty because of its easy distribution and epidemic character. The Gestapo offices in Baden solemnly filed any examples they came across. In October 1934

Jewish schoolchildren were overheard singing a vulgar but cryptic ditty about the dead German president: 'Hindenburg, the great rider, has a lightning conductor on his arse and a pickled gherkin in front, which is why he's called Hindenburg.'[112] Jokes about Hitler had to be made with great care, but other leaders were the regular butt of mockery and lewdness. Göring carried a special calf-bound book in which he recorded all the jokes he heard about himself.[113] In the Soviet Union scatological verses and riddles were characteristic forms for mediating discontent which long pre-dated Stalinism. In the Soviet countryside traditional rhymes or *chastushki* were adapted in the 1930s to illuminate the harsh conditions on the new collective farms: 'I arrived at the *kolkhoz*/ With a new skirt/ I left the *kolkhoz*/ Completely naked.' Others had a direct political message: 'Kirov's been killed/ Stalin will be killed/ All the peasants will rejoice/ And the communists will cry.'[114] Jokes and riddles revolved around the same themes: 'Lenin died and we had a rest; if another good chap dies, we'd rest even more.'[115] One popular tale says much about the nature of the relationship between people and rulers. Stalin is rescued from drowning by a passing peasant: 'Now,' said Stalin, 'ask whatever you wish. Your desire is granted in advance. I am Stalin.' To which the anxious peasant replies: 'Little father, I don't want anything, but please don't tell anyone that I have saved you. They will murder me for that.'[116]

More open criticism of the regimes was possible beyond the daily grumbles about shortages of food or consumer goods, on issues that the population found genuinely difficult to understand or to accommodate. The signing of the Soviet–German pact on 23 August 1939, after years of public vilification of fascism, provoked widespread uneasiness and hostility in the Soviet population when the purposes of the treaty were discussed at party meetings.[117] The discovery in 1941 that the German government was systematically killing handicapped children provoked so much evident public outrage that the programme was officially suspended. The decision to remove crucifixes from schools in Catholic Bavaria in 1941 prompted enough popular, sometimes violent protest that this decision, too, had to be reversed.[118] Both systems monitored popular opinion on a daily basis in order to anticipate popular reactions. The Security Service (*Sicherheitsdienst*) in Germany, set up originally to monitor opinion in the party, became the source after 1933 of home intelligence reports on the whole population. These regular reports were used to alert the regime to potential difficulties, to test the public mood and to underpin shifts in the emphasis of propaganda.[119] The Soviet authorities observed public opinion with equal care. The crisis over the 1939 Pact was met by renewed agitational effort to explain to the Soviet people that Britain was really the common enemy of dictatorship. A crude triangular diagram was distributed with 'London' at the apex and 'Berlin' and 'Moscow' on the base, under the caption 'What did Chamberlain want?' A second triangle with 'Moscow' at the top and the other two capitals below was captioned 'What did Comrade Stalin do?', though whether this enlightened ordinary Russians a great deal is open to conjecture.[120]

These many forms of popular opinion were tolerated by the regimes. Occasionally those who joked too openly or whose satire was deemed to be too seditious were arrested, but the regimes could not and did not persecute everyone who mocked or carped. This gave ordinary people an outlet for their feelings in a situation where open manifestations of protest were too dangerous. They broadly understood the limits, and operated within them to construct small counter-cultures to reinforce a sense of surviving autonomy, but with restricted subversive effect. Both populations came to understand, as the labour force did, that they were not entirely powerless either to shape their own lives or to place some distance between themselves and the totalitarian imperatives of the regimes. Neither population was simply passive or inert. Most people, like the bulk of the schoolchildren in the school in Bielefeld with which this chapter opened, neither opposed nor wildly applauded but adapted their expectations to existing possibilities. The fraction that opposed or resisted faced daunting inhibitions and an implacably repressive state. Since so much was defined as 'political', ordinary people clung to those aspects of their lives that were relatively free of politics, but at the price of a depoliticized existence, punctuated by occasional episodes of protest or dissent. The popular response to dictatorship was prudent and opportunistic, as well as enthusiastic or hostile. There was a profound rationality in the behaviour of the majority, faced as they were with systems that won broad, if conditional, approval and were praeternaturally vigilant. Habits of

347

submission and dissembling were learned quickly, but disappeared swiftly too when dictatorship disappeared. Opposition and resistance were exceptional, courageous and easily confined. Compliance meant inclusion, non-compliance meant exclusion. Faced with such stark moral choices, even in the most difficult or desperate of circumstances most people preferred to be friend rather than foe.

9

Cultural Revolutions

When the Regime commanded that books with harmful
    knowledge
Should be publicly burned and on all sides
Oxen were forced to drag cartloads of books
To the bonfires, a banished
Writer, one of the best, scanning the list of the
Burned was shocked to find that his
Books had been passed over. He rushed to his desk
On wings of wrath, and wrote a letter to those in power
Burn me! He wrote with flying pen, burn me! Haven't my
    Books
Always reported the truth?
    Bertolt Brecht, *The Burning of the Books* (1937/8)[1]

In 1937, two magnificent art exhibitions were planned, one in the
Soviet Union, one in Hitler's Germany. Each was intended as a cultural
landmark. The 'Industry of Socialism' exhibition in Moscow was to
be the first all-Union event since the revolution. It was the brainchild
of the Commissar for Heavy Industry, Sergo Ordzhonikidze, who in
1935 set up a committee to plan the exhibition under the chairmanship
of the editor of the journal *Industriia*. It was scheduled for autumn
1937, to mark the twentieth anniversary of the revolution and the end
of the Second Five-Year Plan.[2] The Exhibition of German Art was to
be the first national display of contemporary painting and sculpture
since Hitler took power. It was to take place in the new House of
German Art in Munich, the foundation stone of which Hitler had laid

on 15 October 1933, the date of the first official Day of Art in the Third Reich. The vast exhibition hall was the first piece of monumental architecture Hitler commissioned. Its long pseudo-classical façade, dominated by twenty-one stone columns, was completed in 1937 in time for the first Exhibition of German Art in July.[3]

The 'Industry of Socialism' exhibition was a deliberate celebration of the economic and social achievements of the Soviet state. Artists were invited to contribute works on set themes, described in detail in an eighty-page guide. Each theme was to have its own exhibition room, one for consumer goods, one for metals, one for food, and so on. All Soviet artists were invited to contribute their proposals by January 1936, and several thousand pieces were commissioned. The plans soon ran into difficulties. A new exhibition centre to house the show could not be completed on time, and it had to be housed in the Permanent Construction Exhibition Hall. There was a dearth of canvases for the chosen artists to work on, and for many of them virtually no studio space. Rooms for artists were freed in schools and public buildings. The Leningrad factory assigned to supply paint for the exhibitors produced products so poor in quality that the white never dried, and the coloured paints began to turn black after six months.[4] Heroic efforts finally produced an exhibition in time for the November opening, but the doors remained sealed to the public. Too many of the pictures displayed portraits of 'enemies of the people' unmasked and purged while the paintings were completed. Artists had to paint over the offending figures; a large group portrait of Ordzhonikidze's commissariat had to be begun again entirely from scratch.

The replacement pictures satisfied the censors enough for the exhibition to open sixteen months late, on 18 March 1939. Visitors were supplied with a small handbook of exhibition notes drafted by the party's All-Union Arts Committee, a scrutinizing body set up at Stalin's behest three years before. They were led by official guides through the seventeen themed rooms, from 'Old and New', contrasting the Tsarist and Soviet experience, on through 'The USSR has become Metallic', full of worthy paintings of steel mills, to the final rooms grouped under Stalin's well-known quotation 'Life has got better, life has got jollier', where pictures of shops bursting with good things to buy and peasants harvesting ripe, mouth-watering produce showed less fortunate spectators a glimpse of the socialist future.[5] There were two large portraits of Stalin with his people, Vasilii Efanov's *Unforgettable Meeting* and Grigorii Shegal's *Leader, Teacher, Friend*; and there were images of lesser political figures with less memorable titles, among them Fedor Modorov's admired *Comrade Mikoyan at the Astrakhan Fish Processing Plant*. The entire exhibition contained an exhausting 2,000 paintings and sculptures by 700 registered Soviet artists.[6]

The Exhibition of German Art opened exactly on time, on 18 July 1937, in the presence of Hitler and a corps of party leaders and art experts. Ethnic German artists had been invited to submit finished pieces to a jury headed by Adolf Ziegler, a favoured artist and president of the Reich Chamber of Visual Arts. Over 15,000 entries were received, which were reduced down to 900 paintings and sculptures before being displayed to Hitler for his final approval. He was outraged at some of the paintings that were so modernist he found it impossible to tell which way up they were supposed to hang. Some of those that had been rejected as too dull or sentimental were rescued by the dictator and others purged. Ziegler's assistant resigned at once in protest. In the end 884 works were displayed, grouped by theme.[7] Two-fifths were landscapes, two-fifths portraits, but Hitler allowed only one image of the Leader into the exhibition. He bought 202 of the paintings himself, despite his initial reservations. Outside the House of Art he watched a pageant illustrating 2,000 years of German history in a sea of swastikas, party banners and fancy dress. The party newspaper assured readers the following day that visitors to Munich 'sat as spectators in the theatre of our own time and saw greatness'.[8]

The success of the two exhibitions was mixed. Around 600,000 Germans filed through the House of German Art before the exhibits were distributed to those who had bought them, but only 162,000 visitors went to see 'The Industry of Socialism'. The Arts Committee was disappointed with the response to the display and closed it in 1940. Some exhibits were intended for a permanent Museum of Soviet Art, but it was never built. Some critics whispered that the exhibition was dull. The first prize was awarded not to a picture of worthy Soviet achievements but to Johanson's *At an Old Urals Works*, a picture inspired by Tsarist industrialization; Stalin liked the image of class tension generated by the juxtaposition of sneering plutocrat and contemplative workman.[9] Hitler was unimpressed by much of what he saw in Munich ('no artists whose work is worthy'), though he admired the hall of neo-classical, larger-than-life statues of stately Aryan men and women.[10] The official reaction was, nonetheless, ecstatic in both capitals. One Soviet critic thought that the show put Soviet culture on the 'threshold of a new Renaissance'. The German exhibition was lauded as the 'foundation of a new and genuine German art', in which the artist had finally turned his back on vain self-expression and had become, in Goebbels' words, 'a true servant of the people'.[11]

Both exhibitions were manifestations of official art. The pictures and statues were the product not of spontaneous artistic expression but of state guidance and approval. Hitler and Stalin each played a part in selecting the exhibits and awarding prizes; each helped to shape the entire world of cultural production permitted by the two regimes. These grandiose pretensions resulted in a prescriptive art; culture was seen as a central element in the construction of the new orders, as capable of political regimentation as any other area of society. The two dictatorships were united by a conviction that culture had an extraordinary capacity to affect the state of mind and beliefs of the beholder. Had it not been so, the efforts to regiment every single manifestation of the printed word, or the pictorial image, or the built environment would have been redundant. The criteria for measuring the worth of artistic or literary output reflected the social aspirations and political needs of dictatorship. Official art was not entirely blind to aesthetic achievement, but the principal purpose of art was to express approved social values and political ideals in ways that could be appreciated by the ordinary public rather than the narrower world of art critics and patrons. All culture under the dictatorships was intended to be democratic rather than self-indulgently elitist.

Official art was representational, didactic and heroic. The Moscow exhibition was a major demonstration of the virtues of what was called 'socialist realism'. The term was applied indiscriminately to all forms of culture under Stalin. Although the dictator was credited with formulating the principle, its first use dates from a speech given to a literary assembly by Ivan Gronsky, editor of *Izvestiia*, on 20 May 1932. A few days later the Soviet *Literary Gazette* took up the theme, urging artists to recognize that what the Soviet masses wanted from artists and writers was 'the sincerity and truthfulness' of socialist realism, when representing the revolutionary achievement.[12] A few months later, on 26 October, at the apartment of the author Maxim Gorky, Stalin was a guest at a late night discussion with fifty writers on what was understood by socialist realism. His definition was simple and circular: if an artist 'truthfully depicts our life' he can do no other than 'depict in it that which leads to socialism'. 'This exactly,' he continued, 'will be socialist art.' Gorky, who had been made honorary chairman of the Union of Soviet Writers, formed in 1932, added that socialist realism was to illustrate 'the heroic present' with optimism and dignity.[13]

Socialist realism was, in effect, an invitation to paint or describe the Stalinist utopia, not the underlying reality of life in the 1930s. This was to be done by permitting only those forms of representation that were straightforward cultural accounts of everyday life, with simple themes and simple heroes. The limits of Stalinist art were set by 'a beautiful socialist reality' and 'great deeds of socialist construction'.[14] Any form of art that challenged that straightforward reality was deemed to be 'bourgeois formalism', a self-regarding art that ignored the necessity of binding culture and people together. Stalin himself helped to promote the ideal of cheerful populist art. Two days after he visited, with evident displeasure, the Shostakovich opera *Lady Macbeth of Mtsensk* in January 1936, *Pravda* published a savage review, under the headline A MESS INSTEAD OF MUSIC: 'intentionally dissonant, confused stream of sounds . . . The music shouts, quacks, explodes, pants and sighs . . .' Composers were warned that music, like all art, had to grasp the principles of 'simplicity, realism, comprehensibility of image'.[15] The simplification of art in the Soviet Union did not stem entirely from a failure of aesthetic appreciation or crass philistinism. Stalin wanted operas that could establish a Soviet classical tradition to match the great classical composers of the nineteenth century. Culture was simplified and prettified because, under communism, it was understood to be a reflection of the whole society, the property of peasant and worker as well as art critic. Lenin in 1920 had pronounced that 'art belongs to the people'.[16] Under socialist realism the idea of art as something universal and accessible was part of the wider social revolution ushered in by Stalinist modernization, though its roots lay in the 1920s. Artists were regularly reminded that the priority in their work was 'people-mindedness', as well as the obligatory 'party-mindedness'.[17] Andrei Zhdanov, who was the leading party spokesman on all cultural issues in the 1930s and 1940s, announced in 1948 that music 'incomprehensible to the people is not needed by the people'.[18] Stalin liked concert pieces that the audience could whistle afterwards.

For Marxists it was also axiomatic that art should reflect social reality rather than personal artistic choice: 'Life itself is the crystallizer – life, the source of all art,' wrote the biographer of Nikolai Ostrovsky, one of the great literary heroes of socialist realism, whose best-selling novel *How the Steel Was Tempered* was serialized during the months in 1932 when socialist realism was first defined.[19] Stalin told the socialist realist artist Isaak Brodskii that he most liked paintings that showed 'living people' in forms that were 'living and comprehensible'. Artistic anguish, ambiguity, irresolution and despair were the enemies of 'real' life and a betrayal of the revolutionary state. The official handbook on permitted literary themes in the 1940s did not even include the category 'struggle'.[20] Socialist realism was, at the same time, intentionally educative and exemplary, both inspired by life and an inspiration for living. In 1928 the Central Committee resolved that all artistic production should be exploited 'in the fight for a new cultural outlook, a new way of life'.[21] At the meeting in Gorky's house Stalin was said famously to have defined artists as 'engineers of human souls', and when Zhdanov officially launched socialist realism in August 1934, he told his audience of writers that socialist realism was the vehicle for 'ideological refashioning', for the 'education of labouring people in the spirit of socialism', and these injunctions were included in the official regulations governing the Union of Soviet Writers set up in 1934.[22] Socialist realism was to be both cause and effect of the transformation of Soviet society.

The official art of the Third Reich displays many similarities with the Soviet model. In Germany, too, art for art's sake was rejected in favour of the idea, expressed by Joseph Goebbels, overlord of the entire cultural apparatus, that 'art is a function of the life of the people'. Art was supposed to be 'heroic and romantic' like socialist realism.[23] Hitler's address at the annual party rally in Nuremberg in September

1934 contained a definition of culture that almost exactly matched the speech given by Zhdanov the month before: '. . . art, since it forms the most uncorrupted, the most immediate reflection of the people's soul, exercises unconsciously by far the greatest influence upon the masses of the people.' The function of art was nonetheless conditional: 'that it draws a true picture of that life and of the inborn capacities of a people and does not distort them'.[24] For Hitler art was married to the people, not independent of it. When he opened the exhibition in 1937 he declared that any art is intolerable that 'cannot rely on the joyous, heartfelt assent of the broad and healthy mass of the people'. Art was meant to 'confirm the sound instinct of the people'.[25] The principles of simplicity and accessibility that feature so frequently in Soviet statements on culture were central to Hitler's artistic prejudices: 'art that is in our blood,' he continued, 'art that people can comprehend, because only art that the simple man can understand is true art.'[26]

Hitler's relationship with culture was more direct than Stalin's, for although Stalin read almost all the literature, watched all the films and viewed thousands of paintings generated during his dictatorship, he was not the self-conscious 'artist-ruler' that Hitler pretended to be. The young Hitler had flirted with an artistic career in pre-war Vienna, where he eked a living out of producing simple watercolours and dreamt of a place at the Vienna Academy of Art to train as an architect. This was enough to turn the later politician into a self-appointed authority on culture. In *Mein Kampf* he argued that all forms of art had become corrupted by modernity and would have to be cleansed before they could serve a renewed 'moral, political and cultural idea'.[27] That idea was the revival and enlargement of the German race, and of those elements within it which 'bestow culture and create beauty'.[28] For Hitler, artistic creation was an expression of racial health and eternal racial value. From 1933 he made regular public pronouncements about his view of art, and these informally became the 'principles of the *Führer*', based on his personal tastes and political prejudices.[29] In sculpture he insisted on copying the 'physical beauty' of Greek statues, which, despite their exaggerated anatomy, he regarded as an expression of 'real', scientifically verifiable physique. In art he preferred the simple representational landscapes of the nineteenth century and painting that 'draws a true picture of life' without blue fields, yellow clouds, green skies and pink trees.[30] In architecture the Romano-Greek world supplied the model of 'clarity, light, beauty'.[31] Literature interested him much less than it concerned Stalin.

These preferences might be described as 'nationalist realism', though realism as a term was not officially used to describe National Socialist art because of its socialist connotations. Nonetheless, the public identification of art as something uplifting and heroic, a strenuously optimistic and uncomplicated view of reality, was common to both dictatorships. Official art was, in practice, idealist and romantic rather than realist. Any hint of conflict or anxiety or meanness was removed. The 'enemy' of the revolution or of the race was seldom depicted. Gorky spoke of a 'revolutionary romanticism' in art which lifted images of collective farms and steel works out of the category of mere illustration, and depicted 'the heroic present in brighter tones'.[32] Goebbels, writing in 1933, stated that the arts in Germany would be 'romantic' and 'sentimental' as well as 'factual'.[33] The consequence for both regimes was the deliberate restriction of cultural horizons and the promotion of a single, drably conventional artistic and literary genre.

The enemy of official, collectivist culture was artistic individualism. In the thirty years before the dictatorships emerged, Europe experienced the flowering of an extraordinary age of cultural self-expression. Russia and Germany were at the forefront of the artistic avant-garde. The revolution in 1917 was hailed by many Russian artists and writers as an act of artistic emancipation and in the 1920s an experimental, pluralist culture emerged, encouraged by the aggressively anti-bourgeois outlook of the regime. The republican years in Germany after 1919 witnessed a rich variety of artistic expression; liberated from the old empire, profoundly influenced by the experience of war, defeat and revolution, uninhibited by popular prejudice or taste, many German artists and writers welcomed the opportunity to push art to the limits of social protest or morbid nihilism or indulgent innovation.

The explosion of experimental culture in the 1920s reflected a profound defence of artistic autonomy, for the avant-garde was subversive and independent, deliberately challenging and uncontrollable, self-consciously revolutionary and iconoclastic. 'It's time for bullets/

to pepper the museums' walls/Hundred-throat guns to shoot the old junk', wrote the futurist poet Vladimir Mayakovsky.[34] The regimentation of culture in the 1930s was a reaction against the disintegrative and restless effects of the avant-garde, which neither dictatorship was willing to indulge despite the fact that prominent modernists could be found in the Soviet Union and in Germany, including Mayakovsky, willing to offer support to the new political orders. Boris Pasternak, the Russian poet and novelist, described in 1942 the tension between artistic creation and political control that accounted for the dictatorships' complete distrust of artistic independence (and for his own literary silence): 'Art is inconceivable without risk . . . without freedom and boldness of imagination. Real art always comes as a surprise. You cannot foresee the unpredictable, or regulate the unruly.'[35]

The tension between free artistic expression and political regulation was already evident in the 1920s in both Germany and the Soviet Union. Even before the official sponsorship of socialist realism, the Soviet state placed obvious limits upon what was acceptable as revolutionary culture. In the first three years after the revolution a popular movement of authentic proletarian culture, known by the acronym 'Proletkult', recruited thousands of workers to be trained as revolutionary writers and artists to take the place of bourgeois artists and end the divide between high art and popular culture. The regime disliked the democratic and autonomous character of the movement and it declined sharply after 1921.[36] Various forms of modernism – cubism, constructivism, impressionism, surrealism – were also the object of close state scrutiny on suspicion that they represented some form of bourgeois deviation. Russian Futurists, many on the far left of the Bolshevik party, organized themselves as the Left Front of the Arts in 1922, but their aggressive artistic activism, inspired by the first futurist, the Italian Filippo Marinetti, was out of step with the economic priorities of the regime, and by 1928 the movement was doomed. Mayakovsky, perhaps Futurism's most famous name, shot himself two years later, leaving a brief suicide note with the laconic conclusion: 'Seriously, there is nothing to be done. Goodbye.'[37] 'Formalism', a method as much as a movement, was also suspect because of its central claim that the 'form' of a book, building or picture was more important than the content and had nothing to do with the social environment. The formalist slogan 'art is always free of life' was a direct challenge to Marxism, and became one of the chief accusations laid against any deviant artist under the reign of socialist realism.[38]

In 1928 the onset of collectivization and the First Five-Year Plan finally pushed the regime to a more direct supervision of the arts in order to overcome the 'slavish imitation of bourgeois culture'.[39] In December of that year a Central Committee resolution 'on the serving of the mass reader with literature' ordered publishers to supply books predominantly by communists on themes of economic mobilization, and to stop producing literature full of 'bourgeois influences' or 'decadence'.[40] The deliberate proletarianization of culture was promoted by two institutions, the Russian Association of Proletarian Writers (RAPP) and Proletarian Musicians (RAPM); both insisted on nothing less than the silencing of all forms of art other than the art necessary to carry forward the economic and social transformation. Art was to respond to 'social command', rather than its own creative impulses. Social origin became a stigma for any writer or musician not drawn from the toiling classes.[41] Cultural modernism rapidly disappeared. By the time socialist realism was declared the orthodoxy in 1932, the many strands of cultural experiment in the 1920s were close to extinction.

In Germany the conflict between modernity and convention long pre-dated 1933. It reflected a widespread popular concern that modern culture somehow symbolized Germany's debilitated post-war condition and moral bankruptcy. Hitler's was one voice among thousands of outraged Germans who saw in the artistic revolution evidence of racial degeneration, alien subversion or straightforward pornography. The artistic avant-garde self-consciously chose to undermine or challenge popular morality and cherished values. At his trial in 1924 on charges of publishing obscene drawings, the artist George Grosz confronted the morally affronted prosecutor with the argument that his 'negative and sceptical' view of the world reflected an aesthetic reality: he could see in humankind 'no beauties and delicate forms'. The judge disagreed, declared the content of the pictures to be smut and fined him 6,000 marks.[42] Nationalist sensibilities were affronted in turn by the realistic portrayal of the horrors of the recent war. 'Lice, rats, barbed wire, fleas, shells, bombs ... corpses, blood ... that is what war is!' wrote the artist Otto Dix. 'It is all the work of the

Devil!'[43] The film of Erich Remarque's disturbing novel of the real face of war, *All Quiet on the Western Front*, screened in 1930, provoked nationalist demonstrations and had to be withdrawn from cinemas in Berlin. National Socialist cultural policy typically reflected the prejudices and prudishness of a great many Germans. In May 1928 the party ideologue, Alfred Rosenberg, co-founded with non-party intellectuals the *Kampfbund für deutsche Kultur* (Combat League for German Culture) to defend the 'German essence' against 'cultural decadence'.[44] When in 1930 Wilhelm Frick became the first National Socialist to be appointed to public office as interior minister in Thuringia, he replaced Walther Gropius, the founder of the progressive Bauhaus school of architecture and director of the Weimar Academy of Arts, with the author Paul Schultze-Naumburg, whose recent book *Art and Race* summed up the popular belief that modern art was the product of diseased minds. Frick ordered all modernist paintings (dubbed 'nigger culture') to be removed from the Weimar museum of art.[45]

From 1933 these prejudices were able to flower unchecked. All modern culture was suspect as 'hostile to the *Volk*': impressionism, futurism, cubism, Dadaism. The most intemperate language was reserved for expressionism, a defiantly unorthodox, freely constructed, richly imaginative art which, in the hands of Max Beckmann and Ernst Kirchner, produced work of startling originality. Expressionism was dismissed as 'sub-human', 'alien', 'negroid', 'half-idiotic' and, most commonly, 'degenerate' (*entartete*). It was also defined as politically tendentious. The term 'culture-bolshevism' was used to describe any art that did not conform to the regime's standards. The first exhibition of degenerate art, held in Karlsruhe in 1933, was given the title 'Government Art 1919–1933' to make clear the connection between modern art and failed republicanism.[46] Small exhibitions of 'art horrors' flourished all over Germany. In 1937 the regime ordered a major Exhibition of Degenerate Art to be held in Munich, close to the display of German art. It was exploited as an opportunity to remove from the public domain all remaining examples of artistic modernism.

The committee set up by Goebbels to organize the parallel exhibition confiscated 16,000 drawings, paintings and sculptures from museums, galleries and public buildings. A total of 650 exhibits were chosen, a veritable who's who of modern art – Dix, Grosz, Kirchner, Beckmann, Kokoschka, Kollwitz, Chagall, Kandinsky. They were displayed higgledy-piggledy from floor to ceiling to accentuate the sense of confusion and disorder. Each group of exhibits was given an aggrieved title – 'insolent mockery of the divine', 'revelation of the Jewish soul' (though only six of the artists in the whole show were Jewish), 'nature as seen by sick minds' – and so on.[47] The objects taken from public galleries had a red sticker next to them with the words 'Paid for from the taxes of the labouring German people'. Jumbled up with the artworks were drawings and paintings by psychiatric patients to demonstrate to the visitor that the avant-garde had indeed been deranged. The exhibition was opened by Adolf Ziegler on 19 July 1937, a day after the exhibition of German art, with a jeremiad against 'the monstrous offspring of insanity, impudence, ineptitude and sheer degeneracy'.[48] The display was an instant success. Over two million visitors in four months walked through the crowded, airless rooms, a bizarre mixture of morally repelled conservative Germans, guffawing and exclaiming as they went, and silent enthusiasts for artistic modernity. The exhibition was then moved around Germany, where it was seen by another million visitors.[49] Soon 'degenerate art' was joined on tour by an Exhibition of Degenerate Music, arranged by Goebbels in May 1938 as an assault on modern, dissonant 'Jewish' music and 'black' jazz. A catalogue of degenerate films, Film-'Art', Film-Cohen, Film-Corruption, was published by the party to show that expressionist and experimental film was a Jewish invention.[50]

The permanent suppression of artistic modernity and experiment and the reassertion of conservative artistic values were made possible in both systems by establishing formal, all-embracing institutions for the regimentation of cultural output. In the Soviet Union new organizations were introduced for each artistic medium, beginning in 1930 with the cinema. In place of the state film corporation, Sovkino, and smaller, experimental studios of the 1920s, a single All-Union Soviet Film Trust was set up, responsible for producing every Soviet film and vetting every script for political correctness.[51] In 1932 the axe fell on RAPP, RAPM and a host of official and unofficial cultural organizations. A Central Committee resolution of 23 April ordered the liquidation of all existing literary associations and the establishment of a single Union of Soviet Writers. The other branches of the arts were ordered to fall into line. On 25 June a Moscow-based Union of Soviet Artists was constructed from a host of smaller artistic circles. A Union of Soviet Composers followed in 1933, a Union of Soviet Architects and a Union of Soviet Journalists in 1934. Each artistic sector was obliged to follow the statutes drawn up for the official launch of the Union of Writers, in August 1934, which included the promotion of 'the great wisdom and heroism of the Communist Party' and active participation, through socialist realist art, 'in the class struggle of the proletariat and in socialist construction'.[52] Early in 1936 the Central Committee upgraded its own arts section by appointing an All-Union Committee for the Arts under Platon Kerzhentsev, with the power to supervise and, when necessary, direct the political and artistic behaviour of all the separate unions.[53] After the war the regime strengthened its grip on the arts even more. In 1946 Zhdanov launched the so-called *Zhdanovschina*, a ruthless suppression of any remaining hint of modern, formalist or foreign influence in the arts, which lasted until the onset of a cultural thaw three years after Stalin's death, in 1956.[54]

The organization of culture in Germany became, if anything, even more centralized than the Soviet model. In the autumn of 1933 almost all cultural associations were forced into liquidation and their activities transferred to a new Reich Chamber of Culture, legally established on 22 September and officially launched on 13 November under the auspices of Goebbels' Ministry of Propaganda and Popular Enlightenment and the executive presidency of the young journalist Hans Hinkel, a former Freikorps fighter and early party member. The national chamber had seven subordinate chambers for music, visual arts, theatre, literature, press, radio and film. Every aspect of artistic and literary creation and distribution was anticipated. The chamber for the visual arts was in turn subdivided into seven branches: administration; press and propaganda; architecture, landscaping and interior design; painting, sculpture and graphic arts; commercial illustration and design; art promotion, artistic and craft associations; publication, sales and auctions.[55] The chambers were also geographically organized into thirty-one districts, each represented by a local cultural administrator responsible to the ministry; within each district there were regional associations for every branch of activity. The press chamber alone had 134 local associations, including everything from railway station bookstores to press stenographers.[56]

Three further laws followed the establishment of the chamber structure. The 'Law for Literary Leaders' published on 4 October 1933, the Cinema Law of 16 February and the 'Unified Theatre Law' of 15 May 1934 each gave the chamber power to dictate the content of what could be written and performed. The chamber's own statutes stated in unambiguous terms the regime's ambition to subject cultural output to strict political control: 'it is the business of the state to combat injurious influences and encourage those that are valuable, actuated by a sense of responsibility for the wellbeing of the national community'.[57] The aim was to co-ordinate all national cultural production, 'to merge together the creative elements from all fields for carrying out, under the leadership of the state, a single will'.[58] In practice it took some time before Goebbels could impose a single will. Rosenberg's *Kampfbund* sprang from a modest membership of 6,000 in January 1933 to 38,000 by October, and expected to play a large part in defining acceptable National Socialist art. In 1934 it was renamed the National Socialist Community of Culture and worked closely with Ley's Labour Front in pursuing the ideal of authentic German drama, where its influence gradually dwindled away.[59] The difficulty of bringing artists and intellectuals under unitary control led Goebbels to appoint a Senate of Culture in 1935, to advise the Reich chamber and to pamper the creative but critical egos of those invited to participate. By 1936 the chambers were paramount in the cultural life of the new Germany.

The apparatus in each system approached the task of constructing a politically co-ordinated culture in positive as well as negative ways. Cultural policy was never simply a war on modernism. A politically acceptable cultural content had to be defined and support given to those artists officially sanctioned to execute or perform it; at the same time, any attempt to defy the new cultural norms was suppressed through a combination of official censorship, exclusion and terror. The unions and chambers were never starved of active and voluntary participants who were enthusiastic or prudent enough to see that they could only sustain their art through collaboration. Control of the arts did not necessarily mean the stifling of any artistic enthusiasm or inspiration. Most cultural producers in Germany and the Soviet Union continued to write, paint, carve or compose within the parameters of form and content permitted. Most of those who chose not to do so went voluntarily into exile. The Reich Chamber of Music had 95,600 members in 1937, the Chamber of Visual Arts 35,000, the Chamber of Theatre 41,000.[60] The Soviet Union of Writers boasted 3,700 members in 1953. Since anyone who wanted to remain a publicly active creator had to be registered and approved, artists soon adjusted to the new circumstances. There were substantial advantages from doing so. The Soviet culture unions provided a central meeting place, bursaries, artistic retreats, and the prospect for the fortunate few of real fame. The Stalin Prize, instituted in 1939 and first awarded in 1941 retrospectively to thirteen pieces of post-1934 socialist realism, had a top value of 100,000 roubles.[61] The unions were also the source of all materials. In an economy of absolute scarcity, control over the supply of paints, marble, paper, canvases, brushes and musical instruments gave an exceptional power to the cultural authorities to promote and restrict the very act of artistic creation. The German chambers were welcomed by many artists, actors and musicians not only because they not uncommonly shared the anti-modernist bias of their political masters, but because cultural unemployment and artistic insecurity were overcome by economic revival, official patronage and rising incomes.[62] The young architect Albert Speer was rescued from the enforced idleness of the slump by a contract from Goebbels that opened the door on a glittering career. There were thousands of Speers who found the regimentation of culture to be a source of security as much as menace, and welcomed the elimination of artistic rivals and flamboyant modernism.

It is easy to forget that in both systems official patronage created new literary and artistic elites drawn from the ranks of party activists and supporters. They were in most cases promoted because they exemplified the ideals of the movement in their life as well as their art. The young German poet Gerhard Schumann was typical. Growing up in the Weimar years, Schumann was obsessed with Germany's defeat and apparent cultural decay; he joined the party in 1930, the SA in 1931. His early poetry reflected a conventional longing among many cultured

Germans for a new Reich, a heroic messiah and a single people united by blood and comradeship. After 1933 he became, in his early twenties, a nationally famous party poet, writing glum and predictable verses in praise of the *Führer*, the German countryside, blood and death. In 1936 he won the National Book Prize for a book of verse, which included 'Festival of Heroes' for the sixteen party 'martyrs' who fell during the Putsch of 1923, which was set to music and played in front of Hitler at the Berlin Opera. When Germany occupied Austria in March 1938, it was Schumann's poem 'After suffering the wounds of a thousand years/Blood has returned to blood . . .' that was broadcast across Greater Germany day after day.[63] That year he was appointed to head the writers' section of the chamber of literature. His play *Entscheidung* (*Decision*), staged in 1939 to wide public acclaim, was a quintessential statement of nationalist realism: two wartime comrades take different paths in the 1920s, one to the nationalist Freikorps, the other to the communist party; in the final scene the communist realizes his error, hears the song of the Freikorps ('The heavens are bloody red . . . We want to die for Germany'), and is somehow inspired to change sides. His dying comrade tells him 'The new *Führer* is coming.'[64] Schumann's resolute morbidity reflected the regime's desire to merge art and violent, heroic experience. 'Where could German men better learn the quiet, unexplainable power of a poem,' he asked in 1940, 'than in the face of death?'[65]

The Soviet Union produced a crop of workers who were turned into literary stars by their capacity to ape socialist realism through experience. Nikolai Ostrovsky, the author of *How the Steel Was Tempered*, fought in the civil war, joined the young communist league, helped in industrial reconstruction, and faithfully recorded all these activities in his novel, which he wrote, blind and bedridden before his early death, worn out, so it was said, by an excess of youthful revolutionary zeal.[66] The writer Vasilii Azhaev, who shot to fame in 1948 with his best-selling novel *Far from Moscow*, was a model product of Stalinist culture. Azhaev began his literary career in a GUlag camp in the Soviet far east. He was arrested shortly after Kirov's murder, sent to a camp in Baikal-Amur where a second Trans-Siberian railway was being built, and after serving four years remained there as a free worker and camp official. He began writing short stories as a prisoner and in 1939 began a correspondence course with the Gorky Literary Institute to become a trained writer. His novel was written over the war period; it relates in idealized and heroic terms the building of an oil pipeline through the bleak, often uncharted reaches of the Siberian tundra, with the usual cast of hesitant engineers and brave communist workers working faster than the Plan requires, though with none of the miseries of GUlag life that Azhaev witnessed at first hand. Workers labour joyfully, nature is humbled and mastered, and an area once exotic and primitive is rescued for Soviet civilization. In 1949 the novel was awarded the Stalin Prize (first class), and Azhaev became a firm part of the literary canon, a member of the Writers' Union board and editor of the journal *Soviet Literature*. He was presented as a triumphant example of the capacity of very ordinary Soviet citizens to create their own exhilarating culture out of the most mundane material.[67]

The question of what was acceptable as art under the new dispensation was more contentious, because it involved decisions about dead composers, writers and artists as well as the living. The establishment of an exemplary literary and artistic canon was a process fraught with unexpected ambiguity. The composer Richard Wagner, whose operas had fascinated the youthful Hitler and were extravagantly celebrated once a year in the dictator's presence at Bayreuth, was claimed by both sides, Soviet and German. In the 1920s Wagner was regularly staged in Moscow and Leningrad. His brief flirtation with revolution in 1848, his ideas of art for the people and the social function of theatre, made it possible to regard him, in the words of *Pravda* on the occasion of the 125th anniversary of his birth in 1938, as a 'fighter and revolutionary'. In November 1940 Sergei Eisenstein staged a sumptuous revival of *Die Walküre* as a symbol of reconciliation in the age of the German–Soviet Non-Aggression Pact. The war brought an abrupt end to the Wagner revival and he was not staged again until a month after Stalin's death, in April 1953.[68]

There existed other ambiguities under socialist realism. Stalin was the driving force behind rehabilitating the classics in literature and music. In music the nineteenth-century Russian composers Tchaikovsky, Rimsky-Korsakov, Glinka and Borodin were revived after their eclipse by musical modernists in the 1920s, but so too were Beethoven,

Brahms and Schubert. The Russian classics of Tolstoy, Pushkin, Chekhov and Turgenev (but not Dostoevsky, considered too 'complex') were issued in millions, including half-a-million copies of *War and Peace* distributed to the population of Leningrad during the wartime siege to keep up their resolve, when what they desperately needed was fuel and food.[69] Simultaneously, the regime sponsored the ideal of the new Soviet 'classic'. From the 1930s authors were trained to replicate the master plot: young proletarian hero (rarely a heroine), devious bourgeois expert, apparently insurmountable production challenge, the support of a good woman (rarely a man) and no sex. They were told to read Stalin's speeches for the 'terseness, clarity and crystal purity of his language'.[70] A list of twelve exemplary socialist realist texts was drawn up, which included pedestrian dramas of industrial construction (Fyodor Gladkov's *Cement*, Nikolai Ostrovsky's *How the Steel was Tempered*), accounts of civil war heroism (Alexander Fadayev's *The Rout*, Dmitrii Furmanov's *Chapaev*), as well as two novels by Maxim Gorky, *Mother* and *Klim Samgin*, the first published in 1907, the second in 1928, his last novel.[71] Gorky was included despite the fact that he had chosen to turn his back on the revolution and move to Mussolini's Italy for most of the 1920s. Stalin liked his work, and encouraged Gorky to return from Capri for carefully staged visits in which he was lionized as 'the innovator, the founder' of Soviet literature. He returned for good in 1933 and was given a large house in Moscow and a smart dacha; the city of his birth, Nizhny Novgorod, was renamed Gorky in his honour. He became a prisoner of the socialist realism he helped to construct. Denied the return of his passport, he was trailed by NKVD agents until his death in 1936.[72]

The positive canon in Germany was also open to wide interpretation. Even Goebbels was uncertain about what was acceptable. For some time he kept paintings by the expressionist and pro-Nazi artist Emil Nolde in his ministerial office, until he was told by Hitler to remove them. In order to strengthen the credibility of the new chambers, Goebbels invited prominent artists to lead them, whose work was certainly modern. The elderly composer Richard Strauss accepted the presidency of the Chamber of Music; the expressionist film director Fritz Lang was invited by Goebbels at some point in the summer of 1933 to head the film chamber, at exactly the same time that his newly completed and starkly gothic film, *The Testament of Dr Mabuse*, was banned from German cinemas for glamorizing crime.[73] Lang went to Hollywood instead. As in the Soviet Union, approved art became a mixture of old and new, as long as it was predominantly German, though even this did not prevent the work of the émigré Russian composer Igor Stravinsky from being performed regularly in German concert repertoire in the 1930s when he was ignored as a cosmopolitan formalist in the Soviet Union. Nor could it prevent Italian opera from replacing Wagner in German theatres. In 1932–3 four of Wagner's operas featured among the top ten most regularly performed; in 1938–9 there was not one, and the top three places were all Italian.[74] The classics of German literature were permitted if the authors were neither Jewish nor evidently un-German; modern literature was indulged if it fitted standard themes of nationalist realism. German classical music was heavily patronized, except for German-Jewish composers. Beethoven's *Fidelio* was staged in ways that glossed over its message of emancipation from petty tyranny; Brahms and Bruckner remained the most popular choices. New musical classics were encouraged, among them Gottfried Müller's *Requiem for German Heroes*, first performed in 1934 in honour of the German war dead, and Carl Diem's *Olympic Youth*, staged for the 1936 Berlin Olympics.[75] However, the establishment of a strict canon proved impossible given the variety and depth of German cultural output, old and new; acceptable culture came to be determined more by what was excluded on grounds of race or politics or the subjective 'Principles of the *Führer*'.

The control of culture in its negative aspect took many forms, from direct state censorship to self-imposed artistic silence. Exclusion was directed across the cultural spectrum, from high art to popular entertainment. Soviet censorship dated from 1920, when the State Publishing House was given the right to vet everything for ideological purity before it could be set in type. A formal national structure was established on 6 June 1922 under the title Main Administration for Literary and Publishing Affairs, generally known as Glavlit. Its early role was political as much as cultural, for it had to prevent anything from being published that undermined state secrecy, encouraged sedition, inspired national or religious fanaticism or moral degeneration. It drew up an index of proscribed books, the *Perechen'*, which at first covered publications that had to be kept secret, but came to include any books from which it was thought the public should be sheltered.[76] In 1923 a separate Main Administration for Repertory (Glavrepertkom) was set up to censor everything that was staged. In 1936 both branches were brought under the direct supervision of the Central Committee. Regional offices were set up throughout the union and by 1939 the censor organization employed a little over 6,000 people.[77]

The censors in the 1920s were chiefly concerned with banning what could not be viewed or read; but in the age of socialist realism they were also made responsible for 'reforming' literature or film so that they reflected the current party line. Suppressed books, Soviet and foreign, were placed on a blacklist, copies seized and handed to the NKVD, who placed them solemnly in sealed premises. Larger quantities had to be destroyed. In 1938–9 alone 16,453 titles were withdrawn from circulation and over 24 million copies pulped.[78] In libraries censors combed through books to erase the names of disgraced citizens with black ink. They were remorselessly thorough. One day in October 1934 an issue of the farm journal *Kolkhoznik* in a village in Karelia was found to contain censorable material. Censors rushed out to retrieve the 1,900 copies: 1,507 were confiscated from the village post office, 300 were taken from news-stands, 50 copies had already been used as improvised wallpaper, 12 as toilet paper. Eleven subscribers refused to part with their copies and were given a formal warning. The rest were burned by the censor board.[79] Poorly trained but anxiously vigilant censors left no stone unturned: swastikas were found by scrutinizing the most innocent of illustrations; papers were held up to the light to ensure that pictures of Stalin did not reveal the unfortunate juxtaposition of images from the page behind; one well-meaning censor wrote to Moscow that a portrait of Stalin published in a pamphlet in December 1937 showed an unmistakable outline of Mussolini on the sleeve, and the faint letters HITLER across the chest.[80]

The reformation of books, scripts and images was as important as simple proscription. Under socialist realism censors were to ensure that everything should reveal a clear and unambiguous message or 'one-meaningness'.[81] There was always scope for ambiguity. Some of the pictures from the 'Industry of Socialism' exhibition were withdrawn because they juxtaposed trivial images with portraits of party leaders (though this did not prevent the display of Nikolai Denisovski's commended painting of Stalin, Molotov, Kaganovich and Mikoyan, the Commissar for Trade, inspecting a small table of women's toiletries).[82] The printed word was easier to police; censors went through everything, recommended changes in red pen, returned them to publishers and authors, and then re-read them before permitting publication to ensure that the alterations had been made. Only then was the Glavlit 'visa' granted. Even books in the Soviet canon were not immune. *Cement* had small changes made with every printing; Fadeyev's *The Young Guard*, published in 1945, was redrafted on Stalin's recommendation. Stalin was the Soviet Union's unofficial chief censor. He was the inspiration behind the decision that under socialist realism books should be cleansed of profanities, blasphemy, sex and, as far as possible, the natural functions of the body. The growing coyness was part of the general policy of 'culturedness' in the 1930s. In 1935 censors were sent instructions from Glavlit 'About the struggle for the purity of the Russian language', which included the injunction to fight against 'coarse expressions, swearwords'.[83] The word for whore was first reduced to 'w . . .', but by the 1940s was deleted altogether. Any word indicating sexual organs was removed; attempts to use the four-letter Russian word for horseradish (*khren*) as a pun for the word penis (*chlen*) were detected and eliminated.[84] By the 1940s authors and editors censored themselves rather than wait for the inevitable deletion.

Censorship in Germany differed from Soviet practice in one important respect. There was no attempt to reform artistic output since anything likely to be proscribed was, by definition, the product of 'cultural bolshevism', or Jewish or alien. Cultural products were divided up into those that were acceptable and those that were not. The latter were banned or destroyed. In March 1933 Goebbels instructed the librarian Wolfgang Herrmann to draw up a blacklist of Jewish, Marxist and un-German literature. The list was sent to the student unions in German universities and high schools; it was the student activists in the *Deutsche Studentenschaft*, rather than the rival National Socialist Student League, who declared a four-week programme of cultural cleansing from 12 April to 10 May, which culminated with the mass-burning of blacklisted books. Books were seized from university libraries and bookshops; professors who protested were boycotted. On the final day of the programme huge bonfires were lit in Berlin, Munich, Breslau, Frankfurt and Dresden and crowds of students, SA men and academic staff threw the offending literature into the flames, including the plays and poetry of Bertolt Brecht, who had already left Germany for Austria in March 1933. In the autumn Brecht settled in Denmark, and it was here that he wrote the satirical poem *The Burning of the Books* for the writer Oskar Maria Graf, who did complain that he had been omitted from the first list of proscribed books drawn up in March 1933. The first books thrown onto the pyres were those of Karl Marx.[85]

Censorship was never usually so violent, though it was crude. Goebbels' ministry ordered publishers and booksellers to remove all proscribed books from their lists and bookshelves. The press was cleansed of anti-party publications. By April 1934 1,000 newspapers had been closed down, and 350 voluntarily wound up.[86] All published cultural material, artistic or literary, was vetted by the censorship departments of each chamber or by the party's own Checking Commission, whose limp imprimatur appeared inside the front cover: 'the NSDAP has raised no objection against the publication of this volume'.[87] At local level official commissars watched over provincial theatres, concert programmes and galleries. At the party's headquarters in Munich a large library of all banned material was kept and catalogued. Current artistic output was censored before it reached the public. Film censorship was particularly thorough; every approved film had a member of the film censorship board assigned to watch every day of filming. In June 1935 Goebbels gave himself the legal right to overrule the censors if he did not like a film that they had certified. He saw every finished product, Hitler a great many. Even under these circumstances it was possible for ambiguity to elude the censor. A film set in medieval Germany, Frank Wysbar's *Ferryman Maria*, had the right ingredients – an Aryan hero rediscovering his homeland, a romantic historical setting – but the finished product was condemned as decadent because the German homeland was under foreign rule and the hero in love with a non-German.[88] Foreign films were cut or banned before German audiences could see them. To prevent the public discussion of films or art from fuelling ambiguity,

Goebbels took the step on 26 November 1936 of banning all artistic criticism. The press was allowed only to print 'art reports' or 'the contemplation of art'. The critical evaluation of artistic output was permitted only to those who were judged to display a National Socialist 'purity of heart and outlook', and would say what the regime wanted.[89]

The termination of free expression ultimately rested in both dictatorships not on formal systems of censorship but on the physical and psychological coercion of artists, writers, directors and publishers who challenged the values of official culture. Thousands were purged under both cultural regimes. To be expelled from or refused membership of the union or chamber was artistic death, though it could not prevent people from writing or drawing in private, except in those cases where the security services continued to keep a close watch on what the banned artist was doing. The aftermath of Stalin's attack on Shostakovich in 1936 was a wave of purges directed at all composers, artists, directors and filmmakers accused of 'formalism', though Shostakovich survived. Even before this, the coercive silencing of artistic output was widespread. The playwright Nikolai Erdman, author of several successful modernist plays in the 1920s, was banned from the stage in the late 1920s, arrested in 1933, forced to confess that he was the author of 'counter-revolutionary literary productions' and exiled to Siberia for three years. He was not allowed to return to Moscow or to resume his work, but was not killed. To confirm his literary demise, he was later recruited to write sketches for the NKVD wartime variety shows.[90] His patron, the remarkable stage director Vsevolod Meyerhold, was less fortunate. Condemned as formalist, he struggled to maintain his experimental theatre throughout the 1930s until it was closed down in January 1938. Unpopular with the regime, he was arrested in June 1939 after two Lubyanka prisoners, one a Japanese communist, the other a Moscow journalist, had been forced to confess that Meyerhold was a spy for both the French and the Japanese secret services. Under interrogation past misdemeanours were dredged up – acquaintance with 'enemies of the people', support for a Trotskyite poet, and so on – and after days of savage physical beating and enforced sleeplessness the 66-year-old Meyerhold was finally made to confess that he had indeed been the leader ten years before of an anti-Soviet, Trotskyite (and hence avant-garde) conspiracy representing all

Soviet arts. He was tried in camera on 1 February 1940, pleaded his innocence, bravely withdrew all his confessions, and was shot the following day.[91]

Artistic survival in the Soviet Union under Stalin was entirely capricious. The writers Isaak Babel and Osip Mandelstam were arrested and murdered, but most of those named by Meyerhold under torture as his co-conspirators remained unmolested if Stalin liked their work – the film director Sergei Eisenstein, who was constantly at odds with the artistic authorities but died in his bed in 1948; or the anti-Bolshevik poet Ilya Ehrenburg, who left Russia for Paris in 1921 with the help of Bukharin, had once worked briefly with Trotsky, returned to Moscow in 1940 after the fall of France, and ended up as the leading propagandist and poet of the Soviet war effort.[92] The most remarkable survivor was the playwright, poet and novelist Mikhail Bulgakov, whose curriculum vitae ought to have brought him to the front of the purge queue. Born in 1891 in Kiev, he graduated as a doctor and served in the army medical corps during the First World War. In 1918 he became a medical officer in the White armies fighting the civil war in the Caucasus, and remained hostile to Bolshevism throughout his life. In the 1920s he adopted a provocatively anti-proletarian style with neat bow-ties, stiff collars, a monocle and an uncompromising commitment to Russian literary traditions. He turned his civil war experience into his only successful play, *The Days of the Turbins*, which explored the complex pressures forcing people to choose one side over the other, but after that all his work was suppressed.

In 1930 Bulgakov sent a brave letter to the Soviet government condemning its crude efforts to stifle literary freedom, and the 'helots, panegyrists and frightened lackeys' who pandered to Soviet artistic taste.[93] During the 1930s he worked continuously on projects that were never staged or published; in 1934, obsessed with fear of death and the reality of creative imprisonment, he experienced a prolonged psychological collapse. In 1939 he told a friend, 'However much you might try to throttle yourself, it is difficult to stop seizing the pen.' He was tormented, he continued, 'by an obscure desire to settle my final account in literature'.[94] He was an uncompromising commentator on Soviet literary corruption. In 1938 he wrote a biting satire of Soviet cultural life, *Richard I*, in which a cultural apparatchik, Richard Richardovich, recruits a frustrated author to write official literature before himself being purged, leaving the writer as powerless as before, but more morally tainted.[95] Yet Bulgakov was both fascinated and repelled by Stalin. In 1939 he fulfilled a hope he had long cherished of writing about the dictator when he was commissioned to script a play on Stalin's early political life. It was finished in July 1939; after trying fifteen titles, the Caucasian city name *Batum* was chosen as sufficiently uncontroversial. Stalin read the script at once and rejected it as an inappropriate embellishment of his revolutionary adolescence. Bulgakov rapidly declined, spiritually and physically, and died in March 1940. A few days before his death his wife promised to type out the final version of a novel he had been working on since 1928: 'To be known . . . To be known!' muttered Bulgakov.[96] The novel, *The Master and Margarita*, first published in 1966, was an epitaph for Soviet literary repression, a fantastical rendering of the guilt-ridden tension between mischievous and diabolical power on one side and unnatural authorial silence on the other. For reasons that remain obscure, it was Stalin who allowed Bulgakov to survive and Stalin who destroyed his artistic integrity and psychological health.

The elimination of artists in the Third Reich was less evidently unpredictable. In 1933 the first wave of purges eliminated most of the German-Jewish and anti-party artistic intelligentsia. Artists were asked to make a specific pledge to the regime. In March 1933 the President of the Prussian Academy of Arts wrote to all its members, asking them to answer with a simple 'yes' or 'no' the question whether they were prepared to eschew any anti-government activity and to work loyally for the new 'national cultural programme' imposed by the regime.[97] Among those who refused were the novelists Thomas Mann and Alfred Döblin; fourteen other members were expelled, including the German-Jewish composer Arnold Schoenberg. Jewish artists were purged from any artistic contact with Germans. Among the demands of the students who burned books in May 1933 was a refusal to allow any Jewish writer to use German script or to be translated into German. 'Jews cannot be interpreters of Germanness,' announced Goebbels in 1933.[98] Most of those employed by the state in orchestras, theatres, opera houses or galleries who were defined as Jewish under the terms of the public employment law of April 1933 were sacked. When the music chamber was opened in November, anyone with Jewish ancestry was debarred from membership. The process continued throughout the 1930s as registered artists and musicians had their genealogies checked. By 1938 2,310 musicians had been expelled, together with 1,657 artists, 1,303 authors and 1,285 from film and theatre.[99] Eventually any Jewish artist left in Germany, or captured in Europe after 1939, was dragged into the genocide. Jewish musicians in the camps were not killed at once but were forced to play 'German' music to their captors, while a few defiantly wrote their own compositions on hidden scraps of paper.

There were also those, as in the Soviet Union, who were initially indulged by the regime only to be expunged or silenced at a later stage. The composer Richard Strauss welcomed the reorganization of the music profession in 1933 but was soon enmeshed in the coils of the new political system. He was banned from the Salzburg Festival in 1934 because of German–Austrian tensions, a new Strauss opera with words by the exiled German-Jewish poet Stefan Zweig was cancelled in the summer of 1935 and the Gestapo intercepted a letter from Strauss to Zweig the same month. Two party officials visited Strauss's home and told him to retire on grounds of 'ill-health'. Gustav Havemann, a party member and professor at the *Hochschule für Musik*, was sacked from his position in the music chamber in 1935 for supporting the modernist composer Paul Hindemith, and for his unsavoury reputation as a drunk and a womanizer; Friedrich Mahling was sacked as the chamber press secretary after making the mistake of allowing a magazine advertisement for the Moscow Theatre Festival; and so on. They were all replaced by more reliable party stalwarts.[100]

In literature a similar fate befell the expressionist poet Gottfried Benn. Like Bulgakov, Benn was a trained doctor who saw service in the war; he, too, dressed smartly in dapper suit and tie, the antithesis of the bohemian anti-bourgeois suggested by his poetry. His aesthetic views were scarcely those of the party cultural establishment, hovering between a profound nihilism and a striving for artistic autonomy, but in 1933, deeply disillusioned with the republic, he initially welcomed the new Reich and its commitment to firm authority and racial purity. The party intellectuals did not trust him and by 1934 he was already under attack for his expressionist degeneracy and his open links with Italian Futurism. Press articles speculated that he was Jewish, and a puzzled Benn wrote to a friend to ask if the name 'Benn' was derived from the Jewish 'Ben- . . .', but was assured that it could not be.[101] 'The times have become so dark,' he wrote to a friend in January 1938, 'and the world so empty, one must experience everything alone, with a chain on the door and bars in front of your mind and your words.'[102] In March 1938 the campaign of vilification ended with a terse official letter from the writers' chamber notifying him that his membership was cancelled and that if he tried to write and publish anything, he would be punished.[103] Benn continued to write in secret, a series of savage attacks on the party and its cultural barbarism and 'criminal society', but he was not published again until 1949.[104]

Official suppression was complemented by a widespread self-censorship. This took a great many forms. Publishers and editors did much of the censors' work for them. Artists chose to write on themes they knew would be acceptable, or produced much less, or produced in secret, or remained silent. The lesbian poet Sophia Parnok published her last collection of poems in 1928 under the title *Halfvoiced* to reflect the official stifling of her poetry, but wrote a hundred more unpublished poems before her death in 1933.[105] Boris Pasternak abandoned his own writing in the 1930s and instead undertook translation, including Russian versions of Shakespeare's *Hamlet* and Goethe's *Faust*. Avant-garde architects in the Soviet Union chose to give up their work altogether. Exile or suicide was a possibility, though escape from the Soviet Union was rare. Thousands of German intellectuals and artists left Germany between 1933 and 1939, the majority in the early months. The expressionist artist Max Beckmann, though sacked from teaching in 1933, stayed in Germany until the opening day of the Exhibition of Degenerate Art, when the honour of having two large pictures in the opening room finally persuaded him to leave for the Netherlands.[106] Exile brought personal safety, but exiled artists could have little if any effect on the cultural battleground they abandoned, while it weakened the resistance and provoked the resentment of those who stayed behind. 'No foreign sky protected me/no stranger's wing shielded my face', wrote the Russian poet Anna Akhmatova, whose lyric poetry was condemned as the work of a 'half nun, half harlot' by

Zhdanov in 1946.[107] The final retreat was suicide, though remarkably few did kill themselves. Akhmatova, in a black poem written in 1939, begged for death ('You will come in any case – so why not now?/How long I wait and wait'), but survived until 1966.[108] Ernst Kirchner, on learning that no fewer than thirty-two of his pieces were to appear in the 1937 exhibition alongside Beckmann, and that 639 of his paintings had been seized from museums, was thrown into a prolonged despair, from which he released himself on 18 June 1938, after destroying his woodblocks and burning his remaining paintings, with a bullet through his head.[109]

The ambition to shape and control all culture was never limited by the common distinction between 'high art' and popular, mass entertainment. The new classics of Soviet and German literature, music and art were supposed to be read and admired by all. The publication of *Far From Moscow* was followed by organized meetings in party branches, factories and offices where the public was encouraged to voice their opinions about the novel's qualities and drawbacks. In the first year alone 150,000 copies were printed.[110] In 1950 the Soviet Union published a staggering 180 million copies of books of fiction or poetry.[111] Gerhard Schumann's poems and songs were recited and sung by the Hitler Youth or the SA at party festivals and meetings. Culture was treated as something that belonged to the entire community as part of its collective endeavour and the fabric of everyday life, not as something abstracted from it. This wider conception of 'culture' meant that even the most innocuous popular pastime had to conform to the cultural guidelines of the regime. People were little freer when they listened to light music, visited the dance hall or sat in front of a film than they were in a library or an art gallery.

The official attitude to jazz demonstrated the extent to which cultural ideology was used to shape the entire cultural environment. From the early 1930s jazz in the Soviet Union was treated as a form of cultural sabotage and the dancing it inspired as degenerately bourgeois. Since jazz was evidently widely popular, state jazz orchestras were formed that were allowed to play only smooth ballroom numbers, or tunes that drew on Russian folk traditions. After 1945 the association of jazz with the American Cold War enemy brought further restrictions, until in 1949 the production and sale of saxophones was out-lawed altogether.[112] Jazz fared even less well in Hitler's Germany, where it was defined, along with popular dances such as the tango and the Charleston, as racially degenerate 'nigger-music', entirely alien to German musical tastes. It was banned from the radio in 1935, and from many other places, but a sanitized dancehall version was allowed that used violins and cellos instead of saxophones, and where mel-odious rather than discordant tunes and 'provocative rhythms' were played.[113] Official efforts were made through public music compe-titions to construct a distinctive German dance band music that sup-plied bland and decorous entertainment in a German style, and in 1942 Goebbels established the German Dance and Entertainment Orchestra to play the permitted music on the radio.[114] Under both dictatorships listening to or playing authentic, discordant, syncopated jazz was an act of political defiance.

These values were extended to the expanding field of film and radio. Both regimes attached particular importance to radio broadcasting. Radio was developed in the Soviet Union as early as 1919 and regular broadcasts began by 1924. There were sixty radio stations by 1933, ninety by 1940; the number of government-licensed receivers grew steadily over the same period, from 1.3 million to 7 million. Under socialist realism the radio provided a regular diet of music (which supplied about three-quarters of all programmes), readings from the classics, drama and political education, all under the watchful eye of Glavlit.[115] Radio broadcasting began in Germany in 1923, and by 1933 there existed a plethora of small local stations loosely supervised by a Reich Radio Society (RRG). Goebbels centralized the whole system under the control of his ministry. In July 1933 the powers of the RRG were strengthened and it was brought under the supervision of the Broadcasting Division of the Propaganda Ministry. Each local station was subject to political vetting by the Interior Ministry, and had a Cultural Council attached to monitor the quality and suitability of programmes. National programming was organized by Eugen Hadamowsky, who saw radio as a propaganda instrument 'to mould the character and will of the German nation'.[116] The parameters of broadcasting were set, according to one official, by the words '"German", "race", "blood" and "Volk"'.[117] Music nevertheless made up around 70 per cent of German programming too, a combination of classics and light music that was, according to Goebbels, 'pleasing and accessible'. In order to widen the radio audience rapidly the regime organized the mass production of a cheap 'People's Radio' (*Volksempfänger*). Production began in May 1933 of the first model – the VE301 or '30 January', to honour the day Hitler became Chancellor – which sold at 76 marks; a smaller, compact version was on the market by 1938, retailing at 35 marks. In 1933 there were 4.5 million registered radio sets, by 1941 15 million.[118]

The cinema was also central to the development of an acceptable mass culture, particularly with the advent of sound in the early 1930s (though this had less impact in the Soviet Union, where in 1934 only 1 per cent of the country's 30,000 projectors could relay sound, and silent film was made into the 1940s).[119] In the Soviet Union the number of cinemas, often little more than a wooden hall with a portable screen, increased from 17,000 in 1927 to 31,000 a decade later, while ticket sales trebled. By 1952 there were 49,000 projectors throughout the Soviet Union, even in the most remote reaches of the tundra, though the average Soviet citizen in 1950 still watched a film only six times a year.[120] The importance attached to the cinema in the age of socialist realism did not derive entirely from the official assertion that film 'easily communicates its ideological value'. Soviet films were also intended to amuse as well as educate, to be '100 per cent ideologically correct and 100 per cent commercially viable'.[121] Musicals, comedies and historical dramas far outnumbered films set in factories or on collective farms, which made up only 9 per cent of all films produced between 1933 and 1940. Exhaustive censorship of film in the 1930s and 1940s nevertheless reduced the range of entertainment as producers struggled to find scripts and settings that met the stiff requirements of a socialist realist age. Igor Pyriev's film about the evils of western capitalism, *Conveyor-Belt of Death*, had to be re-made fourteen times. In the 1920s around 120 films a year had been made; under Stalin, who watched every single film produced, the number dropped to an average of 35 a year in the 1930s, 25 a year in the 1940s, and in 1951 just 9 films were made in 12 months. Some 2,700 films of all kinds made before 1935, including newsreels, were banned from theatres. Foreign films almost entirely disappeared: in 1927 there were on average eleven Soviet and twenty foreign titles screened each week; by 1937 the figure was just eleven Soviet.[122] There was a brief revival between 1945 and 1950 when Soviet cinema-goers were allowed to view a clutch of romantic German films (and a single copy of *Tarzan*) seized from Goebbels' personal film archive in Berlin. In 1947 the glamorous German wartime romance, *Girl of My Dreams*, topped the Soviet Union's box office sales.[123]

Film under Hitler was also meant to amuse and divert as well as educate. Like the organizers of the Soviet cinema, Goebbels accepted that film had a 'political function to fulfil', and was an ideal means 'for influencing the masses'. He also recognized that film had to entertain, and only around 14 per cent of the 1,094 films made were overt propaganda; an average of 47 per cent of films screened between 1934 and 1940 were comedies. Only ninety-six were state-commissioned films, intended to carry a more weighty ideological message.[124] The German industry was second only to Hollywood in 1933 in size and technical capability, and there already existed a national cinema network and a vast established cinema audience. Ticket sales nonetheless expanded more than fourfold between 1933 and 1944, when the average German made 14.4 visits to the cinema in the year instead of the modest 4 in 1933.[125] Official 'Film Days' were used to promote cinema-going, and villages remote from a theatre were served with mobile cinemas. Special 'Youth Film Hours' were introduced by the Hitler Youth; didactic in purpose, screened once a month on a Sunday, the number of performances rose from 905 in 1935 to more than 45,000 in 1942.[126] The screening of foreign films dropped away rapidly, including all the comedies and light romances, because they could not be censored at each stage of production like German-made films. There were 64 American films on show in 1933, but only 39 four years later and a mere 5 in 1940. Most of the films made in Germany before 1933 were denied official approval and disappeared even from private cinemas except for a handful of heroic films on flight and mountain-climbing.[127] One exception was the film *Dawn*, made in 1932 but shown in Berlin on 2 February 1933 to an ecstatic reception in front of an enthusiastic Hitler. The film, set in a doomed German submarine, is about sacrifice in war: 'Perhaps we Germans do not know how to live,' remarks the sailor hero to his mother, 'but how to die, this we know incredibly well.'[128]

The combination of entertainment and instruction in the popular films of both dictatorships was intended to win audiences over to particular social values without repelling them with cinematic sermons. This involved a much more careful and deliberate process of ideological selection, adjustment and redrafting than the artistically successful end-product might suggest. To take one example: in both dictatorships the role of women inside and outside the home was made to conform rigorously to regime guidelines, though these reflected gender stereotypes that were certainly not confined only to the two dictatorships. In each system a new puritanism prevailed after the freer mood of the 1920s. Female screen stars were denied the right to dress skimpily or behave immodestly or immorally; instead they had to display healthy instincts and a tame sentimentality. In the Soviet Union films about complex dilemmas of family life (*Two Mothers* in 1931, on the moral problems of adoption, or *Five Wives* in 1930, on issues of rape within the family) were banned by popular demand as 'unproletarian'.[129] The female film director Esfir' Shub, who made the successful film *KshE* in 1932 about young communists helping to electrify the Soviet Union – the boys building generators, the girls making light bulbs – tried a year later to make a film simply called *Women*, but the script was rejected as too socially complex. Under socialist realism women could play a role in building communism, but only under the guidance of a (usually older) man, and as long as their role as mothers was not neglected or trivialized. Dziga Vertov's 1937 film of contented Soviet mothers and infants, *Lullaby*, ends appropriately with the appearance of Stalin himself as the iconic father-figure.[130] Alexander Zarkhi's 1939 film *Member of the Government* and Grigori Alexandrov's 1940 highly successful film fairytale *The Radiant Path* (originally titled *Cinderella*, but altered at Stalin's suggestion) both star humble Soviet women, one on a collective farm, the other a maidservant turned textile-worker, who overcome every obstacle with the help of calm and solidly competent men (peasant worker, party secretary, engineer), unmask wreckers (a murderous agronomist on the farm, a warehouse arsonist in the factory), and both enjoy a fairy-tale ending as deputies to the Supreme Soviet.[131]

German films about the place of women after 1933 did not ignore the working woman but usually resolved the dilemmas posed by the tension between family and profession by standard romantic or comic devices. The popular wartime romance *The Great Love*, made in 1942 as a state-commissioned film, reveals the capacity of a self-absorbed celebrity, who falls for an air force pilot, to set aside her own romantic yearnings and send him bravely back to his squadron singing 'The World's Not Going to End because of This'.[132] The working woman, like her Soviet counterpart, appears in numerous films supported in the dilemmas presented by her new role or new technology by a man. In *Woman at the Crossroads*, made in 1938, a woman doctor whose marriage fails is rescued from uncertainty by an older (male) medical professor, who takes her under his wing and gives her a sense of purpose and direction. The ambiguous position of the woman professional was explored in *The Impossible Woman*, made in 1936, in which an ill-tempered spinster in charge of an ailing business is saved from commercial disaster and a life without love by an obliging male engineer.[133] Few films explored realistic dilemmas like the 1932 film *Eight Girls in a Boat*, in which a student who becomes pregnant seeks an abortion, or *The Dreaming Mouth*, made the same year, where an adulterous woman, unable to cope with losing her illicit lover, drowns herself.[134] After 1933 women become wholesome members of the community as mothers, workers or farm-girls, but they cannot become deputies to the all-male Reichstag. The escapism and sentimentality of German cinema after 1933 left women adrift from politics, whereas in Soviet cinema party politics even in the utopian genre of the 1930s was presented as part of the fabric of life for men and women alike.

In neither dictatorship was popular culture confined to the passive act of listening to the radio or watching films. The aim of both dictatorships was to develop positive forms of cultural participation for those who were not necessarily professional artists. Amateur or 'people's' culture was a way to sustain the populist ideal that culture in some sense belonged collectively to the people and was not simply imposed by the system. Popular cultural initiatives had also to conform to the parameters of official art, since unsupervised they offered considerable scope for subversion or mockery, but for many of those who willingly participated in making their own culture the organic bonds between politics, art and society were seldom obtrusive or inhibiting, and in many, perhaps most cases the ideological purposes of official art met with willing endorsement, approval or imitation. The construction of a 'people's culture' was a two-way process, neither monolithically dictated nor uncontrollably spontaneous, but a mixture of the two.

This process went further in the Soviet Union, where popular cultural life had been under-developed before the revolution. Communists were generally hostile to the inherited folk traditions and archaic rites that lingered on in much of Russia after 1917. Popular Soviet culture developed as a direct consequence of opportunities opened up by the revolution, even in those cases where it remained symbolically attached to pre-revolutionary cultural forms. By 1952 there were 123,000 clubs or houses of culture throughout the Soviet Union, where local groups could practise and present plays, choral work or concerts, or discuss the latest novel, or run poetry competitions. In the 1930s under Stalin there came a revival of folk music and folk tales, though now cast in an idiom that was recognizably communist. Folk music took the form of the 'mass song', popular, tuneful, revolutionary or patriotic, and they were composed in their thousands. A State Folk Orchestra was founded in 1936 and gave 571 concerts across the Soviet Union in four years. Local folk choirs and bands proliferated and by 1940 production of balalaikas reached one-and-a-half million a year.[135] Folk poets became national stars. The Kazakh Dzhambul Dzhabaev performed for Stalin himself and his effusive paeans to the great leader and the cause of communism were published country-wide (though in this case it was subsequently proved that the poems had been drafted by a Russian journalist who recruited a real but illiterate Kazakh to play the part of folk genius).[136]

During the 1930s traditional folklore was stripped of its superstitious and pagan clothing and slowly turned from oral tradition into written literature. A folklore section was set up in the Soviet Writers' Union under the prominent folklore scholar Yuri Sokolov, who argued in 1931 that folk tales and folksong should also suffer 'systematic class direction'.[137] Throughout the Stalin years folklore was subjected to the same steady political supervision as the rest of the arts. The first volume of Soviet folk literature, a collection of Uzbek epic poems on the revolution and its leaders, was published in 1935 under the title *Verses and Songs of the People of the East Concerning Stalin*. In 1937, to mark the twentieth anniversary of the revolution, there appeared the first anthology of Soviet folk tales, *Creations of the Peoples of the USSR*. The most famous Russian folk performer, Marfa Kryukova, called the Soviet verses *noviny* (new songs). They were for the most part composed (but not necessarily written down) by ordinary peasants, soldiers or workers and then transcribed by Soviet folklorists. They included the ancient form of the *byliny* or epic lament, and the short doggerel *chastushki*, both infused with Soviet content. One of the first, published in *Pravda* in 1936, was a 'Lament for Kirov'. Later laments guilelessly combined the ancient and the modern: 'It's not a prophetic bird talking/it's the Soviet radio'; 'Stars from the heaven have fallen/ into our peasant villages/Our village houses/Have become illuminated by electricity'.[138]

The fusion of old and new was also evident in the spread of popular theatre, which drew in turn on village and small-town traditions of ritualized carnival or mummery. During the 1920s amateur dramatic groups, acting out revolutionary fables or promoting party propaganda, sprang up all over the Soviet Union. By 1931 it was estimated that there were 15,000 groups, reaching an audience of perhaps 100 million a year. The 2 million participants made theatre a genuinely populist medium. In 1932 the state organized an Olympiad of Autonomous Art and over one hundred theatre and choral groups were selected to represent the best of amateur art. The subject matter was derived from the daily lives of those who performed it: the Minsk builders' collective performed 'The Five Year Plan in Four Years', the Izhorsk factory collective presented 'Coal'. During the 1930s the groups became more ambitious and more professional, and in 1938 the winner was a Moscow theatre circle performing Gorky's play *The Philistine*.[139] Popular theatre was adapted to local conditions in every area of the Union. In 1935 a Travelling Arctic Theatre set out from Moscow to reach the most remote and sparsely inhabited areas within the Arctic Circle, giving 400 performances in two years. In remote Igarka local enthusiasts asked to be allowed to set up their own theatre and, after a training course in Moscow, were sent back to open the world's most northerly playhouse. A young northern tribesman, Ankakemen, wrote a play in his far-northern Chukcha language. In Buriat-Mongolia, on the banks of Lake Baikal, a Mongolian version of Shakespeare's *King Lear* was regularly staged because of its close links with themes in local folklore. Shakespeare was widely performed, along with the Soviet canon. At the Moscow Rubber Works the dramatic society performed *The Taming of the Shrew* more than a hundred times.[140]

Popular participation took a different direction in Germany. Here there was already a well-established tradition of active amateur culture. The Union of German Singers had a membership of 800,000 country-wide. Reading societies, theatre groups and amateur musicians faced restrictions on what they could read or play, but they were not com-pelled to act out revolutionary morality plays. There were folklore societies and folkbands, but the German public was by the 1930s too urbanized and too heavily exposed to modern forms of entertainment for folklore to play more than a minor part in the promotion of popular culture. A form of popular National Socialist folk poetry emerged, much though not all of it by professional poets; in 1941 a selection was published under the title *To the Führer. The Words of German Poets*, including sycophantic verses by the German novelist Will Vesper, one of the most prolific producers of German 'new songs'. The language of much of the adulatory poetry had strong elements of folklore (themes of resurrection, redemption, suffering, overcoming) and of folkloric imagery (sun, nature, strength, second sight, etc.).[141] The popular press carried regular examples of amateur poetry and doggerel celebrating the regime, but it lacked the formal support or popular resonance that poetry enjoyed in the Soviet Union.

The failure to produce a distinctively National Socialist popular culture was evident in the theatre. In the first years of the new Reich hundreds of plays on the rise and triumph of National Socialism were written, many by amateur, party-minded enthusiasts. They were collectively described as *Thing* plays ('*thing*' or '*ting*' = 'place of judgement' in Norse) and placed under a Reich League for Outdoor and People's Theatre set up in July 1933 to control the performances of amateur theatre clubs. From October 1933 they could produce plays only with official permission. The League encouraged *Thing* theatre to use large numbers of players and vast choruses to make them purposefully an example of collective drama. The Labour Front organized a competition that year, which produced 489 plays and 694 choral works, all for mass-casts.[142] Special Play Communities were established to stage the large-scale works as forms of popular festival. Goebbels' ministry planned to cover Germany with 400 special out-door amphitheatres to accommodate the new dramas. The plays them-selves were the stock-in-trade of all German nationalist writing, but the effect they achieved was from the collective choral work and the synchronized marching of the actors, which personified the new organic community and its ideals of racial brotherhood. The heroism, like the heroism of socialist realist plays, is one-dimensional and stead-fast; but the remorselessly morbid theme of death and resurrection (Richard Euringer's *Dance of Death* and *German Passion* were the best known and most often performed) seems uniquely a product of nationalist realism.[143] Nonetheless, in 1935 Goebbels suddenly with-drew support, closed down the Play Communities and banned chorus chanting. *Thing* drama disappeared. The strongly religious imagery, constant references to Weimar decadence and a style of staging with echoes of the expressionist or independent worker dramas of the 1920s may all have contributed to its loss of party patronage. *German Passion* was dropped from the repertoire because of its implicit pacifism, despite winning a State Prize in 1934. The overtly political themes were not regarded as suitable as mere entertainment. The decline of the *Thing* theatre coincided with the eclipse of heroic films of the SA during the years of struggle.[144]

In Germany popular participation was more widespread in the theatre of politics itself. The idea of an 'aestheticized politics' was first formulated by the German Marxist philosopher Walter Benjamin, in 1936, to explain the appeal of National Socialism as a mass movement. A year later Brecht, in a satirical poem on Goebbels' decision to ban all arts criticism, described the Third Reich as a vast stage or film set with Hitler 'the Reich's first actor': 'The regime/Dearly loves the theatre. Its accomplishments/Are mainly on the theatrical plane.'[145] The logic of a regime that defined art as politics was to define poli-tics as art. In the 1930s the Reich was sometimes compared to a *Gesamtkunstwerk*, a total work of art. The pervasive image of the social 'body', in the utopian language of the regime, was echoed in the promotion of modern representations of the ideal physical form in art.[146] The National Socialist conception of the organic and collective nature of the social and political system was made deliberately visible in the aesthetic presentation of the movement: the ubiquitous banners, flags, uniforms, festivals, rallies, films and, above all, in the vast, solemn set-piece theatre of the regime's liturgical calendar.

The National Socialist year was punctuated by four major ritual occasions, and a host of more minor ones, organized by an Office of Festivals, Leisure and Celebrations. Each May Day was celebrated as a day dedicated to labour in its broadest sense, a 'Day of National Brotherhood' across the whole Reich. Each autumn the harvest was celebrated in the Lower Saxon town of Bückeburg amidst a sea of flags, banners and folk costume and in the presence of Hitler.[147] In September every year the national party rally was held at Nuremberg. The majestic setting and elaborate rites made the Nuremberg rallies the centrepiece of party political art. In 1937 the architect Albert Speer was invited to create an aesthetic spectacle for the annual congress to eclipse all earlier rallies. He took 130 anti-aircraft searchlights and placed them at 40-metre intervals around the Zeppelin Field stadium. The result was a 'cathedral of light' stretching more than 6,000 metres into the air. Deliberately staged at night to disguise the less-than-aesthetic sight of thousands of ageing, portly party officials, the effect of the massed ranks in the stadium, the thousands of banners and flags, the trumpeters, the high podium with the single figure of the *Führer* picked out by light represented a spectacle of extraordinary theatrical power.[148] By day, despite almost continuous rain on this occasion, the choreographed marchers, the shouts of *Sieg Heil*, the blend of brown, black and red in every corner of the field, the rites observed with strict sanctity and decorum, defined the movement and its collective will more clearly than the dull, ranting speeches. The symbolism was a statement of politics as artifice or design. It is perhaps significant that Speer himself only decided to join the party in 1931 after he watched SA men marching smartly along the street.[149]

The fourth celebration of the year was the most theatrical of all. Each 8 November, from 1926 onwards, the party faithful gathered at Munich to honour on the following day the fallen 'martyrs' of the movement who died in a hail of police fire on 9 November 1923, the day of the Hitler *Putsch* in Bavaria. Each year the revolt was replayed as political pantomime. In 1935 Hitler decided to exhume and rebury the martyrs in a Temple of Honour in the middle of Munich. Architects were asked to design sixteen bronze sarcophagi with ceremonial flags. Pillars with oil lamps burning and vast red flags lined the route through the centre of Munich to the Feldherrnhalle, where the putschists had been killed. The sarcophagi were drawn at night through the torchlit streets surrounded by the party faithful bearing standards and flags and to the sound of hundreds of muffled drums. 'A heroic symphony', recalled the party newspaper.[150] The following day, the dead were laid to rest in the newly constructed temple in a lengthy, carefully rehearsed coda to the night-time rituals. Borne in front of the procession of party leaders was the 'Blood Flag', the banner from the original parade, soaked with blood from the dead putschists, the party's most important and most sacred relic. After the cortège arrived at the temple, the theatrical effect was suddenly heightened as Hitler, alone, bare-headed and simply dressed, entered the sanctuary to commune silently with the dead. The two-day ceremony was captured on film and released the following spring under the title *For Us*, so that the whole of Germany could witness the political performance.[151]

These collective dramas were repeated on a smaller scale throughout Germany. It was the endless patterning of public political life, the omnipresent symbolism, the rhetorical art, the blending of music, poetry, film and theatre with political ritual that created a genuinely popular and participatory culture more immediate and purposeful than *Thing* theatre. There was obvious resemblance in the collective political culture of the Soviet Union, which used the same blend of staged political performance and mass participation. By chance, the key spectacles of the communist calendar also fell in May and November – the May Day celebration of labour and defence and, on 7 November, the anniversary of the Bolshevik revolution. As in Germany, there were numerous lesser festival days, for the Red Army, for Stalin's birthday, and so on. In the Soviet Union ritual and festival were built into the daily life of the party and the population and, like their German counterparts, were self-consciously a blend of artistic political display and cultural participation. Political celebrations were

387

marked with choirs, orchestras and recitations as well as party speeches. The annual May Day parades were less extravagantly choreographed and sacral than the German rallies, but were by the 1930s spectacular in scale. An English visitor to the 1936 parade in Leningrad watched for five hours as first 40,000 soldiers and sailors, then thousands of workers, sports clubs, young pioneers, students and trade unions marched past with red banners and standards, flowing into and out of Uritsky Place in front of the Winter Palace. There were opera singers, gypsy choruses, acrobats, mass callisthenics. In the evening the Leningrad sky was filled with fireworks and the streets with dancing. A year before Speer, the centre of the city was illuminated with anti-aircraft searchlights.[152]

The roots of Stalinist political display lay in carnival. It lacked the solemn memorialization and morbidity of National Socialist ritual. The purpose was to involve the whole people in periodic, extravagant, visually exciting celebration of the revolutionary achievement, to dissolve the separate sphere of spectator and artist. This was carried much further than in Germany, where participants in political theatre were often distinct from the audience, even if they were drawn from it. At the May Day parade in Leningrad the English visitor realized that there were 'no onlookers' because 'all were active participants'.[153] In the 1920s the public festival was seen as a necessary release for revolutionary enthusiasm. A Central Holidays Commission was set up under the Agitprop department of the Central Committee, to supervise public events. They were to be known by the western term 'carnival' to distinguish them from the peasant carnivals, *maslyanitsa*, which had strong religious links and were occasions for indulgent drinking and bawdy disorder.[154] From the outset the major socialist celebrations were to be observed with a certain dignity and earnestness, but there were many smaller carnivals where theatres, film shows, music and dancing were jumbled together with political displays and party propaganda. In the 1920s great efforts were made to get wide popular participation by involving the cultural clubs of factories and co-operatives in planning and designing popular festivals. They were gradually subjected to greater regulation. The wearing of masks was proscribed in 1927; so-called 'friendly caricature' of public figures was banned in 1929.[155] As the festivals became larger, and the celebration of

Soviet achievements more significant, their form became more clearly prescribed and their structure and content professionalized. Parades were separated from the festivals, and the festival songs and plays were directed by artists rather than workers.

Stalinist political ritual nevertheless involved millions each year. Every province had its own cultural spectacles. Every branch of the party, as in Germany, had its own symbols, songs, imagery and choreography, from keep-fit clubs to air defence. They became after 1934 elements of socialist realism, participants in the utopian metaphors that popular culture and the arts alike sustained, just as ordinary Germans became caught up as actors rather than audience in the public theatre of nationalist realism. It is difficult to find ways of assessing the extent to which the populations in the Soviet Union and Germany willingly collaborated in sustaining the artistic illusion, since there were in both states wide variations in the response, but it would be wrong to assume a priori that the public was, as Brecht assumed, invited to the political performance 'on a compulsory basis'.[156] Public participation was regulated and encouraged but was not entirely passive. The 1936 diary of Galina Shtange, an activist in the Moscow women's movement, shows how easily socialist realism was absorbed by ordinary people. In December she was invited as a delegate of the wives of the Commissariat of Transport and Communications to sing in front of Stalin himself on the occasion of the presentation of an armoured train bought with their savings. The delegation was rehearsed repeatedly on their opening song ('A Spacious Land, My Native Land'). A second song had been composed for the occasion: 'The Transport Section and the Army – the Dearest of Brothers'. Shtange was then told she could not be included on the rostrum as there were too many delegates. She confided to her journal her devastation at being robbed of the chance to see Stalin close to, 'whom I love so dearly'.[157] She sat in the audience with a feeling of 'intense pride' and when she saw Stalin embrace two young children she was close to tears. She found it all a beautiful sight: 'A whole sea of flowers, ribbons, banners etc. Music, singing and prolonged cheering.' In her diary a few weeks later she wrote: 'our life isn't a whole lot of fun, in spite of all the indicators saying how happy we should be', but her realization remained unrelated to the spectacle she had recently witnessed.[158] Socialist realism and private hardships could be kept apart in order to sustain the artistic metaphor, not only for Galina Shtange but for millions of Soviet and German citizens who identified with and were nourished by the new realities.

There were great expectations in both dictatorships that the cultural revolutions that ushered in the politics of socialist and nationalist realism would transform the relationship between art and people and between politics and art. Maxim Gorky, who played a central role in pushing Stalin towards socialist realism, was strongly influenced by ideas of thought transference pioneered by the Russian psychologist Naum Kotik, who in 1904 claimed to have discovered what he called 'N-Rays', invisible psychic threads that explained mind-reading and thought-transference, and helped to bind together people in mobs and mass movements.[159] These insights were sustained after 1917 by the scientist Vladimir Bekhterev, who saw Bolshevism as a form of mass-hypnosis; his Committee for the Study of Mental Suggestion developed in the 1920s a general theory of mass telecommunication of thought, which Gorky hoped might be exploited by literature to produce an optimistic revolutionary society.[160]

Ideas of social psychology also underlay some of Hitler's view of the function of culture and propaganda, but they do not explain the decision in either dictatorship to try to regulate so absolutely the nature of all cultural output, high and low, professional and amateur in order to exclude any influence defined at the time as subversive, decadent or ambiguous. This decision stemmed first from the central utopian ideologies of the two systems, which deliberately constructed a particular version of reality for which there could not be an alternative. The result was a deliberate cultural autarky or self-sufficiency, sheltering both populations as far as possible from external cultural influences and encouraging the development of popular domestic art. Although the lives of many of those who lived through the dictatorships bore little relation to the stated reality, neither system was prepared to tolerate a single violation of the artistic or, by implication, the political norms. The deep fear of exposure to reality explains why the regulation was so thorough and absurd. The attempt to discipline an entire culture, artistic and popular, could not be from its very nature entirely

absolute; there remained ambiguities, contradictions, shifts of emphasis in cultural policy, even authorial deceit, explicit, for example, in
Osip Mandelstam's 1937 *Ode to Stalin*, which was manifestly faceti-
ous and won him no reprieve from arrest and death. Nevertheless,
there existed very little cultural resistance in either state to the stifling
of artistic experiment and openness, and the occasional cracks made
little difference to the overall cultural strategy.

One of the chief reasons for this success lies not in the apparatus of
cultural repression, but in the extent to which the great majority of
those engaged in all the many forms of cultural expression participated,
willingly or otherwise, in sustaining the new artistic reality. In 1938
the Reich chamber of literature had to vet no fewer than 3,000 drama
scripts; a national music festival in 1939 attracted 1,121 compositions,
including 36 operas and 631 symphonies.[161] Popular culture, like
popular justice, was not simply an invention of the system. Nor did
official patronage fail to produce art that was approved of as well as
approved art. Though the genre adopted in each dictatorship was
narrow, the bulk of the plays, films and books were accepted by
viewers and readers as their own culture, and were in many cases
widely popular. In the Soviet Union socialist realism can be interpreted
as a form of escapism, just as Hollywood films in the 1930s offered
impoverished Americans a glimpse of a bright consumer future. Soviet
culture, Stalin claimed in 1951, was 'the art of the new world, gazing
boldly into the future'.[162] In Hitler's Germany national realism was, in
many respects, more challenging because of its emphasis on historical
grandeur, self-sacrifice and the immanence of glorious death, but the
sentiments and imagery produced a wide resonance precisely because
National Socialist culture did reflect the wider values and interests of
significant sections of the population. However utopian the new art
might be, its roots lay in the societies at which it was directed.

10

Commanding the Economy

'Soon Germany will not be any different from Bolshevik Russia; the heads of enterprises who do not fulfil the conditions which the "Plan" prescribes will be accused of treason against the German people, and shot.'   Fritz Thyssen, 1940[1]

Few German businessmen were more enthusiastic about Hitler's appointment as Chancellor in 1933 than the steel magnate Fritz Thyssen. The eldest son of August Thyssen, the founder in 1873 of one of the Ruhr's most successful and wealthy businesses, he first met Hitler in October 1923. He had already experienced more than his fair share of politics. In December 1918 he was arrested with three other business leaders by German communist revolutionaries on grounds of treason, though he was released a few days later. In July 1923 he was hauled before a French court martial at Mainz for organizing the passive resistance in the Ruhr to the Franco-Belgian occupation of the region; he was fined and imprisoned again.[2] He became convinced that National Socialism would revive Germany's fortunes and heal the social conflicts of the new republic. A devout Catholic, Thyssen was strongly influenced by the Austrian social theorist Othmar Spann, whose ideas on the corporative organization of society matched Thyssen's social-Catholic views on ending class conflict through a structured estate-based collaboration. In return for his generous donations to the party from his large personal fortune, Thyssen was encouraged to set up an Institute for Corporative Affairs (*Institut für Ständewesen*) when Hitler came to power.

Two years later, in 1935, the director of the Institute, who had fallen foul of the ambitions of the German Labour Front to represent all workers and employers, was sent to Dachau concentration camp. Thyssen grew increasingly disillusioned with the new regime, partly on account of its anti-Catholic and anti-Semitic posture, and partly repelled by the increasing state control of economic life. Although he warmly welcomed the destruction of the Versailles settlement, he was opposed to war. While on holiday in Bavaria in August 1939, Thyssen sent letters to Hermann Göring condemning Hitler's diplomacy as irresponsible and wrong-headed. He also demanded to know the reason why his sister's son-in-law, an Austrian monarchist who had also ended up in Dachau after the union with Austria in 1938, had died suddenly in custody in the late summer of 1939. On 2 September, the day after the German invasion of Poland, Thyssen and his family set off in cars, apparently bound for a daytrip to the Alps. Instead they crossed into Switzerland as refugees. A few months later the Swiss authorities denied him sanctuary and he moved to France, where he dictated his memoirs to an American journalist, Emery Reves. It was during the tape-recorded interviews with Thyssen in the spring of 1940 at Monte Carlo that the comparison with Bolshevik Russia, with which this chapter opens, was given voice. A few weeks after the French defeat in June, Thyssen once again found himself in prison. Gestapo agents were permitted to arrest him in unoccupied France and he was taken back to Germany, where he spent the rest of the war, a man in his early sixties, in concentration camps. His entire fortune had already been sequestrated by the Gestapo in October 1939; it was formally acquired by the state in December, using legislation passed on 26 May 1933 for the confiscation of the property of communists.[3]

In 1944 a prominent Soviet steel industry manager and one-time junior member of the Soviet government defected, like Thyssen, in protest at the crimes and follies of a regime whose aspirations he had once applauded with complete enthusiasm. Viktor Kravchenko, the son of a radical worker from Ekaterinoslav, trained as a metallurgical engineer in the 1920s. By the time of the Second Five-Year Plan (1932–7) he had become a communist party member and the young manager of a steel pipe plant at Nikopol in the industrial heartland of the Donbass. His revolutionary idealism, inherited from his non-party father, was punctured by the reality of the grotesque inequalities in Soviet industry. As a manager at the pipe plant Kravchenko was entitled to one of eight five-roomed houses for top officials; the house had a refrigerator (kept full of caviar, melons and fresh vegetables), a radio and a bath. He was waited on by a state-paid maid, gardener and chauffeur. A car and two horses were at his disposal. He ate in the managers' restaurant, plentifully supplied from the local collective farm. The workers ate in a 'huge, unsanitary, evil-smelling cafeteria'; some 5,000 of them lived in crude wooden barracks next to the plant in conditions 'more fit for animals than for human beings'.[4] He earned five times the wage of a skilled foreman, ten times that of a line worker.

It was these disparities that first provoked Kravchenko's disillusionment with the yawning gap between socialist rhetoric and the naked exploitation of the Soviet industrial workforce. He recalled his revolutionary father complaining that workers were tied to their machines 'like so many serfs'; the 'political tyranny and economic oppression' was no better than capitalism under another name.[5] Kravchenko came to believe that the Soviet Union was again divided into upper and lower classes and had betrayed the promise of a better life for all. He was more fortunate than Thyssen in avoiding prison. During the purges of the 1930s hundreds of Kravchenko's colleagues were spirited away to camps or execution on trumped-up charges of sabotage. He was constantly in trouble with the security police, but managed to avoid anything more than a party reprimand and a brief sentence in 1940 on spurious charges of embezzlement, which he succeeded in reversing on appeal. In 1943, he was sent to the United States as a member of a Soviet lend-lease purchasing commission, but only after enduring a thorough vetting by the NKVD that consisted of months of repeated and futile interrogations. His travel was approved at last by no less a body than the Central Committee of the party. He was given two pamphlets to read, which included instructions not to enter any bars or clubs in America, not to speak to women and to expect his passport to be stolen. Before departing he was subjected to a harangue from a senior party official on an enemy society (the United States, not Germany) 'in the final stages of rotten degeneration', and shipped to America in August 1943 on a timber freighter. On 3 April 1944 he announced to the *New York Times* his defection. In a prepared statement he condemned the oppression and want experienced by ordinary Russians in the face of a cynical tyranny.[6]

Thyssen and Kravchenko were united by their separate beliefs that the economic systems they served, the one capitalist, the other communist, had each become, under dictatorship, more like the other. Their experiences are at odds with the conventional image of two economic systems that were regarded at the time, and have been widely regarded since, as the one unassailable and self-evident difference between the two regimes. Marxists defined the National Socialist economy as an extreme form of capitalism, created out of the pressures of the slump after 1929 and fear of the working class. The Communist International described Hitler's Germany as 'the open terrorist dictatorship of the most chauvinistic and most imperialist elements of finance capitalism'.[7] The German social scientist Fritz Pollock, writing in exile in the United States during the Second World War, defined the German system as 'state capitalism', a term that has been widely used ever since. Pollock described a coercive regime that disciplined labour, helped to steady the market and intervened extensively, but which ultimately protected the generation of private profit, the engine of any capitalist economy. In post-war interpretations, the German economy under Hitler has become a 'dysfunctional capitalism', typical of an age of prolonged crisis.[8]

By contrast the Soviet economy under Stalin was viewed as a system where all private profit had been eliminated, state ownership introduced in place of private enterprise and private property and every element of economic life directed solely by the agencies of state planning. National Socialist economists condemned the Marxist planned economy as a system 'which requires the nationalization of all means of production' and 'stifles all independent existence'.[9] Post-war descriptions of Stalin's economy have been highly critical of the exaggerated claims made for the success of economic planning, but have not doubted the fact that collective ownership, state planning and state control were the characteristic features of the Soviet experiment. Recent interpretations of the failures of the Soviet planned economy under Stalin might well justify its description as 'dysfunctional socialism'.[10]

The distinction between the two economic systems was, in reality, less clear-cut: the National Socialist view of the economy is not easily defined as capitalist, any more than the Soviet system under Stalin can be described as an example of unalloyed socialism. The most obvious distinction between the two economies was the product of the very different circumstances of their economic development. The German economy grew in the forty years before the First World War into the world's second largest industrial power, and the world's second largest trader. Industrial development relied on a highly skilled workforce, the application of science to practical production, and a buoyant world market. The state played a part in supplying protection where it was needed, and assisted the development of infrastructure services, but the economy was dominated by privately owned businesses that regulated their affairs through large trusts and cartels. The war transformed German economic performance. After 1919 the economy struggled to return to the levels of trade and output achieved before the war, with the result that the state came to play a far more prominent part in German economic management, pursuing state employment policies, promoting foreign trade and generating public investment. The inflation of 1923 dispossessed the wealthy classes and left Germany excessively dependent on foreign sources of capital or state-led investment. The slump that began in Germany in early 1929 brought the state willy-nilly to play a direct role in the efforts to salvage the failing German banking system (which was effectively nationalized as a crisis measure) and to try to ameliorate collapsing employment and output levels. By 1932 the private economy in Germany was in exceptionally severe crisis; the output of heavy industry was little higher than the 1890s, trade had fallen by half from 1928 and unemployment reached well over 6 million, more than one-third of the industrial workforce.[11]

The Soviet experience was the opposite. Before the First World War the Russian empire was in the middle of rapid economic modernization, but the pace and nature of this transformation was compromised by the overwhelming size of the rural economy, from which some 80 per cent of the population derived its livelihood, either from farming or from rural crafts. By 1913 industrial output was more than ten-fold the level of 1860 and Russia's aggregate output made her the fifth largest producer in the world. This achievement relied heavily on state orders, particularly for the greatly expanded armed forces, and on extensive state regulation and assistance. The business community was divided between a small native merchant and entrepreneurial class and significant numbers of foreign businessmen and managers who accompanied the large investments made from abroad, treating Russia as if it were an economic colony. Heavy industry was large-scale, organized in marketing syndicates and subject to close regulation by the state. The consumer sectors were privately owned and market-led, but most of them were technically unsophisticated, regional and small in scale.[12]

After the October revolution the young communist state assumed ownership of all heavy industry, the banking sector and railways. Bolsheviks hoped to make land and petty trade a part of the system of social ownership, but the near collapse of consumer supplies and the famine of 1921 persuaded Lenin's government to relinquish these claims, and under the New Economic Policy (NEP) some 80 per cent of small-scale production, and 99 per cent of farming, remained in the private sector.[13] By 1927 industrial output and investment achieved approximately the Tsarist levels of 1913, but unemployment among industrial workers stood at more than a million, while peasants, petty traders and middle-men (the so-called 'nepmen') sustained a thriving and largely private commercial economy. The survival of popular small-scale capitalism and the slow development of modern state-owned heavy industry prompted the party's decision to introduce a state-led industrialization drive. In 1927–8 the Soviet regime, pressed to adopt the course by Stalin, embarked on a second attempt to create a more genuinely socialist economy. Under the First Five-Year Plan private ownership of land and trade was overturned in favour of socially owned collective farms and socially managed retailing. By 1937 93 per cent of peasant households were in the state sector, and two-thirds of all small producers.[14] The heavy industrial sectors, which Lenin had always urged as the first priority in achieving sustainable socialist growth, grew rapidly. While Germany languished in the grip of the worst slump in its history, the Soviet economy expanded industrial output, employment and investment at breathtaking speed. By 1932 the workforce in heavy industry was double that of 1928, with industrial output growing at a little over 10 per cent a year.[15] For a brief moment the Soviet economy almost caught up with Germany's: in 1933 German steel furnaces turned out 7.5 million tonnes, Soviet furnaces around 6 million tonnes.[16]

The history of both economies was transformed under dictatorship. Although they remained at different levels of development, the gap rapidly closed during the 1930s. The distinction between systems that were 'socialist' or 'capitalist' also narrowed, though it did not disappear. Under dictatorship the two became varieties of command economy, subject to coercive economic direction by state agencies, in which the motor force of economic development was supplied not by the market, but by the target-policies of the regime. The command economies each faced very similar problems, and devised very similar economic policies to deal with them. Rapid revival from the slump in Germany and accelerated industrial growth in the USSR promoted an economics of mobilization, in which state energies were focused on achieving exceptional growth rates and an economic restructuring quite distinct from anything the operation of the market alone would have produced. While the developed world struggled to revive from the slump, Germany's national product grew in real terms by more than 70 per cent between 1933 and 1938. The Soviet economy, according to the most recent and reliable estimates, grew by at least 70 per cent between 1928 and 1937.[17]

In both cases this growth was achieved in conditions of relative economic isolation as the rest of the world economy staggered towards recovery during the 1930s. Trade declined by two-thirds in Germany and the Soviet Union between 1928 and 1937; foreign capital, forthcoming for both states in the 1920s, was absent as a factor in the growth of the 1930s and 1940s. Both economies were reconstructed and expanded under conditions of exceptional autarky. This isolation from the wider world economy, though not absolute, reflected the political priorities of the two dictators, who both saw economic independence as politically desirable and militarily essential.

Stalin and Hitler were both anti-capitalists. Neither dictator accepted the unrestricted economic individualism, the free market and the profit motive that defined the contemporary capitalist system. Both, from different vantage points, recognized the need to supersede the age of liberal or bourgeois economics with a new economic order. It was not necessary to be a Marxist in the 1920s to believe that capitalism produced class-conflict, economic selfishness and repeated slumps. Stalin, of course, was a Marxist: he understood that the liberal economic order was doomed to extinction because of its fundamental contradictions. 'To abolish crisis,' he told the Sixteenth Congress of the party, shortly before the assault on Russia's extensive private sector, 'it is necessary to abolish capitalism.'[18] For Hitler, modern capitalism was responsible for holding nations to ransom in the interests of a cosmopolitan, parasitical class of rentiers. 'The economic system of our day,' he told one party leader in 1934, 'is the creation of the Jews.' He recommended 'a radical removal . . . of all unrestricted economic liberalism'. 'Capitalism,' he explained to Mussolini a decade later, 'had run its course.'[19]

Both dictators viewed the economy as a means to an end but not an end in itself. Economics was central to the two systems because Hitler and Stalin regarded a healthy economy as the indispensable foundation for the achievement of other priorities: the construction of the social utopias, the military defence of the dictatorships, the achievement of social peace, a distant future age of perpetual prosperity. These were ambitions which the dictators recognized could not be secured by relying on the willingness of free-market capitalism to abjure its primary, profit-seeking impulses in favour of community goals. Hitler rejected the 'free play of forces' in favour of the idea that 'what was once accident must be planned'; Stalin, in the same Congress speech in 1930, ridiculed the 'childish formula' that predicted Russia's 'capitalist elements peacefully growing into socialism'.[20]

In Stalin's case the central place of the economy in his world view is clear-cut. All Marxists took as axiomatic the materialist view of history: political systems and social orders were derived ultimately from the nature of the mode of production (feudalism, capitalism, and so forth), and from the social relations that each mode generated (serf/lord, capitalist/proletarian, etc.). In the Soviet Union of the 1920s the assumption was that at some point the mode of production would be sufficiently socialist to permit the transition to a classless socialist society. Yet the economic reality under the New Economic Policy was a mixed economy, part socialist, part capitalist, in which more than four-fifths of its members were engaged in some form of private economic activity. The party was divided in its response: some assumed that small-scale private economy contained the possibility of a slow development into more socialist forms; others argued for accelerated industrial development and the elimination of vestigial capitalism. The impact of this debate on the party political conflicts that brought Stalin to prominence has already been described. Here it is only necessary to recall that by the winter of 1927/8 Stalin had finally become convinced that the regime must run the risks of confronting the predominantly non-socialist masses, and the 'new millionaires' who exploited them, with the planned building of a socialist economy. For Stalin the economic reconstruction had one primary purpose: 'full steam ahead along the path of industrialization – to socialism'.[21]

The economic revolution ushered in by the First Five-Year Plan was designed to produce a more effective match between the mode of production and the social system. Stalin articulated a simple Marxist viewpoint, enjoying wide support in the party, that socialism was impossible without a socially owned and socially managed economy. The economy became the sole means to secure the social and political ambitions of the party and to break the surviving power of domestic capitalism. Stalin understood this to mean two distinct but related processes: the construction of a modern industrial and agrarian economy on the one hand, and on the other, the 'abolition of exploitation' and the defeat of the final, desperate counter-offensive of capitalism.[22] Both ambitions were, in reality, difficult to reconcile with conventional Marxism. The construction of an industrial economy from above through the agency of a socialist state planning apparatus replaced the missing bourgeois stage of Russian economic evolution altogether; under Stalin, socialists rather than capitalists would build the modern economy. This could only be achieved through a rigid command economy and high levels of economic coercion directed at ordinary workers and farmers. Secondly, the 'offensive of socialism' against capitalist and imperialist enemies turned the socialist economy into an instrument for waging a war to the death against capitalism, an outcome inconceivable to Marx. Stalin reminded his audience in 1930 that the key issue had been formulated by Lenin rather than by Marx: 'who will beat whom?' In the face of capitalist encirclement and the permanent threat of military intervention, Stalin regarded the economy as the source of the military power necessary to preserve the revolutionary state. In the 1930s he threw his political weight behind a shift in economic planning in favour of defence; the imperative to exploit the command economy as an instrument for revolutionary survival eclipsed all other priorities, and left the Soviet Union saddled for the rest of its existence with top-heavy military production.[23]

Hitler's view of the economy is more problematic. There was no corpus of ready-made theory. National Socialist economists disagreed, often profoundly, about the precise nature of their economic ideology, and it was necessary for the party to be cautious in its public pronouncements in order to avoid alienating their property-owning or enterprising supporters. It has often been suggested that Hitler himself had little interest in, or knowledge of the economy, and left its intricacies to the professionals. Nothing could be further from the truth. Hitler's world view had a profound economic core. Throughout his political career he remained, like Stalin, a consistent advocate of a number of clear if simple economic principles. The most important was his insistence that the economy was always and necessarily subordinate to the needs of the *Volk* and the state that represented it. In this, as in other spheres, the economy was an instrument for the 'preservation of the race'. Capitalism, Hitler announced to an early party rally, 'has to become the servant of the state and not its master'.[24] In an economic programme drawn up by the party economic office in 1931, the economy was defined as 'the property of the people', for which the state as trustee has 'supreme authority'.[25] In 1937 Hitler told the annual party congress that it made no difference whether his ideology was capitalist or socialist, as long as economic policy served the one constant factor – 'the community itself'.[26] The defining term was *Volkswirtschaft*. In the 1920s this was an innocuous synonym for 'economy', but in the mouths of National Socialist economists it was filled with new meaning: an economy for the people, 'the organs and blood-supply' of the racial body.[27] These views were not original to the party, for there was a long tradition of nationalist and dirigiste economic thought in Germany that culminated in a wide intellectual revolt in the 1920s against the idea that unregulated capitalism could meet the real needs of the German people. The instrumental view of national economies in the service of the people as a whole, rather than self-appointed economic cliques, became the stock-in-trade of radical nationalist circles, and was borrowed unreservedly by Hitler.

The idea of 'the primacy of politics' in the economic life of the nation was shackled to Hitler's central social-Darwinist beliefs about racial competition. In 1928 Hitler dictated a sequel to *Mein Kampf* which he never published; the so-called 'Second Book' is preoccupied with the relationship between racial survival, war and economic resources. His conception had more in common with the mercantilist traditions of the early-modern age, when territory, treasure and resources were seized at the point of the sword under the misapprehension that the world's wealth was finite – though infinitely capable of expropriation. Hitler borrowed from the popular geopolitics of the 1920s the idea that the primordial issue facing all nations was the limitation of living-space (*Lebensraum*) – the amount of land and materials necessary to sustain the life of a given nation or race. Space was limited; hence 'the struggle for daily bread stands at the forefront of all vital necessities'.[28] A healthy people, Hitler argued, had to rely on economic resources under its own control: 'World trade, world economy, tourist traffic, etc., are all transient means for securing a nation's sustenance.' The only answer for a nation like Germany that lacked adequate land and resources for its industrious population was to take land by force from someone else. Hitler argued that the earth was not allotted as inviolable property to any particular people, but was awarded by Providence to its conqueror: 'The acquisition of soil is always linked with the employment of force.'[29]

The extraordinary candour of these remarks perhaps explains why they were never published. His assumption that the economy was a function of racial struggle, for which naked warfare and expropriation were the only remedies, relied on the same critique of capitalism used by communists – excessive financial concentration, declining exports, shrinking markets, overproduction – but where the Marxist answer was revolution, Hitler's was conquest.[30] War was the instrument for providing the German people with the economic resources they could not acquire under the conditions of a failing capitalist system. It followed that the state had to be so organized that it could prepare the people for war, seize the living-space necessary for its sustenance, and then protect and defend its renewed prosperity against all-comers. In one of his first cabinet meetings in 1933 Hitler told his ministers that Germany's future 'depends exclusively and alone on rebuilding the armed forces'.[31] Hitler shared the popular view that economic failure had produced the collapse of the German war effort in 1918. The economy was a primary instrument for waging war; it had to be reshaped entirely to avoid another defeat. The concept of the *Wehrwirtschaft*, or 'defence-based economy' – what might now be called the 'military-industrial complex' – was developed in the 1930s to make explicit the dominant part played by economic rearmament in shaping the 'people's economy'.

Hitler did not believe that the capitalist economy could be trusted to put these national priorities first, because capitalism was inherently egoistical. The alternative was an economy directed and planned by the state, even, when necessity dictated, owned by the state. This was the path Hitler followed and he did so in ways consistent with his ideological preferences. He favoured private ownership as a spur to creative competition and technical innovation, as long as it conformed to the national interest, and as long as it was 'productive' (*schaffendes*) rather than 'parasitical' (*raffendes*) capital. He feared the excessive bureaucratization and lack of personal responsibility that would come from a complete state monopoly of economic life, but he was never committed in any sense to defend the liberal capitalist system inherited from the Weimar republic. Many of his followers were positively enthusiastic about unshackling the German economy from its capitalist past by defining the economy as a distinctive German socialism, putting the economy exclusively 'at the service of the state and the people's community'.[32]

In the Third Reich the survival of the private sector was not incompatible with the existence of extensive state planning, economic intervention, or even public ownership of the means of production. Hitler wanted to direct economic resources in ways that matched the many national goals of the regime – defence, city-building, a network of new roads, self-sufficiency in resources, etc. In 1935 he told the annual party congress that 'without a plan we will not come through'. He returned to the theme at the congress a year later: 'the lack of restraints of a free economy had to be ended in favour of planned direction and planned action'. In conversation in July 1942 he reminded his listeners that the nation's economic power had only been mobilized 'with a planned economy from above'; after the war 'state control of the economy' would continue in order to prevent individual interests trespassing on the fundamental interest of the nation.[33] Economists, not all of them National Socialists, deployed the term 'the managed economy' (*die gelenkte Wirtschaft*) to describe an economic form that was neither clearly capitalist nor communist. Otto Ohlendorf, one of a group of economic experts attached to the SS who, during the war, was in command of an *Einsatzgruppe* on the Eastern Front murdering Soviet Jews, defined the economic order that emerged after 1933 as 'fully planned economic management', in which 'the state *leads* the economy'.[34] The German economy under Hitler became, like Stalin's, a command economy.

Stalin and Hitler were, for different reasons, confronted with crisis-ridden economic systems that inhibited the achievement of their political goals. Stalin favoured a new economic order that might overcome the central problem facing Russian economic modernization since the mid-nineteenth century – how to cope with the reality of economic and social backwardness produced by the existence of a numerous and poor population of small farmers and craftsmen whose outlook was hostile to the demands of a modernizing state. The political breakthrough to communism became possible only by resolving the central contradictions of Russian economic development and imposing a socialist industrialization. Hitler's new order was designed to overcome Germany's vulnerable dependence on the wider world economy, alarmingly exposed in the war and the economic crises that had followed, by embracing a predatory neo-mercantilist economics and seizing the territory needed to satisfy the needs of the German population. The breakthrough to a new German racial state, healthy, prosperous and heavily armed, was possible only by transforming free-market capitalism into something else. In both systems economic outcomes were conditioned entirely by political prerogatives.

In the 1930s state economic planning and the macro-economic theory on which it relied were still infants waiting to grow into post-1945 adulthood. The remarkable record of growth and restructuring achieved in the Soviet Union and Germany in the 1930s and 1940s was the outcome of policies that were experimental and improvisatory. The key to commanding the economies owed a great deal to the coercive character of the two political systems. Hitler once boasted that the surest means to beat inflation 'was to be sought for in our concentration camps'.[35] The threat of tough retribution for an act of economic sabotage, enshrined in law in both states, hung over the head of every slacking worker or incompetent engineer.[36] Yet neither economy could have been transformed by political will-power alone.

The chief explanation for the economic outcomes of the 1930s lies with a generation of Soviet and German economic experts – economists, officials, bankers, industrial managers – who attempted the first real experiments in macro-economic planning and macro-economic policy. Experts in both countries were forced to explore novel forms of state economic intervention under pressure from political masters who were not prepared to allow economic constraints to inhibit their political ambitions. The root of both systems lies in the German experience of the First World War. The extensive nationwide planning and organization of the production and distribution of raw materials, food and industrial products, inspired by the German industrialist Walther Rathenau, came to be viewed as a model of modern state economic control. Soviet economists were impressed by German achievements and, in particular, by the German economist Karl Ballod, whose book *The State of the Future*, first published in 1898 but extensively revised in 1919 to take account of the war, was translated into Russian and read enthusiastically by the mainly non-Bolshevik economists and engineers recruited to begin the task of constructing a state economy in the early 1920s.[37]

Soviet commitment to planning dated from the Eighth Party Congress of 1919, when Molotov called for the establishment of a 'national economic plan'. On 22 February 1921 the State General Planning Commission was established as an advisory body to the Council of Labour and Defence, which had been set up in March 1919. Better known by its acronym Gosplan, the organization was run by a small staff of economists who struggled to construct even the most primitive statistical picture of the economy they were supposed to plan. Their most distinguished member was Nikolai Kondratiev, an academic economist and former member of the Socialist-Revolutionary party, who had made no secret of his hostility to Bolshevism, but whose expertise was recruited nonetheless to head a national economic think-tank, the Conjuncture Institute, founded in 1920. He was a well-respected theorist, remembered for his discovery of a historical pattern of long waves of economic development, known now as the 'Kondratiev cycle'. He joined Gosplan and took responsibility for drafting an aggregate picture of the infant Soviet economy, together with a former Menshevik, Vladimir Groman. These first control figures were published only in 1925–6; they were incomplete and, for the statistically less accessible rural economy, speculative.[38] Kondratiev opposed any idea that economic development could be based on mere 'wishes', and with most Gosplan planners he favoured prudent growth, based on realistic statistical forecasts and a residual market economy. He was penalized for his commitment to counter-revolutionary 'equilibrium' theory when the party shifted to a programme of accelerated indus-trialization in 1927. He was sacked in May 1928, arrested in June 1930, charged with being a 'kulak-professor' and jailed, along with Groman and scores of other specialists. He was executed at the height of the terror, in September 1938.[39]

Kondratiev and his colleagues nevertheless laid the foundation for macro-economic planning. The annual control figures were used by the Supreme Council of the National Economy (VSNKh) for drafting the first industrial Five-Year Plan in 1927. The draft of 740 pages contained 340 pages of statistics; the final version stretched to three volumes and 2,000 pages.[40] But this plan was deliberately prescrip-tive, and was no longer a set of mere forecasts or extrapolations: 'Our plans,' Stalin told the Fifteenth Party Congress in 1927, 'are not prognoses, guess-plans, but *instructions* which are *compulsory* . . .'[41] This conception of planning as a set of orders reflected the increasingly militaristic language of battles and campaigns used to define the economic ambitions of the regime. The system commanded; the economy obeyed. As if to emphasize the rejection of economic caution, Stalin recruited his fellow Georgian, the coarse and choleric Sergo Ordzhoni-kidze, to push the First Five-Year Plan into reality. Large and loud, with a shock of unkempt hair and bushy moustaches, Ordzhonikidze displayed the barrack-room manners appropriate for his role as an economic sergeant-major. He shouted and swore at everyone, even Stalin; he manhandled colleagues and subordinates as if they were so many raw recruits. An economic ignoramus, Ordzhonikidze simply bullied and threatened managers and bureaucrats to fulfil their part in the plan, first as chairman of the Workers' and Peasants' Inspectorate (Rabkrin) between 1927 and 1930, then as head of VSNKh during the period in which the Second Five-Year Plan was in preparation. In 1932 he moved again to take over a newly created Commissariat of Heavy Industry, but he was able to use this new office as the engine driving on economic reconstruction until, on 18 February 1937, in declining health, and depressed by arguments with Stalin over the wave of purge arrests among his closest colleagues, he shot himself.[42]

The political take-over of planning was completed by a thorough overhaul of the entire structure in the early 1930s in response to the reality of economic disorder provoked by the First Five-Year Plan. In 1931 Gosplan, shed of its 'bourgeois' experts, was reorganized into eleven divisions to allow it a more complete overview of the economy. An All-Union Planning Academy now turned out a stream of young communist planners to replace those languishing in the camps. In 1935 Gosplan was reformed again, in order to generate planning that was genuinely nationwide; five departments for macro-economic planning were set up, a further sixteen for individual economic branches, and seven autonomous departments for major areas of state policy such as defence and public health.[43] In 1932 the VSNKh was abolished, and Rabkrin two years later, removing any awkward rivals from the planning field. At the same time Gosplan was made more directly responsible to the Politburo, where the chief decisions on economic planning were taken under Stalin's watchful eye. The object was to make clearer the lines of control, and to strengthen the particular role of national planning. In 1934 a Control Commission replaced Rabkrin as the executive arm of the plan, checking on fulfilment and penalizing economic dereliction of duty.[44]

The system of planning began to solidify only by the mid-1930s. The series of five-year plans that began to be drawn up from the mid-1920s were intended to provide a rough framework for government targets, but they proved unworkable in practice. There existed a permanent deficit between planned output and the more modest reality. Long-term targets were replaced, in effect, by a running series of one-year plans, loosely shaped by the aspirations of the five-year schedule. A rough outline of the annual plan was drawn up each July by the Politburo on a few sheets of paper, covering the main categories of physical output and the investment needed to sustain them. Between July and November the industrial commissariats and Gosplan organized conferences at branch and regional level throughout the Soviet Union, to discuss needs and possibilities. Each November the Central Planning division of Gosplan drew up the aggregate plan or *svodny*, now swollen to hundreds of pages, and submitted it to the government. The plan was then formally adopted in December or January, and the targets sent out to the economic commissariats, and from there through to the system of industrial combines (*glavki*), trusts and enterprises set up under the First Five-Year Plan.[45]

The system worked better in theory than in practice. The shadow of the trouble-shooting Ordzhonikidze hung over the whole enterprise, for in reality the efforts to co-ordinate planning and arrive at realizable targets could not be sustained without a situation of constant emergencies, creative improvisation and extravagant penalties. The difficulty of obtaining reliable data from individual enterprises whose managements were under constant threat of investigation and punishment, or too harassed, ill-informed or illiterate to comply with endless form-filling, left Gosplan regularly short of reliable statistics. The first real national plan was drawn up only in 1931, but was deficient in a number of key planning variables. The removal of the economic specialists in the early 1930s diminished economics as an academic subject, and produced planners who were technicians rather than theorists, narrowly knowledgeable in their field but less equipped to understand a whole economy. There existed no adequate review of national accounts, measuring the economy in monetary rather than in crude physical terms; one was in preparation at Gosplan's Institute of Economic Research, but was not ready before the outbreak of war in 1941. In a desperate search for help the Gosplan Institute studied the German economic revival under Hitler, but the subsequent book, *Planning Manoeuvres in Capitalist Countries*, was banned and in 1938 the Institute was closed down.[46] The economy was mobilized more than planned; when shortages or bottlenecks occurred the efforts of the regime were targeted at the current crisis until the next one cried out for remedy. 'A coherent planning system did not exist,' wrote a young American economist after a year spent at the Planning Academy. 'What existed was a priorities system of a simple kind.'[47]

The problems of matching plan to reality led to a final reform of Gosplan in 1938, which laid the foundation for the macro-economic planning system of the post-war Soviet Union. The change is usually associated with the name of Nikolai Voznesensky, one of a new generation of communist-trained economists untainted by the values of pre-revolutionary economics, who became chairman of Gosplan in January 1938 at the start of the Third Five-Year Plan. A child at the time of the revolution, he graduated from life as a labourer to become a leading light of party economics in the 1930s. He was a precocious thirty-four-year-old when he was appointed to head Gosplan. His chief contribution to theory was to make a virtue of necessity by arguing that an economic system based on constant shortages and bottlenecks was more genuinely revolutionary: through 'fighting actively to abolish them' the system engaged in a creative struggle for production. Economic laws were not, in his view, abstract obstacles to development, but were no more and no less than the production goals set down by the proletarian state.[48] Nevertheless, Voznesensky oversaw the transformation of the planning system into a more professional instrument of macro-economic management. On 2 February 1938 Gosplan was divided into two sections. The first dealt with the major macro-economic variables, organized in four departments (national economic balances, investment, finance and regional/sector planning); the second section had twenty departments responsible for each major industrial branch, foreign trade, food and communications. This was the first point at which Gosplan could claim to be supervising the whole economy.[49]

Other changes soon followed. Gosplan now had the right to oversee plan fulfilment as well, and a structure of regional commissions was set up to enforce the plan. In 1939 the national statistical office, the Central Administration of Economic Accounting, was attached to Gosplan, and its practices overhauled to ensure a more reliable supply of lower-level data. For the first time the synoptic plan was expressed in money values, giving aggregates of the population's income and expenditure, and providing aggregate balances of capital formation and industrial resources. Plans had hitherto started with production targets and then extrapolated the necessary money, materials and labour needed to fulfil them; now plans began with the projected money, materials and labour for the following year, in order to see what was possible before deciding what was desirable.[50] The industrial commissariats were expanded in number to take account of the greater complexity of planning. In 1938 their number rose from five to twenty-two, together with six non-industrial commissariats for agriculture and transport. After 1938 they worked closely with Gosplan in formulating and refining the planning process. Each commissariat had *glavki*, or combines, based on functional and territorial divisions, and these operated as the transmission belts between the planning authorities and the individual enterprises.[51] Gradually the character of economic management altered from unplanned state control to controlled state planning. The reformed system remained in place beyond Stalin's death in 1953, but Voznesensky was less fortunate. In 1948 he ran foul of Stalin's jealous nature when he drafted his own textbook of communist economics. Arrested and tortured to confess absurd charges of spying and sabotage, he was shot in 1950.

Economic planning in the Third Reich was, in general, a less risky occupation. It was almost certainly more effective. For this there were good reasons. In the 1920s the state apparatus had already developed the framework of a modern mixed economy, with extensive responsibilities for welfare and housing, as well as policies for economic steering begun in the aftermath of war and extended in the wake of the currency collapse in 1923. There was a rich tradition of academic economics that anticipated the Keynesian revolution by more than a decade. German economists watched closely what was happening in the Soviet Union, and produced pioneering work on the national accounts necessary to pursue effective macro-economic policy. The Reich Statistical Office, founded in 1872, was greatly expanded after 1924 under the leadership of Ernst Wagemann; by the mid-1930s there were 2,800 employees, seven times the number working for Gosplan in the early 1930s.[52] In 1925 an Institute for Business-Cycle Research was set up to monitor fluctuations in national economic growth and to analyse their causes. The tools needed to steer an economy and to control its development were already available before Hitler came to power.

The coming of the dictatorship in Germany strengthened the hand of the central apparatus for economic planning and policy. In March 1933 the influential banker Hjalmar Schacht was appointed President of the *Reichsbank*, the German central bank. He was not a National Socialist, but he sympathized with the new regime's hostility to the old economic order and with its economic nationalism. He was recruited by Hitler as an economic expert who could direct Germany's economic revival more surely than the party's own economists, and so provide the foundation for large-scale rearmament. The fifty-six-year-old Schacht looked oddly out of place among the brown-shirted party elite. A conservative in habit and outlook, his round, bird-like face, obscured by oversize rimless glasses, peers out from photographs uncomfortably perched above an old-fashioned stiff collar and dark city suit. The product of a stiff and conventional bourgeois family, the young Schacht became a moderately successful career banker with a lively interest in politics. The inflationary collapse of the mark after the war brought him to national prominence, when he was appointed currency commissar in November 1923 after two other bankers had turned the job down. He pushed through a currency stabilization and headed the *Reichsbank* until his resignation in 1930 in protest at the continued payment of reparations to the victorious Allied powers. He returned to the bank convinced that Germany had to pursue the course of economic nationalism. 'The age of economic liberalism in itself,' he told an audience in 1934, 'has gone for good.'[53]

Schacht did not introduce a fully planned economy, for which there was little political support. Instead he introduced a system of centralized economic management (*Wirtschaftslenkung*) using a clutch of control mechanisms designed to override the market and stabilize economic development. The controls were prescriptive and coercive, and were backed by what Schacht called 'the firm hand of the state'. The object was to make the economy move in the direction the government wanted, but without a central plan or a central planning agency.[54] In practice Schacht was able to make the *Reichsbank* the hub of the macro-economic project until he was made economics minister in September 1934, when he combined the work of both offices in order to co-ordinate the overall management of the economy. The keys to Schacht's strategy were control over the capital market, control over trade and currency affairs and maintenance of low wages. The first was introduced in 1933. All investment decisions had to be channelled to an office in the *Reichsbank*, which reserved the right to approve all capital issues. Preference was given only to projects that complied with state priorities. Control over foreign trade, which had begun in 1931 to cope with Germany's deteriorating balance of payments, was extended in 1933, and finally turned into a system of state-regulated trade under Schacht's 'New Plan', introduced in the autumn of 1934. Wage rates were fixed at the level of 1933, while labour lost any right to negotiate freely for their improvement.[55]

The system of credit rationing and resource allocation performed something of the same function achieved by target and quota planning in the Soviet economy. It was supplemented by a national organization of industry and agriculture introduced in 1933–4, in a system of chambers and estates whose membership was compulsory. The Reich Food Estate was set up by an enabling law on 15 July 1933 under the leadership of the party's chief agrarian spokesman, Walther Darré. Its character and powers were defined in a second law of 13 September 1933, which introduced a nationwide organization of agricultural production, pricing and marketing both more comprehensive and more efficient than Soviet control of the collective farm sector.[56] On 27 February 1934, under a law for the Organic Reconstruction of Germany's Economic System, a national structure of chambers was established under the umbrella of the Reich Economic Chamber (*Reichswirtschaftskammer*) led by the economist Albert Pietzsch. All previous economic associations were abolished, to be replaced by six national chambers representing industry, commerce, handicrafts, banking, insurance and energy supply. The national chambers were divided again into 43 subsidiary economic groups (*Wirtschaftsgruppen*), and each of these into smaller functional and territorial units, 393 in total.[57]

The function of this corporate structure under Hitler's dictatorship has never been entirely clear since, unlike the Soviet *glavki*, they had no specified planning or executive responsibility. Their significance becomes clearer if the structure is seen in the context of efforts to centralize economic management after 1933 and reduce areas of organizational autonomy. The Reich Economic Chamber operated as a forum to discuss economic policy and co-ordinate its implementation in collaboration with the economics ministry, much like the Economic Council set up in the Soviet Union in November 1937. One of the economists attached to it, Ferdinand Grünig, generated sector-by-sector balance sheets and aggregate national accounts that were distributed throughout the state economic apparatus as a tool in policy formation.[58] The whole complex structure ensured that not a single business or farm would be independent of the central apparatus, and the chambers and groups became critical agents for collecting the data necessary to present a full statistical image of the aggregate economy, and for communicating to their members the direction and consequences of national policy. In turn, the central authorities could be kept informed of problems in the economic foothills through compulsory fortnightly reports sent in from the economic groups.[59]

Schacht's strategy produced a remarkable three-year recovery from the slump, but it proved increasingly difficult to resist the demands of the market through an indirect system of controls. By 1936 there was pressure on the precarious trade balance to supply more food following a poor harvest; industry was keen to exploit the revival by expanding consumer output and restoring normal trade; there was growing dissatisfaction with what were perceived by many businessmen and farmers as an unnecessary restriction of economic choice and excessive bureaucratization. Above all, the growing importance of the defence sector, which Schacht had played a major part in encouraging at Hitler's insistence, threatened to create inflationary pressures as extensive military contracts competed for scarce resources. This Schacht was not willing to risk. He had gambled on high growth and a slow return to a more open market economy. Instead, state control became more extensive while there developed growing political pressure for a genuine 'people's economy' uncoupled from the narrow interests of the capitalist elite. In 1935 Schacht complained that he was forced to operate 'under the primacy of politics'. Party radicals began a strident propaganda campaign against capitalist egoism, and against Schacht in particular. His telephone was tapped by the security police and his office bugged; in February 1936 he narrowly escaped arrest by the

Gestapo after an outspoken attack on the party in a speech at Bremen.[60] However, the threatened crisis over economic policy in the summer of 1936 was resolved by Hitler himself, without warning or consulation.

Late in August Hitler went south to his retreat at Berchtesgaden, where he personally drafted one of the very few documents of any length that he wrote throughout the twelve years of dictatorship. The document dealt with the issue of German survival in a hostile world. The six-page memorandum set out Hitler's view that the future of Germany depended not only on building up armed forces larger than any possible combination of enemies, but on forcing the economy to accept its racial duty by eschewing all inessential tasks in favour of creating the foundation for large-scale war-making: 'The nation does not live for the economy,' wrote Hitler, echoing his views from the 1920s, '... it is finance and the economy, economic leaders and theories, which all owe unqualified service in this struggle for the self-assertion of our nation.'[61] Both aims, rearmament and economic restructuring, were to be achieved in four years. A few days later he summoned Hermann Göring; the two men went for a long ramble on the mountainside. In the course of the walk Hitler explained what he had written and then asked Göring to take on responsibility for what soon became known as the Four-Year Plan.[62] Schacht was not told until the plan was formally announced on 9 September at the annual party rally; though he was minister of economics, he was not given a copy of the memorandum. Hitler's decision proved as important as Stalin's final conversion to a planned industrialization in 1927. The title of Four-Year Plan was not accidental; army leaders had suggested a 'five-year plan' for military and economic revival in 1933, but the title had been turned down in favour of a less evidently Marxist four-year plan to get the economy back to work. The 1936 plan was thus technically the Second Four-Year Plan; a Third Four-Year Plan was approved in October 1940 to continue the work of the second.[63] On 18 October 1936 the Plan was put into law, and Göring installed as its plenipotentiary with absolute power granted by Hitler himself to ride roughshod over any obstacle in his path. 'What the Russians have managed to build up,' Göring told the cabinet, 'we can also achieve.'[64]

If Schacht was the timid bourgeois expert, Göring was the German

Ordzhonikidze. Despite his reputation as an indolent bon vivant, the portly, flamboyant commander-in-chief of the German Air Force was a man of ruthless political energy and great ambition, a charming bully who brooked no opposition. Hitler announced to an audience of business leaders in Berlin the menacing news that their new Plan leader was a man 'of unbending will, for whom the phrase "it won't work" does not exist'.[65] He was not an economic expert but he quickly assembled a team of party economists and businessmen who were. In the palace of the Prussian State Ministry on Leipzigerstrasse in the heart of Berlin's ministerial quarter, Göring set up an organization that soon employed more than a thousand people. An inner economic cabinet was run by two economists, Erich Neumann and Friedrich Gramsch, who unobtrusively co-ordinated the macro-economic policies of the Plan to the point, according to one Plan official, that they eventually 'steered the whole economy'.[66] This was certainly how Göring interpreted the Plan's purpose. In the first edition of a new Four-Year Plan journal published in January 1937, he announced that he intended to exercise 'the unitary leadership and organization of the entire economy'.[67]

The claims made on behalf of the Plan have been viewed sceptically by most critics, but the structure established in the first fifteen months of the Plan's existence is consistent with the view that the regime did treat the Plan like its Soviet counterpart. Hitler moved towards the Stalinist practice of stating in bald terms what his plans were and then matching resources to targets, rather than the other way round. Where Schacht, like Kondratiev, had been concerned with balance, Hitler preferred the expression of sheer economic will-power. Hitler's economic views were instinctively those of a command economy, like Stalin's. His wish list was extensive: a modernized and productive agriculture sector to free Germany from fear of blockade, a network of new motorways, a dozen remodelled cities, a massive programme of import-substitution to supply synthetic strategic materials, and military industries capable of out-producing the largest enemy economy. The emphasis here was on grandiose programmes of direct physical investment, a 'productionist' conception that Hitler also shared with his economically unsophisticated co-dictator.

This hard core of economic objectives could not possibly be met without stricter supervision of the national economy. The structure of the Plan organization established in October 1936 reflected this reality. There were six main divisions: raw material production, raw material distribution, labour, agriculture, price control and foreign exchange, each with its own sub-divisions. The most important office was that of the Price Commissar, set up on 29 October 1936, since price inflation might well have undermined the whole strategy. The *Gauleiter* of Silesia, Josef Wagner, took on the new job and issued a price-stop decree in November. A network of twenty-seven local offices was set up nationwide whose job was to monitor all local prices and to approve or refuse any price increases. Wagner was also allowed to intervene in setting wage-rates, which were closely related to issues of price stability; his officers could also insist that firms adopt new production methods or work practices if they reduced prices.[68] These changes still left economic planning divided with Schacht's ministry. In November 1937 Schacht was compelled to resign as economics minister, and in January 1939 was sacked from the *Reichsbank*. Like the Soviet economic experts, he ended up in a concentration camp. Göring took the opportunity of Schacht's resignation to rationalize the Plan structure by linking it directly to the economics ministry, which he now placed under a party stooge, the bibulous economic journalist Walther Funk. Administrative divisions for trade and commerce, currency and credit, mining, iron and energy supply were added to the Plan. Göring's organization now undertook the annual allocation of industrial investment, prescribed the output of a range of major industries, from bulk chemicals to sausage skins, operated a quota system for the allocation of raw materials, supervised all trade and currency transactions, modernized agricultural output, expanded machinery production, and trained labour. The whole was supported by a statistical effort aimed at identifying to the smallest degree the production, movement and allocation of all goods and services and to monitor plan fulfilment. This was something that Voznesensky's Gosplan could not do in 1938.

The command economies performed the functions of choice and allocation normally associated with the market under liberal capitalism. The consequence of displacing the market was a fundamental restructuring of the two economies so that they more closely matched the political planning preferences of the two dictatorships, rather than the preferences of ordinary consumers, producers and traders. In both regimes this meant not only control of domestic economic variables, but also the reduction of dependence on the wider world market and the elimination of foreign influence on domestic economic conditions.

For Germany and the Soviet Union there were histories of dependence to overcome. The modernization of the Tsarist state had relied on high levels of foreign lending, the forced export of grain and the transfer of experts and technical know-how from the more developed western economies. During the late 1920s the Soviet state was compelled to adopt a similar strategy in order to complete the First Five-Year Plan. Hundreds of foreign experts helped to set up Soviet factories; a slow stream of imported machines and industrial equipment became a flood after 1927, reaching 71 per cent of total imports against the more modest Tsarist total of 21.5 per cent in 1913; foreign debt, which had been repudiated in 1918, reached the high levels of Tsarist days again between 1930 and 1932. The deficit expanded as the Soviet Union urgently imported the technical means to further industrialization at precisely the time that the Great Crash emasculated the capacity of other countries to buy Soviet exports in exchange.[69] Grain, desperately needed by peasants starving as a consequence of collectivization, was dumped on world markets to try to stem the rising tide of debt.

Germany before 1914 was the world's second largest trading nation behind Britain; one-quarter of its industrial workforce produced exports. After the war, trade revived sluggishly, leaving the German economy particularly vulnerable to the international business cycle. Defeat in 1918 also saddled Germany with a bill for wartime reparation scheduled to last until 1988, and brought the loss of resource-rich territory in Alsace-Lorraine and Silesia. The collapse of the currency in 1923 placed Germany in the position of a developing state: its currency was reconstructed with the help of the richer countries of the West, and throughout the 1920s Germany was forced to rely on exceptional levels of foreign lending to make up for the absence of adequate sources of domestic capital. When the world boom ended in 1929, Germany, like the Soviet Union, found herself under pressure to repay the debt without any longer being able to export goods to do so. In 1931 the German balance of payments produced virtual bankruptcy; disaster was staved off only because her creditors agreed temporarily to suspend debt repayment. Trade fell by half, leaving millions of Germans in the export industries unemployed or on short-time. Many German exporters survived only because for three years Soviet importers took more than half German machinery exports to feed the machine-tool shortages of the Five-Year Plan.[70]

Over the course of the 1930s the relationship of the Soviet Union and Germany with the world economy was transformed from a damaging dependence to an insular self-reliance. It is certainly true that the world economic crisis would in itself have altered this relationship, as it did for all industrial states, because of reduced levels of trade and the exceptional decline in foreign direct investment and commercial credits. The international slump accelerated a more general worldwide trend towards economic self-sufficiency, regulated trade and currency controls, generally known by the inter-war term 'autarky'. Germany and the Soviet Union developed extreme versions of the concept. Both deliberately chose to isolate themselves from the world market by substituting domestic sources of capital for foreign credits, and domestic production of essential equipment and materials in place of imports. The residual links with the world economy were controlled absolutely by the state to safeguard its domestic priorities.

The purpose behind Soviet and German autarky was political as much as economic. The concept of autarky, as it was understood in the 1930s, represented more than mere import-substitution; it embraced the idea of national self-dependence and political manoeuvrability instead of remaining, as one National Socialist economist put it, a 'province' of the world economy and the cosmopolitan capitalism that sustained it.[71] For the Soviet Union it was doubly important to reduce foreign dependence, first to distinguish the Soviet industrial drive from that of the Tsarist state, and second to demonstrate that the world's only socialist economy could sustain growth without bourgeois products and bourgeois specialists. The purpose of industrial modernization, Stalin told party delegates in December 1925, was to convert the Soviet Union 'from a country which imports machines and equipment into a country which produces machines and equipment'.[72]

The popular attack on foreign experts that began in 1929 and ended with the 'Metro-Vickers' trial of British engineers in 1933 was an expression of the political resentment felt at having to employ the capitalist enemy to build the socialist future.

The Soviet authorities did not use the term autarky in this wider sense, but the policies pursued in the 1930s were recognizably autarkic. Soviet trade was completely regulated by the state and was based on bilateral trade agreements, principally for products essential to the industrialization drive instead of goods for ordinary consumers. The system was run by the Commissariat of Foreign Trade, established in 1930. Separate export and import trade corporations were set up for each major product category, which were responsible for planning and executing trade operations, but each transaction had to be licensed by the central commissariat. Exports were heavily subsidized in the 1930s because the costs of production exceeded the prices that could be obtained on the world market. The state bank handled all foreign currency transactions.[73] During the 1930s, as industrialization provided substitutes for goods previously imported, the trade ratio was progressively reduced; in 1928 trade made up an estimated 8 per cent of Soviet national income, in 1940 only 4.7 per cent. In 1938 the value of exports and imports was just 28 per cent of the post-war peak reached in 1930–31 (and just one-fifth of the value of Tsarist trade in 1913).[74] Trade with the major capitalist states fell dramatically. Imports from the United States peaked at 1.1 billion roubles in 1930, but fell to a mere 78 million in 1934. The number of American contracts fell from 124 in 1931 to just 46 in 1933; the well-appointed villa occupied by Viktor Kravchenko had been built to house American engineers a few years before.[75] German imports reached 1.8 billion roubles in 1931 but were down to 67 million in 1938. Dependence on foreign machinery imports dropped away. In 1932 the Soviet Union took exactly three-quarters of German machinery exports, but in 1938 only 3.8 per cent.[76] Foreign debt was repaid, much of it in gold bullion, dug miserably from the ground by an army of camp labourers in the new goldfields of Siberia.

Autarky in Germany was a more deliberate policy, and, in the context of a hitherto free-market trading economy, a more radical one. Nationalist economists argued in the 1920s for an autarkic economy to restore to Germany her economic sovereignty and political dignity. Buying German goods, eating German food, building only with German materials became a patriotic obligation. The National Socialist economic programme committed the party to freeing Germany from the economic consequences of Versailles and the 'chains of international capital'. 'We want to secure the existence of the German people,' wrote Göring in 1937, 'independent of all crises in the world.'[77] Among the first acts of the new government were the repudiation of further reparation payments and the reduction or suspension of repayments on foreign loans. Almost no new loans were taken up, while existing loans from the 1920s were reduced substantially because of the willingness of foreign bondholders to dump their German stock once interest payments had been blocked. The bonds were bought back at rock-bottom prices by agents secretly acting for the German government. By 1939 only 15 per cent of the foreign debt outstanding in 1932 still remained in foreign hands. The foreign capital relied on in the 1920s was replaced by capital supplied by the German state, whose debt trebled between 1933 and 1939.[78]

German external trade was subjected to a structure of state supervision remarkably similar to the Soviet model. A close balance between import costs and export earnings was essential because, after near bankruptcy, Germany lacked the gold or foreign exchange needed to finance any balance-of-payments deficit, so that clear priorities had to be defined. In September 1934 Schacht introduced what he called 'The New Plan' for centralized control of German trade. In fact it largely consolidated a set of controls that had been built up piecemeal since 1931. All importers and exporters needed a licence for each foreign trade transaction. They had to apply through one of seventeen (later twenty) control offices (*Überwachungstellen*), which, like the Soviet corporations, were each responsible for a single product range. The system was exploited ruthlessly to ensure that those goods – principally raw materials – essential for the regime's policies of rearmament and heavy industrial development were preferred. Trade was increasingly arranged on a bilateral barter basis, and the value of the mark artificially fixed to boost the exports needed to pay for essential imports. Like Soviet goods, German goods were subsidized by a levy imposed on non-exporters since German prices, like Soviet ones, were above world price-levels.[79] During the 1930s the free transfer of goods was entirely suspended to prevent consumer preferences pushing up the import bill. The trade ratio, already low, fell from 18.2 per cent of the national product in 1933, to 12.2 per cent six years later.

The Second Four-Year Plan carried autarky to new limits by introducing a programme of large-scale import-substitution. The evidence that the West was prepared to use economic sanctions against Italy following the invasion of Ethiopia in 1935 increased the possibility that Germany, too, might become the victim of a future blockade in any crisis. The Plan's first priority was to raise domestic output of food and industrial raw materials. By increasing inputs of chemical fertilizers, raising the number of machines on farms and rationalizing food processing it proved possible to increase German self-sufficiency in foodstuffs from 68 per cent in 1928 to 83 per cent in 1938/9.[80] Raw material output from German sources had already risen by 108 per cent between 1932 and 1937, while the quantity of imported raw materials rose by just 14 per cent. Germany even succeeded in exploiting its own limited supplies of natural oil: production was 102,900 tonnes in 1928, but 445,000 by 1936.[81] Many goods Germany just did not possess, or not in enough quantities. The Four-Year Plan launched major capital projects for the synthetic production of key materials, in particular oil and rubber (both based on experimental breakthroughs by German chemists working at the German chemical giant IG Farben), and for the expansion of domestic production of coal, iron ore and basic industrial chemicals. The first Plan listed nineteen product sectors, with the main emphasis on the chemical industry; included too were large investments in shipbuilding and electricity supply, down to tiny sums for the production of soot, leatherware and fat-free soaps. The sums invested totalled over 8 billion marks, more than half of all industrial investment between 1936 and 1940.[82] Germany, like the Soviet Union, physically expanded its industrial base in the 1930s to avoid being hostage to the rest of the capitalist world.

The Four- and Five-Year Plans made little economic sense in a world of free trade and peaceful economic exchange. In the context of the economic siege mentality and deteriorating international situation of the 1930s they had a greater rationality. In both Germany and the

Soviet Union autarky was a strategic choice. Self-reliance was a neces- sary step for waging a war of defence or aggression. Economic failure was regarded in both states as the explanation for defeat in the First World War. The most significant restructuring carried out under the command economies was the establishment of defence sectors larger than any yet created in peacetime by any major state. The object was to ensure that neither economy entered a future conflict insufficiently prepared or inadequately structured for wartime mobilization.

Military procurement did not cause the command economies, but the scale of defence outlays and preparation in the 1930s led to an intensification of control to ensure that current resources could be released into the defence sector at the expense of current civilian consumption, and to the conversion of existing civilian productive capacity to military use in war. The raw figures of the military budgets in Germany and the Soviet Union show a rapid upward trajectory from the mid-1930s from relatively insignificant levels in the late 1920s. Defence spending in both states increased, coincidentally, by the same factor between 1928 and 1938: 880 million roubles to 23.2 billion in the one case, 650 million marks to 17.3 billion in the other, a twenty-six-fold growth. The decision to expand the Soviet defence sector as a key economic priority was made in the planning for the First Five-Year Plan, but was upgraded by Stalin himself in 1932 and became, in the Third Plan in 1937, the dominant element. The launch of large-scale rearmament in Germany began later, in the first years of Hitler's dictatorship, and reached exceptional levels at the same time as the Soviet Union, from 1937 onwards. The share of defence spending in the state budget in Germany reached 54 per cent in 1938/9; in the Soviet Union it reached one-third of the budget by 1940. In both cases this was a share of a state budget that was very much larger in the late 1930s than it had been in 1931, a sevenfold increase for the Soviet Union, fourfold in the German case.[83]

However it is measured, the commitment to defence in the two economies was historically exceptional, creating by the late 1930s something approaching a war economy in peacetime. The proportion of the national product devoted to military spending in 1913, at the height of the pre-war arms race, was dwarfed by the race run in the 1930s. In 1913 the Tsarist state devoted an estimated 4.8 per cent of the national product to the military, imperial Germany approximately 3 per cent; in 1939 Germany devoted 29 per cent, the Soviet Union 17 per cent, both, again, much larger economies on the eve of the Second World War than they had been on the eve of the First. The claims made by defence on the labour force and on investment funds were also exceptional. By May 1939 over one-fifth of all German industrial workers worked for the armed forces; in the manufacturing and building sectors the figures were close to one-third.[84] Defence sector investment in Germany (weapons production and military construction) was 28 per cent of all investment in 1938. Figures for the Soviet Union show that by 1937 a little over one-fifth of all industrial investment went to the defence industries.[85] The international comparisons are also telling. Between 1933 and 1938 the Soviet Union and Germany each spent on defence almost three times the amount spent by Britain or France or the United States. In 1938 Britain and the United States each produced just 13 per cent of the quantity of weapons produced in Germany.[86]

Weapons, barracks and fortifications – the physical outputs of defence spending – tell only part of the story. In both systems defence planning was based on the assumption that any future war would make far-reaching demands on economic resources and stamina. The programmes of import-substitution and capital goods investment were based partly on this assumption. Aircraft production required an aluminium industry; explosives were produced from basic chemicals; guns, tanks and vehicles were made from steel. The supply of food in wartime was also an indispensable component of any wartime economy, as both Germany and the Soviet Union had found to their cost in the First World War. One of the arguments put forward for collectivization of agriculture by the defence sector of Gosplan was that socialized agriculture would permit greater 'capacity to control' food production and distribution in 'wartime conditions'.[87] The link between agricultural rationalization and future war was also central to the farm programme of the Second Four-Year Plan. Defence preparation on this scale generated secondary claims on the economy, which are usually described by the terms 'indirect' or 'economic' rearmament.

The sum of direct and indirect claims by the defence sector has never been fully computed for either state. In the German case much of the investment in strategic industries was undertaken by private investors and not from the public purse, making it harder to establish aggregate figures. The problem also arises of separating military and civilian production in enterprises where production was undertaken for both simultaneously. By 1939 many German consumer industries were providing extensive quantities of goods for the armed forces – boots, uniforms, mess kit, paper, leatherwork – which were almost identical with the civilian product and which were counted, for statistical convenience, as civilian goods. Conversely, in the Soviet Union designated defence plants might turn out tanks in one workshop, but farm tractors in another.[88] There are nevertheless important examples of indirect rearmament where there is no ambiguity. Germany established in the 1930s the world's largest aluminium industry, two-thirds of whose output was used by the predominantly military aircraft industry.[89] In 1937 the programmes for synthetic oil and rubber, whose chief purpose was to secure the fuel and tyres needed by a modernized German army and air force, required investment totalling 1.9 billion marks in three years, almost half of all investment in the capital goods industry. The 'New Production Programme' announced in July 1938 for basic chemical products (explosives, chemical weapons and synthetics) required more than a million tonnes of steel a year to build, at a cost of 8.6 billion marks between 1938 and 1941.[90] The jewel in the crown was a gigantic integrated iron, steel and armaments corporation, founded in 1937 under the title *Reichswerke 'Hermann Göring'* to produce and exploit Germany's low-grade iron ore at the Salzgitter ore field near Brunswick. The project grew rapidly into a central pillar of the defence economy, with fixed capital assets in Germany of more than a billion marks by the war, and total assets throughout occupied Europe of 3.1 billion, making it the largest industrial combine in Europe.[91] The simple addition of investment in military industries and in war-related heavy industry, most of which would not have been built under normal market conditions, suggests that in excess of 70 per cent of all industrial investment in Germany by 1938–9 anticipated the waging of war.[92]

The figures on defence spending alone would make it difficult to claim, as has often been done, that the German economy was being prepared in the 1930s for short, limited wars, using a small and flexible arms sector.[93] The plans for core chemicals, synthetic production, domestic iron ore, aluminium and machine-building were justified principally on their contribution to German war-making.[94] So large was the planned expansion of the military base that it became clear by 1937 that Germany would need access to other resources in addition to those generated by the programmes of autarky. When Hitler outlined his foreign policy plans to the commanders-in-chief of the armed forces on 5 November 1937 (recorded by his adjutant, Colonel Hossbach), he indicated that Germany would have to take over neighbouring territory to ensure the supply of agricultural land and raw materials: 'The only remedy,' ran the minutes of Hitler's speech, 'lay in the acquisition of more living-space.'[95] The *Anschluss* with Austria in March 1938, the threat of war against Czechoslovakia that resulted in the annexation of the Czech Sudetenland in October 1938, and the subsequent occupation of Bohemia and Moravia in March 1939, were all driven by economic as much as by racial motives. Most heavy industry and raw material production was immediately gobbled up by the *Reichswerke* rather than by private industry; by the end of 1940 the combine employed 600,000 people, and had begun to take control not only of iron, steel and coal production but also the oil resources and refineries of occupied and allied Europe.[96] The economic imperialism was undisguised. Even while German forces were completing the staged occupation in early October 1938 of the areas of Czechoslovakia granted under the terms of the Munich agreement, Göring hosted a meeting in Berlin of high-ranking economic officials where every item of Sudeten economic resources, from lignite (the 'brown' coal used to produce synthetic oil) to margarine, was allocated to the programmes of the Four-Year Plan.[97] Autarkists began to talk about the 'large area economy' (*Grossraumwirtschaft*), the concept of an autarkic territorial bloc rather than a discrete national economy, with Germany at its core. In the summer of 1941 Hitler remarked that if you could just seize resources and land by force – 'what one needs and does not have, one must conquer' – autarky was perhaps a waste of effort after all.[98]

The predatory economics of the Third Reich derived from Hitler's view of national economic competition outlined in the 1920s. It set the German command economy apart from the Soviet experiment, where economic colonization was internal and productive rather than external and piratical. In both cases, however, the effect of choosing an expanded defence sector and heavy industrial development produced the same structural distortions. A *Reichsbank* research report in 1939 showed that the balance between the production of consumer goods and producer goods (machinery, engineering equipment, heavy industry, materials) had altered remarkably in just six years. In 1932 consumer industries accounted for 40 per cent of investment, in 1938 only 17 per cent; in 1932 the consumer industry wage bill was 40 per cent of all wages paid, in 1938 just 25 per cent. These proportions, it was drily observed, were identical with the current situation in the Soviet Union.[99] The altered distribution of the national product reflected this structural shift. In 1928 private consumption made up 69 per cent of the German economy, 83 per cent of the less-developed Soviet one; a decade later, in 1937, the figures had fallen to 56 per cent and 61 per cent respectively. The unprecedented growth of the national product in the 1930s was almost all diverted to state-directed programmes of investment and militarization.[100]

In the 1930s the two dictatorships chose guns before butter, a distinction made famous by Göring during a speech in 1935: 'Ore has always made a state strong, butter and margarine have at the most made people fat . . .' This was a deliberate choice. Hitler, in a candid speech to building workers in 1937, told them that military priorities required the employment of 'millions of German workers on work not in itself productive, in the sense that other workers cannot buy the products of this labour'. Fewer consumer goods and more armaments, Hitler assured them, would make Germany strong and independent and make possible 'a later, better German living-standard'.[101] Neither command economy was set up to satisfy the appetites of consumers; they were introduced for the very reason that, left to themselves, the two populations would seek to maximize their own well-being at the expense of the state. In 1941 Erich Neumann, the head of the Four-Year Plan cabinet, explained that the Plan had never been intended to raise living-standards: 'Before we can begin to favour consumption, the fundamentals of national economy will have to be re-established and permanently secured . . . "Guns instead of butter" is the watchword . . .'[102] In the Soviet Union increased civilian consumption remained a stated goal in the Five-Year Plans, but, in practice, consumer goods were the regular victim of plan rescheduling in favour of heavy industry and building. Real per capita consumption in the Soviet Union was 6 per cent lower in 1937 than in 1928, though real GNP was 71 per cent higher; real per capita consumption in Germany in 1938 was just 4 per cent higher than in 1928, reflecting the shift to full employment, but the real national product was more than 40 per cent higher.[103] Growth on this scale could have made everyone richer had the state willed it.

Wage levels are one way of estimating changes in living standards. In both states wages were closely controlled by the state, following the destruction of the independent trade unions in Germany in May 1933, and the abolition of any independent labour bargaining in the Soviet Union in 1931. Hourly wage rates were fixed in Germany at depression levels by the Law on National Labour in 1934. By 1938 real weekly earnings had expanded well beyond depression levels thanks to longer hours and extensive overtime, but were still fractionally lower than they had been in 1928. In the Soviet Union estimates show real hourly wage rates in 1937 around 40 per cent lower than in 1928; by 1940 they were down by a further 5–10 per cent, and the 1928 level was not reached again until 1949, after which there was sustained real wage growth for the first time in the dictatorship.[104] These are very blunt statistics. Some workers gained from concessions made in war-related sectors short of skilled manpower; other workers, particularly in consumer sectors, found themselves on short-time and low fixed rates of pay. In general, however, there was no sustained earnings growth under the dictatorship compared with the late 1920s; most workers remained little better off than they had been in 1913, some worse off.[105]

In reality earnings bore little relation to living standards under dictatorship. What counted was the availability of goods. Here there existed a wide difference between the German and Soviet experience. For many consumers in the Soviet Union there were long periods of desperate hardship, the result of poor harvests, or poor distribution, or war. Millions died of starvation during the food crisis caused in the wake of collectivization; in the post-1945 period perhaps another million died from the harvest failure of 1946, a human disaster that has failed to attract the same attention as the calamitous famines of 1921 and 1932.[106] For millions of Soviet citizens there were long periods of hunger and malnutrition. Food was the primary concern of all consumers. Between 1931 and 1935 bread was rationed to ensure that all workers got at least something. There was some rationing again between 1939 and 1941, as defence crowded out the civilian economy, and then complete rationing of all basic goods during the war, which lasted until 1947. For most Soviet citizens, work meant food. Non-workers were not entitled to ration cards. Factory and school canteens provided a regular supply of cheap and nourishing meals. The availability of any other goods was quite arbitrary. Vodka dulled the reality of empty shelves and food deprivation and was easily found in stores and kerbside kiosks; sales of vodka made up 38 per cent of the retail trade in 1945.[107]

German consumers were regularly supplied with a minimum level of food and standard consumer products, but few luxuries. There was limited rationing, of butter in particular, before the outbreak of war. The limits on consumption were placed on the producer rather than the consumer. Shortages of raw materials and credit deliberately restricted the output of the main consumer sectors. German customers paid above the world market price for most goods, because controlled trade prevented them from getting the benefit of cheaper foreign products. Food prices were kept artificially high to boost farm incomes. A study of consumption in a group of working-class families found that between 1927 and 1937 there was a sharp fall in the consumption of higher value or imported foodstuffs – 44 per cent less wheat bread, 18 per cent less meat, 37 per cent less fruit, 41 per cent fewer eggs – while standard foods high in carbohydrates, such as potatoes or rye bread, were consumed in greater quantities. But unlike the Soviet experience, German families drank less alcohol: beer consumption fell by more than half.[108]

Living standards can be measured by the quality as well as the quantity of what is consumed. The increasingly stodgy German diet represented a decline of a kind even if rye bread and potatoes kept stomachs full. The quality of Soviet consumer products was low on any list of planning priorities and was generally poor or shoddy.

German products were undermined by the imperatives of autarky, which insisted on the use of substitute or recycled materials. In September 1936, for example, all woollen clothes for men had to be made from at least 25 per cent recycled material; the following November a further decree ordered all uniforms produced for public service to contain at least 50 per cent of the newly developed artificial fibres (*Zellwolle*). The clothes wore badly, and held dye poorly. Soldiers exposed to rain were nicknamed 'Men from Mars' as the stain from their grey-green uniforms spread over their skin.[109] Recycling became a way of life in Germany. On 20 November 1936 a decree on kitchen waste ordered all households to save scraps and peelings. A Commissar for Recycled Material was appointed, who organized exhibitions and talks on the merits of substitute (*ersatz*) products and the virtues of make-do-and-mend. Subsequent decrees in 1937 and 1938 ordered the recycling of paper, tin and scrap metals. Disposal was arranged by door-to-door collections. Households also had to dispose of any surplus clothing. Men could keep no more than two pairs of shoes or two suits of clothes; police had the powers to search apartments and houses for hoarded clothing or metals. Concealment became an act of economic sabotage.[110]

Consumers in both systems had to accept the second-hand economy to make up for shortages, sub-standard goods and low pay. In the Soviet Union informal bazaars re-emerged after the ban on private selling in 1930. Millions of Soviet consumers bought and sold whatever they could of their own possessions. All over the cities of the Soviet Union the street tout and peddler became a universal sight. In 1945 almost half of all trade was conducted in the private street markets. Visitors to Russia were astonished by the willingness of shoppers to buy anything offered for sale, however worn, damaged or contaminated its condition.[111] In shortage economies, consumers sacrifice quality for availability. In both systems consumers reacted opportunistically; they hustled, bargained and occasionally pilfered what they could not afford or find in the shops.

In both command economies the authorities were anxious to control not just what was consumed, but the disposal of any surplus income or 'excess purchasing power' that remained after consumers had bought what they could. Some of this surplus was creamed off in high tax rates. In Germany direct and indirect taxes remained at the high emergency levels set during the depression; tax revenues as a percentage of the national product doubled between 1930 and 1940, from 12.5 to 23.1 per cent. In the Soviet Union the turnover tax, introduced in 1931, and levied at the point of production rather than sale, supplied the largest part of government revenue (59 per cent in 1934); direct taxation supplied only 6 per cent of tax revenue in the same year. The rate of turnover tax was manipulated to ensure that the costs of industrialization would be met by consumers rather than from state loans.[112] The rest of the surplus was siphoned into savings. These were virtually compulsory in the Soviet Union, where monthly sums were deducted from wages. These were 'savings' in a very limited sense, since they could be liquidated and spent only with state permission. The sums saved were taken from the savings banks and used by the state to cover its current expenditure and investment, while retaining the illusion that citizens had a financial stake in their own future.

In Germany savings came to be manipulated in the same way. The savings ratio rose sharply with the recovery, as people were bombarded with state propaganda to save as a patriotic and prudential duty. Savings banks were then compelled to take up government stock or short-term Treasury bills, primarily to fund rearmament and capital projects, and to prevent the surplus from generating a consumer demand that could not be satisfied. This circular form of financing was nicknamed 'noiseless finance' (*geräuschlose Finanzierung*) by the Finance Ministry, since it was conducted without the need for loud public campaigns to get people to buy government bonds.[113] Saving ensured that excess purchasing power did not generate inflationary pressures on a limited supply of consumer goods, and disguised the extent to which the structural distortions of the two command economies penalized their populations by getting them to pay indirectly for the state contracts they worked on.

Economies are notoriously difficult to command. They possess an aggregate momentum that is hard to deflect: the larger the economy, the greater its tendency to inertia or resistance in the face of state policy. The dictatorships possessed no magic formula to transform this reality. The efforts to dominate and redirect the economy in the

1930s prompted persistent social friction, jurisdictional squabbles and political argument, which in some serious cases could only be resolved by Stalin or Hitler. What on paper appears an effortless statistical picture of growth and development was, in practice, a constant cycle of crisis, readjustment, political brokering and naked, militaristic coercion. It was not mere self-interest that drove Thyssen and Kravchenko to abandon the command economy, but when they did so they were treated like deserters from an economic army.[114]

Many of the problems facing the two economies were a consequence of the experimental nature of command economics. The emphasis on the physical construction of factories, canals, roads, military installations and cities produced an accumulating crisis of over-investment, a failure to ensure that the rest of the economy could supply enough labour, construction materials and machinery to complete the projects on schedule. The First Five-Year Plan ended with hundreds of incomplete projects; the relative success of the Second Plan was due to the effort made to bring unfinished capacity into productive use. The German Four-Year Plan made heavy demands on resources already in short supply because of high military spending, with the consequence that most of its programmes were postponed and delayed in the constant scramble for raw materials, building workers and engineering equipment.[115] There are numerous examples from both economies of incompetent or over-optimistic planning. Viktor Kravchenko's experience in Siberia was typical. In 1939 he was sent to Stalinsk to set up a new steel pipe plant. It was a prestige project for the region, planned to turn out 170,000 tonnes of high-quality pipe-work a year. But when Kravchenko arrived he found Stalinsk in chaos, a patchwork of half-completed factories already short of fuel, wood, bricks, cement and labour. The site selected for the steel plant was a bare stretch of river bank miles from the city, with no road, railway, gas or electric power and so waterlogged that it could never hope to support the heavy buildings it was designed for. A two-year-old building further down the bank was already sinking into the muddy earth. Kravchenko succeeded, at great personal risk, in persuading his commissariat to abandon the project after millions of roubles had already been spent on its development. A new site had to be found and the whole process of planning and allocation began anew.[116]

The competence and efficiency of either system was compromised by monopsony – the state was the principal customer in the Soviet Union; it was by far the largest single customer in Germany, not only for armaments but for a whole range of other goods. The absence of conventional market pressures on producers left the issue of value-for-money up to the dominant customer. In Germany the system of cost-plus public contracts actually gave businessmen an incentive to produce at higher cost and less efficiently. Profits were allowed as a percentage of costs; the more expensive the product, the greater the yield to the factory. Since the state was committed to buying the end product there was no market penalty for producing overpriced goods.[117] Cost-reductions were built in to yearly targets for Soviet producers, but this did not prevent embattled managers, through a mixture of fraud and incompetence, from charging as much as possible to provide a cushion of extra funds for the plant. The consequence was the growth of a vast bureaucratic structure to monitor contract performance and examine accounts, forcing managers in both systems to live and labour, as Kravchenko put it, 'in a jungle of questionnaires, paper forms and reports in seven copies'.[118] In Germany the Four-Year Plan authorities struggled to impose proper accounting practice on contractors unwilling to reveal their books to public scrutiny, while in the Soviet Union there simply did not exist a large-enough body of competent accountants to ensure that every factory scrupulously pursued the public interest.[119]

The tension between producers and planners highlights the absence of consensus within command economies. Though there was broad political agreement on the necessity for economic management, arguments about priorities and policies were built into each system. The habit of piling one essential project on top of another, without reconciling them in some order of priority, encouraged every project director to see himself (seldom, if ever, herself) as specially privileged, able to argue with officials about the allocation of labour or materials at the expense of other economic impresarios. The pressure to fulfil the plan was felt even more keenly in the Soviet Union, where every failure might be interpreted as an act of economic sabotage. The command economies were the product not of a smooth process of draughts-manship but of endless, and often bitter, bargaining. In practice this meant a system of priorities based less on economic rationality and more on the degree of political pressure and bureaucratic self-interest a particular bargainer was able to exert.[120] This explains the extraordinary authority given by Hitler to Göring so that he could cut through the bargaining process and give orders to the other economic actors. Yet Göring, too, soon became immersed in the bargaining culture as he staved off the demands of the army, the finance ministry, the plenipotentiary for construction, and private industry.[121] In the Soviet Union the proliferation of industrial commissariats encouraged a sense of planning isolation and bureaucratic egotism as each branch argued its own case with the political authorities. There were too many centrifugal interests to reconcile in each economy to avoid an almost permanent condition of incipient entropy. In the absence of conventional market pressures, the systems were kept in being by political will.

Under these many circumstances it proved difficult to keep the market permanently suppressed. In the state-run sectors of the Soviet economy managers and officials had to find ways of coping with a system that was at times chaotically inefficient, savagely punitive and administratively capricious. The result was the slow emergence of subordinate market mechanisms, which helped to make the system work despite itself. This shadow market was a simple one: enterprises or warehouses had things another manager needed to fulfil the Plan but which he was not entitled to; he in turn had stocks of equipment or tools that he did not need, which could be exchanged for what he did want. This was risky, but the system proved to be sufficiently incompetent in monitoring plan fulfilment, or sufficiently willing to indulge malpractice, for it to work. Two peculiarly Russian institutions were needed to operate the shadow market. The first was *blat*, the use of personal influence (and sweeteners) to get preferential treatment from officials. The second was the *tolkach*, a professional hustler whose job it was to hunt out resources that could be obtained outside the Plan. *Tolkachi* were everywhere in the Soviet Union, doing deals and exchanging products in a black economic underworld based on its own informal rules and market codes.[122] They were tolerated by the authorities, partly because officials too found it convenient to use their own troubleshooters (*otvetrabotniki*) to cut through red tape and skirt regular channels.[123] The *tolkachi* were paid generous commissions out of enterprise funds, which had to be disguised by creative accounting. The government turned a blind eye to the practice. The survival of crude market mechanisms was necessary for the system to work at all. Only when economic leaders openly talked of reviving market practices did the state react. The head of Gosbank, the state central bank, was shot in 1936 after he suggested a relaxation of economic controls.[124]

In Germany the process worked in reverse. Here a predominantly market economy had to adapt to a state-run economic system. As market mechanisms were removed, so German industry and bureaucracy adjusted their behaviour to take account of the changed reality. A pattern very similar to that in the Soviet Union developed; the same patron–client relationships, the same networks of officials and managers who found ways of circumventing controls or rewarding loyalty, the same hoarding and hustling, even a German variety of *blat*, whose dimensions historians are only now beginning to unearth.[125] German business had always been more organized and bureaucratic than its western counterparts, which made the transition to command economy smoother and less uncongenial. Prominent directors from the private sector moved into top positions in the new state-party apparatus, whose values they adopted: Carl Krauch from IG Farben, who ran the Four-Year Plan chemical division; Heinrich Koppenberg, a former Flick employee, who ran large parts of the state-owned aircraft and aluminium sectors; Karl-Otto Saur, a Krupp time-and-motion expert, who became technical director of Speer's armaments ministry in 1942; Paul Pleiger, a small-time Rhenish iron producer, whose party credentials brought him to head the whole *Reichswerke* empire.[126] The informal structures of collaboration and exchange generated by the changed economic environment had little to do with the displaced mechanisms of the market-place or capitalist self-interest. These were pseudo-markets, created to make the planning and priority system work more effectively. As in the Soviet Union, any initiative to restore conventional market rationality was strongly resisted. When the leaders of the Ruhr iron and steel industry met together in the summer of 1937 to discuss their opposition to the mining of more expensive domestic ores by the *Reichswerke*, their meetings were bugged by Göring's intelligence service. He sent all but one a telegram threatening them with prosecution for sabotage; to the one exception he offered the prospect of a fat contract.[127]

Ultimately, both command economies relied on coercion to limit the natural tendency of their populations to put individual economic well-being before their duty to the dictatorial state. The command economies were, first and foremost, systems of power; their instructions, plans and regulations had the force of law. 'Every directive of the government is an operational order that must be unconditionally fulfilled,' announced the prosecutor of a group of Soviet managers in one of the purge trials; 'only complete execution of orders and discipline will ensure total victory in the battle to build a socialist economy'.[128] The concept of economic sabotage was built into the Soviet Criminal Code of 1926 under Article 58 §14. Any act of negligence or obstruction in the process of producing and distributing goods was defined as a counter-revolutionary crime, with penalties ranging from one year in jail to execution by shooting ('the highest measure of social defence').[129] During the period of the First Five-Year Plan additional laws were passed against the production of shoddy goods, against malpractice in retail stores and against state theft, all of them carrying penalties of between five and ten years in a camp.[130] After the war, economic conditions were so poor that economic crime became a widespread reality for millions of hungry Soviet citizens. The commissariat of justice launched a campaign in 1945 against the 'plunderers of socialist property', but thefts rose by almost a quarter the following year. At Stalin's insistence a draconian new law on economic crime was published on 4 June 1947, which led to an increase in sentences of more than six years from 44,552 in 1946 to just over a quarter of a million the following year. Between 1947 and 1952 one and a half million Russians were sent to the camps on charges of state theft.[131] Most of those caught were criminals from sheer desperation, like the woman worker from a Leningrad rubber factory sent to the camps for ten years for stealing three pairs of boots.[132] The Chairman of the Soviet Supreme Court thought that such crimes displayed 'the survivals of capitalism in the consciousness of our people'.[133]

Nothing on this scale occurred in Germany, but the imperatives contained in the economic plan were exploited as a form of social control. The intrusive demands of the legislation on waste and recycling, and the insistent propaganda on buying German goods, were unavoidable. The priority awarded to 'national tasks' ahead of consumer satisfaction made every grumble about shortages or quality potentially treasonable. Under the Four-Year Plan a wave of proscriptive legislation was published that criminalized economic misdemeanour and carried the same wide spectrum of penalities that existed in the Soviet system. On 1 December 1936 a Law against Economic Sabotage was published. Any German citizen who 'inflicts serious harm on the German economy' could be 'punished by death' and his property seized.[134] Black-marketeering, smuggling, currency fraud, even unauthorized price rises, were all subject to long prison terms or execution, as examples of what the law called 'sheer selfishness'. The legislation was used sparingly. The Price Commissioner discovered that simple threats against two businessmen, widely publicized in the press when price legislation was first introduced in 1936, were enough to produce such a 'deterrent effect' that no further 'spectacular action' was required from then until 1945.[135] In Germany exemplary punishment of businessmen, retailers or workers did deter the newly defined categories of economic crime. In the Soviet Union the fear or shame of punishment was never great enough to stimulate obedience.

One of the many victims of economic coercion was the principle of property ownership. This was not an issue confined only to the Soviet Union, as might be supposed. In neither dictatorship was private property regarded as an inviolable right, but as a privilege derived from membership of the community. National Socialism borrowed the idea of a 'Germanic' law of property from nationalist legal theorists. Writing in 1935, Otto Ohlendorf explained that private property did not imply the liberal concept of 'unrestricted dominion over a good', but was instead 'an obligation towards the community' enjoyed in trusteeship for the good of all.[136] In Stalin's Soviet Union a distinction was drawn between private and personal property. The first had been permitted under the 1923 Civil Code as consistent with the New Economic Policy. With the end of NEP the concept of property was changed to one of personal possession and was enshrined in the 1936 constitution. Property in this sense was justified as a derivative of socialist property, earned from doing socialist labour and thus sanctioned by its collectivist character; those individuals still operating their own craft workshops, or the few who owned their own farms, were deemed to own private, not personal, property and had no constitutional protection.[137]

There is a persistent myth that all property in the Soviet Union was state-owned. The state under the Five-Year Plans only undertook to eliminate private property that involved the exploitation of another's labour. Credit banks, peasant farms, retail shops and the majority of artisan workshops were transferred to social ownership after 1929 in the form of collective farms or producer co-operatives, but these were 'owned' only indirectly by the state. There remained in the Stalinist system extensive areas of private ownership, private trade and personal property. Under the farm law of 1935 collective farm workers were granted an allotment each, which they could farm themselves and whose produce they could sell on the free market. By 1950 over 50 per cent of the total value of Soviet farm produce was generated from private gardens filled with animals, hens, fruit trees and vegetables.[138] In 1939 there were still over a million individual artisan producers eking a living as private producers on the fringes of the socialized economy. The ban on bazaars and markets had little effect, and much of the country's trade was carried on in the informal and statistically invisible street stalls and markets that mushroomed again all over the Soviet Union in the 1930s and 1940s.

All except the private producers were entitled to personal property. This could take many forms, and great efforts were made to ensure that the kernel of personal ownership should not grow into a capitalist plant. Under the 1936 constitution people could own farm tools for their own allotments; they were allowed to own a dwelling-place as long as permission was granted from the local Soviet and it did not exceed 60 square metres in extent; the ubiquitous *dacha* was also allowed in most cases; the ownership of bonds and savings accounts was permitted, though they were difficult to access, and in 1947 the post-war currency revaluation reduced their worth to a mere fraction.[139] Goods could also be inherited, though here the authorities were intent on hedging in the development of a wealth culture. The first post-revolutionary regulations stipulated that the family of a working male could inherit tools, a house and goods up to 10,000 roubles in value, but from 1922 these estates were subject to a strict inheritance tax, which peaked at 90 per cent on those (presumably) few estates worth more than half a million roubles. During the 1930s and 1940s inheritance laws were further relaxed, and in 1945 goods could be inherited by individuals other than the immediate household of the deceased. Bonds and cash deposits were free of inheritance tax.[140] None of this made Soviet citizens rich; nor were they ever free of the threat of expropriation. Laws usually specified the confiscation of all property as a penalty for serious crimes, and for all major political offences or military desertion. Nevertheless, personal and private property survived within the limits laid down by the state. The free disposal of goods flourished outside the dominant socialized sector because it posed no serious threat to the political system.

There exists a further myth about the place of property in the National Socialist system. It is commonly assumed that the survival of private property differentiates the German system from any form of socialist economy. While it is evidently the case that private forms of ownership survived in the Third Reich, state ownership spread rapidly, while the principle of the free disposal of property was restricted by the concept of trusteeship. Already, in 1933, the state made substantial claims on the productive economy, but between 1933 and 1939 the state share increased year by year. In 1929 state spending made up 27 per cent of the national product; by 1938 the figure was 36 per cent. In the ten years from 1933 the assets of state-owned businesses doubled to more than 4 billion marks, and the number of state-owned enterprises rose to 531, many of them in the armaments sector.[141] The huge Volkswagen plant was state-owned, as was the *Reichswerke* complex. In 1937 Hitler announced to the party congress that private enterprise would be tolerated only as long as it conformed with the regime's objectives; otherwise the state would step in.[142] The National Socialist economy was not intended to be run for the benefit of private capitalism any more than the Soviet economy.

The restrictions on the free disposal of capital assets were also imposed from national-political motives. Under the terms of the Reich Entailed Farm Law (*Erbhofgesetz*) in 1934, farmers could no longer freely dispose of their estates, and incompetent or politically unreliable farmers could be deprived of their property altogether. The Dividend Law of 1934 restricted profits and dividends to no more than 6 per cent, and required enterprises to reinvest any surplus or forfeit it to the state. Capital could not be freely transferred abroad and its use within Germany was restricted by the Supervisory Office for Credit Affairs (set up in December 1934), so that it might be directed to specific national tasks rather than to the most profitable. Political opposition invited expropriation as it did in the Soviet Union. The property of imprisoned communists could be seized. Fritz Thyssen violated no law when he fled to Switzerland, but the regime deemed his flight to be an act of economic sabotage and first sequestrated, then nationalized, his entire industrial fortune.[143] The most extensive and violent expropriation was directed at Germany's Jews, whose assets were either seized, or bought at greatly deflated prices, or taken as collateral against Jewish emigration.[144] The expansion of the state outside Germany's frontiers increased the opportunities for further spoliation and expropriation of goods, wealth and labour power. Private ownership was never a barrier to the predations of the National Socialist state. Hitler's own perception of economics was based on the idea that the well-being of one nation could only be secured by seizing the assets of another. Although the property of most Germans was not directly threatened by the state, the principle of property rights and the security of private ownership were breached in many ways by the racial or national priorities of the regime. The idea of trusteeship gave the state limitless opportunities to substitute national priorities when it saw fit to do so.

The effort to reconstruct and control the Soviet and German economies in the space of a few years was one of the major projects of the two dictatorships. The promised communist society could not be built without economic transformation, and it could not be properly protected without a powerful military establishment. Germany's national revival and imperial expansion were inconceivable without mobilizing an important share of the national economic effort. Yet the decision to insist on the primacy of politics led each regime to try to mobilize and direct economic systems of enormous size, diversity and complexity. The only way to achieve the restructuring was to suspend the market and greatly strengthen the coercive powers of the state. The narrow, productionist view of economics promoted by both Hitler and Stalin offered simple solutions. The actual process of transformation was, in reality, immensely difficult. It provoked widespread argument and resentment, inherent inefficiencies and, in the Soviet case, a record of extraordinary violence against the very men and women who struggled daily to translate the bland dimensions of the 'Plan' into productive reality.

In 1947 the German economist Arnold Müller-Armack, who was one of those who in the 1930s welcomed the idea that planning might iron out the terrible effects of the capitalist business-cycle, recanted his earlier views in a book titled *Managed Economy or Market Economy*. He argued that the experience of the 1930s in Europe showed that experiments in national economic management that dispensed with the mechanism of free prices, as the German and Soviet models both did, inevitably translated into a 'power mechanism of the authoritarian state', whose purpose was 'to mobilize economic resources to the maximum' to meet political goals. The logical outcome was the suppression of consumption in favour of the state; the consumer became 'an insignificant figure'.[145] In 1943 the young Soviet economist, N. Sazonov, submitted a doctoral dissertation titled 'Introduction to a Theory of Economic Policy', in which he too argued that the absence of free prices and independent markets for labour and trade permanently penalized the Soviet consumer. The Central Committee condemned the thesis as a plea for the restoration of capitalism and Sazonov was forced to renounce it publicly.[146]

The suppression of formal markets and the restriction of private consumption was indeed the logic behind the command economies. Under such conditions the Soviet Union was not demonstrably socialist, though it was clearly not capitalist either. National Socialist Germany was not conventionally capitalist, but neither was it a system that could be described as Marxist. Thyssen and Kravchenko were right to see their two systems as hybrids. The command economies were instruments, first and foremost, for the achievement of particular political outcomes, whose utopian character was defined more by the political ambitions of each dictatorship and less by the prevailing mode of production.

II

Military Superpowers

'Again, as in 1914, the parties of bellicose imperialism, the parties of war and revenge are coming to the foreground. Quite clearly things are heading for a new war.'

Josef Stalin, Report to the
Seventeenth Congress of the CPSU, 1934[1]

'Germany will as always have to be regarded as the focus of the Western world against the attacks of Bolshevism. I only want, in these lines, to express my conviction that this crisis cannot and will not fail to occur. The extent of the military development of our resources cannot be too large, nor its pace too swift.'   Adolf Hitler, August 1936[2]

Hitler and Stalin both anticipated a major war between Germany and the Soviet Union. Hitler, like many other Europeans, regarded Bolshevism as the main threat to the survival of western civilization; Stalin believed that the imperialist powers would inevitably be plunged into further wars for markets and resources, and that Germany under Hitler was the most dangerous and predatory imperialist of all. Both dictators wanted to avoid defeat at all costs. Bolshevik victory, Hitler thought, would be worse for Europe than the fall of the Roman Empire.[3] Imperialist war for Stalin was counter-revolution, the loss of everything achieved since 1917. Since both regarded war as an unavoidable historical necessity, each armed against the other. In the process Germany and the Soviet Union became, under dictatorship, the world's first military superpowers.

441

War was one of the principal elements in the world view of both leaders. They had each experienced four years of warfare, but not the same four. Hitler's intense, messianic nationalism was born on the front line in France between 1914 and Germany's eventual defeat in 1918. Stalin had observed this war in distant exile in Siberia, too dangerous a radical to be conscripted into the Tsar's armies; his war experience was shaped by the bitter four-year civil war that followed the Bolshevik revolution. War for Hitler became inseparable from the contest for national survival that he longed to lead. 'What is ultimately decisive in the life of a people,' he wrote in his second, unpublished book in 1928, 'is the will to self-preservation.' Warfare, Hitler argued, was something 'quite in keeping with nature', desirable for its own sake to keep a people vigorous and healthy.[4] In power, ten years later, he watched the German armed forces complete their summer manoeuvres. As he tramped away from the mock battlefield in an evidently elated mood, he announced to his companions that Clausewitz had been right: 'War is the father of all things; every generation has to go into war once.'[5]

Stalin's view of war was shaped by Lenin's insistence that war and revolutionary politics were inseparable in the modern age. 'Out of the universal ruin caused by the war,' wrote Lenin in 1920, 'a world-wide revolutionary crisis is arising which cannot end otherwise than in a proletarian revolution and its victory.'[6] The party line throughout the 1920s and 1930s insisted that imperialist wars would recur, and that these would provide the final opportunity to complete the revolutionary transformation of the modern world. In a letter written to Maxim Gorky in 1930, Stalin explained that 'questions of war cannot be severed from questions of politics, of which war is an expression'. He continued: 'we are for liberating, anti-imperialist, revolutionary wars', even if such wars 'are not only not exempt from "the horrors of bloodshed" but even abound in them'.[7] The many war scares detected by the Soviet leadership between the civil war and the German invasion of 1941 reflected not simply a misplaced paranoia, but a central element in the revolutionary ideology of Leninism. Stalin's own civil war experience, in which he acted as party representative in some of the key campaigns, stamped in his mind the self-evident connection between revolutionary triumph and uncompromising violence, with profound consequences for Soviet society. Western intervention in the civil war demonstrated that imperialism would never allow the Soviet Union to flourish unmolested. Stalin's was one of the loudest voices prophesying doom. In the most famous war-scare, in the summer of 1927, Stalin announced that there could be no doubt that 'a new imperialist war' was pending: 'the real and actual threat of a new war in general, and of a war against the Soviet Union in particular'.[8]

There existed, nonetheless, a very real difference between Hitler's and Stalin's view of war. Hitler longed for it, not simply as revenge for defeat in 1918 and the punitive peace settlement that followed, but because war would provide the ultimate justification for his self-appointed dictatorial mission, to forge a tough new community of Germans, capable of carving out and defending a new empire and slaying the Jewish-Bolshevik dragon. War was a necessary act of historical regeneration and redemption. For Stalin, war was something imposed by others bent on the destruction of the infant socialist state; the appropriate posture was defence. Despite all attempts to demonstrate that Stalin planned wars of revolutionary conquest in the 1930s and 1940s, the balance of evidence still shows that Stalin's outlook was defensive and reactive. The Soviet preference was for wars between imperial states, which was why the Soviet–German non-aggression pact of August 1939, which apparently defied the logic of the confrontation between communism and fascism, was preferred by Stalin to fighting Germany alongside the western powers. In the late 1920s the Soviet leadership had even speculated on a coming war between the two principal capitalist powers, Britain and the United States, beside which the First World War 'will seem like child's play'.[9]

The different postures, one by nature aggressive and predatory, the second defensive, produced a similar response during the 1930s, as both Germany and the Soviet Union became dominated by military preparations and the mobilization of society along paramilitary lines. Both dictatorships were stamped with a pervasive popular militarism, which existed alongside and helped to support the giant programmes of military preparation ordered in the 1930s. It is not mere accident that both Hitler and Stalin chose to be seen in public wearing simple military-style dress. Stalin's plain high-collar tunic and knee-length boots were modelled on the uniform of the new Soviet army, unadorned and braidless. Hitler wore a simple SA uniform with its distinctive shade of brown; at times he donned more elaborate costume, as he came to assume the mythical image of the people's commander-in-chief, but he was no military peacock like Göring. Wearing uniform was a deliberate choice, indicative of the two men's differing beliefs that revolutionary war, or the struggle for national existence, was in some sense a permanent state of being.

Nor is it an accident that both dictators came to assume the supreme command of their armed forces – Hitler in February 1938, Stalin in June 1941. Though there were motives that derived from distrust of the independence and ambition of the military elite in both states, the assumption of supreme command was entirely consistent with the nature of the wider authority that both men exercised. This responsibility was not merely decorative. Hitler and Stalin assumed supreme command in order to dominate the processes of military and strategic decision-making, and to prevent others from doing so in their stead. The logic of the dictatorship both men practised made it inevitable that in war, as in peace, there would be no proxies. This was the logic also of popular mobilization under both leaders. The explicit militarism of the dictatorships made war-making seem the natural prerogative of leaders whose credentials were, in reality, political and civilian, and whose view of war was shaped by political rather than military priorities.

No one observing the military position of the Soviet Union or Germany in the 1920s would have described either as anything other than a second-rank military state. Both states suffered from a degree of military debilitation that excluded them temporarily from the definition of a great power. The transformation from military enfeeblement to superpower status was achieved at striking speed in the 1930s, but the seeds of that alteration lie in the first difficult post-war years.

German weakness was a direct consequence of defeat in 1918. Under the terms of the Treaty of Versailles signed in June the following year, Germany was effectively disarmed. The large pre-war army was reduced to a policing force of 100,000 men, all of whom had to be long-serving soldiers to prevent Germany from training more men by changing the 100,000 regularly. The German General Staff was disbanded; the leading military academies were shut; the military infrastructure of fortifications, barracks, airfields and stores was destroyed or closed down. Germany was allowed only limited weapons of defence: a number of light guns and small vehicles, a tiny navy of no more than six small capital ships and thirty lesser vessels, but no submarines or marine aircraft; and no air force at all. The Ministry of War was rechristened the Ministry of Defence. These etiolated forces were permitted under the terms of the treaty to perform only two tasks – to maintain domestic order and to police German frontiers. The victorious Allies kept weapons inspectors in Germany until 1926 to verify compliance, and stationed troops in western Germany until 1930. German staff exercises conducted in the early 1930s indicated that Germany could not defend herself even against her smaller but now more heavily armed neighbours created by the peace settlement, Poland and Czechoslovakia.

The Soviet Union could not defeat Poland either. In 1920 Soviet armies tried to capitalize on the successful rout of counter-revolutionary White forces by pushing on into territory formerly belonging to the Tsarist empire, but now claimed by Poland. The Soviet forces led by Mikhail Tukhachevsky were defeated by the Polish army in front of Warsaw, thanks in part to serious strategic misjudgement on the part of Stalin himself, who, as the party's military representative, refused to release the troops under his control to support the offensive. The Red Army remained in control of the rest of the area that became the Soviet Union in 1924, but with little prospect of carrying the revolution into Europe it was largely demobilized, leaving a poorly disciplined rump of 600,000 men out of the 5.3 million fielded in the civil war. Of the 87,000 officers trained during the conflict, 30,000 were dead and only 25,000 remained in post.[10] In January 1924 a special commission was appointed to examine the Soviet Union's defensive position. Its findings concluded that the Red Army was 'not a reliable fighting force'.[11] Under the leadership of Mikhail Frunze, appointed Commissar for the Army and Navy in January 1925 in succession to Trotsky, a new conscription law was introduced to try to get more young Soviet men, and women, into the armed forces, while improvements were made in officer training and in the disciplining and provisioning of the rank-and-file. Morale, however, remained a problem in an army whose citizen character in the civil war had bred habits of familiarity between men and officers and a lack of respect for military spick-and-span. The armed forces had little idea of what strategic profile they should adopt beyond the obvious injunction that it was their task to defend the revolutionary state. Mobilization planning and staff evaluation were in their infancy. Above all, weapons remained scarce. The air force had an establishment of twenty-five squadrons for the whole Soviet area; the army mustered only twenty-eight active, and under-strength, divisions.[12] Tanks and vehicles were few in number and rudimentary in nature. On May Days in the 1920s Red Army men paraded through Red Square on bicycles.

Both states nonetheless had lengthy and elaborate military traditions on which to draw. The enforced disarmament of Germany in the 1920s could not prevent the former military elite from reflecting upon defeat and its lessons, nor from preparing for the day when Germany could recreate the military establishment it enjoyed before 1918. In 1925 one of their number, the First World War army commander Field Marshal Paul von Hindenburg, was popularly elected President of the Reich, and conservative military circles began to explore the possibilities for limited, closet rearmament. A network of informal contacts, based upon the millions of former soldiers recruited into veterans' leagues, kept German military traditions alive among the wider public. In the Soviet Union the shadow of the former Imperial Army lay heavily over the new revolutionary force. At the end of the civil war around one-third of Red Army officers were former specialists (*voenspetsy*) from the Tsarist officer corps; 83 per cent of all divisional and army corps commanders were former Tsarist soldiers.[13] Demands from Bolshevik party radicals for a pure militia system, a genuine 'people's army', were defeated; a decision was made to build a professional armed force that borrowed from the pre-revolutionary army's rich fund of organizational and doctrinal experience. The longest-serving chief-of-staff of the Red Army between 1920 and 1941 was a former Tsarist staff officer, Boris Shaposhnikov, who held the office from 1928 to 1931, and again from 1937 to 1940. In between he remained an important voice in shaping the doctrine and structure of Soviet forces and, above all, in creating a revived General Staff after the long period of revolutionary hostility to rank and authority.[14] He was also one of the few senior army officers that Stalin liked or trusted.

The military leaderships in both states were united in the 1920s by the desire to explain the defeats they had suffered in the First World War, and to avoid any prospect of their repetition. The answers both arrived at were broadly similar: neither state had prepared adequately for what was now described as 'total war'. Military thinking before 1914 had not excluded the possibility of long wars of national attrition. In 1895, a Russian businessman, Ivan Bloch, published a widely read treatise on war in the future, in which he suggested that conflicts between modern industrial states would inevitably degenerate into crude slogging matches so massively destructive and costly that war was all but unthinkable. It was translated into German in 1899.[15] German military thinkers were divided between those who thought in terms of the single, decisive battle of annihilation, and more cautious voices who detected in modern weaponry the possibility of a longer war of attrition.[16] But in 1914 both the Russian and German armies had sought a quick conflict and decisive battles. Instead came a long and devastating war. The disintegration of the Russian war effort in revolution in 1917 was followed a year later by the collapse of German resistance. The post-mortem on defeat in both states focused on the failure to sustain the home front, or to comprehend from the start that modern war was not confined to armies but involved the entire social and economic fabric of the warring state.

This realization shaped the whole period of military revival in the inter-war years. In German military circles the concept of total war became common currency. General Erich Ludendorff, the man who effectively ran the German war effort by 1918, coined the term '*totaler Krieg*' in his post-war memoirs. Ludendorff argued that total war 'literally demands the entire strength of the nation'. Modern war, unlike previous wars, was about the most fundamental issue of all, national survival or destruction. The nation, he continued, must put 'its mental, moral, physical, and material forces in the service of war'.[17] General Wilhelm Groener, Minister of Defence in the Weimar Republic from 1928 to 1932, helped to shape an attitude to war that reflected the changing social and economic reality of industrialized war and mass armies. 'It is necessary,' he wrote in a memorandum on Germany's strategic future, 'to organize the entire strength of the

447

people for fighting and working.' War was now about nothing less than 'the future of the race'.[18]

Soviet thinking about war drew similar conclusions from the failure of the Tsarist state before 1917 and the communist victory in the civil war in 1920. Lenin argued that in order 'to wage war correctly, a strong organized home front is needed'.[19] War was about the survival of the revolution. Soviet leaders took it for granted that war would have to be fought using the whole of Soviet society and the economy, grimly defending their socialist birthright as soldier and worker. When Shaposhnikov published a study of the new Red Army General Staff in 1927, he argued that future wars would be vast, mass-mobilizing wars, which could no longer be the responsibility of the armed forces: 'war preparation and war itself is an affair . . . of the state. Today, strategy encompasses both the use of the armed forces and all other state resources.'[20] By this time it had become axiomatic in the Soviet Union that war with imperialist-capitalist states would be long, large-scale and economically draining. 'The whole of industry,' ran one report in 1927, 'must direct its efforts to supplying war.' Despite its ultimate failure, the German military command economy developed after 1914 was taken as the Soviet model.[21] In 1926 Tukhachevsky, now a very youthful chief-of-staff, asked his staff to prepare a comprehensive study of the nature of modern industrialized conflict. The result, a 735-page study titled *Future War*, was issued in May 1928. Its central recommendation was the desirability of preparing industry and the workforce for military mobilization on the largest scale and well before the onset of hostilities.[22]

In both states preparations began in the 1920s to confront the daunting, morbid prospect of a second total war. In Germany this had to be done in secret. An innocent 'Statistical Society' was established in 1925, which masked a network of contacts between the military and German industry for the purpose of initiating businessmen into the new thinking about total mobilization and the economic front in war. By the early 1930s, the defence establishment in Germany was slowly infiltrating ideas and personalities into the civilian ministries in order to create the skeleton of a future mobilization of the home front. To get around the persistent restrictions on weapons development imposed by the Versailles settlement, the German army took a radical decision to collaborate with the Red Army on Soviet soil, far away from the Allied verification teams. Under the terms of a treaty signed in Berlin in 1926, German forces were allowed to establish experimental centres for tank, chemical weapons and aviation research in the Soviet Union. There followed regular exchanges of personnel. Soviet officers were sent on staff courses in Germany, where they picked up sophisticated ideas about how to wage total war; German officers, travelling incognito in civilian clothes, experimented at spartan bases on the Soviet steppe with the weapons that later became the spearhead of the German assault across the same bleak landscape in 1941. Both sides maintained a wary collaboration, aware, perhaps, that they might one day be using these lessons against each other. Secret collaboration finally ended only after Hitler became Chancellor in 1933.[23]

Large-scale and systematic preparation for waging total war became a reality only under dictatorship. Hitler and Stalin played a pivotal role in turning their two respective states into military superpowers in less than a decade. Though they did so for different reasons, both dictators shared the view of their armed forces that a future conflict between great states would call on the entire military, social and economic resources of the nation. Their willingness to accept the terrible cost of total war reflected the nature of the stakes they saw themselves playing for – German national survival on the one hand, the future of the Soviet revolution on the other.

Hitler's view of the kind of war Germany must fight was shaped by his argument that war was a function of the struggle for racial predominance and national self-assertion that his dictatorship represented. This was a conception that was, at root, economic and social as much as military. In his so-called 'Second Book', Hitler took as his premise that all history is 'the course of a people's struggle for existence'. The struggle was fundamentally about access to economic resources and the seizing of territory appropriate to the size of the race. War was 'the ultimate weapon with which a people fights for its daily bread'. Hitler's answer to the crisis of the race that followed the limitations imposed in the Versailles settlement was to restore the German people's 'inner strength' and then to embark on military campaigns to win the resources needed. This meant mobilizing not just a military arm, but 'the whole strength of the people'. Great

statesmen, Hitler reasoned, could never be content with 'limited preparation for war'. War was something integral to the 'fundamental,
well-grounded, permanent development of a people'.[24] When, eight
years later and in power, he wrote the memorandum that produced
the Second Four-Year Plan, he argued that military preparation for
war had to be large-scale and overriding. The army he envisaged was
to be *the premier army in the world*, and the development of German
resources for war *cannot be too large, nor its pace too swift* (italics
in original). Economic and social priorities were to be defined by the
demands of war preparation: 'all other desires are unimportant'.[25]

Stalin's view of war also had an irreducible economic core. This was
not just good Marxism. When he addressed graduates from the Red
Army Academies in May 1935, he told them that the Soviet Union had
had to face a critical choice, either to remain in the medieval darkness
of small-scale production and primitive technology, or to build up
modern heavy industry as the foundation for the defence of the revolution. Stalin reminded them that the resources used to build up the
modern economy and Soviet military strength could have been used
to make the daily life of each Soviet citizen more pleasant:

But with such a 'plan' we would not now have a metallurgical industry, or a
machine-building industry, or tractors and automobiles, or aeroplanes and
tanks. We would have found ourselves unarmed in face of foreign foes. We
would have undermined the foundations of Socialism in our country.
We would have fallen captive to the bourgeoisie.[26]

The decision to link the economic modernization of the Soviet Union
with its military ability to defend the revolution dated back to the
beginnings of the First Five-Year Plan in 1927–8. But the critical
turning-point came in 1932–3 when Stalin, who had initially favoured
a more modest rate of military expansion at a pace the economy
could manage, threw his weight behind programmes of large-scale
militarization and the economic restructuring necessary to achieve it.
In a speech to the Central Committee in 1933, Stalin expanded on the
theme that the production drive was fundamentally about the defence
of the revolution: 'That is why the Party was obliged to spur on the
country to create in the USSR the basis of industrialization, which is
the foundation of her power.'[27]

Why the change came in the early 1930s is not entirely clear. When Tukhachevsky proposed in 1930, on the basis of the studies in *Future War*, a colossal programme of rearmament – a 260-division army, 40,000 aircraft, 50,000 tanks – to secure the basis for mass industrialized warfare, Stalin rejected it on the grounds that the plan was unrealistic 'red militarism'.[28] Yet a year later Stalin appointed Tukhachevsky Chief of Armaments, and extensive new plans were laid down for Soviet rearmament. Military expenditure in the Second Five-Year Plan rose sharply, though its full extent was disguised, as it was in the first rearmament plans under Hitler, by budgetary sleight-of-hand. Defence outlays in 1931 were 1.8 billion roubles. In 1932 they totalled 4 billion, and by 1936 14.8 billion.[29] Rearmament on this scale required, in turn, a further strengthening of Soviet machinery and materials production, and higher levels of investment in heavy engineering industries and basic chemical production. One explanation for the shift of priorities lies in the deteriorating international situation following the Japanese invasion and occupation of Manchuria in 1931. Japan was a fiercely anti-communist state with imperial ambitions and a large army, and, with the seizure of Manchuria, a long common frontier with the Soviet Union. There were revived fears that imperialist powers, East and West, might use war against the Soviet Union as a form of crisis-management during the world slump. This explains, for example, the decision to relocate much of the new heavy industry in the Second Plan to safer sites in central Russia, and the decision to create defensive buffer zones along the Soviet Union's vulnerable frontiers, which were denuded of their populations and turned into high-security no-man's-lands.[30] The Soviet leadership saw the threat of a new war as a very real one. Stalin accepted the prevailing concerns, and made possible the decision to begin a sharp expansion of the defence sector.[31]

European rearmament in the 1930s is usually presented as a race between Germany and the western powers. In reality, the driving force of rearmament was an early version of the Cold War, a military race between Germany and the Soviet Union. Hitler's 1936 memorandum opened with reflections on the 'menacing extent' of Red Army development; Stalin's report to the Seventeenth Party Congress in 1934 highlighted the particular threat of German fascism and its deliberate

451

'policy of war'.[32] Stalin did not think the threat from western imperialism was very immediate in the mid-1930s, but the menace of German and Japanese imperialism was obtrusive and growing. Hitler, too, expected to conduct his foreign policy in the belief that the western powers could be overtaken militarily and be forced to accept German treaty revision and the domination of eastern Europe, as the only means to keep Soviet communism away from Europe.[33] It was no accident that when the German Air Force began to develop a long-range bomber in the mid-1930s, it was nicknamed the 'Ural Bomber'.[34]

The statistical record of the military build-up in both states in the 1930s reveals an extensive remilitarization achieved in a remarkably short period of time. This was not an entirely smooth process. German rearmament slowed down in 1936–7 as it competed for resources with the expansion of the industrial base (steel, chemicals, machine-tools, etc.) necessary for future war. Soviet military production slowed in 1934–6 under similar constraints, but the trajectory was relentlessly upward. Between 1933 and 1938 Germany and the Soviet Union spent approximately the same amounts on the defence sector (£2.9 billion and £2.8 billion respectively); in contrast Britain spent only £1.2 billion and France £1.1 billion.[35] The ratio of military spending to national product also rose sharply, reaching 17 per cent in Germany in 1938 and 13 per cent in the Soviet Union (see Table 11.1). These are exceptional peacetime figures by the standard of the rest of the twentieth century. On the eve of the First World War Germany spent approximately 3 per cent of the national product on defence, the Tsarist empire around 5 per cent. In the 1960s, Cold War expenditure in the West averaged around 6 per cent of the national product.[36]

In terms of weapons and manpower both military systems were transformed from their relatively disarmed positions of the 1920s. In the Soviet Union the armed forces grew from 562,000 in 1931 to 4.2 million in 1940. Germany's 100,000-man army of 1933 became an army of more than 2 million by 1939. Both had larger numbers of trained reserves.[37] The Soviet aircraft industry turned out 860 aircraft in 1931, but 10,382 in 1939; Soviet tank output was 740 in 1931 (many no more than an armoured car with a light gun), but in 1939 it was 2,950 heavy tanks of advanced design and performance. Artillery output increased a hundred-fold between 1931 and 1939. Much of

Table 11.1: Defence Expenditure in Germany and the Soviet Union 1928–1939

Budget year	Germany (bn RM)	Soviet Union (bn rbls)
1928	0.75	0.88
1929	0.68	1.05
1930	0.67	1.20*
1931	0.61	1.79
1932	0.62	4.03**
1933	0.75	4.30**
1934	4.09**	5.40**
1935	5.49**	8.20
1936	10.27**	14.80
1937	10.96**	17.48
1938	17.25	27.04
1939	38.00	40.88

* Figure for 1930 is an estimate.
** These figures include expenditure outside the regular budget. Special armaments bills (so called 'Mefo-bills') covered the additional German expenditure. These totalled 2.1 billion marks in 1934, 2.7 billion in 1935, 4.45 billion in 1936 and 2.7 billion in 1937. Soviet expenditure for 1932–4 includes additional non-budget funds, which remained, like the 'Mefo-bills', secret.

Note: Soviet budget figures do not reflect the high level of inflation. Calculated in prices of 1937 the figure for 1928 is 1.7 billion, that for 1937 17.0 billion and in 1940 45.2 billion. There was price deflation in Germany between 1929 and 1936, so the expenditure figures in those years are higher in real terms.

Source: R.W. Davies 'Defence spending and defence industry in the 1930s' in J. Barber and M. Harrison (eds) *The Soviet Defence-Industry Complex from Stalin to Khrushchev* (London, 2000), pp. 73, 81; Bundesarchiv-Berlin, R2/21776–81, Reichsfinanzministerium, 'Entwicklung der Ausgaben in der Rechnungsjahren 1934–1939', 17 July 1939. Higher figures for total defence outlays are given in BA R3102/3602, Statistisches Reichsamt, 'Die gesteuerte Wehrwirtschaft 1933–1939', 25 February 1947, p. 135, where the total for 1932/3–1938/9 is given as 57.8 billion marks, against the 49.3 billion in the Finance Ministry files.

this increase came during the years 1937–9, when the Third Five-Year Plan laid the basis for the heavily armed superpower of the 1940s. In Germany, too, the level of military output rose steadily after 1933, and then more rapidly in 1937–9, once the industrial resources and new military infrastructure were in place. The 368 light aircraft of 1933 became the 8,295 high-quality bombers, fighters and trainers produced in 1939 by the world's best-endowed aviation industry; 5,667 military vehicles produced in 1934 grew to 66,930 by 1939.[38] Plans laid down late in 1938 promised to create a huge air force by 1942, with a core of 4,300 heavy and medium bombers for long-range bombing. In October 1938 Hermann Göring, in his capacity as head of the Four-Year Plan, announced Hitler's decision to try to raise armaments production overall by a factor of three.[39] In both the Soviet Union and Germany the target date for the completion of the military build-up was the period 1943–5.

Significantly, the later phase of rearmament was designed to provide weapons that would give the two states a global reach. For much of the 1930s the navy was the Cinderella service in both states. Modern navies, based on large ocean-going vessels, were expensive. Little effort had been made to revive the imperial Russian navy after 1917, and the German navy had been reduced to a rump by disarmament. When large-scale rearmament began the navies were given only a small share of the enhanced military budget. This situation changed thanks to the direct intervention of the two dictators. In late 1935 Stalin backed a decision to create what was called a 'Big Ocean-Going Fleet'. Until then the navy had confined itself to planning small-scale naval warfare in the Baltic or the Black Sea, using submarines and small, fast vessels. However, with Stalin's support, the idea of a fleet of major surface vessels was resuscitated, capable of intervening in eastern Asia or the Mediterranean. The plans were approved in May 1936, and work began over the next three years on a fleet of twelve cruisers, four battleships and two battlecruisers. In August 1939 the plans were revised for an even larger fleet of fifteen new battleships, sixteen battlecruisers and twenty-eight new cruisers, to be completed by 1947, though all the plans proved to be well beyond the capacity of Soviet dockyards.[40] In 1938 Hitler also began to think about Germany's wider strategic requirements once her status as a great power was restored, and encouraged those in the German navy who still favoured traditional big-ship naval strategy to present a plan. The subsequent Z-Plan (Z for *Ziel* or 'goal') was approved in January 1939 for

6 battleships, 4 aircraft carriers, 8 heavy cruisers and 233 submarines, to be completed in stages by 1949.[41]

The delusions of superpower strategy also fuelled ideas about inter-continental aircraft for attacks on the United States. In the late 1930s the German Messerschmitt company worked on a long-range bomber, the Me 264, with a range of 6,000 kilometres carrying a one-tonne bomb, nicknamed the 'America Bomber'; in the late 1940s Stalin ordered the development of a long-range bomber, the Mya-4 'Bison', capable of attacking American targets from bases in the Soviet Union, though it failed to meet its specification.[42] By this stage Stalin was on the point of developing nuclear weapons to fight the Cold War.

The raw statistics of military production tell only a part of the story. In both dictatorships the construction of what is now called the 'military-industrial complex' was accompanied by large investments in the raw materials of war-making, such as steel and chemicals, and in the numerous consumer goods, from uniforms to bicycles, which every armed force needs in order to function. These indirect forms of rearmament have already been explored in Chapter 10, but the scale of these requirements is worth reiterating. By May 1939 German industry reported that one-fifth of all workers in the raw-material sector, one-third of all construction workers, and 29 per cent of all manufacturing labour were working directly on orders from the defence sector.[43] Investment in future war-making capacity between 1937 and 1939 amounted to an estimated two-thirds of all industrial investment; Four-Year Plan programmes alone cost 5.5 billion marks, more than the value of all investment in heavy industry since 1933. During 1938–9 shortages of the appropriate labour for the defence sector prompted retraining schemes for 736,000 workers, sponsored by the Four-Year Plan and the Labour Front; a further half-a-million were retrained by industrial firms themselves.[44] The priorities of the Soviet Third Five-Year Plan, begun in 1938, were unabashedly stra-tegic. The output of the defence sector industries increased from 7.7 billion roubles in 1937 to 25.9 billion in 1940, growing at 41 per cent a year – an exceptional figure for peacetime. Investment in the defence sectors totalled 1.6 billion roubles in 1936, but the Plan projected investment totalling 21.9 billion for the years 1938–42, and substantial increases in the output of machine tools, electricity supply, vehicles and chemicals, on which future war-making depended.[45] In both Germany and the Soviet Union hundreds of thousands of workers, many of them conscripted or assigned from local camps, toiled away building huge physical fortifications. The German 'Westwall', along the frontier with France, was designed to protect the German rear while Germany conquered the East; the 'Stalin Line', built along the whole of the Soviet Union's exposed western border, was designed to keep Germany out.[46]

The scale of these military preparations can be gauged from the plans for wartime mobilization. In Germany the entire population was viewed as potential fighters or workers in a future total war effort. In June 1939 at a meeting of the Reich Defence Council, set up in 1938 under Göring's chairmanship to co-ordinate the whole military and economic effort, new guidelines were approved for the exploitation of the German population in wartime. The total active population capable of mobilization was calculated at 43.5 million, out of a population (including Austria and the recently acquired Sudetenland) of 79 million (only the very young, the old and 11 million women with children under 14 years of age were excluded). From the 26 million men, 7 million would be claimed for the armed forces if war broke out. The rest, and 17 million women, were to work in industry, agriculture and essential services. Working women were to be transferred from shops and offices to industry (although this process was already under way in the late 1930s, as women volunteered or were drafted into industrial labour); one-third of the men working on the land would be drafted into the army, and their place taken by women. Even the concentration camp prisoners, approximately 20,000 in number, were to be forced to work for the German war effort, in small workshops to be set up inside the camps.[47] Throughout the discussions in 1938 and 1939 about the nature of Germany's war effort, it was assumed that the whole nation would fight as one, some at the fighting front, others in the workshops and on the farms. In May 1939 Hitler warned the commanders-in-chief of the armed forces that the government had to be prepared 'for a war of ten to fifteen years' duration', for which 'the unrestricted use of all resources is essential'.[48]

In the Soviet Union plans for future war were likewise expressed in terms of national mobilization. Industry was subject to extensive preparatory planning for conversion to war production if war broke out, with general-purpose machine tool equipment capable of being used to produce tractors one day, but tanks the next. Military mobilization anticipated the raising of an army of 5 million men in the first weeks of war, to add to the existing peacetime force of conscripts (5.2 million in 1941). Successive conscription laws in 1936 and 1939 increased the age-range for recruitment to cover all men of nineteen to fifty years of age. The millions of men in the reserve had to undertake ten hours of compulsory training a month, and each year an additional 650,000 men were pushed through training schools. From Soviet agriculture 730,000 horses and 30,000 tractors were to follow the millions of peasant workers into the Red Army. The MP-1 mobilization plan for industry projected an annual output of more than 60 billion roubles-worth of war-related production, more than double the peacetime level.[49] The terms of the vast conflict fought on the Eastern Front during the Second World War were set well before 1941, by two states in which war was seen as a contest between the sinews of a whole society. In the end, to sustain this vision of total war, the Soviet Union mobilized 29 million soldiers between 1941 and 1945. Germany mobilized 18 million, supported by millions more from her allies and from the conquered territories. These figures dwarfed the mobilization efforts of the other great powers.[50]

Why did both dictatorships strive to become superpowers in the 1930s? The obvious explanation – that they feared for their international security – on its own is not sufficient, for they could have rearmed more slowly and on a smaller scale to be able to defend themselves against external threats. Both shared the idea that future war would be like the Great War, only perhaps worse, but this view was common outside Germany and the Soviet Union, and prompted widespread pacifism in Europe after 1919. What was distinctive about the German and Soviet dictatorships was a pervasive militarism derived not from the ambitions or influence of the armed forces, but from the very nature of the two regimes. The dictatorships were military metaphors, founded to fight political war.

War both gave rise to the dictatorships, and shaped their political purposes. The Bolshevik revolution was made possible by the collapse of the Tsarist war effort, and was secured and consolidated only through four years of bitter civil war. Stalin, and most of the leading cohort around him in the 1930s, had experienced that war at first hand. The triumph of the revolution and the defeat of bourgeois enemies were regarded as a historically necessary contest, in which no moral scruples or humanitarian instincts should deflect the dedicated communists from their bloody cause. Throughout the decades that followed, Soviet communists perceived themselves to be permanently embattled against the remnants of the bourgeoisie. It was a system always apparently on the edge of renewed war against the counter-revolution.

The Hitler dictatorship was a direct product of German defeat in 1918 and the violent political civil war between nationalists and the German left that followed it. Nationalist veterans fought a merciless war against German communism; the violence continued spasmodically throughout the 1920s, but resurfaced in the economic crisis of the late 1920s and early 1930s. Hitler's self-proclaimed manifest destiny was to turn German defeat in 1918 into German victory over the forces that he believed had subverted her war effort, and continued to throttle German revival in the 1920s. His eventual triumph in 1933 was presented as if it were a consequence of this struggle, and it opened the way to the prospect of revenge for 1918. The Third Reich was at war from the start against communism and the Jews; at some point this civil war was expected to grow into a larger European conflict along the same political lines. Hitler represented all those nationalist elements for whom 1918 had been only a postponement. 'Peace must be subordinated to the requirements of war', ran an editorial in the military magazine *Deutsche Wehr*. 'War is the secret ruler of our century; peace no longer signifies more than a simple armistice between two wars.'[51]

The two dictatorships created metaphors of permanent conflict as a means to legitimize the regime. The result was a widespread militarization of political life, in which distinctions between the military and civilian spheres became blurred and indeterminate amidst the prevailing idioms of war. The root of militarized politics lay in the 1920s. In the Soviet Union the revolutionary struggles were carried out by revolutionaries in uniform – 'the people armed', as Lenin put it.[52] Leon

Trotsky, Commissar for the Red Army until 1925, treated workers during the civil war as if they were subject to martial law: no 'desertion from labour', 'tireless energy in work – just as on the march, just as in battle'. The ideal Bolshevik was the worker-warrior, building and defending socialism simultaneously. May Day became early on an occasion for military ritual, rather than a festival of pacifism, internationalism and proletarian solidarity. 'Not a demonstration against militarism,' wrote Trotsky before May Day 1920, 'but a strengthening of our army.' Throughout the 1920s, May Day and the celebration of the anniversary of the revolution in November became opportunities to make statements about Soviet power in the face of the perennial threat of counter-revolution. 'Wars are profoundly inevitable so long as class society exists,' wrote Trotsky two years later. 'For us war is the continuation of revolution.'[53]

The idea that the revolutionary state was organized to supervise a permanent state of civil war, in which poor peasants and workers stood on the frontline against class enemies, was illustrated by the terms in which the struggle to eliminate the kulaks was conducted in the Soviet countryside from late 1929. 'In order to oust the kulaks as a class,' wrote Stalin, 'the resistance of the class must be smashed in open battle.'[54] This was a war for food, as well as social reorganization, and the campaign had strong echoes of the civil war regimentation of peasant producers and the punitive expeditions to seize hoarded grain. In November 1929 the regime called for 25,000 volunteers from among the most trustworthy and communist of the industrial workforce, who could bring the programme of collectivization to the villages. More than 70,000 volunteered; 27,219 were selected as the so-called '25,000ers' on the basis of their political loyalty and proletarian origins. Many were veterans of the civil war. One recruit, sent off to the area he had fought in ten years previously, recalled his earlier fighting: 'Here now before me arises an image of '19, when I was in this same district, climbing along snow drifts with rifle in hand and blizzard raging, like now. I feel that I am young again.'[55] Many of the workers accepted the language of mobilization and frontline service. One named his collective farm 'Death to Kulaks'. The poet Vladimir Mayakovsky penned the march of the 25,000ers: 'Onward 25! Onward 25! . . . The enemy advances, it's time to finish off/This band of priests and kulaks./To the front, 25!/Onward 25!'[56] The high death toll on both sides showed that talk of battle was anything but mere rhetoric. The war on the kulaks was unfinished business from the civil war.

The militarization of German politics in the 1920s represented unfinished business as well. The revolution and civil conflict in Germany after 1918 produced a political war of particular savagery, unknown in the political world of pre-war imperial Germany. To keep the communist revolution at bay, the government in 1919 recruited returning veterans to help keep order. These militia units, known as Freikorps, were given free rein to terrorize the working population. Fiercely nationalist, brutalized by war, the volunteers murdered and tortured communists, fought against Polish encroachments on German territory, and assassinated those they regarded as enemies of the people, including the German Foreign Minister, Walther Rathenau, who was gunned down in 1922 on his way to work by two former members from one of the most notorious and vicious groups, the Reinhardt Brigade.[57] Though the Freikorps were disbanded, with difficulty, in 1922, the parties of the nationalist right developed paramilitary political militia to keep alive the struggle on the streets. Included in their number was the National Socialist Sturm-Abteilung (SA), created by the fledgling party in 1921.

The growth of political 'armies' in the 1920s was characteristic of all German political parties. The social-democrats organized the *Reichsbanner* as a uniformed wing of the movement, the communists the Red Front, echoing the Soviet sense of class war as civil war. 'War is for us not a matter of "once upon a time",' wrote the communist Johannes Becher in 1929, 'but a living reality in our midst.'[58] The National Socialist SA was 60,000-strong by the late 1920s, 450,000-strong by 1932. It was organized on strictly military lines, with uniforms, ranks and insignia. SA men saw themselves as political soldiers in the frontline against Marxism, and they fought a murderous street war against the left throughout the 1920s. Alongside the political armies, German men could join nationalist youth groups or veterans' associations which encouraged paramilitary activities – the *Jungdeutscher Orden*, the *Wehrwolf*, the *Burgerwehr*, and many more. The largest was the Steel Helmet (*Stahlhelm*), which recruited around

300,000 former soldiers by the mid-1920s, half a million by 1933. Pictures of its many ceremonies honouring the dead of the war, or demonstrating on nationalist anniversaries, confirm that in Germany popular militarism flourished defiantly in the face of Germany's enforced disarmament.[59]

The rise of German popular militarism was more overt and autonomous than it was in the Soviet Union. Though there were pacifist movements in Weimar Germany, and a strong cultural rejection of war (though not of violence) among the German artistic avant-garde, millions of Germans kept alive their *Fronterlebnis* (experience of the front) as a shared identity of comradeship and sacrifice in a disintegrating world. Many came to accept the more dangerous assertion among a generation of radical conservative intellectuals that war was both natural and the one truly authentic human experience. 'In the beginning was war', wrote the chief philosopher of the conservative revolt, Oswald Spengler.[60] The writers that followed Spengler revelled in a fatalistic, nihilistic acceptance of man's primitive urge to test himself in battle. They celebrated the idea that life was raw, unmediated struggle; they interpreted the violence of combat as a sublime expression of the human will. 'We are not bourgeois, we are sons of war and civil wars,' wrote Ernst Jünger in a denunciation of the new republican age, 'and only when this spectacle circling in the void is swept away can there unfold within us that which is natural, elemental, truly wild, primitive in speech.' Wilhelm von Schramm longed for war, 'the solemn, elevated and bloody game', which, since the beginning of time, 'has been making men of men'.[61] It is possible to exaggerate the influence of the many other radical nationalists like Jünger or von Schramm, who dreamt of war as a purification of the spirit, but there is no doubt that Germany before Hitler was obsessed with war and military life. Millions of Germans wore uniforms voluntarily in the 1920s. For every book on peace written in the early 1930s, there were twenty written on war.[62] In the four years before Hitler became Chancellor, German politics descended into a wave of savage violence that lasted until the consolidation of the dictatorship in 1934. Popular militarism traded on a shared exaltation of war and violence as the instrument of national redemption.

Militarism was not an invention of the two dictatorships, but it was exploited widely under Stalin and Hitler in a variety of cultural and social contexts. Soviet culture in the 1930s was permeated by images and themes drawn from memories of the civil war and the idea of sacrifice on the battlefields of revolution. *The Last Decisive*, a play by Vsevolod Vishnevsky, ran for several seasons in the early 1930s. Its final scene depicts a group of twenty-seven Soviet soldiers and sailors defending the border against an imperialist enemy. The theatre fills with the roar of artillery and the rat-tat-tat of machine-gun fire; twenty-six of the twenty-seven are wiped out. A lone survivor staggers to a blackboard, on which he scrawls '162,000,000 minus 27 leaves 161,999,973' before dying too. A man with a commanding voice then steps out onto the stage and bellows: 'Who in the audience is in the army?' A few stand. Next he shouts, 'Who is in the reserve?' A larger number stands. Finally he asks, 'Who will defend the Soviet Union?' Everyone else leaps to attention. The giant voice concludes with the words: 'The performance is finished. The continuation – on the front!'[63]

Combat, heroism and redemption feature as the central themes in *Hans Westmar*, a propaganda film made by Goebbels' ministry early in the dictatorship. Screened in December, 1933, the film is a fictionalized story of the Hitler Youth hero Horst Wessel, who wrote the party anthem before being killed in a brawl with young communists in 1928. The film shows Westmar as an idealistic young student, determined to rid Germany of the shame of defeat and to fight for her resurrection against the communist menace. He goes out to fight what he calls 'the real battle' on the streets and is gunned down by a communist gang. He dies of his wounds in hospital, but not before a visit from Joseph Goebbels himself, who tells Westmar that his fever is like that of the movement: 'it is healing and moving towards victory'. The youth raises his arm in a final salute, mutters 'Deutschland!' and dies.[64] In the film's stylized conclusion, Westmar is seen ascending heavenwards, a swastika banner in his hand, resurrected like Hitler's Germany. Wessel became the symbol of heroic combat. 'The spirit of Horst Wessel,' ran a later wartime radio programme in 1941, celebrating his martyrdom, 'is today the driving force behind the struggle for freedom of the armed services and the homeland.' Wessel memorial occasions became so popular that Goebbels eventually banned all of them except the celebration of the anniversary of his death on the political battlefield.[65]

The presentation of politics as if it were a form of warfare was characteristic of the Third Reich, though no less so in Stalin's Soviet Union. The obsession with uniform was one expression of the desire to turn civilians into pseudo-soldiers. Uniforms were found for every party-led institution. The *Organisation Todt*, set up to build the German motorways, had an elaborate uniform indistinguishable from formal military dress. Even Joachim von Ribbentrop's foreign ministry was compelled to adopt a new diplomatic uniform in 1939 so that officials would not feel out of place among the bevy of militarized institutions whose retinues dressed up as soldiers on every public occasion. The Hitler Youth, in which boys between fourteen and eighteen were given preliminary military training along with rough-and-tumble games and gruelling country hikes, were decked out exactly like military cadets. There were different uniforms for each of the five Hitler Youth ranks, from chief-of-staff down to *Unterbannführer*; each rank enjoyed its own military-style peaked cap, complete with different markings in braid and piping, and different badges. Members of the League of German Girls (BDM) wore a more discreet uniform of suedette jacket, long skirt and blouse, but they were also supposed to keep themselves fully fit through running, swimming, walking and gymnastics. By 1940 60,000 badges had been awarded to girls for exceptional sporting achievement; girls went on long hikes with weighty packs on their backs, and BDM summer camps mirrored the military routines and layout of those for boys.[66]

After membership in the Hitler Youth came a year of labour service, also organized on entirely military lines. Labour Service (*Arbeitsdienst*) was made compulsory for all eighteen-year-olds in June 1935, as a form of 'service to the *Volk*'.[67] Each year hundreds of thousands of young men went off to work camps in order to dig ditches, repair roads, fell trees and, above all, to become familiar with the rigours and routines of military life. A lively description of one such camp has been left by a young Englishman who volunteered to spend a three-week holiday in 1934 doing German labour service. Reveille sounded at 4.30 in the morning, followed by exercises and a company parade. Work lasted from 6.40 to 2.00, to allow for an afternoon of sport. For an hour every evening there was political instruction, followed by the playing of the Last Post at 9.30 and lights out at 9.45. For any infractions of discipline – a poorly made bed, poor time-keeping – the company commander doled out penalties in extra work or a loss of leave. Work uniforms were pale grey battledress and army boots; for drill there were brown uniforms, military caps and smarter army boots. For formal occasions recruits wore full ceremonial dress in military khaki with cap and swastika badge.[68] When the Labour Service paraded at the major party rallies, it did so in solemn military style, tools held like rifles, ready for the order: 'Present spades!'

For many young Germans after 1933 this paramilitarism was all they knew. Boys joined the *Jungvolk* at ten, graduated to the Hitler Youth four years later, undertook labour service at eighteen and, following the reintroduction of conscription in 1935, an additional two years of military service. Soviet youth was only a little less regimented than this, but the *Komsomol* youth organization also sought to instil an ethos of national service with a strongly military aspect. 'The *Komsomol* is not a school', ran a slogan in the 1920s. 'Its most important tradition is struggle.'[69] Hundreds of thousands took shooting courses, along with other more conventional sports, and were presented at the end of the course with badges declaring 'Ready for Labour and Defence'. In 1933 alone 215,000 qualified as sharpshooters, girls as well as boys. All students in universities, higher and middle schools were obliged to undertake regular military training. Rifle practice and lessons in handling weapons were organized in factories and colleges; in the countryside the Motor Tractor Stations set up for each group of collective farms also ran courses to familiarize villagers with primitive lessons in self-defence and popular resistance, using their farm implements. In addition to the regular army, which introduced two-year conscription for most nineteen-year-olds in 1925, there were territorial forces, which received from one to three months' training over a five-year period, under the direct supervision of members of the regular army. Finally, there were two volunteer organizations, one for chemical weapons defence, one for air civil defence, set up in 1923, both of which became important vehicles in the 1930s for preparing the Soviet people for the kind of war they might face in the future. The two organizations joined forces under the title *Osaviakhim* in 1927, and by 1933 boasted 13 million members, including 3 million women. By the 1930s many *Osaviakhim* members received rudimentary military instruction, and thousands of future pilots began their air training on the gliders and aircraft operated by the organization.[70]

These forms of popular mobilization kept the Soviet and German populations in a state of permanent alert. The dictatorships presented each policy initiative as if it were a rallying cry for battle, a political call to arms. This deliberate cultivation of a culture of mobilization was reflected in the language of the two regimes. In Germany the word *Kampf* was applied to numerous public campaigns. The word can be translated as either 'battle' or 'struggle'. The word 'front' was commonly used to inject into policy a sense of urgent combat. 'Battle', 'enemy', 'victory' were commonplaces in public rhetoric. The word 'march' had a special resonance. Life in Germany, claimed the party ideologue, Alfred Rosenberg, adopted 'the style of a marching column'.[71] The National Socialist movement generated endless parades in military style, in order to ram home the idea that the party really had put the German people in step. Their destination was the many battlegrounds of the regime, against unemployment, slackers, the childless couple, the hoarder, and so on. These crude military metaphors were reinforced by a vocabulary of violence that elevated virtues deemed to be soldierly, and denigrated the vices of liberal gentility. When Hitler told the assembled Hitler Youth at Potsdam in 1936 that he wanted 'a cruel, unflinching youth hard as steel – Krupp steel', he was using a language that permeates to a remarkable degree the public utterances of hundreds of party leaders.[72] The party deliberately encouraged verbal brutality and barrack-room manners. The culture of male toughness was magnified and exploited by the aggressive militarism of the regime. Its baleful echoes could be heard in the exhortations to soldiers and security police as they butchered populations in eastern Europe in the early 1940s.

The Soviet Union was not immune from the perversion of public language. The ideal of virtuous revolutionary violence, on which the regime had been built, was manifested in a persistently militaristic vocabulary, which took its cue from Lenin himself: 'In an epoch of civil war, the ideal of the party of the proletariat must be that of a belligerent party.'[73] Trotsky was famously dismissive of bourgeois humanitarianism, and an advocate of 'stern, uncompromising struggle'.[74] The party adopted and never lost the fighting language of the civil war, and Stalin repeatedly reached for military metaphors in the speeches of the 1930s to describe the party faithful and the many tasks they confronted. Policy was defined in terms of 'battle', 'campaign' and 'fighting front'. The word 'front' was also applied remorselessly to all areas of Soviet public life. Socialists stormed ramparts, mounted offensives, launched attacks. The word 'enemy', used in every description of the class struggle, invited the use of such language. Soviet artists, commissioned to paint pictures on civil war themes in the 1930s, wrote to the Commissar of Defence, Kliment Voroshilov: 'We artists with our works want to shoot at our class enemies as Red Army soldiers have shot and will shoot. You have taught us fighting art.'[75]

Two purposes were served by popular militarization. First, it was a form of social discipline; second, it encouraged active psychological preparation for the great phantom wars of the future. Discipline could be imposed on the workforce by inculcating the language of conscription and military service. The Soviet workforce in the First Five-Year Plan came to be organized in 'shock brigades', reminiscent of the 'shock troops' of the civil war. In 1932 in the Soviet Union and 1938 in Germany both governments created the legal right to conscript labour for tasks deemed essential for defence. The labour codes in the Soviet Union treated the workforce as so many recalcitrant recruits, trying to dodge drill or go absent without leave. The code of 1940 placed the industrial workforce on a virtual war footing, with longer overtime and heavy penalties for slackness. Among German workers it was observed that those who had been through the youth movements and labour service more readily accepted the changed political reality and the harsher discipline than did older workers, accustomed to greater independence of action. At the vast new Volkswagen plant set up in 1939, the young apprentices were trained under the title of 'soldiers of labour' in a special training centre (*Ordensburg*), with military routines and a militarized uniform, and lectures on loyalty to the 'work front'.[76] The ultimate instruments of repression in each state, the concentration camps, were set up in imitation of military bases. The parody of military routines – the daily roll call on the parade ground, the marching columns in crude uniforms, the barrack blocks, the structures of cruel command – could be seen as part of the wider process of mobilizing every member of the community for national service, including political opponents and so-called 'asocials'.

The mobilizing priorities of both regimes ensured that their populations should be prepared in time of peace to meet the demands of future war. German schoolteachers were instructed to make their charges 'self-confident, militant (*wehrhaft*), and ready for action'. In October 1937 the Education Ministry issued 'Guidelines for bodily education', to ensure that all boys had an hour of 'keep fit' a day to prepare them for military service.[77] In the 1920s Soviet leaders looked for a revolutionary society that made little distinction between education for work and education for defending the revolution: 'The more knowledge and skills the worker and the peasant youth master at school, the more pre-call-up preparation they are given, the better will the young Red Army man master the soldier's trade.'[78] Both regimes expected the discipline and commitment instilled by the party and its many subsidiary associations to provide a set of values that could be exploited in defence of the revolutionary state or in the conquest of living-space and a war of revenge. War-making was perceived to be a universal civilian duty, as much a political and party responsibility as a military one. Lazar Kaganovich told the Seventeenth Party Congress in 1934 that communists were 'an army of revolutionary warriors'.[79] The idea that the party was a political army, representative of a militarized society, raised fundamental issues about the relationship between the armed forces and the dictatorship.

In 1933, shortly after Hitler had become Chancellor, Colonel Walther Reichenau wrote triumphantly that 'Never were the armed forces more identical with the state than today.'[80] Not all of the German army felt the same way, but there was a widespread hope that the armed forces could recover the place they had occupied under the Wilhelmine Empire, a position summarized by General Kurt von Schleicher a few years before as a 'pre-eminent, determining role in the areas of foreign and domestic policy'.[81] Hitler pampered these expectations by announcing that the armed forces were one of the two 'pillars of state', alongside the party. When the 4-million-strong SA was decapitated with the murder of Ernst Röhm and other SA leaders in June 1934, the army stood ready to support the new leader against his own radical supporters. Yet the same day that Röhm was arrested, SS killers gunned down von Schleicher as well. This murder heralded a slow change in the relationship between the new regime and its armed forces, which ended with their almost complete subjection to the dictatorship.

Circumstances in the Soviet Union dictated a closer link between the military and politics from the outset. The armed forces were established as the armed wing of the proletarian revolution, subject, like the rest of Soviet society, to the political will of the party vanguard. When the first full Field Regulations of the Red Army were published in 1929, there was included a formal political apparatus working alongside the military commanders to guarantee and strengthen 'the combat readiness of the Red Army as the armed support of the dictatorship of the proletariat'.[82] Some Bolsheviks wanted to replace the army from the start with a popular militia of workers and peasants. Party leaders demurred, but the issue rumbled on until 1924, when arguments for a truly socialist militia ('real worker-and-peasant democratization', as Trotsky described it, 'deeply rooted, and armed with rifle and sabre') were rejected, and a mixed system instituted, part regular army, part territorial units under army control.[83]

The armed forces were supervised by the Revolutionary Military Council of the Soviet Union, a committee of civilians and soldiers drawn from the party and army (and later the navy) elite, which established early in the regime the principle that the armed forces were not an autonomous component of the revolutionary state, but one entirely joined to it. In 1918 a Political Administration (PUR) was set up to undertake the political education of the armed forces. The PUR became the instrument for party influence over the armed forces; the political commissar assigned by the PUR to every army, division and regiment became the key figure linking the armed forces to the centre of the Soviet party system. The PUR was responsible not to the army command, but directly to the Central Committee. From 1924, under the direction of A.S. Bubnov, the political wing began to expand its activities and to trespass increasingly on the prerogatives of the regular soldiers. The party saw the armed forces as a 'school for socialism', and encouraged officers to join party associations, even the party itself.

In 1926 40 per cent of army officers were communists; by the 1940s, approximately 70 per cent.[84]

The close marriage between party and military produced among Soviet officers quite different ambitions from the German military elite. In 1927 the army chief-of-staff, Boris Shaposhnikov, published a major study of the new Soviet general staff, under the title *The Brain of the Army*. He took as his starting point the assumption that the Soviet army should not try to emulate the pre-war German army by claiming any major role in politics or society. Instead he argued that the army should reflect the socialist society of which it was a part. The role of the general staff was a functional one: 'Preparation of the army for victories in the theatre of military activities.'[85] The insistence on the purely technical prerogatives of the armed forces implied their complete subordination to the Soviet state and, ultimately, the party, but it also prompted growing pressure in the army and the navy to produce more professional, functionally proficient armed forces. One of the leading spokesmen for professionalization was Tukhachevsky. He favoured the creation of modernized, better-trained and larger armed forces, which would enjoy within the narrow sphere of military organization, planning and technology a greater autonomy.

The drive to reform and professionalize the armed forces in the 1930s, under the shadow of Stalin's emerging dictatorship, had immediate political repercussions. The initiatives were taken by the military leadership, whose relationship with the Commissar for Defence, Voroshilov, deteriorated steadily. He was one of the close coterie around Stalin, with little military experience or understanding. He mistrusted those who drove on the reorganization of the armed forces because the process widened the gap between military functionaries and their party overseers. The first test of this changing relationship came over the issue of Tukhachevsky's plans for military expansion, presented to Stalin in person in 1930. Stalin rejected the proposal as un-Marxist and reprimanded Tukhachevsky for presenting 'purely military' considerations, independent of the 'economic and cultural condition of the country'.[86] Stalin retreated two years later, when he authorized the rearmament drive and put Tukhachevsky in charge of it as Chief of Armaments. Tukhachevsky gathered a group of military modernizers about him, who were committed to his ideas on creating a thoroughly professional, technically trained armed force, with proper levels of discipline and modern armament. These reforms challenged the close political supervision of the armed forces. In 1934 the party agreed to remove political commissars from all field formations of the armed forces, and the influence of the PUR diminished. In 1935 the pre-revolutionary ranks were restored, including the highest rank of Marshal. Tukhachevsky was among the first five to be promoted, along with Voroshilov.[87] In April 1936 Tukhachevsky was appointed First Deputy Commissar of Defence. That same spring the professionalizers tried, unsuccessfully, to oust Voroshilov on the grounds that he was incompetent to run the defence department. During 1936 the balance of power in military affairs swung for the first time since the revolution towards the armed forces and away from the party.[88]

In Germany the situation was almost entirely the reverse. From a position of relative autonomy, in an institution where the process of *Gleichschaltung* (co-ordination) had made few inroads, the German army found its independence progressively eroded. At first the army's position was safeguarded by the survival of the presidential system. Hitler's dictatorship was never secure enough in the first two years of the regime to challenge von Hindenburg, even if Hitler had chosen to do so. Instead, the army command was given considerable independence in devising plans for rearmament and in reorganizing the armed forces, following the decision taken in December 1933 to violate the Versailles settlement by trebling the size of the 100,000-man army.[89] Hitler inherited Colonel Werner von Blomberg as his first Minister of Defence, an officer who had already helped to organize the closet rearmament of Germany before 1933, and who embraced Hitler's ideas on rearmament with enthusiasm. In 1934 von Blomberg was appointed to chair a newly created Reich Defence Council, which brought together military chiefs and civilian ministers; but unlike the Revolutionary Military Council in the Soviet Union, von Blomberg hoped to be able to use it as the means to extend military interests and influence into the civilian establishment. He succeeded in persuading Hitler to appoint a Plenipotentiary for War Economy to oversee the mobilization preparations for the economy. The job was given to Hjalmar Schacht, the minister of economics, though von Blomberg would have preferred a military commissar. In November 1935 von

Blomberg published 'Guidelines for the unitary preparation of the defence of the Reich', which made clear that this was the exclusive function of the armed forces alone if war should come.[90] Von Blomberg, like Tukhachevsky, whom he had met during the Soviet–German exchange of personnel in the late 1920s, was a military modernizer who saw the army as a professional tool and its leadership as technical functionaries of a special sort. He did not want to interfere in politics, but he hoped that politics would not interfere with the army.

The death of President Hindenburg on 2 August 1934 ushered in political changes that ultimately frustrated the wider ambitions of Germany's generals. That same day von Reichenau sent instructions to all units of the armed forces to swear a personal oath of loyalty to Hitler. Many senior officers were unenthusiastic. The new oath required a soldier to offer 'unconditional obedience' to Adolf Hitler to the point of death. The oath of the republic had obliged soldiers to 'protect the German nation and its lawful establishments'.[91] Hitler also combined the offices of Chancellor and President into the single office of *Führer* and became technically supreme commander of the armed forces. At a stroke the army lost the protection of its presidential patron, and gained as its nominal commander-in-chief the leader of the National Socialist party. Though Hitler took pains to assure the army leadership that he would secure the 'existence and inviolability' of the army, the relationship between the political and the military in the Third Reich was transformed.[92]

This relationship was compromised further by divisions within the armed forces' establishment. The army was not the sole bearer of arms after 1933. On 27 April that year Hermann Göring was appointed Minister of Aviation. The army wanted to keep control of military aircraft, which it had been developing in secret before 1933, but was overruled. The fledgling air force, cautiously nurtured by the Defence Ministry, was turned over to one of the most popular and powerful men in the party. The new air ministry was filled with senior officials loyal to National Socialism, including a former director of Lufthansa, Erhard Milch, and the flamboyant former air ace, stuntman and cartoonist, Ernst Udet, who as an SA officer narrowly escaped death in the Röhm purge, only to be rescued by Göring and appointed to control the development of German air technology in 1936.[93] Göring wanted the air force to be the symbol of the new state, and although many of its senior commanders and officers were drawn at first from army circles, the air force became largely independent of the influence of the army and of von Blomberg's ministry, to which the air force was technically subordinate until 1938. Only members of the air force greeted each other with the Hitler salute, or 'German greeting'.

The air force soon competed directly with the army for resources. Between 1933 and 1939 around 40 per cent of the military budget was devoted to air power.[94] Göring ordered a magnificent ministerial building on the Leipzigerstrasse in Berlin, its 4,500 offices a monument to the new military order. On 1 April 1935 Hitler formally announced the re-establishment of the German armed forces outside the terms permitted by the Versailles settlement, and the German Air Force was officially created with Göring as its commander-in-chief. In October 1936 he was appointed to run the Second Four-Year Plan, which directly challenged the monopoly that the Defence Ministry (renamed the War Ministry in 1935) had enjoyed in organizing Germany's rearmament. The tough jurisdictional battles that followed in 1937 over who had the right to prepare Germany for war were not a product of simple bureaucratic rivalry, but represented a political conflict between the ambitions of the army leadership and the desire of party politicians to have a decisive say in the formation of German military policy and strategy.

The attitude of the army was itself divided on the issue of its function in the state. Many senior officers favoured the technocratic path, creating a highly effective fighting force but leaving the politics of war to the politicians. Others, including the army chief-of-staff Colonel Ludwig Beck, wanted to preserve and enlarge what they saw as the special place of the German army in national politics. Few of the traditionalists were enthusiastic about the National Socialist movement, though they were profoundly nationalist in outlook. They were able to prevent the excessive intrusion of the party and its symbols into the armed forces (save for the swastika on the tailplanes of German military aircraft and a number of party badges that could be worn with military uniform), but there were many recruits to the expanding armed forces who shared National Socialist values unconditionally. In 1935 von Blomberg issued instructions to soldiers not to buy goods in

Jewish-owned shops, and in April 1936 he asked soldiers to marry only 'Aryan' women.[95] In January 1936, General Friedrich Dollmann, commander of the military district of Thuringia, issued a set of guidelines for his troops directing them to put portraits of Hitler in the mess and to put images of the Kaiser into storage. Officers were instructed 'by education and example' to become 'positively National Socialist'.[96]

The slow infiltration of National Socialist values and supporters into the armed forces was scarcely surprising. The German army of the 1920s was very small and long-service. In 1933 the regular army had only 4,000 officers. The political paramilitary organizations were very much larger, and the SA the largest of all by 1934. As the armed forces began to expand in 1933 it was inevitable that many of those who entered did so after an apprenticeship in one or other of the radical nationalist or youth movements of the pre-Hitler period. The reintroduction of conscription on 14 March 1935 brought waves of young recruits from a background in the Hitler Youth or the Labour Service or the SA. This created fresh friction between the older career soldiers and eager young National Socialists with a nose for smelling out old-fashioned values and half-hearted loyalty among their superiors.[97] The army came to reflect the wider society, as it did in the Soviet Union, and the younger generation was of all the elements of that society the most self-consciously National Socialist.

The most significant challenge to the monopoly of the armed forces came, in both dictatorships, not from the party but from the security apparatus. In the Soviet Union the Commissariat for the Interior (NKVD) had 750,000 men under its control. They included police and militia men, and armed security officers. This apparatus stood above the army itself and was directly responsible to the interior commissar, not to Voroshilov. Security officials were also posted, along with political commissars, to army units down to the divisional and regimental level. Their task was not to make good communists out of rank-and-file recruits, but to isolate and identify anti-communists and counter-revolutionaries. Every officer knew that he risked more than a reprimand for slack political education; every time he made a mistake or flouted the current party line, he risked accusations of sabotage or political dissent. In Germany the security apparatus did not act as a higher law above the armed forces (although von Blomberg agreed in 1936 that soldiers who allegedly committed political crimes should be handed over to the Gestapo rather than the military justice system), but the SS, whose leaders came to dominate the security apparatus in 1936, did have pretensions to compete with the army. The SS was defined by its leader, Heinrich Himmler, as 'guard of the nation, a guard of the Nordic race'.[98] In 1936 the SS was given the right to carry arms when guarding the concentration camps. Three years later, Himmler succeeded in persuading Hitler that separate SS units should be formed in the armed forces as the Armed SS (*Waffen SS*). Relations between the armed forces and the SS were poor in the mid-1930s. There were regular brawls and insults traded between soldiers and SS men. Himmler made no secret of his distrust of senior officers, or of his ultimate ambition to create a model force of SS units to supplant the army as the chief defender of the nation. The deliberate cultivation of the SS as the party and national elite, military in every aspect, was the most direct threat posed by the party to the armed forces, because of the exceptional powers enjoyed by the security apparatus and Himmler's close relationship with Hitler.[99]

It was thus no mere chance that led the NKVD and Himmler's security apparatus to play central roles in the crises in civil–military relations that emerged in both dictatorships during the years 1937–8. In these two years the Soviet armed forces and the German army saw their senior leadership purged and any claims to professional autonomy or political influence decisively quashed, with profound consequences in both dictatorships. The purge of the senior military leadership in the Soviet Union was part of the wider terror that engulfed Soviet society in 1937, but it had its own particular causes. The security police had had suspicions about the army leadership that dated back to the early 1930s and the period of Soviet–German collaboration. During the years 1930–32 the Red Army was purged of former Tsarist specialists; more than 3,000 were sacked or sent to camps. In the course of the regular interrogations of those purged, two victims hinted that Tukhachevsky himself had discussed setting up a military dictatorship. At Stalin's insistence, the OGPU was asked to investigate, but reported back that he was '100% clean'.[100] Almost certainly the security police kept senior army commanders under close surveillance, but Tukhachevsky made his own case worse by his brusque and intolerant attitude towards the politicians, Voroshilov in particular, whose military ignorance he deplored in outspoken terms.

Tukhachevsky was a popular figure in army circles; hero of the civil war, young, handsome, confident of his opinions, he was the very model of a Bonaparte-in-waiting. His forthright style was uninhibited in Stalin's presence. When he organized war games in November 1936 around the contingency of a German attack, Stalin ordered them to be demonstrated at the Kremlin. Tukhachevsky turned up late to find that his colleagues had obligingly staged a simulation for Stalin already, in which Soviet forces had repelled a German attack, stormed into Poland, linked hands with anti-fascist revolutionary forces and achieved a triumphant table-top victory. Tukhachevsky told them that they were wrong: Germany would attack without warning, with overwhelming strength, and force a long and bitter defensive conflict. 'What are you trying to do?' Stalin snapped back, 'frighten Soviet authority?'[101] When, a few weeks later, the NKVD under Ezhov began a whispering campaign about the political unreliability of the army leadership, Tukhachevsky was an obvious target. There was enough about his presumptuous personality and ideological irreverence to persuade Stalin that the military might indeed hatch a plot along the lines he first suspected in 1930, 'to install even a military dictator-ship'.[102] The example of military revolt in Spain was fresh in Stalin's mind, and in March 1937 the NKVD began arresting Soviet officers who were serving there, on the grounds that they were politically contaminated. When an unfortunate brigade commander named Medvedev was tortured by the security police into confessing an army plot, the evidence was sent straight to Stalin.

The result, according to Mikhail Shpigelglaz, head of foreign intelli-gence in the NKVD, was a Kremlin panic that 'a real conspiracy' had been unearthed. NKVD troops were put on full alert. The source of the alleged plot was almost certainly Ezhov himself. His deputy instructed a security police detective in the spring of 1937 to 'develop a line about an important, deep-seated plot in the Red Army', which would magnify Ezhov's personal role.[103] Documents concerning an army conspiracy purporting to come from German counter-intelligence (whose provenance has never been satisfactorily proved) were used by the NKVD to give plausibility to what was almost certainly an invention. Records of the contact with German soldiers in the 1920s and 1930s under the terms of the Berlin Treaty were unearthed as further evidence of the duplicity of army leaders. Tukhachevsky was followed everywhere; his visit to London to attend the coronation of King George VI was suddenly cancelled, with the excuse that an assassination plot had been discovered aimed at the Soviet marshal; in May he was suddenly sacked as chief-of-staff and demoted to command the Volga Military District, an almost certain prelude to arrest. A few days later he was summoned to meet local political commissars, arrested and sent to Lefortovo prison in Moscow. Seven other senior commanders were arrested with him. Not even soldiers could withstand days of torture. Tukhachevsky crumbled completely, admitted his crimes and incriminated ever-wider circles among his colleagues in the army and the navy. At a Central Committee meeting on 24 May the politicians insisted on a vote for trial. No one dissented, and on 11 June the eight military leaders were tried and found guilty on the same day. Stalin signed their death warrants and that same night they were all shot. Tukhachevsky died professing loyalty to the man who had, only hours before, approved his death.[104]

There has been much speculation about the motives for removing the military leadership at a time when the Soviet Union faced a deteriorating international situation. The least convincing explanation is that Tukhachevsky and other soldiers were actually plotting to overthrow Stalin, and somehow the NKVD found out. In 1956 a former NKVD officer, Alexander Orlov, who had defected to the United States, published the claim that Red Army leaders planned to arrest Stalin and Voroshilov at a Kremlin meeting, surround the building with two regiments of troops loyal to the generals, and either shoot Stalin on the spot, or haul him before the Central Committee to expose his crimes to public scrutiny. Orlov's sources were second-hand, and no other evidence has surfaced since to support the story.[105] The point is not whether Tukhachevsky did or did not conspire to overthrow Stalin, but that the Soviet leadership believed that he had. Forty years afterwards, Molotov remained convinced that the evidence exposed by the NKVD was real, and that the army generals were in league with the Germans to transform the Soviet Union into a German colony: 'as to whether Tukhachevsky and his group in the military were preparing a coup, there is no doubt'.[106] In late 1936 and early 1937 there was a panic in the Kremlin about German provocation and spying; Germans working in Moscow were expelled. The Anti-Comintern Pact signed between Germany and Japan on 15 November 1936 fuelled the alarm. Tukhachevsky had links with the German embassy in 1936, and had even put out friendly feelers to German representatives.[107] When Tukhachevsky's name was mentioned in the interrogation of the disgraced Bolshevik leader Karl Radek in January 1937, Stalin's perennially suspicious mind began to make connections. Tukhachevsky was originally a protégé of the disgraced Trotsky; Tukhachevsky had been a leading advocate of Soviet–German collaboration. Though the only 'evidence' was beaten out of prisoners in State Security cells, it all supported the idea of a 'Trotskyist-fascist' conspiracy. The military purge was directed at those officers who had worked with the Germans before 1933. Only one escaped execution in 1937. The murky climate of treason made the irrational seem plausible. 'Everything was strained to breaking point,' Molotov recalled in 1977. 'In that period it was necessary to act mercilessly.'[108]

Over the following eighteen months thousands of officers were expelled from the army and navy, some to arrest and eventual execution, some to camps, some to short periods of retirement before being reinstated later. In all, 45 per cent of the most senior military officers and PUR commissars were purged, including 71 of the 85 officers on the Revolutionary Military Council, and 720 out of 837 commanders, from colonel to marshal, appointed under the new table of ranks drawn up in 1935. Shaposhnikov was one of the few survivors. For the rest of the army the picture was less catastrophic than was once thought. Roger Reese has calculated that 34,501 officers were expelled, of whom 11,596 were reinstated by 1940, leaving 22,705 men out of an officer corps of around 144,000 in 1937 and 179,000 in 1938 still purged. Of those sacked only 4,474 were arrested by the NKVD in 1937 and 5,032 in 1938, representing just 5.4 per cent of all officers. In 1940 only 3.7 per cent of the 1938 officer corps was still discharged as a result of the purges.[109] All those convicted of complicity in Tukhachevsky's 'fascist-Trotskyist plot' were shot, but precisely how many may never be known. Most officers remained in post, and most of those purged were not killed. These conclusions put the military purge into perspective, but they do not alter its political significance. The crisis was used to restore political domination over Soviet armed forces at the expense of the military modernizers.

The problem facing the German army in 1938 – generally known as the Blomberg-Fritsch crisis after its two principal victims – also began with whispering campaigns about the army's reliability. During 1936 relations between the army and leading party figures began to deteriorate. The Gestapo kept files on senior officers; Himmler's SS encouraged a press campaign suggesting that the army was an old-fashioned barrier to building a truly National Socialist state. Telephones were tapped and mail intercepted. Much of the mud stuck, for Hitler became noticeably cooler towards army leaders during 1937. A year later his army adjutant heard him claim that the army had been 'an uncertain element in the state'.[110] Later still, in August 1942, in one of his afternoon monologues, Hitler complained to his chief of operations, Alfred Jodl, that in the mid-1930s the army had 'a mass of people working against me behind my back and sabotaging my efforts'.[111] When Hitler announced to his commanders-in-chief his plans for German territorial expansion, at the meeting on 5 November 1937 recorded in the Hossbach memorandum, their lukewarm response (from all but Göring, who is said to have leapt on a table and pledged his support) ignited what was already a smouldering resentment at the army's evident ambivalence about risking war, and the slow pace of military rebuilding. Nevertheless, there is no evidence that Hitler planned to sack von Blomberg or other senior officers at once. This was achieved by Himmler and Göring, both ambitious to replace the war minister and both hostile to an army leadership whose conservative background and political pretensions they regarded as insufficiently National Socialist.

The occasion for the crisis was banal enough. Werner von Blomberg, a good-looking man of sixty, jovial, young for his age, decided to marry the pretty twenty-four-year-old Eva Gruhn, a charwoman's daughter from the wrong side of the tracks, a waitress who had made money posing in the nude for calendars and pornographic folios. She was several months pregnant. When von Blomberg imprudently confessed to Göring in December 1937 his unfortunate liaison, he little could have realized the consequences. Göring told him to go ahead with the marriage, while the Gestapo compiled a dossier, complete with three sets of compromising photographs, on the war minister's bride-to-be.[112] At the same time Göring, working closely with Reinhard Heydrich, Himmler's deputy, decided to revive an old Gestapo file on General Werner von Fritsch, commander-in-chief of the army, which alleged, on the basis of mistaken identity, that Fritsch was homosexual. A quiet, withdrawn, solitary man, whose monocle made him a caricature of a Prussian general, Fritsch was regarded by the party as a symbol of the older Germany they wanted to sweep aside. The temptation to bring down both von Blomberg and von Fritsch at the same time on grounds of moral turpitude was irresistible to the plotters. The conspiracy against them was deliberately orchestrated and manipulated by Heydrich and Göring. In January 1938 von Blomberg married Eva Gruhn, with Hitler as his witness. Over the next two weeks the truth was revealed to Hitler, along with the dossier on von Fritsch, which was used as incriminating evidence of his alleged homosexuality. Von Blomberg was forced to resign, and was sent with his young bride into exile for a year by an infuriated Hitler. Von Fritsch resigned in humiliation, protesting his innocence, and died eighteen months later when he walked straight towards Polish guns in September 1939 to expiate his humiliation.[113]

The political consequences of the Blomberg-Fritsch crisis were profound for the future role of the armed forces. There were fears among party leaders that the crisis might provoke an army coup, and one witness later recalled that 20,000 SS men were surreptitiously stationed around Berlin in case civil war should result.[114] This failed to materialize, though there were genuine opponents of Hitler's policy in the German army, including the chief-of-staff, Ludwig Beck, who thought Hitler ran too many risks in foreign policy. Hitler moved to consolidate his position against the conservative leadership in the armed forces. On 4 February 1938, following advice from von Blomberg himself, who did not want to see any of the conspirators rewarded by replacing him, Hitler announced that there would no longer be a war minister and that he would assume an active role as Supreme Commander of the Armed Forces, a position he had nominally held since the publication of the defence law of 21 May 1935. The decree appointing him as supreme commander in 1938 spelt out his intention to transform the office: 'From now on I will directly exercise command authority over the entire armed forces personally.'[115] The three branches of the armed forces were from this point onwards formally subordinate to Hitler, who now enjoyed and practised what his military headquarters chief, Wilhelm Keitel, described as 'an immediate power of authority'.[116] On the day of his appointment, Hitler addressed senior officers at the War Ministry building, where he blamed the pre-1933 100,000-man army for failing to produce any leaders worth the name, and announced that he would now approve all appointments in the armed forces. The same day he authorized the retirement of fourteen senior generals and the demotion of forty others, whose reliability or outlook clashed with the new military regime.[117]

These initiatives altered the relationship between party and military completely. For several months the army argued back, in the hope that after the dust of the scandals had settled Hitler would leave things much as they were. Instead, each demarcation dispute left Hitler more firmly in control and the army leadership forced into a sulky collaboration. The terms of the new relationship were defined in a statement Hitler made to the Reichstag on 20 February, in which he assured deputies that no problems any longer existed between the National Socialist state and 'the National Socialist armed forces'.[118] The Supreme Command (OKW) grew rapidly into an apparatus with an operational staff reporting directly to Hitler, twelve major departments and 1,500 officials and military administrators drawn mainly from the former War Ministry.[119] A few weeks later Hitler had his first test as Supreme Commander when he oversaw the military occupation of Austria. When in May he announced his ambition to fight Czechoslovakia in the autumn, a group of senior commanders grouped around Beck explored the possibility of overturning the government if Hitler went to war, but in August Beck was also forced to resign because of his consistent opposition to the risk of war. The coup he helped to plan for late September (to seize the Reich chancellery building and execute Hitler) broke down after Hitler won his bloodless victory at the Munich conference.[120]

At the same time practical efforts were made to link the armed forces more closely with the party. The 'German greeting' of upheld arm was added to the conventional military salute. A decree in April called for

'comradely relations' between military units and the party organization. The new army commander-in-chief, General Walther von
Brauchitsch, was chosen as a less independent spirit than von Fritsch.
He became a model of co-operation, bringing National Socialism more
obtrusively into the army than had been possible hitherto. Political
education was stepped up, and in April 1939 a Department for Armed
Forces Propaganda was set up inside the OKW organization.[121] When
von Brauchitsch issued guidelines for officer training in December
1938, he insisted that the officer corps 'must not be surpassed by
anybody in the purity and genuineness of its National Socialist outlook'.[122] During the summer of 1938 the SS won a further battle with
the army. On 17 August Hitler issued a decree confirming Himmler's
control over armed SS men in peacetime, and removing any limitations
on the number of SS men who could bear arms.[123]

The communist party also increased its surveillance of the post-purge
armed forces in the Soviet Union. On 8 May 1937, as the hapless
Tukhachevsky was tortured into confession, Stalin authorized the
reintroduction of political officers in all military units above the size
of a division. In August 1937 PUR was placed under the control of a
stalwart Stalinist, Lev Mekhlis, a *Pravda* editor and a former member
of Stalin's party secretariat in the 1920s. A crude propagandist and a
man of great energy and ruthlessness, Mekhlis saw it as his mission to
'bolshevize' the army. Soon political officers were placed in even the
smallest military units. An estimated 73 per cent of the new wave of
political commissars had no military training. Military commanders
now found their every order scrutinized, and usually co-signed, by the
political commissar. The purges continued in a lower key during
1939 and 1940, but all officers knew that the party and the security
apparatus had restored a political grip on the armed forces as tight as
that during the civil war.[124]

The two victors from the purge of their armies were Hitler and
Stalin. Both removed a possible challenge to the dictatorship from the
one element in each system potentially capable of seizing power, and
both brought the armed forces under the close supervision of the party
and its leadership. Two eulogies from the late 1930s, one for Hitler's
birthday in April 1938, one for Stalin's sixtieth birthday in December
1939, reveal the extent to which the cult of personality both men

enjoyed came to reflect the military pretensions of the two dictators. Hitler was hailed as a political and military genius, 'the spiritual creator and inspirer' of German military revival: 'In his immeasurable labour on the military strength of the Reich, in his care for its defences and its arms . . . he is the true soldier-leader of his people!'[125] In *Pravda*, Voroshilov described the name of Stalin as 'a synonym for the Red Army'. He continued: 'The armed defence of victorious socialism, the development of the Red Army of the Soviet Union, its history, its strength and might, its solid steeled ranks, are all inseparably linked with the name of Stalin.'[126] Both states had been turned into major military powers by the late 1930s, and the dictators acted to prevent the great expansion of the military establishment from puffing up the political pretensions of the armed forces, on which that power ultimately rested. The logic of dictatorship, particularly of systems where popular militarization derived from a civilian political party rather than the armed forces, was to arrogate to the dictators an exceptional degree of military responsibility, and to bring the armed forces in line with the political revolution.

This proved ultimately a dangerous outcome for world history. Both dictators had at their disposal by the late 1930s the means to fight the civil war confrontation on which their dictatorships were predicated, communism against capitalist imperialism, National Socialism against Jewish-Bolshevism. The language and metaphors of violence and belligerency were eventually mobilized for a conflict of exceptional scale and savagery between the two states. Both dictators saw this contest as historically unavoidable, though Stalin wished to avoid it if he could. Hitler wanted to use the military power at his disposal to fight other states. 'He simply could not understand a soldier who feared war', wrote an adjutant in his diary.[127] Stalin did all he could in the 1930s to ensure that the Soviet Union could respond to any threat with massive violence of its own. Rearmament and the militarization of politics underscored the fact that violence was central to both systems. A violent political vocabulary and violent political solutions were defining features of two revolutionary orders that were both directly and indirectly the offspring of war. Both systems eventually rose or fell on their capacity to wage a second world war with greater success than the first.

I2

Total War

'The enemy is cruel and implacable. He is out to seize our lands, watered with our sweat, to seize our grain and oil secured by our labour. The issue is one of life or death for the Soviet State, for the peoples of the USSR; the issue is whether the peoples of the Soviet Union shall remain free or fall into slavery.'   Josef Stalin, radio address, 3 July 1941[1]

'The *Führer* says: right or wrong, we must win. It is the only way. And victory is right, moral and necessary. And once we have won, who is going to question our methods? In any case, we have so much to answer for already that we must win, because otherwise our entire nation – with us at its head – and all we hold dear will be eradicated.'
                              Joseph Goebbels, diary, 16 June 1941[2]

The lengthy, bitter, bloody war fought between Germany and the Soviet Union from the summer of 1941 until the spring of 1945 would determine the survival of one or other of the two dictatorships. The stakes for each side were absolute. German destruction of the Soviet Union and the communist system was the whole purpose of the war launched by Germany and a string of smaller allies and co-belligerents – Finland, Romania, Hungary – on 22 June 1941 under the codename Operation 'Barbarossa'. The communist revolution would not have survived Soviet defeat. 'The German invaders,' warned Stalin in a broadcast in November 1941, 'want a war of extermination against the peoples of the U.S.S.R.'[3] German leaders thought that a Soviet victory would mean the end not only of National Socialism, but of the German people – even of European civilization. Writing in his diary in January 1942, Joseph Goebbels concluded that if the 'conglomeration of animals' that composed the Russian people ever came westward into Europe, 'the human mind cannot possibly imagine what it would mean'.[4] In April 1945, as the Red Army approached Berlin, Hitler reflected that once Germany was beaten, 'our defeat will be utter and complete'. He continued: 'In a ghastly conflict like this, in a war in which two so completely irreconcilable ideologies confront one another, the issue can inevitably only be settled by the total destruction of one side or another.'[5] Rather than risk capture, he killed himself a few weeks later. The war the two dictatorships waged was a total war, not only because it was waged using the mobilization of all the material and social resources at their disposal, but because the stark division between total victory and total defeat was built into the very ideological fabric of the two systems.

If the general terms in which the conflict was understood had deep ideological roots that reached back to the earlier Great War, the timing and nature of the German–Soviet confrontation in 1941 owed much to the shifting circumstances of the war that broke out on 3 September 1939 between Germany, Britain and France. Ideological perception and political calculation were not alternatives in 1941, but operated in tandem. Indeed, from August 1939 to June 1941 politics succeeded in masking how wide the ideological chasm was that separated the two dictatorships. A number of politically expedient agreements turned the rivals into temporary collaborators. On 23 August 1939 a Non-Aggression Pact was signed between the two states; on 28 September a second treaty of friendship was sealed, which divided Poland and parts of eastern Europe into spheres of influence, one German, one Soviet; on 11 February 1940 a comprehensive trade treaty was agreed, exchanging Soviet raw materials and food for German machinery and military equipment; finally, on 10 January 1941, a supplementary treaty was signed in Moscow confirming the economic relationship for another year.[6] Neither side entered the brief period of détente with any illusions about the reasons for agreement. It was sealed because, in 1939, neither wanted a war with the other. Hitler hoped that the pact would weaken the resolve of Britain and France to confront him over the German–Polish war, launched on 1 September 1939; when it did not, the pact helped to secure the German rear and supplied the German war economy with a large list of essential supplies. Stalin approved the pact, despite the shock it represented to the many thousands of communists worldwide who took Soviet anti-fascism for granted, because it allowed the Soviet Union to consolidate its security position in eastern Europe, acquire vanguard technologies from German industry, and, above all, to avoid war at the side of two capitalist empires, Britain and France, against another capitalist state, Germany.[7]

The agreements also allowed the Soviet Union to seize additional territory in spheres of influence sketched out in a secret protocol to the pact in August, and confirmed in the treaty of friendship signed in Moscow a month later. The Soviet Union invaded Poland on 17 September and occupied the eastern half of the country; during the autumn months the Baltic States were converted into virtual satellites. In December a short war was waged against Finland to bring the former Tsarist province under Soviet control, but stiff Finnish resistance forced the Soviet Union to be content with annexing an area of territory in the Karelian Isthmus west of Leningrad, to improve the city's security. In June 1940, with Germany occupied in the west, the Baltic States were fully incorporated into the Soviet Union, and the Romanian provinces of Bessarabia and northern Bukovina were forcibly occupied. The territorial gains were hailed as a triumph for Soviet strategy. According to the chairman of the Supreme Soviet foreign policy committee, Andrei Zhdanov, it had proved possible to exploit 'the contradictions among imperialists' in order 'to extend the position of socialism',[8] a view consistent with the whole thrust of Soviet thinking on international affairs. The Soviet Union was regarded as morally neutral in its relations with non-socialist states, since all were manifestations of greater or lesser forms of capitalist exploitation. Lenin's argument that capitalism, in its late stage, was forced to stave off collapse by active imperialism and war was the foundation of Stalin's own theoretical outlook, but it was important to ensure that capitalist states devoured each other rather than the Soviet Union; in the final stages of any great war the Soviet Union would 'take action last'.[9] The pact with Germany was designed to keep the Soviet Union away from the conflict, but not to prevent war. On 1 July 1940, Stalin told the

Soviet ambassador to Tokyo that the non-aggression pact 'was dictated by the desire to unleash war in Europe'.[10] The Soviet Union had no interest in maintaining the status quo, but every prospect of gaining from a war kept distant from Soviet soil. Stalin censured Comintern in October 1939 for preferring democratic states to fascist states: 'We are not opposed [to war], if they have a good fight and weaken each other.'[11]

The policy of encouraging capitalist war in order to emasculate capitalism hinged on one critical premise: the new war, like the last, had to be a long and exhausting war of attrition. It was initially assumed that the military balance between what Zhdanov called the two 'opposing capitalist groups' would produce a stalemate. In June 1940 Molotov talked candidly to the Lithuanian foreign minister about the Soviet vision of the future, when the warring populations, driven to desperate revolt by the terrible costs of a prolonged and unresolved war, would be liberated by the Red Army as the capitalist military effort crumbled: a final battle between bourgeoisie and proletariat in the Rhine basin 'will decide the fate of Europe once and for all'.[12] This was, in practice, a vision of the past, for it was coloured entirely by the experience of the Great War and the Russian revolution. It reflected the dangerous reality that the Soviet Union could not afford either capitalist side to win a quick or decisive victory. Stalin wanted Germany not beaten, but 'so weakened that years would be required for it to risk unleashing a great war against the Soviet Union'.[13] German defeat, it was realized, might expose the Soviet Union to two heavily armed, predatory empires, which might find it hard to resist an assault on communism. German victory, on the other hand, might provoke Hitler into a new adventure in the east. The Soviet Union hoped for a stalemate. The rapid destruction of the French and British armies in May and June 1940 unexpectedly exposed the Soviet state to the renewed threat of war. Stalin was stunned by news of the French surrender. 'How could they allow Hitler to defeat them, to crush them?' he asked Khrushchev.[14] In order to delay the day when Germany might turn on the Soviet Union, Stalin was forced into appeasement. A steady stream of resources flowed from the Soviet Union to bolster the German war effort; in the seventeen months of the agreement Germany received 1.4 million tonnes of grain, 1 million tonnes of timber, large quantities of scarce metals, and 212,000 tonnes of supplies from Japan shipped across the Trans-Siberian railway.[15] Soviet propaganda orchestrated extravagant displays of sympathy for the German cause. Stalin sent his personal congratulations to Hitler for his lightning victory.

German reactions to the pact with the Soviet Union were equally cynical and ambiguous. Hitler needed Soviet neutrality as long as he was forced to fight the western powers, and he bought it with the prospect of significant economic assistance from his new Soviet partner. The issue of German–Soviet relations was put on ice in September 1939 until the unwanted war with Britain and France was concluded, but Soviet expansion against Finland, the Baltic States and Romania put German security at risk. At the end of June 1940, German army commanders began to develop contingency plans to reduce the threat from an encroaching Red Army. On 3 July the army chief-of-staff, General Franz Halder, asked his staff to consider a 'military blow' in the east, to keep the Soviet armed forces at arm's length. The subsequent plan for an operation in the Baltic States and the Ukraine was presented to Hitler by the army commander on 21 July; its purpose was to inflict a sharp reminder of 'Germany's dominant position in Europe', and to do so within four to six weeks while army units were still mobilized after defeating France.[16] Though at first he made no response to the army's suggestion, Hitler had also been considering the Soviet question during July. On 29 July his chief of operations, Colonel-General Alfred Jodl, summoned his colleagues to a conference in a converted railway car, where he announced that Hitler was resolved 'once and for all' to rid the world of the Soviet menace. Two days later German military commanders made their way to a room in Hitler's Bavarian retreat, where the full scale of Hitler's plans was revealed. He wanted nothing less than an end to the Soviet system, 'to smash the state heavily in one blow'. The campaign was scheduled for the spring. It was to be short, sharp and fatal.[17]

Some of the arguments that Hitler elaborated to justify the war against the Soviet Union were products of circumstance. At the meeting on 31 July, he made it clear that invasion was a way of securing complete mastery of Europe as a springboard for the war against the British empire, and perhaps the United States. War would also end the uncertainty and speculation about Stalin's motives as the communist frontier crept stealthily closer to central Europe. Hitler also understood that Soviet raw materials, oil and foodstuffs could relieve the German war economy in any future contest with the resource-rich West.[18] For Hitler, however, these were factors that he could use to persuade party and military leaders, and perhaps himself, that war had an immediate and sensible strategic purpose. Behind all the expressions of rational strategic necessity, however, lurked the more fantastic ambitions to complete the national revolutionary war waged since 1933 against communism and its alleged Jewish allies, and to free up the limitless geography of the east for a permanent German empire.

Throughout the life of the German–Soviet pact Hitler never made any secret that an eventual war with Soviet communism was still his intention. In the autumn of 1939 his army adjutant, Nicolaus von Below, heard Hitler on several occasions argue that war in the west was a brief diversion 'to free his back for the confrontation with Bolshevism'. On 23 November, Hitler confided to von Below that he needed a quick victory in the west because he needed the army 'for a great operation in the East against Russia'.[19] Party leaders were told, during the course of a four-and-a-half hour speech late in October 1939, that only 'current necessity' kept him from 'turning back again to the East'.[20] The decision to prepare for war taken in July 1940 must be understood in this context. Hitler hoped that Britain would abandon the war and allow him to take up a conflict for which his whole career had prepared him. Hitler viewed the decision in grandiose, world-historical terms; it was, he later confessed in his testament in 1945, 'the hardest decision' he had to take.[21] Bolshevism, he told Goebbels in August 1940, 'was enemy number one'. In December he returned to the theme that the great contest with the Soviet Union 'will decide the question of hegemony in Europe'.[22] On 30 March 1941 he assembled his commanders again, in the Cabinet Room of the chancellery, where he explained in another lengthy speech that this was no ordinary war but a 'struggle of two opposing world views', which had to be fought mercilessly to 'exterminate' communism ('an asocial criminal system') 'for all time'.[23] The war with the Soviet Union was not a product of mere strategic calculation; had it been so then the army plan for a short strike in autumn 1940 to wound the Red Army enough to keep it out of Europe made greater sense. Though he looked for ways of justifying aggression, Hitler's plan for a final settlement of accounts had its own trajectory. Almost a year was to elapse between his decision to prepare for war, taken in July 1940, and the campaign launched in June the following year. This can hardly be regarded as a short-term reaction to the unpredictable circumstances of war.

From August 1940 the German armed forces set about preparing the great blow against the Soviet Union. Codenamed 'Fritz', the planning was taken over in September by a team led by General Friedrich Paulus, the German commander later encircled and captured at Stalingrad. In November, on the eve of a visit from the Soviet Foreign Minister, Molotov, Hitler signed a directive that preparation for war in the east should continue. The meetings with Molotov, who asked for Soviet bases in Bulgaria and Turkey, to dominate the mouth of the Danube and the Bosporus Straits, had about them an air of unreality. Hitler was prepared to make no further concessions, and Molotov's written request a week later for clarification of what the Germans might offer went unanswered.[24] The visit may well have been used to convince waverers that the Soviet Union did constitute a real threat to German interests in eastern Europe; it may have been necessary for Hitler to convince himself that the course he had adopted was the right one. Only after Molotov had returned to Moscow was the plan for war confirmed. A few days later Hitler ordered work to begin on a large eastern headquarters. Under the supervision of Fritz Todt, who had masterminded the building of the *Autobahnen*, an area of 250 hectares was chosen in a forest close to the East Prussian town of Rastenburg. Work began at once on a vast complex of offices, bunkers and conference rooms, masquerading as a new chemical works – Askania Nord. Hitler chose the name *Wolfschanze* (Wolf's Lair) for the headquarters of his predatory war. Directly overhead, airliners from Aeroflot cruised back and forth on the Moscow–Berlin route, oblivious of the work going on beneath them.[25]

On 5 December Hitler received the military plans in conference. He approved them all, and proposed a timetable for invasion in May the following year. On 18 December he signed War Directive 21 for an operation now called 'Barbarossa', 'to crush Soviet Russia in a rapid campaign'. The object was to smash the Red Army in a matter of weeks and to occupy the vast area west of a so-called 'AA Line', from Archangel in the far north to Astrakhan at the mouth of the Volga in the far south. 'Asiatic Russia' would be cooped up behind the line; the remaining industry of the Urals region was to be destroyed by bombing to prevent any Soviet revival.[26] The whole campaign was predicated on the assumption that Soviet forces were no match for the Germans and would be swiftly defeated. On 5 December Hitler argued that by the spring German military units would be 'visibly at their zenith', the enemy's forces 'at an unmistakable nadir'.[27] The idea of the quick war was never countered. German commanders endorsed it in their own dismissive assessments of the enemy. In April 1941 General Blumentritt told the General Staff that Soviet officers were so incompetent that defeat might be achieved in 'fourteen days of heavy fighting'; a month later he spoke of 'eight to fourteen days' against an army of 'ill-educated, half-Asiatic' fighters. The army commander-in-chief thought the war would take 'up to four weeks' of fighting, followed by simple mop-up operations.[28] The final directive Hitler gave before the start of the campaign, eventually postponed to 22 June 1941, called for total victory by the autumn. Joseph Goebbels recorded in his diary the final discussions with Hitler: 'The enemy will be driven back in one, smooth movement. The *Führer* estimates that the operation will take four months. I reckon on fewer. Bolshevism will collapse like a pack of cards.'[29]

The Soviet Union, for all the talk of a new era in Soviet–German friendship, did not ignore the German problem. The danger of a German war was never overlooked. Following the defeat of France the commissar for defence, Marshal Semyon Timoshenko, reported that Germany was now 'the most important and strongest enemy'.[30] In July 1940, the army chief-of-staff, Boris Shaposhnikov, produced, sooner than the Germans, a detailed plan of what a German invasion might look like. His suggested three-pronged assault closely resembled the eventual attack.[31] Soviet military strategy was based on the idea that in any war light covering forces on the border would hold up invasion long enough to enable the bulk of the army to mobilize its forces for a massive offensive, to drive the enemy back onto his own territory and to annihilate him there. During the first months of 1941 efforts were made to improve the preparation of border areas to receive the first shock of German attack, but full guidelines were only issued in early May, and by June the border areas were still awaiting a comprehensive plan.[32] The general plan for mobilization in 1941 in the event of war also took time to work out, and was still incomplete when war arrived. On 26 April the army chief-of-staff, the recently appointed General Georgi Zhukov, ordered a creeping mobilization to begin, in response to widespread evidence that German forces were moving eastwards. On 13 May the redeployment of substantial forces to the western frontier areas was ordered, but out of thirty-three divisions only four or five were fully equipped when war broke out. On 1 June 793,500 conscripts were called up, and on the 15th they were ordered into forward positions. The process was to be completed by July or August. On 19 June orders went out to start camouflaging airfields, but this had scarcely begun when German aircraft destroyed thousands of Soviet planes stranded in plain view on the ground.[33]

Soviet leaders also began to express these preparations in terms of a coming settlement of accounts with the imperial enemy. In September 1940 Stalin approved the plan to repulse a German attack, though he hoped that war could be averted to at least 1942, when Red Army preparations would be complete and the frontier fortifications built along the borders of the newly acquired territories.[34] From October 1940 the possibility of war was firmly considered, and the first signals were given in a speech by Zhdanov to prepare the population for 'self-sacrifice and heroism', and to reject any idea of a 'war with little bloodshed'. In the spring Stalin himself indicated the change in the Soviet position, when he decided to announce at a passing-out ceremony for military cadets on 5 May that there did exist a threat from Germany for which the new Red Army had to prepare itself rapidly. The only surviving notes of the speech – the original has never been published – show that Stalin himself regarded war as highly likely. The German armed forces had won easy victories, but would lose 'a booty-seeking war of conquest'. He considered German forces weaker than they seemed ('nothing special') and many soldiers 'tired of war'.[35] Replying to a toast later in the evening, Stalin declared: 'The Red Army is a modern army, and a modern army is an offensive army!'[36] Over the following month Soviet propaganda began to highlight the theme of a final apocalyptic battle, 'an offensive and annihilating war'. In

June 1941, just days before invasion, the army political education department circulated the view that war with 'the capitalist world is inevitable', and with unintended foresight suggested that the Soviet Union might be forced 'any day now, stubbornly and tenaciously to prepare for a decisive battle with the surrounding capitalist world'.[37]

Some historians have used this sudden shift in Soviet outlook as evidence that Stalin was actually preparing a pre-emptive strike against Germany in the summer of 1941. A document dated 15 May shows a suggestion from military planners that the Soviet Union launch a short strike against any assembling force threatening Soviet territory. The document reflected prevailing military strategy, which was to try to disrupt an enemy attack by short punitive attacks on enemy positions while the rest of the Red Army mobilized and deployed for the decisive battle, a posture of 'aggressive defence'. There is no evidence that this was any more than a suggestion to disrupt German preparations which went unheeded. It is unlikely that Stalin read it, but even if he had his formal position throughout May and June remained consistently opposed to any action that might provoke German retaliation until the Red Army was ready for battle in 1942. He hoped that the limited mobilization westwards would be enough to deter a Germany which he regarded as still too weak and too occupied in the west to risk all-out war. The Soviet Union was much more alert to the German threat in the summer of 1941 than at any time since 1939, but beyond a limited and incomplete preparation of border areas little was done. The German military attaché in Moscow travelled the breadth of the country in late May and could find 'no signs of an offensive intention'.[38] Only the commander of the Soviet Baltic front defied instructions and alerted his forces before 22 June. All along the rest of the Soviet frontier, even though the German army could be seen building rafts and pontoon bridges on the western banks of the river frontier in Poland, even though 236 German agents were arrested in the western border areas, and even though all secret intelligence pointed unambiguously to a German attack, orders from Moscow were to avoid any provocative preparations.[39] Zhukov finally persuaded Stalin, on the night of 21 June, to send out an alert to border units, but by the time the telegrams were decrypted many units were already being bombed by German aircraft.

The war did not unfold to plan for either side. At first the German view that the Red Army would fold up when faced with a modern and sophisticated military machine seemed utterly vindicated. The first six weeks saw Axis forces push deep into Soviet territory, seizing all the areas taken over by the Soviet Union in 1939 and 1940, and pushing on into Belorussia and the Ukraine. By 1 September, German armies had surrounded Leningrad and had taken Kiev, and were at last pressing into the territory of the Russian federation. Large encircling operations destroyed most of the Soviet front line, killed 236,000 Soviet soliders and netted over 2 million Soviet prisoners. An estimated nine-tenths of Soviet tank strength was destroyed in just four weeks; most of the 319 Red Army units committed to the battle were destroyed or badly mauled in the same time.[40] The remarkable rout convinced German generals, and Hitler himself, that the quick war in the east was possible. The military leaders wanted to race on and capture Moscow, but Hitler insisted on switching the priority to seizing the rich economic resources of the Ukraine. In September the axis was switched back to Moscow, where Hitler believed only weak forces remained. On 6 September he issued Directive 35 for Operation Typhoon, which would destroy in a swift blow remaining Soviet resistance. On 30 September German armoured forces drove straight towards Moscow, moving so fast that they entered the city of Orel with the streetcars still running. By 5 October the leading formations were only eighty miles from Moscow; by the end of November the first spearhead was on the outskirts, twelve miles from Stalin's Kremlin.[41] Hitler was now so confident that his three-month campaign had succeeded that he had returned to Berlin on 4 October. In front of an ecstatic audience in the Berlin Sportpalast he announced that he had come back from 'the greatest battle in the history of the world', which was not far from the truth. The Soviet dragon, he assured them, was thoroughly slain and 'would never rise again'.[42]

On the Soviet side the failure to prepare for the German attack, even to alert the vital border forces to stand ready in time, unhinged Soviet strategy within hours. The idea that the light frontier forces would hold and harass an attacking force while the army mobilized, concentrated and attacked to repel the enemy onto his own soil, was exposed as fanciful. The offensive posture of Soviet strategy made sense only if the enemy took time to mobilize and was numerically weaker. The confusion caused through a sudden attack by a great force already at battle stations was complete. From Moscow came frantic calls for Soviet armies to mount paralysing attacks on the enemy to drive him back across the frontier, but they were meaningless. Where Soviet armies tried to stand they were seized in great pincer movements and annihilated as a fighting force. Stalin remained out of touch with military reality for weeks, but not, as Khrushchev asserted during the years of de-Stalinization, because he had completely broken down. The evidence now shows Stalin urgently at work. For the first week of the German attack he cursed and bullied his colleagues and the army generals, but he was very much in charge, if not quite in command of the situation. His office log shows a ceaseless round of visitors and consultations: twenty-nine entries on 22 June from 5.45 in the morning, when news of the German attack broke, to 4.45 in the afternoon; the following day meetings began at 3.00 in the morning until almost 2.00 the following morning; meetings and interviews until 11.30 or 12.00 at night for the next three days.[43] Stalin's haggard and tense appearance was not the result of nervous collapse, but of desperate, frantic overwork. On Sunday 29 June he went to his dacha on the outskirts of Moscow, and stayed there until Monday writing a speech to the Soviet people, and drafting two important directives on the Soviet war effort. By 1 July he was back in the Kremlin as chairman of a new State Defence Committee, set up by law the day before, and two days later he broadcast to the population that the Soviet state had 'come to death grips with its most vicious and perfidious enemy'; it was not 'an ordinary war' but a war to be waged to the death.[44]

In the first months of war Stalin insisted that the Red Army stand and fight or counter-attack, when withdrawal to a more defendable line made greater operational sense. The chief-of-staff, Zhukov, was sacked for suggesting that Soviet forces abandon territory and draw back to dig in and consolidate. Stalin assumed the Supreme Command of the Armed Forces himself, and made his Kremlin office the centre of the Soviet war effort, but his military inexperience and habitual distrust of army commanders helped to make a difficult situation worse. Soon German forces of Army Group Centre began the final assault on Moscow; most of the Soviet government was evacuated to the city of Kuibyshev. While Hitler gloated in Berlin, Stalin faced a hard choice. He was not a courageous personality, by all accounts. A decision to remain in Moscow, with German armoured units, unstoppable all summer and autumn, only eighty miles away from the capital, exposed Stalin to considerable risk. Some of the city population panicked; thousands fled the capital, others looted food shops or robbed the apartments of those who had already left. Smoke and flames from German air attacks mingled with the large bonfires of state documents, hastily burnt to avoid them falling into enemy hands. But thousands of Muscovites also flocked to the city centre, demanding that the government make a firm stand. On 19 October a state of siege was declared in the capital. The same day, Stalin made the historic decision that he would stay in the Kremlin come what may, influenced perhaps by the example of the ordinary people, whose demonstrations of loyalty were reported to him. He told the guards at his dacha: 'We will not surrender Moscow.'[45] He returned to the capital and ordered harsh measures to restore order.

A few days before this decision, Stalin had appointed Zhukov, back in favour after arguing with Stalin in July, to command the defensive positions in front of the capital. Only 90,000 tired and poorly equipped forces stood between Moscow and the Germans. Somehow Zhukov scraped together enough forces to hold a perimeter around the city while reserves were brought up from the eastern Soviet Union, where it was gambled the Japanese would not intervene. The line held by the finest of margins, and on 5 December a counter-offensive was mounted, which drove the exhausted, frostbitten German forces back far enough to end the threat to the Soviet capital for the moment, finally creating the conditions for a long war of attrition and averting a rapid German victory. Hitler, like many of his generals, had treated the invasion of the Soviet Union as if it had been a larger version of the brief Polish campaign two years previously and had been contemptuous of Soviet prospects for resistance. The failure to take Moscow forced Hitler to accept a second year of war, though he remained confident that the Soviet Union could be defeated once better fighting weather was restored in the spring and summer. On 19 December he relieved von Brauchitsch as army commander-in-chief and took over command of the army himself, promising 'to educate it to be National Socialist'.[46]

Stalin, too, was reluctant to admit that the war could not be won there and then, by what he called 'victory soon', and drove his armies on again in January and February, only to subject them to terrible losses for little strategic purpose.[47] Both dictators now controlled their military effort directly – two amateur warlords commanding the largest forces in history.

The war of attrition between the two sides was uneven from the start. German forces and their allies enjoyed many obvious advantages. Though their units took high casualties in the autumn and winter of 1941, they were only a fraction of the losses inflicted on the enemy. Between June and December 1941 the Red Army lost 2.6 million killed and 3.3 million taken prisoner; the German armed forces had 164,000 killed. For every dead German soldier there were twenty Soviet.[48] German military equipment and levels of training were, in general, very much better, while operational understanding and tactical skill greatly exceeded that of a Red Army unprepared for modern, mobile ground warfare and poorly prepared to fight a modern air war over the battlefront. The chief disparity lay in the quantity of military, industrial and agricultural resources available to the two sides. The swift Axis assault seized a large part of the Soviet bread-basket in the Ukraine, whose food surplus fed much of the rest of the country. The occupied regions contained 60 per cent of Soviet livestock supplies, 40 per cent of the grain area, and 84 per cent of sugar production. These were also the main centres of Soviet industrial output, containing approximately two-thirds of the coal, pig-iron and aluminium capacity of the Soviet Union, most of it in the rich industrial region of the Donbass. The occupied zone contained more than 40 per cent of the Soviet population, and 32 per cent of the industrial workforce, many of them potential soldiers and workers lost to the Soviet war effort. Eventually millions of the captured population worked for the German armed forces in the east, and more than 2 million were sent back to labour in the Reich.[49] The amount of railway track available to the Soviet Union fell from 106,000 km to 63,000 km between December 1940 and December 1942.[50] Many of the captured resources were exploited by the occupying forces, a net gain to Germany, a net loss to the Soviet Union.

In 1942 the imbalance of resources was at its widest; the losses experienced by the Soviet Union were exceptionally debilitating for a long war of attrition. The Soviet economy was reduced to a rump of the system built up under the Second and Third Five-Year Plans. Soviet coal mines in 1942 produced just 23 per cent of the amount produced by the Greater German Reich; Soviet steel mills just 28 per cent of German steel supplies. The Soviet industrial workforce was reduced from 8.3 million in 1940 to 5.5 million in 1942; the native German industrial workforce was 13.6 million in 1940, 11.5 million in 1942.[51] Yet over the course of the war the Soviet Union succeeded in producing more tanks, guns and aircraft than Germany by a wide margin, even within a year of the catastrophic defeats of 1941 (see Table 12.1). The ability to squeeze extraordinary quantities of equipment out of a shrunken economy and workforce is a central explanation for the eventual victory of the Soviet Union on the Eastern Front, and a striking contrast with the productive performance of her more technically advanced and richly endowed opponent.

From the very start of the war with Germany the organization of the Soviet war effort was completely centralized. On 30 June 1941 the State Defence Committee (GKO) was established under Stalin's chairmanship. The small 'war cabinet' initially had four other members – Molotov, Malenkov, Beria and Voroshilov – but its deliberations were dominated by Stalin. The committee was granted 'the entire plenitude of power in the country', though Stalin already enjoyed authority not very different.[52] It ran roughshod over established bureaucratic and commissarial procedure, encouraging an exceptional degree of improvisation and flexibility, as long as the activities of those mandated on its behalf were reported back directly to the committee. There were no set hours. Anyone who had something to say was encouraged to enter the GKO office in the Kremlin at any time. Decisions could be made by GKO members on the spot and were binding. Established commissariats and soviets carried out the committee's instructions, but they had to focus all their energies on war production and mobilization. The Commissariat for General Machine Building was turned into the Commissariat for Mortars; the Construction Commissariat was responsible only for the building of factories and installations necessary for the war, and enjoyed extraordinary

Table 12.1: Resources and Military Output of the Soviet Union and Germany 1941–1945

		1941	1942	1943	1944	1945
Resources						
Coal (m.t.)	SU	151.4	75.5	93.1	121.5	149.3
	Germany	315.5	317.9	340.4	347.6	–
Steel (m.t.)	SU	17.9	8.1	8.5	10.9	12.3
	Germany	28.2	28.7	30.6	25.8	–
Oil (m.t.)	SU	33.0	22.0	18.0	18.2	19.4
	Germany*	5.7	6.6	7.6	5.5	1.3
Aluminium (thous.t)	SU	–	51.7	62.3	82.7	86.3
	Germany	233.6	264.0	250.0	245.3	–
Industrial Labour**(m)	SU	11.0	7.2	7.5	8.2	9.5
	Germany	12.9	11.6	11.1	10.4	–
Foreign Labour***	SU	–	0.05	0.2	0.8	2.9
	Germany	3.5	4.6	5.7	7.6	–
Weapons						
Aircraft	SU	15,735	25,436	34,900	40,300	20,900
	Germany	11,776	15,409	28,807	39,807	7,540
Tanks#	SU	6,590	24,446	24,089	28,963	15,400
	Germany	5,200	9,300	19,800	27,300	–
Artillery##	SU	42,300	127,000	130,000	122,400	62,000
	(over 76 mm)	–	49,100	48,400	56,100	28,600
	Germany	7,000	12,000	27,000	41,000	–

* Synthetic oil products, natural crude oil production and imports.
** Figures for German industry include those classified as handworkers.
*** Figures for Soviet Union for POWs at end of year, figures for Germany include foreign labour (voluntary and coerced) and POW labour.
# Figures for Soviet Union include self-propelled guns. German figures include self-propelled guns for 1943 and 1944.
Artillery pieces of all calibres for Soviet Union (with separate figures over 76 mm); German figures include all pieces over 37 mm.

Sources: for Soviet Union POW figures, S. Karner, *Im Archipel GUPVI: Kriegsgefangenschaft und Internierung in der Sowjetunion 1941–1956* (Vienna, 1995), p. 90; for German forced labour and POWs, U. Herbert, *Fremdarbeiter: Politik und Praxis des 'Ausländer-Einsatzes' in der Kriegswirtschaft des Dritten Reiches* (Berlin, 1985), pp. 99, 180–2, 271; on labour supply, M. Harrison, *Soviet Planning in Peace and War 1938–1945* (Cambridge, 1985), pp. 138–40 (for rather different figures see R. W. Davies, M. Harrison and S.G. Wheatcroft, *The Economic Transformation of the Soviet Union 1913–1945* (Cambridge, 1994), p. 322, which gives figures from 1941 to 1945 of 12.8 m, 8.8 m, 9.1 m, 10.3 m and 11.7 m). German industrial employment from IWM FD 3056/49 'Statistical Material on the German Manpower Position during the War Period 1939–1944', 31 July 1945.

powers to requisition the labour and materials it needed. The system was simple but effective. A blockage in production or a crisis in the transport system was recognized immediately and could be acted upon at once by the highest authorities. The balance between centralization and flexible delegation proved a better instrument for wartime emergency than it had done during the industrialization drive of the 1930s.[53]

The economic plan was put in the hands of the young economist Nikolai Voznesensky, who had been made head of Gosplan in 1938. On 9 July 1941 he was given responsibility for drafting a war production plan for the whole economy. When German victories rendered the plan redundant, a new plan was published on 25 October for what was left of Soviet territory in the centre and east of the country. Plans were made for monthly, quarterly and annual production of a range of standard weapons, and all the supporting equipment needed to produce them. Detailed balance sheets were drawn up to ensure that the main elements of production – machine-tools, energy supply, labour and raw materials – were distributed rationally among the most important users. These balances did not work perfectly, but thanks to the recent experience of national economic planning, an overall picture of the war economy was possible, and the processes of production greatly simplified.[54] The plans gave maximum weight to defence production and expenditure and reduced civilian consumption to the absolute minimum; from two-thirds of national income in 1940 civilian consumption was just one-third by 1944. Defence expenditure rose from 17 per cent of national income in 1940 to a peak a little under 60 per cent in 1943. Retail trade declined during the war, to reach in 1943 just 36 per cent of its volume in 1940, supplying the Soviet people with a bare minimum for survival.[55]

War production was concentrated from the outset in large work halls, where primitive forms of mass production were possible using large numbers of scantily trained new workers, predominantly women and young boys. Women made up 38 per cent of the industrial workforce in 1940, but 52 per cent by 1943; more than one-third of construction workers were women by the end of the war.[56] Industrial regions in the Urals, Kazakhstan and western Siberia were quickly expanded to supply the chemicals, raw materials and armaments lost in the west. In some cases the new plants were married to equipment and workers that had been evacuated from the battle zone. Up to 25 million people were evacuated, either in railway trucks or vehicles, or on foot, trudging hundreds of miles to safety, sometimes driving herds of cattle and goats before them. A Council of Evacuation was set up two days after the German attack, on 24 June. Armed with emergency powers, the council and its eighty-five full-time officials succeeded in organizing the withdrawal of machinery, skilled workers and food-stuffs on a large scale. An estimated 50,000 small workshops and factories, including 2,593 major enterprises, were shipped eastwards, dumped often in open ground, and re-assembled in harsh winter conditions by the evacuated workforce.[57] Almost half of Soviet indus-trial investment was devoted to restarting the transported factories and building new ones in the eastern territories. Workers lived there in primitive, improvised housing. More than 2 million were retrained as machinists to cope with work in military factories in Trade and Industrial Schools, first established in October 1940. All planning was devoted to turning the unoccupied area into what Stalin called 'a single war camp'.[58]

The conditions for the Soviet workforce were tough in the extreme. Among the first wartime decrees came an extension of the working day for up to three hours; in December 1941 a decree ordered all workers to stay in the job they were in for as long as the war lasted. Local authorities had the power to conscript labour, and in February 1942 all men of 16 to 55 years of age, and all women from 16 to 45, were obliged to do labour service, often working late at night to dig defences or fill sandbags after a gruelling ten-hour shift in the factory. As military work expanded, so the supply of consumer goods and food contracted. The government responded by introducing a comprehen-sive system of rationing, based rigidly on the principle that only work earned food. Rationing of basic foodstuffs began in Moscow, Leningrad and other major cities on 8 July 1941, but by November rationing was country-wide in 115 major cities and settlements, though not in rural areas. Rations were distributed in four categories, from a meagre 750 calories for dependants, to higher, precisely calculated rations of 1,387 calories for ordinary workers, 1,913 for heavy work, and 4,418 calories for coal-miners. Those who did not work, or were not part of a worker's household, got nothing. An unknown, and unacknowledged, number of elderly, ill or isolated Russians died of starvation during the war, unable to buy on the free or black markets, where food prices increased sixteen-fold between 1940 and 1943; bread prices twenty-three-fold.[59]

Food dominated the strategies for survival worked out by ordinary Soviet people faced with the rigours of the Soviet war effort. For regular workers the factory was the source of food, with one, sometimes two warm meals a day at subsidized prices. State-run canteens increased from 51,600 in 1941 to 73,400 by the end of the war, serving food to an estimated 25 million people. Factories developed their own farms to cater for the workforce, but the shortages of food and the low calorie-levels of official rations led local authorities to allocate small plots of land to workers on the outskirts of the industrial cities. A decree of 7 April 1942 permitted them to distribute uncultivated land and by the end of 1942 there were 5.9 million allotments, by 1944 16.5 million. Here, after work, tired labourers produced limited amounts of meat, fruit and vegetables, eventually supplying one-quarter of the Soviet potato crop. An army of 600,000 'social controllers' volunteered in what spare time they had to guard the allotments against the ever-present threat of pilfering.[60] The standard diet was composed mainly of carbohydrates – potatoes and coarse bread. Bread rations ranged from 800 grams a day for the most strenuous work, down to 400 grams. By 1944 the average annual consumption of meat and fats was just seven kilograms per head. Rationing did not guarantee that food would be available, only personal entitlement. On one occasion in Kuibyshev, chocolate was substituted when there was no bread available, though luxury foodstuffs were in general almost unobtainable. Blood donors were a special exception. They were given a three-course meal, a worker's ration card for a month and 500 grams of butter and sugar. In Moscow alone there were between 200,000 and 300,000 volunteers.[61]

Life was grimmest in the Soviet countryside. A large part of the army was made up of peasant conscripts, leaving farm work largely in the hands of women, who made up half the collective farm workers in 1941 and four-fifths in 1945. The compulsory workdays were increased to 150 a year, and severe punishments introduced for failure to comply. Horses disappeared from the farms to the army, and tractors broke down or were short of fuel. Teams of women and young boys hauled ploughs, in improvised harnesses. In 1942 four-fifths of the grain was harvested by sickle, and average yields per hectare were little more than half the pre-war level.[62] Farm workers were paid almost nothing for the hours of back-breaking and dispiriting labour: a potato and 200 grams of bread a day, but sometimes less. The regime was suspicious of the peasants' opportunity to hold the cities and the army to ransom and took almost everything the collective farms produced. Rural workers were given 10 million tonnes of the grain they harvested in 1940, but only 2.24 million tonnes in 1942, and no more than 3.79 million in 1945 when conditions in the countryside were starting to improve. The rural workforce was expected to make do from the small household plots they had been allocated in the 1930s, but much of the livestock they raised on them was requisitioned, and food sales were subject to a high tax.[63] Rural workers were, in the context of the Soviet war effort, marginal. Some made money from selling on the black market, some from bartering with hungry townspeople, but the regime's determination to avoid the crippling food crises that had toppled the monarchy in 1917 made peasant enrichment or hoarding risky. The key to the survival of the war effort was the ability to extract and distribute sufficient food to keep workers working and soldiers fighting.

The exceptional efforts to transform the remaining territory of the Soviet Union into a single integrated war economy would have been severely hampered had it not been for foreign aid. The role played by American and British economic assistance supplied under the terms of 'Lend-Lease' agreements reached in 1941 and 1942 has always been subject to contention. Relatively little of it came in the form of finished armaments, and some of the military equipment, including British Matilda tanks, was regarded (not unreasonably) as second-rate. Only four per cent of Soviet weapons were supplied by her two western allies, and this, so ran the official post-war Soviet history of the war, 'could have had no decisive influence'.[64] However, the bulk of assistance came in the form of food, raw materials, machinery and industrial equipment. Lend-Lease allowed Soviet factories to concentrate on the large-scale production of weapons of Soviet design, rather than having to produce other forms of equipment. The United States supplied 409,500 vehicles (mostly the well-known Studebaker truck), but the

Soviet Union produced only 265,000. In addition 43 per cent of Soviet tyres came from America, and 56 per cent of rails for the Soviet railway network. America supplied 1,900 locomotives, while the Soviet Union produced only 92 throughout the war. Without Lend-Lease, Soviet transportation would have become a crisis sector. The supply of raw materials was as vital. Though the Soviet Union was well-endowed with crude oil deposits, the war disrupted refineries and the supply of refining equipment, and sharply reduced high-grade oil production. The United States supplied 58 per cent of the high-octane fuel needed for Soviet aircraft and approximately one-third of Soviet explosives, four-fifths of all copper, and 328,000 tonnes of aluminium against Soviet output of 283,000 tonnes, most of which was produced in 1944 and 1945.[65] Enough canned food was supplied to have provided every Soviet soldier with a meal a day, though accounts from the fighting fronts make it clear that soldiers were not the regular beneficiaries.

The Soviet war effort focused above all on the prosecution of war at the expense of everything else. Weapons were produced in the kind of quantities that Tukhachevsky had talked about when he suggested the industrialization of warfare in the early 1930s. Anyone who failed to work, or was guilty of neglect or incompetence, lost rations or could be sent to a camp, whose inmates laboured all over the Soviet area as forced workers. Yet it would be wrong to assume that coercion was the only means to commit the Soviet home front to total war. Work meant survival, not only for the individual, who might otherwise face slow debilitation through hunger, but for the Soviet Union or Mother Russia. A real enemy at last, in the shape of Germany, galvanized Soviet society into efforts that would have seemed all but impossible when the Soviet industrial economy and food supply were pulled in half by the invader in 1941.

The gulf that temporarily separated the Soviet and German economies in the middle years of the war was never fully exploited by the German dictatorship. German industry continued to produce equipment of very high technical quality throughout the war. By comparison with the Soviet Union, Germany was rich in resources and free to exploit them fully before the onset of large-scale allied bombing in 1944. Moreover, if the Soviet Union had Lend-Lease, by 1941 Germany had access to the resources of much of Europe occupied by her forces since 1938, or supplied by neutral or allied states under special trade treaties, including large quantities of coal, iron-ore, oil and non-ferrous ores. This 'large area economy', as German planners called it, provided a potentially vast resource base. Some of these resources were exploited where they stood, some taken back to the Reich. An estimated 20 million workers outside Germany were employed for the German war effort by 1943–4; around 6 million workers were transferred from the occupied areas, largely by force, to work in Germany.[66] The entire economic base available to the Third Reich was, with the single exception of oil, immensely greater than that available to the Soviet Union. Yet between 1941 and 1945 German-dominated Europe produced 103,000 aircraft against the 137,000 produced in the Soviet Union, 61,000 tanks and self-propelled guns against 99,500, 87,000 heavy artillery pieces against 182,000.

The principal explanation for this paradox has focused on the apparent unwillingness of the German government to mobilize the economy very fully from fear that civilian morale would collapse as it was alleged to have done in 1918. Hitler's personal obsession with the 'stab-in-the-back' legend has been used to justify the argument that the German war effort constituted a 'peace-like' war economy until at least 1942, and was not fully mobilized for total war until 1944.[67] This is an argument that fits poorly with the already exceptional levels of military preparedness and economic diversion achieved under the Four-Year Plan before 1939, or with the reality of large-scale economic and social mobilization introduced immediately in Germany and the occupied territories in the autumn of 1939. On 4 September 1939 a War Economy Decree was published that laid down guidelines for the rapid mobilization of civilian resources and the conversion of the economy to war. In December 1939 Hitler ordered an armaments programme 'with the highest possible figures'. The army procurement office compared Hitler's targets with German production at the height of the war effort in 1918 and found in all cases that Hitler wanted more: 151,780 artillery pieces a year instead of 15,550, 2,179,000 machine guns instead of 196,600, and so on. All this required, as a later wartime report indicated, 'a throttling of civilian consumption' and the conversion of the national economy 'rapidly and comprehensively to the demands of war'. Walther Funk, head of the central bank, told its directors in February 1940 that economic mobilization was 'based on the assumption of a total war'.[68]

Although these figures were not realized even by 1942, the conversion of the civilian economy to cope with them went ahead from autumn 1939 and was mostly completed by the time of Barbarossa. In May 1941, 55 per cent of the workforce was producing equipment for the armed services. The increase in German labour working for defence was 149 per cent between 1939 and 1941, but only 11 per cent between 1941 and 1943. The shape of the economy under the impact of war altered as it did in the Soviet Union. Defence expenditure was approximately 20 per cent of national income in 1938/9, but reached 60 per cent by 1941, and 73 per cent by 1943/4. Consumer expenditure fell from 71 billion marks in 1939 to 57 billion in 1942 and 53 billion by 1944 – four-fifths of the fall coming before 1942. Consumption per head fell by approximately one-fifth by 1941. The consumer industries swiftly converted to war production; by 1940 most were devoting half or more of their output to the forces or the government.[69] The armed forces took the lion's share of the quotas for iron, steel and a range of scarce metals. German civilians came a poor second to the demands of war.

Unlike the Soviet war effort, no attempt was made to build a centralized wartime administration when war broke out. Military decision-making was the task of Hitler's supreme headquarters. The wider war effort was initially to be the responsibility of a Reich Defence Council, chaired by Hermann Göring, but it lacked the powers enjoyed by the GKO and was too distant from Hitler. Within weeks it had collapsed as a central forum. The regular ministries, the Four-Year Plan organization and the technical and procurement divisions of the armed forces shared the work of mobilization uncertainly between them. The organization of the economic resources of occupied Europe, despite their importance to the war effort, was also divided between competing authorities and never centralized. The armed forces, the army in particular, were keen to take over the organization of war production, having lost responsibility to the Four-Year Plan during the late 1930s, and resisted what they saw as civilian encroachment. In the spring of 1940 the engineer Fritz Todt was appointed Minister of Munitions to try to bring some organization to the production of army weapons, but he had no say in aircraft production, which constituted two-fifths of all war production, and his relations with army leaders and industrialists were ill-defined and fractious. The combination of central control and flexible response characteristic of the Soviet system was entirely absent. The German war economy produced weapons of high quality, but in numbers far smaller than the allocation of resources should have merited.

In 1941 Hitler became fully aware of the growing gap between his targets and the actual level of output. Those trying to mobilize the war economy complained by the summer that there were no more resources to conscript, even with the wealth of occupied Europe. In July 1941 Hitler authorized higher production targets to meet the projected military situation once the Soviet Union had been defeated in the autumn. These plans for air and naval forces to fight Britain and the United States, combined with Hitler's requirement for a large permanent, fully motorized army, finally exposed how ineffectively the German war economy had been mobilized. Lack of central control encouraged exceptional levels of waste and misallocated effort; it also encouraged the armed forces to order short production runs and regular technical modifications as they sought to exploit a lead in quality rather than quantity. Hitler insisted that the armed forces accept 'crude mass production' and 'primitive, robust construction' instead of the small batches of high-quality weapons, expensive in labour and materials.[70] On 3 December 1941 he signed a decree on 'Simplification and Increased Efficiency in our Armaments Production', which was known popularly as the 'Rationalization Decree'. He chided German firms for failing to adopt the practice of large factories and simple production methods, and ordered the military to simplify and standardize the design of all weapons to make possible 'mass production on modern principles'.[71]

In the spring of 1942 Hitler acted to overhaul the way the domestic war effort was organized. After Fritz Todt was killed in an air crash in February 1942, Hitler appointed as his successor his architect Albert Speer, who happened to be passing through headquarters just hours after Todt's death. Hitler wanted Speer, a man whose work he admired and whose links to the military were negligible, to enjoy complete authority, derived from the *Führer* himself, for the 'greater centralization and streamlining of the entire economy'.[72] Speer was appointed to a new Ministry of Armaments and Munitions. Like Vosnesensky, he set out to plan war production in detail. In March he established a new Central Planning apparatus, a small economic cabinet where every element of the economy could be discussed and a proper balance established between resources and the manufacture of weapons. A nation-wide system of specialist main committees (*Hauptauschüsse*) was set up for every major branch of military production, and industrialists and engineers recruited to bring a fresh expertise to bear. Considerable success followed, for Speer's assistants unearthed a remarkable degree of inefficiency and waste in the industrial economy. By 1944 it proved possible to produce four times as many weapons from the same quantity of allocated steel. Costs and production times were slashed thanks to new standard work practices and long production runs. In 1941 the Messerschmitt Me 109 fighter was produced at a rate of 180 a month in seven separate factories; two years later 1,000 per month were produced in three large plants. In 1944, with a small overall increase in resources, three times as many armaments were produced as in 1941, though still less than the Soviet Union.[73]

The greater rationalization of the German war effort was limited by numerous factors. The occupied areas were never fully exploited. Aircraft production remained independent until 1944; labour allocation was placed outside Speer's direct control when in March 1942 Hitler decided to appoint the *Gauleiter* of Thuringia, the old party fighter Fritz Sauckel, as Plenipotentiary for Labour Supply. Over-bureaucratized structures produced a system that was too planned for its own good. The army accepted Speer as armaments minister with great reluctance, since he was a civilian, and tried to maintain their commitment to vanguard technologies and small production runs. The weapons produced remained, on balance, superior to the Soviet equivalent, but there were too few of them to equip a vast army whose losses of men and materials accelerated through 1943 and 1944. In 1944 the onset of heavy Allied bombing began to erode any possibility of utilizing resources fully, and encouraged Hitler's search for wonder-weapons (the so-called 'Vengeance weapons'), which diverted vast resources away from standard but mass-produced weapons at a critical juncture of the war. In the summer of 1944 Joseph Goebbels was appointed Plenipotentiary for Total War as Speer's star began to decline, but Goebbels saw his task principally in propaganda terms. From the summer of 1944 the organization of the war economy became ever more improvised and dispersed, forced, as the Soviet economy was in 1941 and 1942, to simplify production and to mass-produce cruder but proven weapons, like the hand-held anti-tank *Panzerfaust*, and to increase the regimentation and exploitation of an armaments workforce now made up of a majority of forced foreign workers.

Conditions on the German home front were always more favourable than in the Soviet Union, where living standards were already very low before 1941. But the German experience too was one of immediate and permanent reductions in standards of diet and household consumption, and harsher conditions of labour as the structure of the labour force altered. There still exists a popular myth that German women were not recruited to war work as they were in the other warring powers, an assertion that rests largely on a statistical illusion. Women in Germany had always made up a large proportion of the workforce, particularly in agriculture, where, as in the Soviet Union, they ran the farms while the men worked in industry or transport. In 1939, on the eve of war, women made up 37 per cent of the German workforce, or more than 14 million workers; by the war's end they comprised 51 per cent, a figure not far short of the figure in the Soviet Union, and very much greater than in Britain or the United States. In agriculture they constituted 65 per cent of the native rural workforce in 1944. The large number of foreign forced labourers who were female increased the proportion of women in industry substantially. Women had to accept longer hours of work, as well as more dangerous and arduous work. The number working in heavy industry doubled from 760,000 to 1.5 million between 1939 and 1943. Illness and absenteeism were persistent problems, made worse by the experience of bombing. More than 3 million women with children worked six-hour shifts, which classified them as part-time; taken together with the regular workforce, there were over 17 million women working by 1944, and millions more engaged in voluntary work as welfare workers, teachers or party activists.[74] Women in Germany played a major part in keeping the war effort going, as they did in the Soviet Union.

For the home population the supply of food was as important as it was for the Soviet enemy. The German regime wanted to avoid the problems of the mass hunger experienced in the Great War, and made every effort to stamp out black-marketeering and hoarding. Rationing and rigid price controls ensured a more equal distribution of opportunities and sacrifices than in 1914. The rationing system was planned before the outbreak of war and was introduced immediately in the autumn of 1939 for a whole range of products, except for potatoes. Luxury foods disappeared, and for most of the war period the German public ate a monotonous diet of potatoes, coarse bread and limited quantities of meat and sugar products, not very different from the ingredients of the Soviet diet (which also allowed the average consumer three kilograms of bread a week), though with a fractionally higher calorific content. When customers ate in a restaurant they had to supply ration coupons for each of the food items on their plate: one for the peas, one for the meat and so on. Many foods were produced in substitute (*ersatz*) forms even before 1939, but the quality of most foodstuffs deteriorated in wartime as the state insisted on a single standard product and permitted adulteration. Coffee was made from roast barley, tea from a variety of herbs and plants. Cigarettes were rationed to one-and-a-half a day for women, three for men. Fresh foods disappeared, either to the canning industry or to the much-better-fed armed forces. The supply of standard rationed goods was maintained during the war by exploiting European resources (though the captured Soviet agricultural area mainly supplied the millions of men and horses in the east), but save for potatoes and beet sugar, the main ingredients of the German diet were steadily cut except for those engaged in the most strenuous jobs. Only the army of forced labourers and prisoners was worse off.[75]

The experience of total war for both populations was never uniform. Conditions in the Soviet Union were harsher at the start of the war than they were by 1944, when large areas had been recaptured and the improvised economy replaced by a more fixed and predictable system. In Germany, on the other hand, conditions worsened steadily as the war continued and bombing became a regular occurrence. Life in the German countryside was generally preferable to life in the city, and food more plentiful. By contrast, life in most Soviet cities was safer and less wretched, and, since the government was determined to use force to ensure that food reached the towns, the urban populace was generally better fed. Social status brought advantages in access to food and consumer goods, particularly for party officials in both systems. Workers could earn bonuses in food for exceptional efforts, but white-collar workers had less claim. Camp prisoners in each system experienced total war as an intensification of their hardships, with declining diet, non-existent medical supplies and a regime of gruelling work under the supervision of agents instructed to extract the maximum labour at minimum cost. In each dictatorship the degree of regimentation and organization of the domestic population was extreme, and penalties for law-breaking or slacking or acts of casual dissent severe. A Polish doctor on a train going through Siberia in 1942 observed that at every river crossing or bridge the passengers in the train were obliged for security reasons to shut the windows and to stare straight in front of them. Apart from an occasional tussle between a drunken passenger and the guards, he observed that 'the rule is carried out by everyone without a murmur'.[76]

Perhaps nowhere was the reality of total war more absolute than in the city of Leningrad during the more than 900 days of siege to which it was subjected from the autumn of 1941. The civilian population of the city became part of a web of soldiers, nurses, fire-fighters, workers and militia who constituted their own enclosed war effort, producing weapons, digging trenches, extinguishing fires and scrounging desperately for food. More than a million people perished from cold and hunger, while the rest coped with 200,000 small allotments carved out in and around the city limits and a thin lifeline to the rest of the Soviet Union across the 'ice-road' on Lake Ladoga. They were subject to regular bombing and shelling from German artillery and aircraft, and produced the shells that filled their own guns in reply. For the first nine months of siege conditions of life were almost unendurable. In freezing temperatures, with no electricity or paraffin, householders hunted for any wood that would burn or stole it from those who were too tired or weakened to resist. The few medicines were soon exhausted. The starving dropped in the streets and froze there. Agents of the party and NKVD tried to instil discipline, arresting and deporting victims even as German forces closed the ring around the city. 'We are all on death row,' confided a Leningrad nurse in her diary, 'we just don't know who is next.'[77] Extreme hunger created a single obsession in the population. A doctor, whose small son died in the winter of 1941/2, observed that 'wherever two or three people meet, at work, at the office, in line, the talk is only of food. What are they giving us on the ration cards, how much, what is available etc. – it is life's most vital question.' When a former ballerina reported to a local party organizer that she had shared enough food to allow her elderly mother to survive the winter, she was told that she was tactless and sentimental: 'For a young life is needed by the government, but an old life is not!'[78] A Leningrad artist, Anna-Petrovna Ostroumova-Lebedeva, saw the fate of the city as somehow representative of a collective insanity that had overtaken mankind and plunged innocent populations into a furnace. 'Our Leningrad,' she wrote in her journal in March 1942, '– we are only a tiny detail in this entire, horrible, nightmarish but grandiose and amazing war.' She confessed to herself that she felt a 'satanic romanticism', a kind of 'grandeur', a 'head-long irrepressible rush to death and destruction'.[79]

Leningrad lay in the main battleground of the giant civil war between Germany and the Soviet Union. The war was fought across the broad borderlands that separated the two dictatorships – Poland, the Baltic States, the Ukraine, Belorussia. In 1941 and 1942 Axis forces fought their way into the western fringes of the Russian federation itself, but were expelled from these areas first; in 1945 the Red Army penetrated only as far as the eastern provinces of the Reich, to reach a little beyond Berlin. In the lands between, millions of soldiers and millions of civilians lost their lives in history's largest and costliest war. It was a conflict that raged twice across the same terrain, first as Axis forces swarmed across in 1941, then when the Red Army drove them back again between 1943 and 1945. Each time the retreating armies destroyed much of what they had to leave behind; each time the attacking armies destroyed more. The area became a human desert of abandoned villages, crushed cities, and numberless mass graves. It was in these borderlands that the genocide of the Jews was sited. It was here that millions of Soviet prisoners of war starved to death. It is here that most German and Soviet soldiers who died during the war still lie.

The term now commonly used to describe the degeneration into unrestricted mass violence on the Eastern Front is 'the barbarization of warfare'.[80] The concept suggests a level of deliberate, atrocious violence greater than the normally barbarous conditions under which modern war was fought on all fronts between 1939 and 1945, and it has been applied in particular to the behaviour of German forces in the occupied east. 'Barbarization' suggests a process of degeneration from conventional warfare to forms of ill-disciplined, routine barbarity, even to the systematic, violent racism that resulted in genocide. The pattern of violence was, in reality, more complex than this. The Eastern Front hosted a number of distinct confrontations, each with its own history of exceptional lethality. There were forms of violence between opposing armed forces that violated the contemporary conventions of the rules of war governing the battlefield and the taking and incarceration of prisoners. There was violence between armed forces, security forces and civilians as a result of irregular, guerrilla warfare. This took the form of military conflict between regular soldiers and partisans, but also of reprisals by the military and security forces against (usually) unarmed civilians in retaliation for partisan attacks. Both of these forms of violence involved the two sides, Axis and Soviet. Axis forces were a mixture of regular soldiers, policemen, security officers and local militia recruited and supplied by the occupier. Then there was violence directed deliberately at civilian populations, who were besieged, shelled, bombed, starved or deported by the enemy armed forces. Finally there was violence displayed by the occupying power and native collaborators against racial minorities, predominantly Jews, who were to be placed in ghettos or exterminated. This violence was chiefly conducted against unarmed civilians by the German security apparatus (SS, SD, Gestapo, police) with the aid of thousands of native collaborators, and help from the regular armed forces; it is dealt with in more detail in the chapters that follow. The borders between these different forms of violence were not closely defined, for perpetrators could move across them at will, but each had separate reasons for the nature and escalation of violence, which are not clearly conveyed by using the umbrella term 'barbarization'.

Explanations for some of the forms of violence distinguished here generally divide into two camps: the first sees a predisposition to excessive violence produced by ideological indoctrination or deliberate brutalization; the second focuses on the demoralizing environment of combat – high losses, fierce fighting, poor climate, hunger and fear.[81] These factors unquestionably played a part, but the excessive violence displayed in the east was a direct consequence of the way the two dictatorships shaped the conflict from its outset, Hitler as the conqueror of racial empire, Stalin as the defender of the revolutionary state against German violation. The entire German campaign in the east was defined by Hitler's claim in March 1941 that he was waging a 'war of extermination'.[82] Between March and June a series of directives from Hitler's supreme headquarters, generally known as the 'criminal orders', gave German forces permission to execute the 'Jewish-Bolshevik' intelligentsia, political commissars and Soviet security officers. 'Force,' Hitler told the army chief-of-staff, 'must be used in its most brutal form.'[83] On 13 May 1941, a decree on wartime military jurisdiction was published, which removed crimes against civilians from the sphere of courts martial and suspended any obligation to punish offences against 'hostile civilian persons' committed by soldiers. 'Irregulars,' ran the decree, 'are to be mercilessly executed in battle or on the run.' Any other hostile acts by civilians were 'to be silenced on the spot by the most extreme methods'; in localities whence attacks came 'collective reprisal measures' were permitted if the culprits could not be caught.[84] 'Guidelines for the behaviour of the troops in Russia' followed on 19 May. Paragraph I (2) read '[Germany's] struggle demands ruthless and energetic action against Bolshevik agitators, guerrillas, saboteurs, Jews' and approved 'the complete liquidation of any active or passive resistance'.[85] On 6 June the supreme command issued 'Guidelines on the treatment of political commissars', which first offered a lurid description of the 'hate-filled, cruel and inhuman treatment' that German soldiers could expect from them, and then ordered that commissars captured in battle or resisting 'are as a matter of principle to be finished off by weapon at once'. The army commander von Brauchitsch added a rider to the instructions to read that commissars should, if possible, be killed 'inconspicuously'.[86]

Hitler's views on how to treat the Soviet enemy were the views of Germany's Supreme Commander; they gave unambiguous permission to act with extreme harshness against the Soviet civilian population and to murder certain categories of captives out of hand, and granted German forces immunity from prosecution in advance if they did so. The army made little protest because many senior officers accepted the necessity for special measures against the new enemy, and willingly passed on the prejudices of their commander to the troops under their control. Typical was a study produced by General Hoepner for *Panzergruppe* 4 in early May 1941, which began with the statement that the war against Russia was an essential part 'of the struggle for existence of the German *Volk*' against 'Jewish-Bolshevism'. The campaign had to be led, Hoepner continued, 'with unheard-of harshness'. Soldiers had to arm themselves with 'an iron, pitiless will' and show 'no mercy for the bearers of today's Russian-Bolshevist system'.[87] Franz Halder, chief-of-staff of the army and a member of the circle which had contemplated a coup against Hitler in 1938, took upon himself to add the categories 'Jew and Communist' to a list of those targeted during the campaign against Yugoslavia in April 1941; he helped draw up instructions for the Barbarossa campaign a few weeks later, demanding 'iron severity' in dealing with a civilian population 'deluded' by the 'exponent of the Jewish-Bolshevik ideology'.[88] At a meeting of military judges in June, General Eugen Müller told them that it was Hitler's intention that in the coming invasion 'legal considerations have to step back behind the necessities of war'. Von Brauchitsch was concerned only to avoid 'the degeneration of the troops' as a result of their unrestricted licence to kill, and insisted that reprisal and murder should only be carried out on the orders of an officer.[89]

The troops themselves were warned in advance to expect the enemy to behave in ways that clearly made legitimate any acts of retaliatory and systematic violence. All Soviet soldiers, even prisoners, were to be treated with extreme caution. The army guidelines on combat warned that 'the Asiatic soldiers of the Red Army are particularly impenetrable, unpredictable, underhand and callous'.[90] An instruction sheet under the title 'Do You Know the Enemy?' pointed out that Russians could not be expected 'to behave as decent soldiers and chivalrous opponents'. Many senior officers recalled the war in the east between 1914 and 1918, where they learned how Russian soldiers would play dead, or continue to fight while wounded, or dress in enemy uniform before murdering German soldiers. Russians were expected to kill or torture their prisoners, and the German soldier was bound in honour to ensure that 'he allows none of his comrades to fall into the hands of the enemy!' Among the other dangers to guard against were enemy parachutists in civilian dress, poisoned food and water supplies, and chemical weapons, which, it was claimed, the Soviet side would use first. Later in the war, German recruits arriving at the front were routinely told to assume that surrendering soldiers were likely to attack at any opportunity and that 'dead' soldiers often revived to shoot German soldiers in the back.[91] When German soldiers entered the Soviet Union in 1941 they were already primed to expect the worst. Albert Neuhaus, a travelling salesman from Münster called up for the invasion, wrote to his wife a week after the start of the campaign that the Russians did not know what had struck them: 'And they certainly deserve it, this riff-raff have earned nothing better.'[92] The young machine-gunner Günther Koschorrek described in a secret journal his first impressions of 'the dirty brown heap of destruction' represented by the Soviet soldiery in his line of fire.[93]

The Soviet reaction to German invasion was to issue a call to arms for the whole of Soviet society. The pre-war ideal of the soldier-citizen, which dated back to the civil war, was deeply embedded in popular Soviet culture. Every citizen was expected to become a fighter if the moment demanded; to repel the invader, and if possible to kill him, was regarded not as an act of suicidal desperation, but a high civic obligation. Stalin in his first wartime speech, broadcast to universal relief on 3 July 1941, announced that beside the Soviet armed forces 'all citizens of the Soviet Union must defend every inch of Soviet soil, must fight to the last drop of their blood for our towns and villages'. The war, he said, was not an ordinary war but 'a great war of the entire Soviet people', and he summoned up partisan forces to hound and annihilate the enemy, and a popular *levée en masse* of ordinary working people to defend the threatened cities.[94] In November Stalin addressed the Moscow Soviet, where he told its members that because of the unrestricted violence shown by German forces, the people's task 'consists of annihilating to the last man all Germans'.[95] The same ruthlessness was applied to all those who threatened the Soviet home front, and to soldiers who surrendered rather than fight to the last bullet and the last breath. Order No. 270, issued in August 1941, condemned all captured Soviet soldiers as 'traitors to the motherland' and penalized their families. When Stalin's own son, Yakov, was captured in July, his wife spent two years in a camp.[96]

The call to arms for the whole society exposed thousands of irregular forces to the savage reprisals of the advancing German armies. Militia units hastily raised in Moscow and Leningrad were thrown into front-line battles, where they took devastating casualties. Some 130,000 were sent to the Leningrad front, while 500,000 Leningraders prepared the city's defences and 14,000 were trained as partisans and sent behind enemy lines.[97] The early months of the German invasion showed a widespread response to Stalin's call for popular participation and a popular ethos of sacrifice, for this had been the central message of the progressive militarization of Soviet society before 1941. During 1942 the emphasis in wartime propaganda shifted from heroic sacrifice to bloody reprisal as news of German atrocities spread through the Soviet population. By the summer months an orchestrated campaign of hatred was used to spur the population on to new efforts. The poet Ilya Ehrenburg, who returned to Moscow from Paris in 1940, turned out regular hate propaganda: 'Let us kill! If you haven't killed a German in the course of the day, your day has been wasted.' The enemy was reduced to a core of animal images, favourite among them the snake/ reptile and dog. In 'Partisan', published in *Pravda* in July 1942, the Germans were 'executioners, bloodsuckers, cannibals, killers, thieves, dogs'. In another poem in late August the German became a 'fascist snake': 'We should pull out its teeth/pull out its insides/smash its spine.'[98] The theme of German rape of Soviet women featured regularly, and ordinary Soviet soldiers were told atrocity stories concerning children and women and passed on these stories to each other. German soldiers were presented to the Soviet public as depraved beasts, to be put down without mercy – mirroring the negative stereotype of the Red Army man in German military propaganda. The effect was to render inevitable an escalation of violence: German forces were given permission to act with exceptional brutality against civilians and to treat the military with a wary contempt; the Soviet people were expected to resist by every means and Soviet soldiers to exact grim revenge on the invader when he retaliated. The image each side created of the other became a self-fulfilling prophecy.

Nonetheless, not every German or Soviet soldier committed atrocities because they were permitted or encouraged to do so. On the battlefield between the two armies, conditions of combat provoked exceptional levels of violence. Soviet forces took extravagant losses, but fought with a determination that astonished German troops. The bravery of individual Soviet soldiers was often suicidal, but it produced much higher losses on the German side. The ever-present reality of violent death produced both fear and fatalism. The soldiers on both sides faced the prospect of violence from their own side if they deserted or panicked. The German armed forces judged 35,000 cases of alleged desertion, condemned 22,000 to death and executed somewhere between 15,000 and 20,000 of their own soldiers; like the Red Army, they put shirkers and criminals in penal battalions. Soldiers fought in the frontline, if they survived, for months on end with declining prospects of leave. Death was immanent, casual and arbitrary. An Italian liaison officer in the Ukraine, Giorgio Geddes, witnessed a small group of Axis soldiers who had lost their units walking along a dirt track away from Stalingrad. When two German field police stopped them to check their papers, one of them fired a burst from the heavy machine gun he was carrying and killed them both. As he turned to walk on 'as if nothing had happened', one of his German companions pulled out a pistol and killed him. The group carried on down the road, leaving the dead where they had fallen.[99]

In battle the laws of war were disregarded by both sides. Soviet soldiers fought with skills that exposed them to harsh reprisals. They were adept at concealment and infiltration, hiding in foxholes or copses, silent and completely still until German infantry, oblivious of the hidden enemy, found themselves attacked from behind. Soviet soldiers were more willing to engage in hand-to-hand combat; they used knives to kill sentries and lookouts; the silence and stealth with which Soviet soldiers learned to move forward was unnerving; Red Army sniper fire was deadly. In combat they fell down during attacks and lay still amongst those who were really dead until they could use their weapons again. German forces learned to kill anyone on the ground, even the wounded. Koschorrek, in his first engagement near Stalingrad, watched in horror as his sergeant placed a sub-machine gun barrel against the heads of apparently dead soldiers and fired.

Other men did the same, kicking the corpses for a sign of life and firing at those that moved. But a few months later he watched with indifference as a wounded Soviet officer was machine-gunned for trying to fire at the men who were dressing his wounds.[100] German soldiers were told that the Red Army did not take prisoners; Soviet soldiers were told the same about the German forces. Atrocity became routine. Evgeni Bessonov, a Soviet tank officer, recalled in his memoirs a German raid on a makeshift hospital where all but one of the wounded were killed; Koschorrek, retreating in 1944, came across the mutilated bodies of his companions, their heads crushed and their stomachs slit open.[101] Prisoners were taken, by both sides, but thousands of captured soldiers were killed out-of-hand by forces on the move, or desperate or consumed by sudden hatreds. Atrocious behaviour produced a circle of fear and retaliation that could not be broken.

Millions of prisoners of war were taken by both sides, but their treatment shows a clear difference in the way the two dictatorships approached the war. By the summer of 1944 the German armed forces had captured a total of 5.2 million Soviet soldiers. Of these 2.2 million were reported as dead. Estimates for the death of Soviet prisoners over the whole war period range from 2.54 million to 3.3 million.[102] Soviet records show that from the 2.88 million German prisoners taken 356,000 died, a loss rate of 14.9 per cent.[103] The high losses of Soviet prisoners occurred mainly during the winter of 1941/2, when the German army captured very much larger numbers of the enemy than they had anticipated. They were herded into makeshift camps behind barbed wire and machine-gun emplacements, often with little or no shelter and inadequate food supplies. Hitler was adamant at first that they were not to be brought into Europe to be used as forced labour, for they were regarded as both a biological and a political threat. When in late June 1941 the Soviet government, which had not signed the 1929 Geneva Convention on prisoners of war, tried to involve the International Red Cross in defining the treatment of prisoners by both sides, Germany refused. In the early stages of the war Hitler's view of the conquered Slavic peoples was overtly genocidal. The general plan for the east expected millions of Slavs to perish as the new empire was constructed. Hitler ordered the troops besieging Leningrad to be entirely indifferent to the fate of its 3 million inhabitants; he told his entourage that Moscow would be wiped from the face of the earth, together with its inhabitants. While Soviet prisoners starved to death, thousands died in the German-occupied cities from disease and hunger.[104]

Not all Soviet prisoners died of deliberate neglect. Approximately 600,000 were killed by German forces and security men on grounds of race or because they were communists. Others were killed for breaking the rules or for trying to escape from the deadly camps. A camp commandant in Smolensk wrote in his diary in January 1942 about the execution 'before the eyes of the others' of two starving prisoners accused of eating their dead comrades.[105] Few Soviet prisoners were recruited and sent to Germany until, under pressure on all sides to ease the labour shortages, Hitler agreed on 31 October 1941 that Soviet prisoners of war could be used in the Reich, as long as they were isolated from the home population. But by March only 166,800 had been sent. Not until April 1942 did large-scale transports begin, by which time two-thirds of the prisoners were dead.[106] The rest were in little condition for labour. 'From the millions of prisoners,' wrote the same camp commandant, 'only a few thousand can be regarded as capable of work . . . first unbelievably many died from typhus fever and the remainder are so weak and wretched.'[107] During 1942 new prisoners were transported back to Germany and by the autumn almost half-a-million were employed, by 1944 631,000. They were given a deliberately poor diet and severely punished for any infraction. Thousands ended up in concentration camps. The SD reported in August 1942 that anti-Soviet propaganda had created anxieties among the German population about the 'animal-like' Russian beast. 'Many members of the *Volk*,' ran the report, 'imagine that they must be radically exterminated.'[108]

The treatment of German prisoners in the Soviet Union was governed by the severe labour shortages experienced in the Soviet war economy. Like the German armed forces, the Red Army had made only limited provision for prisoners. There were only three camps capable of housing 8,000 available in the autumn of 1941. By 1943 there were thirty-one camps, and a capacity of 200,000. Most prisoners were allocated to work camps in agriculture, construction and heavy industry under the provisions of a law of 1 July 1941 on the use of prisoner labour.

They were classified in the same four categories as GUlag labour, from fully healthy to invalid. Death rates were high at first from inadequate food supplies, cold and disease. During the first winter of 1941/2 the rate was 15 per cent, but during the winter of 1942/3 it rose to 52 per cent; most of the 119,000 died from the consequences of extreme dystrophy. From 1943 the authorities made great efforts to raise prisoner productivity and to improve their provisioning, and the death rate fell by the end of the war to only 4 per cent.[109] The prisoners were isolated from the rest of the population. The camps of tents or rough barracks were run by German officers. The men worked ten or twelve hours a day, and had the same diet of bread and soup given to Soviet GUlag prisoners. Those strong enough to exceed the work norms earned more bread. German prisoners were encouraged to compete with each other to become Stakhanovite prisoners. They were subject to the same security screening as regular prisoners. Cases of sabotage were treated as 'fascist resistance' and severely punished; at the same time a programme of re-education was begun, which led to one-fifth of the prisoners enrolling in the 'Free Germany' movement. Some were trained in three-month courses of 'anti-fascist propaganda' run by the NKVD, and sent back to the Soviet zone of Germany in 1945 as agitators. Eventually over 2 million prisoners were repatriated to Germany, 1.4 million by 1948, the last not until 1956.[110]

The one area of the war in which few prisoners were taken and no quarter given was the war between the Axis armies and the irregular forces that fought them behind German lines. This was a war the German army expected to fight, though few preparations were made for conducting it. The harsh measures ordered before the invasion were invoked at once. Corporal Werner Bergholtz witnessed two weeks after the start of the campaign the shooting of 100 hostages after the death of two sentries: 'They all had to be Jews,' he wrote in his diary.[111] The anti-guerrilla instructions were applied remorselessly. From Hitler's headquarters came a stream of new directives to the armed forces and the security troops to act ever more barbarously. On 23 July a decree permitted forces 'to spread the kind of terror' that would make the Soviet people 'lose all interest in insubordination'.[112] On 16 September Keitel, chief-of-staff at Hitler's Supreme Command, distributed the Hostage Order, allowing troops to execute between 50 and 100 Soviet citizens for every German killed. Human life, he asserted, counted for little in the Soviet Union.[113] All over the occupied area, even including those regions recently occupied by the Soviet Union, Axis forces were attacked by *francs-tireurs*, small pockets of isolated and encircled Soviet troops or political officers, *Komsomol* recruits, irregular militia. This was scarcely organized partisan activity, but they were hunted down by policemen and soldiers and murdered in their thousands. Their bodies, with hand-scrawled placards around their necks, were left hanging for days as a warning to others. In July 1942 anti-guerrilla operations were taken under Himmler's jurisdiction; he immediately ordered the term 'partisan' to be dropped and the enemy to be described by the term 'bandit'. On 16 December 1942 new guidelines for the conduct of anti-guerrilla War were published, which spelled out that the war against irregulars was to be fought regardless of any conventional legality or morality, 'without limitation, even against women and children'.[114]

The Soviet government had made no provision for a partisan war. When Stalin called for a partisan uprising against the invader in July 1941, he knew that preparations for possible partisan operations had been suspended because of his own distrust of the political reliability of an irregular force. Irregulars were issued with copies of Lenin's 1906 pamphlet on 'Partisan Warfare' and limited supplies of weapons. Not until 30 May 1942 did Stalin finally approve the establishment of a Central Staff for Partisan Warfare under the direction of the Belorussian Communist Party Secretary, Pantelymon Ponomarenko. The units were organized on military lines, with infiltrated Red Army commanders and NKVD officials to run them. Partisans were encouraged to see themselves as avengers as well as fighters. The partisan oath bound them to pursue 'a terrible, merciless, and unrelenting revenge upon the enemy . . . Blood for blood! Death for death!'[115] By the end of 1942 there were an estimated 300,000 partisans, but the numbers are impossible to calculate with any accuracy. Thousands were killed in the large German anti-partisan sweeps carried out by the ten security divisions allocated to the German army rear areas. Others moved in and out of partisan activity. Many were genuine bandits, preying on the native population and terrorizing whole areas. Giorgio Geddes witnessed the execution of a local partisan leader in the Ukraine who, under the guise of collaborating with the Germans as a Ukrainian militiaman, had killed more than thirty local villagers. His death drew an appreciative crowd who regarded him 'as a vulgar criminal and an assassin', but as he was executed he shouted 'Long live Stalin!', and succeeded in calling out 'Long live Russia!' in the face of the German officer who delivered the *coup de grâce*.[116]

This story exemplifies the complex battle lines that crossed and re-crossed the partisan war. The areas under Axis occupation were mainly non-Russian, and local anti-Soviet collaborators could be found in their thousands. Some were recruited as anti-guerrilla units, hunting down Red Army stragglers and deserters or genuine partisans and slaughtering them. In the Ukraine an estimated 300,000 nationalist guerrillas fought a war against both the German occupier and the partisans and the Red Army when it re-entered the country. Violent crime flourished in areas remote from the main power centres; casual violence was built into the efforts of the hungry population to survive at all under occupation. The one common thread running through the war between irregular and regular forces was the willingness of German military and security units to impose exceptional terror on the civilian population. The dangerous conditions of guerrilla warfare encouraged German soldiers to be trigger-happy and brutal. Partisan attacks were unpredictable and deadly, and the partisan difficult to distinguish from the rest of the population. The reprisal methods were routinely murderous. A diary entry in January 1943 recorded: '15 men, 41 women, 50 children – altogether 106 people as sympathetic to the partisans or accessories given special treatment [*sonder-behandelt*]. All inhabitants driven together and finished off.'[117] A partisan ambush in November 1941 outside the village of Velyka Obukhivka in the Ukraine brought instant retaliation. The German infantry unit surrounded the village, burned all the buildings except the ones they wanted, and shot around 200–300 men, women and children.[118]

The war against the partisans was controlled by SS general Erich von dem Bach-Zelewski, who also directed the *Einsatzgruppen* security units used to murder Soviet Jews and communists from the first days of the campaign. He made little distinction between the two: 'Where the partisan is, there the Jew is too, and where the Jew is, there is the partisan also.'[119] Thousands of those caught up in anti-partisan sweeps were innocent Jewish communities, which were singled out at first for reprisal actions. But anti-partisan violence continued to be visited on the local civilian population even after the Jewish populations had been largely liquidated. The organized security sweeps produced high levels of civilian casualties, although the dead were reported by German officials as 'bandits'. Operation 'Malaria' in August 1942 pitted a mixed force of 3,750 SS infantry, policemen and local Lithuanian and Russian militia against a partisan stronghold. Some 1,274 'suspects' were shot and 389 partisans killed in combat. Many, perhaps most of those killed in operations were unarmed. Another operation, in November 1942, resulted in 2,975 deaths for the loss of 2 on the German side, another a month later produced 6,172 dead against 7, a major operation in February 1943 12,897 against 29 German losses.[120] Over 100,000 'bandits' were recorded as killed in the area of Army Group Centre. In all these engagements the number of guns found was tiny in proportion to those killed. In one operation in 1942, 928 'bandits' were killed but only 201 guns discovered.[121] The overwhelming majority of those killed in the long irregular war in the east were innocent civilians, thousands of whom were driven to join the partisans in reaction to German violence. The total civilian dead on the Soviet side has been estimated at 16 or 17 million. They were the victims of violence of many kinds, and from all sides, but the common denominator was the 'war of extermination' unleashed by Hitler in June 1941 that provoked the wave of violence in the first place.

The perpetrators of violence were driven by a variety of motives. Any attempt to classify motivation in simple terms – the result of indoctrination, or the consequence of a military ethos of masculine values, group loyalty and heartlessness – breaks down on the sheer number and variety of perpetrators and the very great range of behaviour and attitude that they brought with them. In many cases ideology and the cult of soldierly manliness, or *Kampfmoral*, went hand-in-hand. Karl Kretschmer, an SS officer in charge of a killing unit in late 1942, wrote to his wife that 'the sight of the dead (including women and children) is not very cheering. But we are fighting this war for the survival or non-survival of our people.' He regretted his scruples, 'stupid thoughts' he called them, but wrote again: 'it is a weakness not to be able to stand the sight of dead people; the best way of overcoming it is to do it more often. Then it becomes a habit.' On the other hand were those for whom violence became unthinkingly a way of life. A Waffen-SS soldier in a camp after the war boasted of how he had killed civilians and Red Army prisoners, 700 on one occasion, 'because he got cigarettes and schnapps for it'.[122] The argument that this kind of brutality was the product of a long war in the east, where conditions produced moral degeneration, does not fit with the evidence of excessive German violence in other theatres of war, carried out both by the armed forces and by the security services, or with the knowledge that atrocities against Jews and other civilians were also committed systematically and on the largest scale during the period of easy Axis victories in 1941, and from the first days of the campaign.[123] Indeed, for the cohort of young German soldiers who went east later in the war, most of the atrocities had already taken place two or three years before. The degeneration of military behaviour can be understood more easily in terms of the political and racial prejudices generated by the regime, the climate of legal permission for atrocity, which soldiers were well aware of, and the unusually harsh traditions of German military justice, which were invoked to justify reprisal, hostage-taking and military murder. This was what 'total war' was expected to be like.

On the Soviet side violence is easier to comprehend, not only because the Red Army and the thousands of civilian volunteers were fighting to free their homeland from invasion and violation, but also because the system itself justified and exploited extreme forms of violence in defence of the revolutionary state. Violence against the invader took place alongside the Soviet state's violence against its own soldiers and population. In Moscow, for example, under martial law from October 1941, 83,060 people were detained in a nine-month period: 13 were shot on the spot, 887 were sentenced to death and 44,168 imprisoned.[124] When Soviet soldiers reached Germany they engaged in an orgy of reprisal killings and mass rapes against a population that they had been taught to hate as animals, and after they had traversed the ruins of their western borderlands. This is violence easier to understand than the violence visited on the populations of the east because it was driven by the simple but vicious lusts of victory and revenge. At the same time Soviet soldiers and security forces were locked in a brutal partisan war of their own, against the Ukrainian and Baltic nationalists once again under Soviet rule. Here guerrilla war generated another savage cycle of unrestrained violence. Between February 1944 and May 1946 Soviet forces killed 110,000 nationalists, arrested a further 250,000 and deported to the camps a total of 570,826 people, many of them the families and children of nationalists killed or imprisoned.[125] Because many were suspected collaborators, it was possible to emphasize their treachery rather than their nationalism. Few prisoners were taken, and those captured were hanged as an example, with placards detailing their 'crimes' around their necks. Many of the groups that hunted them down were former partisans who had once been the victims of Ukrainian nationalist vendetta.[126] Violence in the shattered borderlands did not disappear entirely until the early 1950s.

In the final weeks of 1940 both the German armed forces and the Red Army staged table-top war games to see which of them would win a German–Soviet military confrontation. The German games were held in Berlin in November, and resulted in a swift and annihilating defeat of Soviet forces. The war games in Moscow were staged after a week of staff discussions in late December. The first game was played between Zhukov and General Dmitri Pavlov, chief of Soviet mechanized forces. Zhukov represented the Germans. After an initial Soviet thrust, Zhukov won a resounding victory. When Stalin asked about the outcome, the chief of the general staff could not bring himself to state the truth, and was sacked the following day. Pavlov was shot in July after failing to stem the real German attack.[127]

Hitler's Germany did not win the war against Stalin's Soviet Union, a fact for which Zhukov takes much credit. The reasons for German defeat in the east are many. Some stem from differences in the way the two systems made war, some from the contrasting reactions of the two dictators to the demands of supreme military leadership. The starting point lies on the battlefield, for, despite the numerous handicaps that inhibited Red Army performance in the first eighteen months of the war, Soviet forces succeeded in outfighting their attacker, not, as is often supposed, simply by swamping the enemy with greater manpower. The idea that the Soviet Union had the endless spaces of Eurasia to draw upon to replenish the armies annihilated in the first years of the conflict presents a completely distorted view of the contrast in available human resources for the two sides. The areas occupied by Axis forces by mid-1942 contained approximately 66 million people, reducing the Soviet pool of potential soldiers and workers substantially. In contrast, Germany could draw not only on the manpower of the enlarged Reich, but also from the occupied areas of Europe and the Soviet Union. Germany was supported in the east by Finland, Hungary, Romania, Slovakia and, to a limited extent, Italy, adding a great deal to the potential population pool. During the critical central years of the war, before German forces were tied down in Italy and France fighting Britain and the United States, the population balance between the two sides in the east reveals surprising figures. Greater Germany had a population of over 96 million, the rump Soviet state around 120 million. The combined populations of Finland, Romania and Hungary amounted to approximately 29 million in 1941.

From these core populations, each side in 1943 and 1944 sustained approximately 11 million men in the armed forces, not including for the German side the Finnish, Hungarian, Slovakian and Romanian armies, volunteer divisions from the rest of Europe and several million former Soviet citizens, 300,000 of whom bore arms, while others became supply troops and auxiliaries for the German front.[128] The Soviet Union lost more than 5 million trained soldiers in the first year of war, including the hard core of the regular army. Loss rates continued to be exceptionally high throughout the war, though they declined as the Red Army learned to fight better. Total military losses were 11,444,100, of whom 8,668,400 were killed. Another 18 million were medical casualties of one kind or another, from battle wounds, illness, frostbite or psychiatric breakdown – an extraordinary 84 per cent of all those mobilized.[129] German losses in the east totalled around 6 million killed or taken prisoner, the large part in the last two years of the campaign.[130] Since Soviet troops sustained unnecessarily high casualties due at first to poor combat tactics, then to an often reckless disregard for losses, the balance of manpower says little about the fighting power of the two sides. Soviet divisions were formed and re-formed with ever smaller numbers of troops, which explains their proliferation during the war. The average division size of 10,000–12,000 fell over the war to levels often little more than 3,000, sometimes even less. Battlefield accounts by Soviet survivors show that they nonetheless continued fighting even when reduced to a mere rump representing an entire military unit. The Red Army lieutenant Evgeni Bessonov fought in a brigade reduced from 500 men to 50, but still in the front line. Accounts show that many Soviet military units were scraped together using men who were over-age (and often more reluctant warriors), or men who were poorly trained and difficult to discipline. Bessonov found even the regular eighteen-year-old recruits 'not strong physically, mostly small and frail youngsters'.[131]

What changed the balance in fighting power between the two adversaries was a very sharp increase in the number of battlefront weapons on the Soviet side, and great improvements in the way those weapons were organized and exploited. The balance between military capital and military labour swung heavily in favour of the Red Army during 1942 and 1943. Like the Western Front in the First World War, the critical balance was in artillery. Soviet factories produced artillery pieces in hundreds of thousands, German factories in tens of thousands. The balance of tank production was also heavily in the Soviet favour in 1942 and 1943. Red Army mobility was higher than German, with hundreds of thousands of Soviet-built and American trucks and jeeps. Battlefield memoirs from both sides demonstrate that artillery and tanks supplied the means to break through enemy positions and confirm the complete ineffectiveness of unsupported infantry. The increased modernization and mechanization of Soviet forces took place against a declining level of supply on the other side. The long distances, poor terrain, and problems of repair, routine maintenance and fuelling contributed to German difficulties and widened an already existing gap in the military capital available to each side, though German weapons continued to be in general better made and more effectively operated, gun for gun or tank for tank, than Soviet ones.[132] It was not the Soviet 'masses' that defeated Axis forces, but ever-larger numbers of the weapons of modern warfare.

Not even this advantage would have been sufficient without major changes in the way the Red Army organized operations and deployed modern weaponry. This was a remarkable transformation, all the more so since it was conducted against a background of constant defeats and emergency measures. The Soviet General Staff set out in 1942 to learn the lessons of early defeats. The principal weakness was keeping control of the battlefield. Significant improvements were made in the management of large-scale operations. The centralization of control was imperative, together with effective concentration of effort. This meant reforming entirely the organization of military units. Hard-hitting, heavily armed and motorized tank armies were formed, which mirrored the German *Panzer*-armies. They were mobile, self-contained units, with their own infantry, artillery, anti-tank guns and armour. They formed the spearhead in any attack, followed by less well-armed rifle divisions, whose job was to mop up and hold ground.[133] Air forces in 1941 were divided up along the whole front, assigned to individual armies rather than co-ordinated. Under a young air force officer, Alexander Novikov, who distinguished himself in the defence of Leningrad, the Red Air Force was centralized, its forces concentrated for use at critical points in the battle, and its operations monitored as a whole from control centres set up behind the front line.[134] The key component in the reforms was radio communication, which had been primitive or, in some cases, non-existent before 1942. Neither tanks nor aircraft had been fitted routinely with radios, or kept in contact with battlefield commanders. Under Lend-Lease, the Soviet Union was supplied with 35,089 radio stations, 380,000 field telephones, 5,900 radio receivers and almost a million miles of telephone wire.[135] These supplies revolutionized Soviet battlefield performance. The movement of tank armies and aircraft fleets could be controlled by two-way radio links. Great efforts were made to keep good security in communications, in contrast with practice in 1941 when messages were often broadcast uncoded and openly for German radio intelligence to intercept. Radio counter-measures were developed to a sophisticated level on the Soviet side, blocking German radio traffic or transmitting confusing or mischievous messages.[136]

The tactical performance of Soviet forces was also greatly improved, though hasty training or poor officer quality sometimes annulled these improvements in combat. Günter Koschorrek, now fighting on the approaches to Stalingrad, observed in front of him a large pocket of Soviet infantry caught in a small depression in the ground. Their officer, with shrill blasts on a whistle, forced his men to run forward through a field of machine-gun fire with appalling and unnecessary losses, until they were all agonisingly consumed in the fire of a German flame-thrower tank.[137] But in general Soviet infantry was no longer thrown forward in great waves to be mown down by entrenched German machine-gun fire, but instead advanced under the protection of tanks, artillery and rocket fire. Soviet forces became expert at concealment and deception, moving with exceptional stealth and rigidly maintained silence. The battle that led to the encirclement of Stalingrad in November 1942, Operation 'Uranus', was preceded by a massive build-up of Red Army forces that went almost entirely undetected by German intelligence. One of the largest battles of the eastern war, Operation 'Bagration', launched in June 1944 against German Army Group Centre, saw the Red Army muster 5,000 aircraft, 5,200 tanks and 1.4 million men, and move into place 300,000 tonnes of oil and 1 million tonnes of supplies, and yet achieve complete surprise. The head of German military intelligence in the east, Colonel Reinhard Gehlen, told Army Group Centre to 'expect a quiet summer'.[138] Soviet battlefield intelligence also improved greatly. Using tactics of aggressive scouting, infiltration and spying, as well as radio interception and decryption, Soviet forces had by 1943 a much better grasp of the nature of the enemy they faced. The gap in fighting effectiveness was glaring in 1941, but Soviet forces made the most of their particular skills to narrow the gap to acceptable dimensions two years later.

These many fundamental improvements in the way the Soviet forces fought were displayed fully in the battles that rescued Stalingrad between November 1942 and January 1943, when the German Sixth Army under General Friedrich Paulus was forced to capitulate. The turning-point came six months later, when the German armed forces launched Operation 'Citadel' to seize a major salient around Kursk to try to unhinge the Soviet front and create the possibility for a renewed assault on Moscow. The thick defensive field created at Zhukov's insistence withstood the German assault, and for the first time the Red Army did not retreat when faced by a German summer-time attack. The subsequent counter-offensive drove German forces back to their starting positions and then initiated the long German retreat. This withdrawal did not imitate the rout of the Soviet armies in the summer of 1941. The German armed forces remained a formidable enemy, whose own battlefield performance was also continually modified and improved, and whose new weapons, like the 75-tonne Ferdinand tank-destroyer, could eliminate the standard Soviet T-34 tank at will. The defeat of German forces took almost two further years of costly warfare, in which another 4.52 million Soviet soldiers were killed or captured. Heavy bombing of Germany reduced the possibility for greater mass-production of battlefield weapons, denuded the German front in the east of aircraft, and opened the way for a second front in the west, in June 1944. But the critical years were 1942 and 1943, when the Red Army succeeded in holding German forces long enough for the reform of its own practices, organization, training and equipment to bear successful operational fruit.

The changing fortunes of military combat reflected something about the way the two dictators approached their responsibilities as supreme commanders. Both took the role seriously. Neither man took a single day away from the war effort throughout the four years of conflict. Hitler forswore his evening film shows for the duration of the war. It was usual for each man to meet at least twice every day with operational or command staff to be briefed on developments and to confirm or modify military directives. Stalin's headquarters in the Kremlin combined the work of both the State Defence Committee and the Supreme Command (Stavka), which provided a close link between supervision of the home front and the fighting front. Stalin regularly sent out top-ranking troubleshooters to monitor what was happening in any sector of the war effort, and these reported back directly to him. Sometimes he would make direct contact by telephone with a general or official to issue instructions or to encourage their fulfilment.[139] Hitler chiefly ran the military war effort from his headquarters, though he would also meet regularly with civilian officials or ministers to discuss economic or technical questions.[140] There was less direct supervision of the fighting front or the home front once Hitler's decisions were made, and no systematic use of special emissaries or delegates from supreme headquarters to check that orders were fulfilled or problems identified and acted upon. The German structure was centralized but not centrally controlled, an important distinction from the more improvised, more responsive and less bureaucratic structures established under Stalin.

There were other important contrasts between the two men. As the war progressed Stalin came to recognize his limitations as a military strategist and to rely more on the advice of the professional soldiers. The turning point came in the late summer of 1942, when German forces, unleashed towards Stalingrad and the Caucasus oilfields on 28 June 1942 in Operation 'Blue', threatened once again to sweep all before them. On 27 August Stalin summoned Zhukov to meet the State Defence Committee at the Kremlin. He told Zhukov that it was his responsibility to save the city of Stalingrad, and then announced that he was to be appointed Deputy Supreme Commander to Stalin himself. The plan to cut off German forces and save the southern front was worked out by Zhukov and the General Staff; the plan to defeat German forces at Kursk also derived from the military leadership. In both cases Stalin had to be persuaded, cajoled and convinced, but Zhukov learned that firmness, clear arguments and a mastery of detail could allay Stalin's doubts. Stalin accepted the new balance of power, since he had little choice, and focused his own efforts on mobilizing the domestic economy and workforce, for which he had much more experience. The victories from Stalingrad onwards reflected a balance of responsibility between the armed forces and the dictator that reduced, though it did not completely eliminate, the damaging effects of Stalin's naïve grasp of operational planning.[141]

Hitler, on the other hand, developed a growing faith in his own strategic capabilities. He was not a military simpleton, any more than Stalin. His chief of operations, Colonel-General Alfred Jodl, when asked by his interrogators in 1945 how he judged Hitler as a military commander, replied that 'many of the major decisions made by the Führer prevented us from losing the war sooner'. He considered that Hitler 'was a great military leader', but one whose early successes, often achieved in the face of resistance from the German General Staff, encouraged the delusion that he understood warfare better than the military experts.[142] Hitler came to regard his senior staff officers as unnecessarily conservative or prudent, even disloyal or cowardly. 'I've noticed,' he remarked about the army's dismay at the reverses before Moscow, 'that when everybody loses his nerves, I'm the only one who keeps calm.'[143] His decision to take over direct command of the army in December 1941 was the first of many instances where senior soldiers were sacked or redeployed for failing to accept or understand their commander's wishes. In August 1942 Hitler insisted that every decision he made at headquarters should have a stenographic record, so that there could be no doubt about what he had ordered and when.[144] There was never any question that Hitler would appoint a deputy supreme commander. In October 1941 he told Himmler: 'if I apply my mind to military problems, it is because for the moment I know that nobody would succeed better at this than I can.'[145] As the war progressed, the balance of power between dictator and armed forces in Germany tilted towards Hitler, who insisted, according to Jodl's testimony, on taking 'all decisions that were of any importance'. This placed an extraordinary strain on one man. By the war's end, Hitler became so suspicious about delegating responsibility that he took it upon himself to order the deployment of even the smallest military units. His greatest weakness, Jodl concluded, was his grasp of operational realities, as it was with Stalin. Hitler refused to accept his limitations, perhaps because he saw his calling as Germany's warlord as the central purpose of a dictatorship based on the ideal of violent self-assertion of the race, where for Stalin supreme command was above all a political necessity.

The changing relationship between dictator and armed forces was reflected in the role of the party in military affairs. In the Soviet Union the party was represented by the political commissar attached to each military unit, who was responsible for the political education of the services and held dual command with his military opposite number. This role had been strengthened during the purges of 1937, and reasserted during the catastrophic defeats in 1941, which were blamed partly on the failure to make the army sufficiently communist. During 1942 the party began to loosen its grip as greater responsibility passed to the military. In June Lev Mekhlis was sacked as head of the Political Directorate. On 9 October the post of political commissar was scrapped in smaller military units. In larger units they lost the right to countersign orders in October, and in December were demoted to assistant to the commander they served with. In 1943 122,000 former commissars were drafted to the front line as junior officers, where they were forced to become real soldiers.[146] The use of the term 'comrade' became less common and officer ranks replaced it. Officers were allowed to wear braid and epaulettes, and military awards from the pre-revolutionary years were reinstated. Distinguished conduct on the battlefield was rewarded with membership of the party, though this brought no immunity from combat. Many millions of Red Army men qualified as party members, but more than 3.5 million communists died during the war.[147] Party education in the armed forces did not disappear, but the emphasis throughout the Soviet Union was on popular military education and patriotic revival at the expense of political formalism.

In the German armed forces the party played a more limited role in the early stages of the war, although many regular soldiers were either former National Socialists or identified with the values of the movement. The Department for Armed Forces Propaganda, set up in April 1939, organized Propaganda Companies to raise morale among the troops and to supply front-line newspapers. In May 1940 the army commander, von Brauchitsch, published a decree on 'Unity in National Socialism' to encourage closer identification between army and party, and in October 1940 new guidelines on army education were published, based under four headings: 'The German *Volk*'; 'The German Reich'; 'German Living Space'; and 'National Socialism as the Foundation'.[148] The armed forces were resistant to further encroachment, but when morale in the east became more brittle during the long retreat after Kursk, the party reacted by a programme to raise the National Socialist level of the armed forces, and to communicate to the troops the political character of their struggle. In October 1943 Hitler ordered officers to become like political commissars, and on 22 December 1943 he instituted a National Socialist Leadership Staff at supreme headquarters under General Hermann Reinecke. In collaboration with the party chancellery, Reinecke appointed political officers to all major military units. By December there were 1,047 full-time commissars, and 47,000 other officers who combined political education with regular military responsibilities.[149] They were granted equivalent command status with the front-line officers, and subjected to courses of political training. Hitler wanted to avoid what he saw as the mistakes of the Great War. 'Back then,' he told Reinecke at the founding meeting of the new political staff, 'it was real nonsense; there was no morale.' He reminded his audience that victory in the east was possible only 'as an absolutely united ideological body'.[150]

The impact of increased party indoctrination may have helped to sustain morale, though evidence from the front line suggests that many soldiers continued to fight from dread of a Soviet invasion of the homeland and fear for their own survival. Günther Koschorrek noted in his diary on 26 July 1944, as his unit retreated across Poland back towards the Reich, that German soldiers 'are only fighting because of the sense of duty which has been drummed into them . . . more and more of them only go forward reluctantly'. A few days later Koschor-rek's morale had 'sunk to zero level' as he came to realize 'that our leaders are no longer able to do anything'.[151] Army censors found little evidence in letters from the front even for belief in Hitler. Out of 38,000 letters sent during September 1944 by the men of the 14th Army, only 2 per cent displayed faith in the *Führer*, and only 5 per cent in the prospect of a final victory.[152] As in the Soviet Union in the early stages of Barbarossa, the security services began to use greater measures of terror to keep soldiers fighting, while party enthusiasts watched for evidence of disloyalty or faint-heartedness among the officer corps. The SS played an ever larger role. In July 1944 Himmler was appointed to command the Replacement Army, the organization for reserve-building and training. SS forces fought with an increasingly savage and nihilistic contempt for the enemy and for the regular, less Nazified German army that they fought alongside. Koschorrek, still in the front line in March 1945, wounded seven times, confessed in his journal that he no longer believed any of the propaganda, but dared not express such views openly because of the military policemen 'who would brutally shoot dissenters, or even hang them publicly'.[153] On 1 May he heard of Hitler's suicide. He and his companions 'were shocked that the proud leader had decided to shirk his responsibilities', but 'within a couple of hours he is forgotten'.[154]

The effort to keep German soldiers fighting highlights an important moral contrast between the two sides, Soviet and German, which in its simplest form derives from the difference between fighting an aggressive and a defensive war. This was a contrast appreciated from the outset by Soviet leaders and exploited relentlessly to keep Soviet society fighting. In a speech in Moscow in November 1941, Stalin observed that 'the morale of our army is higher that that of the German, for our army is defending its country against foreign invaders and believes in the justness of its cause'. By contrast, he continued, 'the German army is waging a war of conquest', which creates the moral outlook of 'professional robbers' and leads inexorably to 'the deterioration of the German army'.[155] Soviet wartime propaganda traded on the defence of the Soviet homeland and memories of the historic defence of Russia, and these views were in many cases accepted and internalized by Soviet soldiers and workers.[156] When the German assault on Stalingrad created growing panic in southern Russia, Stalin was forced to issue Order 227 'Not One Step Backward', which promised stern punishment for any commander or commissar who ordered an unauthorized retreat, and exhorted the ordinary soldier 'to fight for our soil, to save the Motherland'.[157] Special blocking units (*zagraditel'nye otriady*) were created from security troops to prevent soldiers from fleeing the front line. Dereliction of duty carried the risk of execution, and estimates suggest that 158,000 Soviet soldiers were condemned to death during the war. Lesser infractions carried a prison sentence or service in a penal battalion; 442,000 served in these punishment units and 436,000 served, usually brief, periods of confinement.[158]

The harsh discipline did not necessarily reflect a lack of patriotism but the exceptional battlefront conditions, which encouraged panic or temporary moments of demoralization and dissent. Both at the front and among the home population there were complaints and grumbles about the hardships of war, the lack of information, or the insidious presence of state power. But there is a great deal of evidence to suggest that a large part of the population came to terms with the terrible levels of sacrifice and personal loss, and fought and worked from simply expressed patriotic resentment against the invader. Such sentiments often had little to do with enthusiasm for Stalin or the Soviet state, but did not exclude genuine conviction that this was a revolutionary war of the proletarian state against the forces of naked imperialism. The military censors in Moscow, in the weeks when the German army was approaching in November 1941, checked over 5 million items of mail, but confiscated only 6,912 pieces and deleted passages in a further 56,808. In general, views were reported as 'positive'.[159] In Leningrad in the early months of the war, before the siege, the evidence from workers' meetings or from letters to the authorities and army newspapers displays a genuine desire to defend the revolution. One worker, who joined the militia in July 1941, sent an 'Address to all Toilers' for publication: 'We, workers at the bench, go – and old men, and grandfathers – . . . to overthrow fascism, to liquidate the exploiters . . .'[160] The letter was not published, on the grounds that it was not very politically literate. Another, more critical worker in Leningrad distinguished between fighting for the leadership and fighting for the revolution, which was 'ours'.[161] The Soviet authorities responded to the evident desire to fight a 'people's war' by relaxing the tight control of the party and the security apparatus (a directive to party cadres in 1942 ran: 'stop instructing the masses, learn from them') and allowing society to collaborate with authority in defeating Germany. This relaxation proved temporary, but it encouraged a widespread popular belief that after the war the Soviet system would change for the better. A young Siberian soldier, in January 1944, told the Ukrainian writer Alexander Dovzhenko, 'You know, every one of us looks forward to some changes and revisions in our life.'[162] The sense that the war greatly simplified the relationship between people and system, both intent on defeating the German enemy, meant an end to the evident gap between social reality and the official line on the Soviet utopia. The war, wrote Yeygenii Yevtushenko in his memoirs, 'lightened the Russians' spiritual burden, for they no longer needed to be insincere'. This, Yevtushenko believed, 'was one of the chief causes of our victory'.[163]

The German presence in the Soviet Union had a different purpose. The war in the east was a war of imperial aggression to destroy the Bolshevik state and create an area of German racial domination. This could be presented in ideological terms that ordinary soldiers and workers could identify with, but it was inherently a more difficult programme to explain and to justify than was patriotic defence. The Soviet belief in a better future once the enemy was driven back was for the aggressor a more ambiguous ambition, since the exact nature of that future was unclear and, as the war turned against Germany, increasingly distant. The conception of racial empire and economic exploitation contained in the detailed thinking of the SS or Göring's Four-Year Plan was difficult to convey to either the home population or the armed forces, save through simple ideas of 'living-space'. One German army unit in Belorussia in 1941 had a large board displayed with the slogan 'The Russian must perish that we may live'.[164] Soldiers' memories of the war in the east indicate that the idea of keeping the 'Asiatic' enemy away from Europe had as much resonance as promises of a German model empire in the future. The failure to defeat the Soviet Union in 1941 complicated the process of sustaining popular morale. Goebbels already noted in the winter of 1941/2 a sharp decline in the public mood as they realized for the first time that the swift victories of the first two years of war were over. 'The anxiety of the German people about the Eastern Front is increasing . . . Words cannot describe what our soldiers are writing home from the front.'[165] By the time of the German defeat in the Kursk offensive, Goebbels recorded a growing volume of letters 'with an unusual amount of criticism' directed not only at the party leadership but at Hitler himself.[166] German propaganda was switched during 1943 more and more to the idea that Germany was leading a crusade against Bolshevism to save not just German culture, but European civilization itself. The fanaticism displayed by German soldiers, party members and ordinary civilians in the months leading to defeat derived from the desperate efforts to prevent German destruction and to sustain the idea of a righteous violence against Asian Bolshevism, a view that was easier to fight for than the policies of racial destruction and economic plunder with which the conflict began.[167]

These differences help to explain why it was so much more difficult to export Hitlerism to Eastern Europe than Stalinism. Although the German armed forces were at first greeted as liberators, and popular demonstrations, complete with placards and icons bearing Hitler's image, were mounted in areas in the east only recently taken under Soviet rule, the harsh treatment of local nationalists, the seizure of food and labour, and the unremitting violence of the occupier against the civilian population alienated much of the potential for political collaboration. The German authorities made little effort to pretend that the areas they had conquered were not German colonies, outposts of a new German racial empire. When the Red Army recaptured the occupied areas they were not necessarily greeted as liberators, particularly in the areas taken under Soviet rule before 1941. But in general, the Soviet authorities were able to pose as the instrument of liberation, and to present the Soviet presence as something distinct from German rule. In the aftermath of war the Soviet authorities established nominally independent states in Eastern Europe, dominated by native communist parties which were committed to the Stalinist model of rapid heavy industrial growth, communal farm ownership and a single political movement. For all the many hardships characteristic of Stalin's system, the cultural authoritarianism, the political persecutions, the destruction of social classes deemed unacceptable to the revolutionary state, the 'people's democracies' were not colonies, but sovereign states. Soviet propaganda made much of this distinction. Though the states of Eastern Europe might well have preferred complete independence, the conditions of their existence under Soviet domination were demonstrably different from their condition under the Third Reich.

Hitler slowly came to realize that the war was lost during 1944 and early 1945. Rather than indulge in self-recrimination he accepted the logic of racial conflict, which remained central to his intellectual outlook. His Darwinian view of the world had assumed that the Germans would win because they were by nature more worthy, but he saw struggle itself as a natural condition: 'Who wants to live, must also fight,' he wrote in 1944, 'and whoever does not want to take up the eternal struggle of this world, does not deserve life.'[168] If that meant defeat, he said in one of his evening monologues, 'Then, I am ice-cold here too: If the German people is not prepared to engage in its own survival, so be it: Then it must disappear!'[169] Consistent to the end, in one of his last recorded conversations in February 1945 Hitler came back to the contest with world Jewry: 'it will mean that we have been defeated by the Jews'.[170] In March 1945 he ordered a policy of scorched earth to prevent the victorious enemy from gaining anything from its conquest, but the directive was largely ignored. With the Soviet seizure of Berlin in early May 1945, the Hitler dictatorship came to an end.

Victory in 1945 secured the Soviet system and Stalin's personal rule. Stalin emerged from the war with his cult of personality enlarged and his authority unchallengeable. The Soviet system was suffused with a popular militarism. A visiting British journalist in 1945 was struck by the extent to which the whole of Soviet society was focused on military issues, military training and military schooling. He found that school-children aged from seven to fourteen were supposed to have 916 hours of instruction a year on military questions. Young girls were taught Morse-code and radio transmission; boys of thirteen were familiarized with rifles and machine-guns. The standard school song-book had twenty-six songs. The first was a 'Song for Stalin'; the second a 'Song of Happiness' about the achievements of the Soviet Union. The other twenty-four were war songs, ranging from 'Tankists' March', 'Song of a Partisan', 'Song of the Front' to 'I am Thirteen (soon I'll go to a mobilization centre)'.[171] Victory allowed military preparedness to be built into the system, and by the time of Stalin's death in 1953 the Soviet Union remained the most heavily armed state in the world. The commemoration of Victory Day on 9 May each year was treated as the most serious celebration of the party calendar. Victory provided a new foundation myth for the system more immediate and more potent than recollections of the Revolution, which for anyone younger than forty-five was already a dimly perceived event.

What was not redeemed for the Soviet people was the implicit promise that the state would relax its vigilant grip on Soviet society after the end of the war. Even before the final defeat of Germany, the regime re-imposed the security net, and strengthened party power. In 1946 cultural control was tightened and any hint of cosmopolitanism or wartime liberalization stamped out. The system moved effortlessly from confrontation with Hitler to the Cold War confrontation with American and British imperialism. The enemy was once again 'masked', infiltrating the party as fascist spies had done before 1939. In January 1953 *Izvestiia* warned readers that 'the spies and saboteurs sent to us by the imperialist intelligence services operate "on the sly" ', and demanded the same rigorous vigilance practised against enemies of the people in the 1930s.[172] War remained in the Soviet mind a total war between two irreconcilable systems. Stalin's dictatorship was stamped by central metaphors of struggle as clearly as Hitler's, and continued to be so as it strove to reconstruct a country shattered by three years of towering violence, and to restore a society recovering from the traumatic effects of loss unprecedented in the modern age.

13

Nations and Races

'But it is a scarcely conceivable fallacy of thought to believe that a Negro or a Chinese, let us say, will turn into a German because he learns German and is willing to speak the German language in the future . . . nationality or rather race does not happen to lie in language but in the blood . . .'

Adolf Hitler, *Mein Kampf*, 1925[1]

'. . . if a person who by blood is a Negro was brought up in such a society and with such a language and culture that he calls himself Russian, there is nothing incorrect about this even if his skin colour is black.' V. N. Starovski, 1938[2]

On 12 August 1941 the Central Committee of the Soviet Communist Party published resolution number 2060–935s, ordering the security forces to deport the entire population of the Volga German Autonomous Republic to destinations in central Asia and Siberia. The reasons for the order were largely fanciful. In Moscow the German invasion two months before had provoked widespread fear of a fifth column of fascist sympathizers eager to give succour to the invading armies. There were almost one-and-a-half million immigrants of German descent living within the Soviet Union. They became the regime's prime target, even though the NKVD had so far unearthed only twelve alleged cases of spying and sabotage from among the entire German population. In August the NKVD dressed Soviet paratroopers in German uniforms and dropped them into the German-populated farmland of the lower Volga to test the villagers' loyalty. Where they were welcomed, whole villages were liquidated. Stalin was advised that all Germans were suspect, not only those who might act as 'saboteurs and diversionists' (in the words of the resolution) but also the rest of the population, men, women and children, for failing to denounce sabotage in the first place.[3]

On 3 September the equivalent of a whole division of the Red Army was sent south to round up all the Soviet Germans they could find. Commanded by NKVD security officers, the soldiers first arrested the adult males, and then ordered the households to gather food and clothing before being marched or driven in trucks to waiting trains. Though Moscow had decreed the right of each household to take up to a ton of goods and as much of their money as they wanted, the troops were only interested in getting the Germans to the railway, and many arrived with little more than a bundle of possessions. So swift was the round-up in some villages that Russian refugees brought in to take over the farms later that same day found half-finished meals and cows unmilked.[4] The trigger-happy security men, primed to hunt out any hint of diversion, found small swastika flags in some houses, and shot the owners on the spot. The flags had been handed out a year before when there had been talk of a Hitler state visit to keep alive the German–Soviet pact.[5] Within three weeks the whole population of more than 366,000 had been shipped in overcrowded and unsanitary trainloads to remote areas of central and northern Russia, where they were unceremoniously dumped to build a new life from scratch. By January 1942 800,000 Germans from all parts of the Soviet Union had been shipped eastwards.[6]

Germans living under Russian rule were no strangers to deportation. During the First World War 200,000 had been deported east from the areas bordering the Russian–German front. During the 1930s thousands more were forcibly removed, often at a few hours' notice, from a 100-kilometre zone behind the western Soviet frontier. In 1934 security police compiled as complete a list as they could of all ethnic Germans in the Soviet population in case war with Hitler's Germany ever became a reality. The long history of the German community under Russian rule was one of slow decline from the privileged status, low taxes and exemption from military service that had lured thousands of Germans as settlers to the Russia of Catherine the Great in the eighteenth century. More German immigrants followed over the next century to the Ukraine, the Crimea and the Caucasus, and by 1914 there were more than 2 million throughout the Russian Empire. Their settlements were small Germanies: neat cottages and well-tended farms, Lutheran churches, German spoken in a distinctive local patois. They intermarried little with the Russian population. This exclusiveness helped them after the revolution. The Bolshevik regime classified them as a separate nationality, and allowed the Germans to maintain their cultural identity and a good measure of self-government. In 1924 the Volga Germans were granted the title of an Autonomous Soviet Socialist Republic, with their seat of self-government in the city of Engels, named in honour of the great German co-founder of communism. The republic had a German-language radio station, German newspapers and a German administration.

Under Stalin much of this changed. By 1939 German communities outside the Volga German republic had had their autonomous status revoked; in the Ukraine the 451 German-language schools were closed down; German newspapers were suspended; Germans were over-represented in the GUlag population.[7] By the time of the German invasion in 1941 there was no German-language teaching, culture, administration or religion left for the million Soviet Germans living outside the Volga republic. Even here the authorities had begun to clamp down well before the war by arresting and executing prominent community leaders and inflicting NKVD patrols and curfews. In 1934 the Politburo issued a decree 'On the Battle with Counter-Revolutionary Fascist Elements' in what the regime insisted on calling 'the German colonies'.[8] Because of Hitler, all Germans, even enthusiastic communists, as many were, came to be regarded as a standing threat to the regime. The war completed the destruction of the old communities. The autonomous republic was formally abolished on 7 September; all German males were formed into construction brigades, working as forced labourers wherever the regime directed them in conditions little different from the GUlag camps, where an estimated 175,000 men died. After the war German speaking declined and inter-marriage increased sharply. Not until after Stalin's death were the Germans freed from the special labour settlements, and not until 1964 did the Soviet government finally issue a decree removing the charge of wartime treason from its now scattered and impoverished German communities.[9]

This was very different from the fate allotted to them in the plans drawn up in Hitler's Germany for the ethnic remodelling of the conquered East. There had been talk in the First World War of bringing the Volga Germans back to the Reich as settlers to replace Poles under German rule. In the late 1920s the German public donated money to help Soviet Germans emigrate to Germany to escape collectivization.[10] In 1941 the idea of reuniting all expatriate Germans with their distant fatherland was central to the extravagant schemes dreamt up by Heinrich Himmler in his capacity as Reich Commissar for the Protection of the German Race, a new office created for him by Hitler in October 1939. Himmler's ambition in the East was to ensure that 'no drop of German blood be lost or left behind for an alien race'.[11] The German settlers in the Crimea, the Ukraine and along the Volga were to become the racial outposts of the new Germanic empire, the unwitting raw material for the Germanization of the East. The announcement in Moscow in September 1941 of the mass deportation of all Soviet Germans produced an angry response from the authorities in Berlin. The Minister for the East, the party ideologue Alfred Rosenberg, issued instructions for German radio propaganda to broadcast a counterthreat: 'If the crimes against the Volga Germans are carried out, then Jewry will have to settle the account of these crimes many times over.'[12]

The German occupiers were not left entirely empty-handed. So swiftly did Axis forces push into Soviet territory that a total of more than 300,000 Soviet Germans came under their jurisdiction, over 183,000 of them in the Ukraine.[13] The first step was to define precisely who among the population of the new eastern empire was a true 'German'. This process was far from straightforward. All over German-occupied Europe Himmler's commissariat was busy compiling a list of ethnic Germans. The list detailed distinct categories for the populations of the East and these were applied remorselessly by German officials as they scoured the ethnic melting-pot for signs of Germanness. Groups I and II on the list were racially pure Germans with two German parents, the two groups distinguished from each other by the degree to which the individual had retained a true German consciousness. Group III included those with a predominance of

German blood, and whose bearing and behaviour made it clear that 're-Germanization' was possible. The final classification included all those who had some German blood, but who had become merged with the alien racial environment to such an extent that they had lost any urge to remain German and were beyond effective 're-Germanization'.[14] There remained anomalies even to this extensive catalogue. Soviet Germans with Jewish blood were excluded from the list altogether, and executed. Officials had to be specially vigilant that Russians who had learned German or adopted a German lifestyle should not slip through the net as sham Germans; by the same token, ethnic Germans who spoke only Russian and had adopted Russian habits could nonetheless qualify as a genetic addition under the long-winded category 'German origin, capable of being re-Germanized'.[15]

When the screening began it was soon discovered that two centuries of life in Russia had changed the Germans into something rather less than the SS ideal. Officials complained that the language was not simply a distinct dialect but had made compromises with Russian; the habits and outlook of the Soviet Germans were not those of European Germans; there was plenty of evidence that communism was preferred to fascism, and Soviet German communists were singled out for elimination. When local Soviet Germans were made to join the details rounding up and murdering Jews, there were protests and mutinies. Large numbers were sent westward to settle the conquered areas of Poland; others were sent to the Crimea as the advance guard of a programme of German colonization. When the German army retreated, 300,000 Soviet Germans followed them, but most were captured at the end of the war and handed back to Soviet rule, where they ended up in camps and special labour settlements in Siberia. Their descendants were finally united with their fellow Germans in the 1990s, when more than a quarter-of-a-million emigrated from post-communist Russia to the recently re-unified German state.[16]

The fate of the Soviet Germans highlights the extraordinarily complex and ambiguous nature of the issues of race and nation under Stalin and Hitler. For the unfortunate Soviet Germans this ambiguity imposed on them a double jeopardy. The more the Soviet regime allowed them to retain their German identity, the more attractive they appeared to Hitler's Germany, and the more dangerous to Stalin. The consequence for these innocent populations was a decade of unmerited victimization and the complete eradication of their traditional cultures and communities.

The definition of nation, race and state was a central political question in both dictatorships. National and racial issues spawned much of the excessive violence and social victimization of the two regimes. In neither case was the issue of national identity clear cut. Indeed, the two dictatorships emerged in states where national identity was unclear, contradictory or fragile. Stalin and Hitler had to confront the legacy of an unstable identity by imposing, often by force, and in differing ways, a version that they regarded as consistent with the ideological priorities and historical circumstances of the two systems.

Pre-revolutionary Russia was an imperial state, not a nation. Around 45 per cent of the population of the empire was made up of non-Russian peoples, many of them conquered only in the course of the nineteenth century, grouped around an ethnic Russian core. The distinction between the state as a Russian-centred empire and the idea of a distinct 'Russian' nationality and culture was captured semantically in the difference between the adjectives *rossiiskii* (state, empire) and *russkii* (people, language), and politically by the difference between 'westernizers', who preferred the state definition, and 'Slavophiles', who preferred a cultural and ethnic definition of nationhood. The primary allegiance of the empire's subjects was to the crown, as the central institution of state. Ethnic Russians, or 'Great Russians' as they were known, regarded themselves – if they considered it at all – as the state's senior nationality, but they did not constitute a national state; on the wide non-Russian periphery a separate and developed sense of national identity was either non-existent or in its infancy in the nineteenth century. The term for 'nation' gave rise to further confusion: the Russian term *natsiia* (nation) was used by ethnographers to define distinct ethnic categories within the empire; the word *narod* (people), used by Slavophile nationalists, suggested a distinct cultural and linguistic community, but not necessarily a developed sense of nationality, or even a common geographical territory. The weakness of political nationalism was reflected in the first Duma elections in 1905, where only 9 per cent of the votes went to nationalist parties.[17] In the Russian empire the connections between state, nation and territory were ill-defined. For most inhabitants of the empire identity was determined chiefly by the immediate context of work and place and a greater or lesser loyalty to the Tsar.

After 1917 the Bolshevik regime was confronted with a clear paradox. On the one hand Marxism dictated that the revolutionary state would be internationalist and sociological. 'The working men have no country,' wrote Marx.[18] National identity was generally regarded as the product of a specific bourgeois stage of historical development, destined to melt away as the population recognized their identity as members of a socialist commonwealth. On the other hand, Lenin viewed national emancipation as a legitimate ambition for colonial peoples struggling against capitalist imperialism. Radical political movements had flourished before 1917 in the non-Russian periphery of the Tsarist empire; some of them had national aspirations, and could be said to resemble the overseas colonies of the other great European empires. In 1918 an ideological compromise was reached. The regime granted national self-expression as a right for all formerly subject people, but recognized that this was in some sense a temporary stepping-stone towards a mature stage of socialist consciousness uniting all peoples in fraternal collaboration. During the civil war national concessions were made to win allies against counter-revolutionary forces, but when the new Soviet state was finally defined constitutionally, those components classified as nationalities were given no right to separate political development. Separatist movements in Georgia and the Ukraine were stamped out. Stalin wanted to describe the new state as the Russian Federation, but when the constitution was finally ratified in January 1924 the state was defined as Lenin wanted it: the Union of Soviet Socialist Republics.[19]

Even this formulation begged a great many questions. The Union's inhabitants were expected to have several overlapping identities, first as an inhabitant of one of the thirty-seven federal republics or autonomous regions confirmed in 1924, then as the member of a distinct ethnographic group, and finally as a Soviet citizen. The link between nationality and territory remained very imperfect. Over 20 million people lived as ethnic minorities in republics dominated by a different ethnic category. In some of the small republics, the native people were outnumbered by resident ethnic Russians.[20] Millions more now inhabited lands that had once belonged to the Russian empire, but were joined to the newly independent states in Eastern Europe, which Soviet leaders hoped might one day be brought under Soviet rule. The idea that the revolution would eventually engulf other parts of Europe gave the Soviet Union itself a temporary aspect as it waited for a brotherhood of socialist states to emerge. The internationalism of the regime, expressed in the deliberate choice of the 'Internationale' as the state's 'national' anthem and the red flag of international socialism as its emblem, had to be reconciled with the proliferation of distinct national units within the Soviet federal state and, by the early 1920s, with the evident failure of the revolution to materialize outside its borders.

German national identity was the product of an equally complex history. The German state created in 1871 was a federation of formerly independent states dominated by the largest, Prussia. The federal character of the new constitution allowed powerful provincial loyalties to survive right through to the 1930s. The new state, like the Russian empire, was a constitutional rather than a national entity, united by loyalty to the crown and the new constitution. The term chosen to define Germany was deliberately ambiguous. The *Deutsches Reich* echoed the medieval Germanic 'empire', or the defunct Holy Roman Empire, but conveyed little sense of nationhood. The German word for nation, like its Russian counterpart, had two versions: *Nation* was chiefly an ethnographic term, but the word most commonly used in the nineteenth century to define the German nation, *Volk*, implied not just 'people' but a unique community of shared values, common language, culture and even blood. The concept of nationality was a deeply contested area. Many German nationalists, inspired by the idea of a single *Volk*, had sought a 'Great German' solution before 1871 based on a union of all the Germanic peoples in an ethnically defined state. Yet the Germany that emerged in 1871 excluded millions of Germans living in the Habsburg empire, while it included within its borders millions of Poles, Danes and Frenchmen, who were citizens of the new state as the result of conquest or annexation but shared no common nationality. This 'Lesser German' solution suited the conservative elites who had constructed the German empire, but not the pan-German aspirations of many German nationalists, who still hoped for a nation based upon ethnic and cultural affinity rather than on shared territory or common imperial institutions. The symbols of the new Reich were equally contentious. No national anthem was approved until the 1920s. The flag was the Prussian black, white and red, dominated by the imperial eagle, but the flag of the German national movement, raised during the revolution of 1848, was a tricolour of black, gold and red. Politics divided the two banners: the Prussian standard demonstrated the conservative credentials of the post-1871 Reich; the rejected tricolour signified the forces of social progress.

These differing versions of Germany were thrown into sharp relief in the aftermath of the First World War. The imperial German state was eliminated and a new republican state established. The Weimar Republic, founded in a Thuringian rather than a Prussian city, adopted yet another version of German nationhood, rooted in the quest for a united, constitutional and liberal polity that had first surfaced in the failed German revolution of 1848. The republican nation was a community of free and equal citizens, an all-inclusive *Staatsnation*. The symbols echoed this liberal heritage. The republic adopted the German tricolour. In 1924 the popular nationalist song 'Deutschland, Deutschland, über alles' was adopted as the national anthem. 'Germany above all', too readily mistranslated as 'Germany over everyone', had been sung as the unofficial anthem of the Frankfurt Assembly in 1848. Written in 1841 as a radical challenge to monarchical despotism by an exiled German poet, its three verses celebrate every aspect of German identity, from love of nature to love of wine.[21] It was regarded by German democrats as an expression of revolutionary patriotism, the German equivalent of the 'Marseillaise'.

The nation of the republic was never accepted by much of the population it claimed to represent. Conservatives hankered after the old Reich of monarchy and tradition; they resented the social-democratic origins of the new state and the implicit internationalism of German socialists and communists. Some Germans wanted a return to the pre-1871 federal structure, with virtual independence for the major provinces. Most German nationalists assumed that the central national question – the future of 'Germany' after defeat and territorial fragmentation – could not be solved by the republic. The very issue of what constituted 'Germany' remained as unresolved as ever. Pan-Germans wanted a union between Germany and the German-populated territory that became Austria in 1919, but union was denied by the terms of the Versailles Treaty. Border territories were handed over to France, Poland and Denmark, though they contained sizeable German minorities. Millions of Germans from the former Habsburg empire now lived under Czech or Italian rule. During the 1920s German geographers tried to draw an agreed map of what a true German nation should look like, but the results were inconclusive. It was possible to map Germany ethnically, but it was difficult to decide whether the map should be stretched even as far as the Volga Germans; German linguistic, cultural and commercial influence could be mapped to the east and south of the existing borders, but as a territory such a Germany was indeterminate.[22]

By the 1920s the prevailing view in nationalist circles was neither geographical nor constitutional. They drew on the traditional concept of the *Volk* to define the German nation as a unique and exclusive community, incorporating all Germans, inside and outside the frontiers of the state. By defining the German nation in narrowly ethnic and cultural terms, nationalists could include all the pockets of German populations stranded in neighbouring states, but they could also deny nationality to anyone who was formally a citizen but not a German. 'Our supreme object,' wrote the Austrian pan-German, Georg von Schönerer, in 1921, 'is national exclusiveness.'[23] In the 1920s the idea of the *Volk* was given a pseudo-scientific underpinning by marrying it to popular social biology. Nationalists saw the *völkisch* community as a racial unit, linked not only by a powerful sense of cultural distinctiveness and spiritual affinity, but by common physical origin. The hereditarian interpretation of nationhood was central to all radical nationalist thought in Germany. The principle of *Artgleichheit*, or similarity of kind, was at the heart of this new view of the nation, and it is here that the contrast with issues of identity in the Soviet Union is most evident, for in none of the arguments about the competing identities of Soviet citizens was the issue of racial exclusiveness either relevant or practicable.[24]

The problem of national identity was one on which Stalin and Hitler had a great deal to say. Both were national 'outsiders' themselves – Stalin a Georgian who adopted Russia as his political home before the war, Hitler an Austrian who preferred in 1914 to fight for Germany rather than for the Habsburg empire, and ended up staying there after 1918. Hitler was technically stateless for eight years between 1925 and 1932, stripped of his Austrian citizenship but denied German. It is tempting to argue that as a result both men were prone to exaggerate their adopted Russian or German identity, but this is difficult to demonstrate convincingly. There were many other non-Russians in the Soviet leadership, drawn to Bolshevism by their hostility to the chauvinism of the Tsarist state; Austrian Germans moved across the frontier as easily as Germans the other way, and many more beside Hitler shared his pan-German sentiments. Both men no doubt realized that they could be much more successful politicians in an arena larger than Georgia or Austria, but the main point is that ideas about nation, nationality and statehood were central to the ideological outlook of the two politicians.

In 1913 Lenin asked Stalin to write a pamphlet on *Marxism and the National Question* to define where the Bolshevik party stood on nationalism. It is perhaps Stalin's most important and original contribution to theory; it is also a remarkably clear statement of what constitutes a nation. Stalin rejected a priori the view that the nation was racial or tribal in character or that 'national seclusion' made practical political sense. Most modern nations were the product of a long history of racial mixing. Nations, Stalin insisted, were constructed historically rather than biologically. Nationhood was expressed in common language, a unitary territory, a shared economic life and, above all, in a common culture and mentality.[25] All nations defined in this way had an equal right to the self-expression of their nationality. The self-determination of national groups was a form of emancipation from oppression: the condition of cultural freedom for one nationality was their willingness to allow the same condition to all others.[26]

The free expression of cultural and linguistic diversity was not the same thing as bourgeois nationalism. Stalin's interpretation distinguished between nationalism as a ruling-class strategy of separatism and chauvinism intended to divide national proletariats from each other, and nationalism as 'the right of nationalities to develop freely' within a framework of international proletarian solidarity.[27] Stalin did not favour the unlimited right to political self-determination if autonomy ran counter to the interests of the revolutionary movement. Bourgeois nationalities were segregationist and tribal; Bolshevik nationalities were internationalist and fraternal.[28] The contradictory idea that nations could both assert their cultural uniqueness and remain members of a broader socialist brotherhood remained the central plank of Bolshevik nationality policy after 1917. It was summed up by Stalin in 1925 in a simple formula: 'national in form, but socialist in content'.[29]

Stalin was always clear in his mind that the Soviet Union did not in any sense constitute a nation. It was, like the Tsarist monarchy, a state with many nationalities within its borders. As a multi-national polity Stalin was able to claim that the Soviet Union – 'that remarkable organization for the collaboration of peoples' – was genuinely internationalist, 'the living prototype of the future union of peoples'.[30] Eventually nationalism would become less important as the nationalities merged into a single classless community. This would represent what came to be known as building 'socialism in one country'. This idea, first articulated by Lenin in 1915, has often been misrepresented as an expression of 'national' socialism – a shift away from the internationalist aspirations of true Marxism inspired by the more 'nationalist' Stalin. Yet the ambition was not nationalist in any recognizable sense. When Stalin claimed in 1924 that 'we can build socialism ... by our own efforts', he was expressing a social, not a national ambition.[31] The failure of revolution outside Soviet borders forced most Bolsheviks to take the sensible view that socialism would have to be built without the assistance of other proletariats, but the existence of so many national groups within the USSR allowed the regime to maintain the appearance that it remained internationalist in substance as well as intent. Stalin never turned his back on the idea that the Soviet Union should continue to combat capitalism and encourage revolution abroad; 'socialism in one country' gave the Soviet Union a special place in leading the world struggle, but it was not a declaration of national independence. If Stalin in the 1930s expected Soviet citizens to express a Soviet patriotism, it was from love of the only socialist motherland, not from national hubris. In 1930 Stalin told the Sixteenth

Party Congress that there was no question of forcing the distinct national units of the Soviet Union into a 'common *Great Russian* nation'.[32] Although from the mid-1930s the dictatorship began to identify more with a specifically Russian past, Stalin always maintained the distinction between the Soviet Union as a socialist state of many nationalities and the nation as an expression of a particular and unique culture.

Hitler did not produce as systematic a definition of nationhood as Stalin, but he described what he meant by it both in *Mein Kampf*, written in 1924, and in his so-called 'second' book, dictated in 1928, but not published. Nation for Hitler was inseparable from the idea of race. Each nation, he wrote, 'is only a multitude of more or less similar individual beings'; these beings were 'linked by blood', a similarity of values and a developed racial consciousness. Where Stalin argued that 'each nation is equal to any other nation', Hitler insisted that they existed historically in a state of permanent inequality.[33] He divided nations into two categories: higher races imbued with the urge to 'self-preservation and continuance' and capable of both creating and sustaining a superior culture; lower races destined for biological degeneration and cultural sterility. Hitler's nations were communities locked into permanent confrontation, exclusive and belligerent from nature and necessity. They could not be defined by a common territory, since a vigorous but geographically restricted people had the right to seize all the additional land it needed for its long-term sustenance.

The state, in Hitler's view, should be coterminous with nation or race. The only purpose of the state was to protect the biological purity of its population, raise levels of racial awareness and organize itself to fend off other nations that trespassed on its vital interests. All non-Germans were, by definition, incapable of being or becoming full members of Hitler's 'Germanic state of the German nation'.[34] He rejected out of hand any idea of internationalism, regarding it as the mortal enemy of the true racial state and an inspiration of the Jews. In its place Hitler expected 'the whole life and action' of a people to be devoted to asserting its own national values at the expense of other, alien cultures.[35] The chief enemy of this ambition was the Jewish people because they alone, the 'mightiest counterpart' of the racial state, had throughout history been the instrument of what Hitler called 'denationalization'.[36] Without a fixed territory themselves – 'the race without roots' – Jews flourished parasitically on the body of the unsuspecting host nation, sucking its culture dry, polluting its biological heritage.[37] Hitler's nationalism was exclusive and defensive, an expression of cultural superiority and racial affinity, whereas Stalin's was expressed as an instrument for cultural emancipation and political convergence. Stalin's state was a multi-national reality sustained by a distinctly non-national social and political vision; Hitler's concept of the state was based solely on the 'preservation and intensification' of a single nation to which end all political and social ambitions were to be ruthlessly subordinated.[38]

Soviet nationality policy closely followed the lines set down by Stalin in 1913, which the party broadly endorsed. No nationality was allowed to break away from the new revolutionary state and pursue its own politics, since this was branded as bourgeois separatism. Nationalists who were not also committed communists were removed from office or imprisoned. On the other hand the regime pursued an energetically ethnocentric programme. Major nationalities were allowed a separate party 'section', including Soviet Jews, who lacked a distinct territory. This decision highlighted the difficulty of deciding which ethnic fractions of the Soviet population did constitute a nation. There was a genuine will to encourage ethnic diversity since it was widely assumed that developing a sense of national cultural identity would speed up the process of social and political modernization, while at the same time encouraging the nationalities to identify with the broader goals of Soviet socialism. The first step to emancipating national culture was taken in 1923 when a policy of 'indigenization' (*korenizatsiia*) was introduced. The object was to encourage the 'taking root' of local expressions of ethnic identity. The 1924 constitution gave formal shape to the multi-national state: alongside four major republics (Ukraine, Belorussia, the Russian Federation and the Transcaucasian Federal Republic) were smaller autonomous republics and autonomous regions. Ethnic communities living outside their designated national territory were allowed to organize autonomous provinces or districts to protect their separate national identity.[39]

This process pushed the Soviet state into the paradoxical position that it had, in many cases, to identify and construct national identities for populations that had little or no sense of their own ethnic character, sometimes even no written language. Soviet geographers and ethnographers spent years classifying every ethnic minority they could find even in the remotest reaches of the Article Circle. By 1927 they had found 172, all of them granted official status. The first full list of nationalities was published a year earlier, but it included a section of 'questionable nationalities', some of which had populations of fewer than fifty people.[40] Research on languages was yet more thorough; 192 distinct languages were identified, all of which were entitled to some kind of institutional representation even where they existed as small linguistic islands surrounded by a sea of other tongues. Where there was no written language, one had to be devised. It was decided that the Latin alphabet was less imperialistic than Russian Cyrillic script, and the first transcribed languages were written with roman letters based on symbols devised by the International Phonetic Association, but without capitals or punctuation.[41] Linguistic modernization also drove the decision to Latinize the Arabic scripts of the southern Soviet Union under the auspices of an All-Union Committee for the New Alphabet, established in 1927. In the Caucasus and central Asia poorly qualified teachers struggled to get their illiterate populations to read in a script thoroughly unfamiliar to them all. One Kyrgyz instructor, having successfully instilled the letters of the alphabet in her class by rote, sent off to Moscow for another set.[42] With the obscure languages, spoken by small numbers, the Latin alphabet could not convey the sheer diversity of sounds and in the end 125 different alphabet signs were devised for 92 distinct languages.[43]

Even with larger ethnic populations the process of 'indigenization' had to be encouraged by the state. The eastern areas of White Russia were converted into the Belorussian republic in 1924, but most native Belorussians were peasants with a very limited sense of ethnic identity and many spoke a language other than Belorussian. In the 1926 census 80 per cent claimed to be Belorussian, but only 67 per cent claimed to speak it.[44] There was not a single newspaper in Belorussian before the revolution, but thanks to official promotion there were 30 by 1928 and 149 a decade later. The key to successful *korenizatsiia* was education in native languages and rising literacy rates. In his 1913 pamphlet Stalin had suggested that nationalist aspirations could all be met by giving every minority 'its own schools'.[45] By 1927 38 per cent of Belorussian children were being taught in their native language; by 1939 the figure was 93 per cent.[46] All over the Soviet Union schools teaching the local languages were set up in direct proportion to the ethnic distribution in each region. Uzbekistan, a 'nation' artificially created in 1924 out in many different peoples, boasted twenty-two official languages, tiny Daghestan twenty. By 1934 school textbooks were available in over a hundred different tongues.[47]

Internal nation-building had contradictory effects. On the one hand it did encourage the modernization of Soviet society by raising literacy levels and promoting modern forms of communication. The Soviet population was 56 per cent literate in 1926, but 89 per cent by 1939. The non-Russian regions produced their own elites, whose primary interest was in exploiting Soviet programmes of economic development and welfare reform for their own populations. In Ukraine and Belorussia the urban population had had a high proportion of non-native, chiefly Russian, inhabitants. By the end of the 1920s cities began to fill up with Belorussian and Ukrainian peasants attracted by higher industrial wages. In 1926 for every Russian inhabitant of Kiev there were 1.7 Ukrainians; by 1941 the ratio was one to 5.6.[48] The shifting national composition of local communist parties also reflected the ethnocentric priorities of the state. In 1922 only 23 per cent of Ukrainian Communist Party members were native Ukrainians, more than half were Russian; in 1931 58 per cent were Ukrainians and only 24 per cent Russians.[49] In the late 1920s the Ukrainian party requested the transfer of Russian territory mainly inhabited by Ukrainians back to the Ukraine. Moscow refused, but awarded 130 ethnic 'regions' and 4,000 ethnic townships to the Ukrainian population living within the borders of the Russian Federation.[50]

A policy that had begun by granting nationalist concessions in order to stifle local separatism instead deepened the sense of nationality and weakened the links between socialist centre and nationalist periphery. This contradiction proved intolerable in the context of the economic revolution launched in 1928. The widespread resistance to collectivization in the non-Russian regions culminated in the decision to compel

Ukrainian and Kazakh peasants to part with their grain in 1932, even at the cost of a massive famine that took the lives of an estimated 4 million people, most of them non-Russian. From the early 1930s, under pressure from Stalin to ensure that the slogan 'national in form, socialist in content' could really be enforced, the exaggerated nationality policy of the 1920s was slowed down, and in some cases reversed. In 1933 *korenizatsiia* was formally abandoned: less attention was paid to the 'indigenization' of local cultures and more effort made to promote a Soviet-Russian identity.[51]

The ethnographers who had busily defined so many national fractions in the 1920s were ordered to simplify their classification. By 1937 the list of nationalities had been reduced from 172 to 107 by lumping together small groups with clear ethnic affinities. For the 1939 census the number was further reduced to 98. Of this number some 59 were identified as major nationalities, 39 as ethnographic groups.[52] The exaggerated pursuit of linguistic autonomy was also decelerated. In 1937 the 40 million non-Russians who had been forced to adopt the Latin alphabet were told that their languages would now be written in Cyrillic script instead and the change was enforced the following year, leaving them once again bewilderingly illiterate. On 13 March 1938 it was decreed that Russian should henceforth be a compulsory second language in all schools. In most higher-grade schools and universities Russian had persisted as the language of instruction even in non-Russian areas. Compulsory bilingualism was a way of widening access to higher education, but it was also a means to ensure that the Soviet Union had a single, common means of communication. Russian was hailed as 'the international language of socialist culture'.[53] Russian was re-introduced as the language of command in the Red Army. Local languages could still be used by officials and party leaders, but Russian was an essential tool for communicating with Moscow, and indispensable for any non-Russian with ambitions to climb further up the career ladder.[54]

From the early 1930s the regime began to unravel the complex web of separate ethnic identities in favour of a policy of greater assimilation. Stalin wanted to reduce the centrifugal tendencies encouraged by *korenizatsiia* by asserting a common Soviet identity derived not from nation, but from class. In 1930 the Central Committee dissolved all the national sections in the party apparatus. In 1934 many of the local committees set up to safeguard the affairs of national minorities were wound up. Over the next five years thousands of schools, soviets, autonomous national regions or townships that had been assigned to specific nationalities were converted into multi-ethnic institutions or closed down. The centre tightened its economic grip on the periphery as well. With the introduction of the Five-Year Plans, the state budget was centralized on Moscow at the expense of the non-Russian republics and regions. The centre accounted for an average of 55–60 per cent of the state budget in the 1920s; in 1930 the figure was 74 per cent and by the end of the dictatorship almost 80 per cent.[55] The closure in 1932 of the Supreme Economic Council, which had branches in all the major national republics, ended local responsibility for economic planning and construction in everything save a narrow range of consumer goods. The Stalin Constitution four years later removed most of the responsibilities previously enjoyed by the national republics and regions except for the administration of welfare and education; the role of the Council of Nationalities within the Supreme Soviet was emasculated when its praesidium was abolished.[56]

It is tempting to argue that the centralizing trend of the 1930s reflected the re-assertion of Russian nationalism after its eclipse in 1917. Stalin has often been presented as a Great Russian nationalist, intent on using Russian history and Russian culture as a means to stifle the recrudescence of non-Russian nationalism, to betray the multi-cultural aspirations of the revolution and to underpin the centralizing tendency of the dictatorship. The issue is more complex than this. There had existed a real contradiction in Soviet nationality policy since the Union's establishment in 1924. Consistent with Lenin's fears about the survival of pre-1917 Great Russian chauvinism, there was no distinct Russian nationality. The words 'Russia' or 'Russian' were deliberately left out of the title of the new Soviet state. There was no separate Russian Communist Party. Postmen were instructed not to deliver mail from abroad with the word 'Russia' on the front. The territory covered by the Russian Federation was as ethnically diverse as the Union as a whole, and was as a consequence host to numerous autonomous regions or townships inhabited by national minorities. The word used for 'Russian' in Russian Federation was *rossiiskii*, indicating 'state' rather than people or culture. Russia was clearly the dominant territory from its sheer size and historic situation, yet the Russian people were trapped between an unacknowledged national identity and the novel reality of Soviet citizenship.[57]

Stalin understood the contradiction. He was not a Russian nationalist, though he admired Russian culture and was fascinated by Russia's history. He promoted a limited Russification in the 1930s from political motives. Russia was presented as the Soviet Union's most advanced model for socialist development, an older brother to the infant and adolescent national republics grouped around its borders. The Russian example was also used as a model for a new Soviet patriotism, which the regime regarded as a necessary counterweight to the unintended creation of local patriotism in the national republics. To be Russian was to be at the same time the ideal socialist citizen, committed not to chauvinistic fantasies of national superiority but to a deep awareness of the progressive character of the socialist state he or she was helping to construct.

Soviet patriotism was intended to unite all nationalities in a common commitment to building socialism, but in the 1930s it had a more immediate purpose. With the growing threat of war from Japan in the east and Germany in the west, the regime sought to mobilize popular enthusiasm for the defence of what was now once again called the 'motherland' (*rodina*). Russian history was recruited to supply the patriotic symbols and heroic past that a shared Soviet identity could not entirely satisfy. The change in emphasis was signalled by the reintroduction of conventional narrative history into Soviet classrooms in 1934 to replace the teaching of historical materialism, which was now rejected as too dry and passionless. The standard textbook, M. Pokrovsky's *Brief History of Russia*, was replaced in 1937 by a more patriotic version of the past. The opening page contained the motto: 'We love our country and we must know its wonderful history.'[58] In 1940 Alexandra Pankratova published a new *History of the USSR*, which appropriated the great military victories of the past as stepping-stones to the modern socialist state. The Battle of Borodino of 1812, in which Napoleon's invading army was held at bay, was described in terms that could only have had a contemporary purpose: 'the Russian nation once more demonstrated to the world the heroism and self-sacrifice of which it was capable when the defence of the country and national independence were at stake'.[59]

The link between the official indulgence of patriotism and the wider international crisis was self-evident. The revival of interest in the great military heroes of Russian history did not imply the rehabilitation of the villains of the Tsarist past. History was selective. Peter the Great was hailed as a modernizer and state-builder. The sixteenth-century tsar Ivan IV, the 'Terrible', was allowed back into the Soviet pantheon, after a decade of vilification, on the ground that he had laid the first primitive foundation for the modern Soviet state. He was officially rehabilitated by the Central Committee in 1940, and an approving report prepared two years later praised his 'stunning political skills' and the necessity for 'harsh measures' against internal traitors.[60] The new history was self-consciously didactic. It was important to show that the common people played an important part in the heroic struggles of the past, while the gentry and merchants hesitated to fight or betrayed their state. This was the central theme of Sergei Eisenstein's film *Alexander Nevsky*, commissioned in 1937 and produced in six months during 1938. Originally titled *Rus*, the medieval name for Russia, the film narrates the history of the thirteenth-century Muscovite prince who roused the people to defeat the German Teutonic Knights in the famous 'battle on the ice' of Lake Peipus in 1242. No imaginative leap was required to understand the message. Eisenstein's original script saw Nevsky killed just before his people's army routs the Germans, but Stalin told him he liked his heroes alive. The film was made across the summer months of 1938; the winter battle had to be simulated by suspending lumps of ice on the lake using gas-filled balloons and painting all the vegetation white. When the film was finished Eisenstein wrote a propaganda piece under the title 'My Subject is Patriotism', which explained that Nevsky's famous final words – 'Should anyone raise his sword against us, he shall perish by the sword' – expressed 'the feelings and will of the masses of the Soviet people'.[61]

Russia's rediscovered past was used to make Soviet allegiance more secure. In the late 1930s the 'Song of the Motherland' from *Circus*, a film about racial tolerance, sold 20 million copies, but the motherland in question was the Soviet state, not Russia.[62] The Russification policies of the 1930s should not be exaggerated. There was no intention of reviving the chauvinist legacy of the Tsarist empire. Russia's history provided Soviet patriotic propaganda with heroes everyone could remember, but there were many Soviet heroes too. There were practical reasons for expanding Russian language-teaching, or introducing a common command language in the Soviet armed forces or the bureaucracy, but in other ways the commitment to a multi-ethnic state was maintained. The number of newspapers and books in non-Russian languages continued to expand in the 1930s and 1940s. The celebration of the centenary of the Russian poet Pushkin in 1937 saw the publication of 27 million copies of his poetry in no fewer than sixty-six languages.[63] New homelands continued to be granted. A Jewish Autonomous Republic was founded in Birobidzhan in the Soviet far east to encourage a fuller sense of Jewish national identity. The proportions of non-Russians in local or national government tended to expand throughout the Stalin years.

Far more important than Russification was Stalinist antinationalism. In the 1930s and 1940s this led to the deportation of more than 2 million non-Russians to camps and special settlements, the mass murder of thousands more in the purges of 1936–8 and the pursuit of an increasingly violent policy towards Soviet Jews. The evident contradiction between the ethnocentrism of the regime and the terrible violence done to a great many national minorities has its source in the distinction between two kinds of nationalism drawn by Stalin in his 1913 pamphlet. Reactionary nationalism was incompatible with socialism because it preached a separate, tribal identity; socialist nationalism was acceptable because it was based on ideas of equality and liberation. The dividing line was political, not ethnic. In the 1930s and 1940s Stalin defined these political categories very broadly indeed to include nationalities whose loyalty was suspect because of their common ethnic link with foreign populations presumed to be hostile to the Soviet state. He objected not to the principle of national development as such (some of the deported peoples were allowed to retain a form of ethnic identity in their new homeland), but to those peoples who were alleged to have failed the political test of fealty to the communist cause, as with the Soviet Germans.

Most of the ethnic deportations were the result of war or fear of war. On the Soviet borders to east, west and south there were sizeable national minorities who shared a common ethnic origin with the Soviet Union's anti-communist neighbours, Finland, Poland, the Japanese empire, Iran, Turkey, and the Baltic states. A border zone twenty-two kilometres deep set up in 1923, patrolled by NKVD troops, was supposed to ensure that any irredentist ambitions could be isolated and enclosed. Soviet xenophobia was part and parcel of a collective paranoia about protecting 'socialism in one country'. In 1929 a second zone was defined further from the frontier, and from 1930 onwards populations deemed likely to be hostile to Soviet security interests were moved to the interior, first Poles, Belorussians and Ukrainians, then Finns in Karelia and Leningrad, later on Germans in the Ukraine.[64] In 1932 60,000 Kuban Cossacks were moved, and five years later 6,000 Iranians and almost 1,000 Kurds. In August 1937 the Central Committee decreed the first large-scale deportation of 171,000 Koreans from the Soviet far east, all of whom were regarded as a security risk because of the proximity of Japan. In September they were moved in trainloads to forty-four different locations in central Asia. Those willing to leave were paid a bounty of 370 roubles and their train fare; the rest were bundled into trains by NKVD militia. The measures were pointlessly thorough: 700 Koreans already imprisoned in special labour settlements in the east were identified in the camps and sent to join their compatriots in Kazakhstan.[65]

Fear of the enemy within explains the high proportion of non-Russians who were victims of the wave of mass arrests and executions between 1936 and 1938. Hundreds of thousands of Russians shared the same fate, but the non-Russian peoples were more heavily penalized. The NKVD described many of them as 'nationalities of foreign governments' to justify their victimization. Of the 681,000 shot during the *Ezhovschina* of 1937 and 1938, 247,000 came under the umbrella of anti-nationalist operations. It is estimated that 73 per cent of those arrested from the non-Russian areas were shot, a higher proportion than among ethnic Russians; between 1936 and 1938 around 800,000 non-Russians were executed, sent to camps or deported to central Asia.[66] The Ukrainian Communist Party was singled out by Moscow as a seedbed of irredentism and bourgeois nationalism, reversing a decade of official encouragement for a distinct Ukrainian national identity. In 1930 the independent Ukrainian Auto-cephalous Church, established in 1921, was forced to rejoin Russian Orthodoxy.[67] Ukrainian resistance to collectivization was savagely suppressed. In 1937 the axe fell on the Ukrainian Communist Party, but, in particular, on the ethnic Ukrainians who increasingly domin-ated it. In spring 1937 two-thirds of senior officials and one-third of local party functionaries were purged. Between August 1937 and the summer of 1938 all Ukrainian government commissars and all but three of the 102 members of the Ukrainian party central committee were arrested; most of them were shot. In the spring of 1938 Stalin sent to the Ukraine the young Russian Nikita Khrushchev, a rising star of the party who, as party boss in Moscow, had already purged most of the city's senior communists, with instructions to root out any remaining Ukrainian 'resistance'. A model over-achiever, he ordered the arrest of the entire government once again, and sacked the party secretaries hastily appointed to replace those purged or shot in 1937. In the course of 1938 1,600 new party secretaries were appointed to the cities and districts of the republic.[68] 'Our hand must not tremble,' Khrushchev had said in August 1937, '. . . we must march across the corpses of the enemy . . .'[69]

The regime's anti-nationalism ripened with the coming of war. Between 1940 and 1948 more than 3 million non-Russians were uprooted from their homelands and sent to the Soviet interior. Here they shared the same fate as the Soviet Germans, left in special settle-ments in remote and desolate areas of Kazakhstan and Siberia without food or water supply, little or no housing and few amenities. Ten per cent of all those sent to special settlements – around 377,000 people – died of disease, malnutrition or hypothermia.[70] Thousands more died en route to the settlements in long, slow train journeys or gruelling forced marches. The deportations had no particular pattern; there was no central, premeditated plan. Each wave occurred in response to circumstances outside the Soviet Union, the first during the period of collaboration with Germany, the second as a response to fears of wartime treachery in the non-Russian borderlands, the third in the aftermath of war as hundreds of thousands accused of collaboration with the German enemy were sent to GUlag camps or special settlements. Only the second wave involved the methodical transplantation of entire ethnic groups. Before 1941 and after 1945 the exiles were selected on political criteria as 'socially dangerous' or anti-Soviet, elastic categories that stretched from the obvious (nationalist politicians, churchmen, soldiers and merchants) to the absurd (philatelists and Esperanto speakers, victims of the cosmopolitan character of their hobby). Nationality as such was not the sole cause; had it been so millions more might well have joined the involuntary exodus.[71]

The victims of the first wave included Poles, Latvians, Estonians and Lithuanians in the former Tsarist territories that fell to Soviet control under the terms of the Soviet–German pact signed on 28 September 1939 to confirm the division of Poland between the two states. The precise number of deportees is uncertain, since hundreds of thousands either moved voluntarily to seek work in the industrial centres of the western Soviet Union, or were drafted as conscripts into the Red Army. The number of Polish deportees to camps and special settlements is estimated at approximately a million men, women and children, including 336,000 refugees from the western German-occupied zone of Poland, but not all were ethnic Poles. Only 58 per cent spoke Polish; one-fifth was Jewish and 15 per cent were Russians or Ukrainians, caught up in the net because of their politics or social position.[72] In the Baltic states, occupied by the Soviet Union in June 1940, the same socio-political elements were targeted: 30,000 from Lithuania, 16,000 from Latvia and 10,000 Estonians.[73] They were deported in freight cars, with a crude hole cut in the wooden floor to serve as a latrine, and a tiny barred window. Trucks that were supposed to hold forty were filled to breaking point. Food was supplied for each journey, but its distribution depended on the guards, who pilfered or sold the supplies for themselves. The diet of soup, bread and salt fish was served once every few days, but little water; the result was a high death rate from dehydration among the most vulnerable deportees, infants and the elderly. Escape was possible by smashing the worn or rotten floors of the trucks, but after a time the guards fitted an improvised steel scythe beneath the last freight car to cut escapees in half as they lay on the track.[74]

The second wave of deportations had a different cause. Following the invasion on 22 June 1941, populations in the border areas ethnically linked with the invading armies were moved away for security reasons: the fate of the Soviet Germans has already been told, but they were joined by 89,000 Finns sent to Kazakhstan in August and September 1941, despite the fact that trains and manpower were desperately needed to stem the enemy's precipitous advance. Two years later ten smaller national minorities from the southern borderlands were collectively punished on Stalin's direct instructions for collaboration with the invader. All were regarded as a potential security risk, but since there was no way of identifying which individuals either had collaborated or might do so in the future, the entire population was pre-emptively deported and their lands granted to ex-soldiers or Russian settlers. In 1943 93,000 Kalmyks and 69,000 Karachai were sent eastwards; a year later 387,000 Chechens, 91,000 Ingushi, 38,000 Balkars, 183,000 Tatars from the Crimea, 15,000 Greeks and 95,000 Turks and Kurds.[75] The justification for deportation was slender indeed, but many of the smaller nationalities had been in dispute with Moscow well before the war. They were vulnerable from their limited size and, thanks to the policy of *korenizatsiia*, easily identified. Many Ukrainians had also collaborated with the German invader, or joined anti-Soviet nationalist armies fighting both the Germans and the Russians, but Stalin's appetite for vengeance could not swallow the transfer of 40 million Ukrainians from the most fertile and industrially advanced republic.[76] Instead, in the three years after the end of the war a third wave of deportees arrived in the labour camps and special settlements. Some were Ukrainians and Belorussians who had willingly worked for the Germans; others had worked or fought on the German side to avoid starvation or imprisonment; some were the unwilling *Ostarbeiter*, eastern workers, 2 million of whom had been shipped to Germany to labour in war industries and agriculture. Since their number included many ethnic Russians, this third wave was, like the first, not determined by race. The numbers are difficult to hazard, but by 1949 there were 2.3 million special settlers, almost all of them from the national minorities; four-fifths of them were condemned, in a decree in November 1948, to spend the rest of their lives in the settlements. In the first five post-war years 219,000 of the southern deportees died.[77]

Although ethnic deportation on a large scale in the Soviet Union ebbed away after 1945, evidence of its close connection with the circumstances of war, Stalinist anti-nationalism still had one more chapter. In the years up to the dictator's death in 1953 it was the turn of the Soviet Jews to be victimized. The Jewish community in the Soviet Union posed particular problems for Soviet nationality policy. 'I can't swallow them, I can't spit them out,' Stalin was said to have exclaimed after an ecstatic crowd of 50,000 Jews greeted Golda Meir, Israel's first ambassador to Moscow, in October 1948. 'They are the only group that is completely unassimilable.'[78] The unique character of Jewish identity had been recognized by Stalin when he wrote on nationalism in 1913. Out of the eighty-one pages of *Marxism and the National Question*, seventeen were devoted to the Jewish question. Stalin considered the Jews to possess 'national character', but because they lacked any close link with the land, and hence possessed no clearly defined territory, they did not 'constitute a nation'. He deplored what he called Jewish 'segregation' and 'demarcation', and saw Jewish 'national exclusion' as pretentious and hostile to socialism.[79]

The Jewish population of the Tsarist state was predominantly non-peasant, and in this sense had no defined territory, but it was geographically concentrated. Most of the empire's 5 million Jews lived in the Pale of Settlement, a wide arc of territory stretching from the Baltic states to the Crimea, where Jews had been permitted to settle in the eighteenth century. They were confined to particular regions in which they constituted a high proportion of the population of cities and townships. Victimized both by the state and popular local anti-Semitism, Russia's Jews were the first in Europe to develop a distinct Zionist outlook. From the first congress of the Lovers of Zion in 1884 to the Zionist Convention of May 1917, after the fall of the Tsar, Jewish nationalists demanded the right to a national homeland and the protection of Jewish cultural and religious identity. In 1917 there were 300,000 Zionists in Russia, organized in 1,200 local groups.[80] Very few of Russia's Jewish population were Bolsheviks; only 958 had joined the party before 1917. By contrast, the main Jewish socialist organization, the Bund, had 33,000 members.[81] In the early 1920s thousands of socialist Jews joined the communist party; the party established a national section for Jews, the *evsektsiia*, even though the Jews were not defined as a distinct nationality with their own autonomous territory. Communist Jews played the lead in isolating and attacking Zionists, whose support of a segregated identity, Jewish faith and Jewish internationalism violated in obvious ways the political priorities of the regime. In 1920 the Zionist movement went underground, where it lived in dangerous and clandestine defiance. Throughout the 1920s Zionists were subject to mass arrests and imprisonment. Efforts to leave the Soviet Union for Palestine were deliberately restricted; 21,157 emigrated in 1925–6, but for the eight years between 1927 and 1934 (the year when all emigration was terminated) only 3,045 were allowed to leave.[82]

Soviet Jewish policy in the 1920s was divided between the harsh repression of Zionism and the ideological commitment to the cultural autonomy and social development of ethnic minorities. Anti-Semitism was formally proscribed as part of the official policy against the Tsarist heritage of discrimination and chauvinism; the term 'Yid' was outlawed. The regime drew an arbitrary distinction between Yiddish and Hebrew on the ground that the first was the language of the Jewish masses, the second of the Jewish religious and cultural elite. By 1931 there were 1,100 Yiddish schools and 40 daily papers in Yiddish.[83] Soviet Jews were also encouraged to leave the small-town life of the traditional *shtetl* in the Pale of Settlement (which had finally been abolished in 1915, before the revolution) so that they could adopt a more modern social outlook. Thousands were resettled on farms in the southern Ukraine and the Crimea, raising the Jewish rural population from 75,000 to 396,000 by the end of the 1930s, around 13 per cent of the total Jewish population. The number of Jews in industry more than doubled between 1926 and 1931; there was a marked drift to the larger cities outside the Pale.[84] The hope was that Soviet Jews would be rapidly assimilated into the secular, proletarian world under construction. By 1939 77 per cent of Jewish workers were wage-earners in industry and offices; only 16 per cent still maintained traditional craft work, and of those only a tiny 3 per cent were private traders.[85]

Conditions for many Soviet Jews altered sharply in the 1930s under Stalin. It is important to distinguish here between policies that were generally applied to the Soviet population and policies directed specifically at Jews. In most cases Soviet Jews suffered the same penalties as non-Jews. In 1930 the *evsektsiia* was closed down, together with other national party sections, and most of its officials were later killed in the purges. The ending of the New Economic Policy brought an end to most independent Jewish businesses and craft shops, but this was also the case for non-Jewish producers. The intensification of the anti-religious campaigns in 1929 led to the closure of 100 synagogues and the banning of Sabbath observance for Jewish workers; but Christian and Muslim churches were also closed, and the working week altered to prevent the Christian Sunday.[86] Jews who were arrested, imprisoned or murdered by the state in the 1930s were persecuted as counter-revolutionaries or reactionary nationalists, along with millions of non-Jews. In the GUlag population of the late 1930s Jews were actually under-represented in terms of their numbers in the population as a whole.[87] In 1928 the government decided to create an area of special settlement for Soviet Jews in Birobidzhan on the distant Soviet–Manchurian border, in the hope that this might divert Jewish aspirations for a homeland from the focus on Palestine. In 1936 it was given official status as an autonomous republic. The area was as bleak and inhospitable as any in the Soviet Union; to make such an unenticing homeland more appealing private land-ownership was permitted. However, there was no question of compelling or deporting Jews to Birobidzhan. A slow trickle of settlers arrived, but by 1939 there were still only 108,000, many of them non-Jews attracted by the prospect of a free farm. The 1959 census showed that only 8.8 per cent of the region's population was Jewish.[88]

It was once again the circumstances of war that provoked the regime into a more aggressive anti-nationalism directed, at first, towards the Jewish elites in the Soviet Union, then at the Jewish population as a whole, who, like the Soviet Germans or the Chechens, came under collective political suspicion. The war years altered the situation of Soviet Jews violently and permanently. In 1939 and 1940 the Soviet Union acquired almost 2 million additional Jews in eastern Poland and the Baltic states. These were areas where Zionism was strongly represented and Jewish culture distinctive and pervasive. In less than two years of occupation an independent Jewish life was emasculated: synagogues were closed down, the Sabbath officially ignored, Jewish shops and workshops turned into compulsory state co-operatives, and the public rituals of Jewish religious and family life driven into the privacy of the home and illicit prayer-house.[89] Thousands of rabbis and community leaders and intellectuals were arrested and deported. Estimates suggest that around 250,000 of those deported from eastern Poland were Jews, some of them refugees from German-occupied western Poland.[90] When the war came in June 1941 an unknown number of Jews from the region fled eastwards with the retreating Red Army, but almost all of those who remained were killed in the ensuing German genocide. When the Red Army re-entered Kiev in November 1943 they found only one Jew still alive. When refugees finally returned in 1944 and 1945 to the towns and villages they had vacated, Jewish life had effectively vanished.

During the war Stalin exploited German hostility towards the Jews for his own purposes. Prominent Jewish intellectuals formed a Jewish Anti-Hitler Committee in August 1941, but its independence and internationalism proved too much for a distrustful and embattled regime. Its two exiled Polish leaders were spirited away by the NKVD; one committed suicide in prison, the other was shot. In April 1942 a state-sponsored Jewish Anti-Fascist Committee was set up to mobilize Jewish enthusiasm for the war and to tap foreign sources of funds to support the Soviet war effort. It was nominally headed by a well-known Soviet actor, Solomon Mikhoels, but was in reality a tool of the regime, constantly monitored by a watchful NKVD. The committee lived on after the war, tolerated as long as it could win support for the Soviet cause abroad. The revival of Jewish identity after the war, stimulated by the creation of the state of Israel in 1948, was cautiously welcomed by Stalin as a means to put pressure on western imperialism in the Middle East, but when it became evident that many Soviet Jews expected the revival of Zionism to enhance their own aspirations for separate cultural and religious development in the Soviet Union, a wave of repression was unleashed. Thousands of Jewish intellectuals and spokesmen were arrested and imprisoned for alleged 'cosmopolitanism' in their relations with foreign Jewish communities. Emigration to Israel was banned; four elderly women and a disabled veteran were the only ones to get through the net between May 1948, when the ban was imposed, and the end of 1951.[91] Stalin's inveterate fear of an ethnic fifth-column, which had provoked the deportations of the 1930s and early 1940s, was now transferred to the context of the Cold War.

1 Adolf Hitler on the path to power. He combined an exceptional self-belief with a keen instinct for manipulation. History, he thought, had always been shaped by 'the magic power of the spoken word'.

2 Hitler voting in the general election of March 1936 in a polling office in Potsdam. The regime boasted that 'German democracy', even with only one party, was more sensitive to the people's will than a conventional parliamentary system.

3 The cult of personality in Germany played on the idea of Hitler as an ordinary man called to perform extraordinary deeds. He liked to be seen mixing with his people as here, welcoming a group of Hitler Youth in 1936.

4 Hitler retained around him a small cohort of leaders to whom he remained remarkably loyal and who played a key part in promoting policy. Hitler is seen here in 1935 with his deputy, Rudolf Hess (*right*), in SS uniform and Joseph Goebbels (*centre*), the Minister for Propaganda and Popular Enlightenment.

5 Youth played a special part in National Socialist Germany. Here young girls from the *Bund deutscher Mädel* are addressed by Hitler Youth officials and leaders. The BDM had strict rules and a full monthly schedule of activities.

6 Adolf Hitler with Heinrich Himmler, head of the Reich security services, police forces and the SS. By the late 1930s Himmler was a major influence on Hitler, promoting not only a nation-wide terror but also the race and medical policies of the regime.

7 The National Socialist lawyer Roland Freisler, who played a key role in undermining the established legal system and replacing it with a 'Germanic law'. In 1943 he became president of the People's Court in Berlin, where he presided over the trial of the July plotters in 1944, from which this picture is taken.

8 The social utopia envisaged by National Socialism was to be run by a technocratic and party elite. Here Hitler is examining a model of an *Autobahn* bridge with the engineer Fritz Todt (*centre*) and his deputy Albert Speer (*far right*). The motor-roads were to be a symbol of the new German empire.

9 Hitler had extravagant plans for the remodelling of Berlin. The great Congress Hall pictured above was only built as a model. The planned hall had a dome seven times larger than St Peter's in Rome, and was to house 200,000 people.

10 The mother and child were idealized in the Third Reich as well. Here an appeal for family welfare highlights the importance of reproduction and the link between 'blood and soil' in the regime's propaganda.

Unterstützt das Hilfswerk
Mutter und Kind

generation (F₂) fpaltet jedes der beiden Merkmalpaare nach dem 1. Mendelſchen Geſetz: Schwarze und Rote erſcheinen im Verhältnis ³/₄ · ¹/₄, ebenſo Ganzgefärbte und Geſcheckte ³/₄ · ¹/₄ (Abb. 31). Dabei treten in der F₂ Tiere mit ſämtlichen Zuſammenſtellungen der gegenſätzlichen Ausgangsmerkmale auf: ſchwarz-weiß Geſcheckte, wie die eine P-Raſſe, ganzgefärbte Rote, wie die andere P-Raſſe und zwei

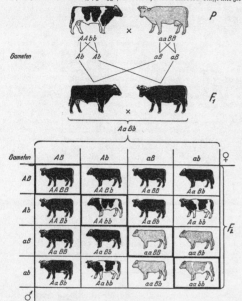

Abb. 31. Zweipaarige Kreuzung einer ſchwarz-weiß geſcheckten und einer rot-ganzfarbigen Raſſe.
(Nach Lauprecht.)

11 In Germany Mendelian genetics w
seen as central to understanding the
importance of heredity in determini
racial purity. A book published in 19
showed how cross-breeding produce
genetic deviation, and went on to wa
that racial mixing between Germans
and Jews 'brings the danger of interr
disharmony'.

12 The ideal National Socialist fami
The picture shows children in the
Hitler Youth, the *Jungvolk*, the *Bun*
deutscher Mädel and the Luftwaffe.
Uniform was an obsession in the Thi
Reich, a visible indication of
commitment to the new order.

13 Anti-Soviet Russians in exile applauded Hitler's anti-Marxism. Here a member of the Russian National Socialist Party poses in Berlin, complete with imitation Hitler moustache. Despite the Russian opposition's sympathy with the new Germany, the Russian movement was closed down in 1939.

4 The expressionist poet Gottfried Benn was initially an enthusiast for the national revolution in 1933, but his work was distrusted by the party as too avant-garde and 'Jewish', and he was banned from publishing in 1938.

15 Hitler visits the Exhibition of Degenerate Art in Munich in 1937. Hundreds of modern pictures were displayed randomly, interspersed with the drawings of psychiatric patients to demonstrate the crazed nature of modern art.

16 The National Socialist movement developed an 'aesthetic politics' in which ritual, symbolism and choreography played a key role. In this still from the film of the 1935 ceremony honouring the martyrs of the movement in Munich, Hitler Youth present party flags before the party temple.

17 Keep fit was a central message of the new society. Young Germans were encouraged to participate in organized displays of callisthenics to symbolize the importance of the healthy body for the racial community. Here German girls from the Sudetenland take to the field.

18 In 1934 labour service was made compulsory for all boys of 18. Here a labour battalion returns home after a day's work, spades on shoulders like rifles. The boys were given a military-style schedule and regular political pep-talks.

19 The Third Reich developed many forms of compulsory labour. Women at the Ravensbrück concentration camp stand ready to begin work in the camp factory. The long hours of work we rewarded with a meagre diet and regular punishments.

20 German nationalist politics were completely militarized in the inter-war years. The gathering he includes Hermann Göring (*centre, front row*) and the SA leader Ernst Röhm (*third from left*), wh was later murdered. Hitler described his followers as 'political soldiers'.

21 Hitler Youth in full voice. 'Youth! Youth!' runs the caption, 'We are soldiers of the future.' Young Germans were brought up after 1933 to think of military service as the highest honour, and self-sacrifice for the race as their principal ambition.

„Jugend! Jugend! Wir sind
der Zukunft Soldaten . . ."

22 Hitler a few months after assuming supreme command of the armed forces in February 1938. He is seen here at the annual army manoeuvres near Stettin in August 1938. Hitler 'could not understand a soldier who feared war'.

23 A woodcut from 1942, based on a drawing by the Soviet artist Mikhail Pikov, shows German forces routed in front of Moscow, a curious blend of modern war and traditional art. The failure to capture Moscow doomed Hitler's war on the Soviet Union.

24 The Soviet Union suffered massive destruction as the German armed forces seized the richest and most populated areas in 1941 and 1942. Here stand the bombed ruins of the Guinsburg House in Kiev after German attacks in the summer of 1941.

Befehl.

Das Dorf ......*Zizicha.*......

ist sofort vor der Zivilbevölkerung zu räumen. Wer sich

ab ..*15.8.1941*.*00*" noch dort aufhält wird erschossen.

den 11.8.41

o b e r s t

ПРИКАЗ.

Гражданское население деревни *ЦИЦИХА* подлежит немедленной эвакуации. Все лица не покинувшие деревни к *15.8_941* _*00*" — будут расстреляни

11 8. 41

Полковник

25 German soldiers entered the Soviet Union with orders to act harshly against any kind of resistance. Here an army order published in German and Belorussian in August 1941 requires the population of the village of Zizicha to leave or be shot.

26 A Red Army soldier murdered on the Eastern Front. Both sides fought a barbarous war against enemy soldiers. Of the 5.7 million Soviet prisoners of war, 57 per cent died or were killed during the war.

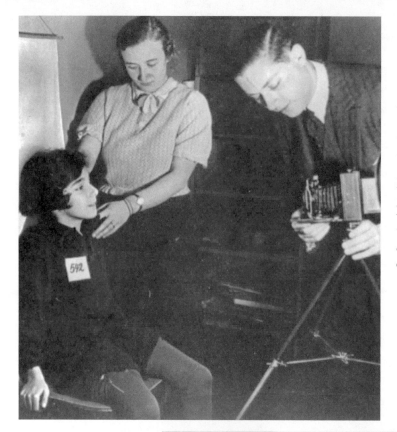

27 A young Jewish ch
is assessed racially by
German officials. All
over occupied Europe
army of scientists and
bureaucrats compiled
racial profile of the
population to find the
who could be
'Germanised' and thos
destined, from 1941, f
extermination.

28 A gypsy baby at
Auschwitz, with the camp
tattoo on its forearm.
Himmler ordered a special
camp for gypsies where
they could be studied, but
thousands died or were
gassed. One-quarter of all
Europe's gypsies perished
during the war.

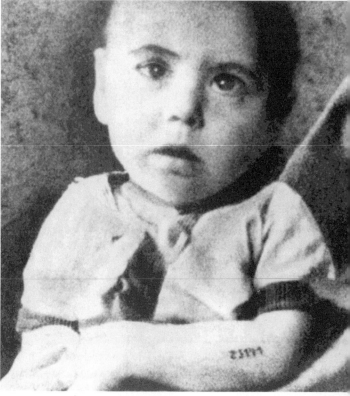

29 A camp drawing of lice inspection from the Buchenwald concentration camp in 1944. There were regular medical examinations to determine how much labour power was left in the emaciated prisoners. Those too weak to work were killed.

30 A group of European Jews waiting after arrival at Auschwitz-Birkenau. Around one-fifth were kept for labour on the new 'model city' planned by Himmler, the rest were killed in the gas chambers of Birkenau and cremated. More than a million died at the camp.

31 Two women liberated by the Red Army from a camp in Pomerania at the
end of the war. The older woman was an elderly German from Cologne, the
other a young Polish girl. One-quarter of the camp population was female.

32 Three women truck drivers for the German air force, captured by the
American 7th Army at the end of the war, sit next to a box of *Panzerfaust* anti-tank
weapons. Hitler saw war as a test for his people. Loss of the war, he said in February 1945,
'means we have been defeated by the Jews'.

For the first time all Jews came under suspicion of being agents of an American international Zionist conspiracy. Mikhoels was the victim of a clumsy assassination ordered directly by Stalin in January 1948. First bludgeoned and then shot by NKVD agents, he was laid out on a road, run over by a truck to simulate a traffic accident, and given a splendid state funeral.[92] Over the next five years, until Stalin's death in 1953, thousands more from a Jewish elite of doctors, artists and intellectuals were murdered or imprisoned as spies, saboteurs or assassins working for American imperialism. There is strong, though not yet complete evidence that Stalin was preparing to order the mass deportation of Soviet Jews in 1953, as punishment for their political unreliability and obdurate 'national seclusion'.[93]

Was this wave of anti-Jewish repression racially inspired? The same question might be asked of the other deportations and the pervasive anti-nationalism of the years of high Stalinism. There is no doubt that popular racism did exist in the Soviet Union towards the Jews and between other ethnic minorities. But the formal position of the Soviet state was against all forms of overt or violent racial discrimination. When two visiting white American engineers threw a black American worker out of the works canteen in a tractor plant in Stalingrad in 1930, they were arrested, charged with 'white chauvinism' and deported back to the United States.[94] The small black community in the Caucasus – descendants of deserters from the multi-racial Ottoman army – was encouraged by the regime to intermarry and assimilate. The concept of 'race' (*rasa*) was regarded by Soviet scientists as an anthropological phenomenon, and was studied separately from ethnography, which concerned itself with nations. During the 1920s Soviet and German anthropologists collaborated on the physiological classification of races, but when German scientists began to embrace National Socialist arguments about the political character of racial difference, their Soviet colleagues abandoned collaboration and emphasized instead that all races were equal: race was a product of changing historical conditions, not of inner essence. In the 1930s Soviet researchers were sent off to the remotest parts of the Soviet Union to demonstrate that so-called 'backward' races were not biologically doomed as long as the Soviet state could alter their external social conditions.[95] Miscegenation, the curse of racial degeneration for

German social biologists, was scientifically tested in the Buriat-Mongol autonomous republic to demonstrate the common-sense conclusion that workers of mixed race were the equal in stamina and physical capacity of ethnically pure Russians.[96]

The chief explanation for the Soviet regime's hostility to particular nationalities, in a political context where ethnic diversity was deliberately promoted and constructed, is political rather than biological. In 1934 internal passports were introduced in which holders had to enter in box five their nationality. The purpose was not to produce a comprehensive ethnic profile of the population, since it applied only to those over sixteen years of age living in cities, but to be able to track down members of nationalities deemed to be a potential security risk who had disappeared into urban areas. It was an imperfect tool at best, for passport holders could choose either parent's nationality, or declare a preferred nationality if it seemed prudent to do so. Those ethnic fractions that became the butt of Stalinist anti-nationalism were the victims not of racism but of xenophobia, a fear that particular peoples with links to the outside world represented so many political Trojan horses bent on undermining the Soviet experiment. This was scarcely more rational than biological racism, but its root was political and its object was to preserve Soviet communism under any circumstances.

Nationality policy under National Socialism appears at first sight a more straightforward question. Few descriptions of Hitler's Reich fail to describe its ultra-nationalism and, in a very real sense, all policy between 1933 and 1945 was causally related to the central objective of preserving, enlarging and defending the German nation. Hitler himself regarded the foreign policy, the military build-up, the economic revival and the social ambitions of the regime as all of a piece. 'The aim of German policy,' Hitler was minuted as saying in November 1937, 'was to make secure and to preserve the racial mass and to enlarge it.'[97] The German *Volk*, the preferred term throughout the dictatorship, conflating both the idea of 'nation' and of 'race', was the touchstone of everything the regime did, reducing the complex nationalist heritage to its simplest expression.

However, the national question was not so easily solved. For a regime so stridently assertive about nationhood there was strikingly little discussion about what constituted the nation. The language and symbols of nationality and statehood were as ambiguous as they had been since the German state was founded in 1871. The very term chosen to describe the new state, the 'Third Reich' (*Das Dritte Reich*), had unfortunate origins, for it was coined by a colourful radical nationalist, Moeller van den Bruck, whose book *The Third Reich* was published in 1923. Two years later van den Bruck was confined to a psychiatric hospital suffering from the effects of syphilis contracted during his bohemian youth, and there, on 30 May 1925, he shot himself. The book's call for a revived, authoritarian Germany made it a bestseller, and National Socialists appropriated the term, but van den Bruck was among those authors whose books were burned by gleeful National Socialist students in May 1933.[98] The word 'Reich' again carried connotations of empire rather than nation, but Third Reich was never the official description of the state, which remained the same 'German Reich' (*Deutsches Reich*) it had been in 1871. The term 'nation' was seldom used because of its link with the western liberal tradition. In most political discourse after 1933 terms like 'race' (*Rasse, Volk*) or 'racial state' (*Volksstaat*) were preferred. In August 1936 a directive from Goebbels proscribed the use of the word *Volk* in any other context: 'There is only a German *Volk*.'[99]

The symbols of the national revival were also ambiguous. The regime rejected the republican tricolour flag, and substituted not the national flag of the pre-1919 Reich, but a flag designed by Hitler himself with the swastika in the centre. The four armed, jagged cross, ancient Indian in origin, was familiar by the late nineteenth century to a coterie of mystical race-theorists and 'Aryanists' on the radical wing of German nationalism, who used it as an 'Aryan' talisman. A curved, left sloping swastika was introduced to the German Workers' Party in 1919 by a dentist, Friedrich Krohn, as a mark of its Aryan, anti-Semitic outlook. When the party became the NSDAP, Hitler took the symbol over, straightened the arms, turned them rightwards and set a black swastika on a white background surrounded by red. This became the standard formula for flag, banner and armband. After 1933 the flag was used on all public occasions, and in May of that year Goebbels published guidelines that banned any commercial exploitation of the swastika except for the badges, bunting and banners that dominated every public ritual during the dictatorship.[100] The colours of the new flag had echoes of the imperial black, white and red, but were not intended to revive the old empire.

The choice of a swastika flag highlighted the extent to which the national symbols of the dictatorship were derived not from the nationalist past but from the National Socialist present. The national anthem was one such instance. After 1933 the regime insisted that only the first of the three verses could be sung; the second was regarded as trivial, and the third verse recalled the nineteenth-century liberal longing for 'freedom and justice'. Instead the single verse was to be followed on all public occasions by the singing of the two verses of the Horst Wessel Song, the party anthem written by a young SA man murdered by communists in 1928 in the Berlin room he shared with a prostitute.[101] The Wessel song, 'Raise the Banner', is a call to arms for the National Socialist movement, but not the nation. The subversion of national symbols by the party had the effect of reducing rather than enhancing any traditional sense of national allegiance. In 1934 the annual festivals organized to commemorate Bismarck as the founder of modern Germany were suspended.[102] The same year the oath sworn by all soldiers entering service was changed from commitment to uphold the constitution and 'protect the German nation' to a personal declaration of 'unconditional obedience' to the person of Adolf Hitler, 'Leader of the German People'.[103] When the oath of the Soviet army was changed in January 1939 from a vow to 'fight for the Soviet Union, for socialism', it was not to swear loyalty to Stalin, but to the more patriotic 'people and homeland'.[104]

The idea of the party as the embodiment of the nation and Hitler as the personification of the national struggle offered a distinct version of German nationhood in direct competition with other conceptions of the nation. The federal nation-state inherited from the republic was set aside by the reform of local government in 1934, which ended the independence of the provinces and centralized all decision-making in Berlin. Conservative versions of the German future were also set aside. In 1933 the German National People's Party (DNVP), for most of the 1920s the main nationalist party in Germany, committed to a conservative reconstruction of the republic, was forced into self-liquidation. In March the name was changed to the German National Front to make it appear less like an old-fashioned party. Two months later the paramilitary wing of the movement, the green-shirted *Kampfring*, was banned as a hotbed of anti-Nazism and its leader, Herbert von Bismarck, nephew of the great Bismarck, arrested. On 27 June 1933 the party voted to dissolve itself before dissolution was compelled by Hitler.[105] The patriotic Pan-German League, founded in 1889 to promote the union of all Germans, also found itself in trouble with the new authorities because, like the DNVP, its aspirations were too reactionary and its distrust of National Socialism unconcealed. After six years of intermittent harassment from the party, its offices across Germany were sealed by the Gestapo on 13 March 1939; a number of its leaders were arrested for their contacts with the conservative resistance, and the League was wound up.[106]

The National Socialist image of the nation as the *Volk* was also subject to the same uncertainties of definition characteristic of earlier *völkisch* nationalism. The issue of territoriality remained unresolved for most of the life of the dictatorship. National Socialists knew that the Germany of the Versailles settlement was not the German nation as they understood it because it did not include all Germans or historic areas of German settlement. Hitler always intended to extend German territory, but the ambition was left deliberately vague, since a demand for the return of the areas lost at Versailles simply restored the old Bismarckian Reich, while it excluded Germans from the former Habsburg empire. Cartographers found themselves subject to constant scrutiny by party offices if they tried to define German claims too narrowly, or to suggest a clearly defined ethnic or cultural area of Germanness outside existing boundaries. Maps of the racial composition of Europe were banned from school instruction. In March 1938 a final attempt was made by geographers and ethnographers to construct an acceptable map of the full extent of German national territory (*Volksboden*). Three distinct territorial categories were agreed: category I for the German core area, category II for mixed areas between the German core and the core areas of other peoples, and category III for all the German enclaves stranded among distant and alien cores. However, on 4 November 1938 the party's censorship office, the *Prüfungskommission*, banned all general maps of putative national territory.[107]

By this stage Greater Germany, incorporating the Germans of the former Habsburg empire, had already been created following the union with Austria in March 1938 and the occupation of the Sudeten areas of Czechoslovakia in early October. The party radicals were already looking towards the next stage of Greater German empire in the east.[108]

Blood rather than soil was the defining characteristic of the National Socialist nation. The use of the word 'blood' rather than 'genes' was a semantic choice; when nineteenth-century German scientists classified races according to quality they talked about 'blood' as the key variable. The metaphor of blood was easily understood and fitted with a more mystical nationalism that saw blood as the vehicle of a particular national spirit flowing on from one generation to the next. The 1913 Nationality Law in Germany defined those of German nationality exclusively in terms of blood.[109] A common 'racial blood' (*Volksblut*) was regarded by Hitler as the fundamental precondition for the German nation.[110] German national identity in the nineteenth century had used metaphors of the body to suggest the common union of the *Volk*; under Hitler the regime set out to define that national body not as a metaphorical device, but as a biological certainty. Nationhood in the Third Reich was less concerned with issues of culture or a shared history, which was open to wide interpretation, and more with the idea of what was called a 'genealogical community'.[111]

The national community was defined in the first years of the regime by specific legislation laying down who was and who was not a racial German. The first law was published on 14 July 1933 'for the Annulment of Naturalization and the Stripping of German Citizenship'. The targets were mainly, but not exclusively, Jewish. Jews from Eastern Europe recently naturalized had their status revoked; Germans abroad who were enemies of the new Reich could be 'denaturalized'. It was under this law that the physicist Albert Einstein, who had exiled himself to the United States in March 1933, was deprived of his German citizenship.[112] In 1935 the first comprehensive nationality legislation was announced by Hitler at the Nuremberg Party Rally. On 15 September 1935 the Reichstag met in special session in Nuremberg, where it approved two separate laws, the first 'for the Protection of German Blood and German Honour', the second, a new Reich Citizenship Law. The laws were directed mainly at German Jews whose status as 'Germans' was still technically intact. Marriage between Germans and Jews was forbidden; so too were sexual relations outside marriage in order to protect 'the purity of German blood'. The second law granted citizenship only to those of 'German or related blood', as long as they were 'willing and suitable to serve the German *Volk* and Reich'.[113] This second law did not specify Jews as such, and under its provisions other non-Germans could no longer be citizens, including the small German black population which had come from the German pre-war African colonies, and the 600 offspring of unions between German women and black French soldiers during the Ruhr occupation of 1923. In 1937 these children were compulsorily sterilized to remove any prospect of the further contamination of German blood.[114] Even ethnic Germans who were not 'willing or suitable' could lose their citizenship; under the law thousands of communist exiles were made into non-Germans.

Hitler left definitions open in the law on German blood by striking out the final sentence of the draft prepared for him at Nuremberg: 'This law is for full Jews only.' The next months saw lengthy arguments about whether half or quarter-Jews qualified under either piece of legislation. On 14 November a supplement to the Citizenship Law was published that laid down that a German with two Jewish grandparents, who was himself an orthodox Jew, or was married to a Jew, or was the offspring of a marriage with a Jew, was Jewish; all other half or quarter-Jews were still German citizens.[115] The convoluted efforts on the Soviet steppe seven years later to define who was a racial German have their root in the ambition to give very precise legal form to Jewish nationality. Throughout the remaining ten years of the Reich the exact definition of German blood occupied many hours of legal and medical scrutiny. But it was the key to determining the full extent of the German body; in 1938 Hitler suggested that as many as 30 million ethnic Germans (*Volksdeutsche*) lay outside German territory. As German expansion after 1938 drew many of them into the German net, they qualified for citizenship under the 1935 law in all cases where German blood and correct racial behaviour could be demonstrated.

The responsibility for defining and guarding German blood devolved early in the dictatorship to Heinrich Himmler's SS. The original SS Race Office, founded in 1932, was primarily concerned with the biological condition of its own recruits. In November 1933 the office moved from Munich to Berlin, where it was renamed the Main Office for Race and Settlement under the direction of Walther Darré, the party's agricultural expert and leading exponent of ideas about what he called the 'blood-consciousness of the Germanic peoples'.[116] Until his resignation in 1938, the early activity of the office reflected Darré's own views on breeding a healthy peasantry and encouraging SS families to live in the countryside. His successor, the SS race expert Günther Pancke, supervised the transition of the office into the central instrument of racial planning. The Race Office promoted research into 'racial science' and collected scientific and medical data intended to confirm the biological superiority of the Germanic peoples and the permanent genetic inferiority of all others. It became the principal agency for recovering for the *Volk* the thousands of racial Germans who were brought under German control by occupation and invasion. The war opened up for the SS extraordinary and unexpected opportunities to realize the idea of 'nation' as 'race'. On Himmler's birthday, 7 October 1939, Hitler named him Reich Commissar for the Protection of the German Race, and the following year Himmler established a German Racial Register (*Deutsche Volksliste*) as the first step in identifying anyone who might qualify from blood, rather than culture or language, as ethnically German.[117]

The register eventually covered some 1.5 million Europeans who were interrogated, measured, photographed and medically examined as part of the scientific effort to construct a single and exclusive national body. Each one of the potential Germans was recorded on a 'race card'. On the front were details of parents and grandparents, and a box for 'judgement about race' based first on the physical evidence, then on the interviewee's own opinion. The reverse of the card listed the main physical characteristics – hair colour, eyes, etc. – in four columns. The first column was the Aryan ideal: tall, long-limbed, blond, blue-eyed, thin-lipped, rosy-faced. The features in the fourth column described a short, swarthy-skinned, full-lipped, dark-haired, Mongol-eyed creature. Nose categories extended from 'high, straight and narrow' to 'squat, broad and hooked'.[118] All of these race records were faithfully stored on the most up-to-date automatic punched-card Hollerith machines, ancient forerunner of the modern computer. SS race scientists were also interested in a more exact ethnic classification of the populations under their control, to isolate those with greater potential for Germanization or re-Germanization. The Poles were divided into five distinct categories: Nordic, sub-Nordic, Dinarian, Praeslavic and Oriental; Poland itself was divided into five racial zones, each one subject to its own racial profiling. The Western Ukraine was designated as a zone with seven racial sub-types.[119]

This classification was done not to satisfy scientific curiosity but to justify a policy of racial hierarchy. In occupied Poland only 3 per cent of those examined were deemed biologically suitable for the German nation. On Hitler's express instructions the Polish national elite was to be liquidated to prevent any nationalist revival. In the spring of 1940 6,000 Polish intellectuals were selected and murdered; during the war 45 per cent of all doctors, 57 per cent of lawyers, 40 per cent of professors were killed.[120] Where Stalin hesitated to deport the Ukrainian population, German planners had no such scruples. Plans for the ethnic reconstruction of the East assumed fantastic proportions. Four-fifths of all Poles, 75 per cent of Belorussians and 64 per cent of Western Ukrainians were to be deported to Siberia, an area deemed to be more appropriate to the primitive nature of their racial character, and where millions were expected to perish. Estimates for those to be moved varied from 31 million in the General Plan East, drafted in 1941, to 46–51 million in the plans of Rosenberg's Eastern Ministry, founded the same year to co-ordinate the ethnic cleansing and political reform of the occupied East.[121] The plan was to relocate an estimated 650–750,000 ethnic Germans from the east and south-east of Europe to a new homeland in the areas conquered in Poland, where Himmler hoped to build what he called a *Blutswall* (wall of blood) to mark off German Europe from Slavic Asia. This number included 187,000 Germans in the areas annexed by the Soviet Union in 1940, who were deported to Germany under the terms of the German–Soviet agreement of 28 September 1939, and 77,000 living in Romania. The plan was greatly enlarged in 1941 when it was decided to settle 3.3 million Germans in the East, among them 770,000 from the Reich itself, chosen on the basis of their assessed 'blood-value'. To make room for the influx of the new racial material Poles and Polish Jews were moved eastwards, but the whole vast programme of resettlement and deportation was ill-planned, improvised and costly. In the winter of 1940/41 200,000 of the ethnic Germans still languished in a network of 1,500 refugee camps.[122]

The result of the efforts to construct a nationality on strictly biological terms, ridiculed by Soviet scientists, resulted in policies that were confused, contradictory, discriminatory and, ultimately, lethal for those excluded from the national body. Among those ethnic groups that became part of Himmler's extravagant programme for national consolidation were the 26,000 gypsies (Sinti and Roma) living in Germany. They were not at first considered a serious racial threat. They were harried by the criminal police as vagrants or habitual offenders, and from 1937 they were victimized because of Himmler's decision to fill up the concentration camps with so-called 'asocials'. Their racial victimization only followed the establishment by the Interior Ministry in the spring of 1936 of a Research Institute for Racial Hygiene and Population Biology under Robert Ritter, a child psychologist with an academic interest in hereditary criminality. Ritter tramped from gypsy camp to gypsy camp cataloguing around 77 per cent of the gypsy population; his assistants took blood samples and compiled complex genealogies. By 1938 Ritter concluded that the gypsy population was not Aryan, despite its Indian origins, because, in his view, approximately 90 per cent were of mixed race (*Mischlinge*). 'Here we know we are dealing,' he wrote, 'with primitive nomads of an alien race.'[123] He suggested that the gypsies' 'asocial' behaviour was a consequence of their inferior mixed-racial status. Growing popular hostility to the different populations of gypsies, including the itinerant *Jenische*, or 'white gypsies' (who were in fact ethnically German), finally resulted in a decree on 'Combating the Gypsy Plague', published on 8 December 1938 by Himmler as Chief of the Reich Police. The decree was based on 'the inner characteristics of the race'. It authorized the compilation of a national register of all pure-blood gypsies, *Mischlinge* and non-gypsy itinerants, and their compulsory racial-biological examination. All itinerants were forbidden from entering border areas for security reasons. The application of the Nuremberg law on mixed marriage was finally imposed on the gypsies as 'an alien race'.[124]

Conditions for gypsies deteriorated in 1939 as local authorities interpreted the police decree generously. In Austria the large sedentary population of gypsies in the Burgenland had already lost voting rights and the right to schooling, and the public performance of their music was banned in 1938. In 1939 all adult males were subjected to compulsory forced labour.[125] The coming of war altered the gypsies' situation radically. After the defeat of Poland, Hitler gave authorization for the deportation of all the Reich's gypsies to conquered Polish territory, partly for security reasons, since gypsies were popularly regarded as potential spies, partly because they were, like the German Jews who would be sent with them, an 'alien' nationality. On 17 October 1939 Himmler's deputy, Reinhard Heydrich, ordered all gypsy populations to cease travelling or face a concentration camp. Gypsy men were used as forced labour; those in military service were removed from the ranks. Gypsy women were banned from fortune-telling in case they alarmed the German population with unfounded rumours. Those who were caught ended up in the women's concentration camp at Ravensbrück.[126]

The mass deportation never took place because of over-crowding in the Polish reception areas. In 1940 only 2,500 German gypsies were sent to Poland to work, but they were not imprisoned; in November 1941 5,000 Burgenland gypsies were sent to the Lodz ghetto, where many contracted typhus and became among the first victims exterminated in gas vans at Chelmno, to prevent the spread of the disease.[127] Finally, in March 1943, Himmler ordered a special gypsy camp to be established at Auschwitz to house 'asocial' mixed-race gypsies. Approximately 5,000 gypsies classified as pure-blood were permitted to stay in Germany as an object of SS racial study. Those mixed-race gypsies who were in war work, or married to ethnic Germans, or who could prove they had had a steady job and a permanent home before 1939 were granted amnesty. Only mixed-race gypsies whose style of life was deemed a permanent threat to the host race were supposed to be deported, but local policemen and officials were less sensitive to the racial nuances of the SS, and thousands were shipped eastwards or sent to camps regardless of their circumstances. Some 13,080 German gypsies were sent to Auschwitz, and a further 10,000 from other parts of Europe. There was no general plan of extermination. Most gypsies at Auschwitz died from the effects of debilitating labour or disease;

around 5,600 were gassed. Soviet and Polish gypsies, however, were treated differently. At first they were killed as potential partisans or spies, but their murder soon became routine racial killing. Hinrich Lohse, German commissar of the Baltic Ostland, ordered the gypsies 'to be treated like Jews'.[128] An estimated 64,700 died in the East. Out of a gypsy population in Europe of 872,000 in 1939, 212,000 (24 per cent) died or were killed.[129]

The gypsies were the target of a popular social resentment which made it simple for the authorities to isolate and penalize them with widespread public approval. Race became the excuse for punishing what was widely regarded as social deviancy rather than ethnic threat. The situation with Germany's Jews was different. 'The racial problem,' wrote two Interior Ministry race experts in 1938, 'is *the Jewish question*.'[130] German Jews were regarded by the authorities as the only alien race of any significance within the German national body and they were the principal object of a systematic policy of official racial discrimination after 1933. Little in their recent history suggested that this should be the case. In 1932 there were 525,000 Jews in Germany; most were settled families, many of them assimilated Christianized Jews, some more recent refugees from the pogroms and racism of Eastern Europe. There was a long and rich tradition of Jewish-German culture; since their civic emancipation in 1812, many German Jews had integrated with German elites in business and intellectual life. There was sporadic anti-Semitic protest against Jewish immigration and Jewish shopkeepers in the late 1890s. The term 'anti-Semitism' itself was coined by a German in 1879. Among educated Germans there existed an important fraction who saw 'the Jew' as an enemy of German culture and German values; some regarded the Jews as a biological threat when hereditarian social biology became fashionable before 1914. Both intellectual traditions flourished after 1919. This made little difference to Jewish Germans. There was little sense of a separate political or social identity, though there were obvious distinctions of culture and of religion, for those who still practised it. Zionism became briefly popular after 1918, but from 23,000 Zionists in 1923 the number fell to 17,000 in 1929, of whom a much smaller proportion was politically active.[131] Palestine held only limited appeal, and by 1933 fewer than 2,000 German Jews had moved there.[132] During the

1920s the radical nationalist right had absorbed anti-Semitism as a central element of their political outlook, but until the NSDAP broke through electorally in 1930, they remained a small but conspicuous minority. A casual anti-Semitism existed widely in German society, as it did throughout non-Jewish Europe.

In this sense 1933 represented a complete break with the past. The frontier dividing ethnic German and German Jew, which had been permeable and hazy, became a high wall. A few days after the appointment of Hitler as Chancellor a young German law student, Raimund Pretzel, deeply hostile to the new leader, sat at a desk in the main law library in Berlin. Young SA men broke into the building hunting for Jewish lawyers. One stood in front of his desk, arms akimbo, legs apart, and asked him if he was Aryan; he mumbled 'yes' and the thug moved on.[133] Racial identity was from the very start of the Third Reich a litmus test of inclusion and exclusion; it was also physically dangerous. Hitler's characterization of the 'Jew' as the enemy defined the confrontation from the start as a racial war. Pretzel not only reluctantly endorsed the ethnic categories of the new regime, he avoided a beating.

These are obvious but important points. The anti-Semitic attitudes of the National Socialist movement were popular knowledge throughout Germany and in 1933 immediately infected every area of public life. Some government effort was made to rein back the wave of anti-Semitic violence unleashed against German Jews in the spring of 1933 by the large number of racists in the party and the SA because of the effect abroad. Only three months after Hitler's appointment there were limited unofficial boycott actions in Britain, Canada, South Africa, Australia, the Netherlands, France, Sweden and the United States.[134] But the widespread and vicious manifestation of anti-Semitism left its mark. 'I am almost used to the condition of being without rights,' wrote the Jewish philologist Victor Klemperer only weeks after Hitler's electoral success in March 1933. 'I simply am not German and Aryan, but a Jew and must be grateful if I am allowed to stay alive. . . .'[135] Over the next six years the German Jewish population was deprived of citizenship, expelled from professional life and subjected to state-orchestrated expropriation of their assets. This was a slow and cumulative process, but it was widely trumpeted by the regime and the party, and won extensive public endorsement. More than 250 laws and decrees excluding and stigmatizing the Jews appeared between 1933 and 1939, beginning with the Law for the Restoration of the Professional Civil Service published on 7 April 1933. Paragraph 3 of this law announced that civil servants not of Aryan origin 'are to retire'; four days later a supplementary decree defined 'non-Aryan' as anyone with one parent or grandparent who was not Aryan.[136] There were exceptions for Jewish veterans and those with records of long service.

The inspiration behind the legislation was a Ministry of the Interior official, Achim Gercke, who, as a student at Göttingen University in the 1920s, had tried to create a card index of all Jews living in Germany. In May 1933 he justified the law on the grounds that the German population would now realize that 'the national community is a community of blood'.[137] Hundreds of officials all over Germany hastily drafted regulations excluding or discriminating against Jews. University and higher school places were closed to Jews; cinemas, swimming pools, theatres, parks were 'Aryanized'. Jews were not allowed to own radios; successive pieces of legislation removed their right to a driving licence, or to own a car, or a motorcycle or even, with remorseless consistency, to possess a motorcycle sidecar.[138] The response of many German Jews was to emigrate. In June 1933 there were 499,682 Jews in Germany; of this number 98,747 were nationals of another country. By May of 1939 there were 213,457 left, 25,783 of them non-German.[139] Around 60,000 left for Palestine under the terms of an agreement drawn up in August 1933 between the Ministry of Economics and German Zionists – the so-called Haavarah Agreement – which tied Jewish emigration to the export of German goods to the Middle East. All Jewish emigrants had to pay a high tax levy to the state as a kind of public ransom for their release from Germany. Emigration continued until the autumn of 1941, at which point there were still 164,000 German Jews in the Reich.[140]

The primary aim of National Socialist policy was to exclude German Jews from the national body, first by placing them in quarantine within Germany, then by expelling them abroad. Paradoxically, Jewish identity in the 1930s was strengthened by the forced development of an exclusively Jewish cultural, educational and economic life, and by the party's sponsorship of official links with Zionism. German race experts argued about how German Jews should be defined, but in general they followed Hitler's view that they did constitute a 'nation'. Yet the more distinctive and separate Jewish identity became, the more it fuelled the racism of the party faithful. From the mid-1930s the idea that Germany should become completely *judenrein*, 'cleansed of Jews', was undisguised. 'The Jews must get out of Germany,' Hitler told Goebbels in November 1937, 'in fact out of the whole of Europe.'[141] The takeover of Austria in March 1938 brought millions of Germans into the *Volk*, but an additional 190,000 Jews as well. A comprehensive programme of anti-Semitic 'cleansing' was imposed at once by Austrian National Socialists working with SS and Gestapo advisers. Emigration was organized by the Gestapo's Jewish expert, Adolf Eichmann. Jewish businesses and housing were 'Aryan-ized' within months. By August 1939 all 33,000 Jewish businesses in Vienna had been liquidated or transferred to German hands. The practice in Germany of making Jews pay for their release and emi-gration was extended to Austria. By May 1939 100,000 of Austria's Jews had moved abroad.[142]

Jews were the victims of a popular racial hatred and a developed theory of racial nationalism. They were not yet the object of physical extermination. Much of the discussion of anti-Semitism in Germany in the pre-war years has focused on the search for the roots of the subsequent wartime genocide. So-called 'intentionalist' historians find clues in Hitler's private comments and occasional public threats against the Jews; 'functionalist' or 'structuralist' writers see anti-Semitic policy in the 1930s as a series of unplanned steps, a 'cumulative radicalization' towards a distant genocide, but no clear evidence of a genocidal impulse before 1939.[143] Both approaches to the hunt for genocide divert attention from the central reality for all Jews after 1933: whether or not the later genocide was explicit or merely implicit in the anti-Jewish policies of the 1930s, the entire system that emerged after 1933 was fundamentally anti-Semitic in its outlook, purpose and practices. The vengeful and violent xenophobia promoted by the regime had the Jews as its primary object throughout the whole life of the dictatorship.

The relationship between German nationalism and Jewish identity is central to any understanding of the subsequent decisions that led to genocide. Some of the anti-Semitic sentiment in Germany is recogniz-able as conventional prejudice – Christian condemnation for the Christ-slayers, professional envy at Jewish intellectual and cultural success, or popular resentment against Jewish small business. But for Hitler and thousands of German anti-Semites both inside and outside the party, the terms of the conflict between German *Volk* and Jewish identity was an ineluctable, transcendent struggle for mastery between elemental forces of light and darkness. The Jew represented for Hitler 'the anti-man', a 'creature outside nature, alien to nature'.[144] Jews promoted the degeneration of nations; they represented in all their many guises the 'anti-nation'. Jews could be capitalists in London or New York, or Bolsheviks in Moscow, but their different activities served the common and primordial ambition to undermine pure nations and to destroy civilized life. The Jewish threat, in National Socialist eschatology, was profound and limitless, but above all it provoked an enervating sense of insecurity in the threatened nation. The Jew was regarded not only as the instrument of internal national decomposition, but also as the agent of worldwide forces bent on destroying Germany's national existence. Under Hitler, German national identity was shaped by reference to the Jewish 'other'; argu-ments about that identity could be set aside in the face of a common racial enemy.

Hitler interpreted the national struggle in the bleakest historical terms. The German nation was engaged in nothing less than the final battle for its survival. This starkly Manichaen view of the world, the division into 'them or us', German triumph and Jewish catastrophe, permeated all anti-Semitic discourse in the 1930s, and was central to Hitler's own sense of history. When he sketched out a synopsis for a 'Monumental History of Mankind' in 1919 or 1920, the notes are filled with repetitive antonyms – 'Aryan – Jew', 'Workers and drones', 'Builders and destroyers' – which are used to explain nothing less than the entire course of human history. Past nations 'could not save themselves' from collapse, but the Jew, with no state of his own, 'saved himself'.[145] This vast historical canvas was recalled sixteen years later when Hitler wrote the secret memorandum in 1936 that became the basis of German preparations for war. His subject was 'the struggle of nations for life'. The world was poised for a historic conflict against the forces of Jewish Bolshevism. Only German revival stood between the weakened nations of Europe and a new Dark Age, 'the most gruesome racial catastrophe' since 'the downfall of the states of antiquity'. If Germany failed, the consequence would be the 'final destruction' or 'annihilation' of the German *Volk*.[146] This was Hitler's private view, not a piece of public rhetoric. A copy of the memorandum was given to only two other party leaders, on pain never to reveal its contents. The language and intent are unambiguous. The terms in which Hitler's anti-Semitism was expressed were world-historical, violent and German: national survival or national extinction.

The war with the Jews was an expression of fear, not power. The fantasies of worldwide Jewish conspiracy were woven in such a way that Jewish strength was made to appear monstrous and irrepressible. 'We were on the defensive,' wrote Robert Ley in his Nuremberg prison cell in 1945, reflecting on the Jewish catastrophe.[147] National Socialism was presented as the last heroic bulwark against an encroaching 'Jewification' of the world. The Jews in Germany were, in the words of the SS journal *Das Schwarze Korps*, 'part of world Jewry, and they partake in the responsibility for everything that world Jewry initiates against Germany'.[148] The contest with 'world Jewry' for German survival was regarded by the regime's leaders as intimately connected with the course of German foreign policy. Ley again in 1945: 'We National Socialists saw in the struggles which now lie behind us, a war solely against the Jews – not against the French, English, Americans or Russians.'[149] From late 1938 onwards, as German expansion and rearmament provoked serious international crisis, the language of German anti-Semitism became sharper and more violent. 'Annihilation' was used by Hitler in the speech to the Reichstag in January 1939, when he warned the Jews at home and abroad that if Germany found herself faced with a new 'world war' the Jewish race in Europe would be the losers. This has sometimes been taken as a diplomatic gambit, to warn Britain and America to stay out of German affairs. Yet the word 'annihilation' (*Vernichtung*) was being widely used among the party's racist apparatus by 1939. The connection between war and a future settlement of accounts with 'world Jewry' was essential to the regime's view of the impending world-historical crisis, the age of what Himmler called 'race-wars'.[150]

When war broke out in September 1939 it was seen not as an accidental or unplanned opportunity for a more vigorous policy of Jewish deportation, but as an extension and intensification of an anti-Semitic 'Cold War' that Germany had been engaged in since at least her defeat in 1918. On 7 October 1939 Hitler issued a decree empowering Himmler to deport all Jews from Greater Germany to the east, where they would be resettled together with almost 2 million Polish Jews now under German rule. Only 4,700 were deported from Austria and Bohemia before Hitler suddenly put a stop to the transfers, from fear that a large Jewish presence would pose a serious risk if he wanted to assemble troops in Poland for an assault on the Soviet Union.[151] Defeat of France in June 1940 produced a brief flirtation with the idea of shipping European Jews to the African island of Madagascar, where it was hoped that the conditions of a tropical ghetto would decimate the population. The failure to defeat the British empire rendered the 'Madagascar Plan' inoperable. Instead, Polish Jews were pushed into hastily constructed ghetto prisons on Polish soil. The decision finally taken in November 1940, to launch all-out war against the Soviet Union in the summer of 1941, opened up a new and violent dimension to the war with the Jews. In May and June 1941 Hitler issued the first of many orders sanctioning the murder of certain categories of the enemy population, including Jewish men in the service of the Soviet state, armed forces or the communist party. This was the first time that the killing of Jews was specifically and publicly ordained, though it was not the first time that Hitler had ordered the mass murder of national enemies.[152]

From the moment of the invasion on 22 June 1941 the security police units (the four *Einsatzgruppen*) and the armed forces began the extermination not only of Jews in state and party service, but of any Jews deemed to be a security threat to the invading armies. This has been shown to be a messy and unco-ordinated process, fuelled by local initiatives and differing interpretations of the broad and permissive instructions issued from Hitler's headquarters. It was assisted by the recruitment of enthusiastic anti-Semites in the areas quickly occupied by the German army (and by the violent anti-Semitism of the Romanian and Hungarian armies fighting alongside the German). The German security units immediately established contact with local anti-Semitic groups. Only three days after the invasion, Lithuanian militiamen in Kovno were encouraged by German security officers to stage a pogrom, and that night 1,500 Jews were murdered with particular savagery. On 2 July, the local police in Riga were organized by a German commander to murder 400 Jews and burn down all Riga's synagogues.[153] In Belorussia and Ukraine thousands of Jews were slaughtered by non-Germans, sometimes prompted, sometimes not. In the end an estimated 1.4 million Jews were murdered in the so-called 'wild killings', and hundreds of thousands more were forced into makeshift ghettoes, where, denied the means for sustaining life, they died of starvation, disease and cold.[154]

The subsequent extension of the programme of murder in 1942 to cover all the Jews of Germany and occupied Europe was not, therefore, a decision about genocide, but about its scale. The fundamental decision to murder certain categories of Jews because they represented the German people's most dangerous racial enemy was made in the spring of 1941. The mass murder of Jews as Jews began in June 1941 and continued throughout the remaining life of the Reich. In July 1941 Hermann Göring authorized Heydrich to find a 'Final Solution' (*Endlösung*) for the Jewish population, which, even on the most benign interpretation, meant the destruction of their communities and mass deportation, and the physical elimination of those elements judged most dangerous. The transition to a genocidal solution in the summer of 1941 was evidenced in the hundreds of hastily dug pits, ditches and tank traps that served as makeshift mass graves all over the conquered East.

There is no single document or single decision that explains the gradual extension of a policy of extermination to cover all Jewish populations. The Final Solution became a comprehensive genocide step-by-step, the pace quickening with every murderous stride. In autumn 1941, with growing American involvement in the war, symbolized by the publication, on 14 August, of the Anglo-American Atlantic Charter, which Hitler interpreted as evidence of Jewish efforts to create a global anti-German coalition, the murders in the East escalated.[155] In mid-August the *Einsatzgruppen* were instructed by Himmler to start killing women and children as well as all male Jews. In Serbia Jewish men were slaughtered from September. Jewish communities in Galicia and the Warthegau, areas of occupied Poland, were rounded up and murdered during the autumn months. In September Hitler finally approved the deportation of German and Austrian Jews, which had been postponed in 1939. The first deportations began on 15–18 October, and by early November almost 20,000 had been sent to ghettoes, where non-German Jews were murdered to release room for the newcomers. One of the first transports of 5,000 German Jews was murdered at Kovno in November 1941, though no authority had been given from Berlin. By that stage thousands of Jews unfit for slave labour were being systematically murdered as 'useless eaters' all over the occupied East.[156]

After Germany declared war on the United States on 10 December 1941, Hitler announced publicly and privately that the final coming of global war would see the realization of the prophecy he had made in January 1939 about annihilating Europe's Jews. This was a view consistent with the long history of his anti-Semitism, which was always expressed in the idiom of war to the death. 'The World War is here,' observed Goebbels in his diary on 13 December, the day after Hitler made a speech to party leaders, 'the extermination of the Jews must be the necessary consequence.'[157] Hitler may have decided to move from the disorganized and unco-ordinated killings to a systematic camp-based programme of mass killing some weeks earlier, but the firm evidence is lacking. Already, on 18 November, Rosenberg noted that the 'biological extermination of the whole of European Jewry' was to take place on Soviet territory.[158] Adolf Eichmann, the Gestapo official responsible for shipping all Jews to the East, remembered after the war that he had been told of an order for general extermination at some point in the autumn of 1941, but could not be more precise.[159] Whenever the private decisions were made, the mass murders of 1941 in the East gave way by the spring of 1942 to a systematic programme to identify, deport and murder every Jew in Europe. All public discussions of Jewish policy remained cloaked in the deliberately ambiguous language reserved for policies to be shielded from public scrutiny. Hitler continued to talk as though he had in mind mass deportations to the East, when the mass-murder of Jews had been taking place every day for months with his approval. Deportation of European Jews to the East was, at least on the surface, the subject-matter of the infamous

Wannsee Conference called initially for early December, then post-poned until 20 January 1942, by which time the first Polish Jews were already being gassed in the Chelmo extermination camp. Around one-fifth of Jewish deportees were used as forced labour until they died, but the rest were shipped to the camps and murdered within hours of their arrival.[160] The killing continued without interruption until the autumn of 1944, by which point around 5.7 million Jews from all over Europe had been exterminated.

There were many strands that converged to produce the genocide. Some have been explored in other chapters: the barbarous conditions of the war in the East, the Germanization project set in motion by Himmler in 1939, the bio-medical policies pursued against race-defilement in Germany, the self-interest of the security and racist apparatus whose power and influence expanded in step with the poli-cies of deportation and murder, all contributed to the Jewish genocide. But the issue of national survival in the face of the Jewish threat was the bond that linked them all together. The treatment of the Jews was intelligible only in the distorted mirror of German national anxieties and national aspirations. The system deliberately set out to create the idea that Germany's survival was contingent entirely on the exclusion or, if necessary, the annihilation of the Jew. 'For us,' Hitler told Bormann in February 1945, 'this has been an essential process of disinfection, which we have prosecuted to its ultimate limit and with-out which we should ourselves have been asphyxiated and de-stroyed.' Popular German anti-Semitism was mobilized to support these national ambitions; the pervasive brutality and discrimination was not an invention of the party, and it swiftly became embedded in German public life long before war in 1939 changed the nature of the perceived 'Jewish threat'. The war was presented as a desperate war for national survival and the Jew as the malign and hidden hand behind its origin and its escalation. 'Never before,' Hitler continued, 'has there been a war so typically and at the same time so exclusively Jewish.'[161] The terrible convergence of prejudice, self-justification and opportun-ity could only produce such lethal effects because of the uncompromis-ing and fearful terms in which Hitler's dictatorship presented the apocalyptic battle between 'Aryan' and 'Jew'.

*

There is little common ground between the two dictatorships on issues of race and nation. Both sought to construct a consensual identity in states where consensus was lacking, but they did so in entirely distinct contexts. These were not varieties of a common strain of 'nationalist socialism' but distinct species. The Soviet Union was a federation of nationalities, whose national identities were respected to the extent that they did not compromise the central political ambitions of the regime. The long-term aim was assimilation around a set of shared social revolutionary ambitions and a common Soviet patriotism. Nationality was treated in Hitler's Germany as the element that alone determined the character of the state. Xenophobic and exclusive, Hitler's Germany saw itself in direct, violent competition with all other nationalities, locked into a perpetual history of racial struggle (*Völkerringen*).[162] Alien races could not be assimilated under any circumstances.

This contrast did not prevent Stalin's Soviet Union from penalizing nationality. Millions from the national minorities were deported from their homelands; tens of thousands perished in prison and in camps. But so, too, did millions of ethnic Russians. There was nothing ethnically specific about victimization in the Soviet Union. The national victims were penalized for political reasons, either because their loyalty to the communist state was called into question or because they were considered incapable of assimilation into the communist federation. The consequences for the stigmatized minorities were universally wretched. They were torn from their homes, sent on long and debilitating treks to central Asia or Siberia, and left with the barest resources to reconstruct their lives. The language used by the regime to describe its enemies was inseparable from the language of the Third Reich: 'parasites', 'vermin', 'sources of pollution', 'filth'.[163] They were the victims of the general coarseness and brutality of the officials and policemen who ran the deportations and special settlements. Thousands were murdered in the purges for their alleged political unreliability. A crude racism was never far below the surface; Jews regularly suffered at the hands of a popular anti-Semitism inherited from the Tsarist past. But none of the deportations or ethnic actions of the regime was intended to be genocidal. The official orders from the centre concerned the displacement of populations, but not their eradication.

Elaborate efforts were made to dictate reasonable conditions under which these population transfers were to be made. Trains were to have two nursing staff attached, adequate and regular food supplies, and a limited number of passengers in each truck, though few of these conditions seem ever to have been met.[164] Most memoirs of deportation paint a picture of universal misery for the deported peoples, a consequence of the incompetence, corruption, casual violence or deliberate malice of those who deported them: but the final destination was not the railway sidings at Auschwitz.

What made the difference between Soviet national victimization and National Socialist genocide? The willing collaboration of many Soviet citizens with the German mass-murder not only of Jews, but also of gypsies, indicates that there was nothing entirely unique to German society to explain the contrast between the two systems. The difference lay in the political priorities of the two regimes. Under Hitler, German policy was reduced to simple mechanisms of national survival. The system, with Hitler at its head, gave explicit permission first for racial abuse, then for racial exclusion, and finally for mass-murder. The orders handed down from Hitler's wartime headquarters legitimized genocide. 'We should shoot the Jews?' asked one Gestapo officer after a briefing by Heydrich in June 1941. 'Of course,' was the reply.[165] In occupied Ukraine the German authorities organized a wide propaganda campaign to get ethnic Ukrainians to identify with German anti-Semitism, because they, too, were counted as victims of 'Jewish-Bolshevism'. In a German-sponsored newspaper in Kiev, *New Ukrainian Word*, 576 issues out of 700 carried articles on the Jewish menace; propaganda films were shown on *Stalin and the Jews*, and *The Jews and the NKVD*.[166] Rewards were granted for turning Jews over to the authorities. Thousands of Ukrainians worked for the Germans as militiamen, rounding up and executing Jews. Even when Soviet Jews fled to the forests to join the partisans they found a hostile, sometimes murderous reception from the non-Jewish resistance.[167]

The readiness of Ukrainians to confine and to murder the Ukrainian Jewish population when they were given authority to do so highlights the extent to which murderous racism was kept in check by the Soviet authorities. Stalin's Soviet Union did give permission to arrest, deport, even to murder those defined as political enemies of communism, including nationalities alleged to be of doubtful Soviet allegiance, victims of a political xenophobia that was largely prompted by the fear of war and war itself. As a multi-ethnic polity the Soviet state was formally committed to racial tolerance; the evident racial intolerance of the German dictatorship was highlighted by the Soviet authorities as a distinctive characteristic of fascism. After 1945 the Soviet Union ignored the specific fate of the Jews in order to demonstrate the multi-ethnic character of the Soviet war effort and of Soviet sacrifices. The civilian dead from the war with Germany were described as 'Soviet citizens of many nationalities', to ensure that the millions of Slavs murdered between 1941 and 1945 would also be acknowledged as the object of German racial hatred.[168] An ecumenical Soviet identity was forged in the war; German identity under Hitler was reduced to a raw expression of ethnic difference.

14

Empire of the Camps

'What Mostovsky found most sinister of all was that National Socialism seemed so at home in the camp: rather than peering haughtily at the common people through a monocle, it talked and joked in their own language. It was down-to-earth and plebeian. And it had an excellent knowledge of the mind, language and soul of those it deprived of freedom.'

Vasily Grossman, *Life and Fate*, 1960[1]

In the early summer of 1945, an eighteen-year-old German soldier, recently returned to his home town in the Soviet zone of occupation, was picked up by Soviet state security on suspicion of anti-Soviet resistance. Albert Kilian was sent to Special Camp No. 1 at Mühlberg, on the river Elbe. Run by the KGB, the camp was a tough *Schweige-lager*, isolated from the outside world, with no letters or visits. What was different about this outpost of the vast GUlag organization was the fact that only a few weeks before it had been a German camp, housing Soviet prisoners. Now the watchtowers were manned by KGB troops rather than German guards.[2]

The transfer from German camp to Soviet was almost seamless, imperceptible. The same crude barracks, with their tiers of wooden bunks and patched blankets, the same filthy latrines, the same foul food, the same Sisyphean routine of work, breaking stones. The camp was run by 'functionaries' chosen from among the prisoners themselves, distinguished by thick red armbands edged in black, bearing, instead of the insignia of the Third Reich, three large Soviet stars. They drove the prisoners from their barracks at six each morning for

593

roll-call; they bullied and beat the prisoners as they staggered to work for twelve hours a day, every day of the week save Sunday afternoon; they stole the food, and looted possessions. So thorough was the expropriation that there was left not a single watch or clock, and one trusty prisoner was deputed to walk through the camp as an 'hour-shouter'. All the camp supplies were threadbare; each day a twelve-hour shift earned a litre of watery soup and 600 grammes of bread. Very soon the weaker internees – editors, judges, lawyers, bureaucrats and Nazi party officials – were debilitated by hunger, cold and dysentery. Out of 122,671 prisoners who passed through the camp, 42,889 died; 756 more were shot as enemies of the Soviet state.[3]

After a few weeks Kilian witnessed Soviet guards install a large notice at the camp gates, written in German and Russian. In large letters at the top, he read: ORDER, DISCIPLINE, CLEANLINESS. Underneath were the camp rules. Every Soviet soldier and officer had to be given a military salute. No pencils, no paper, no letter-writing, and no talking with women in the camp; above all, amongst the squalor and shortages, with no towels, no brushes, no soap, prisoners had to keep themselves and their bunks hygienic and tidy. Kilian reflected, as well he might, that in the stark contradictions between official regulations and wretched reality, between self-righteous declarations of order and the chaos and the violence of camp society, in the efforts to squeeze labour from prisoners too weak and sick to withstand its destructive effects, there was little to separate the Soviet camp system from the one it had so recently replaced.

The very idea of the 'camp' is central to the popular perception of both dictatorships. Hitler's system is inseparable from the concentration and extermination camps, where the terror and racial violence were distilled and imposed with a savage absolutism. The camps are what make the Hitler and Stalin dictatorships appear so distinctive from other forms of modern authoritarianism. The Soviet GUlag symbolizes the political corruption and hypocrisy of a regime formally committed to human progress, but capable of enslaving millions in the process. Here, too, Stalin's dictatorship is to be found in its most lethal and inhuman shape. There can be no question that the camps were not in some sense representative of the two systems. When Vasily Grossman said that National Socialism seemed so 'at home' in the camp he was writing about the Soviet experience as much as the German. No Russian was allowed to read what Grossman wrote in 1960 on account of the censors, because the sub-text would have been evident to all.[4]

Yet however useful the generic term 'camp' has become as a shared emblem of the two dictatorships, the purpose, structure and development of each camp organization has its own distinct history. Camp does not equal camp. There were differences between the two systems, as well as striking homologies. There were many separate types of camp within each system. Conditions in the camps were never constant, but altered in response to external pressures or circumstances, part ideological and political, part a consequence of the practical demands of economic development or war. The camps, despite their isolation and restrictions, their secrecy and exclusiveness, reflected wider processes at work in state and society. They were never simply a by-product of crass authoritarianism, but cruel mirrors in which dictatorship confronted its own hideously magnified and distorted image.

The immense complexity of the camp system in Germany and the Soviet Union makes impossible any simple answer to the question 'what were they for?' The emergence and growth of the two camp empires had no single cause, and no single outcome. At one juncture of the Second World War German-occupied Poland was simultaneously host to concentration camps for political prisoners, prisoner-of-war camps, extermination camps, and private labour camps serving wartime industry, each a distinct category with its own origins and history. There were even camps for ethnic Germans who had been railroaded in from eastern Europe to colonize conquered Poland, only to find instead of the promised farms and homesteads long months spent in rough barracks, short of food and medical provisions. Camp life was ubiquitous and multifarious, both in Hitler's German empire and in the Soviet Union. The capacity of the camps was vast. Quite literally millions of prisoners from all over Europe experienced life and death in the two camp systems.

The origins of the Soviet concentration camp are to be found, like so much else in the dictatorship, in the Russian civil war. There had been penal colonies and internment centres under the Tsars, but they little resembled the makeshift concentration camps set up under the

Cheka secret police by the infant Bolshevik regime in July 1918. The camps were for class enemies, rounded up and herded into any buildings large enough to house them – barracks, factories, even the manor houses of the dispossessed gentry – where they were subjected to a regime of terror and deprivation by guards who were poorly supervised, and often little better fed than the prisoners. Hunger, disease and a regime of beatings and abuse produced mortality rates estimated at one-third. Some prisoners were put to back-breaking work, and died all the faster as a result. They had the aspect, recalled one witness, of 'pitiful, intimidated slaves'.[5] The number of camps ran to an estimated 300.

These early camps were the product of the civil war confrontation. Most of those in the camps were regarded as class enemies; some were socialist rivals, put there without trial to prevent them from undermining the revolutionary struggle. In May 1919 the Commissariat of Justice set up what became formally known a year later as the Main Administration of Forced Labour (GUPR), and more camps were created, also run by the Cheka, where prisoners were to pay for their own incarceration by work. In 1922, with the civil war won, the Soviet government began to scale down what was now regarded as a redundant camp apparatus. The 300 Cheka camps were either closed or transferred to the Commissariat of Justice. The prison system was centralized under the Commissar of the Interior. The GPU/OGPU, successor to the Cheka in the 1922 reorganization, was left with only a handful of sites: two prisons in Moscow and Leningrad, ten small camps used as 'isolators' for the most dangerous prisoners, and a network of concentration camps in the far north of the Soviet Union known by the bland acronym SLON (Northern Special Purpose Camps).[6]

It was these arctic camps that formed the core of what was to become the notorious GUlag a decade later. They were set up far from the centres of Russian life, in Arkhangel'sk province. The main site was a disused monastery on the island of Solovetsky. Here were sent not only counter-revolutionaries and political rivals, but ordinary criminals deemed 'incorrigible' by a regime that only a few years before had released all common prisoners on the ground that it was capitalism that had made criminals of them. The number sent to the north rose steadily over the 1920s; year by year the OGPU succeeded in undermining the moderate reforms of 1922 by expanding the number of camps and persuading the government to send fresh categories of prisoner. The official line throughout the 1920s stressed the value of camps as places for re-education, where prisoners could be prepared for a life committed to communism. 'The Soviet government does not punish,' ran a slogan displayed on a camp wall, 'it reforms.'[7] Most prisoners were compelled to undertake hard labour – the notorious *katorga* – as the instrument of their conversion into good communists. The Soviet camp system was transformed by the introduction of the First Five-Year Plan in 1928. Prisoner labour was exploited with ever greater vigour and the number of young, fit prisoners allocated to the OGPU camps reflected the growing economic significance of the camp system. Numbers were expanded by handing over to the OGPU camps all criminals whose sentences exceeded three years, and expanded further still when courts were instructed to increase custodial sentencing by abandoning the practice, widespread in the 1920s, of imposing labour service 'while at liberty' for the majority of those convicted in the regular courts. Stalin was a leading supporter of the use of camp labour to fulfil the economic goals of socialism. The camps were never regarded as pure instruments of terror.

On 7 April 1930 the prison and camp system was reformed under the Law on the Corrective Labour Camps. The OGPU camps were grouped under the Main Administration of Corrective Labour Camps and Labour Settlements. The title produced the unpronounceable acronym GUITLTP, and it was informally shortened to GUlag or Main Administration of Camps, by which it has been known ever since. The system was placed under an OGPU official, Lazar Kogan, but he was replaced in 1932 by his deputy, Matvei Berman, who played the main part in creating and expanding the vast GUlag system. The law of 1930 was the only public acknowledgement of the existence and purpose of the camps throughout the Stalin period. The term 'corrective labour' neatly married together two different conceptions of what the camps were for. They were, in the first place, institutions for rehabilitation, engaged in 'a struggle for Communist morals' against common criminals and counter-revolutionaries alike; but at the same time prisoners were supposed to work enthusiastically like everyone else as active participants 'in socialist construction'. Political prisoners, who had not hitherto been required to work, became part of the army of inmates who joined what the Act called 'the society of toiling people'.[8] Camp slogans, daubed on placards and walls by the camps' political bureaux, reflected the shift in emphasis: 'Soviet society rewards your work!'; 'Work will earn your place in socialist society'.[9] There was in this a harsh but understandable Marxist logic: those who had committed crimes should not be absolved from useful labour while the virtuous citizens outside worked heroically to build socialism. This would make a mockery of the revolution. It was not only economic expediency that produced the tough regime of camp labour, but communist morality.

The GUlag controlled a network of many different kinds of camp. The arctic camps remained a separate though subordinate Administration of Solovetsky Camps (USLAG). In 1931 a new network was set up in eastern Siberia, the Far-Eastern Construction Administration (*Dal'stroi*), to mine the world's largest gold deposits in one of the world's least habitable regions. At first an autonomous division of the camp system, it was brought under GUlag control in 1937. Here grew up the notorious Kolyma camps, where around one-third of the country's gold was mined, and which for twenty years remained the most lethal division of the GUlag empire. The rest of the camps came under the general title of 'corrective labour camp' (ITL); some of these camps were redefined in 1943 as *katorga* camps for the most socially dangerous criminals; in 1948 Special Camps were set up for political prisoners, who were, at last, separated from the common criminals they had shared the camps with since the 1920s. One women's camp was created in 1937 to house the wives and daughters of men convicted and shot as enemies of the people, but most camps held both men and women in separate barrack areas.[10] The GUlag also took responsibility for so-called 'special settlements' in the more remote and barren parts of the Soviet Union, where kulak families were sent in the early 1930s. These were not camps as such. In many cases settlers were simply dumped in forests and steppes without food or shelter and told to build a new community with their bare hands. The settlers worked in agriculture, heavy industry and tree-felling under the loose supervision of the GUlag authorities. Freer than the population of the camps, without the watchtowers and barbed wire, the exiles were modern serfs: they were not free to leave or move; their labour was obligatory and closely supervised.

In July 1934 the NKVD took over unified control of the entire security and prison system. The GUlag added to its empire of camps and settlements a third category, the corrective labour colonies formerly run by the Commissariat of Justice since 1919. The labour colony (ITK) had been set up for prisoners convicted for petty crimes and sentenced to less than three years' confinement. Here the prison regime was less arduous; colonists worked side-by-side with criminals who were sentenced to labour duty but not to prison custody. So limited were the resources to guard the colonies that escapes were routine, and it was for this reason that all colonies were handed over to the NKVD. What had been in effect open prisons now came to resemble more closely the sterner camp structure. The colony guards were militarized, and camp security tightened up. Escape from the GUlag, which had been common before 1934, dwindled to a mere trickle. Colonies became little better than camps, though labour was less murderous than in the lumber camps of the arctic or the mines of Kolyma, and release more regular. They were also more numerous and more geographically dispersed, their workers distributed to wher-ever the programme of economic construction required them. By 1940 there were fifty-three corrective labour camps (each one in reality a network of camps or 'points' built around a central administration), organized on a regional basis by the central GUlag authorities in Moscow; there were 425 corrective labour colonies, run by local branches of the NKVD.[11]

The early history of the German camp system differed in one import-ant respect from its Soviet counterpart. In Germany the camps were regarded as prisons for political opponents first and foremost, and their function was to concentrate and isolate political enemies as an instrument of protection for German society and the dictatorship. The term 'concentration camp' was coined in Germany before 1914, to describe the improvised camps used by the British in the Boer War to house the enemy population, and the labour camps set up in the German colony of South West Africa. The idea of using concentration camps as a temporary measure against political unrest in Germany can be traced back at least to the revolution of 1919, and it was during the years of post-war crisis that the term 'camp' entered the German political vocabulary. Communists were rounded up and placed in 'collection camps' (*Sammellager*) under the watchful eye of local militia and demobilized soldiers. In 1923, at the height of the inflation crisis, communists were once again herded into former prisoner-of-war camps in response to the threat of insurrection. Camps were set up in Prussia and Hanover; at Sennelager near Bielefeld the now familiar apparatus of barbed wire, watchtowers and brutal supervision was introduced.[12] All these camps were quickly shut down once the political crisis had ebbed. But the idea of using concentration camps against political enemies lodged in the popular political mind. Hitler made his first recorded reference to camps in March 1921; at a party rally in September 1922 he explained that the 'November criminals' – Jews and Marxists – 'must feel what it is like to live in a concentration camp [*Konzentrationslager*]'.[13] A decade later, when National Socialism had become a mass movement arguing for a share of political power, the party made no secret of its intention to carry through this threat. In August 1932 the Nazi newspaper explained that on the day the party took over the government, it would round up communists and social-democrats and put them in concentration camps.

The party was as good as its word. Within days of Hitler's appointment to the chancellorship, the SA began to seize political enemies and put them in rough-and-ready confinement. Like the Cheka camps of 1918, these were improvised, poorly supervised and intentionally brutal, but unlike the Cheka, the SA acted on its own behalf, ignoring the state apparatus at will. Only gradually, during the first half of 1933, did the local authorities begin to take the camps under their own responsibility. The lawless regime of SA terror was brought under control. The number of camps was progressively reduced and the prisoners concentrated in a number of larger centres. During 1933 a total of at least 157 camps were set up. Some were little more than overcrowded jails; some, like the notorious Oranienburg camp outside Berlin, were set up in large factories; still others were housed in disused barracks. Between May and October 1933, thirty-four camps were closed down. Almost all the remainder were closed during the course of 1934 as political prisoners were freed from direct terrorization. They held an estimated 25,000 prisoners in summer 1933, but no more than 3,500 by 1935.[14] The emergency character of this period of camp history was evident.

The foundation of the future camp system lay in a small group of camps that were given formal state recognition and state funding during the course of 1933. They were administered by local offices of the Ministries of Justice or the Interior. The most important was the camp set up at a factory barracks outside Munich, at Dachau. This camp, first established in March 1933 by the leader of the SS and chief of the Bavarian political police, Heinrich Himmler, became the model for the future camp system. It was operated not by the regular police force but by SS guards, whose responsibility was to Himmler rather than the state judicial authorities, an anomaly that gave the guards the opportunity to terrorize their prisoners at will. In June 1933 Himmler appointed the first camp commandant, an SS officer named Theodor Eicke, who had previously helped to run the security department of the country's largest chemical combine, IG Farbenindustrie.

Eicke was a man with a chip on his shoulder. The eleventh child of a station master, the 41-year-old commandant had a long history of violent behaviour. Himmler plucked him from a psychiatric hospital where he had been forcibly sent by the local Nazi leadership to have his sanity tested. After an army career in the pay corps, he had drifted in and out of police jobs, where he was discriminated against for his extreme right-wing views, until he secured the job at IG Farben. He joined the party in 1928, the SS in 1930. He had a fierce temper and a brutal hatred of the left. His picture shows a humourless, heavy-featured face with grim, unyielding eyes, the model camp commander. He took his task with immense seriousness. Dachau was run with military precision and calculated cruelty. Eicke it was who drafted the regulations governing the operation of the whole camp system. He introduced regimes of tough, remorseless work; he drew up detailed disciplinary codes, and undertook to train guards in the techniques of daily oppression, including the delicate art of shooting prisoners while trying to escape. 'Tolerance,' so ran Eicke's instructions, 'means weakness.'[15] So successful did he prove to be that shortly after Himmler took over the Prussian political police in April 1934, Eicke was invited to supervise the organization and operation of all the remaining camps. His official title was Inspector of Concentration Camps.

In the summer of 1934 the camp system was at a crossroads. Eicke's new empire was dwindling rapidly as small camps were closed down and the number of inmates reduced month by month. The remaining political prisoners could have been dealt with by the normal prison and justice system, and there was strong pressure from the Justice and Interior Ministries to end what was seen as an improvised response to a period of exceptional crisis, much as the camps of 1919 had been. In addition to Dachau, Eicke ruled over four other camps: Oranienburg-Columbiahaus in Berlin, Esterwegen in the Emsland, Sachsenburg in Thuringia and Lichtenburg on the Elbe. In December 1934 his jurisdictional position was strengthened by the establishment of a formal inspectorate office set up in the Gestapo headquarters in Berlin, but by June 1935, Eicke's new department mustered only five police officers and eight SS men for the whole of the Reich.[16]

The camps survived largely because Hitler approved of them. In February 1935 he announced that the number of prisoners would be reduced no further. In June 1935 he authorized Reich funding for the camps, endorsed Eicke's proposals for camp organization and agreed that the camps should be guarded exclusively by armed SS men; in November 1935 he rejected the efforts of the Justice Ministry to introduce normative law into the camps. Finally, in the spring of 1936 Hitler confirmed that the camps were exclusively the responsibility of the SS, and when he appointed Himmler as Reich security and police chief in June, the camps were placed under his direct authority.[17] Only in 1936 did the system of concentration camps become organizationally secure. Himmler regarded the camps as a permanent and necessary feature of a system where unreformed enemies and racial undesirables could be sealed from the rest of the national community. At first the camps, like their Soviet counterparts, were expected to re-educate prisoners through a disciplined daily routine and political indoctrination. When released, prisoners had to sign an undertaking not to engage in any form of political activity hostile to the regime. Only prisoners whose behaviour appeared to be politically incorrigible were never to be released. On Eicke's instructions they were to be organized in special punishment companies, subject to measures of particular severity.[18]

From 1936 the character of the camp system began to alter in line with Germany's accelerated rearmament and social preparations for war. The fear that a domestic conspiracy might undermine any future German war effort encouraged the physical expansion of camp capacity so that traitors could be subject to conditions of harsh and isolated imprisonment. The choice of a central German site for a new camp at Buchenwald, near Weimar, was based on Eicke's bizarre belief that before a war enemies of the state would literally hide away here, in 'the heart of Germany'; biding their time, they would strike when war broke out unless they could be pre-emptively incarcerated.[19] Himmler, in a speech in January 1937, linked the expanding camp system directly with a future war in which 'a considerable number of unreliable types' would have to be rounded up, perhaps as many as 50,000.[20] He explained to the Reich Finance Minister, who had to pay for the new camps, that a second camp at Sachsenhausen outside Berlin was to be built in response to a demand from the armed forces for a large prison for potential enemies of the national war effort, whose capacity could easily be expanded when war broke out. He planned a camp to hold 7,500.[21]

The second function of the camps was economic. Since 1933 the camps had forced prisoners to work, producing small items for the use of the SS, or undertaking construction. But the work was neither very productive nor economically essential, and the number of prisoners involved too small to have any effect on the economic revival of Germany even if they had been used more effectively. By 1937 the situation had changed. Unemployment had all but disappeared, and labour shortages had set in. The economy was now geared to accelerated war preparation under Göring's Four-Year Plan. An office for the Plan was attached to Himmler's personal staff under the direction of Ulrich Greifert. In 1939 he announced that the expanded concentration camp system was 'the most ideal realization' of the aim to ensure that every able-bodied German, including prisoners, should be forced into performing the 'life work of the Nation'.[22]

To achieve these two aims, to provide against wartime demoralization and to promote war preparation, Himmler wanted to replace what he called the 'simple camps', built in the crisis year of 1933, with a new generation of 'completely new, modern and up-to-date camps, capable at any time of expansion'.[23] During 1936 and 1937 all the old camps except Dachau were closed down, and even Dachau was built completely anew, using its own prisoners as labour. In their place came Sachsenhausen and Buchenwald, both built with extensive industrial facilities, both completed in 1938; in occupied Austria a special punishment camp was built at Mauthausen, where prisoners were worked to death in the stone quarries. A fourth camp only for women was built north of Berlin at Ravensbrück. Both were completed in 1939. To expand the camp populations quickly new categories of prisoner – habitual criminals, 'asocials' and the work-shy – were rounded up or transferred from the regular prisons. In order to employ them more productively, the SS desired to establish its own industrial undertakings. In the spring of 1938 the *Deutsche Erd-und Steinwerke* (German Earth and Stone Works) was founded under an SS economics officer, Oswald Pohl. It supplied quarried raw materials for the rebuilding of Berlin and other German cities. A year later the SS set up its own armaments business to supply the armed SS. In the end over forty businesses were run by the SS, from jam-making to the construction of V2 rockets.[24]

There was an iron logic also to the transformation of German camps into prisons based on productive labour. No case could be made to allow groups regarded by the SS (and many others) as the dregs of society to sit in idle confinement while honest German workers toiled away arming the fatherland. A binding link between imprisonment and labour brought the German system closer to its Soviet counterpart. In both it was the gruelling, physically insupportable conditions of harsh labour that gave the camps their special lethality; in both systems it was thought necessary to ensure that unfree labour should suffer economic exploitation of greater intensity than free workers. The SS enterprises were expected to sustain the dual purpose of the new camps whose labour they used, by ensuring that productive work should also be a means of debilitating or annihilating repression. In neither system were these ambitions, as it is sometimes suggested, alternatives. Work, however rational in terms of German rearmament or Soviet industrialization, was another form of punishment for social deviancy or political resistance.

The history of one of the large new camps built in 1940 after the defeat of France and the occupation of Alsace illustrates the close relationship between labour and repression. The camp location was determined by deposits of rare red granite found in the northern Vosges mountains, which Albert Speer needed for the victory buildings planned for Berlin. He agreed that the deposits should be exploited by the SS quarrying company, using concentration camp labour. A site was found at Natzweiler, next to the red stone, and construction began in the spring of 1941 using prisoners. Half of the 900 camp building workers were invalided or died in the first year. When the camp was completed the SS employed it as an instrument of special repression. Natzweiler became an isolation camp for political enemies from western and northern Europe confined under the 1941 *Nacht und Nebel* (Night and Fog) decree. It was also designated a site for special executions, where SS prisoners could be brought and murdered in secret. Hundreds more were worked to death quarrying the stone for Hitler's cities or producing armaments for a victory whose prospect diminished year by year.[25] Wartime economic necessity did not in any way diminish the lethal character of the camp regime, but merely increased its appetite for victims.

The war did transform the German camp system in one important aspect: from a small group of five main camps with perhaps 25,000 prisoners in 1939, there grew a continent-wide net of camps scattered across the face of occupied Europe. By 1944 there were 20 main camps surrounded by 165 sub-camps. There were at least another 78 camps in occupied Europe run by the police where prisoners were collected for transfer or interned without trial.[26] These many camps were filled with thousands of 'race' enemies, principally Jews, and thousands of political and criminal prisoners from among the conquered peoples, principally from Poland and the Soviet Union. In September 1939 Eicke went off to fight (he was killed in Russia in 1943), but not before leaving to his successor, Richard Glücks, the injunction that 'every enemy of the state, every saboteur of the war is to be destroyed'.[27] The camp inspectorate was transferred from the Gestapo to Himmler's SS

Head Office, but in the spring of 1942 the growing economic role of the camps was recognized by placing them under a newly founded SS economic division, the Main Office of Economic Administration (WVHA), run by Oswald Pohl. The camps were run from Office D, where they continued to be administered by Glücks, a man scarcely more amiable than Eicke, until the end of the war.

With the pressing demands of production, the camp inspectorate lost its monopoly of camp administration. In autumn 1942 Speer called for more camp labour to meet the enlarged armament programmes. Some businesses set up their own camps. The Hasag company ran six camps on its own behalf in Poland, using predominantly Jewish labour. There were no Schindlers here. The camps were run by a militia recruited from local Poles who introduced a reign of awesome terror. Conditions were far worse than the concentration camps. Prisoners were given just 200 grammes of bread and a litre and a half of watery soup for twelve hours of work. Jews who collapsed from malnutrition were worked to death in a special part of the factory known as Camp C. In the process, the hapless prisoners helped to produce around one-third of the ammunition used on the Eastern Front.[28]

The SS and the Gestapo ran their own camps for recalcitrant or insubordinate workers. At Hinzert near Trier the SS built what was called a 'Special Camp' for construction workers who fell foul of the authorities. By the end of the war this camp alone controlled 33 other camps, 27 sub-camps and 6 police camps.[29] The Gestapo began to take workers into custody for short spells of 're-education' through work after the outbreak of war. These Work Education Camps (*Arbeitserziehungslager*) proliferated with the influx of forced workers into the Reich. By the end of the war there were 106 of them, some set up within existing concentration camps, all of them supplying workers for war work.[30] By the end of the war every small factory had its quota of camp labourers, often housed in makeshift conditions, short of every amenity and food. In the Berlin area alone there were over 1,100 small camps. At Buchenwald, near Weimar, prisoners were regularly hired out in small groups to help local firms or state offices with small construction projects, gardening or repair work.[31] No one in Germany could ever pretend that the camps were hidden from view. By the war's end Germany was divided visibly into the free and the unfree, a *Brave New World* of slaves and exploiters.

The wartime German camp system contained one central paradox. The more the camps were supposed to support the war effort, the more lethal they became. Workers in the worst camps often survived little more than a few weeks. Camp records show that adults of twenty to thirty tended to survive longest, but this age-group was in demand everywhere. Many camp prisoners were already weakened by shortages of food, age or disability before they entered the camp, and for them death came quickly. Nowhere was the tension more evident between the political purposes of the camps and the practical necessities of war than in the treatment of the Jewish population of Europe. While state security organized the mass murder of millions of Jews in purpose-built extermination camps, the economic authorities of the Reich were scouring Europe for additional manpower.

This schizophrenic reality was encapsulated in the terrible history of the camp at Auschwitz-Birkenau, half of which was built to supply labour for war production, and half for the mass extermination of millions. Auschwitz began its bleak career in April 1940 when a former barracks there was chosen as a camp for Polish political prisoners. Six months later Pohl visited the camp and decided to use it to work the local gravel pits. In 1941, as the result of a decision taken by the chemical corporation IG Farben to build a large synthetic rubber plant at Auschwitz, the camp complex was expanded. In March 1941 Himmler ordered work on a camp to house 30,000 prisoner-labourers for work in the rubber factory. At Monowitz, across the river from the camp, a vast industrial site was planned. Eventually he hoped to house 100,000 camp prisoners for the reconstruction of the entire region. In September of that year the German army, by now deep in Soviet territory, promised Himmler 100,000 Soviet prisoners to build the larger camp and the factories, and the first contingent of 10,000 arrived in October 1941. In 1942 it was decided to replace Soviet prisoners with deported Jews.[32] For the next four years an estimated 405,000 workers toiled to construct a factory that failed to supply a single pound of synthetic rubber throughout the war because of problems in supplying equipment and skilled engineers, and the inhuman conditions of work. Only 144,000 of the labourers survived. Of the initial batch of 10,000 Soviet prisoners-of-war, 8,000 were dead in three months, the other 2,000 by the end of January.[33]

Side-by-side with the growth of the slave-labour camp, Auschwitz-Birkenau became a killing centre. This programme began in 1940, when Polish prisoners in the first concentration camp were murdered or died from mistreatment. The existing crematorium had to be supplemented by a second in 1940, and a third was ordered in November 1941. Auschwitz, like Natzweiler, was a special killing site for the East, first for Polish nationalists, then for communists among the Soviet prisoners, 950 of whom were crushed into the first improvised gas chamber at Auschwitz in September 1941 to test the effects of the pesticide Zyklon B on human victims.[34] During the latter part of 1941 the supply of Soviet prisoners from the East dried up. In January 1942 Himmler ordered Glücks to prepare for the transport of up to 150,000 Jews to the concentration camps in the East. Auschwitz-Birkenau became the eventual destination for an estimated 1.2 million Jews, around two-thirds of whom were murdered immediately on their arrival at the camp in gas chambers set up in the Birkenau area of the camp complex.[35] Those men and women deemed capable of labour were selected on arrival and sent to work at Monowitz and other labour sites. The first group of 400 elderly Jews was murdered in mid-February 1942. The building of new gassing facilities in 1942 and 1943 increased the capacity of the extermination process. The killing continued without interruption until November 1944, at an average of more than 30,000 a month. To cope with the millions of Jews doomed to genocide the regime built other camps – at Chelmno, Belzec, Treblinka, Maidanek and Sobibor – where a further 2.6 million are thought to have perished. Smaller facilities at Riga and Maly-Trostenets, near Minsk, accounted for at least another 250,000.[36] These camps were never camps in the conventional sense. They were killing-factories. When the killing was done those that were not also work camps, like Auschwitz and Maidanek, were torn down and the sites returned to Polish ploughland.

Though Soviet camps were prisons of a particularly brutal and despairing character, they were never designed or intended to be centres of extermination. The war brought important but different changes to the Soviet camp structure. Even before the war, in 1940 and early 1941, a process of decentralizing and rationalizing the GUlag system was introduced by Beria. Each of the major economic branches supported by GUlag forced labour was placed under a separate Main Administration, whose job it was to ensure that production quotas were met and output maximized. There were five in all, one each for industrial construction, mining and metallurgy, railway construction, lumber and road construction, producing a bewildering array of new acronyms in a system already burdened with administrative abbreviation.[37] These changes indicate the extent to which the logic of using camp labour for economic ends eventually turned GUlag into a socialist industrial trust vital to economic development, and after 1941 vital to the economic war effort. During the war, camp labour made up around one-tenth of the entire non-farming workforce. The prisoners produced 8.9 million tonnes of coal, 30.2 million mortar shells (13 per cent of all production), 25.5 million large-calibre shells, 9.2 million anti-personnel mines and 1.7 million un-needed gas masks. They also produced food for the prisoners and guards, and for the wider population, on prison farms: in 1941 alone this amounted to 140,000 tonnes of grain, 203,000 tonnes of potatoes, 225,000 tonnes of fodder and 366,500 animals.[38]

The German invasion threatened a disaster for the whole camp administration, for many camps were in the path of the oncoming enemy. Alongside the skilled workers, machinery and tools evacuated eastward in the wake of the retreating Red Army, the NKVD managed to organize the removal of 27 concentration camps and 210 labour colonies with altogether more than 750,000 prisoners.[39] The hapless prisoners were crammed into the remaining camps until new ones could be built, and this perhaps explains the willingness of the GUlag to hire prisoners out to more than forty different commissariats working on war contracts. These forced workers were assigned to individual enterprises, and a large network of temporary sub-camps developed like those in Germany, close to where the work had to be done. Some 380 of these camps were in place by the war's end, and more than 200,000 prisoners lived in them. By 1945 the GUlag also controlled 53 major construction camps, with 667 sub-camps and 475 colonies.[40] The decentralization of the prison population took a further twist with the desperate shortages of manpower experienced by the armed forces.

Between 1941 and July 1944 figures show a flow of 975,000 prisoners released into the armed forces. These were mainly common criminals; political prisoners had their sentences frozen for the duration. As in Germany, the regime wanted to run no risk that resistance might be sapped by internal defeatism. The prisoner-soldiers found freedom a mixed blessing. They were organized into special penal units and sent to do the most dangerous work.[41]

The releases and hiring-out produced a sharp fall in the size of the camp population, in complete contrast to Germany. In 1939 Soviet camps held sixty-six times as many prisoners as the German ones; in 1944, when the German camp population reached its height, GUlag camps held only one and a half times as many. However, new categories of camps were introduced during the war to cope with defeatism and counter-revolutionary threat among the armed forces, and among the millions of Soviet citizens unfortunate enough to become German prisoners and compulsory labourers. The prisoner-of-war administration (UPWI) activated not only camps for the enemy's soldiers, but twenty-six special camps for Soviet troops; Soviet soldiers returning from the German side of the line were incarcerated in the camps as potential spies and saboteurs.[42] These camps were run by the NKVD until they were absorbed by the GUlag in July 1944. The NKVD also operated what were called Proof and Filtration camps (PFI) set up for the same purpose on 27 December 1941 for civilians as well as soldiers. These camps investigated around half a million people during the war, and the prisoners were forced to work while under investigation. In May 1945 161,000 were working for the Soviet war effort. In January 1946 these camps were abolished and the remaining prisoners transferred to GUlag camps, their cases still pending.[43]

The high point of the GUlag system was achieved after the war. A sharp increase in the camp population reflected a fresh drive against the internal enemy, now in the guise of 'cosmopolitans' or American spies, and a renewed call from Stalin for heavier sentencing for crimes that had previously carried brief confinements or community labour. The number of camps increased to cope with the influx. In 1947 the GUlag controlled 63 concentration camps (22 of them designated as severe punishment camps) and 1,016 labour colonies. Only on Stalin's death was the grip relaxed. Within a year around 70 per cent of the prisoners had been freed, though ominously 589,000 new ones were added.[44] Camps remained a permanent feature of the post-Stalin penal system down to the 1980s.

It is well known that millions lived and died in the two camp regimes. But how many millions? And what kind of prisoner? These are difficult questions to subject to narrow statistical scrutiny, not simply because many of the surviving figures are of doubtful reliability, but because it might seem a historical impertinence to describe the long years of servitude and the millions of lives lost or blighted through the camps with mere numbers and percentages. The statistical recovery of the camp experience nonetheless reveals important truths and dispels many myths about the nature of each system; the statistics illuminate a number of profound differences between the two systems, which a mere description of their establishment and operation might otherwise disguise.

The total number of those imprisoned fluctuated according to the circumstances and intentions already described. The German camp population is more difficult to calculate than the Soviet because of the different categories of camp outside the jurisdiction of the SS camp inspectorate, where records were less scrupulously maintained, but global figures do exist for those camp prisoners working for the SS, and for the size of the camp populations at points in the 1930s. Table 14.1 shows that from the lowest point in 1934, with around 3,000 prisoners, the population grew to at least 715,000 by the beginning of 1945. Most of this increase occurred between 1943 and 1945. As late as the summer of 1942 there were still only around 100,000 camp prisoners. The numbers in the camps controlled by the police or under Gestapo supervision are not known. By contrast there are very full figures on the Soviet camp population because, in almost all cases, the prisoners went through some kind of formal judicial process before incarceration, which was meticulously recorded by the NKVD and the GUlag authorities. The Soviet statistics are reproduced in Table 14.2. They show that most prisoners between 1930, when the GUlag was founded, and 1953, when Stalin died, were in the camps rather than the milder colonies. The large increase in colony population after 1947 was a consequence of new laws on state crime, which resulted in

Table 14.1 German Concentration Camp Population 1933–1945

Year	Total	Year	Total
1933 (July)	26,789	1939 (Aug)	21,400
1934 (Aug)	c.3,000	1940	c.60,000
1935	c.3,500	1942 (Aug)	115,000
1936 (Nov)	4,761	1943 (June)	199,500
1937 (Jan)	7,500	1944 (Aug)	524,286
1938 (Oct)	24,000	1945 (Jan)	714,211
1939 (early)	60,000*		

* This number included around 35–40,000 Jewish Germans briefly imprisoned following the Kristallnacht pogrom on 9/10 November 1938.
Source: W. Sofsky *The Order of Terror: the Concentration Camp* (Princeton, NJ, 1997) pp. 28–9, 34–5, 38; J. Tuchel 'Dimensionen des Terrors: Funktionen der Konzentrationslager in Deutschland 1933–1945' in D. Dahlmann and G. Hirschfeld (eds) *Lager, Zwangsarbeit, Vertreibung und Deportation: Dimensionen der Massenverbrechen in der Sowjetunion und in Deutschland* (Essen, 1999), pp. 372, 383.

more custodial sentences for trivial offences, but usually a sentence in a colony rather than a camp. The Soviet figures should also include up to half a million held in NKVD camps during and after the war, who were not formally prisoners but returnees under scrutiny.

The chief difficulty in describing the camp population in yearly statistics is obvious. To understand the impact of the camps on the German and Soviet populations it is essential to reconstruct the *flow* of prisoners in and out of them. Each year some prisoners were released (a fact that is easy to overlook, but nevertheless statistically significant); each year a certain number died (no less significant statistically). The prisoner body at the end of the year was different from the year before. It is these dynamic statistics that are particularly elusive. In the German camps of the 1930s, for example, the majority of political prisoners were detained for periods of six months to one year. A single annual figure at a particular point in time understates significantly the grand total of all those Germans who passed through the hands of the SS, year by year. The few available figures on admissions to German camps show totals very much greater than the resulting camp population. At

Table 14.2 Number of Prisoners in ITLs (GUlag labour camps) and ITKs (labour colonies) 1930–1953

Year	ITL camps	ITK colonies	Total
1930	179,000	—	179,000
1931	212,000	—	212,000
1932	268,700	—	268,700
1933	334,300	—	334,300
1934	510,307	—	510,307
1935	725,483	240,259	965,742
1936	839,406	457,088	1,296,494
1937	820,881	375,488	1,196,369
1938	996,367	885,203	1,881,570
1939	1,317,195	355,243	1,672,438
1940	1,344,408	315,584	1,659,992
1941	1,500,524	429,205	1,929,729
1942	1,415,596	361,447	1,777,043
1943	983,974	500,208	1,484,182
1944	663,594	516,225	1,179,819
1945	715,506	745,171	1,460,677
1946	746,871	956,224	1,703,095
1947	808,839	912,704	1,721,543
1948	1,108,057	1,091,478	2,199,535
1949	1,216,361	1,140,324	2,356,685
1950	1,416,300	1,145,051	2,561,351
1951	1,533,767	994,379	2,528,146
1952	1,711,202	793,312	2,504,514
1953	1,727,970	740,554	2,468,524

Source: J. P. Pohl The Stalinist Penal System (London, 1997), pp. 10–11.

Buchenwald between 1937, when it opened, and 1942 43,502 prisoners were admitted, yet the camp population at the end of 1942 was only around 10,000. Over the same period the camp records show 8,246 deaths, but also very high numbers of departures.[45] Some must be presumed to have been released, which was more likely before 1940 but rare during the war, or transferred to other work camps and prisons, in which case a proportion would show up as admissions in the records of another camp, and be counted twice. There is no way out of this statistical conundrum. The only sure conclusion is that the figures for the camp population at any given time substantially understate the actual number of all those who passed through the camp gates. The best estimate of total admissions suggests that around 1,650,000 were sent to the major camps (excluding the camps set up purely for extermination). Estimates of total deaths vary widely, from 400,000 to as many as 1,100,000. Monthly statistics for four camps – Auschwitz, Buchenwald, Sachsenhausen and Mauthausen – show a total of 1,046,000 admissions and 409,000 deaths during the whole period of their existence. This is a death rate of 40 per cent. Understated or not, this raw statistic still shows an exceptional level of lethality in the German system.[46]

For all its many cruelties, the GUlag system was less deadly than the German camps. The number of prisoners flowing into and out of the GUlag system is known with more precision than in the German case, as is the number of deaths. The figures are set out in Table 14.3. Between 1934 and 1947 6,711,037 entered the camps; the number who died or were killed totalled 980,091, a proportion of 14.6 per cent. There were also 4,182,135 prisoners released during the period, either because they had served their sentence, or were transferred into the armed forces. Almost two-thirds of those who died did so in the four years from 1941 to 1944, largely as a consequence of the sharp deterioration in food and medical supplies caused by wartime short-ages. The death rate in the non-war years was substantially lower, averaging 38,600. It is true that the worst years of camp deaths in Germany, in 1944 and 1945, were also the result of military defeat, bombing and the collapse of food supplies, as well as deliberate neglect and brutality, particularly on the many forced marches imposed on tired and sick prisoners, but the gap between 40 and 14 per cent remains significant. Evidence of death rates at three German camps between 1938 and 1940 shows that even before the wartime crisis mortality was exceptional. At Mauthausen the death rate was 24 per cent in 1939, 76 per cent in 1940; at Buchenwald it was 21 per cent in 1940, at Sachsenhausen 33 per cent.[47] The German camps were created

Table 14.3 Admissions, Escapes, Deaths and Releases in the GUlag Camps
1934–1947

Year	Admissions*	Escapees	Deaths	Releases
1934	493,313	83,490	26,295	147,272
1935	457,063	67,493	28,328	211,035
1936	468,714	58,313	20,595	369,544
1937	673,325	58,264	25,376	364,437
1938	836,444	32,033	90,546	279,966
1939	401,230	12,333	50,502	223,622
1940	660,003	11,813	46,665	316,825
1941	854,699	10,592	100,997	624,276
1942	559,774	11,822	248,877	509,538
1943	363,023	6,242	166,967	336,750
1944	331,161	3,586	60,948	152,131
1945	364,210	2,196	43,848	336,750
1946	463,344	2,642	18,154	115,700
1947	626,987	3,779	35,668	194,886

* Admissions include those recaptured after escape.
Source: E. Bacon *The Gulag at War: Stalin's Forced Labour System in the Light of the Archives* (London, 1994), p. 167.

with the intention of violence against enemies of the nation and the war effort. Work was often a deliberate path to destruction. Work in the GUlag could be destructive, but the object was to keep prisoners alive and well enough to continue working in all but the most sinister punishment camps. If the regime had wanted them dead, it would have killed them, just as all those prisoners convicted of Trotskyism were murdered in 1942 to prevent them from contaminating the camps in wartime.

There are equally striking contrasts between the dictatorships in the social statistics of the camps. Two are of particular importance. The German camps were overwhelmingly populated by non-Germans for more than half their life. During the war years an estimated 90–95 per cent of camp prisoners were drawn from the rest of Europe. The great majority of those who died or were killed in the camps were drawn from their non-German populations. The SS sub-camp at Gusen contained only 4.9 per cent ethnic Germans in 1942 (half the prisoners were Spanish republicans, over a quarter Russians). At Natzweiler only 4 per cent of the political prisoners by 1944 were German; at Buchenwald only 11 per cent were German in May 1944.[48] By 1944 there were more Soviet citizens in captivity in Germany than in the USSR. In the Soviet camps the proportions were almost entirely the other way round. In 1939 fewer than half a per cent of prisoners came from ethnic groups outside the Soviet Union. Most prisoners were ethnic Russians or Ukrainians, who comprised 77 per cent of inmates.[49] The proportion of foreigners rose during and after the war, when Poles and Germans were taken to work in camps and special settlements. But in the main the Soviet state incarcerated its own people, while German camps held the citizens of other states.

The greater contrast stems from the Soviet practice of sending ordinary criminals to the camps. From the late 1920s the camps were intended to be an extension of the conventional penal and prison system. The popular image of the GUlag as home to a generation of Soviet dissidents misses out the largest proportion of the camp population. Between 1934 and 1953 there were only two years – 1946 and 1947 – when the proportion of counter-revolutionary prisoners, convicted under the provisions of Article 58, exceeded that of ordinary criminals. At the height of the purges in the 1930s political prisoners made up only 12 per cent of the GUlag; at the time of Stalin's death they comprised just over one-quarter, 582,522 'politicals' as against 1,920,553 criminal prisoners. These political prisoners were divided into distinct categories of political crime: the great majority were held for treason and nationalist resistance, the rest for spying, terrorism, 'diversion' and lesser counter-revolutionary acts.[50] The rest of the camp population was a mix of habitual criminals and petty delinquents. These included the ferocious *urki* or *blatnye*, convict clans that had existed before the revolution. The clans were instantly recognizable, not simply from their perpetually vicious behaviour but from the colourful tattoos that covered every part of their bodies, sometimes with portraits of Stalin or Lenin. They terrorized the other prisoners, whom they murdered and robbed at will; even the guards were fearful of them and colluded in their murderous regime. Alongside hardened criminals were hundreds of thousands of small-time crooks, or *byto-viki*, whose cases in the 1920s might have brought no more than a fine or a spell of labour duty. They were the victims of harsher sentencing from the early 1930s, driven, in part, by the need for more prison-camp labour. Many were scarcely criminals by any conventional definition – women who had stolen a bag of grain for their hungry families, workers who grumbled more than they should. The greater part were imprisoned for state theft; in 1952 1 million of the 1.9 million criminals had been sentenced under the state theft law of 4 June 1947, but only 19,925 were in prison for stealing from other people.[51]

The German camps contained very few criminals. Several thousand habitual criminals were sent to the camps in the mid-1930s; in 1942 thousands of allegedly incorrigible prisoners were sent to Mauthausen, to be worked to death in a matter of weeks. Most camps had a small hard core of criminal toughs, German *urki*, but they were never able to dominate the huge multi-national camp populations with impunity. Most of the German prisoners in the camps from 1937 onwards were there because of a social or biological stigma, not for perpetrating specific crimes. They included the thousands of homosexuals, vagrants, alcoholics and 'parasites' who were hauled into the camp net on moral as much as criminal grounds – some 70 per cent of the camp population by 1939. There were also Jehovah's Witnesses, who refused to compromise their faith by acknowledging Hitler's authority. These were often the weakest elements in the hierarchies of the camp, dying faster than the rest. When the camps filled up with non-Germans after 1939, the majority of prisoners were there as political or racial enemies. At Ravensbrück 83 per cent of prisoners came under the broad heading of politicals; only 12 per cent were 'asocials', 2 per cent criminals and just over 1 per cent were Jehovah's Witnesses.[52] The trawl across Europe no doubt brought criminals into the camps under one guise or another, but most criminals convicted of penal offences ended up in prisons rather than camps.

In one respect the two systems converged: both imprisoned large numbers of women as well as men. In the Soviet Union women were brought into the camps in the drive against the kulaks in the early 1930s. There are photographs of long chains of women in headscarves

and worn tunics toiling with shovels and huge wheelbarrows to exca-
vate the White Sea canal. They worked and lived alongside the men,
separated only by a compound fence in the camps, occasionally not
separated at all. In the purges thousands of women were sent to the
Akmolinsk internment camp for 'Wives of Traitors to the Motherland'.
After 1946 some all-female sub-camps were created, where women
were employed producing textiles and other consumer products.
Women were no more immune than men from wild accusations of
counter-revolution. Nor were they any less liable for the harshest
prison regime. Women could be sent to the worst prisons in the far north
or the far east to do the same hard labour as the men. The proportion of
women in the camps and colonies steadily increased. By 1948 almost
one-fifth of the camp population was female, 208,000 women. The
proportion in the milder labour colonies was even higher. In 1945
there were 246,000 in the colonies, 38 per cent of all colony convicts.[53]

The German camps also witnessed a slow but steady growth in
the numbers of women. In the early period the state workhouse at
Moringen, near Hanover, was used as a temporary camp for women
in protective custody. It was a relatively mild regime, where women
were held for short spells of 're-education'. Their number included a
communist romantic who was caught placing flowers on the grave
of the communist leader Rosa Luxemburg, murdered by German
nationalists in 1919. In 1938 Moringen was closed down and the small
number of women transferred to Lichtenburg fortress, one of the
first concentration camps set up in 1933. Here the camp's female
population soon filled up with 'asocials'. In May 1939 a purpose-built
women's camp was opened at Ravensbrück, eighty kilometres north
of Berlin. The camp opened with 867 prisoners, but so rapidly did it
begin to fill with non-German women that the original buildings for
4,000 had to be expanded in 1942. By 1944 Ravensbrück and its
sub-camps housed more than 50,000 women, most of them Poles and
Russians.[54] By 1945 there were an estimated 203,000 women prisoners
throughout the shrunken German empire, working in numerous sub-
camps and labour camps. This figure represented 28 per cent of the
whole camp population, a higher proportion than in the GUlag.[55]

There is little information on the age-profile in the camps. The
testimony of survivors confirms that age was no barrier to incarcer-

ation. Older and younger age-groups died faster, which suggests that the age profile of most camps would be heavily weighted towards the 20–50 age-range. Both systems made special provision for juveniles. The SS set up eight *Jugendschutzlager* (Youth Protective Camps) in Germany and Poland for young delinquents, but teenage boys and girls ended up in the regular camp system as well. In the Soviet Union the number of young offenders, both regular criminals and counter-revolutionaries, expanded greatly from the late 1930s with tougher sentencing for petty crime. Many were simply described as 'socially harmful elements', and sent to prison for being the adolescent offspring of former gentry or priests. From a little over 10,000 in 1939, the GUlag population of 12- to 18-year-olds grew to 35,500 in 1953. Some were the children of female prisoners, some had been born in the GUlag, others were the victim of Stalin's insistence that hooliganism and vandalism should be treated not by official remonstrance but by real punishment.[56]

The social pattern of the camp populations is impossible to reconstruct further. They housed as wide an array of social and occupational groups as the society they came from. No social group was immune from the threat of imprisonment, since many of the crimes defined as political were applied quite arbitrarily. In the camps social class meant nothing. The social structure of the camp was reduced immediately on entry to a simple division between prisoners and guards. The routines of registration reduced newcomers in a matter of hours from the individual they once were to just one of the thousands of shaven-headed, crudely uniformed, undernourished numbers on the camp list. Once in the camp, prisoners found themselves in another world. The complex hierarchies and collectives established by the prison population were, in general, unrelated to the outside world, the 'big zone' as Soviet prisoners called it. Life in the 'little zone' was a society apart.[57]

No two concentration camps were exactly the same. Their operation was affected by climate, topography, the nature of the work assigned to prisoners, the behaviour of the guards and the divisions and hierarchies among the camp population. There were regular camps where a tough but settled existence could be built up; there were punishment camps, with intensified brutality and killing work. Nonetheless, a great many common characteristics can be found not only among camps in the same organization, but between the German and Soviet camp systems. The narratives written by survivors unfortunate enough to be imprisoned in both camp systems show how familiar camp life could be from one prison to the next.

Almost all accounts of the first hours of a prisoner's life in the camp focus on the sudden and profound loss of personal identity. All newcomers had already experienced a journey either by lorry or train, overcrowded, short of food or water, stifling and airless in summer, freezing in winter. Soviet prison trains had a bucket in each car for use as a latrine; hard bread and salt fish were given every couple of days, but little fresh water. Most accounts of German prison trains show no provisioning at all, so that passengers arrived at camps already famished, exhausted and soiled. Prisoners went through a standard routine on arrival. At Auschwitz those chosen for camp labour rather than extermination handed over all their possessions on arrival; they were registered and a number tattooed on their forearm; after a bowl of watery soup, too hot to drink in the time allotted, prisoners were stripped, doused with cold water and had their heads shaved. Crude prison uniforms with the familiar thick grey stripes were then issued and prisoners were led to their barracks, where they would be assigned a bunk consisting of nothing but a narrow plank and a thin blanket, a prisoner's living space.[58] For women these rituals involved deliberate sexual degradation. At Ravensbrück women were stripped and shaved, both head and pubic hair, and then made to stand naked in the open for hours, in full view of male guards, for a medical inspection that consisted of little more than a rough search of the vagina for hidden valuables, all carried out with the same unwashed probe.[59]

Arrival at a Soviet camp involved a performance that differed only in details. At the Temnikovsky camp in southern Russia, after a long journey in freezing cattle wagons, in which the prisoners were forced to remain for two extra days without food or exercise because the camp officials had gone home for the weekend, one Finnish prisoner recalled the slow march through a high gate adorned with socialist slogans; the process of registration; the cold water wash; the shaven head; the mug of hot water; the barracks where newcomers were forced to take the blanketless bunk furthest from the two small stoves.[60]

Prisoners were, however, allowed to keep their own clothes. By the 1940s the Soviet authorities had given up issuing standard working clothes; even the German camps abandoned handing out uniforms in 1944 as they were swamped by numbers.[61] Living quarters were the same in both systems – long barrack rooms (in the USSR sometimes tents, or deep earth trenches with a thatched covering) with two tiers of wooden bunks set so close together that movement was almost impossible. In Auschwitz the need to bring in more labour than the barracks were designed to hold was solved by reducing the living space still further, so that up to five people would be crammed together on a wooden bed little more that a metre wide.[62] As both systems expanded, the space allotted each prisoner declined.

The camp geography and rituals were not random. They were the product of regulations and instructions that emanated from the centre on how prisoners were to be housed, disciplined and worked. The German system was deliberately designed to be physically tough and psychologically destructive. The original instructions drawn up by Theodor Eicke for Dachau in 1933 remained in force down to 1945. Inmates were supposed to have a hard wooden bunk and poor food rations; their work was designed to be punitive and degrading; guards were instructed in a range of torturous penalties long before the war.[63] There were instructions on food rations, labour norms and discipline procedures in the GUlag camps, handed down from the NKVD. These rules and regulations were enforced by the camp commandant – the same title was used in both systems – and the administrative and guard details under his command. Each camp had its own bureaucracy. Soviet camps had a cultural and educational department (a thin residue of the initial idea of 'correction'), which organized displays on communist holidays and the painting of slogans, and ran the camp library. In one camp prisoners could earn extra rations by painting portraits of Stalin to decorate the camp walls. Slogans proclaiming the socialist paradise were painted on boards and coarse cloth with red paint made from ground-up bricks and water.[64] Culture was absent from the German camps.

The most feared branch of the administration was the political office. Camps in both systems operated a 'double terror' on prisoners already victimized by the system. The German camp political department was linked to the Gestapo; its job was to monitor the camp population for any signs of political resistance or 'clique-building', and to recommend transfer or execution, carried out in the camp. The GUlag special departments, run by an NKVD plenipotentiary, expected the political prisoners to continue their wrecking and terrorist activities even in the remote wastelands of the tundra. They employed prisoners as spies or *stuchki*, in return for better rations or a privileged workload. In 1940 there were 10 *stuchki* for every 1,000 prisoners; in 1947 there were 139,000 of them, 80 for every 1,000.[65] A word from an informer would mean a summary GUlag hearing and an inevitable additional sentence. One prisoner at Temnikovsky, eight years into a ten-year sentence, was heard to mutter that boots were better made under the Tsars; eight more years were added to his remaining two.[66]

Below the camp administration lay a second layer of camp authority. In both systems the prisoners were made to govern themselves. The main functions of the camp were run by prisoners chosen by the camp commandant; in some cases even the camp guards were former inmates. The prisoner-supervisors were more feared than the camp authorities because they enjoyed a daily power of life or death over all the prisoners under their control. They meted out arbitrary justice, bullied and beat their fellows, and forced the pace of work, from fear of their own punishment or demotion. In the German camp the system was run like a military unit. The camp trusties were, Himmler told a group of senior generals in 1944, 'the non-commissioned officers' of the camp hierarchy.[67] At the top of the hierarchy came the camp senior or *Lagerältester*. Each barrack was run by a *Blockältester*. The work commands were each run by a *Kapo* or boss. In addition there were much sought-after white collar jobs, working as a barrack clerk or in the camp labour office. These office-holders were known collectively as the *Prominenten* and were usually appointed from among the longest-serving prisoners. Sometimes these were criminals, who ran the camps like mafia bosses; sometimes they were drawn from among the 'politicals'. When the camps expanded the best jobs were usually given to ethnic Germans from either group, who could liaise more effectively with the SS overseers. The functionaries carried clubs or rubber truncheons, or, in the case of one *Kapo* at Auschwitz, a notorious whip nicknamed 'Interpreter' because it could speak to the multi-national workforce in any language.[68] They were free to use these as they saw fit. For disobedient prisoners there existed the 'punishment company', a unit distinguished by the exceptional levels of savagery visited on its unfortunate recruits.

The Soviet camps also made use of prisoners in all the main camp functions, almost always criminals, often the merciless *urki* who robbed, raped and extorted to keep the camp in order. The chief functions were to organize the workforce. Each work brigade had a leader and a foreman who hustled the prisoners onto the parade ground at six in the morning to carry out *rasvod*, the allocation of work. They kept close watch on what the workers were doing, noted down any dereliction, meted out a rough justice with clubs and sticks and filled out details on the brigade's work norms at the end of the day.[69] Since over- or under-achievement affected food rations, their power in the camps was immense. These were the Soviet 'prominents', the *predurki*.

Every morning of every day in the camp except Sunday, which was usually a day (sometimes only a half day) of rest, the *Kapos* and foremen led the prisoners off to work. Labour dominated the routine of camp life and the work brigade or command was the core social unit, usually based on a single barrack block. It made little difference what economic objectives were set in Moscow or Berlin. Guards and functionaries usually saw to it that the work was punishing, repetitive and continuous. The prisoners' ideal was industrial work, indoors, and this became common later in the war with frantic efforts to produce more military equipment. But here too the conditions imposed on the prisoners were intentionally worse than on the free workers who often worked alongside, though with regular breaks and solid meals. The Soviet camps were linked closely to the culture of plan-fulfilment and over-achievement generated by the Stalinist industrial drive of the 1930s. The camps became a grotesque parody of socialist emulation. For those who completed the work norms assigned there was extra bread, even the chance to live in one of the Stakhanovite barracks, with straw pillows and blankets. The GUlag set the bread ration against work performance – 1,000 grammes a day for achieving the norm, and a sliding scale for anyone who failed or exceeded it. Those unfortunate enough to achieve only 75 per cent got 400 grammes. Those who achieved less than 30 per cent were deemed to be work-shy 'refusers' and usually shot. Since those who performed poorly got less bread, their chances of reaching the norms diminished day by day. They were known in the camps by the term *dokhodyaga*, 'dying away' or 'concluded'.[70]

Work in German camps varied. In the hard-regime camps the work was exceptionally heavy and prisoners died within weeks. In the factory labour camps armaments work was easier to do and to survive. From 1943 onwards greater efforts were made to keep the fit and capable workers alive for longer, and prisoner productivity began to rise in some sectors. A premium system was introduced like that of the GUlag, extra food for outstanding labour. But in too many camps the guards and *Kapos* had come to regard work as the most severe form of punishment and degradation, not as a contribution to the war economy. Norms were meaningless in conditions where workers could barely walk. Early in the morning at Auschwitz men and women lined up for roll-call at six o'clock. A band played light dance music. Slowly the work commands set out in rows of five abreast, compelled to march in military style past the band, and out of the gates. Men and women had to trudge in crude clogs and filthy clothes infested with lice and covered in faeces to distant work sites. Those who collapsed or were beaten senseless during the day were dragged back in the evening on makeshift stretchers. Women workers were treated with a particular harshness. They were sent to move stones for road building with nothing but their bare hands, or to widen the river Vistula in winter with light clothes and no shoes. When a party of eighty French Jewish women refused they were beaten to death by their female guards with poles and axes.[71]

'A day without a dark cloud. Almost a happy day,' reflects Ivan Denisovich at the end of Solzhenitsyn's novel of camp life.[72] This is not mere irony. Solzhenitsyn himself survived years in the GUlag camps. A majority of prisoners survived the Soviet concentration camp system. Amongst the horrors of forced labour and summary punishment, inmates constructed small, usually temporary societies, with their own routines, their own hierarchies, their own crude systems of camp trade. Prisoners who survived the first months learned how to avoid punishment and victimization, how to have 'a happy day' in the camps.

The first thing prisoners had to learn was the structure of social power in the camp population. In the German camps this structure was made instantly recognizable by the insistence that every prisoner wear a distinguishing triangle and a letter indicating their nationality. Criminals wore a green triangle, political prisoners a red one. Jews wore either a yellow triangle, or a Star of David created by superimposing a second triangle in a different category colour on top of the yellow. 'Asocials' wore black, returning emigrant prisoners blue, Jehovah's Witnesses lavender, and homosexuals pink. Prisoners for special punishment had a black mark on the top of their triangle, or prominent red stripes and circles drawn on their tunics.[73] The different categories were treated differently by guards and *Kapos*. Ethnic Germans had no distinguishing letter inside their triangles and were treated better than non-Germans. By the war many were long-serving prisoners, which also brought a higher status with both guards and newcomers. As the camps filled with non-Germans and Jews, ethnic Germans were given jobs as functionaries, at the top of the camp hierarchy. At the bottom of the hierarchy stood the Jewish prisoners, whose treatment was always more vindictive and dehumanizing than that of other victims, as it was throughout the German 'New Order'. Russians and Poles, who made up the majority of the camp population by 1944, were treated scarcely better. Prisoners marked for punishment could be kicked and abused more vigorously than the rest. Asocials and homosexuals were the victims of a different set of prejudices shared by many of the other prisoners. Homophobia was international and classless.

The GUlag camps had a more simplified hierarchy. The *urki* and *predurki* were the camp elite, though they could also be divided into distinct and warring clans. There were no distinguishing badges for 'politicals' and criminals, but a few hours in the camp were enough to show the innocent newcomer which was which. Criminals dominated the political prisoners, whom they regarded not as fellow-villains but as traitors or class-enemies. There was less overt racism in Soviet camps, though Jews could be singled out. The tensions and conflicts were more a product of the social prejudices generated by the Soviet regime. Political prisoners disliked the incorrigible coarseness and vice of the criminals; they in turn saw 'politicals' as bourgeois snobs whose class habits would be stamped out by tough labour. The result was a parody of Stalinist revolutionary class-conflict.

The balance of power between criminal and political prisoners was different in the German camps, where the proportion of political prisoners was greater. The criminal 'greens' dominated Auschwitz, but at Buchenwald and Sachsenhausen the balance shifted back and forth between the two prisoner communities. Where there were substantial numbers of communists it proved possible to create camp 'collectives', which either dominated the appointment of functionaries, or ameliorated the harsh criminal regime by helping weaker prisoners and keeping the thieves and extortionists at bay. Prisoners who belonged to neither group, without affiliation, were the most vulnerable, trapped in a lethal no-man's land. The camp authorities knew of these tensions, but seldom interfered. In some cases the SS and the criminals collaborated in corruption. A special commission of the Criminal Police sent to investigate the Sachsenhausen camp in March 1944 found not only a flourishing communist collective in the camp, but criminal collusion between SS personnel and the dominant 'greens'.[74]

Prisoners had no choice but to inhabit the world of prison hierarchies and prison discrimination. The unwritten rules of camp society were understood and obeyed alongside the formal instructions of the camp administration. The official schedule was the same in both systems: reveille at between 4.30 and 6.00 a.m., depending on the season, breakfast, work until evening, supper, evening roll-call (which could last for as long as it took to account for everyone who had died or fallen ill during the day), finally an exhausted, impoverished sleep. In the interstices between work, sleep and food the prisoners' time was their own. In these brief interludes flourished the secret life of the camp. There were camp markets where goods were traded, stolen or extorted. In the Soviet camps prisoners were sometimes paid in roubles, which would buy a few more ounces of bread, or copies of *Pravda*, which were torn up to make cigarette papers.[75] In some of the German camps there existed a clandestine world of politics, where resistance and escape were discussed, self-help networks set up, small acts of protest organized. The camp cabals were routinely betrayed by camp informers, and their members murdered or transferred.[76]

Here and there in both systems existed brief opportunities for hidden intimacy. Testimony from Ravensbrück has revealed the widespread existence of lesbian relationships between prisoners, even between overseers and their charges, and it is difficult to believe that sex was entirely absent from the male camps, even if it is largely absent from the testimony.[77] In the GUlag system, where men and women shared the same site, sexual intimacy was more common, and the attitude of the authorities generally more tolerant. Guards and commandants took concubines from among the female prisoners. In 1950 there were almost 12,000 pregnancies in the GUlag.[78] Soviet camps had a blacker side to this history. The *urki* engaged in violent mass rapes of women prisoners, amidst scenes so depraved as to defy the imagination. Rape appears to have been much less common in the German camps, although at Auschwitz there was a small room adjacent to the entrance to the gas chamber where Ukrainian guards would drag and rape naked girls before murdering them minutes later. At Ravensbrück drunken Soviet soldiers gang-raped the starving, listless women they liberated.[79]

One elemental urge united all prisoners. 'All the vital energy I have left,' wrote a Jewish prisoner at Auschwitz, 'is mobilized for my own survival.'[80] The margin between life and death depended principally on the supply of food. In neither system was it intended simply to starve the prisoners to death; the food was supposed to be sufficient to allow the system to extract labour, and in the GUlag the quantity of food depended entirely on labour performance. In practice the food was seldom adequate to sustain work. In the Soviet camps food consisted principally of hard bread, watery soup and occasional packets of crude sugar, salt fish or sausage. In the northern camps prisoners were given a shot of neat alcohol each day before work in the winter for warmth.[81] In the German camps the diet was the same: thin gruel, bread in the morning and evening, occasional chunks of salami. It was possible in both systems for food for some categories of prisoner to be supplemented by parcels from relatives or friends. These additional supplies were purloined by guards or looted by the criminals, but survivor narratives confirm that some of the parcels were distributed, and that they could make the difference between rapid physical decline and longer-term survival.[82] A crisis in food supply was usually a consequence of external circumstances. In the Soviet Union the disruptions caused by overcrowding and the breakdown of supply services in 1937–8 and in the early years of war produced exceptional death rates from hunger and disease. In the last year of war food supplies to the German camps broke down under the impact of bombing and defeat, and a high proportion of all those who died did so in the months before and after liberation from the many debilitations induced by starvation.

Poor diet made disease and disablement more deadly still. Foul, infected water made dysentery unavoidable. Scabies, scurvy, typhus and a host of other parasitic diseases were epidemic. The heavier and more dangerous work meant broken limbs and dislocated joints. The winter weather produced frostbite and hypothermia not only in Siberia but in the camps in central Europe. The camp officials made regular checks of the state of the workforce. In the Soviet camps prisoners were divided into five categories from 'fit for all kinds of work' to 'invalid, second class'.[83] The weakest prisoners were fed less, but usually given a lighter workload. Camp doctors and orderlies, from most accounts of the camps, supplied what remedies they could (including a foul-tasting distillation of pine-needles for the treatment of scurvy). More serious cases of disablement or disease were sent from the camp points to the central hospital. In the GUlag prisoners were not lightly dispensed with if they could still work. Months of convalescence could be granted in local hospitals, where the battered and filthy prisoners could enjoy a brief interlude of clean sheets and a full diet before being sent back to camp.[84] Only the 'concluded' ones were abandoned. They were distinguished by their expression of vacant despair, an absence of will that accelerated physical decline. They died at work, at roll-call, in their sleep. In summer the bodies were buried in shallow pits. In the winter both corpse and ground were frozen stiff. Bodies were taken out and left like macabre statuary in nearby woods, upright or prostrate, where they would be mauled by wolves and bears. Guards were instructed to check all the bodies to ensure that no escapees were feigning death. Remorselessly obedient to the state, they crushed the skulls with a hammer and applied hot irons to the frozen body.[85]

Prisoners were checked for their labour power in the German camps every month. The consequences were far more lethal than in the GUlag.

There was no predisposition to keep the debilitated prisoners alive. The 'goners' in the German camps were nicknamed *Muselmänner* or Muslims; like the 'concluded' ones, they were utterly drained physically, apathetic, involuntarily psychotic. Their condition was evident. At Auschwitz men and women were made to haul down their filthy underwear to display their buttocks to the camp doctors, who could tell from their degree of emaciation whether there was any work left in the prisoner in front of them.[86] Those who failed the test were not sent to convalescent homes, but to the gas chambers. Most camps had an infirmary, but prisoners tried at all costs to avoid being sent there. Sympathetic prisoner-doctors made efforts to save prisoner lives, but regular SS patrols through the hospitals picked out patients who were to be exterminated. Little effort was made to keep prisoners alive. As the war went on, demands for rising productivity were satisfied by killing the weaker prisoners to make room for workers with more strength to exploit. At Ravensbrück an improvised gas chamber was made in 1944 that could kill 150 sick and disabled women at a time. Smaller groups were dispatched with a bullet in the back of the head.[87] Crematoria and gas chambers were introduced at other camps to cope with the debilitation of the camp populations, turning the regular camps step-by-step into extermination centres.

The chances of survival could be extended in a number of ways. In the GUlag prisoners and overseers sometimes colluded in rigging the norms, a ruse known in the camps (and in the regular economy) as *tufta*. If the norms were regularly met, the bread ration was substantial, and work easier to sustain. It was possible for camp functionaries to engage in barter with cooks and storekeepers; criminals stole what they could not extort.[88] Escape was also a possibility. The number of escapes from the laxer Soviet camp regimes of the early 1930s reached a peak in 1934, with 83,490 recorded. By 1953, however, the system was so secure that only 785, or 0.045 per cent of the camp population got away. Escapees were always hunted down. At the Temnikovsky camp a small group of escapees was caught and mutilated by the camp dogs, and shot repeatedly in the back. Their bodies were left in a cart by the camp gate for three days as a warning. Escape from German camps, with high electrified fences, machine-gun posts and dogs, was almost impossible. Those who escaped did so from less well-guarded sub-camps, or in transit. Between 1938 and 1945 only 31 prisoners managed to escape from Mauthausen, but 353 from the smaller out-stations of the main camp. Few escapees remained at large. They were either turned over to the authorities by the local population or hunted down and killed, sometimes in hideous staged reprisals before the eyes of the prisoner population.[89]

Death in the camps came in countless guises. To the predatory effects of hunger and disease must be added the fundamental lawlessness of the camps. Prisoners killed other prisoners for profit or revenge. The leading *Kapo* at Auschwitz, a giant of a man feared by all the prisoners, was demoted to Buchenwald, where he was strangled in his barrack by ten of his new companions.[90] Former interrogators incarcerated in the GULag were routinely assassinated by those who had been at the receiving end of Soviet interrogation. Prisoners in both systems were the victims of unpredictable and arbitrary violence from guards and prisoner-functionaries who treated all rule-breaking and disrespect as potentially capital offences. There are numerous accounts of prisoners bludgeoned to death, drowned head-down in latrines or soup caul-drons, or simply shot down in cold blood. Punishments were experi-ments in carefully calibrated sadism that permeated every aspect of camp life in both systems. There were special isolation cells in each camp where minor rule-breaking would earn a week or more in tiny, cramped, dark and airless rooms or lockers with little or no food; in the Soviet isolators, the prisoners' warm clothing and boots were removed. At the Solovetsky camps in the early 1930s delinquent pris-oners were tied naked to trees during summer nights to be eaten alive by mosquitoes; in winter a favourite penalty was the ice staircase, 273 steps leading down to a frozen lake. Prisoners were forced to climb down barefoot to fetch two buckets of water; if they spilled any as they struggled up the icy stairway, they were sent down again. The object was to get the prisoner's feet to stick fast to the frosty steps, where he would be left to freeze to death.[91] Savage punishments were meted out under Eicke's regime set up at Dachau in 1933, and barbar-ous practices marked the system until its collapse in 1945. A favourite was the *Pfahlbaum* torture, where prisoners would be suspended with their arms above and behind them on a long pole. Hours hung in this position dislocated the shoulders; days produced a slow death. At one camp during the war Soviet prisoners were stripped naked and tied on tip-toe with a wire noose to a high fence. As exhaustion forced their feet to slump down they were slowly strangled with the wire.[92]

These atrocities were not always tolerated. Complaints about camp conditions reached the authorities in Moscow, and did produce efforts to curb the sadism and debilitating living conditions.[93] The first generation of GUlag bosses, Berman included, disappeared in the purges of 1938 accused of running a regime of crime and violence. In German camps control over camp violence was laxer, partly because it was indulged in by so many, including senior officials, officers and doctors, who routinely experimented on prisoners under the most barbarous conditions. Accounts of GUlag life focus on harsh efforts to extract labour and to keep men working; but numerous recollections of camp life under the SS suggest that the violence was an end in itself, embedded in the system long before the demands of the war economy began to trespass on the prerogatives of unrestricted oppression. The SS guards regularly imposed hardships and penalties on entire barracks or camp populations as expressions of their absolute authority. When there was no work at Sachsenhausen camp early in the war, prisoners did not have free time but were forced to stand all day, or even to lie prone on the floor for hours, during which time SS visitors amused themselves forcing the elderly prisoners to do press-ups until they collapsed from exhaustion.[94] This pattern of undifferentiated victimization set the German camp experience apart.

It is impossible to avoid the question of why the two camp systems generated a culture of such deliberate cruelty and indifference. There are different kinds of explanation. First it should be recalled that prison regimes all over Europe in the 1930s were tough; many aspects of camp life shared common features with prison for convicts sentenced to hard labour. Second, the systems for monitoring or controlling camp lawlessness in Germany and the Soviet Union were weak and seldom imposed. The message emanating from the centre was to make camp life exceptionally brutal, since many of the prisoners were alleged to be traitors. The attitude of guards and prisoner-functionaries intensified the brutality. Criminal functionaries used their position to criminalize the camps; non-criminals used the jobs as a means to survival, and acted viciously in order to keep themselves safer; guards were often ill-educated, unwilling exiles themselves, and took out their frustrations on the prisoners; other guards, particularly the SS Death's Head Division that guarded the 1930s camps, were specifically trained in techniques of soul-destroying routine and sadistic terror. Finally, the relationship was one of limitless inequality. Prisoners could find all kinds of ways to ameliorate their conditions, but they had no power and no rights. Hitler insisted early on that lawyers would be permanently denied access to the prisoners.[95] Nothing stood between the individual prisoner and his wilful mistreatment in either system.

The camps reflected the very worst sides of human nature. They have been described as institutions of 'absolute power', in which state terror reached its logical apogee by applying an 'absolute terror'.[96] Though this may be a satisfactory description of the way the camps operated, the part they played in the functioning of dictatorship is more obscure. Both regimes could have employed regular prison systems for the same purpose, but set up camps instead. In neither system was the deterrent effect of the camps evident: the longer they lasted, the larger the population of political prisoners and convicts became.

One explanation lies with the sheer magnitude of the problem of confinement. The Soviet prison system could not hope to house the millions of men and women who were victimized by state policy in the 1930s. At one point in 1930 massive overcrowding forced Stalin to order half the prisoners to be released. In Germany in August 1934 a partial amnesty was declared to clear room in overcrowded cells.[97] Camps were an answer to the crisis of the prison system: they were cheap, flexible, quickly constructed and easily movable. German camps were a small part of the regular German prison system in the mid-1930s, but both institutions were swamped after 1939 by the hundreds of thousands of wartime convicts who were treated as prisoners of a political war, and incarcerated like regular POWs in crude, quickly constructed barracks behind barbed wire. The sheer number of prisoners could have been housed in no other way.

The role of economics is also central. In the Soviet case the relationship between the expansion of the camp population and the demands of industrial construction in the 1930s, and reconstruction after 1945, is so close as to be almost self-evident. It has often been suggested that the regime cynically expanded the categories of crime and the number of criminals convicted in order to supply the essential labour to open up inhospitable regions or build massive infrastructure projects. There can be little doubt that the exploitation of prison labour was irresistible to a regime desperate to speed up industrial change by any means and at the swiftest pace; the labour function of the camps became primary from the early 1930s. In Germany the link is less clear-cut until the shortages of wartime labour encouraged both state and private industry to exploit prison labour more productively. Most of that labour was employed outside the camps and the SS industries.[98]

There is something in both these explanations. Camps were an answer to the flood of prisoners, political and non-political. Camp labour became indispensable to both economies at moments when the regular labour market could not supply enough free labour. But in both cases the camp as an institution of dictatorship pre-dated the crisis in numbers, and pre-dated its large-scale economic exploitation. The function of the camp system was related more to strategies of isolation or annihilation practised by both regimes against those deemed to be its enemies. There was in this a central ideological consistency. Himmler wanted to keep camps going in 1935, when the Interior Ministry hoped to shut them down, because he wanted somewhere under effective party jurisdiction where all those excluded from the *Volksgemeinschaft* on grounds of political resistance, social delinquency or race could be isolated entirely, experimented on or exterminated.[99] It is from this period that release from camp became quite exceptional, and it is from this period that the idea of 'extermination through labour' – the antithesis of a strategy of rational economic exploitation – was first mooted. The German concentration camp was an instrument of ideological warfare. Its justification lay in the wilder fantasies of racial hygiene that informed the vision of a German utopia, but also from the exaggerated fears of wartime conspiracy and national collapse on the home front.

The Soviet camp was also a child of the ideological war. The campaign against the kulak in the early 1930s and the later war against Trotskyites and wreckers in 1936–8 were too elaborate and too politically charged to have been mere devices for rounding up forced labour. The expansion of the number of common prisoners in the camps reflected changes in penal policy, of which enhanced labour-power was a consequence rather than a cause. Soviet concentration camps were also designed to isolate enemies from wider society, though unlike the German camps, prisoners were released once they had served their time, except for a smaller group of enemies deemed too incorrigible to be trusted back into regular life. Even then political prisoners, when they were released, were compelled to sign a paper stating that they would never again engage in counter-revolutionary activity. They had to live away from a specified list of major cities, and to report to NKVD police stations every week for years after their release.[100] The 'double terror' of denunciation and re-punishment in the GUlag was redundant if the primary purpose was a regime of forced labour. Camps were seen as dangerous places, full of those whom the regime defined as a threat.

The camps functioned as the logical outcome of ideologies rooted in the dichotomy between belonging and exclusion. That most victims of political or racial exclusion were innocent was immaterial. The regimes defined their enemies and destroyed or removed them. In the German dictatorship the language of annihilation and destruction was employed indiscriminately and literally. Primo Levi, an Italian Jewish chemist who survived Auschwitz, observed that the SS used the ashes from the crematoria where prisoners were burned after gassing as surfacing for the paths and roads around the SS quarters. Here was the ultimate expression of that urge to humiliate and destroy, to trample underfoot the wretched cohort of prisoners in their power, evident in all the daily routines and continual cruelties of the concentration camp. The camps were not just a product of circumstance and utility, nor simply an expression of pure terror. They were the direct consequence of the ideological driving-force of the two dictatorships, which rested, like most modern authoritarianism, on the allocation of blame and the redemptive destruction of the enemy.

Two Dictatorships

'People are bewitched by great illusions. They are hypno-
tized and do not see what actually takes place around
them. All around, ferocity and slaughter reign supreme. They
don't perceive it and believe that on the morrow the revolution will bring not only plenty, but the beatitude of paradise
to all. All around morality crumbles away, license, sadism,
and cruelty are everywhere – the masses call it a moral
regeneration.'

Pitrim Sorokin, 1967[1]

The Soviet interpreter Valentin Berezhkov found himself working in
Berlin in the spring and summer of 1940 as part of the commission
sent to monitor deliveries of German technology to the Soviet Union
under the terms of the trade agreement recently signed between the
two dictatorships. He was surprised by the familiarity of his surround-
ings: 'The same idolization of the "leader", the same mass rallies
and parades . . . Very similar, ostentatious architecture, heroic themes
depicted in art much like our socialist realism . . . massive ideological
brainwashing.'[2] He watched the adulation of the German crowds when
Hitler addressed them and recalled Stalin standing on the platform
above the Lenin mausoleum to wave at the marching columns of
enthusiastic communists. Yet this was a comparison, Berezhkov later
recalled, which he could not make at the time, 'even to myself'. The
gulf that separated the two dictatorships he well understood. Stalin
wanted the Soviet people to construct a socialist future 'where all
people would be equal and happy'. Hitler was bent on creating 'the

empire of the master race', and wanted his people to build it from 'the carnage of war'.[3]

This difference remains fundamental. For all the similarities in the practice of dictatorship, in the mechanisms that bound people and ruler together, in the remarkable congruence of cultural objectives, strategies of economic management, utopian social aspirations, even in the moral language of the regime, the stated ideological goals were as distinct as the differences that divided Catholic from Protestant in sixteenth-century Europe. The brief popularity of the idea of 'national-bolshevism' that flourished in the 1920s might have bridged the gulf between the two ideologies, but it did not appeal to either dictator.[4] Stalin, for all the terrible cost of pursuing the socialist paradise, maintained throughout his dictatorship that he was fighting for the world-wide triumph of the underprivileged and exploited even while the overwhelming majority of his own people suffered political regimentation and economic deprivation. Hitler, for all the millions of his countrymen killed, maimed and victimized, remained convinced to the very end in 1945 that an ideal racial empire had been worth fighting for. What united the two systems was the unresolved and permanent gap between ideal and reality, and the common instruments exploited by each system to mask the distortions of the truth.

The starting point in any comparison is to try to answer the question why, in the years after the First World War, there emerged two extreme forms of dictatorship, widely and popularly endorsed, whose leaders preached the idea of an exclusive, holistic community, bound collectively in the pursuit of an absolute utopia. Neither system was an abstraction; neither was imposed by external force. The two dictatorships were the product of a particular political culture and social environment, not historical aberrations beyond explanation. They were also unique. No modern European state had attempted, or had the means before 1914, to embrace the totality of society – to control or monitor all cultural output, to command the economy, to regiment society, to define the parameters of private life and the terms of public behaviour. The First World War prompted the first (limited) efforts to manage whole societies and organize their economy and culture, but on nothing like the scale attempted by the post-war dictatorships, including that of Mussolini, which first gave birth in the 1920s to the term 'totalitarian' to describe systems that embraced the totality of society.

One answer to the broader question of the roots of political holism may lie in what Tzvetan Todorov has called 'the cult of science'. A confident belief in the power of science to understand and then transform the human condition was widespread from the middle of the nineteenth century onwards.[5] The claims of 'scientism' (though not science as such) could be distilled down to a belief that society should be organized around objective scientific principles, and that those principles were exclusive and monistic. Individuals mattered little, but the social organism mattered a great deal. Popular scientific discourse had strongly utopian overtones. Science was expected to solve the problems of the real world through planning, medical reform, eugenics, social engineering and technical innovation.

Faith in science did not necessarily produce dictatorship, though its disciples had a strong predisposition to see science in authoritarian terms. But scientific arguments did underlie the political ideology and social aspirations of the two dictatorships, Soviet and German. The first culprit was Marxism, with its vision of a sociological utopia rooted in the application of modern economic and social science. The claims of scientific socialism, the product of the work of Friedrich Engels as much as Karl Marx, rested on belief that the laws of economic development necessarily produced the conditions for a unique social system resting on the abolition of class and the appropriation of property for social use. Its claims were total, since communist society would not only embrace all, it would at the same time eradicate any manifestations of 'false' social consciousness through what Marx (and, with greater force, Lenin) called 'the dictatorship of the proletariat'. Social development, according to Marx, produced a form of modern absolutism, while at the same time promising complete social emancipation – a paradox that lay at the heart of the Stalinist dictatorship.

The scientific roots of the German dictatorship could be found in the biological sciences. The development of a popular social biology in the late nineteenth century, associated with the work of Ernst Haeckel and his many disciples, constructed a view of the world based on preserving the race or nation as a pure and exclusive 'species', and the application of strict rules to govern its long-term health and strength. Hitler was familiar with the race theories of Ludwig Woltmann, whose book *Political Anthropology*, published in 1903, reappears in a vulgar scientific form in *Mein Kampf*.[6] The idea of racial struggle hygiene was intertwined by Woltmann and others with more conventional evolutionary science, by asserting the unavoidability of racial struggle as the central historical reality, where Marxists saw class struggle. The end product was a biological utopia, its holistic claims based on the preservation of the species and its authoritarianism derived from the merciless medical intervention necessary to preserve the gene pool.

The importance of these scientific imperatives in explaining the claims made by both dictatorships to be creating an organic community shielded from social or racial contamination has been a central theme of the book. Science helps to explain the absolute nature of the collectivist communities, and the grotesque lengths to which each went to extirpate elements regarded as social or racial outcasts. But science alone does not explain why dictatorship emerged when and where it did, even if it supplies a framework for understanding its remorseless efforts at scientific perfection. The two dictatorships represented the fruit of a profound rejection in Germany and Russia of the western liberal ideal of progress, with its emphasis on the sovereignty of the individual, the virtues of civil society and toleration of diversity. Marxists rejected the liberal-bourgeois age because in their view it manifestly represented the exclusive interests of the possessing classes. National Socialists rejected it because it produced social antagonism, encouraged racial impoverishment in the sprawling, unsupervised industrial cities and led to an exaggerated worship of economic selfishness. It is important to realize just how irrelevant modern liberalism or ideas of civic virtue were to Stalin and Hitler at the start of their political careers, the one engaged in the violent subversion of a very illiberal authoritarian monarchy, the other obsessively concerned with national struggle and racial hygiene. War and revolution, midwives to their world view, destroyed liberal claims about the nature of historical development. Liberal values never detained either politician when in power; they were intrinsically regarded as evidence of the political weakness and social fragmentation of a past age.

The anti-liberalism expressed by both dictators, and by the movements they represented, was part of a broader interpretation of the development of world history. In their differing ways both Stalin and Hitler saw themselves as actors in an extraordinary historical drama. They each argued that their dictatorship represented a fundamental turning point in the history of the modern world. Stalin defended the revolution as a world-shattering event, which threatened to undermine and then transcend the entire bourgeois era, born, as Marx had argued, in the French Revolution. In an article in *Pravda* marking the tenth anniversary of the revolution, Stalin wrote that October 1917 was 'a revolution of an international world order', which did nothing less than signify 'a radical turn in the world history of mankind'. Stalin compared the shock that the Jacobins presented to the aristocracy after 1789 with the shock of Bolshevism, 'which evokes horror and loathing among the bourgeois of all countries'.[7] Stalin wanted to complete the destruction of the bourgeois stage of history, as Marx's economic science had predicted. The alternative was unthinkable for Stalin, and for every other Bolshevik. 'Between our proletarian state and all the remaining bourgeois world,' wrote Mikhail Frunze, Voroshilov's predecessor as commissar for the Red Army, 'there can only be one condition of long, persistent, desperate war to the death.'[8] This overawing sense that they were somehow responsible for the fate of the world's underprivileged and exploited was a heavy historical burden. Soviet leaders acted as though the weight of historical development was on their side, and justified their actions by constant reiteration of the uncompromising nature of historical change and the world-historical nature of their mission.

National Socialism was also regarded as a world-historical phenomenon, acting to reverse the tide of historical change which had produced Marxism and revolution, and to rescue Europe from the greatest crisis it had faced since at least the French Revolution. Writing in 1938, Hans Mehringer celebrated the success of the movement in producing a historical 'turning-point' against the long march since 1789 towards 'Bolshevism, nihilism and anarchy'. Mehringer thought the movement would change the very circumstances of life in Europe, and give 'a meaning to existence for centuries'.[9] Hitler, very early in his career, developed extraordinary delusions of historical grandeur by marrying his personal destiny with the course of German history. In 1936, in the memorandum on Germany's geopolitical future, he sketched out terms that exactly mirrored those of Stalin: 'Since the outbreak of the French Revolution the world has been moving with ever increasing speed towards a new conflict, the most extreme solution of which is Bolshevism.' Hitler hoped this conflict would be won by Germany, fighting for the entire legacy of civilized Europe; otherwise the world would experience 'the most gruesome catastrophe since the downfall of the states of antiquity'.[10] At the party congress in 1934 he told delegates that the National Socialist movement was pitted against the French Revolution and its legacy of 'international-revolutionary dogma' which for a hundred and fifty years had been broadcast by Jewish intellectuals.[11] This, too, was a heavy historical responsibility. 'I do not regard this as an agreeable task,' Hitler wrote in his memorandum, 'but a serious handicap and burden for our national life.'[12] Such sentiments nevertheless gave to both Soviet communism and National Socialism an inflated sense of self-importance. The dictators could appeal to populations who also felt themselves to be making history, along with their leaders.

The collectivist ambitions of both dictatorships were defined by these various impulses. Science gave them a rational legitimacy, in keeping with the fundamental claims of the science community about possibilities for the future of modern society. History demonstrated the necessity for a revolutionary transformation of the conditions of existence in the face of a damaging capitalist modernity, and reinforced the legitimacy derived from science. The anti-liberal and anti-humanist revolt freed the dictatorships from conventional moral scruples and endorsed their distinctive anti-individualist moral outlook. The resulting systems were exclusive and all-embracing and morally absolute. They were communities regarded as sacrosanct by the parties that constructed them, which explains why they were so obsessive about any breach, however trivial or benign, in the unitary organism. There can be no other explanation for the fact that local censors in the Soviet Union searched for signs of subversion on every printed page produced, even among works written on behalf of the communist party itself. The frantic efforts of the Gestapo to track every single surviving Jew in Germany, even issuing detailed instructions about how to detect partition walls and hidden trapdoors, cannot be understood without the exaggerated holism of the system.[13]

The conventional description of both systems has focused on the rigorous character of state repression as evidence of their unrestricted power. In reality it was an expression of weakness. Both dictatorships were infused with profound fears and uncertainties. The 'enemy' in each was presented as if he enjoyed extraordinary powers that were secretive, subversive and socially corrosive. The 'masked' enemy in the Soviet Union of the 1930s, hidden away among the party apparatus, was regarded as the greatest menace faced by the regime; the 'Jew' was presented in National Socialist Germany as an almost unstoppable force, who had hijacked world history for his own designs and whose destruction would call on the most intense efforts of the German people and their allies. In both cases it was a profound fear of loss that prompted the savage regime of discrimination. Hitler persuaded himself, and millions of his adopted countrymen, that Germany's many enemies meant to secure the end of German culture and the emasculation of the German people. The evidence from the aftermath of the First World War, and from the catastrophe of inflation and slump in the 1920s, gave an apparent historical validation to the claim that Germany was teetering on the edge of chaos. In the Soviet Union fears that the revolution would go the way of the abortive revolts in 1919 in the rest of Europe, that counter-revolution was an ever-present reality ready to exploit the first sign of vacillation and compromise, fuelled paranoia about revolutionary survival which was party-wide, not just confined to Stalin. Loss was taken in both cases to be absolute. The death of the race was presented by National Socialists as the end of everything for Germany; successful counter-revolution in the Soviet Union was regarded as a disaster that would confirm the malign and unrelenting power of the bourgeoisie even in the face of their historical collapse. These unhappy scenarios made both systems promote an exaggerated state of defence against the supposed internal enemy and the threat of dissolution he represented, which explains why the apparatus of state security acted with such rigour and severity in exposing and destroying him.

Fear of the hidden enemy helps to explain one of the central characteristics of the two dictatorships. Both were animated by profound hatreds and resentments. The two dictators led the way by expressing their politics in terms which were to leave no doubt in the public mind that the enemies of the regime were unquestionably hateful. Hitler and Stalin's hate was born of their own historical experience. Hitler learned to hate the enemies of the nation during the First World War, not only the external enemy, but, more importantly, the enemy within, whom he thought sapped the national will to win. Hermann Rauschning, writing about the Hitler he knew in the early 1930s, was struck by the fact that 'hatred is like wine to him'.[14] Hitler's *Mein Kampf* contains statement after statement about institutions, classes and ideas that inspired in its author a profound historical resentment. Hating was infectious in Weimar Germany. It suffused the nationalist writing of the 1920s. Oswald Spengler observed at the end of the Great War 'an indescribable hatred' forged from defeat.[15] Soviet leaders peppered their public utterances with calls to hate the enemy and arguments that hatred was a virtuous revolutionary quality. Andrei Vyshinsky, the leading Soviet jurist in the 1930s, accepted that 'an irreconcilable hatred against enemies' was 'one of the most important principles of communist ethics'.[16] Stalin's resentments, like Hitler's, were on regular public display. They derived from his experience in the revolutionary underworld, which traded on bitter hostility to the powers of the Tsarist state, and equally bitter resentment of the other revolutionary factions that failed to accept the rightness of the Bolshevik cause, or had failed the test of uncompromising revolutionary struggle.[17]

The combination of historical and moral certainty, together with implacable hatred of the enemy, produced an institutionalized dichotomy between friend and foe, expressed explicitly in the political thought of the German jurist Carl Schmitt, who saw modern politics unavoidably defined by the division between those who were included in a particular political community and those who were excluded. His idea of 'friend or foe' (*Freund oder Feind*) reflected a widespread reality in European politics in the 1920s and was not merely an academic invention. The division suggested an absolute distinction, which left no room for the many millions of German or Soviet citizens who, if they thought about it at all, lay somewhere between these two poles. Very early in his career Stalin observed that anyone 'who did not submit their "I" to our sacred cause' was an enemy.[18] National

Socialism saw everything in black or white. There were, Gregor Strasser told a party rally in 1929, 'two categories in Germany'. On the one hand were 'those who believe in a German future, the Germans'; on the other were 'those who, for whatever reasons, are against, the non-Germans'.[19] In 1934 Gerhard Neesse wrote that any German reading *Mein Kampf* could give 'only a yes or a no', nothing in between.[20] Soviet rhetoric also left no space for the undecided. The world was divided along Manichean lines, good and evil, socially acceptable and socially corrupt, a division captured in the term 'socially dangerous' used to describe all those who had some genetic connection with the former dominant classes.[21] The division between those who were included and those who were excluded was a complex one, but all Soviet citizens, like all Germans, had to belong to either one category or the other. This explains the extraordinary lengths to which the National Socialist regime went in trying to define precisely the status of those who were part-Jewish. It explains, too, the policy in the Soviet Union of tracking down the sons and daughters of 'socially dangerous' individuals and denying them full civil rights or social opportunities on grounds of genetic or environmental contamination.[22]

Hatred also accounts, at least in part, for the pervasive violence of the two dictatorships. Violence inhabits the pages of this and of every account of the two dictatorships. Murder, or assassination, or suicide were routine; other forms of violent exclusion, deportation and camp imprisonment were meted out to millions. The violence was too widespread and continuous to be explained only by the fact that these were repressive, authoritarian regimes. Violence was built into the world view of each dictator and each dictatorship; it was essential to the system, not a mere instrument of control, and it was practised at every level of society. An argument can be made that acceptance of violence as inescapable, even, under certain circumstances, welcome, derived from the trauma of the Great War and the civil wars to which it gave rise. Hitler and the many other veterans in the party were exposed to death for years in a form that was harrowing and direct and bloody. Some, though not all, carried with them into peacetime an easy tolerance for physical brutality, and a morbid obsession with the virtue of violence (and violent death) that later permeated the entire culture of the Third Reich. The anthem written for 'Olympic youth' in 1936 celebrated not the joy of sport but the lure of a heroic end: 'The Fatherland's chief gain / The Fatherland's highest demand / in necessity: sacrificial death!'[23]

The civil war in the Soviet Union bloodied Bolshevik leaders. The violence was widespread and barbarous on both sides, blunting moral sensibilities and forging the belief that violent defence of the revolution was both righteous and historically necessary.[24] Yet in the Soviet case the language of political violence long pre-dated the experience of war. It was central to the Bolshevik conception of revolutionary struggle, which by definition would be destructive and bloody. Lenin in 1905 saw the task of the revolutionary masses in terms of 'ruthless destruction of the enemy', a theme to which he returned again and again during the revolution and civil war, and which was echoed in the language of his revolutionary colleagues.[25] Stalin later described in his *Foundations of Leninism* how 'the law of violent proletarian revolution, the law of the smashing of the bourgeois state machine is an inevitable law of the revolutionary movement'.[26] Both Stalin and Hitler saw violence as an unavoidable consequence of their political mission. Revolutionary conflicts necessitated the physical removal or constraint of those forces defined as counter-revolutionary; racial conflict was nature applied to human populations, where violence was instinctive and merciless. The dictators' expectations of politics and social reconstruction were deliberately, almost exultantly, anti-humanist. Neither man considered himself a murderer, though they ran murderous regimes. Violence was instead regarded as redemptive, saving society from imaginary enemies to whom murderous violence was thought to be second nature. The long-term consequences were disastrously destructive, beyond what either dictator could ever have imagined. The two dictatorships did not just crush lives in their prisons and camps; one or the other, they destroyed entire ancient communities, exterminated millions, deported millions from their homelands, uprooted religious belief, destroyed churches, smashed cities into premature ruins and eradicated some of the richest culture of Europe. For different reasons, the two systems directly or indirectly caused the deliberate death of millions more through starvation, neglect, disease, or state murder; Germany's attack on the Soviet Union cost the lives of 11 million servicemen, most of them Soviet. The mere reiteration of these unimaginable statistics sets the two dictatorships apart from anything else in the modern age. The human cost of constructing utopia and fighting to preserve it seems inexplicably disproportionate with what was gained or lost. It was a consequence of the terrible logic of systems stamped by an unrestrained battle for existence that called for violence without limit until that existence was secure, and removed all moral restraints which might have held back its perpetrators.

The bleak downward spiral from social exclusion, through hatred, to perpetual violence is difficult to reconcile with the utopian aspirations of the two systems. The two elements were united by the common concept of struggle. The utopia promised in the 1930s to both populations was always in the process of 'becoming', a distant ideal dimly visible through the day-to-day reality of struggle against what the systems regarded as the shackles of the old order and the social values and moral outlook that had sustained it. Stalin expressed this paradox in a speech in 1934, in which he explained that the current power of the state was a necessary transitional phase to a freer system: 'The highest development of state power with the object of preparing the conditions for the withering away of state power . . .' Stalin added that anyone who did not understand the contradictory character of the historical process 'is dead as far as Marxism is concerned'.[27] Hitler's sense of the future was also conditional on further struggle before the basis for a settled racial state could be guaranteed.[28] The two utopian states led a metaphorical existence, justifying present policy in pursuit of a distant goal, and persuading their populations that the postponed ideal was worth fighting for.

The metaphorical character of the two dictatorships was a feature which has always been difficult to understand. The gap between what was real and what was claimed to be real now appears so self-evident that it seems implausible the regimes would sustain the illusion, or that the populations would in any sense believe it. Yet the schizophrenic nature of the two dictatorships defined the terms of their operation. Both leaders and led engaged in collective acts of misrepresentation so that truth became untruth and untruths masqueraded as truth. 'People have grown cunning,' wrote a disillusioned German businessman in September 1939, 'and know how to dissemble. We have become a fine community of liars.'[29]

The metaphors of dictatorship were many. The leaders were presented as mythic symbols of the regime and the humdrum aspects of their personalities suppressed. The cults turned both figures into unreal versions of themselves, which were then appropriated by the rest of the system as if the ascribed virtues were in some sense real. The societies were presented as parodies of social reality. At just the point that Stalin made his claim that 'life has become more joyous' the regime embarked on two years of exceptional terror, and living-standards dropped to their lowest level of the dictatorship. The many images of smiling collective farmers and bountiful harvests were peddled at the same time that millions of peasants were in labour camps and millions more dying in the worst famine of the century. The Third Reich built the ideal society on the foundation of racial intimidation and discrimination, that led 300,000 to be compulsorily sterilized and the suggestion that a further 1.6 million with biological defects should be added to the list. Democracy in both systems was presented as something other than the exercise of free and open political choice. The enemies of each system were defined in ways that made them seem a looming and frightful menace, when in most cases they represented no threat at all. Political prisoners in the Soviet Union were forced to confess to the most absurd crimes and the confessions were then used to magnify the fantastic nature of the counter-revolution. Confession was beaten out of prisoners who in some cases subsequently found themselves uncertain as to whether they had or had not committed the crimes of which they were accused. In court they spoke as if the many falsehoods were historically true; when a few attempted to revoke their statements they were routinely shouted down by the prosecution or the tribunal judges as liars. Soviet leaders seem actually to have believed the accusations. Molotov, who signed many of the lists of those executed in 1937, could still make the following claim in an interview more than thirty years later: 'It was shown in court that the right-wingers had Gorky poisoned. Yagoda, the former chief of the secret police, was involved in the poisoning of his own predecessor.'[30] Similar psychological contortions were made by millions of ordinary German and Soviet citizens who suspended their disbelief in order that the utopian metaphors of the system should be sustained.

The success of both dictatorships in creating and promoting illusions about their true nature lies at the heart of their widespread affirmation by the public. All political systems indulge in some degree of subterfuge, but the Stalin and Hitler regimes did so systematically in ways that permitted no single chink of light through the curtains drawn tightly around them. They were both subject to an exceptional degree of international isolation, control of information and cultural autarky. Not a single hostile reference to either regime was permitted, though many were made when the risk could be taken; information about the outside world or about the true conditions of dictatorship was unobtainable except on the political black market, where those involved risked a concentration-camp sentence or death; a large part of the process of policy-making was kept entirely secret and the penalties for divulging it were severe. Isolation, limited access to information mainly pre-selected by the state, and exaggerated campaigns of propaganda and party education made it difficult for much of the public to know the truth, and predisposed them to accept either all, or important parts, of the official line. The public language of the two dictatorships reinforced the absence of criticism and the narrowness of vision. 'In the USSR,' wrote the French novelist André Gide, after a disillusioning visit in 1936, 'everyone knows beforehand that on any and every subject there can be only one opinion. Every time you talk to one Russian you feel as if you were talking to them all.' Gide observed that criticism amounted to nothing more than asking 'if this, that or the other is "in the right line". The line itself is never discussed.'[31] This conformity entered by stealth, so 'easy, natural and imperceptible that I do not think any hypocrisy enters into it'.[32] The German philologist Viktor Klemperer observed the same process at work in Germany. 'Nazism,' he wrote in his notebooks of the 1930s, 'enters into people's very flesh and blood through individual words, turns of speech and linguistic forms.' The endless repetition of the new language was absorbed, Klemperer believed, 'mechanically and unconsciously'.[33] His daily contact with his fellow Germans persuaded him that 'the masses believe everything' and did so willingly. 'The main thing for tyrannies of any kind,' he reflected on the day of the plebiscite for union with Austria, 10 April 1938, 'is the suppression of the urge to ask questions.'[34]

The powerful appeal of the two systems relied on the extent to which the populations could identify with the central message. In each case there were important historical circumstances that facilitated willingness to accept distorted versions of the truth. The promises made by the dictatorships were seductively attractive because they reflected aspirations already shared by an important fraction of the population, and easily communicated to the rest. In the Soviet Union the promise of a revolutionary paradise through redemptive struggle was central to the Bolshevik cause and was used to justify all the sacrifices of the present. For the party faithful it was essential to believe it; for millions of ordinary people struggling to come to terms with the post-revolutionary world the distant utopia provided a subliminal goal in the face of otherwise inexplicable hardships. 'It's all very well to build for the future,' explained a young factory official to a visiting American journalist. 'And we are doing great things – we are building a society that in time will make the civilization of Western Europe and America seem like barbarism.' Nevertheless, he continued, 'I'd like to have a little leisure and beauty now'.[35] Not every Soviet citizen fully understood the nature of what was promised, or accepted its necessity or its human cost, but the framework within which the work of the dictatorship was accomplished was a powerful popular belief, embedded in everyday life, that the future would yield a remarkable harvest.

In Germany the longing to reverse the judgement of the Great War, to expunge war guilt, to resurrect a powerful and respected state, to reverse the threat of communism, to reassert Germany's distinctive values and culture was overwhelmingly appealing not only to the activists in the nationalist revolution, but to many Germans who were hostile or indifferent to the National Socialist party. The collective psychological trauma of defeat and shame was abruptly reversed in 1933; the more evident it became that Hitler, apparently, could redeem the promises of German political revival, moral renewal and cultural awakening, the more readily the population identified with the dictatorship and the German new age. The need to believe in the possibility of redemption reflected a collective desperation, whose psychological dimension is impossible to measure historically, but was evident in the willingness to accept as true the claims of the regime and to become submerged in its language, values and behaviour. This was a process of sublimation that occurred in a remarkably short period of time, an indication that popular endorsement did not come just in response to the language and propaganda of the regime, but from the insecurities and resentments of those who supported Hitler as the German messiah even before 1933. In this, and in the Soviet case, the dictatorships reduced allegiance to very simple formulae of belief in a better future, a more secure identity and the transformative effect of the new politics. The power of this appeal, even for those not seduced by it, was irresistible; those who resisted were regarded as heretics who failed to understand the new faith.

This does not mean that every German became a National Socialist or every Soviet citizen a communist. Endorsement of the central myths of the dictatorship was, for most ordinary citizens, an indirect process, and in many cases not something that was even thought about clearly. A great many people in each system had no particular grounds for not believing the reality they were presented with. The historian's ability to reject the distorted or mendacious evidence in the speeches and propaganda sheets of the dictatorships is a privileged reaction which understates the extent to which these documents were used at the time as if the sentiments they expressed were valid.[36] The tendency to see the population under dictatorship in a perpetual state of critical engagement – enthusiastic, repelled, or resistant – exaggerates the degree of popular political consciousness and ascribes a degree of knowledge about the wider processes of state of which even party officials were often in ignorance. The great majority of Soviet and German citizens were not excluded from the new society. They remained relatively distant from the central political process; their view of political reality was parochial, ill-informed and unreflective; they were not touched by the terror unless they were defined as the enemy; everyday life lay under the shadow of politics, but was not necessarily joined to it. The local party supplied the party line, monitored non-compliance and encouraged enthusiasm for the cause. The metaphors of the regime were distant aspirations, the leaders themselves reduced to iconographic images, glimpsed briefly in newsreels or newspaper articles, but physically remote from the bulk of the population. Hitler and Stalin were idealized as phenomena capable of supplying the central promise of utopia through struggle. These political ambitions were appropriated and internalized as a framework for the conduct of ordinary lives. Seema Allan, an American living in the Soviet Union in the 1930s, recorded many conversations with ordinary Russians which reflected how easily the myths of the regime were borrowed in everyday discourse. 'If we hadn't built up our industries we'd have been crushed by some foreign power long ago'; 'let me tell you, Russia is developing as it never could in the old days! Life is a little hard now but it's getting better fast'; a Tatar folksong 'tells of everything that is new and good in our world and how we are changing the old'.[37]

Rulers and ruled in Germany and the Soviet Union colluded in creating societies that struggled collectively to achieve the promised new age. This was a mutual relationship in which Hitler and Stalin presented themselves as representative of the broader historical interests and social aspirations of the people they ruled, and were accepted on that basis by significant fractions of the population. However different in origin, all holistic dictatorships – and there have been many more in the years since 1945 – rely on creating complicity, just as they operate by isolating and destroying a chosen minority, whose terrorized status confirms the rational desire of the rest to be included and protected. The Stalin and Hitler dictatorships were populist dictatorships, nourished by mass acclamation and mass participation, and by fascination with unrestricted power. The many accounts of those who lived through the two dictatorships make clear that such fascination existed; it took the form of an emotional bond, by turn exhilarating, disturbing, even repellent, which lasted only as long as the object of that fascination still existed (though its echoes linger on in an apparently inexhaustible popular appetite for their history). The dictatorships cannot be understood only as systems of political oppression, since so many who participated in them willingly saw them as instruments of emancipation or security or enhanced identity or personal advantage. The barbarously destructive war waged between the two populations between 1941 and 1945 derived its savage character from the depths of social support and psychological identification with the two dictatorships that fought it, and the odium, indifference and fear towards the enemy instilled by the relentless propaganda directed against the 'other'. This war could not have been fought by democratic states.

The relationship between dictator and population was complex, diverse, ambivalent, even, at times, contradictory. It was a relationship governed in each case by different circumstances, differing milieus and widely different aspirations. Yet the European crisis that gave rise to them both, and the intellectual and cultural heritage on which each of them drew, created two systems sustained by remarkably similar political and social strategies and common patterns of authority, participation and popular response. In this sense Valentin Berezhkov's feeling of unease on finding 'how much there is in common' when he arrived in Berlin from Moscow in 1940 was not misplaced.[38]

Bibliography

I   Published documents, reference works
II Works by Hitler and Stalin
III Memoirs, diaries, literature
IV Contemporary publications
V   Publications since 1960

I PUBLISHED DOCUMENTS, REFERENCE WORKS

Adibekov, G. M. 'Special Settlers – Victims of "Complete Collectivisation"': from the Documents of "Osobaya Paplea" Political Bureau', *Istoricheskii Archiv*, no. 3 (1994), pp. 145–81.

Benn, G. *Briefe an F. W. Oetze 1932–1945* (Wiesbaden, 1977).

Benn, G. *Briefe an Tilly Wedekind 1930–1955* (Stuttgart, 1986).

Bugai, N. 'Crammed into Freight Cars and Deported to Place of Destination: L. Beria Reports to I. Stalin', *Istoria SSSR*, no. 1 (1994), pp. 143–61.

Burdick, C. and Jacobsen, H.-A. (eds) *The Halder Diary, 1939–1942* (London, 1988).

Chizhova, L. M. 'Unheard War Warnings, April–June 1941', *Istoricheskii Archiv*, no. 2 (1995), pp. 4–23.

Constitution (Fundamental Law) of the Union of Soviet Socialist Republics (Moscow, 1937).

Corley, F. (ed.) *Religion in the Soviet Union: an Archival Reader* (New York, 1996).

Curtis, J. E. (ed.) *Mikhail Bulgakov: Manuscripts Don't Burn. A Life in Diaries and Letters* (London, 1991).

Davies, R. W., Khlevniuk, O. V., Rees, E. A., Liudmila, P. K. and Larisa, A. R. (eds) *The Stalin–Kaganovich Correspondence 1931–1936* (New Haven, Conn., 2003).

Domarus, M. *Hitler: Reden und Proklamationen 1932–1945* (3 vols, Munich, 1965).

Ehrenburg, I. and Grossman, V. *The Complete Black Book of Russian Jewry* ed. D. Patterson (New Brunswick, NJ, 2002).

Franklin, B. (ed.) *The Essential Stalin: Major Theoretical Writings 1905–52* (London, 1973).

Fröhlich, E. *Die Tagebücher Joseph Goebbels: sämtliche Fragmente* (4 vols, Munich, 1987).

Genoud, F. (ed.) *The Testament of Adolf Hitler: The Hitler–Bormann Documents* (London, 1961).

Gruchmann, L. and Weber, R. (eds) *Der Hitler-Prozess 1924: Wortlaut der Hauptverhandlung vor den Volksgericht München I* (4 vols, Munich, 1997).

Hazard, J. (ed.) *Soviet Legal Philosophy* (Cambridge, Mass., 1951).

Heiber, H. and Glantz, D. (eds) *Hitler and his Generals: Military Conferences 1942–1945* (London, 2002).

Hess, W. R. (ed.) *Rudolf Hess: Briefe, 1908–1933* (Munich, 1987).

Jochmann, W. (ed.) *Adolf Hitler: Monologe im Führerhauptquartier 1941–1944* (Hamburg, 1980).

Kaden, H. and Nestler, L. (eds) *Dokumente des Verbrechens: aus Akten des Dritten Reiches 1933–1945* (3 vols, Berlin, 1993).

Kogon, E., Langbein, H. and Rückerl, A. (eds) *Nazi Mass Murder: a Documentary History of the Use of Poison Gas* (New Haven, Conn., 1993).

Kotze, H. von (ed.) *Heeresadjutant bei Hitler 1938–1945: Aufzeichnungen des Majors Engel* (Stuttgart, 1974).

Kotze, H. von and Krausnick, H. (eds) *'Es spricht der Führer': 7 exemplarische Hitler-Reden* (Gütersloh, 1966).

Lawton, A. (ed.) *Russian Futurism through Its Manifestoes, 1912–1928* (Ithaca, NY, 1988).

Lih, L. T., Naumov, O. V. and Khlevniuk, O. V. (eds) *Stalin's Letters to Molotov* (New Haven, Conn., 1995).

Loza, D. *Fighting for the Soviet Motherland: Recollections from the Eastern Front* (Lincoln, Nebr., 1998).

The Military Writings and Speeches of Leon Trotsky (4 vols, London, 1981).

Miller-Kipp, G. (ed.) *'Auch Du gehörst dem Führer': Die Geschichte des Bundes Deutscher Mädel (BDM) in Quellen und Dokumenten* (Weinheim, 2001).

Moll, M. (ed.) *'Führer-Erlasse', 1939–1945* (Stuttgart, 1997).

Owings, A. *Frauen: German Women Recall the Third Reich* (London, 1993).

Reddemann, K. (ed.) *Zwischen Front und Heimat: Der Briefwechsel des münsterischen Ehepaares Agnes und Albert Neuhaus 1940–1944* (Münster, 1996).

Report of Court Proceedings in the Case of the Anti-Soviet Trotskyite Centre, January 23–30 1937 (Moscow, 1937).

Runciman, W. G. (ed.) *Max Weber: Selections in Translation* (London, 1974).

Russkii Archiv 13: nemetskii Voennoplennye v SSSR (Moscow, 1999).

Schrader, F. E. *Der Moskauer Prozess 1936: zur Sozialgeschichte eines politischen Feindbildes* (Frankfurt am Main, 1995).

Semin, I. V., Sigachev, I. and Chuvashin, G. 'At the Battle-Front – Documents from the Central Archives, 1941–1945', *Istoricheskii Archiv*, no. 2 (1995), pp. 40–86.

Seraphim, H.-G. *Das politische Tagebuch Alfred Rosenbergs aus dem Jahren 1934/35 und 1939/40* (Göttingen, 1956).

Shapovalov, V. (ed.) *Remembering the Darkness: Women in Soviet Prisons* (Lanham, Md., 2001).

Short History of the Communist Party of the Soviet Union (Moscow, 1942).

Siegelbaum, L. and Sokolov, A. (eds) *Stalinism as a Way of Life* (New Haven, Conn., 2000).

Simmons, C. and Perlina, N. (eds) *Writing the Siege of Leningrad: Women's Diaries, Memoirs and Documentary Prose* (Pittsburgh, 2002).

Stalinskoye Politburo v 30-ye gody ed. O. Khlevniuk *et al.* (Moscow, 1995).

Suny, R. G. (ed.) *The Structure of Soviet History: Essays and Documents* (Oxford, 2003).

Taylor, F. (ed.) *The Goebbels Diaries 1939–1941* (London, 1982).

Treue, W. 'Hitlers Denkschrift zum Vierjahresplan 1936', *Vierteljahreshefte für Zeitgeschichte*, 3 (1955) pp. 184–210.

Trevor-Roper, H. (ed.) *Hitler's War Directives* (London, 1964).

Uncensored Germany: Letters and News Sent Secretly from Germany to the German Freedom Party (London, 1940).

Vollnhals, C. (ed.) *Hitler: Reden, Schriften und Anordnungen Februar 1925 bis Januar 1933* (12 vols, Munich, 1992).

Wehrmachtsverbrechen: Dokumente aus sowjetischen Archiven (Cologne, 1997).

Werth, N. and Moullec, G. *Rapports secrets soviétiques: La société russe dans les documents confidentiels 1921–1991* (Paris, 1994).

Widerstand und Exil der deutschen Arbeiterbewegung 1933–1945 (Bonn, 1982).

Wilhelm, H.-H. (ed.) *Rassenpolitik und Kriegführung: Sicherheitspolizei und Wehrmacht in Polen und der Sowjetunion* (Passau, 1991).

Zile, Z. L. (ed.) *Ideas and Forces in Soviet Legal History: a Reader on the Soviet State and the Law* (Oxford, 1992).

II CONTEMPORARY WORKS BY HITLER AND STALIN

Hitler, A. *Mein Kampf* (2 vols, Munich, 1926–7).

Hitler, A. *The Secret Book* ed. T. Taylor (New York, 1961).

Stalin, J. *Economic Problems of Socialism in the U.S.S.R.* (Peking, 1972).

Stalin, J. *Foundations of Leninism* (New York, 1939).

Stalin, J. *The Great Patriotic War of the Soviet Union* (New York, 1945).

Stalin, J. *Leninism: Selected Writings* (New York, 1942).

Stalin, J. *Problems of Leninism* (Moscow, 1947).

Stalin, J. *The War of National Liberation* (New York, 1942).

Stalin, J. *Works* (13 vols, Moscow, 1953–55 edition).

Stalin, J. *et al. From the First to the Second Five-Year Plan: a Symposium* (New York, n.d.).

III MEMOIRS, DIARIES, LITERATURE, ETC

Allan, S. R. *Comrades and Citizens: Soviet People* (London, 1938).

Baikoff, A. V. *I Knew Stalin* (London, 1940).

Bardach, J. and Gleeson, K. *Man is Wolf to Man: Surviving the Gulag* (Berkeley, Calif., 1998).

Bazhanov, B. *Avec Staline dans le Kremlin* (Paris, 1930).

Below, N. von *At Hitler's Side: The Memoirs of Hitler's Luftwaffe Adjutant 1937–1945* (London, 2003).

Berezhkov, V. M. *At Stalin's Side* (New York, 1994).

Beria, S. *Beria, My Father: Inside Stalin's Kremlin* (London, 2001).

Bessonov, E. *Tank Rider: into the Reich with the Red Army* (London, 2003).

Brecht, B. *Poems 1913–1956* (London, 1976).

Brown, E. J. *The Proletarian Episode in Russian Literature 1928–1932* (New York, 1953).

Brunovsky, V. *The Methods of the OGPU* (London, 1931).

Bulgakov, M. *The Master and Margarita* (London, 1997).

Cassidy, H. *Moscow Dateline 1941–1943* (London, 1944).

Chamberlin, W. H. *Soviet Russia: a Living Record and a History* (Boston, Mass., 1938).

Davies, J. E. *Mission to Moscow* (London, 1942).

Deriabin, P. with Evans, J. C. *Inside Stalin's Kremlin* (Washington, DC, 1998).

Djilas, M. *Conversations with Stalin* (New York, 1962).

Duranty, W. *Stalin and Co: The Politburo and the Men who Rule Russia* (London, 1949).

Ehrenburg, I. *Men – Years – Life, volume 5: The War Years 1941–1945* (London, 1964).

Engelmann, B. *In Hitler's Germany: Everyday Life in the Third Reich* (London, 1988).

Fadeev, A. *The Rout* ed. R. Cockrell (London, 1995).

François-Poncet, A. *The Fateful Years. Memoirs of a French Ambassador in Berlin* (London, 1949).

Geddes, G. *Nichivó: Life, Love and Death on the Russian Front* (London, 2001).

Geissmar, B. *The Baton and the Jackboot: Recollections of Musical Life* (London, 1988).

Gidé, A. *Back from the U.S.S.R.* (London, 1937).

Giesler, H. *Ein anderer Hitler: Bericht seines Architekten Hermann Giesler* (Leoni, 1977).

Ginzburg, E. *Into the Whirlwind* (London, 1967).

Gladkov, N. *Cement* (London, 1980).

Gorky, M. *Mother* (London, 1949).

Grigorenko, P. *Memoirs* (London, 1983).

Grossman, V. *Life and Fate* (London, 1985).

Hanfstaengl, E. *Hitler: the Missing Years* (London, 1957).

Hoess, R. *Commandant of Auschwitz* (London, 1959).

Junge, T. *Until the Final Hour: Hitler's Last Secretary* (London, 2003).

Jünger, E. *Storm of Steel* (London, 2003).

Khrushchev, N. *Khrushchev Remembers* (London, 1971).

Kilian, A. *Einzuweisen zur völligen Isolierung NKWD-Speziallager Mühlberg/Elbe 1945–1948* (Leipzig, 1993).

Klemperer, V. *I Shall Bear Witness: The Diaries of Viktor Klemperer 1933–1941* (London, 1998).

Klukowski, Z. *Diary from the Years of Occupation 1939–1944* (Chicago, 1993).

Koschorrek, G. K. *Blood Red Snow: The Memoirs of a German Soldier on the Eastern Front* (London, 2002).

Krause, K. *Zehn Jahre Kammerdiener bei Hitler* (Hamburg, 1950).

Kravchenko, V. *I Chose Freedom: The Personal and Political Life of a Soviet Official* (London, 1947).

Krivitsky, W. *I Was Stalin's Agent* (2nd edn, Cambridge, 1992).

Lengyel, E. *Secret Siberia* (London, 1947).

Levi, P. *The Drowned and the Saved* (London, 1988).

Leyda, J. *Kino: a History of Russian and Soviet Film* (Princeton, NJ, 1983).

The Life of Stalin: a Symposium (London, 1930).

Lorant, S. *I Was Hitler's Prisoner* (London, 1935).

Luck, S. I. *Observation in Russia* (London, 1938).

Lunacharsky, A. *Revolutionary Silhouettes* (London, 1967).

Lyons, E. *Assignment in Utopia* (London, 1937).

Lyons, E. *Stalin: Czar of all the Russias* (London, 1940).

Maks, L. *Russia by the Back Door* (London, 1954).

Mandelstam, N. *Hope Against Hope* (London, 1970).

Mikoyan, A. *Memoirs of Anastas Mikoyan, vol I* (Madison, Conn., 1988).

Nahon, M. *Birkenau: Camp of Death* (Tuscaloosa, Ala., 1989).

Parvilahti, U. *Beria's Gardens: Ten Years' Captivity in Russia and Siberia* (London, 1959).

Platanov, A. *Happy Moscow* (London, 2001).

Price, G. Ward *I Know These Dictators* (London, 1937).

Reck-Malleczewen, F. *Diary of a Man in Despair* (London, 1995).

Resis, A. (ed.) *Molotov Remembers: Inside Kremlin Politics* (Chicago, 1993).

Romano-Petrova, N. *Stalin's Doctor, Stalin's Nurse: A Memoir* (Princeton, NJ, 1984).

Serge, V. *The Case of Comrade Tulayev* (London, 1968).

Serge, V. *Memoirs of a Revolutionary 1901–1941* (Oxford, 1967).

Simonov, K. *Kriegstagebücher 1942–1945* (2 vols, Berlin, 1979).

Smith, A. *I Was a Soviet Worker* (London, 1937).

Solzhenitsyn, A. *One Day in the Life of Ivan Denisovich* (London, 1963).

Speer, A. *Inside the Third Reich: Memoirs* (London, 1970).

Steinberg, P. *Speak You Also: a Survivor's Reckoning* (London, 2001).

Steinhoff, J., Pechel, P. and Showalter, D. (eds) *Voices from the Third Reich: an Oral History* (Washington, DC, 1989).

Stieber, J. *Against the Odds: Survival on the Russian Front 1944–1945* (Dublin, 1995).

Street, L. *I Married a Russian: Letters from Kharkov* (London, 1944).

Tennant, E. W. *True Account* (London, 1957).

Turner, H. A. (ed.) *Hitler: Memoirs of a Confidant* [Otto Wagener] (New Haven, Conn., 1985).

Warlimont, W. *Inside Hitler's Headquarters* (London, 1964).

White, W. *Report on the Russians* (New York, 1945).

Yevtushenko, Y. (ed.) *Twentieth-Century Russian Poetry* (London, 1993).

Zbarsky, I. and Hutchinson, S. *Lenin's Embalmers* (London, 1998).

Zhukov, G. K. *Reminiscences and Reflections* (2 vols, Moscow, 1985).

IV CONTEMPORARY PUBLICATIONS (PRE-1960)

Abel, T. *Why Hitler Came into Power: An Answer Based on the Original Life Stories of Six Hundred of His Followers* (New York, 1938).

Alexander, E. *Der Mythos Hitler* (Zurich, 1937).

Alexandrov, G. L. *et al. Joseph Stalin: a Short Biography* (Moscow, 1939, 2nd edn, 1947).

Barton, P. *L'Institution concentrationnaire en Russe 1930–1957* (Paris, 1959).

Bauer, R. A. *The New Man in Soviet Psychology* (Cambridge, Mass., 1952).

Baykov, A. *The Development of the Soviet Economic System* (Cambridge, 1947).

Belli, E. von *Der Krieg der Zukunft im Urteil des Auslandes* (Berlin, 1936).

Bettelheim, C. *La planification soviétique* (Paris, 1939).

Borland, H. *Soviet Literary Theory and Practice during the First Five-Year Plan, 1928–32* (New York, 1950).

Brady, R. A. *The Spirit and Structure of German Fascism* (London, 1937).

Brausse, H. *Die Führungsordnung der deutschen Volkes: Grundlegung einer Führungslehre* (Hamburg, 1940).

Bromage, B. *Molotov: the Story of an Era* (London, 1956).

Brutzkus, B. *Economic Planning in Soviet Russia* (London, 1934).

Carson, G. B. *Electoral Practices in the USSR* (New York, 1955).

Coates, W. P. and Coates, Z. K. *From Tsardom to the Stalin Constitution* (London, 1938).

Dallin, D. and Nicolaevsky, B. *Forced Labor in Soviet Russia* (London, 1947).

Douglas, P. F. *God Among the Germans* (Philadelphia, 1935).

Fraenkel, E. *The Dual State: A Contribution to the Theory of Dictatorship* (New York, 1941).

Gachkel, S. *Le mécanisme des finances soviétiques* (Paris, 1946).

Graham, S. *Stalin: An Impartial Study of the Life and Work of Joseph Stalin* (London, 1931).

Gregory, J. S. *Land of the Soviets* (London, 1946).

Grothe, H. (ed.) *Kleines Handwörterbuch des Grenz-und Ausland-Deutschtums* (Munich, 1932).

Guillebaud, C. W. *The Economic Recovery of Germany* (London, 1939).

Guins, G. C. *Soviet Law and Soviet Society* (The Hague, 1954).

Haydu, J. *Russland 1932* (Vienna, 1932).

Hodgman, D. R. *Soviet Industrial Production 1928–1951* (Cambridge, Mass., 1954).

Horrabin, J. F. and Gregory, J. S. *An Atlas of the U.S.S.R.* (London, 1945).

Hubbard, L. E. *Soviet Labour and Industry* (London, 1942).

Hubbard, L. E. *Soviet Money and Finance* (London, 1936).

Hubbard, L. E. *Soviet Trade and Distribution* (London, 1938).

Hudson, G. F. *Questions of East and West: Studies in Current History* (London, 1953).

Inkeles, A. *Public Opinion in Soviet Russia: a Study in Mass Persuasion* (Cambridge, Mass., 1950).

Jones, J. W. *The Nazi Concept of Law* (Oxford, 1939).

Kautsky, K. *Thomas More and His Utopia* (London, 1927).

Koerber, L. von *Sowjetrussland kämpft gegen das Verbrechen* (Berlin, 1933).

Kohn, H. *The Twentieth Century: a midway account of the western world* (London, 1950).

Kolnai, A. *The War Against the West* (London, 1938).

Kruck, A. *Geschichte des Alldeutschen Verbandes 1890–1939* (Wiesbaden, 1954).

Kühn, A., Staemmler, M. and Burgdörfer, F. (eds) *Erbkunde. Rassenpflege. Bevölkerungspolitik. Schicksalsfragen des deutschen Volkes* (Leipzig, 1936).

Labin, S. *Stalin's Russia* (London, 1949).

Leites, N. and Bernant, E. *Rituals of Liquidation: The Case of the Moscow Trials* (Glencoe, Ill., 1954).

Lewis, W. *The Hitler Cult* (London, 1939).

Macleod, J. *The New Soviet Theatre* (London, 1943).

Mehringer, H. *Die NSDAP als politische Ausleseorganisation* (Munich, 1938).

Meissner, B. *The Communist Party of the Soviet Union* (New York, 1956).

Metalnikov, S. *La lutte contre le mort* (Paris, 1937).

Mirbt, R. (ed.) *Das deutsche Herz: Ein Volksbuch deutscher Gedichte* (Berlin, 1934).

Morgan, J. H. *Assize of Arms: being the Story of the Disarmament of Germany and her Rearmament* (2 vols, London, 1945).

Müller-Armack, A. *Wirtschaftslenkung und Marktwirtschaft* (Hamburg, 1947).

Münz, L. *Führer durch die Behörden und Organisationen* (Berlin, 1939).

Neesse, G. *Die NSDAP: Versuch einer Rechtsdeutung* (Stuttgart, 1935).

Neumann, F. *Behemoth: the Structure and Practice of National Socialism* (London, 1942).

Nicolai, H. *Der Neuaufbau des Reiches nach dem Reichsreformgesetz vom 30. Januar 1934* (Berlin, 1934).

Nissen, O. *Germany – Land of Substitutes* (London, 1944).

Öhquist, J. *Das Reich des Führers* (Bonn, 1943).

Prokopovicz, S. N. *Russlands Volkswirtschaft unter den Sowjets* (Zurich, 1944).

Rauschning, H. *The Conservative Revolution* (New York, 1941).

Rauschning, H. *Germany's Revolution of Destruction* (London, 1938).

Roberts, S. *The House that Hitler Built* (London, 1938).

Royal Institute of International Affairs *Nationalism* (London, 1939).

Serge, V. *Portrait de Staline* (Paris, 1940).

Shabad, T. *Geography of the USSR: a Regional Survey* (New York, 1951).

Sorokin, P. *The Crisis of Our Age: the Social and Cultural Outlook* (New York, 1945).

Spinka, M. *The Church in Soviet Russia* (Oxford, 1956).

Stern, B. J. and Smith, S. (eds) *Understanding the Russians: a Study of Soviet Life and Culture* (New York, 1947).

Trotsky, L. *The Revolution Betrayed: What is the Soviet Union and where is it going?* (London, 1937).

Van Paassen, P. *Visions Rise and Change* (New York, 1955).

Voroshilov, K. *Stalin and the Armed Forces of the U.S.S.R.* (Moscow, 1951).

Voznesensky, N. *War Economy of the USSR in the Period of the Patriotic War* (Moscow, 1948).

Weber, A. *Marktwirtschaft und Sowjetwirtschaft* (Munich, 1949).

Wetter, G. *Dialectical Materialism: A Historical and Systematic Survey of Philosophy in the Soviet Union* (New York, 1958).

White, W. L. *Report on the Russians* (New York, 1945).

Winterton, P. *Report on Russia* (London, 1945).

V PUBLICATIONS SINCE 1960

Absolon, R. *Die Wehrmacht im Dritten Reich: Band IV, 5 Februar 1938 bis 31 August 1939* (Boppard a Rh, 1979).

Acton, E. *Russia: the Tsarist and Soviet Legacy* (2nd edn, London, 1995).

Adam, P. *Arts of the Third Reich* (London, 1992).

Addison, P. and Calder, A. (eds) *Time to Kill: The Soldier's Experience of War in the West 1939–1945* (London, 1997).

Agursky, M. 'An Occult Source of Socialist Realism: Gorky and Theories of Thought Transference', in B. G. Rosenthal *The Occult in Russian and Soviet Culture* (Ithaca, NY, 1997), pp. 225–46.

Alexopoulos, G. 'Exposing Illegality and Oneself: Complaint and Risk in Stalin's Russia', in P. H. Solomon *Reforming Justice in Russia 1864–1996* (New York, 1997), pp. 168–89.

Alexopoulos, G. *Stalin's Outcasts: Aliens, Citizens, and the Soviet State 1926–1936* (Ithaca, NY, 2003).

Allen, M. T. 'The Banality of Evil Reconsidered: SS Mid-level Managers of Extermination through Work', *Central European History*, 30 (1997), pp. 253–94.

Allen, M. T. *The Business of Genocide: The SS, Slave Labor, and the Concentration Camps* (Chapel Hill, NC, 2002).

Altshuler, M. *Soviet Jewry on the Eve of the Holocaust* (Jerusalem, 1998).

Aly, G. *'Final Solution': Nazi Population Policy and the Murder of the European Jews* (London, 1999).

Aly, G. and Heim, S. *Architects of Annihilation: Auschwitz and the Logic of Destruction* (London, 2002).

Amis, M. *Koba the Dread: Laughter and the Twenty Million* (New York, 2002).

Anderson, T. 'Incident at Baranivka: German Reprisals and the Soviet Partisan Movement in Ukraine, October–December 1941', *Journal of Modern History*, 71 (1999), pp. 585–623.

Andrew, C. and Gordievsky, O. *KGB: the Inside Story* (London, 1990).

Andreyev, C. *Vlasov and the Russian Liberation Movement: Soviet Reality and Émigré Theories* (Cambridge, 1987).

Andrle, V. *A Social History of Twentieth-Century Russia* (London, 1994).

Andrle, V. *Workers in Stalin's Russia: Industrialization and Social Change in a Planned Economy* (New York, 1988).

Antonov-Ovseyenko, A. *The Time of Stalin: Portrait of a Tyranny* (New York, 1981).

Applebaum, A. *Gulag: a History of the Soviet Camps* (London, 2003).

Arbogast, C. *Herrschaftsinstanzen der württembergischen NSDAP: Funktion, Sozialprofil und Lebenswege einer regionalen NS-Elite 1920–1960* (Munich, 1998).

Armstrong, J. A. (ed.) *Soviet Partisans in World War II* (Madison, Wisc., 1964).

Armstrong, J. A. *Ukrainian Nationalism* (3rd edn, Englewood, Colo., 1990).

Attwood, L. (ed.) *Red Women on the Silver Screen: Soviet Women and Cinema from the beginning to the end of the Communist era* (London, 1993).

Audoin-Rouzeau, S., Becker, A., Ingrao, C. and Rousso, H. (eds) *La Violence de guerre 1914–1945* (Brussels, 2002).

Avtorkhanov, A. *The Communist Party Apparatus* (Chicago, 1961).

Axell, A. *Stalin's War Through the Eyes of his Commanders* (London, 1997).

Axell, A. *Zhukov* (London, 2003).

Ayass, W. *Asoziale im Nationalsozialismus* (Stuttgart, 1995).

Bacon, E. *The Gulag at War: Stalin's Forced Labour System in the Light of the Archives* (London, 1994).

Bacon, E. T. 'Soviet Military Losses in World War II', *Journal of Slavic Military Studies*, 6 (1993), pp. 613–33.

Baigent, M. and Leigh, R. *Secret Germany: Claus von Stauffenberg and the Mystical Crusade against Hitler* (London, 1994).

Bailes, K. E. 'The American Connection: Ideology and the Transfer of American Technology to the Soviet Union, 1917–1941', *Comparative Studies in Society and History*, 23 (1981), pp. 421–48.

Bailes, K. E. 'Stalin and the Making of a New Elite: A Comment', *Slavic Review*, 39 (1980), pp. 286–9.

Bailes, K. E. *Technology and Society under Lenin and Stalin: Origins of the Soviet Technical Intelligentsia* (Princeton, NJ, 1978).

Baird, J. W. *To Die for Germany: Heroes in the Nazi Pantheon* (Bloomington, Ind., 1990).

Bajohr, F. *'Arisierung' in Hamburg; Die Verdrängung der jüdischen Unternehmer 1933–1945* (Hamburg, 1997).

Bajohr, F. *Parvenüs und Profiteure. Korruption in der NS-Zeit* (Frankfurt am Main, 2001).

Bakels, F. B. *Nacht und Nebel: Das Bericht eines holländischen Christen aus deutschen Gefängnissen und Konzentrationslagern* (Frankfurt am Main, 1979).

Baldauf, I. 'Some Thoughts on the Making of the Uzbek Nation', *Cahiers du monde russe*, 32 (1991), pp. 79–96.

Balderston, T. *Economics and Politics in the Weimar Republic* (Cambridge, 2002).

Balfour, M. *Withstanding Hitler in Germany 1933–1945* (London, 1988).

Ball, A. M. *Russia's Last Capitalists: The Nepmen, 1921–1929* (Berkeley, Calif., 1987).

Banach, J. *Heydrichs Elite: Das Führerkorps der Sicherheitspolizei und des SD 1936–1945* (Paderborn, 1998).

Barber, J. 'The Moscow Crisis of October 1941', in J. Cooper, M. Perrie and E. A. Rees (eds) *Soviet History 1917–1953: Essays in Honour of R. W. Davies* (London, 1995).

Barber, J. and Harrison, M. (eds) *The Soviet Defence-Industry Complex from Stalin to Khrushchev* (London, 2000).

Barber, J. and Harrison, M. *The Soviet Home Front 1941–1945* (London, 1991).

Barkai, A. *From Boycott to Annihilation: The Economic Struggle of German Jews, 1933–1943* (Hannover, NJ, 1989).

Barkai, A. *Nazi Economics: Ideology, Theory, and Policy* (Oxford, 1990).

Barnes, J. J. and Barnes, P. P. *Hitler's* Mein Kampf: *Britain and America: a Publishing History 1930–39* (Cambridge, 1980).

Barnett, V. *For the Soul of the People: Protestant Protest against Hitler* (Oxford, 1992).

Barnett, V. *Kondratiev and the Dynamics of Economic Development: Long Cycles and Industrial Growth in Historical Context* (London, 1998).

Barron, S. (ed.) *'Degenerate Art': The Fate of the Avant-Garde in Nazi Germany* (New York, 1991).

Barros, J. and Gregor, R. *Double Deception: Stalin, Hitler and the Invasion of Russia* (Dekalb, Ill., 1995).

Bärsch, C.-E. *Die politische Religion des Nationalsozialismus* (Munich, 1998).

Bartlett, R. *Wagner in Russia* (Cambridge, 1995).

Bartov, O. *The Eastern Front 1941–1945: German Troops and the Barbarization of Warfare* (New York, 1985).

Bartov, O. *Hitler's Army: Soldiers, Nazis and War in the Third Reich* (Oxford, 1991).

Bartov, O. 'The Missing Years: German Workers, German Soldiers', in D. Crew (ed.) *Nazism and German Society 1933–1945* (London, 1994), pp. 41–66.

Bashalov, A. *General Vlasov – predatel' ili geroi?* (St Petersburg, 1994).

Baykov, A. *The Development of the Soviet Economic System* (Cambridge, 1947).

Beachley, D. R. 'Soviet Radio-Electronic Combat in World War II', *Military Review*, 61 (1981), pp. ???.

Beaumont, J. *Comrades in Arms: British Aid to Russia 1941–1945* (London, 1980).

Beetham, D. *Max Weber and the Theory of Modern Politics* (London, 1974).

Behrenbeck, S. *Der Kult um die toten Helden: nationalsozialistische Mythen, Riten und Symbole* (Vierow bei Greifswald, 1996).

Beier, G. *Die illegale Reichsleitung der Gewerkschaften 1933–1945* (Cologne, 1981).

Beirne, P. (ed.) *Revolution in Law: Contributions to the Development of Soviet Legal Theory, 1917–1938* (New York, 1990).

Bendersky, J. W. *Carl Schmitt: Theorist for the Reich* (Princeton, NJ, 1983).

Benvenuti, F. 'A Stalinist Victim of Stalinism: "Sergo" Ordzhonikidze', in J. Cooper, M. Perrie and E. A. Rees (eds) *Soviet History 1917–1953: Essays in Honour of R. W. Davies* (London, 1995), pp. 134–57.

Benvenuti, F. 'Industry and Purge in the Donbass 1936–37', *Europe–Asia Studies*, 45 (1993), pp. 57–78.

Bergan, R. *Sergei Eisenstein: a Life in Conflict* (New York, 1997).

Bergen, D. 'The Nazi Concept of the Volksdeutsche and the Exacerbation of Anti-Semitism in Eastern Europe 1939–1945', *Journal of Contemporary History*, 29 (1994), pp. 569–82.

Berghahn, V. *Der Stahlhelm: Bund der Frontsoldaten 1918–1935* (Düsseldorf, 1966).

Bergmeier, H. and Lotz, R. E. *Hitler's Airwaves: the Inside Story of Nazi Radio Broadcasting and Propaganda Swing* (New Haven, Conn., 1997).

Berschel, H. *Bürokratie und Terror: Das Judenreferat der Gestapo Düsseldorf 1935–1945* (Essen, 2001).

Berthold, W. *Die 42 Attentate auf Adolf Hitler* (Wiesbaden, 2000).

Berton, K. *Moscow: An Architectural History* (London, 1977).

Bessel, R. *Germany after the First World War* (Oxford, 1993).

Bessel, R. (ed.) *Life in the Third Reich* (Oxford, 2001).

Beyerchen, A. 'Rational Means and Irrational Ends. Thoughts on the Technology of Racism in the Third Reich', *Central European History*, 30 (1997), pp. 386–440.

Bezyminsky, L. A. 'Stalins Rede vom 5. Mai 1941 – neu dokumentiert', in G. R. Ueberschär, and L. A. Bezyminsky (eds) *Der deutsche Angriff auf die Sowjetunion 1941* (Darmstadt, 1998).

Biesemann, J. *Das Ermächtigungsgesetz als Grundlage der Gesetzgebung im nationalsozialistischen Staat* (Münster, 1985).

Bilas, I. 'Le KGB et la destruction de l'église catholique ukrainienne', *L'est européen*, 31 (1993), pp. 50–63.

Billington, J. H. *The Face of Russia* (New York, 1998).

Birken, L. *Hitler as Philosophe: Remnants of the Enlightenment in National Socialism* (Westport, Conn., 1995).

Birkenfeld, W. 'Stalin als Wirtschaftsplaner Hitlers', *Vierteljahrshefte für Zeitgeschichte*, 51 (1966), pp. ???

Blakely, A. *Russia and the Negro* (Washington, DC, 1986).

Blank, S. 'Soviet Institutional Development during NEP: A Prelude to Stalin', *Russian History*, 9 (1982), pp. 325–46.

Blasius, D. *Carl Schmitt: Preussischer Staatsrat im Hitlers Reich* (Göttingen, 2001).

Bleuel, P. *Strength through Joy: Sex and Society in Nazi Germany* (London, 1973).

Bloch, M. *Ribbentrop* (London, 1992).

Boas, J. *Boulevard des misères: The Story of Transit Camp Westerbork* (Hamden, Conn., 1985).

Bociorkiw, B. R. 'Religion and Atheism in Soviet Society', in R. H. Marshall *Aspects of Religion in the Soviet Union 1917–1967* (Chicago, 1971).

Bock, G. 'Racism and Sexism in Nazi Germany: Motherhood, Compulsory Sterilization and the State', in R. Bridenthal, A. Grossmann and M. Kaplan (eds) *When Biology became Destiny: Women in Weimar Germany and Nazi Germany* (New York, 1984).

Bonnell, V. *Iconography of Power: Soviet Political Posters under Lenin and Stalin* (Berkeley, Calif., 1997).

Boog, H. *et al. Der Angriff auf die Sowjetunion* (Stuttgart, 1983).

Bordiugov, G. A. 'The Bolsheviks and the National Banner', *Russian Studies in History*, 39 (2000), pp. 79–90.

Bordiugov, G. A. 'The Transformation of the Policy of Extraordinary Measures into a Permanent System of Government', in N. Rosenfeldt, B. Jensen and E. Kulavig (eds) *Mechanisms of Power in the Soviet Union* (London, 2000), pp. 122–44.

Boshyk, Y. (ed.) *Ukraine During World War II: History and its Aftermath* (Edmonton, Alberta, 1986).

Boterbloem, K. *Life and Death under Stalin: Kalinin Province, 1945–1953* (Montreal, 1999).

Bougai, N. *The Deportation of Peoples in the Soviet Union* (New York, 1996).

Bourdeaux, M. *Opium of the People: the Christian Religion in the USSR* (London, 1965).

Bowlt, J. and Drutt, M. (eds) *Amazons of the Avant-Garde* (Royal Academy, London, 1999).

Bracher, K. D. *The German Dictatorship: the Origins, Structure, and Effects of National Socialism* (London, 1971).

Brahm, H. (ed.) *Opposition in der Sowjetunion* (Düsseldorf, 1972).

Brandenberger, D. *National Bolshevism: Stalinist Mass Culture and the Formation of Modern Russian National Identity 1931–1956* (Cambridge, Mass., 2002).

Brandenberger, D. and Dubrovsky, A. ' "The People need a Tsar": the Emergence of National Bolshevism as Stalinist Ideology 1931–1941', *Europe–Asia Studies*, 50 (1998), pp. 873–92.

Brechtefeld, J. *Mitteleuropa and German Politics: 1848 to the Present* (London, 1996).

Brenner, M. *After the Holocaust: Rebuilding Jewish Lives in Postwar Germany* (Princeton, NJ, 1997).

Bridenthal, R., Grossmann, A. and Kaplan, M. (eds) *When Biology became Destiny: Women in Weimar Germany and Nazi Germany* (New York, 1984).

Brooks, J. 'Socialist Realism in *Pravda*: Read All About It!', *Slavic Review*, 53 (1994), pp. 973–91.

Brossat, A. (ed.) *Ozerlag, 1937–1964. Le système du Goulag: traces perdues, mémoires reveilles d'un camp stalinien* (Paris, 1991).

Broszat, M. *Hitler and the Collapse of Weimar Germany* (Leamington Spa, 1987).

Broszat, M. *The Hitler State: the foundation and development of the internal structure of the Third Reich* (London, 1981).

Brotherstone, T. and Dukes, P. (eds) *The Trotsky Reappraisal* (Edinburgh, 1992).

Browder, G. C. *Foundations of the Nazi Police State: the Formation of Sipo and SD* (Lexington, Ky, 1990).

Browning, C. 'Hitler and the Euphoria of Victory: the Path to the Final Solution', in D. Cesarani (ed.) *The Final Solution: Origins and Implementation* (London, 1994), pp. 137–47.

Browning, C. *Ordinary Men: Reserve Police Battalion 101 and the Final Solution* (Cambridge, 1992).

Browning, C. *The Path to Genocide: Essays on Launching the Final Solution* (Cambridge, 1992).

Brumfield, W. C. *A History of Russian Architecture* (Cambridge, 1993).

Brunner, G. *Das Parteistatut der KPdSU 1903–1961* (Cologne, 1965).

Brustein, W. *The Logic of Evil: The Social Origins of the Nazi Party 1925–1933* (New Haven, Conn., 1996).

Buckley, M. *Women and Ideology in the Soviet Union* (New York, 1989).

Bullock, A. *Hitler and Stalin: Parallel Lives* (London, 1991).

Burbank, J. 'Lenin and the Law in Revolutionary Russia', *Slavic Review*, 54 (1995) pp. 23–44.

Burden, H. T. *The Nuremberg Party Rallies: 1923–39* (London, 1967).

Burleigh, M. *Death and Deliverance: 'Euthanasia' in Germany 1900–1945* (Cambridge, 1994).

Burleigh, M. *Ethics and Extermination: Reflections on Nazi Genocide* (Cambridge, 1997).

Burleigh, M. 'National Socialism as a Political Religion', *Totalitarian Movements and Political Religions*, 1 (2000), pp. 1–26.

Burleigh, M. *The Third Reich: a New History* (London, 2000).

Burleigh, M. and Wippermann, W. *The Racial State: Germany 1933–1945* (Cambridge, 1991).

Butler, R. *An Illustrated History of the Gestapo* (London, 1992).

Butler, W. E. *Soviet Law* (2nd edn, London, 1988).

Campbell, B. *The SA Generals and the Rise of Nazism* (Lexington, Ky, 1998).

Caplan, J. 'National Socialism and the Theory of the State', in T. Childers, and J. Caplan (eds) *Reevaluating the Third Reich* (New York, 1993), pp. 98–113.

Carlebach, E. *Tote auf Urlaub: Kommunist in Deutschland, Dachau und Buchenwald 1937–1945* (Bonn, 1995).

Caroe, O. *Soviet Empire: the Turks of Central Asia and Stalinism* (London, 1967).

Carsten, F. L. *The German Workers and the Nazis* (Aldershot, 1995).

Cary, N. D. 'Antisemitism, Everyday Life, and the Devastation of Public Morals in Nazi Germany', *Central European History*, 55 (2002), pp. 551–89.

Cassinelli, C. W. *Total Revolution: A Comparative Study of Germany under Hitler, the Soviet Union under Stalin and China under Mao* (Santa Barbara, Calif., 1976).

Chapman, J. G. *Real Wages in Soviet Russia since 1928* (Cambridge, Mass., 1963).

Chegodneva, M. 'Mass Culture and Socialist Realism', *Russian Studies in History*, 42 (2003), pp. 49–65.

Chichlo, B. 'Histoire de la formation des territoires autonomes chez les peoples turco-mongols de sibérie', *Cahiers du monde russe*, 28 (1987), pp. 361–402.

Chor'kov, A. G. 'The Red Army during the Initial Phase of the Great Patriotic War', in B. Wegner (ed.) *From Peace to War: Germany, Soviet Russia and the World 1939–1941* (Providence, RI, 1997).

Ciszek, W. and Flaherty, D. *With God in Russia* (London, 1964).

Clark, K. 'Engineers of Human Souls in an Age of Industrialization: Changing Cultural Models, 1929–31', in W. Rosenberg and L. Siegelbaum (eds) *Social Dimensions of Soviet Industrialization* (Bloomington, Ind., 1993).

Clark, K. *The Soviet Novel: History as Ritual* (3rd edn, Bloomington, Ind., 2000).

Clark, K. 'Utopian Anthropology as a Context for Stalinist Literature', in R. Tucker (ed.) *Stalinism: Essays in Historical Interpretation* (New York, 1977).

Clemens, W. C. 'The Burden of Defense: Soviet Russia in the 1920s', *Journal of Slavic Military Studies*, 9 (1996), pp. 786–99.

Cohen, A. (ed.) *The Shoah and the War* (New York, 1992).

Cohen, S. F. *Bukharin and the Bolshevik Revolution: a Political Biography 1888–1938* (New York, 1980).

Cohen, S. F. *Rethinking the Soviet Experience: Politics and History after 1917* (Oxford, 1985).

Colton, T. J. *Moscow: Governing the Socialist Metropolis* (Cambridge, Mass., 1995).

Connelly, J. 'Nazis and Slavs: From Racial Theory to Racist Practice', *Central European History*, 32 (1999), pp. 1–34.

Connelly, J. 'The Uses of Volksgemeinschaft: Letters to NSDAP Kreisleitung

Eisenach, 1939–1940', *Journal of Modern History*, 68 (1996), pp. 899–930.

Conquest, R. (ed.) *Justice and the Legal System in the USSR* (London, 1968).

Conquest, R. *The Great Terror* (London, 1971).

Conquest, R. *Stalin: Breaker of Nations* (London, 1991).

Conquest, R. *Stalin and the Kirov Murder* (London, 1989).

Constantini, A. *L'union soviétique en guerre 1941–1945* (Paris, 1968).

Conway, J. *The Nazi Persecution of the Churches* (London, 1968).

Cooper, J., Perrie, M. and Rees, E. A. (eds) *Soviet History 1917–1953: Essays in Honour of R. W. Davies* (London, 1995).

Cooper, M. *The Phantom War: The German Struggle Against Soviet Partisans* (London, 1979).

Cornwell, J. *Hitler's Scientists: Science, War and the Devil's Pact* (London, 2003).

Crew, D. (ed.) *Nazism and German Society 1933–1945* (London, 1994).

Cristi, R. *Carl Schmitt and authoritarian liberalism* (Cardiff, 1998).

Crome, L. *Unbroken: Resistance and Survival in the Concentration Camps* (London, 1988).

Curtiss, J. S. *The Russian Church and the Soviet State* (Gloucester, Mass., 1965).

Dahlmann, D. and Hirschfeld, G. (eds) *Lager, Zwangsarbeit, Vertreibung und Deportation* (Essen, 1999).

Dallin, A. *German Rule in Russia 1941–1945* (2nd edn, London, 1981).

Daniels, R. V. *The Conscience of the Revolution: Communist Opposition in Soviet Russia* (Cambridge, Mass., 1960).

Daniels, R. V. *Trotsky, Stalin and Socialism* (Boulder, Colo., 1991).

Daniels, R. V. 'Trotsky's conception of the revolutionary process', in T. Brotherstone and P. Dukes (eds) *The Trotsky Reappraisal* (Edinburgh, 1992), pp. 145–55.

Dann, O. *Nation und Nationalismus in Deutschland 1770–1990* (Munich, 1993).

David-Fox, M. 'Memory, Archives, Politics: The Rise of Stalin in Avtorkhanov's *Technology of Power*', *Slavic Review*, 54 (1995), pp. 988–1003.

David-Fox, M. *Revolution of the Mind: Higher Learning among the Bolsheviks 1918–1929* (Ithaca, NY, 1997).

David-Fox, M. and Hoffmann, D. 'The Politburo Protocols, 1919–40', *Russian Review*, 55 (1996), pp. 99–103.

Davies, R. W. (ed.) *From Tsarism to the New Economic Policy* (Ithaca, NY, 1991).

Davies, R. W. 'The Socialist Market: A Debate in Soviet Industry 1932–1933', *Slavic Studies*, 43 (1984), pp. 201–23.

Davies, R. W. *Soviet Economic Development from Lenin to Khrushchev* (Cambridge, 1998).

Davies, R. W. 'Soviet Military Expenditure and the Armaments Industry 1929–1933', *Europe–Asia Studies*, 45 (1993), pp. 577–608.

Davies, R. W. and Harrison, M. 'Defence spending and defence industry in the 1930s', in J. Barber and M. Harrison *Soviet Defence-Industry Complex from Stalin to Khrushchev* (London, 2000), pp. 70–95.

Davies, R. W., Harrison, M. and Wheatcroft, S. G. *The Economic Transformation of the Soviet Union 1913–1945* (Cambridge, 1994).

Davies, S. *Popular Opinion in Stalin's Russia: Terror, Propaganda and Dissent, 1934–1941* (Cambridge, 1997).

Day, R. B. *The 'Crisis' and the 'Crash': Soviet Studies of the West 1917–1939* (Ithaca, NY, 1984).

Dean, M. *Collaboration in the Holocaust: Crimes of the Local Police in Belorussia and Ukraine, 1941–44* (London, 2000).

Dean, M. 'The Development and Implementation of Nazi Denaturalization and Confiscation Policy up to the Eleventh Decree of the Reich Citizenship Law', *Holocaust and Genocide Studies*, 16 (2002), pp. 217–42.

Degras, J. and Nove, A. (eds) *Soviet Planning: Essays in Honour of Naum Jasny* (Oxford, 1964).

Deist, W. (ed.) *The German Military in the Age of Total War* (Oxford, 1985).

Deist, W. *The Wehrmacht and German Rearmanent* (London, 1981).

Deist, W. *et al. Das Deutsche Reich und der Zweite Weltkrieg: Band I* (Stuttgart, 1979).

D'Encausse, H. C. *The Great Challenge: Nationalities and the Bolshevik State 1917–1930* (New York, 1992).

Depretto, J.-P. *Les Ouvriers en U.R.S.S. 1928–1941* (Paris, 1997).

Depretto, J.-P. 'L'opinion ouvrière (1928–1932)', *Revue des Études Slaves*, 66 (1994), pp. 55–60.

Deutscher, I. *Stalin: a Political Biography* (London, 1966).

Dewhirst, M. and Farrell, R. *The Soviet Censorship* (New York, 1973).

Diewald-Kerkmann, G. 'Denunziantentum und Gestapo. Die freiwilligen 'Helfer' aus der Bevölkerung', in G. Paul and K.-M. Mallmann (eds) *Die Gestapo: Mythos und Realität* (Darmstadt, 1995).

Die Weisse Rose. Student Resistance to National Socialism 1942/1943: Forschungsergebnisse und Erfahrungsberichte (Nottingham, 1991).

Dlugoborski, W. 'Das Problem des Vergleichs von Nationalsozialismus und

Stalinismus', in D. Dahlmann and G. Hirschfeld (eds) *Lager, Zwangsarbeit, Vertreibung und Deportation* (Essen, 1999) pp. 19–28.

Dohan, M. R. 'The Economic Origins of Soviet Autarky 1927/28–1934', *Slavic Review*, 35 (1976), pp. 603–35.

Dörner, B. *'Heimtücke': Das Gesetz als Waffe: Kontrolle, Abschreckung und Verfolgung in Deutschland 1933–1945* (Paderborn, 1998).

Dove, R. and Lamb, S. (eds) *German Writers and Politics 1918–39* (London, 1992).

Dreier, R. and Sellert, W. *Recht und Justiz im 'Dritten Reich'* (Frankfurt am Main, 1989).

Drobisch, K. and Wieland, G. *System der NS-Konzentrationslager 1933–1939* (Berlin, 1993).

Droste, M. *Bauhaus 1919–1933* (Cologne, 1998).

Dunin-Wasowicz, K. *Resistance in the Concentration Camps* (Warsaw, 1982).

Dunmore, T. *The Stalinist Command Economy: the Soviet State Apparatus and Economic Policy 1945–1953* (London, 1980).

Dunn, W. S. *Hitler's Nemesis: the Red Army, 1930–1945* (Westport, Conn., 1994).

Dunn, W. S. *The Soviet Economy and the Red Army 1930–1945* (London, 1995).

Durgan, A. 'Trotsky, the POUM and the Spanish Revolution', *Journal of Trotsky Studies*, 2 (1994), pp. 43–74.

Dwork, D. and Pelt, R. J. van *Auschwitz: 1270 to the Present* (New York, 1996).

Dyakov, Y. and Bushuyeva, T. *The Red Army and the Wehrmacht: How the Soviets Militarized Germany 1922–1933* (New York, 1995).

Eaton, K. B. (ed.) *Enemies of the People: The Destruction of Soviet Literary, Theater, and Film Arts in the 1930s* (Evanston, Ill., 2002).

Eaton, R. *Ideal Cities: Utopianism and the (Un) Built Environment* (London, 2001).

Echevarria, A. J. *After Clausewitz: German Military Thinkers before the Great War* (Lawrence, Kans., 2000).

Edele, M. 'Strange Young Men in Stalin's Moscow', *Jahrbücher für Geschichte Osteuropas*, 50 (2002), pp. 22–36.

Edmondson, L. and Waldron, P. (eds) *Economy and Society in Russia and the Soviet Union 1860–1930: Essays for Olga Crisp* (London, 1992).

Elleinstein, J. *Staline* (Paris, 1984).

Ellman, M. 'The Soviet 1937 Provincial Show Trials: Carnival or Terror?', *Europe–Asia Studies*, 53 (2001), pp. 1221–34.

Elon, A. *The Pity of it All: A Portrait of Jews in Germany 1743–1933* (London, 2002).

El-Tayeb, F. ' "Blood is a very special Juice": Racialized Bodies and Citizenship in Twentieth-Century Germany', *International Review of Social History*, 44 (1999), pp. 149–69.

Engerman, D. C. 'William Henry Chamberlin and Russia's Revolt Against Western Civilization', *Russian History*, 26 (1999), pp. 45–64.

Erickson, J. (ed.) *Barbarossa: the Axis and the Allies* (Edinburgh, 1994).

Erickson, J. 'Red Army Battlefield Performance, 1941–1945; the System and the Soldier', in P. Addison and A. Calder (eds) *Time to Kill: The Soldier's Experience of War in the West 1939–1945* (London, 1997).

Erickson, J. *The Road to Berlin: Stalin's War with Germany* (London, 1983).

Erickson, J. *The Road to Stalingrad* (London, 1975).

Erickson, J. *The Soviet High Command: a Military-Political History 1918–1941* (London, 1962).

Erickson, J. 'Soviet Women at War', in J. Garrard and C. Garrard (eds) *World War 2 and the Soviet People* (London, 1993), pp. 50–76.

Ericson, E. E. *Feeding the German Eagle: Soviet Economic Aid to Nazi Germany, 1933–1941* (Westport, Conn., 1999).

Erlich, V. *Russian Formalism. History-Doctrine* (3rd edn, New Haven, Conn., 1981).

Ermolaev, H. *Censorship in Soviet Literature* (Lanham, Md., 1997).

Ermolaev, H. *Soviet Literary Theories 1917–1934: the Genesis of Socialist Realism* (New York, 1977).

Fainsod, M. *How Russia Is Ruled* (Cambridge, Mass., 1967).

Fainsod, M. *Smolensk under Soviet Rule* (Boston, Mass., 1989).

Falter, J. and Kater, M. H. 'Wähler und Mitglieder der NSDAP', *Geschichte und Gesellschaft*, 19 (1993), pp. 155–77.

Farber, S. *Before Stalinism: The Rise and Fall of Soviet Democracy* (Cambridge, 1990).

Feinstein, M. M. 'Deutschland über alles? The National Anthem Debate in the Federal Republic of Germany', *Central European History*, 33 (2000), pp. 505–31.

Felshtinsky, Y. 'Lenin, Trotsky, Stalin and the Left Opposition in the USSR 1918–1928', *Cahiers du monde russe*, 31 (1990), pp. 569–78.

Fenander, S. 'Author and Autocrat: Tertz's Stalin and the Ruse of Charisma', *Russian Review*, 58 (1999), pp. 286–97.

Fenner, J. *Le Goulag des Tsars* (Paris, 1986).

Fenske, H. *Bürokratie in Deutschland von späten Kaiserreich bis zur Gegenwart* (Berlin, 1985).

Fieberg, G. *Justiz im nationalsozialistischen Deutschland* (Bundesministerium der Justiz, Cologne, 1984).

Figes, O. *A People's Tragedy: the Russian Revolution 1891–1924* (London, 1996).

Figes, O. *Natasha's Dance: a Cultural History of Russia* (London, 2002).

Figes, O. and Kolonitskii, B. *Interpreting the Russian Revolution: the Language and Symbols of 1917* (New Haven, Conn., 1999).

Filtzer, D. *Soviet Workers and Stalinist Industrialization* (London, 1986).

Filtzer, D. 'Stalinism and the Working Class in the 1930s', in J. Channon *Politics, Society and Stalinism in the USSR* (London, 1998), pp. 163–84.

Filtzer, D. 'The Standard of Living of Soviet Industrial Workers in the Immediate Postwar Period, 1945–1948', *Europe–Asia Studies*, 51 (1999), pp. 1013–38.

Fischer, C. *The Rise of the Nazis* (Manchester, 2002).

Fischer, C. *Stormtroopers: a Social, Economic and Ideological Analysis 1929–1935* (London, 1983).

Fitzpatrick, S. 'Ascribing Class: The Construction of Social Identity in Soviet Russia', *Journal of Modern History*, 65 (1993), pp. 745–70.

Fitzpatrick, S. *The Cultural Front: Power and Culture in Revolutionary Russia* (Ithaca, NY, 1992).

Fitzpatrick, S. *Everyday Stalinism. Ordinary Life in Extraordinary Times: Soviet Russia in the 1930s* (Oxford, 1999).

Fitzpatrick, S. 'How the Mice Buried the Cat: scenes from the Great Purges of 1937 in the Russian Provinces', *Russian Review*, 52 (1993), pp. 299–320.

Fitzpatrick, S. 'Ordzhonokidze's Takeover of Vesenkha: a Case Study in Soviet Bureaucratic Politics', *Soviet Studies*, 37 (1985), pp. 153–72.

Fitzpatrick, S. *The Russian Revolution* (Oxford, 1994).

Fitzpatrick, S. 'Signals from Below: Soviet Letters of Denunciation of the 1930s', *Journal of Modern History*, 68 (1996), pp. 831–66.

Fitzpatrick, S. 'Stalin and the Making of a New Elite, 1928–1939', *Slavic Review*, 38 (1979), pp. 377–402.

Fleischauer, I. and Pinkus, B. *The Soviet Germans: Past and Present* (London, 1986).

Fleming, G. *Hitler and the Final Solution* (London, 1985).

Flores, M. and Gori, F. (eds) *GULag: il sistema dei lager in URSS* (Milan, 1999).

Förster, J. 'Hitler Turns East – German War Policy in 1940 and 1941', in B. Wegner (ed.) *From Peace to War: Germany, Soviet Russia and the World 1939–1941* (Providence, RI, 1997), pp. 115–34.

Förster, J. 'Ludendorff and Hitler in Perspective: The Battle for the German Soldier's Mind, 1917–1944', *War in History*, 10 (2003), pp. 321–34.

Förster, J. 'The Relation between Operation Barbarossa as an Ideological War of Extermination and the Final Solution', in D. Cesarani (ed.) *The Final Solution: Origins and Implementation* (London, 1994), pp. 85–102.

Förster, J. and Mawdsley, E. 'Hitler and Stalin: Secret Speeches on the Eve of Barbarossa', *War in History*, 11 (2004), pp. 61–103.

Frei, N. *National Socialist Rule in Germany: the Führer State 1933–1945* (Oxford, 1993).

Frei, N., Steinbacher, S. and Wagner, B. (eds) *Ausbeutung, Vernichtung, Öffentlichkeit: neue Studien zur nationalsozialistischen Lagerpolitik* (Munich, 2000).

Freifeld, A. 'Nietzscheanism and Anti-Nietzscheanism in East Europe', in A. Freifeld, P. Bergmann and B. C. Rosenthal (eds) *East Europe Reads Nietzsche* (New York, 1998) pp. 1–19.

Friefeld, A., Bergmann, P. and Rosenthal, B. G. (eds) *East Europe reads Nietzsche* (New York, 1998)

Frevert, U. *Women in German History* (Oxford, 1989).

Friedlander, H. *The Origins of Nazi Genocide: From Euthanasia to the Final Solution* (Chapel Hill, NC, 1995).

Friedländer, S. *Nazi Germany and the Jews: The Years of Persecution 1933–1939* (London, 1997).

Fröhlich, E. 'Die kulturpolitische Pressekonferenz des Reichspropagandaministeriums', *Vierteljahrshefte für Zeitgeschichte*, 22 (1974), pp. 347–81.

Füllberg-Stolberg, C., Jung, M., Riebe, R. and Scheitenberger, M. (eds) *Frauen in Konzentrationslagern Bergen-Belsen, Ravensbrück* (Bremen, 1994).

Garrard, J. and Garrard, C. *Inside the Soviet Writers' Union* (London, 1990).

Garrard, J. and Garrard, C. (eds) *World War 2 and the Soviet People* (London, 1993).

Gasman, D. *The Scientific Origins of National Socialism* (London, 1971).

Gay, P. *Weimar Culture* (London, 1968).

Geifman, A. *Thou Shalt Kill: Revolutionary Terrorism in Russia, 1894–1917* (Princeton, NJ, 1993).

Geiger, H. K. *The Family in Soviet Russia* (Cambridge, Mass., 1968).

Gellately, R. *Backing Hitler: Consent and Coercion in Nazi Germany* (Oxford, 2001).

Gellately, R. *The Gestapo and German Society: Enforcing Racial Policy 1933–1945* (Oxford, 1990).

Gellately, R. and Stoltzfus, M. (eds) *Social Outsiders in Nazi Germany* (Princeton, NJ, 2001).

Gentile, E. 'The Sacrilisation of Politics: Definitions, Interpretations and Reflections on the Question of Secular Religion and Totalitarianism',

Totalitarian Movements and Political Religions, 1 (2000), pp. 18–55.

Gerlach, C. 'The Wannsee Conference, the Fate of the German Jews, and Hitler's Decision in Principle to Exterminate All European Jews', *Journal of Modern History*, 70 (1998), pp. 759–812.

Getty, J. A. *The Origin of the Great Purges: The Soviet Communist Party Reconsidered 1933–1938* (Cambridge, 1985).

Getty, J. A. 'Samokritika Rituals in the Stalinist Central Committee, 1933–38', *Russian Review*, 58 (1999), pp. 49–70.

Getty, J. A. and Manning, R. (eds) *Stalinist Terror: New Perspectives* (Cambridge, 1993).

Getty, J. A., Rittersporn, G. T. and Zemskov, V. N. 'Victims of the Soviet Penal System in the Pre-War Years: A First Approach on the Basis of Archival Evidence', *American Historical Review*, 98 (1993), pp. 1017–47.

Gill, G. *The Origins of the Stalinist Political System* (London, 1990).

Gill, G. *The Rules of the Communist Party of the Soviet Union* (London, 1988).

Gill, G. *Stalinism* (2nd edn, London, 1998).

Gispen, K. 'Visions of Utopia: Social Emancipation, Technological Progress and Anticapitalism in Nazi Inventor Policy 1933–1945', *Central European History*, 32 (1999), pp. 35–51.

Gladkov, A. *Meetings with Pasternak* (London, 1977).

Glantz, D. M. *Before Stalingrad: Barbarossa – Hitler's Invasion of Russia 1941* (Stroud, 2003).

Glantz, D. M. *Soviet Operational Art: in Pursuit of Deep Battle* (London, 1991).

Glantz, D. M. *Stumbling Colossus: The Red Army on the Eve of World War* (Lawrence, Kans., 1998).

Glantz, D. M. and House, J. *When Titans Clashed: How the Red Army Stopped Hitler* (Lawrence, Kans., 1995).

Gooding, J. *Rulers and Subjects: Government and People in Russia 1801–1991* (London, 1996).

Gorlizki, Y. 'Party Revivalism and the Death of Stalin', *Slavic Review*, 54 (1995), pp. 1–22.

Gorlizki, Y. 'Rules, Incentives and Soviet Campaign Justice after World War II', *Europe–Asia Studies*, 51 (1999), pp. 1245–65.

Gorodetsky, G. *Grand Delusion: Stalin and the German Invasion of Russia* (New Haven, Conn., 1999).

Gorsuch, A. E. ' "NEP Be Damned". Young Militants in the 1920s and the Culture of Civil War', *Russian Review*, 56 (1997), pp. 564–80.

Gossweiler, K. *Die Strasser-Legende* (Berlin, 1994).

Gottfried, P. *Thinkers of Our Time: Carl Schmitt* (London, 1990).

Goure, L. *The Siege of Leningrad* (Stanford, 1962).

Graham, L. R. *Science, Philosophy and Human Behaviour in the Soviet Union* (New York, 1987).

Graml, H. (ed.) *Widerstand im Dritten Reich: Probleme, Ereignisse, Gestalten* (Frankfurt am Main, 1994).

Grau, G. (ed.) *Hidden Holocaust? Gay and Lesbian Persecution in Germany 1933–1945* (London, 1995).

Graziosi, A. *A New, Peculiar State: Explorations in Soviet History 1917–1937* (Westport, Conn., 2000).

Great Patriotic War of the Soviet Union 1941–1945 (Moscow, 1970).

Gregory, P. R. *Before Command: an Economic History of Russia from Emancipation to the First Five-Year Plan* (Princeton, NJ, 1994).

Gregory, P. R. (ed.) *Behind the Façade of Stalin's Command Economy* (Stanford, 2001).

Grekhov, V. N. 'Massacre of the Komsomol Leaders in 1937–38', *Voprosii Istorii*, 11 (1990), pp. 136–45.

Grenkevich, L. *The Soviet Partisan Movement 1941–1944* (London, 1999).

Grill, J. H. *The Nazi Movement in Baden 1920–1945* (Chapel Hill, NC, 1983).

Gritschner, O. *Der Hitler-Prozess und sein Richter Georg Neithardt* (Munich, 2001).

Gronov, E. S. *Stalin: vlast' iskussvo* (Moscow, 1998).

Gross, J. *Revolution from Abroad: the Soviet Conquest of Poland's Western Ukraine and Western Belorussia* (Princeton, NJ, 1988).

Grunwald, C. de *God and the Soviets* (London, 1961).

Guerin, D. *Fascism and Big Business* (New York, 1973).

Günther, H. (ed.) *The Culture of the Stalin Period* (London, 1990).

Günther, H. *Walter Benjamin und der humane Marxismus* (Freiburg im Breisgau, 1974).

Gutkin, I. 'The Magic of Words: Symbolism, Futurism, Socialist Realism', in B. G. Rosenthal *The Occult in Russian and Soviet Culture* (Ithaca, NY, 1997), pp. 225–46.

Gutman, Y. and Berenbaum, M. (eds) *Anatomy of the Auschwitz Death Camp* (Bloomington, Ind., 1994).

Hachtmann, R. *Industriearbeit im 'Dritten Reich'* (Göttingen, 1989).

Hachtmann, R. 'Industriearbeiterinnen in der deutschen Kriegswirtschaft 1936–1945', *Geschichte und Gesellschaft*, 19 (1993), pp. 322–66.

Hackett, D. A. (ed.) *The Buchenwald Report* (Boulder, Colo., 1995).

Hagen, M. von *Soldiers in the Proletarian Dictatorship: the Red Army and the Soviet Socialist State 1917–1930* (Ithaca, NY, 1990).

Hagendoorn, L., Csepeli, G., Dekker, H. and Farnen, R. (eds) *European Nations and Nationalism: Theoretical and historical perspectives* (Aldershot, 2000).

Hahn, W. *Postwar Soviet Politics: the Fall of Zhdanov and the Defeat of Moderation 1946–1953* (Ithaca, NY, 1982).

Hake, S. *Popular Cinema of the Third Reich* (Austin, Tex., 2001).

Halfin, I. *From Darkness to Light: Class Consciousness and Salvation in Revolutionary Russia* (Pittsburgh, 2000).

Halfin, I. 'Poetics in the Archives: the Quest for "True" Bolshevik Documents', *Jahrbücher für die Geschichte Osteuropas*, 51 (2003), pp. 84–9.

Hamburger Stiftung zur Förderung von Wissenschaft und Kultur (ed.) *'Deutsche Wirtschaft': Zwangsarbeit von KZ-Häftlingen für Industrie und Behörden* (Hamburg, 1991).

Hamerow, T. S. *On the Road to the Wolf's Lair: German Resistance to Hitler* (Cambridge, Mass., 1997).

Hancock, E. *National Socialist Leadership and Total War 1941–1945* (New York, 1991).

Hanser, R. *Prelude to Terror: The Rise of Hitler 1919–1923* (London, 1970).

Harasymiw, B. *Soviet Communist Party Officials: A study in organizational roles and change* (New York, 1996).

Hardesty, V. *Red Phoenix: the Rise of Soviet Air Power* (London, 1982).

Harrison, M. *Accounting for War: Soviet production, employment and the defence burden 1940–1945* (Cambridge, 1996).

Harrison, M. 'Counting Soviet Deaths in the Great Patriotic War: a Comment', *Europe–Asia Studies*, 55 (2003), pp. 939–44.

Harrison, M. (ed.) *The Economics of World War II: Six great powers in international comparison* (Cambridge, 1998).

Harrison, M. 'Soviet National Accounting for World War II: an Inside View', in J. Cooper, M. Perrie and E. A. Rees (eds) *Soviet History 1917–1953: Essays in Honour of R. W. Davies* (London, 1995), pp. 219–42.

Harrison, M. *Soviet Planning in Peace and War 1938–1945* (Cambridge, 1985).

Harrison, M. and Davies, R. W. 'The Soviet Military-Economic Effort during the Second Five-Year Plan', *Europe–Asia Studies*, 49 (1997), pp. 369–406.

Hartmann, C. *Halder Generalstabschef Hitlers 1938–1942* (Paderborn, 1991).

Hartmann, C. 'Massensterben oder Massenvernichtung? Sowjetische Kriegsgefangene im "Unternehmen Barbarossa"', *Vierteljahrshefte für Zeitgeschichte*, 49 (2001), pp. 97–158.

Haslam, J. 'Political Opposition to Stalin and the Origins of the Terror in Russia, 1932–1936', *The Historical Journal*, 29 (1986), pp. 395–418.

Häufele, G. 'Zwangsumsiedlung in Polen 1939–1941: zum Vergleich sowjetischer und deutscher Besatzungspolitik', in D. Dahlmann and G. Hirschfeld (eds) *Lager, Zwangsarbeit, Vertreibung und Deportation* (Essen, 1999), pp. 515–34.

Haynes, J. *New Soviet Man: Gender and Masculinity in Stalinist Soviet Cinema* (Manchester, 2003).

Hayward, M. *Writers in Russia 1917–1978* (London, 1983).

Hayward, M. and Labedz, L. (eds) *Literature and Revolution in Soviet Russia 1917–1962* (Oxford, 1963).

Hazard, J. N., Shapiro, I. and Maggs, P. B. (eds) *The Soviet Legal System* (New York, 1969).

Heer, H. *Tote Zonen: Die deutsche Wehrmacht an der Ostfront* (Hamburg, 1999).

Heer, H. and Naumann, K. *War of Extermination: The German Military in World War II 1941–1944* (Oxford, 2000).

Heiden, D. and Mai, G. (eds) *Nationalsozialismus in Thüringen* (Weimar, 1995).

Heilbronner, O. 'From Antisemitic Peripheries to Antisemitic Centres: The Place of Antisemitism in Modern German History', *Journal of Contemporary History*, 35 (2000), pp. 559–76.

Hein, D. 'Partei und Bewegung: Zwei Typen moderner politischer Willensbildung', *Historische Zeitschrift*, 263 (1996), pp. 69–98.

Heinemann, I. *'Rasse, Siedlung, deutsches Blut': Das Rasse-& Siedlungshauptamt der SS und die rassenpolitische Neuordnung Europas* (Göttingen, 2003).

Heinsohn, K., Vogel, B. and Weckel, U. (eds) *Zwischen Karriere und Verfolgung: Handlungsräume von Frauen im ns-en Deutschland* (Frankfurt am Main, 1997).

Hellbeck, J. 'Working, Struggling, Becoming: Stalin Era Autobiographical Texts', *Russian Review*, 60 (2001), pp. 340–59.

Heller, L. 'Le réalisme socialiste comme organisation du champ culturel', *Cahiers du monde russe*, 33 (1992), pp. 307–44.

Heller, L. 'Nécro-, retro-, ou post? Modernismes, modernité et réalisme socialiste', *Cahiers du monde russe*, 33 (1992), pp. 5–22.

Heller, M. *Cogs in the Soviet Wheel: the Formation of Soviet Man* (London, 1988).

Heller, M. and Nekrich, A. *Utopia in Power: The History of the Soviet Union from 1917 to the Present* (London, 1982).

Herb, G. and Kaplan, D. (eds) *Nested Identities: Nationalism, Territory and Scale* (Lanham, Md, 1999).

678

Herb, G. H. *Under the Map of Germany: Nationalism and Propaganda 1918–1945* (London, 1997).

Herbert, U. *Best: Biographische Studien über Radikalismus, Weltanschauung und Vernunft 1903–1989* (Bonn, 1996).

Herbert, U. *Fremdarbeiter: Politik und Praxis des 'Ausländer-Einsatzes' in der Kriegswirtschaft des Dritten Reiches* (Berlin, 1985).

Herbert, U. *National Socialist Extermination Policies: Contemporary German Perspectives and Controversies* (Oxford, 2000).

Herf, J. *Reactionary Modernism: Technology, Culture, and Politics in Weimar and the Third Reich* (Cambridge, 1984).

Hermand, J. *Der alte Traum vom neuen Reich. völkische Utopien und Nationalsozialismus* (Frankfurt am Main, 1988).

Hermann, U. and Nassen, U. (eds) *Formative Ästhetik in Nationalsozialismus. Intentionen, Medien und Praxisformen totalitärer ästhetischer Herrschaft und Beherrschung* (Weinheim, 1994).

Herzstein, R. *When Nazi Dreams Come True* (London, 1982).

Hesse, E. *Der sowjetrussische Partisanenkrieg 1941 bis 1944* (Göttingen, 1969).

Hessler, J. 'Postwar Normalisation and its Limits in the USSR: the Case of Trade', *Europe–Asia Studies*, 53 (2001), pp. 445–71.

Higham, R. and Kagan, F. W. (eds) *The Military History of the Soviet Union* (New York, 2002).

Hildermeier, M. *Geschichte der Sowjetunion 1917–1991* (Munich, 1998).

Hill, R. and Frank, P. *The Soviet Communist Party* (London, 1983).

Hingley, R. *Russian Writers and Soviet Society 1917–1978* (London, 1979).

Hirsch, F. 'Race without the Practice of Racial Politics', *Slavic Review*, 61 (2002), pp. 30–43.

Hirschfeld, G. *The Politics of Genocide: Jews and Soviet POWs in Nazi Germany* (London, 1988).

Hirschfeld, G. and Kettenacker, L. (eds) *Der 'Führerstaat': Mythos und Realität* (Stuttgart, 1981).

Hoffmann, D. L. *Stalinist Values: the Cultural Norms of Soviet Modernity 1917–1941* (Ithaca, NY, 2003).

Hoffmann, D. L. and Kotsonis, Y. (eds) *Russian Modernity: Politics, Knowledge and Practices* (London, 2000).

Hoffmann, J. *Die Geschichte der Wlassow-Armee* (Freiburg im Breisgau, 1984).

Hoffmann, J. *Stalins Vernichtungskrieg 1941–1945* (Munich, 1995).

Höhne, H. *The Order of the Death's Head: the Story of Hitler's SS* (New York, 1969).

Hollander, G. D. *Soviet Political Indoctrination: Developments in Mass Media and Propaganda since Stalin* (New York, 1972).

Holloway, D. *Stalin and the Bomb: The Soviet Union and Atomic Energy* (New Haven, Conn., 1994).

Hooton, E. *Phoenix Triumphant: the Rise and Rise of the Luftwaffe* (London, 1994).

Hopkins, M. W. *Mass Media in the Soviet Union* (New York, 1970).

Hosking, G. *A History of the Soviet Union* (London, 1985).

Hosking, G. 'The Second World War and Russian National Consciousness', *Past & Present*, 175 (2002), pp. 162–87.

Hosking, G. and Service, R. (eds) *Russian Nationalism Past and Present* (London, 1998).

Hubbard, W. B. *'Godless Communists': Atheism and Society in Soviet Russia 1917–1932* (DeKalb, Ill., 2000).

Hubert, P. *Uniformierte Reichstag: Die Geschichte der Pseudo-Volksvertretung 1933–1945* (Düsseldorf, 1992).

Hughes, J. 'Re-evaluating Stalin's Peasant Policy in 1928–30', in J. Pallot (ed.) *Transforming Peasants: Society, State and the Peasantry 1861–1930* (London, 1998), pp. 238–57.

Hughes, J. *Stalin, Siberia and the crisis of the New Economic Policy* (Cambridge, 1991).

Husband, W. B. 'Soviet Atheism and Russian Orthodox Strategies of Resistance 1917–1932', *Journal of Modern History*, 70 (1998), pp. 74–107.

Ilic, M. 'The Great Terror in Leningrad: a Quantitative Analysis', *Europe-–Asia Studies*, 52 (2000), pp. 1515–34.

Ilic, M. *Women Workers in the Soviet Interwar Economy* (London, 1999).

Ivanov, M. 'The Conditions of Russian Labour in the 1920s–early 1930s', *Voprosii Istorii*, 5 (1998), pp. 28–44.

Jäckel, E. *Hitler's World View: a Blueprint for Power* (Middleton, Conn., 1981).

Jahn, E. 'Zum Problem der Vergleichbarkeit von Massenverfolgung und Massenvernichtung', in D. Dahlmann and G. Hirschfeld (eds) *Lager, Zwangsarbeit, Vertreibung und Deportation* (Essen, 1999), pp. 29–51.

Jakobsen, M. *Origins of the Gulag: the Soviet Prison Camp System 1917–1934* (London, 1993).

James, H. *The Deutsche Bank and the Nazi Economic War against the Jews* (Cambridge, 2001).

James, H. *The German Slump: Politics and Economics, 1924–1936* (Oxford, 1986).

Jasny, N. *Soviet Economists of the Twenties* (Cambridge, 1972).

Jersak, T. 'Die Interaktion von Kriegsverlauf und Judenvernichtung: ein Blick auf Hitlers Strategie im Spätsommer 1941', *Historische Zeitschrift*, 268 (1999), pp. 311–74.

Joachimsthaler, A. *Korrektur einer Biographie. Adolf Hitler 1908–1920* (Munich, 1989).

Johnson, E. A. *Nazi Terror: The Gestapo, Jews and Ordinary Germans* (New York, 1999).

Kagan, F. 'The Evacuation of Soviet Industry in the Wake of Barbarossa: a Key to Soviet Victory', *Journal of Slavic Military Studies*, 8 (1995), pp. 387–414.

Kaienburg, H. (ed.) *Konzentrationslager und deutsche Wirtschaft 1939–1945* (Opladen, 1996).

Kaienberg, H. *'Vernichtung durch Arbeit': Der Fall Neuengamme* (Bonn, 1990).

Kallis, A. A. 'To Expand or not to Expand? Territory, Generic Fascism and the Quest for an "Ideal Fatherland" ', *Journal of Contemporary History*, 38 (2003), pp. 237–60.

Kaminsky, U. *Zwangssterilisation und 'Euthanasie' im Rheinland* (Cologne, 1995).

Kane, M. *Weimar Germany and the Limits of Political Art: a Study of the Work of George Grosz and Ernst Toller* (Fife, 1987).

Karay, F. *Death Comes in Yellow: Skarzysko-Kamienna Slave Labor Camp* (Amsterdam, 1996).

Karner, S. *Im Archipel GUPVI: Kriegsgefangenschaft und Internierung in der Sowjetunion 1941–1956* (Vienna, 1995).

Kater, M. 'Forbidden Fruit? Jazz in the Third Reich', *American Historical Review*, 94 (1989), pp. 11–43.

Kater, M. *The Nazi Party: A Social Profile of Members and Leaders, 1919– 1945* (Oxford, 1983).

Katsenelinbolgen, A. *Soviet Economic Thought and Political Power in the USSR* (New York, 1980).

Kelly, A. *The Descent of Darwin. The Popularization of Darwinism in Germany, 1860–1914* (Chapel Hill, NC, 1981).

Kelly, C. *A History of Russian Women's Writing 1820–1992* (Oxford, 1994).

Kenez, P. *Cinema and Soviet Society: From the Revolution to the Death of Stalin* (London, 2001).

Kerber, L. L. *Stalin's Aviation Gulag: a Memoir of Andrei Tupolev and the Purge Era* (Washington, DC, 1996).

Kershaw, I. *Hitler: Hubris 1889–1936* (London, 1998).

Kershaw, I. *The 'Hitler Myth': Image and Reality in the Third Reich* (Oxford, 1987).

Kershaw, I. *Hitler: Nemesis, 1936–1945* (London, 2000).

Kershaw, I. *The Nazi Dictatorship* (London, 2003).

Kershaw, I. *Popular Opinion and Political Dissent in the Third Reich: Bavaria, 1933–1945* (Oxford, 1983).

Kershaw, I. and Lewin, M. (eds) *Stalinism and Nazism: Dictatorships in Comparison* (Cambridge, 1997).

Khlevniuk, O. 'The Objectives of the Great Terror 1937–38', in J. Cooper, M. Perrie and E. A. Rees (eds) *Soviet History 1917–1953: Essays in Honour of R. W. Davies* (London, 1995), pp. 158–76.

Khlevniuk, O. *In Stalin's Shadow: the Career of 'Sergo' Ordzhonikidze* (London, 1995).

Khlevniuk, O. *Politburo – mekhanizmy politicheskoi vlasti v 1930 ye gody* (Moscow, 1996).

Kienitz, S. 'Der Krieg der Invaliden. Helden-Bilder und Männlichkeitskonstruktion nach dem Ersten Weltkrieg', *Militärgeschichtliche Zeitschrift*, 60 (2001), pp. 367–402.

Kinz, G. *Der Bund Deutscher Mädel: Ein Beitrag zur ausserschulischen Mädchenerziehung im Nationalsozialismus* (Frankfurt am Main, 1990).

Kirstein, W. *Das Konzentrationslager als Institution totalen Terrors: Das Beispiel des Konzentrationslager Natzweiler* (Pfaffenweiler, 1992).

Kissenkoetter, U. *Gregor Strasser und die NSDAP* (Stuttgart, 1978).

Klaus, M. *Mädelen im Dritten Reich: Der Bund Deutscher Mädel* (Cologne, 1983).

Kline, G. L. 'The Defence of Terrorism: Trotsky and his major critics', in T. Brotherstone and P. Dukes (eds) *The Trotsky Reappraisal* (Edinburgh, 1992), pp. 156–65.

Knight, A. *Beria: Stalin's First Lieutenant* (London, 1993).

Knight, A. *Who Killed Kirov? The Kremlin's Greatest Mystery* (New York, 1999).

Koch, H. W. *In the Name of the Volk: Political Justice in Hitler's Germany* (London, 1989).

Kochan, L. (ed.) *The Jews in Soviet Russia since 1917* (Oxford, 1978).

Koehl, R. *The Black Corps: The Structure and Power Struggles of the Nazi SS* (Madison, Wisc., 1983).

Koenen, A. *Der Fall Carl Schmitt: sein Aufstieg zum 'Kronjuristen des Dritten Reiches'* (Darmstadt, 1995).

Kokusin, A. I. 'The Gulag during the war', *Istoricheskii Arkhiv*, (1994–5), pp. 60–87.

Kolloquien des Instituts für Zeitgeschichte: NS-Recht in historischer Perspecktive (Munich, 1981).

Koonz, C. *The Nazi Conscience* (Cambridge, Mass., 2003).

Kopperschmidt, J. (ed.) *Hitler der Redner* (Munich, 2003).

Kopperschmidt, J. 'Hitler vor Gericht. Oder: Rede als "Arbeit am Mythos"', in *idem, Hitler der Redner* (Munich, 2003), pp. 327–58.

Koshar, R. *Social Life, Local Politics, and Nazism: Marburg 1880–1935* (Chapel Hill, NC, 1986).

Kostyrchenko, G. V. 'Soviet Censorship in 1945–52', *Voprosii istorii*, 11–12 (1996), pp. 87–95.

Kotkin, S. *Magnetic Mountain: Stalinism as Civilization* (Berkeley, Calif., 1995).

Kozlov, V. 'Denunciation and its Functions in Soviet Governance: a Study of Denuciations and their Bureaucratic Handling from Soviet Police Archives 1944–1953', *Journal of Modern History*, 68 (1996), pp. 867–98.

Kracauer, S. *From Caligari to Hitler: a Psychological History of the German Film* (Princeton, NJ, 1974).

Krausnick, H. and Broszat, M. *Anatomy of the SS State* (London, 1970).

Krivosheev, G. F. (ed.) *Soviet Casualties and Combat Losses in the Twentieth Century* (London, 1997).

Kroll, F. L. *Utopie als Ideologie: Geschichtsdenken und politisches Handeln im Dritten Reich* (Paderborn, 1998).

Kubatzki, R. *Zwangsarbeiter-und Kriegsgefangenenlager: Standorte und Topographie in Berlin und im brandenburgischen Umland 1939 bis 1945* (Berlin, 2001).

Kube, A. *Pour le mérite und Hakenkreuz: Hermann Göring im Dritten Reich* (Munich, 1986).

Kuhn, U. 'Rede als Selbstinszenierung – Hitler auf der "Buhne"', in J. Kopperschmidt (ed.) *Hitler als Redner* (Munich, 2003), pp. 159–82.

Kuhr-Korolev, C., Plaggenborg, S. and Wellmann, M. (eds) *Sowjetjugend 1917–1941: Generation zwischen Revolution und Resignation* (Essen, 2001).

Kumanev, G. A. 'The Soviet Economy and the 1941 Evacuation', in J. Wieczynski, (ed.) *Operation Barbarossa: The German Attack on the Soviet Union, June 22 1941* (Salt Lake City, 1993) pp. 163–93.

Kumanev, G. A. 'Sudibi Sovetskoi Intellegentsii (30e gody)', *Istoriia SSSR*, 1 (1990), pp. 23–40.

Kuromiya, H. *Stalin's Industrial Revolution: Politics and Workers, 1928–1932* (Cambridge, 1988).

Kuschpèta, O. *The Banking and Credit System of the USSR* (Leiden, 1978).

Lahusen, T. *How Life Writes the Book: Real Socialism and Socialist Realism in Stalin's Russia* (Ithaca, NY, 1997).

Laqueur, W. *Russia and Germany: a Century of Conflict* (London, 1965).

Laqueur, W. *Stalin: the Glasnost Revelations* (London, 1990).

Large, D. C. (ed.) *Contending with Hitler: Varieties of German Resistance in the Third Reich* (Cambridge, 1991).

Lastours, S. de *Toukhatchevski: le bâtisseur de l'Armée Rouge* (Paris, 1996).

Lattek, C. 'Bergen-Belsen: From "Privileged" Camp to Death Camp', in J. Reilly *et al.* (eds) *Belsen in History and Memory* (London, 1997), pp. 37–71.

Latzel, K. *Deutsche Soldaten – nationalsozialistischer Krieg?* (Paderborn, 1998).

Lauryssens, S. *The Man who Invented the Third Reich* (Stroud, 1999).

Lebedeva, V. G. 'Totalitarian and Mass Elements in Soviet Culture of the 1930s', *Russian Studies in History*, 42 (2003), pp. 66–96.

Lenoe, M. 'Did Stalin Kill Kirov and Does it Matter?', *Journal of Modern History*, 74 (2002), pp. 352–80.

Leo, R. di *Occupazione e salari nell'URSS 1950–1977* (Milan, 1980).

Levi, E. *Music in the Third Reich* (London, 1994).

Levin, N. *Paradox of Survival: The Jews in the Soviet Union since 1917* (2 vols, London, 1990).

Lewin, M. *The Making of the Soviet System: Essays in the Social History of Interwar Russia* (London, 1985).

Lewin, M. *Russian Peasants and Soviet Power: a Study of Collectivization* (New York, 1975).

Lewis, D. C. *After Atheism: Religion and Ethnicity in Russia and Central Asia* (New York, 2000).

Lewy, G. 'Gypsies and Jews under the Nazis', *Holocaust and Genocide Studies*, 13 (1999), pp. 383–404.

Lewy, G. *The Nazi Persecution of the Gypsies* (Oxford, 2000).

Liebermann, S. R. 'Crisis Management in the USSR: The Wartime System of Administration and Control', in S. Linz (ed.) *The Impact of World War II on the Soviet People* (Totowa, NJ, 1985), pp. 59–76.

Lifton, R. J. *The Nazi Doctors: Medical Killing and the Psychology of Genocide* (London, 1986).

Linden, C. A. *The Soviet Party-State: the Politics of Ideocratic Despotism* (Westport, Conn., 1983).

Lindenmeyr, A. 'The First Political Trial: Countess Sofia Panina', *Russian Review*, 60 (2001), pp. 505–25.

Linz, S. (ed.) *The Impact of World War II on the Soviet Union* (Totowa, NJ, 1985).

Loe, M. L. 'Gorky and Nietzsche: The Quest for a Russian Superman', in B. G. Rosenthal (ed.) *Nietzsche in Russia* (Princeton, NJ, 1986), pp. 251–74.

Loginov, V. *Tene' Stalina* (Moscow, 2000).

Löhmann, R. *Der Stalinmythos: Stalin zur Sozialgeschichte des Personenkults in der Sowjetunion (1929–1935)* (Münster, 1990).

Longerich, P. *Die braunen Bataillone: Geschichte der SA* (Munich, 1989).

Longerich, P. *The Unwritten Order: Hitler's Role in the Final Solution* (Stroud, 2001).

London, J. (ed.) *Theatre under the Nazis* (Manchester, 2000).

Lotfi, G. *KZ der Gestapo: Arbeitserziehungslager im Dritten Reich* (Stuttgart, 2000).

Löwenhardt, J. *Decision Making in Soviet Politics* (London, 1981).

Löwenhardt, J., Ozinga, J. and van Ree, E. *The Rise and Fall of the Soviet Politburo* (London, 1992).

Lozowick, Y. *Hitler's Bureaucrats: The Nazi Security Police and the Banality of Evil* (London, 2000).

Lucas, J. *War on the Eastern Front: The German Soldier in Russia 1941–1945* (London, 1991).

Lüdtke, A. 'The "Honor of Labor": Industrial Workers and the Power of Symbols under National Socialism', in D. Crew (ed.) *Nazism and German Society 1933–1945* (London, 1994), pp. 67–109.

Lukes, R. *The Forgotten Holocaust: the Poles under German Occupation 1939–1944* (Lexington, Ky, 1986).

Lumass, V. *Himmler's Auxiliaries: the Volksdeutsche Mittelstelle and the German National Minorities of Europe 1939–1945* (Chapel Hill, NC, 1993).

Lutzel, K. *Deutsche Soldaten – nationalsozialistischer Krieg? Kriegserlebnis und Kriegserfahrung* (Paderborn, 1998).

Luukkanen, A. *The Religious Policy of the Stalinist State* (Helsinki, 1997).

Lydolph, P. E. *Geography of the USSR* (2nd edn, New York, 1970).

Lynn, N. and Bogorov, V. 'Reimaging the Russian Past', in G. Herb and D. Kaplan (eds) *Nested Identities: Nationalism, Territory and Scale* (Langham, Md, 1999).

Lyons, G. (ed.) *The Russian Version of the Second World War* (London, 1976).

Mai, U. *'Rasse und Raum': Agrarpolitik, Sozial- und Raumplanung im NS-Staat* (Paderborn, 2002).

Main, S. J. 'The Arrest and "Testimony" of Marshal of the Soviet Union M. N. Tukhachevsky', *Journal of Slavic Military Studies*, 10 (1997), pp. 151–95.

Main, S. J. 'Stalin in June 1941', *Europe–Asia Studies*, 48 (1996), pp. 837–9.

Maiwald, S. and Mischler, G. *Sexualität unter dem Hakenkreuz: Manipulation und Vernichtung der Intimsphäre im NS-Staat* (Hamburg, 1999).

685

Majer, D. *Grundlagen des nationalsozialistischen Rechtssystems* (Stuttgart, 1987).

Malcher, G. *Blank Pages: Soviet Genocide against the Polish People* (Woking, 1993).

Mally, L. 'Autonomous Theatre and the Origins of Socialist Realism: the 1932 Olympiad of Autonomous Art', *Russian Review*, 52 (1993), pp. 198–212.

Mally, L. *Culture of the Future: The Proletkult Movement in Revolutionary Russia* (Berkeley, Calif., 1990).

Mangan, J. A. (ed.) *Shaping the Superman: Fascist Body as Political Icon – Aryan Fascism* (London, 1999).

Manuel, F. E. (ed.) *Utopias and Utopian Thought* (Cambridge, Mass., 1966).

Marchand, S. 'Nazi Culture: Banality or Barbarism?' *Journal of Modern History*, 70 (1998), pp. 108–18.

Marples, D. *Stalinism in the Ukraine in the 1940s* (Cambridge, 1992).

Marsh, R. *Images of Dictatorship: Stalin in Literature* (London, 1989).

Marshall, R. H. (ed.) *Aspects of Religion in the Soviet Union 1917–1967* (Chicago, 1971).

Marten, H.-G. 'Racism, Social Darwinism, Anti-Semitism and Aryan Supremacy', in J. A. Mangan (ed.) *Shaping the Superman: Fascist Body as Political Icon – Aryan Fascism* (London, 1999), pp. 23–41.

Martens, L. *Un autre regard sur Staline* (Brussels, 1994).

Maser, W. *Mein Kampf: Der Fahrplan eines Welteroberers: Geschichte, Auszüge, Kommentare* (Esslingen, 1974).

Mason, T. W. *Social Policy in the Third Reich: the Working Class and the 'National Community'* (Oxford, 1993).

Matheson, P. *The Third Reich and the Christian Churches* (Edinburgh, 1981).

Mawdsley, E. *The Russian Civil War* (London, 1987).

Mawdsley, E. *The Stalin Years: the Soviet Union 1929–1953* (Manchester, 1998).

Mawdsley, E. and White, S. *The Soviet Elite from Lenin to Gorbachev: The Central Committee and its Members 1917–1991* (Oxford, 2000).

Mazower, M. 'Military Violence and National Socialist Values: The Wehrmacht in Greece 1941–1944', *Past & Present*, 134 (1992), pp. 129–58.

McCagg, W. O. *Stalin Embattled 1943–1948* (Detroit, 1978).

McCauley, A. *Women's Work and Wages in the Soviet Union* (London, 1981).

McClelland, J. C. 'Utopianism versus Revolutionary Heroism in Bolshevik

Policy: the Proletarian Culture Debate', *Slavic Review*, 39 (1980), pp. 403–25.

McDermott, K. and Agnew, J. (eds) *The Comintern: A History of International Communism from Lenin to Stalin* (London, 1996).

McGilligan, P. *Fritz Lang: the Nature of the Beast* (London, 1997).

McKale, D. M. *The Nazi Party Courts: Hitler's management of conflict in his Movement 1921–1945* (Lawrence, Kans., 1974).

McKenzie, K. *Comintern and World Revolution* (New York, 1964).

McNeal, R. H. *Stalin: Man and Ruler* (London, 1988).

Medvedev, R. *Let History Judge: the Origins and Consequences of Stalinism* (London, 1971).

Medvedev, R. *Nikolai Bukharin: The Last Years* (New York, 1980).

Meissner, B., Brunner, G. and Löwenthal, R. (eds) *Einparteisystem und bürokratische Herrschaft in der Sowjetunion* (Cologne, 1978).

Merkl, P. H. *Political Violence under the Swastika: 581 Early Nazis* (Princeton, NJ, 1975).

Merridale, C. *Moscow Politics and the Rise of Stalin: The Communist Party in the Capital 1925–32* (London, 1990).

Merridale, C. *Night of Stone: Death and Memory in Russia* (London, 2000).

Merridale, C. 'The Reluctant Opposition: The Right "Deviation" in Moscow, 1928', *Soviet Studies*, 41 (1989), pp. 382–400.

Merson, A. *Communist Resistance in Nazi Germany* (London, 1985).

Merz, K.-U. *Das Schrecksbild: Deutschland und der Bolschewismus 1917 bis 1921* (Frankfurt am Main, 1995).

Michel, A. *Des Allemands contre le Nazisme: oppositions et resistances 1933–1945* (Paris, 1997).

Mickiewicz, E. P. *Soviet Political Schools: the Communist Party Adult Instruction System* (New Haven, Conn., 1967).

Mil'bakh, V. S. 'Repression in the 57th Special Corps (Mongolian People's Republic)', *Journal of Slavic Military Studies*, 15 (2002), pp. 91–122.

Millar, J. R. *The Soviet Economic Experiment* ed. S. J. Linz (Urbana, Ill., 1990).

Miller, F. J. *Folklore for Stalin: Russian Folklore and Pseudofolklore of the Stalin Era* (New York, 1990).

Miller, F. J. 'The Image of Stalin in Soviet Russian Folklore', *Russian Review*, 39 (1980), pp. 50–67.

Milne, L. *Mikhail Bulgakov: a Critical Biography* (Cambridge, 1990).

Milward, A. S. *The German Economy at War* (London, 1965).

Milward, A. S. *War, Economy and Society 1939–1945* (London, 1987).

Miner, S. M. *Stalin's Holy War: Religion, Nationalism and Alliance Politics, 1941–1945* (Chapel Hill, NC, 2003).

Miskolczy, A. *Hitler's Library* (Budapest, 2003).

Moll, M. 'Steuerungsinstrument im "Ämterchaos"? Die Tagungen der Reichs- und Gauleiter der NSDAP', *Vierteljahrshefte für Zeitgeschichte*, 49 (2001), pp. 215–73.

Mommsen, H. 'Hitlers Stellung im nationalsozialistischen Herrschaftssystem', in G. Hirschfeld and L. Kettenacker (eds) *Der 'Führerstaat': Mythos und Realität* (Stuttgart, 1981).

Mommsen, H. (ed.) *The Third Reich between Vision and Reality: New Perspectives on German History 1918–1945* (Oxford, 2001).

Montefiore, S. S. *Stalin: The Court of the Red Tsar* (London, 2003).

Moorsteen, R. and Powell, R. *The Soviet Capital Stock 1928–1962* (Homewood, Ill., 1966).

Morsey, R. (ed.) *Das 'Ermächtigungsgesetz' vom 24 März 1933* (Düsseldorf, 1992).

Moskoff, W. *The Bread of Affliction: The Food Supply in the USSR during World War II* (Cambridge, 1990).

Mosse, G. L. *Fallen Soldiers: Reshaping the Memory of the World Wars* (Oxford, 1990).

Müller, I. *Hitler's Justice: The Courts of the Third Reich* (London, 1991).

Müller, K.-J. *Das Heer und Hitler: Armee und ns Regime 1933–1940* (Stuttgart, 1969).

Müller, R.-D. *Hitlers Ostkrieg und die deutsche Siedlungspolitik* (Frankfurt am Main, 1991).

Müller, R.-D. and Ueberschär, G. R. *Hitler's War in the East 1941–1945: a Critical Assessment* (Oxford, 1997).

Müller, R.-D. and Volkmann, H.-E. (eds) *Die Wehrmacht: Mythos und Realität* (Munich, 1999).

Müller-Dietz, H. *Recht im Nationalsozialismus* (Baden-Baden, 2000).

Munting, R. *The Economic Development of the USSR* (London, 1982).

Naiman, E. *Sex in Public: The Incarnation of Early Soviet Ideology* (Princeton, NJ, 1997).

Naimark, N. and Gibianski, L. (eds) *The Establishment of Communist Regimes in Eastern Europe 1944–1949* (Boulder, Colo., 1997).

Nation, R. C. *Black Earth, Red Star: A History of Soviet Security Policy 1917–1991* (Ithaca, NY, 1992).

Nekrich, A. M. *Pariahs, Partners, Predators: German–Soviet Relations 1922–1941* (New York, 1997).

Neurohr, J. F. *Der Mythos vom Dritten Reich* (Stuttgart, 1957).

Nevezhin, V. A. 'The Pact with Germany and the Idea of an "Offensive War" (1939–1941)', *Journal of Slavic Military Studies*, 8 (1995), pp. 811–33.

Nevin, T. *Ernst Jünger and Germany: Into the Abyss 1914–1945* (London, 1997).

Nicholls, A. *Freedom with Responsibility: The Social Market Economy in Germany 1918–1963* (Oxford, 1994).

Nichols, T. M. *The Sacred Cause: Civil–Military Conflict over Soviet National Security, 1917–1992* (Ithaca, NY, 1993).

Nicosia, F. R. and Stokes, L. D. (eds) *Germans Against Nazism: Nonconformity, Opposition and Resistance in the Third Reich* (New York, 1990).

Nove, A. *An Economic History of the USSR* (3rd edn, London, 1992).

Nove, A. 'The peasantry in World War II', in S. Linz (ed.) *The Impact of World War II on the Soviet Union* (Totowa, NJ, 1985), pp. 79–90.

Nove, A. *Stalinism and After* (London, 1975).

Nove, A. (ed.) *The Stalin Phenomenon* (London, 1993).

Nove, A. 'Terror Victims – Is the Evidence Complete?' *Europe–Asia Studies*, 46 (1994), pp. 535–7.

O'Neill, R. J. *The German Army and the Nazi Party 1933–1939* (London, 1966).

Orlow, D. *The History of the Nazi Party* (2 vols, Newton Abbot, 1973).

Orth, K. *Das System der ns Konzentrationslager: Eine politische Organisationsgeschichte* (Hamburg, 1999).

Orth, K. 'Gab es eine Lagergesellschaft? "Kriminelle" und politische Häftlinge im Konzentrationslager', in N. Frei, S. Steinbacher and B. Wagner (eds) *Ausbeutung, Vernichtung, Öffentlichkeit: neue Studien zur nationalsozialistischen Lagerpolitik* (Munich, 2000), pp. 109–33.

Osokina, E. *Our Daily Bread: Socialist Distribution and the Art of Survival in Stalin's Russia, 1927–1941* (New York, 2001).

Otto, R. *Wehrmacht, Gestapo und sowjetische Kriegsgefangene im deutschen Reichsgebiet 1941/42* (Munich, 1998).

Oved, Y. 'The Future Society according to Kropotkin', *Cahiers du monde russe*, 33 (1992), pp. 303–20.

Overy, R. J. 'The Four-Year Plan', in T. Gourvish (ed.) *European Yearbook of Business History: Number 3* (Aldershot, 2000), pp. 87–106.

Overy, R. J. 'Germany and the Munich Crisis. A Mutilated Victory?' *Diplomacy and Statecraft*, 10 (2000), pp. 191–215.

Overy, R. J. *Interrogations: the Nazi Elite in Allied Hands, 1945* (London, 2001).

Overy, R. J. *The Nazi Economic Recovery 1932–1938* (2nd edn, Cambridge, 1996).

Overy, R. J. *Russia's War* (London, 1998).

Overy, R. J. *War and Economy in the Third Reich* (Oxford, 1994).

Overy, R. J. *Why the Allies Won* (London, 1995).

Overy, R. J., Ten Cate, J. and Otto, G. (eds) *Die Neuordnung Europas: NS-Wirtschaftspolitik in den besetzten Gebieten* (Berlin, 1997).

Pabst, M. *Staatsterrorismus: Theorie und Praxis kommunistischer Herrschaft* (Graz, 1997).

Padfield, P. *Himmler: Reichsführer SS* (London, 1990).

Panayi, P. (ed.) *Weimar and Nazi Germany: Continuities and Discontinuities* (London, 2001).

Parrish, M. 'The Downfall of the "Iron Commissar": N. I. Ezhov 1938–40', *Journal of Slavic Military Studies*, 14 (2001), pp. 71–104.

Parrish, M. *The Lesser Terror: Soviet State Security 1939–1953* (Westport, Conn., 1996).

Paul, G. (ed.) *Die Täter der Shoah: fanatische Nationalsozialisten oder ganz normale Deutsche?* (Munich, 2002).

Paul, G. and Mallmann, K.-M. (eds) *Die Gestapo – Mythos und Realität* (Darmstadt, 1995).

Paul, G. and Mallmann, K.-M. (eds) *Die Gestapo im Zweiten Weltkrieg: Heimatfront und besetztes Europa* (Darmstadt, 2000).

Pavlov, D. V. *Leningrad 1941: the Blockade* (Chicago, 1965).

Pavlova, I. V. 'The Machinery of Political Power in the USSR of the 20s and 30s', *Voprosii istorii*, 11–12 (1998), pp. 49–67.

Pavlova, I. V. 'The Strength and Weakness of Stalin's Power', in N. Rosenfeldt, B. Jensen and E. Kulavig (eds) *Mechanisms of Power in the Soviet Union* (London, 2000), pp. 23–39.

Peris, D. 'Commissars in Red Cassocks: Former Priests in the League of the Militant Godless', *Slavic Review*, 54 (1995), pp. 342–64.

Peris, D. *Storming the Heavens: the Soviet League of the Militant Godless* (Ithaca, NY, 1998).

Perrie, M. 'Nationalism and History: the Cult of Ivan the Terrible in Stalin's Russia', in G. Hosking and R. Service (eds) *Russian Nationalism Past and Present* (London, 1998), pp. 107–27.

Perz, B. *Projekt Quarz: Steyr-Daimler-Puch und das Konzentrationslager Melk* (Vienna, 1991).

Peschanski, D. *La France des Camps: L'internement 1938–1946* (Paris, 2002).

Petrone, K. *Life Has Become More Joyous, Comrades: Celebrations in the Time of Stalin* (Bloomington, Ind., 2000).

Petropoulos, J. *The Faustian Bargain: the Art World in Nazi Germany* (London, 2000).

Petsch, J. 'Architektur und Städtebau im Dritten Reich – Anspruch und Wirklichkeit', in D. Peukert and J. Reulecke (eds) *Die Reihen fast geschlossen: Beiträge zur Geschichte des Alltags unterm Nationalsozialismus* (Wuppertal, 1981).

Peukert, D. 'The Genesis of the "Final Solution" from the Spirit of Science', in D. Crew (ed.) *Nazism and German Society 1933–1945* (London, 1994), pp. 274–99.

Peukert, D. *Inside Nazi Germany: Conformity, Opposition and Racism in Everyday Life* (London, 1987).

Pfaff, D. *Die Entwicklung der sowjetischen Rechtslehre* (Cologne, 1968).

Pinchuk, B.-C. *Shtetl Jews under Soviet Rule: Eastern Poland on the Eve of the Holocaust* (London, 1990).

Pine, L. 'Creating Conformity: the Training of Girls in the Bund Deutscher Mädel', *European History Quarterly*, 33 (2003), pp. 367–85.

Pine, L. *Nazi Family Policy 1933–1945* (Oxford, 1997).

Pingel, F. *Häftlinge unter SS-Herrschaft: Widerstand, Selbstbehauptung und Vernichtung im Konzentrationslager* (Hamburg, 1978).

Pini, U. *Erotik im Dritten Reich* (Munich, 1992).

Pinkus, B. *The Jews of the Soviet Union: the History of a National Minority* (Cambridge, 1993).

Pinkus, B. 'La participation des minorities nationals extra-territoriales à la vie politique et publique de l'Union Soviétique, 1917–1939', *Cahiers du monde russe*, 36 (1995), pp. 297–318.

Pinnow, K. 'Cutting and Counting: Forensic Medicine as a Science of Society in Bolshevik Russia, 1920–29', in D. Hoffmann and Y. Kotsonis (eds) *Russian Modernity: Politics, Knowledge, Practices* (London, 2000).

Pisiotis, A. K. 'Images of Hate in the Art of War', in R. Stites *Culture and Entertainment in Wartime Russia* (Bloomington, Ind., 1995), pp. 141–56.

Plaggenborg, S. 'Gewalt und Militanz in Sowjetrussland 1919–1930', *Jahrbücher für die Geschichte Osteuropas*, 44 (1996), pp. 409–30.

Platt, K. E. and Brandenberger, D. 'Terribly Romantic, Terribly Progressive, or Terribly Tragic: Rehabilitating Ivan IV under I. V. Stalin', *Russian Review*, 58 (1999), pp. 635–54.

Plöckinger, O. 'Rhetorik, Propaganda und Masse in Hitlers Mein Kampf', in J. Kopperschmidt (ed.) *Hitler als Redner* (Munich, 2003), pp. 115–42.

Plumper, J. 'Abolishing Ambiguity: Soviet Censorship Practices in the 1930s', *Russian Review*, 60 (2001), pp. 526–44.

Poeppel, D. H., Prinz Wilhelm von Preussen and von Hase, K.-G. *Die Soldaten der Wehrmacht* (Munich, 1998).

Pohl, J. *Ethnic Cleansing in the USSR, 1927–1949* (Westport, Conn., 2002).

Pohl, J. *The Stalinist Penal System* (Jefferson, NC, 1997).

Pons, S. *Stalin and the Inevitable War 1936–1941* (London, 2002).

Pons, S. 'Stalinism and Party Organisation (1933–48)', in J. Channon (ed.) *Politics, Society and Stalinism in the USSR* (London, 1998), pp. 93–114.

Porter, C. and Jones, M. *Moscow in World War II* (London, 1987).

Pospielovsky, D. V. *A History of Marxist-Leninist Atheism and Soviet Anti-Religious Policies: Volume I. A History of Soviet Atheism in Theory and Practice* (London, 1987); *Volume II. Soviet Anti-Religious Campaigns and Persecutions* (London, 1988).

Potthoff, H. *Freie Gewerkschaften 1918–1933: Der Allgemeine Deutsche Gewerkschaftsbund in der Weimarer Republik* (Düsseldorf, 1987).

Prantl, H. (ed.) *Wehrmachtsverbrechen: eine deutsche Kontroverse* (Hamburg, 1997).

Pulzer, P. *The Rise of Political Anti-Semitism in Germany and Austria* (London, 1988).

Pyta, W. ' "Menschenökonomie": Das Ineinandergreifen von ländlicher Sozialraumgestaltung und rassenbiologischer Bevölkerungspolitik im nationalsozialistischen Staat', *Historische Zeitschrift*, 273 (2001), pp. 31–94.

Quinn, M. *The Swastika: Constructing the Symbol* (London, 1994).

Raddatz, F. J. *Gottfried Benn: Leben – niederer Wahn: Eine Biographie* (Munich, 2001).

Radosh, R. and Habeck, M. R. *Spain Betrayed: The Soviet Union in the Spanish Civil War* (New Haven, Conn., 2001).

Radzinsky, E. *Stalin* (London, 1996).

Rapaport, Y. *The Doctors' Plot: Stalin's Last Crime* (London, 1991).

Rebentisch, D. 'Die "politische Beurteilung" als Herrschaftsinstrument der NSDAP', in D. Peukert and J. Reulecke (eds) *Die Reihen fast geschlossen: Beiträge zur Geschichte des Alltags unterm Nationalsozialismus* (Wuppertal, 1981), pp. 107–28.

Redell, C. (ed.) *Transformations in Russian and Soviet Military History* (Washington, DC, 1990).

Ree, E. van *The Political Thought of Joseph Stalin* (London, 2002).

Ree, E. van 'Stalin's Organic Theory of the Party', *Russian Review*, 52 (1993), pp. 43–57.

Rees, E. A. (ed.) *Decision-Making in the Stalinist Command Economy, 1932–37* (London, 1997).

Rees, E. A. 'Stalin and Russian Nationalism', in G. Hosking and R. Service (eds) *Russian Nationalism Past and Present* (London, 1998), pp. 77–105.

Reese, R. R. *Stalin's Reluctant Soldiers: a Social History of the Red Army 1925–1941* (Lawrence, Kans., 1996).

Reibel, C.-W. *Das Fundament der Diktatur: Die NSDAP-Ortsgruppen 1932–1945* (Paderborn, 2002).

Reichel, P. 'Festival and Cult: Masculine and Militaristic Mechanisms of National Socialism', in J. A. Mangan (ed.) *Shaping the Superman: Fascist Body as Political Icon – Aryan Fascism* (London, 1999), pp. 153–68.

Reid, S. 'Socialist Realism in the Stalinist Terror: the Industry of Socialism Art Exhibition, 1935–41', *Russian Review*, 60 (2001), pp. 153–84.

Reidel, P. 'Aspekte ästhetischer Politik im nationalsozialistischen Staat', in U. Hermann and U. Nassen (eds) *Formative Ästhetik im Nationalsozialismus. Intentionen, Medien und Praxisformen totalitärer ästhetischer Herrschaft und Beherrschung* (Weinheim, 1994).

Reilly, J. *et al.* (eds) *Belsen in History and Memory* (London, 1997).

Reinhardt, K. *Moscow – the Turning Point: the Failure of Hitler's Strategy in the Winter of 1941–1942* (Oxford, 1992).

Renner, A. 'Defining a Russian Nation: Mikhail Katkov and the "Invention" of National Politics', *Slavonic and East European Review*, 81 (2003), pp. 659–82.

Reuth, R. *Goebbels* (London, 1993).

Rhodes, R. *Masters of Death: The SS Einsatzgruppen and the Invention of the Holocaust* (New York, 2002).

Rich, N. *Hitler's War Aims* (2 vols, London, 1973–4).

Rigby, T. H. *The Changing Soviet System: Mono-organisational Socialism from its Origins to Gorbachev's Restructuring* (London, 1990).

Rigby, T. H. *Communist Party Membership in the USSR 1917–1967* (Princeton, NJ, 1968).

Rigby, T. H. 'Staffing USSR Incorporated: The Origins of the Nomenklatura System', *Soviet Studies*, 40 (1988), pp. 523–37.

Rigby, T. H. 'Was Stalin a Disloyal Patron?' *Soviet Studies*, 38 (1996), pp. 311–24.

Ritchie, J. M. *German Literature under National Socialism* (London, 1983).

Rittersporn, G. T. 'Extra-Judicial Repression and the Courts: Their Relationship in the 1930s', in P. H. Solomon (ed.) *Reforming Justice in Russia 1864–1996* (New York, 1997), pp. 207–27.

Rittersporn, G. T. *Stalinist Simplifications and Soviet Complications: Social Tensions and Political Conflict in the USSR, 1933–1953* (Reading, 1991).

Rizzi, B. *The Bureaucratisation of the World. The USSR: Bureaucratic Collectivism* (London, 1985).

Roberts, C. A. 'Planning for War: the Red Army and the Catastrophe of 1941', *Europe–Asia Studies*, 47 (1995), pp. 1293–326.

Roberts, G. 'The Soviet Decisions for a Pact with the Soviet Union', *Soviet Studies*, 44 (1992), pp. 67–87.

Roberts, G. *The Soviet Union and the Origins of the Second World War 1933–1941* (London, 1995).

Roberts, J. *Walter Benjamin* (London, 1982).

Robin, R. *Socialist Realism. An Impossible Aesthetic* (Stanford, 1992).

Rogovin, V. Z. *1937: Stalin's Year of Terror* (Oak Park, Mich., 1998).

Rogovin, V. Z. *Vlasti i oppozi'tsii* (Moscow, 1993).

Rohwer, J. and Monakov, M. *Stalin's Ocean-Going Fleet: Soviet Naval Strategy and Shipbuilding Programme 1935–1953* (London, 2001).

Rosefielde, S. 'Stalinism in Post-Communist Perspective: New Evidence on Killings, Forced Labor and Economic Growth in the 1930s', *Europe–Asia Studies*, 48 (1996), pp. 959–87.

Roseman, M. 'Recent Writing on the Holocaust', *Journal of Contemporary History*, 36 (2001), pp. 361–72.

Roseman, M. *The Villa, the Lake, the Meeting: Wannsee and the Final Solution* (London, 2002).

Rosenberg, W. and Siegelbaum, L. (eds) *Social Dimensions of Soviet Industrialization* (Bloomington, Ind., 1993).

Rosenfeldt, N. ' "The Consistory of the Communist Church": The Origins and Development of Stalin's Secret Chancellery', *Russian History*, 9 (1982), pp. 300–324.

Rosenfeldt, N., Jensen, B. and Kulavig, E. (eds) *Mechanisms of Power in the Soviet Union* (London, 2000).

Rosenthal, B. G. *New Myth, New World: from Nietzsche to Stalin* (Pittsburgh, 2002).

Rosenthal, B. G. 'Nietzsche, Nationality, Nationalism', in A. Freifeld, P. Bergmann and B. G. Rosenthal (eds) *East Europe reads Nietzsche* (New York, 1998), pp. 181–206.

Rosenthal, B. G. (ed.) *The Occult in Russian and Soviet Culture* (Ithaca, NY, 1997).

Rossi, J. *The Gulag Handbook* (New York, 1989).

Rossman, J. J. 'The Teikovo Cotton Workers' Strike of April 1932: Class, Gender and Identity Politics in Stalin's Russia', *Russian Review*, 56 (1997), pp. 44–69.

Roth, C. *Parteikreis und Kreisleiter der NSDAP unter besonderer Berücksichtigung Bayerns* (Munich, 1997).

Roth, K. H. *Facetten des Terrors. Der Geheimdienst der 'Deutsche Arbeitsfront'* (Bremen, 2000).

Rousso, H. (ed.) *Stalinisme et Nazisme. Histoire et mémoire comparées* (Paris, 1999).

Rowley, D. G. 'Imperial versus national discourse: the case of Russia', *Nations and Nationalism*, 6 (2000), pp. 23–42.

Roxburgh, A. *Pravda: Inside the Soviet News Machine* (London, 1987).

Rubinstein, J. *Tangled Loyalties: The Life and Times of Ilya Ehrenburg* (London, 1996).

Rummell, R. *Lethal Politics: Soviet Genocide and Mass Murder since 1917* (New Brunswick, NJ, 1990).

Russell, E. P. ' "Speaking of Annihilation": Mobilizing for War against Human and Insect Enemies', *Journal of American History* (1996), pp. 1505–29.

Rzhevsky, N. (ed.) *Modern Russian Culture* (Cambridge, 1998).

Sabrin, B. *Alliance for Murder: the Nazi Ukrainian-Nationalist Partnership in Genocide* (London, 1991).

Salkeld, A. *A Portrait of Leni Riefenstahl* (London, 1997).

Samuelson, L. 'Mikhail Tukhachevsky and War-Economic Planning: Reconsiderations on the Pre-War Soviet Military Build-Up', *Journal of Slavic Military Studies*, 9 (1996), pp. 804–47.

Samuelson, L. *Plans for Stalin's War Machine: Tukhachevskii and Military-Economic Planning, 1925–1941* (London, 2000).

Samuelson, L. 'The Red Army and economic planning, 1925–40', in J. Barber and M. Harrison (eds) *The Soviet Defence-Industry Complex from Stalin to Khrushchev* (London, 2000), pp. 47–69.

Sapir, J. *Les fluctuations économiques en URSS 1941–1945* (Paris, 1989).

Sapir, J. 'The Economics of War in the Soviet Union during World War II', in I. Kershaw and M. Lewin (eds) *Stalinism and Nazism: Dictatorships in Comparison* (Cambridge, 1997), pp. 208–36.

Saur, C. 'Rede als Erzeugung von Komplizentum. Hitler und die öffentliche Erwähnung der Judenvernichtung', in J. Kopperschmidt (ed.) *Hitler als Redner* (Munich, 2003), pp. 413–40.

Schaer, R., Claeys, G. and Sargent, L. T. (eds) *Utopia: the Search for the Ideal Society in the Western World* (New York, 2000).

Schapiro, L. *The Communist Party of the Soviet Union* (London, 1960).

Schauff, F. 'Company Choir of Terror: The Military Council of the 1930s – the Red Army Between the XVIIth and XVIIIth Party Congresses', *Journal of Slavic Military Studies*, 12 (1999), pp. 123–63.

Schechter, J. and Luchkov, V. (eds) *Khrushchev Remembers: the Glasnost Tapes* (New York, 1990).

Scherer, K. *'Asoziale' im Dritten Reich* (Münster, 1990).

Schieder, W. 'Die NSDAP vor 1933. Profil einer faschistischen Partei', *Geschichte und Gesellschaft*, 19 (1993), pp. 141–54.

Schley, J. *Nachbar Buchenwald: Die Stadt Weimar und ihr Konzentrationslager 1937–1945* (Cologne, 1999).

Schmid, H.-D. (ed.) *Zwei Städte unter dem Hakenkreuz: Widerstand und Verweigerung in Hannover und Leipzig 1933–1945* (Leipzig, 1994).

Schmider, K. 'No Quiet on the Eastern Front: the Suvorov Debate in the 1990s', *Journal of Slavic Military Studies*, 10 (1997), pp. 181–94.

Schmidt, H. *'Beabsichtige ich die Todesstrafe zu beantragen': die nationalsozialistische Sondergerichtsbarkeit im Oberlandesgerichtsbezirk Düsseldorf 1933 bis 1945* (Essen, 1998).

Schmiechen-Ackermann, D. 'Der "Blockwart" ', *Vierteljahrshefte für Zeitgeschichte*, 48 (2000), pp. 575–602.

Schmiechen-Ackermann, D. *Diktaturen im Vergleich* (Darmstadt, 2002).

Schmiechen-Ackermann, D. *Nationalsozialismus und Arbeitermilieus: Der nationalsozialistische Angriff auf die proletarischen Wohnquartiere und die Reaktion in den sozialistischen Vereinen* (Bonn, 1998).

Schmölders, C. *Hitlers Gesicht: Eine physiognomische Biographie* (Munich, 2000).

Schneider, J. and Harbrecht, H. (eds) *Wirtschaftsordnung und Wirtschaftspolitik in Deutschland (1933–1993)* (Stuttgart, 1996).

Schneider, M. *Unterm Hakenkreuz: Arbeiter und Arbeiterbewegung 1933 bis 1939* (Bonn, 1999).

Schoenbaum, D. *Hitler's Social Revolution: Class and Status in Nazi Germany 1933–1939* (New York, 1966).

Scholder, K. *A Requiem for Hitler and Other New Perspectives on the German Church Struggle* (Philadelphia, 1989).

Scholder, K. 'Die evangelische Kirche in der Sicht der nationalsozialistischen Führung', *Vierteljahrshefte für Zeitgeschichte*, 16 (1968), pp. 15–35.

Schubert-Weller, C. *Hitler-Jugend: Vom 'Jungsturm Adolf Hitler' zur Staatsjugend des Dritten Reiches* (Weinheim, 1993).

Schulte, J. E. *Zwangsarbeit und Vernichtung: Das Wirtschaftsimperium der SS* (Paderborn, 2001).

Schulte, T. *The German Army and Nazi Policies in Occupied Russia* (Oxford, 1989).

Schumann, D. 'Europa, das Erste Weltkrieg und die Nachkriegszeit: eine Kontinuität der Gewalt?' *Journal of Modern European History*, 1 (2003), pp. 24–43.

Schwaab, E. H. *Hitler's Mind: a Plunge into Madness* (New York, 1992).

Schwarz, G. *Die nationalsozialistischen Lager* (Frankfurt am Main, 1990).

Schweller, R. L. *Deadly Imbalances: Tripolarity and Hitler's Strategy of World Conquest* (New York, 1998).

Schwendemann, H. *Die wirtschaftliche Zusammenarbeit zwischen dem Deutschen Reich und der Sowjetunion von 1939 bis 1941* (Berlin, 1993).

Seidler, F. W. and Zeigert, D. *Die Führerhauptquartiere: Anlagen und Planungen im Zweiten Weltkrieg* (Munich, 2000).

Sella, A. *The Value of Human Life in Soviet Warfare* (London, 1992).

Semiryaga, M. 'The USSR and the Pre-War Political Crisis', *Voprosii Istorii*, 9 (1990), pp. 49–65.

Sengotta, H. J. *Der Reichsstatthalter in Lippe 1933 bis 1939. Reichsrechtliche Bestimmungen und politische Praxis* (Detmold, 1976).

Seurot, F. *Le système économique de l'URSS* (Paris, 1989).

Shearer, D. *Industry, State, and Society in Stalin's Russia* (Ithaca, NY, 1996).

Shearer, D. 'Wheeling and Dealing in Soviet Industry: syndicates, trade and political economy at the end of the 1920s', *Cahiers du monde russe*, 36 (1995), pp. 139–60.

Shepherd, B. 'The Continuum of Brutality: Wehrmacht Security Divisions in Central Russia, 1942', *German History*, 21 (2003), pp. 49–81.

Shklovsky, V. *Mayakovsky and his Circle* (London, 1972).

Shtemenko, S. M. *The Soviet General Staff at War* (Moscow, 1970).

Shukman, H. (ed.) *Stalin's Generals* (London, 1993).

Shymko, Y. (ed.) *For This Was I Born* (Toronto, 1973).

Siegelbaum, L. 'Production Collectives and Communes and the "Imperatives" of Soviet Industrialization', *Slavic Review*, 45 (1986), pp. 65–84.

Siegelbaum, L. *Stakhanovism and the Politics of Productivity in the USSR, 1935–1941* (Cambridge, 1988).

Siegelbaum, L. and Suny, R. G. (eds) *Making Workers Soviet: Power, Class and Identity* (Ithaca, NY, 1994).

Simonov, N. 'The "war scare" of 1927 and the birth of the defence-industry complex', in J. Barber and M. Harrison (eds) *The Soviet Defence-Industry Complex from Stalin to Khrushchev* (London, 2000), pp. 33–46.

Simonsen, S. G. 'Raising "The Russian Question": Ethnicity and Statehood – Russkie and Rossiya', *Nationalism and Ethnic Politics*, 2 (1996), pp. 91–110.

Skalnik, P. 'Soviet etnografiia and the nation(alities) question', *Cahiers du monde russe*, 31 (1990), pp. 183–93.

Slepyan, K. 'The Soviet Partisan Movement and the Holocaust', *Holocaust and Genocide Studies*, 14 (2000), pp. 1–27.

Smelser, R. *Robert Ley: Hitler's Labor Front Leader* (Oxford, 1988).

Smith, G. (ed.) *The Nationalities Question in the Soviet Union* (London, 1990).

Sofsky, W. *The Order of Terror: The Concentration Camp* (Princeton, NJ, 1997).

Sohn-Rethel, A. *Economy and Class Structure of German Fascism* (London, 1978).

Sokolov, B. 'The Cost of War: Human Losses for the USSR and Germany 1939–1945', *Journal of Slavic Military Studies*, 9 (1996), pp. 152–93.

Sokolov, B. 'Lend Lease in Soviet Military Efforts 1941–1945', *Journal of Slavic Military Studies*, 7 (1994), pp. 120–51.

Solomon, P. H. *Soviet Criminal Justice Under Stalin* (Cambridge, 1996).

Solomon, S. G. 'The demographic argument in Soviet debates over the legalization of abortion in the 1920s', *Cahiers du monde russe*, 33 (1992), pp. 59–82.

Solzhenitsyn, A. *The Gulag Archipelago* (3 vols, London, 1973–8).

Sorenson, J. B. *The Life and Death of Soviet Trade Unionism 1917–1928* (New York, 1969).

Sorokin, P. *The Sociology of Revolution* (New York, 1967).

Soyfer, V. N. *Lysenko and the Tragedy of Soviet Science* (New Brunswick, NJ, 1994).

Spotts, F. *Hitler and the Power of Aesthetics* (London, 2002).

Stachura, P. *Gregor Strasser and the Rise of Nazism* (London, 1983).

Starkov, B. 'The Trial that was not Held', *Europe–Asia Studies*, 46 (1994), pp. 1297–315.

Starkov, B. 'Trotsky and Ryutin: from the history of the anti-Stalin resistance in the 1930s', in T. Brotherstone and P. Dukes (eds) *The Trotsky Reappraisal* (Edinburgh, 1992), pp. 70–83.

Staudinger, H. *The Inner Nazi: a critical analysis of Mein Kampf* (London, 1981).

Steinbach, P. and Tuchel, J. (eds) *Widerstand in Deutschland 1933–1945* (Munich, 1994).

Steinberg, M. D. *Proletarian Imagination: Self, Modernity and the Sacred in Russia, 1910–1925* (Ithaca, NY, 2002).

Steinweis, A. E. *Art, Ideology and Economics in Nazi Germany: the Reich Chambers of Music, Theater, and the Visual Arts* (Chapel Hill, NC, 1993).

Steinweis, A. E. 'Weimar Culture and the Rise of National Socialism: the Kampfbund für deutsche Kultur', *Central European History*, 24 (1991), pp. 402–23.

Stephan, J. J. *The Russian Fascists: Tragedy and Farce in Exile 1925–1945* (London, 1978).

Stephens, F. J. *Hitler Youth: History, Organisation, Uniforms and Insignia* (London, 1973).

Stephenson, J. *The Nazi Organisation of Women* (London, 1981).

Stephenson, J. 'Propaganda, Autarky and the German Housewife', in D. Welch (ed.) *Nazi Propaganda* (London, 1983), pp. 117–42.

Stephenson, J. *Women in Nazi Germany* (London, 1975).

Stern, J. P. *Hitler, the Führer, and the People* (London, 1976).

Stettner, R. *'Archipel GULag': Stalins Zwangslager – Terrorinstrument und Wirtschaftsgigant* (Paderborn, 1996).

Stites, R. (ed.) *Culture and Entertainment in Wartime Russia* (Bloomington, Ind., 1995).

Stites, R. *Revolutionary Dreams: Utopian Vision and Experimental Life in the Russian Revolution* (Oxford, 1989).

Stites, R. *Russian Popular Culture: Entertainment and Society since 1900* (Cambridge, 1992).

Stollies, M. *The Law under the Swastika: Studies in Legal History in Nazi Germany* (Chicago, 1998).

Stoltzfus, M. *Resistance of the Heart: Intermarriage and the Rosenstrasse Protest in Nazi Germany* (New York, 1996).

Stommer, R. ' "Da oben versinkt einem der Alltag . . .," Thingstätten im Dritten Reich als Demonstration der Volksgemeinschaftsideologie', in D. Peukert and J. Reulecke (eds) *Die Reihen fast geschlossen: Beiträge zur Geschichte des Alltags unterm Nationalsozialismus* (Wuppertal, 1981), pp. 149–74.

Stone, D. R. *Hammer and Rifle: the Militarization of the Soviet Union 1926–1933* (Lawrence, Kans., 2000).

Storr, A. (ed.) *The Essential Jung: Selected Writings* (London, 1983).

Strätz, H. W. 'Die studentische Aktion wider den undeutschen Geist', *Vierteljahrshefte für Zeitgeschichte*, 16 (1968), pp. 347–72.

Straus, K. M. *Factory and Community in Stalin's Russia: The making of an industrial working class* (Pittsburgh, 1997).

Streim, A. *Sowjetische Gefangene in Hitlers Vernichtungskrieg: Berichte und Dokumente* (Heidelberg, 1982).

Streit, C. *Keine Kameraden: die Wehrmacht und die sowjetischen Kriegsgefangenen 1941–1945* (Stuttgart, 1978).

Streit, C. 'Die sowjetischen Kriegsgefangenen in den deutschen Lagern', in D. Dahlmann and G. Hirschfeld (eds) *Lager, Zwangsarbiet, Vertreibung und Deportation* (Essen, 1999), pp. 403–14.

Sutela, P. *Socialism, Planning and Optimality: a Study in Soviet Economic Thought* (Helsinki, 1984).

Sutton, A. C. *Western Technology and Soviet Economic Development 1930 to 1945* (Stanford, 1971).

Swayze, H. *Political Control of Literature in the USSR 1946–1959* (Cambridge, Mass., 1962).

Sword, K. *Deportation and Exile: Poles in the Soviet Union, 1939–48* (London, 1994).

Sword, K. (ed.) *The Soviet Takeover of the Polish Eastern Provinces 1939–1941* (London, 1991).

Syring, E. *Hitler: seine politische Utopie* (Frankfurt am Main, 1994).

Szamuely, T. 'The Elimination of Opposition between the Sixteenth and Seventeenth Congresses of the CPSU', *Soviet Studies*, 17 (1966), pp. 318–38.

Szejnmann, C.-C. *Nazism in Central Germany: the Brownshirts in 'Red' Saxony* (Oxford, 1999).

Szöllösi-Janze, M. (ed.) *Science in the Third Reich* (Oxford, 2001).

Szporluk, R. 'Nationalism and communism: reflections: Russia, Ukraine, Belarus and Poland', *Nations and Nationalism*, 4 (1998), pp. 301–20.

Tait, A. L. 'Lunacharsky: a "Nietzschean Marxist"?' in B. G. Rosenthal *Nietzsche in Russia* (Princeton, NJ, 1986), pp. 275–92.

Tarleton, R. E. 'What Really Happened to the Stalin Line?' *Journal of Slavic Military Studies*, 6 (1993), pp. 21–61.

Taylor, B. and van der Will, W. (eds) *The Nazification of Art: Art, Design, Music, Architecture and Film in the Third Reich* (Winchester, 1990).

Taylor, R. *Film Propaganda in Soviet Russia and Nazi Germany* (London, 1998).

Taylor, R. *Literature and Society in Germany 1918–1945* (Brighton, 1980).

Taylor, R. *The Politics of the Soviet Cinema* (London, 1979).

Taylor, R. and Spring, D. (eds) *Stalinism and Soviet Cinema* (London, 1993).

Temin, P. 'Soviet and Nazi economic planning in the 1930s', *Economic History Review*, 44 (1991), pp. 573–93.

Thamer, H.-U. *Verführung und Gewalt: Deutschland 1933–1945* (Berlin, 1986).

Theweleit, K. *Male Fantasies. Male bodies: psychoanalysing the white terror* (Oxford, 1989).

Thies, J. 'Nazi Architecture – a Blueprint for World Domination: the Last Aims of Adolf Hitler', in D. Welch (ed.) *Nazi Propaganda* (London, 1983), pp. 45–64.

Thurner, E. *National Socialism and Gypsies in Austria* (Tuscaloosa, Ala., 1998).

Thurston, R. W. *Life and Terror in Stalin's Russia 1934–1941* (London, 1996).

Thurston, R. W. 'Social Dimensions of Stalinist Rule: Humor and Terror in the USSR, 1935–1941', *Journal of Social History*, 24 (1990/1), pp. 541–62.

Todorov, T. *Facing the Extreme: Moral Life in the Concentration Camps* (New York, 1996).

Todorov, T. *Hope and Memory: Reflections on the Twentieth Century* (London, 2003).

Tolz, V. 'New Information about the Deportations of Ethnic Groups in the USSR during World War 2', in J. Garrard and C. Garrard (eds) *World War 2 and the Soviet People* (London, 1993), pp. 161–79.

Tompsen, W. *Khrushchev* (London, 1994).

Tooze, J. A. *Statistics and the German State, 1900–1945: the Making of Modern Economic Knowledge* (Cambridge, 2001).

Tregub, S. *The Heroic Life of Nikolai Ostrovsky* (Moscow, 1964).

Tröger, A. 'The Creation of a Female Assembly-Line Proletariat', in R. Bridenthal, A. Grossmann and M. Kaplan (eds) *When Biology became Destiny: Women in Weimar Germany and Nazi Germany* (New York, 1984), pp. 237–70.

Tuchel, J. 'Dimensionen des Terrors: Funktionen der Konzentrationslager in Deutschland 1933–1945', in D. Dahlmann and G. Hirschfeld (eds) *Lager, Zwangsarbeit, Vertreibung und Deportation* (Essen, 1999), pp. 371–91.

Tuchel, J. *Konzentrationslager: Organisationsgeschichte und Funktion der 'Inspektion der Konzentrationslager' 1934–1938* (Boppard am Rhein, 1991).

Tucker, R. *Stalin as Revolutionary, 1879–1929* (New York, 1974).

Tucker, R. *Stalin in Power: the Revolution from Above, 1928–1941* (New York, 1990).

Tucker, R. (ed.) *Stalinism: Essays in Historical Interpretation* (New York, 1977).

Tumarkin, N. *Lenin Lives! The Lenin Cult in Soviet Russia* (Cambridge, Mass., 1997).

Ueberschär, G. and Bezymenski, L. A. (eds) *Der deutsche Angriff auf die Sowjetunion 1941: Die Kontroverse um die Präventivkriegsthese* (Darmstadt, 1998).

Ueberschär, G. and Wette, W. (eds) *'Unternehmen Barbarossa': Der deutsche Überfall auf die Sowjetunion* (Paderborn, 1994).

Ulam, A. *Lenin and the Bolsheviks* (London, 1965).

Ulam, A. *Stalin: The Man and His Era* (London, 1973).

Usborne, C. *The Politics of the Body in Weimar Germany: Women's Reproductive Rights and Duties* (London, 1992).

Vaksberg, A. *The Prosecutor and the Prey: Vyshinsky and the 1930s Moscow Show Trials* (London, 1990).

Vaksberg, A. *Stalin against the Jews* (New York, 1994).

Van Dyke, C. 'The Timoshenko Reforms March–July 1940', *Journal of Slavic Military Studies*, 9 (1996), pp. 69–96.

Vardys, V. 'The Baltic States under Stalin: the First Experience 1939–1941', in K. Sword (ed.) *The Soviet Takeover of the Polish Eastern Provinces 1939–1941* (London, 1991), pp. 268–90.

Vieler, E. H. *The Ideological Roots of German National Socialism* (New York, 1999).

Viola, L. *The Best Sons of the Fatherland: Workers in the Vanguard of Soviet Collectivization* (New York, 1987).

Viola, L. (ed.) *Contending with Stalinism: Soviet Power and Popular Resistance in the 1930s* (Ithaca, NY, 2002).

Viola, L. *Peasant Rebels under Stalin: Collectivization and the Culture of Peasant Resistance* (New York, 1996).

Volkogonov, D. *Stalin: Triumph and Tragedy* (London, 1991).

Volkogonov, D. *Trotsky: the Eternal Revolutionary* (London, 1996).

Volkov, V. K. 'Soviet–German Relations during the Second Half of 1940', *Voprosii istorii*, 2 (1997), pp. 3–18.

Vopel, S. 'Radikaler, völkischer Nationalismus in Deutschland 1917–1933', in H. Timmermann (ed.) *Nationalismus und Nationalbewegung in Europa 1914–1945* (Berlin, 1999).

Vorländer, H. *Die NSV: Darstellung und Dokumentation einer national-sozialistischen Organisation* (Boppard am Rhein, 1988).

Vorsin, V. F. 'Motor Vehicle Transport Deliveries through "Lend-Lease"', *Journal of Slavic Military Studies*, 10 (1997), pp. ?

Voslensky, M. *Nomenklatura: Anatomy of the Soviet Ruling Class* (London, 1984).

Wachsmann, N. ' "Annihilation through Labor": The Killing of State Prisoners in the Third Reich', *Journal of Modern History*, 71 (1999), pp. 624–59.

Watson, D. *Molotov and Soviet Government: Sovnarkom, 1930–41* (London, 1996).

Wegner, B. (ed.) *From Peace to War: Germany, Soviet Russia and the World 1939–1941* (Providence, RI, 1997).

Wegner, B. *Hitlers politische Soldaten: Die Waffen-SS 1933–1945* (Paderborn, 1992).

Weinberg, R. 'Purge and Politics on the Periphery: Birobidzhan in 1937', *Slavic Review*, 52 (1993), pp. 13–27.

Weindling, P. *Health, Race and German Politics between National Unification and Nazism 1870–1945* (Cambridge, 1989).

Weiner, A. 'The Making of a Dominant Myth: the Second World War and the Construction of Political Identities within the Soviet Polity', *Russian Review*, 55 (1996), pp. 638–60.

Weiner, A. *Making Sense of War: The Second World War and the Fate of the Bolshevik Revolution* (Princeton, NJ, 2001).

Weiner, A. 'Nothing but Certainty', *Slavic Review*, 61 (2002), pp. 44–53.

Weisbrod, B. 'Violence and Sacrifice: Imagining the Nation in Weimar Germany', in H. Mommsen, (ed.) *The Third Reich between Vision and Reality: New Perspectives on German History 1918–1945* (Oxford, 2001), pp. 5–22.

Weitz, E. D. 'Racial Politics without the Concept of Race: Reevaluating Soviet Ethnic and National Purges', *Slavic Review*, 61 (2002), pp. 1–29.

Weitz, J. *Hitler's Banker: Hjalmar Horace Greeley Schacht* (London, 1998).

Welch, D. (ed.) *Nazi Propaganda* (London, 1983).

Welch, D. *Propaganda and the German Cinema* (London, 2001).

Wellers, G. *Les chambers à gaz ont existé: Des documents, des temoignages, des chiffres* (Paris, 1981).

Werle, G. *Justiz-Strafrecht und polizeiliche Verbrechenskämpfung im Dritten Reich* (Berlin, 1989).

Werth, A. *Russia at War 1941–1945* (London, 1964).

Wheatcroft, S. 'More Light on the Scale of Repression and Excess Mortality in the Soviet Union in the 1930s', in J. A. Getty and R. Manning (eds) *Stalinist Terror: New Perspectives* (Cambridge, 1993), pp. 275–90.

Wieczynski, J. (ed.) *Operation Barbarossa: the German Attack on the Soviet Union, June 22 1941* (Salt Lake City, 1993).

Wiesen, S. J. 'Morality and Memory: Reflections on Business Ethics and National Socialism', *Journal of Holocaust Education*, 10 (2001), pp. 60–82.

Wild, D. *Fragments of Utopia* (London, 1998).

Wilhelm, F. *Die Polizei im NS-Staat: Die Geschichte ihre Organisation im Überblick* (Paderborn, 1997).

Wilhelm, H.-H. (ed.) *Rassenpolitik und Kriegsführung: Sicherheitspolizei und Wehrmacht in Polen und der Sowjetunion* (Passau, 1991).

Winkler, D. *Frauenarbeit im 'Dritten Reich'* (Hamburg, 1977).

Winkler, H. A. *Der Weg in die Katastrophe: Arbeiter und Arbeiterbewegung in der Weimarer Republik 1930 bis 1933* (Berlin, 1987).

Wolf, N. *Kirchner* (London, 2003).

Woll, H. *Die Wirtschaftslehre des deutschen Faschismus* (Munich, 1988).

Wysocki, G. *Die Geheimestaatspolizei im Land Braunschweig* (Frankfurt am Main, 1997).

Yakupov, N. M. 'Stalin and the Red Army', *Istoriia SSSR*, 5 (1991), pp. 170–76.

Yedlin, T. *Maxim Gorky: a Political Biography* (Westport, Conn., 1999).

Yekelchyk, S. 'The Making of a "Proletarian Capital": Patterns of Stalinist Social Policy in Kiev in the mid-1930s', *Europe–Asia Studies*, 50 (1998), pp. 1229–44.

Young, G. *Power and the Sacred in Revolutionary Russia: Religious Activists in the Village* (University Park, Pa., 1997).

Young, J. W. *Totalitarian Language: Orwell's Newspeak and its Nazi and Communist Antecedents* (Charlottesville, Va., 1991).

Zaleski, E. *Planning for Economic Growth in the Soviet Union 1918–1932* (Chapel Hill, NC, 1962).

Zaleski, E. *Stalinist Planning for Economic Growth 1933–1952* (London, 1980).

Zarubinsky, O. 'Collaboration of the Population in Occupied Ukrainian Territory: Some Aspects of the Overall Picture', *Journal of Slavic Military Studies*, 10 (1997), pp. 138–52.

Zayas, A. M. de *The Wehrmacht War Crimes Bureau, 1939–1945* (Lincoln, Nebr., 1989).

Zehnpfennig, B. *Hitler's Mein Kampf: Eine Interpretation* (Munich, 2000).

Zeidler, M. *Reichswehr und Rote Armee 1920–1933* (Munich, 1993).

Zelenin, I. 'The Implementation of Politics of the Elimination of the Kulaks as a Class (Autumn 1930-1932)', *Istoriia SSSR*, 6 (1990), pp. 172–91.

Zeman, Z. *Nazi Propaganda* (Oxford, 1973).

Zetterling, N. 'Loss Ratios on the Eastern Front during World War II', *Journal of Slavic Military Studies*, 9 (1996), pp. 895–906.

Zhukrai, V. *Stalin: Pravda i loch'* (Moscow, 1996).

Ziegler, H. F. *Nazi Germany's New Aristocracy: the SS Leadership, 1925–1939* (Princeton, NJ, 1989).

Ziemann, B. 'Germany after the First World War – A Violent Society?' *Journal of Modern European History*, 1 (2003), pp. 80–95.

Zitelmann, R. *Hitler: the Politics of Seduction* (London, 1999).

Zuckermann, F. S. *The Tsarist Secret Police in Russian Society, 1880–1917* (London, 1996).

Notes

Introduction

1. H. Kohn *The Twentieth Century: a Midway Account of the Western World* (London, 1950), p. 65.

2. T. Todorov *Hope and Memory: Reflections on the Twentieth Century* (London, 2003), pp. 75–7.

3. Todorov, *Hope and Memory*, p. 82.

4. A. Besançon 'Nazisme et communisme, également criminels', *L'est européen*, 35 (1997), pp. 3–6. See also W. Dlugoborski 'Das Problem des Vergleichs von Nationalsozialismus und Stalinismus' in D. Dahlmann and G. Hirschfeld (eds) *Lager, Zwangsarbeit, Vertreibung und Deportation* (Essen, 1999), pp. 19–28; E. Jahn 'Zum Problem der Vergleichbarkeit von Massenverfolgung und Massenvernichtung' in *ibid.*, pp. 29–51.

5. S. Courtois, N. Werth, *et al. The Black Book of Communism: Crimes, Terror, Repression* (Cambridge, Mass., 1999).

6. D. Rayfield *Stalin and his Hangmen* (London, 2004). On Hitler, R. G. Waite *The Psychopathic God: Adolf Hitler* (New York, 1978); E. H. Schwaab *Hitler's Mind: A Plunge into Madness* (New York, 1992); F. Redlich *Hitler: Diagnosis of a Destructive Prophet* (Oxford, 1999), esp. ch. 9.

7. A. Bullock *Hitler and Stalin: Parallel Lives* (London, 1991).

8. On Hitler there is the standard two-volume biography by I. Kershaw *Hitler: Hubris 1889–1936* (London, 1998) and *Hitler: Nemesis 1936–1945* (London, 2000). On Stalin, D. Volkogonov *Stalin: Triumph and Tragedy* (London, 1991); S. Sebag Montefiore *Stalin: The Court of the Red Tsar* (London, 2003).

9. On Germany see M. Burleigh *The Third Reich: a New History* (London, 2000); on the Soviet Union, R. Service *A History of Twentieth-Century Russia* (London, 1997).

10. R. H. McNeal *Stalin: Man and Ruler* (London, 1988), p. 237.

11. F. Genoud (ed.) *The Testament of Adolf Hitler* (London, 1960), p. 100, entry for 26 February 1945.

12. H. Heiber and D. M. Glantz (eds) *Hitler and His Generals: Military Conferences 1942–1945* (London, 2003), p. 388, meeting of the *Führer* with General Reinecke, 7 January 1944.

13. On Stalin see E. van Ree *The Political Thought of Joseph Stalin* (London, 2002). On Hitler, R. Zitelmann *Hitler: the Politics of Seduction* (London, 1999); F. L. Kroll *Utopie als Ideologie: Geschichtsdenken und politisches Handeln im Dritten Reich* (Paderborn, 1998).

14. On German inflation G. Feldman *The Great Disorder: Politics, Economics, and Society in the German Inflation 1914–1924* (Oxford, 1993); on Soviet inflation L. E. Hubbard *Soviet Money and Finance* (London, 1936), chs. 1, 4.

15. V. Serge, *The Case of Comrade Tulayev* (London, 1968), p. 88.

Chapter 1

1. A. Hitler *Mein Kampf*, ed. D. C. Watt (London, 1969).

2. R. Service *Lenin* (London, 2000), pp. 462–5.

3. Service, *Lenin*, p. 467; E. Radzinsky *Stalin* (London, 1996), pp. 193–4.

4. Service, *Lenin*, p. 469.

5. B. Bazhanov *Avec Staline dans le Kremlin* (Paris, 1930), p. 43.

6. D. Volkogonov *Stalin: Triumph and Tragedy* (London, 1991), pp. 93–4; Bazhanov, *Avec Staline*, p. 48.

7. E. Hanfstaengl *Hitler: the Missing Years* (London, 1957), p. 108.

8. L. Gruchmann and R. Weber (eds) *Der Hitler-Prozess 1924: Wortlaut der Hauptverhandlung vor den Volksgericht München* (4 vols, Munich, 1997) vol. i, pp. xxxv–xxxvii.

9. O. Gritschner *Der Hitler-Prozess und sein Richter Georg Neithardt* (Munich, 2001), p. 42.

10. Gruchmann and Weber, *Der Hitler-Prozess*, vol. iv, p. 1591.

11. Hanfstaengl, *Hitler*, p. 114; W. R. Hess (ed.) *Rudolf Hess: Briefe, 1908–1933* (Munich 1987), p. 322, letter from Hess to Ilse Pröhl, 12 May 1924.

12. Gritschner, *Der Hitler-Prozess*, p. 62.

13. On Stalin, W. Duranty *Stalin and Co: The Politburo and the Men who Rule Russia* (London, 1949), p. 39; on Hitler, Imperial War Museum, Speer Collection, Box 369, Part III, exploitation of Albert Speer, 'Adolf Hitler', 19 Oct 1945, p. 19. See too, T. Junge *Until the Final Hour. Hitler's Last Secretary*

(London, 2003), p. 130, who recalled Hitler's comment after the bomb exploded at his headquarters in July 1944: 'Well, ladies, everything turned out all right again. Yet more proof that Fate has chosen me for my mission.' See too, W. S. Allen (ed.) *The Infancy of Nazism: The Memoirs of Ex-Gauleiter Albert Krebs 1923–1933* (New York, 1976), p. 181: 'Providence,' Hess told Krebs in 1931, 'has always inspired him [Hitler] to do the right thing.'

14. Duranty, *Stalin and Co*, p. 38.

15. On his medical history N. Romano-Petrova *Stalin's Doctor: Stalin's Nurse: A Memoir* (Princeton, NJ, 1984), pp. 5–6.

16. On Stalin's many revolutionary nicknames see *The Life of Stalin: a Symposium* (London, 1930), p. 3; on Siberia A. V. Baikaloff *I Knew Stalin* (London, 1940), pp. 27–9.

17. See for example *Joseph Stalin: a Short Biography* (Moscow, 1949), p. 55, 'Stalin was Lenin's closest associate. He had direct charge of all the preparations for the insurrection [in 1917]' or p. 76, 'It was Stalin who directly inspired and organized the major victories of the Red Army [in the civil war]'. The same portrait appears in *Short History of the Communist Party of the Soviet Union* (Moscow, 1942) (so-called 'Short Course') pp. 206–7.

18. Joseph Stalin *Works*, vol. iii, p. 67, 'What did we expect from the conference?' in *Soldatskaya Pravda*, 6 May 1917.

19. Stalin, *Works*, vol. iii, p. 408, Speech at a meeting of the Central Committee, 16 October 1917.

20. R. Tucker, *Stalin as Revolutionary 1879–1929* (New York, 1973), pp. 179–82.

21. Cited in Tucker, *Stalin*, pp. 178–9; Trotsky's remark in D. Volkogonov *Trotsky: The eternal revolutionary* (London, 1996), p. 322.

22. Baikaloff, *I Knew Stalin*, p. 29.

23. Tucker, *Stalin*, p. 181; S. Graham *Stalin: an Impartial Study of the Life and Work of Joseph Stalin* (London, 1931), p. 39.

24. M. Voslensky *Nomenklatura: Anatomy of the Soviet Ruling Class* (London, 1984), p. 47.

25. Duranty, *Stalin and Co*, p. 30; E. Lyons *Stalin: Czar of all the Russians* (London, 1940), pp. 176–7; Baikaloff, *I Knew Stalin*, p. 28, 'He spoke haltingly, with a strong Georgian accent; his speech was dull and dry'; Graham, *Stalin*, pp. 117–19.

26. Volkogonov, *Stalin: Triumph and Tragedy*, pp. 225–9.

27. Tucker, *Stalin*, p. 175. 'There is a dogmatic Marxism,' Stalin said in a debate in August 1917, 'and a creative Marxism. I stand on the ground of the latter.'

28. The story of the cutlery in A. H. Birse *Memoirs of an Interpreter* (London, 1967), p. 160.

29. Tucker, *Stalin*, p. 212.

30. Baikaloff, *I Knew Stalin*, p. 85, repeating a story told by Noah Dzhordania.

31. Baikaloff, *I Knew Stalin*, p. 84.

32. Lyons, *Stalin: Czar*, p. 175; see too his account in E. Lyons *Assignment in Utopia* (London, 1937), pp. 381–9: 'his swarthy face' had, Lyons recalled, 'a friendly, almost benignant look'.

33. Graham, *Stalin*, p. 119: 'Calm and immobile sits Stalin,' wrote one observer, 'with the stone face of a prehistoric dragon, in which alone the eyes are living.'

34. Graham, *Stalin*, p. 79; Tucker, *Stalin*, pp. 210ff.

35. S. Sebag Montefiore *Stalin: the Court of the Red Tsar* (London, 2003), pp. 1–18 on the suicide of his second wife; A. Reiss (ed.) *Molotov Remembers: Inside Kremlin Politics. Conversations with Felix Chuev* (Chicago, 1993), pp. 177–8 on Stalin's drinking habits: 'Stalin didn't drink much, although he pushed others to do it. Apparently he considered it a useful way to test people.'

36. Interview with Dmitri Volkogonov, episode 1, *Russia's War* documentary, 1997.

37. Tucker, *Stalin*, p. 209.

38. Graham, *Stalin*, p. 93.

39. A. Amba *I Was Stalin's Bodyguard* (London, 1952) p. 69.

40. E. W. Tennant *True Account* (London, 1957), pp. 182–3.

41. On his liking for the Austrian Jewish composer before 1914 see B. Hamann *Hitler's Vienna: a Dictator's Apprenticeship* (London, 1999), pp. 64–6, 349.

42. Hamman, *Hitler's Vienna*, pp. 398–402; W. Maser (ed.) *Hitler's Letters and Notes* (New York, 1977), pp. 27–31.

43. Maser, *Letters and Notes*, p. 45, letter from Hitler to Anna Popp, 20 October 1914.

44. Maser, *Letters and Notes*, pp. 52–5, letter from Hitler to Joseph Popp, 1 November 1914.

45. Hitler, *Mein Kampf*, p. 150.

46. Hitler, Mein Kampf, pp. 186–7. See an analysis of Hitler's psychological state in F. Redlich *Hitler: Diagnosis of a Destructive Prophet* (New York, 1999), pp. 286–317.

47. A. Joachimsthaler *Korrektur einer Biographie: Adolf Hitler 1908–1920* (Munich, 1989), pp. 250–53.

48. F. Reck-Malleczewen *Diary of a Man in Despair* (London, 1995), pp. 22–3.

49. H. Rauschning *Hitler Speaks* (London, 1939), p. 68; see too the description by one of his interpreters, Eugen Dollmann, in Public Record Office, London, WO 218/4475 Interrogation Report on SS Oberfüehrer Dollmann [n.d. Aug. 1945], pp. 1–2.

50. H. Hoffmann *Hitler Was My Friend* (London, 1955), p. 196.

51. Junge, *Until the Final Hour*, p. 44.

52. Hitler, *Mein Kampf*, p. 98.

53. IWM Speer Collection, Box S366, Evaluation Report 241, First Preliminary Report on Hjalmar Schacht, 31 July 1945, p. 1.

54. A. Miskolczy *Hitler's Library* (Budapest, 2003), ch. 1.

55. F.-L. Kroll *Utopie als Ideologie: Geschichtsdenken und politisches Handeln im Dritten Reich* (Paderborn, 1998), pp. 32–4, 56–64; E. Syring *Hitler: seine politische Utopie* (Frankfurt am Main, 1994), pp. 22–9, 51–93; J. Hermand *Der alte Traum vom neuen Reich: völkische Utopien und Nationalsozialismus* (Frankfurt am Main, 1988), pp. 147–56, 215ff.

56. See for example P. Pulzer *The Rise of Political Anti-Semitism in Germany and Austria* (London, 1988), pp. 121ff., 195–207. In May 1918 the small Austrian 'Workers' Party' changed its name to German National Socialist Workers' Party. 'National socialist' ideas were central to much Austrian radical nationalism before 1914. See too, K. D. Bracher *The German Dictatorship: the Origins, Structure and Consequences of National Socialism* (London, 1971) pp. 72–9.

57. Kroll, *Utopie als Ideologie*, pp. 49–56; Syring, *Hitler*, pp. 40–4; P. Longerich *The Unwritten Order: Hitler's Role in the Final Solution* (Stroud, 2001), pp. 15–26; K.-U. Merz *Das Schreckbild: Deutschland und der Bolschewismus 1917 bis 1921* (Frankfurt am Main, 1995), pp. 457–71.

58. Rauschning, *Hitler Speaks*, pp. 208–9; Hitler, *Mein Kampf*, pp. 96–7.

59. Rauschning, *Hitler Speaks*, p. 211.

60. Hitler, *Mein Kampf*, p. 269.

61. On Hitler's medical history Redlich, *Hitler: Diagnosis*, pp. 223–54.

62. G. Ward Price *I Know These Dictators* (London, 1937), pp. 9–10; PRO, WO 218/4775, Dollmann interrogation, p. 1.

63. Ward Price, *I Know These Dictators*, pp. 16–17; see too the account in K. Krause *Zehn Jahre Kammerdiener bei Hitler* (Hamburg, 1990), pp. 14–21. On champagne over Pearl Harbor see Liddell Hart Archive, King's College, Hechler Collection, file 1, 'The enemy side of the hill', p. 93.

64. Krause, *Zehn Jahre*, pp. 31–2; Junge, *Until the Final Hour*, pp. 67–70 on Hitler's eating habits and hostility to meat-eaters.

65. Junge, *Until the Final Hour*, p. 114.

66. Miskolczy, *Hitler's Library*, pp. 3–5.

67. E. H. Schwaab *Hitler's Mind: a Plunge into Madness* (New York, 1992), p. 29.

68. Schwaab, *Hitler's Mind*, p. 43.

69. F. Genoud (ed.) *The Testament of Adolf Hitler: the Hitler–Bormann Documents* (London, 1961), p. 95, entry for 25 February 1945.

70. Allen (ed.), *Infancy of Nazism*, p. 165.

71. Tucker, *Stalin*, pp. 309–10 on the collective leadership principle; p. 319 for Bukharin quotation.

72. Graham, *Stalin*, p. 121.

73. I. Zbarsky and S. Hutchinson *Lenin's Embalmers* (London, 1998), pp. 11–12; N. Tumarkin *Lenin Lives! The Lenin Cult in Soviet Russia* (Cambridge, Mass., 1997), pp. 174–5.

74. J. Stalin *Problems of Leninism* (Moscow, 1947), pp. 13–93, 'The Foundations of Leninism'; Tucker, *Stalin*, pp. 316–24; R. W. Daniels *The Conscience of the Revolution: Communist Opposition in Soviet Russia* (Cambridge, Mass., 1960), pp. 236–8.

75. Stalin, *Works*, vol. vi, p. 48, 'On the death of Lenin', speech of 26 January 1924 to Second All-Union Congress of Soviets.

76. Stalin, *Works*, vol. vi, pp. 189–90, 'Foundations of Leninism', *Pravda*, May 1924.

77. Stalin, *Works*, vol. vi, p. 47.

78. Stalin, *Works*, vol. vi, pp. 191–2.

79. Graham, *Stalin*, pp. 78–9.

80. Volkogonov, *Stalin: Triumph and Tragedy*, pp. 104–5. On the contest with Trotsky see too R. W. Daniels *Trotsky, Stalin and Socialism* (Boulder, Colo., 1991); Y. Felshtinsky 'Lenin, Trotsky, Stalin and the Left Opposition in the USSR, 1918–1928', *Cahiers du Monde russe et soviétique*, 31 (1990), pp. 570–73.

81. Stalin, *Works*, vol. vi, p. 373, 'Trotskyism or Leninism?' speech 19 November 1924; Tucker, *Stalin*, pp. 340–44.

82. Tucker, *Stalin*, pp. 353–4.

83. Volkogonov, *Stalin: Triumph and Tragedy*, p. 134.

84. Volkogonov, *Stalin: Triumph and Tragedy*, p. 113.

85. Volkogonov, *Stalin: Triumph and Tragedy*, p. 135.

86. L. Trotsky *My Life: an Attempt at an Autobiography* (London, 1970), p. 554.

87. Stalin, On the Opposition, p. 865, speech at plenum of the Central Committee, 23 October 1927.

88. Stalin, On the Opposition, pp. 867, 883.

89. Volkogonov, *Stalin: Triumph and Tragedy*, pp. 175–8; Zbarsky and Hutchinson, *Lenin's Embalmers*, pp. 61–2 for the description of Bukharin. See too S. Cohen *Bukharin and the Bolshevik Revolution: A Political Biography 1888–1938* (New York, 1980) for the standard account.

90. On the emergence of the 'right opposition' see C. Merridale, 'The Reluctant Opposition: the Right "Deviation" in Moscow 1928', *Soviet Studies*, 41 (1989), pp. 382–400.

91. Volkogonov, *Stalin: Triumph and Tragedy*, p. 177.

92. Merridale, 'Reluctant Opposition', pp. 384–8; see too idem, *Moscow Politics and the Rise of Stalin: the Communist Party in the Capital 1925–32* (London, 1990) esp. chs 2–3; R. Medvedev *Nikolai Bukharin: The Last Years* (New York, 1980), pp. 17–18.

93. A. Avtorkhanov *Stalin and the Soviet Communist Party: a Study in the Technology of Power* (Munich, 1959) pp. 117–18.

94. Volkogonov, *Stalin: Triumph and Tragedy*, p. 186; Avtorkhanov, *Stalin and the Communist Party*, pp. 124–5, 152–3. For a more critical assessment of the claim for a right 'deviation' see M. David-Fox 'Memory, Archives, Politics. The Rise of Stalin in Avtorkhanov's *Technology of Power*', *Slavic Review*, 54 (1995), pp. 988–1003. On Molotov's elevation, see D. Watson *Molotov and Soviet Government: Sovnarkom, 1930–41* (London, 1996), pp. 27–44; R. G. Suny 'Stalin and his Stalinism: power and authority in the Soviet Union, 1930–53' in I. Kershaw and M. Lewin (eds) *Stalinism and Nazism: Dictatorships in Comparison* (Cambridge, 1997), pp. 33–5.

95. Avtorkhanov, *Stalin and the Communist Party*, pp. 156–7; J. Brooks *Thank You, Comrade Stalin! Soviet Public Culture from Revolution to Cold War* (Princeton, NJ, 2000), pp. 59–61; J. Gooding *Rulers and Subjects: Government and People in Russia 1801–1991* (London, 1996), pp. 199–200.

96. D. Orlow *The History of the Nazi Party: Volume I, 1919–1933* (Newton Abbot, 1973), p. 49.

97. Orlow, *History of the Nazi Party: I*, pp. 52–3.

98. Hess, *Rudolf Hess: Briefe*, p. 363, letter from Hess to Klara and Fritz Hess, 2 March 1925. Speech in C. Vollnhals (ed.) Hitler: *Reden, Schriften und Anordnungen Februar 1925 bis Januar 1933* (12 vols, Munich, 1992), i, p. 14–28.

99. P. Stachura *Gregor Strasser and the Rise of Nazism* (London, 1983), pp. 11–26; U. Kissenkoetter *Gregor Strasser und die NSDAP* (Stuttgart, 1978), pp. 22–5.

100. Stachura, *Strasser*, p. 38.

101. Hess, *Rudolf Hess: Briefe*, p. 368, letter from Hess to Klara and Fritz Hess, 24 April 1925.

102. Orlow, *History of the Nazi Party: I*, pp. 68–70; I. Kershaw *Hitler: Hubris 1889–1936* (London, 1998), pp. 274–7.

103. Stachura, *Strasser*, p. 51; see too Kissenkoetter, *Gregor Strasser*, p. 24.

104. Stachura, *Strasser*, pp. 51–3; see on Hitler's economic views R. Zitelmann *Hitler: The Politics of Seduction* (London, 1999), esp. part iv, pp. 198–269.

105. Orlow, *History of the Nazi Party: I*, pp. 135–6, 143.

106. P. Longerich *Die braunen Bataillone: Geschichte der SA* (Munich, 1989), pp. 15–33; Orlow, *History of the Nazi Party: I*, pp. 211–13.

107. K. Gossweiler *Die Strasser-Legende* (Berlin, 1994), p. 19; Kissenkoetter, *Gregor Strasser*, pp. 41–7.

108. C. Fischer *Stormtroopers: a Social, Economic and Ideological Analysis 1929–1935* (London, 1983) pp. 5–6; H. A. Turner (ed.) *Hitler: Memoirs of a Confidant* (New Haven, Conn. 1985), pp. 28–31.

109. Stachura, *Strasser*, p. 101.

110. Stachura, *Strasser*, pp. 101–13; Kissenkoetter, *Gregor Strasser*, pp. 123–30, 162–77.

111. Avtorkhanov, *Stalin and the Communist Party*, p. 124.

112. S. Cohen *Rethinking the Soviet Experience: Politics and History since 1917* (Oxford, 1985), ch. 3. See the discussion in S. Blank 'Soviet Institutional Development during NEP: A Prelude to Stalinism', *Russian History*, 9 (1982), pp. 325–46; Daniels, *Conscience of the Revolution*, pp. 398–401, 408–11; S. Farber *Before Stalinism: the Rise and Fall of Soviet Democracy* (Cambridge, 1990) pp. 149 ff. on the absence of any independent political activity long before Stalinism.

113. Stachura, *Strasser*, p. 124; Medvedev, *Nikolai Bukharin*, p. 161.

114. Stalin, *Works*, vol. xiii, p. 41, speech to First All-Union Conference of Leading Personnel of Socialist Industry, 4 February 1931.

115. Stalin, *Works*, vol. xiii, p. 42.

116. H. Kuromiya *Stalin's Industrial Revolution: Politics and Workers, 1928–1932* (Cambridge, 1988), p. 5.

117. Kuromiya, *Stalin's Industrial Revolution*, p. 17; J. Hughes 'Capturing the Russian Peasantry: Stalinist Grain Procurement Policy and the "Urals-Siberian" Method', *Slavic Review*, 53 (1994), pp. 77–8. See too J. Hughes *Stalin, Siberia and the crisis of the New Economic Policy* (Cambridge, 1991), esp. chs 5–6.

118. Hughes, 'Capturing the Peasantry', p. 87; J. Hughes 'Re-evaluating Stalin's Peasant Policy 1928–30' in J. Pallot (ed.) *Transforming Peasants: Society, State and the Peasantry 1861–1930* (London, 1998), pp. 242–50, 255–6.

119. Hughes, 'Capturing the Peasantry', pp. 80–81; M. Lewin *Russian Peas-*

ants and Soviet Power: a Study of Collectivization (New York, 1975) chs 16–17.

120. R. C. Nation *Black Earth, Red Star: A History of Soviet Security Policy 1917–1991* (Ithaca, NY, 1992), p. 61; Kuromiya, *Stalin's Industrial Revolution*, p. 15; on the fate of bourgeois experts see N. Jasny *Soviet Economists of the Twenties* (Cambridge, 1972), pp. 119, 127, 144.

121. R. W. Davies, M. Harrison and S. G. Wheatcroft (eds) *The Economic Transformation of the Soviet Union 1913–1945* (Cambridge, 1994), pp. 113–14, 290.

122. L. Viola *Peasant Rebels under Stalin: Collectivization and the Culture of Peasant Resistance* (Oxford, 1996), pp. 105, 139–40; see too T. Macdonald 'A Peasant Rebellion in Stalin's Russia' in L. Viola (ed.) *Contending with Stalinism: Soviet Power and Popular Resistance in the 1930s* (Ithaca, NY, 2002), pp. 84–108.

123. Viola, *Peasant Rebels*, pp. 171–2.

124. Davies, Harrison and Wheatcroft, *Economic Transformation*, p. 68.

125. R. W. Davies, O. V. Khlevniuk, E. A. Rees, L. P. Kosheleva and L. A. Rogovaya (eds) *The Stalin–Kaganovich Correspondence 1931–1936* (New Haven, Conn. 2003) pp. 180–81, letter from Stalin to Kaganovich, 11 August 1932. On the famine see S. G. Wheatcroft 'More Light on the Scale of Repression and Excess Mortality in the Soviet Union in the 1930s' in J. A. Getty and R. Manning (eds) *Stalinist Terror: New Perspectives* (Cambridge, 1993) pp. 278–89. Extrapolations from the demographic data suggest excess mortality of 4–5 million in total attributable to famine and its effects.

126. J. Rossman 'A Workers' Strike in Stalin's Russia' in Viola (ed.), *Contending with Stalinism*, pp. 45–6; J. Haslam 'Political Opposition to Stalin and the Origins of the Terror in Russia, 1932–1936', *The Historical Journal*, 29 (1986), pp. 396–9; B. Starkov 'Trotsky and Ryutin: from the history of the anti-Stalin resistance in the 1930s' in T. Brotherstone and P. Dukes (eds) *The Trotsky Reappraisal* (Edinburgh, 1992), pp. 71–3.

127. Kuromiya, *Stalin's Industrial Revolution*, p. 21.

128. R. G. Suny 'Stalin and his Stalinism', in I. Kershaw and M. Lewin (eds) *Stalinism and Nazism: Dictatorships in Comparison* (Cambridge, 1997), pp. 46–7.

129. Lewin, *Russian Peasants*, p. 448.

130. R. Gaucher *Opposition in the USSR, 1917–1967* (New York, 1969), p. 270.

131. The standard work is H. James *The German Slump: Politics and Economics 1924–1936* (Oxford, 1986); see too J. von Krüdener (ed.) *Economic Crisis and Political Collapse: the Weimar Republic 1924–1933* (Oxford, 1990).

132. S. Haffner *Defying Hitler: a Memoir* (London, 2002), p. 68.

133. D. Schumann *Politisches Gewalt in der Weimarer Republik 1919–1933* (Essen, 2000), pp. 320, 335–7.

134. Zitelmann, *Hitler*, pp. 33–53, 62–75. 'Our Party,' Hitler announced in a speech in 1920, 'must have a revolutionary character'; or in 1921, 'The salvation of Germany can only come . . . through revolution' (p. 62).

135. T. Abel *Why Hitler Came into Power: an Answer Based on the Original Life Stories of Six Hundred of his Followers* (New York, 1938), p. 93.

136. Haffner, *Defying Hitler*, p. 71.

137. Stachura, *Strasser*, p. 76.

138. See P. Fritzsche *Germans into Nazis* (Cambridge, Mass., 1998), pp. 209ff. In general see C. Fischer *The Rise of the Nazis* (Manchester, 2002); M. Broszat *Hitler and the Collapse of Weimar Germany* (Leamington Spa, 1987); H. A. Turner *Hitler's Thirty Days to Power: January 1933* (London, 1996).

139. Avtorkhanov, *Stalin and the Communist Party*, pp. 1–2.

140. J. Biesemann *Das Ermächtigungsgesetz als Grundlage der Gesetzgebung im nationalsozialistischen Staat* (Münster, 1985), pp. 279–82.

141. Stalin, *Works*, vol. xiii, p. 354.

142. Volkogonov, *Stalin: Triumph and Tragedy*, p. 198.

143. J. Toland *Adolf Hitler* (New York, 1976), p. 361; H. Burden *The Nuremberg Party Rallies: 1923–39* (London, 1967), pp. 76, 80–81.

144. Longerich, *Die braunen Bataillone*, p. 184. By mid-1934 the SA numbered 4.5 million. On the background see K. Heiden *The Führer* (New York, 1944), pp. 570–82; Kershaw, *Hitler: Hubris*, pp. 500–507.

145. Kershaw, *Hitler: Hubris*, p. 517.

146. Details in H.-G. Seraphim (ed.) *Das politische Tagebuch Alfred Roenbergs aus den Jahren 1934/35 und 1939/40* (Göttingen, 1956), pp. 33–5.

147. M. Domarus *Hitler: Reden und Proklamationen 1932–1945: Band I Triumph* (Munich, 1965), p. 405.

148. Domarus, *Hitler: Reden*, p. 406.

149. Domarus, *Hitler: Reden*, pp. 424–5.

150. A. Knight *Who Killed Kirov? The Kremlin's Greatest Mystery* (New York, 1999), p. 115.

151. Knight, *Who Killed Kirov?*, pp. 172–4; Volkogonov, *Stalin: Triumph and Tragedy*, p. 200.

152. Knight, *Who Killed Kirov?*, pp. 169–70; Volkogonov, *Stalin: Triumph and Tragedy*, pp. 205–6.

153. Knight, *Who Killed Kirov?*, p. 183.

154. Knight, *Who Killed Kirov?*, pp. 197–8; Getty and Manning, *Stalinist Terror*, pp. 45–9; M. Lenoe 'Did Stalin Kill Kirov and Does it Matter?', *Journal of Modern History*, 74 (2002), pp. 352–80.

155. On the 'Lex Kirov' Volkogonov, *Stalin: Triumph and Tragedy*, p. 208.

156. V. M. Berezhkov *At Stalin's Side* (New York, 1994), p. 10.

Chapter 2

1. D. Beetham *Max Weber and the Theory of Modern Politics* (London, 1974), p. 236.

2. A. Avtorkhanov *The Communist Party Apparatus* (Chicago, 1966), p. 52.

3. V. Garros, N. Korenevskaya and T. Lahusen (eds) *Intimacy and Terror: Soviet Diaries of the 1930s* (New York, 1995), pp. 205–6, diary of Galina Shtange, 12 December 1937, p. 357, diary of Lyubov Shaporina, 12 December 1937.

4. Garros *et al.*, *Intimacy and Terror*, p. 206.

5. Garros *et al.*, *Intimacy and Terror*, p. 357.

6. S. Labin *Stalin's Russia* (London, 1949), p. 34.

7. L. Siegelbaum and A. Sokolov (eds) *Stalinism as a Way of Life* (New Haven, Conn., 2000), pp. 159–63; K. Petrone *Life Has Become More Joyous, Comrades: Celebrations in the Time of Stalin* (Bloomington, Ind., 2000), p. 175.

8. S. Davies *Popular Opinion in Stalin's Russia: Terror, Propaganda and Dissent 1934–1941* (Cambridge, 1997), pp. 102–12.

9. Davies, *Popular Opinion*, p. 112.

10. P. Hubert *Uniformierter Reichstag: Die Geschichte der Pseudo-Volksvertretung 1933–1945* (Düsseldorf, 1992), pp. 88, 265; R. Gellateley *Backing Hitler: Consent and Coercion in Nazi Germany* (Oxford, 2001), pp. 15–16.

11. Hubert, *Uniformierter Reichstag*, p. 281.

12. Hubert, *Uniformierter Reichstag*, pp. 249–51, 274; IWM, FO 645, Box 156, testimony of Albert Göring, 25 September 1945, for details on voting 'no'.

13. Hubert, *Uniformierter Reichstag*, p. 237.

14. J. Stalin *Problems of Leninism* (Moscow, 1947), p. 557, 'On the Draft Constitution of the U.S.S.R.', speech of 25 November 1936.

15. *Ibid.*

16. H. von Kotze and H. Krausnick (eds) '*Es spricht der Führer*': 7 *exemplarische Hitler-Reden* (Gütersloh, 1966), p. 142, speech by Hitler to party district leaders, 29 April 1937.

17. Stalin, *Problems*, pp. 550–51; see too G. B. Carson *Electoral Practices in the USSR* (New York, 1955), pp. 50–52.

18. Hubert, *Uniformierter Reichstag*, pp. 61, 87; Kotze and Krausnick, '*Es spricht der Führer*', p, 120.

19. Kotze and Krausnick, '*Es spricht der Führer*', p. 140.

20. G. Neesse *Die NSDAP: Versuch einer Rechtsdeutung* (Stuttgart, 1935), pp. 143–5; Hubert, *Uniformierter Reichstag*, p. 240.

21. H. Rauschning *Hitler Speaks* (London, 1939), p. 199. Hitler told Rauschning that 'there is no such thing as unlimited power . . . Even the most extreme autocrat is compelled to correct his absolute will by existing conditions.'

22. A. L. Unger *Constitutional Development in the USSR: a Guide to Soviet Constitutions* (London, 1981), pp. 50–52, 59–72.

23. *The Constitution of the U.S.S.R.* (Moscow, 1937), pp. 7–9.

24. Hubert, *Uniformierter Reichstag*, pp. 59–61; J. Biesemann *Das Ermächtigungsgesetz als Grundlage der Gesetzgebung im nationalsozialistischen Staat* (Münster, 1985), pp. 51–4, 381–2. On Hitler's ideas of an advisory senate, *Mein Kampf*, vol. ii, pp. 501–2.

25. Hubert, *Uniformierter Reichstag*, pp. 58–63; M. Domarus (ed.) *Hitler: Reden und Proklamationen 1932–1945: Band I, Triumph* (Munich, 1965), p. 429; M. Moll (ed.) '*Führer-Erlasse*', *1939–1945* (Stuttgart, 1997), pp. 49–50.

26. Labin, *Stalin's Russia*, p. 31.

27. E. Lyons *Assignment in Utopia* (London, 1937).

28. E. van Ree *The Political Thought of Joseph Stalin* (London, 2002), pp. 148–9; see too J. Stalin *Works* (13 vols, Moscow, 1953–55), vol. i., pp. 371–2 for his early views in 'Anarchism or Socialism', December 1906/January 1907. He distinguished two kinds of dictatorship – of the majority, 'dictatorship of the street, of the masses, a dictatorship directed against all oppressors', and a dictatorship of a minority or clique, which 'tightens the noose around the neck of the majority'.

29. E. Mawdsley and S. White *The Soviet Elite from Lenin to Gorbachev: The Central Committee and its Members 1917–1991* (Oxford, 2000), pp. 126–7; D. Volkogonov *Stalin: Triumph and Tragedy* (London, 1991), p. 217.

30. M. David-Fox and D. Hoffmann 'The Politburo Protocols 1919–40', *Russian Review*, 55 (1996), pp. 99–100; I. Pavlova 'The Strength and Weakness of Stalin's Power', in N. Rosenfeldt, B. Jensen and E. Kulavig (eds) *Mechanisms of Power in the Soviet Union* (London, 2000), p. 30; O. V. Khlevniuk *Politburo – mekhanizmy politicheskoi vlasti v 1930-ye gody* (Moscow, 1996), pp. 330–31.

31. Mawdsley and White, *Soviet Elite*, p. 126; Khlevniuk, *Politburo*, pp. 288, 332–3; J. Löwenhardt, J. Ozinga and E. van Ree *The Rise and Fall of the Soviet Politburo* (London, 1992), pp. 34–5.

32. Khlevniuk, *Politburo*, pp. 246–52.

33. See for example the effects of a long Stalin holiday, from 30 June to 31 October 1935, in R. W. Davies, O. V. Khlevniuk, E. A. Rees, P. K. Liudmila and A. R. Larisa (eds) *The Stalin–Kaganovich Correspondence 1931–1936* (New Haven, Conn., 2003), pp. 209–35.

34. T. J. Colton *Moscow: Governing the Socialist Metropolis* (Cambridge, Mass., 1995), p. 324–5, for Stalin's close attention to the rebuilding of Moscow.

35. Khlevniuk, *Politburo*, pp. 290–91; see too M. Djilas *Conversations with Stalin* (New York, 1962), pp. 76–7: 'It was at these dinners that the destiny of the vast Russian land, of the newly acquired territories, and, to a considerable degree, of the human race was decided.' Djilas concluded, 'At these dinners the Soviet leaders were at their closest, most intimate with each other.'

36. N. Rosenfeldt ' "The Consistory of the Communist Church": The Origins and Development of Stalin's Secret Chancellery', *Russian History*, 9 (1982), pp. 308–15, 318; N. Rosenfeldt 'The Importance of the Secret Apparatus of the Soviet Communist Party during the Stalin Era', in Rosenfeldt, Jensen and Kulavig, *Mechanisms of Power*, pp. 40–59; Pavlova, 'Strengths and Weaknesses', pp. 29–36. On Stalin's regular access to secret intelligence on states abroad see V. V. Poznyakov 'The Soviet Intelligence Services and the Government: Information and Military-Political Decisions from the early 1920s to the early 1950s', in Rosenfeldt, Jensen and Kulavig, *Mechanisms of Power*, p. 107.

37. Rosenfeldt, ' "The Consistory of the Communist Church" ', pp. 315–17, 321.

38. S. S. Montefiore *Stalin: the Court of the Red Tsar* (London, 2003), pp. 59–60.

39. A. Knight *Beria: Stalin's First Lieutenant* (London, 1993), pp. 172–3; Montefiore, *Court of the Red Tsar*, p. 559.

40. Rosenfeldt, ' "The Consistory of the Communist Church" ', pp. 320–23.

41. V. Serge *The Case of Comrade Tulayev* (London, 1968), pp. 257–8. See too V. Serge *Memoirs of a Revolutionary 1901–1941* (Oxford, 1967), pp. 284 ff.

42. Kotze and Krausnick, '*Es spricht der Führer*', p. 117.

43. J. Öhquist *Das Reich des Führers* (Bonn, 1943), p. 157.

44. H. Brausse *Die Führungsordnung des deutschen Volkes: Grundlegung einer Führungslehre* (Hamburg, 1940), pp. 54–60; Neesse, *Die NSDAP*, pp. 145–7: 'The Führer is the living embodiment of the majority of the people.'

45. Hubert, *Uniformierter Reichstag*, pp. 132–7.

46. Moll, *Führer Erlasse*, pp. 48–9; E. H. Schwaab *Hitler's Mind: a Plunge into Madness* (New York, 1992), p. 43 cites Hans Frank: 'In the formulation of the law, the historical will of the Führer is implemented, and the fulfilment of this historical will of the Führer is not contingent on any prerequisites of the laws of the state.'

47. IWM, FO 645 Box 161, testimony of Baldur von Schirach, 15 September 1945, p. 5.

48. Kotze and Krausnick, *'Er spricht der Führer'*, p. 160.

49. D. Orlow *The History of the Nazi Party. Vol. 2: 1933–1945* (Newton Abbot, 1973), pp. 333–6.

50. Orlow, *History of the Nazi Party*, pp. 422–3, 458–9, 466.

51. Hubert, *Uniformierter Reichstag*, pp. 57, 220–26.

52. A. Resis (ed.) *Molotov Remembers: Inside Kremlin Politics* (Chicago, 1993), pp. 38–9.

53. See the discussion of 'weak dictator' in Moll, *Führer Erlasse*, pp. 9–29; see too D. Rebentisch *Führerstaat und Verwaltung im Zweiten Weltkrieg* (Stuttgart, 1989).

54. H. Mommsen 'Hitlers Stellung im nationalsozialistischen Herrschaftssystem', in G. Hirschfeld and L. Kettenacker (eds) *Der 'Führerstaat': Mythos und Realität* (Stuttgart, 1981), pp. 43–70.

55. See, for example, J. P. Duffy *Hitler Slept Late And Other Blunders That Cost Him the War* (New York, 1991), esp. ch 11 'profile of a bungler'. On Hitler's work pattern in the 1930s see K. Krause *Zehn Jahre Kammerdiener bei Hitler* (Hamburg, 1950), pp. 13–22, who describes his daily routine in the 1930s and early in the war.

56. See Pavlova, 'Strengths and Weaknesses', pp. 23–37; S. Pons 'Stalinism and Party Organisation (1933–48)', in J. Channon (ed.) *Politics, Society and Stalinism in the USSR* (London, 1998), pp. 93–4.

57. G. A. Bordiougov 'The Transformation of the Policy of Extraordinary Measures into a Permanent System of Government', in Rosenfeldt, Jensen and Kulavig, *Mechanisms of Power*, pp. 122–40.

58. See for example I. Kershaw 'Working Towards the Führer: reflections on the nature of the Nazi dictatorship', in I. Kershaw and M. Lewin (eds) *Stalinism and Nazism: Dictatorships in Comparison* (Cambridge, 1997), pp. 88–107.

59. See, for example, S. Fitzpatrick *'Blat* in Stalin's Time', in S. Lovell, A. Ledeneva and A. Rogachevskii (eds) *Bribery and Blat in Russia: Negotiating Reciprocity from the Middle Ages to the 1990s* (London, 2000), pp. 169–76;

E. Belova 'Economic Crime and Punishment', in P. R. Gregory *Behind the Façade of Stalin's Command Economy* (Stanford, 2001), pp. 133–42.

60. See, for example, Belova, 'Economic Crime', pp. 134–5; D. R. Shearer *Industry, State, and Society in Stalin's Russia, 1926–34* (Ithaca, NY, 1996), pp. 196–203, 208–10.

61. Resis, *Molotov Remembers*, p. 181.

62. Resis, *Molotov Remembers*, pp. 181–3.

63. Montefiore, *Court of the Red Tsar*.

64. Ironically one of the few people he did address with the familiar 'Du' was Ernst Röhm, murdered on his orders in 1934.

65. R. J. Overy *Interrogations: the Nazi Elite in Allied Hands* (London, 2001), pp. 132–40.

66. Resis, *Molotov Remembers*, p. 183.

67. B. Bromage *Molotov: the Story of an Era* (London, 1956); Montefiore, *Court of the Red Tsar*, pp. 34–5.

68. S. Beria *Beria, My Father: Inside Stalin's Kremlin* (London, 2001), p. 165; Volkogonov, *Triumph and Tragedy*, pp. 249–52.

69. Davies *et al.*, *The Stalin–Kaganovich Correspondence*, pp. 21–36.

70. Resis, *Molotov Remembers*, p. 232.

71. Beria, *Beria, My Father*, p. 160; on Zhdanov's death see J. Brent and V. Naumov *Stalin's Last Crime: the Plot against the Jewish Doctors, 1948–1953* (London, 2002).

72. Beria, *Beria, My Father*, pp. 141–2.

73. T. H. Rigby 'Was Stalin a Loyal Patron?' *Soviet Studies*, 38 (1986), pp. 313–14, 17–19.

74. See A. Kube *Pour le mérite und Hakenkreuz: Hermann Göring im Dritten Reich* (Munich, 1986).

75. R. Reuth *Goebbels* (London, 1993).

76. T. Junge *Until the Final Hour: Hitler's Last Secretary* (London, 2003), p. 94. On Himmler, P. Padfield *Himmler: Reichsführer SS* (London, 1990).

77. F. Genoud (ed.), *The Testament of Adolf Hitler: the Hitler–Bormann Documents* (London, 1961), p. 104.

78. IWM, Speer Collection, Box S369, FIAT Report 19, 'Adolf Hitler', pp. 3–4.

79. P. Huttenberger 'Nationalsozialistische Polykratie', *Geschichte und Gesellschaft*, 2 (1976), pp. 419–42; K. Hildebrand 'Monokratie oder Polykratie? Hitlers Herrschaft und das Dritte Reich', in Hirschfeld and Kettenacker, *Der 'Führer-straat'*, pp. 73–96.

80. Beria, *Beria, My Father*, p. 157; Resis, *Molotov Remembers*, p. 181.

81. IWM, Speer Collection, Box 5369, FIAT Report, 19, p. 3.

82. Dollmann in PRO, WO 218/4475, interrogation of Eugen Dollmann (August 1945), p. 1; G. W. Price *I Know These Dictators* (London, 1937), pp. 9–10: 'His bearing remains tranquil until his attention is aroused by some political remark. Then his eyes light up, his relaxed frame stiffens, and in a hoarse, sombre voice, he pours forth a voluble reply.'

83. IWM, Speer Collection, Box S369, FIAT Report 19, Albert Speer 'Adolf Hitler' 19 October, 1945, p. 9.

84. Junge, *Until the Final Hour*, p. 85.

85. *Reichsgesetzblatt*, 1936, Part I, p. 887; BA-B, R26 IV/4, 'Sitzung des kleinen Ministerrats', 21 October 1936, p. 2: 'the full power of the Minister President [Göring] is unlimited'. Heinrich Lammers, head of the Reich Chancellery, described the nature of this power after the war: 'Göring . . . under whose jurisdiction all Government and Party units were subordinate'. See IWM, FO645 Box 159, 'Notes on Legislation and Measures for the Defence of the Reich', 17 October, 1945.

86. IWM, Speer Collection, Box S369, FIAT Report 19, Part III, 'Exploitation of Albert Speer', pp. 9–10.

87. Volkogonov, *Triumph and Tragedy*, pp. 240–41.

88. Resis, *Molotov Remembers*, pp. 179–80.

89. Krause, *Zehn Jahre*, p. 22.

90. Resis, *Molotov Remembers*, p. 180.

91. Resis, *Molotov Remembers*, p. 29.

92. R. J. Overy *Goering the 'Iron Man'* (London, 1984), pp. 59–75.

93. G. P. Megargee *Inside Hitler's High Command* (Lawrence, Kans., 2000), pp. 44–8; IWM, FO 645, Box 158, memorandum by Wilhelm Keitel 'The position and powers of the Chief of OKW', 9 October 1945, pp. 1–4; W. Deist 'Die Wehrmacht des Dritten Reiches', in W. Deist *et al. Das Deutsche Reich und der Zweite Weltkrieg: Band I* (Stuttgart, 1979), pp. 501–20.

94. 'Weisung Adolf Hitlers an die Wehrmacht von 3 April 1939', H. Michaelis and E. Schraepler (eds) *Ursachen und Folgen vom deutschen Zusammenbruch 1918 bis 1945* (Berlin, 1967), vol. xiii, p. 212.

95. See R. J. Overy 'Strategic Intelligence and the Outbreak of the Second World War', *War in History*, 5 (1998), pp. 456–64.

96. IWM, Case XI, document book 1b, p. 133, Fritzsche affidavit, 29 June 1948; E. Fröhlich (ed.) *Die Tagebücher von Joseph Goebbels: Teil I, Aufzeichnungen 1923–1941*, vol. vii (Munich, 1998), p. 87.

97. H. von Kotze (ed.) *Heeresadjutant bei Hitler 1938–1945: Aufzeichnungen des Majors Engel* (Stuttgart, 1974), p. 60; H. Groscurth *Tagebuch eines Abwehroffiziers* (Stuttgart, 1970), p. 128, entries for 28, 30 September 1938.

98. J. Toland *Adolf Hitler* (London, 1976), p. 571.

99. B. Whaley *Codeword Barbarossa* (Cambridge, Mass., 1973), p. 211.

100. On Stalin's letter see A. M. Nekrich *Pariahs, Partners, Predators: German–Soviet Relations 1922–1941* (New York, 1997), p. 22; C. Roberts 'Planning for War: the Red Army and the Catastrophe of 1941', *Europe–Asia Studies*, 47 (1995), p. 1319.

101. R. McNeal *Stalin: Man and Ruler* (London, 1988), p. 238.

102. Resis, *Molotov Remembers*, p. 22; Knight, *Beria*, p. 109.

103. On Stalin, Resis, *Molotov Remembers*, p. 25; O. Dietrich *The Hitler I Knew* (London, 1955), p.47. Also L. E. Hill (ed.) *Die Weizsäcker-Papiere 1933–50* (Frankfurt am Main, 1974), p. 164, entry for 7 September 1939.

104. N. von Below *At Hitler's Side: The Memoirs of Hitler's Luftwaffe Adjutant 1937–1945* (London, 2003), pp. 32–3.

105. E. Radzinsky *Stalin* (London, 1996), pp. 451–2.

106. von Below, *At Hitler's Side*, p. 33.

107. On the office see Brausse, *Führungsordnung*, p. 52; on the succession N. Zitelmann *Hitler: the Politics of Seduction* (London, 1999), p. 383.

108. Zitelmann, *Hitler*, pp. 383–7; on the special nature of Hitler's leadership Brausse, *Führungsordnung*, pp. 54–5, 60.

109. W. Taubman *Khrushchev: the Man and his Era* (New York, 2003), pp. 3–17.

Chapter 3

1. *Pravda*, 19 December 1939, 'About Stalin'.

2. *Uncensored Germany: Letters and News Sent Secretly from Germany to the German Freedom Party* (London, 1940), pp. 23–4.

3. I. Zbarsky and S. Hutchinson *Lenin's Embalmers* (London, 1998), pp. 164–5; S. Fenander 'Author and Autocrat: Tertz's Stalin and the Ruse of Charisma', *Russian Review*, 58 (1999), p. 295.

4. P. Grigorenko *Memoirs* (London, 1983), p. 219; P. Deriabin with J. C. Evans *Inside Stalin's Kremlin* (Washington, DC, 1998), pp. x–xi.

5. A. Speer *Inside the Third Reich: Memoirs* (London, 1970), pp. 488–9.

6. Imperial War Museum, London, *Aus deutsche Urkunden*. Letters from British censor's office, n.d. but *c.* 1945.

7. I. Kershaw *The 'Hitler Myth': Image and Reality in the Third Reich* (Oxford, 1987), pp. 264–6.

8. W. Lewis *The Hitler Cult* (London, 1939); E. Alexander *Der Mythos Hitler* (Zurich, 1937).

9. See S. Labin *Stalin's Russia* (London, 1949), pp. 61ff for contemporary views of the Stalin cult.

10. A. Hitler *Mein Kampf* (ed. D. C. Watt, London, 1969), pp. 403, 408–9; R. Zitelmann *Hitler: the Politics of Seduction* (London, 1999), p. 391.

11. H. Trevor-Roper (ed.) *Hitler's Table Talk, 1941–1944* (London, 1973), pp. 385–6, 508, conversation of 31 March 1942 and 31 May 1942.

12. G. Macdonogh *The Last Kaiser: William The Impetuous* (London, 2000), p. 453.

13. J. Stalin *Foundations of Leninism* (New York, 1939), p. 59.

14. Stalin, *Foundations*, pp. 110, 118.

15. J. Stalin *Works* (13 vols, Moscow, 1952–55), vol. xiii, pp. 107–9, 'Talk with the German author Emil Ludwig', 13 December 1931.

16. D. Brandenberger and A. Dubrovsky ' "The People need a Tsar": the Emergence of National Bolshevism as Stalinist Ideology 1931–1941', *Europe–Asia Studies*, 50 (1998), pp. 873–92; see too D. Brandenberger *National Bolshevism: Stalinist Mass Culture and the Formation of Modern Russian National Identity 1931–1956* (Cambridge, Mass., 2002), pp. 56–8, 86–90, 100–03.

17. A. Resis (ed.) *Molotov Remembers: Inside Kremlin Politics. Conversations with Felix Chuev* (Chicago, 1993), pp. 181, 213.

18. E. van Ree *The Political Thought of Joseph Stalin* (London, 2002), p. 163.

19. *Voprosy Istorii*, 1953, no. 11.

20. B. Rosenthal *New Myth, New World: from Nietzsche to Stalin* (Pittsburgh, 2002), p. 377.

21. R. Bendix *Max Weber: an Intellectual Portrait* (London, 1966), pp. 299–307; J. Winckelmann (ed.) *Max Weber: gesammelte politische Schrifte* (Tübingen, 1958), pp. 505ff, 'Politik als Beruf', October 1919.

22. D. Beetham *Max Weber and the Theory of Modern Politics* (London, 1974), p. 227.

23. W. G. Runciman (ed.) *Max Weber: Selections in Translation* (London, 1974), p. 226.

24. Rosenthal, *New Myth, New World*, p. 377.

25. A. Storr (ed.) *The Essential Jung: Selected Writings* (London, 1983), pp. 191, 202–3.

26. A. Kolnai *The War Against the West* (London, 1938), p. 159.

27. G. Scheele *The Weimar Republic: Overture to the Third Reich* (London, 1946), pp. 229–30.

28. B. G. Rosenthal 'Nietzsche, Nationality, Nationalism', in A. Freifeld, P. Bergmann and B. G. Rosenthal (eds) *East Europe reads Nietzsche* (New York, 1998), pp. 190–97; M. L. Loe 'Gorky and Nietzsche: the Quest for a Russian

Superman', in B. G. Rosenthal (ed.) *Nietzsche in Russia* (Princeton, NJ, 1986), pp. 251–2.

29. Y. Yevtushenko (ed.) *Twentieth-Century Russian Poetry* (London, 1993), p. 81; on the use of religious imagery and metaphor see N. Tumarkin *Lenin Lives! The Lenin Cult in Soviet Russia* (Cambridge, Mass., 1997), pp. 18–23; M. D. Steinberg *Proletarian Imagination: Self, Modernity, and the Sacred in Russia, 1910–1925* (Ithaca, NY, 2002), pp. 254–5, 273–8.

30. Tumarkin, *Lenin Lives!*, p. 21; on Lunacharsky see A. L. Tait 'Lunacharsky: a "Nietzschean Marxist"?', in Rosenthal, *Nietzsche in Russia*, pp. 275–92.

31. On the Tsar cult and its decline see O. Figes and B. Kolonitskii *Interpreting the Russian Revolution: the Language and Symbols of 1917* (New Haven, Conn., 1999), chs 1–2; Tumarkin, *Lenin Lives!*, pp. 6–12.

32. *Pravda*, 18 December 1939.

33. W. Laqueur *Stalin: the Glasnost Revelations* (London, 1990), p. 180.

34. Tumarkin, *Lenin Lives!*, pp. 54–5.

35. I. Bonnell *Iconography of Power: Soviet Political Posters under Lenin and Stalin* (Berkeley, Calif., 1997), pp. 140–54; S. Davies *Popular Opinion in Stalin's Russia: Terror, Propaganda and Dissent, 1934–1941* (Cambridge, 1997), pp. 147–9.

36. Tumarkin, *Lenin Lives!*, p. 80.

37. Tumarkin, *Lenin Lives!*, p. 82.

38. B. Ennker 'The Origins and Intentions of the Lenin Cult', in I. D. Thatcher (ed.) *Regime and Society in Twentieth-Century Russia* (London, 1999), pp. 119–25; Zbarsky and Hutchinson, *Lenin's Embalmers*, pp. 9–25 for details on the decision.

39. Ennker, 'Lenin Cult', pp. 123–4; Zbarsky and Hutchinson, *Lenin's Embalmers*, pp. 25–31; Tumarkin, *Lenin Lives!*, pp. 191–6, 205.

40. Bonnell, *Iconography of Power*, pp. 148, 150; Tumarkin, *Lenin Lives!*, pp. 126–7; R. Löhmann *Der Stalinmythos: Studien zur Sozialgeschichte des Personenkultes in der Sowjetunion (1929–1935)* (Münster, 1990), pp. 47–56.

41. Storr, *The Essential Jung*, p. 210, 'The Development of Personality', 1934.

42. Lewis, *Hitler Cult*, p. 47.

43. IWM, FO 645/161, interrogation of Christa Schroeder, 13 September 1945, p. 5.

44. See for example, G. Ueding 'Rede als Führerproklamation' in J. Kopperschmidt (ed.) *Hitler der Redner* (Munich, 2003), pp. 441–53.

45. M. Dodd *My Years in Germany* (London, 1939), p. 180.

46. M. Loiperdinger ' "Sieg des Glaubens" – Ein gelungenes Experiment national-sozialistischer Filmpropaganda', in U. Hermann and U. Nassen (eds)

Formative Ästhetik in National-Sozialismus (Weinheim, 1994), pp. 40–45.

47. V. Cowles *Looking for Trouble* (London, 1941), pp. 153–4.

48. Lewis, *Hitler Cult*, p. 39.

49. J. H. Billington *The Face of Russia* (New York, 1998), p. 210.

50. See for example J. Stalin *Problems of Leninism* (Moscow, 1947), pp. 250, 285, 439.

51. Resis, *Molotov Remembers*, pp. 175–6.

52. Hitler's model was the unmarried mayor of pre-war Vienna, Karl Lueger. See B. Hamann *Hitler's Vienna: a Dictator's Apprenticeship* (Oxford, 1999), pp. 375–8; See too Public Record Office, Kew, London FO 1031/102 'Women around Hitler', Memorandum by Karl Brandt, 6 February 1946: 'Hitler wished to keep the mystic legend alive in the hearts of the German people that so long as he remained a bachelor, there was always the chance that any out of the millions of German women might possibly attain the high distinction of being at Hitler's side.'

53. Speer, *Inside the Third Reich*, p. 114.

54. E. Barker *Reflections on Government* (Oxford, 1942), p. 375.

55. Kolnai, *War against the West*, p. 153.

56. Kolnai, *War against the West*, pp. 156, 158.

57. Stalin, *Foundations*, pp. 109–10.

58. Bonnell, *Iconography of Power*, pp. 157–9.

59. Tumarkin, *Lenin Lives!*, pp, 252–3; Rosenthal, *New Myth, New World*, pp. 375, 379; S. Davis 'The Leader Cult: Propaganda and its Reception in Stalin's Russia', in J. Channon (ed.) *Politics, Society and Stalinism in the USSR* (London, 1998), pp. 117–18.

60. Labin, *Stalin's Russia*, p. 71; see too van Ree, *Political Thought of Joseph Stalin*, p. 162.

61. Bonnell, *Iconography of Power*, pp. 162–4; Labin, *Stalin's Russia*, p. 67.

62. van Ree, *Political Thought of Joseph Stalin*, p. 165.

63. C. Schmölders *Hitlers Gesicht: Eine physiognomische Biographie* (Munich, 2000), p. 145.

64. Schmölders, *Hitlers Gesicht*, pp. 39–40; on the presentation of the image see too U. Kühn 'Rede als Selbstinszenierung – Hitler auf der "Bühne"', in Kopperschmidt, *Hitler der Redner*, pp. 368–79; K. Protte 'Hitler als Redner in Fotografie und Film', in Kopperschmidt, *Hitler der Redner*, pp. 243–54.

65. Schmölders, *Hitlers Gesicht*, p. 104.

66. Schmölders, *Hitlers Gesicht*, pp. 148–9; see too C. Koonz *The Nazi Conscience* (Cambridge, Mass., 2003), pp. 77–9.

67. Bonnell, *Iconography of Power*, p. 137.

68. Bonnell, *Iconography of Power*, p. 157.

69. Rosenthal, *New Myth, New World*, pp. 380, 386.

70. Löhmann, *Der Stalinmythos*, p. 27.

71. G. F. Alexandrov *et al. Joseph Stalin: a Short Biography* (Mocow, 1949); see too van Ree, *Political Thought of Joseph Stalin*, pp. 162–5.

72. J. J. Barnes and P. P. Barnes *Hitler's* Mein Kampf: *Britain and America: a Publishing History 1930–39* (Cambridge, 1980), pp. 1–2; see too W. Maser *Mein Kampf: Der Fahrplan eines Welteroberers: Geschichte, Auszüge, Kommentare* (Esslingen, 1974) and, more recently, B. Zehnpfennig *Hitler's* Mein Kampf: *Eine Interpretation* (Munich, 2000).

73. Laqueur, *Glasnost Revelations*, p. 182.

74. *History of the Communist Party of the Soviet Union: short course* (Moscow, 1942), p. 206.

75. Fenander, 'Author and Autocrat', p. 297.

76. Fenander, 'Author and Autocrat', p. 297.

77. Davies, *Popular Opinion in Stalin's Russia*, p. 149.

78. Labin, *Stalin's Russia*, p. 68.

79. H. G. Baynes *Germany Possessed* (London, 1941), pp. 107–8.

80. Schmölders, *Hitlers Gesicht*, p. 145.

81. Bonnell, *Iconography of Power*, pp. 148, 166.

82. Labin, *Stalin's Russia*, pp. 64–5.

83. Davies, *Popular Opinion in Stalin's Russia*, p. 161.

84. F. J. Miller *Folklore for Stalin: Russian Folklore and Pseudofolklore of the Stalin Era* (New York, 1990), ch. 2.

85. Miller, *Folklore for Stalin*, p. 69; F. J. Miller 'The Image of Stalin in Soviet Russian Folklore', *Russian Review*, 39 (1980), pp. 57–8.

86. Miller, *Folklore for Stalin*, p. 143.

87. Baynes, *Germany Possessed*, p. 107.

88. R. Marsh *Images of Dictatorship: Stalin in Literature* (London, 1989), p. 31.

89. Marsh, *Images of Dictatorship*, p. 39.

90. Marsh, *Images of Dictatorship*, p. 27.

91. Labin, *Stalin's Russia*, p. 65.

92. Davies, *Popular Opinion in Stalin's Russia*, p. 165; Laqueur, *Glasnost Revelations*, p. 183.

93. Davies, *Popular Opinion in Stalin's Russia*, p. 174.

94. G. Neesse *Die NSDAP: versuch einer Rechtsdentung* (Stuttgart, 1935), pp. 196–7; see too H. Brausse *Die Führungsordnung des deutschen Volkes: Grundlegung einer Führungslehre* (Hamburg, 1940) pp. 14–25, 52–5.

95. Storr, *Essential Jung*, p. 201.

96. M. Perrie 'Nationalism and History: the Cult of Ivan the Terrible in

Stalin's Russia', in G. Hosking and R. Service (eds) *Russian Nationalism: Past and Present* (London, 1998), p. 120.

97. *Joseph Stalin: a Short Biography*, pp. 201–3.

98. Kolnai, *War against the West*, p. 20.

99. Davies, *Popular Opinion in Stalin's Russia*, p. 172.

100. Kershaw, *The 'Hitler Myth'*, p. 60.

101. In general on the cult see Kershaw, *The 'Hitler Myth'*; G. Gill 'The Soviet Leader Cult: Reflections on the Structure of Leadership in the Soviet Union', *British Journal of Political Science*, 10 (1980), pp. 167–86; R. H. Tucker 'The Rise of Stalin's Personality Cult', *American Historical Review*, 84 (1979), pp. 347–66; S. Davies, 'The Leader Cult: Propaganda and its Perception in Stalinist Russia', in J. Channon (ed.) *Politics, Society and Stalinism in the USSR* (London, 1988), pp. 115–38.

102. Davies, *Popular Opinion in Stalin's Russia*, p. 170.

103. Davies, *Popular Opinion in Stalin's Russia*, p. 174.

104. N. Mandelstam *Hope against Hope* (London, 1970), p. 203; see too Marsh, *Images of Dictatorship*, pp. 36–8.

105. Marsh, *Images of Dictatorship*, pp. 45–50.

106. J. Brooks *Thank you, Comrade Stalin: Soviet Public Culture from Revolution to Cold War* (Princeton, 2000), p. 60.

107. G. Prokhorov *Art under Socialist Realism: Soviet Painting 1930–1950* (Roseville East, Austr., 1995), p. 101.

108. IWM, Speer Collection, Box S369, FIAT Report 19, exploitation of Albert Speer, 19 October 1945, pp. 3–4

109. C. Haste *Nazi Women* (London, 2001), p. 78.

110. F. Reck-Malleczewen *Diary of a Man in Despair* (London, 1951), p. 19.

111. Resis, *Molotov Remembers*, pp. 189–90; on Hitler's retirement, IWM, Speer Collection, Box S369, FIAT Report 19, p. 15.

112. Löhmann, *Der Stalinmythos*, p. 6.

113. Marsh, *Images of Dictatorship*, p. 28.

114. Fenander, 'Author and Autocrat', p. 295.

Chapter 4

1. J. Öhquist *Das Reich des Führers* (Bonn, 1943), p. 161.

2. J. Stalin *Works* (13 vols, Moscow, 1953–55), vol. viii, p. 43, 'Concerning Questions of Leninism', January 1926.

3. 'Der Schlussrede des Führers auf dem Parteikongress' 10 September 1934,

in G. Neesse *Die Nationalsozialistische Deutsche Arbeiterpartei* (Stuttgart, 1935), pp. 194–6.

4. J. Stalin *Problems of Leninism* (Moscow, 1947), pp. 80–81, 'Foundation of Leninism', April 1924.

5. Stalin, *Problems of Leninism*, pp. 81–2; Neese, *Nationalsozialistische Partei*, pp. 196–7; D. Hein 'Partei und Bewegung. Zwei Typen moderner politischer Willensbildung', *Historische Zeitschrift*, 263 (1996), pp. 85–7, 90–91.

6. Neesse, *Nationalsozialistische Partei*, p. 202; Stalin, *Problems of Leninism*, p. 80.

7. Neesse, *Nationalsozialistische Partei*, p. 202; Stalin, *Problems of Leninism*, p. 139, 'On the Problems of Leninism', 26 January 1926; H. Mehringer *Die NSDAP als politische Ausleseorganisation* (Munich, 1938), p. 14.

8. Stalin, *Problems of Leninism*, p. 84; Neesse, *Nationalsozialistische Partei*, p. 202; L. Münz *Führer durch die Behörden und Organisationen* (Berlin, 1939), p. 2a.

9. Stalin, *Problems of Leninism*, p. 153; *Works*, vol. viii, p. 43.

10. Stalin, *Problems of Leninism*, p. 82; Stalin, *Works*, vol. viii, pp. 44–5.

11. Neesse, *Nationalsozialistische Partei*, p. 22; Mehringer, *Die NSDAP*, p. 14; W. Schieder 'Die NSDAP vor 1933. Profil einer faschistischen Partei', *Geschichte und Gesellschaft*, 19 (1993), pp. 145–7; J. Caplan 'National Socialism and the Theory of the State', in T. Childers and J. Caplan (eds) *Reevaluating the Third Reich* (New York, 1993), pp. 105–7.

12. T. H. Rigby *Communist Party Membership in the USSR 1917–1967* (Princeton, NJ, 1968), p. 52; M. Kater *The Nazi Party: A Social Profile of Members and Leaders, 1919–1945* (Oxford, 1983), p. 263; B. Meissner *The Communist Party of the Soviet Union* (New York, 1956), pp. 4–5.

13. A. Avtorkhanov *The Communist Party Apparatus* (Chicago, 1961), pp. 76, 79–80; M. Fainsod *How Russia is Ruled* (Cambridge, Mass., 1967), pp. 248–50, 262; G. Gill *The Rules of the Communist Party of the Soviet Union* (London, 1988), pp. 40–42.

14. R. Taylor *Film Propaganda in Soviet Russia and Nazi Germany* (London, 1998), p. 63.

15. Meissner, *Communist Party*, p. 40; Gill, *Rules of the Communist Party*, pp. 163–4.

16. C.-W. Reibel *Das Fundament der Diktatur: Die NSDAP-Ortsgruppen 1932–1945* (Paderborn, 2002), pp. 232–3.

17. Details on membership from Rigby, *Communist Party Membership*,

pp. 190–91, 197–200, 256–63; see too Fainsod, *How Russia is Ruled*, pp. 248–70.

18. Rigby, *Communist Party Membership*, pp. 275–80.

19. D. Orlow *The History of the Nazi Party: Volume II 1933–1945* (Newton Abbot, 1973), pp. 55–6, 202.

20. Kater, *The Nazi Party*, p. 263; Orlow, *Nazi Party: II*, pp. 203–5, 253, 323.

21. Rigby, *Communist Party Membership*, p. 73; D. Schmiechen-Ackermann 'Der "Blockwart"', *Vierteljahrshefte für Zeitgeschichte*, 48 (2000), pp. 584–5.

22. Rigby, *Communist Party Membership*, pp. 204–13; Fainsod, *How Russia is Ruled*, 260–61, 262; see too J. A. Getty *The Origin of the Great Purges: The Soviet Communist Party Reconsidered 1933–1938* (Cambridge, 1985).

23. Fainsod, *How Russia is Ruled*, pp. 177, 196.

24. Rigby, *Communist Party Membership*, pp. 263–75.

25. Schmiechen-Ackermann, 'Der "Blockwart"', pp. 596–7.

26. Calculated from Kater, *Nazi Party*, p. 263.

27. Orlow, *Nazi Party: II*, pp. 124–5.

28. Schmiechen-Ackermann, 'Der "Blockwart"', p. 587.

29. D. Mühlberger 'The Pattern of the SA's Social Appeal', in C. Fisher (ed.) *The Rise of National Socialism and the Working Classes in Weimar Germany* (Oxford, 1996), pp. 99–116.

30. A. Graziosi *A New, Peculiar State: Explorations in Soviet History 1917–1937* (Westport, Conn., 2000), pp. 196–7.

31. Fainsod, *How Russia is Ruled*, p. 251; R. Hill and P. Frank *The Soviet Communist Party* (London, 1983), pp. 33–6.

32. K. Boterbloem *Life and Death under Stalin: Kalinin Province, 1945–1953* (Montreal, 1999), p. 102; Fainsod, *How Russia is Ruled*, p. 264.

33. C.-C. Szejnmann *Vom Traum zum Alptraum: Sachsen in der Weimarer Republik* (Dresden, 2000), pp. 114–16.

34. Kater, *The Nazi Party*, pp. 264–7; D. Mühlberger (ed.) *The Social Basis of European Fascist Movements* (London, 1987), pp. 76–94: C. Roth *Parteikreis und Kreisleiter der NSDAP unter besonderer Berücksichtigung Bayerns* (Munich, 1997), p. 182; H.-U. Thamer *Verführung und Gewalt: Deutschland 1933–1945* (Berlin, 1986), p. 175.

35. J. Falter and M. H. Kater 'Wähler und Mitglieder der NSDAP', *Geschichte und Gesellschaft*, 19 (1993), p. 165.

36. Roth, *Parteikreis und Kreisleiter*, p. 183; Meissner, *Communist Party*, p. 10.

37. Fainsod, *How Russia is Ruled*, pp. 254, 271; Rigby, *Communist Party Membership*, p. 361.

38. Rigby, *Communist Party Membership*, p. 354; Fainsod, *How Russia is Ruled*, pp. 257, 274.

39. Roth, *Parteikreis und Kreisleiter*, p. 180; Thamer, *Verführung und Gewalt*, p. 178; Kater, *The Nazi Party*, p. 257.

40. Gill, *Rules of the Communist Party*, pp. 162–3, Rules of the All-Union Communist Party, 1934.

41. Avtorkhanov, *Communist Party Apparatus*, pp. 119, 122; Fainsod, *How Russia is Ruled*, pp. 229–30.

42. Avtorkhanov, *Communist Party Apparatus*, pp. 153–4; Fainsod, *How Russia is Ruled*, p. 196; M. Fainsod *Smolensk under Soviet Rule* (Boston, Mass., 1989), pp. 63, 113; L. Schapiro *The Communist Party of the Soviet Union* (London, 1960), pp. 444–5.

43. Reibel, *Fundament der Diktatur*, pp. 32–5.

44. Reibel, *Fundament der Diktatur*, pp. 121, 123; Schmiechen-Ackermann, 'Der "Blockwart"', p. 586.

45. Münz, *Führer durch die Behörden und Organisationen*, pp. 6–8.

46. Reibel, *Fundament der Diktatur*, pp. 50–51, 56–63.

47. Fainsod, *How Russia is Ruled*, pp. 284–91; Avtorkhanov, *Communist Party Apparatus*, pp. 256–7; see too I. Tirado, 'The Komsomol and the Bright Socialist Future', in C. Kuhr-Korolev, S. Plaggenborg and M. Wellmann (eds) *Sowjetjugend 1917–1941; Generation zwischen Revolution und Resignation* (Essen, 2001), pp. 217–32.

48. G. Kinz *Der Bund Deutscher Mädel: Ein Beitrag zur ausserschulischen Mädchenerziehung im Nationalsozialismus* (Frankfurt am Main, 1990), pp. 3–12, 25; C. Schubert-Weller *Hitler-Jugend: Vom 'Jungsturm Adolf Hitler' zur Staatsjugend des Dritten Reiches* (Weinheim, 1993), pp. 13–15, 33–4.

49. H. Vorländer *Die NSV: Darstellung und Dokumentation einer national-isozialistischen Organisation* (Boppard am Rhein, 1988), pp. 1–14, 96; J. Stephenson *The Nazi Organisation of Women* (London, 1981), pp. 50–55, 140.

50. Avtorkhanov, *Communist Party Apparatus*, p. 13.

51. E. van Ree 'Stalin's Organic Theory of the Party', *Russian Review*, 52 (1993), p. 54.

52. S. Allan *Comrades and Citizens: Soviet People* (London, 1938), pp. 88–9, 94–5.

53. Fainsod, *How Russia is Ruled*, pp. 260–61; Fainsod, *Smolensk under Soviet Rule*, pp. 220–22.

54. Allan, *Comrades and Citizens*, pp. 257–9.

55. Fainsod, *Smolensk under Soviet Rule*, p. 230; S. Pons 'Stalinism and Party Organisation (1933–1948)', in J. Channon (ed.) *Politics, Society and Stalinism in the USSR* (London, 1998), pp. 96–7.

56. D. M. McKale *The Nazi Party Courts: Hitler's management of conflict in his Movement 1921–1945* (Lawrence, Kans., 1974), pp. 77–8, 123.

57. McKale, *Nazi Party Courts*, p. 55.

58. McKale, *Nazi Party Courts*, p. 22–3.

59. McKale, *Nazi Party Courts*, pp. 144–5, 164, 178–80; M. Moll, 'Steuerungsinstrument im "Ämterchaos"? Die Tagungen der Reichs-und Gauleiter der NSDAP', *Vierteljahrshefte für Zeitgeschichte*, 49 (2001), pp. 236–8.

60. Allan, *Comrades and Citizens*, p. 88.

61. E. P. Mickiewicz, *Soviet Political Schools: the Communist Party Adult Instruction System* (New Haven, Conn., 1967), pp. 3–9, 89–101; M. David-Fox *Revolution of the Mind: Higher Learning among the Bolsheviks, 1918–1929* (Ithaca, NY, 1997), pp. 84–7; T. Kirstein, 'Das sowjetische Parteischulsystem', in B. Meissner, G. Brunner and R. Löwenthal (eds) *Einparteisystem und bürokratische Herrschaft in der Sowjetunion* (Cologne, 1978), pp. 204–16.

62. Orlow, *Nazi Party: II*, pp. 188–92; Schmiechen-Ackermann, 'Der "Blockwart"', p. 589.

63. Schubert-Weller, *Hitler-Jugend*, pp. 182–3; on selection and admission see the testimony of P. Peterson in J. Steinhoff, P. Pechel and D. Showalter (eds) *Voices of the Third Reich: an Oral History* (Washington, DC, 1989), pp. 8–9.

64. Avtorkhanov, *Communist Party Apparatus*, pp. 79–80; Schmiechen-Ackermann, 'Der "Blockwart"', p. 586; M. Voslensky *Nomenklatura: Anatomy of the Soviet Ruling Class* (London, 1984), pp. 48–9.

65. Allan, *Comrades and Citizens*, p. 242.

66. Schmiechen-Ackermann, 'Der "Blockwart"', p. 589.

67. Gill, *Rules of the Communist Party*, pp. 165–6.

68. Schmiechen-Ackermann, 'Der "Blockwart"', pp. 581–3; Reibel, *Fundament der Diktatur*, pp. 104–5; Stephenson, *Nazi Organisation of Women*, p. 155; L. Pine 'Creating Conformity: the Training of Girls in the Bund Deutscher Mädel', *European History Quarterly*, 33 (2003), pp. 367–85.

69. Schmiechen-Ackermann, 'Der "Blockwart"', pp. 590–95; J. Noakes (ed.) *Nazism 1919–1945: a Documentary Reader: Volume 4* (Exeter, 1998), pp. 96–100, 'Service Instructions for Block Leaders. 1 June 1944'.

70. Reibel, *Fundament der Diktatur*, pp. 104–5, 191.

71. D. Rebentisch 'Die "politische Beurteilung" als Herrschaftsinstrument der

NSDAP', in D. Peukert and J. Reulecke (eds) *Die Reihen fast geschlossen: Beiträge zur Geschichte des Alltags unterm Nationalsozialismus* (Wuppertal, 1981), pp. 107–28; Roth, *Parteikreis und Kreisleiter*, pp. 269–70.

72. Rebentisch, 'Die "politische Beurteilung"', p. 114.

73. Rebentisch, 'Die "politische Beurteilung"', pp. 108, 117–18.

74. Roth, *Parteikreis und Kreisleiter*, pp. 282–3.

75. S. Labin, *Stalin's Russia* (London, 1949), p. 149; Tirado, 'The Komsomol', pp. 220–22.

76. Labin, *Stalin's Russia*, p. 153.

77. Boterbloem, *Life and Death under Stalin*, p. 125.

78. A. Smith *I Was a Soviet Worker* (London, 1937), p. 242.

79. Noakes, *Nazism: Volume 4*, pp. 97–8.

80. Vorländer, *Die NSV: Dokumente*, pp. 53–4.

81. G. Miller-Kipp (ed.) *'Auch Du gehörst dem Führer': Die Geschichte des Bundes Deutscher Mädel in Quellen und Dokumenten* (Munich, 2001), p. 62.

82. See for example C. Arbogast *Herrschaftsinstanzen der württembergischen NSDAP: Funktion, Sozialprofil und Lebenswege einer regionalen NS-Elite 1920–1960* (Munich, 1998), pp. 116–22.

83. On the development of German bureaucracy J. Caplan 'Profession as Vocation: The German Civil Service', in G. Cocks and K. Jarausch (eds) *German Professions, 1800–1950* (Oxford, 1990), pp. 163–82.

84. T. H. Rigby 'Staffing USSR Incorporated: The Origins of the Nomenklatura System', *Soviet Studies*, 40 (1988), pp. 526–30.

85. Labin, *Stalin's Russia*, p. 50; Rigby, 'Staffing USSR Incorporated', pp. 531–3.

86. Labin, *Stalin's Russia*, p. 50.

87. R. Koshar *Social Life, Local Politics, and Nazism: Marburg 1880–1935* (Chapel Hill, NC, 1986), pp. 247–50.

88. J. H. Grill *The Nazi Movement in Baden 1920–1945* (Chapel Hill, NC, 1983), pp. 247–8, 257, 265.

89. H. Fenske *Bürokratie in Deutschland von späten Kaiserreich bis zur Gegenwart* (Berlin, 1985), pp. 40–43.

90. Fenske, *Bürokratie in Deutschland*, pp. 44, 48; M. Broszat *The Hitler State: the foundation and development of the internal structure of the Third Reich* (London, 1981), pp. 242–3.

91. Orlow, *Nazi Party: II*, pp. 226–7; H. Mommsen *Beamtentum in Dritten Reich: mit ausgewählten Quellen zur nationalsozialistischen Beamtenpolitik* (Stuttgart, 1966), pp. 103–4.

92. Roth, *Parteikreis und Kreisleiter*, pp. 234–5.

93. Roth, *Parteikreis und Kreisleiter*, p. 195.

94. Roth, *Parteikreis und Kreisleiter*, pp. 213, 215.
95. Orlow, *Nazi Party: II*, pp. 228–9.
96. Schmiechen-Ackermann, 'Der "Blockwart"', p. 586; Orlow, *Nazi Party: II*, pp. 72–3.
97. Avtorkhanov, *Communist Party Apparatus*, pp. 143, 199.
98. Münz, *Führer durch die Behörden*, pp. 6–9.
99. Roth, *Parteikreis und Kreisleiter*, pp. 122–3.
100. Roth, *Parteikreis und Kreisleiter*, pp. 139–44.
101. Broszat, *Hitler State*, pp. 112–17; on the *Reichsstatthalter* see H.-J. Sengotta *Der Reichsstatthalter in Lippe 1933 bis 1939. Reichsrechtliche Bestimmungen und politische Praxis* (Detmold, 1976), pp. 41–59, 408–9.
102. Moll, 'Steuerungsinstrument', pp. 215–72; more generally on the *Gauleiter* see P. Hüttenberger *Die Gauleiter* (Stuttgart, 1969).
103. Fainsod, *How Russia is Ruled*, p. 199.
104. Fainsod, *Smolensk under Soviet Rule*, p. 98.
105. Mommsen, *Beamtentum*, p. 103.
106. Gill, *Rules of the Communist Party*, pp. 44–7.
107. Avtorkhanov, *Communist Party Apparatus*, pp. 103–4; Pons, 'Stalinism and Party Organisation', pp. 108–9
108. B. Harasymiw *Soviet Communist Party Officials: A study in organizational roles and change* (New York, 1996), pp. 85–8.
109. B. Meissner 'Die besonderen Wesenszüge der sowjetschen Bürokratie und die Wandlungsmöglichkeiten des Einparteisystems' in Meissner, Brunner and Löwenthal, *Einparteisystem*, pp. 73–4; R. di Leo *Occupazione e salari nell'URSS 1950–1977* (Milan, 1980), pp. 38–9, 50.
110. Harasymiw, *Communist Party Officials*, p. 30.
111. Fenske, *Bürokratie in Deutschland*, pp. 45–7.
112. Fenske, *Bürokratie in Deutschland*, pp. 48–51.
113. See R. Koehl *The Black Corps: the Structure and Power Struggles of the Nazi SS* (Madison, Wisc., 1983); the process of infiltration and control is charted in A. Speer *The Slave State: Heinrich Himmler's Masterplan for SS Supremacy* (London, 1981).
114. Meissner, 'Der besonderen Wesenzüge', p. 77.
115. Fenske, *Bürokratie in Deutschland*, p. 45.
116. The party revived after Stalin's death. See Y. Gorlizki 'Party Revivalism and the Death of Stalin', *Slavic Review*, 54 (1995), pp. 1–22.
117. See for example A. Unger *The Totalitarian Party: Party and People in Nazi Germany and Soviet Russia* (London, 1974).
118. Roth, *Parteikreis und Kreisleiter*, p. 143.
119. Harasymiw, *Communist Party Officials*, pp. 136–7.

120. Boterbloem, *Life and Death under Stalin*.

121. S. Davies '"Us Against Them": Social Identity in Soviet Russia, 1934–41', *Russian Review*, 56 (1997), pp. 70–89.

Chapter 5

1. M. Fainsod *How Russia is Ruled* (Cambridge, Mass., 1967), p. 424.

2. N. Baynes (ed.) *Hitler's Speeches 1919–1939* (2 vols, Oxford, 1942), vol i., p. 504.

3. R. Tucker and S. Cohen (eds) *The Great Purge Trial* (New York, 1965), p. xv.

4. Fainsod, *How Russia is Ruled*, p. 423.

5. N. Leites and E. Bernant *Rituals of Liquidation: the Case of the Moscow Trials* (Glencoe, Ill., 1954), pp. 318, 322–3; see too People's Commissariat of Justice of the USSR *Report of Court Proceedings in the case of the Anti-Soviet 'Bloc of Rights and Trotskyites'* (Moscow, 1938), pp. 625–7.

6. J. Stalin *Works* (13 vols, Moscow, 1952–5), vol. xiii, pp. 110–11, 'talk with the German author Emil Ludwig', 13 December 1931.

7. T. Rees and A. Thorpe (eds) *International Communism and the Communist International 1919–1943* (Manchester, 1998), p. 35.

8. Fainsod, *How Russia is Ruled*, p. 159.

9. Leites and Bernant, *Rituals of Liquidation*, p. 12.

10. E. Alexander *Der Mythos Hitler* (Zurich, 1937), p. 395.

11. Baynes, *Hitler's Speeches*, vol. i, p. 504, proclamation at the party congress, 1 September 1933.

12. Baynes, *Hitler's Speeches*, vol. i, p. 299, Hitler speech to the Reichstag, 13 July 1934. Hitler reminded his audience that communism had brought 'mass-terrorism' to all parts of the world.

13. P. Weindling *Health, Race and German Politics between National Unification and Nazism 1870–1945* (Cambridge, 1989), pp. 382–5.

14. F. S. Zuckermann *The Tsarist Secret Police in Russian Society, 1880–1917* (London, 1996), pp. 19–27; J. Daly 'The Security Police and Politics in Late Imperial Russia', in A. Geifman (ed.) *Russia under the Last Tsar: Opposition and Subversion* (Oxford, 1999), pp. 217–34.

15. M. Broszat *The Hitler State: the foundation and development of the internal structure of the Third Reich* (London, 1981), p. 332. On political police forces see F Wilhelm *Die Polizei im NS-Staat* (Paderborn, 1997), pp. 24–35.

16. G. Leggett *The Cheka: Lenin's Political Police* (Oxford, 1981), pp. 16–22,

342–6, 351–2; R. Conquest (ed.) *The Soviet Police System* (London, 1968) pp. 13–18.

17. Fainsod, *How Russia is Ruled*, pp. 425–8.

18. R. Sharlet 'Stalinism and Soviet Legal Culture', in R. Tucker (ed.) *Stalinism: Essays in Historical Interpretation* (New York, 1977), pp. 164–6.

19. R. W. Thurston *Life and Terror in Stalin's Russia 1934–1941* (London, 1996), pp. 22–3; J. A. Getty and O. V. Naumov (eds) *The Road to Terror: Stalin and the Self-Destruction of the Bolsheviks 1932–1939* (New Haven, Conn., 1999), pp. 145–7; D. Rayfield *Stalin and his Hangmen* (London, 2004), pp. 239–40.

20. K. McDermott and J. Agnew *The Comintern: A History of International Communism from Lenin to Stalin* (London, 1996), pp. 148, 151.

21. B. A. Starkov 'The Trial that was not Held', *Europe–Asia Studies*, 46 (1994), pp. 1308–9.

22. E. Ginzburg *Into the Whirlwind* (London, 1967), pp. 130–37.

23. V. Z. Rogovin *1937: Stalin's Year of Terror* (Oak Park, Mich., 1998), pp. 286–8.

24. Starkov, 'The Trial that was not Held', pp. 1304–5; Rogovin, *1937*, pp. 497–9.

25. Starkov, 'The Trial that was not Held', p. 1300; Thurston, *Life and Terror*, pp. 59–60.

26. Thurston, *Life and Terror*, pp. 124–5, 129–31; A. Knight *Beria: Stalin's First Lieutenant* (London, 1993), pp. 90–93; G. T. Rittersporn 'Extra-Judicial Repression and the Courts: Their Relationship in the 1930s', in P. H. Solomon (ed.) *Reforming Justice in Russia, 1864–1996* (New York, 1997), pp. 216–19.

27. S. Beria *Beria, My Father: Inside Stalin's Kremlin* (London, 2001), p. 44.

28. In general see M. Parrish *The Lesser Terror: Soviet State Security 1939–1953* (Westport, Conn., 1996).

29. Baynes, *Hitler's Speeches*, vol. i., p. 220.

30. J. Biesemann *Das Ermächtigungsgesetzt als Grundlage der Gesetzgebung im nationalsozialistischen Staat* (Münster, 1985), pp. 250–53.

31. H. Kaden and L. Nestler (eds) *Dokumente des Verbrechens: aus Akten des Dritten Reiches 1933–1945* (3 vols, Berlin, 1993), vol. i, p. 29, Verordnung zum Schutz von Volk und Staat, 28 February 1933; see too Biesemann, *Das Ermächtigungsgesetz*, pp. 253–63.

32. Kaden and Nestler, *Dokumente des Verbrechens*, vol. i., p. 31; Broszat, *Hitler State*, p. 329.

33. Kaden and Nestler, *Dokumente des Verbrechens*, vol. i, pp. 34–8; Broszat, *Hitler State*, pp. 330–31. On the courts H. Koch *In the Name of the Volk: Political Justice in Hitler's Germany* (London, 1989), p. 4; H. Schmidt 'Beab-

sichtige ich die Todesstrafe zu beantragen': *die nationalsozialistische Sondergerichtsbarkeit im Oberlandesgerichtsbezirk Düsseldorf 1933 bis 1945* (Essen, 1998), pp. 27–9; B. Dörner *'Heimtücke': Das Gesetz als Waffe* (Paderborn, 1998), pp. 20 ff.

34. Koch, *In the Name of the Volk*, pp. 45–8.

35. I. Müller *Hitler's Justice: the Courts of the Third Reich* (London, 1991), pp. 86–7.

36. G. Werle *Justiz-Strafrecht und polizeiliche Verbrechenskämpfung im Dritten Reich* (Berlin, 1989), pp. 533–42; U. Herbert *Best: Biographische Studien über Radikalismus, Weltanschauung und Vernunft 1903–1989* (Bonn, 1996), pp. 150–51, 169. See also J. Tuchel 'Dimensionen des Terrors: Funktionen der Konzentrationslager in Deutschland 1933–1945', in D. Dahlmann and G. Hirschfeld (eds) *Lager, Zwangsarbeit, Vertreibung und Deportation* (Essen, 1999), p. 374, who estimates that 80,000 were held in protective custody for some period in 1933.

37. S. Lorant *I Was Hitler's Prisoner* (London, 1935), pp. 32–42, 275–8.

38. Broszat, *Hitler State*, p. 333; H.-U. Thamer *Verführung und Gewalt: Deutschland 1933–1945* (Berlin, 1986), p. 385.

39. Kaden and Nestler, *Dokumente des Verbrechens*, vol. i, pp. 183–4, Bestimmungen zur Durchführung von Exekutionen in 'Sonderbehandlungsfälle', 6 January 1943; N. Frei *National Socialist Rule in Germany: the Führer State 1933–1945* (Oxford, 1993), pp. 114–15.

40. Broszat, *Hitler State*, p. 342.

41. J. Noakes and G. Pridham (eds) *Nazism 1919–1945: a Documentary Reader* (Exeter, 1984), p. 519.

42. A. Antonov-Ovseyenko *The Time of Stalin: Portrait of a Tyranny* (New York, 1981), pp. 211–13.

43. S. G. Wheatcroft 'The Scale and Nature of German and Soviet Repression and Mass Killings', *Europe-Asia Studies*, 48 (1996), pp. 1332–3. A. Nove 'Terror Victims – Is the Evidence Complete?', *Europe–Asia Studies*, 46 (1994), pp. 535–7.

44. Getty and Naumov, *Road to Terror*, p. 588; J. O. Pohl *The Stalinist Penal System* (Jefferson, NC, 1997), p. 8.

45. Pohl, *Stalinist Penal System*, pp. 11, 15; E. Bacon *The Gulag at War: Stalin's Forced Labour System in the Light of the Archives* (London, 1994), pp. 28–30.

46. Nove, 'Terror Victims', p. 536; GUlag deaths in Pohl, *Stalinist Penal System*, pp. 48–9.

47. On estimates for German camps see Wheatcroft, 'German and Soviet Repression', pp. 1328–9; camp figures in W. Sofsky *The Order of Terror: the*

Concentration Camp (Princeton, NJ, 1997), pp. 28–9, 34–5, 38; Tuchel, 'Dimensionen des Terrors', 372, 383.

48. Koch, *In the Name of the Volk*, p. 132.

49. Schmidt, '*Beabsichtige ich die Todesstrafe*', p. 91.

50. Kaden and Nestler, *Dokumente des Verbrechens*, vol. i., pp. 162–3, Erlass Hitlers über die Verfolgung von Straftaten gegen das Reich, 7 December 1941; for a case study see F. B. Bakels *Nacht und Nebel: Das Bericht eines holländischen Christen aus deutschen Gefängnissen und Konzentrationslagern* (Frankfurt am Main, 1979).

51. On differing estimates of Jewish deaths see Wheatcroft, 'Ausmass und Wesen', p. 75.

52. F. Pingel *Häftlinge unter SS-Herrschaft: Widerstand, Selbstbehauptung und Vernichtung im Konzentrationslager* (Hamburg, 1978), p. 230.

53. McDermott, 'The History of the Comintern', p. 35; A. Resis (ed.) *Molotov Remembers: Inside Kremlin Politics* (Chicago, 1993), p. 277–8.

54. Ginsburg, *Into the Whirlwind*, p. 44.

55. V. S. Mil'bakh 'Repression in the 57th Special Corps (Mongolian People's Republic)', *Journal of Slavic Military Studies*, 15 (2002), pp. 108–9.

56. Mil'bakh, 'Repression in the 57th Corps', pp. 109–11.

57. D. Volkogonov *Stalin: Triumph and Tragedy* (London, 1991), p. 373.

58. Volkogonov, *Stalin*, p. 374.

59. N. Werth 'A State against its People: Violence, Repression and Terror in the Soviet Union', in N. Werth *et al. The Black Book of Communism: Crimes, Terror, Repression* (London, 1999), pp. 190–93.

60. M. Ilič 'The Great Terror in Leningrad: a Quantitative Analysis', *Europe–Asia Studies*, 52 (2000), pp. 1518–20.

61. McDermott, 'History of the Comintern', p. 35.

62. McDermott and Agnew, *The Comintern*, pp. 145–9.

63. A. Lindenmeyr 'The First Political Trial: Countess Sofia Panina', *Russian Review*, 60 (2001), pp. 505–25.

64. Mil'bakh, 'Repression in the 57th Corps', p. 117. Accident rates were regularly reported to the army authorities as evidence of negligence and poor leadership before the terror. See F. Schauff 'Company Choir of Terror: The Military Council of the 1930s – the Red Army Between the XVIIth and XVIIIth Party Congresses', *Journal of Slavic Military Studies*, 12 (1999), pp. 132, 136, 142.

65. F. F. Benvenuti 'Industry and Purge in the Donbass 1936–37', *Europe–Asia Studies*, 45 (1993), pp. 60–63; see too D. L. Hoffmann 'The Great Terror on the Local Level: Purges in Moscow Factories', in J. A. Getty and R.

Manning (eds) *Stalinist Terror: New Perspectives* (Cambridge, 1993), pp. 163–7.

66. Werth, 'A State Against its People', pp. 200–201; on the killing of clergy see M. Pabst *Staatsterrorismus: Theorie und Praxis kommunistischer Herrschaft* (Graz, 1997), p. 67.

67. M. Parrish 'The Downfall of the "Iron Commissar": N. I. Ezhov 1938–40', *Journal of Slavic Military Studies*, 14 (2001), pp. 72–99; Getty and Naumov, *Road to Terror*, p. 561.

68. Baynes, *Hitler's Speeches*, p. 221.

69. P. Longerich *The Unwritten Order: Hitler's Role in the Final Solution* (Stroud, 2001), pp. 19–26 on Hitler's early views. On the conspiracy theory see K.-U. Merz *Das Schreckbild: Deutschland und der Bolschewismus 1917 bis 1921* (Frankfurt am Main, 1995), pp. 457–71.

70. Kaden and Nestler, *Dokumente des Verbrechens*, vol. i, pp. 78–9, Vortrag Heinrich Himmlers über Wesen und Aufgaben der SS und der Polizei, January 1937.

71. A. Merson *Communist Resistance in Nazi Germany* (London, 1985), p. 32; Müller, *Hitler's Justice*, p. 56.

72. Lorant, *Hitler's Prisoner*, pp. 92–3, 155.

73. K. Orth *Das System der ns Konzentrationslager: Eine politische Organisationsgeschichte* (Hamburg, 1999), pp. 47, 51–3; Pingel, *Häftlinge unter SS-Herrschaft*, pp. 69, 71.

74. Pingel, *Häftlinge unter SS-Herrschaft*, pp. 70–71.

75. N. Wachsmann ' "Annihilation Through Labor": The Killing of State Prisoners in the Third Reich', *Journal of Modern History*, 71 (1999), p. 625.

76. G. J. Giles 'The Institutionalization of Homosexual Panic in the Third Reich', in R. Gellately and N. Stoltzfus (eds) *Social Outsiders in Nazi Germany* (Princeton, NJ, 2001), p. 235.

77. Giles, 'Homosexual Panic', pp. 242–4.

78. G. Grau (ed.) *Hidden Holocaust? Gay and Lesbian Persecution in Germany 1933–45* (London, 1995), pp. 4–7, 248–9, 251; Giles, 'Homosexual Panic', pp. 244–5; H.-G. Stümke 'From the "People's Consciousness of Right and Wrong" to "The Healthy Instincts of the Nation": The Persecution of Homosexuals in Nazi Germany', in M. Burleigh (ed.) *Confronting the Nazi Past* (London, 1996), pp. 154–65.

79. N. Wachsmann 'Reform and Repression: Prisons and Penal Policy in Germany, 1918–1939', University of London, PhD thesis, 2000, p. 215.

80. Wachsmann, 'Reform and Repression', p. 206.

81. G. Bock 'Racism and Sexism in Nazi Germany: Motherhood, Compulsory

Sterilization and the State', in R. Bridenthal, A. Grossman and M. Kaplan (eds) *When Biology became Destiny: Women in Weimar Germany and Nazi Germany* (New York, 1984), pp. 276–80.

82. Y. Lozowick *Hitler's Bureaucrats: The Nazi Security Police and the Banality of Evil* (London, 2000), pp. 20–21, 46–8. See too H. Benschel *Bürokratie und Terror: Das Judenreferat der Gestapo Düsseldorf 1935–1945* (Essen, 2001).

83. E. A. Johnson *Nazi Terror: the Gestapo, Jews, and Ordinary Germans* (New York, 1999), pp. 408–11.

84. Johnson, *Nazi Terror*, pp. 385–7; K. Kwiet 'Nach dem Pogrom: Stufen der Ausgrenzung', in W. Benz (ed.) *Die Juden in Deutschland 1933–1945: Leben unter nationalsozialistischer Herrschaft* (Munich, 1988), pp. 596–614.

85. I. Erhenburg and V. Grossman *The Complete Black Book of Russian Jewry* (New Brunswick, NJ, 2002), pp. 423–4.

86. Johnson, *Nazi Terror*, pp. 322–8.

87. Lorant, *Hitler's Prisoner*, p. 123.

88. Stalin, *Works*, vol. xiii, p. 111.

89. R. W. Thurston 'Fear and Belief in the USSR's "Great Terror": Response to Arrest 1935–1939', *Slavic Review*, 45 (1986), p. 228.

90. H. Arendt *Eichmann in Jerusalem: a Report on the Banality of Evil* (London, 1963), p. 22; C. Browning *Ordinary Men: Reserve Police Battalion 101 and the Final Solution in Poland* (London, 1992).

91. K.-M. Mallmann and G. Paul 'Omniscient, Omnipotent, Omnipresent? Gestapo, Society and Resistance', in D. Crew (ed.) *Nazism and German Society 1933–1945* (London, 1994), pp. 173–4; R. Gellately *The Gestapo and German Society: Enforcing Racial Policy 1933–1945* (Oxford, 1990), pp. 44–6; G. Browder *Foundations of the Nazi Police State: the Formation of Sipo and SD* (Lexington, Kty, 1990), p. 235, who gives a figure of 7,000 for the Gestapo detective force in 1936.

92. On police routine see Wilhelm, *Die Polizei im NS-Staat*. In 1938 Interior Minister Wilhelm Frick asked the police to compile a card index (*Volkskartei*) on every inhabitant aged 5 to 70, a task completed by 1940 (pp. 109–10).

93. Mallmann and Paul 'Gestapo, Society and Resistance', pp. 175–7. During the war the Gestapo spent most of its time pursuing non-German political 'enemies'. See for example R. Otto *Wehmacht, Gestapo und sowjetische Kriegsgefangenen im deutschen Reichsgebiet 1941/42* (Munich, 1998).

94. R. Conquest *Justice and the Legal System in the USSR* (London, 1968), p. 6.

95. Thurston, *Life and Terror*, pp. 70–71.

96. See C. Graf 'Kontinuitäten und Brüche. Von der Politischen Polizei der

Weimarer Republik zur Geheimen Staatspolizei', in G. Paul and K.-M. Mallmann (eds) *Die Gestapo – Mythos und Realität* (Darmstadt, 1995), pp. 73–83; J. Tuchel 'Gestapa und Reichssicherheitshauptamt, Die Berliner Zentralinstitutionen der Gestapo', in Paul and Mallmann, *Gestapo*, pp. 84–100.

97. Merson, *Communist Resistance*, pp. 50–51; on factory monitoring see K.-H. Roth *Facetten des Terrors: Der Geheimdienst der 'Deutsche Arbeitsfront' und die Zerstörung der Arbeiterbewegung 1933–1938* (Bremen, 2000), pp. 13–21.

98. S. Fitzpatrick 'Signals from Below: Soviet Letters of Denunciation of the 1930s', *Journal of Modern History*, 68 (1996), p. 834; Thurston, *Life and Terror*, p. 71.

99. Fitzpatrick, 'Signals from Below', p. 835.

100. V. Kozlov 'Denunciation and its Functions in Soviet Governance: a Study of Denunciations and their Bureaucratic Handling from Soviet Police Archives 1944–1953', *Journal of Modern History*, 68 (1996), p. 876.

101. Gellately, *Gestapo and German Society*, p. 162; see too Johnson, *Nazi Terror*, p. 365, who shows that in Krefeld civilian denunciations began 24 per cent of cases, while 32 per cent were initiated by the police.

102. Mallmann and Paul, 'Gestapo, Society and Resistance', p. 179.

103. R. Gellately 'Denunciations in Twentieth-Century Germany: Aspects of Self-Policing in the Third Reich and the German Democratic Republic', *Journal of Modern History*, 68 (1996), p. 939.

104. Fitzpatrick, 'Signals from Below', p. 861.

105. J. Connelly 'The Uses of *Volksgemeinschaft*: Letters to the NSDAP Kresileitung Eisenach, 1939–1940', *Journal of Modern History*, 68 (1996), p. 926. On motivation see C. Arbogast *Herrschaftsinstanzen der württembergischen NSDAP: Funktion, Sozialprofil und Lebenswege einer regionalen NS-Elite 1920–1960* (Munich, 1998), pp. 102–11.

106. Fitzpatrick, 'Signals from Below', p. 848.

107. For example, Benvenuti, 'Industry and Purge', pp. 61–3, 68–9.

108. R. Evans 'Social Outsiders in German History: From the Sixteenth Century to 1933', in Gellately and Stoltzfus, *Social Outsiders*, pp. 20–44; see too G. Alexopoulos *Stalin's Outcasts: Aliens, Citizens and the Soviet State, 1926–1936* (Ithaca, NY, 2003), pp. 3–11.

109. S. Fitzpatrick 'How the Mice Buried the Cat: scenes from the Great Purges of 1937 in the Russian Provinces', *Russian Review*, 52 (1993), p. 319.

110. Baynes, *Hitler's Speeches*, vol. i., p. 230.

111. R. Gellately *Backing Hitler: Consent and Coercion in Nazi Germany* (Oxford, 2001), pp. 51–69. See too B. Engelmann *In Hitler's Germany:*

Everyday Life in the Third Reich (London, 1988), pp. 34–5. Engelmann, discussing the camps with acquaintances after the war, records the following: 'My parents spoke of the camps as having an important educational function. Of course in my house there was more talk of "dangerous enemies of the state", and I also heard that they were dealt with severely.'

112. M. Ellman 'The Soviet 1937 Provincial Show Trials: Carnival or Terror?', *Europe–Asia Studies*, 53 (2001), pp. 1221, 1223–33.

113. I. Zbarsky and S. Hutchinson *Lenin's Embalmers* (London, 1998), pp. 108–9.

114. Connelly, 'Uses of *Volksgemeinschaft*', p. 917.

115. I. Gutkin 'The Magic of Words: Symbolism, Futurism, Socialist Realism', in B. G. Rosenthal (ed.) *The Occult in Russian and Soviet Culture* (Ithaca, NY, 1997), pp. 241–4.

116. E. Lyons *Assignment Utopia* (London, 1937), p. 372.

117. R. Rhodes *Masters of Death: the SS Einsatzgruppen and the Invention of the Holocaust* (New York, 2002), p. 219.

118. Kaden and Nestler, *Dokumente des Verbrechens*, vol. i., pp. 245, 247, Rede Heinrich Himmlers in Posen, 4 October 1943.

119. Resis, *Molotov Remembers*, pp. 265, 270.

Chapter 6

1. J. Thies 'Nazi Architecture – a Blueprint for World Domination: the Last Aims of Adolf Hitler', in D. Welch (ed.) *Nazi Propaganda* (London, 1983), pp. 46–7.

2. T. J. Colton *Moscow: Governing the Socialist Metropolis* (Cambridge, Mass., 1995), p. 280.

3. Colton, *Socialist Metropolis*, p. 218.

4. K. Berton *Moscow: an Architectural History* (London, 1977), pp. 222–4.

5. Colton, *Socialist Metropolis*, p. 332; Berton, *Moscow*, p. 224.

6. R. Eaton *Ideal Cities: Utopianism and the (Un) Built Environment* (London, 2001), pp. 183–96 on Soviet utopianism; Colton, *Socialist Metropolis*, p. 333.

7. A. Speer *Inside the Third Reich: Memoirs* (London, 1970), pp. 74, 132–3.

8. D. Münk *Die Organisation des Raumes im Nationalsozialismus* (Bonn, 1993), p. 304; A. Scobie *Hitler's State Architecture: the Impact of Classical Antiquity* (London, 1990), pp. 110–12; H. Weihsmann *Bauen unterm Hakenkreuz: Architektur des Untergangs* (Vienna, 1998), pp. 19–20.

9. Weihsmann, *Bauen unterm Hakenkreuz*, p. 272; Scobie, *Hitler's State Architecture*, p. 112.

10. W. C. Brumfield *A History of Russian Architecture* (Cambridge, 1993), p. 486; Colton, *Socialist Metropolis*, p. 332.

11. E. Forndran *Die Stadt-und Industriegründungen Wolfsburg und Salzgitter* (Frankfurt am Main, 1984), pp. 67–8.

12. L. E. Blomquist 'Some Utopian Elements in Stalinist Art', *Russian Review*, 11 (1984), pp. 298–301; Colton, *Socialist Metropolis*, p. 223. See too A. J. Klinghoffer *Red Apocalypse: the Religious Evolution of Soviet Communism* (Lanham, Md, 1996), pp. 48 ff.

13. Scobie, *Hitler's State Architecture*, p. 97.

14. Forndran, *Die Stadt-und Industriegründungen*, pp. 67–8.

15. Colton, *Socialist Metropolis*, p. 200.

16. S. F. Starr 'Visionary Town Planning during the Cultural Revolution', in S. Fitzpatrick (ed.) *Cultural Revolution in Russia, 1928–1931* (Bloomington, Ind., 1978), p. 218.

17. R. Stites *Revolutionary Dreams: Utopian Vision and Experimental Life in the Russian Revolution* (Oxford, 1989), p. 202.

18. M. Droste *Bauhaus, 1919–1933* (Cologne, 1998), pp. 227–8, 233–5.

19. H. Giesler *Ein anderer Hitler: Bericht seines Architekten Hermann Giesler* (Leoni, 1977), pp. 199, 206; G. Troost (ed.) *Das Bauen im neuen Reich* (Bayreuth, 1939), p. 131.

20. Weihsmann, *Bauen unterm Hakenkreuz*, pp. 274–5.

21. Thies, 'Nazi Architecture', pp. 45–6.

22. Colton, *Socialist Metropolis*, p. 254.

23. Colton, *Socialist Metropolis*, pp. 277–8.

24. Berton, *Moscow*, p. 226.

25. Berton, *Moscow*, pp. 228–9; V. Paperny 'Moscow in the 1930s and the Emergence of a New City', in H. Günther *The Culture of the Stalin Period* (London, 1990), pp. 233–4

26. Colton, *Socialist Metropolis*, pp. 257–9.

27. Colton, *Socialist Metropolis*, p. 327.

28. Brumfield, *History of Russian Architecture*, p. 49.

29. Münk, *Die Organisation des Raumes*, p. 304.

30. Forndran, *Die Stadt-und Industrigründungen*, pp. 88–9; M. Cluet *L'Architecture du IIIe Reich: Origines intellectuelles et visées idéologiques* (Bern, 1987), pp. 201–4.

31. Weihsmann, *Bauen unterm Hakenkreuz*, p. 28.

32. Münk, *Die Organisation des Raumes*, pp. 306–7; on Wolfsburg see C.

Schneider *Stadtgründung im Dritten Reich: Wolfsburg und Salzgitter* (Munich, 1979).

33. Weihsmann, *Bauen unterm Hakenkreuz*, p. 22.

34. Speer, *Inside the Third Reich*, p. 140. The calculation was in current (1960s) marks.

35. T. Harlander and G. Fehl (eds) *Hitlers sozialer Wohnungsbau 1940–1945: Wohnungs politik, Baugestaltung und Siedlungsplanung* (Hamburg, 1986), p. 111: Memorandum of DAF 'Die sozialen Aufgaben nach dem Kriege', 1941.

36. Harlander and Fehl, *Hitlers sozialer Wohnungsbau*, p. 116: DAF Homesteads Office 'Totale Planung und Gestaltung', 1940.

37. Harlander and Fehl *Hitlers sozialer Wohnungsbau*, pp. 131–2: Hitler Decree 'Das Grundgesetz des sozialen Wohnungsbau', 25 November 1940.

38. On the plans for the new economy area see for example H. Kahrs 'Von der "Grossraumwirtschaft" zur "Neuen Ordnung"', in H. Kahrs (ed.) *Modelle für ein deutsches Europa: Ökonomie und Herrschaft im Grosswirtschaftsraum* (Berlin, 1992), pp. 9–26.

39. Thies, 'Nazi Architecture', pp. 54–8.

40. S. Steinbacher *'Musterstadt Auschwitz': Germanisierungspolitik und Judenmord in Ostoberschlesien* (Munich, 2000), pp. 223–4, 238.

41. D. Dwork and R. J. van Pelt *Auschwitz: 1270 to the Present* (New York, 1996), p. 156.

42. Dwork and van Pelt, *Auschwitz*, pp. 241–4.

43. Steinbacher, *'Musterstadt Auschwitz'*, p. 224; G. Aly and S. Heim *Architects of Annihilation: Auschwitz and the Logic of Destruction* (London, 2002), pp. 106–12.

44. Colton, *Socialist Metropolis*, p. 284.

45. Starr, 'Visionary Town Planning', pp. 208, 210; Stites, *Revolutionary Dreams*, pp. 197–8.

46. Starr, 'Visionary Town Planning', p. 238; Stites, *Revolutionary Dreams*, pp. 97–8.

47. Blomquist, 'Utopian Elements in Stalinist Art', p. 298; on the ambiguity between modernity and progress see C. Caldenby 'The Vision of a Rational Architecture', *Russian Review*, 11 (1984), pp. 269–82.

48. Brumfield, *History of Russian Architecture*, pp. 486–7.

49. Colton, *Socialist Metropolis*, p. 223.

50. S. Kotkin *Magnetic Mountain: Stalinism as Civilization* (Berkeley, Calif., 1995), pp. 34, 397.

51. Kotkin, *Magnetic Mountain*, pp. 116–17, 120; see too Caldenby, 'Rational Architecture', pp. 270–71.

52. Kotkin, *Magnetic Mountain*, p. 117.

53. Kotkin, *Magnetic Mountain*, pp. 125, 134–5.

54. F. Rouvidois 'Utopia and Totalitarianism', in R. Schner, G. Claeys and L. T. Sargent (eds) *Utopia: the Search for the Ideal Society in the Western World* (New York, 2000), p. 330.

55. D. Schoenbaum *Hitler's Social Revolution: Class and Status in Nazi Germany 1933–1939* (New York, 1966), p. 38.

56. R. Zitelmann *Hitler: the Politics of Seduction* (London, 1999), pp. 109, 127; E. Syring *Hitler: seine politische Utopie* (Frankfurt am Main, 1994), pp. 170–71.

57. Zitelmann, *Hitler*, pp. 145, 147.

58. S. Fitzpatrick 'Ascribing Class: The Construction of Social Identity in Soviet Russia', *Journal of Modern History*, 65 (1993), pp. 749–50; see too G. Alexopoulos *Stalin's Outcasts: Aliens, Citizens, and the Soviet State 1926–1936* (Ithaca, NY, 2003), pp. 14–17, 21–5.

59. Zitelmann, *Hitler*, pp. 127, 145; Schoenbaum, *Hitler's Social Revolution*, pp. 65–6; F. L. Kroll *Utopie als Ideologie: Geschichtsdenken und politisches Handeln im Dritten Reich* (Paderborn, 1998), pp. 35–9.

60. A. Kolnai *The War Against the West* (London, 1938), pp. 73, 80.

61. Münk, *Organisation des Raumes*, p. 67.

62. F. Janka *Die braune Gesellschaft: ein Volk wird formatiert* (Stuttgart, 1997), pp. 172–85, 196–7; see too Syring, *Hitler: seine politische Utopie*, pp. 22–9, 210.

63. Münk, *Organisation des Raumes*, p. 63

64. Schoenbaum, *Hitler's Social Revolution*, p. 62.

65. Schoenbaum, *Hitler's Social Revolution*, p. 57.

66. A. Lüdtke 'The "Honor of Labor": Industrial Workers and the Power of Symbols under National Socialism', in D. Crew (ed.) *Nazism and German Society 1933–1945* (London, 1994), pp. 67–109.

67. Zitelmann, *Hitler*, pp. 154–6.

68. Schoenbaum, *Hitler's Social Revolution*, p. 67; see too the statistical analyses in D. Mühlberger (ed.) *The Social Basis of European Fascist Movements* (London, 1987), pp. 76–94.

69. Fitzpatrick, 'Ascribing Class', pp. 749–50.

70. Alexopoulos, *Stalin's Outcasts*, pp. 24–8, 70–73, 90–95; Fitzpatrick, 'Ascribing Class', pp. 756–7.

71. L. Siegelbaum 'Production Collectives and Communes and the "Imperatives" of Soviet Industrialization', *Slavic Review*, 45 (1986), pp. 65–79.

72. J. C. McClelland 'Utopianism versus Revolutionary Heroism in Bolshevik Policy: the Proletarian Culture Debate', *Slavic Review*, 39 (1980), pp. 404–7, 415.

73. J. Stalin *Problems of Leninism* (Moscow, 1947), pp. 421–2, 424, 'Results of the First Five-Year Plan', CC Plenum, 7 January 1933.

74. Stalin, *Problems of Leninism*, pp. 498–9, 'Report on the Work of the Central Committee to the 17th Congress', 26 January 1934.

75. K. E. Bailes *Technology and Society under Lenin and Stalin* (Princeton, NJ, 1978), p. 166.

76. Stalin, *Problems of Leninism*, p. 502.

77. Stalin, *Problems of Leninism*, pp. 544–6, 'On the Draft Constitution of the USSR', 25 November 1936: '. . . all the exploiting classes have been eliminated. There remains the working class. There remains the peasant class. There remains the intelligentsia.'

78. Stalin, *Problems of Leninism*, p. 503.

79. Zitelmann, *Hitler*, p. 164.

80. Zitelmann, *Hitler*, p. 168; see too Syring, *Hitler: seine politische Utopie*, pp. 184–7.

81. See for example A. Angelopoulos *Planisme et progres social* (Paris, 1951) esp. Ch. 3; E. Lederer *Planwirtschaft* (Tübingen, 1932); F. Lenz *Wirtschaftsplanung und Planwirtschaft* (Berlin, 1948).

82. Zitelmann, *Hitler*, p. 321.

83. P. Kluke 'Hitler und das Volkwagenprojekt', *Vierteljahrshefte für Zeitgeschichte*, 8 (1960), p. 349.

84. On Todt see J. Herf *Reactionary Modernism: Technology, Culture, and Politics in Weimar and the Third Reich* (Cambridge, 1984), pp. 199–200; on the *Westwall* see J. Heyl 'The Construction of the *Westwall*: An Example of National Socialist Policy-Making', *Central European History*, 14 (1981), p. 77.

85. Herf, *Reactionary Modernism*, pp. 200, 204–6.

86. Herf, *Reactionary Modernism*, p. 168. An interesting example of the new view of technology and the people's community is given in K. Gispen 'Visions of Utopia: Social Emancipation, Technological Progress and Anticapitalism in Nazi Inventor Policy, 1933–1945', *Central European History*, 32 (1999), pp. 35–51.

87. Bailes, *Technology and Society*, pp. 160–63.

88. Colton, *Socialist Metropolis*, p. 259; K. Clark 'Engineers of Human Souls in an Age of Industrialization: Changing Cultural Models, 1929–31', in W. Rosenberg and L. Siegelbaum (eds) *Social Dimensions of Soviet Industrialization* (Bloomington, Ind., 1993), p. 249.

89. Bailes, *Technology and Society*, p. 163.

90. Clark, 'Engineers of Human Souls', pp. 250–51; Bailes, *Technology and Society*, pp. 176–7.

91. Bailes, *Technology and Society*, p. 289; K. E. Bailes 'Stalin and the

Making of a New Elite: A Comment', *Slavic Review*, 39 (1980), pp. 268–9; S. Fitzpatrick 'Stalin and the Making of a New Elite, 1928–1939', *Slavic Review*, 38 (1979), pp. 385–7, 396–8.

92. Zitelmann, *Hitler*, p. 182.

93. On Eichmann and the security bureaucracy see Y. Lozowick *Hitler's Bureaucrats: the Nazi Security Police and the Banality of Evil* (London, 2000); H. Safrian *Die Eichmann Männer* (Vienna, 1993).

94. M. Kater *The Nazi Party: a Social Profile of Members and Leaders, 1919–1945* (Oxford, 1983), pp. 252–3, 264 (figures based on statistical sampling); H. F. Ziegler *Nazi Germany's New Aristocracy: the SS Leadership, 1925–1939* (Princeton, NJ, 1989), pp. 102–5.

95. Ziegler, *Nazi Germany's New Aristocracy*, p. 73.

96. I. Halfin 'The Rape of the Intelligentsia: A Proletarian Foundation Myth', *Russian Review*, 56 (1997), pp. 103, 106; A. Lunacharsky *On Education: Selected Articles and Speeches* (Moscow, 1981), lecture on 'Education and the New Man', 23 May 1928.

97. S. Fitzpatrick *Everyday Stalinism: Ordinary Life in Extraordinary Times: Soviet Russia in the 1930s* (Oxford, 1999), pp. 75–6.

98. H. Rauschning *Hitler Speaks* (London, 1939), pp. 241–3.

99. Rauschning, *Hitler Speaks*, p. 247; Janka, *braune Gesellschaft*, pp. 183–91, 200–201.

100. P. Weindling *Health, Race and German Politics between National Unification and Nazism 1870–1945* (Cambridge, 1989), pp. 7–8; P. Weingart 'Eugenic Utopias: Blueprints for the Rationalization of Human Evolution', *Sociology of the Sciences Yearbook: Vol VIII* (Dordrecht, 1984), p. 175.

101. L. R. Graham 'Science and Values: The Eugenics Movement in Germany and Russia in the 1920s', *American Historical Review*, 82 (1977), pp. 1132, 1145–7.

102. J. Stalin *Works* (13 vols, Moscow 1953–55), vol. i, p. 316, 'Anarchism or Socialism?' 1906–7; see too V. N. Soyfer *Lysenko and the Tragedy of Soviet Science* (New Brunswick, NJ, 1994), pp. 200–203.

103. Graham, 'Science and Values', pp. 1139–43, 1151; F. Hirsch 'Race without the Practice of Racial Politics', *Slavic Review*, 61 (2002), pp. 32–4.

104. Sofer, *Lysenko*, chs 8–11; L. R. Graham *Science, Philosophy and Human Behaviour in the Soviet Union* (New York, 1987), pp. 221–2.

105. Weindling, *Health, Race and German Politics*, pp. 436–7; R. Proctor *Racial Hygiene: Medicine under the Nazis* (Cambridge, Mass., 1988), p. 286.

106. Graham, 'Science and Values', p. 1143.

107. Rauschning, *Hitler Speaks*, p. 243.

108. Weindling, *Health, Race and German Politics*, pp. 522–7; H. Friedlander

'The Exclusion and Murder of the Disabled', in R. Gellately and N. Stoltzfus (eds) *Social Outsiders in Nazi Germany* (Princeton, NJ, 2001), pp. 146–8; Weingart, 'Eugenic Utopias', pp. 183–4.

109. Friedlander, 'Murder of the Disabled', p. 148.

110. Weindling, *Health, Race and German Politics*, pp. 529–30, 533; G. Bock 'Racism and Sexism in Nazi Germany: Motherhood, Compulsory Sterilization and the State', in R. Bridenthal, A. Grossmann and M. Kaplan (eds) *When Biology became Destiny: Women in Weimar Germany and Nazi Germany* (New York, 1984), pp. 276–7, 279–80. Some 2000 were also castrated by 1940, including women, who were subjected to overectomies. See U. Kaminsky *Zwangssterilisation und 'Euthanasie' im Rheinland* (Cologne, 1995), pp. 535–7, whose figures show that sterilization proceeded most rapidly between 1934 and 1936, and H. Friedlander *The Origins of Nazi Genocide: From Euthanasia to the Final Solution* (Chapel Hill, NC, 1995), pp. 26–30.

111. Proctor, *Racial Hygiene*, pp. 203–4; Weindling, *Health, Race and German Politics*, pp. 526–9.

112. Weindling, *Health, Race and German Politics*, pp. 530–32. See too S. Maiwald and G. Mischler *Sexualität unter dem Hakenkreuz* (Hamburg, 1999), pp. 105–16.

113. P. Bleuel *Strength through Joy: Sex and Society in Nazi Germany* (London, 1973), p. 194; Weingart, 'Eugenic Utopias', pp. 178–80.

114. K. H. Minuth (ed.) *Akten der Reichskanzlei: Regierung Hitler 1933–1938* (Boppard am Rhein, 1983) vol. ii, pp. 1188–9; Maiwald and Mischler, *Sexualität*, pp. 108–9.

115. L. Pine *Nazi Family Policy 1933–1945* (Oxford, 1997), p. 132.

116. U. Frevert *Women in German History* (Oxford, 1989), pp. 232–3; R. Grunberger *A Social History of the Third Reich* (London, 1968), p. 300.

117. Frevert, *Women in German History*, p. 237; on the *Pflichtjahr* see F. Petrick 'Eine Untersuchung zur Beseitigung der Arbeitslosigkeit unter der deutschen Jugend in den Jahren 1933 bis 1935', *Jahrbuch für Wirtschaftsgeschichte*, Part I (1967), pp. 291, 299; on employment see S. Bajohr *Die Hälfte der Fabrik: Geschichte der Frauenarbeit in Deutschland 1914 bis 1945* (Marburg, 1979), p. 252.

118. Frevert, *Women in German History*, pp. 236–7; Grunberger, *Social History of the Third Reich*, pp. 312–13.

119. Proctor, *Racial Hygiene*, pp. 283–4.

120. Bleuel, *Strength through Joy*, p. 111.

121. On Himmler see Kroll, *Utopie als Ideologie*, pp. 213–22; see too J. Hoberman 'Primacy of Performance: Superman not Superathlete', in J. A.

Mangan (ed.) *Shaping the Superman. Fascist Body as Political Icon – Aryan Fascism* (London, 1999), pp. 78–80.

122. I. Heinemann '*Rasse, Siedlung, deutsches Blut': Das Rasse-& Siedlungshauptamt der SS und die rassenpolitische Neuordnung Europas* (Göttingen, 2003), pp. 64–5; on race classification in Europe see I. Heinemann ' "Another Type of Perpetrator": The SS Racial Experts and Forced Population Movements in the Occupied Regions', *Holocaust and Genocide Studies*, 15 (2001), pp. 389–93, 395–9.

123. R. J. Lifton *The Nazi Doctors: Medical Killing and the Psychology of Genocide* (London, 1986), pp. 25, 41–5, 469–87; D. Peukert 'The Genesis of the "Final Solution" from the Spirit of Science', in Crew (ed.), *Nazism and German Society*, p. 285.

124. Lifton, *Nazi Doctors*, p. 477.

125. Proctor, *Racial Hygiene*, p. 196.

126. E. P. Russell ' "Speaking of Annihilation": Mobilizing for War against Human and Insect Enemies', *Journal of American History*, 82 (1996), pp. 1519–22; E. Kogon, H. Langbein and A. Rückerl (eds) *Nazi Mass Murder: A Documentary History of the Use of Poison Gas* (New Haven, Conn., 1993), pp. 146–7, 193–5, 206–9.

127. Friedlander, 'Murder of the Disabled', pp. 150–52; Proctor, *Racial Hygiene*, p. 186; see too M. Burleigh *Death and Deliverance: 'Euthanasia' in Germany 1900–1945* (Cambridge, 1994), pp. 96–7, 112–13; Friedlander, *Origins of Nazi Genocide*, pp. 37–40.

128. Lifton, *Nazi Doctors*, p. 45; Friedlander, 'Murder of the Disabled', p. 151; S. Kühl 'The Relationship between Eugenics and the so-called "Euthanasia Action" in Nazi Germany', in M. Szöllösi-Janze (ed.) *Science in the Third Reich* (Oxford, 2001), pp. 201–3, who argues that war was the primary incentive to start killing.

129. Friedlander, 'Murder of the Disabled', pp. 154–5; Friedlander, *Origins of Nazi Genocide*, pp. 83–8.

130. Friedlander, 'Murder of the Disabled', pp. 155–6; Proctor, *Racial Hygiene*, pp. 206–8.

131. K. Pinnow 'Cutting and Counting: Forensic Medicine as a Science of Society in Bolshevik Russia, 1920–29', in D. Hoffmann and Y. Kotsonis (eds) *Russian Modernity: Politics, Knowledge, Practices* (London, 2000), p. 123.

132. Fitzpatrick *Everyday Stalinism*, pp. 117–22, 130–32; Alexopoulos, *Stalin's Outcasts*, pp. 169–75.

133. P. Barton *L'institution concentrationnaire en Russe 1930–1957* (Paris, 1959), p. 56.

134. S. Allan *Comrades and Citizens: Soviet People* (London, 1938), pp. 122, 155–6.

135. A. E. Gorsuch 'NEP Be Damned! Young Militants in the 1920s and the Culture of Civil War', *Russian Review*, 56 (1997), pp. 576–7. Smoking was also condemned as harmful to the Soviet 'body'.

136. H. K. Geiger *The Family in Soviet Russia* (Cambridge, Mass., 1968), pp. 88–90.

137. Geiger, *Family in Soviet Russia*, p. 190; M. Buckley *Women and Ideology in the Soviet Union* (New York, 1989), pp. 134–5.

138. Geiger, *Family in Soviet Russia*, p. 94.

139. Geiger, *Family in Soviet Russia*, p. 95; on attitudes to sexual emancipation see E. Naimark *Sex in Public: the Incarnation of Early Soviet Ideology* (Princeton, NJ, 1997).

140. Allan, *Comrades and Citizens*, pp. 84–5; Geiger, *Family in Soviet Russia*, p. 92.

141. Buckley, *Women and Ideology*, pp. 128–9; Fitzpatrick, *Everyday Stalinism*, p. 152.

142. Geiger, *Family in Soviet Russia*, p. 194.

143. Buckley, *Women and Ideology*, pp. 129–31; Fitzpatrick, *Everyday Stalinism*, p. 155; Geiger, *Family in Soviet Russia*, pp. 193–5; S. G. Solomon 'The demographic argument in Soviet debates over the legalization of abortion in the 1920s', *Cahiers du monde russe*, 33 (1992), pp. 60–65.

144. Halfin, 'Rape of the Intelligentsia', p. 104; McClelland, 'Utopianism versus Revolutionary Heroism', p. 405.

145. R. A. Bauer *The New Man in Soviet Psychology* (Cambridge, Mass., 1952), pp. 124, 132, 143–50.

146. Stalin, *Problems of Leninism*, pp. 522–33.

147. L. Siegelbaum *Stakhanovism and the Politics of Productivity in the USSR, 1935–1941* (Cambridge, 1988), pp. 68–71.

148. Siegelbaum, *Stakhanovism*, p. 73.

149. V. Bonnell 'The Iconography of the Worker in Soviet Political Art', in L. Siegelbaum and R. Suny (eds) *Making Workers Soviet: Power Class and Identity* (Ithaca, NY, 1994), pp. 361–2; Fitzpatrick, *Everyday Stalinism*, pp. 73–5; K. Clark 'Utopian Anthropology as a Context for Stalinist Literature', in R. Tucker (ed.) *Stalinism Essays in Historical Interpretation* (New York, 1977), pp. 185–6.

150. Clark, 'Utopian Anthropology', pp. 183–4; Fitzpatrick, *Everyday Stalinism*, p.77; Bonnell, 'Iconography of the Worker', pp. 367–9.

151. Buckley, *Women and Ideology*, pp. 108–9, 112; Geiger, *Family in Soviet Russia*, p. 187.

152. Buckley, *Women and Ideology*, pp. 118–19; Siegelbaum, *Stakhanovism*, pp. 190–91.

153. Geiger, *Family in Soviet Russia*, p. 177.

154. Buckley, *Women and Ideology*, p. 117.

155. J. E. Bowlt and M. Drutt (eds) *Amazons of the Avant-Garde* (London, 1999), pp. 54–5; Bonnell, 'Iconography of the Worker', pp. 369, 71.

156. K. Theweleit *Male Fantasies. Male bodies: psychoanalysing the white terror* (Oxford, 1989), p. 163; B. Taylor and W. van der Will (eds) *The Nazification of Art: Art, Design, Music, Architecture and Film in the Third Reich* (Winchester, 1990), p. 63. See too J. A. Mangan 'Icon of Monumental Brutality: Art and the Aryan Man', in Mangan, *Shaping the Superman*, pp. 139–49.

157. Fitzpatrick, *Everyday Stalinism*, p. 46.

158. Blomquist, 'Utopian Elements', p. 300; Rouvidois, 'Utopia and Totalitarianism', p. 322.

159. Stalin, *Problems of Leninism*, p. 531.

160. Rouvidois, 'Utopia and Totalitarianism' p. 324.

161. Fitzpatrick, *Everyday Stalinism*, p. 68.

162. Allan, *Comrades and Citizens*, pp. 208–9.

163. See R. Gellately *Backing Hitler: Consent and Coercion in Nazi Germany* (Oxford, 2001) and C. Koonz *The Nazi Conscience* (Cambridge, Mass., 2003), which both explore different ways in which ordinary Germans came to accept and justify the dictatorship.

164. Rouvidois, 'Utopia and Totalitarianism', p. 330.

165. E. Kamenka 'Soviet Philosophy', in A. Smirenko (ed.) *Social Thought in the Soviet Union* (Chicago, 1969), pp. 89–90; K. Bayertz 'From Utopia to Science? The Development of Socialist Theory between Utopia and Science', *Sociology of the Sciences Yearbook: Vol VIII* (Dordrecht, 1984), pp. 93–110. See too L. R. Graham *Science, Philosophy and Human Behaviour in the Soviet Union* (New York, 1987), esp. Chs. v–vii.

166. The complex relationship between modern science and the regime is explored in Szöllösi-Janze, *Science in the Third Reich*; see too M. Renneberg and M. Walker (eds) *Science, Technology and National Socialism* (Cambridge, 1994).

167. J. W. Baird *To Die for Germany: Heroes in the Nazi Pantheon* (Bloomington, Ind., 1990).

168. Bauer, *New Man*, pp. 144–5; on abortion see Geiger, *Family in Soviet Russia*, p. 195.

Chapter 7

1. G. C. Guins *Soviet Law and Soviet Society* (The Hague, 1954), p. 29.

2. A. Koenen *Der Fall Carl Schmitt; sein Aufstieg zum 'Kronjuristen des Dritten Reiches'* (Darmstadt, 1995), p. 612.

3. J. Stalin *Problems of Leninism* (Moscow, 1947), pp. 569–78, 'Dialectical and Historical Materialism', September 1938; see too E. Kamenka 'Soviet Philosophy 1917–1967', in A. Smirenko (ed.) *Social Thought in the Soviet Union* (Chicago, 1969), p. 53. Primers on dialectical materialism were issued in printruns of 250,000 to 500,000.

4. N. Harding *Leninism* (London, 1996), p. 226.

5. R. T. de George *Patterns of Soviet Thought* (New York, 1966), pp. 171–2.

6. G. Wetter *Dialectical Materialism: A Historical and Systematic Survey of Philosophy in the Soviet Union* (New York, 1958), pp. 219–20.

7. A. Hitler *Mein Kampf*, ed. D. C. Watt (London, 1968), p. 258; W. Maser (ed.) *Hitler's Letters and Notes* (New York, 1977), p. 280; D. Gasman *The Scientific Origins of National Socialism* (London, 1971), pp. 47–9.

8. Hitler, *Mein Kampf*, p. 260; Maser, *Hitler's Letters and Notes*, p. 280.

9. E. Jäckel *Hitler's World View: a Blueprint for Power* (Middleton, Conn., 1981), p. 94.

10. A. Hitler *The Secret Book*, ed. T. Taylor (New York, 1961), p. 6; see too E. Fraenkel *The Dual State. A Contribution to the Theory of Dictatorship* (New York, 1941), pp. 108–9, citing Hans Gerber's view that National Socialist political thought was 'existential and biological, its data being the primal unique life process'.

11. Hitler, *Mein Kampf*, pp. 268–9.

12. Stalin, *Problems of Leninism*, p. 578; Hitler, *Mein Kampf*, p. 262.

13. P. van Paassen *Visions Rise and Change* (New York, 1955), pp. 100–106.

14. J. Bergman 'The Image of Jesus in the Russian Revolutionary Movement. The Case of Russian Marxism', *International Review of Social History*, 25 (1990), p. 226.

15. P. J. Duncan *Russian Messianism: Third Rome, Revolution, Communism and After* (London, 2000), pp. 51–2; D. G. Rowley *Millenarian Bolshevism, 1900–1920* (New York, 1987), pp. 355–72; W. B. Hubbard *'Godless Communists': Atheism and Society in Soviet Russia 1917–1932* (Dekalb, Ill., 2000), pp. 30–35.

16. V. Lenin *Collected Works* (45 vols., Moscow, 1963), vol. xxxv, p. 121, letter to Maxim Gorky, 13 or 14 November 1913, pp. 127–8, letter to Maxim Gorky, November 1913. See too D. V. Pospielovsky *A History of Marxist-*

Leninist Atheism and Soviet Anti-Religious Policies: Vol I: A History of Soviet Atheism in Theory and Practice (London, 1987), pp. 1–17.

17. Hubbard, '*Godless Communists*', p. 47.

18. M. A. Meerson 'The Political Philosophy of the Russian Orthodox Episcopate in the Soviet Period', in G. Hosking (ed.) *Church, Nation and State in Russia and Ukraine* (London, 1991), p. 217.

19. van Paassen, *Visions Rise and Change*, p. 63; E. Trubetskoy 'The Bolshevist Utopia and the Religious Movement in Russia', in M. Bohachevsky-Chomiak and B. G. Rosenthal (eds) *A Revolution of the Spirit: Crisis of Values in Russia 1890–1918* (Newtonville, Mass., 1982), pp. 331–2, 336–8.

20. M. Bourdeaux *Opium of the People: the Christian Religion in the USSR* (London, 1965), p. 51; Hubbard, '*Godless Communists*', pp. 58–9; J. S. Curtiss *The Russian Church and the Soviet State* (Gloucester, Mass., 1965), pp. 200–203; A. J. Klinghoffer *Red Apocalypse: the Religious Evolution of Soviet Communism* (Lanham, Md, 1996), pp. 113–14.

21. Pospielovsky, *Marxist-Leninist Atheism: I*, pp. 30–34.

22. Hubbard, '*Godless Communists*', pp. 62–3; D. Peris *Storming the Heavens: the Soviet League of the Militant Godless* (Ithaca, NY, 1998), pp. 48–9.

23. D. V. Pospielovsky *A History of Marxist-Leninist Atheism and Anti-Religious Policies, Vol II: Soviet Anti-Religious Campaigns and Persecutions* (London, 1988), p.19; C. de Grunwald *God and the Soviets* (London, 1961), pp. 46–7, 79.

24. de Grunwald, *God and the Soviets*, pp. 73–9; F. Corley (ed.) *Religion in the Soviet Union* (New York, 1996), p. 119, instructions from Roslavl District Committee to Party officials and the League of the Militant Godless, 15 April 1937.

25. Bergman, 'The Image of Jesus', pp. 240–42.

26. Pospielovsky, *Marxist-Leninist Atheism: II*, pp. 48–9.

27. M. Spinka *The Church in Soviet Russia* (Oxford, 1956), p. 38.

28. Bourdeaux, *Opium of the People*, p. 54; G. L. Freeze 'Counter-reformation in Russian Orthodoxy: Popular Response to Religious Innovation, 1922–1925', *Slavic Review*, 54 (1995), pp. 305–39.

29. Spinka, *Church in Soviet Russia*, pp. 62–6; Bourdeaux, *Opium of the People*, p. 54.

30. Pospielovsky, *Marxist-Leninist Atheism: I*, p. 51.

31. Pospielovsky, *Marxist-Leninist Atheism: II*, p. 34.

32. W. H. Chamberlin *Soviet Russia: a Living Record and a History* (Boston, 1938), p. 318; Pospielovsky, *Marxist-Leninist Atheism: I*, pp. 44–5.

33. de Grunwald, *God and the Soviets*, p. 54; Pospielovsky, *Marxist-Leninist Atheism: II*, p. 67.

34. Pospielovsky, *Marxist-Leninist Atheism: II*, pp. 66–8.

35. Curtiss, *The Russian Church*, pp. 228–9.

36. Pospielovsky, *Marxist-Leninist Atheism: I*, pp. 61–4; Curtiss, *The Russian Church*, p. 232.

37. A. Luukkanen *The Religious Policy of the Stalinist State* (Helsinki, 1997), pp. 53–4; Corley, *Religion in the Soviet Union*, p. 118. Other subjects included 'The tale of christ and other dying and allegedly risen gods', 'Religion and the church in the service of international fascism'; and so on.

38. Pospielovsky, *Marxist-Leninist Atheism: I*, p. 55; Curtiss, *The Russian Church*, pp. 212, 253; see too G. Young *Power and the Sacred in Revolutionary Russia: Religious Activists in the Village* (University Park, Pa., 1997).

39. van Paassen, *Visions Rise and Change*, pp. 44–5, 72–3.

40. Peris, *Storming the Heavens*, p. 224 for the census result. Out of 98,410,000 census returns, 42,243,000 defined themselves as atheists. On bishops see Pospielovsky, *Marxist-Leninist Atheism: II*, pp. 67–8.

41. The Moscow Patriarchate *The Truth about Religion in Russia* (London, 1944); Spinka, *Church in Soviet Russia*, pp.82–6; S. M. Miner *Stalin's Holy War: Religion, Nationalism and Alliance Politics, 1941–1945* (Chapel Hill, NC, 2003), pp. 96–8.

42. Bourdeaux, *Opium of the People*, p. 234; Miner, *Stalin's Holy War*, p. 99.

43. Pospielovsky, *Marxist-Leninist Atheism: II*, p. 96; I, p. 71; Peris, *Storming the Heavens*, p. 222.

44. B. R. Bociorkiw 'Religion and Atheism in Soviet Society', in R. H. Marshall (ed.) *Aspects of Religion in the Soviet Union 1917–1967* (Chicago, 1971), pp. 45–6.

45. van Paassen, *Visions Rise and Change*, p. 60; Duncan, *Russian Messianism*, p. 58.

46. S. Roberts *The House that Hitler Built* (London, 1938), p. 268; M. Bendiscioli *The New Racial Paganism* (London, 1939), p. 22.

47. Meerson, 'Russian Orthodox Episcopate', p. 218.

48. P. F. Douglas *God Among the Germans* (Philadelphia, 1935), pp. 278–9.

49. K. Scholder *A Requiem for Hitler and Other New Perspectives on the German Church Struggle* (Philadelphia, 1989), pp. 54–5; Douglas, *God Among the Germans*, pp. 19–21.

50. A. Kolnai *The War Against the West* (London, 1938), pp. 247, 267: 'no brave man wants another life', claimed one German theologian.

51. Scholder, *Requiem for Hitler*, pp. 41–2.

52. Douglas, *God Among the Germans*, pp. 72–4; W. Künneth and H. Schreiner (eds) *Die Nation vor Gott* (Berlin, 1937), pp. 403–22.

53. Kolnai, *War Against the West*, pp. 233–4; Douglas, *God Among the Germans*, p. 74.

54. Künneth and Streiner, *Nation vor Gott*, pp. 444 ff; Kolnai, *War Against the West*, p. 283; Douglas, *God Among the Germans*, p. 58.

55. K. Scholder 'Die evangelische Kirche in der Sicht der nationalsozialistischen Führung', *Vierteljahrshefte für Zeitgeschichte*, 16 (1968), p. 18–19; Douglas, *God Among the Germans*, pp. 87–91; on Hauer see Kolnai, *War Against the West*, p. 283.

56. H. Trevor-Roper (ed.) *Hitler's Table Talk 1941–1944* (London, 1984), p. 191, 8–9 January 1942.

57. Trevor-Roper, *Hitler's Table Talk*, p. 59, 14 October 1941; p. 125, 11 November 1941.

58. Trevor-Roper, *Hitler's Table Talk*, p. 314, 8 February 1942: 'The evil that's gnawing our vitals is our priests, of both creeds.'

59. Douglas, *God Among the Germans*, pp. 2–3; Trevor-Roper, *Hitler's Table Talk*, pp. 60–61, 14 October 1941; on Hitler's religiosity see too H. Buchheim *Glaubenskrise im Dritten Reich: Drei Kapitel nationalsozialistischer Religionspolitik* (Stuttgart, 1953), pp. 9–16.

60. Douglas, *God Among the Germans*, pp. 14–17; Trevor-Roper, *Hitler's Table Talk*, p. 59; D. Gasman *The Scientific Origins of National Socialism* (London, 1971), pp. 162–9.

61. Roberts, *House that Hitler Built*, p. 270; on Rosenberg see Douglas, *God Among the Germans*, pp. 30 ff.

62. M. Burleigh *The Third Reich: a New History* (London, 2000), p. 253; Hitler, *Mein Kampf*, pp. 419–20.

63. Douglas, *God Among the Germans*, pp. 212–13, 217; V. Barnett *For the Soul of the People: Protestant Protest against Hitler* (Oxford, 1992), pp. 32–4.

64. Scholder, *Requiem for Hitler*, pp. 101–2; Barnett, *Soul of the People*, pp. 34–5.

65. Scholder, *Requiem for Hitler*, pp. 77–9, 90–92, 103.

66. Scholder, *Requiem for Hitler*, p. 93.

67. Text in P. Matheson (ed.) *The Third Reich and the Christian Churches* (Edinburgh, 1981), pp. 39–40, speech by Dr Krause, 13 November 1933; Douglas, *God Among the Germans*, pp. 81–4.

68. Trevor-Roper, *Hitler's Table Talk*, p. 7, 11–12 July 1941; on Kerrl see Scholder, 'Die evangelische Kirche', pp. 26–8.

69. Douglas, *God Among the Germans*, p. 26.

70. Buchheim, *Glaubenskrise im Dritten Reich*, p. 16.

71. Bendiscioli, *New Racial Paganism*, pp. 3, 32.

72. Douglas, *God Among the Germans*, p. 21.
73. Scholder, *Requiem for Hitler*, pp. 110–11.
74. Bendiscioli, *New Racial Paganism*, pp. 67–85; Scholder, *Requiem for Hitler*, p. 112; Matheson, *Third Reich and the Christian Churches*, pp. 67–71, 'With Burning Concern', 14 March 1937. There was no room, the encyclical ran, 'for an *ersatz* or substitute religion based on arbitrary *revelations*, which some contemporary advocates wish to derive from the so-called myth of blood and race'.
75. J. Conway *The Nazi Persecution of the Churches* (London, 1968), pp. 298–9. The figure is an estimate only. The exact number is not known.
76. Scholder, 'Die evangelische Kirche', pp. 23–4.
77. Barnett, *Soul of the People*, pp. 43–4.
78. Scholder, *Requiem for Hitler*, pp. 163–6.
79. Barnett, *Soul of the People*, pp. 87, 93.
80. F. Reck-Malleczewen *Diary of a Man in Despair* (London, 1995), p. 22.
81. Trevor-Roper, *Hitler's Table Talk*, p. 6, 11–12 July 1941; p. 343, 27 February 1942.
82. S. A. Golunskii and M. S. Strogovich 'The Theory of the State and the Law', in J. Hazard (ed.) *Soviet Legal Philosophy* (Cambridge, Mass., 1951), pp. 366–77; D. Hoffmann *Stalinist Values: the Cultural Norms of Soviet Modernity 1917–1941* (Ithaca, NY, 2003), pp. 58–9.
83. Guins, *Soviet Law and Soviet Society*, p. 27.
84. M. Stolleis *Public Law in Germany 1880–1914* (Oxford, 2001), pp. 422–3, 430–31; I. Müller *Hitler's Justice: The Courts of the Third Reich* (London, 1991), p. 71.
85. Fraenkel, *Dual State*, p. 109. See too J. W. Bendersky *Carl Schmitt: Theorist for the Reich* (Princeton, NJ, 1983), pp. 35, 87; B. Rüthers *Carl Schmitt in Dritten Reich. Wissenschaft als Zeitgeist-Verstärkung* (Munich, 1989), pp. 41–4.
86. J. W. Jones *The Nazi Concept of Law* (Oxford, 1939), p. 19.
87. R. Conquest (ed.) *Justice and the Legal System in the USSR* (London, 1968), p.13; J. Hazard, I. Shapiro and P. B. Maggs (eds) *The Soviet Legal System* (New York, 1969), pp. 5–6; P. Beirne and R. Sharlet 'Toward a General Theory of Law and Marxism: E. B. Pashukanis', in P. Beirne (ed.) *Revolution in Law: Contributions to the Development of Soviet Legal Theory, 1917–1938* (New York, 1990), pp. 23–4.
88. Conquest, *Justice and the Legal System*, p. 13; R. Sharlet, P. B. Maggs and P. Beirne 'P. I. Stuchka and Soviet Law', in Beirne, *Revolution in Law*, pp. 49–50. See too J. Burbank 'Lenin and the Law in Revolutionary Russia', *Slavic Review*, 54 (1995), pp. 23–44.

89. Beirne and Sharlet, 'Toward a General Theory', p. 36.

90. P. H. Solomon *Soviet Criminal Justice Under Stalin* (Cambridge, 1996), pp. 20–24, 34–8. By 1928 100 per cent of procurators were party members, and 85 per cent of judges in people's courts.

91. Hazard *et al.*, *Soviet Legal System*, p. 6.

92. D. Pfaff *Die Entwicklung der sowjetischen Rechtslehre* (Cologne, 1968), pp. 115–21; Beirne and Sharlet, 'Toward a General Theory', pp. 34, 39.

93. Guins, *Soviet Law and Soviet Society*, p. 31.

94. R. Sharlet and P. Beirne 'In Search of Vyshinsky: the Paradox of Law and Terror', in Beirne, *Revolution in Law*, pp. 150–51; Guins, *Soviet Law and Soviet Society*, pp. 30–31.

95. Sharlet and Beirne, 'In Search of Vyshinsky', pp. 138–40.

96. Pfaff, *sowjetischen Rechtslehre*, p. 115.

97. Pfaff, *sowjetischen Rechtslehre*, p. 118; see too I. P. Trainin 'The Relationship between State and Law', 1945 in Hazard, *Soviet Legal Philosophy*, pp. 444–5, 446–8.

98. Z. L. Zile (ed.) *Ideas and Forces in Soviet Legal History: a Reader on the Soviet State and the Law* (Oxford, 1992), p. 277; E. Huskey 'Vyshinsky, Krylenko, and Soviet Penal Policies in the 1930s', in Beirne, *Revolution in Law*, pp. 184–6; P. H. Solomon 'The Bureaucratization of Criminal Justice under Stalin', in P. H. Solomon (ed.) *Reforming Justice in Russia, 1864–1996* (New York, 1997), pp. 229–32.

99. Bendersky, *Carl Schmitt*, p. 35.

100. Koenen *Der Fall Carl Schmitt*, p. 609; H. Müller-Dietz *Recht im Nationalsozialismus* (Baden-Baden, 2000), p. 5; G. Fieberg *Justiz in nationalsozialistischen Deutschland* (Bundesministerium der Justiz, Cologne, 1984), pp. 28–9.

101. Rüthers, *Carl Schmitt im Dritten Reich*, p. 60.

102. Müller, *Hitler's Justice*, p. 76.

103. Roberts, *House that Hitler Built*, p. 285; Müller, *Hitler's Justice*, p. 72; D. Majer *Grundlagen des nationalsozialistischen Rechtssystems* (Stuttgart, 1987), p. 104; Koenen, *Der Fall Carl Schmitt*, p. 608.

104. On Schmitt see Bendersky, *Carl Schmitt*, pp. 38–9, 87–8; R. Cristi *Carl Schmitt and authoritarian liberalism* (Cardiff, 1998), pp. 5–15. For a general biography D. Blasius *Carl Schmitt: Preussischer Staatsrat im Hitlers Reich* (Göttingen, 2001).

105. Rüthers, *Carl Schmitt im Dritten Reich*, p. 53.

106. Koenen, *Der Fall Carl Schmitt*, p. 608; Müller, *Hitler's Justice*, p. 71.

107. Rüthers, *Carl Schmitt im Dritten Reich*, pp. 59–66; Cristi, *Carl Schmitt*, pp. 12–15.

108. Rüthers, *Carl Schmitt im Dritten Reich*, pp. 53–5; Koenen, *Der Fall Carl Schmitt*, p. 601.

109. E. Rabofsky and G. Oberkofler *Verborgene Wurzeln der NS-Justiz: Strafrechtliche Rüstung für zwei Weltkriegen* (Vienna, 1985), p. 97.

110. Müller, *Hitler's Justice*, pp. 68–9; Rabofsky and Oberkofler, *Verborgene Wurzeln*, pp. 83–4.

111. Müller, *Hitler's Justice*, pp. 60–65.

112. Majer, *Grundlagen des nationalsozialistischen Rechtssystems*, p. 103.

113. Majer, *Grundlagen des nationalsozialistischen Rechtssystems*, pp. 101–2; Fraenkel, *Dual State*, pp. 40, 107–12.

114. Majer, *Grundlagen des nationalsozialistischen Rechtssystems*, p. 103.

115. Roberts, *House that Hitler Built*, p. 286.

116. Koenen, *Der Fall Carl Schmitt*, p. 612. The attribution was made by Göring in July 1934.

117. Hazard, *Soviet Legal Philosophy*, p. 370.

118. Fieberg, *Justiz im ns Deutschland*, p. 28.

119. Conquest, *Justice and the Legal System*, p. 17.

120. Majer, *Grundlagen des nationalsozialistischen Rechtssystems*, p. 104.

121. Rabofsky and Oberkofler, *Verborgene Wurzeln*, pp. 96–7; Müller, *Hitler's Justice*, pp. 76–7.

122. Zile, *Ideas and Forces*, pp. 265–6, decree 'On Protecting and Strengthening Public (Socialist) Property', 7 August 1932.

123. Zile, *Ideas and Forces*, pp. 297–8, decree 'On Supplementing the Statute on Crimes Against the State . . . with Articles Covering Treason'.

124. Hazard *et al.*, *Soviet Legal System*, pp. 5–6; E. Ginzburg *Into the Whirlwind* (London, 1967), p. 131.

125. Rabofsky and Oberkofler, *Verborgene Wurzeln*, pp. 85–6; Müller, *Hitler's Justice*, p. 74.

126. Pfaff, *sowjetischen Rechtslehre*, p. 117.

127. Royal Institute of International Affairs *Nationalism* (London, 1939), p. 72.

128. Wetter, *Dialectical Materialism*, p. 176.

129. Guins, *Soviet Law and Soviet Society*, p. 32.

130. Scholder, *Requiem for Hitler*, pp. 47–8.

131. Kolnai, *War Against the West*, pp. 55–6.

132. Bendersky, *Carl Schmitt*, pp. 38–9; Müller, *Hitler's Justice*, p. 72.

133. Kolnai, *War Against the West*, p. 289.

134. G. Neesse *Die Nationalsozialistische Deutsche Arbeiterpartei* (Stuttgart, 1935), p. 10.

135. Majer, *Grundlagen des nationalsozialistischen Rechtssystems*, p. 103.

136. Wetter, *Dialectical Materialism*, p. 268.

137. Douglas, *God among the Germans*, p. 25.

138. V. Kravchenko *I Chose Freedom: The Personal and Political Life of a Soviet Official* (London, 1947), p. 275.

139. de George, *Soviet Ethics and Morality*, p. 83.

140. Guins, *Soviet Law and Soviet Society*, p. 30.

141. Kolnai, *War Against the West*, pp. 291, 293–4; on the ideal of hardness see J. Hoberman 'Primacy of Performance: Superman not Superathlete', in J. A. Mangan (ed.) *Shaping the Superman: Fascist Body as Political Icon – Aryan Fascism* (London, 1999), pp. 78–9.

142. Imperial War Museum, London, FO 645, Box 157, testimony of Rudolf Höss taken at Nuremberg, 5 April 1946, p. 11.

143. Trevor-Roper, *Hitler's Table Talk*, p. 304; Pfaff, *sowjetischen Recht-slehre*, p. 111.

Chapter 8

1. *Uncensored Germany: Letters and News Sent Secretly from Germany to the German Freedom Party* (London, 1940), pp. 71–3, letter from a teacher, 14 August 1939.

2. *Uncensored Germany*, pp. 69–73. See too B. Engelmann *In Hitler's Germany: Everyday Life in the Third Reich* (London, 1988), p. 38. Engelmann estimated that between 10 and 18 per cent of his classmates at school were 'real Nazis'.

3. See for example R. Gellately *Backing Hitler: Consent and Coercion in Nazi Germany* (Oxford, 2001); N. Frei 'People's Community and War: Hitler's Popular Support', in H. Mommsen (ed.) *The Third Reich between Vision and Reality: New Perspectives on German History 1918–1945* (Oxford, 2001), pp. 59–74; D. Hoffmann *Stalinist Values: the Cultural Norms of Soviet Modernity 1917–1941* (Ithaca, NY, 2003).

4. G. M. Ivanova *Labor Camp Socialism: the Gulag in the Soviet Totalitarian System* (New York, 2000), p. 51: a farmworker was found to have 850 grammes of rye concealed, and was sentenced by the Belgorod District Court to five years in a camp in 1947. H. James 'The Deutsche Bank and the Dictatorship 1933–1945', in L. Gall *et al. The Deutsche Bank, 1870–1945* (London, 1995), p. 350. The bank director Hermann Kohler was executed for saying that National Socialism was 'nothing more than a fart'.

5. See I. Kershaw *The 'Hitler Myth': Image and Reality in the Third Reich* (Oxford, 1987), pp. 83–104; I. Kershaw 'The Führer-Image and Political Integration: the Popular Conception of Hitler in Bavaria during the Third

Reich', in G. Hirschfeld and L. Kettenacker (eds) *Der 'Führerstaat': Mythos and Realität* (Stuttgart, 1981), pp. 133–60.

6. Engelmann, *In Hitler's Germany*, p. vii.

7. A. Solzhenitsyn *The Gulag Archipelago 1918–1956* (London, 1974), pp. 18–20.

8. See for example the political police reports in J. Schadt (ed.) *Verfolgung und Widerstand unter dem Nationalsozialismus in Baden. Die Lageberichte der Gestapo und des Generalstaatsanwalts Karslruhe 1933–1940* (Stuttgart, 1976). These reports were structured to report any manifestations of hostility or non-compliance, but not evidence of complicity or enthusiasm.

9. J.-P. Depretto 'L'opinion ouvrière (1928–1932)', *Revue des Études Slaves*, 66 (1994), pp. 59.

10. For example Schadt, *Verfolgung und Widerstand in Baden*, p. 107, 'Stand und Tätigkeit der staatsfeindlichen Betätigungen', 4 October 1934.

11. D. Schmiechen-Ackermann *Nationalsozialismus und Arbeitermilieus: Der nationalsozialistische Angriff auf die proletarischen Wohnquartiere und die Reaktion in den sozialistischen Vereinen* (Bonn, 1998), p. 756.

12. L. Siegelbaum 'Soviet Norms Determination in Theory and Practice 1917–1941', *Soviet Studies*, 36 (1984), pp. 46–8; on worker legal protection in the 1920s see M. Ilič *Women Workers in the Soviet Inter-War Economy: From 'Protection' to 'Equality'* (London, 1999), pp. 46–52.

13. J.-P. Depretto *Les Ouvriers en U.R.S.S. 1928–1941* (Paris, 1997), pp. 276–7; T. Szamuely 'The Elimination of Opposition between the Sixteenth and Seventeenth Congresses of the CPSU', *Soviet Studies*, 17 (1966), pp. 335–6; A. Graziosi *A New, Peculiar State: Explorations in Soviet History 1917–1937* (Westport, Conn., 2000), pp. 179–83; J. B. Sorensen *The Life and Death of Soviet Trade Unionism 1917–1928* (New York, 1969), pp. 245–53.

14. Graziosi, *New, Peculiar State*, pp. 190–91.

15. Graziosi, *New, Peculiar State*, pp. 192–4; D. Filtzer 'Stalinism and the Working Class in the 1930s', in J. Channon (ed.) *Politics, Society and Stalinism in the USSR* (London, 1998), pp. 172–8; Szamuely, 'Elimination of Opposition', pp. 336–7; D. Filtzer *Soviet Workers and Stalinist Industrialization: the Formation of Modern Soviet Production Relations 1928–1941* (London, 1986), pp. 107–15, 135–46.

16. V. Kravchenko *I Chose Freedom: The Personal and Political Life of a Soviet Official* (London, 1947), pp. 311–15; L. E. Hubbard *Soviet Labour and Industry* (London, 1942), pp. 96–7.

17. J. Harrer 'Gewerkschaftlicher Widerstand gegen das "Dritte Reich"', in F. Deppe, G. Fülberth and J. Harrer (eds) *Geschichte der deutschen Werkschaftsbewegung* (4th edn, Cologne, 1989), pp. 349–56; S. Mielke and M. Frese

(eds) *Die Gewerkschaften im Widerstand und in der Emigration 1933–1945* (Frankfurt am Main, 1999), pp. 13–17; G. Mai ' "Warum steht der deutsche Arbeiter zu Hitler?" Zur Rolle der Deutschen Arbeitsfront im Herrschaftssystem des Dritten Reiches', *Geschichte und Gesellschaft*, 13 (1987), pp. 215–17.

18. C. W. Guillebaud *The Economic Recovery of Germany, 1933–1938* (London, 1939), pp. 110–11.

19. Harrer, 'Gewerkschaftlicher Widerstand', p. 344.

20. Harrer, 'Gewerkschaftlicher Widerstand', pp. 346–9; Mielcke and Frese, *Gewerkschaften in Widerstand*, pp. 13–16.

21. Harrer, 'Gewerkschaftlicher Widerstand', pp. 372–7; G. Beier *Die illegale Reichsleitung der Gewerkschaften 1933–1945* (Cologne, 1981), pp. 41–3, 73.

22. A. Merson *Communist Resistance in Nazi Germany* (London, 1985), p. 182. The figure of 60,000 includes all those estimated to have been active after 1933. In January 1933 the party had 360,000 members.

23. Schadt, *Verfolgung und Widerstand in Baden*, pp. 106–9, 'Lagebericht des Gestapa Karlsruhe', 4 October 1934.

24. G. Plum 'Die KPD in der Illegalität', in H. Graml (ed.) *Widerstand im Dritten Reich: Probleme, Ereignisse, Gestalten* (Frankfurt am Main, 1994), pp. 167–70.

25. Harrer, 'Gewerkschaftlicher Widerstand', p. 369; K. H. Roth *Facetten des Terrors: Der Geheimdienst der 'Deutsche Arbeitsfront' und die Zerstörung der Arbeiterbewegung 1933 bis 1938* (Bremen, 2000), pp. 36–8.

26. Roth, *Facetten des Terrors*, pp. 9–21; Harrer, 'Gewerkschaftlicher Widerstand', p. 370; G. Lotfi *KZ der Gestapo: Arbeitserziehungslager im Dritten Reich* (Stuttgart, 2000), pp. 25–42, 114–21.

27. Depretto, 'L'opinion ouvrière', pp. 53–8; E. Osokina *Our Daily Bread: Socialist Distribution and the Art of Survival in Stalin's Russia* (New York, 2001), pp. 53–6.

28. Filtzer, 'Stalinism and the Working Class', pp. 168–9.

29. J. J. Rossman 'The Teikovo Cotton Workers' Strike of April 1932: Class, Gender and Identity Politics in Stalin's Russia', *Russian Review*, 56 (1997), p. 44.

30. Rossman, 'Teikovo Cotton Workers' Strike', pp. 46–63; see too J. J. Rossman 'A Workers' Strike in Stalin's Russia: the Vichuga Uprising of April 1932', in L. Viola (ed.) *Contending with Stalinism: Soviet Power and Popular Resistance in the 1930s* (Ithaca, NY, 2002), pp. 44–80. This strike, too, was defeated by police repression, though it brought some economic alleviation.

31. See J. Falter and M. H. Kater 'Wähler und Mitglieder der NSDAP', *Geschichte und Gesellschaft*, 19 (1993), pp. 155–77.

32. Mielke and Frese, *Gewerkschaften im Widerstand*, pp. 13–15.

33. On the fate of the other socialist parties see V. N. Brovkin *The Mensheviks after October: Socialist Opposition and the Rise of the Bolshevik Dictatorship* (Ithaca, NY, 1987); V. N. Brovkin (ed.) *The Bolsheviks in Russian Society: the Revolution and the Civil Wars* (New Haven, Conn., 1997), esp. chs 2, 4 and 7; A. Liebich 'The Mensheviks', in A. Geifman (ed.) *Russia under the Last Tsar: Opposition and Subversion 1894–1917* (Oxford, 1999), pp. 19–33.

34. R. Löhmann *Der Stalinmythos: Studien zur Sozialgeschichte des Personenkultes in der Sowjetunion* (Münster, 1990), p. 205; Depretto, *Les Ouvriers en U.R.S.S.*, p. 367.

35. Löhmann, *Stalinmythos*, pp. 206–15; V. Andrle *Workers in Stalin's Russia: Industrialization and Social Change in a Planned Economy* (New York, 1988), p. 35; Ilič, *Women Workers*, p. 185; Filtzer, *Soviet Workers*, pp. 57–65.

36. K. M. Strauss *Factory and Community in Stalin's Russia: the Making of an Industrial Working Class* (Pittsburgh, 1997), pp. 23–4, 268–81.

37. H. Potthoff *Freie Gewerkschaften 1918–1933: Der Allgemeine Deutsche Gewerkschaftsbund in der Weimarer Republik* (Düsseldorf, 1987), p. 346.

38. W. Benz 'Vom freiwilligen Arbeitsdienst zur Arbeitsdienstpflicht', *Vierteljahrshefte für Zeitgeschichte*, 16 (1968), pp. 317–46; D. P. Silverman *Hitler's Economy: Nazi Work Creation Programs, 1933–1936* (Cambridge, Mass., 1998), pp. 168–72, 195–8.

39. Schmiechen-Ackermann, *Nationalsozialismus und Arbeitermilieus*, pp. 432–4, 487–90, 674–84; M. Schneider *Unterm Hakenkreuz: Arbeiter und Arbeiterbewegung 1933 bis 1939* (Bonn, 1999), pp. 347–411, 736–51.

40. Strauss, *Factory and Community*, pp. 272–4; L. Siegelbaum *Stakhanovism and the Politics of Productivity in the USSR, 1935–1941* (Cambridge, 1988) pp. 146–8, 163–8, 179–90. By the late 1930s there were 3 million workers classified as Stakhanovites, but mobility into and out of the category was high.

41. Strauss, *Factory and Community*, p. 195.

42. Filtzer, 'Stalinism and the Working Class', pp. 172–4.

43. Siegelbaum, 'Soviet Norms Determination', pp. 53–6; on the breakdown of collectives L. Siegelbaum 'Production Collectives and Communes and the "Imperatives" of Soviet Industrialization', *Slavic Review*, 45 (1986), pp. 67, 73–81.

44. M. Lewin *The Making of the Soviet System: Essays in the Social History of Interwar Russia* (London, 1985), p. 250.

45. R. Smelser 'Die Sozialplanung der Deutschen Arbeitsfront', in M. Prinz and R. Zitelmann (eds) *Nationalsozialismus und Modernisierung* (Darmstadt, 1991), pp. 75–77; Mai, ' "Warum steht der deutsche Arbeiter zu Hitler?" ', pp. 220–26; U. Herbert 'Arbeiterschaft im "Dritten Reich": Zwischenbilanz

und offene Fragen', *Geschichte und Gesellschaft*, 15 (1989), pp. 323–31. See too R. Hachtmann *Industriearbeit im 'Dritten Reich'* (Göttingen, 1989), pp. 54–66; J. Gillingham 'The "Deproletarianization" of German Society: Vocational Training in the Third Reich', *Journal of Social History*, 19 (1985/6), pp. 423–32.

46. Smelser, 'Sozialplanung der Deutschen Arbeitsfront', p. 75.

47. See for example U. Hess 'Zum Widerstand gegen den Nationalsozialismus in Leipziger Betrieben 1933–1939. Bedingungen, Möglichkeiten, Grenzen', in H.-D. Schmid (ed.) *Zwei Städte unter dem Hakenkreuz: Widerstand und Verweigerung in Hannover und Leipzig 1933–1945* (Leipzig, 1994), pp. 148–51.

48. Bundesarchiv-Berlin, R3101/11921, Reich Economics Ministry, weekly report, 18 December 1944. Some of the women would also be foreign workers. See also A. Tröger 'Die Planung des Rationalisierungsproletariats: Zur Entwicklung der geschlechts-spezifischen Arbeitsteilung und das weibliche Arbeitsmarkt im Nationalsozialismus', in A. Kuhn and J. Rüsen (eds) *Frauen in der Geschichte* (Düsseldorf, 1982), pp. 245–313.

49. Strauss, *Factory and Community*, pp. 224–30; Ilič, *Women Workers*, pp. 96–103; on canteen food, P. Francis *I Worked in a Soviet Factory* (London, 1939), pp. 80–82.

50. Andrle, *Workers in Stalin's Russia*, pp. 46–9; Hubbard, *Soviet Labour and Industry*, pp. 192, 211–14.

51. M. Klürer *Von Klassenkampf zur Volksgemeinschaft: Sozialpolitik im Dritten Reich* (Leoni, 1988), pp. 167–9; Herbert, 'Arbeiterschaft im "Dritten Reich"', p. 137. On the social spending of German businesses see H. Pohl, S. Habeth and B. Brüninghaus *Die Daimler-Benz AG in den Jahren 1933 bis 1945* (Stuttgart, 1986), pp. 172–80.

52. Smelser, 'Sozialplanung der Deutschen Arbeitsfront', pp. 78–9; Herbert, 'Arbeiterschaft im "Dritten Reich"', p. 342; Mai, '"Warum steht der deutsche Arbeiter zu Hitler?"', pp. 226–8.

53. Schmiechen-Ackermann, *Nationalsozialismus und Arbeitermilieus*, p. 642.

54. Filtzer, 'Stalinism and the Working Class', pp. 177–8; Siegelbaum, 'Soviet Norms Determination', pp. 57–8; Hubbard, *Soviet Labour and Industry*, pp. 105–9.

55. BA-Berlin, R2501/65, Reichsbank report, 'Steigende Arbeiterlöhne', 19 June 1939, pp. 2–7.

56. Mai, '"Warum steht der deutsche Arbeiter zu Hitler?"', pp. 216–20, 228; W. Zollitsch 'Die Vertrauensratswahlen von 1934 und 1935', *Geschichte und Gesellschaft*, 15 (1989), pp. 363–4, 378–9.

57. Mai, '"Warum steht der deutsche Arbeiter zu Hitler?"', p. 222. See too

G. Mai 'Die nationalsozialistische Betriebszellen-Organisation: Arbeiterschaft und Nationalsozialismus 1927–1934', in D. Heiden and G. Mai (eds) *Nationalsozialismus in Thüringen* (Weimar, 1995), p. 165.

58. F. Carsten *The German Workers and the Nazis* (Aldershot, 1995), pp. 44, 46.

59. Carsten, *German Workers*, p. 37.

60. J. Falter 'Warum die deutsche Arbeiter während des "Dritten Reiches" zu Hitler standen', *Geschichte und Gesellschaft*, 13 (1987), pp. 217–31. Hess, 'Zum Widerstand gegen den Nationalsozialismus', p. 149, who notes that in Leipzig factories three-quarters of party cell members were wage-earners.

61. A. Geifmann *Thou Shalt Kill: Revolutionary Terrorism in Russia, 1894–1917* (Princeton, NJ, 1993).

62. I. Zbarsky and S. Hutchinson *Lenin's Embalmers* (London, 1998), p. 93.

63. D. Volkogonov *Trotsky: the Eternal Revolutionary* (London, 1996), pp. 377–8.

64. A. V. Baikaloff *I Knew Stalin* (London, 1940), pp. 78–9.

65. See for example T. J. Colton *Moscow: Governing the Socialist Metropolis* (Cambridge, Mass., 1995), pp. 323–4.

66. Volkogonov, *Trotsky*, pp. 379, 392; V. Serge *Memoirs of a Revolutionary 1901–1941* (Oxford, 1967), p. 344.

67. R. J. Overy *Interrogations: the Nazi Elite in Allied Hands, 1945* (London, 2001), pp. 132–4, 460–67.

68. R. W. Whalen *Assassinating Hitler: Ethics and Resistance in Nazi Germany* (Toronto, 1993), pp. 36–7.

69. J. P. Duffy and V. L. Ricci *Target Hitler: the Plots to Kill Adolf Hitler* (Westport, Conn., 1992), pp. 26–8; W. Berthold *Die 42 Attentate auf Adolf Hitler* (Wiesbaden, 2000), pp. 126–45.

70. Berthold, *42 Attentate*, pp. 102–13; Duffy and Ricci, *Target Hitler*, pp. 19–21.

71. F. von Schlabrendorff *The Secret War Against Hitler* (London, 1966), pp. 229–40, 276–92; M. Baigent and R. Leigh *Secret Germany: Claus von Stauffenberg and the Mystical Crusade against Hitler* (London, 1994), pp. 46–58; Berthold, *42 Attentate*, pp. 214–36.

72. Carsten, *German Workers*, pp. 17–19.

73. Carsten, *German Workers*, pp. 105–6; H. Mehringer 'Sozialdemokrat-ischer und sozialistischer Widerstand', in P. Steinbach and J. Tuchel (eds) *Widerstand und Nationalsozialismus* (Berlin, 1994), pp. 126–36.

74. Merson, *Communist Resistance*, pp. 85–7, 162–3; Carsten, *German Workers*, pp. 70–71; on problems of communist resistance see Hess 'Zum

Widerstand gegen den Nationalsozialismus', pp. 148–9, 152; Plum, 'KPD in der Illegalität', pp. 157–70.

75. Merson, *Communist Resistance*, pp. 160–63; Carsten, *German Workers*, pp. 110–11.

76. T. Hamerow *On the Road to The Wolf's Lair: German Resistance to Hitler* (Cambridge, Mass., 1997), pp. 9–11. See too M. Meyer-Krahmer *Carl Goerdeler und sein Weg in den Widerstand* (Freiburg im Braisgau, 1989).

77. Hamerow, *Road to the Wolf's Lair*, pp. 13–14.

78. A. Speer *Inside the Third Reich: Memoirs* (London, 1970), pp. 379–81, 392; H. Schacht *76 Jahre meines Lebens* (Bad Wörishofen, 1953), pp. 533–7.

79. Hamerow, *Road to the Wolf's Lair*, pp. 320–21.

80. Hamerow, *Road to the Wolf's Lair*, p. 334.

81. K. von Klemperer *German Resistance Against Hitler: the Search for Allies Abroad* (Oxford, 1992), pp. 432–3.

82. B. Scheurig *Verräter oder Patrioten. Das Nationalkomitee 'Freies Deutschland' und der Bund deutscher Offiziere in der Sowjetunion 1943–1945* (Berlin, 1993), p. 138.

83. J.P. Stern 'The White Rose', in *Die Weisse Rose. Student Resistance to National Socialism 1942–1943: Forschungsergebnisse und Erfarhrungsberichte* (Nottingham, 1991), pp. 11–31.

84. Serge, *Memoirs of a Revolutionary*, p. 275.

85. S. Davies *Popular Opinion in Stalin's Russia: Terror, Propaganda and Dissent, 1934–1941* (Cambridge, 1997), pp. 122–3. See too B. Starkov 'Trotsky and Ryutin: from the history of the anti-Stalin resistance in the 1930s', in T. Brotherstone and P. Dukes (eds) *The Trotsky Reappraisal* (Edinburgh, 1992), pp. 73, 77–6.

86. R. Gaucher *Opposition in the U.S.S.R. 1917–1967* (New York, 1969), pp. 123–7.

87. G. Fischer *Soviet Opposition to Stalin: a Case Study in World War II* (Cambridge, Mass., 1952), p. 146.

88. J. J. Stephan *The Russian Fascists: Tragedy and Farce in Exile, 1925–1945* (London, 1978), pp. 49–51, 55–8.

89. Stephan, *Russian Fascists*, pp. 159–66, 168–9.

90. Stephan, *Russian Fascists*, pp. 338–40, 351–4, 357–64.

91. Volkogonov, *Trotsky*, pp. 320–22.

92. Volkogonov, *Trotsky*, pp. 328–9, 337–9, 401–6; on the influence of Trotsky see Starkov, 'Trotsky and Ryutin', pp. 74, 78–9. See too A. Durgan 'Trotsky, the POUM and the Spanish Revolution', *Journal of Trotsky Studies*, 2 (1994), pp. 56–7, 64–5; on Trotsky's view of terrorism G. L. Kline 'The

Defence of Terrorism: Trotsky and his major critics', in Brotherstone and Dukes, *The Trotsky Reappraisal*, pp. 156–63.

93. Gaucher, *Opposition in the U.S.S.R.*, pp. 273–80; V. Rogovin *1937: Stalin's Year of Terror* (Oak Park, Mich., 1998), pp. 328–44.

94. Volkogonov, *Trotsky*, pp. 463–6; Durgan, 'Trotsky and the POUM', p. 43 on Mercader. On Trotsky's view of terrorism see Kline, 'The Defence of Terrorism'.

95. Fischer, *Soviet Opposition*, pp. 42–3.

96. Gaucher, *Opposition in the U.S.S.R.*, p. 321; C. Andreyev *Vlasov and the Russian Liberation Movement: Soviet Reality and Émigré Theories* (Cambridge, 1987), pp. 2–4.

97. Andreyev, *Vlasov*, pp. 206–8; M. Parrish *The Lesser Terror: Soviet State Security 1939–1953* (Westport, Conn., 1996), pp. 151–3.

98. Andreyev, *Vlasov*, pp. 210–14.

99. J. Hoffmann *Die Geschichte der Wlassow-Armee* (Freiburg im Breisgau, 1984), pp. 205–6.

100. Parrish, *Lesser Terror*, pp. 148–50.

101. R. W. Thurston 'Social Dimensions of Stalinist Rule: Humor and Terror in the USSR, 1935–1941', *Journal of Social History*, 24 (1990/91), p. 541.

102. Fischer, *Soviet Opposition*, pp. 115–16.

103. J. Fürst 'Re-Examining Opposition under Stalin: Evidence and Context – A Reply to Kuromiya', *Europe–Asia Studies*, 55 (2003), pp. 795–9.

104. D. Peukert *Inside Nazi Germany: Conformity, Opposition and Racism in Everyday Life* (London, 1987), p. 154–9.

105. Peukert, *Inside Nazi Germany*, p. 161.

106. Thurston, 'Social Dimensions', p. 553.

107. *Pravda*, 12 June 1937.

108. L. Siegelbaum and L. Sokolov (eds) *Stalinism as a Way of Life* (New Haven, Conn., 2000), p. 239.

109. Davies, *Popular Opinion in Stalin's Russia*, p. 135.

110. Siegelbaum and Sokolov, *Stalinism as a Way of Life*, p. 176.

111. Siegelbaum and Sokolov, *Stalinism as a Way of Life*, p. 241.

112. Schadt, *Verfolgung und Widerstand*, p. 117.

113. D. Kahn *Hitler's Spies: German Military Intelligence in World War II* (London, 1978), pp. 181–2.

114. Davies, *Popular Opinion in Stalin's Russia*, pp. 52, 177.

115. Davies, *Popular Opinion in Stalin's Russia*, p. 177.

116. S. Graham *Stalin: An Impartial Study of the Life and Work of Joseph Stalin* (London, 1931), pp. 78–9; see too Thurston, 'Social Dimensions', pp. 544–7.

117. V. A. Nevezhin 'The Pact with Germany and the Idea of an "Offensive

War" (1939–1941)', *Journal of Slavic Military Stduies*, 8 (1995), pp. 813–15.

118. I. Kershaw *Popular Opinion and Political Dissent in the Third Reich: Bavaria, 1933–1945* (Oxford, 1983), pp. 334–57.

119. H. Boberach (ed.) *Meldungen aus dem Reich: Auswahl aus den geheimen Lageberichten der Sicherheitsdienst der SS, 1939–1945* (Berlin, 1965).

120. E. Radzinsky *Stalin* (London, 1996), p. 429.

Chapter 9

1. B. Brecht *Poems 1913–1956* (London, 1976), p.294.

2. S. Reid 'Socialist Realism in the Stalinist Terror: the Industry of Socialism Art Exhibition, 1935–41', *Russian Review*, 60 (2001), pp. 153–6.

3. S. Barron (ed.) *'Degenerate Art': the Fate of the Avant-Garde in Nazi Germany* (New York, 1991), p. 17; P. Adam *Arts of the Third Reich* (London, 1992), pp. 36–7.

4. Reid, 'Socialist Realism', pp. 161–4.

5. Reid, 'Socialist Realism', pp. 169–72.

6. Reid, 'Socialist Realism', pp. 169, 173–4, 179.

7. Barron, *'Degenerate Art'*, p. 17; F. Spotts *Hitler and the Power of Aesthetics* (London, 2002), pp. 171–2; Adam, *Arts of the Third Reich*, p. 94.

8. Spotts, *Hitler and the Power of Aesthetics*, pp. 171, 176; Barron, *'Degenerate Art'*, p. 18; R. S. Wistrich *Weekend in Munich: Art, Propaganda and Terror in the Third Reich* (London, 1995), pp. 80, 82–3.

9. Reid, 'Socialist Realism', pp. 182–3.

10. Spotts, *Hitler and the Power of Aesthetics*, p. 172.

11. Adam, *Arts of the Third Reich*, p. 114; Spotts, *Hitler and the Power of Aesthetics*, p. 169; Reid, 'Socialist Realism', p. 168.

12. H. Ermolaev *Soviet Literary Theories 1917–1934: the Genesis of Socialist Realism* (New York, 1977), pp. 144, 147; K. Clark *The Soviet Novel: History as Ritual* (Bloomington, Ind., 2000), pp. 27–31.

13. Ermolaev, *Soviet Literary Theories*, p. 145; T. Yedlin *Maxim Gorky: a Political Biography* (Westport, Conn., 1999), pp. 198–9.

14. Ermolaev, *Soviet Literary Theories*, pp. 166–7.

15. S. Fitzpatrick *The Cultural Front: Power and Culture in Revolutionary Russia* (Ithaca, NY, 1992), pp. 187–8; *Pravda*, 28 January 1936. Attacks on Shostakovich were followed by an article in *Pravda* on 6 February 1936 on modern ballet ('ballet's trickery') and, in the issue for 20 February, on modern building, 'cacophony in architecture'.

16. I. Golomstock *Totalitarian Art* (London, 1990), p. 174.

17. R. Hingley *Russian Writers and Society 1917–1978* (London, 1979), pp. 198–200.

18. Golomstock, *Totalitarian Art*, p. 179.

19. S. Tregub *The Heroic Life of Nikolai Ostrovsky* (Moscow, 1964), pp. 4, 38, 47.

20. W. N. Vickery 'Zhdanovism (1946–1953)', in M. Hayward and L. Labedz (eds) *Literature and Revolution in Soviet Russia 1917–1962* (Oxford, 1963), p. 110.

21. E. J. Brown *The Proletarian Episode in Russian Literature 1928–1932* (New York, 1953), p. 88.

22. Golomstock, *Totalitarian Art*, p. 86; Ermolaev, *Soviet Literary Theories*, p. 197.

23. M. Meyer 'A Musical Façade for the Third Reich', in Barron '*Degenerate Art*' p. 174; Golomstock, *Totalitarian Art*, p. 169.

24. Golomstock, *Totalitarian Art*, pp. 184–5.

25. Barron, '*Degenerate Art*', p. 46; Golomstock, *Totalitarian Art*, p. 83; D. Welch 'Nazi Film Policy: Control, Ideology, and Propaganda', in G. R. Cuomo (ed.) *National Socialist Cultural Policy* (London, 1995), p. 98.

26. Adam, *Arts of the Third Reich*, p. 94.

27. E. Bahr 'Nazi Cultural Politics: Intentionalism vs. Functionalism', in Cuomo, *National Socialist Cultural Policy*, p. 9.

28. A. Steinweis *Art, Ideology, and Economics in Nazi Germany* (Chapel Hill, NC, 1993), p. 22.

29. Golomstock, *Totalitarian Art*, pp. 82–3; L. Richard *Le Nazisme et la Culture* (Brussels, 1988), pp. 184–90.

30. Golomstock, *Totalitarian Art*, p. 83.

31. Spotts, *Hitler and the Power of Aesthetics*, p. 176; Golomstock, *Totalitarian Art*, pp. 150–51.

32. Yedlin, *Maxim Gorky*, p. 199; Golomstock, *Totalitarian Art*, pp. 183, 191.

33. Barron, '*Degenerate Art*', p. 174.

34. A. Lawton (ed.) *Russian Futurism through its Manifestoes, 1912–1928* (Ithaca, NY, 1988), p. 253.

35. A. Gladkov *Meetings with Pasternak: a Memoir* (London, 1977), p. 72.

36. L. Mally *Culture of the Future: the Proletkult Movement in Revolutionary Russia* (Berkeley, 1990), pp. 246–50, 253–5.

37. Lawton, *Russian Futurism*, p. 48.

38. V. Erlich *Russian Formalism: History – Doctrine* (3rd edn, New Haven, Conn., 1981), pp. 99–103, 118.

39. Brown, *Proletarian Episode*, p. 88.

40. Brown, *Proletarian Episode*, p. 89.

41. Ermolaev, *Soviet Literary Theories*, pp. 94–5.

42. M. Kane *Weimar Germany and the Limits of Political Art: a Study of the Work of George Grosz and Ernst Toller* (Fife, 1987), pp. 51–3.

43. M. Tatar *Lustmord: Sexual Murder in Weimar Germany* (Princeton, NJ, 1995), p. 69.

44. A. E. Steinweis 'Weimar Culture and the Rise of National Socialism: the *Kampfbund für deutsche Kultur*', *Central European History*, 24 (1991), p. 405; Barron, '*Degenerate Art*', p. 11.

45. Steinweis, 'Weimar Culture', p. 414; J. Hermand 'Bewähre Tümlichkeiten: Der völkisch-nazistische Traum einer ewig-deutschen Kunst', in H. Denkler and K. Prümm (eds) *Die deutsche Literatur im Dritten Reich* (Stuttgart, 1976), p. 102.

46. Hermand, 'Bewähre Tümlichkeiten', pp. 102–3.

47. M. A. von Lüttichen '*Entartete Kunst*, Munich 1937: a Reconstruction', in Barron, '*Degenerate Art*', pp. 45–6; S. Barron 'Modern Art and Politics in Pre-War Germany', in *ibid.*, pp. 9–10.

48. von Lüttichen, '*Entartete Kunst*', p. 45.

49. Barron, 'Modern Art and Politics', p. 9; for a memoir of the exhibition see P. Guenther 'Three Days in Munich, July 1937', in Barron, '*Degenerate Art*', pp. 33–43.

50. W. Moritz 'Film Censorship during the Nazi Era', in Barron, '*Degenerate Art*', p. 190; Meyer, 'Musical Façade', pp. 180–82.

51. O. Figes *Natasha's Dance: a Cultural History of Russia* (London, 2002), pp. 476–7; P. Kenez *Cinema and Soviet Society: From the Revolution to the Death of Stalin* (London, 2001), pp. 94–5.

52. J. Garrard and C. Garrard *Inside the Soviet Writers' Union* (London, 1990), pp. 31–2; Golomstock, *Totalitarian Art*, pp. 93–4.

53. Fitzpatrick, *Cultural Front*, pp. 197–8.

54. Vickery, 'Zhadanovism', pp. 101–5.

55. R. A. Brady *The Spirit and Structure of German Fascism* (London, 1937), pp. 90–91; Barron, 'Modern Art and Politics', p. 10; E. Fröhlich 'Die kultur-politicische Pressekonferenz des Reichspropagandaministeriums', *Vierteljahrs-hefte für Zeitgeschichte*, 22 (1974), pp. 353–6; V. Dahm 'Der Reichs-kulturkammer als Instrument Kulturpolitischer Stenerung und Sozialer Reglementierung', *Vierteljahrsheft für Zeitgeschichte*, 34 (1986) pp. 53–84; J. Petropoulos 'A Guide through the Visual Arts Administration of the Third Reich', in Cuomo, *National Socialist Cultural Policy*, pp. 121–52.

56. Brady, *Spirit and Structure*, p. 92.

57. S. Roberts *The House that Hitler Built* (London, 1937), p. 242; J. London (ed.) *Theatre Under the Nazis* (Manchester, 2000), pp. 8–9, 12.

58. Brady, *Spirit and Structure*, p. 88.

59. Steinweis, 'Weimar Culture', pp. 406–19.

60. Steinweis, *Art, Ideology, and Economics*, pp. 4–6.

61. Golomstock, *Totalitarian Art*, pp. 220–22; Garrard and Garrard, *Soviet Writers' Union*, p. 24; Hingley, *Russian Writers and Society*, p. 207.

62. Steinweiss, *Art, Ideology and Economics*, pp. 74–9, 81–95.

63. J. W. Baird *To Die for Germany: Heroes in the Nazi Pantheon* (Bloomington, Ind., 1990), p. 145.

64. Baird, *To Die for Germany*, pp. 146–7.

65. Baird, *To Die for Germany*, p. 148.

66. E. J. Simmons 'The Organization Writer (1934–46)', in Hayward and Labedz, *Literature and Revolution*, pp. 84–5; Tregub, *The Heroic Life of Nikolai Ostrovsky*, pp. 7, 14, 38.

67. T. Lahusen *How Life Writes the Book: Real Socialism and Socialist Realism in Stalin's Russia* (Ithaca, NY, 1997), pp. 13–15, 48–50, 53, 64–8, 79–80, 189–91.

68. R. Bartlett *Wagner in Russia* (Cambridge, 1995), pp. 227, 259–67, 271–2, 288–9.

69. Figes, *Natasha's Dance*, pp. 480–81; Simmons, 'The Organization Writer', p. 96; Fitzpatrick, *Cultural Front*, p. 207.

70. H. Ermolaev *Censorship in Soviet Literature* (Lanham, Md, 1997), p. 53.

71. Clark, *The Soviet Novel*, p. 4; M. Gorky *Mother* (Moscow, 1949). The introduction claimed: 'though it was written ten years before the establishment of Soviet power in Russia, we count it the first stone laid in the foundations of Soviet literature' (p. 5).

72. Yedlin, *Maxim Gorky*, pp. 178, 180–83, 186, 192–3, 209 ff.

73. E. Levi *Music in the Third Reich* (London, 1994), pp. 178–82; P. McGilligan *Fritz Lang: the Nature of the Beast* (London, 1997), pp. 173, 174–6.

74. Levi, *Music in the Third Reich*, pp. 98–9, 192–3.

75. Meyer, 'Musical Façade', p. 175; on literary conventions see J. M. Ritchie *German Literature under National Socialism* (London, 1983), pp. 96–101; T. Alkemeyer and A. Pichantz 'Insezenierte Körperträume: Reartikulation von Herrschaft und Selbstbeherrschung in Körperbildern des Faschismus', in U. Hermann and U. Nassen (eds) *Formative Ästhetik im Nationalsozialismus. Intentionen, Medien und Praxisformen totalitärer ästhetischer Herrschaft und Beherrschung* (Weinheim, 1994), p. 88; R. Taylor *Literature and Society in Germany 1918–1945* (Brighton, 1980), pp. 236–44.

76. Ermolaev, *Censorship in Soviet Literature*, pp. 1–6; G. V. Kostyrchenko 'Soviet Censorship in 1945–52', *Voprosii istorii*, 11–12 (1996), pp. 87–8.

77. Ermolaev, *Censorship in Soviet Literature*, pp. 7, 57; Kostyrchenko,

'Soviet Censorship', p. 92, gives the number of censors in the organization as 1,000; J. Plumper 'Abolishing Ambiguity: Soviet Censorship Practices in the 1930s', *Russian Review*, 60 (2001), pp. 527–8, 533.

78. Ermolaev, *Censorship in Soviet Literature*, p. 57; Kostyrchenko, 'Soviet Censorship', p. 92, gives the following figures for censorship work during the war: 235,031 newspaper editions checked; 207,942 journal articles; 71,740 books; 158,998 brochures.

79. Plumper, 'Abolishing Ambiguity', pp. 530–31.

80. Plumper, 'Abolishing Ambiguity', pp. 535–7.

81. Plumper, 'Abolishing Ambiguity', p. 527.

82. Reid, 'Socialist Realism', p. 179.

83. Ermolaev, *Censorship in Soviet Literature*, pp. 43–5, 56; V. G. Lebedeva 'Totalitarian and Mass Elements in Soviet Culture of the 1930s', *Russian Studies in History*, 42 (2003), pp. 81–4. On Fadayev see Vickery, 'Zhdanovism', pp. 114–15; R. Cockrell (ed.), introduction to A. Fadeev *The Rout* (London, 1995), pp. xi–xii.

84. Ermolaev, *Censorship in Soviet Literature*, p. 46.

85. H.-W. Strätz 'Die studentische "Aktion wider den undeutschen Geist" im Frühjahr 1933', *Vierteljahrshefte für Zeitgeschichte*, 16 (1968), pp. 347–53; Brecht, *Poems*, pp. 294, 568; Richard, *Nazisme et la Culture*, p. 211; Ritchie, *German Literature*, p. 68–9. Strictly speaking there were two first authors, Marx and the German socialist Karl Kautsky.

86. Roberts, *House that Hitler Built*, p. 248.

87. See for example G. Neesse *Die NSDAP: Versuch einer Rechtsdeutung* (Stuttgart, 1935), frontispiece.

88. Moritz, 'Film Censorship', p. 188; R. Taylor *Film Propaganda – Soviet Russia and Nazi Germany* (London, 1998), pp. 145–6.

89. D. Welch *Propaganda and the German Cinema 1933–45* (London, 2001), p. 14.

90. K. B. Eaton (ed.) *Enemies of the People: the Destruction of Soviet iterary, Theater, and Film Arts in the 1930s* (Evanston, Ill., 2002), pp. xx–xxi.

91. E. Braun 'Vsevolod Meyerhold: the Final Act', in Eaton, *Enemies*, pp. 151–9.

92. J. Rubinstein *Tangled Loyalties: the Life and Times of Ilya Ehrenburg* (London, 1996), pp. 45, 49–50, 69, 176.

93. Ermolaev, *Censorship in Soviet Literature*, p. 50.

94. J. E. Curtis (ed.) *Mikhail Bulgakov: Manuscripts Don't Burn. A Life in Diaries and Letters* (London, 1991), p. 284, letter from Bulgakov to V. Veresayev, 11 March 1939.

95. L. Milne *Mikhail Bulgakov: a Critical Biography* (Cambridge, 1990), pp. 259–60.

96. Milne, *Bulgakov*, pp. 220–25; Curtis, *Manuscripts Don't Burn*, pp. 229–30.

97. Taylor, *Literature and Society*, p. 215.

98. Strätz, '"Aktion wider den undeutschen Geist"', p. 350; Taylor, *Literature and Society*, p. 218. In general see A. E. Steinweis 'Cultural Eugenics: Social Policy, Economic Reform, and the Purge of Jews from German Cultural Life', in Cuomo, *National Socialist Cultural Policy*, pp. 23–37.

99. Levi, *Music in the Third Reich*, p. 48.

100. Levi, *Music in the Third Reich*, pp. 30–31; E. Levi 'Music and National Socialism: The Politicisation of Criticism, Composition and Performance', in B. Taylor and W. van der Will (eds) *The Nazification of Art: Art, Music, Architecture and Film in the Third Reich* (Winchester, 1990), pp. 162–4; B. Geissmar *The Baton and the Jackboot: Recollections of Musical Life* (London, 1988), p. 69.

101. G. Benn *Briefe an F. W. Oetze 1931–1945* (Wiesbaden, 1977), pp. 33–5, letter from Benn to Oetze, 25 April 1934.

102. G. Benn *Briefe an Tilly Wedekind 1930–1955* (Stuttgart, 1986), pp. 267–8, letter from Benn to Tilly Wedekind, 11 January 1938.

103. Benn, *Briefe an F. W. Oetze*, pp. 186–7, President, Reich Chamber of Writers, to Benn, 18 March 1938; see too F. J. Raddatz *Gottfried Benn: Leben – niederer Wahn: Eine Biographie* (Munich, 2001), pp. 168–73.

104. Taylor, *Literature and Society*, pp. 271–3.

105. D. L. Burgin 'Sophia Parnok and Soviet-Russian Censorship, 1922–1933', in Eaton (ed.), *Enemies*, pp. 44–5; Gottfried Benn described his years in the wilderness as a 'double life', *Doppelleben*.

106. On Beckmann see Barron, '*Degenerate Art*', p. 203; on Pasternak, Gladkov, *Meetings with Pasternak*, pp. 88–90; on exile see M. Durzak (ed.) *Die deutsche Exilliteratur 1933–1945* (Stuttgart, 1973), pp. 10–19. Some German artists and writers moved to the Soviet Union. See K. Kudlinska 'Die Exilsituation in der USSR', in Durzak, *deutsche Exilliteratur*, pp. 159–72.

107. Y. Yevtushenko (ed.) *Twentieth-Century Russian Poetry* (London, 1993), p. 180, 'Requiem. 1935–40', written 1961.

108. Yevtushenko, *Russian Poetry*, p. 184, 'To Death', 19 August 1939.

109. Barron, '*Degenerate Art*', pp. 203, 269–70; N. Wolf *Kirchner* (London, 2003), pp. 86–90.

110. Lahuson, *How Life Writes the Book*, pp. 152–9.

111. G. D. Hollander *Soviet Political Indoctrination: Developments in Mass Media and Propaganda since Stalin* (New York, 1972), p. 210.

112. R. Stites *Russian Popular Culture: Entertainment and Society since 1900* (Cambridge, 1992), pp. 74–6; Fitzpatrick, *Cultural Front*, p. 212.

113. M. Kater 'Forbidden Fruit? Jazz in the Third Reich', *American Historical Review*, 94 (1989), pp. 16–20; H. Bergmeier and R. E. Lotz *Hitler's Airwaves: the Inside Story of Nazi Radio Broadcasting and Propaganda Swing* (New Haven, Conn., 1997), pp. 138–44; C. Lusane *Hitler's Black Victims* (New York, 2002), pp. 201–3.

114. Bergmeier and Lotz, *Hitler's Airwaves*, p. 139, 145; Lusane, *Hitler's Black Victims*, pp. 202–3.

115. Stites, *Russian Popular Culture*, p. 82; M. W. Hopkins *Mass Media in the Soviet Union* (New York, 1970), p. 94; A. Inkeles *Public Opinion in Soviet Russia: a Study in Mass Persuasion* (Cambridge, Mass., 1950), pp. 226–7, 235–6, 255. In 1947 music supplied 60 per cent of programmes, political broadcasts 19.4 per cent, literary programmes 8.6 per cent, children's programmes 7.9 per cent.

116. Bergmeier and Lotz, *Hitler's Airwaves*, p. 6.

117. Bergmeier and Lotz, *Hitler's Airwaves*, p. 7.

118. Bergmeier and Lotz, *Hitler's Airwaves*, p. 8.

119. M. Turovskaya 'The 1930s and 1940s: cinema in context', in R. Taylor and D. Spring (eds) *Stalinism and Soviet Cinema* (London, 1993), p. 43.

120. Turovskaya, 'The 1930s and 1940s', p. 42; Hollander, *Soviet Political Indoctrination*, pp. 214–15; Inkeles, *Public Opinion*, pp. 301–3.

121. Turovskaya, 'The 1930s and 1940s', pp. 43, 45.

122. P. Kenez 'Soviet cinema in the age of Stalin', in Taylor and Spring *Stalinism and Soviet Cinema*, pp. 56–7, 61; Turovskaya, 'The 1930s and 1940s', p. 42; R. Taylor 'Red stars, positive heroes and personality cults', in Taylor and Spring, *Stalinism and Soviet Cinema*, p. 95.

123. Turovskaya, 'The 1930s and 1940s', p. 51.

124. Moritz, 'Film Censorship', p. 188; Taylor, *Film Propaganda*, pp. 145, 151; Welch, *Propaganda and the German Cinema*, p. 43.

125. Welch, *Propaganda and the German Cinema*, pp. 31, 35.

126. D. Welch 'Nazi Film Policy: Control, Ideology, and Propaganda', in Cuomo, *National Socialist Cultural Policy*, p. 113; Welch, *Propaganda and the German Cinema*, p. 14.

127. S. Hake *Popular Cinema of the Third Reich* (Austin, Tex., 2001), pp. 130–31; Moritz, 'Film Censorship', pp. 186–7.

128. S. Kracauer *From Caligari to Hitler: a Psychological History of the German Film* (Princeton, NJ, 1974), pp. 269–70.

129. E. Khokhlova 'Forbidden films of the 1930s', in Taylor and Spring, *Stalinism and Soviet Cinema*, p. 94.

130. J. Haynes *New Soviet Man: Gender and Masculinity in Stalinist Soviet Cinema* (Manchester, 2003), p. 52; L. Attwood 'The Stalin Era', in Attwood (ed.) *Red Women on the Silver Screen: Soviet Women and Cinema from the beginning to the end of the Communist era* (London, 1993), pp. 57–8.

131. Attwood, 'Stalin Era', p. 65; M. Enzensberger ' "We were born to turn a fairy tale into reality": Grigori Alexandrov's *The Radiant Path* ', in Taylor and Spring, *Stalinism and Soviet Cinema*, pp. 97–108.

132. Welch, 'Nazi Film Policy', p. 109.

133. Hake, *Popular Cinema of the Third Reich*, pp. 192–9.

134. Kracauer, *Caligari to Hitler*, pp. 255–6.

135. Stites, *Russian Popular Culture*, pp. 73–9; Hollander, *Soviet Political Indoctrination*, pp. 214–15.

136. Marsh, *Images of Dictatorship*, pp. 27–8.

137. F. J. Miller *Folklore for Stalin: Russian Folklore and Pseudofolklore of the Stalin Era* (New York, 1990), p. 7.

138. Miller, *Folklore for Stalin*, pp. 69, 71; R. Robin 'Stalin and Popular Culture', in H. Günther (ed.) *The Culture of the Stalin Period* (London, 1990), p. 29.

139. L. Mally 'Autonomous Theatre and the Origins of Socialist Realism: the 1932 Olympiad of Autonomour Art', *Russian Review*, 52 (1993), pp. 198–211; see too Lebedeva, 'Soviet Culture of the 1930s', pp. 68–76, 83–5.

140. J. Macleod *The New Soviet Theatre* (London, 1943), pp. 53–7, 65.

141. Taylor, *Literature and Society*, pp. 246–61.

142. W. Niven 'The Birth of Nazi Drama', in London (ed.), *Theatre under the Nazis*, pp. 54–5.

143. E. Levi 'Opera in the Nazi Period', in London (ed.), *Theatre under the Nazis*, pp. 62–73; see too R. Stommer ' "Da oben versinkt einem der Alltag . . .": Thingstätten im Dritten Reich als Demonstration der Volksgemeinschaftsideologie', in D. Peukert and J. Reulecke (eds) *Die Reihen fast Geschlossen: Beiträge zur Geschichte des Alltags unterm Nationalsozialismus* (Wuppertal, 1981), pp. 154 ff.

144. B. Drewniak 'The Foundations of Theater Policy in Nazi Germany', in Cuomo, *National Socialist Cultural Policy*, pp. 68, 82–3; Stommer, 'Thingstätten im Dritten Reich', pp. 170–72.

145. Brecht, *Poems*, p. 299. On Benjamin see B. Taylor and W. van der Will 'Aesthetics and National Socialism', in Taylor and van der Will, *Nazification of Art*, p. 11. On the role of aesthetics in politics see P. Reidel 'Aspekte ästhetischer Politik im NS-Staat', in Hermann and Nassen, *Formative Ästhetik*, pp. 14–21; P. Labanyi 'Images of Fascism: Visualization and Aestheticization in the Third Reich', in M. Lafann (ed.) *The Burden of German*

History: 1919–1945 (London, 1988), pp. 156–60, 170–72. See too S. Behrenbeck *Der Kult um die toten Helden: nationalsozialistische Mythen, Riten und Symbole* (Vierow bei Greifswald, 1996).

146. Labanyi, 'Images of Fascism', p. 169.

147. Spotts, *Hitler and the Power of Aesthetics*, pp. 100–101.

148. A. Speer *Inside the Third Reich: Memoirs* (London, 1970), pp. 58–9.

149. H. T. Burden *The Nuremberg Party Rallies: 1923–39* (London, 1967), pp. 138–43.

150. Baird, *To Die for Germany*, pp. 58–6.

151. Baird, *To Die for Germany*, pp. 62–5.

152. S. I. Luck *Observation in Russia* (London, 1938), pp. 30–39.

153. Luck, *Observation in Russia*, p. 33.

154. R. Sartorti 'Stalinism and Carnival: Organisation and Aesthetics of Political Holidays', in Günther, *Culture of the Stalin Period*, pp. 49–50.

155. Sartorti, 'Stalinism and Carnival', pp. 58, 71.

156. Brecht, *Poems*, p. 299.

157. V. Garros, N. Korenevskaya and T. Lahusen (eds) *Intimacy and Terror: Soviet Diaries of the 1930s* (New York, 1995), pp. 181–2, diary of Galina Shtange, 25 December 1936.

158. Garros *et al.*, *Intimacy and Terror*, pp. 183, 191, Shtange diary, 25 December, 1936, 8 May 1937.

159. M. Agursky 'An Occult Source of Socialist Realism: Gorky and Theories of Thought Transference', in B. G. Rosenthal (ed.) *The Occult in Russian and Soviet Culture* (Ithaca, NY, 1997), p. 250.

160. Agursky, 'Occult Source of Socialist Realism', pp. 249, 252–8.

161. Meyer, 'Musical Façade', p. 182.

162. Golomstock, *Totalitarian Art*, p. 179.

Chapter 10

1. F. Thyssen *I Paid Hitler* (London, 1941), p. 187.

2. H. A. Wessel *Thyssen & Co, Mülheim a.d.Ruhr: die Geschichte einer Familie und ihrer Unternehmnung* (Stuttgart, 1991), pp. 47–8, 162–3, 171.

3. Wessel, *Thyssen & Co*, pp. 48. 171; Thyssen, *I Paid Hitler*, pp. 30–41, 49–50; A. Barkai *Nazi Economics: Ideology, Theory, and Policy* (Oxford, 1990), pp. 120–21.

4. V. Kravchenko, *I Chose Freedom: the Personal and Political Life of a Soviet Official* (London, 1947), pp. 174–5.

5. Kravchenko, *I Chose Freedom*, pp. 203–4.

6. Kravchenko, *I Chose Freedom*, pp. 2–4, 216–22, 226–30, 347–51.

7. K. McKenzie *Comintern and World Revolution* (New York, 1964), p. 144.

8. F. Pollock 'Staatskapitalismus', in H. Dubied and A. Sollner (eds) *Wirtschaft, Recht und Staat im Nationalsozialismus: Analysen des Instituts für Sozialforschung* (Frankfurt am Main, 1981), pp. 81–106; 'dysfunctional capitalism' in A. Sohn-Rethel *Economy and Class Structure of German Fascism* (London, 1978), pp. 128–31.

9. Bundesarchiv-Berlin, R7/2149 Ohlendorf papers 'Grundsätze der Volkswirtschafts-politik' [September 1935], p. 9.

10. See for example P. R. Gregory (ed.) *Behind the Façade of Stalin's Command Economy* (Stanford, 2001).

11. In general see T. Balderston *Economics and Politics in the Weimar Republic* (Cambridge, 2002); H. James *The German Slump: Politics and Economics, 1924–1936* (Oxford, 1986); H.-J. Braun *The German Economy in the Twentieth Century* (London, 1990); R. J. Overy 'The German Economy, 1919–1945', in P. Panayi (ed.) *Weimar and Nazi Germany: Continuities and Discontinuities* (London, 2001), pp. 33–73.

12. See in general R. W. Davies (ed.) *From Tsarism to the New Economic Policy* (Ithaca, NY, 1991); R. Munting *The Economic Development of the USSR* (London, 1982); P. Gatrell *The Tsarist Economy, 1850–1917* (London, 1986).

13. A. M. Ball *Russia's Last Capitalists: the Nepmen, 1921–1929* (Berkeley, Calif., 1987), pp. 162–5; on small-scale trade A. Baykov *The Development of the Soviet Economic System* (Cambridge, 1947), p.107. Out of 165,781 enterprises in the production census in 1923, 147,471 (88.5 per cent) were in private hands. In 1922–3, some 75 per cent of the retail trade was also in private hands (p. 55).

14. Munting, *Economic Development*, p. 97.

15. R. W. Davies, M. Harrison and S. G. Wheatcroft (eds) *The Economic Transformation of the Soviet Union* (Cambridge, 1994), pp. 36–7, 292. There is no agreed figure on the annual rate of industrial growth. The Soviet official figure was 16.8 per cent a year.

16. Davies, Harrison and Wheatcroft, *Economic Transformation*, p. 296; *Statistisches Jahrbuch für das Deutsche Reich, 1933* (Berlin, 1934).

17. On Russia see Davies, Harrison and Wheatcroft, *Economic Transformation*, p. 269. Soviet GNP was 123.7 bn rbls. in 1928, 212.3 bn in 1937 (1937 prices); German GNP from A. Ritschl and M. Spoerer 'Die Bruttosozialprodukt in Deutschland nach den amtlichen Volkseinkommens-und Sozialproduktstatistiken 1901–1995', *Jahrbuch für Wirtschaftsgeschichte*, 37 (1997),

pp. 51–2. Growth between 1928 and 1938 was 39 per cent in real terms, from 90.8 bn RM in 1928 to 126.2 bn in 1938.

18. J. Stalin *Works* (13 vols, Moscow, 1952–55), vol. xii, p. 252, political report of the CC to the XVI Congress of the CPSU, 27 June 1930.

19. R. Zitelmann *Hitler: the Politics of Seduction* (London, 1999), p. 224; H. Rauschning *Hitler Speaks* (London, 1939), p. 235.

20. Zitelmann, *Hitler*, p. 215; Stalin, *Works*, vol. xi, p. 314; Rauschning, *Hitler Speaks*, p. 34.

21. J. Stalin *Problems of Leninism* (Moscow, 1947), p. 300, 'A Year of Great Change' *Pravda*, 7 November 1929.

22. Stalin, *Works*, vol. xii, pp. 314–20, political report to the XVI Congress; J. Stalin *Economic Problems of Socialism in the U.S.S.R.* (Peking, 1972), p. 5.

23. Stalin, *Works*, vol. xii, pp. 311–15.

24. Zitelmann, *Hitler*, pp. 206, 207.

25. Barkai, *Nazi Economics*, p. 37.

26. NSDAP *Parteitag der Arbeit von 6 bis 13 September 1937* (Munich, 1938), p. 38.

27. O. Wagener *Das Wirtschaftsplan der NSDAP* (Munich, 1932), p. 5.

28. A. Hitler *The Secret Book* ed. T. Taylor (New York, 1961), pp. 5–6, 13.

29. Hitler, *Secret Book*, pp. 14, 24.

30. Hitler, *Secret Book*, pp. 21–3.

31. K.-H. Minuth (ed.) *Akten der Reichskanzlei: Regierung Hitler 1933–1938* (Boppard am Rhein, 1983), vol. i, p. 62, committee for work-creation, 9 February 1933.

32. F. Nonnenbruch *Die Wirtschaft in der NS Politik* (Berlin, 1935), p. 16.

33. Zitelmann, *Hitler*, p. 226–7, 232; on planning BA-B, R7/2149, Ohlendorf memorandum, 'Grundsätze der Volkswirtschaftspolitik', p. 9; see too A.-I. Berndt (ed.) *Gebt mir vier Johre Zeit: Dokumente zum ersten Vierjahresplan des Führers* (Munich, 1937), pp. 233–5, Hitler speech 30 January 1937.

34. BA-B R7/2149, Ohlendorf papers, 'Unsere Wirtschaftsauffassung. Das Program der NSDAP', p. 9.

35. H. Trevor-Roper (ed.) *Hitler's Table Talk, 1941–1944* (Oxford, 1984), p. 65.

36. See for example D. L. Hoffmann 'The Great Terror on the Local Level: Purges in Moscow Factories, 1936–1938', in J. A. Getty and R. Manning (eds) *Stalinist Terror: New Perspectives* (Cambridge, 1993), pp. 163–8.

37. F. Seurot *Le système économique de l'URSS* (Paris, 1989), pp. 55–7; J. Schneider and W. Harbrecht (eds) *Wirtschaftsordnung und Wirtschaftspolitik in Deutschland (1933–1993)* (Stuttgart, 1996), pp. viii–xxii.

38. V. Barnett *Kondratiev and the Dynamics of Economic Development: Long Cycles and Industrial Growth in Historical Context* (London, 1998), pp. 21–2, 171; N. Jasny *Soviet Economists of the Twenties* (Cambridge, 1972), pp. 103–5.

39. Barnett, *Kondratiev*, pp. 190–96; Jasny, *Soviet Economists*, pp. 119, 127.

40. Jasny, *Soviet Economists*, p. 141; E. Zaleski *Planning for Economic Growth in the Soviet Union, 1918–1932* (Chapel Hill, NC, 1962), p. 58.

41. Baykov, *Soviet Economic System*, p. 424.

42. Details in E. A. Rees *State Control in Soviet Russia: the Rise and Fall of the Workers' and Peasants' Inspectorate 1920–1934* (London, 1987), pp. 190–231; O. K. Khlevniuk *In Stalin's Shadow: the Career of 'Sergo' Ordzhonikidze* (London, 1995), pp. 41–52, 167; S. Fitzpatrick 'Ordzhonikidze's Takeover of Vesenkha: a Case Study in Soviet Bureaucratic Politics', *Soviet Studies*, 37 (1985), pp. 154–67.

43. C. Bettelheim *La planification soviétique* (Paris, 1939), pp. 72–3.

44. Rees, *State Control in Soviet Russia*, p. 231; Baykov, *Soviet Economic System*, pp. 453–5.

45. J. Millar 'Soviet Planners 1936–37', in J. Degras and A. Nove (eds) *Soviet Planning: Essays in Honour of Naum Jasny* (Oxford, 1964), pp. 127–9.

46. Miller, 'Soviet Planners', pp. 120–21; Baykov, *Soviet Economic System*, pp. 441, 444.

47. Miller, 'Soviet Planners', p. 120; see too H. Hunter 'Priorities and Shortfalls in Prewar Soviet Planning', in Degras and Nove, *Soviet Planning*, pp. 3–31.

48. P. Sutela *Socialism, Planning and Optimality: a Study of Soviet Economic Thought* (Helsinki, 1984), pp. 13–15, 57–8; M. Harrison *Soviet Planning in Peace and War, 1938–1945* (Cambridge, 1985), pp. 14–16, 18–19.

49. Bettelheim, *planification soviétique*, pp. 74–5; Baykov, *Soviet Economic System*, pp. 455–7.

50. Baykov, *Soviet Economic System*, pp. 457–60.

51. T. Dunmore *The Stalinist Command Economy: the Soviet State Apparatus and Economic Policy 1945–1953* (London, 1980), pp. 6–10.

52. J. A. Tooze *Statistics and the German State, 1900–1945: the Making of Modern Economic Knowledge* (Cambridge, 2001), p. 186; Gosplan figures in E. Zaleski *Stalinist Planning for Economic Growth 1933–1952* (Chapel Hill, NC, 1980) pp. 49–50.

53. BA-B R2/540 Schacht speech on 'Ziele deutscher Wirtschaftspolitik', 11 December 1934.

54. BA-B R2/540 'Die Ansprache Dr Schachts' 23 January 1937; R11/318 'Ansprache Dr Schachts', Berlin 10 May 1938, pp. 12–14. Economic manage-

ment, said Schacht, 'must only lead to a healthy and life-sustaining economic order, but not to a schematic economic bureaucratism'.

55. R. J. Overy *The Nazi Economic Recovery 1932–1938* (Cambridge, 1996); for a critical assessment of growth strategy see C. Buchheim 'The Nazi Boom: An Economic Cul-de-Sac', in H. Mommsen (ed.) *The Third Reich between Vision and Reality: New Perspectives on German History 1918–1945* (Oxford, 2001), pp. 79–92.

56. G. Corni and H. Giess *Brot, Butter, Kanonen: Die Ernährungswirtschaft in Deutschland unter der Diktatur Hitlers* (Berlin, 1997), pp. 81–6, 87–98, 133. By 1938 there were 17,300 officials running the Food Estate, with 57,400 farmers used as local 'farm leaders'.

57. R. A. Brady *The Spirit and Structure of German Fascism* (London, 1937), pp. 266–72.

58. Tooze, *Statistics and the German State*, pp. 202–3; see BA-B R11/11 for reports from Grünig on national income estimates and economic balances. See too BA-B R43 II/301, Dr Grünig, 'Probleme der Wirtschaftslenkung'.

59. BA-B R11/77 Reichswirtschaftskammer, economic situation reports. The chamber produced composite quarterly reports, and regular digests of the economic group reports organized into sections on labour, raw materials, industry, wages and prices, trade, etc.

60. On 'primacy of politics' F. Marx *Government in the Third Reich* (New York, 1936), p. 150; telephone tapping in H. B. Gisevius *To the Bitter End* (London, 1948), pp. 200–201; on Bremen speech H. Heiber (ed.) *Reichsführer! Briefe an und von Himmler* (Stuttgart, 1968), p. 44, Aktennotiz 1 May 1936.

61. W. Treue 'Hitlers Denkschrift zum Vierjahresplan 1936', *Vierteljahrshefte für Zeitgeschichte*, 3 (1955), p. 206.

62. Imperial War Museum, London, FO 645, Box 156, Göring interrogation, 17 October 1945, p. 8.

63. Berndt, *Gebt mir vier Jahre Zeit*, p. 211; P. Schmidt *Deutsche Wirtschaftsfreiheit durch den Vierjahresplan* (Breslau, n.d.), pp. 2–8; G. Thomas *Geschichte der deutschen Wehr-und Rüstungswirtschaft 1918–1943/5* ed. W. Birkenfeld (Boppard am Rhein, 1966), p. 111.

64. 'Niederschrift über die Sitzung des Ministerrats 4 September 1936', in H. Michaelis and E. Schraepler (eds) *Ursachen und Folgung vom deutschen Zusammenbruch 1918 bis 1945* (Berlin, 1968), vol.x, p. 545.

65. M. Domarus *Hitler: Speeches and Proclamations* (4 vols., Wauconda, Ill., 1990–2004), vol. ii, p. 853.

66. BA-B R26/II Anh/2 W. Rentrop, 'Materialen zur Geschichte des Reichskommissars für die Preisbildung', pp. 8–13.

67. *Der Vierjahresplan* 1 (1937), p. 277.

68. BA-B R26/II Anh/1 H. Dichgans 'Zur Geschichte des Reichskommissars für Preisbildung' n.d., pp. 4–6, 9–11.

69. Davies, Harrison and Wheatcroft, *Economic Transformation*, p. 313; M. Dohan 'Foreign Trade', in Davies, *Tsarism to the New Economic Policy*, pp. 224–33, 326–7; W. Beitel and J. Nötzold *Deutsch-sowjetische Wirtschaftsbeziehungen in der Zeit der Weimarer Republik* (Baden-Baden, 1979), p. 206.

70. Beitel and Nötzold, *Deutsch-sowjetische Wirtschaftsbeziehungen*, p. 217.

71. L. Prager *Nationalsozialismus gegen Liberalismus* (Munich, 1933), p. 3. On autarky in Germany see D. Petzina *Autarkiepolitik im Dritten Reich* (Stuttgart, 1968); A. Teichert *Autarkie und Grosswirtschaftsraum in Deutschland 1930–1939* (Munich, 1984). For a contemporary analysis H. Kremmler *Autarkie in der organischen Wirtschaft* (Dresden, 1940).

72. R. W. Davies and O. K. Khlevniuk 'Gosplan', in E.A. Rees (ed.) *Decision-Making in the Stalinist Command Economy, 1932–37* (London, 1997), p. 34.

73. L. E. Hubbard *Soviet Money and Finance* (London, 1936), pp. 290–96; Baykov, *Soviet Economic System*, pp. 264–72. In general on Soviet autarky M. R. Dohan 'The Economic Origins of Soviet Autarky 1927/28–1934', *Slavic Review*, 35 (1976), pp. 603–35.

74. Calculated from Davies, Harrison and Wheatcroft, *Economic Transformation*, pp. 272, 312.

75. K. E. Bailes 'The American Connection: Ideology and the Transfer of American Technology to the Soviet Union, 1917–1941', *Comparative Studies in Society and History*, 23 (1981), pp. 443–8.

76. Beitel and Nötzold, *Deutsch-sowjetische Wirtschaftsbeziehungen*, pp. 208, 210, 217.

77. E. von Mickwitz (ed.) *Aussenhandel unter Zwang* (Hamburg, 1938), pp. 5, 41; on Hitler's conversion to autarky E. Syring *Hitler: seine politische Utopie* (Frankfurt am Main, 1994), pp. 173–4.

78. See in general S. Lurie *Private Investment in a Controlled Economy: Germany 1933–1939* (London, 1947); N. Forbes 'London Banks, the German Standstill Agreement and Economic Appeasement in the 1930s', *Economic History Review*, 40 (1987).

79. On the control offices BA-B R3101/8445 Economics Ministry 'Bekanntmachung über die Reichsstellen zur Überwachung und Regelung des Warenverkehrs'; on the operation of the system G. R. von Radiis *Die deutsche Aussenhandelspolitik unter dem Einfluss der Devisenbewirtschaftung con 1931 bis 1938* (Vienna, 1939). See too W. A. Boelcke *Deutschland als Welthandelsmacht 1930–1945* (Stuttgart, 1994), pp. 13–43.

80. Petzina, *Autarkiepolitik*, p. 95.

81. L. Zumpe *Wirtschaft und Staat in Deutschland 1933 bis 1945* (Berlin, 1979), p. 221; H.-E. Volkmann 'Die NS-Wirtschaft in Vorbereitung des Krieges', in W. Deist *et al.* (eds) *Das Deutsche Reich und der Zweite Weltkrieg: Band I* (Stuttgart, 1979), p. 262; W. Jungermann and H. Krafft *Rohstoffreichtum aus deutscher Erde* (Berlin, 1939), p. 69 on oil.

82. Details in R. J. Overy 'The Four Year Plan', in T. Gourvish (ed.) *European Yearbook of Business History: Number 3* (Aldershot, 2000), pp. 101–2.

83. R. W. Davies and M. Harrison 'Defence spending and defence industry in the 1930s', in J. Barber and M. Harrison (eds) *The Soviet Defence-Industry Complex from Stalin to Khrushchev* (London, 2000), p. 73; German figures in National Archives, Microcopy T178, Roll 15, Reich finance ministry 'Statistische Übersichten zu den Reichshaushaltsrechnungen 1938 bis 1943', November 1944.

84. IWM FD 3056/49 'Statistical Material on the German Manpower Position during the war period 1939–1944', 31 July 1945, table 7.

85. B. H. Klein *Germany's Economic Preparations for War* (Cambridge, Mass., 1959), p. 14; Davies and Harrison, 'Defence spending', pp. 87–8.

86. J. Sapir *Les fluctuations économiques en URSS 1941–1945* (Paris, 1989), p. 47.

87. N. Simonov 'The "war scare" of 1927 and the birth of the defence-industry complex', in Barber and Harrison, *Soviet Defence-Industry Complex*, p. 44.

88. In May 1939 1 in 8 German workers in the consumer industries worked directly on military orders. See R. J. Overy *War and Economy in the Third Reich* (Oxford, 1994), pp. 27–9 on the conversion of consumer sectors.

89. United States Strategic Bombing Survey, Report 20 'Light Metal Industry in Germany', Part I Aluminium, p. 2.

90. BA-B Reichsamt für Wirtschaftsausbau, New Production Plan, 12 July 1938, 'Finanzbedarf der Projekte des Vierjahresplan'.

91. R. J. Overy 'The Reichswerke Hermann Göring: a Study in German Economic Imperialism', in Overy, *War and Economy*, pp. 144–74.

92. This excludes investment in areas such as the railways, whose overhaul in the late 1930s also had a strategic purpose; so too the expansion of basic electric power.

93. This view was formulated in United States Strategic Bombing Survey Overall Report, September 1945, p. 31: 'The Germans did not plan, nor were they prepared for, a long war'. See too N. Kaldor 'The German War Economy', *Review of Economic Statistics*, 13 (1946); A. S. Milward 'Hitlers Konzept des Blitzkrieges', in A. Hillgruber (ed.) *Probleme des Zweiten Weltkrieges* (Cologne, 1967), pp. 19–40.

94. For a survey of all these preparations see BA-B R26 I/18 'Ergebnisse der Vierjahresplan-Arbeit', spring 1942, pp. 5–95. 'He [Hitler] gave economic policy the task of making the economy ready for war in the space of four years . . .' (p. 1).

95. *Akten zur deutschen auswärtigen Politik* Ser. D., vol.i (Baden-Baden, 1950), p. 27, 'Niederschrift über die Besprechung in der Reichskanzlei', 5 November 1937.

96. Overy, *War and Economy*, pp. 148–59.

97. BA-B R26 IV/4 'Besprechung über die Eingliederung Sudetendeutschlands in die reichsdeutsche Wirtschaft', 3 October 1938.

98. IWM, EDS AL/1571 Thomas minute, 20 June 1940.

99. BA-B R2501/6585, Reichsbank memorandum 24 August 1939, appdx 1.

100. P. Temin 'Soviet and Nazi economic planning in the 1930s', *Economic History Review*, 44 (1991), p. 585.

101. H. von Kotze and H. Krausnick (eds) *'Es spricht der Führer': 7 exemplarische Hitler-Reden* (Gütersloh, 1966), pp. 176–7, speech of 24 Febuary 1937 to construction workers.

102. IWM Case XI Pros. Doc. Book 112, Neumann lecture 'The Four Year Plan', 29 April 1941, p. 294.

103. Temin, 'Soviet and Nazi planning', p. 584; J. Chapman *Real Wages in Soviet Russia since 1928* (Cambridge, Mass., 1963), p. 166.

104. Chapman, *Real Wages*, pp. 144, 146–8. R. di Leo *Occupazione e salari nell'URSS 1950–1977* (Milan, 1980), p. 122 calculates that average monthly wages rose in money terms by a factor of 10.8 from 1928 to 1950, but prices by a factor of 11.8. D. Filtzer 'The Standard of Living of Soviet Industrial Workers in the Immediate Postwar Period, 1945–1948', *Europe–Asia Studies*, 51 (1999), pp. 1015–16. On German wages G. Bry *Wages in Germany 1871–1945* (Princeton, NJ, 1960), pp. 264, 362. On wage policy T. Siegel 'Wage Policy In Germany', *Politics and Society*, 14 (1985), pp. 5–37.

105. See BA-B R2501/6581 Reichsbank 'Zur Entwicklung des deutschen Preis-und Lohnstandes seit 1933', appdx 6, which shows a range of increased weekly earnings against 1933 of –0.8 per cent (book production) to 26.0 per cent (metalworking).

106. Filtzer, 'Standard of Living', p. 1019.

107. J. Hessler 'Postwar Normalisation and its Limits in the USSR: the Case of Trade', *Europe–Asia Studies*, 53 (2001), pp. 445–8.

108. O. Nathan and M. Fried *The Nazi Economic System* (London, 1944).

109. On textiles League of Nations *World Economic Survey 1936/7* (Geneva, 1937), p. 150; H. Hauser, *Hitler against Germany: a Survey of Present-day Germany from the Inside* (London, 1940) p. 109.

110. On the legal framework BA-B R3102/3602, A. Jessen 'Die gesteuerte Wehrwirtschaft 1933–1939', pp. 61–2. See too J. Stephenson 'Propaganda, Autarky and the German Housewife', in D. Welch (ed.) *Nazi Propaganda* (London, 1983), pp. 117–38; F. Grube and G. Richter *Alltag im 'Dritten Reich': so lebten die Deutsche 1933–1945* (Berlin, 1992), pp. 169–71; W. Bayles *Postmarked Berlin* (London, 1992), pp. 40–41.

111. Hessler, 'Postwar Normalisation', p. 448.

112. A. Sommariva and G. Tullio *German Macroeconomic History, 1880–1979* (London, 1987), p. 59; Hubbard, *Soviet Money and Finance*, pp. 111–13.

113. On noiseless finance L. Schwerin von Krosigk *Statsbankrott: Finanzpolitik des Deutschen Reiches 1920–1945* (Göttingen, 1974), pp. 297–9; W. A. Boelcke *Die Kosten von Hitlers Krieg* (Paderborn, 1985), pp. 103–4. On increased saving see BA-B R7 XVI/22 O. Donner 'Die Grenzen der Staatsverschuldung'.

114. Kravchenko, *I Chose Freedom*, p. 476; Thyssen, *I Paid Hitler*, pp. 47–9.

115. See for example J. Heyl 'The Construction of the Westwall: an Example of National Socialist Policy-making', *Central European History*, 14 (1981), pp. 71–4.

116. Kravchenko, *I Chose Freedom*, pp. 323–5.

117. Zumpe, *Wirtschaft und Staat*, pp. 341–2.

118. Kravchenko, *I Chose Freedom*, p. 328.

119. Tooze, *Statistics and the German State*, pp. 239–44, on problems of data collection; Harrison, *Soviet Planning*, pp. 26–7.

120. See for example Fitzpatrick, 'Ordzhonikidze's Takeover of Vesenkha', pp. 158–67.

121. R. J. Overy *Goering: the 'Iron Man'* (London, 1984), pp. 53–60, 62–8; on his special powers *Reichsgesetzblatt*, 1936, Part I, p. 887.

122. Munting, *Economic Development*, p. 105; Dunmore, *Stalinist Command Economy*, pp. 19–20; Temin, 'Soviet and Nazi Planning', p. 575; S. Fitzpatrick '*Blat* in Stalin's Time', in S. Lovell, A. Ledeneva and A. Rogachevskii (eds) *Bribery and Blat in Russia: Negotiating Reciprocity from the Middle Ages to the 1990s* (London, 2000), pp. 169–76.

123. D. R. Shearer *Industry, State, and Society in Stalin's Russia 1928–1934* (Ithaca, NY, 1996), pp. 235–6.

124. R. W. Davies 'Making Economic Policy', in Gregory, *Behind the Façade*, p. 75.

125. See for example F. Bajohr *Parvenüs und Profiteure. Korruption in der NS-Zeit* (Frankfurt am Main, 2001).

126. Overy, *War and Economy*, pp. 14, 164–6.

127. T. Emessen (ed.) *Aus Göring's Schreibtisch: ein Dokumentenfund* (Berlin, 1947), pp. 81–3.

128. Khlevniuk, *In Stalin's Shadow*, pp. 51–2.

129. S. N. Prokopovicz *Russlands Volkswirtschaft unter den Sowjets* (Zurich, 1944), p. 257.

130. E. Belova 'Economic Crime and Punishment', in Gregory (ed.), *Behind the Façade*, pp. 145–52.

131. Y. Gorlizki 'Rules, Incentives and Soviet Campaign Justice after World War II', *Europe–Asia Studies*, 51 (1999), pp. 1247–52, 1260.

132. Filtzer, 'Standard of Living', p. 1027.

133. Gorlizki, 'Rules, Incentives and Campaign Justice', p. 1253.

134. *Reichsgesetzblatt*, 1936 Part I, p. 1015, 'Gesetz gegen Wirtschafts-sabotage'.

135. BA-B R26/II Anh./1 H. Dichgans 'Zur Geschichte des Reichskommissars für die Preisbildung', pp. 4–6.

136. BA-B R7/2149, Otto Ohlendorf, 'Grundsätze der nationalsozialistischen Wirtschaftspolitik', p. 4. See too D. Majer, *Grundlagen des nationalsozial-istischen Rechtssystems* (Stuttgart, 1987), pp. 152–3; H. Woll *Die Wirtsch-aftslehre des deutschen Faschismus* (Munich, 1988), pp. 92–6.

137. J. N. Hazard, I. Shapiro and P. B. Maggs (eds) *The Soviet Legal System* (New York, 1969), pp. 384–6.

138. A. Nove, *An Economic History of the USSR* (London, 1992).

139. W. E. Butler *Soviet Law* (London, 1988), pp. 180–85; J. R. Millar *The Soviet Economic Experiment* ed. S. Linz (Urbana, 1990), pp. 115–20.

140. Hazard *et al.*, *Soviet Legal System*, pp. 402–3; Butler, *Soviet Law*, p. 189.

141. G. Ambrosius *Der Staat als Unternehmer: öffentliche Wirtschaft und Kapitalismus seit dem 19. Jahrhundert* (Göttingen, 1984), pp. 64, 79; NA Microcopy T83, Roll 74, Economics Ministry memorandum 'Der Zuwachs an staatlichen Unternehmungen in Privatrechtsform'.

142. NSDAP, *Der Parteitag der Arbeit*, pp. 36–8, Hitler's speech to the party congress, 13 September 1937.

143. Thyssen, *I Paid Hitler*, p. 49.

144. A. Barkai *From Boycott to Annihilation: the Economic Struggle of German Jews, 1933–1943* (Hannover, NJ, 1989); F. Bajohr *'Arisierung' in Hamburg: Die Verdrängung der jüdischen Unternehmer 1933–1945* (Hamburg, 1997).

145. A. Müller-Armack *Wirtschaftslenkung und Marktwirtschaft* (Hamburg, 1947).

146. G. Bordiugov 'The Bolsheviks and the National Banner', *Russian Studies in History*, 39 (2000), pp. 82–3, 89.

Chapter 11

1. J. Stalin *Problems of Leninism* (Moscow, 1947), pp. 460–61.

2. W. Treue 'Hitlers Denkschrift zum Vierjahresplan 1936', *Vierteljahrshefte für Zeitgeschichte*, 3 (1955), pp. 204–5.

3. Treue, 'Hitlers Denkschrift', p. 205.

4. A. Hitler *The Secret Book* ed. T. Taylor (New York, 1961), p. 25.

5. Imperial War Museum, FO 645 Box 162, testimony of Fritz Wiedemann at Nuremberg, 9 October 1945, p. 23.

6. V. I. Lenin *Imperialism, the Highest Stage of Capitalism* (Peking, 1965), p. 6: preface to the French and German editions.

7. J. Stalin *Works* (13 vols, Moscow, 1952–55), vol. xii, p. 182, letter to A. M. Gorky, 17 January 1930.

8. M. von Boetticher *Industrialisierungspolitik und Verteidigungskonzeption der UdSSR 1926–1930* (Düsseldorf, 1979), pp. 164–6; J. Erickson *The Soviet High Command: a Military-Political History 1918–1941* (London, 1962), p. 284.

9. Boetticher, *Industrialisierungspolitik*, p. 166.

10. M. von Hagen *Soldiers in the Proletarian Dictatorship: the Red Army and the Soviet Socialist State, 1917–1930* (Ithaca, NY, 1990), pp. 204–5.

11. von Hagen, *Soldiers in the Proletarian Dictatorship*, p. 203.

12. R. Pennington 'From Chaos to the Eve of the Great Patriotic War, 1922–41', in R. Higham, J. T. Greenwood and V. Hardesty (eds) *Russian Aviation and Airpower in the Twentieth Century* (London, 1998), p. 39; see too W. S. Dunn *Hitler's Nemesis: the Red Army, 1930–1945* (Westport, Conn., 1994), p. 27.

13. J. W. Kipp 'Mass, Mobility, and the Origins of Soviet Operational Art, 1918–1936', in C. W. Reddel (ed.) *Transformations in Russian and Soviet Military History* (Washington, DC, 1990), p. 95.

14. H. Shukman (ed.) *Stalin's Generals* (London, 1993), pp. 220–23; P. A. Bayer *The Evolution of the Soviet General Staff, 1917–1941* (New York, 1987), pp. 152 ff.

15. I. S. Bloch *Modern Weapons and Modern War: Is War Now Impossible?* (London, 1900).

16. A. J. Echevarria *After Clausewitz: German Military Thinkers before the Great War* (Lawrence, Kans., 2000), pp. 85–7, 201–4.

17. E. Ludendorff *The Nation at War* (London, 1935), pp. 22–3.

18. D. Fensch and O. Groehler, 'Imperialistische Ökonomie und militärische Strategie: eine Denkschrift Wilhelm Groeners', *Zeitschrift für Geschichtswis-*

senschaft, 19 (1971), pp. 1170–77, 'Bedeutung der modernen Wirtschaft für die Strategie', *c.* 1927/8.

19. Boetticher, *Industrialisierungspolitik*, p. 209.

20. Bayer, *Evolution of Soviet General Staff*, pp. 152–3; Erickson, *Soviet High Command*, pp. 293–4.

21. L. Samuelson *Plans for Stalin's War Machine: Tukhachevskii and Military-Economic Planning, 1925–1941* (London, 2000), pp. 11–15, 17–18, 37–8; Boetticher, *Industrialisierungspolitik*, p. 207.

22. Samuelson, *Plans for Stalin's War Machine*, pp. 22–3.

23. Y. Dyakov and T. Bushuyeva (eds) *The Red Army and the Wehrmacht: How the Soviets Militarized Germany, 1922–1933* (New York, 1995) pp. 18–26; on the 'Statistical Society' see B. A. Carroll *Design for Total War: Arms and Economics in the Third Reich* (The Hague, 1968), pp. 54–7, 64–71. See too E. W. Hansen *Reichswehr und Industrie: Rüstungswirtschaftliche Zusammenarbeit und wirtschaftliche Mobilmachungsvorbereitungen, 1923–1932* (Boppard am Rhein, 1978).

24. Hitler, *Secret Book*, pp. 5, 15.

25. Treue, 'Hitlers Denkschrift', p. 206.

26. Stalin, *Problems of Leninism*, pp. 520–21, 'Address to graduates from Red Army Academies', 4 May 1935.

27. Stalin, *Problems of Leninism*, p. 405, 'The Results of the First Five-Year Plan', report to the CC Plenum, 7 January 1933.

28. L. Samuelson 'Mikhail Tukhachevsky and War-Economic Planning: Reconsiderations on the Pre-War Soviet Military Build-Up', *Journal of Slavic Military Studies*, 9 (1996), p. 828.

29. R. W. Davies and M. Harrison 'Defence spending and defence industry in the 1930s', in J. Barber and M. Harrison (eds) *The Soviet Defence-Industry Complex from Stalin to Khrushchev* (London, 2000), p. 73; R. W. Davies 'Soviet Military Expenditure and the Armaments Industry 1929–1933: A Reconsideration', *Europe–Asia Studies*, 45 (1993), pp. 577–86.

30. Samuelson, *Plans for Stalin's War Machine*, pp. 128–43; T. Martin 'The Origins of Soviet Ethnic Cleansing', *Journal of Modern History*, 70 (1998), pp. 837–47.

31. D. Stone *Hammer and Rifle: the Militarization of the Soviet Union 1926–1933* (Lawrence, Kans., 2000), pp. 185–6: Stalin told Voroshilov after the Manchurian invasion that 'things with Japan are complicated, serious'.

32. Treue, 'Hitlers Denkschrift', p. 204; Stalin, *Problems of Leninism*, p. 461, Report to the Seventeenth Congress of the CPSU, 26 January 1924.

33. B.-J. Wendt *Grossdeutschland: Aussenpolitik und Kriegsvorbereitung des Hitler-Regimes* (Munich, 1987).

34. R. J. Overy 'From "Uralbomber" to "Amerikabomber": the Luftwaffe and Strategic Bombing', *Journal of Strategic Studies*, 1 (1978), pp. 155–6.

35. W. S. Dunn *The Soviet Economy and the Red Army 1930–1945* (London, 1995), p.21; see too R. L. Schweller *Deadly Imbalances: Tripolarity and Hitler's Strategy of World Conquest* (New York, 1998), pp. 206–7. Schweller calculates a 'power weight' in 1938/9, based on resources and military spending, of 100 for Germany, 72.5 for the USSR, 29.0 for Britain, 20.2 for the USA and 15.3 for France.

36. Davies, 'Soviet Military Expenditure', pp. 590–91, 601; G. Kennedy *The Economics of Defence* (London, 1975), p. 79; S. Andic and J. Veverka 'The Growth of Government Expenditure in Germany', *Finanzarchiv*, 25 (1964), p. 261. The figure in 1913 was 3.6 per cent.

37. Dunn, *Hitler's Nemesis*, pp. 26–32; W. Deist 'Die Aufrüstung der Wehrmacht', in W. Deist *et al. Das Deutsche Reich und der Zweite Weltkrieg* (Stuttgart, 1979), p. 447. The figure by September 1939 was 2.87 million men.

38. M. Harrison *Soviet Planning in Peace and War, 1938–1945* (Cambridge, 1985), pp. 250–53; Samuelson, 'Mikhail Tukhachevsky', pp. 805–9; R. Wagenführ *Die deutsche Industrie im Kriege* (Berlin, 1963), p. 74.

39. Overy, 'From "Uralbomber" to "Amerikabomber" ', pp. 155–7; A. Bagel-Bohlan *Hitlers industrielle Kriegsvorbereitung im Dritten Reich 1936 bis 1939* (Koblenz, 1975), pp. 117–21.

40. J. Rohwer and M. Monakov *Stalin's Ocean-Going Fleet: Soviet Naval Strategy and Shipbuilding Programme 1935–1953* (London, 2001), pp. 54–62, 103, 229–56.

41. J. Dülffer *Weimar, Hitler und die Marine: Reichspolitik und Flottenbau 1920–1939* (Düsseldorf, 1973), pp. 488–504; W. Deist *The Wehrmacht and German Rearmament* (London, 1981), pp. 82–4.

42. T. M. Nichols *The Sacred Cause: Civil-Military Conflict over Soviet National Security, 1917–1992* (Ithaca, NY, 1993), p. 50; A. van Ishoven *Messerschmitt* (London, 1975), pp. 115, 172.

43. IWM, FD 3056/49 'Statistical Material on the German Manpower Position', 31, July 1945, Table 7, based on returns from Reichsgruppe Industrie to the statistical office.

44. J. Gillingham 'The "Deproletarianization" of German Society: Vocational Training in the Third Reich', *Journal of Social History*, 19 (1985/6), pp. 427–8.

45. Samuelson, *Plans for Stalin's War Machine*, pp. 191–5; N. S. Simonov 'Mobpodgotovka: mobilisation planning in interwar industry', in Barber and Harrison, *Soviet Defence-Industry Complex*, pp. 216–17.

46. J. Heyl 'The Construction of the *Westwall*: an Example of National-Socialist Policy-making', *Central European History*, 14 (1981), p. 72; R. E. Tarleton 'What Really Happened to the Stalin Line?', *Journal of Slavic Military Studies*, 6 (1993), pp. 21–61.

47. R. Absolon *Die Wehrmacht im Dritten Reich: Band IV, 5 Februar 1938 bis 31 August 1939* (Boppard am Rhein, 1979), pp. 9–11; see too IWM, EDS Mi 14/478 Heereswaffenamt 'Die personelle Leistungsfähigkeit Deutschlands im Mob.-Fall', March 1939.

48. *Akten zur deutschen auswärtigen Politik*, Ser D, vol. vi (Baden-Baden, 1956), p. 481.

49. Dunn, *Hitler's Nemesis*, pp. 27, 29, 57; Simonov, 'mobilisation planning', pp. 211–215; D. M. Glantz *Stumbling Colossus: The Red Army on the Eve of World War* (Lawrence, Kans., 1998), pp. 100–101.

50. On Soviet manpower mobilization G. F. Krivosheev (ed.) *Soviet Casualties and Combat Losses in the Twentieth Century* (London, 1997), p. 91; B. V. Sokolov 'The Cost of War: Human Losses for the USSR and Germany, 1939–45', *Journal of Slavic Military Studies*, 9 (1996), p. 165.

51. H. Rauschning *Germany's Revolution of Destruction* (London, 1938), p. 133.

52. Stone, *Hammer and Rifle*, pp. 3–5; I. Getzler 'Lenin's Conception of Revolution as Civil War', in I. D. Thatcher (ed.) *Regime and Society in Twentieth-Century Russia* (London, 1999), pp. 109–17.

53. *The Military Writings and Speeches of Leon Trotsky* (6 vols, London, 1981), vol. iii, pp. 56, 374–5; vol. v, pp. 24–5.

54. Stalin, *Works*, vol. xii, p. 189, 'Concerning the policy of eliminating the kulaks as a class', 21 January 1930.

55. L. Viola *The Best Sons of the Fatherland: Workers in the Vanguard of Soviet Collectivization* (New York, 1987), p. 62.

56. Viola, *Best Sons of the Fatherland*, p. 64.

57. R. Hanser *Prelude to Terror: The Rise of Hitler 1919–1923* (London, 1970), pp. 266–71; in general see D. Schumann *Politisches Gewalt in der Weimarer Republik 1919–1933* (Essen, 2001); B. Ziemann 'Germany after the First World War – a Violent Society?' *Journal of Modern European History*, 1 (2003), pp. 80–95.

58. R. Taylor *Literature and Society in Germany 1918–1945* (Brighton, 1980), p. 119.

59. V. Berghahn *Der Stahlhelm: Bund der Frontsoldaten 1918–1935* (Düsseldorf, 1966), pp. 275–7, 286; P. Longerich *Die braunen Bataillone: Geschichte der SA* (Munich, 1989), pp. 159, 184. On the ambiguity of this identification with war see S. Kienitz 'Der Krieg der Invaliden. Helden-Bilder und Männlich-

keitskonstruktion nach dem Ersten Weltkrieg', *Militärgeschichtliche Zeitschrift*, 60 (2001), pp. 367–402.

60. W. Wette 'From Kellogg to Hitler (1928–1933). German Public Opinion Concerning the Rejection and Glorification of War', in W. Deist (ed.) *The German Military in the Age of Total War* (Oxford, 1985), p. 83.

61. T. Nevin *Ernst Jünger and Germany: Into the Abyss 1914–1945* (London, 1997), p. 108; Wette, 'From Kellogg to Hitler', p. 85. See too G. Mosse *Fallen Soldiers: Reshaping the Memory of the World Wars* (Oxford, 1990), pp. 159–80; K. Theweleit *Male Fantasies: Volume II. Male Bodies: psychoanalysing the white terror* (Oxford, 1989), pp. 143–76.

62. Wette, 'From Kellogg to Hitler', pp. 88–9.

63. W. H. Chamberlin *Russia's Iron Age* (London, 1934), p. 193–4.

64. J. W. Baird *To Die for Germany: Heroes in the Nazi Pantheon* (Bloomington, Ind., 1990), pp. 101–3.

65. Baird, *To Die for Germany*, p. 106.

66. F. J. Stephens *Hitler Youth: History, Organisation, Uniforms, Insignia* (London, 1973), pp. 5–7, 10–14, 37, 44–5; C. Schubert-Weller *Hitler-Jugend: Vom 'Jungsturm Adolf Hitler' zur Staatsjugend des Dritten Reiches* (Weinheim, 1993), pp. 165–88; L. Pine 'Creating Conformity: the Training of Girls in the *Bund Deutscher Mädel*', *European History Quarterly*, 33 (2003), pp. 371–5, 377–80.

67. W. Benz 'Vom freiwilligen Arbeitsdienst zur Arbeitsdienstpflicht', *Vierteljahrshefte für Zeitgeschichte*, 16 (1968), pp. 317–46.

68. Bank of England, German files E8/56 204/8 C. A. Gunston 'The German Labour Service', *The Old Lady*, 10 (December, 1934), pp. 277–87.

69. A. E. Gorsuch ' "NEP Be Damned": Young Militants in the 1920s and the Culture of Civil War', *Russian Review*, 56 (1997), pp. 566–8, 576.

70. Chamberlin, *Russia's Iron Age*, pp. 200–202; Erickson, *Soviet High Command*, pp. 307–8.

71. J. W. Young *Totalitarian Language: Orwell's Newspeak and its Nazi and Communist Antecedents* (Charlottesville, Va., 1991), p. 92.

72. Stephens, *Hitler Youth*, p. 5; on the idealization of the warrior see P. Reichel 'Festival and Cult: Masculine and Militaristic Mechanisms of National Socialism', in J. A. Mangan (ed.) *Shaping the Superman: Fascist Body as Political Icon – Aryan Fascism* (London, 1999), pp. 153–67.

73. Getzler, 'Lenin's Conception of Revolution', p. 109.

74. *Military Writings of Leon Trotsky*, vol. iii, p. 374.

75. Chamberlin, *Russia's Iron Age*, p. 299.

76. M. Kipp 'Militarisierung der Lehrlingsausbildung in der "Ordensburg der Arbeit" ', in U. Hermann and U. Nassen (eds) *Formative Ästhetik im*

Nationalsozialismus (Weinheim, 1994), pp. 209, 216–17. See too O. Bartov 'The Missing Years: German Workers, German Soldiers', in D. Crew (ed.) *Nazism and German Society, 1933–1945* (London, 1994), pp. 54–60; W. Wette 'Ideologien, Propaganda und Innenpolitik als Voraussetzung der Kriegspolitik des Dritten Reiches', in Deist *et al.*, *Deutsche Reich und der Zweite Weltkrieg*, pp. 152–4, 166–73.

77. L. Peiffer ' "Soldatische Haltung in Auftreten und Sprache ist beim Turnunterricht selbstverständlich" – Die Militarisierung und Disziplinierung des Schulsports', in Hermann and Nassen, *Formative Ästhetik in Nationalsozialismus*, pp. 181–3.

78. *Military Writings of Leon Trotsky*, vol. v, p. 24.

79. S. Fitzpatrick *Everyday Stalinism. Ordinary Life in Extraordinary Times: Soviet Russia in the 1930s* (Oxford, 1999), p. 17.

80. K.-J. Müller *Das Heer und Hitler. Armee und nationalsozialistisches Regime 1933–1940* (Stuttgart, 1969), p. 63.

81. P. Hayes 'Kurt von Schleicher and Weimar Politics', *Journal of Modern History*, 52 (1980), pp. 37–40 for Schleicher's view of politics.

82. Erickson, *Soviet High Command*, pp. 316–17.

83. von Hagen, *Soldiers in the Proletarian Dictatorship*, pp. 206–9; *Military Writings of Leon Trotsky*, vol. v, p. 23.

84. Erickson, *Soviet High Command*, p. 309; von Hagen, *Soldiers in the Proletarian Dictatorship*, pp. 94–100, ch. 5 passim.

85. Bayer, *Evolution of the Soviet General Staff*, p. 162.

86. Samuelson, *Plans for Stalin's War Machine*, pp. 108–9

87. E. O'Ballance *The Red Army* (London, 1964), pp. 116–18.

88. V. Rapaport and Y. Alexeev *High Treason: Essays on the History of the Red Army, 1918–1938* (Durham, NC, 1985), p. 12.

89. H. J. Rautenberg 'Drei dokumente zur Planung eines 300,000-Mann Friedenheeres aus dem Dezember 1933', *Militärgeschichtliche Mitteilungen*, 22 (1977), pp. 103–39; M. Geyer 'Das Zweite Rüstungsprogramm (1930–1934)', *Militärgeschichtliche Mitteilungen*, 17 (1975), pp. 25–72; W. Bernhardt *Die deutsche Aufrüstung 1934–1939* (Frankfurt am Main, 1969), pp. 72–4, 84.

90. Carroll, *Design for Total War*, pp. 91–2, 108–9, 120.

91. R. J. O'Neill *The German Army and the Nazi Party, 1933–1939* (London, 1966), p. 87.

92. O'Neill, *German Army*, p. 90.

93. E. R. Hooton *Phoenix Triumphant: the Rise and Rise of the Luftwaffe* (London, 1994), pp. 94–9, 110–11; E. Homze *Arming the Luftwaffe: the Reich Air Ministry and the German Aircraft Industry, 1919–39* (Lincoln,

Nebr., 1976), pp. 51–60, 98–103; A. van Ishoven *The Fall of an Eagle: the Life of Fighter Ace Ernst Udet* (London, 1977), pp. 152–3, 161–2.

94. Bundesarchiv-Berlin, R2/21776–81, Reich finance ministry 'Entwicklung der Ausgaben in der Rechnungsjahren 1934–1939', 17 July 1939.

95. O'Neill, *German Army*, p. 115; A. W. Zoepf *Wehrmacht zwischen Tradition und Ideologie: Der NS-Führungsoffizier im Zweiten Weltkrieg* (Frankfurt am Main, 1988), pp. 24–9.

96. O'Neill, *German Army*, pp. 119–20.

97. See on tensions between old and new elements M. Geyer 'Traditional Elites and National Socialist Leadership', in C. Maier (ed.) *The Rise of the Nazi Regime: New Perspectives* (London, 1986), pp.57–68; Deist *et al.*, *Deutsches Reich und der Zweite Weltkrieg*, pp. 500–17.

98. On army/SS relations O'Neill, *German Army*, pp. 143–52.

99. B. Wegner *Hitlers politische Soldaten: die Waffen-SS 1933–1945* (Paderborn, 1992), pp. 104–14.

100. Samuelson, *Plans for Stalin's War Machine*, pp. 113–15. Officers continued to be investigated in the early 1930s, and party membership withdrawn. See F. Schauff 'Company Choir of Terror: The Military Council of the 1930s – the Red Army Between the XVIIth and XVIIIth Party Congresses', *Journal of Slavic Military Studies*, 12 (1999), pp. 136–7, 141–2.

101. Rapaport and Alexeev, *High Treason*, pp. 15–19.

102. Samuelson, *Plans for Stalin's War Machine*, p. 114; Nichols, *Sacred Cause*, pp. 42–3.

103. D. Volkogonov *Stalin: Triumph and Tragedy* (London, 1991), p. 319; C. Andrew and O. Gordievsky *KGB: the Inside Story* (London, 1990), p. 106.

104. S. Main 'The Arrest and "Testimony" of Marshal of the Soviet Union M. N. Tukhachevsky (May–June 1937)', *Journal of Slavic Military Studies*, 10 (1997), pp. 152–5.

105. V. Rogovin *1937: Stalin's Year of Terror* (Oak Park, Mich., 1998), pp. 470–82; see too L. Martens *Un autre regard sur Staline* (Brussels, 1994), pp. 185–90.

106. A. Resis (ed.) *Molotov Remembers: Inside Kremlin Politics* (Chicago, 1993), p. 280.

107. A. M. Nekrich *Pariahs, Partners, Predators: German–Soviet Relations 1922–1941* (New York, 1997), pp. 88–9, 99–100.

108. Resis, *Molotov Remembers*, p. 275; Nekrich, *Pariahs, Partners*, p. 100; R. C. Nation *Black Earth, Red Star: a History of Soviet Security Policy 1917–1991* (Ithaca, NY, 1992), pp. 90, 96. Rykov also confirmed a 'plot': see N. Leites and E. Bernant *Rituals of Liquidation: the Case of the Moscow Trials* (Glencoe, Ill., 1954), p. 317.

109. R. Reese *Stalin's Reluctant Soldiers: a Social History of the Red Army, 1925–1941* (Lawrence, Kans., 1996), pp. 134–46; N. M. Yakupov 'Stalin and the Red Army', *Istoria SSSR*, 5 (1991), pp. 170–2.

110. H. Deutsch *Hitler and his Generals: the Hidden Crisis, January–June 1938* (Minnesota, 1974), p. 40.

111. H. Trevor-Roper *Hitler's Table Talk, 1941–1944* (London, 1974), p. 633, 16 August 1942.

112. Deutsch, *Hitler and his Generals*, pp. 80–87, 98–104.

113. Deutsch, *Hitler and his Generals*, p. 111; F. Hossbach *Zwischen Wehrmacht und Hitler 1934–1938* (Göttingen, 1965), pp. 123–4.

114. Deutsch, *Hitler and his Generals*, p. 251.

115. G. P. Megargee *Inside Hitler's High Command* (Lawrence, Kans., 2000), pp. 44–5; Absolon, *Wehrmacht im Dritten Reich*, pp. 156–7.

116. IWM, FO 645 Box 158, memorandum by Wilhelm Keitel, 'The position and powers of the Chief of OKW', 9 October 1945, pp. 1–2.

117. Deutsch, *Hitler and his Generals*, p. 307.

118. Deist, 'Aufrüstung der Wehrmacht', p. 512.

119. Absolon, *Wehrmacht im Dritten Reich*, pp. 161–70

120. K.-J. Müller 'Über den "Militärischen Widerstand"', in P. Steinbach and J. Tuchel (eds) *Widerstand gegen den Nationalsozialismus* (Berlin, 1994), pp. 270–75.

121. Zoepf, *Wehrmacht zwischen Tradition und Ideologie*, pp. 32–8.

122. O'Neill, *German Army*, p. 103.

123. Wegner, *Hitlers politische Soldaten*, pp. 114–15.

124. H. Holdenhauer 'Die Reorganisation der Roten Armee vor der "Grossen Säuberung" bis zum deutschen Angriff auf die UdSSR (1938–1941)', *Militärgeschichtliche Mitteilungen*, 55 (1996), p. 137; Reese, *Stalin's Reluctant Soldiers*, p. 144.

125. Rauschning, *Germany's Revolution of Destruction*, pp. 166–7.

126. K. E. Voroshilov *Stalin and the Armed Forces of the U.S.S.R.* (Moscow, 1951), p. 53.

127. G. Engel *Heeresadjutant bei Hitler 1938–1943: Aufzeichnungen des Majors Engel*, ed. H. von Kotze (Stuttgart, 1974), p. 59.

Chapter 12

1. J. Stalin *The War of National Liberation* (New York, 1942), p. 13, speech on the German invasion of the Soviet Union, 3 July 1941.

2. F. Taylor (ed.) *The Goebbels Diaries 1939–1941* (London, 1982), p. 415.

3. Stalin, *War of Liberation*, p. 29, speech on the anniversary of the revolution, 6 November 1941.

4. L. Lochner (ed.), *The Goebbels Diaries* (London, 1948), p. 18.

5. F. Genoud (ed.) *The Testament of Adolf Hitler: the Hitler–Bormann Documents* (London, 1961), pp. 103–4, 2 April 1945.

6. E. E. Ericson *Feeding the German Eagle: Soviet Economic Aid to Nazi Germany, 1933–1941* (Westport, Conn., 1999), pp. 104–5, 152; S. Pons *Stalin and the Inevitable War 1936–1941* (London, 2002), p. 197.

7. Pons, *Stalin and War*, pp. 186–96; G. Roberts 'The Soviet Decision for a Pact with Nazi Germany', *Soviet Studies*, 44 (1992), pp. 66–8.

8. A. M. Nekrich *Pariahs, Partners, Predators: German-Soviet Relations 1922–1941* (New York, 1997), p. 230.

9. R. Tucker *Stalin in Power: the Revolution from Above, 1928–1941* (New York, 1990), p. 49.

10. V. A. Nevezhin 'The Pact with Germany and the Idea of an "Offensive War"', *Journal of Slavic Military Studies*, 8 (1995), p. 811; Pons, *Stalin and War*, pp. 202–3.

11. Nekrich, *Pariahs, Partners*, p. 137.

12. Nevezhin, 'Pact with Germany', p. 821.

13. R. E. Tarleton 'What Really Happened to the Stalin Line?' *Journal of Slavic Military Studies*, 6 (1993), p. 29.

14. J. Schechter and V. Luchkov (eds) *Khrushchev Remembers: the Glasnost Tapes* (New York, 1990), p. 46; see too Pons, *Stalin and War*, pp. 198–9. On fear of Britain see G. Gorodetsky *Grand Delusion: Stalin and the German Invasion of Russia* (New Haven, Conn., 1999), pp. 14–19.

15. Ericson, *Feeding the Eagle*, p. 209; Nekrich, *Pariahs, Partners*, p. 156; H. Schwendemann *Die wirtschaftliche Zusammenarbeit zwischen dem Deutschen Reich und der Sowjetunion von 1939 bis 1941* (Berlin, 1993), pp. 373–5.

16. J. Förster 'Hitler Turns East – German War Policy in 1940 and 1941', in B. Wegner (ed.) *From Peace to War: Germany, Soviet Russia and the World, 1939–1941* (Providence, RI, 1997), p. 120; C. Hartmann *Halder. Generalstabschef Hitlers 1938–1942* (Paderborn, 1991), pp. 225–6.

17. Hartmann, *Halder*, p. 226; J. Förster 'Hitler's Decision in Favour of War Against the Soviet Union', in H. Boog *et al. Germany and the Second World War: Volume IV: the Attack on the Soviet Union* (Oxford, 1998), pp. 25–9.

18. G. Ueberschär and W. Wette (eds) *'Unternehmen Barbarossa': Der deutsche Überfall auf die Sowjetunion* (Paderborn, 1994), pp. 98–100.

19. Ueberschär and Wette, *'Unternehmen Barbarossa'*, p. 90; N. von Below

At Hitler's Side: the Memoirs of Hitler's Luftwaffe Adjutant 1937–1945 (London, 2001), pp. 42–3, 46–7.

20. Ueberschär and Wette, '*Unternehmen Barbarossa*', p. 91.

21. Genoud, *Testament of Adolf Hitler*, p. 63, 15 February 1945. In 1945 Hitler maintained that his primary motives were strategic and economic: 'War with Russia had become inevitable, whatever we did' (p. 66).

22. Förster, 'Hitler Turns East', pp. 121, 126.

23. Ueberschär and Wette, '*Unternehmen Barbarossa*', p. 107; von Below, *At Hitler's Side*, pp. 91–2.

24. H. Trevor-Roper (ed.) *Hitler's War Directives 1939–1945* (London, 1964), p. 86; Gorodetsky, *Grand Delusion*, pp. 67–75.

25. F. W. Seidler and D. Zeigert *Die Führerhauptquartiere: Anlagen und Planungen im Zweiten Weltkrieg* (Munich, 2000), pp. 193–6.

26. Trevor-Roper, *Hitler's War Directives*, pp. 93–4.

27. Förster, 'Hitler Turns East', p. 127.

28. Förster, 'Hitler Turns East', p. 129; A. Hillgruber 'The German Military Leaders' View of Russia prior to the Attack on the Soviet Union', in Wegner, *From Peace To War*, pp. 172, 182.

29. Trevor-Roper, *Hitler's War Directives*, pp. 130–31, Directive no. 32 'Preparations for the Period after Barbarossa'; Taylor, *Goebbels Diaries*, p. 414.

30. K. Alt 'Die Wehrmacht im Kalkül Stalins', in R.-D. Müller and H.-E. Volkmann (eds) *Die Wehrmacht: Mythos und Realität* (Munich, 1999), pp. 107–9.

31. D. Glantz *Stumbling Colossus: the Red Army on the Eve of World War* (Lawrence, Kans., 1998), pp. 90–93.

32. Glantz, *Stumbling Colossus*, pp. 95–6.

33. Tarleton, 'Stalin Line', p. 50; C. Roberts 'Planning for War: the Red Army and the Catastrophe of 1941', *Europe–Asia Studies*, 47 (1995), p. 1319; Glantz, *Stumbling Colossus*, pp. 103–4.

34. Nevezhin, 'Pact with Germany', p. 821.

35. Alt, 'Die Wehrmacht', p. 111; L. A. Bezyminsky 'Stalins Rede vom 5 Mai 1941 – neu dokumentiert', in G. R. Ueberschär and L. A. Bezminsky (eds) *Der deutsche Angriff auf die Sowjetunion 1941: Die Kontroverse um die Präventivkriegsthese* (Darmstadt, 1998), pp. 136–41; see too J. Förster and E. Mawdsley 'Hitler and Stalin: Secret Speeches on the Eve of Barbarossa', *War in History*, 11 (2004), pp. 88–100 for recent versions of the 5 May speech.

36. Förster and Mawdsley, 'Hitler and Stalin', pp. 101–2.

37. V. A. Nevezhin 'The Making of Propaganda concerning USSR Foreign

Policy, 1939–1941', in N. Rosenfeldt, J. Jensen and E. Kulavig (eds) *Mechanisms of Power in the Soviet Union* (London, 2000), pp. 159–60; Nekrich, *Pariahs, Partners*, p. 241; Förster and Mawdsley, 'Hitler and Stalin', pp. 86–7 for the reaction to the 5 May speech.

38. Nekrich, *Pariahs, Partners*, pp. 228–9.

39. Glantz, *Stumbling Colossus*, pp. 239–43.

40. G. F. Krivosheev *Soviet Casualties and Combat Losses in the Twentieth Century* (London, 1997), p. 98; R. Stolfi *Hitler's Panzers East: World War II Reinterpreted* (Norman, Okl., 1991), pp. 88–9; A. G. Chor'kov 'The Red Army during the Initial Phase of the Great Patriotic War', in Wegner, *From Peace to War*, p. 416.

41. For details see D. M. Glantz *Before Stalingrad: Barbarossa – Hitler's Invasion of Russia 1941* (Stroud, 2003), chs 7–8; Trevor-Roper, *Hitler's War Directives*, pp. 152–5, Directive no. 35, 6 September 1941.

42. J. Toland *Adolf Hitler* (London, 1976), pp. 684–5.

43. V. P. Yampolsky (ed.) *Organy Gosudarstvennoi Bezopasnosti SSSR v Velikoi Otechestvennoi voine* (Moscow, 2000), vol. ii, pp. 98–104.

44. Yampolsky, *Organy*, p. 107.

45. D. Volkogonov *Stalin: Triumph and Tragedy* (London, 1991), pp. 434–5; G. A. Bordiugov 'The Popular Mood in the Unoccupied Soviet Union', in R. Thurston and B. Bonwetsch (eds) *The People's War: Responses to World War II in the Soviet Union* (Chicago, 2000), pp. 58–9; M. M. Gorinov 'Muscovites' Moods, 22 June 1941 to May 1942', in Thurston and Bonwetsch, *People's War*, pp. 123–4; J. Barber 'The Moscow Crisis of October 1941', in J. Cooper, M. Perrie and E. A. Rees (eds) *Soviet History 1917–1953: Essays in Honour of R.W. Davies* (London, 1995), pp. 201–18.

46. M. Cooper *The German Army 1933–1945* (London, 1978), p. 344.

47. Alt, 'Die Wehrmacht', p. 111.

48. *Kriegstagebuch des Oberkommandos der Wehrmacht* 5 vols (Frankfurt am Main, 1961–3), vol. i, pp. 1120–21; Soviet figures calculated from J. Erickson 'Soviet War Losses', in J. Erickson and D. Dilks (eds) *Barbarossa: the Axis and the Allies* (Edinburgh, 1994), pp. 264–5.

49. E. Zaleski *Stalinist Planning for Economic Growth 1933–1952* (London, 1980), p. 291; S. Linz 'World War II and Soviet Economic Growth, 1940–1953', in S. Linz (ed.) *The Impact of World War II on the Soviet Union* (Totowa, NJ, 1985), p. 13.

50. W. S. Dunn *The Soviet Economy and the Red Army 1930–1945* (London, 1995), p. 195.

51. Linz, 'Soviet Economic Growth', p. 18; Imperial War Museum, London, FD 3056/49 'Statistical Material on the German Manpower Position During

the War', 31 July 1945. These figures are based on the annual labour balances produced by the Reich Statistical Office. The German manpower figure includes those classified as 'handworkers' as well. Industrial wage-earners numbered 8.37 million in 1942.

52. S. R. Lieberman 'Crisis Management in the USSR: The Wartime System of Administration and Control', in Linz, *Impact of World War II*, pp. 60–61.

53. Zaleski, *Stalinist Planning*, pp. 287–8; M. Harrison *Soviet Planning in Peace and War, 1938–1945* (Cambridge, 1985), pp. 94–9; Lieberman, 'Crisis Management', pp. 60–66.

54. Zaleski, *Stalinist Planning*, pp. 286, 289–90.

55. Zaleski, *Stalinist Planning*, p. 317; M. Harrison 'The Soviet Union: the defeated victor', in M. Harrison (ed.) *The Economics of World War II: Six great powers in international comparison* (Cambridge, 1998), pp. 275–8.

56. Linz, 'Soviet Economic Growth', p. 20; Harrison, 'The Soviet Union', p. 286.

57. F. Kagan 'The Evacuation of Soviet Industry in the Wake of Barbarossa: a Key to Soviet Victory', *Journal of Slavic Military Studies*, 8 (1995), pp. 389–406; G. A. Kumanev 'The Soviet Economy and the 1941 Evacuation', in J. L. Wieczynski (ed.) *Operation Barbarossa: The German Attack on the Soviet Union, June 22 1941* (Salt Lake City, 1993), pp. 161–81, 189.

58. Linz, 'Soviet Economic Growth', p. 17 on investment; on schools M. Hindus *Russia Fights On* (London, 1942), pp. 63–4; W. Moskoff *The Bread of Affliction: The Food Supply in the USSR during World War II* (Cambridge, 1990), p. 83.

59. Linz, 'Soviet Economic Growth', pp. 19–20; J. Barber and M. Harrison *The Soviet Home Front 1941–1945* (London, 1991), pp. 147–52 on labour mobilization. On rationing *Zaleski*, Stalinist Planning, pp. 328–30; Moskoff, *Bread of Affliction*, pp. 143–55; Barber and Harrison, *Soviet Home Front*, pp. 214–15 for ration levels in 1944.

60. Zaleski, *Stalinist Planning*, pp. 333, 336–7; Moskoff, *Bread of Affliction*, pp. 108–9, 175.

61. Moskoff, *Bread of Affliction*, pp. 136–42.

62. A. Nove 'The peasantry in World War II', in Linz, *Impact of World War II*, pp. 79–84.

63. Zaleski, *Stalinist Planning*, pp. 337–40.

64. B. V. Sokolov 'Lend Lease in Soviet Military Efforts 1941–1945', *Journal of Slavic Military Studies*, 7 (1994), pp. 567–8.

65. Sokolov, 'Lend Lease', pp. 570–81; V. Vorsin 'Motor Vehicle Transport Deliveries Through "Lend-Lease"', *Journal of Slavic Military Studies*, 10

(1997), pp. 164, 172–3; H. P. van Tuyll *Feeding the Bear: American Aid to the Soviet Union 1941–1945* (New York, 1989), pp. 156–7.

66. U. Herbert *Fremdarbeiter: Politik und Praxis des 'Ausländer-Einsatzes' in der Kriegswirtschaft des Dritten Reiches* (Berlin, 1985), pp. 270–72.

67. The term was used by Rolf Wagenführ, a Reich Statistical Office official, when he wrote a history of the German war economy for the Allies in 1945. See IWM, FD 3057/49 FIAT Report 1312 'Economic History of the Second World War', pp. 6–8.

68. Hitler's plan in IWM, MI 14/521 (Part I) 'Munitionslieferung im Weltkrieg'; War Economy decree *Reichsgesetzblatt* 1939, Part I, p. 1609 'Kriegswirtschaftsverordnung', 4 September 1939. Total war references in Bundesarchiv-Berlin R2501/7132, Reichsbank, notes for a speech by Director Lange, November 1941; R2501/7041, Report of speech by Reichsbank President 2 February 1940, p. 2.

69. R. J. Overy *War and Economy in the Third Reich* (Oxford, 1994), pp. 275–81; Soviet comparison in Harrison, 'The Soviet Union', p. 291.

70. Overy, *War and Economy*, p. 352.

71. IWM, EDS Mi 14/433 (file 2), Führer decree 'Vereinfachung und Leistungssteigerung unserer Rüstungsproduktion', 3 December 1941, p. 1.

72. IWM AL/1571, Col. Thomas, 'Aktennotiz über Besprechung mit Minister Speer, 3 March 1942', p. 1.

73. Overy, *War and Economy*, pp. 356–64.

74. D. Winkler *Frauenarbeit im 'Dritten Reich'* (Hamburg, 1977), pp. 196–8; S. Bajohr *Die Hälfte der Fabrik: Geschichte der Frauenarbeit in Deutschland 1914 bis 1945* (Marburg, 1979), p. 252; R. Wagenführ *Die deutsche Industrie im Kriege* (Berlin, 1963), pp. 145–7; F. Wunderlich *Farm Labor in Germany 1810–1945* (Princeton, NJ, 1961), pp. 297–9; on part time work IWM Box S368, Report 69, p. 5. See too E. Hancock 'Employment in Wartime: the experience of German women during the Second World War', *War & Society*, 12 (1994), pp.43–68.

75. On rationing see Overy, *War and Economy*, pp. 170–71, 282–4; H. Focke and U. Reimer *Alltag unterm Hakenkreuz: Wie die Nazis das Leben der Deutschen veränderten* (Hamburg, 1980), pp. 179–81.

76. L. Maks *Russia by the Back Door* (London, 1954), p. 169.

77. C. Simmons and N. Perlina *Writing the Siege of Leningrad: Women's diaries, memoirs and documentary prose* (Pittsburgh, 2002), p. 23, diary of Liubov Shaporina, 12 September 1941.

78. Simmons and Perlina, *Siege of Leningrad*, p. 60, diary of Anna Likhacheva, 16 May, 1942; p. 50, diary of Vera Kostrovitsknia [n.d.].

79. Simmons and Perlina, *Siege of Leningrad*, pp. 30–31, diary entry, 8 March 1942.

80. See O. Bartov *The Eastern Front 1941–1945: German Troops and the Barbarization of Warfare* (New York, 1985).

81. See in general T. Schulte *The German Army and Nazi Policies in Occupied Russia* (Oxford, 1989); H. Heer *Tote Zonen: Die deutsche Wehrmacht an der Ostfront* (Hamburg, 1999); H. Heer and K. Naumann (eds) *Vernichtungskrieg, Verbrechen der Wehrmacht 1941–1944* (Hamburg, 1995). On the debate over Wehrmacht criminality K. H. Pohl ' "Vernichtungskrieg. Verbrechen der Wehrmacht 1941–1944', in K. H. Pohl (ed.) *Wehrmacht und Vernichtungspolitik. Militär im nationalsozialistischen System* (Göttingen, 1999), pp. 141–60.

82. Ueberschär and Wette, '*Unternehmen Barbarossa*', p. 107; Förster and Mawdsley, 'Hitler and Stalin', pp. 70–78 for text of notes of the speech.

83. J. Förster 'Operation Barbarossa as a War of Conquest and Annihilation', in Boog *et al.*, *Germany and the Second World War: Vol IV*, p. 485.

84. Schulte, *The German Army*, pp. 321–2.

85. Förster, 'Operation Barbarossa', p. 514.

86. Förster, 'Operation Barbarossa', p. 510.

87. H.-H. Wilhelm (ed.) *Rassenpolitik und Kriegführung: Sicherheitspolizei und Wehrmacht in Polen und der Sowjetunion* (Passau, 1991), p. 140, 'Barbarossa-Studie', Generaloberst Hoepner, 2 May 1941.

88. Förster, 'Operation Barbarossa', pp. 492, 500.

89. E. Hesse *Der sowjetrussische Partisanenkrieg 1941 bis 1944* (Göttingen, 1969), p. 36; Förster, 'Operation Barbarossa', p. 504.

90. Schulte, *German Army*, p. 317.

91. Schulte, *German Army*, pp. 319–20; Wilhelm, *Rassenpolitik*, p. 138, General von Küchler, lecture to divisional commanders, 25 April 1941; Förster, 'Operation Barbarossa', p. 516. See too G.K. Koschorrek *Blood Red Snow: The Memoirs of a German Soldier on the Eastern Front* (London, 2002), pp. 67–9.

92. K. Reddemann (ed.) *Zwischen Front und Heimat: Der Briefwechsel des münsterischen Ehepaares Agnes und Albert Neuhaus 1940–1944* (Münster, 1996) p. 227, letter from Albert Neuhaus, 30 June 1941.

93. Koschorrek, *Blood Red Snow*, p. 64.

94. Stalin, *War of Liberation*, pp. 14–16.

95. Stalin, *War of Liberation*, p. 30.

96. A. Sella *The Value of Human Life in Soviet Warfare* (London, 1992), pp. 100–102; Volkogonov, *Triumph and Tragedy*, p. 430 for story of Yakov.

97. R. Bidlack 'Survival Strategies in Leningrad during the First Year of the Soviet–German War', in Thurston and Bonwetsch, *People's War*, pp. 86–7.

98. *Pravda*, 17 August, 30 August 1942; A. Werth *Russia at War 1941–1945* (London, 1964), p. 414; A. Weiner *Making Sense of War: the Second World War and the Fate of the Bolshevik Revolution* (Princeton, NJ, 2001), pp. 162–3.

99. G. Geddes *Nichivó: Life, Love and Death on the Russian Front* (London, 2001), p. 40; on German treatment of their own soldiers see M. Messerschmidt 'Deserteure im Zweiten Weltkrieg', in W. Wette (ed.) *Deserteure der Wehrmacht: Feiglinge – Opfer – Hoffnungsträger* (Essen, 1995), pp. 61–2; O. Hennicke and F. Wüllner 'Über die barbarischen Vollstreckungsmethoden von Wehrmacht und Justiz im Zweiten Weltkrieg', in Wette, *Deserteure*, pp. 80–81.

100. Koschorrek, *Blood Red Snow*, p.69; see too J. Stieber *Against the Odds: Survival on the Russian Front 1944–1945* (Dublin, 1995), pp. 18–19.

101. Koschorrek, *Blood Red Snow*, p. 275; E. Bessonov *Tank Rider: into the Reich with the Red Army* (London, 2003), p. 118; Stieber, *Against the Odds*, pp. 169–70.

102. A. Streim *Sowjetische Gefangenen in Hitlers Vernichtungskrieg: Berichte und Dokumente* (Heidelberg, 1982), p. 175; C. Streit 'Die sowjetische Kriegsgefangenen in den deutschen Lagern', in D. Dahlmann and G. Hirschfeld (eds) *Lager, Zwangsarbeit, Vertreibung und Deportation* (Essen, 1999), pp. 403–4. See more recently C. Hartmann 'Massensterben oder Massenvernichtung? Sowjetische Kriegsgefangenen im "Unternehmen Barbarossa"', *Vierteljahrshefte für Zeitgeschichte*, 49 (2001).

103. *Russkii Arkhiv 13: Nemetskii Voennoplennye v SSSR* (Moscow, 1999), Part I, p. 9.

104. *Russkii Arkhiv 13*, Part I, p. 17, document 1, Molotov to International Red Cross, 27 June 1941. For Hitler's views see Toland *Adolf Hitler*, p. 685. See too C. Streit 'Die Behandlung der verwundeten sowjetischen Kriegsgefangenen', in Heer and Naumann, *Vernichtungskrieg*, pp. 78–91.

105. Hartmann, 'Massensterben oder Massenvernichtung?', p. 157.

106. Hartmann, 'Massensterben oder Massenvernichtung?', p. 158; Herbert, *Fremdarbeiter*, pp. 148–9.

107. Hartmann, 'Massensterben oder Massenvernichtung?', p. 158.

108. Herbert, *Fremdarbeiter*, p. 136.

109. S. Karner *Im Archipel GUPVI: Kriegsgefangenschaft und Internierung in der Sowjetunion 1941–1956* (Vienna, 1995), pp. 90–94, 194; *Russkii Arkhiv 13*, Part 2, pp. 69, 76, 159–60.

NOTES

110. Karner, *Archipel GUPVI*, pp. 94–104, 195; *Russkii Arkhiv 13*, Part 2, pp. 171–9, 265–74; R. J. Overy *Russia's War* (London, 1998), pp. 297–8.

111. Heer, *Tote Zonen*, p. 101.

112. C. Streit 'Partisans – Resistance – Prisoners of War', in Wieczynski, *Operation Barbarossa*, p. 271.

113. H. Heer 'Die Logik des Vernichtungskrieges: Wehrmacht und Partisanen- kampf', in Heer and Naumann, *Vernichtungskrieg*, pp. 112–13.

114. Hesse, *Partisanenkrieg*, pp. 178–80; L. Grenkevich *The Soviet Partisan Movement 1941–1944* (London, 1999), pp. 77–9; *Wehrmachtsverbrechen: Dokumente aus sowjetischen Archiven* ed. L. Besymensky (Cologne, 1997), p. 116, OKW Befehl, 16 December, 1942; K.-M. Mallmann ' "Aufgeräumt und abgebrannt": Sicherheitspolizei und "Bandenkampf" in der besetzten Sowjetunion', in G. Paul and K.-M. Mallmann (eds) *Die Gestapo im Zweiten Weltkrieg: Heimatfront und besetztes Europa* (Darmstadt, 2000), pp. 506–7.

115. J. A. Armstrong (ed.) *Soviet Partisans in World War II* (Madison, Wisc. 1964), pp. 98–103, 662; Grenkevich, *Soviet Partisan Movement*, pp. 92–3.

116. Geddes, *Nichivó*, pp. 87–95.

117. Mallmann, 'Sicherheitspolizei und "Bandenkampf" ', p. 503.

118. T. Anderson 'Incident at Baranivka: German Reprisals and the Soviet Partisan Movement in the Ukraine, October–December 1941', *Journal of Modern History*, 71 (1999), pp. 611–13.

119. K. Lutzel *Deutsche Soldaten – nationalsozialistischer Krieg? Kriegser- lebnis und Kriegserfahrung* (Paderborn, 1998), p. 184.

120. Mallmann, 'Sicherheitspolizei und "Bandenkampf" ', pp. 513–14; see too B. Shepherd 'The Continuum of Brutality: *Wehrmacht* Security Divisions in Central Russia, 1942', *German History*, 21 (2003), pp. 60–63.

121. R. Rhodes *Masters of Death: the SS Einsatzgruppen and the Invention of the Holocaust* (New York, 2002), pp. 219–20.

122. Public Record Office, London, WO 311/45, letter from Judge-Advocate General Western Command Branch to Military Dept., Judge-Advocate Gen- eral's office, 1 May 1945, p.1.

123. See for example M. Mazower 'Military Violence and National Socialist Values: The *Wehrmacht* in Greece 1941–1944', *Past & Present*, 134 (1992), pp. 129–58; W. Manoschek 'The Extermination of Jews in Serbia', in U. Herbert (ed.) *National Socialist Extermination Policies: Contemporary Ger- man Perspectives and Controversies* (Oxford, 2000), pp. 163–85.

124. Gorinov, 'Muscovites' Moods', p. 119.

125. Weiner, *Making Sense of War*, pp. 172–3.

126. Weiner, *Making Sense of War*, pp. 177–9.

127. S. Bialer (ed.) *Stalin and his Generals: Soviet Military Memoirs of World War II* (New York, 1969), pp. 140–41, 143–8.

128. Soviet figures in Harrison, 'The Soviet Union', p. 285. The armed forces employed 7.1 million in 1941, 11.3 million in 1942, 11.9 million in 1943 and 12.2 million in 1944. German figures from H.-U. Thamer *Verführung und Gewalt: Deutschland 1933–1945* (Berlin, 1986), p. 718. The numbers conscripted by 1942 were 9.4 million, 1943 11.2 million, 1944 12.4 million.

129. Krivosheev, *Soviet Casualties*, pp. 85–91.

130. Sokolov, 'The Cost of War', pp. 175–6, 187.

131. Bessonov, *Tank Rider*, p. 44; W. S. Dunn *Hitler's Nemesis: the Red Army 1933–1945* (Westport, Conn., 1994), pp. 62–4; R. Thurston 'Cauldrons of Loyalty and Betrayal: Soviet Soldiers' Behaviour 1941 and 1945', in Thurston and Bonwetsch, *People's War*, pp. 239–40; J. Erickson 'Red Army Battlefield Performance, 1941–45: the System and the Soldier', in P. Addison and A. Calder (eds) *Time to Kill: the Soldier's Experience of War in the West, 1939–1945* (London, 1997), pp. 237–41, 247–8.

132. On the Soviet balance between men and military equipment see J. Sapir 'The Economics of War in the Soviet Union during World War II', in I. Kershaw and M. Lewin (eds) *Stalinism and Nazism: Dictatorships in Comparison* (Cambridge, 1997), pp. 219–21; S. J. Zaloga and J. Grandsen *Soviet Tanks and Combat Vehicles in World War II* (London, 1984), pp. 146–9, 160–62. On Germany's capital–manpower ratio see, for example, R. L. di Nardo *Mechanized Juggernaut or Military Anachronism: Horses and the German Army in World War II* (London, 1991), pp. 37–56, 92–7; R. M. Orgorkiewicz *Armoured Forces: a history of armoured forces and their vehicles* (London, 1970), pp. 74–9. In general O. Bartov *Hitler's Army: Soldiers, Nazis and War in the Third Reich* (Oxford, 1991), ch. 2.

133. Ogorkiewicz, *Armoured Forces*, pp. 123–4; Zaloga and Grandsen, *Soviet Tanks*, pp. 146–9, 160–62.

134. V. Hardesty *Red Phoenix: the Rise of Soviet Air Power 1941–1945* (London, 1982), pp. 83–8; M. O'Neill 'The Soviet Air Force, 1917–1991', in R. Higham and F. W. Kagan (eds) *The Military History of the Soviet Union* (New York, 2002), pp.159–62.

135. van Tuyll, *Feeding the Bear*, pp. 156–7; J. Beaumont *Comrades in Arms: British Aid to Russia, 1941–1945* (London, 1980), pp. 210–12.

136. D. R. Beachley 'Soviet Radio-Electronic Combat in World War II', *Military Review*, 61 (1981), pp. 67–8.

137. Koschorrek, *Blood Red Snow*, p. 64.

138. D. Kahn *Hitler's Spies: German Military Intelligence in World War II* (New York, 1978), pp. 440–41.

139. Liebermann, 'Crisis Management', pp. 61–6; Bialer, *Stalin and his Generals*, pp. 352–4, 350–51.

140. See P. Schramm *Hitler the Man and the Military Leader* (London, 1972), pp. 194–205, Appendix II 'Memorandum on Hitler's Leadership, 1946' by Col. A. Jodl; W. Warlimont 'The German High Command during World War II', in D. Detweiler (ed.) *World War II German Military Studies* (24 vols, New York, 1979) vol. vi, pp. 6–59. On the record of his meetings on technical and economic issues see W. A. Boelcke (ed.) *Deutschlands Rüstung im Zweiten Weltkrieg: Hitlers Konferenzen mit Albert Speer* (Frankfurt am Main, 1969); IWM, Box S363, Kartei des Technischen Amtes, 1941–4, pp. 1–24: 'Liste von Rüstungs-Besprechungen bei Adolf Hitler, 1940–1945'.

141. B. Bonwetsch 'Stalin, the Red Army, and the "Great Patriotic War"' in Kershaw and Lewin, *Stalinism and Nazism*, pp. 203–6; Overy, *Russia's War*, pp. 187–90.

142. National Archives, College Park, MD, RG332 USSBS, interview 62, Col-Gen. A. Jodl, 29 June 1945, pp. 6–7.

143. H. Trevor-Roper (ed.) *Hitler's Table Talk, 1941–1944* (London, 1973), p. 340, 26–27 February 1942.

144. NA, RG332, Jodl interview p. 3.

145. Trevor-Roper, *Hitler's Table Talk*, p. 82, 21–22 October 1941. See too the remark recalled in T. Junge *Until the Final Hour: Hitler's Last Secretary* (London, 2003), p. 83. Hitler wanted to 'never see any more officers' after the war: 'They're all stubborn and thick-headed, prejudiced and set in their ways.'

146. Bonwetsch, 'Stalin, the Red Army', p. 203; E. O'Ballance *The Red Army* (London, 1964), p. 179.

147. M. Fainsod *How Russia is Ruled* (Cambridge, Mass., 1967), pp. 269, 480–1; T. H. Rigby *Communist Party Membership in the USSR 1917–1967* (Princeton, NJ, 1968), pp. 249–6.

148. A. W. Zoepf *Wehrmacht zwischen Tradition und Ideologie: Der NS Führungsoffizier im Zweiten Weltkrieg* (Frankfurt am Main, 1988), pp. 35–9.

149. H. Heiber and D. M. Glantz (eds) *Hitler and his Generals: Military Conferences 1942–1945* (London, 2002), p. 386; J. Förster 'Ludendorff and Hitler in Perspective: The Battle for the German Soldier's Mind, 1917–1944', *War in History*, 10 (2003), pp. 329–31.

150. Heiber and Glantz, *Hitler and his Generals*, pp. 393, 396, meeting of 7 January 1944.

151. Koschorrek, *Blood Red Snow*, pp. 275–6, 278–9.

152. Förster, 'Ludendorff and Hitler', p. 333.

153. Koschorrek, *Blood Red Snow*, pp. 305–6.

154. Koschorrek, *Blood Red Snow*, p. 311.

155. Stalin, *War of Liberation*, p. 23, speech of 7 November 1941.

156. See the many examples of popular enthusiasm in D. Loza (ed.) *Fighting for the Soviet Motherland: Recollections from the Eastern Front* (Lincoln, Nebr., 1998); on propaganda J. Barber 'The Image of Stalin in Soviet Propaganda and Public Opinion during World War 2', in J. Garrard and C. Garrard (eds) *World War 2 and the Soviet People* (London, 1993), pp. 38–48; J. Brooks *Thank You, Comrade Stalin: Soviet Public Culture from Revolution to Cold War* (Princeton, NJ, 2000), pp. 165–84; D. Brandenberger *National Bolshevism: Stalinist Mass Culture and the Formation of Modern Russian National Identity* (Cambridge, Mass., 2002), pp. 161–80.

157. Loza, *Fighting for the Soviet Motherland*, pp. 220–21, appdx B. 'Order of the People's Commissar of Defense, no. 227', 28 July 1942.

158. Erickson, 'Soviet Losses', p. 262. Figure of those condemned to death in review by E. Mawdsley, *War in History*, 4 (1997), p. 230.

159. Gorinov, 'Muscovites' Moods', p. 126.

160. A. R. Dzeniskevich 'The Social and Political Situation in Leningrad in the First Months of the German Invasion: the Social Psychology of the Workers', in Thurston and Bonwetsch, *People's War*, pp. 77–9.

161. Bordiugov, 'Popular Mood', pp. 59–60.

162. Bordiugov, 'Popular Mood', p. 68.

163. B. Bonwetsch 'War as a "Breathing Space": Soviet Intellectuals and the "Great Patriotic War"', in Thurston and Bonwetsch, *People's War*, p. 146.

164. *Wehrmachtsverbrechen*, p. 20.

165. Lochner, *Goebbels Diaries*, pp. 4–5, entry for 22 January 1942.

166. Lochner, *Goebbels Diaries*, p. 320, entry for 25 July 1943.

167. Z. Zeman *Nazi Propaganda* (Oxford, 1968), pp. 165–6.

168. J. Hermand *Der alte Traum von neuen Reich: Völkische Utopien und NS* (Frankfurt am Main, 1988), p. 341.

169. Hermand, *alte Traum von Reich*, p. 342.

170. Genoud, *Hitler's Testament*, p. 89.

171. P. Winterton *Report on Russia* (London, 1945), pp. 108–12.

172. Weiner, *Making Sense of War*, p. 37.

Chapter 13

1. A. Hitler *Mein Kampf* (ed. D. C. Watt, London, 1969), pp. 353–4.

2. F. Hirsch 'Race without the Practice of Racial Politics', *Slavic Review*, 61 (2002), pp. 30–31.

3. J. O. Pohl *Ethnic Cleansing in the USSR, 1937–1949* (Westport, Conn.,

2002), p. 33; M. Parrish *The Lesser Terror: Soviet State Security 1939–1953* (Westport, Conn., 1996), pp. 100–03.

4. I. Fleischhauer ' "Operation Barbarossa" and the Deportation', in I. Fleischhauer and B. Pinkus *The Soviet Germans: Past and Present* (London, 1986), pp. 78–80.

5. Fleischhauer, 'Deportation', p. 80.

6. Pohl, *Ethnic Cleansing*, pp. 42–4; V. Tolz 'New Information about the Deportations of Ethnic Groups in the USSR during World War 2', in J. Garrard and C. Garrard (eds) *World War 2 and the Soviet People* (London, 1993), pp. 161–5.

7. Pohl, *Ethnic Cleansing*, pp. 29–30; T. Martin 'The Origins of Soviet Ethnic Cleansing', *Journal of Modern History*, 70 (1998), pp. 853–5.

8. Fleischhauer, 'Deportation', pp. 78–9; Martin, 'Soviet Ethnic Cleansing', p. 853.

9. Pohl, *Ethnic Cleansing*, p. 56.

10. M. Burleigh *Germany Turns Eastwards: a Study of* Ostforschung *in the Third Reich* (Cambridge, 1988), pp. 16–17; Martin, 'Soviet Ethnic Cleansing', p. 836.

11. I. Heinemann *'Rasse, Siedlung, deutsches Blut': Das Rasse-& Siedlungshauptamt der SS und die rassenpolitische Neuordnung Europas* (Göttingen, 2003), pp. 1909–91, 449.

12. Fleischhauer, 'Deportation', p. 83.

13. Pohl, *Ethnic Cleansing*, p. 44; Fleischhauer, 'Deportation', pp. 86–7.

14. Heinemann, *'Rasse, Siedlung'*, pp. 260–61; I. Fleischauer 'The Ethnic Germans under Nazi Rule', in Fleischhauer and Pinkus, *The Soviet Germans*, pp. 95–6; J. Connelly 'Nazis and Slavs: From Racial Theory to Racist Practice', *Central European History*, 32 (1999), pp. 15–19.

15. Heinemann, *'Rasse, Siedlung'*, pp. 449–50.

16. Pohl, *Ethnic Cleansing*, p. 60.

17. T. R. Weeks 'National Minorities in the Russian Empire, 1897–1917', in A. Geifman (ed.) *Russia under the Last Tsar: Opposition and Subversion 1894–1917* (Oxford, 1999), pp. 112–14, 117–21; A. Renner 'Defining a Russian Nation: Mikhail Katkov and the "Invention" of National Politics', *Slavonic and East European Review*, 81 (2003), pp. 661–5; G. Hosking and R. Service (eds) *Russian Nationalism Past and Present* (London, 1998), pp. 2–3; A. N. Sakharov 'The Main Phases and Distinctive Features of Russian Nationalism', in Hosking and Service, *Russian Nationalism*, pp. 14–15; D. G. Rowley 'Imperial versus national discourse: the case of Russia', *Nations and Nationalism*, 6 (2000), pp. 23–35.

18. S. Avineri 'Marxism and Nationalism', *Journal of Contemporary History*, 26 (1991), pp. 630–39.

19. J. Smith *The Bolsheviks and the National Question 1917–1923* (London, 1999), p. 240.

20. G. Simon 'Nationsbildung und "Revolution von oben": Zur neuen sowjetischen Nationalitätenpolitik der dreissiger Jahre', *Geschichte und Gesellschaft*, 8 (1992), p. 46; B. Chiclo 'Histoire de la formation des territoires autonomes chez les peoples turco-mongols de sibérie', *Cahiers du monde russe*, 28 (1987), pp. 390–92.

21. M. M. Feinstein 'Deutschland über alles? The National Anthem Debate in the Federal Republic of Germany', *Central European History*, 33 (2000), pp. 506–9.

22. G. H. Herb *Under the Map of Germany: Nationalism and Propaganda 1918–1945* (London, 1997), pp. 136–9.

23. A. Kolnai *The War Against the West* (London, 1938), p. 394.

24. S. Vopel 'Radikaler, völkischer Nationalismus in Deutschland 1917–1933', in H. Timmermann (ed.) *Nationalismus und Nationalbewegung in Europa 1914–1945* (Berlin, 1999), pp. 162–75.

25. J. Stalin *Works* (13 volumes, Moscow, 1952–55), vol. ii, pp. 303–7, 'Marxism and the National Question', January 1913.

26. Stalin, *Works*, vol. ii, p. 321.

27. Stalin, *Works*, vol. ii, p. 296, 'On the Road to Nationalism: a Letter from the Caucasus', 12 January 1913.

28. Stalin, *Works*, vol. ii, pp. 322, 359, 375–7.

29. E. Koutaissoff 'Literacy and the Place of Russian in the Non-Slav Republics of the USSR', *Soviet Studies*, 3 (1951), p. 115. Stalin formulated the phrase in a speech given on 18 May 1925.

30. Stalin, *Works*, vol. vi, p. 153, 'Foundations of Leninism', April 1924.

31. Stalin, *Works*, vol. vi, p. 109.

32. G. Simon *Nationalism and Policy Toward the Nationalities in the Soviet Union* (Boulder, Colo., 1991), p. 248; Y. Slezkine 'The USSR as a Communal Apartment, or How a Socialist State Promoted Ethnic Particularism', *Slavic Review*, 53 (1994), p. 437; see too P. Skalnik 'Soviet etnografiia and the nation(alities) question', *Cahiers du monde russe*, 31 (1990), pp. 183–4.

33. Hitler, *Mein Kampf*, p. 348; A. Hitler, *The Secret Book* (ed. T. Taylor, New York, 1961), pp. 6, 29, 44; Stalin's remark in Slezkine, 'The USSR as Communal Apartment', p. 445.

34. Hitler, *Mein Kampf*, pp. 299, 339–40.

35. Hitler, *Secret Book*, p. 29.

36. Hitler, *Mein Kampf*, pp. 272–7; Hitler, *Secret Book*, pp. 212–13.

37. W. Maser (ed.) *Hitler's Letters and Notes* (New York, 1974), p. 221; Hitler, *Mein Kampf*, p. 273.

38. Hitler, *Mein Kampf*, p. 355.

39. H. C. D'Encausse *The Great Challenge: Nationalities and the Bolshevik State 1917–1930* (New York, 1992), pp. 135–7, 217; Simon, *Nationalism and Policy*, pp. 23–4.

40. F. Hirsch 'The Soviet Union as a Work-in-Progress: Ethnographers and the Category Nationality in the 1926, 1937 and 1939 Censuses', *Slavic Review*, 56 (1997), pp. 251–64.

41. S. Crisp 'Soviet Language Planning 1917–1953', in M. Kirkwood *Language Planning in the Soviet Union* (London, 1989), pp. 26–7.

42. Simon, *Nationalism and Policy*, p. 50.

43. Koutaissoff, 'Literacy and the Place of Russian', pp. 120–21.

44. S. L. Guthier 'The Belorussians: National Identification and Assimilation 1897–1970: Part I', *Soviet Studies*, 29 (1977) p. 55.

45. Stalin, *Works*, vol. ii, p. 376.

46. J. Smith 'The Education of National Minorities: the Early Soviet Experience', *Slavonic and East European Review*, 75 (1997), p. 302; Y. Bilinsky 'Education and the Non-Russian Peoples in the USSR, 1917–1967: an Essay', *Slavic Review*, 27 (1968), pp. 419–20.

47. Simon, *Nationalism and Policy*, p. 240; Crisp, 'Soviet Language Planning', p. 38; I. Baldauf 'Some Thoughts on the Making of the Uzbek Nation', *Cahiers du monde russe*, 32 (1991), pp. 86–9.

48. G. O. Liber *Soviet Nationality Policy, Urban Growth, and Identity Change in the Ukrainian SSR 1923–1935* (Cambridge, 1992), p. 187.

49. Liber, *Soviet Nationality Policy*, appendix 14.

50. Martin, 'Soviet Ethnic Cleansing', pp. 842–4.

51. Simon, 'Nationsbildung und "Revolution von oben" ', pp. 233–4, 247–9.

52. Hirsch, 'The Soviet Union as a Work-in-Progress', pp. 271–4.

53. Royal Institute of International Affairs *Nationalism* (London, 1939), p. 78.

54. Crisp, 'Soviet Language Planning', pp. 28–9; Bilinsky, 'Education and the Non-Russian Peoples', p. 428; Koutaissoff, 'Literacy and the Place of Russian', p. 114; Simon, *Nationalism and Policy*, pp. 150–51.

55. Details in Simon, *Nationalism and Policy*, pp. 142–5.

56. Simon, *Nationalism and Policy*, pp. 144–5, 148.

57. Royal Institute of International Affairs, *Nationalism*, p. 74; S. G. Simonsen 'Raising "The Russian Question": Ethnicity and Statehood – Russkie and Rossiya', *Nationalism and Ethnic Politics*, 2 (1996), pp. 96–110. See too N. Lynn and V. Bogorov 'Reimaging the Russian Idea', in G. Herb and D. Kaplan

(eds) *Nested Identities: Nationalism, Territory and Scale* (Lanham, Md, 1999), pp. 101–7; R. Szporluk 'Nationalism and Communism: reflections: Russia, Ukraine, Belarus and Poland', *Nations and Nationalism*, 4 (1998), pp. 308–11.

58. Royal Institute of International Affairs, *Nationalism*, p. 79.

59. A. Powell 'The Nationalist Trend in Soviet Historiography', *Soviet Studies*, 2 (1950/1), pp. 373–5; D. Brandenberger *National Bolshevism: Stalinist Mass Culture and the Formation of Modern Russian National Identity 1931–1956* (Cambridge, Mass., 2002), pp. 71–6, 86–94.

60. M. Perrie 'Nationalism and History: the Cult of Ivan the Terrible in Stalin's Russia', in Hosking and Service (eds), *Russian Nationalism*, pp. 107–13; K. E. Platt and D. Brandenberger 'Terribly Romantic, Terribly Progressive, or Terribly Tragic: Rehabilitating Ivan IV under I. V. Stalin', *Russian Review*, 58 (1999), pp. 637–8.

61. R. Bergan *Sergei Eisenstein: a Life in Conflict* (New York, 1997), pp. 296–306; see too D. Brandenberger 'Soviet social mentalité and Russocentrism on the eve of war', *Jahrbuch für die Geschichte Osteuropas*, 44 (1996), pp. 388, 392–4.

62. R. Stites *Russian Popular Culture: Entertainment and Society since 1900* (Cambridge, 1992) p. 57.

63. Royal Institute of International Affairs, *Nationalism*, p. 79; see too Lynn and Bogorov, 'Reimaging the Russian Idea', pp. 107–8.

64. Martin, 'Soviet Ethnic Cleansing', pp. 830–31, 837, 845–9.

65. N. Bugai *The Deportation of Peoples in the Soviet Union* (New York, 1996), pp. 28–31; Simon, *Nationalism and Policy*, pp. 199–200; Pohl, *Ethnic Cleansing*, pp. 9–19.

66. Martin, 'Soviet Ethnic Cleansing', pp. 853–7.

67. P. J. Duncan 'Ukrainians', in G. Smith (ed.) *The Nationalities Question in the Soviet Union* (London, 1990), pp. 96–7.

68. Simon, *Nationalism and Policy*, pp. 162–3.

69. W. Taubman *Khrushchev: the Man and his Era* (New York, 2002), p. 99.

70. Pohl, *Ethnic Cleansing*, pp. 1–3.

71. On Esperanto speakers see K. Sword (ed.) *The Soviet Takeover of the Polish Eastern Provinces, 1939–1941* (London, 1991), appendix 3c 'NKVD Instructions Relating to "Anti-Soviet Elements"'.

72. K. Sword *Deportation and Exile: Poles in the Soviet Union, 1939–48* (London, 1994), pp. 25–7; J. Gross *Revolution from Abroad: the Soviet Conquest of Poland's Western Ukraine and Western Belorussia* (Princeton, NJ, 1988), pp. 193–4.

73. Tolz, 'Deportations of Ethnic Groups', p. 162.

74. Sword, *Deportation and Exile*, p. 22.

75. Pohl, *Ethnic Cleansing*, p. 5; Tolz, 'Deportation of Ethnic Groups', pp. 161–7; Bougai, *Deportation of Peoples*, passim.

76. Tolz, 'Deportation of Ethnic Groups', p. 164.

77. Tolz, 'Deportation of Ethnic Groups', p. 166.

78. N. Levin *Paradox of Survival: the Jews in the Soviet Union since 1917* (2 vols, London, 1990), vol. i, pp. 477–9, 484.

79. Stalin, *Works*, vol. ii, pp. 307–8, 345, 359; J. Miller 'Soviet Theory on the Jews', in L. Kochan (ed.) *The Jews in Soviet Russia since 1917* (Oxford, 1978), pp. 49–52.

80. J. B. Schechtman 'The USSR, Zionism and Israel', in Kochan, *Jews in Soviet Russia*, pp. 106–8.

81. Z. Gitelman 'Soviet Jewry before the Holocaust', in Z. Gitelman (ed.) *Bitter Legacy: Confronting the Holocaust in the USSR* (Bloomington, Ind., 1997), p. 5; B. Pinkus 'La participation des minorities nationals extra-territoriales à la vie politique et publique de l'Union Soviétique, 1917–1939', *Cahiers du monde russe*, 36 (1995) pp. 299–300.

82. Schechtman, 'The USSR, Zionism and Israel', p. 118.

83. Gitelman, 'Soviet Jewry', p. 6; Smith, 'Education of National Minorities', p. 30; see too S. W. Baron *The Russian Jew under Tsars and Soviets* (2nd edn, New York, 1987), pp. 226–34.

84. M. Altshuler *Soviet Jewry on the Eve of the Holocaust* (Jerusalem, 1998), pp. 30, 146; Levin, *Paradox of Survival*, pp. 134–43, 233; E. Lohr 'The Russian Army and the Jews: Mass Deportations, Hostages, and Violence during World War I', *Russian Review*, 60 (2001), p. 408 on the Pale.

85. Altshuler, *Soviet Jewry*, p. 146.

86. Levin, *Paradox of Survival*, pp. 275–6.

87. Altshuler, *Soviet Jewry*, p. 26.

88. C. Abramsky 'The Biro-Bidzhan Project, 1927–1959', in Kochan, *Jews in Soviet Russia*, pp. 70–71, 73–7.

89. B.-C. Pinchuk *Shtetl Jews under Soviet Rule: Eastern Poland on the Eve of the Holocaust* (London, 1990), pp. 55, 129–31.

90. Pinchuk, *Shtetl Jews*, p. 39.

91. Schechtman, 'The USSR, Zionism and Israel', p. 124.

92. S. Sebag Montefiore *Stalin: the Court of the Red Tsar* (London, 2003), pp. 509–10; A. Vaksberg *Stalin against the Jews* (New York, 1994), pp. 159–81; Levin, *Paradox of Survival*, pp. 393–4.

93. For details see B. Pinkus *The Jews of the Soviet Union: the History of a National Minority* (Cambridge, 1993), pp. 142–50, 174–7; Y. Rapaport *The Doctors' Plot: Stalin's Last Crime* (London, 1991); J. Brent and V. Naumov

Stalin's Last Crime: the Plot against the Jewish Doctors, 1948–1953 (London, 2002).

94. A. Blakely *Russia and the Negro* (Washington DC, 1986), p. 101.

95. Hirsch, 'Race without Racial Politics', pp. 32–5; A. Weiner 'Nothing but Certainty', *Slavic Review*, 61 (2002), pp. 44–51. See for a different view E. D. Weitz 'Racial Politics without the Concept of Race: Reevaluating Soviet Ethnic and National Purges', *Slavic Review*, 61 (2002), pp. 1–29.

96. Hirsch, 'Race without Racial Politics', p. 36.

97. *Akten zur deutschen auswärtigen Politik, Ser. D*, vol. I (Baden-Baden, 1950), p. 25, 'Niederschrift über die Besprechung in der Reichskanzlei', 5 November 1937.

98. S. Lauryssens *The Man who Invented the Third Reich* (Stroud, 1999), pp. 140, 146, 151.

99. J. W. Young *Totalitarian Language: Orwell's Newspeak and its Nazi and Communist Antecedents* (Charlottesville, Va., 1991), p. 108.

100. M. Quinn *The Swastika: Constructing the Symbol* (London, 1994), pp. 21, 116, 130–33.

101. Feinstein, 'Deutschland über alles?', pp. 506–9; J. W. Baird *To Die for Germany: Heroes in the Nazi Pantheon* (Bloomington, Ind., 1990), pp. 79–80, 264–5.

102. A. Kruck *Geschichte des Alldeutschen Verbandes 1890–1939* (Wiesbaden, 1954), p. 216.

103. R. J. O'Neill *The German Army and the Nazi Party 1933–1939* (London, 1966), p. 87.

104. Royal Institute of International Affairs, *Nationalism*, p. 78.

105. J. A. Leopold *Alfred Hugenberg: The Radical Nationalist Campaign against the Weimar Republic* (New Haven, Conn., 1977), pp. 149–63.

106. Kruck, *Geschichte des Alldeutschen Verbandes*, pp. 216–17.

107. Herb, *Under the Map of Germany*, pp. 132–40.

108. F. L. Kroll *Utopie als Ideologie: Geschichtsdenken und politisches Handeln im Dritten Reich* (Paderborn, 1998), pp. 217–20; see too A. A. Kallis 'To Expand or not to Expand? Territory, Generic Fascism and the Quest for an "Ideal Fatherland" ', *Journal of Contemporary History*, 38 (2003), pp. 237–60; J. Hermand *Der alte Traum vom neuen Reich: Völkische Utopien und Nationalsozialismus* (Frankfurt am Main, 1988), pp. 321–33.

109. F. El-Tayeb ' "Blood is a very special Juice": Racialized Bodies and Citizenship in Twentieth-Century Germany', *International Review of Social History*, 44 (1999), Supplement, pp. 149–53, 162.

110. E. Syring *Hitler: seine politische Utopie* (Frankfurt am Main, 1994), p. 210.

III. Vopel, 'Radikaler, völkischer Nationalismus', p. 164.

112. M. Dean 'The Development and Implementation of Nazi Denaturalization and Confiscation Policy up to the Eleventh Decree of the Reich Citizenship Law', *Holocaust and Genocide Studies*, 16 (2002), pp. 218–20.

113. H. Kaden and L. Nestler (eds) *Dokumente des Verbrechens: aus Akten des Dritten Reiches 1933–1945* (3 vols., Berlin, 1993), vol. i, pp. 60–62, Reichsbürgergesetz, 15 September 1935; Gesetz zum Schutze des deutschen Blutes und der deutschen Ehre, 15 September 1935.

114. P. Weindling *Health, Race and German Politics between National Unification and Nazism 1870–1945* (Cambridge, 1989), p. 530; C. Lusane *Hitler's Black Victims* (New York, 2002).

115. *Dokumente des Verbrechens*, vol. i, pp. 66–7, Erste Verordnung zum Reichsbürgergesetz, 14 November 1935.

116. B. Miller-Lane (ed.) *Nazi Ideology before 1933: A Documentation* (Manchester, 1978), p. 115 from 'Marriage Laws and the Principles of Breeding'; Heinemann, '*Rasse, Siedlung*', pp. 62–6; D. Bergen 'The Nazi Concept of "Volksdeutsche" and the Exacerbation of Anti-Semitism in Eastern Europe 1939–1945', *Journal of Contemporary History*, 29 (1994), pp. 569–72 for details of the 'Volksliste'.

117. Heinemann, '*Rasse, Siedlung*', pp. 190–95.

118. Heinemann, '*Rasse, Siedlung*', pp. 64–5; on the figures for those recorded, pp. 600–602.

119. Connelly, 'Nazis and Slavs', pp. 18–19; see too G. Bock 'Gleichheit und Differenz in der nationalsozialistischen Rassenpolitik', *Geschichte und Gesellschaft*, 19 (1993), pp. 277–310.

120. R. Lukes *The Forgotten Holocaust: the Poles under German Occupation 1939–1944* (Lexington, Kty, 1986), p. 8; see too J. T. Gross *Polish Society under German Occupation: the Generalgouvernement, 1939–1944* (Princeton, NJ., 1979), pp. 195–8 on German nationality policy.

121. Connelly, 'Nazis and Slavs', p. 10.

122. Lukes, *Forgotten Holocaust*, p. 8; G. Aly *'Final Solution': Nazi Population Policy and the Murder of the European Jews* (London, 1999), pp. 108–13; Kroll, *Utopie*, p. 220. See too W. Pyta '"Menschenökonomie": Das Ineinandergreifen von ländlicher Sozialraumgestaltung und rassenbiologischer Bevölkerungspolitik im nationalsozialistischen Staat', *Historisches Zeitschrift*, 273 (2001), pp. 31–94.

123. G. Lewy *The Nazi Persecution of the Gypsies* (Oxford, 2000), pp. 43–5, 47.

124. Lewy, *Persecution of the Gypsies*, pp. 52–3; E. Thurner *National Socialism and Gypsies in Austria* (Tuscaloosa, Ala., 1998), pp. 11–12.

125. Thurner, *Gypsies in Austria*, pp. 38–9.

126. Lewy, *Persecution of the Gypsies*, pp. 66–9.

127. G. Lewy 'Gypsies and Jews under the Nazis', *Holocaust and Genocide Studies*, 13 (1999), pp. 385–7.

128. Lewy, 'Gypsies and Jews', pp. 388–93.

129. B. D. Lutz and J. M. Lutz 'Gypsies as victims of the Holocaust', *Holocaust and Genocide Studies*, 9 (1995), p. 356.

130. Lewy, *Persecution of the Gypsies*, p. 43.

131. A. Elon *The Pity of it All: a Portrait of Jews in Germany 1743–1933* (London, 2002), pp. 210, 378; O. Heilbronner 'From Antisemitic Peripheries to Antisemitic Centres: The Place of Antisemitism in Modern German History', *Journal of Contemporary History*, 35 (2000), pp. 560–75.

132. Elon, *Pity of it All*, p. 379; F. Nicosia *The Third Reich and the Palestine Question* (London, 1985), p. 212 for figures from 1932 onwards.

133. S. Haffner *Defying Hitler: a memoir* (London, 2002), pp. 121–2.

134. Bundesarchiv, Berlin R2501/6601, Reichsbank research department, 'Bedenkliche wirtschaftliche Auswirkungen des Judenboykotts', appendix, pp. 1–5.

135. V. Klemperer *I Shall Bear Witness: the Diaries of Viktor Klemperer 1933–41* (London, 1998), p. 13.

136. S. Friedländer *Nazi Germany and the Jews: the Years of Persecution 1933–1939* (London, 1997), pp. 27–9.

137. Friedländer, *Nazi Germany and the Jews*, p. 28; see too C. Koonz *The Nazi Conscience* (Cambridge, Mass., 2003), pp. 166–7.

138. H. Michaelis and E. Schraepler (eds) *Ursachen und Folgen vom deutschen Zusammenbruch 1918 bis 1945* (Berlin, 1968), vol. xi, p. 605, Himler decree, 3 December 1938.

139. W. Benz (ed.) *Die Juden in Deutschland 1933–1945: Leben unter nationalsozialistischer Herrschaft* (Munich, 1988), p. 783.

140. Friedländer, *Nazi Germany and the Jews*, pp. 62–3; Nicosia, *Third Reich and Palestine*, pp. 41–9, 212; Benz, *Juden in Deutschland*, pp. 733, 738. Benz gives a figure of 168, 972 for May 1941 and 163, 696 for October that year.

141. Friedländer, *Nazi Germany and the Jews*, p. 177.

142. Friedländer, *Nazi Germany and the Jews*, pp. 242–6; B. F. Pauley *From Prejudice to Persecution: a History of Austrian Anti-Semitism* (Chapel Hill, NC, 1992), pp. 284–97.

143. H. Mommsen *Von Weimar nach Auschwitz. Zur Geschichte Deutschlands in der Weltkriegsepoche* (Stuttgart, 1999), pp. 268–82.

144. Connelly, 'Nazis and Slavs', p. 33.

145. Maser, *Hitler's Letters and Notes*, pp. 279–83; see too K.-U. Merz *Das*

Schreckbild: Deutschland und der Bolschewismus 1917 bis 1921 (Frankfurt am Main, 1995), pp. 457–71 for Hitler's view of the Jews in the early 1920s.

146. W. Treue 'Hitlers Denkschrift zum Vierjahresplan 1936', *Vierteljahrshefte für Zeitgeschichte*, 3 (1955) pp. 204–5.

147. National Archives II (College Park, MD) RG 238, Jackson papers, Box 3, translation of letter from Robert Ley to Dr Pflücker, 24 October 1945.

148. Friedländer, *Nazi Germany and the Jews*, pp. 3, 12.

149. National Archives, RG 238, Jackson papers, Box 3, Robert Ley to Dr Pflücker.

150. Hitler's speech in M. Domarus *Hitler's Speeches and Proclamations 1939–1940* (Würzburg, 1997), pp. 1448–9, Hitler's speech to the Reichstag, 30 January 1939; Himmler in Kroll, *Utopie*, pp. 213–16.

151. P. Longerich *The Unwritten Order: Hitler's Role in the Final Solution* (Stroud, 2001), pp. 51–3.

152. Longerich, *Unwritten Order*, pp. 63–5; see the discussion of recent debates in M. Roseman 'Recent Writing on the Holocaust', *Journal of Contemporary History*, 36 (2001), pp. 361–72.

153. R. Breitman 'Himmler and the "Terrible Secret" among the executioners', *Journal of Contemporary History*, 26 (1991), pp. 436–7.

154. See for example W. Benz, K. Kwiet and J. Matthäus *Einsatz im 'Reichskommissariat Ostland': Dokumente zum Völkermord im Baltikum und in Weissrussland 1941–1944* (Berlin, 1998) for a detailed documentation of the process of ghettoization and mass shootings. See too Aly, '*Final Solution*', chs 3, 7 and 8 on ghettos and deportation.

155. T. Jersak 'Die Interaktion von Kriegsverlauf und Judenvernichtung: ein Blick auf Hitlers Strategie im Spätsommer 1941', *Historisches Zeitschrift*, 268 (1999), pp. 345–60.

156. P. Witt 'Two Decisions Concerning the "Final Solution to the Jewish Question": Deportation to Lodz and Mass Murder in Chelmno', *Holocaust and Genocide Studies*, 9 (1995), p. 319; C. Gerlach 'The Wannsee Conference, the Fate of the German Jews, and Hitler's Decision in Principle to Exterminate All European Jews', *Journal of Modern History*, 70 (1998), pp. 762–8.

157. Gerlach 'Wannsee Conference', pp. 784–5.

158. Gerlach, 'Wannsee Conference', pp. 807–8; for other views on the significance of the meeting on 12 December see M. Moll 'Steuerungsinstrument im "Ämterchaos"? Die Tagungen der Reichs-und Gauleiter der NSDAP', *Vierteljahrshefte für Zeitgeschichte*, 49 (2001), pp. 240–43; see too U. Herbert (ed.) *National Socialist Extermination Policies: Contemporary German Perspectives and Controversies* (Oxford, 2000), pp. 38–41.

159. J. von Lang (ed.) *Das Eichmann-Protokoll: Tonbandaufzeichnungen der israelischen Verhörer* (Berlin, 1982), pp. 69, 86.

160. M. Roseman *The Villa, the Lake, the Meeting: Wannsee and the Final Solution* (London, 2002), chs 3–4.

161. F. Genoud (ed.) *The Testament of Adolf Hitler: the Hitler–Bormann Documents* (London, 1961), pp. 51–2, entry for 13 February 1945.

162. Hitler, *Mein Kampf*, p. 403.

163. Weitz 'Racial Politics', p. 23.

164. Pohl, *Ethnic Cleansing*, pp. 2–3.

165. Breitman 'Himmler and the "Terrible Secret"', p. 234.

166. M. I. Koval 'The Nazi Genocide of the Jews and the Ukrainian Population 1941–1944', in Gitelman, *Bitter Legacy*, pp. 52–3.

167. K. Slepyan 'The Soviet Partisan Movement and the Holocaust', *Holocaust and Genocide Studies*, 14 (2000), pp. 2–6.

168. Z. Gitelman 'Soviet Reactions to the Holocaust 1945–1991', in L. Dobroszycki and J. Gurock (eds) *The Holocaust in the Soviet Union: Studies and Sources on the Destruction of the Jews in Nazi-Occupied Territories of the USSR 1941–1945* (New York, 1993), pp. 3, 13–18.

Chapter 14

1. V. Grossman *Life and Fate* (London, 1985), p. 23.

2. A. Kilian *Einzuweisen zur völligen Isolierung NKWD-Speziallager Mühlberg/Elbe 1945–1948* (Leipzig, 1993), pp. 79 ff.

3. Kilian, *NKWD-Speziallager Mühlberg/Elbe*, p. 7.

4. N. Tumarkin *The Living and the Dead: the Rise and Fall of the Cult of World War II in Russia* (New York, 1994), pp. 113–15.

5. M. Jakobsen *Origins of the Gulag: the Soviet Prison Camp System 1917–1934* (London, 1993), pp. 17–41.

6. Jakobsen, *Origins of the Gulag*, pp. 112–14; R. Stettner '*Archipel GULag*': *Stalins Zwangslager – Terrorinstrument und Wirtschaftsgigant* (Paderborn, 1996), pp. 66–76; G. M. Ivanova *Labor Camp Socialism: the Gulag in the Soviet Totalitarian System* (New York, 2000), pp. 13–15. In 1921 there were approximately 50,000 prisoners in Cheka camps. See too A. Applebaum *Gulag: a History of the Soviet Camps* (London, 2003), chs 1–2.

7. Jakobsen, *Origins of the Gulag*, pp. 69, 91.

8. Jakobsen, *Origins of the Gulag*, pp. 125–6; J. Pohl *The Stalinist Penal System* (Jefferson, NC, 1997), p. 12.

9. U. Parvilahti *Beria's Gardens: Ten Years' Captivity in Russia and Siberia* (London, 1959), p. 94.

10. Jakobsen, *Origins of the Gulag*, pp. 119–21; Stettner, '*Archipel GULag*', pp. 76–87; M. Flores and F. Gori (eds) *GULag: il sistema dei lager in URSS* (Milan, 1999), pp. 25–6.

11. Pohl, *Stalinist Penal System*, pp. 14–15; Ivanova, *Labor Camp Socialism*, pp. 23–5.

12. K. Drobisch and G. Wieland *System der NS-Konzentrationslager 1933–1939* (Berlin, 1993), pp. 16–18.

13. Drobisch and Wieland, *NS-Konzentrationslager*, p. 16.

14. G. Schwarz *Die nationalsozialistischen Lager* (Frankfurt am Main, 1990), pp. 139–41, who counts 59 camps set up in 1933 and 1934; J. Tuchel 'Dimensionen des Terrors: Funktionen der Konzentrationslager in Deutschland 1933–1945', in D. Dahlmann and G. Hirschfeld (eds) *Lager, Zwangsarbiet, Vertreibung und Deportation* (Essen, 1999), pp. 374, 383; Drobisch and Wieland, *NS-Konzentrationslager*, pp. 73–5.

15. Eicke in J. Tuchel (ed.) *Die Inspektion der Konzentrationslager 1938–1945: Eine Dokumentation* (Berlin, 1994), pp. 36–7, 'Disziplinar-und Strafordnung für das Gefangenenlager', 1 August 1934; Drobisch and Wieland, *NS-Konzentrationslager*, pp. 98–9; W. Sofsky *The Order of Terror: The Concentration Camp* (Princeton, NJ, 1997), pp. 31–2. On Eicke see C. W. Sydnor *Soldiers of Destruction: The SS Death's Head Division, 1933–1945* (Princeton, NJ, 1977), pp. 3–13.

16. Tuchel, *Inspektion der Konzentrationslager*, p. 34; Sofsky, *Order of Terror*, pp. 30–31.

17. Tuchel, *Inspektion der Konzentrationslager*, p. 40; Drobisch and Wieland, *NS-Konzentrationslager*, pp. 186–91; Tuchel, 'Dimensionen des Terrors', p. 379.

18. F. Pingel *Häftlinge unter SS-Herrschaft: Widerstand, Selbstbehauptung und Vernichtung im Konzentrationslager* (Hamburg, 1978), pp. 39–40.

19. Pingel, *Häftlinge unter SS-Herrschaft*, p. 62.

20. H. Kaienberg '*Vernichtung durch Arbeit*': *Der Fall Neuengamme* (Bonn, 1990), p. 33; Pingel, *Häftlinge unter SS-Herrschaft*, pp. 61–2; K. Orth *Das System der nationalsozialistischen Konzentrationslager: Eine politische Organisationsgeschichte* (Hamburg, 1999), p. 32.

21. H. Kaienberg *Konzentrationslager und deutsche Wirtschaft 1939–1945* (Opladen, 1996), pp. 24–5; Pingel, *Häftlinge unter SS-Herrschaft*, p. 62.

22. Kaienberg, *Konzentrationslager*, p. 26.

23. Pingel, *Häftlinge unter SS-Herrschaft*, pp. 61–2.

24. Orth, *Das System der Konzentrationslager*, pp. 47–51; on SS economic

activities see J. E. Schulte *Zwangsarbeit und Vernichtung: Das Wirtschaft-simperium der SS* (Paderborn, 2001).

25. W. Kirstein *Das Konzentrationslager als Institution totalen Terrors: Das Beispiel des Konzentrationslager Natzweiler* (Pfaffenweiler, 1992), pp. 1–33.

26. H. Kaienberg 'KZ-Haft und Wirtschaftsinteresse: Das Wirtschaftsverwal-tungshauptamt der SS als Leistungszentrale der Konzentrationslager und der SS-Wirtschaft', in Kaienberg, *Konzentrationslager*, p. 51.

27. Kirstein, *Konzentrationslager Natzweiler*, p. 8. The remark was overheard by Rudolf Höss, the future commandant of Auschwitz, who personally killed the first victim of accusations of sabotage, a Junkers aircraft worker who refused to comply with air-raid drill.

28. F. Karay *Death Comes in Yellow: Skarzysko-Kamienna Slave Labor Camp* (Amsterdam, 1996), pp. 235–46.

29. Schwarz, *nationalsozialistischen Lager*, p. 86.

30. G. Lotfi *KZ der Gestapo: Arbeitserziehungslager im Dritten Reich* (Stuttgart, 2000), pp. 114–28, 440–41; Schwarz, *nationalsozialistischen Lager*, pp. 82–3.

31. R. Kubatzki *Zwangsarbeiter-und Kriegsgefangenenlager: Standorte und Topographie in Berlin und im brandenburgischen Umland 1939 bis 1945* (Berlin, 2000), p. 250 (the total was 1,175 camps); J. Schley *Nachbar Buchenwald: Die Stadt Weimar und ihr Konzentrationslager 1937–1945* (Cologne, 1999), pp. 139–44.

32. Pingel, *Häftlinge unter SS-Herrschaft*, pp. 120–21; D. Dwork and R. J. van Pelt *Auschwitz: 1270 to the Present* (New York, 1996), pp. 202–7, 261–3; G. Aly and S. Heim *Architects of Annihilation: Auschwitz and the Logic of Destruction* (London, 2002), pp. 106–12.

33. Pingel, *Häftlinge unter SS-Herrschaft*, p. 230; Dwork and van Pelt, *Auschwitz*, p. 272.

34. E. Kogon, H. Langbein and A. Rückerl (eds) *Nazi Mass Murder: a Documentary History of the Use of Poison Gas* (New Haven, Conn., 1993), pp. 145–6.

35. Dwork and van Pelt, *Auschwitz*, p. 299.

36. Schwarz, *nationalsozialistischen Lager*, p. 211.

37. E. Bacon *The Gulag at War: Stalin's Forced Labour System in the Light of the Archives* (London, 1994), pp. 73–6; Ivanova, *Labor Camp Socialism*, pp. 82–5 for full details of GUlag camp economic organization and output before 1941.

38. Bacon, *Gulag at War*, pp. 139–44; Ivanova, *Labor Camp Socialism*, pp. 94–5.

39. Pohl, *Stalinist Penal System*, p. 16.

40. Bacon, *Gulag at War*, pp. 142–3.

41. Pohl, *Stalinist Penal System*, p. 17.

42. Stettner, '*Archipel GULag*', pp. 181, 205–6.

43. Stettner, '*Archipel GULag*', pp. 203–4; Pohl, *Stalinist Penal System*, pp. 50–52.

44. Pohl, *Stalinist Penal System*, pp. 17–18; Ivanova, *Labor Camp Socialism*, pp. 65–7.

45. Sofsky, *Order of Terror*, pp. 35–6; D. A. Hackett (ed.) *The Buchenwald Report* (Boulder, Colo., 1995), pp. 112–13.

46. Pingel, *Häftlinge unter SS-Herrschaft*, p. 230.

47. Kaienberg, '*Vernichtung durch Arbeit*', p. 60.

48. Kirstein, *Konzentrationslager Natzweiler*, p. 65; K. Orth 'Gab es eine Lagergesellschaft? "Kriminelle" und politische Häftlinge im Konzentrationslager', in N. Frei, S. Steinbacher and B. Wagner (eds) *Ausbeutung, Vernichtung, Öffentlichkeit: neue Studien zur nationalsozialistischen Lagerpolitik* (Munich, 2000), p. 119.

49. Pohl, *Stalinist Penal System*, pp. 35–7; Bacon, *Gulag at War*, p. 153. In 1944 60.9 per cent were Russians, 11.1 per cent Ukrainians.

50. Pohl, *Stalinist Penal System*, p. 22; J. A. Getty, G. T. Rittersporn and V. N. Zemskov 'Victims of the Soviet Penal System in the Pre-war Years: A First Approach on the Basis of the Archival Evidence', *American Historical Review*, 98 (1993), p. 1031–3; N. Werth and G. Moullec (eds) *Rapports secrets soviétiques: La société russe dans les documents confidentiels 1921–1991* (Paris, 1994), p. 386, Report of the chief of the GUlag on the work of the GUlag during the Great Patriotic War, 10 March 1945, which gives figures for 'counter-revolutionaries' and common criminals, 1941–45.

51. Pohl, *Stalinist Penal System*, p. 25.

52. C. Füllberg-Stolberg, M. Jung, R. Riebe and M. Scheitenberger (eds) *Frauen in Konzentrationslagern Bergen-Belsen, Ravensbrück* (Bremen, 1994), p. 79. On the proportion of 'asocials' see Orth, *Das System der Konzentrationslager*, pp. 51–3. In the late 1930s this proportion was high: 58 per cent at Sachsenhausen in 1938.

53. Pohl, *Stalinist Penal System*, pp. 30–31; Stettner, '*Archipel GULag*', pp. 202–3; On Akmolinsk camp, V. Shapovalov (ed.), *Remembering the Darkness: Women in Soviet Prisons* (Lanham, Md, 2001), p. 207.

54. J. Morrison *Ravensbrück: Everyday Life in a Woman's Concentration Camp* (London, 2000), pp. 27–9, 86.

55. Kaienberg, 'KZ-Haft und Wirtschaftsinteresse', p. 51.

56. Pohl, *Stalinist Penal System*, pp. 32–3; Schwarz, *nationalsozialistischen Lager*, pp. 84–6; Werth and Moullec, *Rapports secrets*, p. 387.

57. Shapovalov, *Remembering the Darkness*, p. 206.

58. M. Nahon *Birkenau: Camp of Death* (Tuscaloosa, Ala., 1989), pp. 37–9.

59. Morrison, *Ravensbrück*, pp. 33–4.

60. Parvilahti, *Beria's Gardens*, pp. 93–7.

61. Pingel, *Häftlinge unter SS-Herrschaft*, p. 135.

62. Dwork and van Pelt, *Auschwitz*, pp. 263–4.

63. M. T. Allen 'The Banality of Evil Reconsidered: SS Mid-level Managers of Extermination Through Work', *Central European History*, 30 (1997), p. 263; see too A. Beyerchen 'Rational Means and Irrational Ends: Thoughts on the Technology of Racism in the Third Reich', *Central European History*, 30 (1997), pp. 386–402.

64. Parvilahti, *Beria's Gardens*, p. 95; D. Dallin and B. Nicolaevsky *Forced Labor in Soviet Russia* (London, 1947), pp. 13–14.

65. Pohl, *Stalinist Penal System*, pp. 15–17.

66. Parvilahti, *Beria's Gardens*, p. 126.

67. Pingel, *Häftlinge unter SS-Herrschaft*, pp. 164–5.

68. Nahon, *Birkenau: Camp of Death*, p. 53.

69. Dallin and Nicolaevsky, *Forced Labor*, pp. 6–7; Parvilahti, *Beria's Gardens*, p. 98.

70. P. Barton *L'institution concentrationnaire en Russe 1930–1957* (Paris, 1959), p. 80; on norm competition in the camps see L. von Koerber *Sowjetrussland kämpft gegen das Verbrechen* (Berlin, 1933), pp. 24–5.

71. Dwork and van Pelt, *Auschwitz*, pp. 194–6; P. Steinberg *Speak You Also: a Survivor's Reckoning* (London, 2001), pp. 66–71.

72. A. Solzhenitsyn *One Day in the Life of Ivan Denisovich* (London, 1963), p. 143.

73. Sofsky, *Order of Terror*, p. 118; Nohan, *Birkenau: Camp of Death*, p. 39.

74. Pingel, *Häftlinge unter SS-Herrschaft*, pp. 114–16.

75. Parvilahti, *Beria's Gardens*, pp. 109, 125.

76. See for example K. Dunin-Wasowicz *Resistance in the Concentration Camps* (Warsaw, 1982).

77. Morrison, *Ravensbrück*, pp. 130–33.

78. Pohl, *Stalinist Penal System*, p. 31.

79. Morrison, *Ravensbrück*, p. 365; J. Bardach and K. Gleeson *Man is Wolf to Man: Surviving the Gulag* (Berkeley, Calif., 1998) pp. 191–3.

80. Steinberg, *Speak You Also*, p. 72.

81. Bardach and Gleeson, *Man is Wolf to Man*, pp. 227–8.

82. For example Parvilahti, *Beria's Gardens*, pp. 118, 125; see too, Pingel, *Häftlinge unter SS-Herrschaft*, p. 135.

83. Dallin and Nicolaevsky, *Forced Labor*, p. 6.

84. Bardach and Gleeson, *Man is Wolf to Man*, pp. 247–9.

85. Y. Shymko (ed.) *For This Was I Born* (Toronto, 1973), p. 41; D. Panin *The Notebooks of Sologdin* (New York, 1976).

86. Steinberg, *Speak You Also*, p. 77.

87. Morrison, *Ravensbrück*, pp. 289–91.

88. Parvilahti, *Beria's Gardens*, pp. 99–100; Bardach and Gleeson, *Man is Wolf to Man*, p. 236.

89. Pohl, *Stalinist Penal System*, pp. 14–16; B. Perz *Projekt Quarz: Steyr-Daimler-Puch und das Konzentrationslager Melk* (Vienna, 1991), p. 300; Parvilahti, *Beria's Gardens*, pp. 132–3.

90. Steinberg, *Speak You Also*, p. 22.

91. Barton, *L'institution concentrationnaire*, pp. 78–9; Bardach and Gleeson, *Man is Wolf to Man*, p. 213.

92. L. Crome *Unbroken: Resistance and Survival in the Concentration Camps* (London, 1988), pp. 54, 56–7; see too Kaienberg, '*Vernichtung durch Arbeit*', p. 56.

93. Werth and Moullec, *Rapports secrets*, pp. 377–82: Report from N. Ezhov, March 1938 'on the state of a number of labour camps'; Report of the GUlag operational department, 17 May 1941 on the camp at Sredne-Belsk; Report of deputy chief of GUlag operational department, 23 October 1941 on rising mortality at Aktiubinsk.

94. Crome, *Unbroken: Resistance and Survival*, p. 62.

95. U. Herbert *Best: Biographische Studien über Radikalismus, Weltanschauung und Vernunft 1903–1989* (Bonn, 1996), p. 151; Tuchel, 'Dimensionen des Terrors', p. 381.

96. Sofsky, *Order of Terror*, p. 16.

97. I. Müller *Hitler's Justice: the Courts of the Third Reich* (London, 1991), p. 56.

98. M. Kárný 'Das SS-Wirtschafts-Verwaltungshauptamt', in Hamburger Stiftung zur Förderung von Wissenschaft und Kultur (ed.) '*Deutsche Wirtschaft*': *Zwangsarbeit Von KZ-Häftlingen für Industrie und Behörden* (Hamburg, 1991) pp. 160–64; F. Piper 'Industrieunternehmen als Initiatoren des Einsatzes von KZ-Häftlingen', in Hamburger Stiftung, '*Deutsche Wirtschaft*', pp. 97–103. Out of 500,000 workers approximately 230–250,000 worked in private sector firms.

99. Herbert, *Best*, pp. 169–70.

100. Barton, *L'institution concentrationnaire*, p. 56; Shapovalov, *Remembering the Darkness*, p. 207.

101. P. Levi *The Drowned and the Saved* (London, 1988), p. 100.

Conclusion

1. P. Sorokin *The Sociology of Revolution* (New York, 1967) pp. 185–6.

2. V. M. Berezhkov *At Stalin's Side* (New York, 1994), pp. 7, 72.

3. Berezhkov, *At Stalin's Side*, p. 7.

4. See for example L. Dupeux *Strategie communiste et dynamique conservatrice: essai sur les differents sens de l'expression 'National-Bolchevisme'* (Paris, 1976).

5. T. Todorov *Hope and Memory: Reflections on the Twentieth Century* (London, 2003), p. 25 ff.

6. E. H. Vieler *The Ideological Roots of German National Socialism* (New York, 1999), p. 125; see also D. Gasman *The Scientific Origins of National Socialism* (London, 1971), pp. 147–65.

7. 'The International Character of the October Revolution' in J. Stalin *Problems of Leninism* (Moscow, 1947), pp. 198–203.

8. A. Ulam *Expansion and Co-Existence: a History of Soviet Foreign Policy 1917–1967* (London, 1968) p. 78.

9. H. Mehringer *Die NSDAP als politische Ausleseorganisation* (Munich, 1938), p. 5.

10. W. Treue 'Hitlers Denkschrift zum Vierjahresplan 1936', *Vierteljahreshefte für Zeitgeschichte*, 3 (1955), p. 201.

11. 'Der Schlussrede des Führers auf dem Parteikongress 1934' in G. Neesse *Die Nationalsozialistische Deutsche Arbeiterpartei* (Stuttgart, 1935), p. 195.

12. Treue, 'Denkschrift', p. 202.

13. For details on the Gestapo's Jewish offices see H. Berschel *Bürokratie und Terror: Das Judenreferat der Gestapo Düsseldorf 1935–1945* (Essen, 2001).

14. H. Rauschning *Hitler Speaks* (London, 1939), p. 257.

15. P. Reidel 'Aspekte ästhetischer Politik im NS-Staat' in U. Hermann and U. Nassen (eds.) *Formative Ästhetik im Nationalsozialismus. Intentionen, Medien und Praxisformen totalitärer ästhetischer Herrschaft und Beherrschung* (Weinheim, 1994), p. 14.

16. G. C. Guins *Soviet Law and Soviet Society* (The Hague, 1954), p. 30. In a teacher's manual from 1940 schoolchildren were to be instructed 'to hate their country's enemies'. See D. Brandenberger *National Bolshevism: Stalinist Mass Culture and the Formation of Modern Russian National Identity 1931–1956* (Cambridge, Mass., 2002), p. 65.

17. See in general J. Stalin *On the Opposition* (Peking ed., 1974), speeches and articles from the 1920s on problems of party unity and party disagreements.

18. E. van Ree 'Stalin's Organic Theory of the Party', *Russian Review*, 52 (1993), p. 52.

19. P. Stachura *Gregor Strasser and the Rise of Nazism* (London, 1983), p. 75.

20. Neesse, *Nationalsozialistische Partei*, p. 10.

21. See for example the discussion in I. Gutkin 'The Magic of Words: Symbolism, Futurism, Socialist Realism' in B. G. Rosenthal *The Occult in Russian and Soviet Culture* (Ithaca, NY, 1997), pp. 241–4.

22. G. Alexopoulos *Stalin's Outcasts: Aliens, Citizens, and the Soviet State 1926–1936* (Ithaca, NY, 2002) esp. ch. 2.

23. T. Alkemeyer and A. Richantz 'Inszenierte Körperträume: Reartikulation von Herrschaft und Selbstbeherrschung in Körperbildung des Faschismus' in Hermann and Nassen, *Formative Ästhetik*, pp. 82–3.

24. See for example S. Plaggenborg 'Gewalt und Militanz im Sowjetrussland 1919–1930', *Jahrbücher für die Geschichte Osteuropas*, 44 (1996), pp. 409–30.

25. M. Pabst *Staatsterrorismus: Theorie und Praxis kommunistischer Herrschaft* (Graz, 1997), p. 15.

26. Stalin, *Works*, vol. 6, p. 121.

27. G. A. Wetter *Dialectical Materialism: a Historical and Systematic Survey of Philosophy in the Soviet Union* (New York, 1958), pp. 221–2.

28. F. Kroll *Utopie als Ideologie: Geschichtsdenken und politisches Handeln im Dritten Reich* (Paderborn, 1998), pp. 56–64, 84–8.

29. *Uncensored Germany: Letters and News Sent Secretly from Germany to the German Freedom Party* (London, 1940), p. 80, 'Letter from a Tradesman', September 1939.

30. A. Resis (ed.) *Molotov Remembers: Inside Kremlin Politics* (Chicago, 1993), p. 264, interview 12 April 1973.

31. A. Gide *Back from the U.S.S.R.* (London, 1937), pp. 45, 48.

32. Gide, *Back from the U.S.S.R.*, p. 45.

33. M. Heller *Cogs in the Soviet Wheel: the Formation of Soviet Man* (London, 1988), p. 287; see also the discussion on language in E. Naiman 'Introduction' to A. Platonov *Happy Moscow* (London, 2001), pp. xxxi–xxxvii.

34. V. Klemperer *I Shall Bear Witness: the Diaries of Viktor Klemperer 1933–41* (London, 1998), pp. 227, 243.

35. S. Allen *Comrades and Citizens* (London, 1938), pp. 244, 301.

36. This is a point well-made in I. Halfin 'Poetics in the Archives: the Quest for "True" Bolshevik Documents', *Jahrbücher für die Geschichte Osteuropas*, 51 (2003), pp. 84–9. Language, Halfin argues, is itself 'constitutitive'.

37. Allen, *Comrades and Citizens*, pp. 229, 244, 301.

38. Berezhkov, *At Stalin's Side*, p. 117.

Index

power and influence, 172; terrorism and victims, 197, 208, 512; in repression of Jews, 208; social origins of members, 241; on motherhood, 248; armed (*Waffen SS*), 474, 481; rivalry with army, 474, 478, 481; fighting in war, 534; Race Office, 575–7; manages concentration camps, 601, 604–6, 626, 631–2; runs businesses and industries, 604
science: and totalitarianism, 637–8, 640
SD *see Sicherheitsdienst*
Secret Sector (*earlier* Department; Stalin's), 67–8
Sedov, Lev (Trotsky's son): killed, 327
Sedov, Sergei (Trotsky's son): killed, 338
Sekchow, Bogislav von, 231
Seldte, Franz, 45–7
Semenov, Vladimir, 222
Serge, Viktor, 68
Sergius of Radonezh, St, 272
Sevastopol, 137
Shakhty coal mines, Ukraine, 41; show trial (1928), 177
Shaposhnikov, Boris, 446, 448, 477, 490; *The Brain of the Army*, 469
Shostakovich, Dmitri: *Lady Macbeth of Mtsensk*, 353, 371
show trials, 41, 177–8, 185, 214–16, 335
Shpigelglaz, Mikhail, 475
Shtange, Galina, 389–90
Shub, Esfir', 380
Shvernik, Nikolai, 316
Sicherheitsdienst (SD; Germany), 191, 345, 512, 519
Siebert, Wilhelm, 300

Simplicissimus (magazine), 117
Sinyavsky, Andrei, 99, 119
Slavs: repressed by Nazis, 261; Hitler despises, 518
Smirnov, Ivan, 43
'Smolensk Declaration', 340
Sochi, 52
Social Democratic Party (Russian), 6
Social-Democratic Party (German), 310, 313, 325, 329–30, 460
'socialism in one country', 551, 561
Socialist Courier (Menshevik journal), 334
socialist realism, 352–3, 363, 366, 389–90
Socialist Revolutionaries (Russian), 7, 336
Society for the Dissemination of Political and Scientific Knowledge (Soviet Union), 277
Society of Militant Materialists (Soviet Union), 271
Sokolov, Yuri, 121, 382
Solovetsky (island), 596, 598, 630
Solzhenitsyn, Alexander, 309, 624
Sombart, Werner, 105
'Song of the Motherland' (Soviet Union), 559–60
Soviet Union: civil war (1917–21), 12, 442–3, 644; social upheaval and class revolution, 37–41, 75; grain supplies and rural policy, 39–43; cultural and artistic revolution, 40; show trials, 41, 177–8, 185, 214–16, 335; famines, 42; constitutions (1936–37), 54–5, 60–1, 158, 160, 277, 557; elections and democracy in, 54–5, 58–9; Secret Sector, 67–8; planning control and administration, 76–7; ruling